BREYER
MOLDS & MODELS
Horses, Riders, & Animals

1950 - 1995

Nancy Atkinson Young

Schiffer Publishing Ltd

4880 Lower Valley Road, Atglen, PA 19310 USA

To Chuck

Many of the designations of products mentioned in this book are claimed by
the manufacturers, sellers, or creators as trademarks. Such designations
include, but are not limited to, the names Breyer, Breyer Animal Creations,
Traditional, Classic, Little Bits, Stablemates, Dapples, and B Ranch, which are
trademarks of Reeves International, Inc. The Saddle Club is a registered
trademark of Bonnie Bryant Hiller.

Though the author and publisher have prepared this book with great care,
they make no guarantee against errors or omissions and assume no liability for
any damage resulting from the use of information or opinions provided herein.

Corrections and suggestions welcome. Please send self-addressed, stamped
envelope with all inquiries. No appraisal requests or sales-related inquiries,
please. Nancy A. Young, 268 Ross Ct., Claremont, CA 91711-3139.

Designed by Bonnie Hensley

ISBN: 0-88740-943-1
Printed in China

Library of Congress Cataloging-in-Publication Data

Young, Nancy Atkinson
    Breyer molds & models : horses, riders, & animals : 1950-1995 /
Nancy Atkinson Young. -- 4th ed.
        p.   cm.
    Includes bibliographical references
    ISBN: 0-88740-943-1 (hard)
    1. Breyer Animal Creations--Catalogs. 2. Toy horses--Collectors and
collecting--United States--Catalogs. I. Title.
NK9509.95.H67Y68   1997
688'.1--dc21   97-818
                                                          CIP

Published by Schiffer Publishing Ltd.
4880 Lower Valley Road
Atglen, PA 19310
Phone: (610) 593-1777; Fax: (610) 593-2002
E-mail: schifferbk@aol.com
Please write for a free catalog.
This book may be purchased from the publisher.
Please include $2.95 for shipping.
Try your bookstore first.

We are interested in hearing from authors
with book ideas on related subjects.

Contents

Acknowledgments

Many generous people have helped me with this book. I am grateful to Peter Stone, former Breyer executive and now owner of The Peter Stone Company, for contributing the foreword as well as a wealth of information on Breyer history that no one else could have provided. The collection of photographs published for the first time here owes much to Sheryl Leisure and Heather Wells, who lent me hundreds of their models, filling the large gaps in my own herd, for an intense five-day photo shoot at my home in October 1994. Heather also organized and dusted models during the first days of the shoot, while Leslie Bockol, a photographer and editor for Schiffer Publishing, began taking some 1,400 pictures. Sande Schneider, among her innumerable contributions to this book, proofread a late draft of the fourth edition. Stephanie Macejko at Breyer has graciously answered my unceasing questions. Megan Thilman Quigley, formerly of Breyer, has also provided much information. Stuart Bentley, of Bentley Sales Company, kindly sent me a bounty of archival materials from his files. Werner Fleischmann, president of Reeves International, kindly permitted me to visit the Breyer factory in November 1994 to study the archives and tour the production areas. Many other people have helped me with this fourth edition or previous editions of the book. For earlier permission to draw upon their publications for information on special runs, I thank Paula DeFeyter and Lynn Luther (*The Model Trading Post Insurance Guide*, 1991), Laura Diederich (*The Model Book*, 1988), Karen Grimm (*Breyer Collector's Video*, 1991), Jill Gutierrez (list of test runs, one-of-a-kinds, special runs; 1989), and Jeanette Hollansky ("Breyer Current and Discontinued Models," 1990). Among numerous others who have provided information, photos, or other materials, I am grateful to Lisa Barnett, Linda Bell, Alison Beniush, Joan Berkwitz, Robin Briscoe, Connie Bryan, Ardith Carlton, Karen Crossley, Judy Davinich, Denise Deen, Linda Desmarais, Jolie Devereux, Tina Dils, Kim Fairbrother, Joan Fauteux, Mary Margaret Fox, Chelle Fulk, Karen Gerhardt, Gale Good (who proofread the second edition of this book), Leslie Granger, Andrea Gurdon, Paula Hecker, Lynn Hiersche, Kim Lory Jones, Lani Keller, Blain Kukevitch, Jo Kulwicki, Sue Lehman, Elaine Lindelef, Daphne Macpherson, Lorraine Mavrogeorge, Judith Miller, Chris Nandell, Karen Oelkers, Lori Ogozalek, Tanya Parker, Billie Parsons, Karen Perkins, Robert Peterson, Jack Rodibaugh, Ida Santana, Kay Schlumpf, Joy Sheesley, Liz Strauss, Lillian Sutphin, Debbie Vandegrift, Bonnie Vavra, Ruth-Ann Wellman and family, Georgeanne Wilcox, and Pam Young. Many other kind people who have contributed information are acknowledged throughout the book. They cannot all be listed here, but I wish to express my appreciation to every one. I am grateful as well to my editor at Schiffer Publishing, Nancy Schiffer, who patiently dealt with vast quantities of new and emended text that I sent to her months after submitting the "final" draft of the book early in 1996.

Finally, I would like to thank my husband, Charles Young. Though incredulous that an apparently grown-up woman could be so fascinated by plastic horses as to write a book about them, he helped it happen. He subsidized my repeated bouts of time off from gainful employment to research and write the book. He also solved my computer problems, offered excellent design suggestions, and proofread portions of the text. And he only occasionally protests my dipping into the coffers to buy yet another Breyer.

Foreword
Peter A. Stone

We are just here for a spell and pass on.
—Will Rogers

I was ten years old when my father, Sam Stone, and his partner, Charles Schiff, produced the first Breyer plastic horse—the Western Horse. Forty-six years have passed since this simple beginning. Today Breyer has become a subculture of collecting and horse-related activity.

Breyer is a living tradition. And we who have taken part in that tradition are only sojourners, some for a moment, others for a lifetime. Nancy Young's *Breyer Molds & Models* chronicles the history of Breyer to date, and it is my pleasure to share here a few memories of people, places, and events that I regard as mileposts along my Breyer journey, from 1965, when I first hired on with the company in an official capacity, to 1995, when my time with Breyer came to an end.

Sam Stone had and held the ultimate vision: People love horses! How did he come by this notion? Was it Saturday afternoons with matinee idols such as Roy Rogers and Trigger, Gene Autry and Champion? Dad and I used to enjoy them so much! Was it his daughter Jo's riding lessons, or the trip to the Chief Mountain Ranch in Montana? Or was it the Woolworth's buyer's phone call, "The horses are selling, make more horses!" that convinced him?

We held our board of directors meetings over lunch at a restaurant called Petricca's, not far from the Breyer Molding Company plant in Chicago. Chuck Schiff, the early Breyer missionary, loved to regale us with stories of his sales trips—the times that buyers canceled appointments, wanted ceramic not plastic, complained that the packaging was wrong, the prices too high, not high enough . . . I didn't appreciate it much then, but I understand it now.

Getting the product into stores is an often forgotten but very important process. Two independent sales leaders, both gone now, helped Breyer with this work in the early days. Californian Jules Unger, whose son Henry would create the Brenda Breyer doll years later, was known by almost everyone in the "trade" west of the Rockies. Jules pulled, pushed, and shoved Breyer into the toy industry, where it flourishes to this day. Chicagoan Sam Barth was responsible for selling to national mail-order accounts like Sears. As gentle a man as Jules was tough, Sam taught me a lot about selling and about the value of Breyer, too.

His tutelage would eventually pay off. The year was 1967. Breyer sales were lackluster and declining. The activity in the custom-molding business of Breyer Molding Company had always taken precedence over the Breyer Animal Creations division, but now Sam Stone and Chuck Schiff were actually discussing discontinuing production of the horses and other animals. I raised my hand, volunteered to promote the line, and never looked back. Willie Nelson's "On the Road Again" could have been my theme song. During those early years my family often accompanied me on trips to promote sales of Breyer models. First it was my wife Mary Ellen, son Peter, daughter Missy, and our beagle, Maggie. (Once we left Maggie tied to a fence post in Charlotte, North Carolina, traveled quite a distance before realizing our mistake, and turned back to retrieve her.) Then came sons John, Paul, and Justin. The station wagon was overflowing with children and model horses. Sales too began to grow, after much hard work. Often the children participated in Breyer advertising, and eventually Missy became the model for Bitsy Breyer.

For a time, finding a selection of Breyer in retail stores remained difficult. Letters poured into Breyer from enthusiastic consumers, asking "Where can I buy your horses?" Two companies pioneered a response to that need and continue today among dozens of others. Mission Supply House, originally of Floral City, Florida, established in 1954, began selling Breyers mail-order in the late 1960s. Bentley Sales Company, of Des Plaines, Illinois, was founded in 1969 in order to sell Breyers by mail. Both companies are a testament to capitalism at work!

Above all, in spite of what many may think, Breyer is a business: creating, manufacturing, distributing, and selling a product that generates profit. When I first started selling Breyer models, they were considered to be novelties or souvenirs or toys. Serious collecting, model showing, repainting and remaking—these were concepts Breyer never imagined in the early days. I was first made aware of the model-horse hobby by some remarkable young women who were helping the hobby grow. Two of them were sisters, Sandra and Karen Baehr, who published a little newsletter called *Plastic Horse World* in the late 1960s and early 1970s. The late Marney Walerius too helped introduced me to this Breyer hobby I had never known about. Throughout the following years, plagued with diabetes, Marney continued to contribute ideas and enthusiasm to the Breyer journey and was probably best known for the Model Horse Congress shows of the 1970s and 1980s. Near the end of her lifetime, at BreyerFest 1990 in Lexington, Kentucky, the company presented Marney with a special one-of-a-kind black and white Saddlebred Weanling model. Exhausted by heat and the ramblings of the day, she almost missed this great surprise. The standing ovation she received from fellow collectors and friends that night touched us all.

Just About Horses, created in the mid-1970s as a free newsletter distributed by Breyer to collectors, has grown into a magazine. It was born to respond to the many questions the company received daily from passionate horse-lovers and collectors. How we enjoyed those wonderful *Horsetails* cartoons by Richard Lewis (who was active in Breyer marketing with his wife, Diane) published in many early issues, as well as the hundreds of contributions from subscribers over the years.

Many of the early subscribers were youngsters who have now grown to adulthood and had children of their own, with whom they share their love of horses and the fun of Breyer collecting.

Who among all the participants in the Breyer tradition most understood and had the greatest empathy for the children that love horses? Marguerite Henry showed and expressed this common thread best in story after story as she followed her own trail. Breyer's efforts to make a model of Marguerite's most famous and beloved character, "Misty" of Chincoteague, first brought me in contact with this renowned author. I was so fearful of failure. Marguerite did not acknowledge receipt of those very first samples of the model. Was my attempt at licensing over before it began? Fortunately not—all we had to do was change the model's pinto pattern, which we hadn't gotten right! We went on to create models of most of the equine characters in Marguerite's many stories. Her book *Our First Pony* holds particular meaning for me. I asked her one day to write a pony story, an original, to accompany a set of Breyer models. When the book appeared, what a surprise it was to find that the story concerned a real pony well known to me, my son's pony "Midge," and that it took place on a real farm, our family farm in Wisconsin! Other highlights in my memories of Marguerite include the making of the feature film *King of the Wind*, which unfortunately was never distributed, and the establishment of the Misty of Chincoteague Foundation to preserve the island farm where "Misty" was raised. What fun Marguerite and I had dreaming and scheming on my visits to her hilltop home in Rancho Santa Fe, California!

It was also thanks to Marguerite that I met another character from my Breyer story: Neil Ul Breaslain, Spanish Mustanger from the Cayuse Ranch, Oshoto, Wyoming. I first met Neil at the ranch, also called the True Blood Reserve. Bob Brislawn was the hero of Marguerite's book *San Domingo, the Medicine Hat Stallion*, and this was his son, striding up the canyon trail, shoulder-length red hair and cape flowing in the prairie wind. In that moment Neil made a lasting impression, speaking the Celtic language and dressed in the old Irish way. That night under the stars, we showed Marguerite's film *The Making of a Book* to an avid audience of mustangers gathered at the ranch for the annual meeting of the Spanish Mustang Registry. Neil and I later collaborated on a first-person biography of Bob and his horses, which may yet be published.

I crossed paths with plenty of other characters, too, on my Breyer journey. Otha Calvert was a small man in stature, raised on an Iowa farm. We hit it off and had a good time on his several trips to the Breyer factory to supervise the production of special-run hog models. Otha sold them to his fellow farmers. He is gone now, and I miss his phone calls—"Hey, remember me? Are you ready to make a Breyer chicken yet?"

A guy from Indiana named Mel Riegsecker hitched Breyer to wheeled vehicles. Those first Riegsecker products of the mid-1980s—the flocked Breyer horses, many with intricate leather harnesses and hand-made buggies and wagons—were created in his garage. You should see his flourishing crafts business now!

And of course there were and are the artists. In this reminiscence I must devote a special place to them, for their contributions form the heart of the Breyer tradition. The creation of Breyer models is an art form. Capturing the magic and spirit of living creatures in clay is the richest expression of that art.

Among all the artists who have created Breyer models over the decades, Chris Hess stands out as the most prolific and productive. He created well over 100 Breyer molds and engineered many more, starting with the Western Horse back in 1950. Chris's talents were unique. He was the only one who could take an idea, draft it on paper, sculpt the model, make the patterns, cast the mold, and assemble it into a working tool for plastic injection-molding. Chris is gone now, but fond memories of him will always remain with me—memories of the days discussing projects in his dusty shop in Chicago, accompanied by Bud, Chris's son; memories of our trips together to many different parts of the country to view the living horses of Chris's art . . . and "Benji," the movie dog, too!

I can't mention Chris Hess without acknowledging as well two other craftsmen from the early days, Paul Olson and Gordon Johnson. These men's artistry, although technical rather than aesthetic, was just as essential to the life of Breyer. Paul, an industrial pattern maker with a Chicago company founded by his father, the Englewood Pattern Company, contracted his services to Breyer Animal Creations starting in 1950. He was needed to do something Chris couldn't do—design and create the cooling, soaking, and cementing fixtures for bonding the two halves of the Western Horse models together after molding. He made similar fixtures for every Breyer Animal Creations mold until the later 1980s. Gordy Johnson, a tool engineer, hired on with Breyer in the early to mid 1950s and remained until Breyer Molding Company was liquidated in January 1986. Gordy figured out how all the pieces of the molding equipment would fit together—how big the cavities in the injection molds would be, how they would seat onto the mold bases, how the melted plastic would flow into the molds, and so on—and he supervised all the machining to make the system work. Recently I had the pleasure of meeting up with Paul and Gordy again in Chicago. Eagerly they shared their memories of the old days, both of them proud of their contributions to the art of Breyer.

The Proud Arabian Mare and Foal . . . both offspring of a controversy early in Breyer's history. Their creator, Maureen Love Calvert, the Hagen-Renaker company's primary equine sculptor, remained unknown to us and unapproachable for so many years, even after the two companies signed an agreement allowing Breyer to issue many of her horses in plastic. I had the privilege of meeting Maureen at the 1994 West Coast Model Horse Collector's Jamboree. What a love affair Breyer collectors have had with Maureen's creations!

And with those of the famous Edward Marshall Boehm, another figure from Breyer's early history. Years later, in the early 1970s, came Marv Morin, Native American from Montana, hell-bent on self-destruction but a fine artist. His Saddlebred Weanling mold is still a favorite today.

The introduction of the Artist Series in 1984 gave Breyer an opportunity to present the styles of several more American artists. For me, each of their contributions evokes a tale of its own, a passage in the Breyer tradition. What special memories I have of the late Rich Rudish, "Sham's" creator—of evening trail rides on Rich's Arabs in the San Bernardino Mountains of Southern California. "Buckshot," created by Bob Scriver, reminds me of trips to Browning, Montana, and the Spanish Mustang from Trego trailered to Bob's studio as a model. I often wonder what happened to the little bobcat kit that scurried about in Bob's museum. Did he ever run free in that beautiful mountain countryside? (And how collectible are those limited-edition brass belt buckles that Bob and I created in 1984 for the Fort Benton Jaycees and the Cut Bank Chamber of Commerce?) Summer days in upstate New York at Jeanne Mellin Herrick's studio, surrounded by purebred "old-time" Morgan horses and lush green valleys—Jeanne, a breeder, show trainer, and judge, brought the qualities of the professional horseperson to her artworks, such as Breyer's "Sherman Morgan."

With Rowland Cheney, creator of the Messenger Series models celebrating the wild Kiger Mustangs of southeast Oregon, I shared television interviews and excursions into the Steens Mountain mustang area. At BreyerFest I met Josh Warburton, Rowland's colleague in the effort to preserve the Kigers. Folks call Josh the caretaker in honor of his work in behalf of these magnificent animals. Following him through the rugged mustang country on hands and knees with binoculars and spotting scope, I hoped to see the stallion Mesteño but never did. But just being there was enough.

Artists from the East and West, North and South—each corner of the country holds memories for me that could fill a book. Francis Eustis, draft-horse fancier from Ohio; Martha White, Welsh aficionado from Texas; the elusive Kitty Cantrell from California; Pam Talley Stoneburner of Virginia, who especially loved quarter horses. In Arizona's Valley of the Sun, Kathleen Moody combines horse art with child rearing. Bless her patience and her skill. So easy to spot the models sculpted by Kathleen, a blending of the real and the fanciful.

The story doesn't end. In 1984 the Breyer Animal Creations division of the Breyer Molding Company of Chicago, Illinois, was purchased by Reeves International, Inc., of Pequannock, New Jersey, and today, under Reeves's direction, Breyer produces more models than ever before. An aura of pride and spirit lives on with Breyer!

The Breyer road leads here, there, and everywhere. For those of you that shared with me a tale or two along this journey but find it untold here, please forgive me. There have been hundreds of you along the way—friends, familiar faces, and fans of Breyer. Enjoy each page of this book and your personal memories. Know that I am grateful to each of you and count myself lucky knowing we shared that special time together. And as ol' Will would say, "We are just here for a spell and pass on."

May, 1996
Upper Montclair, New Jersey

Preface

A colorful toy... A collector's joy... An authentic room decoration for every girl and boy.
  — From the boxes of Breyer rider models made in the mid-1950s

Horses are great collectors items—bought mostly by girls. They keep buying them until they complete their collection.
  —From a 1972 Breyer Showcase Assortment wholesale order form

Plastic horses. Not porcelain, not ceramic, not carved wood or cast iron. Nothing respectable, nothing evocative of the antique, nothing with a foot wedged in the door of Art. Plastic. It is a term of abuse in modern society. ("That politician is totally plastic!") Yet for the collector of Breyer models, the medium of her cherished *objets*, far from being an aesthetic drawback (though it may be a social one), is an essential ingredient of their allure. There is something inexpressibly charming about a plastic horse. Indeed the first thing many a Breyer collector does upon acquiring a new model is to plunge her nose into the box and take deep whiffs of that mystical perfume of cellulose acetate.

Breyer plastic horses and other animals have populated the toy boxes of America for decades, and many of their young owners retain or rekindle their interest in collecting as they become adults and have families of their own. Breyer enthusiasts range in age from 5 to 95 and boast (or conceal) herds numbering anywhere from a few pieces to a few thousand. Empty shelves are not a common problem in Breyer households. I have visited homes in which the very concept of an unoccupied horizontal surface had been lost. While some collectors specialize, limiting themselves to models of certain breeds or colors or molds or scales, many others are generalists, acquiring whatever grabs their fancy (most of it does). And not a few collectors are unrepentant completists, determined to acquire at least one example of every model ever issued by Breyer Animal Creations. In many cases, people begin their collecting careers as specialists but gradually succumb to generalism and even completism as they learn to admire other categories of models and lose their sense of how many plastic horses are too many.

Breyer collecting is just one facet of the flourishing model-horse hobby, an international community of equine miniaturists brought together by magazines and newsletters, model-horse events such as BreyerFest in Kentucky, and on-line forums such as the Internet model-horse mailing list, nicknamed the Haynet. Hobby activities include not only collecting factory-finish models of various brands and media but also customizing models, creating original equine sculptures, crafting miniature tack and other equipment, and competing in photo shows held by mail and in live shows held at private homes and community halls across the land. Hobbyists also share a love of real horses—many people own and show the real McCoy as well as the model variety—and knowledge of the horse world is widely cultivated in the pursuit of model-horse realism.

But undoubtedly the most pervasive activity in the model-horse hobby is Breyer collecting. And along with the herds of Breyer models there grows a craving for knowledge about them. When were they issued? What are their names and model numbers? How do they vary in color or mold? What real horses do they represent? Who sculpted them? In the years since the first edition of this book appeared, my fellow collectors have continually amazed me by their quest for detailed information. It is a quest that I share, and *Breyer Molds & Models* is my ongoing record of what I discover and what others teach me. This fourth edition of the book covers everything that the previous, self-published editions covered and much more. New entries have been added for the 1994 and 1995 models, and many entries on older models have been revised and expanded in light of newly unearthed information. In the Traditionals section particularly, numerous entries on topics of interest have been expanded or newly added in alphabetical order to give the book the utility of an encyclopedia: entries on Commemorative Editions, Decorators, Display Boxes, Display Units, Flocked Models, Limited Editions, Presentation Collection, Riegseckers Models, Showcase Collection, Special Runs, Woodgrains, and other subjects provide background discussion as well as cross-references to individual models.

Nonetheless, despite its Percheron proportions, the book is not yet complete and may never be. Not only does Breyer Animal Creations continue to introduce new models each year—more now than ever before—but the long and often murky history of older models continues to come to light. There are many Breyer mysteries yet to be solved and surprises yet to be discovered. The more I learn about Breyers, the more I realize I will never know everything. The instant I get a tad smug, along comes a banana peel with my name on it—another obscure special run I had never heard of, another striking color variation of a model I thought I had pegged, another old magazine ad or Breyer box or price list that turns my latest theory to compost. Consequently, although this book is as comprehensive and accurate as I could make it with regard to catalog runs and special runs 1950-95, I do not claim that it is exhaustive or infallible. If something is not mentioned in these pages, this by no means implies that it doesn't exist or is a fake. I should also note here that while I do mention a few test-color and one-of-a-kind pieces in the course of discussion, I have made no attempt to provide a catalog of these types of models and do not plan to do so in the future.

This is a project for someone more interested in and knowledgeable about such models than I am. Nor does this book cover the various lines of leather tack, wooden stables and jumps, and other accessories that Breyer has issued since the 1970s. I hope eventually to catalog these items, either in a future edition of this book or in a separate publication.

Molds and Models This book is entitled *Breyer Molds & Models*. What is the difference between a mold and a model? A "mold" strictly speaking is a metal form into which melted plastic is injected to produce a plastic figure of a particular shape. So when collectors speak of the "mold" of a model, they mean *its particular shape, regardless of its color.* A "model" is *a particular shape in a particular color.* If two horses differ either in mold or in color, they are different models. For example, the alabaster Running Stallion and the charcoal Running Stallion are different models because they are different colors, though they are the same mold. The alabaster Running Stallion and the alabaster Fighting Stallion are different models because they are different molds, though they are the same color. The difference between "mold" and "model" is important to collectors for the reason that over the years Breyer has produced more than one model from nearly all of its molds. To this day the company regularly makes "new" models by issuing new colors (and often new names) on molds that have been in existence for years. Indeed, among the annual bonanzas of new models, typically only a few are new molds. There is good reason for this practice. The creation of metal injection-molds is a complicated and expensive process, so it only makes sense for Breyer to get as much use as it can from them by painting the molded figures in a variety of colors.

Regular Runs and Special Runs Also important to collectors is the distinction between "regular-run," or as I call them, "catalog-run" models on the one hand and "special-run" models on the other. A regular or catalog run is a model advertised in Breyer's annual catalog and sold through any Breyer retailer who wishes to offer it. (For discussion of the slight difference between "regular run" and "catalog run" as I define these terms, see Abbreviations, Symbols, & Terms below.) A special run is a model painted in a special-order color and sold as an exclusive at model-horse events or through selected retail outlets, such as department-store holiday catalogs. Overruns or leftovers of specials are, however, sometimes sold through retailers other than the one that ordered the special. Special runs are generally not advertised in Breyer catalogs and are produced in much smaller quantities than catalog runs.

Scales Another basic fact about Breyer models is that they come in various sizes or scales. To put the matter oversimply, Breyers come in five different scales, four of them pertaining to realistic molds. From largest to smallest, the four realistic scales are the Traditional (averaging roughly 8" or 9" at the eartips), which is the original scale; Classic (roughly 6"), introduced in 1973; Little Bits (roughly 4.5"), introduced late in 1983; and Stablemates (roughly 2.75"), introduced in 1975. The Traditional and Classic scales might more accurately be called scale groups since the models included in them vary somewhat in scale. The fifth scale, introduced in 1995, is that of the Dapples horses, a line of children's fantasy-style models that fall between the Traditionals and Classics in size.

In a sense, the scale names just given are collectors' fictions; the scales per se have no "official" names. Breyer company catalogs that explicitly identify scales by means of "size charts"—namely, the catalogs for 1985 and 1989 on—typically designate the scales by reference to "series" of models: the Traditional Series, Classic Series, and so on. This designation system works well for the Stablemates, Little Bits, and Dapples scales, which comprise all and only the models in the series of those names. It works less well for the Traditional scale because the Traditional Series includes some models, such as the Bucking Bronco, that are indisputably Classic scale. The system founders on the Classic scale, the majority of whose models are not part of the Classic Series and never even had the term "Classic" in their names. Many of these closet Classics, such as the U.S.E.T. and Black Stallion Returns sets, regularly appeared intermingled with sets of Traditional-scale pieces on Breyer catalog pages headed simply "Gift Sets." In 1995, this irregular but at least familiar landscape of scales and series changed drastically. The names "Classic" and "Little Bits" disappeared altogether from the Breyer

The scales of realistic Breyer models, from smallest to largest Stablemate, Little Bit, Classic, and Traditional

catalog, these series of models (but not the molds) having been discontinued. The catalog's size chart designates what collectors think of as the Classic scale by reference to the B Ranch and Messenger Series, the Little Bits scale by reference to The Saddle Club, and the Stablemates scale by reference to Stablemates and The Saddle Club. The "Gift Set" pages, with their commingling of Classics and Traditionals, are still there, with a couple of Little Bits tossed in.

In the interest of sanity, this edition of *Breyer Molds & Models*, like the previous editions, sticks to the long-standing scale names, collectors' fictions though they be. Both the photo and the text portions of the book are divided into sections covering the five different scales of horses, as well as sections on riders and other animals. A General Note at the beginning of each text section provides background on the given scale or group of models. Rectifying previous editions, the present book takes a strict view of scales: the listings for the (so to speak) "Traditional-Series Classics"—Bucking Bronco, "Hobo," Polo Pony, and Rearing Stallion—have been moved into the Classics section, and Performing "Misty" has been put into the Little Bits section. The Dapples section, which is new, has been inserted after the Stablemates section to avoid disrupting the customary sequence of scales with a group of pieces that may not be of compelling interest to many collectors.

Organization of the Entries Within each section of the book, all models of the given scale or group are listed alphabetically by name. Model names are cross-referenced to the mold name (which is followed by a dash and the symbol ♞). In this book, the mold name is usually the same as the name of the earliest model made from the mold. The mold-name symbol is immediately followed by basic information on the mold, such as gender, pose, sculptor, and catalog-run production dates. (These dates combine the dates of all the catalog-run models made from the mold.) Below this information, all the models of the given mold are again listed by name—first the catalog-run models and sets, then the special runs—and full information is given for each. Model names preceded by the dingbat ♠ (which indicates catalog runs) are full names as shown in Breyer dealer catalogs and collector manuals. A model name preceded by the dingbat ♤ (which indicates special runs) is either just the mold name or else the name, if there was one, by which the special was advertised. At the end of the model entries for each mold come notes on the mold, which discuss such topics as mold variations, unusual mold features such as brands, and points of interest in the mold's history. The last note for each mold identifies the mold's copyright stamps and other mold marks. Dates and histories of the various marks are provided in the Mold Marks section in the Appendix near the end of the book.

Sources Catalog-run models have been recorded in Breyer dealer catalogs and price lists published by Breyer since the 1950s and in collector's manuals published by the company since 1968. I have compiled my basic information on catalog runs from these company publications. No such systematic Breyer company documentation exists for special-run models. I have gathered information on specials from department store holiday catalogs, mail-order company fliers, Breyer's *Just About Horses* magazine, Breyer company computer printouts, Breyer personnel, and the publications and personal communications of collectors. My citations of Mr. Peter Stone refer to him as "Breyer executive" in cases where he provided information prior to leaving Breyer in October 1995 and as "former Breyer executive" in cases where he provided information after that time. My citations of published hobby sources generally give the last name of the author (or authors) and the date of her (or their) publication, thus: Gutierrez 1989; DeFeyter and Luther 1991. Full information on published sources cited in my text, as well as a full listing and discussion of Breyer company publications, is provided in the References section at the end of this book.

Dates Date spans given in this book are inclusive. For example, the date span "1968-75" means that the model was produced in 1968 and in 1975 as well as in the intervening years. Production dates for each model are given in parentheses as the last item of the main description of the model. For models that were sold in a set as well as separately, the set is mentioned and its dates are given in square brackets immediately following the main description. Some dates in this book incorporate slashes, as for example in the date span "1961/63 - 1967." Here the slashed date "1961/63" means that the model was introduced sometime in the period 1961-63. Similarly, the date span "mid-1950s - 1958/59" indicates that the model's last year of production was either 1958 or 1959. As these examples suggest, date spans with slashed dates, as well as "fudge dates" such as "mid-1950s," are rampant in the entries for early catalog-run models. This is because Breyer evidently did not publish a catalog or even a price list every year in the 1950s and early 1960s, so in the absence of other evidence, it is impossible to give precise years for models that might have been introduced or discontinued in the noncatalog years. Slashed dates also occur in the entries for some special-run models. In these cases the slashes indicate either that I am uncertain about the precise year or that the model was announced or produced in one year but not made available to purchasers until the following year. The specific circumstances are noted in the entries for the individual models.

Although this book does not list new models and molds introduced in 1996, it does indicate the 1996 status of older models and molds. For example, a catalog-run model introduced in 1993 and still in production in 1996 is dated in this book as "1993 - current as of 1996," and the mold's catalog-run production dates (which, as noted above, combine the dates of all the catalog-run models of the mold) accordingly end with "current as of 1996." A catalog-run model introduced in 1993 but discontinued at the end of 1995 is dated "1993-95," and the mold's dates accordingly end with "-95" *if* no new catalog-run model of the mold was introduced in 1996. But if a new catalog-run model of that mold was introduced in 1996, the mold is dated to 1996 even though the new 1996 model itself is not listed. (The 1996 dating takes the form "current as of 1996" if the mold was also in production in 1995; otherwise the dating takes the form "1996," or "1996-," depending on whether the new 1996 model is or is not limited to 1996 production.)

Characteristic of the Models The gaits, colors, and genders of Breyer models are in many cases debatable. Is Classic "Keen" cantering or walking? Was any real grulla horse ever colored like Breyer's "Rarin' To Go," whose brown dorsal "stripe" is so wide that it looks more like the result of a nice roll in the manure? What can it mean to label "Pluto" a stallion when he has nary a vestige of genital anatomy? In view of these ambiguities, not to mention the limitations of my own horse knowledge, I wish to stress that the designations of gaits, colors, and genders in this book are not meant to be final or to carry the authority of a show judge. They are intended merely to help identify the models. My designations derive from several sources: Breyer's own descriptions, common usage in the hobby, horse reference books, consultation with fellow collectors, and a good dose of ad hoc invention, a recourse especially useful in the color department.

Values What are second-hand Breyer models worth? New collectors tend to ask this question as though experienced hobbyists were privy to mysterious stone tablets engraved with The Real True Values. Experienced collectors, attempting to correct this notion, often reply, "A model is worth what you are willing to pay for it." While perhaps not hugely helpful to the novice, this epigram aptly conveys that Breyer values are at bottom a subjective matter—a matter of obsession with toy plastic ponies—and that the most important question when contemplating giving up a portion of your paycheck for such an item is "What is it worth *to me?*" But value is also a community question, a question of how much money other plastic-obsessed people think the models are worth. Knowledgeable collectors base their sense of the worth of a model on many criteria: condition (degree of damage), age, rarity, popularity, similarity to other models, quality (shading and detail of the paintwork, smoothness of the seams, etc.), equine and artistic beauty (this judgment of course varies with personal tastes), asking prices they have seen advertised in hobby magazines and on price tags at model-horse events, actual purchase prices they know of for the same or similar models, the model's original retail price, the size of the model (generally speaking, the smaller the piece, the lower the value), and the size of their own budgets. Thus value is by no means just the latest high-end asking price that sends eyebrows soaring throughout the hobby. Nor is value the same as average asking price. For one thing, averages can give a false picture when they derive from numbers that vary widely, as do model-horse asking prices. More importantly, to equate value with average asking price is to believe that only sellers' opinions of value matter, not buyers' opinions, which is ludicrous. Furthermore, asking price often exceeds purchase price, that is, the cash actually handed over. It is not uncommon for sellers to offer a below-sticker price to tempt an interested shopper, or give a discount on a purchase of several models, or accept an offer from a shopper who thinks a model is over-priced.

Condition is the most important criterion weighing into the assessment of value of a particular piece. "Condition is everything!," as Breyer collectors like to say. Collectors have the luxury of being picky since most Breyer models, even special runs, have been produced by the thousands. People unfamiliar with Breyer collectors' persnickety standards can easily misjudge condition toward the favorable side. I have even heard tales of antique dealers who assumed that scuffs and rubs (areas of missing paint), yellowing, and other defects add to the value of a Breyer, just as "distress" can add to the value of an antique table or chair. Nothing could be further from the truth. What collectors seek in a Breyer model is factory-original perfection, a condition they refer to as "mint." Defects as seemingly insignificant as a missing eartip, a heat-bloated neck, a split seam, or a handful of rubs, scratches, stains, or similar insults on the body can cut a model's value by more than a half. Moreover, collectors generally regard touch-ups of rubs and scratches as further damage to the model—anything added to the factory finish, even if it makes the horse look better, compromises his status as an original-finish piece and thus degrades his collectibility. A broken leg or tail, even if it has been mended, renders most models virtually worthless, suitable only for the custom artist's "body box."

Original retail prices, although they are perhaps not always consciously considered in second-hand transactions, play a significant role in defining the level of second-hand values. After all, plastic horses are not automobiles or archeological treasures, and if new Breyers cost $2,000 rather than $20, second-hand values would look a lot different than they do. Original retail prices for Breyer models have of course increased over the decades. For plastic adult Traditionals, retail has averaged from about $2-$3 in the 1950s to $20-$25 in 1996; for adult Classics, from about $3-$5 in the 1970s to $15-$20 in 1996; for Little Bits, from about $3.50-$5.50 in the 1980s to $8-$10 in 1995 and back to $6-$7 in 1996, thanks to Chinese manufacture; and for Stablemates, from about $1-$2 in the 1970s to $4.50-$5.50 in 1991 and down to $2.50-$3.50 in 1996, thanks to ABS plastic and Chinese manufacture since 1992. For pieces other than normal painted plastic models—flocked models, sets with handmade vehicles, and models produced in fine porcelain, ceramic, and cold-cast porcelain (resin)—original retail prices are noted in the main listings in this book.

Packaging is not important to the value of Breyers. Second-hand models are typically bought and sold without their boxes, and when the box is included, it generally adds little to the model's value. This is particularly true of the plastic-fronted yellow boxes in which most Breyers have been sold since 1986 and toward which Breyer collectors nurse bitter feelings on account of the boxes' propensity to damage the models. A model sold in such a box should be carefully wrapped to prevent staining by the box's yellow backing. A yellow box may add about $2 to the value of a special-run, Limited Edition, or Commemorative Edition piece; it adds $1 at best to the value of common regular-run models. Pre-1986 boxes add more to a model's value, about $3-$10, depending on the age, rarity, and elaborateness of the box. Pre-1986 boxes include heavy white or brown cardboard mailer cartons, some with and some without line drawings of the models printed on them (Breyer used such cartons for many models from the 1950s into the 1970s and for at least some non-horse animals into the 1990s); lighter-weight cardboard boxes with color photos of the models printed on them (used from the 1950s into the 1980s, and into the 1990s for sets); and specialty packaging such as Showcase Collection plastic cases or other exotic display boxes (used periodically in the late 1960s and the 1970s; see Display Boxes in the Traditionals section of this book for details).

The values in this book are given in the photo captions. Values are provided for discontinued models only, that is, models no longer in production by the Breyer factory and thus usually no longer available retail. (Recently discontinued models may of course linger on store shelves.) The values are given in ranges—for example, $15-$30—to allow for variations in color, finish, quality, and (for Stablemates) type of plastic, and also, most crucially, variations in condition from fair to mint. A model in *fair* condition may have a scattering of small rubs, scratches, or other flaws on the extremities (ears, nose, lower legs, hooves, and tail) and three or four pinhead-sized rubs or other flaws on the body (torso, neck, main part of the head, and upper legs). A flaw on an extremity is less serious than a flaw on the body, but no rub or similar flaw anywhere on a model in fair condition should be larger than George Washington's nose on the face of a quarter. A somewhat healthier model, in *good* condition, has fewer and smaller flaws on the extremities and no more than one or two pinhead-sized rubs or other flaws on the body. A model in *excellent* condition has no more than two or three tiny rubs or other flaws on the extremities and none on the body. A model in *mint* condition, as the term is used in this book and commonly in the model-horse hobby, has no flaws. (Note that according to this definition of "mint," a model new in its box is not necessarily mint—indeed it may be very far from mint. Breyers are notorious for emerging new from the factory with rubs, scratches, drips in the paint, riffles in the plastic, tweaked ears and nostrils, yellow stains from the box, and other defects, all of which must be reckoned into the model's value.) Proportionally, the value I assign for fair condition ranges from roughly 50 percent of mint value for the most common, least valuable models up to about 70 percent of mint value for the rarest, most valuable pieces, flaws being more forgivable in models that are harder to come by ("She's got a barrel rub, but hey, she's an SR palomino 'Lady Phase'!").

The values given in this book reflect my own sense of reasonable prices to pay. I worked the values out by grouping all the models in the book according to the number of years they were issued, the decades in which they were issued, their size (adults vs. foals, Traditionals vs. Classics, etc.), their material or finish (plastic vs. porcelain; flocked vs. painted; woograin vs. realistic, etc.), and, when known, the quantities produced. These groupings allowed me to assign comparable values to comparable models, adjusting up or down for considerations such as the popularity of the piece, unusual retail price (e.g., BreyerFest models cost more to buy new than Sears models), and similarity to other pieces (e.g., the value of the rare 1978 SR solid black Mustang is reduced by the fact that a nearly identical model, the 1993 SR black Mustang with one stocking, was issued in a sizable quantity). The result is a system of values that is, I believe, rational, consistent, and fair. The maximum value given in this book for a single model is $300. (Some sets with handmade vehicles are valued higher, on account of their high original retail prices.) The $300 figure is in line with the system of values overall and is also my personal ceiling for the purchase of a single Breyer—it is in fact more than I have ever paid for a model. Certainly there are collectors with higher ceilings. There are also many collectors who would choke at the thought of spending as much as $300 on one plastic horse-shaped object, no matter how rare. Thus I do not expect that all collectors will agree with all the values listed in this book. I would only stress that the book is intended not as a Bible of Values but as a guide, an aid for developing an independent sense of value geared to one's own circumstances and adaptable to the ever-changing world of model horses. No responsibility for monetary or trade transactions based on the values or other information in this book is accepted by the author, the publisher, or the people acknowledged in the photo credits.

Abbreviations, Symbols, & Terms

ABBREVIATIONS

ca. = circa, as in "ca.1954," meaning "around 1954"
CE = Commemorative Edition
CWP = Cantering Welsh Pony
FA = Family Arabian
FAF = Family Arabian Foal
FAM = Family Arabian Mare
FAS = Family Arabian Stallion
H-R = The Hagen-Renaker company, maker of ceramic horse and other figurines, many of whose molds Breyer issues in plastic
JAH = *Just About Horses*, the Breyer company's magazine for collectors. A citation such as "JAH 15/#3 1988 (p. 5)" refers to volume 15, issue 3, published in 1988.
LE = Limited Edition
OF = Original finish; that is, the paint job put on the model at the factory
PA = Proud Arabian

PAF = Proud Arabian Foal
PAM = Proud Arabian Mare
PAS = Proud Arabian Stallion
POA = Pony of the Americas
QH = Quarter Horse
SB = Saddlebred
SHF = Stock Horse Foal, standing
SHM = Stock Horse Mare
SHS = Stock Horse Stallion
SR = special run

SYMBOLS

🐴 = A mold counted in the Mold Totals table in this book.
🐴 = A catalog-run model counted in the Model Totals table in this book.
🐴 = A special-run model counted in the Model Totals table.
• = A model not counted in the Model Totals table, either because it is counted by another name (e.g., "Misty" Gift Set #2055 is not counted because the model in this set is counted as "Misty" #20) or because it probably does not exist.
/ = In quotations, a slash flanked by spaces indicates a line break or space break in the source text. For example, in "1995 Limited Edition / Limited to 1995 Orders / Princess Of Arabia / Princess Brenda, Poised . . . ," the slashes indicate that the separated phrases occur on different lines on the box-sticker from which the quote is taken. The slashes themselves do not appear in the source text. In this book, such slashes are generally used only to make the quotation comprehensible in the absence of punctuation in the source text; not every line or space break in the source is indicated. For the use of slashes in dates, see the discussion of dates above in the Preface.

TERMS

Alabaster— Breyer's usual term for white models. Typically such models have gray mane and tail and gray shading, but some have white mane and tail. The term "alabaster" first occurs in the 1963 Breyer catalog, where it is used for the Running Mare and Foal and the Fighting and Rearing stallions. Breyer was not consistent in its use of this term, sometimes using the word "white" for the same color. The uses of these terms in this book do not necessarily follow the Breyer catalogs.

Bald face—In this book, this term is used fairly loosely to refer to a white area, usually unstenciled, covering most or all of the model's face. The white may extend down the sides of the face or be restricted to the frontal plane. Bald faces are unstenciled unless stenciling is specified; blazes, stripes, and stars on the other hand are always stenciled.

Bay—In normal horse parlance, a bay horse is brown with a black mane and tail *and* black on the legs, at least on the knees and hocks. Breyer is notorious for its "bays" that have no black on the legs; typically these are older models. This book follows traditional Breyer usage in calling brown horses with black manes and tails "bay" whether or not they have any black on the legs.

Catalog—Breyer company dealer catalog (unless otherwise specified, e.g., as Sears or Penney's holiday catalog). For a full list and description of catalogs, see the References section at the end of this book.

Catalog run—A model listed in Breyer dealer catalogs and collector's manuals. Thus "catalog run" is a general term covering regular runs, Limited Editions, and all but one of the Commemorative Editions.

Commemorative Edition—A model with special paint detailing, produced only for one year in a pre-announced limited quantity. All CE models but the first have been listed in Breyer catalogs and manuals. See Commemorative Editions below in the Traditionals section for further discussion and a full listing of CE models.

Glossy—Shiny factory finish created by a coating of clear varnish over the painted model. This finish typically has a silky smooth feel and a sparkling shine. Most glossy models are from the 1950s and 1960s. See Finishes in the Appendix near the end of this book for further discussion.

Limited Edition—A model advertised in Breyer catalogs and manuals as a Limited Edition. Most LEs have no special paint detailing but are produced only for one year and come in boxes with a "Limited Edition" label. See Limited Editions below in the Traditionals section for further discussion and a full listing of LE models.

Manual—Breyer company collector's manual. These are the small pamphlets found in the boxes with new models. For a full list and description of manuals, see the References section at the end of this book.

Matte—Non-shiny factory finish, which can be smooth or textured. Even though it is not actually shiny, matte finish can have a lot of sheen, and the line between it and semigloss finish (see below) is very indefinite. Every collector, it seems, draws the line differently, and some collectors use the term "matte" as a general term meaning simply "non-glossy" (non-varnished), without regard to the nuance of semigloss. To make matters worse, the degree of sheen or shine varies greatly from model to model, so it is very difficult to accurately characterize a given run of models as being matte as opposed to semigloss, or vice versa. The entries in this book specify finish on the basis of particular specimens I have seen or heard about. But because finish is so variable, and because I have seen only a minuscule fraction of Breyers ever made, my specifications of finish emphatically do not mean that a different finish was not issued on any specimens in the run in question. See Finishes in the Appendix near the end of this book for further discussion.

Model—This term has two senses, specific and generic. Specifically, a model is an individual specimen, such as this particular bay "Halla" #63 clutched in your right hand. In this sense, your "Halla" #63 and your pal Susie Creamcheese's "Halla" #63 are different models. Generically, a model is a production run of specimens of the same shape and color. In this sense your and Susie's "Halla" #63s are the same model. One could say without contradiction, "Breyer made one million models last year" and "Breyer made forty models last year."

Mold—A mold strictly speaking is a metal form into which melted plastic is injected to produce a plastic figure of a particular shape. Derivatively, when collectors speak of the "mold" of a model, they mean its particular shape regardless of its color. Thus, a Stock Horse Stallion in bay and a Stock Horse Stallion in buckskin are the same mold.

Points—Mane, tail, and lower legs (knees and hocks only in the case of horses with stockings). This is a simplified definition pertaining only to Breyers in the listings in this book. In reference to real horses, "points" often includes nose and eartips as well as mane, tail, and lower legs.

Price list—Breyer company price list. These are distributed to dealers each year along with Breyer dealer catalogs. For a full list and description of price lists, see the References section at the end of this book.

Regular run—All models listed in Breyer catalogs, manuals, and price lists except for CEs and LEs.

Semigloss—Shiny factory finish due to shiny paint or plastic. Semigloss models can be nearly as shiny as true glossies, but the shine of a semigloss model is from the paint or the plastic itself, not from an added varnish coating. Semigloss finish can have a smooth or textured look and feel. See Finishes in the Appendix near the end of this book for further discussion.

Special run—Models painted in special-order colors, produced in limited quantities for sale as exclusives at model-horse events or through mail-order companies, toy stores, and department store holiday catalogs. Special runs (SRs) are generally not listed in Breyer catalogs or manuals. For further discussion see Special Runs below in the Traditionals section.

Stenciled—Created by means of a paint mask. The white areas on Breyer models (blazes, pinto patterns, etc.) are often created by placing a metal mask over the area of unpainted white plastic that is to be kept white while paint is airbrushed onto the model. The resulting white area has a more or less crisp and well-defined outline. Unstenciled white areas have a vaguer, more gradual outline. See Production Process in the Appendix near the end of this book for further discussion.

Stockings—In this book this term is used loosely to refer to white on the lower legs without reference to the height of the white area. Thus a "stocking" may cover only the pastern or may reach onto the knee or hock.

Test color—A trial model painted by Breyer to test out an idea for a color on a new regular run or SR. Test-color models are produced either as one-of-a-kind pieces or in small runs ("test runs") of a few pieces. Test-color models are often shown in Breyer catalogs in the first year of issue of a new model, and they sometimes differ in detail from the models produced for sale. In this book, test-color models are not listed systematically but are occasionally mentioned. See Production Process in the Appendix near the end of this book for further discussion.

Breyer Mold Totals

1950 - 1995

NOTE: In this table, mold variations—for instance, the foreleg-raised and foreleg-down versions of the Stock Horse Mare—are counted as the same mold. For a full list of such variations see Mold Variations in the Appendix near the end of this book; for details, see the notes for the individual molds in the main sections of the book.

HORSES:

Traditional horse molds:	91
Classic horse molds:	39
Little Bits horse molds:	8
Stablemates horse molds:	16
Dapples horse molds:	5
Total horse molds:	159

RIDERS:

Hard-plastic rider molds (1950s):	6
Soft or jointed plastic rider molds:	6
Total rider molds:	12

OTHER ANIMALS:

cattle molds:	10
hog molds:	1
dog molds:	8
cat molds:	1
donkey and mule molds:	3
wildlife molds:	15
Total other animal molds:	38

GRAND TOTAL BREYER MOLDS: 209

Breyer Model Totals

1950 - 1995

NOTE: In this table, variations of color, finish, and mold are counted as the same model. For instance, #96 honey sorrel Shires with blaze and with bald face are counted as a single model, as are #5 palomino Family Arabian Mares in matte and in glossy, #227 sorrel Stock Horse Mares with foreleg raised and with foreleg down, and so forth. Models that are identical to each other but have different names or numbers—for example, Clydesdale Mare #83 and the mare in the #8384 Clydesdale Gift Set—are also counted as the same model. The count of catalog runs includes regular runs, Limited Editions, and all but one of the Commemorative Editions. The count of special runs includes the 1989 Commemorative Edition.

Rider dolls are counted as different models if they wear different outfits, even if the dolls themselves are identical.

Catalog Runs

HORSES:

Traditional catalog runs:	406
Classic catalog runs:	113
Little Bits catalog runs:	39
Stablemates catalog runs:	67
Dapples catalog runs:	5
Total catalog-run horses:	630

RIDERS:

Hard-plastic catalog runs (1950s):	10
Soft or jointed plastic catalog runs:	27
Total catalog-run riders:	37

OTHER ANIMALS:

cattle catalog runs:	25
hog catalog runs:	1
dog catalog runs:	18
cat catalog runs:	4
donkey and mule catalog runs:	6
wildlife catalog runs:	28
Total other animal catalog runs:	82

TOTAL CATALOG RUNS: 749

Special Runs

HORSES:

Traditional special runs:	326
Classic special runs:	76
Little Bits special runs:	22
Stablemates special runs:	66
Dapples special runs:	0
Total special-run horses:	490

RIDERS:

Hard-plastic special runs (1950s):	0
Soft or jointed plastic special runs:	9
Total special-run riders:	9

OTHER ANIMALS:

cattle special runs:	13
hog special runs:	3
dog special runs:	1
cat special runs:	0
donkey and mule special runs:	6
wildlife special runs:	3
Total other animal special runs:	26

TOTAL SPECIAL RUNS: 525

GRAND TOTAL BREYER MODELS: 1,274

HORSES - TRADITIONALS

Action Stock Horse Foal *text p. 145*

Action American Appaloosa Stock Horse Foal #238, gray blanket appaloosa with solid face. Fair to mint condition: $5-$12.

Action Appaloosa Foal #810, red leopard appaloosa. Fair to mint condition: $5-$12.

Action Stock Horse Foal SR, bay. *Model courtesy of Heather Wells.* Fair to mint condition: $13-$22.

Chestnut Stock Horse Foal #236, red sorrel. Fair to mint condition: $8-$15.

Action Stock Horse Foal SR, bay peppercorn leopard appaloosa. Fair to mint condition: $10-$17.

Action American Buckskin Stock Horse Foal #225. *Model courtesy of Joy Sheesley.* Fair to mint condition: $5-$12.

"Cricket" Quarter Horse Foal #934, chestnut. Still available retail in 1996.

Action Stock Horse Foal SR, black paint. Fair to mint condition: $8-$15.

Action Stock Horse Foal SR, buckskin. Fair to mint condition: $8-$15.

Action Stock Horse Foal SR, pale yellow dun. Fair to mint condition: $10-$17.

Action American Paint Horse Foal #237, bay paint. *Model courtesy of Heather Wells.* Fair to mint condition: $5-$12.

"Sunny" Action Foal #891, yellow dun. Fair to mint condition: $5-$12.

"Adios" text pp. 145-147

"Adios" Famous Standardbred #50, dark bay. Fair to mint condition: $12-$25. For the Presentation Collection edition (on base) add $50.

"Clayton" Quarter Horse #911, dappled palomino, darker and lighter color variations. Still available retail in 1996.

"Mesa" The Quarter Horse #853, dark mahogany bay. Fair to mint condition: $15-$30.

Quarter Horse Stallion #830, blue roan. Fair to mint condition: $20-$35.

"Rough 'N' Ready" Quarter Horse #885, pale yellow dun. Fair to mint condition: $12-$25.

Standing Quarter Horse Stallion #705, apricot dun. Fair to mint condition: $15-$30.

"Yellow Mount" Famous Paint Horse #51, chestnut paint, versions with and without forearm spot. Fair to mint condition: $12-$25. For the Presentation Collection edition (on base) add $50.

Breyer Rider Gift Set #3095, palomino horse and his box. *Model courtesy of Sheryl Leisure.* Fair to mint condition: $220-$300.

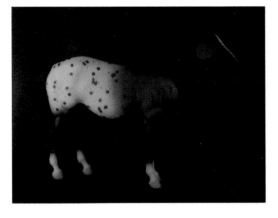

"Adios" SR, bay blanket appaloosa. Fair to mint condition: $25-$40.

"Adios" SR, buckskin. Fair to mint condition: $145-$200.

"Adios" SR #410151, dapple gray. Fair to mint condition: $40-$60.

"Adios" SR, unpainted white. Fair to mint condition: $10-$20.

Belgian text pp. 148-149

Belgian #92, smoke. Note the eyewhites on th specimen. *Model courtesy of Heather Wells.* Fair mint condition: $40-$60.

"Adios" SR #410251, palomino. Fair to mint condition: $35-$55.

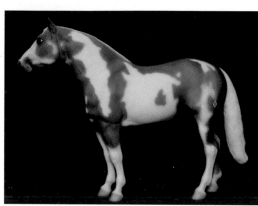

"Mego" SR #707595, palomino paint. Fair to mint condition: $35-$55.

Not shown:
"Adios" SR black. Fair to mint condition: $70-$100.

"Adios" SR #51-1, red chestnut. *Model and photo courtesy of Stephanie Macejko / Reeves International.* Fair to mint condition: $100-$140.

"Aristocrat" text pp. 147-148

Belgian #93, dapple gray. *Top,* a typical dapple gray; *model courtesy of Sheryl Leisure. Bottom,* black dapple variation; *model courtesy of Heather Wells.* Fair to mint condition: $80-$115, black dapple $100-$140.

Belgian #94, chestnut. *Model courtesy of Sheryl Leisure.* Fair to mint condition: $12-$25.

"Adios" SR, red dun semi-leopard appaloosa. Fair to mint condition: $25-$40.

"Aristocrat" Champion Hackney #496, dark reddish bay. Still available retail in 1996.

Belgian #992, woodgrain. *Model courtesy of Heather Wells.* Fair to mint condition: $100-$140.

Belgian SR, black, blue tail ribbon with white criss-crosses. *Model courtesy of Heather Wells.* Fair to mint condition: $40-$60.

"Goliath" The American Cream Draft Horse #906, pale palomino. Fair to mint condition: $20-$35.

Belgian SR, black, white tail ribbon with red criss-crosses. Fair to mint condition: $40-$60.

Belgian SR, alabaster. Fair to mint condition: $30-$50.

Belgian SR, chestnut, lighter chestnut mane and tail. Fair to mint condition: $12-$25.

Belgian SR, dapple gray, yellow tail ribbon with red crisscrosses (1979).*Top,* version A; *center,* version B; *bottom,* version C. Overruns of one of these may have been released in 1984. *Version B model courtesy of Heather Wells.* Fair to mint condition: any version $60-$90.

Belgian SR, bay. Fair to mint condition: $40-$60.

Belgian SR, chestnut/dark palomino with white mane and tail. *Model courtesy of Heather Wells.* Fair to mint condition: $90-$130.

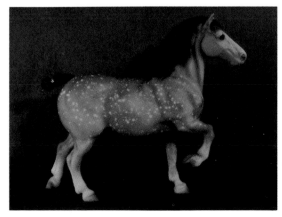

Belgian SR, dapple gray, metallic gold tail ribbon (1986). *Model courtesy of Heather Wells.* Fair to mint condition: $50-$75.

Belgian SR, dapple gray, yellow tail ribbon with red crisscrosses (1986/87). Fair to mint condition: $40-$60.

Percheron SR, black, yellow ribbon with red crisscrosses. Fair to mint condition: $30-$50.

"Donovan" Running Appaloosa Stallion #919, gray dun roan blanket appaloosa. Still available retail in 1996.

Belgian SR, palomino with bald face. *Model courtesy of Heather Wells.* Fair to mint condition: $145-$200.

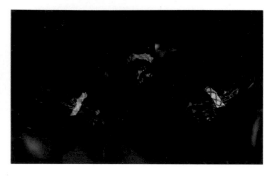

Tail ribbons galore: *left,* Belgian SR black (1979-82); *center,* Percheron SR black (1982-83); *right,* Belgian SR black (1986/87).

Not shown:
Belgian SR, unpainted white. Fair to mint condition: $10-$20.

"Dream Weaver" #833, sorrel. Fair to mint condition: $20-$35.

Belgian SR, red roan. Fair to mint condition: $85-$120.

Belgian SR, "smoke" blue-gray semi-leopard blanket appaloosa. Fair to mint condition: $40-$60.

"Black Beauty" text p. 150

"Black Beauty" #89, black, 4-stocking and right-front-stocking versions. Fair to mint condition: any version $12-$25.

"Fade To Gray" #802, dark dapple gray. Fair to mint condition: $20-$35

"Black Beauty" SR, bay. Fair to mint condition: $35-$55.

Not shown:
"Black Beauty" SR, unpainted white. Fair to mint condition: $10-$20.

Black Stallion text *pp. 150-151*

Walter Farley's Black Stallion #401, black. Fair to mint condition: $12-$25. In set #2095 with poster, book, and box, add $10. For set #3000 with doll and tack, see the photos of the Alec Ramsey doll mold.

"Ofir," Sire of "Witez II," SR #700694, dark plum bay. Fair to mint condition: $25-$40.

Breyer Lapel Pins *text p. 151*

Breyer lapel pins. *Top row, from left*: 1988 Running Stallion, 1989 Black Beauty, 1990 Mustang, and 1990 "Misty." *Bottom row, from left*: 1990 BreyerFest vendor button and 1990 "Misty" button. Fair to mint condition: $4-$8 per pin or button.

Breyer Neckties text *pp. 151-152*

"Greystreak" Action Arabian #899, shaded smoke gray. Fair to mint condition: $12-$25.

"Hyksos" The Egyptian Arabian #832, "ageless bronze." Fair to mint condition: $30-$50.

Majestic Arabian Stallion #811, leopard appaloosa. *Top,* normal version with black and brown spots; *bottom,* variation with brown spots only. Fair to mint condition: $15-$30, variation $20-$35.

Princess Of Arabia set #905, light dapple gray horse. Fair to mint condition: horse alone $20-$35, full set $40-$60.

Princess Of Arabia set #905, red roan horse. Fair to mint condition: horse alone $20-$35, full set $40-$60.

Black Stallion SR, light coffee bay. Fair to mint condition: $25-$40.

Breyer necktie #2035, with "Sham" designs, modeled here by Mr. Biff Young.

15

"Buckshot" *text p. 152*

"Winchester" SR #411194, charcoal brown. Fair to mint condition: $220-$300.

"Buckshot" Famous Spanish Barb #415, grulla semi-leopard appaloosa. Fair to mint condition: $15-$30.

Cantering Welsh Pony *text pp. 152-153*

"Cody" #922, dark bay pinto. Fair to mint condition: $20-$35.

Cantering Welsh Pony #105, chestnut. *Top,* version with bald face and red ribbons; *bottom,* version with solid face and no ribbons. Fair to mint condition: $20-$35.

"Hickok" #923, blue roan pinto. Fair to mint condition: $20-$35.

Spanish Barb #416, chestnut pinto. Fair to mint condition: $20-$35.

Cantering Welsh Pony #104, bay, yellow-ribbon and blue-ribbon versions. *Blue-ribbon model courtesy of Heather Wells.* Fair to mint condition: $40-$60.

Cantering Welsh Pony #106, seal brown, solid-faced and bald-faced versions. *Bald-faced pony courtesy of Heather Wells.* Fair to mint condition: $35-$55.

"Plain Pixie" #866, red roan. Fair to mint condition: $12-$25.

Cantering Welsh Pony SR #410107, dapple gray, metallic gold mane braids. Fair to mint condition: $90-$130.

Cantering Welsh Pony SR #413107, dark chestnut. Fair to mint condition: $55-$80.

Cantering Welsh Pony SR #411107, fleabitten gray. Fair to mint condition: $55-$80.

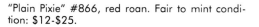

"Tara" Welsh Pony #892, dappled bay, heavily dappled and nearly solid versions. Fair to mint condition: $10-$20.

Cantering Welsh Pony SR #107, dapple gray with red mane braids. *Top,* the common version, with dappled face, head, and neck. *bottom,* the rare version, with bald face and no dapples on the head and neck; shown here with the common-version pony. *Rare-version model courtesy of Sue Lehman.* Fair to mint condition: common version $45-$70, rare version $55-$80.

Cantering Welsh Pony SR, red bay. *Model courtesy of Heather Wells.* Fair to mint condition: $220-$300.

Cantering Welsh Pony SR, bay roan. Fair to mint condition: $25-$40.

Cantering Welsh Pony SR, black. Fair to mint condition: $30-$50.

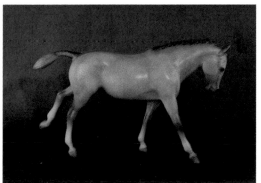

Cantering Welsh Pony SR, dappled rose gray. Fair to mint condition: $30-$50.

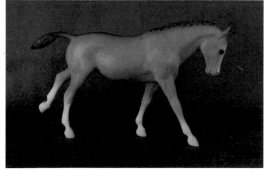

Cantering Welsh Pony SR #414107, red dun. Fair to mint condition: $55-$80.

Right:Cantering Welsh Pony SR #412107, red roan. Fair to mint condition: $55-$80.

Not shown:
Cantering Welsh Pony SR, red-tan dun (1987). Fair to mint condition: $220-$300.
Cantering Welsh Pony SR, unpainted white. Fair to mint condition: $10-$20.

Clydesdale Foal *text pp. 153-154*

Clydesdale Foal #84, chestnut. Fair to mint condition: $5-$12.

Clydesdale Foal #826, light golden bay. Fair to mint condition: $8-$15.

"Satin Star" Drafter Foal #894, dark chestnut. Fair to mint condition: $5-$12.

Clydesdale Foal SR #410384, black. Fair to mint condition: $25-$40.

Clydesdale Foal SR, dapple gray (1980). Fair to mint condition: $40-$60.

Clydesdale Foal SR #410184, dapple gray (1988). Fair to mint condition: $25-$40.

Clydesdale Foal SR #410284, steel gray. Fair to mint condition: $25-$40.

Clydesdale Foal SR, true bay. *Model courtesy of Heather Wells.* Fair to mint condition: $15-$30.

Clydesdale Mare *text pp. 154-155*

Clydesdale Mare #83, chestnut. *Top,* normal version; *bottom,* chalky variation, which has a basecoat of white paint under the chestnut. Fair to mint condition: normal $12-$25, chalky $15-$30.

Clydesdale Mare #825, light golden bay. Fair to mint condition: $15-$30.

Shire Mare #856, liver chestnut. Fair to mint condition: $15-$30.

Clydesdale Gift Set #8384, mare and foal, both chestnut, with blankets. *Set courtesy of Sheryl Leisure.* Fair to mint condition: mare with blanket $14-$27; foal with blanket $7-$14.

Clydesdale Mare SR, true bay. *Model courtesy of Heather Wells.* Fair to mint condition: $30-$50.

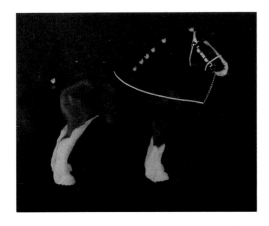

Clydesdale Gelding/Stallion SR, flocked bay. *Model courtesy of Heather Wells.* Fair to mint condition: $35-$55.

Clydesdale Mare SR, unpainted white. Fair to mint condition: $10-$20.

Clydesdale Stallion *text pp. 155-156*

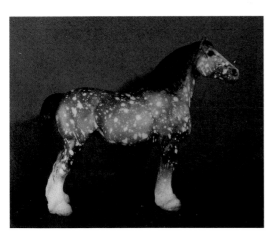

Clydesdale #80, bay. *Top,* version C (gold bobs); *center,* version D (red and white bobs, unstenciled white markings); *bottom,* version E (red and white bobs, stenciled white markings). All have pink hooves. *Version C and D models courtesy of Heather Wells.* Fair to mint condition: version C $20-$35, versions D and E $12-$25.

Clydesdale Mare SR, dapple gray (1979), darker version. Fair to mint condition: $85-$120.

Clydesdale Mare SR, dapple gray (1986/87). Fair to mint condition: $40-$60.

Clydesdale #80, bay. *Top,* version A, no-muscle glossy; *bottom,* version B, muscled glossy. Both have gray hooves. *Version B model courtesy of Sheryl Leisure.* Fair to mint condition: version A $60-$90, version B $75-$110.

Highland Clydesdale #868, bay. Fair to mint condition: $12-$25.

Clydesdale #82, dapple gray. *Top*, no-muscle version; *model courtesy of Sheryl Leisure. bottom*, normal muscled version; *model courtesy of Heather Wells.* Fair to mint condition: no-muscle $90-$130, muscle $60-$90.

Circus Extravaganza set #3170, grulla large horse. Fair to mint condition: $15-$30.

Clydesdale #980, woodgrain, no-muscle version. *Model courtesy of Sheryl Leisure.* Fair to mint condition: muscle or no-muscle version $85-$120.

Clydesdale Stallion SR, dapple gray with gold bobs (1979). *Top*, pink-hoofed version; *center*, gray-hoofed version B; *bottom*, gray-hoofed version C. Overruns of one of these may have been released in 1984/85. *Version B model courtesy of Heather Wells.* Fair to mint condition: any version $60-$90.

Clydesdale Stallion SR, dapple gray, red and white bobs (1986/87). Fair to mint condition: $35-$55.

Clydesdale Stallion SR, true bay. *Model courtesy of Heather Wells.* Fair to mint condition: $25-$40.

Clydesdale Stallion #824, light golden bay. Fair to mint condition: $15-$30.

Clydesdale Stallion SR, grulla, with metallic sheen. Fair to mint condition: $30-$50.

"Grayingham Lucky Lad" SR #410393, black. Fair to mint condition: $50-$75.

Display Boxes *text pp. 157-158*

An example of Breyer's earliest display packaging, the "touchability" box. Note that this box probably did not come with the Western Prancer shown here but with a palomino Family Arabian Stallion "Faith," as indicated by the model number 4 SP stamped on the right end of the bottom of the box. *Box and model courtesy of Sheryl Leisure.* Fair to mint condition: box alone $4-$6.

Left: The third generation of display packaging, the blister-wrap box. The example shown here is a mahogany bay Proud Arabian Foal. The number 1219 assigned to the foal as packaged in this box is visible on the label beneath her belly. *Model courtesy of Sheryl Leisure.* Fair to mint condition: box alone $3-$4.

"El Pastor" *text pp. 158-159*

"El Pastor" Famous Paso Fino #61, bay, star and solid-faced versions. *Star-faced model courtesy of Sheryl Leisure.* Fair to mint condition: star version $15-$30, solid face $25-$40.

"Precipitado Sin Par" ("Cips"), #116, bay pinto. Fair to mint condition: $25-$40.

"Tesoro" #867, palomino. Fair to mint condition: $12-$25.

"Tobe" Rocky Mountain Horse #914, dappled liver chestnut. Still available retail in 1996.

"El Pastor" SR #410116, bay, solid face. *Model courtesy of Heather Wells.* Fair to mint condition: $35-$55.

Family Arabian Foal *text pp. 159-160*

Family Appaloosa Foal "Spot" #39, gray blanket appaloosa. *Left,* glossy belly-striped version; *model courtesy of Heather Wells. Right,* matte small-butt-blanket version; *model courtesy of Sheryl Leisure.* Fair to mint condition: any version $5-$12.

Ara-Appaloosa Foal #874, "bay" leopard appaloosa. *Model courtesy of Sheryl Leisure.* Fair to mint condition: $5-$12.

Family Arabian Foal "Charity" #6, palomino. *Left,* glossy version with blue-ribbon sticker; *model courtesy of Sheryl Leisure. Right,* matte version. Fair to mint condition: glossy $5-$12; matte $2-$5.

Family Arabian Foal SR, alabaster, glossy. Fair to mint condition: $5-$12.

Family Arabian Foal #708, chestnut. *Model courtesy of Sheryl Leisure.* Fair to mint condition: $10-$17.

Family Arabian Foal "Doc" #203, charcoal. *Left,* glossy; *right,* matte. *Models courtesy of Heather Wells.* Fair to mint condition: glossy or matte $5-$12.

Family Arabian Foal SR #12, black. *Model courtesy of Heather Wells.* Fair to mint condition: $20-$35.

Family Arabian Foal #816, bay. *Model courtesy of Sheryl Leisure.* Fair to mint condition: $8-$15.

Family Arabian Foal "Joy" #9, alabaster, matte. *Model courtesy of Heather Wells.* Fair to mint condition: glossy or matte $5-$12.

Family Arabian Foal SR, chestnut pinto on Ford "Pinto" base. *Model and photo courtesy of Lynn Hiersche.* Fair to mint condition: $50-$75.

Family Arabian Foal "Shah" #15, bay. *Left,* glossy; *right,* matte. *Models courtesy of Heather Wells.* Fair to mint condition: glossy or matte $5-$12.

Family Arabian Foal #841, red chestnut. *Model courtesy of Lani Keller.* Fair to mint condition: $5-$12.

Right: Family Arabian Foal #909, woodgrain. *Model courtesy of Heather Wells.* Fair to mint condition: $15-$30.

Right: Family Arabian Foal SR, dapple gray. Fair to mint condition: $10-$17.

Family Arabian Foal SR, dark chestnut with long stripe. *Model courtesy of Heather Wells.* Fair to mint condition: $13-$22.

Family Arabian Mare #815, bay. Fair to mint condition: $15-$30.

Family Arabian Foal SR, medium chestnut with bald face. *Model courtesy of Joy Sheesley.* Fair to mint condition: $25-$40.

Family Arabian Mare #908, woodgrain. *Model courtesy of Heather Wells.* Fair to mint condition: $30-$50.

Family Appaloosa Mare "Speck" #38, gray blanket appaloosa. *Top,* glossy big-blanket version; *center,* glossy belly-striped version; *bottom,* matte small-butt-blanket version. *Belly-striped model courtesy of Sheryl Leisure; other models courtesy of Heather Wells.* Fair to mint condition: any version $12-$25.

Family Arabian Foal SR, light chestnut with long stripe. *Model courtesy of Heather Wells.* Fair to mint condition: $13-$22.

Family Arabian Mare *text pp. 160-162*

Family Arabian Mare #707, chestnut. Fair to mint condition: $20-$35.

Right: Ara-Appaloosa Mare #873, "bay" leopard appaloosa. Fair to mint condition: $12-$25.

Family Arabian Mare "Dickory" #202, charcoal. *Top,* glossy; *bottom,* matte. *Models courtesy of Heather Wells.* Fair to mint condition: glossy or matte $12-$25.

Family Arabian Mare SR, alabaster, glossy. *Model courtesy of Sheryl Leisure.* Fair to mint condition: $15-$30.

Family Arabian Mare "Hope" #5, palomino. *Bottom,* an old glossy honey-tan mare with unstenciled mane; *top,* a newer matte mare with stenciled mane. Fair to mint condition: glossy $12-$25; matte $10-$20.

Family Arabian Mare SR #11, black. *Model courtesy of Heather Wells.* Fair to mint condition: $30-$50.

Family Arabian Mare "in-between" mold, woodgrain, shown from both sides and in comparison to a normal-mold palomino Family Arabian Mare. For discussion, see note 1 for the Family Arabian Mare mold. *In-between mare courtesy of Bonnie Driskill Vavra.*

Family Arabian Mare SR, dapple gray. Fair to mint condition: $25-$40.

Family Arabian Mare SR, dark chestnut with blaze. *Model courtesy of Heather Wells.* Fair to mint condition: $25-$40.

Family Arabian Mare "Pride" #8, alabaster, glossy. *Model courtesy of Sheryl Leisure.* Fair to mint condition: glossy or matte $12-$25.

Family Arabian Mare "Sheba" #14, bay. Top, glossy; bottom, matte. *Models courtesy of Heather Wells.* Fair to mint condition: glossy or matte $12-$25.

Family Arabian Mare SR, light chestnut with blaze. *Model courtesy of Heather Wells.* Fair to mint condition: $25-$40.

Not shown:
Family Arabian Mare SR, medium chestnut with bald face. Fair to mint condition: $60-$90. For the color, see the photos of the Family Arabian Foal and Stallion SR, medium chestnut with bald face.

Family Arabian Stallion
text pp. 162-163

Ara-Appaloosa Stallion #872, "bay" leopard appaloosa. Fair to mint condition: $12-$25.

Family Arabian Stallion #706, chestnut. *Model courtesy of Sheryl Leisure.* Fair to mint condition: $20-$35.

Family Appaloosa Stallion "Fleck" #37, gray blanket appaloosa. *Top,* glossy big-blanket version; *center,* glossy belly-striped version; *boottom,* matte small-butt-blanket version. *Big-blanket model courtesy of Heather Wells; other models courtesy of Sheryl Leisure.* Fair to mint condition: any version $12-$25.

Family Arabian Stallion #907, woodgrain. *Model courtesy of Sheryl Leisure.* Fair to mint condition: $30-$50.

Left: Family Arabian Stallion #814, bay. *Model courtesy of Sheryl Leisure.* Fair to mint condition: $15-$30.

Family Arabian Stallion "Faith" #4, palomino. *Top,* an old glossy honey-tan stallion with unstenciled mane; *bottom,* a newer matte stallion with stenciled mane. Note the mane "wisps" on the matte stallion. *Models courtesy of Heather Wells.* Fair to mint condition: glossy $12-$25; matte $5-$12.

Family Arabian Stallion "Hickory" #201, charcoal. *Top,* glossy with eyewhites; *model courtesy of Heather Wells. bottom,* a matte stallion; *model courtesy of Sheryl Leisure.* Note the mane "wisp" on the glossy stallion. Fair to mint condition: glossy or matte $12-$25.

Family Arabian Stallion SR, dark chestnut with blaze. *Model courtesy of Heather Wells.* Fair to mint condition: $25-$40.

Family Arabian Stallion "Prince" #7, alabaster. *Top,* glossy with charcoal lip line; *bottom,* matte. *Matte model courtesy of Heather Wells.* Fair to mint condition: glossy or matte $12-$25.

Family Arabian Stallion SR, medium chestnut with bald face. Fair to mint condition: $60-$90.

Family Arabian Stallion "Sheik" #13, bay. *Top,* glossy caramel bay; *center,* glossy reddish bay with eyewhites; *bottom,* matte bay with blue ribbon sticker. *Glossy models courtesy of Heather Wells; matte model courtesy of Sheryl Leisure.* Fair to mint condition: glossy or matte $12-$25.

Family Arabian Stallion SR, alabaster with black points. Fair to mint condition: $25-$40.

Family Arabian Stallion SR, light chestnut with long star. *Model courtesy of Heather Wells.* Fair to mint condition: $25-$40.

Fighting Stallion text pp. 163-165

"Chaparral" The Fighting Stallion #855, buckskin pinto. Fair to mint condition: $20-$35.

Family Arabian Stallion SR, alabaster, glossy. Fair to mint condition: $15-$30.

Family Arabian Stallion SR, black. *Model courtesy of Heather Wells.* Fair to mint condition: $30-$50.

Fighting Stallion #709, black leopard appaloosa. Fair to mint condition: $15-30.

Fighting Stallion #4031, Wedgewood Blue decorator. *Model courtesy of Joy Sheesley.* Fair to mint condition: $220-$300.

Fighting Stallion #1031, Copenhagen decorator. *Model courtesy of Heather Wells.* Fair to mint condition: $220-$300.

"King" The Fighting Stallion #33, palomino. *Top,* a glossy model. *Bottom,* a matte horse; *model courtesy of Heather Wells.* Fair to mint condition: glossy or matte $25-$40.

Fighting Stallion #2031, Florentine decorator. *Model courtesy of Heather Wells.* Fair to mint condition: $220-$300.

Fighting Stallion #3031, Golden Charm decorator. *Model courtesy of Joy Sheesley.* Fair to mint condition: $220-$300.

"King" The Fighting Stallion, Alabaster Lipizzan #30, alabaster. *Top,* glossy; *bottom,* matte. Note the orange pads on the bottoms of the matte model's hind hooves. Fair to mint condition: glossy $70-$100, matte $10-$20.

"King" The Fighting Stallion #32, gray appaloosa, glossy. *Model courtesy of Heather Wells.* Fair to mint condition: $60-$90.

"King" The Fighting Stallion #34, charcoal, glossy. *Model courtesy of Heather Wells.* Fair to mint condition: $50-$75.

Bay Fighting Stallion SR #700993, bay. Fair to mint condition: $10-$20; with box, add $2.

"King" The Fighting Stallion #35, bay. *Top*, a 1960s matte with eyewhites and body shading; *bottom*, a later matte with no detailing. *Models courtesy of Heather Wells.* Fair to mint condition: with eyewhites $15-$30, otherwise $10-$20.

"King" The Fighting Stallion #931, woodgrain, lighter and darker versions. *Models courtesy of Heather Wells.* Fair to mint condition: $25-$40.

"Ponokah-Eemetah" The Blackfeet Indian Horse #897, dark bay blanket appaloosa, the 1994 series. Fair to mint condition: $12-$25.

"Ponokah-Eemetah" The Blackfeet Indian Horse #897, dark bay blanket appaloosa, the 1995 series. Fair to mint condition: $12-$25.

Fighting Stallion SR, red sorrel. Fair to mint condition: $30-$50.

"Commander" The Five-Gaiter #51, albino, black-eyed version. Fair to mint condition: either version $65-$95.

"Commander" The Five-Gaiter #1051, Copenhagen decorator. *Model courtesy of Joy Sheesley.* Fair to mint condition: $220-$300.

Rearing Circus Stallion With Ringmaster Set SR, flocked white stallion. *Set courtesy of Heather Wells.* Fair to mint condition: horse alone $50-$75, full set $60-$90.

"Commander" The Five-Gaiter #2051, Florentine decorator. *Model courtesy of Sheryl Leisure.* Fair to mint condition: $220-$300.

"Commander" The Five-Gaiter #53, palomino, in tan and orangy versions. *Models courtesy of Heather Wells.* Fair to mint condition: $35-$55.

"Commander" The Five-Gaiter #3051, Golden Charm decorator. *Model courtesy of Heather Wells.* Fair to mint condition: $220-$300.

"Sierra" SR #400196, red dun. Fair to mint condition: $25-$40.

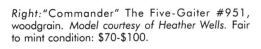

Right: "Commander" The Five-Gaiter #951, woodgrain. *Model courtesy of Heather Wells.* Fair to mint condition: $70-$100.

"Commander" The Five-Gaiter #4051, Wedgewood Blue decorator. *Model courtesy of Joy Sheesley.* Fair to mint condition: $220-$300.

Kentucky Saddlebred #862, red chestnut. Fair to mint condition: $15-$30.

"Moon Shadows" SR #400294, blue roan. Fair to mint condition: $45-$70.

"Commander" The Five-Gaiter #52, sorrel. *Top*, an early model with eyewhites and shading; *bottom*, a later model with less detailing. Fair to mint condition: with eyewhites $15-$30, otherwise $10-$20.

Pinto American Saddlebred #827, black pinto. Fair to mint condition: $20-$35.

The turquoise-and-yellow-striped tassel on the mane ribbon of a glossy albino "Commander" The Five-Gaiter #51, shown from the non-mane side.

Not shown:
Five-Gaiter SR, unpainted white. Fair to mint condition: $10-$20.

Foundation Stallion text pp. 166-167

American Saddlebred #109, dapple gray. Fair to mint condition: $25-$40.

"Project Universe" Premium Pinto American Saddlebred #117, dark chestnut pinto. Fair to mint condition: $20-$35.

"CH Imperator" American Saddlebred #904, liver chestnut. Fair to mint condition: $12-$25.

"Wing Commander" American Saddlebred #140, dark chestnut. Fair to mint condition: $15-$30.

Azteca #85, dapple gray. *Top*, early white-tail version; *bottom*, later gray-tailed version. Fair to mint condition: either version $15-$30.

Black Foundation Stallion #64. Fair to mint condition: $12-$25.

American Indian Pony #710, red roan. Fair to mint condition: $12-$25.

"Fugir Cacador" Lusitano Stallion #870, light buckskin. Fair to mint condition: $20-$35.

Foundation Stallion SR, alabaster. Fair to mint condition: $55-$80.

Right: Foundation Stallion SR, liver-charcoal. Fair to mint condition: $25-$40.

Lakota Pony #869, white with cream shading; the four symbol versions. Fair to mint condition: $20-$35.

Foundation Stallion SR, palomino. Fair to mint condition: $40-$60.

Foundation Stallion SR, bay blanket appaloosa. Fair to mint condition: $25-$40.

Not shown:
Foundation Stallion SR, unpainted white. Fair to mint condition: $10-$20.

Friesian *text p. 167*

Friesian #485, black. Fair to mint condition: $12-$25.

Action Drafters Big And Small set #3175, dark dappled bay big drafter. Fair to mint condition: $15-$30.

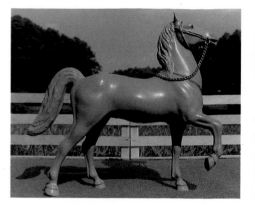

"Fury" Prancer SR, Wedgewood Blue. *Model and photo courtesy of Ruth-Ann, Kirsten, and Sarah Wellman.* Fair to mint condition: $145-$200.

"Black Beauty" Prancer #P40, black. *Left,* earlier version with blaze and black bridle (some have gold bridle); *model courtesy of Heather Wells. Right,* later version with bald face and silver bridle. Fair to mint condition: either version $30-$50; with English saddle and blanket, add $14-$20.

Prancer #P42, brown pinto. *Model courtesy of Heather Wells.* Fair to mint condition: $25-$40; with English saddle and blanket, add $14-$20.

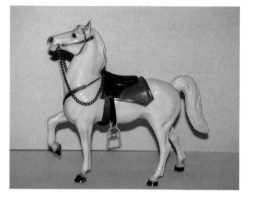

The hard-plastic English saddle and separate red plastic saddle blanket that were available on Prancers without riders. *Model and photo courtesy of Sande Schneider.* Fair to mint condition: each piece $7-$10.

"Fury" #27, black, with original green paper saddle. *Model courtesy of Heather Wells.* Fair to mint condition: $12-$25; with paper saddle, add $10-$15.

Prancer #P40, dark brown. Fair to mint condition: $30-$50; with English saddle and blanket, add $14-$20.

Prancer #P43, palomino. *Model courtesy of Heather Wells.* Fair to mint condition: $20-$35; with English saddle and blanket, add $14-$20.

The rubbery-plastic cavalry-type saddle that came on Prancers in Davy Crockett and Kit Carson rider sets. Fair to mint condition: $7-$10.

Prancer #P41, black pinto. *Model courtesy of Heather Wells.* Fair to mint condition: $25-$40; with English saddle and blanket, add $14-$20.

Prancer #P45, white. Fair to mint condition: $25-$40; with English saddle and blanket, add $14-$20.

The rubbery-plastic medieval saddle that came on Prancers in Robin Hood rider sets. *Model and photo courtesy of Sande Schneider.* Fair to mint condition: $7-$10.

Prancer #P945[?], woodgrain. *Model courtesy of Heather Wells.* Fair to mint condition: $125-$175.

Galiceño *text p. 169*

"Freckle Doll" Galiceno #888, reddish bay pinto. Fair to mint condition: $10-$20.

Galiceno #100, bay. Fair to mint condition: $12-$25.

Grazing Foal *text p. 169*

Grazing Foal "Bows" #151, bay. Fair to mint condition: $5-$12.

Grazing Foal "Bows" #152, black. *Model courtesy of Heather Wells.* Fair to mint condition: $13-$22.

"Buttons" & "Bows" set #3165, apricot dun "Bows" foal. Fair to mint condition: $5-$12.

Grazing Foal SR, bay blanket appaloosa. Fair to mint condition: $10-$17.

"Gem Twist" *text p. 169*

"Gem Twist" Champion Show Jumper #495, white, earliest mane-braid version. Fair to mint condition: any version $12-$25.

Grazing Foal "Bows" #153, palomino. Fair to mint condition: $5-$12.

Grazing Mare *text pp. 169-170*

Grazing Mare "Buttons" #141, bay. Fair to mint condition: $12-$25.

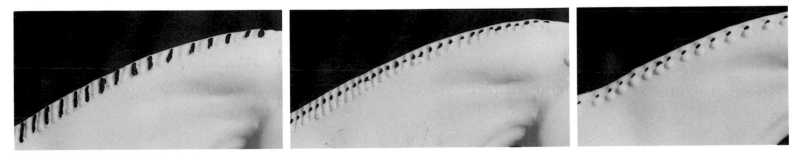

"Gem Twist" Champion Show Jumper #495. *From left*: the early version; the second version, with braids of the same mold but altered paint detailing; and latest version, with differently molded braids.

Grazing Mare "Buttons" #142, black. Fair to mint condition: $35-$55.

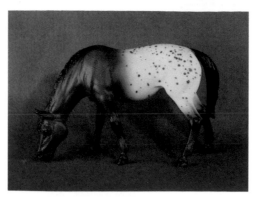

Grazing Mare SR, red bay blanket appaloosa. Fair to mint condition: $15-$30.

"Sargent Pepper" Appaloosa Pony #926, roaned black leopard appaloosa. Still available retail in 1996.

Grazing Mare "Buttons" #143, palomino, bald-faced and solid-faced versions. Fair to mint condition: $12-$25.

Haflinger *text p. 170*

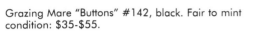

Haflinger #156, chestnut. *Top matte; bottom, semi-gloss.* Fair to mint condition: $10-$20.

"Scat Cat" Children's Pony #883, bay roan leopard appaloosa. Fair to mint condition: $12-$25.

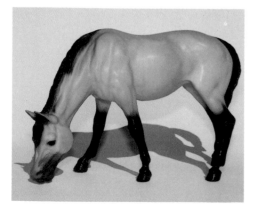

"Buttons" & "Bows" set #3165, apricot dun "Buttons" mare. Fair to mint condition: $12-$25.

Grazing Mare SR, buckskin. Fair to mint condition: $20-$35.

Mountain Pony #850, light chestnut. Fair to mint condition: $12-$25.

Haflinger SR, chestnut with gray mane and tail, versions with and without stockings. *Model without stockings courtesy of Heather Wells.* Fair to mint condition: with stockings $25-$40, no stockings $30-$50.

Haflinger SR, chestnut pinto. Fair to mint condition: $30-$50.

"Halla" *text pp. 170-171*

Noble Jumper #820, dapple gray, darker and lighter variations. Fair to mint condition: $15-$30.

Hanoverian #58, bay, darker and lighter color variations. *Darker model courtesy of Sheryl Leisure.* Fair to mint condition: $25-$40.

Hanoverian SR #410358, alabaster. Fair to mint condition: $70-$100.

"Halla" Famous Jumper #63, bay, solid-faced and star versions. The star-faced mare shown here has an unstenciled snip on the end of her nose. Fair to mint condition: solid-faced $25-$40, star $15-$30

"Halla" SR, fleabitten gray. Fair to mint condition: $25-$40.

Hanoverian *text p. 171*

"Gifted," 1992 Olympic Dressage Bronze Medal Winner #887, bay. Fair to mint condition: $25-$40.

Hanoverian SR #410158, black. *Model courtesy of Heather Wells.* Fair to mint condition: $60-$90.

"Bolya" The Freedom Horse (Akhal-Teke) #490, golden buckskin. Fair to mint condition: $15-$30.

Hanoverian SR #410458, chestnut. Fair to mint condition: $60-$90.

Hanoverian SR, dapple gray. Note the "chalky" appearance of this horse. Fair to mint condition: $105-$150.

Hanoverian SR, dark bay. Fair to mint condition: $30-$50.

Hanoverian SR, dark dapple gray. Fair to mint condition: $30-$50.

Hanoverian SR #410258, red bay. Fair to mint condition: $70-$100.

Vaulting Horse SR #700058, black. Fair to mint condition: $60-$90.

Dressage Horse ("Art Deco") SR #710595, black pinto. Fair to mint condition: $20-$35.

Not shown:
Hanoverian SR, unpainted white. Fair to mint condition: $10-$20.

Icelandic Horse text p. 172

Fine Porcelain Icelandic Horse #79192, buckskin pinto. *Model courtesy of Heather Wells.* Fair to mint condition: $130-$180.

Ideal Quarter Horse text p. 172

AQHA Ideal American Quarter Horse #497, golden-brown chestnut. The horse shown was purchased from the QVC TV Breyer show in August 1995 and thus came in a box labeled with the model number 705695, but he is nonetheless simply a regular-run #497. Fair to mint condition: $15-$30.

AQHA Ideal American Quarter Horse SR #707795, dark red chestnut. Standing behind him for comparison is a #497 golden-brown chestnut. Fair to mint condition: $25-$40; with box $30-$50.

Indian Pony text pp. 172-174

"Cheyenne" American Mustang #929, bay roan. Still available retail in 1996.

Indian Pony #175, chestnut pinto, versions with and without warpaint symbols. Fair to mint condition: with warpaint $40-$60, without warpaint $25-$40. For the Presentation Collection edition (on base) add $50.

"Chinook" SR #700194, dark dapple gray. Fair to mint condition: $55-$80.

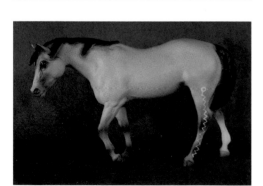

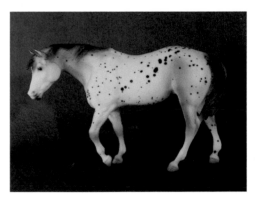

Indian Pony SR #411175, black leopard appaloosa. Fair to mint condition: $60-$90.

"Ichilay" The Crow Horse #882, grulla, the four symbol versions. Fair to mint condition: $20-$35.

Indian Pony #176, buckskin. Fair to mint condition: $70-$100.

Indian Pony #174, bay blanket appaloosa. Fair to mint condition: $12-$25.

Indian Pony SR #414175, blue roan semi-leopard appaloosa. Fair to mint condition: $60-$90.

Indian Pony SR #412175, dapple gray. Fair to mint condition: $60-$90.

Indian Pony SR #413175, red bay. Fair to mint condition: $60-$90.

Indian Pony SR, red dun. Fair to mint condition: $25-$40.

Indian Pony SR #411294, red roan. *Model courtesy of Sheryl Leisure.* Fair to mint condition: $220-$300.

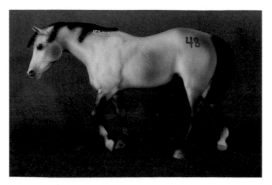

"Mustang Lady" SR #412091, shaded gray. Fair to mint condition: $45-$70.

Not shown:
Indian Pony SR, unpainted white. Fair to mint condition: $10-$20.

"John Henry" *text p. 174*

"Joe Patchen," Sire Of "Dan Patch," #836, black. Fair to mint condition: $12-$25.

"John Henry" Famous Race Horse #445, dark bay, solid dark and brindled versions. Fair to mint condition: either version $15-$30.

Dark Bay Western Horse SR #711594, dark plum bay. Fair to mint condition: $20-$35.

"John Henry" SR, liver chestnut. Fair to mint condition: $30-$50.

Jumping Horse *text pp. 174-175*

"Starlight" #886, seal brown. Fair to mint condition: $20-$35.

Jumping "Gem Twist" SR #702795, white. Fair to mint condition: $30-$50.

Marguerite Henry's "Justin Morgan" #65, medium/dark bay. Fair to mint condition: $10-$20. In set #2065 with book and box, add $8.

Jumping Horse SR, seal brown, star and solid-faced versions. *Models courtesy of Heather Wells.* Fair to mint condition: $45-$70.

Morgan #822, dark seal brown. Fair to mint condition: $12-$25.

Jumping Horse "Stonewall" #300, bay. *Top,* an older model with gray hind legs and blue-ribbon sticker; *model courtesy of Sheryl Leisure. Center,* solid-faced version. *Bottom,* a typical later issue with no dark shading on the legs. Fair to mint condition: solid-faced $40-$60, others $15-$30.

"Mystique" SR #707495, gray appaloosa. *Model courtesy of Heather Wells.* Fair to mint condition: $220-$300.

"Justin Morgan" SR, red chestnut. Fair to mint condition: $25-$40.

"Justin Morgan" *text p. 175*

"Khemosabi" *text p. 175*

"Double Take" Morgan #878, liver chestnut. Fair to mint condition: $12-$25.

"Khemosabi+++" Champion Arabian Stallion #460, bay. Fair to mint condition: $10-$20.

Jumping Horse SR #401291, black. Fair to mint condition: $45-$70.

"Kipper" *text p. 175*

"Kipper" #9960, bay. Fair to mint condition: $15-$30.

Family Appaloosa Mare #860, black leopard appaloosa. Fair to mint condition: $15-$30.

"Lady Phase" SR, bay paint. Fair to mint condition: $25-$40.

"Lady Phase" *text pp. 175-177*

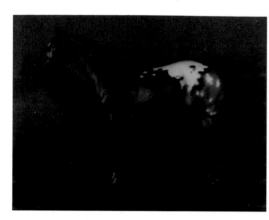

Lynn Anderson's "Lady Phase" #40, red chestnut. Fair to mint condition: $15-$30.

Lynn Anderson's "Lady Phase" Gift Set #3075. Fair to mint condition: full set $20-$35.

"Lady Phase" SR, buckskin with bald face and pink nose (1980), versions with solid black legs and with buckskin shins. *Model with buckskin shins courtesy of Heather Wells.* Fair to mint condition: $65-$95.

"Breezing Dixie" Famous Appaloosa Mare #711, dark bay blanket appaloosa. *Top,* early version with hand-painted hooves and extra thigh spots; *center,* later version with airbrushed hooves; *bottom,* "Breezing Dixie's" tri-color eyes and pink nostrils. Fair to mint condition: early version $45-$70, later version $30-$50.

"Lady Phase" SR, alabaster. Fair to mint condition: $15-$30.

"Lady Phase" SR, chestnut leopard appaloosa. Fair to mint condition: $30-$50.

"Lady Phase" SR #410040, red roan. Fair to mint condition: $45-$70.

"Lady Roxana" *text p. 177*

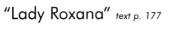

"Lady Phase" SR, buckskin (1983 and 1984). *Top,* solid face and brown hooves; *bottom,* bald face and black hooves. Fair to mint condition: either version $30-$50.

"Night Deck" SR, black. Fair to mint condition: $30-$50.

Marguerite Henry's "Lady Roxana" #425, alabaster. Fair to mint condition: $15-$30.

Prancing Arabian Mare #426, light sorrel. Fair to mint condition: $15-$30.

"Lady Phase" SR, dapple gray. Fair to mint condition: $30-$50.

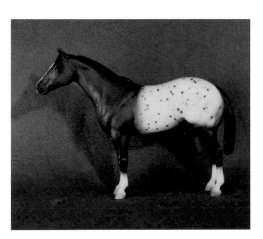

"Prairie Flower" Equitana '93 SR #700193, red bay blanket appaloosa. Fair to mint condition: $50-$75.

Not shown:
"Lady Phase" SR, buckskin with solid face and black nose (1979). *Fair to mint condition: $65- $95.*
"Lady Phase" SR, unpainted white. Fair to mint condition: $10-$20.

Proud Mother And Newborn Foal set #3160, chocolate sorrel Proud Mother. Fair to mint condition: $20-$35.

"Lady Phase" SR #707395, palomino. Model courtesy of Sheryl Leisure. Fair to mint condition: $220-$300.

Proud Mother And Newborn Foal set #3161, tan dun Proud Mother. Fair to mint condition: $20-$35.

"Legionario" *text pp. 177-178*

"Legionario III" Famous Andalusian #68, alabaster. Fair to mint condition: $12-$25. In set #3070 with book and box, add $8.

"Medieval Knight" Andalusian #880, red roan. Fair to mint condition: $15-$30.

"Promenade" Andalusian #918, liver chestnut. Still available retail in 1996.

"Spanish Pride" #851, reddish bay. Fair to mint condition: $15-$30.

"El Campeador" SR #410395, dark dapple gray, lighter and darker variations. Fair to mint condition: $40-$60.

"Legionario" SR, chestnut. Fair to mint condition: $55-$80.

"Legionario" SR #415091, Florentine decorator. *Model courtesy of Heather Wells.* Fair to mint condition: $220-$300.

"Legionario" With Brenda Breyer Rider set SR, flocked white. *Set courtesy of Heather Wells.* Fair to mint condition: horse alone $50-$75, full set $60-$90.

"Llanarth True Briton" Champion Welsh Cob #494, dark chestnut. Still available retail in 1996.

Lying Down Foal *text pp. 178-179*

Lying Down Foal #165, black blanket appaloosa. Fair to mint condition: $5-$12.

Lying Down Foal #166, buckskin. Fair to mint condition: $5-$12.

Lying Down Foal #167, red roan. *Model courtesy of Heather Wells.* Fair to mint condition: $13-$22.

Lying Down Unicorn #245, alabaster. *Model courtesy of Heather Wells.* Fair to mint condition: $5-$12.

"Buster" SR, bay blanket appaloosa. Fair to mint condition: $13-$22.

Lying Down Foal SR, buckskin. Fair to mint condition: $8-$15

Lying Down Foal SR, chestnut. Fair to mint condition: $10-$17

"Man O' War" *text p. 179*

"Man O' War" #47, red chestnut. *Top*, older model with hand-painted hooves and eyewhites; *bottom*, newer model without these details. Fair to mint condition: older version $25-$40, newer version $10-$20. For the Presentation Collection edition (on base) add $50.

"Man O' War" SR, glossy red chestnut. Fair to mint condition: $25-$40.

Left: "Man O' War" SR #413091, Golden Charm decorator. *Model courtesy of Sheryl Leisure.* Fair to mint condition: $220-$300.

Right: "Misty" Of Chincoteague #20, chestnut pinto, glossy version of the first common pattern. Fair to mint condition: $25-$40.

"Misty" *text pp. 180-181*

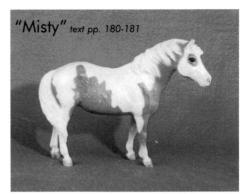

"Misty" Of Chincoteague #20, chestnut pinto. *Top two photos, both sides of the 4-eyed "Misty"; model courtesy of Heather Wells. Bottom two photos, both sides of the early 3-eyed "Misty," matte version; model courtesy of Lani Keller.* Fair to mint condition: either early version $55-$80. In set #2055 with book and box, add $6.

"Misty" Of Chincoteague #20, chestnut pinto. *Top two photos, the first common "Misty"; bottom two photos, the second common "Misty."* Fair to mint condition: first common version $5-$10; in set #2055 with book and box, add $6. Second common version #20 still available retail in 1996.

"Misty" Of Chincoteague SR #715092, chestnut/palomino pinto, cold-cast porcelain. *Model courtesy of Sheryl Leisure.* Fair to mint condition: $85-$120.

"Misty" SR, flocked chestnut pinto. *Model courtesy of Heather Wells.* Fair to mint condition: $25-$35.

Not shown:
"Misty" SR #410020, *Florentine decorator.* Fair to mint condition: $220-$300.

"Misty's Twilight" *text p. 181*

"Misty's Twilight" #470, chestnut pinto. Fair to mint condition: $12-$25.

"Misty's Twilight" SR, black. Fair to mint condition: $30-$50.

Morgan *text pp. 181-182*

"Lippitt Pegasus" Foundation Morgan #901, blood bay. Fair to mint condition: $12-$25.

Morgan #48, black, in bald-faced, star, and solid-faced versions. *Solid-faced model courtesy of Sheryl Leisure.* Fair to mint condition: bald or solid-faced $30-$50, star $12-$25.

Morgan SR, bay, solid face. *Model courtesy of Sheryl Leisure.* Fair to mint condition: $60-$90.

"Morganglanz" *text p. 182*

Morgan #702, light reddish bay. *Top,* normal version; *bottom* buckskin variation. Fair to mint condition: $15-$30.

"Morganglanz" #59, chestnut. Fair to mint condition: $15-$30.

Morgan #49, bay, in three versions: bald-faced, star and gray legs, and star and 4 stockings. *Star model with gray legs courtesy of Heather Wells.* Fair to mint condition: bald-faced $25-$40, star versions $45-$70.

Show Stance Morgan #831, dark red chestnut. Fair to mint condition: $15-$30.

"Black Beauty 1991" #847, black. Fair to mint condition: $10-$20.

Morgan #948, woodgrain. *Model courtesy of Joy Sheesley.* Fair to mint condition: $100-$140.

Vermont Morgan #858, chocolate sorrel. Fair to mint condition: $15-$30.

"Morganglanz" SR, reddish bay with solid face. Fair to mint condition: $25-$40.

45

Appaloosa Sport Horse & Canongate Saddle Set SR #700893, chestnut leopard appaloosa. Fair to mint condition: horse alone $25-$40; with tack, add $10.

"Diablo" The Mustang #85, albino, "red-eyed" version. Fair to mint condition: red or black eyes $65-95.

"Diablo" The Mustang #88, charcoal. *Model courtesy of Heather Wells.* Fair to mint condition: $50-$75.

"Morganglanz" SR, reddish bay with blaze. Fair to mint condition: $25-$40.

"Diablo" The Mustang #985, woodgrain. *Model courtesy of Sheryl Leisure.* Fair to mint condition: $85-$120.

"Pieraz" or "Cash" SR #704695, red fleabit. Fair to mint condition: $30-$50.

Not shown:
"Morganglanz" SR, unpainted white. Fair to mint condition: $10-$20.

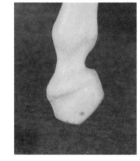

"Diablo" The Mustang #86, gray appaloosa. The detail photo shows the pared toe of the left front hoof, which is typical of early models of the Mustang mold. *Model courtesy of Heather Wells.* Fair to mint condition: $65-95.

"Diablo" The Mustang #1085, Copenhagen decorator. *Model courtesy of Heather Wells.* Fair to mint condition: $220-$300.

Mustang *text pp. 182-183*

Left: American Mustang #118, sorrel/palomino. Fair to mint condition: $15-$30.

"Diablo" The Mustang #87, buckskin. Fair to mint condition: $10-$20.

Right: "Diablo" The Mustang #2085, Florentine decorator. *Model courtesy of Joy Sheesley.* Fair to mint condition: $220-$300.

"Diablo" The Mustang #3085, Golden Charm decorator. *Model courtesy of Joy Sheesley.* Fair to mint condition: $220-$300.

Mustang SR #410287, alabaster. *Model courtesy of Heather Wells.* Fair to mint condition: $45-$70.

Mustang SR #410187, black leopard appaloosa. Fair to mint condition: $45-$70.

"Diablo" The Mustang #4085, Wedgewood Blue decorator. *Model courtesy of Joy Sheesley.* Fair to mint condition: $220-$300.

Mustang SR #410387, bay blanket appaloosa. Fair to mint condition: $55-$80.

Mustang SR #410487, fleabitten gray. Fair to mint condition: $55-$80.

Paint American Mustang #828, bay paint. Fair to mint condition: $20-$35.

Mustang SR #86, black (1978). *Model courtesy of Heather Wells.* Fair to mint condition: $85-$120.

Mustang SR, black (1993). Fair to mint condition: $30-$50.

Mustang SR #410587, palomino. Fair to mint condition: $45-$70.

Mustang SR #410687, red dun. Fair to mint condition: $55-$80.

"Rarin' To Go" #896, grulla. Fair to mint condition: $12-$25.

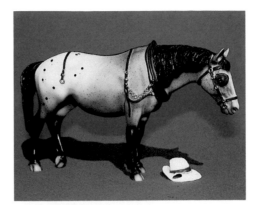

Old Timer *text p. 184*

Old Timer #206, bay. Fair to mint condition: $15-$30.

"McDuff" Old Timer #935, grulla blanket appaloosa. Still available retail in 1996.

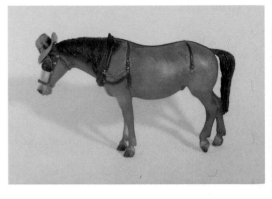

"Rawhide" Wild Appaloosa Mustang SR #702495, chestnut roan blanket appaloosa, wilder and tamer spot variation. Fair to mint condition: $25-$40.

Old Timer #200, alabaster. Fair to mint condition: $15-$30.

Old Timer #834, dark red roan. Fair to mint condition: $12-$25.

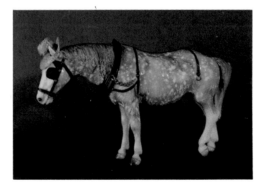

"Ruby" SR #410087, dark red roan. Fair to mint condition: $40-$60.

McCormick Decanter With Old Timer set SR, dapple gray. *Set and photo courtesy of Sande Schneider.* Fair to mint condition: $45-$70.

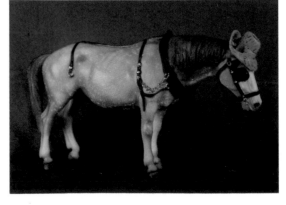

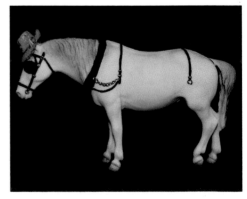

"Turbo" The Wonder Horse SR #410592, golden palomino. Fair to mint condition: $55-$80.

Old Timer #205, dapple gray. *Top,* older glossy model with green hatband. *Bottom,* newer matte model with yellow hatband; *model courtesy of Heather Wells.* Fair to mint condition: glossy $20-$35, matte or semigloss $12-$25.

Old Timer SR, alabaster (1983). *Model courtesy of Joy Sheesley.* Fair to mint condition: $20-$35.

Pacer *text pp. 184-185*

"Dan Patch" Famous Standardbred Pacer #819, red bay. Fair to mint condition: $20-$35.

Pacer SR, dark red chestnut. *Model courtesy of Heather Wells.* Fair to mint condition: $90-$130.

Pacer SR, light bay. Fair to mint condition: $20-$35.

Brenda Breyer Harness Racing Set SR, medium bay Pacer, earlier black-legged and later 4-stocking versions. *Models courtesy of Heather Wells.* Fair to mint condition: black-legged horse alone $40-$60, full set $60-$90; 4-stocking horse alone $25-$40, full set $45-$70.

Pacer #46, liver chestnut. *Top,* older semigloss model with eyewhites; *model courtesy of Heather Wells. Bottom,* newer matte model without eyewhites. Fair to mint condition: with eyewhites $30-$50, otherwise $12-$25.

Brenda Breyer And Sulky Set #2446, alabaster Pacer. Fair to mint condition: horse alone $20-$35, full set $40-$65.

Brenda Breyer Sulky And Pacer Set SR, light golden chestnut Pacer. Fair to mint condition: horse alone $45-$70, full set $65-$100.

Pacer SR, dapple gray. *Model courtesy of Heather Wells.* Fair to mint condition: $100-$140.

Pacer SR, palomino. *Model courtesy of Heather Wells.* Fair to mint condition: $90-$130.

Pacing Horse, Sulky And Harness set SR, black Pacer. Fair to mint condition: horse alone $45-$70, full set $60-$90.

49

Performance Horse *text p. 185*

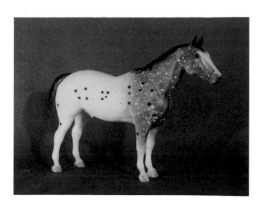

Appaloosa Performance Horse #99, chestnut roan semi-leopard appaloosa. Fair to mint condition: $15-$30.

Brenda Breyer Gift Set #3095, sorrel blanket appaloosa Performance Horse. Fair to mint condition: horse alone $25-$40, full set $40-$60.

Appaloosa Stallion With Western Tack Set SR, gray blanket appaloosa. Fair to mint condition: horse alone $35-$55; with tack, add $10.

Performance Horse SR #410199, alabaster. Fair to mint condition: $55-$80.

Performance Horse SR, black blanket appaloosa. Fair to mint condition: $30-$50.

Performance Horse SR #410099, black leopard appaloosa. Fair to mint condition: $55-$80.

Performance Horse SR #410399, liver chestnut. Fair to mint condition: $55-$80.

Performance Horse SR #410299, red roan. Fair to mint condition: $55-$80.

"Phantom Wings" *text p. 185-186*

"Bright Socks" Pinto Foal #895, black pinto. Fair to mint condition: $5-$12.

"Phantom Wings," "Misty's" Foal, #29, palomino pinto. Fair to mint condition: $5-$12.

"Rough Diamond" #846, dark chestnut pinto. Fair to mint condition: $5-$12.

Stock Horse Foal #17, chestnut blanket appaloosa. Fair to mint condition: $8-$15.

Stock Horse Foal #18, black blanket appaloosa. Fair to mint condition: $8-$15.

"Woodsprite" Pony Foal #875, reddish bay. Fair to mint condition: $5-$12.

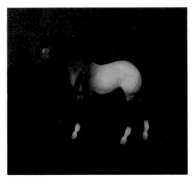

"Phantom Wings" SR, bay blanket appaloosa. Fair to mint condition: $10-$17.

"Phar Lap" *text p. 186*

Galloping Thoroughbred #803, dark dappled bay. Fair to mint condition: $15-$30.

"Hobo" #838, buckskin, lighter and darker color variations. Fair to mint condition: $15-$30.

"Native Diver" Champion Thoroughbred #921, black. Still available retail in 1996.

Wild American Horse #881, shaded brown-gray smoke. Fair to mint condition: $12-$25.

"Phar Lap" Famous Race Horse #90, red chestnut. *Top,* an older, darker, semi-gloss horse; *model courtesy of Heather Wells. Bottom,* a newer, brighter red, matte model. Fair to mint condition: $12-$25.

"Dr. Peaches" SR #410090, medium bay. Fair to mint condition: $55-$80.

"Dustin" SR #700995, red dun, and the gold medallion that came with him. Fair to mint condition: horse alone $20-$35; with medallion, add $1.

"Phar Lap" SR #410390, dark dapple gray. *Model courtesy of Heather Wells.* Fair to mint condition: $55-$80.

"Phar Lap" SR #410490, red bay. *Model courtesy of Heather Wells.* Fair to mint condition: $55-$80.

"Pluto" SR #500493, pale dapple gray. *Model and photo courtesy of Robin Briscoe.* Fair to mint condition: $60-$90.

"Phar Lap" SR, dark mahogany bay. Fair to mint condition: $25-$40.

"Phar Lap" SR #410290, sorrel. *Model courtesy of Heather Wells.* Fair to mint condition: $55-$80.

Pony Of The Americas *text p. 187*

"Just Justin" Quarter Pony #876, dun. Fair to mint condition: $8-$15.

"Phar Lap" SR, medium dapple gray. Fair to mint condition: $20-$35.

"Pluto" *text p. 187*

"Phar Lap" SR #410190, liver chestnut. *Model courtesy of Heather Wells.* Fair to mint condition: $55-$80.

"Pluto" The Lipizzaner #475, alabaster. Fair to mint condition: $12-$25.

"Favory" SR #702595, red fleabit. Fair to mint condition: $50-$75.

"Pantomime" Pony Of The Americas #884, black blanket appaloosa. Fair to mint condition: $12-$25.

Pony Of The Americas #154, bay blanket appaloosa. Fair to mint condition: $10-$20.

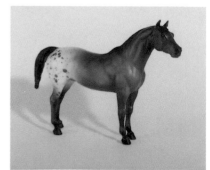

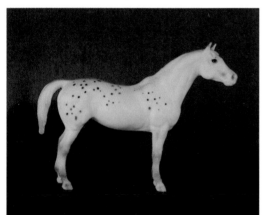

Pony Of The Americas #155, chestnut leopard appaloosa. *Top two photos*, both sides of a normal model; *bottom two photos*, both sides of the 6-spot variation. Fair to mint condition: normal $12-$25, 6-spot $15-$30.

"Rocky" Champion Connemara Stallion #821, dappled buckskin, dark-nosed and light-nosed variations. Fair to mint condition: $10-$20.

Pony Of The Americas SR, black leopard appaloosa. Fair to mint condition: $30-$50.

Not shown:
Pony Of the Americas SR, black blanket appaloosa. Fair to mint condition: $55-$80.

Premier Arabian Mare *text p. 187*

Fine Porcelain Premier Arabian Mare #79195, alabaster. Fair to mint condition: $145-$200.

Presentation Collection *text p. 188*

Presentation Collection Indian Pony #5175. *Model and photo courtesy of Sande Schneider.* Value: for any Presentation Collection piece, add $50 to the value of the regular-issue model.

Proud Arabian Foal *text p. 188-189*

Arabian Foal "Joy" #9, alabaster, glossy with charcoal lip line. Fair to mint condition: $13-$22.

"Joy" grooming-kit set #9548, with regular-run alabaster Arabian Foal "Joy" #9, blue vinyl "pack saddle," packet of girl's hair clips, and original carton. See note 3 for the Proud Arabian Foal mold for discussion. *Set and photo courtesy of Kirsten, Sarah, and Ruth-Ann Wellman.* Fair to mint condition: add $20-$25 to the value of Arabian Foal "Joy" #9.

Proud Arabian Foal SR, red-dish bay. *Model courtesy of Sheryl Leisure.* Fair to mint condition: $10-$17.

Not shown:
Proud Arabian Foal SR, pink. Fair to mint condition: $10-$17.

Arabian Foal "Shah" #15, bay, glossy.*Top,* a typical model. *Bottom,* a model with factory-painted eyewhites, which are highly unusual for #15; *model courtesy of Lani Keller.* Fair to mint condition: $20-$35.

Proud Arabian Foal #220, dapple gray. *Top,* a bevy of variations from the earlier years; *models courtesy of Lani Keller. Left,* a black-point model. *Right,* a soft gray, matte foal from the later years; *models courtesy of Heather Wells.* Fair to mint condition: black-point version $25-$40, others $5-$12.

Proud Arabian Mare *text pp. 189-191*

Left: Proud Arabian Foal #806, dappled rose gray. Fair to mint condition: $8-$15.

Arabian Foal "Spot" #39, gray blanket appaloosa. *Model courtesy of Lani Keller.* Fair to mint condition: $50-$75.

Arabian Mare #908, woodgrain. *Model courtesy of Sheryl Leisure.* Fair to mint condition: $125-$175.

Right: Proud Arabian Foal SR, red bay pinto. Fair to mint condition: $10-$17.

Right: Proud Arabian Foal SR, red chestnut. Fair to mint condition: $10-$17.

Proud Arabian Foal #218, alabaster, matte. Fair to mint condition: $5-$12.

Right: Proud Arabian Foal #219, mahogany bay. *Model courtesy of Heather Wells.* Fair to mint condition: $5-$12.

Arabian Mare "Pride" #8, alabaster, glossy. *Model courtesy of Sheryl Leisure.* Fair to mint condition: $25-$40.

"Pride" grooming-kit set #9547, with regular-run alabaster Arabian Mare "Pride" #8, blue vinyl "pack saddle," packet with various personal items, and original carton. See note 4 for the Proud Arabian Mare mold for discussion. *Set and photo courtesy of Kirsten, Sarah, and Ruth-Ann Wellman.* Fair to mint condition: add $25-$30 to the value of Arabian Mare "Pride" #8.

Arabian Mare "Sheba" #14, bay, glossy. Fair to mint condition: $40-$60.

Arabian Mare "Speck" #38, gray blanket appaloosa. *Model courtesy of Sheryl Leisure.* Fair to mint condition: $100-$140.

Legs of old-mold and new-mold Proud Arabian Mares. The old-mold mare on the left has a straight left foreleg, while the new-mold mare on the right has a splayed left foreleg.

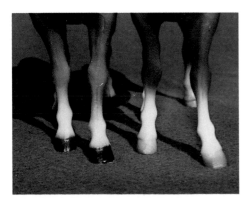

Proud Arabian Mare #215, dapple gray. *Top* a model from the earlier years; *center,* a black-point mare; *bottom,* a soft gray, matte model from the later years. Fair to mint condition: black point $60-$90, others $12-$25. In set #2155 with yarn halter, info sheet, and box, add $10.

Proud Arabian Mare #216, mahogany bay, semi-gloss version. Fair to mint condition: any version $15-$30. In set #2165 with yarn halter, info sheet, and box, add $10.

Proud Arabian Mare #217, alabaster, matte. *Model courtesy of Heather Wells.* Fair to mint condition: $15-$30. In set #2175 with yarn halter, info sheet, and box, add $10.

Proud Arabian Mare #805, dappled rose gray, solid-mane version. Fair to mint condition: solid mane $20-$35, striped mane $25-$40.

Proud Arabian Mare #840, red chestnut. Fair to mint condition: $15-$30.

Proud Arabian Mare SR, black. *Model courtesy of Heather Wells.* Fair to mint condition: $180-$250.

Proud Arabian Mare SR, fleabitten rose gray. Fair to mint condition: $25-$40.

"Steel Dust" SR #400393, pale smoke gray. Fair to mint condition: $35-$55.

Not shown:
Proud Arabian Mare SR, dark rose gray. Fair to mint condition: $220-$300.
Proud Arabian Mare SR, unpainted white. Fair to mint condition: $10-$20.

Proud Arabian Mare SR, reddish bay. *Top, gray-hoofed version; model courtesy of Heather Wells. Bottom, black-hoofed version; model courtesy of Sheryl Leisure.* Fair to mint condition: any version $25-$40.

Proud Arabian Stallion *text pp. 191-193*

Proud Arabian Mare SR, light reddish chestnut. *Model courtesy of Heather Wells.* Fair to mint condition: $85-$120.

Proud Arabian Stallion #211, alabaster. Fair to mint condition: $15-$30.

Proud Arabian Stallion #804, dappled rose gray, solid-mane and striped-mane versions. Fair to mint condition: solid mane $20-$35, striped mane $25-$40.

Proud Arabian Mare SR, red bay pinto. Fair to mint condition: $25-$40.

Proud Arabian Mare SR, sandy bay. Fair to mint condition: $25-$40.

Proud Arabian Mare SR #410293, "silver filigree" decorator. *Model courtesy of Sheryl Leisure.* Fair to mint condition: $220-$300.

Proud Arabian Stallion "Witez II" #212, mahogany bay, matte and semigloss versions. Fair to mint condition: any version $15-$30.

Proud Arabian Stallion #213, dapple gray. *Top*, a semigloss model from the earlier years. *Center*, black-point version; *model courtesy of Heather Wells. Bottom* a later matte stallion with no dapples on the head or neck; *model courtesy of Joy Sheesley.* Fair to mint condition: black-point $60-$90, others $12-$25.

"Sundown" Proud Arabian Stallion #933, light reddish chestnut. Still available retail in 1996.

Arabian Stallion With English Tack Set SR, reddish bay. *Top*, version with stripe and charcoal legs; *model courtesy of Heather Wells. Center*, version with stripe and 4 stockings; *model courtesy of Sheryl Leisure. Bottom*, solid-faced version with 1 stocking; *model courtesy of Lani Keller.* Fair to mint condition: horse alone, any version $25-$40; with tack, add $10.

Proud Arabian Stallion #839, pale dapple gray. Fair to mint condition: $12-$25.

Proud Arabian Stallion SR #412213, black. Fair to mint condition: $45-$70.

Proud Arabian Stallion SR, flocked bay, with halter. *Set courtesy of Heather Wells.* Fair to mint condition: horse alone $45-$70; with tack, add $10.

Not shown:
Open Top Buggy set #19841, flocked chestnut, with buggy and Brenda doll. Fair to mint condition: $255-$350.
Proud Arabian Stallion SR, unpainted white. Fair to mint condition: $10-$20.

Quarter Horse Gelding *text p. 193*

Proud Arabian Stallion SR, flocked chestnut, with buggy. *Set courtesy of Heather Wells.* Fair to mint condition: horse alone $45-$70, full set $240-$330.

Quarter Horse "Two Bits" #99, bay, glossy with eyewhites. Fair to mint condition: $40-$60.

Appaloosa Gelding #97, sorrel blanket appaloosa. Fair to mint condition: $12-$25.

Proud Arabian Stallion SR #413213, light red chestnut. Fair to mint condition: $35-$55.

Quarter Horse "Two Bits" #999, woodgrain. *Model courtesy of Heather Wells.* Fair to mint condition: $70-$100.

"Majesty" Quarter Horse #924, light dapple gray. Still available retail in 1996.

Quarter Horse "Two Bits" #98, buckskin. *Bottom,* an older model with dark brown halter and eyewhites; *model courtesy of Heather Wells. Top,* a newer model with brick-red halter and no eyewhites. Fair to mint condition: with eyewhites $15-$30, otherwise $12-$25.

Proud Arabian Stallion SR, red bay with blaze. Fair to mint condition: $25-$40.

Quarter Horse Gelding SR, bay, matte. *Model courtesy of Sheryl Leisure.* Fair to mint condition: $90-$130.

Quarter Horse Gelding SR, palomino. Fair to mint condition: $25-$40.

Proud Arabian Stallion SR #411213, red bay with solid face. Fair to mint condition: $40-$60.

Quarter Horse Gelding SR, red chestnut. Fair to mint condition: $30-$50.

Quarter Horse Yearling #101, liver chestnut. Fair to mint condition: $12-$25.

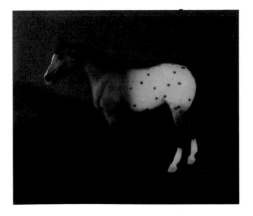

Quarter Horse Yearling SR, bay blanket appaloosa. Fair to mint condition: $25-$40.

"Silver" Quarter Horse SR #700097, steel gray. Fair to mint condition: $35-$55.

A chorus line of #101 and #102 fillies with assorted blaze shapes.

Quarter Horse Yearling SR #400101, blue roan. Fair to mint condition: $40-$60.

Quarter Horse Yearling text pp. 193-194

Appaloosa Yearling #103, sandy bay blanket appaloosa. Fair to mint condition: $10-$20.

Quarter Horse Yearling #102, palomino. Fair to mint condition: $12-$25. For the Presentation Collection edition (on base) add $50.

Quarter Horse Yearling SR #410492, buckskin. Model and photo courtesy of Ida Santana and Craig A. Lamb. Fair to mint condition: $220-$300.

"Calypso" Quarter Horse #937, tan dun. Left, an unusually dark and gray filly; right, a more typical model. Still available retail in 1996.

"Thunder Bay" Quarter Horse #927, dark mahogany bay, lighter and darker color variations. Fair to mint condition: $15-$30.

A test-color model for the SR buckskin Quarter Horse Yearling #410492. This test piece differs from the SR horses in having two hind stockings and a more brown-toned body color. Model courtesy of Paula Hecker; photo courtesy of Laura Hornick Behning.

Race Horse *text pp. 194-195*

"Vandergelder" Dutch Warmblood #900, dappled bay. Fair to mint condition: $12-$25.

Belgian Brabant #837, tan dun. Fair to mint condition: $15-$30.

Race Horse, Derby Winner #36, chestnut, gray-hoofed and black-hoofed versions. *Black-hoofed model courtesy of Sheryl Leisure.* Fair to mint condition: $20-$35; with saddle, add $10.

"Domino" Gift Set SR #700994, black pinto, with saddle and pad. Fair to mint condition: horse alone $25-$40; with tack, add $10.

Race Horse, Derby Winner #936, woodgrain. *Model courtesy of Heather Wells.* Fair to mint condition: $45-$70.

"Roemer" SR, seal brown. Fair to mint condition: $30-$50.

"Roemer" *text p. 195*

"Roy" *text pp. 195-196*

"Roy" SR, liver chestnut. Fair to mint condition: $30-$50.

"Roemer" Champion Dutch Warmblood #465, dark chestnut. Fair to mint condition: $12-$25.

"Roy" Belgian Drafter #455, light sorrel. Fair to mint condition: $15-$30.

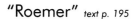

"Rugged Lark" *text p. 196*

"Rugged Lark" Champion American Quarter Horse Stallion #450, bay. Fair to mint condition: $12-$25.

"Rugged Lark" SR, dapple gray. Fair to mint condition: $30-$50.

"Rugged Lark" SR, red chestnut. Fair to mint condition: $25-$40.

Running Foal *text pp. 196-197*

Left: Bluegrass Foal #865, blue roan. Fair to mint condition: $5-$12.

"Little Bub," Young "Justin Morgan," #903, red bay. Fair to mint condition: $5-$12.

Running Foal #849, dark chestnut pinto. Fair to mint condition: $5-$12.

Running Foal #1130, Copenhagen decorator. *Model courtesy of Heather Wells.* Fair to mint condition: $100-$140.

Running Foal #2130, Florentine decorator. *Model courtesy of Joy Sheesley.* Fair to mint condition: $100-$140.

Right: Running Foal #3130, Golden Charm decorator. *Model courtesy of Lani Keller.* Fair to mint condition: $100-$140.

Running Foal #4130, Wedgewood Blue decorator. *Model courtesy of Lani Keller.* Fair to mint condition: $100-$140.

Running Foal "Spice" #130, alabaster with solid gray mane and tail. *Model courtesy of Heather Wells.* Fair to mint condition: $13-$22.

Above and left: Running Foal "Spice" #131, smoke, darker and lighter color variations. *Models courtesy of Heather Wells.* Fair to mint condition: $13-$22.

Running Foal "Spice" #133, dapple gray, glossy. *Model courtesy of Heather Wells.* Fair to mint condition: $10-$17.

Running Foal "Spice" #134, bay with bald face and stockings. *Model courtesy of Heather Wells.* Fair to mint condition: $5-$12.

Running Foal "Spice" #930, woodgrain. *Model courtesy of Heather Wells.* Fair to mint condition: $35-$55.

Running Foal SR, alabaster with striped gray mane and tail. Fair to mint condition: $10-$17.

Left: Running Foal SR, bay with no white markings. Fair to mint condition: $10-$17.

Running Foal SR, black blanket appaloosa. Fair to mint condition: $10-$17.

Running Foal SR, buckskin (1983). *Model courtesy of Heather Wells.* Fair to mint condition: $50-$75.

Running Foal SR, dapple gray with darker gray mane and tail. *Model courtesy of Lani Keller.* Fair to mint condition: $50-$75.

Running Foal SR, flocked white. *Model courtesy of Heather Wells.* Fair to mint condition: $20-$35.

Running Foal SR, dapple gray with white mane and tail, variations with small and large dapples. *Small-dapple model courtesy of Heather Wells.* Fair to mint condition: $13-$22.

Running Foal SR, dark rose gray. Fair to mint condition: $10-$17.

Running Foal SR, flocked palomino. *Model courtesy of Heather Wells.* Fair to mint condition: $20-$35.

Running Foal SR, red roan. *Model courtesy of Heather Wells.* Fair to mint condition: $40-$60.

Running Mare *text pp. 197-199*

Running Mare #1120, Copenhagen decorator. *Model courtesy of Heather Wells.* Fair to mint condition: $220-$300.

Running Mare #3120, Golden Charm decorator. *Model courtesy of Sheryl Leisure.* Fair to mint condition: $220-$300.

Running Mare "Sugar" #121, smoke, darker and lighter color variations. *Darker model courtesy of Heather Wells.* Fair to mint condition: $25-$40.

Running Mare #119, red roan with brown-chestnut dappling. *Top,* a fairly typical mare; *model courtesy of Heather Wells. Bottom* , a more unusual model with large dapples. Fair to mint condition: $45-$70.

Running Mare #848, dark chestnut pinto. Fair to mint condition: $12-$25.

Running Mare "Sugar" #120, alabaster with solid gray mane and tail. Fair to mint condition: $25-$40.

Running Mare "Sugar" #123, dapple gray, glossy. Fair to mint condition: $20-$35.

Running Mare "Sugar" #124, bay with bald face and stockings. Note the factory-painted eyewhites on this specimen. *Model courtesy of Sheryl Leisure.* Fair to mint condition: with eyewhites $12-$25, otherwise $10-$20.

Running Mare "Sugar" #920, woodgrain. *Model courtesy of Heather Wells.* Fair to mint condition: $85-$120.

"Wild Diamond," "Justin Morgan's" Dam, #902, sandy bay. Fair to mint condition: $12-$25.

Running Mare SR, dapple gray with darker gray mane and tail. *Model courtesy of Heather Wells.* Fair to mint condition: $100-$140.

Running Mare SR, flocked white. *Model courtesy of Heather Wells.* Fair to mint condition: $45-$70.

Running Mare SR, alabaster with striped gray mane and tail. Fair to mint condition: $25-$40.

Running Mare SR, palomino (not flocked). *Model courtesy of Heather Wells.* Fair to mint condition: horse alone $40-$60; with tack, add $10.

Running Mare SR, red roan with red-chestnut dappling. In the detail photo at bottom, the light reflection in the mare's right eye (at left in photo) reveals the flattened area that is characteristic of this SR. Some mares have an even more grotesquely flattened eye than this one. *Model courtesy of Heather Wells.* Fair to mint condition: $55-$80.

Running Mare SR, bay with no white markings. Fair to mint condition: $30-$50.

Running Mare SR, dapple gray with white mane and tail, variations with small and large dapples. *Small-dapple model courtesy of Heather Wells.* Fair to mint condition: $30-$50.

Running Mare SR?, buckskin (1960s). *Model and photo courtesy of Laura Hornick Behning.*

Running Mare SR, flocked palomino. *Model courtesy of Heather Wells.* Fair to mint condition: $45-$70.

State Line Tack '95 "Special Delivery" SR #702295, dark plum bay. Fair to mint condition: $25-$40.

The Running Mare's eye problems. *right*, a mare from the 1960s with a normal right eyeball and upper lid, as well as a sharply defined cheekbone. *left*, a 1984 bay SR with a swollen right eye and lid and flattened cheekbone. Note the loss of definition of the eyeball and upper lid folds.

Not shown:
Running Mare #2120, Florentine decorator, dappled gold. Fair to mint condition: $220-$300. For the color, see the photo of the Florentine Running Foal.
Running Mare #4120, Wedgewood Blue decorator, solid blue. Fair to mint condition: $220-$300. For the color, see the photo of the Wedgewood Blue Running Foal.

Running Stallion *text pp. 199-200*

"Lone Star" #928, rose gray snowflake appaloosa. Still available retail in 1996.

"Rumbling Thunder" #879, dark dapple gray. *Top* an early semigloss model with abundant body shading; *Bottom*, a later matte model with flatter coloring. Fair to mint condition: $15-$30.

Running Stallion #125, alabaster. Fair to mint condition: $60-$90.

Running Stallion #126, charcoal. *Model courtesy of Heather Wells.* Fair to mint condition: $70-$100.

Running Stallion #127, black blanket appaloosa. *Top*, an early model with big bald face; *bottom*, a later model with narrow bald face. Fair to mint condition: $12-$25.

Running Stallion #128, red roan, darker and lighter color variations. Fair to mint condition: $35-$55.

Running Stallion #129, bay with bald face. *Model courtesy of Heather Wells.* Fair to mint condition: $15-$30.

Left: Unicorn #210, alabaster with gold-and-white-striped horn. Fair to mint condition: $12-$25.

Running Stallion SR #410212, bay with solid face. *Model courtesy of Heather Wells.* Fair to mint condition: $60-$90.

Unicorn SR #700394, alabaster with silver-and-white-striped horn. Fair to mint condition: $15-$30.

Running Stallion SR #400212, chestnut. Fair to mint condition: $45-$70.

Unicorn II SR #700595, black. Fair to mint condition: $15-$30.

Saddlebred Weanling *text pp. 200-201*

Collector's Rocking Horse #701, flocked chestnut. *Top,* a model with brown glass eyes and brown rockers. *Bottom,* a colorful piece with blue glass eyes and yellow rockers; *model courtesy of Heather Wells.* Fair to mint condition: $45-$70.

Saddlebred Weanling #62, dark chestnut, darker and lighter color variations and a bevy of blaze styles. Fair to mint condition: $15-$30.

Running Stallion SR, palomino blanket appaloosa. Fair to mint condition: $30-$35. Fair to mint condition: $30-$50.

Sky Blue Unicorn SR, flocked sky blue. *Model courtesy of Heather Wells.* Fair to mint condition: $45-$70.

"Kentuckiana" Saddlebred Weanling #915, dappled liver chestnut. Still available retail in 1996.

Saddlebred Weanling #818, caramel pinto. Fair to mint condition: $40-$60.

Saddlebred Weanling SR, chestnut. Fair to mint condition: $70-$100.

Future Champion Show Set SR #494092, bay pinto Saddlebred Weanling. Fair to mint condition: horse alone $30-$50, full set $40-$60.

My Companion Rocking Horse SR, flocked white. *Model courtesy of Sue Lehman.* Fair to mint condition: $50-$75.

My Favorite Rocking Horse SR, flocked mauve. *Top, model and photo courtesy of Sande Schneider; bottom, model courtesy of Heather Wells.* Fair to mint condition: $50-$75.

Our Rocking Horse SR, flocked black blanket appaloosa. *Model and photo courtesy of Sande Schneider.* Fair to mint condition: $50-$75.

"Raven" SR #701091, plum black. Fair to mint condition: $20-$35.

Saddlebred Weanling SR, alabaster. Fair to mint condition: $25-$40.

Not shown:
Saddlebred Weanling SR, unpainted white. Fair to mint condition: $10-$20.

"San Domingo" text pp. 201-202

Blanket Appaloosa #703, dark gray blanket appaloosa. Fair to mint condition: $15-$30.

Comanche Pony #829, dark palomino. Fair to mint condition: $12-$25.

"Oxidol" Rodeo Appaloosa #917, no-spot white. Still available retail in 1996.

"Domino" The Happy Canyon Trail Horse #871, dark olive-brown paint, lighter and darker color variations. Fair to mint condition: $30-$50.

Marguerite Henry's "San Domingo" #67, chestnut pinto. *Top,* an earlier, darker horse; *bottom,* the later, lighter version. Fair to mint condition: earliest, unstenciled version (not shown) $25-$40, others $12-$25.

Right: "San Domingo" SR, red bay. Fair to mint condition: $25-$40.

"Black Gold" SR, black. Fair to mint condition: horse alone $60-$90; with book, add $5.

"Bright Zip" SR #700794, chestnut roan blanket appaloosa. Fair to mint condition: $40-$60.

"San Domingo" SR #416091, Copenhagen decorator. *Model courtesy of Heather Wells.* Fair to mint condition: $220-$300.

"Spotted Bear" Indian Pony SR #490465, black pinto, cold-cast porcelain. Fair to mint condition: $100-$140.

"Wildfire" SR #410067, red chestnut pinto. Fair to mint condition: $40-$60.

Scratching Foal text p. 202

Scratching Foal #168, black blanket appaloosa. *Model courtesy of Sheryl Leisure.* Fair to mint condition: $5-$12.

Scratching Foal #169, liver chestnut. *Model courtesy of Heather Wells.* Fair to mint condition: $30-$50.

Left: Scratching Foal #170, red roan. Fair to mint condition: $20-$35.

"Cochise" SR, chestnut blanket appaloosa, with medallion. Fair to mint condition: foal alone $8-$15; with medallion, add $1.

"Secretariat" SR #410435, Golden Charm decorator. Fair to mint condition: $25-$40. (This is not a typo. This horse is a decorator but is not at all rare.)

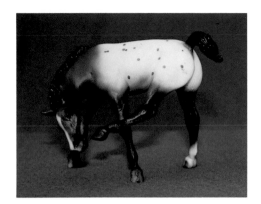

"Brandi" SR, bay blanket appaloosa. Fair to mint condition: $20-$35.

"Secretariat" text pp. 202-203

"Secretariat" Famous Race Horse #435, red chestnut. Fair to mint condition: $10-$20.

"Secretariat" SR #491292, red chestnut, cold-cast porcelain. Model courtesy of Heather Wells. Fair to mint condition: $85-$120.

Scratching Foal SR, alabaster. Fair to mint condition: $10-$17.

"Sea Star" text p. 202

Left: Chincoteague Foal #845, buckskin. Fair to mint condition: $5-$12.

"Burmese" Her Majesty The Queen's Horse SR #700435, black. Fair to mint condition: $40-$60.

"Secretariat" SR, glossy red chestnut. Fair to mint condition: $25-$40.

"Sham" text pp. 203-204

Marguerite Henry's "Sham" The Godolphin Arabian #410, blood bay. Fair to mint condition: wheat-ear version $25-$40, otherwise $12-$25.

The "wheat ear" mold marking on the breast of an early model "Sham" #410.

Right: Marguerite Henry's "Sea Star" #16, red chestnut. Model courtesy of Heather Wells. Fair to mint condition: $5-$12.

Left: "Scribbles" Paint Horse Foal #893, chestnut paint. Fair to mint condition: $5-$12.

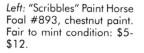

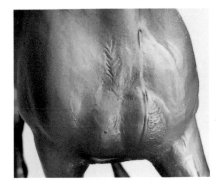

Prancing Arabian Stallion #411, fleabitten gray. *Left*, earlier version with larger, darker flecks and wheat ear (model is slightly yellowed); *right*, a later model with smaller, lighter flecks. Fair to mint condition: wheat-ear version $25-$40, otherwise $15-$30.

Arabian Stallion And Frisky Foal set #3163, dappled dark yellow-gray dun. Fair to mint condition: $20-$35.

"Sham" The Godolphin Arabian Horse SR #701595, blood bay. The detail photo shows the "'95" mold stamp that most of these models have. Fair to mint condition: with stamp $25-$40, without stamp $12-$25.

Prancing Arabian Stallion #812, dark palomino. Fair to mint condition: $15-$30.

"Sham" SR, golden bay (*right*), with a regular-run red bay "Sham" #410 behind him. *Models courtesy of Lani Keller.* Golden Boy, fair to mint condition: $70-$100.

"Rana" The Arab Stallion #863, blue chocolate. Fair to mint condition: $15-$30.

Arabian Stallion And Frisky Foal set #3162, dappled bay Arabian Stallion. Fair to mint condition: $20-$35.

"Galaxias" SR #710410, dapple gray, cold-cast porcelain. *Model courtesy of Heather Wells.* Fair to mint condition: $85-$120.

"Sham" SR #410994, liver chestnut. Fair to mint condition: $45-$70.

"Sham" SR, glossy blood bay. *Top*, a model with normal color; *bottom*, the "Halloween Sham" variation. Fair to mint condition: any version $25-$40.

"Sham" SR #414091, Wedgewood Blue decorator. The specimen shown is named "Smurfy." *Model and photo courtesy of Ida Santana and Craig A. Lamb.* Fair to mint condition: $220-$300.

"Sherman Morgan" text p. 204

Prancing Morgan #835, black. Fair to mint condition: $20-$35.

"Sherman Morgan," Son Of "Justin Morgan," #430, red chestnut. Fair to mint condition: $15-$30.

"Fashionably Late" SR #498092, chocolate sorrel, cold-cast porcelain. *Top,* the version with beige mane and tail and more matte finish; *bottom,* the version with yellow mane and tail and semigloss finish. *Models courtesy of Heather Wells.* Fair to mint condition: either version $100-$140.

"Pride And Vanity" SR #400192, alabaster. Fair to mint condition: $40-$60.

Shetland Pony text p. 205

Shetland Pony #21, black pinto. *Top:* and *center,* a glossy model shown from both sides. *Bottom,* a matte #21; *model courtesy of Sheryl Leisure.* Fair to mint condition: glossy $3-7, matte $13-$22.

Right: Shetland Pony #22, brown pinto, shown here in brown, palomino, and orangy color variations, all with glossy finish. *Models courtesy of Lani Keller.* Fair to mint condition: glossy $5-12, matte $13-$22.

Shetland Pony #23, bay. *Model courtesy of Heather Wells.* Fair to mint condition: $3-$7.

Shetland Pony #25, alabaster. Fair to mint condition: glossy or matte $5-$12.

Shetland Pony #801, bay pinto. Fair to mint condition: $8-$15.

Shetland Pony #857, dark red chestnut. Fair to mint condition: $5-12.

Shetland Pony #925, woodgrain, darker and lighter color variations. *Models courtesy of Heather Wells.* Fair to mint condition: $30-$50.

Shire *text pp. 205-206*

Marguerite Henry's "Our First Pony" Gift Set #3066, black pinto mare "Midge" with pink hooves. Still available retail in 1996.

Shire #95, dapple gray with no dapples on head or upper neck. *Top,* a typical model with dark shading on the hindquarters. *Bottom,* a model with very little shading; *model courtesy of Sheryl Leisure.* Fair to mint condition: $40-$60.

Shire #96, honey sorrel, early darker version with stenciled blaze and later light version with unstenciled bald face. The detail photo shows a jagged stenciled blaze (*left*), unstenciled bald face (*center*), and a stenciled blaze with no jag. Fair to mint condition: stenciled blazes $20-$35, unstenciled bald face $25-$40.

Shire SR, black. *Model courtesy of Heather Wells.* Fair to mint condition: $90-$130.

"Our First Pony" set SR, black pinto mare "Midge" with gray-brown hooves. Fair to mint condition: $10-$17; with tack and book, add $5.

Shire SR, dapple gray with dapples on neck and head. Fair to mint condition: $40-$60.

Shire SR, palomino with bald face. *Model courtesy of Heather Wells.* Fair to mint condition: $70-$100.

Shire SR, palomino with stripe. Fair to mint condition: $30-$50.

Shire SR, reddish bay. Fair to mint condition: $90-$130.

Shire SR, smoke gray. *Model courtesy of Heather Wells.* Fair to mint condition: $90-$130.

Shire Horse *text p. 206*

Fine Porcelain Shire Horse #79193, dark dappled bay. *Model courtesy of Sheryl Leisure.* Fair to mint condition: $160-$220.

Showcase Collection *text p. 206*

Showcase Collection buckskin Western Prancer in his carrying-case box. The model number "#1110#" stamped lightly on the left end of the white Styrofoam insert may be too faint to see here. *Set and photo courtesy of Sande Schneider.* Value of the box: $6-$8.

"Smoky" *text pp. 206-207*

"Smoky" The Cow Horse #69, steel gray, early 4-stocking and late 1-stocking versions. Fair to mint condition: 4-stocking $15-$30, 1-stocking $30-$50. In set #2090 with book and box, add $8.

Spanish Barb *text p. 207*

Fine Porcelain Spanish Barb #79194, pale tan dun. *Model courtesy of Heather Wells.* Fair to mint condition: $130-$180.

Stock Horse Foal *text pp. 207-208*

American Buckskin Stock Horse Foal #224, with solid face. *Model courtesy of Sheryl Leisure.* Fair to mint condition: $5-$12.

Appaloosa Stock Horse Foal #234, gray blanket appaloosa. *Left,* the normal bald-faced version; *model courtesy of Heather Wells. Right,* a solid-faced variation. Fair to mint condition: any version $5-$12.

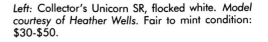

Left: Collector's Unicorn SR, flocked white. *Model courtesy of Heather Wells.* Fair to mint condition: $30-$50.

Stock Horse Foal SR, bay paint. Fair to mint condition: $10-$17.

Stock Horse Mare *text pp. 208-209*

Bay Quarter Horse Stock Foal #228, bay. Fair to mint condition: $5-$12.

Stock Horse Foal SR, buckskin, bald-faced and solid-faced versions. *Solid-faced model courtesy of Sheryl Leisure.* Fair to mint condition: either version $5-$12.

Appaloosa Stock Horse Mare #233, black blanket appaloosa, foreleg-lowered and foreleg-raised versions. Note that the older, foreleg-raised mare has a short blaze while her sister has a star. Fair to mint condition: foreleg lowered $12-$25, foreleg raised $20-$35.

Family Appaloosa Foal #861, bay blanket appaloosa. Fair to mint condition: $5-$12.

Stock Horse Foal SR, gray blanket appaloosa, star-faced version. Fair to mint condition: any version $5-$12.

Paint Horse Foal #809, liver chestnut paint. Fair to mint condition: $8-$15.

Paint Horse Foal #844, light chestnut paint. *Model courtesy of Sheryl Leisure.* Fair to mint condition: $8-$15.

Overo Paint Stock Horse Mare #230, bay paint. *Top,* an early, foreleg-raised mare with normal coloring; *bottom,* an apricot color variation with foreleg down, shown here with the foreleg-raised mare behind her for comparison. Fair to mint condition: foreleg lowered $12-$25, foreleg raised $20-$35.

Stock Horse Foal SR, pale smoke gray. Fair to mint condition: $8-$15.

Pinto Stock Horse Foal #231, black paint. Fair to mint condition: $5-$12.

"Night Vision" SR, bay snowflake leopard appaloosa. Fair to mint condition: $13-$22.

Sorrel Quarter Horse Stock Mare #227, deep red sorrel, foreleg-raised version. Fair to mint condition: foreleg lowered $12-$25, foreleg raised $20-$35.

Right: Stock Horse Foal SR, palomino. *Model courtesy of Heather Wells.* Fair to mint condition: $20-$35.

American Buckskin Stock Horse Mare #222. Fair to mint condition: $15-$30.

Stock Horse Mare SR, black paint. Fair to mint condition: $25-$40.

opy Mare #852, red roan leopard appaloosa. Fair mint condition: $15-$30.

Stock Horse Mare SR, buckskin, gray-hoofed version. *Model courtesy of Heather Wells.* Fair to mint condition: any version $20-$35.

Appaloosa Stock Horse Stallion #232, bay blanket appaloosa, red bay and buckskin color variations. Fair to mint condition: $12-$25.

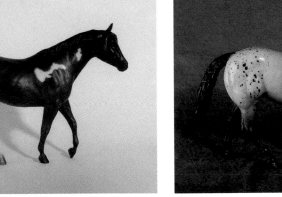

aint Horse Mare #808, liver chestnut paint. Fair to mint condition: $15-$30.

Stock Horse Mare SR, gray blanket appaloosa. Fair to mint condition: $35-$55.

Bay Quarter Horse Stock Stallion #226, bay. Fair to mint condition: $15-$30.

Stock Horse Stallion *text pp. 209-210*

American Buckskin Stock Horse Stallion #221. Fair to mint condition: $15-$30.

tock Horse Mare SR, bay peppercorn leopard appaloosa. Fair to mint condition: $25-$40.

Paint Horse Stallion #807, liver chestnut paint. Fair to mint condition: $15-$30.

"Shane" American Ranch Horse #938, blue roan. Still available retail in 1996.

Kelly Reno And "Little Man" Gift Set #3096, palomino "Little Man." Fair to mint condition: horse alone $35-$55, full set $50-$75.

Stock Horse Stallion SR, buckskin, gray-hoofed version. *Model courtesy of Sheryl Leisure.* Fair to mint condition: any version $20-$35.

"Skipster's Chief" Famous Therapeutic Riding Horse #842, sorrel. Fair to mint condition: $15-$30.

"Sam I Am" SR, dark bay paint. Fair to mint condition: $45-$70.

Stock Horse Stallion SR, dappled reddish chestnut. Fair to mint condition: $20-$35.

Stock Horse Stallion SR, bay paint. Fair to mint condition: $35-$55.

Stock Horse Stallion SR, gray blanket appaloosa. Fair to mint condition: $35-$55.

Tobiano Pinto Stock Horse Stallion #229, black paint. Top, early version with 1 stocking; bottom, the later version with 4 stockings. Fair to mint condition: 1-stocking $25-$40, 4-stocking $12-$25.

Stock Horse Stallion SR, bay peppercorn leopard appaloosa. Fair to mint condition: $25-$40.

Stock Horse Stallion SR, rose alabaster. Fair to mint condition: $35-$55.

Marguerite Henry's "Stormy" #19, chestnut pinto. Still available retail in 1996.

Blanket Appaloosa #823, red bay blanket appaloosa. Fair to mint condition: $12-$25.

"Skeeter" SR, dark bay pinto, and the gold medallion that came in her set. Fair to mint condition: foal alone $8-$15; with medallion, add $1.

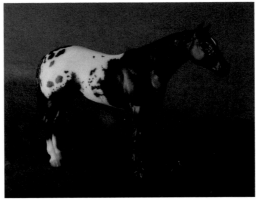

Family Appaloosa Stallion #859, bay blanket appaloosa. Fair to mint condition: $12-$25.

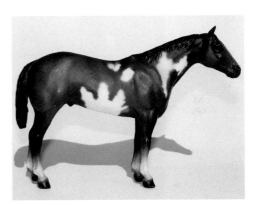

"Stormy" SR, flocked dark chestnut pinto. *Model courtesy of Heather Wells.* Fair to mint condition: $13-$22.

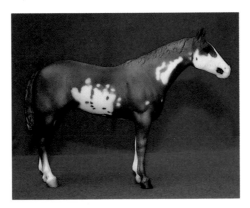

"Mister Mister" Champion Paint #916, medium chestnut paint. Still available retail in 1996.

"Stud Spider" Appaloosa #66, black blanket appaloosa. Fair to mint condition: $12-$25. In set #3080 with book and box, add $8.

Overo Paint #88, dark chestnut paint. *Top two photos,* both sides of the no-forearm-spots pattern (pattern A) with three distinct small spots on the right side of the back. *Bottom two photos,* both sides of another no-forearm-spots horse with two of the small spots on his back merged into one. Fair to mint condition: any version $20-$35.

Suckling Foal SR, bay pinto. Fair to mint condition: $13-$22.

"Stud Spider" SR, blue roan semi-leopard appaloosa. Fair to mint condition: $30-$50.

Not shown:
"Stud Spider" SR, unpainted white. Fair to mint condition: $10-$20.

Suckling Foal *text p. 211*

Medicine Hat Mare And Foal set #3180, chestnut pinto foal. Still available retail in 1996.

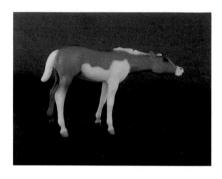

Suckling Foal SR, dark palomino pinto. Fair to mint condition: $10-$17.

Suckling Foal SR, red leopard appaloosa. Fair to mint condition: $8-$15.

Overo Paint #88, dark chestnut paint. *Top two photos,* both sides of the spot-and-crescent pattern (pattern B). *Bottom two photos,* both sides of the one-forearm-spot pattern (pattern C). Fair to mint condition: any version $20-$35.

Thoroughbred Mare And Suckling Foal set #3155, chestnut foal, shown here in red chestnut and sandy "bay" color variations. Fair to mint condition: $5-$12.

Tennessee Walker *text p. 211*

"High Flyer" Tennessee Walker #913, chestnut pinto. Still available retail in 1996.

Left: Bay Stock Horse SR. The hocks and front lower legs on this specimen are dark gray-brown. Fair to mint condition: $40-$60.

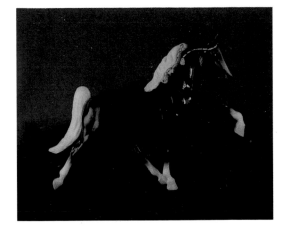

"Memphis Storm" Tennessee Walking Horse #854, charcoal-brown. Fair to mint condition: $30-$50.

Thoroughbred Mare *text pp. 211-212*

Medicine Hat Mare And Foal set #3180, chestnut pinto mare. Still available retail in 1996.

Selle Français #843, shaded liver chestnut. Fair to mint condition: $12-$25.

Thoroughbred Mare #813, black. Fair to mint condition: $15-$30.

"Midnight Sun" Famous Tennessee Walker #60, black, version with brown hooves. Fair to mint condition: $12-$25.

Thoroughbred Mare And Suckling Foal set #3155, bay mare. Fair to mint condition: $12-$25.

"Touch Of Class" Olympic Champion #420, medium/light bay. Fair to mint condition: $12-$25.

Tennessee Walking Horse #704, red bay. Fair to mint condition: $15-$30.

Tennessee Walker SR, light/medium sorrel. Fair to mint condition: $105-$150.

Thoroughbred Mare SR, bay pinto. Fair to mint condition: $35-$55.

"Touch Of Class" *text p. 212*

"Guinevere" English Hack #877, red bay. Fair to mint condition: $10-$20.

Trakehner *text p. 212*

"Abdullah" Champion Trakehner #817, pale dapple gray. Fair to mint condition: $20-$35.

79

"Hanover" Trakehner #912, liver chestnut. Still available retail in 1996.

Trakehner SR, chestnut. Fair to mint condition: $45-$70.

Trakehner SR #400154, golden bay. Fair to mint condition: $55-$80.

Trakehner #54, bay, early seal bay and later medium bay color variations. Fair to mint condition: any version $25-$40.

Trakehner SR, unpainted white. *Model courtesy of Heather Wells.* Fair to mint condition: $10-$20.

"Kaleidoscope" SR #702395, bay pinto. Fair to mint condition: $20-$35.

Right: Western Horse mold versions. *Left,* a normal-mold horse with rounded conchas on the bridle; *right,* an early-mold horse with diamond-shaped conchas flanking a round concha on the bridle.

Western Horse *text pp. 213-216*

Western Horse #59, white. *Top two photos:* "Cream Puff," the diamond-conchas mold version with brown-shaded mane and tail, o-link reins, and old-style Western saddle. Note the saddle's "antique" whitewashing and high-set, nailhead-style grommets that once attached a vinyl girth to the fenders. Also note the characteristic reddish stain left by the saddle on "Cream Puff's" back. *Third photo:* an early normal-mold horse with o-link reins and old-style Western saddle with high-set, donut-style grommets; *model courtesy of Heather Wells. Bottom photo:* a later horse, also normal mold, with twisted-link reins and old-style Western saddle with low-set, donut-style grommets; *model courtesy of Sheryl Leisure.* Fair to mint condition: diamond conchas $45-$70, normal mold with o-links $40-$60, normal mold with twisted-links $25-$40.

"TicToc" #864, alabaster. Fair to mint condition: $12-$25.

Western Horse #55, black pinto. Top, a glossy horse with old-style Western saddle. Bottom, a semigloss model with new-style saddle; model courtesy of Joy Sheesley. Fair to mint condition: either version $15-$30.

Western Horse #50, black with bald face and stockings. Top, the version with unstenciled facial white; model courtesy of Heather Wells. Bottom, the version with stenciled facial white; model courtesy of Joy Sheesley. Fair to mint condition: any version $50-$75.

Western Mount Horse "Black Beauty" #58, black with no white markings. Model courtesy of Heather Wells. Fair to mint condition: $50-$75.

Western Horse #57, palomino. This is the longest-running model in Breyer history, having been issued for 41 years. Top, a very early glossy model with dark coloring, o-link reins, and high-grommet old-style Western saddle. Center, a somewhat later glossy honey-colored model with twisted-link reins and low-grommet saddle; model courtesy of Heather Wells. Bottom, a matte model from the last year of production of #57, with new-style slip-on saddle. Fair to mint condition: with o-links and old saddle $40-$60, twisted-links and old saddle $15-$30, twisted links and new saddle $5-$12.

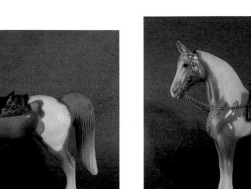

Western Horse #56, brown pinto. Model courtesy of Heather Wells. Fair to mint condition: $25-$40.

Western Horse SR #400057, caramel pinto. Fair to mint condition: $40-$60.

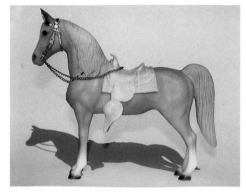

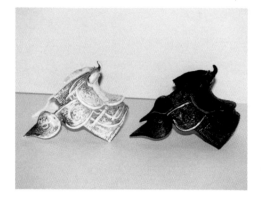

Western Horse SR #701895, palomino. The detail photo shows the "'95" date stamp that is the only physical feature distinguishing this SR from the legions of his matte palomino Western Horse #57 brethren. Fair to mint condition: with stamp $20-$35, without stamp $5-$10.

Western Horse new-style saddles. The tan-shaded and gray-shaded white saddles were the first issues of this saddle and were produced for many years, the tan-shaded one as recently as 1995. The brown and black saddles are both from the 1990s. *Saddles and photos courtesy of Sande Schneider.* Fair to mint condition: $1-$3.

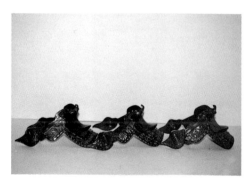

Western Horse old-style saddles. *Top* and *center,* two of the earliest saddles, with white-washed skirts. Both came on horses of the diamond-conchas mold, some of which were mounted on MasterCrafters clocks of the horse-over-the-clock style. The saddle at top has no grommets or cinch; the center saddle has high-set, nailhead grommets and a cinch with slip-through buckle. *Bottom,* a slightly later saddle with high-set donut grommets, snap cinch, and gold-washed skirts. This saddle came on the white Western Horses mounted on MasterCrafters clocks of the horse-beside-the-clock style. The off-white felt saddle pad also came with some of these clocks. *Saddles and photos courtesy of Sande Schneider.*

Western Horse old-style saddles. These black and brown saddles, all with snap cinches, illustrate variations of color and paint detailing. The saddles with high-set grommets are earlier; those with low grommets are later. *Saddles and photos courtesy of Sande Schneider.* Fair to mint condition: $3-$6.

Western Horse reins. *Top,* o-link chain reins, used for the first few years of the mold's existence; *bottom,* twisted-link chain reins, introduced in 1953.

Western Pony *text pp. 216-218*

"Cisco" Western Pony With Saddle #910, buckskin. Still available retail in 1996.

Western Mount Horse "Black Beauty" #44, black with no white markings. Fair to mint condition: $25-$40.

Western Pony "Black Beauty" #40, black. *Top*, the bald-faced version with silver tack; *bottom*, the star-faced version with gold tack. Note the eyewhites on the bald-faced pony; these are unusual for the Western Pony mold. *Models courtesy of Sheryl Leisure.* Fair to mint condition: either version $35-$55.

Western Pony #40, dark brown. *Model courtesy of Joy Sheesley.* Fair to mint condition: $35-$55.

Western Pony #42, brown pinto. *Model courtesy of Heather Wells.* Fair to mint condition: $12-$25.

Western Pony #43, palomino. *Top*, a light honey-tan model with new-style saddle; *model courtesy of Heather Wells. Bottom*, a more yellow-palomino model with old-style saddle; *model courtesy of Joy Sheesley.* Fair to mint condition: with either saddle $5-$12.

Right: Western Pony grooming-kit set #9549, with regular-run palomino Western Pony #43, large "pack saddle," packet of personal items, and original carton. See note 4 for the Western Pony mold for discussion. *Set and photo courtesy of Kirsten, Sarah, and Ruth-Ann Wellman.* Fair to mint condition: add $25-$30 to the value of Western Pony #43.

Western Pony #41, black pinto. *Top* two photos both sides of an old glossy low-spot pattern pony, with old-style saddle. *Bottom two photos*, both sides of a newer matte no-spot pattern pony, with new-style saddle; *model courtesy of Sheryl Leisure.* Fair to mint condition: any version with either saddle $5-$12.

Western Pony grooming-kit set with regular-run palomino Western Pony #43 and a small, tooled "pack saddle" (missing its grooming items). See note 4 for the Western Pony mold for discussion. Fair to mint condition: for any pony kit with small "pack saddle," add $3-$10 to the value of the Western Pony.

Western Pony #45, white. *Top,* an older model with old-style saddle. *Bottom,* a newer model with new-style saddle; *model courtesy of Joy Sheesley.* Fair to mint condition: with either saddle $10-$20.

Western Pony #945, woodgrain. *Model courtesy of Heather Wells.* Fair to mint condition: $70-$100.

Western Horse and Western Pony: the molds are nearly identical except in size.

Old-style snap-cinch saddles for Western Ponies and "Fury" Prancers. *Top,* three brown saddles showing color and mold variations. The one on the left has long fenders with high-set grommets; the other two are short-fender saddles. The dark plum brown saddle in the middle has gold trim even on its latigo ties. *Bottom,* three black saddles, one with long fenders and the others with short fenders. *Saddles and photos courtesy of Sande Schneider.* Fair to mint condition: any saddle $2-$5.

Below: More saddles for Western Ponies. The three on the left are new-style saddles. The gray-shaded and tan-shaded white ones in the middle were the first issues of this style; the black saddle is from 1995. The old-style saddle on the right is the unusual version with no grommets or cinch, which came with some Cowboy rider sets. *Saddles and photo courtesy of Sande Schneider.* Fair to mint condition: new-style $1-$3, cinchless old-style $2-$5.

Western Prancer *text p. 218*

"Ranger" Cow Pony #889, red dun. Fair to mint condition: $12-$25.

Western Prancing Horse "Cheyenne" #110, smoke, light and dark color variations. The darker horse is missing his reins. *Dark model courtesy of Heather Wells.* Fair to mint condition: with eyewhites $20-$35, otherwise $15-$30.

Western Prancing Horse "Cheyenne" #111, buckskin. Fair to mint condition: with eyewhites $20-$35, otherwise $15-$30.

Western Prancing Horse "Cheyenne" #112, palomino. Fair to mint condition: with eyewhites $15-$30, otherwise $12-$25.

Western Prancing Horse "Cheyenne" #115, black leopard appaloosa. Fair to mint condition: with eyewhites $20-$35, otherwise $15-$30.

Western Prancer SR, sorrel. *Model courtesy of Sheryl Leisure.* Fair to mint condition: $50-$75.

Western Prancing Horse "Cheyenne" #113, black pinto. *Model courtesy of Heather Wells.* Fair to mint condition: $

Brenda Western Gift Set #1120, chestnut pinto Western Prancer. Fair to mint condition: horse with saddle $40-$60; with doll, add $3-$7.

Woodgrains *text pp. 218-219*

This detail photo shows the bubbling of the paint finish that has developed on many woodgrain models over the years.

Western Prancing Horse "Cheyenne" #114, bay. *Top,* a coffee-chestnut model with eyewhites and dark brown mane and tail; *Bottom,* a red bay variation with black mane and tail. *Models courtesy of Heather Wells.* Fair to mint condition: with eyewhites $20-$35, otherwise $15-$30.

Western Prancer SR, brown pinto, glossy. *Model and photo courtesy of Judy Davinich.* Fair to mint condition: $220-$300.

HORSES - CLASSICS

Andalusian Family Foal *text p. 219*

Andalusian Family Foal SR, red bay. Fair to mint condition: $5-$9.

Andalusian Family Stallion
text p. 220

Andalusian Family Gift Set #3060, chestnut foal. *Model courtesy of Sheryl Leisure.* Fair to mint condition: $2-$4.

Andalusian Family Gift Set #3060, alabaster stallion. *Model courtesy of Sheryl Leisure.* Fair to mint condition: $5-$12.

Hanoverian Family set #3346, bay foal. *Model courtesy of Sheryl Leisure.* Fair to mint condition: $4-$7.

Spanish-Norman Family Foal SR, steel gray. Fair to mint condition: $6-$10.

Andalusian Family Mare *text pp. 219-220*

Andalusian Family Stallion SR, dapple gray. *Model courtesy of Sheryl Leisure.* Fair to mint condition: $19-$30.

Proud Mother And Newborn Foal set #3160, tan dun foal. Fair to mint condition: $6-$10.

Proud Mother And Newborn Foal set #3161, dark bay foal. Fair to mint condition: $6-$10.

Andalusian Family Gift Set #3060, dapple gray mare. Fair to mint condition: $5-$12.

Spanish-Norman Family Stallion SR, red roan. Fair to mint condition: $10-$17.

Arabian Family Foal *text pp. 220-221*

Andalusian Family Mare SR, alabaster. *Model courtesy of Sheryl Leisure.* Fair to mint condition: $19-$30.

Classic Arabian Foal #4000, alabaster. *Model courtesy of Sheryl Leisure.* Fair to mint condition: $4-$7.

Classic Arabian Foal #4000, black. *Model courtesy of Sheryl Leisure.* Fair to mint condition: $4-$7.

Classic Arabian Foal #4000, chestnut. *Model courtesy of Sheryl Leisure.* Fair to mint condition: $2-$4.

Marguerite Henry's "Our First Pony" Gift Set #3066, bay pinto foal "Friday." Still available retail in 1996.

Arabian Family Foal SR, black. *Model courtesy of Sheryl Leisure.* Fair to mint condition: $6-$10.

Classic Arabian Foal #4000, palomino. *Model courtesy of Sheryl Leisure.* Fair to mint condition: $4-$7.

Classic Arabian Foal #4000, smoke gray. *Model courtesy of Sheryl Leisure.* Fair to mint condition: $4-$7.

Arabian Family Foal SR, bay, solid-faced and bald-faced versions. Fair to mint condition: either version $5-$9.

Arabian Stallion And Frisky Foal set #3162, gray dun foal. Fair to mint condition: $6-$10.

Arabian Stallion And Frisky Foal set #3163, light sandy bay foal. Fair to mint condition: $6-$10.

Arabian Family Foal SR #413155, dapple gray. *Model courtesy of Sheryl Leisure.* Fair to mint condition: $15-$22.

Arabian Family Foal SR, dark rose gray. Fair to mint condition: $5-$9.

Not shown:
Marguerite Henry's "Our First Pony" Gift Set #3066, black pinto foal "Friday" (early 1987). Fair to mint condition: $15-$22.

Bedouin Family Gift Set #3057, chestnut foal. Still available retail in 1996.

Desert Arabian Family set #3056, bay foal. *Model courtesy of Sheryl Leisure.* Fair to mint condition: $4-$7.

Arabian Family Foal SR, dark shaded chestnut. Fair to mint condition: $8-$13.

Arabian Family Mare
text p. 221

Arabian Family Gift Set #3055, chestnut mare. Fair to mint condition: $5-$12.

Bedouin Family Gift Set #3057, black mare. Still available retail in 1996.

Desert Arabian Family set #3056, dark bay mare. *Model courtesy of Sheryl Leisure.* Fair to mint condition: $8-$15.

Arabian Family Mare SR, black. *Model courtesy of Sheryl Leisure.* Fair to mint condition: $12-$20.

Arabian Family Mare SR #413255, dapple gray. *Model courtesy of Sheryl Leisure.* Fair to mint condition: $25-$40.

Arabian Family Mare SR, rose alabaster. *Model courtesy of Sheryl Leisure.* Fair to mint condition: $12-$20.

"Buckaroo" SR, red dun. Fair to mint condition: $10-$17.

Arabian Family Stallion
text p. 221

Bedouin Family Gift Set #3057, dark chestnut stallion. Still available retail in 1996.

Desert Arabian Family set #3056, bay stallion. *Model courtesy of Sheryl Leisure.* Fair to mint condition: $8-$15.

Arabian Family Gift Set #3055, chestnut stallion. *Top,* the early, star-faced version. *Bottom,* the later, solid-faced version; *model courtesy of Sheryl Leisure.* Fair to mint condition: any version $5-$12.

Arabian Family Stallion SR, bay. *Model courtesy of Sheryl Leisure.* Fair to mint condition: $12-$20.

Arabian Family Stallion SR, black. *Model courtesy of Sheryl Leisure.* Fair to mint condition: $12-$20.

Arabian Family Stallion SR #413355, dapple gray. *Model courtesy of Sheryl Leisure.* Fair to mint condition: $25-40.

Arabian Family Stallion SR, smoke gray. Fair to mint condition: $8-$15.

"Black Beauty" text p. 222

"King Of The Wind" Gift Set #3345, golden bay "Lath." *Model courtesy of Sheryl Leisure.* Fair to mint condition: $8-$15.

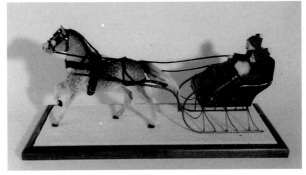

"Black Beauty" Family set #3040, black "Black Beauty." *Top,* the early version with a tiny diamond star; *model courtesy of Sheryl Leisure. Bottom,* the later version with a long star. Fair to mint condition: either version $5-$12.

"Black Beauty" Gift Set SR #700894, black, glossy horse. Fair to mint condition: horse alone $8-$15, full set $15-$30.

Not shown:
"Iltschi" SR #703440, black with long star, 4 stockings. Fair to mint condition: $23-$35.

Collector's One Horse Open Sleigh set SR, flocked dapple gray horse. *Set courtesy of Heather Wells.* Fair to mint condition: full set $370-$500.

Black Stallion text p. 222

"The Black Stallion Returns" Set #3030, black Black Stallion. Fair to mint condition: $5-$12.

"King Of The Wind" Gift Set #3345, blood bay "Sham." *Model courtesy of Sheryl Leisure.* Fair to mint condition: $8-$15.

Not shown:
The Doctor's Buggy set #19842, flocked bay horse, with buggy and doctor doll. Fair to mint condition: $295-$400.

Bucking Bronco text p. 223

Bucking Bronco #190, black. Fair to mint condition: $12-$20.

Bucking Bronco #191, steel gray. *Model courtesy of Heather Wells.* Fair to mint condition: $50-$75.

Bucking Bronco SR #701092, black paint. Fair to mint condition: $15-$25.

"Duchess" *text p. 223*

"Black Beauty" Family set #3040, bay "Duchess." Fair to mint condition: $5-$12.

Bucking Bronco #192, bay. *Model courtesy of Heather Wells.* Fair to mint condition: $25-$40.

Bucking Bronco SR #412190, chestnut. *Model courtesy of Heather Wells.* Fair to mint condition: $30-$50.

"King Of The Wind" Gift Set #3345, alabaster "Lady Roxana." *Model courtesy of Sheryl Leisure.* Fair to mint condition: $8-$15.

"Dakota" Bucking Bronco #932, dappled palomino. Still available retail in 1996.

Bucking Bronco SR #411190, red roan. Fair to mint condition: $30-$50.

Bucking Bronco SR #414190, steel gray. Fair to mint condition: $30-$50.

Trakehner Family set #3347, pale dapple gray mare. *Model courtesy of Sheryl Leisure.* Fair to mint condition: $8-$15.

Bucking Bronco SR #413190, black leopard appaloosa. Fair to mint condition: $30-$50.

Not shown:
Family To Church On Sunday
set #19843, flocked bay
"Duchess" and "Jet Run,"
with buggy and four dolls.
Fair to mint condition:
$425-$575.

"Ginger" text p. 224

"Black Beauty" Family set #3040 chestnut "Ginger." Fair to mint condition: $5-$12.

Hanoverian Family set #3346, light sandy bay mare. *Model courtesy of Sheryl Leisure.* Fair to mint condition: $8-$15.

"A Pony For Keeps" Gift Set #3234, alabaster "Blue" with gray mane and tail. Fair to mint condition: $8-$15.

Spanish-Norman Family Mare SR, alabaster with white mane and tail. Fair to mint condition: $10-$17.

Not shown:
"Hatatitla" SR #703240, medium bay with no white. Fair to mint condition: $23-$35.

"Hobo" text pp. 224-225

"Hobo" The Mustang Of Lazy Heart Ranch #625, buckskin. Fair to mint condition: $17-$27. In #2085 set with book and box, add $8.

"Nevada Star" SR #410493, smoke gray. *Model courtesy of Sheryl Leisure.* Fair to mint condition: $220-$300.

"Riddle" Passing Through Time, Phase One, SR #703595, bay blanket appaloosa. Fair to mint condition: $17-$27.

"Riddle" Passing Through Time, Phase Two, SR #703595, chestnut-point leopard appaloosa. Fair to mint condition: $17-$27.

"Riddle" Passing Through Time, Phase Three, SR #703595, gray-point leopard appaloosa. Fair to mint condition: $17-$27.

"Jet Run" text p. 225

Trakehner Family set #3347, dark chestnut stallion. *Model courtesy of Sheryl Leisure.* Fair to mint condition: $8-$15.

U.S. Equestrian Team Gift Set #3035, bay "Jet Run." Fair to mint condition: $5-$12.

"Jet Run" SR, medium/light chestnut. Fair to mint condition: $10-$17.

"Johar" SR, fleabitten rose gray. Fair to mint condition: $8-$15.

U.S. Equestrian Team Gift Set #3035, red chestnut "Keen." Fair to mint condition: $5-$12.

"Rembrandt" SR #703235, reddish bay. Fair to mint condition: $10-$17.

"Ahlerich" SR #703135, reddish bay. Fair to mint condition: $10-$17.

"Johar" text p. 225

"The Black Stallion Returns" Set #3030, alabaster "Johar." Fair to mint condition: $5-$12.

Eagle And "Pow Wow" set SR #705095, black pinto "Pow Wow." Fair to mint condition: horse alone $10-$17, full set $17-$27.

"Johar" SR, rose alabaster. At bottom is the 2-gallon pail with Sam Savitt illustrations sold in "Foal's First Day" sets. *Pail courtesy of Sheryl Leisure.* Fair to mint condition: horse $15-$25, pail $10-$15.

Not shown:
Drive On A Sunny Day set #19841, flocked chestnut mare, with buggy and woman doll. Fair to mint condition: $295-$400.

"Keen" text pp. 225-226

Hanoverian Family set #3346, black stallion. *Model courtesy of Sheryl Leisure.* Fair to mint condition: $8-$15.

"Keen" SR, steel gray. Fair to mint condition: $10-$17.

Not shown:
Delivery Wagon set #19846, flocked chestnut horse, with wagon and man doll. Fair to mint condition: $330-$450.
Montgomery Ward Delivery Wagon set SR, flocked chestnut horse, with wagon and man doll. Fair to mint condition: $330-$450.

"Kelso" text p. 226

"Blackjack" #263, black pinto. Still available retail in 1996.

"Jeremy" #257, liver chestnut. *Model courtesy of Sheryl Leisure.* Fair to mint condition: $8-$15.

"Citation" SR, medium reddish bay. Fair to mint condition: $15-$25

"Kelso" #601, dark bay. Fair to mint condition: $5-$12.

"Denver" SR, dark bay. Fair to mint condition: $10-$17.

"Norita" #251, dapple gray. *Model courtesy of Sheryl Leisure.* Fair to mint condition: $8-$15.

"Geronimo" SR, chestnut blanket appaloosa. Fair to mint condition: $10-$17.

Fine Horse Family set #3348, red roan mare. Still available retail in 1996.

"Kelso" SR, medium reddish bay. *Model courtesy of Lani Keller.* Fair to mint condition: $15-$25; in set with art book, add $10-$15.

Lipizzan *text pp. 226-227*

Lipizzan Stallion #620, alabaster with pink hooves. Fair to mint condition: $12-$20.

"Pegasus" #209, alabaster. *Model courtesy of Lani Keller.* Fair to mint condition: $17-$27.

Lipizzaner SR #620, alabaster with gray hooves, made for Toys R Us in Germany. Fair to mint condition: $15-$25; with box, add $2.

Lipizzaner SR #700393, alabaster with gray hooves, made for "The Wonderful World of Horses" touring show. Fair to mint condition: $15-$25; with box, add $2. Model may still be available retail in 1996.

"King" #258, dark mahogany brown. Model courtesy of Sheryl Leisure. Fair to mint condition: $8-$15.

"Affirmed" SR, reddish chestnut. Fair to mint condition: $15-$25.

The three alabaster Lipizzans, from left: the German SR, the old regular-run #620, and the touring show SR.

"Merrylegs" text pp. 227-228

"Martin's Dominique" Champion Miniature Horse #898, black. Fair to mint condition: $5-$12.

Sky Blue "Pegasus" SR, flocked sky blue. Model courtesy of Heather Wells. Fair to mint condition: $40-$60.

"Man-O-War" #602, red chestnut. Top, early version with broken stripe and charcoal eartips; model courtesy of Sheryl Leisure. Bottom, later version with roundish star. Fair to mint condition: either version $5-$12.

"Black Beauty" Family set #3040, dapple gray "Merrylegs." Fair to mint condition: $4-$9.

"Man-O-War" text p. 227

"Pepe" #252, reddish chestnut. Model courtesy of Sheryl Leisure. Fair to mint condition: $8-$15.

"A Pony For Keeps" Gift Set #3234, white "Lady Jane Grey." Fair to mint condition: $5-$12.

"Apache" #264, pale grulla. Still available retail in 1996.

Miniature Horse SR, palomino. Fair to mint condition: $12-$20.

Pony Cart And Driver set SR, flocked black pinto "Midge," shown with and without plastic display cover. Covered set and photo courtesy of Sande Schneider; uncovered set courtesy of Heather Wells. Fair to mint condition: set with cover $220-$300.

Not shown:
Joey's Pony Cart set #19845, flocked black pinto "Midge," with cart and boy doll. Fair to mint condition: $220-$300.

"Mesteño" Challenger *text p. 228*

The Challenger Gift Set, "Mesteño" And "Sombra" #4811, reddish dun "Mesteño." Still available retail in 1996.

The Challenger Gift Set, "Mesteño" And "Sombra" #4811, grulla "Sombra." Still available retail in 1996.

"Mesteño" Dawning *text p. 228*

The Dawning Gift Set, "Mesteño" And His Mother #4810, light red dun foal "Mesteño." Still available retail in 1996.

"Mesteño" Messenger *text pp. 228-229*

"Mesteño" The Messenger #480, reddish dun. Still available retail in 1996.

Right: "A Pony For Keeps" Gift Set #3234, light dapple gray "Another." Fair to mint condition: $8-$15.

"Mesteño" Progeny *text p. 229*

The Progeny Gift Set, "Mesteño" And "Rojo" #4812, reddish dun "Mesteño." Still available retail in 1996.

"Mesteño's" Mother *text p. 229*

The Dawning Gift Set, "Mesteño" And His Mother #4810, pale buckskin "Mesteño's" Mother, the early gray-point and later black-point versions. Fair to mint condition: gray-point $20-$25; black-point still available retail in 1996.

"Might Tango" *text p. 229*

U.S. Equestrian Team Gift Set #3035, medium dapple gray "Might Tango." Fair to mint condition: $5-$12.

Fine Horse Family set #3348, chestnut blanket appaloosa foal with no-spot blanket. Still available retail in 1996.

Mustang Family Foal SR, chestnut pinto. Model courtesy of Sheryl Leisure. Fair to mint condition: $8-$13.

"Might Tango" SR, reddish bay with solid face. Fair to mint condition: $10-$17.

Marguerite Henry's "Our First Pony" Gift Set #3066, black pinto foal "Teeny." Still available retail in 1996.

Mustang Family Foal SR, lilac grulla. Fair to mint condition: $6-$10.

Mustang Family Mare text p. 230

"Orchidee" SR #703335, reddish bay with large star. Model courtesy of Sheryl Leisure. Fair to mint condition: $10-$17.

Mustang Family Gift Set #3065, chestnut foal. Fair to mint condition: $2-$4.

Appaloosa Mustang Family Gift Set #3349, black blanket appaloosa mare. Still available retail in 1996.

Mustang Family Foal text pp. 229-230

Appaloosa Mustang Family Gift Set #3349, chestnut blanket appaloosa foal with spotted blanket. Still available retail in 1996.

Mustang Family Gift Set #3065, chestnut pinto mare. Model courtesy of Sheryl Leisure. Fair to mint condition: $5-$12.

Trakehner Family set #3347, bay foal. Model courtesy of Sheryl Leisure. Fair to mint condition: $4-$7.

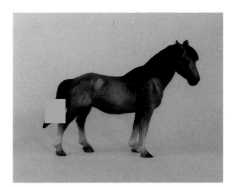

Mustang Family Mare SR, bay. Fair to mint condition: $15-$25.

"A Pony For Keeps" Gift Set #3234, chestnut "Jefferson." Fair to mint condition: $8-$15.

"Silver Comet" SR #700594, dapple gray. Fair to mint condition: $17-$27.

Mustang Family Mare SR, dark bay. Fair to mint condition: $10-$17.

Mustang Family Stallion text p. 230

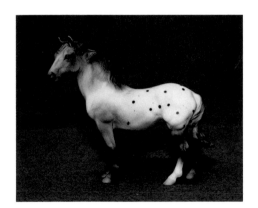

Appaloosa Mustang Family Gift Set #3349, rose dun blanket appaloosa stallion. Still available retail in 1996.

Mustang Family Gift Set #3065, chestnut stallion. The liver-chestnut horse, which has no mold stamps, is a very early piece. The lighter, redder horse at right is a newer piece with a round Breyer stamp. *Models and photo courtesy of Sande Schneider.* Fair to mint condition: any version $5-$12.

Mustang Family Stallion SR, buckskin (1985). Fair to mint condition: $15-$25.

Mustang Family Stallion SR, buckskin (1992). Fair to mint condition: $10-$17.

Polo Pony text pp. 230-231

Polo Pony #626, bay. Fair to mint condition: $17-$27.

Quarter Horse Family Foal

text p. 231

Quarter Horse Foal #4001, bay, shown here in the buckskin color variation. *Model courtesy of Sheryl Leisure.* Fair to mint condition: $2-$4.

Quarter Horse Foal #4001, black. *Model courtesy of Sheryl Leisure.* Fair to mint condition: $4-$7.

Quarter Horse Foal #4001, chestnut. *Model courtesy of Sheryl Leisure.* Fair to mint condition: $4-$7.

Quarter Horse Foal #4001, palomino. *Model courtesy of Sheryl Leisure.* Fair to mint condition: $4-$7.

Quarter Horse Family Foal SR, black blanket appaloosa. *Model courtesy of Sheryl Leisure.* Fair to mint condition: $8-$13.

Quarter Horse Family Mare SR, black blanket appaloosa. *Model courtesy of Sheryl Leisure.* Fair to mint condition: $15-$25.

Quarter Horse Family Gift Set #3045, bay foal, shown here in the red bay color variation. Fair to mint condition: $2-$4.

Quarter Horse Family Foal SR, chestnut blanket appaloosa. Fair to mint condition: $8-$13.

Quarter Horse Family Mare SR, chestnut blanket appaloosa. Fair to mint condition: $15-$25.

"Blaze" SR, dark bay. Fair to mint condition: $6-$10.

Quarter Horse Family Mare

text p. 231

Quarter Horse Family Gift Set #3045, bay mare. Fair to mint condition: $5-$12.

Brown Pinto Mare SR #703245, dark chestnut paint. Fair to mint condition: $17-$27.

Quarter Horse Family Mare SR, liver chestnut. Fair to mint condition: $10-$17.

Quarter Horse Family Stallion

text pp. 231-232

Quarter Horse Family Gift Set #3045, palomino stallion. Fair to mint condition: $5-$12.

Quarter Horse Family Foal SR, alabaster. Fair to mint condition: $6-$10.

Quarter Horse Family Stallion SR #703145, black blanket appaloosa with large blanket (1989). Fair to mint condition: $17-$27.

Quarter Horse Family Stallion SR, black blanket appaloosa with butt blanket (1984). *Model courtesy of Sheryl Leisure.* Fair to mint condition: $15-$25.

Quarter Horse Family Stallion SR, chestnut blanket appaloosa. Fair to mint condition: $15-$25.

Quarter Horse Family Stallion SR, liver chestnut. Fair to mint condition: $15-$27.

Rearing Stallion *text p. 232*

"Promises" Rearing Stallion #890, dark chestnut pinto. Fair to mint condition: $8-$15.

Rearing Stallion "Rex," Alabaster Lipizzan, #180, alabaster. *Top,* a typical horse, whose white color is the color of the plastic; *model courtesy of Heather Wells. Bottom,* a chalky model, whose white color is painted on. Fair to mint condition: normal model $5-$12, chalky version $15-$25.

Right: Rearing Stallion "Rex" #185, bay. Note the blue-ribbon sticker, dating from the 1960s or early 1970s. *Model courtesy of Heather Wells.* Fair to mint condition: $5-$12.

Rearing Stallion "Rex" #183, palomino. *Top,* a typical model. Bottom, a pearly horse, whose white plastic has an iridescent sheen; *model courtesy of Sheryl Leisure.* Fair to mint condition: normal model $5-$12, pearly version $17-$27.

Rearing Stallion (*left*) and Fighting Stallion: the molds are nearly identical except in size.

"Little Chaparral" SR #700293, buckskin pinto. Fair to mint condition: $10-$17.

"Rojo" *text p. 232*

The Progeny Gift Set, "Mesteño" And "Rojo" #4812, light red dun yearling "Rojo." Still available retail in 1996.

"Ruffian" *text pp. 232-233*

"Ruffian" #606, dark brown bay. *Top,* early version with tiny star and half of a sock. *Bottom,* a later mare with larger diamond star and normal stocking; *model courtesy of Sheryl Leisure.* Fair to mint condition: any version $5-$12.

Rearing Stallion SR #410593, buckskin. Fair to mint condition: $30-$50.

"Colleen" #262, red sorrel. *Model courtesy of Sheryl Leisure.* Fair to mint condition: $8-$15.

Willow And "Shining Star" set SR #703495, dark bay blanket appaloosa "Shining Star." Although this special was produced only in 1995, it is still available retail in 1996, offered to dealers through the 1996 Reeves International Mid-Year Introduction brochure.

"Lula" #256, medium reddish bay. *Model courtesy of Sheryl Leisure.* Fair to mint condition: $8-$15.

"Glory" And Plank Jump Gift Set #2003, buckskin "Glory" with her white, blue, and yellow wooden jump. Still available retail in 1996.

Left: "Patches" #268, dark chestnut pinto. Still available retail in 1996.

"Spice" #265, bay blanket appaloosa. Still available retail in 1996.

"Whirlaway" SR, medium/light red chestnut. Fair to mint condition: $15-$25.

"The Black Stallion Returns" Set #3030, red chestnut "Sagr." Fair to mint condition: $5-$12.

"Silky Sullivan" *text p. 233*

"Andrew" #259, shaded smoke gray. *Model courtesy of Sheryl Leisure.* Fair to mint condition: $8-$15.

"T-Bone" #253, fleabitten gray. *Model courtesy of Sheryl Leisure.* Fair to mint condition: $8-$15.

"Swaps" *text pp. 233-234*

"Cloud" #266, dark candy-spot gray. Still available retail in 1996.

"Buck" And Hillary Gift Set #2004, pale buckskin horse "Buck." Still available retail in 1996.

"Hawk" #254, black. *Model courtesy of Sheryl Leisure.* Fair to mint condition: $8-$15.

"Prince" #260, rose alabaster. *Model courtesy of Sheryl Leisure.* Fair to mint condition: $8-$15.

Fine Horse Family set #3348, liver chestnut stallion. Still available retail in 1996.

"Silky Sullivan" #603, medium/dark chestnut. *Top,* early version with small diamond star; *bottom,* later version with larger star. Fair to mint condition: either version $5-$12.

"Azul" #267, blue-bay roan. Still available retail in 1996.

"Swaps" #604, medium chestnut. *Top* a typical model with right hind stocking. *Bottom,* a variation with left hind stocking; *model courtesy of Sheryl Leisure.* Fair to mint condition: any version $5-$12.

"Gaucho" #255, red roan. *Model courtesy of Sheryl Leisure.* Fair to mint condition: $8-$15.

"Terrang" #605, dark/medium bay. Fair to mint condition: $5-$12.

"Seattle Slew" SR, medium/dark chestnut. Fair to mint condition: $15-$25.

"Ten Gallon" #261, pale tan dun. *Model courtesy of Sheryl Leisure.* Fair to mint condition: $8-$15.

"Count Fleet" SR, dark olive chestnut. Fair to mint condition: $15-$25.

Right: "Secretariat" SR, red chestnut. Fair to mint condition: $15-$25.

HORSES - LITTLE BITS
American Saddlebred *text p. 235*

American Saddlebred #9070, black pinto. Fair to mint condition: $3-$7.

American Saddlebred SR, red sorrel. Many models came with a hang tag like the one shown here. *Model courtesy of Sheryl Leisure.* Fair to mint condition: $7-$17.

"Belle" #1021, reddish bay. Still available retail in 1996.

American Saddlebred #9030, medium bay, versions with star and solid face. *Star-faced model courtesy of Sheryl Leisure.* Fair to mint condition: $4-$9.

American Saddlebred SR, seal brown. *Model courtesy of Sheryl Leisure.* Fair to mint condition: $5-$11.

Arabian Stallion *text pp. 235-236*

American Saddlebred #9030, palomino. *Model courtesy of Sheryl Leisure.* Fair to mint condition: $4-$9.

American Saddlebred #9030, red chestnut. *Model courtesy of Sheryl Leisure.* Fair to mint condition: $4-$9.

American Saddlebred SR, dark chestnut pinto. *Model courtesy of Sheryl Leisure.* Fair to mint condition: $5-$11.

Arabian Stallion #9001, chestnut. *Model courtesy of Sheryl Leisure.* Fair to mint condition: $3-$7.

Arabian Stallion #9001, medium bay. *Model courtesy of Sheryl Leisure.* Fair to mint condition: $3-$7.

American Saddlebred SR, palomino pinto. *Model courtesy of Sheryl Leisure.* Fair to mint condition: $5-$11.

Arabian Stallion #9001, smoke gray. Fair to mint condition: $3-$7.

Arabian Stallion SR, dapple gray. Model courtesy of Sheryl Leisure. Fair to mint condition: $5-$11.

Not shown:
Bitsy Breyer Beachcomber Set SR, black horse with black hooves, with doll, bridle, and accessories. Fair to mint condition: horse alone $7-$13, full set $20-$35.

Circus Extravaganza set #3170, dark dappled bay small horse. Fair to mint condition: $4-$9

Arabian Stallion #9045, alabaster. Model courtesy of Sheryl Leisure. Fair to mint condition: $3-$7.

Clydesdale text p. 236

Clydesdale #9025, bay. Model courtesy of Sheryl Leisure. Fair to mint condition: $3-$7.

Charger, The Great Horse, SR #419025, dapple gray. Model courtesy of Sheryl Leisure. Fair to mint condition: $5-$11.

"Starlight" And Carol, Cross Country Set #1016, dark mahogany bay "Starlight." Still available retail in 1996.

Shire #9065, black. Fair to mint condition: $3-$7.

Action Drafters Big And Small set #3175, gray dun small drafter. Fair to mint condition: $4-$9

Clydesdale SR, dapple gray (1990). Model courtesy of Sheryl Leisure. Fair to mint condition: $5-$11.

Arabian Stallion SR, black with tan hooves. Model courtesy of Sheryl Leisure. Fair to mint condition: $5-$11.

Clydesdale SR, golden sorrel. Model courtesy of Sheryl Leisure. Fair to mint condition: $5-$11.

Morgan Stallion *text pp. 236-237*

"Delilah" #1024, palomino. Still available retail in 1996.

Morgan Stallion #9005, dark/medium bay. *Model courtesy of Sheryl Leisure.* Fair to mint condition: $3-$7.

Morgan Stallion #9005, black. *Model courtesy of Sheryl Leisure.* Fair to mint condition: $3-$7.

Morgan Stallion #9005, dark/medium chestnut. *Model courtesy of Sheryl Leisure.* Fair to mint condition: $3-$7.

Morgan Stallion #9050, golden sorrel/palomino. Fair to mint condition: $3-$7.

Bitsy Breyer Stable Set #9950, cardboard stable covered with clear vinyl. Fair to mint condition: stable alone $5-$11.

"Pepper" And Lisa, Hunter/Jumper Set #1018, dapple gray "Pepper." Still available retail in 1996.

Merry-Go-Round Horse SR, mauve. *Model courtesy of Heather Wells.* Fair to mint condition: horse alone $10-$20; with stand and tack $20-$35.

Morgan Stallion SR, dark shaded bay. *Model courtesy of Sheryl Leisure.* Fair to mint condition: $5-$11.

Morgan Stallion SR, light sandy bay. *Model courtesy of Sheryl Leisure.* Fair to mint condition: $10-$20.

Morgan Stallion SR, medium bay. *Model courtesy of Sheryl Leisure.* Fair to mint condition: $5-$11.

Morgan Stallion SR, rose chestnut. Fair to mint condition: $5-$11.

Performing "Misty" *text p. 237*

Performing "Misty" #79293, ceramic, light chestnut pinto. *Model courtesy of Sheryl Leisure.* Fair to mint condition: $28-$45.

Quarter Horse Stallion *text pp. 237-238*

Appaloosa #9040, black blanket appaloosa. *Model courtesy of Sheryl Leisure.* Fair to mint condition: $4-$9.

Appaloosa #9080, chestnut blanket appaloosa. *Model courtesy of Sheryl Leisure.* Fair to mint condition: $3-$7.

Bay Pinto #9035, bay paint. Fair to mint condition: $4-$9.

"Moonglow" #1023, reddish dun. Still available retail in 1996.

Paint #9075, black paint. *Model courtesy of Sheryl Leisure.* Fair to mint condition: $3-$7.

Quarter Horse Stallion #9015, bay. *Model courtesy of Sheryl Leisure.* Fair to mint condition: $3-$7.

Quarter Horse Stallion #9015, buckskin. *Model courtesy of Sheryl Leisure.* Fair to mint condition: $3-$7.

Quarter Horse Stallion #9015, palomino. Fair to mint condition: $3-$7.

Quarter Horse Stallion #9060, blue roan. Fair to mint condition: $3-$7.

"Spot" And Kate, Western Set #1019, black blanket appaloosa "Spot." Still available retail in 1996.

Quarter Horse Stallion SR, black. *Model courtesy of Sheryl Leisure.* Fair to mint condition: $5-$11.

Quarter Horse Stallion SR, black leopard appaloosa. *Model courtesy of Sheryl Leisure.* Fair to mint condition: $5-$11.

Quarter Horse Stallion SR, red leopard appaloosa. *Model courtesy of Sheryl Leisure.* Fair to mint condition: $5-$11.

Quarter Horse Stallion SR, smoke gray. *Model courtesy of Sheryl Leisure.* Fair to mint condition: $5-$11.

Thoroughbred Stallion *text pp. 238-239*

"Prancer" #1022, shaded bay. Still available retail in 1996.

Thoroughbred Stallion #9010, black, version with tan hooves and no stockings. *Model courtesy of Sheryl Leisure.* Fair to mint condition: $3-$7.

Thoroughbred Stallion #9010, chestnut, solid-legged and 1-stocking versions. The 1-stocking horse is from a #1010 Bitsy Breyer And Thoroughbred Jockey Set. *Solid-legged model courtesy of Sheryl Leisure.* Fair to mint condition: $3-$7.

Thoroughbred Stallion #9010, dark/medium bay. *Model courtesy of Sheryl Leisure.* Fair to mint condition: $3-$7.

Thoroughbred Stallion #9055, steel gray. Fair to mint condition: $3-$7.

"Cobalt" And Veronica, Hunter/Jumper Set #1025, black "Cobalt." Still available retail in 1996.

"Topside" And Stevie, Cross Country Set #1017, sandy bay "Topside." Still available retail in 1996.

Thoroughbred Stallion SR, dappled rose gray. *Model courtesy of Sheryl Leisure.* Fair to mint condition: $5-$11.

Thoroughbred Stallion SR, dark bay with baldish face. *Model courtesy of Sheryl Leisure.* Fair to mint condition: $5-$11.

HORSES - STABLEMATES

Arabian Mare *text pp. 239-240*

Arabian Mare #5011, dapple gray. *Model courtesy of Sheryl Leisure.* Fair to mint condition: $10-$15.

Saddle Club Collection, Stablemates #5650, dapple gray Arabian Mare. Fair to mint condition: $2-$4.

Thoroughbred Stallion SR, reddish bay. *Model courtesy of Sheryl Leisure.* Fair to mint condition: $5-11.

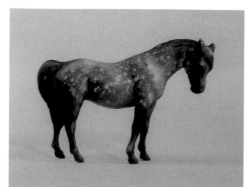

Arabian Mare #5014, bay. *Model courtesy of Sheryl Leisure.* Fair to mint condition: $2-$4.

Arabian Mare SR, black. *Model courtesy of Sheryl Leisure.* Fair to mint condition: $4-$6.

Unicorn *text p. 239*

Unicorn #9020, alabaster. *Model courtesy of Sheryl Leisure.* Fair to mint condition: $2-$6.

Unicorn SR, white with blue mane and tail. *Model courtesy of Sheryl Leisure.* Fair to mint condition: model alone $10-$20; with stand and tack $20-$35.

Arabian Mare #5017 and #5130, alabaster. *Model courtesy of Sheryl Leisure.* Fair to mint condition: $1-$3.

Arabian Mare #5182, palomino. Still available retail in 1996.

Arabian Mare SR, chestnut. Fair to mint condition: $4-$6.

Arabian Mare SR, semi-leopard appaloosa. Fair to mint condition: $2-$4.

Arabian Mare SR, steel gray. *Top,* a 1992 mare; *bottom,* a 1994 mare. Fair to mint condition: $2-$4.

Arabian Stallion *text pp. 240-241*

Arabian Stallion #5013, bay. *Top* the earliest issue of this horse, mislabeled by Breyer as "Citation" #5020. *Bottom,* a normal Arabian Stallion #5013; *model courtesy of Sheryl Leisure.* Fair to mint condition: $2-$4.

Arabian Stallion SR, buckskin. *Model courtesy of Sheryl Leisure.* Fair to mint condition: $4-$6.

Arabian Stallion #5010, dapple gray. *Model courtesy of Sheryl Leisure.* Fair to mint condition: $10-$15.

Arabian Stallion #5120, steel gray. *Model courtesy of Sheryl Leisure.* Fair to mint condition: $2-$5.

Arabian Stallion SR, dappled red chestnut. *Top* a 1992 stallion; *Bottom,* a 1994 stallion. Fair to mint condition: $2-$4.

Arabian Stallion #5016, alabaster. *Model courtesy of Sheryl Leisure.* Fair to mint condition: $2-$4.

Arabian Stallion #5181, medium chestnut. Still available retail in 1996.

Arabian Stallion SR, light dusky chestnut. Fair to mint condition: $2-$4.

"Emperor's Gold Bar" SR, palomino, mounted on paperweight base containing a delightful suppertime conversation piece. *Model courtesy of Jolie Devereux.* Fair to mint condition: horse alone $15-$25; on base $20-$30.

Standing Thoroughbred #5019, chestnut / reddish dun. *Top,* an older, redder model; *bottom,* a newer, browner model. Fair to mint condition: $2-$5.

"Citation" SR, dapple gray. *Top,* a 1992 horse; *bottom,* a 1994 horse. Fair to mint condition: $2-$4.

"Citation" *text p. 241*

"Citation" #5020, bay. *Model courtesy of Sheryl Leisure.* Fair to mint condition: $1-$3.

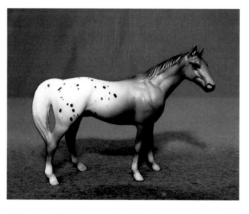

"Citation" SR, brown dun blanket appaloosa. Fair to mint condition: $2-$4.

"Citation" SR, dusty chestnut / olive dun. *Model courtesy of Sheryl Leisure.* Fair to mint condition: $4-$6.

"Citation" SR, dappled gray dun. Fair to mint condition: $2-$4.

"Citation" SR, red roan. *Model courtesy of Sheryl Leisure.* Fair to mint condition: $4-$6.

Left: Standing Thoroughbred #5175, alabaster. At left is a pale gray color variation; the horse at right is the normal alabaster. Still available retail in 1996.

"Citation" SR, steel gray. Fair to mint condition: $4-$6.

Draft Horse *text pp. 241-242*

Draft Horse #5055, sorrel. *Model courtesy of Sheryl Leisure.* Fair to mint condition: $2-$4.

Draft Horse #5187, rose dun. Still available retail in 1996.

Saddle Club Collection, Stablemates #5650, alabaster Draft Horse. Fair to mint condition: $2-$4.

Draft Horse #5180, dapple gray. *Top* and *center,* cellulose acetate drafters in dark and light color variations; *dark model courtesy of Sheryl Leisure. Bottom,* a model made of ABS plastic, with characteristic "polka-dot" dapples. Fair to mint condition: $2-$5.

Draft Horse SR, black with no white markings (1990). *Model courtesy of Sheryl Leisure.* Fair to mint condition: $4-$6.

Draft Horse SR, black with hind stocking (1984). *Model courtesy of Sheryl Leisure.* Fair to mint condition: $15-$25.

Draft Horse SR, buckskin. *Top,* a 1992 model; *bottom,* a 1994 model. Fair to mint condition: $2-$4.

Draft Horse SR, chestnut ("bay"). *Model courtesy of Sheryl Leisure.* Fair to mint condition: $15-$25.

Draft Horse SR, medium/light bay. Fair to mint condition: $4-$6.

Draft Horse SR, smoke gray. *Model courtesy of Sheryl Leisure.* Fair to mint condition: $15-$25.

Draft Horse SR, palomino. *Model courtesy of Sheryl Leisure.* Fair to mint condition: $15-$25.

Draft Horse SR, unpainted white. *Model courtesy of Sheryl Leisure.* Fair to mint condition: $5-$8.

Morgan Mare #5038, bay. *Top,* a typical mare with black-shaded knees and hocks. *Bottom,* a variant mare with no black shading on the legs; *model courtesy of Sheryl Leisure.* Fair to mint condition: $2-$4.

Draft Horse SR, red roan. *Model courtesy of Sheryl Leisure.* Fair to mint condition: $20-$30.

Draft Horse SR, yellow-olive dun. Fair to mint condition: $4-$6.

Morgan Mare *text p. 242*

Morgan Mare #5040, chestnut. The mane and tail on this specimen nearly match the body color, but some #5040s have a darker mane and tail. *Model courtesy of Sheryl Leisure.* Fair to mint condition: $10-$15.

Draft Horse SR, red sorrel. *Model courtesy of Sheryl Leisure.* Fair to mint condition: $15-$25.

Morgan Mare #5039, black. *Top,* a typical 4-stocking mare with gray/black hooves; *model courtesy of Sheryl Leisure. Bottom,* a late-issue 1-stocking mare with a pink hoof. Fair to mint condition: $2-$4.

Morgan Mare #5160, palomino. The yellow-tan mare at the top is a late issue. The sandy-sorrel mare at the bottom came in the 1989 Stablemate Assortment I set; *model courtesy of Sheryl Leisure*. Fair to mint condition: $2-$5.

Morgan Mare #5185, red chestnut. Still available retail in 1996.

Morgan Mare SR, chestnut with bald face (1995). Fair to mint condition: $2-$4.

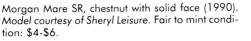

Morgan Mare SR, chestnut with solid face (1990). *Model courtesy of Sheryl Leisure*. Fair to mint condition: $4-$6.

Morgan Mare SR, chocolate sorrel. *Top*, a 1992 mare; *bottom*, a 1994 mare. Fair to mint condition: $2-$4.

Morgan Mare SR, reddish bay. Fair to mint condition: $4-$6.

Morgan Stallion *text pp. 242-243*

Arabian Stallion #5010, dapple gray [Morgan Stallion mold]. *Model courtesy of Sheryl Leisure*. Fair to mint condition: $12-$17.

Arabian Stallion #5016, alabaster [Morgan Stallion mold]. *Model courtesy of Sheryl Leisure*. Fair to mint condition: $12-$17.

Morgan Stallion #5035, bay. *Top*, a dark red variation with matte finish. *Bottom*, a sandy bay with semigloss finish; *model courtesy of Sheryl Leisure*. Fair to mint condition: $2-$4.

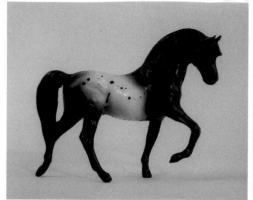

Morgan Stallion #5036 black. *Model courtesy of Sheryl Leisure.* Fair to mint condition: $2-$4.

Morgan Stallion #5037, medium/light chestnut. *Model courtesy of Sheryl Leisure.* Fair to mint condition: $10-$15.

Morgan Stallion SR, black blanket appaloosa. *Top,* a 1992 horse; *Bottom,* a 1994 horse. Fair to mint condition: $2-$4.

Morgan Stallion #5150, medium chestnut / red dun, in three color variations. The lighter red dun horse at the top came in the 1989 Stablemate Assortment I set; *model courtesy of Sheryl Leisure.* The darker red dun in the center was purchased new in a #5150 pack in 1992. The chestnut horse at the bottom was purchased new in #5150 pack in 1995. Fair to mint condition: $2-$5.

Morgan Stallion #5184, light bay. Still available retail in 1996.

Morgan Stallion SR, dark red chestnut. *Model courtesy of Sheryl Leisure.* Fair to mint condition: $4-$6.

Morgan Stallion SR, black with striped mane and tail. Fair to mint condition: $2-$4.

Morgan Stallion SR, palomino. Fair to mint condition: $4-$6.

Saddle Club Collection, Stablemates #5650, medium reddish bay Morgan Stallion. Fair to mint condition: $2-$4.

"Native Dancer" SR, medium bay. Fair to mint condition: $2-$4.

Morgan Stallion SR, seal brown. *Top*, a 1992 horse; *bottom*, a 1994 horse. Fair to mint condition: $2-$4.

"Native Dancer" #5023, steel gray, the early black-point and later 4-stocking versions. Fair to mint condition: $1-$3.

"Native Dancer" SR, red bay. *Model courtesy of Sheryl Leisure*. Fair to mint condition: $4-$6.

Native Dancer *text p. 243*

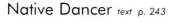

Appaloosa #5178, red bay blanket appaloosa. Still available retail in 1996.

"Native Dancer" SR, white with charcoal/black points. *Model courtesy of Sheryl Leisure*. Fair to mint condition: $4-$6.

Quarter Horse Mare *text pp. 243-244*

Quarter Horse Mare #5048, palomino. Fair to mint condition: $3-$5.

"Native Dancer" SR, palomino. Fair to mint condition: $4-$6.

"Native Dancer" SR, black. *Top*, a 1992 horse; *bottom*, a 1994 horse. Fair to mint condition: $2-$4.

Quarter Horse Mare #5049, golden chestnut. *Model courtesy of Sheryl Leisure.* Fair to mint condition: $10-$15.

Quarter Horse Stallion *text p. 244*

Quarter Horse Stallion #5047, buckskin. Fair to mint condition: $3-$5.

Quarter Horse Mare #5050, buckskin. Fair to mint condition: $3-$5.

Quarter Horse Stallion #5045, palomino. *Top,* a lighter horse with bald face. *Bottom,* a darker horse with solid face; *model courtesy of Heather Wells.* Fair to mint condition: $3-$5.

Quarter Horse Stallion #5186, light bay. Still available retail in 1996.

Stablemates Stable Set #3085, with dark bay Quarter Horse Stallion. *Model courtesy of Sheryl Leisure.* Fair to mint condition: $7-$10.

Stablemates Stable Set #3085, dark bay Quarter Horse Mare and the box for the set of horses and the cardboard stable. *Model and box courtesy of Sheryl Leisure.* Fair to mint condition: $6-$9.

Quarter Horse Stallion #5046, golden chestnut. *Top,* a darker variation; *model courtesy of Heather Wells. Bottom,* a lighter model in his original packaging; *model courtesy of Sheryl Leisure.* Fair to mint condition: $10-$15.

Quarter Horse Stallion SR, medium chestnut. Fair to mint condition: $2-$4.

Saddlebred #5110, black. *Model courtesy of Sheryl Leisure. Fair to mint condition:* $3-$5.

Not shown:
Saddlebred SR, silver plated. Fair to mint condition: $40-$60; *with box. add* $5.

"Seabiscuit" *text p. 245*

Quarter Horse Stallion SR, red leopard appaloosa. *Top,* a 1992 model; *Bottom,* a 1994 model. *Fair to mint condition:* $2-$4.

"Seabiscuit" #5024, dark bay. *Top,* a late-issue matte horse. *Bottom,* an earlier, semigloss horse; *model courtesy of Sheryl Leisure. Fair to mint condition:* $2-$4.

Saddlebred *text pp. 244-245*

Running Paint #5179, chestnut pinto. Still available retail in 1996.

Saddlebred #5001, dapple gray. *Model courtesy of Sheryl Leisure. Fair to mint condition:* $10-$15.

Running Thoroughbred #5025, black. *Fair to mint condition:* $2-$5.

Saddle Club Collection, Stablemates #5650 red chestnut Running Thoroughbred. *Fair to mint condition:* $2-$4.

"Seabiscuit" SR, alabaster. *Top,* a 1992 horse; *bottom,* a 1994 horse. *Fair to mint condition:* $2-$4.

Saddlebred #5002, bay. *Model courtesy of Sheryl Leisure. Fair to mint condition:* $2-$4.

"Seabiscuit" SR, dapple gray. Fair to mint condition: $4-$6.

Thoroughbred Racehorse #5177, black. Still available retail in 1996.

"Silky Sullivan" SR, reddish bay. Fair to mint condition: $4-$6.

"Seabiscuit" SR, palomino. *Model courtesy of Sheryl Leisure.* Fair to mint condition: $4-$6.

"Silky Sullivan" SR, buckskin. *Model courtesy of Sheryl Leisure.* Fair to mint condition: $4-$6.

"Silky Sullivan" SR, reddish dun/chestnut. Fair to mint condition: $4-$6.

"Seabiscuit" SR, red chestnut. *Model courtesy of Sheryl Leisure.* Fair to mint condition: $4-$6.

"Silky Sullivan" SR, dark grulla. Fair to mint condition: $2-$4.

"Silky Sullivan" *text pp. 245-246*

"Silky Sullivan" #5022, dark/medium chestnut. Fair to mint condition: $1-$3.

"Silky Sullivan" SR, pale rose gray. Fair to mint condition: $2-$4.

"Silky Sullivan" SR, rose gray. *Top,* a 1992 horse; *bottom,* a 1994 horse. Fair to mint condition: $2-$4.

"Swaps" text p. 246

"Swaps" SR, steel gray. *Model courtesy of Sheryl Leisure.* Fair to mint condition: $4-$6.

"Swaps" #5021, chestnut, darker and lighter color variations. Fair to mint condition: $1-$3.

Thoroughbred Lying Foal text pp. 246-247

"Swaps" SR, buckskin. *Top,* a 1992 model; *bottom,* a 1994 model. Fair to mint condition: $2-$4.

Thoroughbred Racehorse #5176, red chestnut. Still available retail in 1996.

Stablemates Stable Set #3085, dark bay Lying Foal. Fair to mint condition: $5-$8.

"Swaps" SR, grulla. Fair to mint condition: $2-$4.

Thoroughbred Lying and Standing Foals set #5700, sandy bay Lying Foal. *Model courtesy of Sheryl Leisure.* Fair to mint condition: $5-$8.

"Swaps" SR, blue roan. *Model courtesy of Sheryl Leisure.* Fair to mint condition: $4-$6.

"Swaps" SR, pale rose gray. *Model courtesy of Sheryl Leisure.* Fair to mint condition: $4-$6.

"Swaps" SR, dark liver chestnut. Fair to mint condition: $4-$6.

Thoroughbred Lying and Standing Foals set #5701, black Lying Foal. Fair to mint condition: $5-$8.

Thoroughbred Lying and Standing Foals set #5702, chestnut Lying Foal. The model shown has an unusual roany appearance probably due to spattering of the airbrush. *Model courtesy of Sheryl Leisure.* Fair to mint condition: $5-$8.

Keychain Thoroughbred Lying Foal SR #411494, black. Fair to mint condition: $10-$15.

Keychain Thoroughbred Lying Foal SR #411694, transparent amber. Fair to mint condition: $10-$15.

Thoroughbred Mare text p. 247

Thoroughbred Mare #5026, golden chestnut. Fair to mint condition: $2-$4.

Thoroughbred Mare #5028, black. Fair to mint condition: $2-$4.

Thoroughbred Mare #5030, medium bay, darker brown and lighter red bay color variations. Fair to mint condition: $2-$4.

Thoroughbred Mare #5140, dark/medium bay. Fair to mint condition: $3-$5.

Thoroughbred Mare #5141, medium chestnut, 4-stocking and 2-stocking variations. Fair to mint condition: $2-$5.

Thoroughbred Mare #5183, steel gray. Still available retail in 1996.

Saddle Club Collection, Stablemates #5650, black Thoroughbred Mare. Fair to mint condition: $2-$4.

Thoroughbred Mare SR, alabaster. Fair to mint condition: $4-$6.

Thoroughbred Lying and Standing Foals set #5700, sandy bay Standing Foal. Fair to mint condition: $5-$8.

Thoroughbred Mare SR, dark brown. Fair to mint condition: $2-$4.

Thoroughbred Lying and Standing Foals set #5701, black Standing Foal. *Model courtesy of Sheryl Leisure.* Fair to mint condition: $5-$8.

Thoroughbred Mare SR, red bay. Fair to mint condition: $4-$6.

Thoroughbred Lying and Standing Foals set #5702, chestnut Standing Foal. *Model courtesy of Sheryl Leisure.* Fair to mint condition: $5-$8.

Thoroughbred Standing Foal

text pp. 247-248

Keychain Thoroughbred Standing Foal SR #411394, black. Fair to mint condition: $10-$15.

Keychain Thoroughbred Standing Foal SR #411594, transparent amber. Fair to mint condition: $10-$15.

Stablemates Stable Set #3085, dark bay Standing Foal. Fair to mint condition: $5-$8.

HORSES - DAPPLES

"Amazement" *text p. 248*

"Amazement" #95102, dark chestnut pinto. Still available retail in 1996.

The accessories in Dapples Deluxe Rider Set #95107. Various groups of these items are also included in other Dapples sets.

"Celestria" *text p. 248*

"Dancer" And "Celestria" Set #95105, pearl white filly "Celestria." Still available retail in 1996.

"Dancer" *text p. 248*

"Dancer" #95100, pearl white. Still available retail in 1996.

"Sunny" *text p. 248*

Dapples Deluxe Set #95106, ocher pinto filly "Sunny." Still available retail in 1996.

"Sunny's" Mom *text p. 248*

"Sunny's" Mom #95101, light sorrel. Still available retail in 1996.

RIDERS - HARD PLASTIC
(1950s)

Canadian Mountie *text p. 249*

Canadian Mountie set #P440. The set shown includes a Handsome-mold Mountie and black Prancer. *Set courtesy of Sheryl Leisure.* Fair to mint condition: rider alone, either version, $30-$50. In sets, add the value of the pony and $2-$10 for each accessory.

The same Canadian Mountie, shown full front.

Canadian Mountie versions. *Top,* the Howdy Doody mold version. *Bottom,* two specimens of the Handsome mold version, one without and one with paint detailing. *Models and photos courtesy of Sande Schneider.*

Canadian Mountie accessories. The braided black and gold cloth hatband on the hat is original. *Items and photo courtesy of Sande Schneider.*

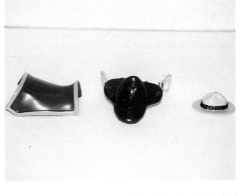

An original 1950s box for Canadian Mountie set #P440. The side panel lists the accessories that came with the set. *Box courtesy of Denise Deen.*

Corky The Circus Boy *text pp. 249-250*

Circus Boy Corky On "Bimbo" set #601. *Set courtesy of Joy Sheesley.* Fair to mint condition: rider alone $55-$65. In set, add the value of Elephant #91.

The same Corky.

Cowboy *text p. 250*

Cowboy & Pinto set #342. The saddle shown is dark brown and has a cinch. *Set courtesy of Sheryl Leisure.* Fair to mint condition: rider alone $35-$45. In sets, add the value of the pony and $2-$10 for each accessory.

The same Cowboy.

Two Cowboy accessories. This saddle is an early version with no grommets or cinch. The hat is dark brown. *Items and photo courtesy of Sande Schneider.*

123

The same Davy Crockett.

The same Kit Carson.

Lucky Ranger set #343. *Set courtesy of Sheryl Leisure.* Fair to mint condition: rider alone $35-$45. In sets, add the value of the pony and $2-$10 for each accessory.

The same Lucky Ranger.

Palomino Prancer music boxes such as this, carrying either Cowboys or Lucky Rangers, were sold through department store holiday catalogs in the mid-1950s. *Model courtesy of Heather Wells.* Fair to mint condition: music-box pony alone $45-$70. In sets, add the value of the rider and accessories.

An original 1950s box for the Davy Crockett set. *Box and photo courtesy of Kim Fairbrother.* Fair to mint condition: $8-$10.

Kit Carson set #542, complete with the elusive removable neckerchief. This soft plastic accessory simply slips onto and off of Kit's neck. *Set and photos courtesy of Ida Santana and Craig A. Lamb.*

Davy Crockett *text pp. 250-251*

Davy Crockett set #P540[?]. *Model courtesy of Sheryl Leisure.* Fair to mint condition: rider alone $35-$45. In sets, add the value of the pony and $2-$10 for each accessory.

Indian *text pp. 252-253*

Kit Carson set #540, rider on black Western Pony. *Set courtesy of Sheryl Leisure.* Fair to mint condition: rider alone $45-$55. In sets, add the value of the pony and $2-$10 for each accessory.

Indian & Pinto set #241. *Set courtesy of Sheryl Leisure.* Fair to mint condition: rider alone $35-$45. In sets, add the value of the pony and $2-$10 for each accessory.

The same Indian.

Indian & Pinto set #242. This Indian is wearing an original paper headdress, which came with some early Indian models. *Set courtesy of Billie Parsons.*

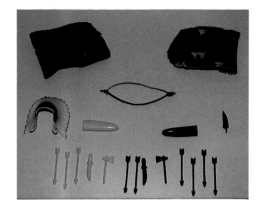

Breyer Indian accessories: two fuzzy-fabric riding blankets; a metal bow (the string is not original); a plastic Chief's headdress; quivers in two colors; a single brave's feather; and an assortment of arrows, knives, and tomahawks. The two red arrows and red knife at the center of the bottom row are transparent plastic; all the other plastic items are opaque. *Accessories and photo courtesy of Sande Schneider.*

Robin Hood *text pp. 253-254*

The same green-cap and red-cap Robin Hoods. This mold, unlike any other old Breyer rider mold, was designed to be able to stand up on its own. *Red-cap photo courtesy of Sande Schneider.*

Indian Chief And Pinto Pony set #P241, made into a music box and sold through department-store holiday catalogs in the mid-1950s. The original wind-up key is shown here beneath the horse. *Set courtesy of Heather Wells.* Fair to mint condition: rider alone $40-$50. In non-music-box sets, add the value of the pony and $2-$10 for each accessory. Music-box pony alone $50-$75.

The same Indian Chief.

Robin Hood set #P145. Top, the version with green cap and boots; *set courtesy of Sheryl Leisure.* Bottom, the version with red cap and boots, often called William Tell by collectors. The bow shown here may not be original. *Set and photo courtesy of Sande Schneider.* Fair to mint condition: rider alone $45-$55. In sets, add the value of the pony and $2-$10 for each accessory.

RIDERS - SOFT OR JOINTED PLASTIC

Alec Ramsey *text p. 254*

Ben Breyer #550. *Doll courtesy of Sheryl Leisure.* Fair to mint condition: $4-$8.

The Black Stallion And Alec Set #3000, with Alec Ramsey doll and racing tack. *Set courtesy of Sheryl Leisure.* Fair to mint condition: doll alone $5-$10. In set, add $12-$25 for the horse and $10 for the tack.

Bitsy Breyer And Arabian Stallion Beach Set #1001. The horse came in chestnut (as shown here), medium bay, or smoke gray. *Set courtesy of Lani Keller.* Fair to mint condition: doll alone $6-$12; full set $12-$25, with box add $2.

Bitsy Breyer And Thoroughbred Jockey Set #1010. The horse came in black (as shown at top, with Bitsy in hot pursuit), chestnut (as shown at bottom), or dark/medium bay. *Black set courtesy of Heather Wells; chestnut set courtesy of Lani Keller.* Fair to mint condition: doll alone $4-$8; full set $10-$20, with box add $2.

Kelly Reno And "Little Man" Gift Set #3096. *Top* Kelly Reno in his gray shirt; *bottom,* Kelly's horse "Little Man" modeling the tack that came with the set. *Doll courtesy of Lani Keller.* Fair to mint condition: doll alone $5-$10. In set, add $35-$55 for the horse and $10 for the tack.

Bitsy Breyer And Morgan English Set #1005. The horse came in dark/medium bay, black (as shown here), or dark/medium chestnut. *Set courtesy of Lani Keller.* Fair to mint condition: doll alone $4-$8; full set $10-$20, with box add $2.

"Pepper" And Lisa, Hunter/Jumper Set #1018. Still available retail in 1996.

Rearing Circus Stallion With Ringmaster set SR. *Set courtesy of Heather Wells.* Fair to mint condition: doll alone $10-$15. In set, add $50-$75 for the horse with tack.

Bitsy Breyer And Quarter Horse Western Set #1015. The horse came in bay, buckskin (as shown here), or palomino. *Set courtesy of Heather Wells.* Fair to mint condition: doll alone $4-$8; full set $10-$20, with box add $2.

"Cobalt" And Veronica, Hunter/Jumper Set #1025. Still available retail in 1996.

"Spot" And Kate, Western Set #1019. Still available retail in 1996.

"Starlight" And Carole, Cross Country Set #1016. Still available retail in 1996.

"Topside" And Stevie, Cross Country Set #1017. Still available retail in 1996.

Not shown:
Bitsy Breyer Beachcomber Set SR, with doll, black Arabian Stallion, bridle, and accessories. Fair to mint condition: doll alone $10-$15; full set $20-$35, with box add $2.

Brenda Breyer *text pp. 255-256*

Brenda Breyer #500, the original long-haired edition. *Left, the normal Brenda with smooth limbs; right, an early Brenda with jointed wrists and ankles. Dolls courtesy of Sheryl Leisure.* Fair to mint condition: normal doll $3-$7; jointed-limbs version $6-$12.

The early Brenda Breyer #500 displays her bionic wrists and rides her cardboard cut-out Western Prancer. *Doll and package courtesy of Sheryl Leisure.*

English Riding Outfit #501, made for Brenda Breyer #500. *Outfit courtesy of Sheryl Leisure.* Outfit in packet $5.

Western Riding Outfit #502, made for Brenda Breyer #500. Outfit in packet $5.

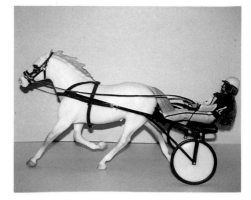

Brenda Breyer And Sulky Set #2446. The black sulky shown here is unusual; most sulkies that came in these sets were blue with transparent spoke-guards. *Set and photo courtesy of Sande Schneider.* Fair to mint condition: doll alone $5-$10, full set $40-$65.

Brenda Breyer Gift Set #3095. *Doll and tack courtesy of Sheryl Leisure.* Fair to mint condition: full set $40-$60.

Brenda Western Gift Set #1120. *Doll courtesy of Sheryl Leisure.* Fair to mint condition: doll alone $3-$7; with horse and saddle, add $40-$60.

Brenda Breyer #500, the big-hair edition. Fair to mint condition: $3-$7.

"Legionario" With Brenda Breyer Rider set SR. *Set courtesy of Heather Wells.* Fair to mint condition: doll alone $10-$15. In set, add $50-$75 for the horse with tack.

"Lassie" #65 mistakes Brenda's outlandish do for an alien intruder.

Left: Dressage Brenda Breyer #510. Still available retail in 1996.

Right: Saddle Seat Brenda Breyer #512. A crop (not shown) also comes with this doll. Still available retail in 1996.

U.S. Equestrian Team Set SR, Brenda in red hunt coat with blue collar. Fair to mint condition: doll alone $6-$12, full set with "Morganglanz" #59, tack, and jump, $40-$60.

Princess Of Arabia set #905. *Top,* Princess Brenda displays her remarkable flexibility. *Center,* the Princess's pale dapple gray mount, issued in the first part of 1995. *Bottom,* the Princess on a bad stirrup day with her red roan steed, issued later in 1995. Fair to mint condition: full set with either horse $40-$60. The doll alone became available retail in 1996 as #518 Arabian Costume Brenda (not listed in this book).

Left: Show Jumping Brenda Breyer #511. *Doll courtesy of Sheryl Leisure.* Still available retail in 1996.

"Black Beauty" Gift Set SR #700894. Fair to mint condition: doll alone $3-$7, full set $15-$30.

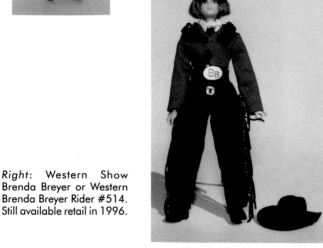

Brenda Breyer Sulky And Pacer Set SR. *Set and photo courtesy of Sande Schneider.* Fair to mint condition: doll alone $5-$10, full set $65-$100.

Right: Western Show Brenda Breyer or Western Brenda Breyer Rider #514. Still available retail in 1996.

Female Rider SR #710995. Fair to mint condition: $6-$12.

Future Champion Show Set SR #494092. Fair to mint condition: full set $40-$60. The doll alone is still available retail in 1996 as Saddle Seat Brenda Breyer #512.

Not shown:
Open Top Buggy set #19841, with flocked Proud Arabian Stallion, Brenda doll, and buggy. Fair to mint condition: $255-$350.
English Brenda Breyer #499, big-hair doll in English outfit #501. Fair to mint condition: $3-$7.
Western Brenda Breyer #498, doll in Western outfit #502. Fair to mint condition: $3-$7.
Brenda Breyer Harness Racing Set SR, jockey Brenda, bay Pacer, sulky, and tack. Fair to mint condition: doll alone $5-$10, full set with no-stockings horse $60-$90, full set with 4-stocking horse $45-$70.

Eagle text p. 257

Eagle And "Pow Wow" set SR #705095. Fair to mint condition: doll alone $5-$10, full set $17-$27.

Willow And "Shining Star" set SR #703495. Although this special was produced only in 1995, it is still available retail in 1996, offered to dealers through the 1996 Reeves International Mid-Year Introduction brochure.

Hillary text p. 257

English Hillary Doll #515. Still available retail in 1996.

Western Hillary Doll #516. Still available retail in 1996.

"Buck" And Hillary Gift Set #2004. Still available retail in 1996.

Darla, in "Amazement's" Riding Set #95104. Still available retail in 1996.

Stampede Riggins text p. 258

Stampede Riggins, Breyer Western Rider, #513. Still available retail in 1996.

Texas Cowboy Replica SR #711294. Fair to mint condition: $10-$15.

CATTLE & HOGS

Black Angus Bull (Standing)

text p. 259

Black Angus Bull #365, black. Still available retail in 1996.

Red Angus Bull SR, nicknamed "The Big Red One," dark red chestnut. *Top*, the version with pink-tan nose. The gloss on the nose and hooves of the specimen shown here is not factory original. *Bottom*, the dark-nosed version; *model courtesy of Sheryl Leisure.* Fair to mint condition: pink-nosed $90-$130, dark-nosed $70-$100.

Black Angus Bull (Walking)

text pp. 259-260

Polled Hereford Bull #73, brown with white, full-rough version. Fair to mint condition: smooth-barrel (not shown) $90-$130, semi-rough (not shown) or full-rough $65-$95.

Black Angus Bull #72, black. *Top*, a glossy smooth-barrel ("poodle cut") bull; *model courtesy of Joy Sheesley. Second*, a glossy semi-rough bull; note the smoothness of his back and croup, contrasting with the roughness of his sides. *Third*, a glossy full-rough bull; note the ridges of his rough coat along his back and croup as well as on his sides. *Bottom* , a matte full-rough bull. Fair to mint condition: smooth-barrel $75-$110, semi-rough or full-rough glossy $25-$40, matte $20-$35.

Brahma Bull *text p. 260*

Brahma Bull #970, woodgrain. *Model courtesy of Sheryl Leisure.* Fair to mint condition: $50-$75.

Brahma Bull #70, shaded gray. *Top*, an old glossy bull with delicate pink shading on nose, dewlaps, and genitals; *bottom*, a much more recent bull with matte finish. Fair to mint condition: glossy $12-$25, matte $8-$15.

Calf *text pp. 260-261*

Ayrshire Calf #350, dark red-brown pinto. *Model courtesy of Sheryl Leisure.* Fair to mint condition: $25-$40.

Brown Swiss Calf #351, medium coffee brown. *Model courtesy of Sheryl Leisure.* Fair to mint condition: $20-$35.

Guernsey Calf #348, dark palomino pinto. Fair to mint condition: $20-$35.

Holstein Calf #347, black pinto. The calf shown is actually from Cow Family set #3447, which included the same model as #347. Fair to mint condition: $3-$7.

Jersey Calf #349, dark palomino with solid face. *Model courtesy of Sheryl Leisure.* Fair to mint condition: $20-$35.

Shorthorn Bull SR, polled dark red chestnut. *Model courtesy of Sheryl Leisure.* Fair to mint condition: $125-$175.

Brown Swiss Cow #345, medium coffee brown. Fair to mint condition: $55-$80.

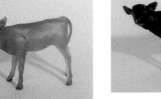

Jersey Cow Family set #3448, dark palomino Calf with large star. Fair to mint condition: $5-$12.

Black Angus Calf SR, black. *Model courtesy of Sheryl Leisure.* Fair to mint condition: $50-$75.

Not shown:
Calf SR, unpainted white. Fair to mint condition: $5-$10.

Guernsey Cow #342, dark palomino pinto. Fair to mint condition: $55-$80.

Charolais Bull text p. 261

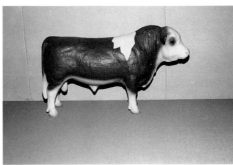

Simmental Bull SR, polled dark reddish-brown pinto. *Top,* a Breyer factory-finish bull. Note the gradual, shaded edge of the brown "blanket"; the completely white crown of the head; and the quite intricate outline of the white spot across the withers, especially the back edge. *Model courtesy of Sheryl Leisure. Bottom,* a bull painted by the National Simmental Association. Note the abrupt, unshaded edge of the brown "blanket"; the brown paint coming onto the crown of the head; and the simplified outline of the white spot across the withers. *Model and photo courtesy of Jo Kulwicki.* Fair to mint condition: Breyer factory-finish bull $125-$175; NSA-painted bull $25-$40.

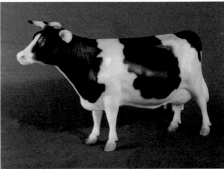

Holstein Cow #341, black pinto. The cow shown is actually from Cow Family set #3447, which included the same model as #341. Fair to mint condition: $10-$20.

Cow text pp. 261-262

Charolais Bull #360, white with horns. *Top,* an old gray-hoofed bull with extraordinary body-shading; *model courtesy of Joy Sheesley. Bottom,* a newer, tan-hoofed bull. Fair to mint condition: $10-$20.

Ayrshire Cow #344, dark red-brown pinto. *Model courtesy of Sheryl Leisure.* Fair to mint condition: $65-$95.

Jersey Cow #343, dark palomino. Fair to mint condition: $55-$80.

A lineup of the regular-run gals, showing the different horn molds. *From left*: Jersey, Guernsey, Holstein, Ayrshire, and Brown Swiss. *Models and photo courtesy of Jo Kulwicki.*

Jersey Cow Family set #3448, polled Jersey Cow, dark palomino. Fair to mint condition: $10-$20.

Guernsey Cow SR, dark red-brown chestnut "pinto." Note the chestnut horns. *Model courtesy of Karen Grimm / Black Horse Ranch.* Fair to mint condition: $55-$80.

Holstein Cow SR #417341, mixed horns, black pinto. The lady on the right is the mixed-horns Holstein; note the upward trajectory of her left horn. The cow on the left is a normal Holstein from Cow Family set #3447. *Models and photo courtesy of Jo Kulwicki.* Fair to mint condition: $20-$35.

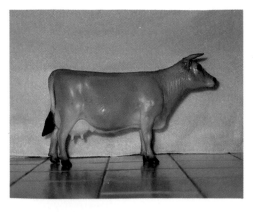

Jersey Cow SR, caramel/palomino. Note the palomino horns. *Model courtesy of Sande Schneider.* Fair to mint condition: $55-$80.

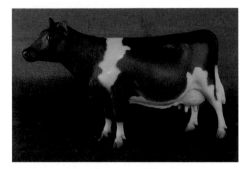

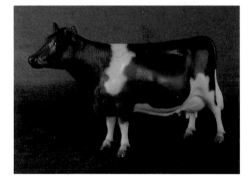

Ayrshire Cow SR #414341, polled, red-brown pinto. *Top*, a 1988 model; *Bottom*, a 1993 model. Fair to mint condition: either year $30-$50.

Brown Swiss Cow SR #413341, polled, medium/light coffee brown. *Top*, a 1988 model; *Bottom*, a 1993 model. Fair to mint condition: either year $30-$50.

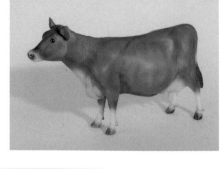

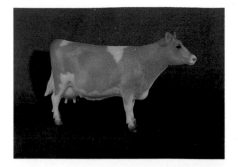

Guernsey Cow SR #415341, polled, dark palomino pinto. *Top*, a 1988 model, an unusually light specimen; *model courtesy of Sheryl Leisure. Bottom*, a 1993 model. Fair to mint condition: either year $30-$50.

Holstein Cow SR #411341, polled, black pinto. *Top*, a 1988 model; *Bottom*, a 1993 model. Fair to mint condition: $12-$25. Model may still be available retail in 1996.

Jersey Cow SR #416341, polled, dark palomino. *Top*, a 1988 model; *bottom*, a 1993 model. *Older model courtesy of Sheryl Leisure.* Fair to mint condition: either year $30-$50.

Hereford Bull *text pp. 262-263*

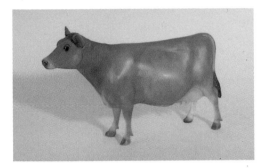

Hereford Bull #71, brown with white. *Top*, an old glossy bull with his brown "blanket" unstenciled along the belly and legs; *bottom*, an old glossy bull with a fully stenciled blanket. Fair to mint condition: unstenciled $15-$30; stenciled $12-$25.

Not shown:
Hereford Bull #971, woodgrain. Fair to mint condition: $100-$140.

"Jasper" *text p. 263*

"Jasper" The Market Hog #355, white with large gray spot; normal stenciled-spot version. Fair to mint condition: early unstenciled and stenciled "pretty" versions $10-$17; later version still available retail in 1996.

Duroc Hog SR, dark red-brown. *Model courtesy of Sheryl Leisure.* Fair to mint condition: $55-$80.

Hampshire Hog SR, black with white band. *Model courtesy of Sheryl Leisure.* Fair to mint condition: $55-$80.

Spotted Poland China Hog SR, white with black spots, shown from both sides. *Model courtesy of Sheryl Leisure.* Fair to mint condition: $55-$80.

An oddball hog, dark red dun with bald face. This hog could well represent a small special run. *Model courtesy of Jo Kulwicki.*

Another oddball hog, light red dun with a dark red dun dorsal band. This pig too may represent a small special run. *Model courtesy of Sue Lehman.*

Polled Hereford Bull *text p. 264*

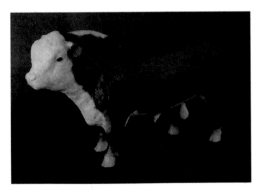

Polled Hereford Bull #74, brown with white; red-brown and dark-brown color variations. Still available retail in 1996.

Spanish Fighting Bull *text p. 264*

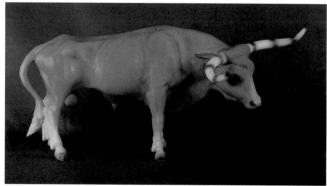

Spanish Fighting Bull #73, black. *Top,* an older model with gray hooves; *bottom,* a newer model with black hooves. Fair to mint condition: $20-$35. For the Presentation Collection edition (on base) add $50.

Texas Longhorn Bull *text p. 264*

Texas Longhorn Bull #370, dark red-brown pinto. Fair to mint condition: $12-$25.

Texas Longhorn Bull #75, light brown. *Top* a 1960s model with eyewhites and stenciled forelock; *center,* a chalky bull from the 1970s; *bottom,* a more recent bull with palomino coloring and brightly striped horns. Fair to mint condition: with eyewhites $15-$30, chalky $20-$35, others $12-$25. For the Presentation Collection edition (on base) add $50.

Texas Longhorn Bull #975, woodgrain. *Model courtesy of Sheryl Leisure.* Fair to mint condition: $85-$120.

DOGS & CATS

"Benji" *text p. 265*

"Benji" #7701, dark yellowy buckskin. *Model courtesy of Sheryl Leisure.* Fair to mint condition: $5-$12.

Boxer *text p. 265*

Boxer #66, some chestnut, some fawn. *Top* an old glossy chestnut specimen with vinyl collar; *bottom,* a more recent matte fawn model with chain collar. *Models courtesy of Sheryl Leisure.* Fair to mint condition: dog alone $12-$25; with either collar, add $5.

Varieties of Boxer eyes. The woodgrain #966 at left has green irises. The chestnut #66 in the center has black irises. The fawn #66 at right has green irises with white "sparkle" dots on top. *Models courtesy of Sheryl Leisure.*

"Pug" Boxer #322, brown brindle. Still available retail in 1996.

Boxer SR, white. *Model and photo courtesy of Robert W. Peterson.* Fair to mint condition: $145-$200.

"Jolly Cholly" *text pp. 265-266*

"Chaser" Hound Dog #324, chestnut and white. *Model courtesy of Sheryl Leisure.* Fair to mint condition: $10-$20.

Left: Boxer #966, woodgrain. *Model courtesy of Sheryl Leisure.* Fair to mint condition: $70-$100.

"Jolly Cholly" Basset Hound #326, tri-color. *Top,* an ordinary #326; *model courtesy of Sheryl Leisure. right,* an "insurance Cholly." Dogs with similar tags are surprisingly common, but the tags were added by an insurance organization, not by Breyer. *Model and photo courtesy of Sande Schneider.* Fair to mint condition: any version $8-$15.

"Jolly Cholly" Bloodhound #325, solid dark brown. *Model courtesy of Sheryl Leisure.* Fair to mint condition: $30-$50.

Kitten *text p. 266*

Left: Calico Kitten #336, orangy-tan tabby with charcoal-brown stripes. This specimen has a factory-original blue-ribbon sticker. *Model courtesy of Sheryl Leisure.* Fair to mint condition: $25-$40.

Right: "Cleopatra" Kitten #337, orange tabby with darker orange stripes. *Model courtesy of Sheryl Leisure.* Fair to mint condition: $10-$20.

Left: "Leonardo" Kitten #338, tawny-gray tabby with darker gray stripes. *Model courtesy of Sheryl*

Siamese Kitten #335, white with dark points. The kitten shown here has an original blue-ribbon sticker. *Model courtesy of Sheryl Leisure.* Fair to mint condition: $35-$55.

Poodle *text pp. 266-267*

A poodle mold made by Breyer in the 1950s but never released for sale. The dog originally had a round "ball" tuft at the end of his tail, but this was broken off and lost. For further discussion, see note 7 for the Poodle mold. *Model and photo courtesy of Robert W. Peterson.*

Poodle #67, black. *Model courtesy of Sheryl Leisure.* Fair to mint condition: $20-$35.

"Lassie" *text p. 266*

"Rin Tin Tin" *text p. 267*

German Shepherd #327, charcoal gray. The model shown has a brown tone. *Model courtesy of Sheryl Leisure.* Fair to mint condition: $25-$40.

"Honey" Collie #323, sandy chestnut. Still available retail in 1996.

Poodle #68, white. *Model courtesy of Sheryl Leisure.* Fair to mint condition: $20-$35.

Poodle #69, silver gray. *Model courtesy of Sheryl Leisure.* Fair to mint condition: $30-$50.

Poodle #967, woodgrain. *Model courtesy of Sheryl Leisure.* Fair to mint condition: $100-$140.

"Lassie" #65, red chestnut with white, and the original "Lassie" box. *Model courtesy of Sheryl Leisure; box courtesy of Jo Kulwicki.* Fair to mint condition: model alone $25-$40.

"Rin Tin Tin" #64, brown and white. *Top,* a dog with a definite "saddle" pattern; *model courtesy of Sheryl Leisure. Bottom,* a dog with a more extensive brown "blanket," shown with his original box and hang tag; *model and photo courtesy of Jo Kulwicki.* Fair to mint condition: model alone $20-$35.

St. Bernard *text p.267*

"Brandy" St. Bernard #321, tawny chestnut with white. Still available retail in 1996.

St. Bernard #328, red-brown with white. *Model courtesy of Sheryl Leisure.* Fair to mint condition: $12-$25.

"Tiffany" *text pp. 267-268*

"Tiffany" And "Benji" Set #3090, white "Tiffany," *shown here slightly smaller than actual size. Model courtesy of Lani Keller.* Fair to mint condition: "Tiffany" alone $10-$17.

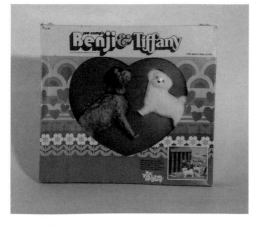

"Tiffany" And "Benji" Set #3090, a set in original box with cellophane wrap still intact. *Set courtesy of Sheryl Leisure.* Fair to mint condition: $35-$55.

"Tiffany" And "Benji" Set #3090, the sweethearts enjoy the ambiance of their cardboard Athens.

DONKEYS & MULES

Balking Mule *text p. 269*

Balking Mule #207, bay. Fair to mint condition: $45-$70.

Balking Mule #208, seal brown. Fair to mint condition: $70-$100.

Balking Mule SR, alabaster. Fair to mint condition: $40-$60.

Balking Mule SR, apricot dun. Fair to mint condition: $40-$60.

Balking Mule SR, black blanket appaloosa. Fair to mint condition: $40-$60.

Balking Mule SR, black leopard appaloosa. Fair to mint condition: $40-$60.

Balking Mule SR, buckskin. Fair to mint condition: $40-$60.

Balking Mule SR, chestnut. Fair to mint condition: $40-$60.

"Brighty" *text p. 269*

"Brighty 1991" #376, grayish brown. *Model courtesy of Sheryl Leisure.* Still available retail in 1996.

Marguerite Henry's "Brighty" #375, gray. *Model courtesy of Sheryl Leisure.* Fair to mint condition: $8-$15. In set #2075 with book and box, add $6.

Donkey *text pp. 269-270*

Donkey #81, most gray. *Top,* battleship-gray donkeys such as this can be either painted or cast in gray plastic; *model courtesy of Heather Wells. Center* and *bottom,* two old gray-brown donkeys, in solid-faced and bald-faced variations; *models courtesy of Sheryl Leisure.* Fair to mint condition: any version $5-$12.

Donkey With Baskets set #82, gray Donkey with removable red plastic baskets. *Set and photo courtesy of Jo Kulwicki.* Fair to mint condition: add $20-$30 to the value of Donkey #81.

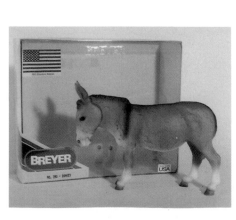

Donkey #390, light gray, with her American-flag box. Fair to mint condition: $10-$20; with box, add $2.

WILDLIFE

Bear text p. 271

Bear #306, black, white-faced and brown-faced versions. Both models shown here have some factory pink in the mouth. *Models courtesy of Joy Sheesley.* Fair to mint condition: any version $15-$30.

Bear #307, brown, white-faced and lighter-brown-faced versions. Both models shown here have some factory pink in the mouth. *Models courtesy of Joy Sheesley.* Fair to mint condition: any version $30-$50.

Bear Family set #3071, white Bear. Fair to mint condition: $10-$20.

Cinnamon Bear And Cub set #3069, medium red-brown Bear. *Model courtesy of Sheryl Leisure.* Fair to mint condition: $15-$30.

Bear Cub text p. 271

Bear Cub #308, black, brown-faced and white-faced versions. Both models shown here have some factory pink in the mouth. *Models courtesy of Joy Sheesley.* Fair to mint condition: $5-$10.

Bear Cub #309, brown, white-faced and lighter-brown-faced versions. Both models shown here have some factory pink in the mouth. *Models courtesy of Joy Sheesley.* Fair to mint condition: $10-$20.

Bear Family set #3071, white Cub. Fair to mint condition: $5-$10.

Cinnamon Bear And Cub set #3069, medium red-brown Cub. *Model courtesy of Sheryl Leisure.* Fair to mint condition: $8-$15.

Bighorn Ram text p. 271

Bighorn Ram #78, brown, version with tan horns. *Model courtesy of Sheryl Leisure.* Fair to mint condition: tan-horn $20-$35, gray-horn or gray-striped-horn $30-$50.

Dall Sheep #85, white, tan-horned and gray-horned versions. *Models courtesy of Sheryl Leisure.* Fair to mint condition: tan-horn $50-$75, gray-horn $45-$70.

Bolo Tie text p. 271

Bolo Tie #501, version with black string tie. Fair to mint condition: $12-$25.

Buck *text pp. 271-272*

Buffalo SR, light smoke gray. *Model courtesy of Sheryl Leisure.* Fair to mint condition: $145-$200.

Not shown:
Buffalo SR, woodgrain. This model may come only on lamps. Fair to mint condition: $145-$200.

Buck #301, tawny. *Model courtesy of Sheryl Leisure.* Still available retail in 1996 in Deer Family set #3123.

Buffalo *text p. 272*

Doe *text p. 272*

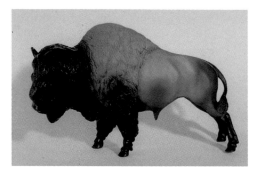

Elephant #92, pink, with original carton. *Model and photos courtesy of Ida Santana and Craig A. Lamb.* Fair to mint condition: $100-$140.

American Bison #381, yellow dun. Still available retail in 1996.

Doe #302, tawny. Note the original blue-ribbon sticker on this specimen. *Model courtesy of Sheryl Leisure.* Still available retail in 1996 in Deer Family set #3123.

Elephant *text pp. 272-273*

Elephant #91, gray. The model shown here is the version cast in white plastic and painted realistic shaded gray, with white tusks. *Model courtesy of Sheryl Leisure.* Fair to mint condition: any version $5-$12.

Although we can't be certain at this point, the model shown may be an Elephant #93, blue. *Model and photo courtesy of Lynn Hiersche.*

Circus Boy Corky On "Bimbo" set #601. The Elephant shown is the solid battleship-gray version with gray tusks. *Set courtesy of Joy Sheesley.* Fair to mint condition: rider alone $55-$65; in set, add the value of Elephant #91.

Buffalo #76, brown. Fair to mint condition: older dark or buckskin versions $20-$35, newer version $10-$20. For the Presentation Collection edition (on base) add $50.

Elephant #391, light/medium gray, with American-flag box. Fair to mint condition: $10-$20; with box, add $2.

"Tatanka" The White Buffalo #380. Fair to mint condition: $20-$35.

Elephant SR, woodgrain. *Model courtesy of Joy Sheesley.* Fair to mint condition: $145-$200.

Not shown:
Elephant With Howdah set #94, gray Elephant with removable howdah. Fair to mint condition: add $20-$30 to the value of Elephant #91.

Elk text p. 273

Elk #77, reddish-brown. *Model courtesy of Sheryl Leisure.* Still available retail in 1996.

Fawn text p. 273

Fawn #303, tawny. *Model courtesy of Sheryl Leisure.* Still available retail in 1996 in Deer Family set #3123.

Golden Buck text p. 273

Golden Buck #101, metallic gold. *Model courtesy of Sheryl Leisure.* Fair to mint condition: $25-$40.

Golden Doe text p. 273

Golden Doe #102, metallic gold. *Model courtesy of Sheryl Leisure.* Fair to mint condition: $25-$40.

Moose text pp. 273-274

Moose #79, brown. *Model courtesy of Sheryl Leisure.* Fair to mint condition: older, dark or tawny versions $20-$35, newer version still available retail in 1996. For the Presentation Collection edition (on base) add $50.

Pronghorn Antelope text p. 274

Pronghorn Antelope #310, brown, with white. *Model courtesy of Sheryl Leisure.* Fair to mint condition: $45-$70.

Rocky Mountain Goat text p. 274

Montana Mountain Goat #312, white with reddish-brown horns. *Model courtesy of Sheryl Leisure.* Fair to mint condition: $25-$40.

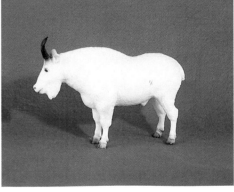

Rocky Mountain Goat #312, white with black or dark gray horns. *Model courtesy of Sheryl Leisure.* Fair to mint condition: $35-$55.

APPENDIX

Hess Wilderness Animal Series
text p. 277

The "© Reeves/Breyer Made in China" stamp on the leg of a Dapples "Sunny's" Mom.

The "B" stamp.

The "PP" stamp on the underside of a Western Prancer saddle.

Wilderness Animal Series by Chris Hess, a selection of the flocked versions. These animals are not Breyer products. Models and photo courtesy of Ida Santana and Craig A. Lamb.

The "© 1984 and TM 20th Century Fox" engraving on the "Phar Lap" mold.

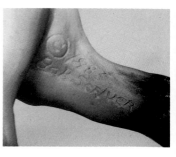

The "© 1985 Bob Scriver" engraving on the "Buckshot" mold.

The "Breyer Molding Co." round stamp. Note the large copyright "C" in the center circle.

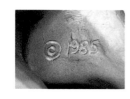

The "©1985" engraving on the "Touch of Class" mold.

The "© 1986 Reeve Intl." engraving on the "Lady Roxana" mold.

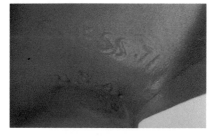

"CHess" mold marks. *Top,* the "C.HESS .71" stamp on the Shire mold; *bottom,* the "CHess" engraving on the Five-Gaiter.

The "Suzann Fiedler" stamp on the Ideal Quarter Horse mold.

The "© Breyer Reeves" stamp.

Six painted (non-flocked) pieces from the Wilderness Animal Series. Again, these animals are not Breyer products. Models courtesy of Joy Sheesley.

Mold Marks *text p. 279-281*

The "Breyer Molding Co. © 1976" and "MEXICO" stamps on the belly of a Stablemate Quarter Horse Mare.

The "U.S.A." stamp, shown here in a typical position beside the round "Breyer Molding Co." stamp.

The "© Reeves Breyer" stamp on the "Llanarth True Briton" mold.

The "'95" stamp, shown here on the "Sham" mold.

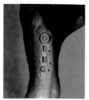

The "© B.M.C." stamp on the leg of a Little Bits Morgan Stallion.

The "© 1986 •thelwell•" engraving on the "Kipper" mold.

The "© MSP 1977" stamp, shown here on the leg of "Benji."

The "AQHA '95" stamp on the 1995 edition of the Ideal Quarter Horse mold.

Chalkies & Pearlies text p. 284

A basecoat chalky Clydesdale Mare (*left*), shown here with a normal mare. Value for chalky models of any mold: add $2-$15 to the value of the ordinary model, depending on the size and beauty of the piece and the extensiveness of the white areas.

A pearly bay Rearing Stallion (*right*), shown here in fetlock-to-fetlock comparison with a normal bay Rearing Stallion. Value for pearly models of any mold: add $10-$15 to the value of the ordinary model, depending on the size and beauty of the piece.

Stickers text p. 285

A gold-foil sticker on an old woodgrain Clydesdale Stallion. *Model and photo courtesy of Sande Schneider.*

A typical blue-ribbon sticker, shown here on the shoulder of a Calico Kitten #336. The model number printed in the center of the sticker has faded. *Model courtesy of Sheryl Leisure.*

Master Crafters Clocks text pp. 285-287

A mirror-image pair of MasterCrafters clocks. On the left is a horse-over-the-clock Hartland Champ clock; on the right is a horse-over-the-clock Breyer Western Horse clock. The hands on these clocks may not be original, but everything else is. *Clocks courtesy of Jo Kulwicki.* Fair to mint condition: Breyer clock $90-$130.

This MasterCrafters horse-over-the-clock with Breyer Western Horse is unusual in having a green base rather than brown. The saddle is Breyer but is probably not original to this clock. *Clock and photo courtesy of Donald and Leslie Granger.* Fair to mint condition: $90-$130.

MasterCrafters horse-beside-the-clock Western Horse clock with palomino horse. *Clock courtesy of Heather Wells.* Fair to mint condition: $80-$120.

MasterCrafters horse-beside-the-clock Western Horse clock with white horse. Note the original felt saddle pad. *Clock and photo courtesy of Sande Schneider.* Fair to mint condition: $80-$120.

MasterCrafters "Fury" Prancer clock with Davy Crockett rider. *Clock and photo courtesy of Sande Schneider.* Fair to mint condition: $80-$120.

MasterCrafters clock with bas-relief resembling Breyer's Quarter Horse Yearling, gold-tone version. *Clock and photo courtesy of Sande Schneider.* Fair to mint condition: $8-$15.

Dunning Industries "Ranchcraft" lamps with burlap shades and Breyer woodgrain models. *Left*, a Fighting Stallion lamp; *courtesy of Sheryl Leisure. Center*, a lamp with Running Mare and Foal, and *right*, a "sconce" lamp with Running Foal; *lamps and photos courtesy of Sande Schneider.* Value: add $15-$30 to the value of the model itself, depending on size and condition of the lamp.

Glen-Tek lamp with a Breyer Classic Lipizzan. *Lamp and photo courtesy of Tina Dils.* Fair to mint condition: $25-$40.

"Fury" Prancer lamps with plaster "desert" base. *Left*, a lamp with a plain shade and Breyer Lucky Ranger rider; *lamp courtesy of Heather Wells. Center* and *right*, a pair of lamps with silhouette shades and Davy Crockett riders; *lamps and photos courtesy of Sande Schneider.* Fair to mint condition: $80-$120.

Glen-Tek lamp with a Breyer Classic "Silky Sullivan." *Lamp and photo courtesy of Tina Dils.* Fair to mint condition: $25-$40.

Conventional nightlights made from Breyer models. *Left*, a glossy gray Brahma Bull on wooden base; *nightlight courtesy of Sheryl Leisure.* Center, a palomino Western Horse on wooden base. *Right*, a free-standing white Western Horse; *nightlight and photo courtesy of Sande Schneider.* Fair to mint condition: light with base, add $20 to the value of the model itself; with no base, add $10.

Car nightlight, the "Ministang," made from a Breyer glossy alabaster Family Arabian Mare. *Nightlight courtesy of Lillian Sutphin; photo courtesy of Sheryl Leisure.* Fair to mint condition: $8-$15.

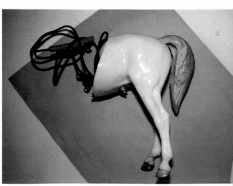

Traditionals

GENERAL NOTE: The Traditional scale is the largest of Breyer's four sizes of realistic models, and includes horses, riders, cattle, and other animals. The adult standing horses average about 8-9 inches tall at the eartips. The first mold ever made by Breyer, the Western Horse, is a large Traditional horse, about 10 inches tall, created in 1950 for wholesale to a clock manufacturer but also sold in 1950 as a free-standing model. (See Breyer Company History in the Appendix near the end of this book.) Although the Traditional scale is the company's original scale, it only received the label "Traditional" years later, in 1975—the year the Stablemate scale was introduced and two years after the debut of the first models designated as Classic. Though many Traditional molds are in proportion to each other, the scale is far from consistent. For example, the horses of the Artist Series, which were reclassified by Breyer as Traditional Series molds starting in 1988, are a bit smaller than the average Traditional-scale horses. The dog molds, though physically smaller than most Traditional horses, are disproportionately large. The Kitten, being life-sized, looks monstrous beside even the biggest Traditional horse or bull. Two of the oldest bull molds— the horned Hereford and the polled walking Black Angus—and a number of horse molds—Bucking Bronco, "Hobo" on stand, Polo Pony, Rearing Stallion, and, until 1995, all the horses of the Messenger Series Of Kiger Mustangs—are listed among the Traditionals in Breyer catalogs but are actually Classic size. Despite Breyer's categorization of these small horses, I have listed them in the Classics section of this book.

A & P Wagon With Old Timer SR — see McCormick Decanter With Old Timer set SR (under Old Timer)

"Abdullah" — see under Trakehner

Action American Appaloosa, Buckskin, and Paint Foals — see under Action Stock Horse Foal

Action Appaloosa Foal — see under Action Stock Horse Foal

Action Drafters, Big And Small set — see under Friesian in the Traditionals section and under Clydesdale in the Little Bits section

Action Stock Horse Foal — Colt, loping on right lead. Sculpted by Chris Hess. Mold in catalog-run production 1984 - current as of 1996.

Catalog-run models made from this mold:

- Action American Appaloosa Stock Horse Foal #238, gray blanket appaloosa, solid face, unstenciled butt blanket, black splashed-on spots, black points, black hooves, matte (1984-88). Called Appaloosa Stock Horse Foal in the 1984-86 catalogs, Action American Appaloosa Stock Horse Foal in 1987-88.
- Action American Buckskin Stock Horse Foal #225, buckskin, solid face, gray nose, black points, black hooves, matte (1987-88). This colt is shown with black legs and hooves in both of the catalogs that list him. He is typically a bit darker than the SR buckskin Action Stock Horse Foal but is otherwise indistinguishable from the black-hoofed version of the SR.
- Action American Paint Horse Foal #237, bay paint, tobiano; solid face; black points; most with 4 stockings and gray hooves; matte (1984-88). Called Bay Pinto Stock Horse Foal in the 1984-86 catalogs, Action American Paint Horse Foal in 1987-88. This foal has the same pinto pattern as the SR black paint Action Stock Foal. *Breyer Collector's Video* shows a variation of this foal with black lower legs and black hooves, no stockings. This variation is not shown in Breyer catalogs, so I don't know when it was issued.
- Action Appaloosa Foal #810, red leopard appaloosa, white foal with splashed-on red chestnut spots, red chestnut mane and tail, charcoal-shaded joints and muzzle, gray hooves, matte (1989-93). Though Breyer catalogs don't say so, this model was patterned after a real foal named "Brother Bold," owned by Black Horse Ranch (per *Breyer Collector's Video*). On many #810s, the nostrils are gray like the muzzle; but on some, the nostrils are pink. I found pink-nostril #810s at several stores in southern California in spring and summer 1991.
- Chestnut Stock Horse Foal #236, red sorrel, solid face, flaxen mane and tail, 1 left hind stocking with gray hoof, other hooves sorrel-gray, matte (1984-86). A variation of this foal has a mane the same color as the body, per collector Gale Good.
- "Cricket" Quarter Horse Foal #934, chestnut, blaze, slightly darker chestnut mane and tail, dorsal stripe, right front and right hind stockings with gray hooves, left lower legs brown-gray with tan-gray hooves, matte (1995 - current as of 1996). This foal is a deep golden brown chestnut with little if any red tone. Some models may have a small white sock on the left hind, as shown in the 1995 catalog; my own foal is light muddy gray in this area.
- "Sunny" Action Foal #891, yellow dun, solid face, gray dun mane and tail, dorsal stripe, gray and charcoal shading on legs, yellow dun "socks," gray dun hooves, matte (1994 - 95). The dorsal stripe can be faint. On some models, the legs have a banded appearance, with gray shading on the knees and hocks, charcoal on the cannons, and yellow dun fetlocks and pasterns. On other models, the gray and charcoal are more blended.

Special-run models made from this mold:

- Action Stock Horse Foal SR, bay, solid face; black mane and tail; black, dark gray, or dark brown lower legs and hooves; some with no stockings, some with 1 left hind stocking with gray hoof; matte (1984). Penney's holiday catalog. Sold in SR "Stallion Mare And Foal Set" (yes, that's how the Penney's catalog reads), with rose-alabaster Stock Horse Stallion. Contrary to the set's name, the set includes only the foal and stallion, no mare. The 1984 Penney's catalog shows the foal with 1 left front and 2 hind stockings; to my knowledge this version was not issued for sale. Collector Sande Schneider's foal has no stockings, but the foals owned by collectors Heather Wells and Linda Bell have 1 left hind stocking. Both versions are also pictured in Maestas 1987a.
- Action Stock Horse Foal SR, bay peppercorn leopard appaloosa, bay foal with darker brown splashed-on spots, solid face, black points, 1 left hind and 2 front stockings, gray hooves, matte (1986). Penney's holiday catalog. Sold in Breyer Traditional Collector's Family Set SR #712459, with bay peppercorn appaloosa Stock Horse Mare and Stock Horse Stallion. My own foal has a white right hind coronary band in addition to the 3 stockings. The number for this set is per a Breyer company computer printout of activity 1985-92 and a Model Horse Collectors Supply price list of July 1987.
- Action Stock Horse Foal SR, black paint, tobiano; solid face; white mane; black tail; 4 stockings; gray hooves; matte (1984 and 1985). Penney's holiday catalog. Sold in Pinto Mare And Foal Set SR with black paint Stock Horse Mare. This foal has the same pinto pattern as regular-run bay paint Action Foal #237. The 1984 Penney's catalog and *JAH* XI/#3 1984 (p. 19) show this SR foal with a black mane, but apparently these are test pieces that were not reproduced for sale. All the collectors' specimens I know of have a white mane, including collector Gale Good's foal, purchased in November 1984. The foal shown in the 1985 Penney's catalog also has a white mane.
- Action Stock Horse Foal SR, buckskin, solid face, gray nose, black mane and tail, black or brownish-charcoal lower legs and hooves, matte (1984). Sears holiday catalog. Sold in Collectible Stock Horse Family set SR with buckskin Stock Horse Mare and buckskin Stock Horse Stallion. This colt is typically somewhat paler and creamier in color than the regular-run buckskin #225. Although my own SR model has black legs and hooves, as do the foals in the Sears catalog and in *JAH* XI/#3 1984 (p. 20), collector Heather Wells's model has brownish-charcoal legs and hooves. There may also be a gray-hoofed version of the SR foal, for gray-hoofed versions of the SR mare and stallion that came in the set are known.
- Action Stock Horse Foal SR, pale yellow dun, solid face, dark brown points, no dorsal stripe, dark brown hooves, matte (1992). Penney's holiday catalog. Sold in Frisky Foals set SR #712092, with red chestnut Proud Arabian Foal, black blanket appaloosa Running Foal, and dark palomino pinto Suckling Foal. 3,000 sets made, per a Breyer company computer printout of activity 1985-92. The number for this set is per the printout and a Bentley Sales price list dated March 15, 1993.

Note: The Action Stock Horse Foal mold has the round "Breyer Molding Co." stamp. Oddly, on the opposite hind leg this mold also has a very faint "© B.-M." stamp, reminiscent of the "© B.M.C." stamp on Little Bits molds. This ghost stamp was pointed out to me by collector Mel Price. It is nearly invisible on my 1992 SR yellow dun, but comparatively clear on my SR foals from 1984-86, though even on them it looks like a pentimento. This mold was never given the "U.S.A." stamp.

"Adios" — Stallion, standing, looking slightly to right. Copied by Chris Hess from a small bronze replica of James Slick's life-sized bronze "Adios." Mold in catalog-run production 1969- current as of 1996.

Catalog-run models made from this mold:

- "Adios" Famous Standardbred #50, dark bay, tiny star, black points, 2 hind striped socks, matte and semigloss (1969-80). In Presentation Collection mounted on American walnut wood base with brass "Adios" nameplate, late 1971-1973. The Presentation Collection is not in the 1971 manual, but "Adios" and five other Presentation models were advertised in the November 1971 *Western Horseman*. The Presentation "Adios" is listed as #5050 (the number later assigned to the buckskin Stablemate Quarter Horse Mare) in the 1973 price list, but prior to that it apparently had the same number as regular-run #50; see Presentation Collection below in this section for discussion. For discussion of other "Adioses" on bases, see note 3 for this mold. The real "Adios," who was foaled in 1940 and died in 1965, was a famous Standardbred pacer that set several world records in the period 1942-46 and sired many champions, such as "Adios Butler" (see Beard 1992). An early "Adios" #50 in my collection (he has no "U.S.A." stamp) has a dorsal stripe, but collector Lynn Isenbarger's early model does not, nor does my later "Adios" or other #50s I've seen. Regarding the release date of #50, see note 1 for this mold. Regarding the origins of Breyer's "Adios" model, see note 2 for this mold. #50 was in the Showcase Collection as #5000 in 1970-72 (see Showcase Collection in this section for discussion). The model number 50 previously belonged to the bald-faced black Western Horse.
- "Clayton" Quarter Horse #911, dappled palomino, dapples on neck, head, and lower part of face; white mane and tail; gray-shaded knees and hocks; 4 stockings; tan hooves; matte (1995 - current as of 1996). The palomino color of this horse is typically dusky in tone, not yellow or golden, and ranges from medium tan to dark chocolate tan. The darker models especially would more accurately be called silver dapple. Some models have an all-white area above the nose; others have only dapples here. In the 1996 catalog, #911's name was expanded to "Clayton" American Quarter Horse.
- "Mesa" The Quarter Horse #853, dark mahogany bay, no white markings, black points, black hooves, slightly semigloss (1991-92).
- Quarter Horse Stallion #830, blue roan, white horse with gray flecks, black points, black hooves, matte (1990). The model number 830 previously belonged to the Showcase Collection issue of the chestnut Clydesdale Mare.
- "Rough 'N' Ready" Quarter Horse #885, pale yellow dun with red-tan flecks, dark red chestnut face with blaze, red chestnut points, 2 hind stockings, 4 brown-gray hooves, matte (1993–95). On some models the front legs, hocks, face, mane, and tail are all the same red chestnut color; on others the face and sometimes the mane and tail are dark chocolate, contrasting with the red chestnut on the legs. One of my #885s has only the tiny red-tan flecks on the body, and his hind hooves are tan-gray, lighter than the brown-gray front hooves. My other #885 has, in addition to red-tan flecks, a light wash of gray shading, which gives him a smutty appearance, as some real dun horses have; and all his hooves are brown-gray. #885's blaze is the same as that on the SR bay blanket appy "Adios."

♠ Standing Quarter Horse Stallion #705, apricot dun, bald face, dark red dun mane and tail, dorsal stripe, 4 stockings, left front hoof gray, other hooves pink, matte (1988-89). Most #705s I've seen have solid dark mane and tail, but in July 1991, at a toy store, I saw several with a light-dark blotchy pattern in the mane and tail. Perhaps these were some of the last models made.

♠ "Yellow Mount" Famous Paint Horse #51, chestnut paint, overo; stenciled extensive bald face, 1 left hind stocking with pink hoof; other hooves peach-tan or gray-brown; matte (1970-87). In Presentation Collection mounted on American walnut wood base with brass "Yellow Mount" nameplate, late 1971-1973. The Presentation Collection is not in the 1971 manual, but "Yellow Mount" and five other Presentation models are announced in an ad in the November 1971 *Western Horseman*. The Presentation "Yellow Mount" is listed as #5051 in the 1973 price list, but previously it apparently had the same number as regular-run #51; see Presentation Collection below in this section for discussion. The body color of #51 varies from dark brown chestnut to medium reddish chestnut. The 1970-75 Breyer catalogs and manuals show a test color "Yellow Mount," with odd-looking rounded white spots, like huge eggs. The test does have a spot on the off forearm, as does the normal model shown in the back pages of the 1974-75 catalogs and in the 1976-80 catalogs. The model has no spot on the off forearm in the 1981-87 catalogs, but otherwise the pinto pattern is the same. My own forearm-spot model has peach-tan hooves on the chestnut legs, while my no-spot horse has gray-brown hooves on those legs. The 1970 and 1974 catalogs show the test-color horse with 4 peach-tan hooves, but other catalog photos don't suggest that the change to dark hooves coincided with the loss of the forearm spot. A few models have a dorsal stripe. The real "Yellow Mount," foaled in 1964 and owned by Mr. and Mrs. Stanley Williamson, won the first American Paint Horse Association Supreme Champion Paint Horse award and was for some years the nation's leading sire of Paint Horse champions. He died in 1990 at the age of 26. (Information is per *The Paint Horse Journal*, Nov. 1974, and *JAH* 18/#1 Spring 1991, p. 5.) #51 was in the Showcase Collection as #5100 in 1970-72 (see Showcase Collection in this section for discussion). The model number 51 previously belonged to "Commander" The Five-Gaiter, albino.

Set:

♠ Breyer Rider Gift Set #3095, palomino horse, solid face, lighter palomino mane and tail, 4 stockings, gray hooves, matte (1976). Never released for sale; only a few pieces made (per *JAH* 15/#2 May/June 1988, p. 15). This set was advertised in the 1976 catalog as including a Western saddle and a Breyer Rider doll. The catalog shows the set's box, which has a photo of the horse and the doll but only a little drawing of the saddle. Although the set was never released, a handful of "jobber samples" were produced (per *JAH* 15/#2 May/June 1988, p. 15). These few "Adioses," which are a beautiful dusky tan color and have solid faces, should not be confused with the SR palomino "Adios," which has a more orangy color, yellowy mane and tail, and bald face. Collector Sheryl Leisure acquired one with its original box, which is different from the box in the 1976 catalog: the photo on Sheryl's box shows not only the horse and doll but also the saddle and a bridle, which are made of a yellow-tan rubbery material (this tack is also shown in the *JAH* article). Sheryl's box also has a sticker with a handwritten note "no rider or saddle." Inside the box was a letter dated December 23, 1977, from the person who bought the horse new to the person she gave it to as a Christmas gift. The letter writer says she got the model at a large toy store in Salinas, California, which had six or seven of these horses, as well as a test color black appy Indian Pony. She learned from the shopkeeper that the horses had been stored in the back room for at least a year and a half (viz., since mid-1976), and that they had come from the factory with no rider or tack "due to some mix-up." I believe the mix-up involved the Mego company, for the Breyer Rider doll shown in the 1976 catalog is identical to dolls manufactured by Mego in Hong Kong. I asked Breyer executive Peter Stone about this in October 1995, but he could not recall who was supposed to supply the dolls or what the snafu was. What he could recall is that he got into trouble for ordering 12,000 boxes for the sets, which then had to be tossed for want of sets to put in them! See the Riders – Soft Or Jointed Plastic section below for details on the Breyer Rider doll. The model number 3095 later belonged to the Brenda Breyer Gift Set with Brenda doll on sorrel blanket appaloosa Performance Horse.

Special-run models made from this mold:

🖎 "Adios" SR, bay blanket appaloosa, blaze, unstenciled blanket covering butt and half of barrel, splashed-on bay spots, black points, 4 stockings, 4 pink-tan hooves, matte (1993). Penney's holiday catalog. Sold in Breyer Three Generations Appaloosa Set SR #710693, with bay blanket appy "Phantom Wings" and bay blanket appy Quarter Horse Yearling. Projected quantity 3,000 sets; no final count was recorded in Breyer's computer when I spoke to *JAH* editor Stephanie Macejko in June 1995. This model's blaze is the same as that on "Rough 'N' Ready." The set's number is per a Breyer company computer printout of 1993 SRs.

🖎 "Adios" SR, black, no white markings, black hooves, semigloss (1985?). Made for Model Horse Congress. About 5-7 models made. Only two sources known to me mention this SR. Gutierrez 1989 lists a run of 7 black "Adioses" sold at Model Horse Congress in Chicago in 1985. *JAH* 23/#2 March/April 1996 (p. 37) has a photo of horse that is presumably from this same Congress run—he is semigloss black, evidently solid (though I'm not sure of his face, which is not visible), and the caption says: "A rare black Adios. One of five made for the Model Horse Congress in the early 1980's." A few earlier black "Adioses" may exist as well, to judge from the following mysterious item in the December 1979 *Model Horse Shower's Journal*: "Another interesting 'find' was by another reader, and purchased it in a Montgomery Ward store? What was it? How about a glossy BLACK 'Adios' #50? orig. fininish [*sic*]!" Collector Margie Langlois wrote to me that she has a black "Adios" with a low stripe and snip. The collector who sold it to Margie told her that she and a friend had each gotten one from longtime collector and Breyer consultant Marney Walerius when she took them on a tour of the Breyer factory in the early 1980s, when it was still located in Chicago. The presentation of a black "Adios" at the end of a tour, the collector told Margie, was a regular practice on Marney's part, and visitors were allowed to specify the white markings they wanted on theirs. To my mind, horses painted by Marney at the factory do not count as true Breyer OFs since she was not a Breyer employee; but opinions differ on this matter.

🖎 "Adios" SR, buckskin, gray nose, no white markings, black points, gray hooves, matte(1984). Made for VaLes Bead Trailer model mail-order company, of Glendale, Arizona. 100-200 models made: Diederich 1988, Section 2, says 200; Pinkham 1988, Gutierrez 1989, Hollansky 1990 all say 100. These sources also conflict about the date and the origin of this special: Diederich says it was sold by VaLes in 1978; Hollansky says it was sold at the Model Horse Congress in 1979; Pinkham says the Congress in 1984; Gutierrez also says 1984 but names no vendor. Perhaps VaLes sold some of these horses at the Congress, but in any case it is certain that VaLes was the vendor and sold the horses in 1984, for collector Heather Wells has her receipt from VaLes for two of these horses, which is dated June 1984. Heather, who has worked for Black Horse Ranch model mail-order company for many years, also told me that BHR ordered a considerable number of these models, at least 20, from VaLes in 1984. So she feels certain that this SR was new in 1984.

🖎 "Adios" SR #410151, dapple gray, no or very few dapples on head and upper neck; bald face; pink ears and nose; gray mane and tail; 4 stockings; gray hooves; matte or semigloss (1987). Made for Black Horse Ranch but distributed to other model mail-order companies as well. 1,000 models made. A BHR ad in the May 1987 *Model Rag* gives the quantity as 500 for this dapple gray horse and 500 for the SR palomino "Adios." Collector Heather Wells, BHR's customer service representative, explained to me that although BHR ordered only 500 models of each color, which they believed would be BHR exclusives, Breyer decided to run 500 additional pieces of each color to be sold through other companies (Bentleys, Horses International, and perhaps one or two others). The model number is per a Breyer company computer printout of activity 1985-92.

🖎 "Adios" SR #410251, palomino, bald face, light palomino mane and tail, 4 stockings, gray hooves; matte (1987). Made for Black Horse Ranch but distributed to other model mail-order companies as well. 1,000 models made. See "Adios" SR dapple gray regarding quantity. This palomino SR differs from the "Adios" in Breyer Rider Gift Set #3095 in having a bald face, orangy body color, and yellowy mane and tail. #3095 has a solid face and a dusky tan color, with the same color shaded lightly onto the mane and tail. The model number for this SR is per a Breyer company computer printout of activity 1985-92.

🖎 "Adios" SR #51-1, red chestnut, short blaze, dark chestnut mane and tail, 1 right front and 2 hind stockings, 4 gray hooves, matte (1986). Made for Potts-Longhorn Leather in Dallas, Texas. Probably about 1,000 models made, per Breyer executive Peter Stone (conversations of Mar. and Oct. 1995). Model number, date, and dealer are per a Breyer company computer printout of activity 1985-92. When I asked Breyer executive Peter Stone about this SR, he had to guess at the quantity on the basis of what he normally tried to sell at that time. He did, however, distinctly remember selling the horses to Bill Hanning, of Potts-Longhorn Leather, which subsequently went out of business. He remarked that Potts-Longhorn used to run ads in *Western Horseman* magazine that were illustrated by Chuck DeHaan. Stone met DeHaan through this "Adios" SR sale to Potts-Longhorn and later commissioned him to sculpt a "Scamper" mold for Breyer (see "Scamper" below for details). *JAH* editor Stephanie Macejko kindly sent me a photo of the specimen horse from this run that is in the sample room at the Breyer plant in Wayne, New Jersey. The blaze is not visible in the photo, but Stephanie described it to me as a short stenciled blaze, wider at the top.

🖎 "Adios" SR, red dun semi-leopard appaloosa, bald face, unstenciled blanket covering butt and barrel, pale dun splashed-on spots, primitive bars on thighs and shoulders, dark red dun mane, tail white on top and dark red dun on bottom, 4 stockings, gray hooves, matte (1987). Penney's holiday catalog. Sold in Breyer Traditional Western Horse Collector Set SR #712848, with liver-charcoal Foundation Stallion and red bay San Domingo. 3,800 sets made. Quantity and set number are per a Breyer company computer printout of activity 1985-92. The Penney's catalog describes the horses as representing particular breeds: "the Appaloosa (speckled horse). The Quarter-horse (brown with white hind legs), and the Mustang (the charcoal brown horse)." So the "Adios" is an appaloosa, the "San Domingo" is a quarter horse, and the Foundation Stallion is a mustang. The Penney's catalog shows the "Adios" with 4 stockings, and I've seen collectors' specimens like this, but my own has no front stockings.

🖎 "Adios" SR, unpainted white (1980). Sold through *JAH* VII/#3 1980 (p. 13). This horse and several other completely unpainted models were offered to hobbyists interested in customizing, but many collectors kept them unpainted. See under Unpainted Models for a complete list.

🖎 "Mego" SR #707595, palomino paint, overo; tri-color eyes; stenciled apron face; white mane and tail; white diamond-D brand hand-painted on left thigh; peach-tan hooves; matte (1995). Dinner model for BreyerFest at the Kentucky Horse Park in Lexington, July 28-30, 1995. Close to 3,000 models made, per JAH editor Stephanie Macejko (conversation of Dec. 1995). Breyer executive Peter Stone announced at BreyerFest that 2,850 models had been sold to attendees; but this figure did not include extras made to give to various volunteers and to cover for defective pieces, etc. The model number is per the label on the model's box. The brand is a capital D inside a diamond shape. Most models that I have seen have at least a bit of gray shading on the tip of their white noses; the shading forms a distinct vertical stripe on some models. This model is a portrait of a real palomino overo gelding named "Mego" (pronounced MEE go), a trick horse and TV star trained by George Taylor. "Mego" co-starred with actor Chuck Norris in the television show *Walker: Texas Ranger* during the 1993-94 seasons (per Snow 1995b; also see see Snow 1995a), but the horse is perhaps best known for his many years of rodeo performing with Mr. Taylor. Unfortunately Mr. Taylor and "Mego" could not attend BreyerFest as scheduled. They traveled from their home in Texas to the Kentucky Horse Park only to learn that the state of Kentucky had just issued a quarantine on horses from several states, including Texas, because of an outbreak of the viral disease vesicular stomatitis. Thus Mr. Taylor and his horse had to return to Texas the following day. Breyer executive Peter Stone and other Breyer personnel conveyed the unhappy news to BreyerFest attendees, for whom Stone signed "Mego" models in lieu of Mr. Taylor.

Notes:

(1) "Adios" #50 is listed as "new for 1970" in the 1970 dealer catalog, but he was actually released in 1969—he is listed in the 1969 collector's manual and pictured in an article in *Craft Model & Hobby Industry*, which states, "The 1969 additions to the fine line of Breyer Animal Creations are ready to enhance the collections of all horse and animal fanciers." Evidently when a new dealer catalog was issued in 1970 for the first time since 1968 (there is no 1969 catalog to my knowledge), Breyer decided to list the 1969 as well as the 1970 models as "new for 1970" to bring them to the attention of dealers, who would naturally suppose that any model not listed as new was something they had seen in 1968.

(2) Breyer's "Adios" mold is a copy of a small bronze replica of a life-sized bronze "Adios" sculpted by James Slick, which stands at the entrance to The Meadows race track in Pennsylvania. Slick's large bronze was unveiled on August 12, 1967, the day of the inaugural Adios Stake race for 3-year-old pacing colts, established in memory of the great Standardbred pacer "Adios" (per Hill 1971, p. 72). Several specimens of the small bronze replica exist, for they have been presented as trophies at many Adios Stakes, including the first one. (Information is per various 1967-91 issues of *Hoof Beats* and *Harness Horse* magazines and other materials, generously provided to me by collector and *Hoof Beats* circulation director Ardith Carlton). The replica is larger than the Breyer and has a slightly less refined head and more pointy tailtip; otherwise the two works are remarkably similar.

Both the large Slick sculpture and the small replica of it were commissioned by Mr. Delvin Miller, a former owner of "Adios" and founder of The Meadows and the Adios Stake. Mr. Miller wrote to me: "When we had it [the large bronze] made I asked what it would cost to have a model likeness of this made into a trophy for the Adios [Stake] and they gave me a pretty good price. . . . We still buy the nice trophy" (letter of March 24, 1995; also see Carlton 1990). In his letter to me, Mr. Miller in fact could not recall for sure what the Breyer was based on (also see Carlton 1990)—he suggested that the Breyer, like the famous porcelain sculpture of "Adios" by Edward Marshall Boehm, was based on pictures of the real "Adios." However, evidence shows that Breyer sculptor Chris Hess based his "Adios" on the bronze replica. In the first place, prior to my correspondence with Mr. Miller, Breyer executive Peter Stone commented to me (conversation of May 1994) that he recalled Miller handing Breyer sculptor Chris Hess a small bronze sculpture back in the late 1960s and saying "Here, copy this." Corroborating Stone's recollection is a letter dated June 28, 1968, to Breyer company attorney Samuel Schiff from Mr. Miller. This letter, a copy of which was kindly provided to me by Gloria Likar, secretary to Mr. Miller, mentions the "small statue" that Miller had loaned to the Breyer company: "Have not heard anything from you since last fall about the plastic Adios mold being made by the Molding Company of Chicago. Are you working on this, and if so when will it be completed? . . . P.S. I will be in Chicago in August and can pick up my small statue." Before learning about this small bronze replica of James Slick's "Adios," I believed, as did some other collectors (see Johnson 1990), that Breyer's "Adios" was copied from the porcelain "Adios" by Boehm, who died on January 29, 1969 (per Palley 1976, p. 40). The first piece of Boehm's porcelain edition of "Adios" ever released was presented to Delvin Miller in October 1968 (per a brochure card of the Boehm piece sent to me by Mr. Miller and per Hill 1971, p. 53). Mr. Miller described the event in his letter to me: "We were racing at Philadelphia and a bunch of the drivers and I were invited out to Ed Boehm's quarters in New Jersey where he raised all things that he made into porcelain[,] so we had a real nice cocktail party and a nice meal and lo and behold that Ed doesn't go up and pull a rope and here is an Adios Boehm that he presented to me. . . . The one that I have . . . was the first porcelain." The Breyer looks remarkably similar to the Boehm but cannot possibly have been based on it, for the Breyer preceded the Boehm: Mr. Miller had loaned the Breyer company the "small statue" some months prior to June 1968, possibly late in 1967, and work on the Breyer was under way by July 1968 (per a letter of July 1, 1968, from Breyer's Charles Schiff to Mr. Miller: "The mold for Adios is being worked on and should be ready in the next few weeks"; copy provided by Gloria Likar). This was some months before the first Boehm "Adios" saw the light of day at the presentation to Miller. If it seems odd that Boehm's sculpture should so closely resemble the Breyer, I would suggest a possible explanation by reference to the photos that Boehm used, as mentioned in Mr. Miller's letter to me. Though Mr. Miller didn't say so, Slick too must have based his large sculpture on photos of the real "Adios," for Mr. Miller commissioned this statue sometime after the death of the horse in 1965. Possibly Slick used the same photos that Boehm would use subsequently, with the result that the two artists' works resemble each other closely. The small bronze trophy of course resembles the large Slick bronze of which it was a replica, and the Breyer inherited the same lines from the replica. A photo of Chris Hess with his clay sculpture of "Adios" appears in the 1985-86 Breyer catalogs, and the unfinished head of the sculpture is shown on the cover of the 1985 catalog.

(3) Not all base-mounted "Adioses" are Breyer Presentation Collection pieces. Many "Adioses" on bases were issued by Delvin Miller, one-time owner of the real "Adios" and founder of The Meadows racetrack in Pennsylvania. These pieces were not mounted on their bases by Breyer but by someone hired by Mr. Miller. The sample piece kindly sent to me by Mr. Miller is quite similar to the Presentation Collection "Adios," but there are differences. The base on Mr. Miller's pieces is made of dark-stained pine or similar wood and has beveled edges, whereas the Presentation base is made of walnut and has squared edges, with the sides angled slightly outward. The brass nameplate on the Miller piece is decoratively rounded on the two ends and is engraved with both the horse's name and the record-breaking pacing time he achieved in 1945 (per House 1995): "Adios 1:57 1/2." The brass nameplate on the Presentation pieces is a simple rectangle and is not engraved with the time but only with the name "Adios," as was clearly visible on the original 1973 Presentation Collection ad flier I saw at the Breyer factory in November 1994 (reprinted in JAH 22/#4 July/Aug. 1995, p. 15). Mr. Miller sold these base-mounted "Adioses" through horse magazines and through Meadowcroft Village, a museum of American history and rural life located near The Meadows and founded by Miller and his brother in 1969. In letters to me (all in 1995), Mr. Miller and his secretary Gloria Likar indicated that they had had a large batch of the base-mounted pieces made when Breyer's "Adios" was first released (1969) and another batch made in 1981. The latter batch actually counts as SR because the models were made after "Adios" #50 was discontinued. (In a letter of July 24, 1981, to Charles Schiff, then president of Breyer, Ms. Likar wrote: "When Mr. Miller returns here will advise him that the Adios statue has been discontinued by your company but because of your friendship for Mr. Miller you will run an order especially and only for him." Copy provided to me by Ms. Likar.) A base-mounted "Adios" identical to the one sent to me by Mr. Miller appeared in the collector's class at BreyerFest 1994. The piece once belonged to collector Karen Perkins, who had been told by long-time collector and Breyer consultant Marney Walerius that it came from a batch made for the Standardbred association in 1969. In all likelihood the models referred to by Marney were in fact the first batch issued by Mr. Miller, who has been a pillar of the Standardbred breeding and racing community for decades.

(4) The earliest models of the "Adios" mold have the round "Breyer Molding Co." stamp only. Slightly later models have the round stamp and the "U.S.A." stamp. The "U.S.A." was probably added at the start of 1970, the year when this stamp was introduced into the Breyer line, for "Adios" #50s without this stamp are scarce, and I don't believe I've ever seen a "Yellow Mount" without it. Some "U.S.A." models have the "B" stamp as well; earlier and later ones do not.

Adorable Horse Foal Set (also called Fun Foal Set) SR — see Grazing Foal SR, bay blanket appaloosa; Lying Down Foal SR, chestnut; Running Foal SR, dark rose gray; and Scratching Foal SR, alabaster

Akhal-Teke — see "Bolya" (under "Halla")

Alabaster Lipizzan — In the Traditionals section see "King" The Fighting Stallion #30 (under Fighting Stallion) and "Pluto." In the Classics section see Lipizzan and Rearing Stallion "Rex" #180.

American Appaloosa Stock Horse Foal — see under Action Stock Horse Foal (#238)

American Appaloosa Stock Horse Mare — see under Stock Horse Mare (#233)

American Buckskin Stock Horse Foal — see under Action Stock Horse Foal (#225)

American Buckskin Stock Horse Mare — see under Stock Horse Mare

American Buckskin Stock Horse Stallion — see under Stock Horse Stallion

American Indian Pony — see under Foundation Stallion

American Mustang — See under Mustang. Also see "Cheyenne" American Mustang (under Indian Pony).

American Paint Horse Foal — see under Action Stock Horse Foal (#237); Stock Horse Foal, standing (#231)

American Paint Horse Mare — see under Stock Horse Mare (#230)

American Paint Horse Stallion — see under Stock Horse Stallion (#229)

American Quarter Horse Foal — see under Stock Horse Foal, standing (#228)

American Quarter Horse Stallion — see under Stock Horse Stallion (#226); also see Ideal Quarter Horse

American Ranch Horse — see "Shane" under Stock Horse Stallion

American Saddlebred — see under Five-Gaiter

Andalusian — In the Traditionals section see all listings under "Legionario." In the Classics section see Andalusian Family Foal, Mare, and Stallion.

Appaloosa-American Classic Set SR — see Performance Horse SR, black blanket appaloosa; Running Stallion SR, palomino blanket appaloosa; and "Stud Spider" SR, blue roan semi-leopard appaloosa

Appaloosa Foal — see under Action Stock Horse Foal (#810)

Appaloosa Gelding — see under Quarter Horse Gelding

Appaloosa Performance Horse — see under Performance Horse

Appaloosa Pony — see "Sargent Pepper" (under Haflinger); also see Pony Of The Americas

Appaloosa Sport Horse & Canongate Saddle Set SR — see under "Morganglanz"

Appaloosa Stallion With Western Tack Set SR — see under Performance Horse

Appaloosa Stock Horse Foal — see under Action Stock Horse Foal (#238); "Phantom Wings"; Stock Horse Foal, standing

Appaloosa Stock Horse Mare — see under Stock Horse Mare (#233)

Appaloosa Stock Horse Stallion — see under Stock Horse Stallion

Appaloosa Yearling — see under Quarter Horse Yearling

Appy Mare — see under Stock Horse Mare

AQHA Ideal American Quarter Horse — see under Ideal Quarter Horse

Ara-Appaloosa Foal — see under Family Arabian Foal

Ara-Appaloosa Mare — see under Family Arabian Mare

Ara-Appaloosa Stallion — see under Family Arabian Stallion

Arabian Family Set With Blue Ribbon SR — see Family Arabian Foal SR, dark chestnut and light chestnut; Family Arabian Mare SR, dark chestnut and light chestnut; Family Arabian Stallion SR, dark chestnut and light chestnut

Arabian Foal "Joy," Shah," and "Spot" — see under Proud Arabian Foal

Arabian Horses Of The World SR — see Family Arabian Stallion SR, alabaster with black points; Proud Arabian Mare SR, fleabitten rose gray; and Proud Arabian Stallion SR, red bay with blaze

Arabian Mare And Foal Set SR — see Proud Arabian Foal SR, red bay pinto; and Proud Arabian Mare SR, red bay pinto

Arabian Mare "Pride," "Sheba," and "Speck" — see under Proud Arabian Mare

Arabian Stallion And Frisky Foal sets #3162 and #3163 — see under "Sham" in the Traditionals section and under Arabian Family Foal in the Classics section

Arabian Stallion With English Tack Set SR — see under Proud Arabian Stallion

Arab Stallion, "Rana" — see under "Sham"

"Aristocrat" — 🐎 Hackney mare, standing in show stance, looking slightly left, braided mane, docked tail. Sculpted by Kitty Cantrell. Mold in catalog-run production 1995 - current as of 1996.
 Catalog-run models made from this mold:
 🐎 "Aristocrat" Champion Hackney #496, dark reddish bay, solid face, black points, 4 stockings, gray or black hooves, matte (1995 - current as of 1996). Models come with a hang tag draped around the neck on a string, which says "Aristocrat / by Kitty Cantrell" on the front. Inside, the tag tells a bit about the Hackney horse and pony breeds, which originated in England. According to JAH 21/#3 Summer II 1994 (inside front cover),

"Aristocrat" is a Hackney pony, as its small stature relative to the Traditional scale also indicates. This *JAH* also has a photo of the unpainted resin casting from which the steel injection-mold would be made. The 1995 catalog shows a hand-painted resin casting of the original sculpture (per *JAH* editor Stephanie Macejko). Some "Aristocrat" models have quite a bit of black shading along the back, shoulders, and haunches, giving a deep, complex look to the bay color. Others have virtually no black shading and are thus a purer, lighter red shade. The basic color was designed by collector Karen Grimm (of Black Horse Ranch model mail-order company), who painted a prototype for Breyer. Sculptor Kitty Cantrell attended a model-horse fair at Black Horse Ranch in spring 1995, where she signed "Aristocrat" models on the belly with a symbol, a kitty's face. On June 1 and August 5, 1995, the QVC home-shopping cable TV channel offered a total of 1,000 "Aristocrats" that were ordinary regular runs but that came in boxes labeled with the special-run model number #703295 (per *JAH* editor Stephanie Macejko).
Note: The "Aristocrat" mold has the "© Breyer Reeves" stamp inside the left gaskin.

'Art Deco" SR — see Dressage Horse SR (under Hanoverian)

Artist Series — See "Buckshot"; "Lady Roxana"; "Secretariat"; "Sham"; "Sherman Morgan"; "Touch Of Class."

This series, launched in 1984 with the introduction of "Sham," showcased the work of four American equine artists. Two of them, Rich Rudish and Jeanne Mellin Herrick, had never before created works for Breyer. The other two, Christian Hess and Bob Scriver, were not new to Breyer, though Scriver had created only one piece previously (the Bolo Tie). All six models in the series are portraits of famous real horses. The series was advertised as the Artist Series, separate from the Traditional Series, in the 1984-87 catalogs. Thereafter, these models were mixed in with the Traditionals and the "Artist Series" rubric was dropped. The models of the Artist Series are a bit smaller than average Traditionals. For discussion of sculptors, see Sculptors in the Appendix near the end of this book.

Assorted Mare And Foals Stable Set SR — see "Phantom Wings" #29; Proud Arabian Foal SR, reddish bay; Proud Arabian Mare SR, reddish bay; and Stock Horse Foal (standing) SR gray blanket appaloosa

Astronaut Watch set — see note 4 for the Western Pony mold

Atlantic & Pacific Tea Co. Wagon With Old Timer SR — see McCormick Decanter With Old Timer set SR (under Old Timer)

Azteca — see under Foundation Stallion

Bay Fighting Stallion SR — see under Fighting Stallion

Bay Pinto Stock Horse Foal — see under Action Stock Horse Foal (#237)

Bay Quarter Horse Stock Foal — see under Stock Horse Foal, standing

Bay Quarter Horse Stock Stallion — see under Stock Horse Stallion

Bay Stock Horse SR — see under "Stud Spider"

Belgian — Stallion, trotting, looking right, tail bundled. Sculpted by Chris Hess. Mold in catalog-run production 1964-80, 1995.

Catalog-run models made from this mold:

- Belgian #92, smoke (solid gray), bald face, white points, gray hooves, yellow tail ribbon with red crisscrosses, matte (1964-71). Some have hand-painted eyewhites. The bald face can be extensive, reaching well down the sides of the face. The model number 92 originally belonged to the pink Elephant.
- Belgian #93, dapple gray, dapples on neck and head; bald face; dark gray mane and tail; 4 stockings; gray hooves; yellow tail ribbon with red crisscrosses; glossy (1964-66). The dappling is heavy and the dapples are large, like white cornflakes. The body and mane/tail color varies from medium gray to black. The latter is referred to by collectors as "black dapple." The model number 93 previously belonged to the blue Elephant.
- Belgian #94, chestnut, lighter chestnut mane and tail, bald face, 4 stockings, gray hooves, yellow tail ribbon with red crisscrosses, matte (1964-80). Reissued as an SR in 1986/87. On earlier #94s the bald face can be extensive, reaching well down the sides of the face. The normal color of #94 ranges from a medium reddish-tan chestnut to a lighter tan chestnut that could be called dark palomino. Collector Joan Fauteux sent me photos of her very unusual Belgian, which is a dark coffee/liver shade with pale cream mane and tail, as well as bald face, 4 stockings, gray hooves, and yellow tail ribbon with red crisscrosses. Joan does not know if her horse is a variation of #94 or something else altogether. The model number 94 previously belonged to the Elephant With Howdah set.
- Belgian #992, woodgrain, black eyes, yellow tail ribbon with red crisscrosses, no other color detailing, matte (1964-65).
- "Goliath" The American Cream Draft Horse #906, pale palomino; blaze; tri-color eyes; white mane and tail, may be lightly oversprayed with pale palomino; 4 stockings; gray hooves; red tail ribbon with blue crisscrosses; matte; Commemorative Edition (1995). 10,000 models made, double numbered by hand on the belly. Although the name "Goliath" is fictional, the model represents a real breed: "The only draft breed to originate in the United States, the Cream descended from a draft mare with a cream-colored coat. . . . The breed earned national recognition when the American Cream Draft Horse Association was formed in 1944" (*JAH* 22/#2 Mar./Apr. 1995, p. 15). The model's box is decorated with a large round gold sticker saying, in full: "1995 Commemorative Edition / Limited to 10,000 Pieces / serially numbered by hand / Goliath / The American Cream Draft Horse, the only breed of draft horses originated in America ... Goliath represents the Ideal" (ellipsis is on the sticker). The 1995 catalog notes of "Goliath": "Heavy as a ton, he is medium cream in color with white mane and tail. His amber-colored eyes are a distinguishing trait of the breed." The brown used for this model's irises is fairly dark, like that used on other Commemorative Edition models.

Special-run models made from this mold:

- Belgian SR, alabaster; light gray mane, tail, knees, and hocks; gray hooves; white tail ribbon with blue crisscrosses; matte (1992). Sears holiday catalog. Sold in Drafters Set SR #497092, with liver chestnut "Roy" and palomino Shire with stripe. 2,250 sets made. Quantity and set number are per a Breyer company computer printout of activity 1985-92. (The number 11216, given for this set on the Bentley Sales price list of March 15, 1993, is the Sears number, not the Breyer number.) Jill Gutierrez 1989 reports two earlier special runs of alabaster Belgians—one run of ordinary alabasters and the other of alabasters with black mane and tail—in the quantity of only 7 models for each run. She does not note the dates, but both runs must have been issued before mid-1985, for Jill reported these same horses in an article in the July/August 1985 *Model Horse Gazette* (p. 17). These reports by Jill are the only sources I know of that mention these early alabaster Belgians.
- Belgian SR, bay, bald face, no black on the legs, 4 stockings, black hooves, yellow tail ribbon with red crisscrosses, matte (1986/87). Made for model mail-order companies. 1,200 models made, per *JAH* 17/#4 Sept./Oct. 1990 (p. 30) and a Breyer company computer printout of activity 1985-92. The printout also gives the number of this SR as #94BY (for "bay"). Sold separately or in SR set with four other Belgians: black with white/red ribbon, chestnut with lighter chestnut mane and tail, dapple gray with yellow/red ribbon, and "smoke" blue-gray semi-leopard blanket appaloosa. *JAH* and the printout give the date of these five SR Belgians as 1986, but they didn't become available from model mail-order companies until early 1987. A Model Horse Collector's Supply price list dated December 22, 1986, states that it "will have" these horses. Bentley Sales Company record cards in my possession show that Bentley's received bays (200 pieces), blacks (100), dapple grays (200), and smokes (200) on December 26, 1986, and these horses are first advertised on a Bentley's list dated January 2, 1987. Collector Heather Wells has her packing-list receipt for this set from Your Horse Source, dated January 22, 1987. The set is pictured in the 1987 Your Horse Source catalog and described in detail on a July 1987 Model Horse Collectors Supply price list. The white on this bay horse's face is fairly restricted and might better be described as a wide unstenciled blaze.
- Belgian SR, black, no white markings, black mane and tail, black hooves, blue tail ribbon with white crisscrosses, semigloss (sometime in the period 1979-82). Made for Disney World in Orlando, Florida. These models were also available at Disneyland in Anaheim, California, according to Walerius 1991 (p. 99). Several sources mention this Disney SR with blue/white tail ribbon, but they conflict about the date: *Breyer Collector's Video* says 1982; Walerius 1991 (who does not mention ribbon color) says 1979-81; Hollansky 1990 says 1981 but notes that her information is not clear. Diederich 1988 and Gutierrez 1989 and 1985 list this horse as a Disney World SR with blue/white ribbon but give no date. In any case it is certain that some of these models were also sold as Percherons through the Ward's holiday catalog in 1982. For discussion of tail ribbon colors on black Belgians, see Percheron SR black, below. Collector Sande Schneider brought it to my attention that at least some black Belgians with blue/white ribbon have glossy hooves. This is true of collector Heather Wells's model, which she purchased directly from Ward's; his raised hoof is very glossy, the other three hooves less so but still distinctly shinier than the body.
- Belgian SR, black, no white markings, black mane and tail, black hooves, white tail ribbon with red crisscrosses, semigloss (1986/87). Made for model mail-order companies. 350 models made, per a Breyer company computer printout of activity 1985-92. (*JAH* 17/#4 Sept./Oct. 1990, p. 30, says 3,500, but that is surely a typo.) The printout also gives the number of this SR as #94BL (for "black"). Sold separately or in SR set with four other Belgians: bay, chestnut with lighter chestnut mane and tail, dapple gray with yellow/red ribbon, and "smoke" blue-gray semi-leopard blanket appaloosa. *JAH* and the printout give the date of this special as 1986, but it didn't become available from model mail-order companies until 1987 (for discussion of date see Belgian SR bay). The set is pictured in the 1987 Your Horse Source catalog and described in a July 1987 Model Horse Collectors Supply price list. The YHS photo conceals the tail ribbons, but the MHCS list specifically mentions the color of the ribbon on the black Belgian in the set: "black is solid black from head to toe with decorative tail piece in white and red." I got a horse with white/red ribbon new from Horses International in July 1989. For more discussion of tail ribbon color see Percheron SR black, below.
- Belgian SR, chestnut, lighter chestnut mane and tail, narrow bald face, pink nose, 4 stockings, gray hooves, yellow tail ribbon with red crisscrosses, matte (1986/87). Made for model mail-order companies. 244 models made, per a Breyer company computer printout of activity 1985-92. (*JAH* 17/#4 Sept./Oct. 1990, p. 30, says 2,440, but that is surely a typo.) The printout also gives the number of this SR as #94CH (for "chestnut"). Sold separately or in SR set with four other Belgians: bay, black with white/red ribbon, dapple gray with yellow/red ribbon, and "smoke" blue-gray semi-leopard blanket appaloosa. *JAH* and the printout give the date of this special as 1986, but it didn't become available from model mail-order companies until 1987 (for discussion of date see Belgian SR bay). The set is pictured in the 1987 Your Horse Source catalog and described in a July 1987 Model Horse Collectors Supply price list. This 1986/87 chestnut Belgian was simply a reissue of regular-run chestnut #94 and was evidently not the first such reissue: price lists and sales record cards from Bentley Sales Company show the receipt of several batches of "#94 chestnut" or "#94C chestnut" models in the period 1982-85, and 1984 price lists from Horses International and Mission Supply House also list #94C chestnut. The Mission Supply list states, "Special run—available in May / #94 chestnut Belgian." Whether these various pre-1986 batches were newly painted or simply leftover regular-run #94s I do not know. But it is quite certain that at least the Bentley's batches are identical to regular-run #94 and are not overruns of the 1984 Belgian in chestnut/dark palomino with white mane and tail (see next entry), for a letter dated April 1, 1986, from Bentley's to collector Kim Jones states, "We didn't have any of the Palomino Belgians or any with the white manes and tails."
- Belgian SR, chestnut/dark palomino, white mane and tail, narrow bald face, 4 stockings, gray hooves, yellow tail ribbon with red crisscrosses, matte (1984). Made for the Riegseckers of Indiana (per Diederich 1988, Section 2, and *Breyer Collector's Video*). 200 models made (per Gutierrez 1989 and DeFeyter and Luther 1991). Diederich and other hobby sources date this horse to 1984, and collector Heather Wells's Riegseckers receipt for this horse is dated February 15, 1985. This SR is very similar in body color to a typical regular-run chestnut #94.
- Belgian SR, dapple gray, dapples on neck and head; bald face; gray or charcoal/black mane and tail; 4 stockings; gray hooves; yellow tail ribbon with red crisscrosses; semigloss (1979).Made for Bentley Sales Company and Mission Supply House. 413-825 or so models made. These two mail-order companies are listed for this SR by both Hollansky 1990 and *JAH* 17/#4 Sept./Oct. 1990 (p. 29). *JAH* also says that each company received 2,000 models, but this quantity seems erroneously high. Old Bentley's sales record cards in my possession show that Bentley's received a total of 413 dapple Belgians in several shipments between mid-1979 and spring 1980. If Mission Supply got about the same quantity, this would mean a total of around 825 models. I do not have any Mission Supply documents from that time, but the earliest Bentley's price list in my possession, dated December 1979, includes "#92 Dapple Belgian $7.95," as well as "#90 Dapple Clydesdale Mare $7.95" and "#82 Dapple Clydesdale Stallion $7.95." These three SRs were also announced by editor Linda Walter in the October 1979

Model Horse Showers Journal: "I've heard reports that there are NEW dapple grey Clydesdales & Belgians being made! Yes, a few are available still possibly at various mail order establishments. They are nos. 92 dap. gr. Belgian, #82 dap. gr. Clydes. stal., & ready for this, #90 dap. gr. Clydesdale MARE! Contact immediately Bentley Sales Co. . . . Their prices were basic Breyer prices. . . . My set of the 3 dapples came in recently (ordered at MHC [Model Horse Congress]) & they are lovely. They are semi-glossy with pink muzzle & ears." This SR Belgian comes in a bewildering array of variations. Adding to the confusion is the 1984 SR dapple Belgian (see next entry), which may have been leftovers of the 1979 horses. The variations I have seen are as follows: [A] Heavy, wild-looking dappling; charcoal/black mane and tail; dark gray hooves. I purchased one of these from an experienced collector who is sure she got it directly from Bentley's in 1979. [B] Heavy, wild-looking dappling; medium-gray mane, tail, and hooves. Collectors Heather Wells and Gale Good have these. [C] Fairly heavy dappling with halo dapples (larger dapples with nimbi of tiny dapples); medium-gray mane, tail, and hooves. I have one of these models, which has a washed-out looking barrel; collector Jo Kulwicki has another, which is less washy looking but has patchier dappling. Both of our specimens have a "B" stamp. [D] Fairly sparse dappling with rounder, simpler dapples; medium-gray mane, tail, and hooves. Collector Sande Schneider has one of these, which I have seen in a photo.

- Belgian SR, dapple gray, dapples on neck and head; bald face; gray mane and tail; 4 stockings; gray hooves; yellow tail ribbon with red crisscrosses; semigloss (1984). The sources that mention this special are *JAH* 17/#4 Sept./Oct. 1990 (p. 29), which gives the surely erroneous quantity of 1,500, and Walerius 1991 (p. 102), which gives the more plausible quantity of 150. Both of these sources give the date as 1984/85 and the dealer to which it was sent as Caauwe Sales—a novelties sales company owned by Don Caauwe of Lincoln, Nebraska, according to former Breyer executive Peter Stone (conversation of Dec. 1995). But a few models were sold through other companies as well. Bentley Sales Company sales record cards in my possession show that Bentley's received a shipment of 18 dapple Belgians early in 1985, and accordingly, "94D Dapple Belgian" turns up on the Bentley's price list dated April 1985 (for $11.99), though it is gone from the June 1985 list. Collector Heather Wells bought two SR dapple Belgians with yellow/red tail ribbon from Riegseckers of Indiana in December 1984, for $12.50 each. I give the date as 1984 on the basis of Heather's dated receipt for these horses. Walerius states that these horses were leftovers from an earlier run; Breyer, which was located in Chicago at the time, sold them and other leftover models in preparation for the company's move to New Jersey. (The move was precipitated by the sale of Breyer Animal Creations to Reeves International in November 1984.) Walerius does not say what year the "1984/85s" were leftovers from, but the 1979 run is the only earlier SR dapple Clydesdale Stallion listed by her or any other source known to me. Which version of the 1979 stallions the 1984/85s were leftovers of I don't know; sadly, Heather cannot recall which of her numerous dapple Belgians came with her Riegseckers receipt.
- Belgian SR, dapple gray, no dapples on neck and head; bald face; charcoal/black mane and tail; 4 stockings; gray hooves; solid metallic gold tail ribbon; matte (1986). Made for Eighmey's Wagon Shop in Waterloo, Iowa. Quantity unknown. Gutierrez 1989 gives the quantity for this gold-ribbon SR as 1,500, but this seems too high in view of the model's evident scarcity. I would guess that a few hundred were made. The 1986 dating is per Mr. Eighmey (conversation of Oct. 1994), who was unsure of the quantity but told me that the gold on the tail ribbon was definitely painted by the Breyer factory. His recollection of the date is consistent with a letter of August 1986 sent to collector Kim Jones by Mrs. Eighmey, who wrote that they had, among other draft models, "Dapple-Greys—Black M & Tail / Gold Bow tail—matte." Collector Heather Wells has her receipt for this SR from Eighmey's, dated November 1986; the receipt lists the horse as "matte D.G. / Gold Tail Ribbon." Except for the ribbon color, this model is like the 1986/87 SR dapple gray matte with yellow/red ribbon.
- Belgian SR, dapple gray, no dapples on neck and head; bald face; charcoal/black mane and tail; 4 stockings; gray hooves; yellow tail ribbon with red crisscrosses; matte (1986/87). Made for model mail-order companies. 450 models made, per a Breyer company computer printout of activity 1985-92. (*JAH* 17/#4 Sept./Oct. 1990, p. 29, says the quantity was 4,500, but this figure is surely a typo.) The printout also gives the number of this SR as #94GR (for "gray"). Sold separately or in SR set with four other Belgians: bay, black with white/red ribbon, chestnut with lighter chestnut mane and tail, and "smoke" blue-gray semi-leopard blanket appaloosa. *JAH* and the printout give the date of this special as 1986, but it didn't become available from model mail-order companies until 1987 (for discussion of date see Belgian SR bay). The set is pictured in the 1987 Your Horse Source catalog and described in a July 1987 Model Horse Collectors Supply price list. The latter list specifies that the dapple gray in this set has yellow/red ribbon (this detail is also mentioned on the printout), black mane and tail, and solid gray neck and head.
- Belgian SR, palomino, bald face, white points, gray hooves, red tail ribbon with white or black crisscrosses, matte (1984). Made for the Riegseckers of Indiana. 150 models made (per *JAH* 17/#4 Sept./Oct. 1990, p. 30; Gutierrez 1985 and 1989; and collector Kim Jones, as reported in Pinkham 1988). Collector Heather Wells's Riegseckers receipt for her palomino Belgians is dated November 5, 1984. An October 1984 Bentley Sales Company price list sent to me by collector Judy Davinich bears the following hand-written note from Stuart Bentley: "Sorry—we didn't get any Red Roan Belgians, or any palomino Belgians, either." This SR is a light, lemony palomino. All the models that I know of have a red tail ribbon, but the crisscross designs on top of the red are sometimes white (as on the models owned by collectors Lynn Luther and Heather Wells) and sometimes black (as on collector Gale Good's model). Diederich 1988, Section 2, shows the version with white crisscrosses but also notes the existence of the black-crisscross version.
- Belgian SR, red roan, tan horse with red chestnut dappling, dappled face, dark red chestnut points, gray hooves, white tail ribbon with red crisscrosses, matte (1984). Made for Horses International, a division of Atlantis International. 600 models made (per *JAH* 17/#4 Sept./Oct. 1990, p. 30, and Gutierrez 1985 and 1989). An October 1984 Horses International ad for this SR says "Limited one to a customer!" Some of these horses were also sold through the Riegseckers, according to collector Judy Davinich (letter of Aug. 1994), who got her red roan as well as her palomino Belgian from them. An October 1984 Bentley Sales Company price list sent to me by collector Judy Davinich bears the following hand-written note from Stuart Bentley: "Sorry—we didn't get any Red Roan Belgians, or any palomino Belgians, either." This SR is the same basic style of red roan as the old regular-run Running Stallion and Mare, but tends to have a more orangy or yellowish cast.
- Belgian SR, "smoke" blue-gray semi-leopard blanket appaloosa, solid blue-gray face, unstenciled blanket covering butt and half of barrel, pale gray splashed-on spots, black points, black hooves, yellow tail ribbon with red crisscrosses, matte (1986/87). Made for model mail-order companies. 1,200 models made, per *JAH* (17/#4 Sept./Oct. 1990, p. 30) and a Breyer company computer printout of activity 1985-92. The printout also gives the number of this SR as #94SM (evidently for "smoke," although the printout describes the color as "blue roan"). Sold separately or in SR set with four other Belgians: bay, black with white/red ribbon, chestnut with lighter chestnut mane and tail, and dapple gray with yellow/red ribbon. *JAH* and the printout give the date of this special as 1986, but it didn't become available from model mail-order companies until 1987 (for discussion of date see Belgian SR bay). The set is described in a July 1987 Model Horse Collectors Supply price list and pictured in the 1987 Your Horse Source catalog. This catalog, however, pictures not the appy Belgian that was actually produced but instead the original test color model, a solid pale bluish gray with charcoal mane and tail. Collector Gale Good told me that before the run was painted, this test piece was rejected by the purchasing dealers as too pale; they wanted the model darker, "more like Buckshot's color." What was conveyed to Breyer's painting department, however, was the less specific request to paint the horses "more like Buckshot." The painting department complied, issuing freakish appy Belgians that resemble Buckshot #415 in both color and pattern. The dealers nonetheless listed him as "smoke."
- Belgian SR, unpainted white (1986). Apparently made for Eighmey's Wagon Shop in Waterloo, Iowa. A Breyer company computer printout of activity 1985-92 lists a 1986 order of unpainted Belgians ("scraped, buffed, unpainted") but does not note the quantity or the customer. However, collector Kim Jones provided me with a copy of a letter she received from the Eighmeys in August 1986, listing various "factory color" draft models they had available. Among them was a "#94" (Belgian mold) in "All white, no paint eyes hooves tail." Collector Heather Wells also provided me with a copy of her Eighmey's receipt for one of these horses (listed as "white"), dated November 12, 1986.
- Percheron SR, black; no white markings; black mane and tail; black hooves; some have blue tail ribbon with white crisscrosses, some have yellow ribbon with red crisscrosses; semigloss (1982 and 1983). Ward's holiday catalog. Sold in SR set with dapple gray Shire. In both *JAH* and the Ward's catalogs, this black Belgian was called a Percheron. The matter of tail-ribbon color on SR black Belgians and Percherons can be confusing. There are three basic ribbon colors on these solid black horses: blue with white crisscrosses, yellow with red crisscrosses, and white with red crisscrosses. The first horses, those made for Disney World sometime in 1979-82, have the blue/white ribbons, according to several sources (see the first entry for Belgian SR, black, above). But some blue/white ribbon horses, undoubtedly leftovers from the Disney run, were also sold through the 1982 Ward's holiday catalog in the set with dapple Shire: collectors Joan Fauteux and Heather Wells got their blue/white ribbon horses from Ward's, and *JAH* IX/#2 1982 (p. 13), which shows the Ward's Percheron among the holiday specials for that year, shows him with blue/white ribbons. The 1982 Ward's catalog photo is small and blurry, but does show some white on the tail ribbon. The majority of Ward's Percherons, however, have yellow/red ribbons; these were sold through both the 1982 and the 1983 Ward's catalogs: collectors Gale Good and Lisa McLeod got such horses new from Ward's, and a sales list in the February 1984 *American Model Horse Collector's Digest* includes a "Black percheron—mint—1982 Christmas special—red/yellow ribbons" (p. 38). The photo in the 1983 Ward's catalog is also small and blurry, but does seem to show the tail ribbon with an orangy color. Leftovers of the yellow/red ribbon horses were sold through Bentley Sales Company starting in 1984: I have Bentley's price lists from August 1984 through October 1985 listing "94B Black Belgian (Percheron)," and collector Heather Wells has her Bentley's receipt, dated November 1984, with the notation "black Belgian—yellow w/red crosses tail ribbon." Last came the black Belgians with white/red ribbon, sold through various model mail-order companies in 1986/87. This is confirmed by a Model Horse Collectors Supply price list of July 1987, which states that the black Belgian issued that year has a white/red tail ribbon (see second entry above for Belgian SR, black). I and other collectors I know got these white/red ribbon horses new from model mail-order companies in the late 1980s. But reportedly some collectors got yellow/red ribbon horses at this time; presumably these were more leftovers of the Ward's run. In case this isn't sufficiently chaotic, Heather Wells has a variation black Belgian with red ribbon with white crisscrosses, reversing the usual color arrangement on the 1986/87 horses.

Notes:

(1) Some Belgians are significantly smaller than others. For discussion of this phenomenon, see Mold Variations in the Appendix near the end of this book.

(2) *JAH* VII/#2 1980 (p. 11) has a photo, unfortunately printed in black and white, of a dappled decorator Belgian. All that the caption says about it is: "Blue and white Copenhagen Belgian. Discontinued in 1965." If "discontinued" here is meant to suggest that a run of such horses was issued for sale, the suggestion is wrong according to the 1960s documents known to me about decorators. I would guess the model was created as a test-color piece. Gutierrez 1985 and 1989 also note the existence of a Copenhagen Belgian, quantity of one, owned by the Breyer company (no date given).

(3) The Belgian mold has the round "Breyer Molding Co." stamp. Some models also have the "B" stamp, which apparently was added to the mold in late 1979 (some but not all 1979 SR dapple Belgians have the "B"). This mold was never given the "U.S.A." stamp.

Belgian Brabant — see under "Roy"

Belgian, "Roy" — see "Roy"

Belt buckles — "Pharaoh's Horses" belt buckle, a cast-metal buckle with pewter finish, was advertised for sale by Breyer Animal Creations in *JAH* Winter 1979 (p. 7). The black and white photo shows the buckle to be a solid round piece with a bas-relief of three Arabian-like horse heads. The buckles were commissioned by Breyer executive Peter Stone from a company called SpecCast, of Loves Park, Illinois, which devised the horse-heads design from a famous artwork and cast about 1,000 buckles. Stone could not recall the name of the artwork in question, but I think it might have been William Morris Hunt's stone frieze *Anahita Flight at Night*, commissioned for the capitol building in Albany, New York, in 1878.

Stone also had three other belt buckles made, in 1984, under the aegis of a business he established called Stone Associates. These three buckles were designed by artist Bob Scriver, who also sculpted Breyer's Bolo Tie and "Buckshot" molds. Two of the buckles were created for the Fort Benton, Montana, Jaycees and the third for the Chamber of Commerce of Cut Bank, Montana. One of the buckles has a steamboat design; Stone could not recall the designs of the other two when he told me about this venture in March 1995.

"Big Ben" — This forthcoming mold by sculptor Kathleen Moody, scheduled for release in 1996, is a portrait of the famous grand-champion jumper from Canada. "Big Ben's" rider, Ian Millar, retired the 17.3–hand gelding from the show circuit in 1994, after many years of competition that included three Olympics and wins of the Volvo World Cup in 1988 and 1989 (per *JAH* 22/#5 Sept./Oct. 1995, pp. 5-7). Moody's sketch of the mold, printed in the same *JAH* (p. 38), shows the horse in a walking position with neck arched and head tucked. The model, like the horse, will be chestnut with hind stockings and a star and stripe.

"Black Beauty"— In the Traditionals section see "Black Beauty" (stallion, cross-galloping); "Black Beauty 1991" (under "Morganglanz"); "Black Beauty" Prancer (under "Fury" Prancer); Western Mount Horse "Black Beauty" #58 (under Western Horse); Western Mount Horse "Black Beauty" #44 and Western Pony "Black Beauty" #40 (both under Western Pony). In the Classics section below see "Black Beauty."

"Black Beauty" — Stallion, cross-galloping. Sculpted by Chris Hess. Mold in catalog-run production 1979-91, 1995 - current as of 1996.

Catalog-run models made from this mold:

- "Black Beauty" #89, black; star; black mane and tail; various stockings; stockinged legs have gray hooves, other hooves usually black; matte (1979-88). Catalogs show this model with 4 stockings in 1979 and probably 1980 (the front legs are hidden), but with only 1 right hind stocking in 1981, and 1 right front stocking in 1982-88. All three of these versions were issued—all are shown on *Breyer Collector's Video*—and a couple other versions as well. Collector Lori Ogozalek, who has all three catalog versions of #89, wrote to me that she got her gray-hoofed 4-stocking horse in the first year of issue. But evidently another version was also produced that year, for collector Delana Metcalf wrote to me that she has a #89 with only a left front stocking, which was purchased new in September 1979 according to her dated purchase receipt. It's hard to be sure which of these two versions came first, but evidence from #89 boxes suggests that the 4-stocking version did. My own 4-stocking #89, purchased from another collector, came in a box picturing a 4-stocking horse. But collector Joan Fauteux's right-front-stocking #89, which is a later version according to catalogs and which Joan purchased new in February 1982, came in a box on which the pictured #89 is the left-front-stocking version, like Delana's horse. (Thanks to Joan for photocopies of her box.) Collector Karen Grimm has a #89 with 1 left front and 1 right hind stocking. Collector Jo Kulwicki's right-front-stocking horse has gray hooves even on his black legs. #89 and Breyer's several other "Black Beauty" models represent the title character of the classic children's book *Black Beauty: The Autobiography of a Horse*, by the English author Anna Sewell. This was Sewell's only book; it was first published in 1877 (per *Oxford Companion to English Literature*). In the 1945 edition of *Black Beauty*, illustrated by Fritz Eichenberg, the text says that "Black Beauty" had a star and "one white foot" (p. 13), partially specifying this in the last chapter as "one white foot on the off side" (p. 299; thanks to Karen Crossley for the reference); it doesn't say which off (right) foot. The illustrations, however, show a stocking on the right hind. A "Black Beauty" #89 was the first model to be produced in the factory in New Jersey where Breyer was moved after being purchased by Reeves International (*JAH* 12/#2 1985, p. 11; also see Breyer Company History in the Appendix near the end of this book). #89 was also sold through the 1979 Sears holiday catalog with leather bridle and canvas stable blanket with leather surcingles; the photo shows the blanket as red and the horse as a 4-stocking version with gray hooves.
- "Donovan" Running Appaloosa Stallion #919, gray-dun roan blanket appaloosa, dappled or bald lower face, unstenciled blanket on butt and loins, splashed-on chestnut spots, black points, 1 left front and 2 hind stockings with tan hooves, right front hoof tan with charcoal stripes, matte (1995 - current as of 1996). The pale dun "roaning" (dappling) on the dun areas of the horse varies widely in quantity; some models have very little, while others are heavily covered. In the 1996 catalog, #919's name was shortened to "Donovan" Appaloosa.
- "Dream Weaver" #833, sorrel, flaxen mane and tail, blaze that covers whole muzzle and chin, regular eyes (not tri-color), 1 right front and 1 right hind stocking, gray hooves, matte, Limited Edition (1991). Limited Edition models are produced only for one year, in quantities sufficient to fill all orders for the model. The real "Dream Weaver" was a Quarter Horse rescued by the Hooved Animal Humane Society in 1977. In articles published in 1991 in *Equus* magazine (Oct.) and *The Western Horse*, the gelding's present owner, Sally Milo, tells how she rescued the badly crippled, starving yearling and slowly nursed him back to health. The real horse is a palomino, although the model has a decidedly red hue that makes him sorrel. The model's big blaze and two right stockings do, however, accurately reflect the real horse's markings. The model's box features a large round gold sticker saying "1991 Limited Edition / Dream Weaver / The 'Miracle Horse' of the Hooved Animal Humane Society / Adopted by Sally and Timm Milo of Illinois."
- "Fade To Gray" #802, dark dapple gray, dapples on neck and head; stripe; charcoal mane and tail; black hooves; slightly semigloss (1989-90). Some of these models have 4 stockings; others have gray legs. The 1989 Sears holiday catalog offered #802 in Majestic Stallion Set with regular-run Majestic Arabian Stallion. The real "Fade To Gray" was a Thoroughbred racing colt owned by Black Horse Ranch. He got his name through a "Name The Foal Contest" announced in *JAH* 15/#2, May/June 1988 (inside front cover); the winning name was thought up by Juanita Snyder (*JAH* 15/#5 Nov./Dec. 1988, p. 19).

Special-run models made from this mold:

- "Black Beauty" SR, bay, no white markings, black points, gray hooves, matte (1984). Sears holiday catalog. Sold in Running Horse Family set SR with bay Running Mare and bay Running Foal. The Sears catalog and *JAH* XI/#3 1984 (p. 20) seem to show this stallion's hooves as black, but my own model and others I know of have gray hooves. Collector Sandy Tomezik's unusual model has brown hooves and a large star like that on regular-run "Black Beauty" #89; her horse is the only one like this that we know of. (Thanks to Sandy for sending me a photo of the model.) *JAH* 17/#4 Sept./Oct. 1990 (p. 30) lists not only this 1984 SR made for Sears but also a 1989 SR bay "Black Beauty" made for export to the English company House of Nisbet. The *JAH* entry describes this 1989 SR as bay with black mane, tail, and legs, and dark hooves; so it would seem to be identical to the 1984 SR. However, a Breyer company printout of activity 1985-92 indicates that the 1989 House of Nisbet horses, 1,000 of which were planned under the model number 400189, were not produced after all: it says "proposal cancelled on Jun. 16, 89."
- "Black Beauty" SR, unpainted white (1980). Sold through *JAH* VII/#3 1980 (p. 13). This horse and several other completely unpainted models were offered to hobbyists interested in customizing, but many collectors kept them unpainted. See under Unpainted Models for a complete list.

Note: The "Black Beauty" mold has the round "Breyer Molding Co." stamp. Some early models have the "B" stamp as well as the round—collector Delana Metcalf's left-front-stocking version of #89 has a "B." But I believe the very earliest models do not have the "B," for I have a 4-stocking #89 (the earliest #89 version) with the round stamp only. This mold was never given the "U.S.A." stamp.

"Black Beauty 1991," trotting — see under "Morganglanz"

Blackfeet Indian Horse — see "Ponokah-Eemetah" (under Fighting Stallion)

Black Foundation Stallion — see under Foundation Stallion

"Black Gold" SR — see under "San Domingo"

Black Stallion — Walking, looking right. Sculpted by Chris Hess. Mold in catalog-run production 1981-91, 1994-95.

Catalog-run models made from this mold:

- "Greystreak" Action Arabian #899, shaded smoke gray, solid pale gray face, black points, 1 left front and 1 right hind stocking with tan hooves, other hooves gray-brown, matte (1994-95). On July 15, 1995, the Q2 home-shopping cable TV channel offered 80 "Greystreaks" that were ordinary #899s but that came in boxes labeled with the special-run model number 704195 (per *JAH* editor Stephanie Macejko). Models that were evidently leftovers from the July show were sold on a Q2 show in November.
- "Hyksos" The Egyptian Arabian #832, "ageless bronze," slightly metallic brown-bronze color; solid face; 2-color eyes (brown and black; no white); mane and tail same color as body; slightly darker brown-bronze hooves; glossy; Commemorative Edition (1991). 7,500 models made, numbered by hand on the belly. The model's box sports a large round gold sticker saying, in full: "1991 Commemorative Edition / Hyksos / The Egyptian Arabian / This year we introduce to you a new Decorator Color—Ageless Bronze. Production is limited to 7,500 pieces and each is hand-numbered." He is described on the Breyer company computer printout of activity 1985-92 as "bronze decorator / high gloss." Collector Lynn Isenbarger sent me photos of her "Hyksos" with chocolate brown mane and tail, which she purchased new from Horses International in April 1991; this is the only such specimen I know of. According to the 1991 Breyer catalog, this model was named for the race of people who introduced horses into Egypt over 3,000 years ago. *Columbia Encyclopedia*, 5th ed., notes that the word "Hyksos" is Egyptian for "rulers of foreign lands." It states further that the Hyksos people were "invaders of ancient Egypt, now substantiated as the XV-XVIII dynasties. They were a northwestern Semitic . . . people who entered Egypt sometime between 1720 and 1710 B.C. and subdued the pharaohs of the Middle Kingdom. They used Avaris-Tanis in the Nile delta as their capital rather than the Egyptian capital of Thebes. . . . They established a powerful kingdom that included Syria and Palestine, and maintained peace and prosperity in their territories. They introduced the horse-drawn chariot." A newspaper article of January 31, 1994, sent to me by collector Liz Strauss, provides more up-to-date information: "Egyptian archeologists have found eight rare tombs from the little-known Hyksos period, including probably the earliest intact skeleton of a horse, an animal introduced to Egypt by Hyksos invaders in about 1750 B.C. . . . The tombs are close to the probable site of the Hyksos capital of Avaris, in the east of the Nile Delta. . . . The origins of the Hyksos puzzled archeologists for years. But it is now widely accepted that they were a race of Indo-Germanic type, related to the Hittites of Asia Minor. They invaded northern Egypt from Asia and ruled for about 180 years until indigenous rulers based in Thebes, the southern capital, defeated them and drove them out in about 1570 B.C. The Egyptians rapidly adopted the Hyksos horses in warfare."
- Majestic Arabian Stallion #811, leopard appaloosa, white horse with mixed brown and black splashed-on spots, black points, gray-shaded forehand and hindquarters, gray hooves, matte (1989-90). I found a #811 with no black spots, only brown, and I know of another collector who has one like this. I have also heard of a #811 with no brown spots, only black (reported to me by Heather Wells). The amount of gray shading on these models varies from heavy to very light. #811 was also sold in Majestic Stallion Set with regular-run "Fade To Gray" through the 1989 Sears holiday catalog.
- Walter Farley's Black Stallion #401, black, no white markings, black mane and tail, tan hooves, semigloss (1981-88). This model was also sold in Black Stallion Gift Set #2095 [1981-83] and Black Stallion And Alec Set #3000 [pre-catalog release 1981, catalog run 1982-85]; see below. This model represents the title character in Farley's book *The Black Stallion*. In the second book of the series, *The Black Stallion Returns*, the stallion is named "Shetan" (thanks to Karen Crossley for the reference; also see *JAH* IX/#4 1982, p. 8).

Sets:

- Black Stallion And Alec Set #3000, black horse; rider; and racing tack (pre-catalog release 1981, catalog run 1982-85). This model was sold separately as Walter Farley's Black Stallion #401 [1981-88]. A set very similar to #3000 was sold through the 1981-82 Sears holiday catalogs, the 1981-82 Ward's holiday catalogs, and the 1982 and possibly the 1981 Penney's holiday catalogs. All of these holiday sets included Walter Farley's book *The Black Stallion*. For details on the doll and tack in these sets, see Black Stallion And Alec Set #3000, under Alec Ramsey in the Riders – Soft Or Jointed Plastic section below.
- Black Stallion Gift Set #2095, black horse, poster, and book *The Black Stallion*, by Walter Farley (1981-83). This model was also sold separately as Walter Farley's Black Stallion #401 [1981-88]. It was also sold in other sets; for dates and names see preceding entry.
- Princess Of Arabia set #905, light dapple gray horse, dapples on neck and head; bald face; regular eyes (not tri-color); white mane and tail touched with gray shading; 4 stockings interrupted by gray fetlocks; hooves tan with short dark-gray stripes; matte; Limited Edition (Jan.-July 1995). Set also includes Princess Brenda doll in beaded pale blue satin Arabian outfit and matching native costume for the horse. For details on the doll and costume, see under Brenda Breyer in the Riders – Soft Or Jointed Plastic section. The dapples on this horse are sparse and round, tending to look like polka dots. The body color varies from soft medium gray to nearly white. The set's box features a large round gold sticker saying, in full: "1995 Limited Edition / Limited to 1995 Orders / Princess Of Arabia / Princess Brenda, Poised with her Arresting Arabian Stallion, resplendently dressed in a striking hand-beaded authentic Bedouin costume." Limited Edition models are normally produced for one year, in quantities sufficient to fill all orders. In previous years, LE models have remained the same throughout the year; but in 1995 Breyer broke with tradition by issuing two completely different colors on the horse: light dapple gray for the first seven months or so and red roan starting in late summer. Only the dapple gray is in the 1995 catalog. For the red roan and further discussion, see the next entry. On June 1, 1995, the QVC home-shopping cable TV channel offered 300 sets that were ordinary #905 light dapple grays but that came in

boxes labeled with the special-run model number 703095 (per *JAH* editor Stephanie Macejko).

▲ Princess Of Arabia set #905, red roan, pale tan horse with tiny chestnut flecks; chestnut mane, tail, and leg joints; 1 right hind stocking with tan hoof; other legs have tan-gray cannons, pale pasterns, and gray hooves; matte; Limited Edition (Aug.-Dec. 1995). Set also includes Princess Brenda doll and pale blue Arabian costume, identical to the doll and costume in the light dapple gray version of set #905 (see preceding entry). This red roan horse, which is not a mere variation of the dapple #905 but a completely different color, should perhaps be categorized as an SR, for he is neither pictured nor mentioned in the 1995 catalog. According to Breyer executive Peter Stone (conversation of Aug. 1995), some months into the year the company simply decided to change the horse's color in order to boost sales. Unfortunately they did not change anything else about the set, so collectors determined to get the new horse had to pay for a duplicate doll and costume. I first heard of the change in mid-August from collector Leslie Granger (Haynet post of Aug. 14), who had just learned from a Breyer/Reeves executive at a trade show in Philadelphia that the first of the new red roans would soon be shipped. *JAH* editor Stephanie Macejko told me near the end of August that she had just seen the new horses in the Breyer warehouse. For details on the doll and costume, see under Brenda Breyer in the Riders – Soft Or Jointed Plastic section.

Special-run models made from this mold:

⚘ Black Stallion SR, light coffee bay, solid face, black points, black hooves, matte (1988). Penney's holiday catalog. Sold in English Horse Collector Set SR #713259, with red chestnut "Justin Morgan" and red dun Indian Pony. The set number is per a Breyer company computer printout of activity 1985-92 and *JAH* 17/#5 Nov./Dec. 1990 (p. 29).

⚘ "Ofir," Sire of "Witez II," SR #700694, dark plum bay, star, many with snip, black points, 4 stockings, tan hooves, matte (1994). Breyer Tour special. 2,350 models made, per *JAH* editor Stephanie Macejko (conversation of June 1995). "Ofir's" star is shaped like a teardrop with the point down. On models with a clear snip, the snip is shaped like a teardrop with the point up. But the snip is faint or partial on some models and nonexistent on others. This horse represents the real Polish Arabian stallion "Ofir," the sire of several famous stallions, including "Witez II" (see Proud Arabian Stallion "Witez II" #212 for Breyer's portrait of this stallion). The 1994 Breyer Tour was a series of seven breakfast, brunch, and barbecue events with Breyer executive Peter Stone, held at toy stores, tack shops, and model-horse shows around the country; a complete list of locations was published in *JAH* 21/#2 Summer I 1994 (p. 5). "Ofir" models were made available only to the seven participating dealers and were included in the price of admission to the events, but leftovers were sold by some of the dealers via mail order. "Ofir's" name and model number are on the model's box.

Note: The Black Stallion mold has the round "Breyer Molding Co." stamp. Early models have the "B" stamp as well as the round. This mold was never given the "U.S.A." stamp.

Blanket Appaloosa — see under "San Domingo"; "Stud Spider"

Blister-wrapped display boxes — see under Display Boxes

Bluegrass Foal — see under Running Foal

Bolo Tie — see below in the Wildlife section

"Bolya" The Freedom Horse — see under "Halla"

"Bows" — see under Grazing Foal

Boxes — see Display Boxes; Showcase Collection

Brabant — see under "Roy"

"Brandi" SR — see under Scratching Foal

"Breakaway" — A large resin-bronze jumping horse sculpture by Breyer sculptor Chris Hess; not a Breyer product. For discussion see the entry on Chris Hess under Sculptors in the Appendix near the end of this book.

"Breakfast with Peter Stone" specials — See in the Little Bits section for a list of these SR models. For discussion see Signing Party Specials / Breyer Show Specials in the Traditionals section.

"Breezing Dixie" — see under "Lady Phase"

Brenda Breyer And Sulky Set — see under Pacer for the horse and under Brenda Breyer in the Riders - Soft Or Jointed Plastic section for the doll, tack, and equipment

Brenda Breyer Gift Set — see under Performance Horse for the horse and under Brenda Breyer in the Riders - Soft Or Jointed Plastic section for the doll and tack

Brenda Breyer Harness Racing Set SR — see under Pacer for the horse and under Brenda Breyer in the Riders – Soft Or Jointed Plastic section for the doll, tack, and equipment

Brenda Breyer horse stickers — In 1980-82 Breyer issued puffy stickers printed with photos of various Breyer Traditional horses. These evanescent items are called Brenda Breyer Horse Stickers #510A in the 1980 catalog but simply Puffy Stickers #510A in 1981-82. Breyer price lists for all three years call them Breyer Fun Stickers #510A. To my knowledge, there were 18 different stickers in all, split into two packets of 9 each, with the assortment in each packet always being the same. The 1980 catalog photo shows one of the two packets as including three stickers—Clydesdale Foal, bay Running Foal, and bay Shetland Pony—that differ from those in my own packets (mahogany bay Proud Arab Stallion, appy Running Stallion, and palomino Family Arab Stallion), but I don't know if those variant stickers were issued for sale. The packets are printed with the label "Brenda Breyer / 9 Horse Stickers," and on the back they say "Made and Printed in Taiwan." In the 1980 catalog photo of the counter display box containing the packets, the box is printed with "Henry Unger Toy Corp." and Unger's jack-in-the-box logo; for discussion see note 3 for the Brenda Breyer mold in the Riders – Soft Or Jointed Plastic section.

Brenda Breyer Sulky And Pacer Set SR — see under Pacer for the horse and under Brenda Breyer in the Riders – Soft Or Jointed Plastic section for the doll, tack, and equipment

Brenda Breyer Sulky Kit #2400 — see Brenda Breyer And Sulky set #2446, under Brenda Breyer in the Riders – Soft Or Jointed Plastic section

Brenda Western Gift Set — see under Western Prancer for the horse and under Brenda Breyer in the Riders – Soft Or Jointed Plastic section for the doll and tack

Breyer Animal Creations display units — see under Display Units

Breyer Anniversary Truck #98453 — In 1995, to celebrate its 45th year of existence, Breyer Animal Creations together with Corgi, a manufacturer of metal toy vehicles, issued a limited-edition Corgi Mack B Series truck bedecked with old and new Breyer logos. Corgi vehicles are among the several toy lines distributed by Reeves International, the company that has owned Breyer Animal Creations since the mid-1980s. According to the Reeves 1995 Mid-Year Introduction brochure, the edition is limited to 10,000 trucks. Painted in bright Breyer yellow and measuring 5.75 inches by 2.5 inches (1:43-scale), the die-cast metal truck looks a little like a small moving van. On one side appears the current "Breyer" cartouche logo and a blue strip with the words "45 years of imaginative play." On the other side appears a logo from earlier decades, which is a logo not of Breyer Animal Creations per se but of the old Breyer Molding Company as a whole. The centerpiece of this logo is a squarish shape with scalloped or wiggly sides, containing the words "Molders of All Plastic Materials." The words "Design" and "Production" flank the square, and the name "Breyer Molding Co." overtops it. The only place I know of where this logo was used was on the company's letterhead stationery of the 1960s and 1970s. The logo does not appear on or in any Breyer catalogs, price lists, or packaging known to me. The wiggly square in the logo does, however, closely resemble the shape of the gold-foil "Tenite" stickers that Breyer put on some models, particularly woodgrains, in the early 1960s (see Stickers & Hang Tags in the Appendix near the end of this book). The truck's model number is per the 1995 Mid-Year Introductions brochure and 1995 Breyer price lists. The truck was offered for sale to Breyer collectors through *JAH* 22/#5 Sept./Oct. 1995 (p. 18 and insert).

Breyer company history — see Breyer Company History in the Appendix near the end of this book

BreyerFest SR models — *Dinner/concert models:* see "Dr. Peaches" SR (1990, see under "Phar Lap"); "Mustang Lady" SR (1991, see under "Indian Pony"); "Turbo" SR (1992, see under Mustang); "Grayingham Lucky Lad" (1993, see under Clydesdale Stallion); "Bright Zip" SR (1994, see under "San Domingo"); and "Mego" SR (1995, see under "Adios"). *Raffle models:* see "Misty" SR, Florentine decorator (1990); "Legionario" SR, Florentine decorator (1991); "Man O' War" SR, Golden Charm decorator (1991); "San Domingo" SR, Copenhagen decorator (1991); "Sham" SR, Wedgewood Blue decorator (1991); Quarter Horse Yearling SR, buckskin (1992); "Nevada Star" SR (1993; see in the Classics section under "Hobo" with stand); "Winchester" SR (1994, see under "Buckshot"); and "Mystique" SR (1995, see under Jumping Horse). *Volunteer special models:* see Proud Arabian Mare SR, "silver filigree" decorator (1993); Indian Pony SR, red roan (1994); and "Lady Phase" SR, palomino (1995). *Other models:* In the Stablemates section see under Thoroughbred Lying Foal and Thoroughbred Standing Foal for the SR black and transparent amber Keychain foals (all 1994). Breyer considered issuing keychain foals in new colors for BreyerFest 1995 (per *JAH* editor Stephanie Macejko), but the plans unfortunately fell through.

BreyerFest is a large 2- or 3-day promotional event that has been put on by the Breyer company each summer since 1990. BreyerFest is usually held at the Kentucky Horse Park in Lexington; the only exception was in 1991, when 4 BreyerFests were held within a few weeks of each other in 4 different sections of the country: Pomona, California; Redmond/ Bend, Oregon; York, Pennsylvania; and Lexington, Kentucky. Activities at BreyerFest include sales of new and vintage models by vendors and hobbyists from across the nation, an auction of test-color models and other factory rarities, a dinner or concert where each attendee receives a BreyerFest exclusive SR model, and a raffle for a different exclusive SR model. Some BreyerFests have included a model-horse show as well, with classes judged by experienced collectors and model customizers. At the 1993, 1994, and 1995 shows, the judges received exclusive SR models in thanks for volunteering their services.

Breyer lapel pins — The Breyer company had several different lapel pins and buttons made in the years 1988-90. Four small pins were made for the national 4-H Club meetings held simultaneously each year in Denver and Louisville (per Breyer executive Peter Stone, conversation of Mar. 1995): (1) 1988: a triangular pin, about a half inch tall, with a drawing of the Running Stallion mold in brown on a cream background and the words "The Running Stallion / Breyer 1988." (2) 1989: a rectangular pin, about an inch long, with a drawing of the Traditional Black Beauty mold in brown on a cream background, with the "Breyer" logo and "1989." A tiny engraving that says "Union Made" is stamped on the back. (3) 1990: a round pin, about an inch in diameter, with a drawing of the Mustang mold in gold on a dark blue background, with the "Breyer" logo and "'90." A tiny engraving that says "Union Made U.S.A." is stamped on the back. And (4) a pin printed with "Breyer Salutes 4-H" and a horse figure. (I have not seen this pin and do not know the date; my information is per Peter Stone.) The first three pins are printed on a gold-tone metal back and are covered on the face by a clear plastic "crystal."

Three more pins were issued at BreyerFest in 1990: (5) The BreyerFest Commemorative Pin, which is enamel on a gold-tone metal back, is roughly triangular in shape and about 1" wide at the base. The shape is made by the oblong "Breyer" logo topped by the head of a palomino pony with white mane. (The pony may represent "Misty" of Chincoteague, but I'm not sure.) The logo is printed in blue with white lettering. A white rim around the logo is printed in gold with the words "BreyerFest / KY Horse Park Lexington KY. July 1990." All proceeds from sales of this pin were donated to the Misty of Chincoteague Foundation. Leftover pins were sold through Bentley Sales Company, as advertised in *JAH* 17/#4 Sept./Oct. 1990 (p. 28); the ad states that 495 pins were produced. (6) The BreyerFest vendor button is a large round pin, 3" in diameter, which was distributed to vendors at BreyerFest (per collector Karen Perkins, from whom I purchased one of these buttons). It has a navy blue background, on which is printed, in pale yellow, a stylized line-drawing of a horse head, the words "BreyerFest 1990," and the oblong Breyer logo. (7) The "Misty" button is also a large round pin, 3" in diameter, which was available at BreyerFest 1990 (per Karen Perkins). It has a white background with "Misty Of Chincoteague" printed in black around the perimeter and, in the center, a line drawing of Misty's head in palomino and white pinto.

Breyer neckties — Among the usual hodgepodge of Breyer promotional items advertised in the back pages of the 1995 dealer catalog—mobiles, window stickers, shelf edgers, posters, videos—something new appears: three silk neckties of different colors, each scattered with images of a different Breyer model. The #2035 red necktie features Traditional "Sham" The Godolphin Arabians; #2036 blue necktie has "Gem Twists" cantering all over it; and #2037 forest green necktie sports Classic "Kelsos." My husband's red "Sham" tie (a forcible birthday gift) has a sewn-on label identifying the maker as Tyler Ties of San Francisco.

Breyer Rider Gift Set — see under "Adios" for the horse and under Breyer Rider in the Riders – Soft Or Jointed Plastic section for the doll and tack

Breyer Show Specials — see Signing Party Specials / Breyer Show Specials

Breyer Three Generations Appaloosa Set SR — see "Adios" SR, bay blanket appaloosa; "Phantom Wings" SR, bay blanket appaloosa; and Quarter Horse Yearling SR, bay blanket appaloosa

Breyer Tour Specials — See "Ofir" SR (1994; under Black Stallion) and "Rawhide" SR (1995; under Mustang). For discussion see Signing Party Specials / Breyer Show Specials.

Breyer Traditional Collector's Family Set SR — see Action Stock Foal SR, bay peppercorn appaloosa; Stock Horse Mare SR, bay peppercorn appaloosa; and Stock Horse Stallion SR, bay peppercorn appaloosa

Breyer Traditional Horse Set SR — see "Lady Phase" SR, dapple gray; Quarter Horse Gelding SR, palomino; and "Rugged Lark" SR, red chestnut

Breyer Traditional Western Horse Collector Set SR — see "Adios" SR, red dun semi-leopard appaloosa; Foundation Stallion SR, liver-charcoal; and "San Domingo" SR, red bay

Breyer truck — see Breyer Anniversary Truck

Breyer Wild Horses Of America Set SR — see Fighting Stallion SR, red sorrel; Foundation Stallion SR, bay blanket appaloosa; and Mustang SR, black with 1 stocking

"Bright Socks" Pinto Foal — see under "Phantom Wings"

"Bright Zip" SR — see under "San Domingo"

"Brother Bold" — see Action Appaloosa Foal #810 (under Action Stock Horse Foal)

"Buckaroo" And "Skeeter" set SR — in the Traditionals sections see "Skeeter" (under "Stormy"); in the Classics section see "Buckaroo" (under Arabian Family Mare)

Bucking Bronco — see below in the Classics section

"Buckshot" — ♞ Stallion, ambling, looking sharply to right. Sculpted by Bob Scriver. Mold in catalog-run production 1985-89, 1995.

Catalog-run models made from this mold:

♞ "Buckshot" Famous Spanish Barb #415, grulla semi-leopard appaloosa, gray forehand, solid face, unstenciled blanket covering butt and barrel, light gray splashed-on spots, black points, primitive bars on forearms, pale dorsal stripe, gray hooves, matte, Artist Series (1985-88). The models came with a small "Artist Series" brochure telling about sculptor Bob Scriver and about the real "Buckshot," "the first horse of the Spanish Mustang Registry." This registry was founded by Robert E. Brislawn, Sr., with his children and colleagues, in 1957 (per the 1985 catalog and *JAH* XII/#2 1985, pp. 12-13). An article about the real "Buckshot," by Brislawn's son Neil Uibreaslain, appears in *JAH* VIII/#1 1981 (p. 2). The model in the 1985 catalog, which is probably Bob Scriver's original sculpture or a plaster casting of it, is painted differently from the horses in the 1986-88 catalogs: it is a darker gray color that covers the body and head evenly, with no appy blanket or spots. To my knowledge no models like this were issued for sale.

♞ "Cody" #922, dark bay pinto, tobiano; low blaze; black mane, tail, and knees; 2 front stockings; white hind legs; 4 tan hooves; matte (Jan. 1 - June 30, 1995). The production dates are per the 1995 catalog. Except for the stockings, this model's pinto pattern is the same as on "Hickok" #923 and Spanish Barb #416. On June 1 and August 5, 1995, the QVC home-shopping cable TV channel offered a total of 1,500 "Cody" models that were ordinary regular runs but that came in boxes labeled with the special-run model number 703195. On July 15, 1995, the Q2 home-shopping channel offered 75 regular "Codys" in boxes with the number 704595. (Information is per *JAH* editor Stephanie Macejko.) Leftover models may have been sold on subsequent programs.

♞ "Hickok" #923, blue roan pinto, tobiano; low blaze; black mane, tail, and front legs; partial stocking on right front leg; front hooves striped tan and black; hind legs white with tan hooves; matte (July 1 - Dec. 31, 1995). The production dates are per the 1995 catalog. Except for the stocking, this model's pinto pattern is the same as on "Cody" #922 and Spanish Barb #416. On August 18-20, 1995, the Q2 home-shopping cable TV channel offered a total of 96 "Hickok" models that were ordinary regular runs but that came in boxes labeled with the special-run model number 707695 (per *JAH* editor Stephanie Macejko). Models that were evidently leftovers from the August shows were sold on a Q2 show in November.

♞ Spanish Barb #416, chestnut pinto, tobiano; low blaze; dark gray-chestnut mane and tail; front legs chestnut with gray-chestnut hooves; hind legs white with gray hooves; matte (1988-89). This model's chestnut areas vary from medium brownish and reddish chestnut shades to bright breakfast-beverage orange, as on the #416s owned by collectors Leslie Granger and Sommer Elaine Prosser, to a realistic yellow dun, as on collector Sandy Tomezik's horse. In the photo Sandy kindly sent me, the model's pinto spots are a light tan-yellow and the mane and tail are yellowish gray.

Special-run models made from this mold:

♘ "Winchester" SR #411194, charcoal brown, bald face, white points, hand-painted eyewhites, tan hooves, glossy (1994). Raffle model for BreyerFest in Lexington, Kentucky. 24 models made, including 21 for the BreyerFest raffle, 1 for the BreyerFest auction, and 2 spares to cover for damage in transport to BreyerFest. The spares were not included in the quantity announcements made by Breyer executive Peter Stone at the raffle and in *JAH* 21/#4 Fall 1994 (inside front cover); *JAH* editor Stephanie Macejko mentioned them to me later and noted that in fact 2 models had been badly rubbed in transport and were taken back to the factory. The model number is also per Stephanie Macejko. Proceeds of the raffle and auction were donated by Breyer to the Misty of Chincoteague Foundation, North American Riding for the Handicapped, Hooved Animal Humane Society, Kentucky Horse Park Foundation, Public Educational Television, and Friends of Wayne, New Jersey, Animals (per the BreyerFest 1994 schedule distributed at the event). "Winchester's" coloration and eyewhites are like those of the old glossy "charcoal" models made in the 1960s.

Notes:

(1) A photo of Bob Scriver working on the unpainted original sculpture of this mold, or a plaster casting of it, is printed in the 1985-87 catalogs. The original sculpture is also shown, along with other Scriver pieces, in a photo of Scriver's Montana studio in *JAH* XI/#3 1984 (p. 11). At various model-horse events, Breyer executive Peter Stone has told how Breyer personnel trailered a real Spanish mustang to Scriver's studio in Montana for him to use in creating his sculpture of "Buckshot" for Breyer.

(2) The "Buckshot" mold has "© 1985 Bob Scriver" engraved inside the near gaskin; it has no other mold marks.

Buckskin Stock Horse Foal — see under Action Stock Horse Foal (#225); Stock Horse Foal, standing (#224)

Buckskin Stock Horse Mare — see under Stock Horse Mare (#222)

Buckskin Stock Horse Stallion — see under Stock Horse Stallion (#221)

"Burmese" SR — see under "Secretariat"

"Buster" SR — see under Lying Down Foal

"Buttons" — see under Grazing Mare

"Buttons" & "Bows" sets — see under Grazing Mare

"Calypso" Quarter Horse — see under Quarter Horse Yearling

Cantering Welsh Pony (CWP) — ♞ Mare, cantering on right lead, head low, mouth open, braided mane and tail. Sculpted by Chris Hess. Mold in catalog-run production 1971-76, 1979-81, 1992–95.

Catalog-run models made from this mold:

♞ Cantering Welsh Pony #104, bay; solid face; most with yellow "bow" ribbons at centers of mane braids and end of dock; black points, with the legs black up to the body; gray hooves; matte (1971-73). The 1974 manual and 1975 manual and catalog have a photo of the bay but do not list it. The 1974 catalog neither shows nor lists the bay; the photo is of chestnut #105. In my dating of this model (and all others) I go by the printed listings rather than the photos. Many #104s have a black band running down the chest, belly, and groin. Some #104s have blue ribbons instead of yellow; collector Jo Kulwicki has a one like this. Gail Allen's daughter found a bay #104 with lime green ribbons; whether these are factory original I am not sure. Collector Julia Harmon sent me her unusual #104 whose legs have no black paint; the bay body color comes down below the knees and hocks, and the hooves and lower legs are gray.

♞ Cantering Welsh Pony #105, chestnut; earlier models have bald face and red "bow" ribbons at centers of mane braids and end of dock; later models have solid face and no ribbons; all have flaxen or pale chestnut mane and tail, 4 stockings, and gray hooves; matte and semigloss (1971-76, 1979-81). The body color varies from medium reddish to a light tan chestnut that could be called dark palomino. The bald-faced ponies often have pinky-orange shading not only on the nose but also in the mouth. The bald-faced version was made 1971-76, according to *Breyer Collector's Video*, and it is shown in the 1972-73 and 1976 Breyer catalogs. The solid-faced version was made 1979-81, as is visible in the catalogs for those years, though the 1979 catalog, in a photo captioned "Brought back by collector demand," shows what could be a test-color model: its mane and tail appear to be the same color as the body rather than flaxen. Collector Lynn Luther has a variant model that conflates the characteristics of the two basic versions: it has a bald face but no ribbons.

♞ Cantering Welsh Pony #106, seal brown, solid or bald face, black-brown mane and tail, blue "bow" ribbons at centers of mane braids and end of dock, 4 stockings, gray hooves, matte and semigloss (1971-74). This model is called "seal brown" in all catalogs and manuals that list her. She is deep coffee brown, darker and less red that the bay #105, and she has no black on the legs. I have seen several specimens of both solid-faced and bald-faced #106s, all with blue ribbons. I've also seen one #106 with a bald face and red ribbons, and *Breyer Collector's Video* mentions a variation with solid face and red ribbons. #106 is not pictured in any of the catalogs or manuals that list her, so I don't know which variation came first.

♞ "Plain Pixie" #866, red roan, beige undercoat with dark red-brown flecks and red chestnut shading on head, belly, butt, and legs; stripe; red chestnut mane and tail; no ribbons; gray hooves; matte (1992-93). The stripe on this model's face is the same as that on the SR black CWP. Most "Plain Pixies" I've seen are like those in the catalogs: predominantly light with lots of dark flecks and scattered splotches of the red chestnut shading. But some models are nearly covered with the shading and have almost no flecks. In 1992, a bay roan variation with bald face and four white socks was produced, according to *JAH* 19/#5 Winter 1992 (p. 33). I've never seen this variation.

♞ "Tara" Welsh Pony #892, dappled bay, large star, black points, no ribbons, 1 right hind stocking with tan hoof, other hooves black, matte (1994–95). The bay color varies from a darker, redder shade to a lighter, more sandy shade. The dapples are always lighter than main body color but vary in intensity from model to model. At one extreme are models with numerous, highly visible dapples; at the other are models with fewer, very muted dapples. The latter models may look solid bay at first glance.

Special-run models made from this mold:

♘ Cantering Welsh Pony SR, bay roan, pale grayish-tan pony with bay flecks; dark bay head with solid face; black points; black hooves; matte (1995). Made for the QVC home-shopping cable TV channel's Breyer hour aired August 5, 1995. Sold in Parade Of Horses Breeds set #705495 with sandy bay Proud Arabian Mare and alabaster Saddlebred Weanling. 1,800 sets made (per *JAH* editor Stephanie Macejko, conversation of Sept. 7, 1995.) Leftovers from this batch were sold on QVC on January 20, 1996. Each model in the set came in a separate Breyer box labeled with the set's name and number. The base body color of the Cantering Welsh varies from a pale tan color with virtually no gray in it to a pale gray dun or grulla color. The black on the lower legs merges into a short stretch of dark bay on or above the knees and hocks.

♘ Cantering Welsh Pony SR, black, stripe, black mane and tail, no ribbons, 4 socks, tan hooves, semigloss (1992). Sears holiday catalog. Sold in Horses Great And Small set SR #496092, with grulla Clydesdale Stallion and palomino Miniature Horse ("Merrylegs" mold). 2,250 sets made. Quantity and set number are per a Breyer company computer printout of activity 1985-92. (The number 11217, given for this set on the Bentley Sales price list of March 15, 1993, is the Sears number, not the Breyer number.) The stripe on this SR is the same as that on #866 "Plain Pixie."

- Cantering Welsh Pony SR #410107, dapple gray, metallic gold mane braids, no dapples on head and upper neck, bald or baldish face, dorsal stripe, black points, gray or black hooves, matte (1987). Made for Small World. 97 made, per *JAH* 19/#5 Winter 1992 (p. 32). The model number and date are per a Breyer company computer printout of activity 1985-92. The printout does not specify quantity. It does, however, specify "dapple gray w/gold ribbon," indicating that the gold was applied by the factory, not by Small World employees as some collectors have speculated. *Breyer Collector's Video* says these ponies were leftovers from the red-braid *JAH* special, with gold painted over the red. Judging from the their dappling style and bald face, I would suggest that the gold-braiders are in particular leftovers of the second batch of *JAH* SRs (see CWP SR dapple gray, red braids, for discussion). I'm not convinced that the gold covers red, however; at least I've never been able to detect even a speck of red peeking out from under the gold on one of these models. The dorsal stripe is very faint on some models. My specimen has gray hooves, but collector Sue Lehman's has black hooves.
- Cantering Welsh Pony SR #107, dapple gray, red mane braids, most with dapples on head and neck, most with solid or dappled face, some with dorsal stripe, black mane and legs, most with tail same gray as body or somewhat darker, most with gray hooves, matte (1985/86). *Just About Horses* subscriber special. A few more than 2,000 models made, per a letter of June 13, 1986, from Breyer employee Jill Göllner to collector Kim Jones. The ad for the model in *JAH* XII/#3 1985 (p. 14) says 2,000, but according to Jill's letter, the company produced a few overruns "as fillers should anything happen to any of our shipments" (Kim's model was one of these overruns). Most of them are numbered by hand on the belly, although a few are not (Kim's overrun model is not numbered). This SR was advertised in 1985 but was not distributed until early 1986 (the *JAH* ad says "Orders will be randomly selected from a central bin . . . on December 18, 1985. . . . Please allow 8 weeks for delivery"), and no other subscriber special was offered in 1986. The model number 107 is per a Breyer company computer printout of activity 1985-92. *Versions*: There are two distinct versions of this SR. By far the more common is the version with dapples on neck and head, solid gray or dappled face, and typically a black mane and legs and gray tail and hooves, though I've seen a specimen (collector Karen Grimm's) with black tail and hooves, and collector Lori Ogozalek wrote to me that her pony has a dark gray mane. The second version is identical, except for its red braids, to the 1987 SR dapple gray with metallic gold braids: no dapples on neck and head, a bald face, and all black points, including the tail. These rarer red-braid ponies are shown in *JAH* 19/#5 Winter 1992 (p. 33) and 22/#1 Jan./Feb. 1995 (p. 17). Collector Sue Lehman notes that the braids on her rare-version pony, which she got from a collector who purchased it from *JAH*, are a deeper, truer red, while the braids on her common version are a more orangy red. The model shown in the 1985 *JAH* ad is the common version except that she seems to have tiny dots and threads of pink sprinkled lightly over her braids; this may be a test-color model. Sue Lehman's rare-version pony is #1,570 (the highest number of all that I've come across on this *JAH* SR), while collector Debbie Vandegrift's common-version pony is #1,452 (the highest number I know of on this version). To judge from these two ponies, this *JAH* special was made in two batches: first the common version, in a batch of roughly 1,500, and then the rare version, in a batch of roughly 500, for a total of 2,000 plus a few. This "batch" theory would help explain why the specials list in *JAH* 17/#5 Nov./Dec. 1990 (p. 29) gives the quantity of the *JAH* dapple SR as 1,500: evidently whoever complied this list found a record only of the initial batch of ponies. In any case, leftovers of the second, rare-version batch must have been the ones used for the gold-braid SR issued in 1987. But the overrun models made as "fillers," as mentioned above, were from the common-version batch, to judge from Kim Jones's overrun pony, which is a common version.
- Cantering Welsh Pony SR, dappled rose gray, darker gray mane and tail, no white markings, no ribbons, gray hooves, semigloss (1990 and 1991). Made for The Country Store, Wisconsin. Sold in Three Piece Horse Set SR #401456, with black leopard appaloosa Pony Of The Americas and chestnut pinto Haflinger. 1,000 sets made. Quantity and set number are per a Breyer company computer printout of activity 1985-92. This Cantering Welsh is the same color as the regular-run Proud Arabians produced 1989-90.
- Cantering Welsh Pony SR #413107, dark chestnut, bald face, flaxen mane and tail, green mane braids, 4 stockings, pinky tan hooves, semigloss (1988). Made for Small World. 500 models made. Sold separately or in SR set with fleabitten gray, red dun with metallic blue-green braids, and red roan CWPs. Models came with certificate of authenticity from Small World. The model number is per this certificate and a Breyer company computer printout of activity 1985-92. The quantity is per the printout and Small World's 1988 ad flier for this special.
- Cantering Welsh Pony SR #411107, fleabitten gray, white horse with gray flecks, gray mane and tail, red mane braids, pink hooves, matte (1988). Made for Small World. 500 models made. Sold separately or in SR set with dark chestnut, red dun with metallic blue-green braids, and red roan CWPs. Models came with certificate of authenticity from Small World. The model number is per this certificate and a Breyer company computer printout of activity 1985-92. The quantity is per the printout and Small World's 1988 ad flier for this special.
- Cantering Welsh Pony SR, red bay, bald face, alternating red and yellow "dot" ribbons at ends of braids, black points, 4 stockings, gray hooves, matte or slightly semigloss (1987). Made for Breyer-sponsored live shows. 10-36 models made. One of the shows to which these models were issued was the 15th I.M.H.C.C. (Congress) show, organized by collector Marney Walerius and held in August 1987. The program for this show states: "Special Cantering Welsh Pony in Bay open to Raffle/Auction . . . to those only to [*sic*] attend the show! There are only ten of these pretty Welshes available this year to the five qualifying shows. [Numeral obscured] each for the host and 1 to raise funds for the show." However, *JAH* 19/#5 Winter 1992 (p. 32) says 2-3 dozen of these bay ponies were made. (An earlier issue, *JAH* 17/#5 Nov./Dec. 1990, said the quantity was 1,000; this figure is certainly wildly amiss and may be a typo for 10.) A Breyer company computer printout of activity 1985-92 also lists this 1987 SR, giving it the model number 107RB (for "red bay") but mentioning no quantity. Also see the discussion for the 1987 SR Cantering Welsh in red-tan dun.
- Cantering Welsh Pony SR #414107, red dun, bald face, darker dun mane and tail, metallic blue-green mane braids, dorsal stripe, 4 stockings, pink hooves, matte (1988). Made for Small World. 500 models made. Sold separately or in SR set with dark chestnut, fleabitten gray, and red roan CWPs. Models came with certificate of authenticity from Small World. The model number is per this certificate and a Breyer company computer printout of activity 1985-92. The quantity is per the printout and Small World's 1988 ad flier for this special.
- Cantering Welsh Pony SR, red-tan dun, bald face, darker dun mane and tail, red mane ribbons (or braids?), brown primitive bars on upper forearms, 2 hind stockings, matte (1987). Made for Breyer-sponsored live shows but not officially released. 10 models made. For some reason the plan to use these horses for the live shows was scuttled, and the SR CWPs in red bay were used instead. Collector Betsy Andrews got hold of five of the unreleased duns and auctioned them through model magazines, including *American Model Horse Collector's Digest* (Sept./Oct. 1990) and *Equine Miniaturist* (Mar./Apr. 1993). Betsy kindly sent me a color photo and the story on the origin of these models. She was uncertain of their precise date. I have given it as 1987 since that is the date given for the red bay in *JAH* and a Breyer company computer printout of activity 1985-92. Neither the printout nor *JAH* lists the SR red-tan dun.
- Cantering Welsh Pony SR #412107, red roan, white pony with chestnut flecks, chestnut mane and tail, yellow mane braids, dark knees and hocks, pink hooves, matte (1988). Made for Small World. 500 models made. Sold separately or in SR set with dark chestnut, fleabitten gray, and red dun with metallic blue-green braids CWPs. Models came with certificate of authenticity from Small World. The model number is per this certificate and a Breyer company computer printout of activity 1985-92. The quantity is per the printout and Small World's 1988 ad flier for this special.
- Cantering Welsh Pony SR, unpainted white (1980). Sold through *JAH* VII/#3 1980 (p. 13). This horse and several other completely unpainted models were offered to hobbyists interested in customizing, but many collectors kept them unpainted. See Unpainted Models for a complete list.

Notes:

(1) Breyer sculptor Chris Hess took his design for the Cantering Welsh Pony from photographs in brochures provided by the Welsh Pony society in Virginia, according to former Breyer executive Peter Stone (conversations of Nov. 1994 and Dec. 1995). The mold represents a Section B Welsh Pony, according to *JAH* editor Megan Thilman (*JAH* 19/#5 Winter 1992, p. 31).

(2) Gutierrez 1989 lists a small special run of 5 Cantering Welsh Ponies in light dapple gray with gray mane and tail and white barrel. I have not heard of such ponies from any other source.

(3) The Cantering Welsh Pony mold has the round "Breyer Molding Co." stamp, the "U.S.A." stamp, and, just above the round stamp, a "CHESS" stamp, which identifies the mold as the design of sculptor Chris Hess. I have never seen a CWP model that lacked any of these stamps, so evidently the mold was introduced with them all. Some models have the "B" stamp in addition.

"Cash" SR — see "Pieraz" SR, under "Morganglanz"

Ceramic models — See Performing "Misty" below in the Little Bits section. Also see Fine Porcelain Models and Cold-Cast Porcelain (Resin) Models in the Traditionals section.

Chalky models — see Chalkies & Pearlies in the Appendix near the end of this book

The Challenger — see below in the Classics section

"Chaparral" — see under Fighting Stallion

"Charity" — see under Family Arabian Foal

Chestnut Pony — see Mountain Pony (under Haflinger)

Chestnut Stock Horse Foal — see under Action Stock Horse Foal

"Cheyenne" — see under Western Prancer

"Cheyenne" American Mustang — see under Indian Pony

Children's Pony — see "Scat Cat" (under Haflinger)

"CH Imperator" American Saddlebred — see under Five-Gaiter

China models — see Fine Porcelain Models; also see Ceramic Models; Cold-Cast Porcelain (Resin) Models

Chincoteague Foal — see under "Sea Star"; also see "Phantom Wings" and "Stormy"

"Chinook" SR — see under Indian Pony

Christmas decorators — see Decorators (1960s)

"Cips" — see under "El Pastor"

Circus Extravaganza set — see under Clydesdale Stallion in the Traditionals section and under Clydesdale in the Little Bits section

Circus Stallion SR — see under Fighting Stallion

"Cisco" - see under Western Pony

"Clayton" Quarter Horse — see under "Adios"

Clocks — see note 1 for the Western Horse mold; also see the Breyer Company History and MasterCrafters Clocks sections in the Appendix near the end of this book

Clydesdale — see under Clydesdale Stallion

Clydesdale Family Set SR — see Clydesdale Foal SR, true bay; Clydesdale Mare SR, true bay; Clydesdale Stallion SR, true bay

Clydesdale Foal — Filly, standing, looking left. Sculpted by Chris Hess. Mold in catalog-run production 1969-91, 1994-95.

Catalog-run models made from this mold:

- Clydesdale Foal #84, chestnut, bald face, dark chestnut or charcoal-chestnut mane and tail, 4 stockings, gray hooves, matte and semigloss (1969-89). This foal was also sold in Clydesdale Gift Set #8384 [1971-90]. Catalogs and manuals 1969-76 show this model with a stenciled-looking extensive bald face, with the white reaching well down the sides of the face. Perhaps the photo model was a test color; in any case, I have not seen a specimen like this. After 1976, the white face looks unstenciled and less extensive. Regarding the release date of this model see note 1 for the Clydesdale Mare mold. #84 was in the Showcase Collection as #840 in 1970-72 (see Showcase Collection in this section for discussion). The number 840 later belonged to the regular-run red chestnut Proud Arabian Mare.

- Clydesdale Foal #826, light golden bay, bald face, black mane and tail, gray-shaded knees, 4 stockings, gray hooves, matte (1990-91). The 1990 catalog and manual show the test run of this model, with a stenciled-looking bald face that covers much of the muzzle. The 1991 catalog shows the model as it was actually produced for sale, with unstenciled bald face that does not cover the chin. See Clydesdale Stallion #824 for further discussion.
- "Satin Star" Drafter Foal #894, dark chestnut, bald face, pale flaxen mane and tail, 4 stockings, gray hooves, matte (1994 -95).

Set: see under Clydesdale Mare.

Special-run models made from this mold:

- Clydesdale Foal SR #410384, black, star, black mane and tail, 4 stockings, gray hooves, semigloss (1988). Made for Horses International, a division of Atlantis International. 500 models made (per Heather Wells, and DeFeyter and Luther 1991). Sold separately or in set with SR Clydesdale Foals in steel gray and dapple gray with little dapples. Model number is per a Breyer company computer printout of activity 1985-92. The printout says these foals were made in 1987; however, they didn't become available at Horses International until 1988.
- Clydesdale Foal SR, dapple gray, heavily dappled, dapples on neck and head, bald or light gray face, gray mane and tail, pink-gray nose and inner ears, 4 stockings, gray hooves, slightly semigloss (1980). Made for Bentley Sales Company and Mission Supply House. About 300-350 models made. Hollansky 1990 and *JAH* 17/#5 Nov./Dec. 1990 (p. 30) both report the quantity as 400, including 200 for each of the two vendors. Hollansky and *JAH* are my only sources for the Mission Supply batch; I have no contemporary documents from this company. But Bentley's sales record cards in my possession show that Bentley's received a total of 148 foals sometime in 1980. Both Hollansky and *JAH* date this foal to 1979, which is also the year of the SR dapple Belgian, Clydesdale Stallion, and Clydesdale Mare. But the Bentley's record cards contradict this dating for the foal, as do other documents from that era. I have Bentley's price lists dated December 1979 and March 1980 that include the three adult SR dapple drafters but not the foal; the foal is, however, on the January 1981 price list, as "#84D Dapple Clydesdale Foal $6.49" (I lack price lists for the balance of 1980). Likewise, two 1979 issues of the *Model Horse Shower's Journal* mention the three adults but omit mention of a foal. First, in the October issue, editor Linda Walter states: "I've heard reports that there are NEW dapple gray Clydesdales & Belgians being made! Yes, a few are available still possibly at various mail order establishments. They are nos. 92 dap. gr. Belgian, #82 dap. gr. Clydes. stal., & ready for this, #90 dap. gr. Clydesdale MARE! Contact immediately Bentley Sales. . . . My set of the 3 dapples came in recently (ordered at MHC [Model Horse Congress]) & they are lovely." Then the November 1979 issue contains numerous ads offering these three SR dapple drafter adults but nary a foal. The same issue also announces: "Attention! The Bentley Sales Company people inform they are sold out of the dapple grey Clydesdales (mare & stallion) as well as the dapple gray Belgian special run horses." The *MHSJ* ceased publication after January 1980, but the *American Model Horse Collector's Digest* contains this item by a collector/dealer in its November/December 1980 issue: "Now Available: Dapple Clydesdale Foal—only $7.50ppd! . . . I can still get all of the above models, but order soon before Christmas rush depletes above supplies. All are brand new!" All the specimens of this SR foal that I've seen have the "B" stamp.
- Clydesdale Foal SR #410184, dapple gray, little dapples, soft looking; some with dapples on head and upper neck, some without; bald or gray-shaded face; gray mane and tail; dark shading on joints, flanks, and shoulders; pink-gray nose; gray inner ears; 4 stockings; pink hooves; matte (1988). Made for Horses International, a division of Atlantis International. 500 models made (per Heather Wells, and DeFeyter and Luther 1991). Sold separately or in set with SR Clydesdale Foals in black and steel gray. Model number is per a Breyer company computer printout of activity 1985-92. The printout says these foals were made in 1987; however, they didn't become available at Horses International until 1988.
- Clydesdale Foal SR #410284, steel gray, solid face, slightly darker mane and tail, 4 stockings, gray hooves, semigloss (1988). Made for Horses International, a division of Atlantis International. 500 models made (per Heather Wells, and DeFeyter and Luther 1991). Sold separately or in set with SR Clydesdale Foals in black and dapple gray with little dapples. Model number is per a Breyer company computer printout of activity 1985-92. The printout says these foals were made in 1987; however, they didn't become available at Horses International until 1988.
- Clydesdale Foal SR, "true bay," bald face, black mane and tail, no black on the legs, 4 stenciled high stockings, white on hind legs up to flanks, 4 gray hooves, matte (1982, 1983, and 1984). Penney's holiday catalog. Sold in Clydesdale Family Set SR #8034, with true bay Clydesdale Mare and Stallion. This set is labeled "true bay" in *JAH* IX/#2 1982 (p. 12), which shows all the Penney's specials for that year. The white on flanks and belly that occurs on many real Clydesdales (as on this model) is called a sabino pattern (per Fitch 1990, 1: 5; and Kathman 1993, p. 22). The number for this set is per a Bentley Sales Company price list dated January 1987.

Notes:

(1) Regarding the release date of this mold, see note 1 for the Clydesdale Mare mold.

(2) The earliest models of the Clydesdale Foal mold have the round "Breyer Molding Co." stamp only (collectors Lynn Isenbarger and Sheri Sommers have models like this, and I have seen other such specimens in person). Later models have the round stamp and the "U.S.A." stamp. The "U.S.A." was probably added in 1970, the year when this stamp was introduced into the Breyer line, for Clydesdale Foals without this stamp are scarce. Some "U.S.A." models also have the "B" stamp.

Clydesdale Gelding/Stallion SR, flocked bay — see under Clydesdale Mare

Clydesdale Gift Set — see under Clydesdale Mare

Clydesdale Mare — Standing, looking right, short tail. Sculpted by Chris Hess. Mold in catalog-run production 1969-93.

Catalog-run models made from this mold:

- Clydesdale Mare #83, chestnut, bald face, dark chestnut or charcoal-brown mane and tail, 4 stockings, gray hooves, matte and semigloss (1969-89). This model was also sold in Clydesdale Gift Set #8384 [1971-90] (see below). The mane and tail often have a very dark charcoal cast. Collector Jeri Harris found a #8384 mare with a solid face (*Model Trading Post*, Mar./Apr. 1994, p. 15). I have seen a few old mares with black ear tips, as occur on some old #80 bay Clydesdale Stallions. Regarding the release date of #83 see note 1 for this mold. #83 was in the Showcase Collection as #830 in 1970-72 (see Showcase Collection in this section for discussion). The number 830 later belonged to blue roan Quarter Horse Stallion ("Adios" mold).
- Clydesdale Mare #825, light golden bay, bald face, black mane and tail, gray-shaded knees, 4 stockings, gray hooves, matte (1990-91). The 1990 catalog and manual show the test run of this model, with a stenciled-looking bald face and muzzle. The 1991 catalog shows the model as it was actually produced for sale, with unstenciled bald face that does not cover the chin. See Clydesdale Stallion #824 for further discussion.
- Shire Mare #856, liver chestnut, nearly black mane and tail, stenciled bald face with white/pink muzzle and chin, 4 stockings, tan hooves, matte (1992-93).

Set:

- Clydesdale Gift Set #8384, mare and foal, both chestnut, with green felt stable-blankets (1971-90). These same models were also sold separately as Clydesdale Mare #83 and Clydesdale Foal #84 [both 1969-89]. The stable blankets are edged and surcingled with white cloth tape. As collector Sheryl Leisure pointed out to me, the surcingles on earlier blankets have metal fasteners; those on later blankets have Velcro closures. The metal fasteners are visible on the foal's blanket in most catalogs from 1972 through 1978; the Velcro closure is first shown in the 1979 catalog.

Special-run models made from this mold:

- Clydesdale Gelding/Stallion SR, flocked bay, blaze and white muzzle, brown glass or painted black eyes, black synthetic hair mane and tail, 4 high stockings, painted black hooves, red ribbons and white floral ornaments along crest and on tail, added male part(s), white leather show halter and lead (1983 and 1984). Sears holiday catalog. About 8,000 models made, per Breyer executive Peter Stone (conversation of Nov. 1994). Sears priced this model at $27.99 in 1983 and $29.99 in 1984. The white stockings on the hind legs go up to the stifles. Some of the models I've seen have brown glass eyes, but collector Heather Wells's model has painted black eyes, as did a specimen I saw at BreyerFest 1994. Despite the female gender of the mold, the Sears catalogs refer to this model with male pronouns, for reasons I learned from collectors Sande Schneider and Gale Good: the model has an added male portion or two, not visible in the Sears catalogs. On some models the addition is only enough to make a gelding, as on Sande's horse; but on others, such as Heather's and collector Sheryl Leisure's, there are two added portions, sufficient for stallionhood. The model shown in *JAH* X/#3 1983 (p. 12) has added white hair feathers on the lower legs, but the caption says "Does not come with fur feathers." The correct model is shown without feathers in the Sears catalogs. The white show halters evidently vary: the 1983 Sears catalog shows it with bit rings, but the 1984 shows it without. The flocking, hairing, eyes, male parts, ornaments, and tack on these models are by the Riegseckers of Indiana (see Riegseckers Models for discussion). Starting in January 1986, leftovers of this SR appeared on the Bentley Sales Company price lists as #83FLK (for "flocked"), complete with halter and ribbons, for $9.99. Bentley's received a total of 186 models, according to old Bentley's sales record cards in my possession. See note 2 for this mold for discussion of other flocked Clydesdale Mares.
- Clydesdale Mare SR, dapple gray, dapples on neck and head; bald face; darker gray mane and tail; 4 stockings; gray hooves; slightly semigloss (1979). Made for Bentley Sales Company and Mission Supply House. At least a few hundred models made. Hollansky 1990 and *JAH* 17/#5 Nov./Dec. 1990 (p. 30) both report the quantity as 400, which includes 200 for each of the two mail-order companies. But old Bentley's sales record cards in my possession show that Bentley's received a total of 291 dapple Clydesdale Mares in several shipments between mid-1979 and spring 1980. If Mission Supply got about the same quantity, this would mean a total of nearly 600 models. I do not have any Mission Supply lists from that time, but the earliest Bentley's price list in my possession, dated December 1979, includes "#90 Dapple Clydesdale Mare $7.95," as well as "#92 Dapple Belgian $7.95" and "#82 Dapple Clydesdale Stallion $7.95." These three SRs were also announced by editor Linda Walter in the October 1979 *Model Horse Showers Journal*: "I've heard reports that there are NEW dapple grey Clydesdales & Belgians being made! Yes, a few are available still possibly at various mail order establishments. They are nos. 92 dap. gr. Belgian, #82 dap. gr. Clydes. stal., & ready for this, #90 dap. gr. Clydesdale MARE! Contact immediately Bentley Sales Co. . . . Their prices were basic Breyer prices. . . . My set of the 3 dapples came in recently (ordered at MHC [Model Horse Congress]) & they are lovely. They are semi-glossy with pink muzzle & ears. . . . The mare never before was released in dapple!" There are two versions of this SR mare: one is darker gray with larger, sparser dapples and very dark mane and tail; the other a lighter gray with smaller, denser dapples and medium/dark gray mane and tail.
- Clydesdale Mare SR, dapple gray, sparsely dappled and soft looking, no dapples on neck and head; bald face; gray mane and tail; pink nose and ears; 4 stockings; gray hooves; matte (1986/87). Made for model mail-order companies. 1,100 models made, per *JAH* 17/#5 Nov./Dec. 1990 (p. 30) and a Breyer company computer printout of activity 1985-92. The printout also gives the model number as #83GR. *JAH* and the printout give the date of this special as 1986, but it didn't become available from mail-order companies until 1987. A Model Horse Collector's Supply price list dated December 22, 1986, states that it "will have" this horse. The first Bentley Sales Company price list to include this SR is dated January 1987. Bentley's sales record cards in my possession show that Bentley's received a total of 100 dapple Clydesdale Mares on December 26, 1986.
- Clydesdale Mare SR, "true bay," bald face, black mane and tail, no black on the legs, 4 stenciled high stockings, white on hind legs goes up to flanks and belly, 4 gray hooves, matte (1982, 1983, and 1984). Penney's holiday catalog. Sold in Clydesdale Family Set SR #8034, with true bay Clydesdale Foal and Stallion. This set is labeled "true bay" in *JAH* IX/#2 1982 (p. 12), which shows all the Penney's specials for that year. The white on flanks and belly that occurs on many real Clydesdales (as on this model) is called a sabino pattern (per Fitch 1990, 1: 5; and Kathman 1993, p. 22). The number for this set is per a Bentley Sales Company price list dated January 1987.
- Clydesdale Mare SR, unpainted white (1980). Sold through *JAH* VII/#3 1980 (p. 13). This horse and several other completely unpainted models were offered to hobbyists interested in customizing, but many collectors kept them unpainted. See Unpainted Models for a complete list.

Notes:

(1) This mold and the Clydesdale Foal are listed as "new for 1970" in the 1970 dealer catalog, but they were actually released in 1969—they are listed in the 1969 collector's manual and pictured in an article in *Craft Model & Hobby Industry*, which states, "The

1969 additions to the fine line of Breyer Animal Creations are ready to enhance the collections of all horse and animal fanciers." Evidently when a new dealer catalog was issued in 1970 for the first time since 1968 (there is no 1969 catalog to my knowledge), Breyer decided to list the 1969 as well as the 1970 models as "new for 1970" to bring them to the attention of dealers, who would naturally suppose that any model not listed as new was something they had seen in 1968.

(2) Two runs of flocked Clydesdale Mares were brought to my attention by collector Gale Good, but I'm not sure whether they should count as actual Breyer SRs, as does the SR flocked bay sold by Sears in 1983 and 1984. First, a run of flocked black Clydesdale Mares, representing the black Percheron team owned by Coors Beer, was sold at the San Diego fairgrounds in 1989 or earlier (Gale bought her mare in 1989 from another collector who had gotten it at the fairgrounds). Second, a run of flocked palomino/light chestnut Clydesdale Mares with low stockings, representing a Belgian team displayed at the Los Angeles County Fair, was sold at the fairgrounds in 1987 (Gale got hers new there). Both models, according to Gale, have floral ornaments on the crest and tail identical to the ornaments on the Sears SR flocked bay, and the palomino/light chestnut mare also has a white headstall with bit rings, identical to that on the Sears SR. (Neither of the fairgrounds models, however, has the added male part sported by the Sears SR.) The identical accessories suggest that these models, like the Sears SR, were flocked and decorated by the Riegseckers of Indiana, but we don't know for sure. Nor do we know if the fairgrounds concessionaires ordered the horses from Breyer (in which case they would count as Breyer SRs) or instead straight from Riegseckers (in which case they wouldn't count as Breyer SRs).

(3) The earliest models of the Clydesdale Mare mold have the round "Breyer Molding Co." stamp only (collector Sheri Sommars and I both have models like this). Later models have the round stamp and the "U.S.A." stamp. My chalky #83 mare has the "U.S.A.," so it is certain that this stamp was added to the mold in the 1970s; and in all likelihood it was added in 1970, the year when this stamp was introduced into the Breyer line, for Clydesdale Mares without this stamp are scarce. Some "U.S.A." models also have the "B" stamp (Chelle Fulk's chestnut #83 is like this).

Clydesdale Stallion — ♞ No stallion parts, starting to jog, bundled tail, eight molded-on mane bobs, molded-on ribbons on tail and forelock. Sculpted by Chris Hess. Mold in catalog-run production 1958 (maybe earlier) - current as of 1996 (no-muscle mold version 1958 [maybe earlier] - 1961; muscle mold version 1962 - current as of 1996).

Catalog-run models made from this mold:

No-muscle and muscle mold versions:

♞ Clydesdale #80, bay, bald face, black mane and tail, no black on the legs, 4 stockings, gray or pink hooves (1958 [maybe earlier] - 1989). Called Clydesdale in catalogs and price lists 1958-72; called Clydesdale Stallion in 1973-89. See note 1 for this mold regarding release date. There are at least five versions of this model. The last three are discernible in catalogs, but as I will discuss in a moment, the catalogs are in error about the ending dates of the third and fourth versions. The five versions, with likely correct dates, are as follows: [A] No muscles (see note 2 for this mold), gold mane bobs and tail ribbon, unstenciled bald face and stockings, gray hooves, many with hand-painted eyewhites, glossy, 1958 (maybe earlier) - 1961. Body color is typically a light orangy bay. [B] Muscles, otherwise identical to the no-muscle version, 1962. I saw one of these glossy, muscled models at BreyerFest 1993, and collectors Joan Fauteux, Sheryl Leisure, Lori Ogozalek, and Sande Schneider have specimens. This horse must have been made only in 1962, for the no-muscle version was still in production in 1961 (see note 2 for this mold), and the 1963, 1966, and 1967 catalogs specify that #80 is matte. The latter two catalogs also show him with pink hooves (#80 isn't pictured but only listed in the 1963 catalog). [C] Muscles, gold bobs and tail ribbon, unstenciled bald face and stockings, pink hooves, some with hand-painted eyewhites, many with black eartips, matte and semigloss, 1963 - 1970/71 (catalogs erroneously show this version through 1975). Body color is typically a medium brownish bay. The 1963, 1966, and 1967 catalogs specify #80 as matte (as opposed to glossy; collectors Betty Mertes and Sande Schneider have version C's that are very high semigloss). The bald face on this version can be extensive, reaching well down the sides of the face. [D] Muscles, alternating red and white bobs, red tail ribbon, unstenciled bald face and stockings, pink hooves, some with black eartips, matte and semigloss, 1971/72 - 1986 (catalogs erroneously show this version as starting in 1976). Body color varies from medium red bay to fairly dark brown bay. The tail ribbon on some version D's is painted as a thin red stripe with central red blob. Normally, the first mane bob near the horse's ears is red and the last one near the withers is white; however, collector Chelle Fulk purchased a new version D in 1977 with the bob colors reversed. Collector Liz Strauss has an unusual version D horse with gray hooves. [E] Muscles, alternating red and white bobs (same order as on version D), red tail ribbon, stenciled blaze, stenciled stockings, pink hooves, matte, 1987-89. Body color varies from medium red bay to fairly dark brown bay (I have one of each extreme). As to the dating of C and D: Although catalogs show version C through 1975 and version D starting in 1976, other evidence indicates that D was introduced no later than 1972. First, collector Leslie Granger has a version D that she is positive she got prior to 1973, when she left the U.S. for an extended period; collector Meg Mac Donald too has a version D that she got in the very early 1970s. Further, the February 1973 *Model Horse Shower's Journal* contains this report by a subscriber: "I have 2 Drafters. They are the Breyer stallion and foal molds. The stallion . . . is the factory color, bay with a white face & feathers. He also has red & white braids in his mane & a red one in his tail." Finally, a color Breyer brochure made for a British distributor (Helmets Limited), which is datable to 1971/73 by other models it pictures, shows a version D, with his red and white bobs. The 1979 Penney's holiday catalog pictures version D in a green stable blanket, along with a Clydesdale Foal #84 in matching blanket. The blankets are the same as those issued on the foal and Clydesdale Mare for many years in regular-run set #8483. Whether Penney's actually sold the blanketed stallion is a question, however, for the text in the Penney's catalog says "Clydesdale Mare and Foal . . . each has stable blanket" and makes no mention of the stallion. #80 was in the Showcase Collection as #800 in 1970-72 (see Showcase Collection in this section for discussion).

♞ Clydesdale #82, dapple gray, dapples on neck and head, bald face, gray mane and tail, 4 stockings, gray hooves, gold mane bobs and tail ribbon, glossy (1961-66). This model is called simply "Clydesdale" in all the Breyer publications that list it. The gray color varies from very pale to medium/dark. The dappling is heavy and the dapples are typically quite large, though some specimens have small dapples. Many #82s have a "cleaned up" look to the hind stockings—the gray paint on the hocks ends in a hard edge as though it had been wiped—but this effect is factory original. The very earliest #82s are the no-muscle version. Collector Sheryl Leisure has one of these, which has pink ears and nose and a round Breyer stamp. The existence of these no-muscle dappled horses indicates that #82 was introduced prior to 1962 (see note 2 for this mold). Most #82s are the muscled mold version. There are some shiny, gray-hoofed SR dapple gray Clydesdales, dating probably to 1979, that are virtually identical to muscled regular-run #82s; the only sure difference between them is that the SRs all have a "U.S.A." stamp whereas all regular-run #82s lack this stamp. The model number 82 originally belonged to the Donkey With Baskets set.

♞ Clydesdale #980, woodgrain; black eyes; woodgrain mane bobs and tail ribbon; no white markings or other color detailing; most matte, a few glossy (1959-64). This model is called simply "Clydesdale" in all the Breyer publications that list it. The name "Clydesdale Stallion" was not introduced in catalogs until 1972, years after #980 was discontinued. *Breyer Collector's Video* mentions that a few glossy woodgrain Clydesdales are known. These and the glossy woodgrain Running Mares and Foals noted in Diederich 1988, Section 1, are the only glossy woodgrains I've heard of. This model came in both no-muscle and muscle versions. The no-muscle horses came first, and the muscled ones succeeded them in 1962. The no-muscle woodgrain Clydesdale Stallion is not in the 1958 catalog or price list but appears with woodgrain Race Horse, Family Arabian Stallion, Proud Arabian Mare, and Brahma Bull in an old undated Ward's catalog ad that I believe dates to 1959. (For discussion of this dating, see under Woodgrains below in this section.) The ad describes the models thus: "Simulated wood grain finish figurines. Beautifully detailed Horses and Brahma Bull. Faithfully copied from original hand-carved wood pieces. Made of Tenite Acetate high quality plastic, carefully hand finished in simulated wood grain. Buy any three figurines—get free 'Album of Horses' book [by Marguerite Henry]." The muscle version of the woodgrain Clydesdale was offered in the 1962 Ward's holiday catalog. The model number 980 later belonged to the Showcase Collection issue of the buckskin Quarter Horse (Quarter Horse Gelding mold).

Muscle mold version only:

♞ Clydesdale Stallion #824, light golden bay, stenciled bald face, black mane and tail, gray-shaded knees, 4 stockings, gray hooves, alternating gold and white mane bobs, gold tail ribbon, matte (1990-91). The 1990 catalog and manual show the test runs of this model and the matching mare and foal, all with stenciled white facial markings. On the stallion and mare, the stenciled white bald face runs all the way down the muzzle and wraps back up over the chin. The test Foal may have a white chin too, but he's shown face-on, so this isn't visible. The models as they were actually produced for sale are shown in the 1991 catalog. The chins are brown, not white; and on the mare and foal, the bald face is unstenciled. Though it's not visible in the 1991 picture, the stallion's bald face is still stenciled.

♞ Highland Clydesdale #868, bay; stenciled bald face with white muzzle; black mane and tail; no black on the legs; 2 front stockings; white hind legs, flanks, and belly; tan-pink hooves; alternating blue and white mane bobs; blue tail ribbon; matte (1992-95). As collector Lynn Isenbarger pointed out to me, the 1992 catalog shows a model whose front stockings go over the knees. This is probably a test-color piece; I don't believe models like this were produced for sale. My own model (purchased in November 1992) and others I've seen have front stockings that end below the knees. The Highland Clydesdale's white facial marking is the same as that on the SR grulla Clydesdale Stallion. The white on flanks and belly that occurs on many real Clydesdales is called a sabino pattern (per Fitch 1990, 1: 5; and Kathman 1993, p. 22).

Set:

♞ Circus Extravaganza set #3170, grulla large horse, medium gray covered with tiny gray flecks; bald face with stenciled white muzzle; 4 stockings; tan hooves with gray stripes; dark gray tail with red, white, and blue ribbon; blue mane; white mane bobs with large red dots; red, white, and blue forelock ribbon; matte (1994-95). Set also includes dark dappled bay small horse (Little Bits Clydesdale mold). This large Clydesdale is the first model of this mold to have the molded-on forelock ribbon regularly painted in ribbon colors. Typically he also has white ribbons painted onto the blue over the withers, but I found a specimen without these white ribbons.

Special-run models made from this mold:

Muscle mold version only:

♘ Clydesdale Stallion SR, dapple gray, dapples on neck and head; bald face; gray mane and tail; 4 stockings; pink or gray hooves; gold mane bobs and tail ribbon; most matte or semigloss (1979). At least a few hundred models made. The specials lists in *JAH* 17/#5 Nov./Dec. 1990 (p. 30) and 17#4 Sept./Oct. 1990 (p. 29) include three 1979 SR dapple drafters—this Clydesdale Stallion, the Belgian, and the Clydesdale Mare—naming both Bentley Sales Company and Mission Supply House as vendors for the mare and the Belgian but naming only Bentley's as the vendor for the Clydesdale Stallion. It seems likely, however, that if the mare and Belgian went to both companies, the Clydesdale Stallion would, too. In any case, *JAH* gives no quantity for this SR, but old Bentley's sales record cards in my possession show that Bentley's received a total of 355 dapple Clydesdale Stallions in several shipments between mid-1979 and spring 1980. I do not have any Mission Supply lists from that time, but the earliest Bentley's price list in my possession, dated December 1979, includes "#82 Dapple Clydesdale Stallion $7.95," as well as "#92 Dapple Belgian $7.95" and "#90 Dapple Clydesdale Mare $7.95." (See the entry for the 1979 SR dapple Clydesdale Mare for a citation from a 1979 model horse magazine.) Like his colleague the dapple Belgian, this Clydesdale Stallion comes in a bewildering array of variations. Adding to the confusion is the 1984/85 SR dapple Clydesdale Stallion (see next entry), which may have been simply leftovers of the 1979 stallions; in any case I do not know how to distinguish the two runs. It is certain that both pink-hoofed and gray-hoofed versions of the Clydesdale Stallion exist (I own one of each), and collector Karen Grimm and others have told me that both versions appeared in 1979. The gray-hoofed horses I have seen come in at least three variations of their own: [A] Heavily dappled, glossy-looking finish. This model, of which I have seen a couple specimens, is virtually indistinguishable from the old regular-run #82 (muscled version). The only clear difference is that the SR has a "U.S.A." stamp, whereas the regular-run lacks this stamp. [B] Heavily dappled, matte. [C] Rather sparse dapples, dishwater-gray tinge to the stockings and face, semigloss (I own this one).

♘ Clydesdale Stallion SR, dapple gray, dapples on neck and head; bald face; gray mane and tail; 4 stockings; hoof color uncertain; gold mane bobs and tail ribbon; matte or semigloss (1984/85). Issued to Caauwe Sales. About 100 models issued. The sources that mention this 1984/85 SR are *JAH* 17/#5 Nov./Dec. 1990 (p. 29), which gives the surely erroneous quantity of 1,000, and Walerius 1991 (p. 102), which gives the more plausible quantity of 100. Both of these sources name the dealer as Caauwe Sales—a novelties sales company owned by Don Caauwe, of Lincoln, Nebraska, per former Breyer executive Peter Stone (conversation of Dec. 1995). Walerius states further that the 1984/85 horses were leftovers from an earlier run; Breyer, which was located in Chicago at the time, sold them and other leftover models in preparation for the company's move to New Jersey. (The move was precipitated by the sale of Breyer Animal Creations to Reeves International in November 1984.) Walerius does not say what year the 1984/

85s were leftovers from, but the 1979 run is the only earlier SR dapple Clydesdale Stallion listed by her or any other source known to me. Which version of the 1979 stallions the 1984/85s were leftovers of I do not know, so I am not sure if the hooves are gray or pink.

- Clydesdale Stallion SR, dapple gray, no dapples on neck and head; bald face; gray mane and tail; 4 stockings; gray hooves; alternating red and white mane bobs; red tail ribbon; matte (1986/87). Made for model mail-order companies. 1,200 models made, per *JAH* 17/#5 Nov./Dec. 1990 (p. 29) and a Breyer company computer printout of activity 1985-92; the printout gives the model number as #80GR. *JAH* and the printout give the date of this special as 1986, but it didn't become available from mail-order companies until 1987: it is not on the Bentley Sales Company price list dated November 1986 but is listed on a January 1987 Bentley's list as "for January delivery"; also a Model Horse Collector's Supply price list dated December 22, 1986, states that it "will have" this horse. Bentley's sales record cards in my possession indicate that Bentley's received a total of 200 pieces. This SR is lighter colored and softer looking (owing to its very matte finish) than the 1979 SR dapple gray. *Breyer Collector's Video* says some of these lighter, matte horses have pink hooves. *JAH* mentions only gray hooves, and my own model and others I've seen have gray hooves. The video also says that some of these matte horses have gold bobs, and in fact the model pictured on the Your Horse Source fliers for this special has gold bobs. But according to collector Gale Good, this was only the test-color piece. Conceivably a few specimens in the production run were given gold bobs before the change was made to red and white. Collector Lindy Pinkham's horse has the normal red and white bobs but has the unusual feature of a red-painted forelock ribbon. This is the only such specimen I know of.
- Clydesdale Stallion SR, grulla, shaded smoke gray with metallic sheen; bald face with stenciled white muzzle; black mane and tail; charcoal shading on head, legs, and belly; 1 right front and 1 right hind stocking with tan hooves; other hooves tannish gray; alternating yellow and blue mane bobs; yellow tail ribbon; matte (1992). Sears holiday catalog. Sold in Horses Great And Small set SR #496092, with black Cantering Welsh Pony and palomino Miniature Horse ("Merrylegs" mold). 2,250 sets made. Quantity and set number are per a Breyer company computer printout of activity 1985-92. (The number 11217, given for this set on the Bentley Sales price list of March 15, 1993, is the Sears number, not the Breyer number.) The Sears holiday catalog calls this stallion's color "grulla." His white facial marking is the same as on #868 Highland Clydesdale. Collector Joan Fauteux got a model with black shading on the face only, none on the legs or body (thanks to Joan for sending a photo).
- Clydesdale Stallion SR, "true bay," unstenciled bald face, black mane and tail, no black on the legs, 4 stenciled stockings, gray hooves, all red mane bobs and tail ribbon, matte (1982, 1983, and 1984). Penney's holiday catalog. Sold in Clydesdale Family Set SR #8034, with true bay Clydesdale Mare and Foal. This set is labeled "true bay" in *JAH* IX/#2 1982 (p. 12), which shows all the Penney's specials for that year. The number for this set is per a Bentley Sales Company price list dated January 1987.
- "Grayingham Lucky Lad" SR #410393, black, stenciled bald face with white muzzle, wishbone-shaped white patch on belly, 4 stockings, tan hooves, red mane, white mane bobs with red stripe over the tops, black tail, white tail ribbon with red center, slightly semigloss (1993). Dinner model for BreyerFest in Lexington, Kentucky. About 1,500 models made, but fewer survived. Breyer employee Megan Thilman told me at this BreyerFest that about 1,420 dinner tickets (one model per ticket) had been sold, and that the leftover models would be destroyed. The models came in normal Breyer boxes (plastic front, yellow backing), with the label "Breyerfest 1993, Grayingham Lucky Lad." No model number is given on the box; the number I've given is per a Breyer company computer printout of 1993 SRs. On most models the right front stocking is only on the sides and front of the leg; the back is black from knee to fetlock. Collector Liz Strauss, however, has seen a model with a full white stocking on the right front. This SR is a portrait of the real Shire stallion "Grayingham Lucky Lad," nicknamed "Laddy," owned by Kristin and Vern Stark, of Star Night Farm in Michigan. The Starks themselves selected the Clydesdale Stallion mold for this special (per *JAH* 20/#2 Summer I 1993, p. 17; for photos of the real horse see *JAH* 20/#4 Fall 1993, p. 18). This magnificent 18-hand, 2,100-pound stallion was presented at BreyerFest sporting red and white mane and tail ribbons matching those on the model. At the West Coast Model Horse Collector's Jamboree in August 1995, Breyer executive Peter Stone announced that the horse had died unexpectedly of an aneurysm just a few days earlier.

Notes:

(1) *JAH* Spring 1978 states, "The first Clydesdale, (#80) was introduced prior to 1958, (we're not sure of the exact year)." The Clydesdale is in the 1958 catalog and price list but not in any of the earlier Breyer publications known to me. So he might have been introduced in 1957 or so, but no earlier than that, I believe.

(2) When the mold was introduced in the late 1950s, it was very smooth, with almost no muscle definition. The 1960 catalog shows the no-muscle version in woodgrain and bay. A short while later the mold was resculpted to add muscling to the neck, shoulders, hindquarters, and legs. The face was also given veins and sharper bone definition, and "wrinkles" were added to the crest of the neck above the withers. The muscled version was certainly in production by 1962, for the woodgrain Clydesdale advertised in the 1962 Ward's holiday catalog is clearly a muscled horse. (The muscling is also plainly visible in the 1963 Breyer catalog.) But the existence of the no-muscle dapple gray regular-run Clydesdale #82 indicates that the muscled version was not yet in production in 1961. Since #82 is not in the 1960 catalog, and since the mold had muscles in 1962, this no-muscle model must have been made in 1961.

(3) Both mold versions have a tiny bow molded onto the forelock, matching the molded-on bow on the tail (thanks to Heather Wells for pointing this out to me). But unlike the tail bow, the forelock bow on almost all models is not painted in ribbon colors but just left the color of the forelock. Aside from a few test-color and oddball pieces with painted bows, the only catalog-run or SR model to have the forelock bow painted in fancy colors is the grulla in the Circus Extravaganza set #3170.

(4) Early models of the Clydesdale Stallion mold have no mold marks. Slightly later models, including the latest no-muscle horses, have the round "Breyer Molding Co." stamp only (Sheryl Leisure's no-muscle regular-run #82 has the stamp, and I have seen a couple of other models like hers as well). Still later models have the round stamp and the "U.S.A." stamp. Some "U.S.A." models have the "B" stamp in addition.

"Cochise" SR — see under "Sea Star"

"Cody" — see under "Buckshot"

Cold-cast porcelain (resin) models — See "Fashionably Late" SR (under "Sherman Morgan"); "Galaxias" SR (under "Sham"); "Misty" Of Chincoteague SR, chestnut/palomino pinto; "Secretariat" SR, red chestnut; and "Spotted Bear" SR (under "San Domingo"). Also see Fine Porcelain Models; Ceramic Models.

Collectible Stock Horse Family SR — see Action Stock Horse Foal SR, buckskin; Stock Horse Mare SR, buckskin; Stock Horse Stallion SR, buckskin

Collector's Mare And Foal Set SR — see Running Foal SR, flocked palomino; and Running Mare SR, flocked palomino

Collector's Rocking Horse — see under Saddlebred Weanling

Collector's Unicorn SR — see under "Smoky"

Comanche Pony — see under "San Domingo"

"Commander" — see under Five-Gaiter

Commemorative Editions — See "Silver" Quarter Horse SR (1989, see under Quarter Horse Gelding); Saddlebred Weanling #818 (1990); "Hyksos" The Egyptian Arabian (1991, see under Black Stallion); "Memphis Storm" (1992, see under Tennessee Walker); "Domino" The Happy Canyon Trail Horse (1993, see under "San Domingo"); "Gifted" (1994, see under Hanoverian); and "Goliath" (1995, see under Belgian).

Commemorative Edition (CE) models have been issued one per year since 1989 but listed in Breyer catalogs only since 1990. The first CE, "Silver" Quarter Horse, was not in the catalog but was marketed as a special through model mail-order companies. CE models are produced in a designated limited quantity—5,000 pieces for the 1989 and 1990 CEs; 7,500 pieces for 1991-93 CEs; 9,000 for the 1994 "Gifted"; and 10,000 for the 1995 "Goliath"—and are numbered by hand on the belly. All have specially painted eyes, either tri-color (brown, black, and white), two color (brown and black, on "Hyksos" and "Gifted"), or, in one case ("Domino"), normal tri-color on one side and blue on the other.

What do Commemorative Editions commemorate? Nothing, according to Breyer executive Peter Stone; the CE concept is merely a marketing tactic with no deeper meaning or unifying principle behind it (conversation of Nov. 1994). The boxes in which CEs are packaged and the Breyer catalogs in which they are advertised bear him out. The "Commemorative Edition" stickers on the boxes of the first two CEs, "Silver" and the Weanling, mention only the CE year of issue, the model's name, and the quantity, giving nary an inkling as to what these pieces commemorate. A July 1989 ad flier from Mission Supply House does comment regarding "Silver" that his mold was "introduced 30 years ago in 1959." But this statement evidently represents that retailer's own attempt to root out some significance to this "commemorative" horse and not anything Breyer said, for the printing on "Silver's" box includes no reference to the mold's age (not to mention that a silver anniversary is the 25th, not the 30th). The CE Weanling offers not even the mold-commemoration straw to grasp at, for in 1990, when she was released, her mold was only 17 years old, hardly antique by Breyer standards. Starting with the third CE, however, the box stickers and catalog blurbs have yielded somewhat more substance, if still no consistent theme, to the "Commemorative Edition" concept. The third and fourth CEs, "Hyksos" and "Memphis Storm," might be said to commemorate Breyer finishes of the 1960s—the decorator colors in the case of "Hyksos" (who sports "a new Decorator Color—Ageless Bronze," as his box sticker notes) and the "collectible, Glossy Charcoal finish" in the case of "Memphis Storm." Subsequent CEs have abandoned allusions to Breyer's past, focusing instead on real horses and breeds, as do the majority of Breyer's ordinary catalog-runs and SRs.

Corgi Breyer truck — see Breyer Anniversary Truck

Country Doctor buggy set — see under Black Stallion below in the Classics section

Cow Pony — see "Ranger" Cow Pony (under Western Prancer)

"Cream Puff" — see Western Horse #59, white

"Cricket" Quarter Horse Foal — see under Action Stock Horse Foal

Crow Horse — see "Ichilay" (under Indian Pony)

"Dakota" Bucking Bronco — see under Bucking Bronco below in the Classics section

"Dan Patch" — see under Pacer

Dark Bay Western Horse SR — see under "John Henry"

The Dawning — see below in the Classics section

Dealer display units — see Display Units

Decorators (1960s) — The original decorators properly so-called are a series of 20 horse models in fantasy colors issued for a short time in the 1960s. The 20 include 5 different molds—Fighting Stallion, Five-Gaiter, Mustang, Running Foal, and Running Mare—each produced in 4 decorator colors, which have their own names: Copenhagen, which is dappled blue; Florentine, dappled metallic gold; Golden Charm, solid metallic gold; and Wedgewood Blue, which is solid blue. These decorator-color terms are used on Breyer's April 1, 1964, Supplemental Price List (discussed below), which lists all and only the decorators. All these models have white points, bald faces, and pale pink or unpainted white hooves. All are glossy except for the Wedgewoods, which are matte. The model numbers of the decorators are all four-digit numbers that start with either 1 (for the Copenhagen models), 2 (the Florentines), 3 (the Golden Charms), or 4 (the Wedgewoods), and end with the number of one of the realistically colored models of the mold. A zero fills in between these starting and ending numbers if the ending number is two-digit. For example, the Five-Gaiter's decorator numbers are #1051, #2051, #3051, and #4051, with 51 being the number of the albino Five-Gaiter model. The decorator Running Mares are #1120, #2120, etc., with 120 being the number of the alabaster Running Mare. The only mold that strays from this tidy fold is the Fighting Stallion, whose decorator numbers end with 31, a number never assigned to any Fighting Stallion model to my knowledge (see note 5 for the Fighting Stallion mold).

Breyer issued a few other models in the 1960s that may also be categorized as decorators. The solid gold Golden Buck and Golden Doe (see below in the Wildlife section)

debuted in 1961 or 1962, a year or two before the decorator horses. Less well known is the SR "Fury" Prancer in Wedgewood Blue, made sometime in the first half of the 1960s. A Copenhagen Belgian model, probably a one-of-a-kind test piece, is also known to exist (see note 2 for the Belgian mold). Beyond these pieces, there is only legend—a tantalizing legend regarding Christmas decorators painted Yuletide red and green. To my knowledge, no collector today owns one of these fabled models or has even seen one, at least not in recent decades. A few longtime collectors—among them Gale Good, a highly intelligent woman of sane mind and sound character—recall seeing Christmas decorator Breyers in stores sometime in the early 1960s. Gale remembers seeing bright dappled red and dappled green Running Mares and Foals in particular, at a shop in Southern California.

Although the original 20 decorator horses are listed as regular runs in this book, they might possibly be specials, as I learned from former Breyer executive Peter Stone in December 1995. These models, according to Stone, were originally produced for a Montgomery Ward's Christmas catalog in the 1960s (probably 1963, as I'll discuss in a moment). Who conceived the idea of blue and gold horses and whether Ward's actually purchased them as exclusives he is not sure, but Stone vividly recalls that a man named Sam Barth, an independent Breyer sales representative who sold models to department stores such as Ward's, Aldens, and Sears, made the decorator deal with Ward's, specifically with the store's stationery division. Stone does not know if Ward's ordered batches of all 20 models—that would be a lot of models for one catalog. But the store had purchased a large selection of novelty Breyers before: the 1962 Ward's holiday catalog offered 9 different woodgrain models, 7 of them in what appears to be the stationery section of that catalog, to judge from my photocopy of that page. In any case, the decorators did not sell well for Ward's, so Breyer offered the horses to other businesses. Longtime collector Kim Jones remembers seeing decorators at a Sav-On store in Downey, her home town in Southern California, and collector Marney Walerius comments in her book that she bought decorators at several stores in Illinois, such as Ben Franklin 5 & 10 and McLeister's Gifts (Walerius 1991, p. 32). Peter Stone does not know whether the models sold by such businesses were all from batches made for Ward's or partially from separate batches, produced perhaps in hopes that these fantastically colored horses would catch on in the wider market. But in either case, the decorators evidently fared no better at other businesses than at Ward's, and Breyer soon discontinued them. Stone's father, Sam Stone, one of the founders of Breyer Animal Creations, had a shelf in his office at the factory in Chicago on which he kept samples of the decorators—a display that prompted jokes about reissuing those duds.

Peter Stone's recollection would explain why the 20 original decorator horses do not appear in any Breyer catalogs: if they were created as holiday specials for Ward's and discontinued shortly thereafter, there would not have been time or occasion to put them in a Breyer catalog. The only 1960s Breyer publication I know of that includes these models is the "Supplemental Price List—April 1, 1964," which lists all and only the 20 individual decorator horses and sets of the decorator Running Mares and Foals. This price list was issued in two versions (as I'll discuss in a moment), both of which state: "All items are individually packed in self-mailer cartons." Apparently made to accompany the price list is a professional, sepia-toned photo of the 20 decorators lined up in rows by color, with a small label printed with the model number placed beside each horse. The original photo that I have examined in person, owned by collector Karen Grimm, of Black Horse Ranch model mail-order company, has no date on it anywhere but does have a rubber-stamped instruction on the back: "Please mail your order to J. C. Unger, . . . Los Angeles 15, Calif." Jules Unger was a Breyer sales representative for many years, followed by his son Henry Unger and grandson Adam Unger (per Peter Stone, conversation of Dec. 1995). The use of a zone number in Unger's address here does not necessarily tell against an early-1964 dating for the photo, for although the zone-number system was replaced by the zip-code system in the U.S. in 1963 (per *Britannica Online*), undoubtedly the transition took time and people continued to use their zone-numbered stationery items for some months.

If the Supplemental Price List and sepia-toned photo are the marketing package that Breyer put together to sell off would-be Ward's models, then the April 1964 dating of the price list would suggest that the Ward's holiday catalog for which the decorators were created was the 1963. I have not seen this Ward's catalog, but as mentioned, I have photocopies of the 1962 Ward's holiday catalog Breyer pages (provided by collector Sande Schneider, who leafed all the way through the original catalog), and there are no decorator horses in them. Nor are there any in the 1964 Ward's holiday catalog, of which I own an original. I have not seen a 1961 Ward's catalog, but such an early date for the decorators, although possible, strikes me as unlikely, if only because no documentation for these models has surfaced except the 1964 Supplemental Price List. Why no 1962 or 1963 price lists with decorators, if Breyer had a load of 1961 Ward's leftovers to peddle? I am not even sure whether all 5 of the molds used for the decorators existed in 1961. The only one I know for a fact came out that year is the Fighting Stallion mold in realistic colors and woodgrain.

As mentioned, I know of two versions of the April 1, 1964, Supplemental Price List, which presumably were sent to different categories of customers (big-volume buyers vs. small-volume buyers). The two versions list all the same individual models and sets but differ in the prices they list: one offers the adult decorators at a net price of $2.50 each and the foals at net $1.50; the other offers the adults at net $2.25 and the foals at net $1.35. Intriguingly, an original of the list with the lower prices in the archives of Reeves International has the term "Disc"—undoubtedly for "discontinued"—jotted by hand in ink beside the listing for the Wedgewood Blue Mustang, which is circled in ink. So apparently he was the first to go. The rest of the models went the way of the Wedgewood Mustang by the end of 1964, to judge from the lack of any 1965 Breyer publication mentioning the decorators.

What quantities of decorator models were produced? We will probably never know. As mentioned, we don't even know if the Ward's batches were the only batches made. But the fact that decorators turned up in various stores in diverse areas of the country indicates that Breyer issued more than a handful of them. And the Supplemental Price List certainly does not suggest that supplies were limited. To the contrary, both versions of the list offer the models only in lots called standard packages ("Std. Pkg."): packages of 12 pieces for each of the decorator foals and packages of 6 pieces for each of the adult decorators. That is, you could order a package of 12 Copenhagen foals, a package of 12 Florentine foals, a package of 6 Wedgewood Five-Gaiters, and so on. Breyer must have had quite a few decorators to unload, or could even have still been producing them in the early months of 1964. Considering that in addition to Ward's, two of the stores known to have carried decorators were chain stores, Sav-On and Ben Franklin, we can reasonably speculate that at least a few hundred pieces of each decorator model were made.

Decorators (post-1960s) — Most of the post-1960 decorator models have been issued as special runs in the 1990s. A couple of them introduce decorator colors that did not exist in the 1960s, and several models that do hark back to the old colors nonetheless differ from the 1960s horses in having manes and tails that match the body color. Such liberties initially provoked much grumbling on the part of collectors to the effect that these upstart models were not "real decorators," but by now the new generation of strangely colored horses has come to be admired in its own right.

See "Hyksos" The Egyptian Arabian #832, ageless bronze (1991); "Legionario" SR, Florentine decorator (1991); "Man O' War" SR, Golden Charm decorator (1991); "Misty" SR, Florentine decorator (1990); Proud Arabian Mare SR, "silver filigree" decorator (1993); "San Domingo" SR, Copenhagen decorator (1991); "Secretariat" SR, Golden Charm decorator (1990); and "Sham" SR, Wedgewood Blue decorator (1991). Also see Elephant SR, metallic gold, in the Wildlife section.

Derby Winner — see under Race Horse

"Diablo" — see under Mustang

"Dickory" — see under Family Arabian Mare

Display boxes — Reeves International, having purchased Breyer Animal Creations in late 1984, introduced the now-ubiquitous Breyer display box with yellow backing and clear plastic front in 1986. Prior to this, the Breyer Molding Company had made three different attempts to promote Traditional-scale models in display packaging—that is, packaging that allows the customer in the shop to see the model itself without opening the box, galloping the horse across the floor with chocolate-smeared fingers, and leaving a mess of dog-eared cardboard and shopworn merchandise on the retailer's shelves. None of the three attempts met with great success, to judge from their brief duration. Breyer issued the first round of display packaging in the period 1968-70 (the "touchability" box), the second in 1970-72 (the Showcase Collection box), and the third in the late 1970s (the blister-wrapped box). Here I will discuss the boxes from the first and third periods; for the middle period, see Showcase Collection below in the Traditionals section.

In 1968, Breyer introduced cardboard display boxes for a very limited selection of Traditional models—specifically, the Family Arabian Stallion, Mare, and Foal in palomino, white, bay, appaloosa, and charcoal. Collector Sheryl Leisure found one of these old boxes at an antique store. It is open-fronted, with the four sides flaring gently outward, as on a square deep-dish pie tin. The box is sturdily made of corrugated cardboard coated with white ink and printed with Breyer cartouche and blue-ribbon logos and a few simple designs—teardrops and scalloped and straight lines—all in blue and dark brown. No date is printed on the box, but a message appears on the back side: "In the creation of these items we bring you truly realistic reproductions of popular animals. Desirable as gifts, toys and art objects, these items are produced of break-resistant molded Tenite and are designed to withstand even the rough handling of children. Breyer Molding Company / Chicago, Illinois." The earliest source known to me that mentions this new display packaging is the 1968 Breyer catalog, which advertises it via a footnote on the page with the above-mentioned 15 Family Arabs: "*These items available in either individual Self-Mailing Corrugated Cartons or individual display Cartons." A Breyer company price list dated November 18, 1968, notifying retailers of price increases for 1969, also mentions the new packaging for those 15 models: "Prices on items in our new DISPLAY carton will be as follows." Neither of these 1968 sources shows the boxes, but a special Breyer price list dated January 1969 features a photo of two stacks of them, with a mightily pleased toddler seated in between. In the photo, the models are set into the middle of the boxes, where they are held by two slender elastic bands—one around the belly and one around the inside hind leg. Amazingly, there appears to be no plastic wrap on the boxes at all—the models seem to be held in only by the elastic bands. The text on the price list alludes to this precarious arrangement as well: "These best selling items are individually packaged in an original display carton incorporating the advantages of visual display while maintaining the unique aspect of touchability inherent in the quality of a Breyer Animal Creation." Evidently the idea was to encourage prospective customers to reach right in and finger the models. Sheryl's box likewise has two elastic bands and nary a shred of plastic wrap, but of course it could have lost whatever wrap it might have had to start with. Oddly, Sheryl's box contains a smoke Western Prancer rather than a Family Arabian, but we believe a previous owner must have switched the models, for as mentioned above, the 1968 catalog and the 1968-69 price lists all indicate that only Family Arabs came in these boxes. The two price lists also give the display-carton horses special model numbers, consisting of the regular model number followed by "SP" (probably meaning "Special" or "Special Packaging"). For example, the charcoal Family Arab Stallion, whose regular number is #201, becomes #201SP as sold in the display carton. Sheryl's box is stamped with the number 4SP, indicating a palomino FAS. The last mention of these display boxes to my knowledge occurs in the 1970 catalog, which has the same footnote as the 1968 catalog, on the page with the same 15 Family Arabs. However, I doubt that the boxes were issued throughout 1970, for in that year Breyer introduced its second generation of display packaging, the clear plastic carrying-case boxes of the Showcase Collection. The Showcase boxes emphatically eliminated "the unique aspect of touchability," initiating a "look but don't touch" concept that the third generation of display packaging would perpetuate with a vengeance.

For a period in the late 1970s, a number of different regular-run Traditional models were sold in open-fronted non-corrugated cardboard display boxes into which the models were tightly swaddled with industrial-strength plastic blister-wrap. The wrap is "blistered" over the horse and bonded smoothly to the surrounding cardboard backing. The boxes are printed with rainbows stripes of dark brown, light brown, and mustard against a background of pale tan.Sheryl Leisure found a mahogany bay Proud Arab Foal and a bay Shetland Pony in blister-wrapped boxes; collector Karen Grimm has a bay Running Foal in the same packaging; and collector Kim Lory Jones got three models new in these boxes from Toys R Us: Overo Paints of two pattern versions, which she bought in 1979 (the year this model debuted), and a "Legionario III," which she got at about the same time. The only Breyer company documentation I know of for this packaging is a chrome (photographic color transparency) unearthed from Breyer's archives by *JAH* editor Stephanie Macejko. The chrome, reprinted in black and white in *JAH 22/#6* Nov./Dec. 1995 (p. 11), shows a dozen different regular-run models in the blister packaging: palomino Family Arabian Foal, Mare, and Stallion; Black Foundation Stallion; bay blanket appaloosa Indian Pony; mahogany bay Proud Arabian Foal and Mare; bay Running Foal and Mare; bay Shetland Pony; black blanket appaloosa Stock Horse Foal ("Phantom Wings" mold); and "Stormy." Of the blister-box collector's specimens known to me, Kim's Overo Paints and "Legionario" are the only ones not represented in the chrome. How many other models Breyer sold in this packaging I do not know. In any case, the models that were blister-boxed were given special model numbers, consisting of the number 1 prefixed to the model's regular number. So, for example, the palomino Family Arabian Foal, whose regular model number would be #6, is #16 according to the label on the display box shown in the chrome; the black blanket appy Stock Foal, normally #18, has #118 on its display box; and Sheryl's mahogany PAF, normally #219, has #1219 on its box, as is also visible on the PAF's box in the chrome. A warning label mounted just under the belly of Sheryl's foal suggests why the packaging was short-lived: "Important: To avoid any possibility of damage upon removal, please see reverse side for simple instructions." If the instructions for removal are simple, removal itself is not, to judge from the fourth and last instruction: "Carefully remove remaining film from horse's legs and tail. Do not roll film down the legs. Remove small pieces rather than attempt to separate the film in one motion." A letter Sheryl received in August 1986 from former Breyer employee Jill Göllner confirms one's worst suspicions: "The blister packaging of the traditionals was discontinued because of breakage to the models when the packaging was opened." The letter also says, "Our blister packaging of traditionals was done in the early '70s—immediately after the 'Showcase' series." Since the Showcase Collection was discontinued at the end of 1972, this would date the blister-wrap packaging to about 1973 or 1974. I have found no dated Breyer price lists for this packaging, nor is it mentioned or shown in catalogs, manuals, or regular price lists of the 1970s or 1980s. But a pre-1975 dating is too early in view of Sheryl's and Kim's boxes, all of which are printed with "© copyright 1978 Breyer Molding Company Chicago, Illinois." Further, the Black Foundation Stallion and black blanket Stock Horse Foal models, both of which are shown in the blister-wrapped boxes in the chrome, did not even exist until 1977 and 1978, respectively; "Legionario III didn't debut until late 1978, and Overo Paint not until 1979. So if the blister-wrapped boxes persisted only for a very few years, those years must have been in the late 1970s and possibly into the very early 1980s.

Display units — These sales-promotional items, offered by Breyer in 1985-88, were made for dealers to display in their shops. Collector Lorraine Mavrogeorge, of Massachusetts, who brought these units to my attention, owns two of them and has seen one other. All three units consist of a solid wood rectangular base, approximately 16" x 38", with various catalog-run Breyer horses screwed onto it and a simulated wood "Breyer Animal Creations" sign pinned onto one front corner. A green felt or fabric surface covers all but the outer inch or so of the wooden base. According to former Breyer executive Peter Stone, the first 50 display units were made for Breyer/Reeves by the Riegseckers of Indiana (see Riegseckers Models for discussion), but Reeves did not care for these pieces and subsequently had units made elsewhere. The Riegseckers units have clear plastic covers, but the subsequent units do not have covers, according to Stone (conversation of Dec. 1995).

One of Lorraine's units has 11 regular-run horses: Action American Buckskin Stock Horse Foal #225, "Cips" #116, dapple gray American Saddlebred #109, "Lady Roxana" #425, sorrel/palomino American Mustang #118, "Secretariat" #435, "Sham" (wheat-ear version) #410, "Sherman Morgan" #430, and the Shetland (with no halter) and foals of "Our First Pony" set #3066 (the Classic Arabian Foal is the bay pinto version). The unit includes no dolls or tack. The "Breyer Animal Creations" sign is a dark mahogany color. The green covering on the base is fuzzy felt. Lorraine's unit came with no cover, but the base has a channel around the perimeter where a cover would fit. Lorraine found the unit in its original box (complete with "Reeves" sealing tape), which has the number 198700 printed on it.

Lorraine's second unit has 10 regular-run Traditional horses, 2 of them ridden by Breyer dolls. The horses are gray blanket Action American Appaloosa Stock Horse Foal #238, Black Stallion #401, chestnut Clydesdale Foal #84, bay Clydesdale Stallion #80 with unstenciled bald face and red and white bobs, "Legionario III" #68, "Man O' War" #47, "Misty" #20, "Sham" (wheat-ear version) #410, black blanket Appaloosa Stock Horse Mare #233, and "Stormy" #19. The Black Stallion is ridden by a Ben Breyer #550 doll (in blue checked shirt), and "Legionario" by a long-haired Brenda Breyer #500; the dolls have their legs tied together under their horses' bellies with string. The "Breyer Animal Creations" sign is a dark mahogany color. The green covering on the base looks like a tight-knit, soft burlap. This unit has a clear hard-plastic cover, which fits into a channel around the perimeter of the base. A covered display unit with these same horses and dolls, though apparently with a narrower base, is shown in a 1980s promotional photo reprinted in *JAH* 22/#6 Nov./ Dec. 1995 (p. 11).

The third unit Lorraine has seen, in a Massachusetts toy store, has most of the same models as the 10-horse, 2-doll unit just described, but the Action Appy Foal, "Sham," and Brenda have been removed (the holes in the base where the models were mounted are visible) and the Clydesdale Stallion is a not a #80 but a #824 with gold and white mane bobs. Undoubtedly the unit originally came with a #80, which was removed by the store owners and replaced with the more recent stallion. The "Breyer Animal Creations" sign on this unit is a lighter "wood" color than the other units' signs. The green covering on the base is fabric with a ribbed texture. This unit too has a clear hard-plastic cover.

No display units are mentioned in Breyer dealer catalogs, but several turn up on Breyer price lists. The 1985 price list, the first to offer a display unit, includes "198500 Display Unit Only w/Orders of $500.00 or more," for $50.00, and "198555 Dealer Asst. w/ Display," for $564.90. The 1986 price list includes only "198655 Dealer Assortment with Display," for $611.59 (this is $53.35 more than the "198650 Dealer Assortment" with no display, for $558.24); there is no display-unit-only option. The 1987 price list includes "198700 Display unit w/order $500.00 or more" (this is the first of Lorraine's units described above), for $75; "198701 Display Unit," for $150; and "198755 Dealer Assortment w/Display," for $686.34. I would suppose that the units in these three 1987 listings are all the same but priced differently as a sales incentive. The 1988 price list, the last price list to offer any display units, includes "198800 Display unit w/order $500.00 or more," for $75.00, and "198801 Display Unit," for $150.00. Here again, the two units are probably the same but priced differently as a sales incentive. Lorraine does not know the number of her second unit and the other she has seen, but they are probably from 1985 or 1986, for the Ben and Brenda dolls on them were discontinued at the end of 1986.

"Doc" — see under Family Arabian Foal

"Domino" Gift Set SR — see under "Roemer"

"Domino" The Happy Canyon Trail Horse — see under "San Domingo"

"Donovan" Running Appaloosa Stallion — see under "Black Beauty" (stallion, cross-galloping)

"Double Take" Morgan — see under "Justin Morgan"

Dressage Horse SR — see under Hanoverian

Drafter Foal — see "Satin Star" Drafter Foal (under Clydesdale Foal)

Drafters Set SR — see Belgian SR, alabaster; "Roy" SR, liver chestnut; and Shire SR, palomino with stripe

"Dream Weaver" — see under "Black Beauty" (stallion, cross-galloping)

Dressage Set Of 2 Horses SR — see Hanoverian SR, dark bay; and "Misty's Twilight" SR, black

Drewry's Beer promotional Mountie set — see Canadian Mountie #P440 (in the Riders - Hard Plastic section)

"Dr. Peaches" SR — see under "Phar Lap"

"Dustin" SR — see under "Phar Lap"

Dutch Warmblood — see "Domino" Gift Set SR, "Roemer," and "Vandergelder" (all under "Roemer")

"El Campeador" SR — see under "Legionario"

"El Morzillo" — see Black Foundation Stallion (under Foundation Stallion)

"El Pastor" — ♞ Stallion, in the paso fino ("fine gait"). Sculpted by Chris Hess. Mold in catalog-run production 1974-81, 1987, 1992 - current as of 1996.

Catalog-run models made from this mold:

♞ "El Pastor" Famous Paso Fino #61, bay; most with star, some with solid face; black points; most with left front and left hind socks; dark gray hooves; matte and semigloss (1974-81). The body color varies from brown to red bay. Some models have white right coronary bands in addition to the left socks. On some models the stockings are so vague as to disappear. Collector Kate Morgan sent me a photo of her "El Pastor" with 4 stockings. Some models have a light area on the tip of the nose. The star comes in at least two versions: a slightly elongated diamond, which is the smaller version, and a diamond with a thick wiggly tail (looks a bit like a fancy dagger), which is larger. Catalog photos are too fuzzy and obscure to show which version came first. The solid-faced "El Pastor" is the earliest issue of #61—collector Gale Good got her solid-faced #61 in March 1974, and this version is shown in the 1974-75 catalogs (it's the same photo in both catalogs). However, I believe the solid face was produced only in the first part of 1974, for collector Andrea Morden-Moore got her star-faced horse in 1974, and a star-faced #61 appears in a group photo at the back of the 1975 catalog. The solid-faced #61 is generally more shaded than the SR "El Pastor" with solid face, which has very little or no shading; but the surest difference between them is that the #61 has a full "U.S.A." stamp, whereas the SR has a periods-only stamp (see note 3 for this mold). The real "El Pastor," whose name means "The Shepherd" in Spanish, was born in Colombia in 1963 and was later brought to the U.S., where he won the highest awards for his breed and was named National Horse of the Year in 1972 (*JAH* July/ Aug./Sept. 1976; 19/#3 Summer II 1992, pp. 32-33). A photo of him with owner Robin Ratliff printed in the 1976 *JAH* shows the horse to have a star and left front and left hind stockings. For discussion of another interesting photo of the real horse, see note 1 for this mold.

♞ "Precipitado Sin Par" ("Cips") Champion Paso Fino, Son Of "El Pastor," #116, bay pinto, tobiano; tri-color eyes; pink in nostrils; black mane with white stripe; black tail; hand-painted pink hooves; matte; Limited Edition (1987). "Cips" is Breyer's first Limited Edition model. His box sports a large round red sticker saying, in full: "1987 Limited Edition / Paso Fino / features special color and detailed eyes, nose and hooves." Limited Edition models are produced only for one year, in quantities sufficient to fill all orders for the model. Collector Jenny Hummel owns a "Cips" model very similar to the one, which is probably a test piece, in the 1987 catalog. The white areas of both horses have extremely crisp, zigzag edges (I saw Jenny's horse at BreyerFest 1994). Jenny got her model new in box from a retail outlet. According to the 1987 catalog, the real "Cips" won the Paso Fino Horse of the Year title for two consecutive years, and stands at stud in Florida. The name "Precipitado Sin Par" means "Hasty Without Equal," as best as I can tell from a word-by-word rendering in my Spanish-English dictionary.

♞ "Tesoro" #867, palomino, blaze ending in pink snip, gray shading on sides of face, 4 stockings, gray hooves, matte (1992-95). Called simply "Tesoro" in the 1992 catalog but "Tesoro" Paso Fino in the 1993-95 catalogs. "Tesoro" is Spanish for "treasure" (*Cassell's Spanish Dictionary*).

♞ "Tobe" Rocky Mountain Horse #914, dappled liver chestnut, star and snip, mane and tail medium chestnut that fades to flaxen ends, 4 stockings, tan hooves with charcoal stripes, matte (1995 - current as of 1996). The dapples are subtle, being only a shade lighter than the basic liver color. This model represents the real horse "Tobe," the chief foundation stallion of the Rocky Mountain Horse breed. These horses travel with a natural ambling gait and are characteristically dark chestnut with light mane and tail. (Information is per *JAH* 22/#2 Mar./Apr. 1995, pp. 14-15.) On August 18-20, 1995, the Q2 home-shopping cable TV channel offered a total of 96 "Tobe" models that were ordinary regular runs but that came in boxes labeled with the special-run model number 707895 (per *JAH* editor Stephanie Macejko). Leftover models may have been sold on subsequent Q2 programs.

Special-run models made from this mold:

♘ "El Pastor" SR #410116, bay, solid face, black points, left fore and left hind socks, black hooves, matte (1987). Made for Henrietta Ratliff Farms, owners of the real "El Pastor." 100 models made. Information per *JAH* 19/#3 Summer II 1992 (p. 33) and a Breyer company computer printout of activity 1985-92. Horse Emporium mail-order company sold what I assume were leftovers of this run in 1988 (per *Model Rag*, Aug. 1988: "Horse Emporium in Florida has a light bay El Pastor, no star and socks on the left side.") The SR tends to be a creamier brown than the solid-faced #61, and has virtually no shading. The mold stamps on the SR and the solid-faced #61 also differ. The three SR models that I've inspected, two of them known to have been purchased directly from Ratliff Farms and one from Horse Emporium, have a periods-only "U.S.A" stamp. Solid-faced #61s on the other hand have a full "U.S.A." stamp.

Notes:

(1) The "El Pastor" mold was one of many that Chris Hess sculpted from photographs of real horses, according to Breyer executive Peter Stone (conversation of Nov. 1994). Stone did not mention which photo of "El Pastor," but the mold strikingly resembles a photo of "El Pastor" printed in *Western Horseman*, October 1969 (p. 414; thanks to Liz Strauss for a copy of this page).

(2) The paso fino is a 4-beat gait natural to the Paso Fino breed, which also performs two other gaits. See *JAH* 19/#3 Summer II 1992 (p. 31).

(3) Models of the "El Pastor" mold have various assortments of mold stamps. In what I believe is chronological order, the assortments are as follows: [A] The early models of the mold have the round "Breyer Molding Co." stamp and a "U.S.A." stamp. Evidently the very

earliest of these early models are the solid-faced "El Pastor" #61s, for the model shown in the 1974-75 catalogs is the solid-faced version. My own and Gale Good's solid-faced #61s do have this stamp grouping. [B] The next models have the round stamp and, nearby on the same leg, a stamp that says "Hecho en Mexico" ("Made in Mexico"), according to former Breyer executive Peter Stone (conversations of Dec. 1995 and Jan. 1996). During a very brief period in the late 1970s, as he recalls, about 2,000 "El Pastors" were molded in Mexico and given this stamp. (*JAH* X/#1 1982, p. 9, gives the quantity as about 3,000 and identifies the stamp incorrectly as "Mexico.") But so far as Stone can recollect, Breyer abandoned the models in Mexico (for reasons discussed in the Mold Stamps section in the Appendix below in this book)—which would explain why none seem to exist in collections in the U.S. If any still exist at all, these models, which according to Stone were unpainted, in all likelihood also have what I call the periods-only "U.S.A." stamp, in which only the punctuation is visible, thus: ". . ." The periods-only stamp, located just above the round stamp and still present on the mold today, must have been created inadvertently when the "U.S.A." was removed from the mold in preparation for production in Mexico—somehow the periods survived the removal. [C] After the Mexico period, production of this mold returned to the U.S. and the "Hecho en Mexico" was removed, but the full "U.S.A." was not restored because the company had completely stopped adding the "U.S.A." to molds after 1975. Thus the next "El Pastors" have just the round stamp and the periods-only stamp. Collector Sande Schneider has a star-faced "El Pastor" with this stamp grouping, and I have seen others. [D] Next are models with the round stamp, the periods-only stamp, and the "B." I have a star-faced #61 like this and have seen others. The "B" stamp dates these models to about 1980-81 (1981 being the last year of #61). [E] Finally, the most recent models of the mold, including "Cips" and the SR solid-faced bay "El Pastor" (both issued in 1987), have just the round stamp and periods-only stamp, no "B." This stamp grouping is identical to that on version C "El Pastors," except that on the version D horses a couple of the periods are often blurred.

English Horse Collector Set SR — see Black Stallion SR, light coffee bay; Indian Pony SR, red dun; and "Justin Morgan" SR, red chestnut

Equitana '93 SR — see "Prairie Flower" Equitana '93 SR (under "Lady Phase")

Evolution Of The Horse series in fine porcelain — This series, Breyer's first venture into fine porcelain figurines, comprises three Traditional-scale horses by sculptor Kathleen Moody: Icelandic Horse (released 1992), Shire Horse (released 1993), and Spanish Barb (released 1994). The series celebrates "breeds which are not necessarily the oldest in the world, but are thought to be the best representation of the three horse types which existed pre-domestication" (*JAH* 20/#1 Spring 1993, p. 17). All of Breyer's fine-porcelain horses are manufactured for Breyer by a Taiwanese firm called Everstream, which is the same firm that makes fine-porcelain pieces for Franklin Mint (per Breyer executive Peter Stone, conversation of July 1995).

Evolution Of The Horse set SR — see Breyer Traditional Horse Set SR for a full cross-listing

Export specials — In the Traditionals section see "Burmese" Her Majesty The Queen's Horse SR (1990-91; under "Secretariat"); Vaulting Horse SR (1990-91; under Hanoverian); "Prairie Flower" Equitana '93 SR (1993; under "Lady Phase"); "Chinook" SR (1994; under Indian Pony); and "Favory" SR (1995; under "Pluto"); also see discussion in the entry for "Black Beauty" SR bay (1984). In the Classics section below see Arabian Family Foal, Mare, and Stallion, all SR dapple gray (1987 and 1988); Brown Pinto Mare SR (1989; under Quarter Horse Family Mare); Quarter Horse Family Stallion SR #703145, black blanket appaloosa (large blanket; 1989); "Ahlerich" SR (1989 and 1990; under "Keen"); "Hatatitla" SR (1989 and 1990; under "Ginger"); "Iltschi" SR (1989 and 1990; under "Black Beauty"); "Orchidee" SR (1989 and 1990; under "Might Tango"); "Rembrandt" SR (1989 and 1990; under "Jet Run"); and Lipizzaner SR #620, alabaster (1992).

Export SRs are made by Breyer for companies located overseas, typically in England and Germany. Although Breyer has been exporting regular-run models since about 1970, to my knowledge the first export special run was issued in 1988—the dapple gray Classic Arabian Family, made for a company in England. In some cases, export specials have been sold through U.S. model mail-order companies as well as the overseas companies for which the specials were made, but in other cases the models have been available only through the overseas companies, such as Modell-Pferde Versand in Germany, owned by Ingrid Muensterer.

"Fade To Gray" — see under "Black Beauty" (stallion, cross-galloping)

"Faith" — see Family Arabian Stallion

Family Appaloosa Foal — see under Stock Horse Foal, standing

Family Appaloosa Foal "Spot" — see under Family Arabian Foal

Family Appaloosa Mare — see under "Lady Phase"

Family Appaloosa Mare "Speck" — see under Family Arabian Mare

Family Appaloosa Stallion — see under "Stud Spider"

Family Appaloosa Stallion "Fleck" — see under Family Arabian Stallion

Family Arabian Foal (FAF) — Filly, standing, left front leg forward. Sculpted by Chris Hess. Mold in catalog-run production 1960-94.

Catalog-run models made from this mold:

- Ara-Appaloosa Foal #874, "bay" leopard appaloosa, white foal with brown splashed-on spots, charcoal or gray points and hooves, matte (1993-94). Some models have a light area near the tip of the tail.
- Family Appaloosa Foal "Spot" #39, gray blanket appaloosa, bald face, black mane and tail, unstenciled blanket, black splashed-on spots, dark gray or charcoal legs, black hooves, early ones glossy, later ones matte (1960-70). The bald face on #39 can be extensive, reaching well down the sides of the face. All the catalogs that list this model are careful not to call her an Arabian, listing her simply as Appaloosa Foal "Spot" under the general heading "Families." Price lists after 1964, however, do get sloppy and list her under the general heading "Arabian" with all the other FAF colors. Regarding gloss finish see note 2 for this mold. For discussion of the "belly striped" and other versions of the appy Family Arabs, see Family Appaloosa Mare "Speck" #38 (under Family Arabian Mare). To my knowledge the appy Family Arabs were never sold in sets, as were the other early "realistic" colors. In 1968-70 "Spot" was available as #39SP in a special cardboard display box; see Display Boxes above in this section for discussion. The model number 39 previously belonged to Arabian Foal "Spot," gray blanket appaloosa (Proud Arabian Foal mold).
- Family Arabian Foal #708, chestnut, bald face, flaxen mane and tail, charcoal-shaded knees and hocks, 4 stockings, light tan hooves, matte (1988). The chestnut color is a medium/dark coffee-with-cream shade, with no red tone.
- Family Arabian Foal #816, bay, solid face, gray-shaded muzzle and eyes, black points, 2 hind stockings, 4 gray or black hooves, matte (1989-90). The body color varies from medium/light rose bay (as shown in catalogs) to a sandy bay that is nearly buckskin. Collector Emily Atkinson's nearly buckskin foal has a gray dorsal band and gray shading on the belly and chest. Emily's foal also has 4 gray hooves and a faint gray dorsal stripe, as shown in the 1989 catalog. The foal in the 1990 catalog has black hooves and no dorsal band.
- Family Arabian Foal #841, red chestnut; no white markings; slightly darker chestnut mane, tail, and hooves; matte (1991-93). Unlike most other Family Arab Foal, #841 was not issued with a matching Family Arab Mare and Stallion. Perhaps the she was intended to go with the red chestnut Proud Arabian Mare #840—their sequential model numbers and their juxtaposition in the 1991-92 catalogs suggests so—but oddly, the mare was discontinued a year before the foal.
- Family Arabian Foal #909, woodgrain, black eyes, no white markings or other color detailing, matte (1960-66).
- Family Arabian Foal "Charity" #6, palomino, bald face, white or light palomino mane and tail, 4 stockings, gray hooves, early ones glossy, later ones matte (1961/62 - 1987). This model was also sold 1961/62 - 1964 in sets #456 and #506; see under Family Arabian Mare. The name "Charity" was dropped from catalogs after 1970/71. The model was called Arabian Foal in 1972-76, Family Foal in 1977-86, Palomino Family Foal in 1987. The glossy models are often a light honey color with light honey mane and tail, but some do have stenciled white mane and tail (collectors Gale Good, Lynn Isenbarger, and Laurie Croddy have such foals) and vary to a dark tan palomino body color (I've seen a glossy white-point foal like this) like this). The later, matte models range from dark tan palomino to a bright orangy shade, and have stenciled white mane and tail. For the dates of gloss finish see note 2 for this mold. On the glossies and some mattes the bald face can be extensive, reaching well down the sides of the face. "Charity" is in the 1963 catalog but not the 1960. I date her release to 1961/62 on the basis of Gale's model, which she received new in July 1962, and on the basis of ads for the palomino FAF in the May 1962 *American Girl* magazine and the 1962 Ward's holiday catalog. In 1968-70 "Charity" was available as #6SP in a special cardboard display box, and for a brief period in the late 1970s she was sold as #16 in another type of display box, one with blister wrap, labeled "No. 16 Palomino Family Foal" (see Display Boxes above in this section for discussion). The number 16 had previously belonged to sets of bay Proud Arabians and Family Arabians, and later was assigned to Marguerite Henry's "Sea Star."
- Family Arabian Foal "Doc" #203, charcoal, bald face, white points, pink hooves, early ones glossy, later ones matte (1961/62 - 1973). This same model was also sold 1961/62 - 1964 in sets #223 and #213; see under Family Arabian Mare. The name "Doc" was dropped from the 1972-73 catalogs, where the model is called simply Arabian Foal. Catalogs describe this model as "charcoal," but her color varies from black to deep brown. The bald face can be extensive, reaching well down the sides of the face. The hooves vary from extremely pale pink (virtually white) to bright pinky peach, and can be touched with gray overspray. A true gray-hoofed variation may also exist; see the entry for Family Arabian Stallion "Hickory." "Doc" is in the 1963 catalog but not the 1960. I date her release to 1961/62 on the basis of collector Gale Good's "Doc," which she received new in December 1962. In 1968-70 "Doc" was available as #203SP in a special cardboard display box; see Display Boxes above in this section for discussion. Regarding gloss finish see note 2 for this mold.
- Family Arabian Foal "Joy" #9, alabaster; gray mane and tail; gray, pink, or white nose and inner ears; gray hooves; early ones glossy, later ones matte (1960-73). This same model was also sold 1960-64 in sets #10 and #11; see under Family Arabian Mare. The name "Joy" was dropped from the 1972-73 catalogs, where the model is called simply Arabian Foal. On collector Sheryl Leisure's pink-nosed glossy foal, the whole muzzle is pink, but on my own glossy foal, only the area between the nostrils is pink. In 1968-70 "Joy" was available as #9SP in a special cardboard display box; see Display Boxes above in this section for discussion. Regarding gloss finish see note 2 for this mold. See Family Arabian Foal SR alabaster for differences between the SR and regular run glossies. The model number 9 previously belonged to Arabian Foal "Joy," alabaster (Proud Arabian Foal mold).
- Family Arabian Foal "Shah" #15, bay, long stripe the widens over the nose, black mane and tail, no black on the legs, 4 stockings, black hooves, early ones glossy, later ones matte (1960-73). This same model was also sold 1960-64 in sets #18 and #16; see under Family Arabian Mare. The name "Shah" was dropped from the 1972-73 catalogs, where the model is called simply Arabian Foal. The body color varies from light caramel bay to reddish bay to dark chocolate bay. Regarding gloss finish see note 2 for this mold. In 1968-70 "Shah" was available as #15SP in a special cardboard display box; see Display Boxes above in this section for discussion. The model number 15 previously belonged to Arabian Foal "Shah," bay (Proud Arabian Foal mold) and in the late 1970s was assigned to the palomino Family Arabian Mare in a special blister-wrapped display box.

Sets: see under Family Arabian Mare.

Special-run models made from this mold:

- Family Arabian Foal SR, alabaster, gray mane and tail, pink nose and inner ears, gray hooves, glossy (1988). Made for Enchanted Doll House. Sold in SR set #400789 with glossy alabaster FAM and FAS. Probably about 1,000 sets made, per Breyer executive Peter Stone (conversation of Oct. 3, 1995), who also explained to me that although the sets were made for Enchanted Doll House, this company wouldn't buy them all, so Breyer sold many sets to other dealers. *Dated and undated models*: The sets from Enchanted Doll House came with the date "88" handwritten in black ink on the bellies (per *JAH* 15/#3 July/Aug. 1988, inside front cover). Some horses sold through other companies are also dated: a 1991 brochure from Horse Emporium lists "Glossy Alabaster Arab Family 1988 on belly $60.00," and a 1991 Small World newsletter says "Family Arab Stallion and Foal in high glossy alabaster (white). Revival of older type finishing technique, hand dated '1989' [*sic*; this must be a typo for '1988'] on underside so not confused with older models. We have approximately 100 sets in stock (Sorry no mares available)." But many of the leftover models sold through other companies have no writing on the bellies—I have a stallion and foal like this from Bentley Sales, and I know of other collectors who got undated models from mail-order companies. The parenthesis in the Small World listing— "(Sorry no mares available)" —brings up another odd aspect of the leftover models: there seem to be fewer mares than stallions and foals. Apparently Bentleys and Small World never had mares but only stallions and foals (Bentleys carried these two as early as April 1990). However, Leonard Huffman (formerly of Model Horse Collector's Supply) did list all three horses on his 1991 price lists, and Horse Emporium sold whole families too, according to their 1991 brochure quoted above. *SR versus regular-run models*: The SR set was made to celebrate the 25th anniversary of Enchanted Doll House (per *JAH*) and commemorated the old regular-run glossy alabaster Family Arabians—"Prince," "Pride," and "Joy." But in addition to commemorating the oldies, the SRs also cause confusion about which is which, for the SRs that lack the "88" on the belly can be mistaken for the pink-nosed version of the old regular runs. Fortunately, there is a clear way to distinguish the undated SR stallions and mares from the oldies: the SRs have a "U.S.A." stamp whereas the old horses do not. Unfortunately, the foal mold was never given the "U.S.A.," so the SR foals are indistinguishable from most regular-run foals on this basis. The only foals whose mold stamps clearly identify them as regular runs are the early foals with the round stamp on the belly, or with the fragmentary "Hess" engraving inside the right hind leg, or with only an ejection-pin circle inside the right hind (see note 3 for this mold). The number for this SR set is per a Breyer company computer printout of activity 1985-92.

- Family Arabian Foal SR #12, black, no white markings, black mane and tail, black hooves, matte (1977). Made in 1977 for retail shops and sold by Bentley Sales at the Model Horse Congress in Chicago in August 1978. Sold separately or in set with SR black Family Arabian Mare #11 and SR black Family Arabian Stallion #10. Precise quantity unknown, but at least several hundred sets were made. See Family Arabian Mare SR #11, black, for discussion.
- Family Arabian Foal SR, chestnut pinto, tobiano; head mostly white; slightly darker chestnut mane and tail; gray hooves; matte; mounted on wood base with the Ford "Pinto" logo in raised silver letters (1970/71). Made for Ford Motor Company to use as sales awards for Pinto car dealers. Quantity unknown. This foal's pinto color and pattern are identical to #175 chestnut pinto Indian Pony's. I first learned about this SR at BreyerFest 1995 from collector Kathleen Rose, who had on display a 3-piece set of horses—the Family Arabian Stallion, Mare, and Foal—all painted in the same chestnut pinto color and pattern as the #175 Indian Pony with no warpaint. The horses were free-standing, not mounted on bases. Kathleen's sister, Karen Perkins, had gotten the set from long-time collector and Breyer consultant Marney Walerius, who told her that this set and one other identical set had been made for Ford when their Pinto car was introduced. (These two sets are also mentioned in Gutierrez 1985 and 1989.) Also made at that time, Marney told her, was a larger batch of the foals only, mounted on wood bases with the "Pinto" logo. Subsequently I learned that collector Lynn Hiersche had found one of the base-mounted foals at a flea market in Portland, Oregon, in spring 1995. (Two other specimens have come to my attention as well: a base-mounted foal like Lynn's, found by collector Annette Chandler, and a "Breyer FAF in OF brown pinto" mentioned in the Sept./Oct. 1986 *Model horse Gazette*, p. 54.) The logo consists of a leaping foal and the word "Pinto," all made of silver metal. According to Lynn, the base itself is walnut with beveled edges and has no sticker or inscription on the bottom. The foal is screwed onto the base through the left front and right rear hooves. I do not know whether Breyer or the Ford company had the foals mounted on the bases, but it is interesting to note that 1971 was also the first year for Breyer's Presentation Collection of models on walnut bases. The Presentation bases, however, do not have beveled edges. The Ford Pinto car debuted in September 1970 (per Motor Vehicle Manufacturers Association 1974, sec. "1970"), but the SR foals may not have been issued immediately, possibly not until 1971. The dating of this SR to 1970/71 is also consistent with the fact that the FAS and FAM in Kathleen's set both have the "U.S.A." stamp, which was introduced by Breyer in 1970. (The FAF was never given this stamp.) Breyer executive Peter Stone had no recollection of these horses when I asked him about them in October 1995.
- Family Arabian Foal SR, dapple gray, dapples on neck and head; pale gray face; black points; black hooves; matte (1991). Sears holiday catalog. Sold in Spirit Of The Wind Set SR #498991, with dapple gray FAM. 4,000 sets made, per a Breyer company computer printout of activity 1985-92. The number for this set is per the printout and a Bentley Sales price list dated March 15, 1993. The Sears catalog shows the foal as slightly darker gray than the mare, and my own set is like this, but Sande Schneider's foal is slightly lighter than her mare.
- Family Arabian Foal SR, dark chestnut, long stripe that widens over nose, darker brown mane and tail, 4 stockings, gray hooves, matte (1982). Penney's holiday catalog. Sold in SR Arabian Family Set With Blue Ribbon, with dark chestnut FAM and light chestnut FAS. For discussion of the ribbon and the two different Penney's chestnut FA sets, see FAF SR light chestnut. Overruns of the dark foal were sold through Bentley Sales Company. She first appears on their November-December 1983 price list, identified as "#6S Dark Chestnut Family Foal." Her number changed to #6S-D (for "dark") on the August 1984 Bentley's list.
- Family Arabian Foal SR, medium chestnut, bald face, dark brown mane and tail, 4 stockings, gray hooves, matte (sometime in the 1960s). Quantity unknown. This foal, with matching FAM and FAS, is shown in Diederich 1988, Section 2. The color details I've given for this foal are based on the foal owned by collector Joy Sheesley. The body color is like that of the older "sorrel" Five-Gaiters, a medium coffee-with-cream shade, with no red tone. See FAM SR medium chestnut for further discussion.
- Family Arabian Foal SR, light chestnut, long stripe that widens over the nose, flaxen mane and tail, 4 stockings, gray hooves, matte (1983). Penney's holiday catalog. Sold in SR Arabian Family Set With Blue Ribbon, with light chestnut FAM and dark chestnut FAS. The blue ribbon, which can fade to purple over the years, is not scaled to the models but is full-sized, like a ribbon awarded at a real horse show. It is identical to the ribbon sold in #3075 Lynn Anderson's "Lady Phase" Gift Set in 1976-81: a rosette with two tails printed in gold, one saying "Breyer" and the other "Champion" (the writing is faintly visible in the 1982-83 Penney's holiday catalogs and was verified by collector Sande Schneider, who got her SR Family Arab set with ribbon from another collector). The rosette's center is printed with a gold horse-head (not a Breyer). There is a lot of confusion about which of the two Penney's FA chestnut sets—the set with light stallion and dark mare and foal, and the set with dark stallion and light mare and foal—came in 1982 and which in 1983. The Penney's catalogs for both years show the same set: dark stallion, light mare and foal. However, *JAH* IX/#2 1982 (p. 12), which shows all the holiday SRs for 1982, shows the set with light stallion and dark mare and foal. An item in the February 1983 *Quequechan Model Horse Collector* explains what happened in 1982: The first sets sold by Penney's had the light stallion and dark mare and foal, as shown in *JAH*. But Penney's received complaints from purchasers because these models differed from those in the 1982 Penney's catalog. So Breyer agreed to produced sets with dark stallion and light mare and foal, as pictured in that Penney's catalog. But it seems these promised sets didn't actually become available until the 1983 holiday season, for subsequent *Quequechan* issues in the spring of 1983 report collectors' failures to secure the new dark stallion/light mare and foal sets from Penney's. The May 1983 issue states: "Oh, as to the chestnut Arabian family, it seems the warehouses must empty before the new ones come through. Hopefully by next year." The dark stallion/light mare and foal sets were finally released, through the 1983 Penney's holiday catalog. Collector Heather Wells has her Penney's receipt, dated August 1984, on which she jotted the following record when she received her horses: "From 1983 Christmas catalog / Dr. Chestnut Family Arabian Stallion / Lt. Chestnut Family Arabian Mare / Lt. Chestnut Family Arabian Foal." Bentley Sales Company sold overruns of the dark mare and foal and light stallion starting in late 1983 and of the dark stallion starting in mid-1984. Old Bentley's sales record cards in my possession show that Bentley's received 240 dark foals, 162 dark mares, 408 light stallions, and at least 80 dark stallions.

Notes:

(1) This mold was introduced when the Proud Arab Foal mold was discontinued because of complaints by Hagen-Renaker Co. For discussion see note 1 for Proud Arabian Mare.

(2) Palomino, charcoal, alabaster, bay, and gray blanket appaloosa Family Arabian Foals were made in glossy finish prior to 1968. The 1968 and 1970 catalogs specify that all colors of Family Arabs are matte only; so evidently 1967 was the last year in which any glossy Family Arabs were made, except for the 1988 alabaster special run. One of the earliest matte alabaster Family Arab sets—purchased in 1968—is pictured in *Quequechan Model Horse Collector* of January 1985.

(3) All Family Arabian Foals have a round "Breyer Molding Co." stamp, but its location and orientation vary on early models, and some models have additional mold marks. *Belly-stamped*: Undoubtedly the first FAFs made in 1960 are those with an odd Breyer stamp: it has no copyright "C" symbol in the center and is located on the belly. Collector Sande Schneider owns a pink-muzzled glossy alabaster with belly stamp and has heard of a woodgrain belly-stamped model. These foals also have a fragmentary "Hess" engraving and round, inward-curving eartips. (These two features were pointed out to me on leg-stamped foals by collector Andrea Gurdon, who also notes some other FAF retooling in *Model Horse Trader*, Jan./Feb. 1997.) The "Hess" engraving, a mark of sculptor Christian Hess, has the left vertical of the "H," a space, and "es" in script. It is inside the right gaskin, below a mold ejection-pin circle. *First leg-stamped foals:* These have a normal Breyer stamp high inside the left hind leg, where it has remained ever since. The stamp, oriented with its central "C" symbol facing backward, was probably put on the leg in 1960, to judge from the rarity of belly-stamped foals and from the fact that some foals of the earliest version of appy #39 are leg-stamped (I own such a foal), as are some glossy bays and alabasters. These foals also have round, inward-curving eartips and the "Hess" engraving. *Second leg-stamped foals:* These lack the "Hess" but retain the other features noted for the first leg-stamped foals, including, I believe, the ejection-pin circle above the site of the engraving. Andrea has a woodgrain like this. The engraving was evidently removed quite quickly, perhaps in 1961. *Third leg-stamped foals:* These, too, retain the ejection-pin circle, but their Breyer stamp is oriented with the "C" symbol facing down. Also, their eartips are molded to end in straight points, as Andrea notes. I own a glossy bay like this and have seen a woodgrain and glossy palominos and alabasters. *Fourth leg-stamped foals*: These foals, the vast majority of FAFs ever made, lack the ejection-pin circle. My old glossy alabaster is like this, which indicates that the circle was removed prior to 1968, when gloss finish was discontinued on all Family Arabs. The Breyer stamp on these foals is oriented with the "C" symbol facing upward. Also these foal's ears, though still straight and pointed, are built up on the back. Some later fourth-generation leg-stamped models also have a "B" stamp (as on collector Chelle Fulk's palomino #6). The FAF mold was never given the "U.S.A." stamp.

Family Arabian Mare (FAM) — Standing, tailtip free of hock. Sculpted by Chris Hess. Mold in catalog-run production 1960-90, 1993-94.

Catalog-run models made from this mold:

- Ara-Appaloosa Mare #873, "bay" leopard appaloosa, white horse with brown splashed-on spots, no or very few spots on head and upper neck, black or gray points and hooves, matte (1993-94). My own specimen (purchased in early spring 1993) and others I've seen have short white streaks in the dark gray tail, near the dock, but the model in the 1993 catalog appears to lack the streaks. Collector Lynn Isenbarger has a mare with black mane and tail (no streaks) and gray legs.
- Family Appaloosa Mare "Speck" #38, gray blanket appaloosa, bald face, black mane and tail, unstenciled blanket, black splashed-on spots, dark gray or charcoal legs, black hooves, early ones glossy, later ones matte (1960-70). The bald face can be extensive, reaching well down the sides of the face. All the catalogs that list this model are careful not to call her an Arabian, listing her simply as Appaloosa Mare "Speck" under the general heading "Families." Price lists after 1964, however, do get sloppy and list her under the general heading "Arabian" with all the other FAM colors. This mare and her companion pieces—the gray appy FAS and FAF—all come in three basic pattern versions: the early "big-blanket" pattern, which comes only in glossy; the slightly later "belly striped" pattern, also glossy; and the "small butt-blanket" pattern, last of the three, which came in glossy and matte. The big-blanket horses have a white appy blanket covering the butt and much of the barrel—the same pattern as on the earlier gray appaloosa Proud Arabian Mare and Foal (1959), with which the #37 big-blanket gray appy FAS was first released. This pattern is shown in the 1960 catalog—the only Breyer catalog that has a photo of any appaloosa Family Arabs. (Regarding the mold oddity of the appy FAM in the 1960 catalog, see note 1 for this mold.) The barrel and hindquarters of a big-blanket FAM appear in the September 1961 *Western Horseman* (p. 83). The "belly-stripe" pattern, as collectors call it, has a white barrel with gray hindquarters and forehand. This pattern debuted in 1961, to judge from the fact that collector Gale Good got a belly-striped FAM new in December 1961. A belly-striped FAF appears in an ad in the May 1962 *American Girl* magazine. Collector Daphne Macpherson got hold of an unusual glossy belly-striped mare with white knees and hocks. The third pattern has a comparatively small white blanket, restricted for the most part to the butt. Since some of the butt-blanket models are glossy, this pattern must have appeared no later than 1967 (see note 2 for this mold). To my knowledge the appy Family Arabs were never sold in sets, as were the other early "realistic" colors. In 1968-70 "Speck" was available as #38SP in a special cardboard display box (see Display Boxes in this section for discussion). She was in the Showcase Collection as #380 in 1970 (see Showcase Collection). The number 380 later belonged to "Tatanka" The White Buffalo. The number 38 belonged to Arabian Mare "Speck," gray blanket

appaloosa (Proud Arabian Mare mold) before being assigned to the appy FAM.

- Family Arabian Mare #707, chestnut, star, flaxen mane and tail, charcoal-shaded knees and hocks, 4 stockings, light tan hooves, matte (1988). The chestnut color is a medium/dark coffee-with-cream shade, with no red tone.
- Family Arabian Mare #815, bay, solid face, gray-shaded muzzle and eyes, black points, 2 hind stockings, 4 black hooves, matte (1989-90). The body color varies from medium/light rose bay, as shown in catalogs (my own mare is like this), to a light sandy bay, as on collector Emily Atkinson's #816 foal that goes with the #815 mare. Some mares may have a gray dorsal stripe, as shown in the 1989 catalog. Some mares may have gray hooves.
- Family Arabian Mare #908, woodgrain, black eyes, no white markings or other color detailing, matte (1960-66). The model number 908 previously belonged to Arabian Mare, woodgrain (Proud Arabian Mare mold).
- Family Arabian Mare "Dickory" #202, charcoal, bald face, white points, pink hooves, early ones glossy, later ones matte (1961/62 - 1973). This same model was also sold 1961/62 - 1964 in sets #223 and #213; see below. The name "Dickory" was dropped from the 1972-73 catalogs, where the model is called simply Arabian Mare. Catalogs describe this model as "charcoal," but her color varies from black to deep brown. Some #202s have hand-painted eyewhites. The bald face can be extensive, reaching well down the sides of the face. I've seen a glossy #202 with an additional white mane wisp above the molded mane wisp on the non-mane side. The hooves vary from extremely pale pink (virtually white) to bright pinky peach, and can be touched with gray overspray. A true gray-hoofed variation may also exist; see the entry for Family Arabian Stallion "Hickory." Regarding gloss finish see note 2 for this mold. "Dickory" is in the 1963 catalog but not the 1960. I date her release to 1961/62 on the basis of Gale's charcoal foal "Doc," which she received new in July 1962; presumably the entire charcoal family was released at the same time. In 1968-70 "Dickory" was available as #202SP in a special cardboard display box (see Display Boxes in this section for discussion). She was in the Showcase Collection as #2020 in 1970-72 (see Showcase Collection).
- Family Arabian Mare "Hope" #5, palomino, bald face, white or light palomino mane and tail, 4 stockings, gray hooves, early ones glossy, later ones matte (1961/62 - 1987). This same model was also sold 1961/62 - 1964 in sets #456 and #506; see below. The name "Hope" was dropped from catalogs after 1970/71. The model was called Arabian Mare in 1972-76; Family Mare in 1977-86; Palomino Family Mare in 1987. The glossy models are light honey colored and usually have light honey mane and tail. Collector Gale Good, however, has a glossy with stenciled white mane and tail, and I've seen others like this. The mare I saw also had an additional white mane wisp above the molded mane wisp on the non-mane side. The later, matte models are darker palomino, often a bright orangy shade, and all have masked white mane and tail. On the glossies and some mattes, the bald face can be extensive, reaching well down the sides of the face. Most palomino Family Arabs do not have hand-painted eyewhites, but collector Lani Keller has a glossy #5 and matching stallion both with hand-painted eyewhites. Regarding gloss finish see note 2 for this mold. "Hope" is in the 1963 catalog but not the 1960. I date her release to 1961/62 on the basis of Gale's "Hope," which she received new in July 1962, and a photo of the palomino FAF in an ad in the May 1962 *American Girl* magazine. In 1968-70 "Hope" was available as #5SP in a special cardboard display box, and for a brief period in the late 1970s she was sold as #15 in another type of display box, one with blister wrap, labeled "No. 15 Palomino Family Mare" (see Display Boxes above in this section for discussion). The number 15 had previously belonged to the old bay Proud Arabian Foal and to the bay Family Arabian Foal. "Hope" was in the Showcase Collection as #500 in 1970-72 (see Showcase Collection). The number 500 later belonged to the Brenda Breyer doll.
- Family Arabian Mare "Pride" #8, alabaster; gray mane and tail; gray, pink, or white nose and inner ears; gray hooves; early ones glossy, later ones matte (1960-73). This same model was also sold in the early 1960s in sets #10, #11, and #12; see below. The name "Pride" was dropped from the 1972-73 catalogs, where the model is called simply Arabian Mare. On my own and collector Sheryl Leisure's pink-nosed glossy mares, the whole muzzle is pink, not just the area between the nostrils. Regarding gloss finish see note 2 for this mold. See Family Arabian Foal SR alabaster for differences between the SR and regular run glossy alabaster Family Arabs. One of the earliest matte alabaster Family Arab sets—purchased in 1968—is pictured in *Quequechan Model Horse Collector*, January 1985. In 1968-70 "Pride" was available as #8SP in a special cardboard display box (see Display Boxes in this section for discussion). She was in the Showcase Collection as #0800 in 1970-72 (see Showcase Collection). The model number 8 previously belonged to Arabian Mare "Pride," alabaster (Proud Arabian Mare mold).
- Family Arabian Mare "Sheba" #14, bay, blaze, black mane and tail, no black on the legs, 4 stockings, black hooves, early ones glossy, later ones matte (1960-73). This same model was also sold in the early 1960s in sets #16, #17, and #18; see below. The name "Sheba" was dropped from the 1972-73 catalogs, where the model is called simply Arabian Mare. Some #14s have hand-painted eyewhites. The body color varies from light caramel bay to reddish bay to dark chocolate bay. The blaze on #14 is very similar in shape to the blaze on SR dark chestnut FAM. Regarding gloss finish see note 2 for this mold. In 1968-70 "Sheba" was available as #14SP in a special cardboard display box (see Display Boxes in this section for discussion). She was in the Showcase Collection as #1400 in 1970-72 (see Showcase Collection). The model number 14 previously belonged to Arabian Mare "Sheba," bay (Proud Arabian Mare mold) and in the late 1970s was assigned to the palomino Family Arabian Stallion in a special blister-wrapped display box.

Sets with FAS, FAM, and FAF:

- "Dickory" And "Doc" set #223, Family Arabian Mare and Foal, both charcoal (1961/62 - 1964). These same models were also sold separately as Arabian Mare "Dickory" #202 and Family Arabian Foal "Doc" #203 [both 1961/62 - 1973].
- "Faith," "Hope," And "Charity" set #456, Family Arabian Stallion, Mare, and Foal, all palomino (1961/62 - 1964). These same models were also sold separately as Family Arabian Stallion "Faith" #4, Family Arabian Mare "Hope" #5, and Family Arabian Foal "Charity" #6 [all 1961/62 - 1987].
- "Hickory," "Dickory," And "Doc" set #213, Family Arabian Stallion, Mare, and Foal, all charcoal (1961/62 - 1964). These same models were also sold separately as Family Arabian Stallion "Hickory" #201, Family Arabian Mare "Dickory" #202, and Family Arabian Foal "Doc" #203 [all 1961/62 - 1973]. The model number 213 later belonged to the dapple gray Proud Arabian Stallion.
- "Hope" And "Charity" set #506, Family Arabian Mare and Foal, both palomino (1961/62 - 1964). These same models were also sold separately as Family Arabian Mare "Hope" #5 and Family Arabian Foal "Charity" #6 [both 1961/62 - 1987].
- "Pride" And "Joy" set #10, Family Arabian Mare and Foal, both alabaster (1960-64). These same models were also sold separately as Family Arabian Mare "Pride" #8 and Family Arabian Foal "Joy" #9 [both 1960-73]. The model number 10 previously belonged to "Pride" And "Joy" Combination, alabaster (Proud Arabian Mare and Foal molds), and much later was assigned to Family Arabian Stallion SR black.
- "Prince" And "Pride" set #12, Family Arabian Stallion and Mare, both alabaster (1960 - 1960/62). These same models were also sold separately as Family Arabian Stallion "Prince" #7 [1959 {possibly late 1958} -1973] and Family Arabian Mare "Pride" #8 [1960-73]. The 1960 catalog does not list this set per se, but it does say, after the listings for the individual bay and alabaster Family Arabs, "Sold also in any combination of two or three." I use the model number 12 for this set since this was the number of the earlier "Prince" And "Pride" set with FAS and PAM. Other bay and alabaster Family Arab sets that are listed in catalogs have the same names and numbers as the earlier sets with FAS, PAM, and PAF. Much later, the number 12 was assigned to Family Arabian Foal SR black.
- "Prince," "Pride," And "Joy" set #11, Family Arabian Stallion, Mare, and Foal, all alabaster (1960-64). These same models were also sold separately as Family Arabian Stallion "Prince" #7 [1959 {possibly late 1958} - 1973], Family Arabian Mare "Pride" #8 [1960-73], and Family Arabian Foal "Joy" #9 [1960-73]. The model number 11 previously belonged to the "Prince," "Pride," And "Joy" set with alabaster FAS, Proud Arabian Mare, and Proud Arabian Foal, and much later was assigned to Family Arabian Mare SR black.
- "Sheba" And "Shah" set #18, Family Arabian Mare and Foal, both bay (1960-64). These same models were also sold separately as Family Arabian Mare "Sheba" #14 and Family Arabian Foal "Shah" #15 [both 1960-73]. The model number 18 previously belonged to the "Sheba" And "Shah" set with bay Proud Arabian Mare and Foal, and much later belonged to the black blanket appaloosa Stock Horse Foal ("Phantom Wings" mold).
- "Sheik" And "Sheba" set #17, Family Arabian Stallion and Mare, both bay (1960 - 1960/62). These same models were also sold separately as Family Arabian Stallion "Sheik" #13 [1959 {possibly late 1958} - 1973] and Family Arabian Mare "Sheba" #14 [1960-73]. The 1960 catalog does not list this set per se, but it does say, after the listings for the individual bay and alabaster Family Arabs, "Sold also in any combination of two or three." I use the number 17 for this set since this is the number of the earlier "Sheik" And "Sheba" set with FAS and PAM [1959]. Other bay and alabaster Family Arab sets that are listed in catalogs have the same names and numbers as the earlier sets with FAS, PAM, and PAF. The model number 17 later belonged to the chestnut blanket appaloosa Stock Horse Foal ("Phantom Wings" mold).
- "Sheik," "Sheba," And "Shah" set #16, Family Arabian Stallion, Mare, and Foal, all bay (1960-64). These same models were also sold separately as Family Arabian Stallion "Sheik" #13 [1959 {possibly late 1958} - 1973], Family Arabian Mare "Sheba" #14 [1960-73], and Family Arabian Foal "Shah" #15 [1960-73]. The model number 16 previously belonged to the "Sheik," "Sheba," And "Shah" set with bay FAS, Proud Arabian Mare, and Proud Arabian Foal; later it belonged to the palomino Family Arabian Foal in a special blister-wrapped display box and then to Marguerite Henry's "Sea Star."

Special-run models made from this mold:

- Family Arabian Mare SR, alabaster, gray mane and tail, pink nose and inner ears, gray hooves, glossy (1988). Made for Enchanted Doll House. Sold in SR set #400789 with glossy alabaster FAF and FAS. Probably about 1,000 sets made, per Breyer executive Peter Stone. See Family Arabian Foal SR alabaster for further information, including differences between the SR and regular-run alabaster Family Arabs. The number for this set is per a Breyer company computer printout of activity 1985-92.
- Family Arabian Mare SR #11, black, no white markings, black mane and tail, black hooves, matte (1977). Made in 1977 for retail shops and sold by Bentley Sales Company at the Model Horse Congress in Chicago in August 1978. Sold separately or in set with SR black Family Arabian Foal #12 and SR black Family Arabian Stallion #10. Precise quantity unknown, but at least several hundred sets were made. Published hobby sources that discuss this SR black family typically mention only the horses at the Congress, saying that about 100-200 sets were made for that event (e.g., *Quequechan Model Horse Collector*, June 1983, says 200). However, solid evidence indicates that the horses sold by Bentley's at the Congress (and via mail order thereafter) were simply leftovers of a larger run produced in 1977. A letter dated May 12, 1980, to collector Kim Jones from Peter Stone, then president of Breyer Animal Creations, states: "The 'black' family stallion, mare and foal were only made for a 'Fall' 1977 promotion, but distributed nationally." This statement is confirmed by several 1978 issues of *Model Horse Shower's Journal* (*MHSJ*), two of which preceded the August 1978 Congress. A sales ad in the March issue includes this item: "Brey. #11 *pure blk.* Arab Fam. mare, few made '77." The July issue contains the following ad and editorial comment: "I can buy a few disc. Breyers, plus the rare PURE BLACK FAMILY ARABS & new '78 releases. . . . (Ed. The black Arabians were something of a test by Breyer to see if they'd sell, but are not true 'test color' horses.)" Finally, the September issue has this item: "Several people now have found the all black Breyer Arabian Family sets. These consist of: #10 foal, #11 mare & #12 stallion. (Ed. I think those are correct.) They come in the regular Arabian boxes, some stated in the 'bay' horse boxes. I don't find them in catalogs, so these are nice additions to your collection if found. They sell for the usual Breyer prices in shops. Look around!" Despite the editorial parenthesis here, the model numbers for the foal and stallion are switched in this quoted passage. Old Bentley's sales record cards in my possession that show Bentley's holdings of these horses as of February 1979 list the models as "#12 All-Black Arabian Foal special," "#11 All-Black Arabian Mare special," and "#10 All-Black Arabian Stallion special." The record cards indicate that Bentley's had at least 70 foals, 92 mares, and 92 stallions for sale in 1979 and received a shipment of 48 more foals in 1982. In all likelihood, quantities this large or larger were sold in 1977-78 as well. Bentley's price lists dated December 1979 and March 1980 list "#11 All-Black Arabian Mare $6.99." The stallion, which sold out earlier in 1979 (as did the 1979 batch of foals), undoubtedly cost the same as the mare. The 1982 foals turn up on Bentley's May 1982 price list as "#12 All-Black Family Foal" for $5.19. The model numbers 10, 11, and 12 were originally used in the late 1950s and early 1960s as the numbers for various Proud Arab and Family Arab sets, all alabaster; see the Models By Number section at the end of this book for specifics.
- Family Arabian Mare SR, dapple gray, no or very few dapples on head and upper neck; bald face; black points; 1 right hind stocking with tan hoof; other hooves black; matte (1991). Sears holiday catalog. Sold in Spirit Of The Wind Set SR #498991, with dapple gray FAF. 4,000 sets made, per a Breyer company computer printout of activity 1985-92. The number for this set is per the printout and a Bentley Sales price list dated March 15, 1993. The Sears catalog shows the mare as slightly lighter gray than the foal, and my own set is like this, but Sande Schneider's mare is slightly darker than her foal.

Family Arabian Mare SR, dark chestnut, blaze, darker brown mane and tail, 4 stockings, gray hooves, matte (1982). Penney's holiday catalog. Sold in SR Arabian Family Set With Blue Ribbon, with dark chestnut FAF and light chestnut FAS. There is a lot of confusion about which of the two Penney's FA chestnut sets— the light stallion and dark mare and foal set, and the dark stallion and light mare and foal set—came in 1982 and which in 1983. For clarification of this issue and for discussion of the ribbon, see FAF SR light chestnut. Overruns of the dark mare were sold through Bentley Sales Company; she first appears on their November-December 1983 price list, identified as "#5S Dark Chestnut Family Mare." Her number changed to #5S-D (for "dark," presumably) on the August 1984 Bentley's list. This mare's blaze is very similar in shape to the blaze on bay FAM #14.

Family Arabian Mare SR, medium chestnut, bald face, dark brown mane and tail, 4 stockings, gray hooves, matte (sometime in the 1960s). Quantity unknown. Some have hand-painted eyewhites. This mare, with matching FAF and FAS, is shown in Diederich 1988, Section 2. The color details I've given for this mare are based on a mare that I saw at BreyerFest 1993. The mare had hand-painted eyewhites, but my stallion does not, nor does the stallion owned by collector Joy Sheesley or any of the models in the set in Diederich 1988. The body color is like that of the older "sorrel" Five-Gaiters, a medium coffee-with-cream shade, with no red tone. Though I know of no contemporary documentation for these models, they are definitely datable to the 1960s by the fact that they lack the "U.S.A." stamp—neither my stallion nor Joy's nor the mare at BreyerFest has this stamp. The hand-painted eyewhites on the BreyerFest mare too date her to the 1960s.

Family Arabian Mare SR, light chestnut, blaze, flaxen mane and tail, 4 stockings, gray hooves, matte (1983). Penney's holiday catalog. Sold in SR Arabian Family Set With Blue Ribbon, with light chestnut FAF and dark chestnut FAS. There is a lot of confusion about which of the two Penney's FA chestnut sets— the light stallion and dark mare and foal set, and the dark stallion and light mare and foal set—came in 1982 and which in 1983. For clarification of this issue and for discussion of the ribbon, see FAF SR light chestnut.

Notes:

(1) It is well-known that the FAM mold was introduced when the PAM was discontinued because of legal complaints by the Hagen-Renaker company (see note 1 for Proud Arabian Mare). It is less well known that Breyer created an early mold version of the FAM, which long-time collector and Breyer consultant Marney Walerius called the "in-between mare," undoubtedly because it was created between the discontinuation of the PAM and the release of the normal FAM (see Walerius 1991, pp. 4-5). The in-between mare looks much like the normal FAM and has her mane on the same side, but she is more finely built overall and has the center of her tail attached to her right buttock, whereas the FAM's tail stands free. Breyer's plans for the in-between mare got far enough along in late 1959 or early 1960 that a steel injection mold was made of her and some trial plastic specimens were produced—Marney's book doesn't say how many, but I would guess a few dozen at most. The mold was then rejected by the company officers, presumably because the mare is giraffe-necked and stands with her front legs a bit out of alignment with her back legs. Some of the plastic in-between mares may have been destroyed at the factory at that time and others sent home with employees for their children. Apparently the steel injection mold itself was preserved—Marney mentions in her book that it was still in storage at the factory in the early 1970s when she visited there. Marney owned one of the only two plastic specimens of the in-between mare known to me—a glossy gray blanket appaloosa, pictured on page 4 of her book (also see Gerhardt 1992). Another specimen, identical to Marney's in mold but painted in woodgrain finish, was found early in 1995 at an antiques market in Southern California by collector Bonnie Driskill Vavra's husband (who was her fiancé at the time). This woodgrain mare, which Bonnie brought to the West Coast Model Horse Collector's Jamboree in August 1995, has the round "Breyer Molding Co." mold stamp, as did Marney's appy mare (per conversation of early 1992). Breyer catalogs do not show the in-between mare, but the 1960 catalog, the first catalog to have the FAM mold, shows models with mold oddities. (Regarding the date of this cataalog, see Breyer Company Publications in the Reference section at the end of this book.) The most strikingly odd is the #38 appaloosa FAM, who has a rounded nose and has her mane on the left side. (This is not a case of a flipped photograph, which would show the horse in complete mirror image. The mare's legs are not reversed in the catalog photo.) The woodgrain and bay FAMs in the 1960 catalog have their manes on the correct side but have rounded noses, and the woodgrain has a bulging windpipe as well. These three models could be merely test or prototype pieces, for so far as I know, models with these oddities were not produced for sale. The FAM models in the 1963 catalog appear completely normal.

(2) Palomino, charcoal, alabaster, bay, and gray blanket appaloosa Family Arabian Mares were made in glossy finish prior to 1968. The 1968 and 1970 catalogs specify that all colors of Family Arabs are matte only; so evidently 1967 was the last year in which any glossy Family Arabs were made, except for the 1988 SR glossy alabaster family.

(3) Collector Marie Spinella-Phillips has an old bay FAM that she got new in March 1962, which is a quarter of an inch shorter in height (hoof to eartip) and in length (face to tail) than her other, more recent FAM. For further discussion of this phenomenon, see Mold Variations in the Appendix near the end of this book.

(4) For the "Ministang" car lights that were made from the rear halves of alabaster, palomino, and appaloosa Family Arab Mares in the late 1960s, see the Lamps & Nightlights section in the Appendix near the end of this book.

(5) 1960s models of the Family Arabian Mare mold have the round "Breyer Molding Co." stamp only. Later models have the round stamp and the "U.S.A." stamp—I have a gray appy #38 with the "U.S.A.," so we know it was added to the mold in 1970, when this stamp was introduced into the Breyer line. Some "U.S.A." mares have the "B" stamp in addition.

Family Arabian Stallion (FAS) — Trotting, neck arched. Adapted by Chris Hess from Maureen Love Calvert's 9-inch "Amir" (produced in ceramic by Hagen-Renaker). Mold in catalog-run production 1959 (possibly late 1958) - 1990, 1993-94, 1996.

Catalog-run models made from this mold:

Ara-Appaloosa Stallion #872, "bay" leopard appaloosa, white horse with brown splashed-on spots, no or very few spots on head and upper neck, black or gray points and hooves, matte (1993-94). My own specimen (purchased in early spring 1993) and others I've seen have short white streaks in the dark gray tail, near the dock, but the model in the 1993 catalog doesn't have the streaks.

Family Appaloosa Stallion "Fleck" #37, gray blanket appaloosa, bald face, black mane and tail, unstenciled blanket, black splashed-on spots, dark gray or charcoal legs, black hooves, early ones glossy, later ones matte (1959-70). The bald face on #37 can be extensive, reaching well down the sides of the face. For discussion of the three pattern versions of "Fleck"—big blanket, "belly striped," and small butt-blanket—see Family Appaloosa Mare "Speck" #38 (under Family Arabian Mare). All the catalogs that list #37 are careful not to call him an Arabian, listing him simply as Appaloosa Stallion "Fleck" under the general heading "Families." Price lists after 1964, however, do get sloppy and list him under the general heading "Arabian" with all the other FAS colors. #37 is not in the 1958 catalog or price list. Nor is he mentioned in September and December 1959 *Western Horseman* ads offering the bay and alabaster sets with FAS, PAM, and PAF. Nonetheless I date "Fleck" to 1959, both because some early-version "Flecks" (with big blanket) have no mold stamps and because it is virtually certain that "Fleck" was issued along with the gray appy Proud Arabian Mare and Foal, which appeared in that year. To my knowledge the appy Family Arabs were never sold in sets, as were the other early "realistic" colors. Regarding gloss finish see note 3 for this mold. In 1968-70 "Fleck" was available as #37SP in a special cardboard display box (see Display Boxes in this section for discussion). He was in the Showcase Collection as #370 in 1970 (see Showcase Collection). The number 370 later belonged to the dark red-brown pinto Texas Longhorn Bull.

Family Arabian Stallion #706, chestnut, stripe, flaxen mane and tail, charcoal-shaded knees and hocks, 4 stockings, light tan hooves, matte (1988). The chestnut color is a medium/dark coffee-with-cream shade, with no red tone. Collector Lorraine Mavro-George found a #706 with gray on the hooves but none on the knees.

Family Arabian Stallion #814, bay, solid face, gray-shaded muzzle and eyes, black points, 2 hind stockings, 4 black hooves, matte (1989-90). The body color varies from medium/light rose bay, as shown in catalogs (my own mare is like this), to a light sandy bay, as on collector Emily Atkinson's #816 foal that goes with the #814 stallion. Some stallions may have a gray dorsal stripe and/or gray hooves.

Family Arabian Stallion #907, woodgrain, black eyes, no white markings or other color detailing, matte (1959-66). The woodgrain FAS appears with woodgrain Race Horse, Brahma Bull, Proud Arabian Mare, and Clydesdale Stallion in an old Ward's catalog ad that I believe dates to 1959. (For discussion of this dating, see under Woodgrains below in this section.) The ad describes the models thus: "Simulated wood grain finish figurines. Beautifully detailed Horses and Brahma Bull. Faithfully copied from original hand-carved wood pieces. Made of Tenite Acetate high quality plastic, carefully hand finished in simulated wood grain. Buy any three figurines—get free 'Album of Horses' book [by Marguerite Henry]." The woodgrain FAS was offered again in the 1962 Ward's holiday catalog.

Family Arabian Stallion "Faith" #4, palomino, bald face, white or light palomino mane and tail, 4 stockings, gray hooves, early ones glossy, later ones matte (1961/62 - 1987). This same model was also sold 1961/62 - 1964 in set #456; see under Family Arabian Mare. The name "Faith" was dropped from catalogs after 1970/71. The model was called Arabian Stallion in 1972-76; Family Stallion in 1977-86; Palomino Family Stallion in 1987. The glossy models are typically light honey colored with light honey mane and tail. Some glossies do, however, have a stenciled white mane and tail; collector Gale Good has such a model. The later, matte models are darker palomino, often a bright orangy shade, and have stenciled white mane and tail. Many stenciled-mane horses have white "wisps" of mane stenciled along the crest on the non-mane side (thanks to Lani Keller for pointing this out to me). The number of wisps varies; I've seen models with just one or two wisps and others with a dozen wisps all up and down the crest. Some models have gray-shaded stallion portions; collector Linda Bell wrote to me that her orangy matte "Faith" has very dark portions, of the round mold version (see note 4 for this mold). On the glossies and some mattes, the bald face can be extensive, reaching well down the sides of the face. Most palomino Family Arabs do not have hand-painted eyewhites, but Lani has a glossy #4 and matching mare, both with hand-painted eyewhites; and collector Chris Wilder also has a #4 with eyewhites. Regarding gloss finish see note 3 for this mold. "Faith" is in the 1963 catalog but not the 1960. I date his release to 1961/62 on the basis of Gale's "Faith," which she received new in December 1962, and a photo of the palomino FAF in an ad in the May 1962 *American Girl* magazine. In 1968-70 "Faith" was available as #4SP in a special cardboard display box, and for a brief period in the late 1970s he was sold as #14 in another type of display box, one with blister wrap, labeled "No. 14 Palomino Family Stallion" (see Display Boxes above in this section for discussion). The number 14 had previously belonged to the old-mold bay Proud Arabian Mare and to the bay Family Arabian Mare. "Faith" was in the Showcase Collection as #400 in 1970-72 (see Showcase Collection). The number 400 was later assigned to the Breyer Rider doll.

Family Arabian Stallion "Hickory" #201, charcoal, bald face, white points, pink hooves, early ones glossy, later ones matte (1961/62 - 1973). This same model was also sold 1961/62 - 1964 in set #213; see under Family Arabian Mare. The name "Hickory" was dropped from the 1972-73 catalogs, where the model is called simply Arabian Stallion. Catalogs describe #201 as "charcoal," but his color varies from black to deep brown. Some #201s have hand-painted eyewhites. The bald face can be extensive, reaching well down the sides of the face. Many #201s, both glossy and matte, have white "wisps" of mane stenciled along the crest on the non-mane side (thanks to Lani Keller for pointing this out to me). The number of wisps varies; I've seen models with just one or two wisps and others with a dozen wisps all up and down the crest. The hooves vary from extremely pale pink (virtually white) to bright pinky peach, and can be touched with gray overspray. Collector Linda Bell wrote to me that her matte black-charcoal #201 has dark gray hooves. Regarding gloss finish see note 3 for this mold. "Hickory" is in the 1963 catalog but not the 1960. I date his release to 1961/62 on the basis of collector Gale Good's charcoal foal "Doc," which she received new in July 1962; presumably the entire charcoal family was released at the same time. In 1968-70 "Hickory" was available as #201SP in a special cardboard display box (see Display Boxes in this section for discussion). He was in the Showcase Collection as #2010 in 1970-72 (see Showcase Collection).

Family Arabian Stallion "Prince" #7, alabaster; gray mane and tail; gray, pink, or white nose and inner ears; gray hooves; early ones glossy, later ones matte (1959 [possibly late 1958] - 1973). This same model was also sold in 1959 (and possibly late 1958) in sets #11 and #12 with PAM and PAF (see under Proud Arabian Mare, old-mold version), and in the early 1960s in sets #11 and #12 with FAM and FAM (see under Family Arabian Mare). He was also sold through the 1962 Ward's holiday catalog with an 8-ounce pack of candies slung over his back, for $1.98. The name "Prince" was dropped from the 1972-73 catalogs, where the model is called simply Arabian Stallion. Some of the oldest glossy models have gray or charcoal lip lines (like lipstick)—my "Prince," which I've had since about 1959 (he has no mold stamps), is like this. Other glossies and matte models have no lip lines but instead either gray or pink or no shading on the nose. One of the earliest matte alabaster Family Arab sets—purchased in 1968—is pictured in *Quequechan Model Horse Collector* of January 1985. Regarding gloss finish see note 3 for this mold. See Family Arabian Foal SR alabaster for differences between the SR and regular-run glossy alabaster Family Arabs. Regarding release date for #7 see note 2 for this mold. In 1968-70 "Prince" was available as #7SP in a special cardboard display box (see Display Boxes in this section for discussion). He was in the

Showcase Collection as #700 in 1970-72 (see Showcase Collection).

♠ Family Arabian Stallion "Sheik" #13, bay, star and stripe, black or charcoal-brown mane and tail, no black on the legs, 4 stockings, black hooves, early ones glossy, later ones matte (1959 [possibly late 1958] - 1973). This same model was also sold in 1959 (and possibly late 1958) in sets #16 and #17 with PAM and PAF (see under Proud Arabian Mare, old-mold version), and in the early 1960s in sets #16 and #17 with FAM and FAF (see under Family Arabian Mare). The name "Sheik" was dropped from the 1972-73 catalogs, where the model is called simply Arabian Stallion. Some #13s have hand-painted eyewhites. The body color varies from light caramel bay to reddish bay to dark chocolate bay. The oldest glossy models have dark gray-brown lip lines; later ones lack this detail. Collector Heather Wells has seen a chalky glossy #13, which evidently dated to pre-1960, for it had no mold stamps. Regarding gloss finish see note 3 for this mold. Regarding release date for this model, see note 2 for this mold. In 1968-70 "Sheik" was available as #13SP in a special cardboard display box (see Display Boxes in this section for discussion). He was in the Showcase Collection as #0130 in 1970-72 (see Showcase Collection).

Sets: see under Family Arabian Mare and under Proud Arabian Mare (old-mold version).

Special-run models made from this mold:

♤ Family Arabian Stallion SR, alabaster, gray muzzle, black points, black hooves, matte (1991 and 1992). Sears holiday catalog. Sold in Arabian Horses Of The World set SR #492091, with fleabitten rose gray Proud Arabian Mare and red bay Proud Arabian Stallion with blaze. 4,350 sets made in all: 3,000 in 1991 and 1,350 in 1992. (Quantity and set number are per a Breyer company computer printout of activity 1985-92.) This FAS represents the Spanish type Arabian, according to the 1992 Sears catalog, which states: "Set includes three types being bred internationally today: the bay American, the fleabitten grey Polish and the alabaster Spanish."

♤ Family Arabian Stallion SR, alabaster, gray mane and tail, pink nose and inner ears, gray hooves, glossy (1988). Made for Enchanted Doll House. Sold in SR set #400789 with glossy alabaster FAF and FAS. Probably about 1,000 sets made, per Breyer executive Peter Stone. See Family Arabian Foal SR alabaster for further information, including differences between the SR and regular-run alabaster Family Arabs. The number for this set is per a Breyer company computer printout of activity 1985-92.

♤ Family Arabian Stallion SR #10, black, no white markings, black mane and tail, black hooves, matte (1977). Made in 1977 for retail shops and sold by Bentley Sales at the Model Horse Congress in Chicago in August 1978. Sold separately or in set with SR black Family Arabian Mare #11 and SR black Family Arabian Foal #12. Precise quantity unknown, but at least several hundred sets were made. See Family Arabian Mare SR #11, black, for discussion.

♤ Family Arabian Stallion SR, dark chestnut, blaze, darker brown mane and tail, 4 stockings, gray hooves, matte (1983). Penney's holiday catalog. Sold in SR Arabian Family Set With Blue Ribbon, with light chestnut FAF and FAM. There is a lot of confusion about which of the two Penney's FA chestnut sets— the light stallion and dark mare and foal set, and the dark stallion and light mare and foal set—came in 1982 and which in 1983. For clarification of this issue and for discussion of the ribbon, see FAF SR light chestnut. Overruns of the dark stallion were sold through Bentley Sales Company; he first appears on their August 1984 price list, identified as "#4S-D Dark Chestnut Family Stallion."

♤ Family Arabian Stallion SR, medium chestnut, bald face, dark brown mane and tail, 4 stockings, gray hooves, matte (sometime in the 1960s). Quantity unknown. This stallion, with matching FAM and FAF, is shown in Diederich 1988, Section 2. The color details I've given for the stallion are based on my own stallion and one owned by collector Joy Sheesley. A matching mare that I saw at BreyerFest 1993 had hand-painted eyewhites, but my stallion and Joy's do not, nor does the set in Diederich 1988. The body color is like that of the older "sorrel" Five-Gaiters, a medium coffee-with-cream shade, with no red tone. See FAM SR medium chestnut for further discussion.

♤ Family Arabian Stallion SR, light chestnut, long star, flaxen mane and tail, 4 stockings, gray hooves, matte (1982). Penney's holiday catalog. Sold in SR Arabian Family Set With Blue Ribbon, with dark chestnut FAF and FAM. There is a lot of confusion about which of the two Penney's FA chestnut sets—the light stallion and dark mare and foal set, and the dark stallion and light mare and foal set—came in 1982 and which in 1983. For clarification of this issue and for discussion of the ribbon, see FAF SR light chestnut. Overruns of the light stallion were sold through Bentley Sales Company; he first appears on their November-December 1983 price list, identified as "#4S Light Chestnut Family Stallion." His number changed to #4S-L (for "light") on the August 1984 Bentley's list to avoid confusion with the dark chestnut stallion #4S-D, which first appears on this list.

Notes:

(1) The FAS mold, like the PAM and PAF, was adapted from a ceramic Hagen-Renaker mold by sculptor Maureen Love Calvert. The H-R mold for the FAS was the 9" "Amir" #656 (see Roller, Rose, and Berkwitz 1989, p. 21). Although the Hagen-Renaker company obliged Breyer to discontinue the PAM and PAF molds, H-R seems not to have complained about the FAS mold—at any rate, the FAS was not discontinued. H-R may have kept quiet about him because his resemblance to "Amir" is not so close as the PAM's and PAF's resemblance to their H-R prototypes. So for example, although the FAS and "Amir" are in the same trotting position, they have opposite legs raised. For comparison shots of FAS and "Amir" see Fitch 1990 (2: C) and *Breyer Collector's Video*.

(2) The FAS mold was issued as a companion piece for the Proud Arabian Mare and Foal but was introduced a year or so after them. Although the H-R "Amir" mold from which Breyer took the design for its FAS was first released by Hagen-Renaker in spring 1957 (per Roller, Rose, and Berkwitz 1989, p. 21), no FAS models are listed in the 1958 Breyer catalog or price list. The FAS mold could conceivably have been introduced late in 1958 but in any case was certainly in production by 1959, for he is advertised, in bay and alabaster sets with PAM and PAF, in the September and December 1959 issues of *Western Horseman*.

(3) Palomino, charcoal, alabaster, bay, and gray blanket appaloosa Family Arabian Stallions were made in glossy finish prior to 1968. The 1968 and 1970 catalogs specify that all colors of Family Arabs are matte only; so evidently 1967 was the last year in which any glossy Family Arabs were made, except for the 1988 alabaster special run.

(4) Like the Fighting Stallion mold, the Family Arab Stallion mold underwent some alteration to his stallion equipment. On early models, the testicles are distinct and realistically rounded. On later models, the scrotum is a solid bar running from thigh to thigh. The alteration was made sometime between the early 1970s and 1983, to judge from my own models. My 1960s glossies are realistic, as are my two matte charcoal #201s, one of which must be an early 1970s piece since he has the "U.S.A." stamp. But my SR dark chestnut stallion from 1983 does have the bar-style scrotum.

(5) The earliest specimens of the Family Arabian Stallion mold—pre-1960 glossy alabaster, glossy bay, glossy big-blanket appy (the earliest version of appy FAS #37), and woodgrain models—have no mold marks. Slightly later models, as collector Denise Deen pointed out to me, have just a tiny portion of what was evidently meant to be a round "Breyer Molding Co." stamp, located inside the left gaskin. The portion consists of two concentric curved lines with three upside-down letters, "MOL" (only the second half of the "M" is present) stamped beneath them. Presumably the letters are from the word "Molding" in the name Breyer Molding.Co. Although this partial stamp is located on these horses where the full round stamp would be located on later FASs, the "MOL" is in a different position from the same letters on the later full round stamp, as though the stamp had been rotated. The partial stamp occurs on slightly later specimens of the same four models that earlier had no stamps: alabaster, bay, big-blanket appy, and woodgrain. My guess is that these partial-stamp models were issued in the first part of 1960 and that the full round "Breyer Molding Co." stamp replaced the partial stamp later in 1960. Still later models have the "U.S.A." stamp as well as the round stamp—collector Sande Schneider has a gray appy #37 with the "U.S.A.," so we know it was added to the mold in 1970, when this stamp was introduced into the Breyer line. Some "U.S.A." models have the "B" stamp in addition.

Fanciful Mare And Pony Set SR — see Running Mare SR, flocked white; and Running Foal SR, flocked white

"Fashionably Late" SR — see under "Sherman Morgan"

"Favory" SR — see under "Pluto"

Fighting Stallion — ♞ Large rearing stallion. Sculpted by Chris Hess. Mold in catalog-run production 1961-90, 1992, 1994 - current as of 1996.

Catalog-run models made from this mold:

♠ "Chaparral" The Fighting Stallion #855, buckskin pinto, tobiano; blaze; black tail with white streaks; mane half black and half white; normal black eyes (not tri-color); black knees; tan hooves; matte; Limited Edition (1992). This model's color and pinto pattern are virtually identical to SR "Little Chaparral's" (see under Rearing Stallion below in the Classics section). "Chaparral's" box sports a large round gold sticker saying, in full: "1992 Limited Edition (Production limited to 1992 orders) / Chaparral / This pinto Fighting Stallion is as rugged as the southwestern plains!" Limited Edition models are produced only for one year, in quantities sufficient to fill all orders for the model.

♠ Fighting Stallion #709, black leopard appaloosa, white horse with black splashed-on spots; pink nose and stallion parts; gray mane, tail, knees, hocks, and hooves; matte (1988-90). Many models also have gray shading around the eyes. The 1988-89 catalogs show this horse with an all-gray tail; the 1990 shows a two-tone tail: the top half is gray, the bottom half white. My #709, purchased in 1992 (so he's probably a 1990 edition), is the two-tone version; I haven't seen an all-gray-tail version.

♠ Fighting Stallion #1031, Copenhagen decorator, dappled blue, bald face, white points, pink hooves, glossy (1963-64). The hooves can be very pale pink or even white. For further discussion see Decorators (1960s) above in the Traditionals section.

♠ Fighting Stallion #2031, Florentine decorator, dappled metallic gold, bald face, white points, pink or white hooves, glossy (1963-64). The hooves can be very pale pink or even white. For further discussion see Decorators (1960s) above in the Traditionals section.

♠ Fighting Stallion #3031, Golden Charm decorator, solid metallic gold, bald face, white points, pink hooves, glossy (1963-64). The hooves can be very pale pink or even white. The gold paint on these horses can darken over time and by now often looks more like tarnished brass. For further discussion see Decorators (1960s) above in the Traditionals section.

♠ Fighting Stallion #4031, Wedgewood Blue decorator, solid blue, bald face, white points, pink hooves, matte (1963-64). The hooves can be very pale pink or even white. For further discussion see Decorators (1960s) above in the Traditionals section.

♠ "King" The Fighting Stallion, Alabaster Lipizzan #30, alabaster; early ones glossy with gray mane and tail; later ones matte with white mane and tail; all with gray hooves (1961-85). The glossy models with gray mane and tail were made only for the first couple of years. Collector Gale Good got her glossy #30 with gray mane and tail in January 1962, and collector Jo Kulwicki has slides dated October 1962 showing her juvenile self with her glossy #30 with gray mane and tail. But the #30s on the cover of the 1963 catalog look matte and definitely have white mane and tail, as do the #30s shown in all subsequent catalogs. This model is called "Alabaster Lipizzan" in catalogs 1963-70; thereafter he is called simply "Alabaster." Many glossies have gray eartips and gray body shading. Some also have pink shading on the inside corners of the eyes (thanks to Liz Strauss for pointing this out to me). Many glossies and mattes have pink and gray stallion parts and pink nose. The gray genital shading is clearly visible as late as the 1976 catalog, but at some point subsequently this detailing was omitted and the models were issued with white under-portions. Collector Delana Metcalf wrote to me that she has a #30 (white mane and tail) with a very shiny semigloss finish rather than the usual matte. The horse must date to the early 1970s since it has a "U.S.A." stamp and scant remnants of hoof pads. Regarding release date for #30 see note 4 for this mold.

♠ "King" The Fighting Stallion #32, gray appaloosa, medium gray horse, typically with white or pale gray belly; black splashed-on spots; bald face; medium or slightly darker gray mane and tail; black or gray lower legs and hooves; glossy (1961-66). The spot pattern varies wildly, ranging from spots only on the rump to spots all over the body. The intensity and distribution of gray and white areas on the body also vary, but the typical model has a "belly stripe" pattern: gray hindquarters and forehand fading into a white or very pale gray barrel. Collector Mary Reardon found an unusual model, heavily spotted all over a virtually alabaster body, with just a slight amount of gray shading on the forehand and hindquarters, and black lower legs and hooves. The bald face on #32 can be extensive, reaching well down the sides of the face. Some models have pink shading by the inside corners of the eyes (thanks to Liz Strauss for pointing this out to me). Some have charcoal-shaded stallion parts. The color of the lower legs varies from medium gray to black. Diederich 1988, Section 1, shows a horse with black legs and hooves, and collectors Jo Kulwicki and Paula DeFeyter both have models of this variation. Collector Sande Schneider owned a #32 with a typical "belly stripe" shading pattern but with the unusual feature of black mane and tail as well as black legs and hooves. Sande's horse (now sold) may be very old, for a #32 that seems to have black points appears in the earliest ads I know of for the Fighting Stallion mold, in the June and December 1961 issues of *Western Horseman*. Regarding release date see note 4 for this mold.

♠ "King" The Fighting Stallion #33, palomino; bald face; white points; most with pink-tan hooves; earlier ones glossy, later ones matte (1961-73). The palomino color of both the glossies and the mattes varies from light honey tan to bright orangy to dark golden tan.

The pink-tan hooves can be very pale; some models even have white hooves. Collector Tanya Parker has a glossy stallion with gray hooves. Many glossies and mattes have gray-shaded genitals. The bald face on #33 can be extensive, reaching well down the sides of the face. Although the matte horses were made later than the glossies, they are less common because they were made for fewer years. Catalogs do not say when the finish was changed, but mold-stamp data indicate that it happened in 1969 or 1970: of the many #33s I have examined, all the glossy #33s have no "U.S.A." stamp, while all but one of the mattes do have the "U.S.A." This stamp was added to the Fighing Stallion mold in 1970 (see note 7 for this mold). Regarding the release date of #33 see note 4 for this mold.

- "King" The Fighting Stallion #34, charcoal, bald face, white points, pink hooves, glossy (1961/63 - 1970). The body color ranges from black to brown, with varying amounts of light body shading. Some models have hand-painted eyewhites. The bald face can be extensive, reaching well down the sides of the face. The hooves can be very pale or even white on some specimens. This model is not in the 1960 catalog but is in the 1963. I have no other evidence to fix the release date more specifically within the 1961-63 period.
- "King" The Fighting Stallion #35, bay; bald face; black mane and tail; no black on the legs; 4 stockings; black hooves; most matte, a few glossy (1961/63 - 1987). Reissued as a special run in 1993. Many of the early #35s have shaded bodies, hand-painted eyewhites, and black shading on the genitals. The bald face can be extensive, reaching well down the sides of the face. I know of two glossy bay Fighting Stallions: one owned by collector Judy Davinich and the other by collector Sande Schneider (thanks to both for photos). Judy's horse has no hand-painted eyewhites, but Sande's horse does have these, as well as foam pads on the bottoms of the hooves and tail (see note 2 for this mold). I don't know about Judy's horse, but Sande's has the round Breyer stamp only, no "U.S.A.," so he is certainly from the 1960s. Since all the early Breyer catalogs that list #35—that is, catalogs 1963-70—specify that he is matte, the glossies were in all likelihood issued prior to 1963, though not earlier than 1961, for #35 is not in the 1960 catalog. Alternatively, the glossies could have been a special run made at any time during the 1960s. An ad for a lamp with a bay Fighting Stallion appears in the September 1964 *Western Horseman;* it is impossible to tell from the small black and white photo whether the horse is matte or glossy. For further discussion see the Lamps &Nightlights section in the Appendix near the end of this book.
- "King" The Fighting Stallion #931, woodgrain, black eyes, painted-on stripe, 4 painted-on stockings, black hooves, matte (1961-73). Regarding release date see note 4 for this mold. Neither the model shown in the 1963 catalog nor the collectors' specimens I know of have eyewhites, but perhaps a few models with this detail exist, to judge from this item on a sales list in the April 1978 *Model Horse Shower's Journal*: "very old disc. woodgrain fight.stal., slight scratch off side, no see in pic, walnut fin., wh. eyeliner."
- "Ponokah-Eemetah" The Blackfeet Indian Horse #897, dark bay blanket appaloosa, solid face, unstenciled blanket covering butt and part of barrel, splashed-on black spots, black points, gray hooves, Indian symbols, matte (1994-95). All models come with a hang tag suspended from the neck on a string, but the tags are different for 1994 and 1995. The 1994 tag explains: "Ponokah-Eemetah (literally translated 'Elk Dog') is the Blackfeet word for 'horse.' Blackfeet grandfathers spin tales to their grandsons of creeping into enemy camps taking prize stallions from war chiefs and riding many exciting chases after Ee-nee, the buffalo. This mount, the buffalo horse, was an especially spirited, long-winded runner." The 1995 tag says "Collect all four Native American designs for 1995" and sets a scenario of a girl being awakened by a spotted stallion. The bay color of #897 varies from very dark charcoal brown to medium/dark bay. Some models have a light bay area on the lower part of the face. The size of the blanket also varies, being restricted to the butt on some models and reaching to the withers on others. Eight different sets of Indian warpaint symbols were issued on #897, four in 1994 and four more in 1995, sufficient to make even the most ardent Breyer completist balk. The 1994 symbols are as follows: [A] yellow sun on forehead, and red and blue arrow on left hindquarter (shaft of arrow is blue; point and feathers are red); [B] 4 parallel white lines on left side of neck, and red handprint on left hindquarter (collector Sande Schneider got a model new in box with the 4 lines but minus the handprint); [C] long, curved yellow zigzag line running from left eye to left knee, and a pair of feathers at the root of the dock on the left side (one feather is brown with red tip, the other white with red tip); [D] a pair of white "open staple" shapes on the left shoulder, and a red zigzag line running from left side of the dock to the left hock. The 1994 catalog pictures only two models, with symbols A and C. Symbols A and B were in fact the first to be widely issued, although I heard reports of a few C models turning up early at toy shops in various parts of the country. Then at mid-year, symbols A and B were discontinued and symbols C and D were released. The 1995 symbols are as follows: [E] white dandelion shape on left cheek, and 4-color semicircular rainbow just behind left shoulder; [F] white dandelion on left cheek, pierced by a thick red-and-white banded arrow running from mouth, up the face, down the neck, to the bottom of the shoulder; [G] white dandelion on left shoulder, and two small red circles, each containing a white curved line, on left hip; [H] white dandelion on left shoulder, and a thick red-and-yellow banded arrow running from mouth, up the face, and down the neck to the dandelion (the general impression is of a schematic diagram for Pepto Bismol). The 1995 catalog pictures all four models, labeling those with symbols E and F "Production 1/1/95 to 6/30/95" and those with symbols G and H "Production 7/1/95 to 12/31/95." Neither the 1994-95 catalogs nor the models' hang-tags mention the meanings of "Ponokah's" warpaint symbols, but clues are available from Breyer's previous warpaint ponies; see Warpaint Indian Ponies below in the Traditionals section for a full list. On January 21 and June 1, 1995, the QVC home-shopping cable TV channel offered a total of 1,637 "Ponokahs" that were ordinary regular runs (E and F symbol versions) but that came in boxes labeled with the special-run model number #701795. On July 15, 1995, the Q2 home-shopping channel offered 75 regular "Ponokahs" (I'm not sure which versions) in boxes with the number 704495. (Information is per *JAH* editor Stephanie Macejko.) Leftover models may have been sold on subsequent programs.

Special-run models made from this mold:

- Bay Fighting Stallion SR #700993, bay, bald face, black mane and tail, no black on the legs, 4 stockings, black hooves, slightly semigloss (1993). Made for Toys R Us. About 6,000 models made (assuming that all the approximately 500 U.S. Toys R Us stores received 12 models each, as did my 2 local stores). This model is a reissue of regular-run bay #35 [1961/63 - 1987], and is nearly indistinguishable from the later, less shaded and less detailed #35s. The only difference is that the stockings on the SR are a bit higher, coming up onto the knees and hocks, whereas the stockings on the regular run generally end below the knees and hocks. This is not a very reliable difference however, since the stockings on the SRs and the regular runs are airbrushed and thus subject to height variation from model to model. The SR's box sports a large round gold sticker that says "1993 Special Collector Edition / Limited Production / Bay Fighting Stallion / Elegant and defiant, this Breyer is a highly collectible edition of a 1980's classic."
- Fighting Stallion SR, red sorrel, bald face, flaxen mane and tail, 4 stockings, pink-tan hooves, slightly semigloss (1993). Penney's holiday catalog. Sold in Breyer Wild Horses Of America Set SR #710493, with bay blanket appaloosa Foundation Stallion and black Mustang with 1 stocking. Projected quantity 1,500 sets; no final count was recorded in Breyer's computer when I spoke to *JAH* editor Stephanie Macejko in June 1995. The set's number is per a Breyer company computer printout of 1993 SRs.
- Rearing Circus Stallion With Ringmaster Set SR, flocked white, brown or blue glass eyes, white synthetic hair mane and tail, painted black hooves (1985). Penney's holiday catalog. Set also includes leather bridle, red feather plume, surcingle, and Ben Breyer doll dressed in ringmaster costume. Sold by Penney's for $44.99 for the set. The models owned by collectors Heather Wells and Kathy Bateman have blue glass eyes, but I have seen one or two others with brown glass eyes. See the under Ben Breyer in the Riders - Soft Or Jointed Plastic section for details on the doll and tack.
- "Sierra" SR #400196, red dun, bald face, darker red dun mane and tail, dorsal stripe, primitive bars on hocks, 1 right front stocking with tan hoof, other hooves gray-dun, matte (1995/96). *Just About Horses* subscriber special. Slightly fewer than 3,000 models made, per *JAH* editor Stephanie Macejko (conversation of May 1996). The certificates of authenticity issued with the models say "3,500 horses produced," but Breyer made only as many as were ordered, which turned out to be fewer than the limit stated in the *JAH* ad for this SR (*JAH* 22/#6 Nov./Dec. 1995, back cover: "limited to 3,500"). Although this SR was advertised in 1995, it was not distributed until February 1996. In view of his late release he will count as the 1996 *JAH* special, according to Stephanie (conversations of Dec. 1995 and Jan. 1996). Unlike previous *JAH* SRs, "Sierra" will have no date or number written on the belly because Stephanie felt that such an inscription would mar his appearance, what with his light-colored underbelly being so visible thanks to the mold's rearing stance. The certificates of authenticity are numbered, however, as well as signed by Stephanie. "Sierra" is not a portrait of any real horse (per Stephanie, conversation of July 1996). A few collectors reported on the Internet that they received models either with no dorsal stripe or with no bars on the hocks.

Notes:

(1) The name "King" was dropped from catalogs after 1970/71; it was never used in manuals.

(2) Breyer glued foam-rubber pads to the bottoms of the hind hooves and underside of the tails of many early Fighting Stallions to avoid scuffing customers' furniture. The pads are often orangy-tan in color and are round, although by now they have usually hardened and half crumbled away. The pads were applied for a number of years, from the early 1960s through the early 1970s. Collector Sande Schneider's glossy bay #35, which may date to 1961/62, and my glossy alabaster #30, dating to no later than 1963, both have pads. Pads are visible on the alabaster and woodgrain stallions in the 1963 catalog, the earliest catalog in which this mold appears, and on the alabaster in the 1966-70 catalogs (the photo is the same in all these years). My matte alabaster #30, whose "U.S.A." stamp dates him to no earlier than 1970, also has pads. Aside from Fighting Stallions, the only models I have heard of with hoof pads are one or two #99 glossy bay Quarter Horse Geldings. The extreme rarity of such models raises the possibility that their pads were added by previous owners rather than the factory.

(3) Chris Hess is identified as the sculptor of this mold in *JAH* XIII/#3 1985 (p. 13). The Fighting Stallion and Rearing Stallion molds are nearly identical to each other except that Fighting Stallion is large and Rearing Stallion is small. There are a few slight differences, however. The muscling on the two molds differs somewhat. The Fighting Stallion's face is straight while the Rearing Stallion's is slightly dished. The Fighting Stallion's head is a bit more tucked. And, as pointed out by Schlumpf 1994, the Fighting Stallion has a more open mouth, a somewhat fuller tail, and a more forward right hind leg than the Rearing Stallion.

(4) The Fighting Stallion mold is not in the 1960 catalog, but it is in the 1963, in all 6 of the early colors. (No catalogs were issued for 1961-62 to my knowledge.) The release date of 1961 that I have given for alabaster #30, gray appy #32, palomino #33, and woodgrain #931 (and for the mold) is per two ads for these models in the June and December 1961 issues of *Western Horseman.* The June ad offered the appy, palomino, and alabaster (called "Albino" in the ad); the December ad offered the appy, palomino, and woodgrain. The palomino and woodgrain horses were also advertised in the 1962 Ward's holiday catalog.

(5) Oddly, the Breyer company often uses the number 31 to refer to the Fighting Stallion mold in computer records and materials such as notices to sales representatives. For example, in a Breyer computer printout of activity 1985-92, the entry for "Chaparral" #855 describes him thus: "Limited edition (limited to 1992 orders). Buckskin pinto. Mold #31. KF box D. Projection Jun 1992: 27000 pcs." Normally, molds are designated by the number of one of the early models made from the mold—for example, the Clydesdale Mare mold is designated as #83, which is the number of the first model of that mold, the chestnut Clydesdale Mare. What is odd about the designation of the Fighting Stallion mold as #31 is that Breyer never issued any Fighting Stallion #31 model. (Indeed, to my knowledge Breyer never issued any model #31 of any mold.) There were Fighting Stallions #30 (alabaster), #32 (appy), #33 (palomino), and #34 (charcoal), but no #31. But intriguingly, the woodgrain Fighting Stallion is #931, and the decorator Fighting Stallions' numbers all end with 31. These numbers too are anomalous, for the numbers of all woodgrain and decorator models of other molds incorporate the number of one of the realistically colored models of the mold—for example, #992 for the woodgrain Belgian incorporates #92, the number of the smoke Belgian, and #1051 for the Copenhagen decorator Five-Gaiter incorporates #51, the number of the albino Five-Gaiter. According to former *JAH* editor Megan Thilman Quigley, the Fighting Stallion mold was referred to as #31 during her whole tenure at Breyer in the early 1990s. The woodgrain and decorator Fighting Stallion numbers suggests that the #31 designation dates back to the very beginnings of this mold in the early 1960s. How this came about I can only guess. Perhaps the "31" began as a Breyer employee's typo for "30" or "32," and the error wasn't noticed until "31" had become too entrenched to be changed. Or perhaps Breyer originally had plans for a #31 Fighting Stallion model but scuttled them for some reason after designating the mold by that model's number.

(6) Collector Kathy Bateman brought it to my attention that this mold's stallion equipment underwent a change at some point. On early models, the testicles are distinct and realistically rounded. On later models, the scrotum is basically a solid bar running from thigh to thigh, with only a hint of roundness remaining on the right side. Evidently the change occurred no later than 1985, for my late-version matte alabaster #30 is the bar version, as are all my subsequent Fighting Stallions. The change may have taken place in stages; I have an old #35 bay, probably from the 1970s, that has an in-between situation: he is nicely bifurcated, but the left testicle is bar-shaped rather than rounded.

(7) Early models of the Fighting Stallion mold have the round "Breyer Molding Co."

stamp only. Later ones have the round stamp and, as mentioned above, the "U.S.A." stamp—I have seen a couple of charcoal #34s with the "U.S.A.," so we know this stamp was added to the mold in 1970, when the "U.S.A." was introduced into the Breyer line generally. Some "U.S.A." models also have the "B" stamp.

Fine porcelain models — See Icelandic Horse; Premier Arabian Mare; Shire Horse; and Spanish Barb. For discussion see Evolution Of The Horse series and Premier Fine Porcelain Series. Also see Ceramic Models; Cold-Cast Porcelain (Resin) Models.

Five-Gaiter — Stallion, racking, right front leg raised high, molded-on ribbons in mane and forelock. Sculpted by Chris Hess. Mold in catalog-run production 1961/62 - 1995 (full-tassel mold version 1961/62 - 1970s; nipped-tassel mold version 1980 [maybe earlier] - 1995).

Catalog-run models made from this mold:

FULL-TASSEL MOLD VERSION:

- "Commander" The Five-Gaiter #51, albino; white horse with white mane and tail; reddish-brown or black eyes; pink nose and ears; gray hooves; turquoise mane ribbons with yellow crisscrosses; glossy (1961/63 - 1966). This model is called "albino" in all catalogs and price lists that include him. True to this labeling, some #51s have so-called "red eyes," which are actually dark reddish-brown. Other models have black eyes. In my experience and that of other collectors, the black-eyed models are more common than the red-eyed version. Many #51s have gray or pink and gray shading on the genitals and subtle gray shading on shoulders and haunches. Collector Jo Kulwicki has a black-eyed #51 whose mane ribbons are yellow with red crisscrosses, the color scheme normally used only on the glossy palomino Five-Gaiter. The model number 51 later belonged to "Yellow Mount" Famous Paint Horse ("Adios" mold).
- "Commander" The Five-Gaiter #53, palomino, bald face, white points, pink hooves, yellow mane ribbons with red crisscrosses, glossy (1961/62 - 1971). The body color varies from a light to medium tan palomino, which is typical of earlier models, to shades of orangy palomino on later specimens. The bald face can be extensive, reaching well down the sides of the face. The model shown in *JAH* 21/#4 Fall 1994 (p. 33) appears to have hand-painted eyewhites, but in my experience this is highly unusual. Some models have subtle pink shading by the inside corners of the eyes; I've seen one like this. Some models have gray-shaded stallion parts, as on collector Linda Bell's tan palomino horse. Linda's model also has yellow-and-pink mane ribbons; I have not seen this in person and can't be sure it is factory original. Collector Judy Miller has a #53 with black hooves, which she believes are factory original, though we can't be sure. Regarding the introduction date of #53, see note 1 for this mold. #53 was in the Showcase Collection as #520 in 1970-71 (see Showcase Collection in this section for discussion).
- "Commander" The Five-Gaiter #951, woodgrain, black eyes, long star painted on, 4 painted-on stockings, black hooves, white mane ribbons with blue crisscrosses, matte (1961/62 - 1965). Regarding the introduction date of #951, see note 1 for this mold. Typically these horses, like all other woodgrain models, have woodgrain mane and tail, but collector Kitty Anderson mentioned to me that her #951 has a black mane and tail, which appear to be factory original.
- "Commander" The Five-Gaiter #1051, Copenhagen decorator, dappled blue, bald face, white points, pink hooves, blue mane ribbons with black crisscrosses, glossy (1963-64). The hooves can be very pale pink or even white. The blue color on the ribbons is the same as the body color. For further discussion see Decorators (1960s) above in the Traditionals section.
- "Commander" The Five-Gaiter #2051, Florentine decorator, dappled metallic gold, bald face, white points, pink hooves, metallic gold mane ribbons with black crisscrosses, glossy (1963-64). The hooves can be very pale pink or even white. For further discussion see Decorators (1960s) above in the Traditionals section.
- "Commander" The Five-Gaiter #3051, Golden Charm decorator, solid metallic gold, bald face, white points, pink hooves, metallic gold mane ribbons with black crisscrosses, glossy (1963-64). The hooves can be very pale pink or even white. The gold paint on these horses can darken over time and by now often looks more like tarnished brass. For further discussion see Decorators (1960s) above in the Traditionals section.
- "Commander" The Five-Gaiter #4051, Wedgewood Blue decorator, solid blue, bald face, white points, pink hooves, blue mane ribbons with black crisscrosses, matte (1963-64). The hooves can be very pale pink or even white. The blue color on the ribbons is the same as the body color. For further discussion see Decorators (1960s) above in the Traditionals section.

FULL-TASSEL AND NIPPED-TASSEL MOLD VERSIONS:

- "Commander" The Five-Gaiter #52, sorrel; bald face; most with charcoal-brown mane and tail, some with reddish-brown; 4 stockings; gray hooves; white mane ribbons with red crisscrosses; matte and semigloss (1961/63 - 1986). Many early ones, both matte and semigloss, have hand-painted eyewhites. On earlier models the bald face can be extensive, with the white extending well down the sides of the face; newer models have a more limited bald face. This model is called "sorrel" in all Breyer catalogs that list him, but his body color varies widely, from very light to quite dark and from reddish sorrel to sepia/coffee shades with no red tones. Collector Sande Schneider owns an old glossy #52 whose sorrel coat was painted over Wedgewood Blue decorator color, as was revealed first by chips in the sorrel layer and then by (ruinous) efforts to remove the sorrel paint completely. As Sande notes, this horse suggests the possibility that in the mid-1960s, when Breyer found itself with a stock of "hideous, unrealistic" decorator models that the public refused to buy, the company decided to repaint some of them in the realistic regular-run sorrel color, perhaps adding the gloss to protect the sorrel paint from chips that would reveal the decorator "undercoat." So there may be more decorators out there hiding under sorrel coats. Collector Heather Wells has heard of a chalky #52 with woodgrain finish hiding beneath the sorrel paint and white basecoat. #52 was in the Showcase Collection as #520 in 1970-72 (see Showcase Collection in this section for discussion).

NIPPED-TASSEL MOLD VERSION:

- American Saddlebred #109, dapple gray, no or very few dapples on head or upper neck; bald face; pink nose and ears; white points; darker gray shading on knees and hocks; pink hooves; red mane ribbons with black crisscrosses; matte (1987-88). The gray body color is soft and fairly light. The gray shading on the legs varies; my own horse has almost none, so that his joints are nearly the same color as his body, but the horses in the 1987-88 catalogs have very dark gray knees and hocks.
- "CH Imperator" American Saddlebred #904, liver chestnut, star, large snip extending up above nose, mane and tail same color as body, dark red mane ribbons with blue crisscrosses, 1 right hind stocking with tan hoof, other hooves liver-charcoal, glossy (1994-95). The model is billed in the catalogs as "high gloss," but some specimens, among them those issued in the first months of release, are more of a high semigloss, or even matte. I have not seen a matte one, but collector Chris Semon and others own such models (per Haynet reports of Aug. 1996). The gloss is applied by spraying, per *JAH* editor Stephanie Macejko at BreyerFest 1994. "CH Imperator" is darker than the dark chestnut matte "Wing Commander" #140. These two models are portraits of related real horses: #904 is a portrait of "CH Imperator," a grandson of the famous five-gaited Saddlebred "Wing Commander." "CH Imperator," who is now retired at the Kentucky Horse Park, has a 12-foot-long natural tail. A photo of him is printed in *JAH* 21/#2 Summer I 1994 (inside front cover).
- Kentucky Saddlebred #862, red chestnut, dark chestnut mane and tail, stripe, 1 right hind and 2 front stockings with tan hooves, other hoof brown, blue mane ribbons with white crisscrosses, semigloss (1992-93).
- Pinto American Saddlebred #827, black pinto, tobiano; stripe; mane half black and half white; white tail; pink hooves; white mane ribbons with red crisscrosses; matte (1990-91). Same pattern as #117 dark chestnut pinto "Project Universe."
- "Project Universe" Premium Pinto American Saddlebred #117, dark chestnut pinto, tobiano; stripe; mane half dark chestnut and half white; white tail; pink hooves; gold mane ribbons with black crisscrosses; matte (1987-89). Same pattern as black pinto Pinto American Saddlebred. #117 represents a real horse named "Project Universe."
- "Wing Commander" American Saddlebred Five-Gaited World Champion 1948-1953 #140, dark chestnut, stripe, darker chestnut mane and tail, left front white pastern, 1 right front and 2 hind stockings, gray hooves, solid red mane ribbons, matte (1988-90). A Breyer company computer printout of activity 1985-92 states that #140 was "issued as a special item with this same number prior to put[ting] the horse in regular line"; the date of this special issue was 1987, and the customer was the American Saddle Horse Museum. This model represents the real horse "Wing Commander," born in 1943, who is widely revered as one of the top five-gaiters ever born. He won the Five-Gaited World's Grand Championship six years in a row, from 1948 through 1953. This champion's white markings were like those on the Breyer model, but the flaxen streaks in the real horse's mane and tail are not represented on the model. This model is somewhat lighter than the glossy liver chestnut "CH Imperator" #904, which is a portrait of "Wing Commander's" grandson. (Information on the real horse is from Beard 1993.)

Special-run models made from this mold:

NIPPED-TASSEL MOLD VERSION:

- Five-Gaiter SR, unpainted white (1980). Sold through *JAH* VII/#3 1980 (p. 13). This horse and several other completely unpainted models were offered to hobbyists interested in customizing, but many collectors kept them unpainted. See Unpainted Models for a complete list. This horse should be the nipped-tassel version (see note 2 for this mold), but the photo of him in the *JAH* issue is small, so I can't be positive.
- "Moon Shadows" SR #400294, blue roan, light gray horse covered with darker gray flecks, black-shaded head with white snip, black mane and tail, 2 hind stockings with tan hooves, front legs and hooves black, blue mane ribbons with silver crisscrosses, matte (1994). *Just About Horses* subscriber special. 2,000 models made, per the ad for the model in *JAH* 21/#4 Fall 1994 (back cover). The model number is per *JAH* editor Stephanie Macejko and a Reeves memo of October 6, 1994, to salespersons. "Moon Shadows" can have a greenish cast to the body. Each horse has "JAH '94" handwritten on the belly. My own models and others I know of have two apostrophes before the "94," but this detail could vary. Certificates of authenticity signed by Breyer executive Peter Stone and Stephanie Macejko were mailed separately from the models. The certificate states: "This limited piece is a blue roan Five Gaiter named Moon Shadows. This horse is ______ of 2,000 produced. These special edition models were hand-crafted at Breyer in Wayne, New Jersey in 1994." In the blank is written the individual model's number, which is a bit confusing. One of my models, for instance, has the number 940628; the "94" here indicates the year of production and "0628" is my horse's number in the run of 2,000.

Notes:

(1) This mold is not in the 1960 catalog; it is in the 1963 (there apparently are no catalogs for 1961-62). It is certain, however, that the mold was introduced no later than 1962, for the woodgrain and palomino Five-Gaiters are advertised in the 1962 Ward's holiday catalog (on pp. 5 and 78 respectively, for $3.98 each). The woodgrain is also in the 1962 Miller's saddlery catalog (p. 25, price $5.95).

(2) The Five-Gaiter mold has been altered in two ways over the years. Most recently, he suffered partial castration, being reduced to a monorchid by the removal of the left testicle. Breyer made this alteration sometime in 1993, to judge from my own models: my #862 Kentucky Saddlebred, purchased in November 1992, is fully endowed, as are all my earlier Five-Gaiter models; but my 1994 SR "Moon Shadows" and "CH Imperator" #904 are monorchid. Breyer previously altered this mold by removing the tassel from the upper mane ribbon (as was brought to my attention by Walerius 1991, p. 46). The upper mane ribbon originally extended well above the top of the mane and ended in a little tuft or tassel. The tassel was carefully painted on both sides with stripes in the colors of the ribbon, so that the colors could be seen clearly on the tassel even from the horse's left (non-ribbon) side. The tassel was eventually done away with, so that on all models made since then the ribbon ends abruptly at the mold seam on top of the mane and no ribbon color is visible from the left side. It is difficult to determine the precise date of the tasselectomy because catalog photos are not always clear and because collector's horses that lack the tassel might have lost it by accident—it is after all small, fragile, and vulnerably positioned, which is undoubtedly one reason why Breyer decided to retool it out of existence (another likely reason being that it was troublesome to paint). Nonetheless, evidence indicates that the tasselectomy happened for sure by 1980 and possibly as early as 1971. The 1980 catalog clearly shows a nipped-tassel sorrel #52—he is pictured from the left side, so there is no ambiguity—and subsequent catalogs show this fairly clearly too. Collectors Linda Desmarais and Lori Ogozalek wrote to me that their sorrel Five-Gaiters purchased in 1980/81 are the nipped-tassel version. Catalogs 1967-79 offer no help in moving the date back: the 1971-79 photos are too unclear to show the tassel-area detail, and the 1967-70 catalogs, although they show the full tassel, all use the 1966 catalog photo, which might not reflect post-1966 horses. However, collector Jo Kulwicki owns a palomino #53 that has not only a full tassel but also a "U.S.A." stamp, which dates the horse to no earlier than 1970. Collector Lynn Isenbarger has a nipped-tassel #52 sorrel with no "U.S.A." stamp which she received sometime prior to 1969, but in view of Jo's horse, I think Lynn's may be an accident victim.

(3) The name "Commander," given to all early Five-Gaiters, was dropped from catalogs after 1970/71; it was never used in manuals.

(4) Five-Gaiters are of different sizes, as are models of many other molds. For discussion of this phenomenon, see Mold Variations in the Appendix near the end of this book.

(5) *JAH* XIV/#3 1987 (p. 13) states that the Five-Gaiter was sculpted by Chris Hess, and

indeed the Five-Gaiter is one of the few Breyer molds with a "CHess" mold mark identifying them as his work. Former Breyer employee Jill Göllner, however, states that the Five-Gaiter was not originally sculpted by Hess but was adapted by him from a larger-scale sculpture by another artist whose name the Breyer company has lost (see Göllner 1989-90). Although Hess certainly based some of his Breyer designs on sculptures by other artists, I'm skeptical that he did so with this mold; in any case I have found no further evidence for Jill's claim.

(6) Early models of the Five-Gaiter mold have a "CHess" engraving (referring to sculptor Chris Hess) inside the right buttock and the round "Breyer Molding Co." stamp on right inner gaskin. Later models have the "U.S.A." stamp in addition to the engraving and the round stamp—I have seen a few glossy palomino #53s with the "U.S.A.," so we know this stamp was added to the mold no later than 1971. Some "U.S.A." models also have the "B" stamp.

Fjord — see "Henry" The Norwegian Fjord

"Fleck" — see Family Appaloosa Stallion "Fleck" (under Family Arabian Stallion)

Flocked models — In the Traditionals section see Clydesdale Gelding/Stallion SR (under Clydesdale Mare), flocked bay (also see note 2 for this mold); Collector's Rocking Horse (under Saddlebred Weanling); Collector's Unicorn SR (under "Smoky"); "Legionario" With Brenda Breyer Rider SR; "Misty" SR, flocked chestnut pinto; My Companion Rocking Horse SR (under Saddlebred Weanling); My Favorite Rocking Horse SR (under Saddlebred Weanling); Open Top Buggy (under Proud Arabian Stallion); Our Rocking Horse SR (under Saddlebred Weanling); Proud Arabian Stallion SR, flocked bay; Proud Arabian Stallion SR, flocked chestnut; Rearing Circus Stallion With Ringmaster Set SR (under Fighting Stallion); Running Foal SR, flocked palomino; Running Foal SR, flocked white; Running Mare SR, flocked palomino; Running Mare SR, flocked white; Sky Blue Unicorn SR (under Running Stallion); and "Stormy" SR, flocked dark chestnut pinto. In the Classics section below, see Sky Blue "Pegasus" SR (under Lipizzan), and see Miniature Collection for a complete list of catalog-run and special-run sets with buggies and flocked and haired horses.

All of Breyer's flockies were issued in the 1980s, the first being the flocked bay Clydesdale Gelding/Stallion SR and the flocked chestnut Proud Arab Stallion SR, both of which appeared in 1983. The last year of issue for any Breyer flockie was 1987. According to Breyer executive Peter Stone (conversation of Nov. 1994), all of Breyer's flockies were flocked, haired, and outfitted by the Riegseckers, an Amish family business in Indiana. Many of the flocked models have glass eyes—either blue or brown, with black pupils—which are inserted into the plastic eye-sockets. Other flockies have their normal molded-plastic eyes, which are painted with black paint. For further discussion see Riegseckers Models below.

Foundation Stallion — ♞ Pawing, looking left, tailtip attached to left hock. Sculpted by Chris Hess, design based on a calendar illustration. Mold in catalog-run production 1977-93, 1996- (mold version without sheath 1977 - 1980/81, 1992-93, and 1996-; version with sheath 1981/82 - 1991).

Catalog-run models made from this mold:

Sheathless and sheath mold versions:

♞ Azteca #85, dapple gray, bald or pale gray face, 4 stockings, gray hooves, semigloss and matte (1980-87). All catalogs that list this model show him with a gray mane and white tail, but in fact only the earlier models have the white tail; later ones have a gray tail. The earlier, white-tailed horses typically have more shaded or variegated body color, dapples on the neck and head, gray nose and ears, and semigloss finish; the mane, knees, and hocks range from medium gray to black. Some white-tailed horses (such as collector Kim Gackowski's) have coloring like the later, gray-tailed models, except of course for the gray tail: a more even, soft-looking body color, no or very few dapples on neck and head, pink nose and ears, matte finish, and a soft medium gray mane and tail, the same shade as or slightly darker than the body. The 1980 Ward's and Penney's holiday catalogs offered white-tailed models in a set with leather Western saddle, breastcollar, and bridle (the white tail is visible in the photos). Azteca horses are a Mexican breed produced from the cross of American Quarter Horses and Andalusians (*JAH* VIII/#2 1981, p. 12). The model number 85 belonged first to "Diablo" The Mustang in albino (Mustang mold) and then to the Dall Sheep (Bighorn Ram mold) before being assigned to the Azteca.

♞ Black Foundation Stallion #64, black, no white markings; black mane and tail; early ones with brown hooves, later ones with black hooves; semigloss (1977-87). The brown hooves are visible in the 1977-78 catalogs; thereafter the hooves appear to be black. This variation was pointed out to me by collector Catherine DeMott, who got her brown-hoofed, sheathless #64 sometime in the period 1977-79. Slightly later sheathless models have black hooves; I've seen specimens like this. No Breyer catalog, manual, or price list in my possession gives a clue as to what real stallion this model might portray or what breed he was supposed to have founded. Nor does the box in which #64 was packaged or any *JAH* issue from the period 1977-87 breathe a word on these topics. Nonetheless, the 1977 price list of the mail-order company R. & J. Distributors lists this model as "#64 'El Morzillo' Foundation Black Stallion." And in the September 1978 *Model Horse Shower's Journal*, editor Linda Walter states: "The Breyer Black Foundation stallion . . . [is] a Barb or Barb/Arab cross & based on Cortez's warhorse 'El Morzillo.' If I recall my Horse History anywhere correctly, this horse was a big black animal Cortez rode many times to victories, and when the horse was injured, left it behind with friendly Indians. The horse then became a local god complete with worshipers & its own monuments which were later destroyed by clergy who converted the Indians." Marney Walerius also lists #64 as Foundation Stallion "El Morzillo" in her book (1991, pp. 47, 89). So how did these people come to believe that #64 is a portrait of Cortez's Barb if Breyer publications never labeled #64 as "El Morzillo" or otherwise associated the model with Barbs, Spanish explorers, or the founding of the Mustang breed? The Breyer company itself was the source of the information, as the June 1979 *Model Horse Shower's Journal* reports: "Model Tidbit: From the Breyer Company to Helga Kartes came this info. The Black Foundation Stallion is an example of the Spanish Conquistador Horse . . An Andalusian with alot of 'Barb' in him." More recently, Breyer's magazine reaffirmed this background in an article on Spanish breeds, by former *JAH* editor Megan Thilman (*JAH* 19/#3 Summer II 1992). The article includes a photo of #64 with the caption "El Morzillo, Cortez's Spanish Barb." Horses of this type brought to America by Spanish explorers, Megan states, were "the major foundation stock of the Spanish Mustangs found in America" (p. 20). For more on the "El Morzillo" connection, see note 1 for this mold; and for another mystery regarding #64, see note 2. The model number 64 previously belonged to the dog model "Rin Tin Tin." For a brief period in the late 1970s #64 was sold in a special blister-wrapped display box with the model number 164. See Display Boxes above in this section for discussion.

Mold version with sheath:

♞ American Indian Pony #710, red roan, white horse with chestnut flecks, chestnut mane and tail, gray-shaded joints, tan hooves, matte (1988-91).

Mold version without sheath:

♞ "Fugir Cacador" Lusitano Stallion #870, light buckskin, solid face, gray facial shading and dorsal stripe, black points, black hooves, matte, Limited Edition (1993). *JAH* 19/#5 Winter 1992 (inside front cover) says this model has tri-color eyes, and the model shown in the 1993 catalog has tri-color eyes; however, the models actually produced for sale have normal monochrome black eyes. Megan Thilman Quigley, who was *JAH* editor when this model was produced, told me that the catalog model, which is a test piece, has tri-color eyes because Breyer originally planned to make "Fugir" the Commemorative Edition (all CE horses have fancy hand-detailed eyes). This plan was scuttled as a labor-saving measure. By switching the Commemorative Edition to "Domino" The Happy Canyon Trail Horse, a model that already required hand-detailing on one eye (his blue one), Breyer could reduce by a third the number of eyes requiring hand-detailing that year. "Fugir Cacador" means "Fleet Hunter" in Portuguese, per the same *JAH*. Neither *JAH* nor the catalog mentions whether the model represents a real horse. The Lusitano is a Portuguese breed somewhat similar to the Andalusian (*Simon & Schuster's Guide*). This model's box sports a large round gold sticker saying, in full: "1993 Limited Edition (Limited to 1993 orders) / Fugir Cacador / Lusitano Stallion / The Lusitano is a Portuguese horse of great speed, courage, and agility." Limited Edition models are produced only for one year, in quantities sufficient to fill all orders for the model.

♞ Lakota Pony #869, white with cream shading; mane and tail white with tan streaks; large blue patches with white dots on chest and buttocks; Indian symbol on face, shoulder, or hip; tan hooves; matte (1992). Plains Indians painted blue patches with white markings on their horses to protect them from arrows and bullets in battle, according to the 1992 catalog. Collector Sande Schneider observed a (live) Indian pony with this blue patch with spots in the movie *Dances With Wolves*. The 1992 Breyer catalog, as well as the small hang tag suspended from the neck of each #869 model, also tells about five different symbols used by Plains Indian horse cultures: a rectangle, meaning "war party leader"; coup marks, which are straight lines stacked atop each other, each line indicating one enemy killed or wounded; a keyhole-shaped "medicine" symbol; a symbol shaped like an unused staple, meaning "Horse taken in raid" (the catalog says, "color of marking showed color of horse taken"); and a symbol shaped like a bunch of grapes without stems, representing a wish for hail to fall on the enemy. Only two symbols were used on the first Lakota Pony models produced: each pony had either [A] the rectangle (in red on the shoulder) or [B] coup marks (three red lines across the nose). The company originally planned to use only these two symbols, but in response to consumer demand decided to use two more (see *JAH* 19/#2 Summer I 1992, inside front cover). Thus the original two were discontinued in July 1992, after only a few months in production, and two new symbols were released: each model has either [C] the keyhole (in red on the neck) or [D] two staple-shapes (in black on the hip). Breyer executive Peter Stone, in his presentation at the West Coast Model Horse Collector's Jamboree (July 18, 1992), said that about 9,000 models were made in the first series of two symbols. To my knowledge no models with the hail symbol were produced. Lakota Pony models have a chalky appearance in that they have a white basecoat with the cream shading and other colors added over it.

Special-run models made from this mold:

Mold version with sheath:

♘ Foundation Stallion SR, alabaster, very light gray shading, pink-gray hooves, matte (1985). Made for Horses International (a division of Atlantis International). 700 models made. The vendor and quantity are per Pinkham 1988 and Walerius 1991 (p. 101). Former Breyer executive Peter Stone did not recall the quantity of this SR when I asked him about it in December 1995. My dating for this SR is based on price lists from Horses International and from Bentley Sales Company, which got a small quantity of the horses. The earliest Horses International list I have that includes this SR is dated November 1985 and states, "Limited to one model per customer!" The earliest Bentley's list that includes it is dated December 1985. Bentley's sales record cards in my possession show that Bentley's received just 51 models, and this small quanity evidently sold out quickly, for the horse is already gone from Bentley's January 1986 list. Reflecting their much larger share of models, Horses International included this SR on their price lists as late as June 1988 (with no limit on orders from 1986 on). Both companies give the model number for this SR as 64W.

♘ Foundation Stallion SR, liver-charcoal, solid upper face, white and pink nose, reddish flaxen mane and tail, 4 stockings, pink-tan hooves, semigloss (1987). Penney's holiday catalog. Sold in Breyer Traditional Western Horse Collector Set SR #712848, with red dun semi-leopard appaloosa "Adios" and red bay "San Domingo." 3,800 sets made. (Quantity and set number are per a Breyer company computer printout of activity 1985-92.) The Penney's catalog describes the horses as representing particular breeds: "the Appaloosa (speckled horse). The Quarter-horse (brown with white hind legs), and the Mustang (the charcoal brown horse)." So the "Adios" is an appaloosa, the "San Domingo" is a quarter horse, and the Foundation Stallion is a mustang.

♘ Foundation Stallion SR, palomino, baldish face, white points, pink nose, gray hooves , matte (1983). Ward's holiday catalog. Sold in Palomino Horse And Foal Set SR with palomino Stock Horse Foal, standing. Bentley Sales Company sold leftovers of these in 1985: 29 stallions and 25 foals, per Bentley's sales record cards in my possession.

Mold version without sheath:

♘ Foundation Stallion SR, bay blanket appaloosa, solid face, unstenciled blanket covering butt and loins, splashed-on bay spots, black points, 1 right hind stocking with pink-tan hoof, other legs and hooves black, matte (1993). Penney's holiday catalog. Sold in Breyer Wild Horses Of America Set SR #710493, with red sorrel Fighting Stallion and black Mustang with 1 stocking. Projected quantity 1,500 sets; no final count was recorded in Breyer's computer when I spoke to *JAH* editor Stephanie Macejko in June 1995. The set's number is per a Breyer company computer printout of 1993 SRs.

♘ Foundation Stallion SR, unpainted white (1980). Sold through *JAH* VII/#3 1980 (p. 13). This horse and several other completely unpainted models were offered to hobbyists interested in customizing, but many collectors kept them unpainted. See Unpainted Models for a complete list. The photo of this model in the above-mentioned *JAH* issue hides the sheath area, but other evidence indicates that he is probably the mold version without sheath. For discussion see note 3 for this mold.

Notes:

(1) Breyer sculptor Chris Hess took his design for this mold from an artist's illustration in a Hallmark calendar, according to Breyer executive Peter Stone (conversation of Nov.

1994). The illustration was titled "El Morzillo," which was the name of a Barb horse brought to the New World by the Spanish conquistador Cortez. Though the name "El Morzillo" was never printed in Breyer literature or on #64 Black Foundation Stallion's box (Breyer wished to avoid attracting Hallmark's attention, according to Stone), the company did communicate it to various hobbyists (see the entry above for #64). Who the artist of the Hallmark illustration was Stone could not recall, but it may well be Rich Rudish, who did a lot of work for Hallmark, including calendars. Collectors Jeanene Mangone and Eleanor Harvey have reproductions of a painting by Rudish titled "El Morzillo"; Jeanene is quite sure hers is in a 1970s Hallmark calendar full of paintings by Rudish (her calendar was packed away and inaccessible at the time Jeanene mentioned this on the Haynet in Nov. 1996). In the mid-1980s, Rudish worked directly for Breyer, creating the "Sham" and "Lady Roxana" molds for the Artist Series.

(2) A mystery concerning the Black Foundation Stallion arises in *JAH* XI/#4 1985 (p. 16). Reprinted here is a newspaper clipping that features a photo of a huge black wooden horse, about life-size, which otherwise looks identical to Breyer's Foundation Stallion #64. According to the newspaper caption, the horse stands on the bar in a hotel in Zurich, Switzerland. An added *JAH* caption teases, "Notice the resemblance to Breyer No. 64?," but offers no explanations. The editor of this *JAH* issue was Breyer executive Peter Stone. When I asked him about this Swiss horse in March 1995, he had forgotten all about it and could shed no further light.

(3) What appears to be a portion of stallion equipment on this mold has come and gone over the years. The portion in question is a sheath—a less than generous extrusion of plastic set at an angle and located a bit further forward on the belly than it should be. (It could be interpreted as an umbilical hernia.) Catalogs and other evidence indicate that the mold was issued without the sheath 1977 - 1980/81; with the sheath 1981/82 - 1991; and again without it from 1992 on. Collector Catherine DeMott wrote to me that her brown-hoof #64 Black Foundation Stallion, purchased sometime 1977-79, came new without a sheath, and that the brown-hoof model pictured on her horse's box (which bears the copyright date 1977) is also sheathless. Breyer catalogs 1977-79 too show the sheathless version of #64, the only model of this mold then in production. In catalogs and *JAH* issues 1980-81 the sheath area isn't visible, but evidence from collectors proves that the mold was still sheathless in 1980: Diederich 1988, Section 1, shows a sheathless #85 Azteca, which was purchased in 1980 (I now own this model), and collector Lynn Weber received a sheathless Azteca for Christmas 1980. The 1982 catalog does show the sheath (on #85; the area is hidden on #64). The 1985-86 and 1991 catalogs also show the sheath. The area is hidden in 1983-84 and 1987-90, but the SRs issued in these periods do have sheaths. Starting in 1992 the mold was again issued without the sheath: as shown in the 1992 catalog, the Lakota Pony was issued minus the sheath (thanks to collector Sue Lehman for pointing this out to me), and all models produced since then have likewise lacked this portion.

(4) The Foundation Stallion mold has the round "Breyer Molding Co." stamp. Some models also have the "B" stamp (my and Kay Schlumpf's white-tailed Aztecas have it, as do Robin Briscoe's and Chelle Fulk's black #64s); earlier and later ones do not. This mold was never given the "U.S.A." stamp.

"Freckle Doll" Galiceno — see under Galiceño

Freedom Horse — see "Bolya" (under "Halla")

Friesian — ♞ Stallion, trotting, looking left, molded-on "shoes." Sculpted by Jeanne Mellin Herrick. Mold in catalog-run production 1992 - current as of 1996.

Catalog-run models made from this mold:

♞ Friesian #485, black, no white markings, black mane and tail, brown hooves, matte (1992-95). Some models have a slightly charcoal-gray cast to the body. The Friesian is a light draft horse developed as a war horse in the Friesland province of Holland during the Middle Ages. It is also an excellent trotting and carriage horse and was at one time called the Harddraver, which means "good trotter" in Dutch. Today only black horses, "very rarely presenting white markings on the head only," are allowed in the Friesian registry. (*Simon & Schuster's Guide*, entry #9.) Models come with a hang tag suspended from the neck with a string; the tag gives the sculptor's name and tells about the Friesian breed, noting: "The world almost lost the Friesian breed to the devastation of World War I; only three stallions survived! Fortunately for horse lovers, this versatile, gentle horse endured."

Set:

♞ Action Drafters Big And Small set #3175, dark dappled bay big drafter, solid face, black points, 1 left hind sock with tan hoof, other hooves black, matte (1994-95). Set also includes gray dun small drafter (Little Bits Clydesdale mold). The large horse's dapples are sparse and extremely muted, being only a slightly lighter shade than the basic body color.

Note: The Friesian mold has the "© Breyer Reeves" stamp only.

Frisky Foals set SR — see Action Stock Horse Foal SR, yellow dun; Proud Arabian Foal SR, red chestnut; Running Foal SR, black blanket appaloosa; and Suckling Foal SR, dark palomino pinto

"Fugir Cacador" Lusitano Stallion — see under Foundation Stallion

Fun Foal Set (also called Adorable Horse Foal Set) SR — see Grazing Foal SR, bay blanket appaloosa; Lying Down Foal SR, chestnut; Running Foal SR, dark rose gray; and Scratching Foal SR, alabaster

"Fury" Prancer — ♞ No stallion parts, prancing, molded-on bridle and breastcollar; most with gold metal chain reins and removable plastic Western saddle. Sculpted by Chris Hess. Mold in catalog-run production 1955-65.

Catalog-run models made from this mold:

♞ "Black Beauty" Prancer #P40, black; earlier ones with stenciled full blaze and gold or black bridle and breastcollar, later ones with unstenciled bald face and silver bridle and breastcollar; black mane; tail solid black or black with white tip; most with 4 stockings; black or gray hooves; glossy; chain reins; black old-style Western snap-on saddle or brown English saddle with separate red plastic saddle blanket (1955/57 - 1960/62). This same model, but with different tack, was also sold in the mid-1950s in some Canadian Mountie #P440 sets and possibly some Kit Carson #P540 sets. This horse is called "'Black Beauty' Prancer" in the 1958 catalog and price list, but simply "Prancer, black" in an old Breyer sheet probably dating to 1955/57 and in the 1960 catalog, the last Breyer publication in which #P40 is listed. There are two basic versions of the black #P40: [A] The earlier version is molded in black plastic and has 4 stockings and a stenciled full blaze, all painted on. The tailtip is sometimes painted white but sometimes left black. The hooves are black. The bottom of the blaze is bluntly rounded, very unnatural looking. The breastcollar and bridle are usually gold, but sometimes black. The saddle is black with gold trim. [B] The later version is molded in white plastic and painted black, and has an unpainted bald face that extends over the nose; the 4 stockings are sometimes painted on and sometimes the natural white plastic. The tailtip is sometimes white, sometimes black. The hooves are painted gray. This version usually or always has silver breastcollar and bridle, and his black saddle has silver trim. On the several specimens I've seen, the reins on this silver-tacked horse have been the usual gold metal chains seen on other Prancers, Western Ponies, etc. Collector Teresa Ward found a silver-tack #P40 with eyewhites, which she says look factory painted; this is an unusual detail on any Prancer model. #P40 is not pictured in either of the catalogs that list him, but there are several reasons for saying A is the earlier version and B the later. For one thing, some version B specimens have the round Breyer stamp (I own one like this); this stamp was first put on Breyer models in 1960. Further, version A definitely came with some pre-1958 Canadian Mountie sets. Finally, version A has the same stenciled, blunt-ended blaze and gold bridle and breastcollar as the dark brown #P40 Prancer and was thus probably made in the same era. The Fall/Winter 1956 Sears catalog shows a Kit Carson set with a blunt-blazed #P40, though I can't tell whether the horse is the dark brown or the black since the photo is printed in sepia.Regarding the English saddle and blanket option, see note 6 for this mold.

♞ "Fury" #27, black, long vee-shaped star, black mane and tail, most with 4 stockings, gray hooves, black bridle and breastcollar, glossy; no reins, green paper saddle with "T.V.'s Fury" printed in white (1957/58 - 1965). This model represents the equine star of the TV show *Fury*, and Breyer catalogs and price lists 1958-65 say "Sold under license arrangements with television producers." The show ran from October 1955 through September 1966 (per Terrace 1979, 1: 355-56), so it is possible that the model was introduced as early as 1956, but I doubt that he was since he is not listed in the old mid-1950s Breyer sheets known to me. All the catalogs that picture "Fury" #27, namely those for 1958, 1960, and 1963, show him with the paper saddle, black bridle and breastcollar, and no reins. Oddly, the 1958 catalog credits him with a "white blaze,"and the pictured model does appear to have a full blaze—but the white could be a light reflection (I can't be sure from my Xerox copy), and "white blaze" could describe the vee-star, which is quite a large marking. I have seen one "Fury" with gold bridle and breastcollar. Some "Furies" are molded in black plastic and have the white markings painted on. Others are molded in white plastic and painted black; on many of these all the white markings are painted on over black paint (my own "Fury" is like this), but on some only the star is painted while the stockings are the natural white plastic. Collector Jo Kulwicki's "Fury" has not only natural stockings but matching unpainted white hooves. Collector Sande Schneider told me of a 2-stocking "Fury" with natural stockings, and collector Brad Leisure found such a model at a flea market in April 1996. Brad's "Fury" has an unpainted white star as well as unpainted hind stockings and hooves; its front hooves are painted only with some overspray from the black canons; and its bridle and breastcollar are the normal black.

♞ Prancer #P40, dark brown, full blaze, 4 stockings, black hooves, solid brown tail, gold bridle and breastcollar, glossy; chain reins, brown or black? old-style Western saddle or brown English saddle with separate red plastic saddle blanket (1955 - 1956/57). This same model, but with different tack, was also sold in the mid-1950s in Davy Crockett #P540[?] sets, at least some Kit Carson #P540 sets, and some Canadian Mountie #P440 sets. This pony's chocolate color is so dark that it may appear black in poor lighting. The pony's blaze, like the blaze on his black twin (#P40 black, version A), is bluntly rounded at the bottom, quite unnatural looking. No Prancers are listed or pictured in the ca. 1954 catalog. I date this dark brown pony's release to 1955 on the basis of an ad in the 1955 Sears holiday catalog for the Davy Crockett set. Although this ad, of which I have a Xerox, shows the pony to be a blunt-blazed #P40, it does not mention his color; but I assume he is dark brown since to my knowledge Davy Crocketts were not issued on black #P40s. The dark brown #P40 Prancer by himself is listed only on an old undated Breyer catalog sheet that probably dates to 1955/57 (partially reprinted in Walerius 1991, p. 25). The sheet doesn't picture this pony, but to my knowledge the version with blunt blaze and 4 stockings is the only dark brown Prancer there is. Most or all of the brown Prancers are made of dark brown plastic with the white markings painted on. The 1955/57 sheet does not specify the color of the Western saddle. It is entirely possible that both black and brown were used. My own brown Prancer has a black Western saddle, while Heather Wells's and Sande Schneider's have brown saddles. (All three horses were acquired second-hand, however, so we can't be positive the saddles are original.) Sande's horse also has hand-painted eyewhites. If they are factory original, they are an oddity, for eyewhites are not normally found on "Fury" Prancers of any color. Regarding the English saddle and blanket option, see note 6 for this mold.

♞ Prancer #P41, black pinto, tobiano; bald face; 4 stockings; gray hooves; white mane; black tail with white tip; gold bridle and breastcollar; glossy; chain reins, black old-style Western saddle or brown English saddle with separate red plastic saddle blanket (1955 - 1960/62). This same horse was also sold in the mid-1950s in Indian Chief And Pinto Pony #P241 and Lucky Ranger #P341 sets. He has the same pinto pattern as brown pinto #P42. No Prancers are listed or pictured in the ca. 1954 catalog. I date the release of this black pinto pony and brown pinto #P42 to 1955 on the basis of an ad in the 1955 Sears holiday catalog for a music box made from an Indian and pinto Prancer set (see Music Boxes below in the Riders - Hard Plastic section). The ad does not note the Prancer's color, but in any case, presumably the two different pinto colors debuted at the same time. The two pinto Prancers without riders are listed for the first time to my knowledge on an old undated Breyer catalog sheet that probably dates to 1955/57 (partially reprinted in Walerius 1991, p. 25). I have a #P41 with hand-painted eyewhites, but I doubt that they are factory original because they softened when soaked; Breyer paint normally remains hard and intact despite any amount of soaking. In any case, if they are factory original, they are highly unusual, for eyewhites are not typically found on "Fury" Prancers of any color. Regarding the English saddle and blanket option, see note 6 for this mold.

♞ Prancer #P42, brown pinto, tobiano; bald face; 4 stockings; gray hooves; white mane; chestnut tail with white tip; gold bridle and breastcollar; glossy; chain reins, brown old-style Western saddle or brown English saddle with separate red plastic saddle blanket (1955 - 1960/62). This same horse was also sold in the mid-1950s in Indian Chief And Pinto Pony #P242 and Lucky Ranger #P342 sets. He has the same pinto pattern as black pinto #P41. Regarding release date, see Prancer #P41. The 1958 and 1960 catalogs list #P42 as "brown pinto," but his color is lighter than this may suggest, varying from light honey tan to darker caramel tan to orangy sorrel to deep reddish sorrel. Some models have gray eyes and some have gold eyes, which are now typically tarnished. Regarding the English saddle and blanket option, see note 6 for this mold.

♠ Prancer #P43, palomino, bald face, palomino-shaded mane and tail, 4 stockings, gray hooves, gold bridle and breastcollar, glossy; chain reins, brown old-style Western saddle or brown English saddle with separate red plastic saddle blanket (1955 - 1960/62). This same horse was also sold in Lucky Ranger #P343 sets in the mid-1950s. The color of this Prancer varies from light to dark palomino. Some models have dark gray eyes and others have gold eyes, which are now typically tarnished. No Prancers are listed or pictured in the ca. 1954 catalog. I date the release of this palomino pony to 1955 on the basis of an ad in the 1955 Sears holiday catalog for a music box made from a Cowboy and palomino Prancer set (see Music Boxes below in the Riders - Hard Plastic section). The palomino Prancer without rider is listed for the first time to my knowledge on an old undated Breyer catalog sheet that probably dates to 1955/57. He is also advertised by the Wiesenfeld Co. in the August/September 1956 *Horse Lover's Magazine*; this ad has a picture of the pony and calls him "Pale Face." Regarding the English saddle and blanket option, see note 6 for this mold.

♠ Prancer #P45, white, white mane and tail, gray hooves, gold bridle and breastcollar, glossy; chain reins, black old-style Western saddle or brown English saddle with separate red plastic saddle blanket (1955/56 - 1960/62). This same horse was also sold in the mid to late 1950s in Canadian Mountie set #P445 and Robin Hood set #P145. No Prancers are listed or pictured in the ca. 1954 catalog. The white Prancer could have been released in 1955, but the earliest evidence I have for him is an ad in the 1956 Sears holiday catalog for the #145 Robin Hood set. The #P45 without rider is listed for the first time to my knowledge on an old undated Breyer catalog sheet that probably dates to 1955/57 (partially reprinted in Walerius 1991, p. 25). Some #P45s have gray/charcoal eyes; others have gold eyes (Sande Schneider has models like this), which are now typically tarnished. Regarding the English saddle and blanket option, see note 6 for this mold..

♠ Prancer #P945[?], woodgrain, black eyes, no white markings or other detailing, woodgrain bridle and breastcollar, no reins or saddle, matte (probably 1959). Several clues point to a 1959 dating for this model. First, neither he nor any other woodgrain model is listed in the 1958 catalog or price list or earlier publications known to me. Second, he is not in the 1960 catalog or later Breyer publications. Third, the several woodgrain "Fury" models I have seen or heard reliable reports of (Jo Kulwicki's, Sheryl Leisure's, and Sande Schneider's, among others) have no mold stamps, which means they antedate 1960, the year the round Breyer stamp was introduced. To my knowledge no 1959 price list or catalog exists, so we can't be sure what the woodgrain "Fury's" number is or even whether he was a regular run; conceivably he was a special. I've suggested the number P945 for this "Fury" because the woodgrain Western Pony is #945, and for all other colors of these two molds, Prancers and Western Ponies of the same color have the same numbers, with "P" prefixed to the Prancer numbers.

Sets (also see note 8 for this mold):

- Canadian Mountie set #P440, rider on dark brown or black Prancer (sometime in the period 1955-57). These same horses were also sold separately as "Black Beauty" Prancer #P40 [1955/57 - 1960/62] and dark brown Prancer #P40 [1955 - 1956/57]. For discussion of dates, set number, and details on the rider and accessories, see the Riders - Hard Plastic section.
- Canadian Mountie set #P445, rider on white Prancer (1957/58 - 1958/59). This pony was also sold separately as Prancer #P45 [1955/56 - 1960/62]. For discussion see the Riders - Hard Plastic section.
- Davy Crockett set #P540[?], rider on dark brown Prancer (1955 - 1956/57). During the same years this pony was also sold separately as dark brown Prancer #P40. For discussion of dates and details see the Riders - Hard Plastic section. MasterCrafters Clock Co. made clocks from this set probably at the same time that the set was in general production; see the MasterCrafters Clocks section in the Appendix near the end of this book.
- Indian Chief And Pinto Pony set #P241, rider on black pinto Prancer (1955 - 1956/57). This pony was also sold separately as Prancer #P41 [1955 - 1960/62]. For discussion see the Riders - Hard Plastic section.
- Indian Chief And Pinto Pony set #P242, rider on brown pinto Prancer (1955 - 1956/57). This pony was also sold separately as Prancer #P42 [1955 - 1960/62]. For discussion see the Riders - Hard Plastic section.
- Kit Carson set #P540, rider on dark brown or black "Fury" Prancer (1955/56 - 1956). These same horses were also sold separately as dark brown Prancer #P40 [1955 - 1956/57] and "Black Beauty" #P40 [1955/57 - 1960/62]. This Kit Carson set was advertised in the Fall/Winter 1956 Sears catalog. The Sears catalog does not mention the Prancer's color, and the photo is printed in sepia, but it shows the pony as very dark, so he has to be either black or dark brown. The photo does clearly show him with 4 stockings and a bluntly rounded stenciled blaze, so whichever color he was, he would also have a gold bridle and breastcoller (see "Black Beauty" Prancer #P40, version A). *Breyer Collector's Video* says the Prancer in this set was dark brown, but it is possible that some sets came with the "Black Beauty" Prancer. For discussion of dates and details on the tack and rider, see the Riders - Hard Plastic section.
- Lucky Ranger set #P341, rider on black pinto "Fury" Prancer (1955/56 - 1957). This pony was also sold separately as Prancer #P41 [1955 - 1960/62]. For discussion see the Riders - Hard Plastic section.
- Lucky Ranger set #P342, rider on brown pinto "Fury" Prancer (1955/56 - 1957). This pony was also sold separately as Prancer #P42 [1955 - 1960/62]. For discussion see the Riders - Hard Plastic section.
- Lucky Ranger set #P343, rider on palomino "Fury" Prancer (1955/56 - 1957). This pony was also sold separately as Prancer #P43 [1955 - 1960/62]. For discussion see the Riders - Hard Plastic section.
- Robin Hood set #P145, rider on white "Fury" Prancer (1956 - 1958/59). This pony was also sold separately as Prancer #P45 [1955/56 - 1960/62]. For discussion see the Riders - Hard Plastic section.

Special-run models made from this mold:

⯈ "Fury" Prancer SR, Wedgewood Blue, solid blue horse; charcoal-gray eyes; no white markings; mane, tail, and hooves same blue color as the body; gold bridle and breastcollar; gold chain reins; no saddle; semigloss (sometime in the period 1960-65). This horse is a slightly grayed sky-blue, very similar to the body color of the regular-run Wedgewood decorator models such as the Five-Gaiter and Mustang. This SR was brought to my attention by collector Sande Schneider and by collectors Ruth-Ann, Kirsten, and Sarah Wellman, who brought to BreyerFest 1994 a blue "Fury" that they had purchased earlier in the year from an antiques vendor in Georgia. Sande, who viewed the Wellmans' horse with me, had told me previously about a blue "Fury" she had seen at an earlier BreyerFest, which was identical to the Wellmans'. Sande had also heard of one other specimen. More recently, in spring 1996, collector Sherry Tuvell found yet another specimen at a flea market in Georgia. To judge from the photos Sherry sent me, her horse is identical to the Wellmans' except that it lacks reins. Both Sherry's model and the Wellmans' have the round "Breyer Molding Co." stamp, which dates the models to no earlier than 1960; but they could possibly have been made as late as 1965. When the Wellmans purchased their horse from the antiques vendor, who had owned the piece for decades, it was still wrapped in the 1965 newspapers that the vendor had put it in when he got it from another person in that year. The vendor also mentioned to the Wellmans that these blue horses were ordered from Breyer by a national company whose logo at the time was a blue horse head; the company used the models as "premium giveaways" to customers. With these clues in hand, the Wellmans are attempting to track down the details on the origins of this SR. Because of his uniformly blue coloration, the horse looks like he might be made of blue plastic, but a tiny chip on his hoof revealed that he is made of white plastic painted blue.

Notes:

(1) Chris Hess is identified as the sculptor of the "Fury" Prancer mold in *JAH* XIII/#2 1985 (p. 13).

(2) The "P" in "Fury" Prancer model numbers undoubtedly stands for "Prancer." This "P" is all that distinguishes the numbers of "Fury" Prancers (#P40, #P41, etc.) from the numbers of Western Ponies of the same color (#40, #41, etc.).

(3) Dating: The earliest records I know of for the "Fury" Prancer mold are ads in the 1955 Sears holiday catalog for the Davy Crockett set, the Cowboy on palomino Prancer music box, and the Indian on pinto Prancer music box (see Music Boxes below in the Riders - Hard Plastic section). The mold also appears in a 1956 Sears holiday catalog ad for the Robin Hood set with white Prancer, a Wiesenfeld Co. ad for the palomino Prancer (the ad calls him "Pale Face") in the August/September 1956 *Horse Lover's Magazine*, and an ad for the Kit Carson set with dark brown or black Prancer (the photo is sepia) in the Fall/Winter 1956 Sears catalog. The "Fury" Prancer is not mentioned in any of the ads I know of from 1950 through 1954 and is not mentioned in a write-up on the Breyer company's toy products in the February 1952 *Playthings* magazine (only the white and palomino Western Horses and the Money Manager toy are mentioned). Nor is the Prancer listed or shown in the ca.1954 catalog. For all these reasons, I believe this mold was first issued no earlier than 1955. It is true that there are MasterCrafters clocks that have Davy Crockett models on "Fury" Prancers, but contrary to Walerius 1991 (pp. 2-3), this in itself by no means implies that the "Fury" Prancer mold dates to 1950 along with the Western Horse, which was on the first MasterCrafters clocks made with Breyer horses. The MasterCrafters company made clocks for many years after 1950 (see MasterCrafters Clocks in the Appendix near the end of this book) and thus could well have made the Davy with Prancer clocks some years after the Western Horse clocks. For another thing, Breyer's own tale of Breyer's origins does not mention Davy or Prancer but only the Western Horse (see Breyer Company History in the Appendix). Thus I see no reason to believe that the clocks with Davy and Prancer were issued earlier than the published evidence for the Prancer mold would indicate.

(4) The old Breyer publications that list this mold call it simply "Prancer," giving the name "Fury" to only one of the several Prancer models. But collectors frequently use the name "'Fury' Prancer" to refer to any of the Prancer models or to the mold generally in order to distinguish it clearly from the Western Prancing Horse "Cheyenne," which collectors call Western Prancer for short. The Western Prancer mold replaced the less realistic "Fury" Prancer mold in the early 1960s, when all of the "Fury" Prancer models except #27 "Fury" were discontinued.

(5) To my knowledge all "Fury" Prancers that came with reins had the twisted-link type gold metal chain reins with a gold wire bit, as on Western Prancers, Western Ponies, and most Western Horses. For the history of these reins, see note 8 for the Western Horse mold.

(6) Saddles: "Fury" Prancers came with four different types of saddles and two different saddle blankets. [A] Brown hard-plastic "English" saddle with brown vinyl cinch (snap-on) and stirrup leathers and pale gray hard-plastic stirrups. This saddle is identical to Race Horse Derby Winner's saddle, but with the Prancer, the saddle also came with a separate hard-plastic saddle blanket. The saddle and blanket came with Prancers without riders and with the Canadian Mountie sets. The blanket with non-rider Prancers is red with a gold border stripe; the blanket in the Mountie sets is usually blue with a yellow border stripe, but may be red with gold stripe in some sets. The blanket comes in two mold versions: one with a ridge line on the underside across the withers and the other without (per Schneider 1993). The riderless Prancers with the English saddle and blanket are listed on an old Breyer company sheet probably dating to 1955/57. The sheet has a color photo of the white Prancer with the saddle and "gay red saddle blanket," but also lists four other Prancer models—black, palomino, black pinto, and brown pinto—which could be ordered with these accessories. Collectors Andrea Gurdon and Sande Schneider have both found white Prancers with the English saddle and red blanket. Oddly, the backside of this 1955/57 sheet, which lists the models on the front side by model number as well as color, lists the dark brown Prancer instead of the black. Be that as it may, the backside also states: "English saddle available. Specify English saddle or Western saddle will be shipped." Apparently not many retailers bothered to specify the English saddle, for the Western saddle is far more commonly found on old Prancers today. [B] Dark brown rubbery cavalry-type saddle, with molded-on saddle blanket and bedroll behind the cantle, and integral rubber girth with self "buckle." This saddle came only on Prancers with Davy Crockett and Kit Carson riders. [C] Dark brown rubbery medieval-type saddle with high pommel and cantle, molded-on rectangular blanket, and integral rubber girth with self "buckle." Two embossed griffins, as on a coat-of-arms, adorn each side of the saddle. This saddle came only with Robin Hood rider sets. [D] Old-style hard plastic Western saddle with tapaderos (pointed stirrup-covers); saddles come in black or brown, with the brown ones ranging from dark chocolate brown to brick red. This is by far the most common type of saddle found on "Fury" Prancers. It is the same as the old-style Western Pony saddle and came in the same variations, as Sande Schneider discusses (see Schneider 1992a): an early variation with no cinch, which came with some Cowboy rider sets; another early variation with long fenders and snap-on vinyl cinch, with the cinch attached to the saddle with grommets high on the fenders; and a later version (visible in the 1960 catalog) with short fenders and snap-on vinyl cinch attached to the saddle with grommets low on the fenders. The amount and style of paint detailing on these Western saddles also varies, but most have at least some touches of gold—or silver, as on one version of "Black Beauty" Prancer #P40—on the "studs" around the edges of the saddle. Sande has also found a brown Western saddle with gold intricately painted on the latigo ties that are molded on the front and back of the saddle skirt. For photos of these saddles, see the photos for the Western Pony mold.

(7) No "Fury" Prancers of any color were regularly issued with factory hand-painted eyewhites. However, a few specimens with eyewhites are known; see "Black Beauty" Prancer #P40, dark brown Prancer #P40, and black pinto Prancer #P41.

(8) It is possible that more Cowboy, Indian, and Lucky Ranger sets than I have listed above were issued by Breyer. For discussion see note 1 for the Cowboy mold in the Riders - Hard Plastic section below.

(9) Early models of the "Fury" Prancer mold have no mold marks. Models produced from 1960 on have the round "Breyer Molding Co." stamp only. This mold was discontinued before the "U.S.A." stamp was introduced. None of the various saddles used on the "Fury" mold has any Breyer stamp or other mold mark.

Future Champion Show Set SR — see under Saddlebred Weanling for the horse and under Brenda Breyer in the Riders - Soft Or Jointed Plastic section for the doll and tack

"Galaxias" SR — see under "Sham"

Galiceño — ♞ Pony mare, standing, looking slightly left, tail attached to left buttock and leg. Sculpted by Chris Hess. Mold in catalog-run production 1978-82, 1994-95.

Catalog-run models made from this mold:

♞ "Freckle Doll" Galiceno #888, reddish bay pinto, overo; blaze; large white patch on left side of barrel; black points; black hooves; matte (1994-95). The white patch on the barrel is the only pinto marking on this horse. The model shown in the 1994-95 catalogs (it's the same photo) appears to be a test color; the white patch has a more intricate outline than the rather blobby patch on the models produced for sale. See Galiceno #100 for discussion of breed.

♞ Galiceno #100, bay, no white markings, black points, black hooves, matte (1978-82). The color varies from a dark brown bay to a rich reddish bay. The Galiceño is a breed of small horse that originated in Galicia, a region of Spain. Galiceños brought to Mexico in the 1500s by the Spanish conquistadors were among the ancestors of mustangs. The Galiceño breed is still maintained in Mexico. (See *JAH* Winter 1978.) Breyer catalogs omit the tilde over the "n" in this breed's name, but this diacritic, indicating the pronunciation "gal-ee-ceen-yo," is correct according to *JAH* and *Simon & Schuster's Guide*, and reflects hobbyists' pronunciation of the name of this model and of the mold.

Note: The Galiceño mold has the round "Breyer Molding Co." stamp. It was never given the "U.S.A." stamp. Some models of this mold might have the "B" stamp as well as the round, but I'm not sure.

Galloping Thoroughbred — see under "Phar Lap"

"Gem Twist"— ♞ Gelding; cantering on left lead; braided mane; large, swirling, unbraided tail. Sculpted by Kathleen Moody. Mold in catalog-run production 1993 - current as of 1996 (39-braid version 1993-94, 20-braid version 1995 - current as of 1996).

Catalog-run models made from this mold:

♞ "Gem Twist" Champion Show Jumper #495, white; gray muzzle, white mane braids with red ribbons, white tail with brown-gray shading, brown-gray shaded kneecaps and points of hock, tan hooves with gray bands at top, matte (1993 -95). Models come with a small hang tag suspended from the neck by a thread; the tag gives the sculptor's name and tells about the real "Gem Twist," a Thoroughbred that has twice been named Horse of the Year by the American Grandprix Association. His rider is Greg Best and his owner is Michael Golden, of New Jersey. A photo of the real "Gem Twist" is printed in *JAH* 19/#5 Winter 1992. There are three versions of this model, distinguished from each other by the number and shape of the molded-on mane braids and the paint design of the ribbons on the braids. The earliest version, issued in 1993 (though not shown in the catalog for that year), has 39 braids, with every other one painted with a red stripe from top to bottom of the braid. These braids are thin, more or less uniform vertical ridges, some of them rather indistinct. The second version, first issued in late spring of 1994 and shown in the 1994 catalog, has the same 39 braids, but with a red dot painted in the center of every braid. The third version, released in January or February 1995 and shown in the 1995 catalog, has 20 braids, with a red dot painted in the center of every braid. These new braids are shaped like tiny hourglasses with round bottoms and are delicately etched with "hairs." The model in the 1993 catalog appears to be a hand-painted plaster or resin casting of the original sculpture. It has dot-style mane ribbons and battleship-gray hooves. What may be the same casting shown from the other side appears in *JAH* 19/#5 Winter 1992 (pp. 16-17); it has battleship gray hooves, but one front hoof sports a vertical tan stripe. Breyer has issued a second portrait of "Gem Twist" on the Jumping Horse mold; see Jumping "Gem Twist" SR in the listings for that mold. On July 15, 1995, the Q2 home-shopping cable TV channel offered 30 "Gem Twists" #495s in a set with leather Canongate English jumping saddle and hunter/jumper bridle; the sets came in boxes labeled with the special-run model number 704295 (per *JAH* editor Stephanie Macejko). Leftover sets were offered on a subsequent Q2 show in December 1995 (per collector Heather Wells) and perhaps other shows as well.

Notes:

(1) Kathleen Moody is identified as the sculptor of "Gem Twist" in the 1993 catalog, in *JAH* 19/#5 Winter 1992 (p. 17), and on the hang tag issued with "Gem Twist" #495.

(2) The "Gem Twist" mold is quite unstable, tending to topple backwards and to the left owing to his unusually weighty tail. Some specimens won't stand up at all. Many models also have an odd facial flaw, a seam that runs down from the right ear, passes just above the right eye, and swoops down and over onto the front of the face. On better prepared models this seam is neatly smoothed off, but on others it is quite obvious. Regarding the mold variations of "Gem Twist," see the entry for #495.

(3) The "Gem Twist" mold has the "© Breyer Reeves" stamp, inside the left gaskin.

"Geronimo" And "Cochise" set SR — In the Traditionals section see "Cochise" SR (under "Sea Star"); in the Classics section see "Geronimo" SR (under "Kelso")

"Gifted" — see under Hanoverian

Glossy finish — see Finishes in the Appendix near the end of this book

Godolphin Arabian — see "Sham"

"Goliath" The American Cream Draft Horse — see under Belgian

"Grayingham Lucky Lad" SR — see under Clydesdale Stallion

Grazing Foal — ♞ Filly, front legs splayed, mouth open. Sculpted by Chris Hess. Mold in catalog-run production 1965-81, 1993- 95.

Catalog-run models made from this mold:

♞ Grazing Foal "Bows" #151, bay; bald face; black mane, tail, and knees; 2 front stockings; gray or black hind legs; gray or black hooves; matte and semigloss (1965-76, 1978-81). This model was also sold in "Buttons" And "Bows" set #1411 [1965]. On earlier models the bald face can be extensive, reaching well down the sides of the face. On the foals with gray hind legs, the gray can be so lightly applied that the foal seems to have dirty white stockings. Collector Cheri Ashe kindly sent me a photo of her variation foal with a solid bay face, which she purchased in the early 1970s. Cheri's is the only solid-faced foal I know of.

♞ Grazing Foal "Bows" #152, black, bald face, black mane and tail, 4 stockings, gray hooves, matte and semigloss (1965-70). This model was also sold in "Buttons" And "Bows" set #1422 [1965]. The bald face can be extensive, reaching well down the sides of the face. A block-footed version of #152 may well exist.

♞ Grazing Foal "Bows" #153, palomino, bald face, white points, gray hooves, matte and semigloss (1965-81). This model was also sold in "Buttons" And "Bows" set #1433 [1965]. The color ranges from medium to dark palomino, and the amount of body shading varies. The bald face can be extensive, reaching well down the sides of the face. For the glossy variation of this model see Grazing Mare "Buttons," palomino.

Sets (for old sets see under Grazing Mare):

♞ "Buttons" & "Bows" set #3165, apricot dun "Bows" foal with stripe, darker red mane and tail, faint dorsal stripe, 2 hind stockings, tan-gray hooves, slightly semigloss (1993-95). Set also includes apricot dun "Buttons" (Grazing Mare mold). The names "Buttons" and "Bows" are a revival of the names used for these molds in the 1960s.

Special-run models made from this mold:

♘ Grazing Foal SR, bay blanket appaloosa, solid face, unstenciled butt blanket, splashed-on bay spots, black points, black hooves, matte (1991). Penney's holiday catalog. Sold in Adorable Horse Foal Set SR #714091, with chestnut Lying Down Foal, dark rose gray Running Foal, and alabaster Scratching Foal. 5,000 sets made. (Quantity and set number are per a Breyer company computer printout of activity 1985-92.) The name Adorable Horse Foal Set is per the Penney's catalog, but the box in which the foals were packed was marked Fun Foal Set. This appaloosa Grazing Foal nicely complements the red bay blanket appaloosa Grazing Mare SR produced in 1989 and 1990 for Sears.

Notes:

(1) Regarding early models, the name "Bows" was dropped from catalogs after 1970/71; it was not used in manuals.

(2) Earlier models of the Grazing Foal mold have the round "Breyer Molding Co." stamp only. Later ones have the round stamp and the "U.S.A." stamp. Some "U.S.A." models have the "B" stamp in addition (Chelle Fulk has a palomino #153 like this).

Grazing Mare — ♞ Mouth open, tailtip attached to right hock. Sculpted by Chris Hess. Mold in catalog-run production 1965-76, 1978-80, 1993-95.

Catalog-run models made from this mold:

♞ Grazing Mare "Buttons" #141, bay; bald face; black mane, tail, and knees; 2 front stockings; gray or black hind legs; gray or black hooves; matte and semigloss (1965-76, 1978-80). This model was also sold in "Buttons" And "Bows" set #1411 set [1965]. The bald face can be extensive, reaching well down the sides of the face. On the models with gray hind legs, the gray can be so lightly applied that the mare seems to have dirty white stockings. #141 was in the Showcase Collection as #1410 in 1970-72 (see Showcase Collection in this section for discussion).

♞ Grazing Mare "Buttons" #142, black, bald face, black mane and tail, 4 stockings, gray or black hooves, matte and semigloss (1965-70). This model was also sold in "Buttons" And "Bows" set #1422 [1965]. The bald face can be extensive. In my experience black hooves are less common than gray. #142 was in the Showcase Collection as #1420 in 1970 (see Showcase Collection in this section for discussion).

♞ Grazing Mare "Buttons" #143, palomino, most with bald face, white points, gray hooves, matte and semigloss (1965-76, 1978-80). This model was also sold in "Buttons" And "Bows" set #1433 [1965]. The color ranges from fairly light palomino to a medium orangy shade to dark palomino, and the amount of body shading varies. The bald face can be extensive, reaching well down the sides of the face. There are also solid-faced and semi-solid versions of this mare—collector Paula DeFeyter has a matte solid-faced one, and collector Linda Bell and I have matte dark palomino mares with a solid face that turns bald (white) just above the nose. Paula also wrote to me that knows of 2 people with glossy palomino Grazing Mare and Foal sets, one set being on a lamp; and Paula herself has a glossy palomino foal. Collector Sande Schneider too used to own a glossy foal, which oddly enough had unpainted eyes and hooves (the foal was from the 1960s; it had no "U.S.A." stamp). #143 was in the Showcase Collection as #1430 in 1970-72 (see Showcase Collection in this section for discussion).

Sets:

♞ "Buttons" & "Bows" set #3165, apricot dun "Buttons" mare, stripe, darker red mane and tail, dorsal stripe, 4 stockings, tan-gray hooves, slightly semigloss (1993-95). Set also includes apricot dun "Bows" (Grazing Foal mold). The names "Buttons" and "Bows" are a revival of the names used for these molds in the 1960s.

- "Buttons" And "Bows" set #1411, both bay (1965). These same models were sold separately as Grazing Mare "Buttons" #141 [1965-76, 1978-80] and Grazing Foal "Bows" #151 [1965-76, 1978-81].
- "Buttons" And "Bows" set #1422, both black (1965). These same models were sold separately as Grazing Mare "Buttons" #142 and Grazing Foal "Bows" #152 [both 1965-70].
- "Buttons" And "Bows" set #1433, both palomino (1965). These same models were sold separately as Grazing Mare "Buttons" #143 [1965-76, 1978-80] and Grazing Foal "Bows" #153 [1965-81].

Special-run models made from this mold:

♘ Grazing Mare SR, buckskin, diamond star, black points, black hooves, matte or somewhat semigloss (1995). Penney's holiday catalog. Sold in Serenity set SR #710195 with SR buckskin Lying Down Foal. 5,200 sets made (per *JAH* editor Stephanie Macejko, conversation of July 2, 1996). The diamond is oddly low on the mare's face owing to the heavy forelock, which covers the prime location for a star. My own mare has gray shading not only on the nose and sides of the face but on the throat.

♘ Grazing Mare SR, red bay blanket appaloosa; solid face; unstenciled blanket covering hindquarters and half of barrel; splashed-on bay spots; black mane and tail; legs red bay with black knees and hocks; black hooves; matte (1989 and 1990). Sears holiday catalog. Sold in Mare And Foal Set SR #494155, with red leopard appaloosa Suckling Foal. 11,000 sets made (1,000 of them for Sears in Canada). Quantity and set number are per a Breyer company computer printout of activity 1985-92. This mare nicely complements the bay blanket appaloosa Grazing Foal SR produced in 1991 for Penney's.

Notes:

(1) Regarding early models, the name "Buttons" was dropped from catalogs after 1970/71; it was not used in manuals.

(2) Early models of the Grazing Mare mold have the round "Breyer Molding Co." stamp

only. Later ones have the round stamp and the "U.S.A." stamp. Some "U.S.A." models might have the "B" stamp too, but I'm not sure.

"Greystreak" Action Arabian — see under Black Stallion

Grooming kits for people — In the 1950s and 1960s Breyer issued a number of regular-run models in sets with flexible vinyl "pack saddles" stuffed with grooming articles, such as combs, toothbrushes, and hair barrettes. Although Breyer undoubtedly did not manufacture the saddles and grooming aids, evidently the company did put the kits together and market them, for grooming-kit sets have been found new in unopened Breyer shipping cartons. Sets with Western Ponies are by far the most common, but sets with other molds are known. In the Traditionals section, see note 3 for the Proud Arabian Foal mold, note 4 for the Proud Arabian Mare mold, note 4 for the Western Pony mold, and the entries for black appy Running Stallion #127 and palomino Western Horse #57. In the Classics section see the entry for the bay Rearing Stallion "Rex" #185. The Hartland company also made grooming-kit sets with palomino Small Western Champs (per Fitch 1993, 2: 27); I am not sure which company had the idea first.

"Guinevere" English Hack — see under "Touch Of Class"

Hackney — see "Aristocrat"

Haflinger — Pony stallion, cantering on left lead, looking right. Sculpted by Chris Hess. Mold in catalog-run production 1979-84, 1991 - current as of 1996.

Catalog-run models made from this mold:

- Haflinger #156, chestnut, no white markings, reddish flaxen mane and tail, charcoal or gray-brown hooves, matte and semigloss (1979-84). The color ranges from medium sorrel to rich chocolate chestnut. This model was also sold through the 1979 Sears holiday catalog in a set with leather bridle and fuzzy cloth bareback pad with leather surcingle (the photo shows the pad as bright red). The Haflinger breed originated in Austria, where it was used for riding and farm work. Austrian Haflingers are bigger than Haflingers bred in the U.S. (*JAH* VIII/#2 1981, p. 12).
- Mountain Pony #850, light chestnut, solid face; pale flaxen mane and tail; gray shading on muzzle, knees, and hocks; dorsal stripe; 3-4 stockings; gray hooves; matte (1991-92). Catalogs show this model with 1 right front and 2 hind stockings, but my own model also has a sock on the left front. At a toy store, collector Kay Schlumpf found a couple of these models with labels on their boxes that said "#850 Chestnut Pony"; the models themselves were identical to ordinary #850 Mountain Ponies. I'm not sure how pervasive this mislabeling is, but I have seen boxes correctly labeled "Mountain Pony #850."
- "Sargent Pepper" Appaloosa Pony #926, roaned black leopard appaloosa, white pony roaned with gray flecks; stenciled black spots on body and head; gray-shaded breast, shoulders, and flanks; gray points; left hooves tan, right hooves brownish-gray; matte (1995 - current as of 1996). The hoof colors may vary—the pony in the 1995 catalog appears to have 4 brownish-gray hooves. The gray mane and tail are softly mottled with lighter and darker areas. Some ponies have a tan nose, others are gray nosed. My own tan-nosed pony also has tan shading on the sheath.
- "Scat Cat" Children's Pony #883, bay roan leopard appaloosa, pale beige body with splashed-on bay spots, head shaded tan and gray with bald face, black points, black hooves, matte (1993-94). This pony is described as "bay roan peppercorn" in *JAH* 19/#5 Winter 1992 (inside front cover).

Special-run models made from this mold:

- Haflinger SR, chestnut; solid face; gray mane and tail; some with 4 socks, some with no socks; gray hooves; matte (1985). Made for Horses International, a division of Atlantis International. 1,000 models made, per Pinkham 1988 and DeFeyter and Luther 1991. I date this horse on the basis of Horses International price lists: he is not on the list dated October 1984, but he is on the one dated November 1985. The latter list describes this SR as "golden brown, white socks and grayish-white mane and tail," but a variation without socks is known and is in fact listed separately from the version with socks on the July 1, 1987 Horses International list. An item in the March 1986 *Quequechan Model Horse Collector* sheds some light on the no-socks models. The item shows a photo of one pony of each version, and notes that the pony with no socks is actually a regular-run chestnut #156 (these models had no socks) with a gray mane and tail painted over the original flaxen. Some of the flaxen is evidently visible under the gray (the photo is inscrutable). The item continues: "HI [Horses International] complained and more were made correctly."
- Haflinger SR, chestnut pinto, overo; half blaze on lower part of face; gray-chestnut mane, tail, and front hooves; gray hind hooves; matte (1990 and 1991). Made for The Country Store, Wisconsin. Sold in Three Piece Horse Set SR #401456, with black leopard appaloosa Pony Of The Americas and dappled rose gray Cantering Welsh Pony. 1,000 sets made. Quantity and set number are per a Breyer company computer printout of activity 1985-92.

Notes:

(1) Breyer sculptor Chris Hess took his design for the Haflinger mold from a photograph or illustration, not from a real horse observed live, according to Breyer executive Peter Stone (conversation of Nov. 1994).

(2) The Haflinger mold has the round "Breyer Molding Co." stamp. At least some early models also have the "B" stamp, though I'm not sure if the very earliest ones do. This mold was never given the "U.S.A." stamp.

Half-year catalog runs — see Lakota Pony #869 (1992, see under Foundation Stallion); Proud Mother And Newborn Foal sets #3160 and #3161 (1993, see under "Lady Roxana" and in the Classics section under Andalusian Family Foal); "Ichilay" The Crow Horse #882 (1993, see under Indian Pony); Arabian Stallion And Frisky Foal sets #3162 and #3163 (1994, see under "Sham" and in the Classics section under Arabian Family Foal); "Ponokah-Eemetah" The Blackfeet Indian Horse #897 (1994 and 1995, see under Fighting Stallion); "Cody" #922 and "Hickok" #923 (1995, see under "Buckshot"); Princess Of Arabia sets, both numbered #905 (1995, see under Black Stallion).

In 1992, Breyer set a new speed record for turnover of catalog-run models. Halfway through the year, the company discontinued the two Indian symbols that had been issued on the Lakota Ponies since the start of the year and released two new symbols on the same ponies, which were then discontinued at the end of the year. The switch was not mentioned in the 1992 catalog, for Breyer had originally planned to issue only the first two symbols and made the change only subsequently, under pressure from consumers who were eager for a greater variety of symbols. Not slow to learn from a windfall, Breyer turned the half-year-production idea into an advertised feature of the catalog line the very next year with the introduction of the two Proud Mother sets, whose six-month production periods were announced in the 1993 catalog. The mares and foals in these sets go beyond the Lakota Ponies in that their entire body color changed at mid-year, not just a small portion of the paint design. The 1993 catalog introduced another half-year piece as well, namely "Ichilay,"; but like the Lakota Pony, "Ichilay" was not advertised as a short-production model and was changed only in Indian symbols (two in each half of the year), not in body color. Breyer repeated its 1993 strategy in 1994, issuing two new announced half-year sets with full color change, namely the "Sham" sets, and an unannounced switch of symbols (two in each half of the year) on a new Indian horse, "Ponokah-Eemetah." In 1995, Breyer brought collectors to the brink of rebellion with two announced half-year models with full color change ("Cody" and "Hickok"), an unannounced full color change on the horse in the Princess Of Arabia set, and another full round of unannounced symbol changes on the very same "Ponokah-Eemetah." Bearing in mind Breyer's accelerated turnover of catalog-run models generally during these years—with 28 new Traditional and Classic models and sets introduced in 1992, 28 in 1993, 32 in 1994, and 44 in 1995, not counting the symbol changes on the various Indian horses (and not mentioning special runs at all)—one has to wonder who will crash and burn first, the company or the collectors.

"Halla" — Mare, standing, looking left, tail attached to left buttock and leg. Sculpted by Chris Hess. Mold in catalog-run production: "Halla" mold version 1977-85, 1990-91; "Bolya" mold version 1992-94.

Catalog-run models made from this mold:

"Halla" mold version:

- "Halla" Famous Jumper #63, bay; most with star, some with solid face; black points; black hooves; matte and semigloss (1977-85). Breyer catalogs that mention #63's color call her chestnut, though the models plainly have black points. The body color is typically medium to dark brown bay but varies to red bay. Some models have a black stripe down the windpipe, and some have black eartips. There are three versions of facial markings that I know of: [A] Solid face. This earliest version must have been issued by mistake, for the real horse "Halla," of which #63 is a portrait, did have a star, as is clearly visible in a photo of the mare in Stoneridge 1972 (p. 414). Although Breyer catalogs 1977-79 do not show the model's face clearly, other evidence indicates that the solid-faced version came first: the picture box that "Halla" came in, which is printed with "© 1977," has a photo of the solid-faced version; also, collector Karen Perkins got her solid-faced mare when #63 was first released. Karen's mare (which I now own) and collector Kay Schlumpf's solid-faced mare are both red bay, with red bay nose, black on the legs that comes up to the body, and a black band running from the throatlatch down the windpipe and onto the chest. I've heard it suggested that solid-faced "Hallas" are chalkies, but my own model is not. [B] Star and black or solid bay nose. Collector Lori Ogozalek wrote to me that she purchased her red bay "Halla" with star and black nose in 1978 (it has a 1978 manual in its box), so I believe this version followed the solid-faced version. The bay-nosed horses may have come later, after version C. [C] Star and "snip" on nose. The "snip" is like that on many "Lady Phases": an unstenciled, slightly oversprayed bald area on the end of the nose. The 1980-85 catalogs show the star but don't show the nose clearly, so I am not sure when the snip version was issued. The real "Halla," a 16.3-hand bay mixed-breed mare foaled in Germany in the mid-1940s, was a high-strung jumper of remarkable talent. With her rider/trainer Hans Winkler, "Halla" won the individual jumping Olympic gold medal in 1956. (Information per Stoneridge 1972.) The "Halla" model is a nearly exact replica of the real "Halla" as posed in the photo in Stoneridge 1972 (p. 414); see note 1 for this mold.
- Noble Jumper #820, dapple gray, no dapples on neck and head, bald face, darker gray shaded muzzle and hindquarters, black front legs and hooves, 2 hind stockings with tan hooves, matte (1990-91). In July 1991 at a toy store, I saw two #820s without shading on the hindquarters; they were just normal Breyer dapple gray. The 1991 catalog shows #820 with the shading, though.
- U.S.E.T. Traditional Assortment #6984, "Halla" #63 with other models (1984). This was an assortment for dealers. I believe the packaging of the models in this assortment included a long paper strip printed with photos and various statements. See discussion under U.S.E.T. Traditional Assortment.

"Bolya" mold version:

- "Bolya" The Freedom Horse (Akhal-Teke) #490, golden buckskin; star; gray shading on face, breast, and belly; 2 front stockings with pink hooves; black hind legs and hooves; semigloss (1992-94). The Akhal-Teke is a light breed from Turkmenistan in the Central Asian region of the former USSR. These horses are now used in endurance riding, jumping, and dressage competition (*Simon & Schuster's Guide*). Per the 1992 catalog, "Bolya" is an Akhal-Teke mare whose name means "freedom" in Russian; she is a shimmering gold buckskin, which is one of the characteristic colors of the Akhal-Teke breed. Breyer produced this model to celebrate the disintegration of the Soviet Union. Models come with a small hang tag suspended from the neck with a string; the tag tells about the mare "Bolya" and about the Akhal-Teke breed. The model number 490 previously belonged to the Showcase Collection issue of the bay Morgan.

Special-run models made from this mold:

"Halla" mold version:

- "Halla" SR, fleabitten gray, white horse with soft gray flecks, gray shading around eyes and nose, gray mane and tail, gray- shaded knees and hocks, pink hooves, matte (1989). Penney's holiday catalog. Sold in International Equestrian Collector Set SR #715963, with dark dapple gray Hanoverian and reddish bay "Morganglanz" with solid face. 3,500 sets made. Quantity and set number are per a Breyer company computer printout of activity 1985-92.

Notes:

(1) Chris Hess sculpted this mold from a photograph of the real "Halla," according to Breyer executive Peter Stone (conversation of Nov. 1994). Stone did not mention which photo, but as *Model Horse Shower's Journal*, January 1979, reported, the mold looks amazingly like the real "Halla" as posed in a photo in *Great Horses of Our Time*, by M. A. Stoneridge (1972, p. 414). The resemblance between the Breyer and the photo is stunning; the lines and stance are virtually identical. The only notable differences are that the real "Halla" in the photo has a bridle on and is slightly over in the knees, a fault Hess's mold corrects.

(2) The "Halla" mold was modified to create the "Bolya" model, which was first released in 1992. The "Halla" version of the mold has no forelock; a braided mane, lying on the right side of her thin neck; a banged tail; and meagerly muscled chest and girth. The "Bolya" version has a forelock; a loose mane, lying on the left side of her beefed-up neck, with both windpipe and crest slightly thicker than "Halla's"; tail tapered at the bottom; and a bit of muscling added to chest and girth. The changes were designed by then Breyer employee Megan Thilman Quigley, who told me that she used a claylike medium called Sculpey to add the mane, muscling, etc., to a plastic "Halla" model. According to Megan, a craftsman then used the resculpted plastic model as a guide in tooling the new contours

into the old metal "Halla" injection mold. (The cost of the conversion was estimated at $5,500.00, per a Reeves memo of Oct. 25, 1991.) Thus, the old "Halla" mold no longer exists as such, as is confirmed by a Reeves memo of October 16, 1991, from Breyer engineer Ted Eng: "As of 10-16-91 mold #63 will no longer exist. It will be converted to #490 Bolya for 1992." Karen Gerhardt, a model-horse hobbyist and artist, wrote to me that she was employed by Breyer to paint Megan's resculpted plastic "Bolya" as the photo model for the 1992 catalog.

(3) The "Halla" version of this mold has the round "Breyer Molding Co." stamp. Some "Hallas" have the "B" stamp as well as the round. This mold was never given the "U.S.A." stamp. The "Bolya" models issued in the first part of 1992 have no mold stamps at all (I got one like this in March 1992; collector Linda Bell also has one). The "© Breyer Reeves" stamp was added to "Bolya" in the latter part of 1992; I have one like this, which I got in November of that year.

Hanoverian — Stallion, in the extended trot. Sculpted by Chris Hess. Mold in catalog-run production 1980-84, 1994, 1996- (version with brand 1980-84; version without brand 1994, 1996-).

Catalog-run models made from this mold:

MOLD VERSION WITH BRAND:

- Hanoverian #58, bay, no white markings, black points, black hooves, matte and slightly semigloss (1980-84). The color ranges from dark to medium bay. This horse was also sold through the 1980 Sears holiday catalog in a set called Hanoverian Horse With English Saddle And Bridle, with leather tack. The bridle has two reins (as on a double bridle) attached to snaffle rings. The model number 58 previously belonged to Western Mount Horse "Black Beauty" (Western Horse mold).
- U.S.E.T. Traditional Assortment #6984, Hanoverian #58 with other models (1984). This was an assortment for dealers. I believe the packaging of the models in this assortment included a long paper strip printed with photos and various statements. See discussion under U.S.E.T. Traditional Assortment.

MOLD VERSION WITHOUT BRAND:

- "Gifted," 1992 Olympic Dressage Bronze Medal Winner #887, bay, blaze, two-color eyes (brown and black), black points, 4 stockings, tan hooves, matte, Commemorative Edition (1994). 9,000 models made (per the 1994 catalog), most of them double numbered by hand in black ink on the belly. The numbering is difficult to see against the models' dark bay bellies. In March 1994, collector Karen Gerhardt and a friend purchased six unnumbered "Gifteds" at a toy store in Denver and heard that more had been sent to a sister store. Possibly more were sent to stores in other parts of the country as well. Reportedly the Breyer factory had sent these unnumbered models out inadvertently and recalled as many of them as had not yet been sold. The hooves on the "Gifteds" I've seen are typically tan (as shown in the catalog), but I got one horse with darker chestnut hooves. The "Gifted" model is a portrait of a famous dressage horse, as is explained by the large round gold sticker on the model's box (I quote in full): "1994 Commemorative Edition / (Limited to 9,000 Pieces serially numbered by hand) / Gifted / USA Olympic Bronze Medal Winner 1992—Barcelona, Spain." The 1994 catalog gives further background: "Standing 17.3 hands and weighing over 1,890 pounds, the mighty Gifted has won nearly every national title in dressage as well as placing strongly in a host of top European events. Piloted by the diminutive Carol Lavell, this popular Hanoverian clinched the Bronze Medal in team dressage with the most outstanding performance of their career at the Barcelona Summer Olympic Games." A photo of the real horse appears in *JAH* 21/#2 Summer I 1994 (inside front cover).

Special-run models made from this mold:

MOLD VERSION WITH BRAND:

- Hanoverian SR #410358, alabaster; pale gray mane, tail, knees, and hocks; pink ears and nose; pale gray hooves; matte (1987). Made for Your Horse Source, of MCS Enterprises, Inc. (per 1987 YHS brochures). 375 models made. Sold separately or in SR set with black, chestnut, and red bay Hanoverians. Quantity and date are per Your Horse Source fliers; model number is per a Breyer company computer printout of activity 1985-92.
- Hanoverian SR #410158, black, no white markings, black mane and tail, black hooves, semigloss (1987). Made for Your Horse Source, of MCS Enterprises, Inc. (per 1987 YHS brochures). 375 models made. Sold separately or in SR set with alabaster, chestnut, and red bay Hanoverians. Quantity and date are per Your Horse Source fliers; model number is per a Breyer company computer printout of activity 1985-92.
- Hanoverian SR #410458, chestnut, bright orange-red; no white markings; slightly darker chestnut mane, tail, and hooves; slightly semigloss (1987). Made for Your Horse Source, of MCS Enterprises, Inc. (per 1987 YHS brochures). 375 models made. Sold separately or in SR set with alabaster, black, and red bay Hanoverians. Quantity and date are per Your Horse Source fliers; model number is per a Breyer company computer printout of activity 1985-92.
- Hanoverian SR, dapple gray, white dapples splashed onto gray horse; dapples on neck and head; face solid gray or slightly dappled; dark gray mane, tail, knees and hocks; 4 painted-on stockings; dark gray hooves; semigloss (1986). Made for Horses International, a division of Atlantis International. About 200 models made. Date, quantity, and distributor information is per an announcement of this special in *Model Horse World News*, Winter/Spring 1986. The announcement has a photo of the model and states: "New from Horses International (these have not been officially released yet) . . . #58S Dapple Grey Hanoverian Special run only about 200." The April 1986 *Quequechan Model Horse Collector* also notes that these models were available from Horses International. These horses were made from #58 regular-run bay Hanoverians that were left over after discontinuation. The SRs were made by covering the bays with a white basecoat, then adding the gray body color, then splashing on the dapples. Because of the white base coat, these SRs look like chalkies. Collector Paula DeFeyter wrote to me that her model has pink dapples, though its painted-on stockings are the usual white; she knows of a few other models like this as well.
- Hanoverian SR, dark bay, red-shaded; solid face; black points; left fore and left hind stockings with tan hooves; other hooves black; slightly semigloss (1993). Spiegel's holiday catalog. Sold in Dressage Set Of 2 Horses SR #500693, with black "Misty's Twilight." 1,130 sets made (per *JAH* editor Stephanie Macejko). The model in the Spiegel catalog has a narrow blaze, but that must be a test color, for all the models received by collectors that I know of have a solid face. The set's number is per a Breyer company computer printout of 1993 SRs.
- Hanoverian SR, dark dapple gray, dark gray horse with slightly lighter gray dapples; dapples on neck and head; solid gray face; black points; black hooves; semigloss (1989). Penney's holiday catalog. Sold in International Equestrian Collector Set SR #715963, with fleabitten gray "Halla" and reddish bay "Morganglanz" with solid face. 3,500 sets made. (Quantity and set number are per a Breyer company computer printout of activity 1985-92.)
- Hanoverian SR #410258, red bay, bald face, black points, 4 stockings, black hooves, slightly semigloss (1987). Made for Your Horse Source, of MCS Enterprises, Inc. (per 1987 YHS brochures). 375 models made. Sold separately or in SR set with alabaster, black, and chestnut Hanoverians. Quantity and date are per Your Horse Source fliers; model number is per a Breyer company computer printout of activity 1985-92. This horse is a medium/light sandy red bay color.
- Hanoverian SR, unpainted white (1980). Sold through *JAH* VII/#3 1980 (p. 13). This horse and several other completely unpainted models were offered to hobbyists interested in customizing, but many collectors kept them unpainted. See Unpainted Models for a complete list.
- Vaulting Horse SR #700058 (or #7000-700058), black, blaze, pink nose with a bit of black freckling, black mane and tail, 4 stockings, tan hooves, matte (1990-91). Export special, made for European companies. 750 models made, per Ingrid Muensterer, owner of the German company Modell-Pferde Versand (email of June 1995). A Breyer company computer printout of activity 1985-92 states that this model was "in line 1990-1991" and indicates that 240 models were made in a batch in 1990. Other batches must have been made subsequently and omitted from the computer records. Some Vaulting Horses also became available through Black Horse Ranch in 1991. This model's box sports a large round gold sticker with phrases in English, French, and German (I quote in full): "Let your imagination play! / Laissez-jouer votre imagination! / Lassen Sie ihrer Phantasie freien lauf! / Voltigier-Pferd." "Voltigier-Pferd" means "Vaulting Horse" in German. The label that gives the model name and number on the front of the box says "No. 7000-700058 Vaulting Horse." The inclusion of the prefix "7000-" here may have been a mistake. This prefix appears on the bar code label on the bottom of all Breyer boxes that have such labels, but is almost always omitted from the name-and-number label on the front of the boxes. (For further discussion of prefixes see the start of the Models By Number section near the end of this book.) Real vaulting horses are of course not horses that vault but horses that are used by riders that vault onto them, off of them, etc. The vaults and other gymnastic maneuvers are performed while the horse walks, trots, or canters on a lunge line. An article on the sport of equestrian vaulting appeared in *JAH* 16/#1 Feb./Mar. 1989 (pp. 19-20).

MOLD VERSION WITHOUT BRAND:

- Dressage Horse ("Art Deco") SR #710595, black pinto, tobiano; two stars; pink chin; mane mostly white; black and white tail; legs mostly white; tan hooves; matte (1995). Penney's holiday catalog. 7,300 models made (per *JAH* editor Stephanie Macejko, conversation of July 2, 1996). This model has a large star between his eyes and a smaller star further down the face. He also has a white spot under his jowls. The model is called simply "Dressage Horse" in the Penney's catalog, but according to Stephanie Macejko, he is meant to be a portrait of the real Dutch Warmblood stallion "Art Deco," a half-brother of "Domino," another black pinto Dutch Warmblood stallion who has been captured in plastic by Breyer (see "Domino" SR, under "Roemer"). The model is also listed as "710595 Art Deco" on a Breyer company "1995 Special Items" printout dated April 5, 1995. A photo of the real "Art Deco" in extended trot and looking very much like his Breyer portrait appears in *JAH* 22/#5 Sept./Oct. 1995 (p. 36).

Notes:

(1) Until 1994 the Hanoverian mold had an "H" brand engraved on the near thigh. The verticals of the "H" curve outward and are bent sharply over at the tips. This brand is an approximation of the brand used on real German Hanoverians registered in the main studbook of the Verband hannoverscher Warmblutzuchter. As shown in a drawing in Coughlin 1994 (p. 8), the German brand is shaped like that on Breyer's Hanoverian, except that the tops of the verticals on the "H" of the German brand are little horse heads. Undoubtedly the tiny scale of the Breyer mold's brand prohibited reproduction of the horse heads. Be that as it may, the brand was removed from the mold prior to the release of "Gifted" #887 in 1994. According to Stephanie Macejko at Breyer (conversation of May 1996), the change was made for the sake of accuracy; the owner of the real horse "Gifted," Carol Lavell, told Breyer that the horse does not have the Hanoverian brand. Oddly, the removal appears to have taken place in phases.On some "Gifteds," the area is smooth and portions of the brand remain: collector Jennifer Barnas's model has fully half of its brand remaining, while one of my models has only two small pits, the remnants of the tips of the "H's" right vertical. But on other "Gifteds," the area of the brand is visibly smeared over, and the brand is completely effaced. I suspect that the models with brand remnants are earlier and were molded with the brand, which was then sanded off each model by hand, and that models with the smear are later, molded after the brand had been rubbed out of the metal injection-mold.

(2) Breyer sculptor Chris Hess took his design for the Hanoverian mold from a photograph or illustration, not from a real horse observed live, according to Breyer executive Peter Stone (conversation of Nov. 1994).

(3) Because this mold is rather unstable, some models have the toe of the near hind hoof slightly pared down to make the model stand up better. The cut toe is not molded but sanded or trimmed during the model-preparation stages at the factory.

(4) The Hanoverian mold has the round "Breyer Molding Co." stamp. Early models have the "B" stamp as well as the round, though I'm not sure if the very earliest ones have it. I have seen one or two old #58s with the "B," and collector Delana Metcalf wrtoe to me that the #58 she got from another collector in 1983 has a "B." This mold was never given the "U.S.A." stamp.

"Hanover" Trakehner — see under Trakehner

Happy Canyon Trail Horse — see "Domino" (under "San Domingo")

Henry, Marguerite — see Marguerite Henry Character Models

"Henry" The Norwegian Fjord — This new Traditional-scale mold is scheduled for release in 1996, according to *JAH* 22/#3 May/June 1995 (p. 2). A photo of a prototype, either the original sculpture or a resin casting, is shown on the back cover of that *JAH* and in the November 1995 issue of *Horse Show*, which identifies the mold as "Henry, the Norwegian Fjord." Breyer executive Peter Stone is responsible for the pun—"Henry Fjord" (per Jennifer Pegg's Haynet report on his remarks at the Puyallup Breyer Roundup event of Aug. 1995). The horse is walking, looking to one side, and is painted in the dun color that is characteristic of the breed. The original sculpture, by artist Kitty Cantrell, was on display at a 1993 open house in Southern California held by Karen Grimm, owner of Black Horse Ranch model mail-order company (see the BHR newsletter in *The Model Horse Trader*, March 1995).

"Hickok" — see under "Buckshot"

"Hickory" — see Family Arabian Stallion

"High Flyer" Tennessee Walker — see under Tennessee Walker

Highland Clydesdale — see under Clydesdale Stallion

"Hobo" — see under "Phar Lap"; also see next entry

"Hobo" The Mustang Of Lazy Heart Ranch (on stand) — see below in the Classics section

"Hope" — see under Family Arabian Mare

Horse and buggy sets — see Miniature Collection below in the Classics section for a full list

Horse Salute Gift Set SR — see "Lady Phase" SR, chestnut leopard appaloosa; "Morganglanz" SR, reddish bay with blaze; and "Phar Lap" SR, dark mahogany bay

Horses Great And Small set SR — see Cantering Welsh Pony SR, black; Clydesdale Stallion SR, grulla; and Miniature Horse SR, palomino (see under "Merrylegs" below in the Classics section)

"Hyksos" — see under Black Stallion

Icelandic Horse — ♞ Stallion, in the toelt gait, looking left, ears back; raised hooves have molded frogs. Sculpted by Kathleen Moody. Mold in catalog-run production 1992-94.

Catalog-run models made from this mold:

♞ Fine Porcelain Icelandic Horse #79192, buckskin pinto, tobiano; star; tri-color eyes with white "sparkle"; top half of mane chocolate, bottom half buckskin; chocolate tail; dorsal stripe on croup; chocolate hocks; pink-tan hooves; matte (1992-94) The total quantity made was 2,300 models (in two batches of 1,500 and 800), per Breyer executive Peter Stone (conversation of Oct. 4, 1995). Models cost $120-160 retail, and came with numbered certificate of authenticity signed by Peter Stone and sculptor Kathleen Moody. This is the first model in the Evolution Of The Horse series of fine porcelain models; for discussion, see Evolution Of The Horse above in the Traditionals section. This model is in the toelt (tølt) gait, a fast, ambling gait natural to Icelandic Horses (*Simon and Schuster's Guide*). To sculpt the piece accurately, Kathleen Moody studied a real Icelandic mare named "Von," owned by Sarah King, of Arizona (see *Equus*, Feb. 1992, p. 96). The bottom of the Icelandic's box says "Made in Taiwan," and at least some models came with a small white "Crafted in Taiwan" sticker on the body or hoof. The model numbers of Breyer's fine porcelains consist of the number 79, which is an abbreviation of the 7900 range number of the porcelains; plus a number designating the model, for instance, 1 for the Icelandic since he is the first porcelain introduced in his year; and finally a number designating the year the model was introduced, 92 in the case of the Icelandic (per *JAH* 19/#5 Winter 1992, p. 3; for discussion of range numbers see the General Note at the start of the Models By Number section near the end of this book).

Note: The Icelandic Horse mold has "© Breyer-Reeves" engraved inside the right thigh and "'92" engraved inside the left thigh.

"Ichilay" The Crow Horse — see under Indian Pony

Ideal Quarter Horse — ♞ Stallion with no genitalia, standing, looking slightly left. Based on a bronze sculpture by Suzann Fiedler. Mold in catalog-run production 1995 - current as of 1996.

Catalog-run models made from this mold:

♞ The AQHA Ideal American Quarter Horse #497, golden-brown chestnut; slightly darker chestnut mane and tail, tail subtly striped with gray; dorsal stripe; brownish-charcoal hooves; matte or slightly semigloss (1995). This model is the first in a series of four differently colored models of the same mold, to be issued one per year through 1998, with each model in the series being produced for only one year. Each model will commemorate one of four major foundation stallions of the American Quarter Horse breed—"Wimpy P-1," in 1995; "Leo," in 1996; "King," in 1997; and "Go Man Go," in 1998 (per the 1995 Breyer catalog). Artist Orren Mixer's famous portraits of these four stallions are printed in the 1995 Breyer catalog. The catalog is unclear about precisely what this series of models represents but tends to give the impression that they are portraits of the four famous stallions (although one then wonders why the #497 model lacks the white star that is prominent in the Mixer portrait of "Wimpy P-1"). But this is evidently a misimpression. The models are not portraits of these stallions themselves but fictitious representations of their offspring, according to the American Quarter Horse Association (AQHA) Registration Application that comes in the box with each model, which the purchaser may fill out and submit to the AQHA to "register" the model. On the form, the space for designating the name of the model's "sire" is already filled in with "Wimpy P-1" for the 1995 models. Obviously the model cannot be "Wimpy P-1" if its sire is "Wimpy P-1." The form also allows the purchaser to specify the model's name, color, gender, dam, and white markings. *JAH* 21/#5 Winter 1994 (p. 5) reports that the real "Wimpy P-1" (1937-59), born at the King Ranch in Texas, was "named grand champion stallion at the 1941 Fort Worth Exposition and Fat Stock Show" and subsequently became the first horse to be registered by the AQHA. The #497 model shown in the 1995 Breyer catalog is actually the bronze statue on which the Breyer model is based; see note 1 for this mold for discussion. The model's box comes decorated with a large round gold sticker saying, in full: "1995 / Ideal American Quarter Horse / Limited Edition Series / Own a Registered American Quarter Horse Model by Breyer / Registration Form Enclosed / AQHA / American Quarter Horse Association." On August 5, 1995, the QVC home-shopping cable TV channel offered 1,200 Ideal American QHs that were ordinary regular runs but that came in boxes labeled with the special-run model number 705695 (number is per the set's box; quantity is per *JAH* editor Stephanie Macejko). These QVC pieces were the first Ideal American Quarter Horse models offered anywhere in the world, according to Breyer executive Peter Stone in his remarks during the show.

Special-run models made from this mold:

♘ The AQHA Ideal American Quarter Horse SR #707795, dark red chestnut; slightly darker chestnut mane and tail, tail subtly striped with gray; dorsal stripe; red-charcoal hooves; matte or slightly semigloss (1995). Sold on Q2 home-shopping cable TV channel, August 18-20, 1995. About 192-221 models made. According to *JAH* editor Stephanie Macejko, who checked Breyer's computer records for me a week before the August 18 Q2 show, 192 pieces had been sent to Q2. I did not see the Q2 show, but at the West Coast Model Horse Collector's Jamboree on August 24-27, Stone told me that 96 pieces had been offered on the show and that approximately 125 more pieces would be sold on a Q2 show in October, for a total of about 221, although in his public remarks at the Jamboree he gave the total as approximately 250. (The October Q2 show was subsequently canceled, but the models eventually sold out nonetheless.) However many of them there are, these models were not intended to be a special run—they were the first pieces made of regular-run #497, painted in the wrong shade of chestnut. According to Peter Stone (conversation of Aug. 2, 1995), Breyer painted a sample #497 in the dark red chestnut shade and sent it to the American Quarter Horse Association for final approval. Not wanting to hold up production on the already delayed #497, Breyer proceeded to paint dark red horses while waiting to hear from the AQHA. Then word came from the AQHA that the shade should be brown, not red. Stone decided to send the reds to Q2 to stimulate collector interest in that station's Breyer shows, which had not previously been scheduled to have any special runs. On the show, Stone explained that these models were collectible "mistakes." The models came in Breyer boxes labeled with the special-run model number given above but decorated with the same large gold sticker as on regular #497 boxes (see above). Of the half dozen SR specimens I have seen, all but one were darker as well as redder than the "correct" regular-run golden-brown chestnuts I've seen; the remaining SR was about as light as the golden brown but redder in hue.

Notes:

(1) The AQHA Ideal American Quarter Horse #497 shown in the 1995 catalog is not a plastic Breyer but a painted bronze statue sculpted by Suzann Fiedler, which was used as the photo model because the plastic Breyer horses were not ready at the time of the catalog photo-session, according to *JAH* editor Stephanie Macejko. This bronze statue is one of several identical pieces that have been used on trophies presented by the AQHA to champion Quarter Horses, often in performance events. Collector and equine artist Laurie Jensen had two of the bronze trophies in her possession late in 1994, when she painted a portrait of the Quarter Horse that had won them for team penning. (Thanks to Laurie for a photo of these trophies.) The trophy bronzes were manufactured by Roger Lawrence & Associates, of Gardena, California, according to Kim Steinman, AQHA marketing services (letter of Sept. 1994). Breyer executive Peter Stone, in his presentation at BreyerFest 1994, stated explicitly that the Breyer mold would be a direct copy of the bronze trophy statue. *JAH* suggests this as well: "Artist Suzanne [*sic*] Fiedler created the American Quarter Horse Association's 'ideal' Quarter Horse stallion in bronze. Now a distinctive Breyer model . . . " (*JAH* 21/#5 Winter 1994, p. 5). But in fact the plastic Ideal QH, although similar to the bronze statue in stance and overall appearance, differs from it substantially. For one thing, the plastic Ideal is a full-sized Traditional model, whereas the bronze, according to Laurie Jensen, is significantly smaller, on the scale of a Breyer Artist Series model. Also, the plastic Ideal has no genitalia, whereas the bronze has a sheath (visible in the side-on photo Laurie provided). From a comparison of the plastic Ideal with the bronze as shown (at an angle) in the Breyer catalog, further differences are readily apparent, perhaps most strikingly in the muzzle, legs, and hooves. Indeed, as collector Megan Thilman Quigley pointed out to me, the plastic Ideal QH appears to be a Breyer "Lady Phase" model modified in some areas to resemble the bronze. The plastic Ideal's tail, neck, mane, and front of the shoulders look like those of the bronze, and his legs have been slightly repositioned from "Lady Phase's." But the muzzles and barrels of the plastic Ideal and "Lady Phase" are identical line for line, dimple for dimple, groove for groove—except for the "Suzann Fiedler" mold stamp that has been added to the Ideal's belly (see note 2 for this mold). Likewise identical are the Ideal's and "Lady Phase's" genitalia-free groins and, particularly from the side view, their shapely legs, right down to the round "Breyer Molding Co." stamp inside the right hind leg—a stamp whose occurrence on a new mold issued in 1995 is otherwise quite unaccountable (see note 2). In view of this ocular proof, it is hard not to believe that Breyer's Ideal QH was cast from a reworked "Lady Phase," a mare mold sculpted by longtime Breyer sculptor Chris Hess and first issued in 1976. Who did the reworking is a question that Breyer executive Peter Stone declined to answer in his discussion session at the West Coast Model Horse Collector's Jamboree in August 1995; nor would he concede that "Lady Phase" was in any way involved.

(2) The Ideal Quarter Horse mold has an assortment of mold stamps. First, on the belly is a "Suzann Fiedler" stamp in script letters; this is an exact replica of Fiedler's own signature, according to Breyer executive Peter Stone (conversation of Aug. 1995). Fiedler is the sculptor of the bronze "ideal American Quarter Horse" statue shown in the 1995 Breyer catalog (for discussion, see note 1 for this mold). Second, inside the left gaskin of the 1995 models is an "AQHA '95" stamp. The earliest releases of the 1996 model #498 Progeny of "Leo" (not listed in this book) also have this stamp, despite the fact that the 1995 and 1996 catalogs say the date in the stamp will be changed each year through 1998 to mark the change in model colors in Breyer's AQHA Ideal American Quarter Horse series (see the entry for #497 above). According to JAH editor Stephanie Macejko (conversation of May 1996), the #498s with the "AQHA '95" stamp were issued inadvertently. The stamp was changed to "AQHA '96" in early spring 1996. Third, inside the right gaskin is the round "Breyer Molding Co." copyright stamp. Although the round stamp is a familiar sight to Breyer collectors, its occurrence on a new mold in 1995 is remarkable, for prior to this the stamp had not been issued on any new Breyer mold since 1985, shortly after Reeves International purchased Breyer Animal Creations from the old Breyer Molding Company. The latter company ceased to exist at the end of 1985. (See the Breyer Company History and Mold Marks sections in the Appendix near the end of this book.) I believe the occurrence of this long-outdated stamp on the Ideal Quarter Horse mold can be explained by reference to a 1976 Breyer mold; see note 1 for discussion.

"Imperator" — see "CH Imperator" (under Five-Gaiter)

In-between Mare — see note 1 for the Family Arabian Mare mold

Indian Pony — ♞ Mare, walking, looking left, tail attached to left buttock and hock. Sculpted by Chris Hess. Mold in catalog-run production 1970-85, 1993, 1995 - current as of 1996.

Catalog-run models made from this mold:

♞ "Cheyenne" American Mustang #929, bay roan, pale grayish-tan horse with bay flecks; dark bay head with blaze; white freeze-brand painted on left side of neck; black points; 1 left front stocking with tan hoof; other hooves black; matte (1995 - current as of 1996). In the 1996 catalog, this model's name was expanded to "Cheyenne" Wild American Mustang Adopt-A-Horse. The base body color of this model varies from a pale tan color with virtually no gray in it to a pale gray dun or grulla color. The freeze-brand on this mare is different from that on SR "Mustang Lady." Freeze-brands are used on all wild mustangs and burros rounded up and put up for adoption by the U.S. Bureau of Land Management. BLM freeze-brands include symbols signifying species, year of birth, and registration number (per *JAH* 17/#2 May June 1990, p. 5). On

January 21, 1995, the QVC home-shopping cable TV channel offered 1,000 "Cheyenne" models that were ordinary regular runs but that came in boxes labeled with the special-run model number 701995. On July 15, 1995, the Q2 home-shopping channel offered 75 regular "Cheyennes" in boxes with the number 704095. (Information is per *JAH* editor Stephanie Macejko.) Leftover models may have been sold on subsequent programs.

- "Ichilay" The Crow Horse #882, grulla, light gray horse covered with brown flecks; solid face; charcoal-brown mane and tail; gray shading on face, knees, hocks, and fetlocks; 1 right hind stocking; 4 brown-gray hooves; Indian symbol; matte (1993). The gray paint on this model is thick looking. Each model comes with a small hang tag suspended from the neck by a string, telling about the general meaning of Indian warpaint and about the word "Ichilay" (pronounced ee-GEE-leh), the Crow Indian term for "horse," which literally means "to search with." Each model has one of four warpaint symbols, three of which are explained in the 1993 catalog: [A] Circled Eye: a red circle around the left eye, which in the Indian tradition was meant to help the horse see danger. [B] Fire Arrow: a red arrow outlined in yellow on the left shoulder, which was meant to enhance the horse's strength. [C] Feather: a 3-color feather, white at the top, brown in the middle, and red a the tip, located on the left side of the neck among the mane wisps, symbolizing a wound received by the warrior in battle. (The catalog says: "If a warrior was wounded in battle, he was entitled to tie a red feather for each wound in his horse's mane.") [D] Medicine Snake: a small white circle on the left stifle, with a long white zigzag line reaching from the bottom of the circle, down the leg, to the fetlock. This symbol is not mentioned in the catalog but it is identified as "Medicine Symbol for Snake" on a Breyer company flyer titled "Native American Painted Horses," which features a color photo of an "Ichilay" model painted with nine different Indian symbols. What the medicine snake signifies the flyer does not say. The two models shown in the 1993 catalog have the circled eye and fire arrow symbols; these were the first released, and were produced only until mid-1993. The feather and medicine-snake symbols were released in July 1993 and discontinued at the end of the year. The January 1994 *Model Horse Trader* contained a report that a collector had found an "Ichilay" with both the feather and medicine-snake symbols.
- Indian Pony #174, bay blanket appaloosa, solid face, black mane and tail, no black on the legs, unstenciled butt blanket, splashed-on bay spots, brown-charcoal hooves, no warpaint symbols, matte and semigloss (1973-85). The brown body color varies from medium bay to nearly black. On some models the mane and tail are charcoal brown rather than true black. The size of the blanket varies somewhat. For a brief period in the late 1970s #174 was sold in a special blister-wrapped display box that was probably labeled with the model number 1174. See Display Boxes above in this section for discussion.
- Indian Pony #175, chestnut pinto, tobiano; head mostly white; slightly darker chestnut mane and tail; gray hooves; earlier ones have warpaint symbols, later ones do not; matte (1970-76). In Presentation Collection mounted on American walnut wood base with brass "Indian Pony" nameplate, 1972-73. This Presentation model is listed as #5175 in the 1973 price list, but previously it apparently had the same number as regular-run #175; see Presentation Collection below in this section for discussion. (The number 5175 was later assigned to the alabaster Stablemates Standing Thoroughbred.) The pinto spots on #175 were airbrushed on by hand without a paint mask (per *JAH* 19/#2 Summer I 1992, p. 32). The warpaint symbols too were hand-painted and thus vary somewhat in size. My own #175 has all the following warpaint symbols: [A] A solid red triangle topped by a red dot, on the right shoulder. Some #175s have this mark on the right thigh instead of the shoulder; collector Sande Schneider's is like this. [B] Two "Z" shapes, one red and one blue, on the left flank. The "Z" represents a lightening bolt, per *JAH* 19/#2 Summer I 1992 (p. 32). And finally, [C] two "U" shapes (like unused staples), one red and one blue, on the left side of the neck. The "U" shapes represent horse tracks, each indicating one horse seized in a raid, per *JAH* 19/#2 Summer I 1992 (p. 32). The #175 shown in the Breyer catalogs has 3 rather than 2 of the "U" shapes on the neck. Evidence indicates that #175's warpaint was discontinued by 1973. For one thing, both of the other warpaint Indian Ponies (alabaster and buckskin) were discontinued by 1973, and the bay appy without warpaint was introduced in that year—so it makes sense that Breyer would discontinue the warpaint on #175 at this time. Further, Sande Schneider has a Presentation Collection pinto Indian Pony with no warpaint, which must have been made no later than 1973 since this was the last year in which this Presentation piece was issued. #175 is shown with warpaint in the 1970-74 catalogs, but these all use the same 1970 photo in their main entries on this mare, and the 1974 catalog shows her apparently without warpaint in a group photo in the back. The 1975 catalog has a different group photo that clearly shows her without warpaint. #175 was in the Showcase Collection as #1750 in 1970-72 (see Showcase Collection in this section for discussion).
- Indian Pony #176, buckskin, most with dark gray dun points and hooves, warpaint symbols, matte and semigloss (1970-72). The buckskin color of this model is typically quite dark and dusky. Some models have a dorsal stripe. Some have black lower legs and hooves along with dark gray dun mane and tail (I've seen photos of a few like this), and some have all black points (collector Paula DeFeyter has one like this), but in my experience dark gray dun points are the norm. I've heard that the kinds of warpaint symbols on #176 vary somewhat (and occasionally a symbol is missing), but my own model and others I've seen have all the following symbols: [A] a red sun with red rays, located below the left hip, and [B] four blue dots on the neck, two on each side. The dots represent hailstones, per *JAH* 19/#2 Summer I 1992 (p. 32). The blue shade varies from light to dark, per Paula DeFeyter, who also wrote to me that #176 comes in semigloss as well as matte. Paula's semigloss model has black lower legs and hooves, though its mane and tail are the normal dark gray dun. The warpaint symbols also vary in size from model to model, for they are hand-painted. #176 was in the Showcase Collection as #1760 in 1970-72 (see Showcase Collection in this section for discussion).
- Indian Pony #177, alabaster, gray mane and tail, gray shading on body, many with dorsal stripe and ventral stripe, gray hooves, warpaint symbols, matte (1970-71). In Presentation Collection mounted on American walnut wood base with brass "Indian Pony" nameplate, late 1971 only. No Presentation Collection models appear in the 1971 manual, but the alabaster Indian Pony and five other Presentation Collection models are announced in an ad in the November 1971 *Western Horseman*. This ad is the only place I know of where the Presentation alabaster Indian Pony is not only pictured but listed as such ("Indian Pony—white ... $15"); see Presentation Collection below in this section for further discussion. The warpaint symbols on #177s may vary somewhat (and occasionally a symbol is missing), but my own model and others I've seen have a red hand-print below the left hip and two "U" shapes (like unused staples), one red and one blue, on each side of the neck (for a total of four "U"s). The "U" shapes represent horse tracks, each indicating one horse seized in a raid, per *JAH* 19/#2 Summer I 1992 (p. 32). The warpaint symbols vary in size from model to model, for they are hand-painted. #177 was in the Showcase Collection as #1770 in 1970-71 (see Showcase Collection in this section for discussion).

Special-run models made from this mold:

- "Chinook" SR #700194, dark dapple gray, dark gray horse with lighter gray dapples, dapples on neck and head, dark dapple gray face, black points, black hooves, matte (1994). Export special, made for Modell-Pferde Versand (MPV), in Germany. 750 models made, per Ingrid Muensterer, owner of MPV (email of June 1995). Sources conflict about the quantity of this SR. MPV's early ad fliers said "limited to 500 pieces," but clearly Breyer increased that figure, for Ingrid wrote to me in May 1994: "So far, 750 Chinooks have been made, so Breyer has told me. . . . Of the 250 I have sold so far we have had a lot of damaged ones already, ears are chipped." Breyer executive Peter Stone said in his BreyerFest presentation in July 1994 that the run total was 900 models. *JAH* editor Stephanie Macejko checked Breyer's computer records in June 1995 but found the "Chinook" entry unclear, though it seemed to indicate 700 models made. In this welter of conflicting reports, I suspect Ingrid's are the most reliable—she is the one who received the models and paid Breyer for them, and her 1994 and 1995 reports to me were consistent. The brightness and quantity of the dapples on these models varies, with some models having such faint dapples that at first they may appear solid dark gray. The model number is per the model's box and ad fliers from Modell-Pferde Versand. The ad fliers note that the name "Chinook" "comes from the wind that sweeps over the Rockies in Alberta."
- Indian Pony SR #411175, black leopard appaloosa, white horse with black splashed-on spots, gray mane and tail, pink nose, gray hooves, matte (1987). Made for Black Horse Ranch model mail-order company. 400 models made. Sold separately or in SR set with dapple gray, blue roan semi-leopard appaloosa, and red bay Indian Ponies. Date and quantity are per BHR ads in the August 1987 *Model Rag* and the September 1987 *Collector's Journal*. Model number is per a Breyer company computer printout of activity 1985-92 (the printout gives the date too).
- Indian Pony SR #414175, blue roan semi-leopard appaloosa, gray forehand, solid face, unstenciled blanket covering butt and half of barrel, black spots splashed onto blanket and shoulders, black points, dark gray hooves, matte (1987). Made for Black Horse Ranch model mail-order company. 375 models made, per Karen Grimm of BHR. 400 models were ordered, but some defective pieces were returned to Breyer. Sold separately or in SR set with black leopard appaloosa, dapple gray, and red bay Indian Ponies. The date is per BHR ads in the August 1987 *Model Rag* and the September 1987 *Collector's Journal*, and per a Breyer company computer printout of activity 1985-92. The printout also gives the model number.
- Indian Pony SR #412175, dapple gray, dapples on neck and head; solid or dappled face; dark gray shading on forehand and hindquarters; dark gray mane and tail; 1 right hind stocking; 4 gray hooves; matte (1987). Made for Black Horse Ranch model mail-order company. 400 models made. Sold separately or in SR set with black leopard appaloosa, blue roan semi-leopard appaloosa, and red bay Indian Ponies. Date and quantity are per BHR ads in the August 1987 *Model Rag* and the September 1987 *Collector's Journal*. Model number is per a Breyer company computer printout of activity 1985-92 (the printout gives the date too). *Breyer Collector's Video* notes that this horse's color is patterned after the color of a real Thoroughbred horse named "Scammer," owned by BHR. The dapples on the head and belly are white, but those on the forehand and hindquarters are light gray owing to the gray overshading in those areas. My own model has a gray mane and tail, just slightly darker than the darkest parts of the body, but collector Lynn Luther's model has a charcoal/black mane and tail.
- Indian Pony SR #413175, red bay, bald face, black mane and tail, charcoal-brown front legs and hooves, 2 hind stockings with gray hooves, semigloss (1987). Made for Black Horse Ranch model mail-order company. 400 models made. Sold separately or in SR set with dapple gray, black leopard appaloosa, and blue roan semi-leopard appaloosa Indian Ponies. Date and quantity are per BHR ads in the August 1987 *Model Rag* and the September 1987 *Collector's Journal*. Model number is per a Breyer company computer printout of activity 1985-92 (the printout gives the date too). This model is a medium/light sandy red bay color.
- Indian Pony SR, red dun, darker red mane and tail, bald face, dorsal stripe, gray/dun-shaded knees and hocks, 2 hind stockings, 4 gray hooves, matte (1988). Penney's holiday catalog. Sold in English Horse Collector Set SR #713259, with red chestnut "Justin Morgan" and light coffee bay Black Stallion. The body shade of this SR pony varies from orangy to a darker, browner dun. *Breyer Collector's Video* refers to this Indian Pony as chestnut. The set number is per a Breyer company computer printout of activity 1985-92 and *JAH* 17/#5 Nov./Dec. 1990 (p. 29).
- Indian Pony SR #411294, red roan, pale tan horse with red chestnut dapples, dappled face, red chestnut mane and tail, red chestnut lower legs, brown hooves (1994). Volunteer special, given to the judging committee of the 1994 BreyerFest live show and to a few other volunteers who helped Breyer in 1994. 30 models made. This model revives Breyer's old style of red roan, which was issued on the Running Stallion, Mare, and Foal and a few other models in the 1970s and 1980s. Model number, quantity, and distribution are per *JAH* editor Stephanie Macejko (conversation of June 1995).
- Indian Pony SR, unpainted white (1980). Sold through *JAH* VII/#3 1980 (p. 13). This horse and several other completely unpainted models were offered to hobbyists interested in customizing, but many collectors kept them unpainted. See Unpainted Models for a complete list.
- "Mustang Lady" SR #412091, shaded gray, bald face, charcoal points, 1 right hind sock, many with white left front coronet band area, tan hooves, white freeze-brand painted on left side of neck, red "48" on each hip, matte (1991). Dinner model for BreyerFest in all four BreyerFest 1991 venues (see BreyerFest above in this section). 2,500 models made. Quantity and model number are per a Breyer company computer printout of activity 1985-92. The 2,500 figure may not reflect the final quantity, however, for former Breyer employee Steve Ryan, in his BreyerFest West presentation, said leftover models would be destroyed after the last of the four 1991 BreyerFests. (See BreyerFest SR Models for a listing of the four events.) The models, which came in plastic bags rather than boxes, vary from lighter to darker shades of gray. This model is a portrait of a real horse, "Mustang Lady," owned by Naomi Tyler, who got the mare through the Bureau of Land Management's Mustang adoption program in 1984, when the mare was two. Like all wild mustangs and burros rounded up by the BLM for adoption, this mare was freeze-branded with symbols signifying species, year of birth, and registration number (per *JAH* 17/#2 May June 1990, p. 5). The red "48"s on the model's hips represent the competitor's number carried by the real horse in the 1990 Tevis Cup 100-mile endurance ride, in which the mare and Tyler placed second. Information on Tyler and the horse is per *JAH* 17/#2 May June 1990 (p. 5) and 18/#2

Summer I 1991 (p. 14; the model appears on p. 16). A photo of Tyler riding "Mustang Lady" is printed on the cover of *JAH* 18/#1 Spring 1991.

Notes:

(1) Chris Hess is identified as the sculptor of the Indian Pony mold in *JAH* XII/#4 1985 (p. 19) and in *JAH* 19/#2 Summer I 1992 (p. 30). When I asked Breyer executive Peter Stone about the origin of this mold in October 1995, he was quite sure that Hess had sculpted it from a photo in one of Stone's art books on the famous Western painter and sculptor Charles Russell (1864-1926). The warpaint symbols on the various Indian Ponies derived from this book as well, he said. Stone's recollection is corroborated by a Breyer Molding Co. news release of which I have a copy. Dated January 20, 1970, the release announced the new Indian Pony mold with the headline "Shades of Charlie Russell." (I had not mentioned this release to Stone when he told me about the Russell art book, so his recollection was independent of it.) "In keeping with the growing interest in Western Art," the release continues, "the Indian Pony is hand decorated with traditional Indian symbols." The release omits mention of the sculptor of the mold, consistent with the fact that Hess was never identified as the sculptor of any mold in Breyer catalogs or manuals until the 1980s.

(2) The June 1979 *Model Horse Shower's Journal* contains this intriguing item by editor Linda Walter: "Ed. Anyone else find the solid black Indian Ponies in their area? Sigh . . ." This is the only reference to black Indian Ponies that I know of, and I have never heard of a specimen in a collection.

(3) The earliest models of the Indian Pony mold have the round "Breyer Molding Co." stamp only—I have seen specimens of all three early ponies (alabaster, buckskin, and pinto) with only this stamp. Later models have the "U.S.A." stamp as well as the round. The "U.S.A." must have been put on the mold no later than 1971, for collector Jo Kulwicki has an alabaster pony with this stamp, as does collector Sheryl Leisure's alabaster Presentation Collection pony. Some "U.S.A." models might have the "B" stamp too, but I am not sure.

International Equestrian Collector Set SR — see "Halla" SR, fleabitten gray; Hanoverian SR, dark dapple gray; and "Morganglanz" SR, red bay

JAH subscriber specials — see *Just About Horses* subscriber specials

Jamboree Specials — In the Traditionals section see "Sham" SR, liver chestnut (1994); and "El Campeador" SR (1995, see under "Legionario"). In the Classics section see Rearing Stallion SR, buckskin (1993). The West Coast Model Horse Collector's Jamboree, which was first held in 1992, is a multifaceted model-horse promotional event organized by collector Sheryl Leisure, who is also the editor of the magazine *The Model Horse Trader* (see the References section at the end of this book). All Jamborees to date have been held in Ontario, California, in the summer, a few weeks after BreyerFest.

"Joe Patchen" — see under "John Henry"

"John Henry" — Gelding, walking, looking right. Sculpted by Jeanne Mellin Herrick. Mold in catalog-run production 1988-93, 1996.

Catalog-run models made from this mold:

- "Joe Patchen," Sire Of "Dan Patch," #836, black, star and blaze, black mane and tail, 4 stockings, tan hooves, semigloss (1991-93). This model's facial markings are the same as those on SR liver chestnut "John Henry." See under Pacer for a description of the real "Dan Patch," a Standardbred pacer.
- "John Henry" Famous Race Horse #445, dark bay; solid face with light russet shading on lower half; light russet shading on belly, upper legs, and sometimes the body; black points; dark gray hooves; slightly semigloss (1988-90). The amount of russet shading on the body varies. My own #445 purchased in February 1989 is very dark, nearly black, with no russet highlights on the body; the model in the 1988 catalog is also like this and seems to lack the red highlights even on the face and legs. The #445s shown in the 1989-90 catalogs have so many russet highlights that they look brindled. I own one of these brindled horses and have seen others; they are very different from the earlier, solid black-bay version. The 1988 catalog states that the real "John Henry" is a Thoroughbred race horse who was the world's top Thoroughbred purse winner. He is now retired at Kentucky Horse Park. (Thanks to Debbie Vandegrift and Nancy Timm for pointing out to me that the horse is a gelding!) The model's box sports a large round gold sticker saying, in full: "Kentucky Horse Park / John Henry / The winner of seven Eclipse Awards, four Champion Turf Horse Awards, and two time Horse of the Year."

Special-run models made from this mold:

- Dark Bay Western Horse SR #711594, dark plum bay, solid face, black points; 4 stockings, tan hooves, matte (1994). Penney's holiday catalog. 6,700 models made (per *JAH* editor Stephanie Macejko, conversation of June 1995). Breyer executive Peter Stone mentioned at his presentation at BreyerFest 1994 that this horse would be called "Long Walker" (a name Stone himself created as an apt description of the mold), but the Penney's catalog used the name Dark Bay Western Horse. The model number is per an information fax of April 11, 1994, from Breyer to dealers; the fax lists the model as "'Lone [*sic*] Walker' - Western horse for J.C. Penney Catalog."
- "John Henry" SR, liver chestnut, star and blaze, darker liver mane and tail, 1 left fore and 1 right hind stocking with tan hooves, other legs light chestnut with gray hooves, semigloss (1992). Sears holiday catalog. Sold in Quiet Foxhunters set SR #491192 with seal brown "Roemer" and dapple gray "Rugged Lark." 1,800 sets made. Quantity and set number are per a Breyer company computer printout of activity 1985-92. (The number 11218, given for this set on the Bentley Sales price list of March 15, 1993, is the Sears number, not the Breyer number.) The facial markings on this SR "John Henry" are the same as those on "Joe Patchen."

Notes:

(1) This mold has a slightly lumpy texturing, as though the clay original hadn't been smoothed off. According to collector Megan Thilman Quigley, who was a Breyer employee when "John Henry" was created, the lumpiness resulted from sculptor Jeanne Mellin Herrick's unfamiliarity with the medium that Breyer required her to use, a spongy, rather difficult material called Sculpey. The 1988 catalog has a photo of Herrick working on either the original sculpture or a plaster casting of it.

(2) The "John Henry" mold has the "© Breyer Reeves" stamp only.

"Joy" — see under Family Arabian Foal; Proud Arabian Foal

Jumper — see Jumping Horse

Jumping "Gem Twist" SR — see under Jumping Horse

Jumping Horse — Stallion jumping over detachable stone-wall jump base (about 5.5" wide). Sculpted by Chris Hess. Mold in catalog-run production 1965-88, 1994.

Catalog-run models made from this mold:

- Jumping Horse "Stonewall" #300, bay, most with bald face, black mane and tail, many with no black or gray on the legs, various stockings, dark gray or black hooves, matte and semigloss; jump is tan on green ground (1965-88). The name "Stonewall" was dropped from catalogs after 1970/71; it was never used in manuals. On early models the bald face can be extensive, reaching well down the sides of the face. Some models have dark-shaded stallion parts, as on collector Linda Bell's #300 from the 1960s (he has no "U.S.A."). Some models have black eartips, as on my post-1970 horse. The number of stockings varies, but the norm is 3: 1 right hind and 2 front. Some #300s have gray or black shading on the joints or lower legs and thus look more like true bays. The model that collector Joan Fauteux got in the late 1960s has an extensive bald face, 2 front stockings topped by black knees, and dark gray back legs (thanks to Joan for photos). I have a similar old 1960s horse, the "ground" of whose jump is a bright grass green rather than the more typical dark green. The tan color of the jump varies from light to medium. Another variation of #300, which is shown in the 1976 catalog, has no white markings at all but a solid bay face and brown legs. Some of these solid bays are chalkies and some are not; I have seen both kinds and own a non-chalky one.
- "Starlight" #886, seal brown, large spiky star, black mane and tail, 1 left front and 2 hind stockings with tan hooves, other leg and hoof dark brown, matte and semigloss; jump is dark brown on gray ground; Limited Edition (1994). Most of the models I've seen are matte, but collector Leslie Granger found three very shiny semigloss specimens in a toy store in Missouri, one of which she purchased and later showed to me. I found a model nearly as shiny at a toy store in southern California. A "Starlight" with a bald face was advertised on a sales list of Gail Hildebrand; this is the only such model I have heard of. "Starlight" #886 represents a character in a popular book series, as the large round gold sticker on the model's box tells (I quote in full): "1994 Limited Edition (Limited to 1994 orders) / Starlight / A majestic jumper, Carole Hanson's horse in The Saddle Club books by Bonnie Bryant." The 1994 catalog explains further: "In Book #12, *Starlight Christmas*, Starlight was given to Carole as a Christmas gift. He was named for the lopsided star on his face. His trot is smooth, his canter gentle, but his greatest strength is his flawless jumping. Carole rode him in his first show in Book #25, *Show Horse*, where he won a reserve championship for a breathtaking performance over jumps." The Saddle Club books are published by Bantam.
- U.S.E.T. Traditional Assortment #6984, 2 Jumping Horses #300 with other models (1984). This was an assortment for dealers. I believe the packaging of the models in this assortment included a long paper strip printed with photos and various statements. See discussion under U.S.E.T. Traditional Assortment.

Special-run models made from this mold:

- Jumping "Gem Twist" SR #702795, white, gray-shaded muzzle, white mane, white tail with tan-gray tip, tan-gray shading on knees and hocks, tan hooves circled with gray at the top, matte; jump is medium gray on medium gray ground (1995). Made for the QVC home-shopping cable TV channel's Breyer hour aired June 1, 1995. 1,000 models made, per Breyer executive Peter Stone (conversation of Oct. 3, 1995). The model number is on the model's box. These models are supposed to be painted white and so have a "chalky" appearance reminiscent of the chalky models of the 1979s, according to an article in *JAH* 23/#2 March/April 1996 (p. 21). A photo of a Jumping "Gem Twist" that accompanies the article bears this caption: "The '95 QVC Jumper was a unique painted-white model." My own two Jumping "Gem Twists" and others I have seen, however, appear to be at most only parially chalky—they have a slight chalkiness on the legs, mane and tail, and nose, but their white body color appears to be the unpainted white plastic. This SR is Breyer's second portrait of the real horse "Gem Twist," a Thoroughbred that has twice been named Horse of the Year by the American Grandprix Association. The first portrait is a cantering mold; see "Gem Twist" above in the Traditionals section.
- Jumping Horse SR #401291, black, bald face, black mane and tail, 4 stockings, tan hooves, semigloss; jump is brick red on black ground (1991/92). *Just About Horses* subscriber special. 1,000 models made (per *JAH* 18/#5 Winter 1991, p. 18). "*JAH* 1991" handwritten on the bottom of the jump. Models came with numbered certificate of authenticity signed by Breyer executive Peter Stone and then-Breyer-employee Steve Ryan. Each certificate bears the number of the particular model (e.g., my certificate says "This horse is No. 0063 of 1,000 produced"). The certificate also says "These models were hand-crafted at Breyer in Wayne, New Jersey at the end of Winter 1991." The horse was advertised as the 1991 *JAH* special, and the issue in which the ad appeared is dated 1991. But the issue was behind schedule; it was not actually printed and distributed until February 1992, and the models were not sent out until mid-1992. The model number is per a Breyer company computer printout of activity 1985-92.
- Jumping Horse SR, seal brown; most with long star, some with solid face; black points; black hooves; matte; jump is light tan on green ground (1982 and 1983). Sears holiday catalog. Some of these models have a solid face, though the 1982 and 1983 Sears holiday catalogs and *JAH* IX/#2 1982 (p. 13) all show the model with a star. Leftovers of the Sears horses were later sold through Bentley Sales Co.; Bentley's January and March 1985 price lists include "300DC Dark Chestnut Jumping Horse." Collector Kim Lory Jones's model from Bentley's has a solid face, whereas her model from Sears has a star. This SR is a much darker horse than the solid bay variation of the regular-run Jumping Horse (see Jumping Horse #300).
- "Mystique" SR #707495, gray appaloosa, bald face, hand-painted eyewhites, pale barrel with darker gray forehand and hindquarters, splashed-on black spots on hindquarters, dark gray points, dark gray hooves, glossy; jump is medium/dark gray on medium/dark gray ground (1995). Raffle model for BreyerFest in Lexington, Kentucky, July 28-30, 1995. 26 models made, of which 25 were raffled and one was sold at the BreyerFest auction (per Breyer executive Peter Stone at the raffle). Proceeds of the raffle were donated by Breyer to the Misty of Chincoteague Foundation, North American Riding for the Handicapped, Hooved Animal Humane Society, Public Educational Television, and Friends of Wayne, NJ, Animals (per *JAH* 22/#3 May/June 1995, inside front cover). This model's color commemorates the glossy gray appaloosa coloring that was used on several models in the 1960s. The model number is per *JAH* editor Stephanie Macejko.

Notes:

(1) *JAH* VIII/#2 1981 (p. 15) has a photo of a dapple gray Jumping Horse with black points. This horse is a one-of-a-kind model won by a collector in a *JAH* subscription contest announced in the VII/#3 1980 issue (p. 14). According to the contest rules, all entrants who recruited 50 or more new subscribers for the magazine would win "any current Breyer model painted to your specifications using standard techniques." Becky Helm Plocek, the collector who won the dapple Jumper, reported on the Haynet (Internet

model-horse group) in spring 1995 and in *JAH* 22/#1 Jan./Feb. 1995 (p. 7) that the model had been lost in a fire.

(2) Early models of the Jumping Horse mold have the round "Breyer Molding Co." stamp only. Later ones have the round stamp and the "U.S.A." stamp—my solid-face bay #300 has the "U.S.A.," so it is certain that this stamp was added to the mold no later than 1976; it may have been added as early as 1970, when the "U.S.A." was first introduced into the Breyer line. Some "U.S.A." models also have the "B" stamp. The jump has only the round stamp; it was never given the "U.S.A."

Just About Horses subscriber specials — *JAH* is the Breyer company's magazine for collectors, which has been published since fall 1975. In 1980, Breyer offered exclusive special-run models through this magazine for the first time: a selection of completely unpainted horses of 15 different Traditional molds. This offer was made specifically with model-horse customizers in mind: "Repainters, Remakers ...," the ad begins (VII/#3 1980, p. 13). *JAH* issued the first SR intended for collectors of factory-painted models in 1984—the chestnut Saddlebred Weanling—and has offered such an SR almost every year since then. In several cases, the models were advertised very late in their designated year and so were not actually issued until the following year. This happened most recently in 1995, with SR "Sierra." Also in 1995, *JAH* offered two SR sets in addition to the almost-annual SR. One set included two SR foals commemorating the magazine's 20th year of publication; see "Brandi" SR (under Scratching Foal) and "Buster" SR (under Lying Down Foal). The other set, designated as a *JAH* Special Retail Set, included a Classic-scale model and doll; see Willow And "Shining Star" set SR (under Rearing Stallion in the Classics section).

For a listing of the 1980 unpainted SRs, see Unpainted Models below in the Traditionals section. For the almost-annual specials, see Saddlebred Weanling SR, chestnut (1984); Cantering Welsh Pony SR, dapple gray with red mane braids (1985/86); Trakehner SR, chestnut (1987); Running Stallion SR, chestnut (1988); Quarter Horse Yearling SR, blue roan (1989); Western Horse SR, caramel pinto (1990); Jumping Horse SR, black (1991/92); "Pride And Vanity" SR, alabaster (1992/93, see under "Sherman Morgan"); "Steel Dust" SR, pale smoke gray (1993/94, see under Proud Arabian Mare); "Moon Shadows" SR, blue roan (1994, see under Five-Gaiter); and "Sierra" SR, red dun (1995/96, see under Fighting Stallion). All these horses have come in plain cardboard mailer cartons. For further discussion of the magazine, see the Just About Horses section in the References at the end of this book.

"Just Justin" Quarter Pony — see under Pony Of The Americas

"Justin Morgan" — Stallion, standing, looking right, tail attached to right hock. Sculpted by Chris Hess. Mold in catalog-run production 1973 - current as of 1996.

Catalog-run models made from this mold:

- "Double Take" Morgan #878, liver chestnut, red shading, short blaze on lower half of face, brown-black mane and tail, 1 right front and 1 left hind stocking with gray-brown hooves, other hooves black, slightly semigloss (1993- 95). Collector Megan Thilman Quigley, who was *JAH* editor when Breyer created this model, mentioned to me that she came up with the name "Double Take" because that is what she did—a double take—when she first saw the test-color sample model. The piece strikingly resembled her own real Morgan horse, a liver chestnut mare.
- Marguerite Henry's "Justin Morgan" #65, medium/dark bay, no white markings, black points, black hooves, matte and semigloss (1977-89). This same model was sold in "Justin Morgan" Gift Set #2065 in 1973-81 and in holiday-catalog sets with book in 1982 and 1985 (see below). The model was also offered in a set with leather English saddle and bridle in the 1980 Penney's holiday catalog. #65 was called simply "Justin Morgan" in Breyer catalogs 1977-86 but Marguerite Henry's "Justin Morgan" in 1987-89. The real "Justin Morgan" was the founding stallion of the Morgan breed. His original owner, a man named Justin Morgan (born in 1747, per Self 1946), named the horse "Figure." Only later, after the horse had been sold and had established a reputation as a sire of fine offspring, did the horse become known as "the Morgan horse" and, eventually, as "Justin Morgan." (Information per Beard 1992.) The stallion's story is also told in Marguerite Henry's book *Justin Morgan Had a Horse*. For Breyer's portrait of "Justin Morgan" as a colt, see "Little Bub" (under Running Foal); also see "Wild Diamond," "Justin Morgan's" Dam (under Running Mare). The model number 65 previously belonged to the dog model "Lassie."
- Morgan #822, dark seal brown, no white markings, black points, black hooves, semigloss (1990-92).

Set:

- "Justin Morgan" Gift Set #2065, bay horse and book *Justin Morgan Had a Horse*, by Marguerite Henry (1973-81). This same model was sold separately as Marguerite Henry's "Justin Morgan" #65 [1977-89]. This #2065 set was also sold through the 1982 Sears holiday catalog and the 1985 Ward's holiday catalog.

Special-run models made from this mold:

- "Justin Morgan" SR, red chestnut, solid face, slightly darker chestnut mane and tail, gray-shaded knees and hocks, 1 left hind stocking with pink hoof, other hooves gray, matte (1988). Penney's holiday catalog. Sold in English Horse Collector Set SR #713259, with light coffee bay Black Stallion and red dun Indian Pony. The set number is per a Breyer company computer printout of activity 1985-92 and *JAH* 17/#5 Nov./Dec. 1990 (p. 29).

Note: The "Justin Morgan" mold has the round "Breyer Molding Co." stamp and the "U.S.A." stamp. Some models have the "B" stamp in addition.

"Justin Morgan's" Dam — see "Wild Diamond" (under Running Mare)

"Kaleidoscope" SR — see under Trakehner

Kelly Reno And "Little Man" Gift Set — for the horse, see under Stock Horse Stallion; for the doll, see under Alec Ramsey in the Riders - Soft Or Jointed Plastic section

"Kentuckiana" Saddlebred Weanling — see under Saddlebred Weanling

Kentucky Saddlebred — see under Five-Gaiter

"Khemosabi" — Stallion, walking. Sculpted by Pam Talley Stoneburner. Mold in catalog-run production 1990-95.

Catalog-run models made from this mold:

- "Khemosabi+++" Champion Arabian Stallion #460, bay, blaze running down over lips to a pink chin, black points, 4 stockings, tan hooves, semigloss (1990-95). At least initially, the model's box sported a large round gold-foil sticker saying, in full: "New Model! Khemosabi... World-renowned Arabian Stallion and Sire of 222+ Champions. Owned by the Khemosabi Syndicate." The 1990 catalog notes that the real "Khemosabi" is "the world's leading sire in the Arabian breed." In his horse-show days in the mid-1970s he won four national championships, according to a stud-service ad in *Arabian Horse World* (July 1978). The three pluses beside the horse's name indicate that he has achieved the highest award for his breed, the Legion of Supreme Merit (per collector and Arabian horse owner and shower Sue Stewart). Collectors Ardith Carlton and Karen Grimm have seen chestnut "Khemosabis" with chestnut points but the same white markings as normal models. The model Ardith knows of has the further variation of gray rather than tan hooves. Presumably these chestnuts are the result of an oversight in the painting department at Breyer—someone forgot to add the black points to a few #460s.

Notes:

(1) A photo of artist Pam Talley Stoneburner with her unfinished clay sculpture of "Khemosabi" appeared in the July 1989 *Arabian Horse World* (p. 153). The accompanying article notes that in creating the Breyer sculpture, Stoneburner worked from *Arabian Horse World* photos and a video of the real stallion "Khemosabi."

(2) Most models of the "Khemosabi" mold have the "© Breyer Reeves" stamp only. At BreyerFest 1993, collector Becky Brooks got an unpainted "Khemosabi" that had no stamp, which suggests the possibility that the very earliest painted models also have no stamp. I have not actually seen one like this, and Becky's own painted #460, purchased in September 1990, does have the stamp—but it is also true that Breyer has previously released new molds without stamps and then added a stamp a few months later (see, e.g., the notes for the "Rugged Lark" mold).

Kiger Mustangs — see Messenger Series below in the Classics section

"King" — see Fighting Stallion

"Kipper" — Pony, standing nearly square, pivoting head/neck, cartoonish, molded-on smile, rooted synthetic hair mane and tail, movable head and neck, bottoms of hooves molded to show frog and hoof wall. Sculpted by an artist in New York, based on Norman Thelwell's illustrations. Mold in production 1986 only.

Catalog-run models made from this mold:

- "Kipper" #9960, bay, solid face, white eyes with large black pupils, black synthetic hair mane and tail, no black on the legs, gray-shaded hooves, in Norman Thelwell's Collection (1986). About 5,000 models made, per former Breyer executive Peter Stone (conversation of Jan. 1996). A few model mail-order companies and retail stores sold this regular-run model, which came in a green cardboard box with plastic front. The same model was also sold through the 1986 Penney's holiday catalog in the "Kipper" And Drawing Book Set SR #712491, with mane brush or comb and Thelwell's book *How to Draw Ponies: All the Secrets Revealed*. The SR set number is per a Breyer company computer printout of activity 1985-92. The printout specifies a "comb," whereas the Penney's catalog says "mane brush." See note 1 for this mold for further discussion.
- "Midget" #9961, black pinto, white synthetic hair mane, black synthetic hair tail, in Norman Thelwell's Collection (1986). This model was never released for sale; see note 1 for this mold.
- "Pumpkin" #9962, palomino, white synthetic hair mane and tail, in Norman Thelwell's Collection (1986). This model was never released for sale; see note 1 for this mold.

Notes:

(1) The 1986 manual pictures three Thelwell ponies: "Midget," "Pumpkin," and "Kipper." The 1986 catalog pictures "Kipper" but only lists the other two. The only one of these three ponies to be released was "Kipper," and he enjoyed only a brief run because he simply did not sell well, according to Breyer executive Peter Stone (conversations of Nov. 1994, March and July 1995). "Kipper" is made of a hard white plastic-like material that smells like vinyl, painted bay, with rooted hair mane and tail. Although the mold bears the trademark stamp of English artist and author Norman Thelwell (see note 3 for this mold), "Kipper" was sculpted not by him but by an artist whose studio was on 24th Street in New York City, according to Peter Stone. (The artist's first name was Carter; Stone couldn't recall the last name.) The mane and tail were designed separately, by a hair designer in another studio in New York City. The ponies were manufactured by a doll-making company located in the Bronx, off of Jerome Avenue, and the manes and tails were added by a company called Dolls Parts, in Long Island City, New York.

(2) The "Kipper" that was actually produced and sold, the "Kipper" in the 1986 Breyer manual, and the "Kipper" in the 1986 Breyer catalog are all different molds. Or more precisely, parts of them are different. All three molds consist of two parts: a body with a hair tail, and a head/neck piece (which swivels) with hair mane and forelock. On the "Kipper" that was actually produced, the body is standing square on very short, straight legs with nearly nonexistent hooves, and the head has its ears forward. The mane and tail are straight, and the pony has no dapples. The catalog "Kipper's" head is virtually identical, but his body has reasonably long legs and adequate hooves, and his right front leg is bent. His mane and tail are curly, and the pony has faint dapples on the hindquarters. The manual "Kipper's" body looks identical to the catalog "Kipper's," but the head has its ears back. The mane and tail are straight, and the pony has faint dapples. The "Kipper" shown in the 1986 Penney's holiday catalog is the manual version (although if the dapples are there, they are impossible to see). Collector Karen Oelkers owns what appears to be the very "Kipper" pictured in the 1986 manual: a red bay with faint dapples. Karen purchased her piece, which is made of resin, at the first BreyerFest auction, where Breyer executive Peter Stone said that it was one of only two in existence, the other one being in his own collection.

(3) The "Kipper" mold has "© 1986 •thelwell•" engraved on the belly. The "thelwell" is in a dot-serif font and is flanked by two dots. Per collector Sue Stewart, this is Norman Thelwell's registered trademark, which also appears on the rubbery Thelwell ponies with riders that were issued by another company in the early 1970s and perhaps earlier. (Sue has one of these mounted ponies, and another is shown in Diederich 1988, Section 4.)

"Lady Phase" — Mare, standing square, looking left. Sculpted by Chris Hess. Mold in catalog-run production 1976-85, 1988, 1992-94.

Catalog-run models made from this mold:

- "Breezing Dixie" Famous Appaloosa Mare #711, dark bay blanket appaloosa, star, tri-color eyes, pink in nostrils, stenciled butt blanket with stenciled dark bay spots, stenciled white spots outside the blanket, black points, gray hooves, matte, Limited Edition (1988). The first models released had hand-painted battleship gray hooves, which looked odd, so subsequent ones were made with airbrushed dark-gray hooves. The mares with hand-painted hooves and the earliest models with airbrushed hooves have a more complex body coloration than later mares, as collector Sande Schneider pointed out to me: they have more small white spots on the left thigh than do the later models, and their bay color is distinctly lighter on the hindquarters than on the forehand. Sande got an airbrushed-hoof mare with this complex coloring at the end of April 1988. Later airbrushed-hoof models are more uniformly dark bay and have fewer white spots on the left thigh; some also have only one small white spot rather than three on the left side of the back. Some of these later models also have a stripe of black shading running down the windpipe from throat to chest and shading on the eyes and nose. Collector Robin Briscoe's model with hand-painted hooves, which she bought new off the shelf at State Line Tack in July 1988, came with 2 vertical black stripes on the front of each hoof and tiny hand-painted bay spots on the outskirts of the white butt blanket. Aside from the test-color model in the 1988 catalog, which also has the tiny spots on the blanket, Robin's model is the only one we have heard of with these extra details; possibly it is a test that got shipped out with hoi polloi. #711's box sports a large round gold sticker saying, in full: "1988 Limited Edition / Breezing Dixie / Champion Appaloosa Mare, special painted eyes, nose and hooves." Clearly this reference to "hooves" became false when the battleship gray went out the window. Limited Edition models are produced only for one year, in quantities sufficient to fill all orders for the model. The real "Breezing Dixie" was a famous cutting horse who won the 1985 Appaloosa World Championships; see the 1988 catalog for further information.

♠ Family Appaloosa Mare #860, black leopard appaloosa, white horse with stenciled black spots on body and head, gray and white striped mane and tail, light gray legs, tan-and-gray striped hooves, matte (1992-94). This gorgeous mare looks as if someone spat watermelon seeds all over her. There is a distinctive heart-shaped spot on the left side of her neck just behind the ear. Her appy pattern is identical to that on the SR chestnut leopard appaloosa "Lady Phase."

♠ Lynn Anderson's "Lady Phase" #40, red chestnut, solid face, flaxen mane and tail, various stockings, gray hooves, matte and semigloss (1976-85). This model was also sold in Lynn Anderson's "Lady Phase" Gift Set #3075 [1976-81]. The real "Lady Phase" belonged to the popular singer Lynn Anderson, who won a Grammy Award in 1973 for her hit song *Rose Garden*. Anderson showed the lovely red chestnut mare to Tennessee State and World Quarter Horse mare championships (*JAH* Jan./Feb./Mar. 1976). The horse died of colic soon after the Breyer model was issued (*JAH* 18/#4 Fall 1991, p. 13). The body color of the models varies from dark red-brown to deep pinky-strawberry to golden chestnut. The strawberries can have a pink cast to the mane and tail, as does collector Tanya Parker's model. Some models have black eartips, as on collector Linda Bell's mare. The white markings also vary. Photos of the real mare in the 1976 dealer catalog show that she had a thin crescent of white hair on her forehead, a white lower lip, 1 left fore and 2 hind white stockings, and, as former *JAH* editor Megan Thilman Quigley pointed out to me, a right front roan "stocking." This roan ankle may account for some of the stocking variation on the models, Breyer rendering the right fore alternately with a white stocking and with a solid leg. To my knowledge no models were issued for sale with the white forehead marking, but a model that is undoubtedly a test piece that appeared in a Breyer ad in the May 1976 *Quarter Horse Journal* does have this marking, as well as a roany right front "stocking" (thanks to Linda Bell for the ad). In my experience the most common assortment of white markings on the models is *1 left fore and 2 hind stockings and a snip* on tip of the nose, the snip being an unstenciled bald area, often lightly oversprayed with chestnut. This typical version is shown in most catalogs that list #40 and set #3075. Some catalogs do show variations, however. The 1976 catalog (p. 5) shows both the original unpainted clay sculpture of this mold and a hand-painted model that seems to be a plaster casting. The casting has *4 stockings and dark nose* (regarding her surprising tail, see note 1 for this mold), and plastic models with these markings were produced for sale—one is shown in *JAH* 16/#2 May/June 1989 (p. 29). In the 1977-78 catalogs, the #3075 model is the typical one, but #40 has *2 hind stockings only* (nose unclear); the 1985 catalog also shows #40 with 2 hind stockings only, and lightish nose. The model pictured on the #3075 box in 1977-81 has *1 left fore and 2 hind stockings and dark nose*. Collector Debbie Vandegrift has a pair of these mares, one a dark red chestnut with dark shading around the eyes, the other a golden chestnut with no eye shading. Maestas 1987a notes an additional "Lady Phase" variation: on early models the crest on the non-mane side is irregular and wide, with the flaxen color extending down onto the neck, whereas on later models the crest is thin and neat. "Lady Phase" was sold through the 1978 Sears holiday catalog in a set with leather bareback pad and bridle, and through the 1980 Sears holiday catalog in a set with leather Western saddle, bridle, breast collar, and "roping rein." Before being assigned to "Lady Phase," the model number 40 belonged first to Western Pony, dark brown, and then to Western Pony "Black Beauty."

Set:

• Lynn Anderson's "Lady Phase" Gift Set #3075, red chestnut mare, blue ribbon, and booklet *I've Always Loved Horses*, by Lynn Anderson (1976-81). This same model was sold separately as Lynn Anderson's "Lady Phase" #40 [1976-85]. The blue ribbon, which can fade to purple over the years, is not scaled to the models but is full-sized, like a ribbon awarded at a real horse show. It is identical to the ribbon sold in the SR chestnut Family Arabian sets through the Penney's holiday catalog in 1982-83: a rosette with two tails printed in gold, one saying "Breyer" and the other "Champion." The rosette's center is printed with a gold horse-head (not a Breyer). The softbound booklet was published by Breyer Animal Creations. "Lady Phase" gift sets sold through the Penney's holiday catalog, I believe in 1976, included a Lynn Anderson record. Collector Kim Lory Jones has the box for this Penney's set, which is the usual #3075 cardboard picture-box but bedecked with a sticker announcing the new item within: "Special Offer from JCPenney / Lynn Anderson's latest hit, "All the King's Horses" 45 rpm record included in this Breyer Set!"

Special-run models made from this mold:

⎋ "Lady Phase" SR, alabaster with gray shading; pink ears and nose; pale gray mane; pale gray and white striped tail; darker gray knees, hocks, fetlocks, and hooves; matte (1993). Made for Toys R Us in the U.S. Sold in The Watchful Mare And Foal set SR #700593 with pale smoke gray standing Stock Horse Foal. 18,000 sets made (per Breyer executive Peter Stone, conversation of Aug. 24, 1995). This set's box sports a large round gold sticker on front saying, in full: "1993 Special Collector Edition / Limited Production / The Watchful Mare & Foal / This highly collectible edition represents the ideal type American Quarter Horse." The stripes on the mare's tail are vertical; those on the foal's tail are horizontal. In the several dozen sets I've seen, the mare is typically lighter than the foal, light enough to be called alabaster. But the amount of shading varies on both mare and foal, so that some mares are pale gray with bald face (I have one like this; she matches the gray foal), and some foals, I've heard, are alabaster. The shading on the mare's leg joints also varies. On mares with darker shading the legs looked striped owing to the alternating zones of gray and white. Some mares totally lack the gray fetlock bands.

⎋ "Lady Phase" SR, bay paint, overo; stenciled bald face with white muzzle and chin; black points; 1 right front and 2 hind stockings with tan hooves; other hoof black, slightly semigloss (1992). Sears holiday catalog. Sold in Spirit Of The West set SR #492092, with bay paint Stock Horse Foal, standing. 4,500 sets made. Quantity and set number are per a Breyer company computer printout of activity 1985-92. The mare shown in the Sears catalog must be a test color since she has two small white spots (right neck and hip) that the mares actually produced do not have. Also the pattern on the photo model's right barrel is more interesting than the big blah blob on the retail mares.

⎋ "Lady Phase" SR, buckskin, bald face, pink nose, black ear tips, black points, black hooves, matte (1980). Made for Bentley Sales Company to sell at Model Horse Congress. Probably 244 models made, per Stuart Bentley, owner of Bentley Sales (conversation of Dec. 1995). Mr. Bentley told me that he recalled these horses as having a "blaze" rather than a solid face. This corroborates Hollansky 1990, which specifies a bald face and pink nose for this Bentley's Congress mare. All the bald-faced, pink-nosed mares I know of have a "B" stamp. Some of them also have buckskin shins on one or two legs, as were common on buckskin models generally in this era; but some mares have solid black legs—I own one of each type and have seen others. The nose on one of my mares is more buckskin than pink. In the November 1980 issue of *The Hobby Horse*, editor Shari Struzan provided a list of "new Breyers," including "#408 Buck. Lady Phase." Presumably she got this model number from Bentley's or from the Breyer company, although I do not have Bentley's sales lists or other records to verify the number.

"Lady Phase" SR, buckskin, solid face, black nose, black points, hoof color uncertain, matte (1979). Made for VaLes Bead Trailer model-horse company, of Glendale, Arizona, to sell at ValSun live show, held in Phoenix (the show was in Aug. 1979, per the June 1979 *Model Horse Shower's Journal*). 200 models made. Quantity is per Hollansky 1990, who specifies solid face and "black nose" for this "VaLes Bead Trailer" mare, and per Walerius 1991 (p. 99). (Walerius lists the VaLes and Bentley Sales buckskin "Lady Phases" in a single entry, saying "These mares came with bald white and solid color faces," without clarifying which version came from which source.) The April 1988 *Model Rag* also specifies this "VaLes 1970s run" as solid faced, and collector Lisa Herndon, who attended the ValSun show and purchased one of the mares, told me via email in March 1996 that the model is indeed solid-faced with black nose. The black nose is to my knowledge all that distinguishes this SR from the solid-faced version of the 1983-84 SR buckskin "Lady Phase," which has a gray nose. Lisa no longer owns the model she got at ValSun, but she kindly shared an intriguing anecdote about this SR: "Patty Brannan [of VaLes Bead Trailer] had the whole run of those horses for her store, but ... a few months after the show I was in Woolco (a now defunct store that was like K-Mart, only better. Woolco always had Breyers for sale.) Guess what was on the shelf? Around 10 buckskin Lady Phases!! Of course I was only 14 and had no money. My mom would not shell out the $7 for her because I already had one. They were identical to the VaLes run." Both Hollansky and Walerius date this SR to 1980, but this date is wrong according to a report on the 1979 ValSun show by editor Linda Walter in the October 1979 issue of *Model Horse Shower's Journal*. Linda notes, "A Mystery Horse was unveiled at ValSun, the Breyer 'Lady Phase'—in buckskin! (See ad next MHSJ possibly.)" This report doesn't mention VaLes as the vendor that sold the models at the show, but the November 1979 *MHSJ* indeed contains the ad mentioned by Linda: "Virginia Brannan, VaLes 'Bead Trailer,' . . . o.f. [original finish] buckskin Lady Phase, perf., $15 & postage (more than 1)."

⎋ "Lady Phase" SR, buckskin; some with bald face, gray nose, and black or gray hooves; some with solid face, gray nose, and brown or black hooves; possibly some with star; all with black points; matte (1983 and 1984). Penney's holiday catalog. Sold in Quarter Horse Mare And Foal Set SR with buckskin standing Stock Horse Foal. About 8,000 sets made, per Breyer executive Peter Stone (conversation of Nov. 1994). There are at least two and perhaps three versions of this Penney's mare. [A] Bald-faced, gray-nosed version: As pictured in *JAH* X/#3 1983 (p. 13), this bald-faced mare has gray hooves. Collector Karen Grimm's mare has gray hooves, but my own bald-faced mare (as well as the matching foal) has black hooves. These mares have no "B" stamp. [B] Solid-faced, gray-nosed version: Collector Sheryl Leisure's mare, which she got from Penney's with a solid-faced foal, has brown hooves and no "B" stamp. My own solid-faced mare (purchased second-hand) is like this too. Collector Karen Malcor's solid-faced mare, which she also got from Penney's with a solid-faced foal, has black hooves and no "B." Sheryl's, Karen's, and my own mares all have a medium gray nose; to my knowledge is the only detail that distinguishes the solid-faced Penney's SR from the 1979 SR solid-faced buckskin SR, which has a black nose. [C] Star-faced version: The 1983 Penney's catalog shows the mare with a charcoal nose and a vague round star. I know of no such mares in collections and thus would have assumed this was a test-color piece, but Maestas 1987a states that in addition to the bald-faced and solid-faced models "there were even some with a star on the face." Also "buckskin Lady Phase w/star" is listed, along with "buckskin Stock Horse Foal (standing) w/star," in a want ad in *Quequechan Model Horse Collector* of January 1985 (want ads often list as many rumors as realities, however, so this "evidence" should be taken with a grain of salt). The mare and standing SHF in the 1984 Penney's catalog are shown from the side in a small photo, so it's impossible to tell about their faces, noses, and hooves. Regarding the foal, the 1983 Penney's catalog shows not the SHF that actually came in the set but instead a solid-faced buckskin Running Foal. This explains why *JAH* X/#3 1983 (p. 13), which shows the correct set, with SHF, has a note by the picture of the foal stating "This is the model available as indicated." The correct set is also shown in the 1984 Penney's holiday catalog. For further discussion, see Running Mare SR buckskin and Running Foal SR buckskin.

⎋ "Lady Phase" SR, chestnut leopard appaloosa, white horse with stenciled chestnut spots on body and head, chestnut mane and tail, chestnut-shaded knees and hocks, gray or chestnut-gray hooves, matte (1994). Penney's holiday catalog. Sold in Horse Salute Gift Set SR #711694, with dark mahogany bay "Phar Lap" and reddish bay "Morganglanz" with blaze. 2,620 sets made (per *JAH* editor Stephanie Macejko, conversations of June and Dec. 1995). This leopard mare has the same appy pattern as the black leopard Family Appaloosa Mare #860. In the two SR sets that I purchased from Penney's, the chestnut leopard mares have different hoof colors: one has gray hooves, the other has chestnut-gray. One of them also has a solid chestnut tail, while the other's tail is chestnut with subtle gray stripes (I've seen another stripe-tail mare as well). The number for this set is per an information fax of April 11, 1994, from Breyer to dealers.

⎋ "Lady Phase" SR, dapple gray, no dapples on neck and head, bald face, most with dorsal stripe, black points, black hooves, matte (1990). Penney's holiday catalog. Sold in Breyer Traditional Horse Set SR #717450, with red chestnut "Rugged Lark" and palomino Quarter Horse Gelding. 3,500 sets made. (Quantity and set number are per a Breyer company computer printout of activity 1985-92.) The Penney's catalog says this set represents "the evolution of the American Quarter Horse," the palomino QH Gelding depicting an "early style" Quarter Horse, the dapple gray "Lady Phase" the "middle style," and the red chestnut "Rugged Lark" the "modern style." Collector Sue Lehman has a mare with no dorsal stripe and with unusually wild dappling.

⌘ "Lady Phase" SR #707395, palomino, tri-colored eyes, diamond snip, white mane and tail, 2 hind stockings with gray hooves, front hooves palomino-gray, matte (1995). Volunteer special, given to the judging committee of the 1995 BreyerFest live show and to other volunteers; one model was auctioned at the same BreyerFest. Approximately 40 models made. Model number and quantity are per JAH editor Stephanie Macejko at BreyerFest 1995. These mares are quite a deep golden shade.

⌘ "Lady Phase" SR #410040, red roan, white horse with reddish-tan flecks; chestnut mane, tail, knees, and hocks; tri-color eyes; pink nose; red in nostrils; tan hooves; matte (1989). Made for signing parties. 2,000 models made. Quantity and model number are per a Breyer company computer printout of activity 1985-92. (This same SR is listed as #19040 on 1990-92 price lists from the German mail-order company Modell-Pferde Versand.) All the ad fliers and Breyer publications that mention this model call her roan, although she has no dark coloring on her head. She would be more accurately described as fleabitten gray.

⌘ "Lady Phase" SR, unpainted white (1980). Sold through JAH VII/#3 1980 (p. 13). This horse and several other completely unpainted models were offered to hobbyists interested in customizing, but many collectors kept them unpainted. See Unpainted Models for a complete list.

⌘ "Night Deck" SR, black, solid face, black mane and tail, 1 left hind sock with tan hoof, other hooves black, matte and slightly semigloss (1992). Made for Black Horse Ranch. Sold in SR set #410392, with bay snowflake leopard appaloosa "Night Vision" (standing Stock Horse Foal mold). 1,500 sets made. Most sets came with a numbered certificate of ownership signed "Karen Grimm" either personally by Karen Grimm, of Black Horse Ranch, who owns the real horses represented by this set, or by BHR employees (employee initials appear on at least some of these certificates). Most of the models are numbered in gold on the belly by BHR (per BHR employee Heather Wells). The style of numbering varies on both the mares and the foals. Many are double-numbered, with the particular set's number followed by a slash and the run total; the abbreviation "S/N," for "set number," is sometimes present and sometimes not. Others are single-numbered, having only the set's number and no run total (e.g., collector Karen Crossley's "Night Vision" is numbered simply "S/N 884"). Approximately 20-30 unnumbered sets and a few sets with mismatched numbers, all without certificates, were sold in the mid-1990s; these were the last of the 1,500-set run (per Heather Wells). The real horses represented by this set are the 1991 world champion appaloosa broodmare "Night Deck" and her first foal, "Night Vision," who was 1991 world champion appaloosa filly. "Night Vision's" sire is world and national champion stallion "Dreamfinder." Information is per the certificate of ownership that came with the models and a BHR ad in Model Horse Trader, May 1992. The set number is per a Breyer company computer printout of activity 1985-92.

⌘ "Prairie Flower" Equitana '93 SR #700193, red bay blanket appaloosa, blaze, unstenciled blanket covering butt and most of barrel, splashed-on red bay spots, black points, 4 stockings, tan hooves, matte (1993). Export special, made for Modell-Pferde Versand, in Germany, to sell at the Equitana horse show held in Germany in March 1993. 900 models made, per Ingrid Muensterer, owner of Modell-Pferde Versand (letter to me of April 21, 1994). Ingrid told me in a phone conversation that she had selected the mold and asked Breyer for a color design similar to "Breezing Dixie's." She and her husband also dreamed up the name "Prairie Flower"; the model is not based on a real horse. Ingrid said this SR had been made for her company as an exclusive, but that one model was reserved by Breyer to sell at BreyerFest 1993. Ingrid's ad flier for this model says that Equitana is the world's biggest horse show. The label on the model's box says "No. 700193 Prairie Flower—Equitana '93."
Notes:
(1) Page 5 of the 1976 catalog has a photo of a hand-painted "Lady Phase" that is either the original clay sculpture of this mold or a plaster casting of it. The photo shows the tip of the tail attached to the point of the left hock. This design must have been changed when the steel injection mold was created, however, for the plastic models produced for sale have the tailtip standing free of the hock. The original unpainted clay sculpture of this mold is shown inside the front cover of the same catalog, but the photo obscures the tailtip, so no attachment can be seen. This photo is also printed in JAH Jan./Feb./Mar. 1976, along with a caption describing the creation of the "Lady Phase" mold. Oddly, sculptor Chris Hess is not mentioned; I suspect his name was omitted in the interest of emphasizing the participation of Lynn Anderson, owner of the real mare: "Lynn gave Breyer many photos of 'Lady Phase' from which the clay model was hand sculpted by our model makers. The next step for the small clay horse was a trip to Nashville. Lynn Anderson spent hours studying the model and sketches were made of the real Lady Phase to work out some of the muscle detail." Breyer executive Peter Stone assured me that Chris Hess did create the "Lady Phase" mold—Stone vividly recalled taking a trip or two with Hess to visit the charismatic star and her mare.
(2) The "Lady Phase" mold has the round "Breyer Molding Co." stamp. Some models also have the "B" stamp. This mold was never given the "U.S.A." stamp.

"Lady Roxana" — ⌘ Mare, trotting, tail touches ground. Sculpted by Rich Rudish. Mold in catalog-run production 1986-89, 1993,1996.
Catalog-run models made from this mold:
⌘ Marguerite Henry's "Lady Roxana" #425, alabaster; gray-shaded eyes and nose; rose gray mane, tail, and hooves; matte; Artist Series (1986-88). This model came with a small folded "Artist Series" brochure telling about sculptor Rich Rudish and about "Lady Roxana," "the elegant and romantic white mare of Marguerite Henry's book 'King of the Wind.'" In this story "Lady Roxana" is the mate of "Sham," the Godolphin Arabian. These equine characters are based on real horses: the Godolphin Arabian and "Roxana," a mare to whom he was bred several times (per Making the American Thoroughbred, by James Douglas Anderson [1916], p. 22; thanks to Jane Chapman for bringing this to my attention). King of the Wind says of the mare, "Except for her tail, which was a smoky plume, Roxana was the shininess of white marble in the sun" (p. 138). The "Lady Roxana" model is shown only in an artist's sketch in the 1986 Breyer catalog. The 1986 manual has a photo, but the horse shown seems to be a test color: her mane is partly dark gray and partly white; her tail has the top half dark gray and the bottom half white; and her knees, hocks, and fetlocks are shaded dark grayish-brown, so that her legs look striped. A similar model, with striped legs but solid gray mane and tail, is pictured in the 1986 Sears catalog. To my knowledge no models like this were actually produced for sale.
⌘ Prancing Arabian Mare #426, light sorrel, light area on lower part of face, flaxen mane

and tail, 1 right front and 2 hind stockings with gray hooves, other hoof gray-chestnut, matte (1988-89). This mare's body color varies from dark golden tan to quite a bright red-orange.
Sets:
⌘ Proud Mother And Newborn Foal set #3160, chocolate sorrel Proud Mother, solid face, dark red mane and tail, 4 stockings, tan hooves, slightly semigloss (Jan. 1 - June 30, 1993). Set also includes tan dun Newborn Foal (Classic-scale Andalusian Family Foal mold). Production dates are per the 1993 catalog.
⌘ Proud Mother And Newborn Foal set #3161, tan dun Proud Mother, solid tan face, darker gray dun mane and tail, dorsal stripe, 1 left front stocking with tan hoof, other legs shaded gray with dark gray hooves, matte (July 1 - Dec. 31, 1993). Set also includes dark bay Newborn Foal (Classic-scale Andalusian Family Foal mold). Production dates are per the 1993 catalog.
Notes:
(1) "Lady Roxana" is the first Breyer mold to exhibit a correct trot. In this gait, no more than 2 hooves are ever on the ground at once—a stance in which a free-standing model is sure to topple over. Sculptor Rich Rudish overcame the problem by giving "Lady Roxana" a tail that reaches the ground, forming a tripod with her two down hooves. In his article "Thoughts on Lady Roxana," Rudish notes that he gained much inspiration for the model from a real horse, "a beautiful Arabian mare named *Dornaba whom I had seen win the 1965 U.S. National Championship for Arabian mares. . . . She was almost pure white and she had an extravagantly long tail. She glided along the ground like a flamingo dancer in a long white dress" (Rudish 1985, p. 20). Although this mold achieves a correct trot, she is heavier bodied than one would expect of a representation of Marguerite Henry's elegant character ("She is built like a fawn!' cried Lord Villiers"; King of the Wind, p. 138). In his article Rudish explains this as follows: "I allowed her to be little plump and well-rounded to reflect the great care which was lavished on her by her wealthy owner." However, he gave a rather different account to some collectors at a model horse event in Southern California. Collector Gale Good, who attended the event, related Rudish's story to me as follows: "Apparently, just before Christmas . . . , Pete Stone [Breyer executive] called him up and wanted him to do a sculpture of an old nag called something like 'Old Bob.' Rich told him that Breyer already had an old nag in the Old Timer mold, and why didn't he do a companion piece to Sham. He had always wanted to do a sculpture where the model had two feet off the ground. Pete apparently agreed, and when Rich asked how soon he wanted it, Pete said two weeks!! Well, that wasn't enough time to do a decent job. Rich took a bundle of pencils, taped them together and put clay around them to form the body. This is why Lady Roxana looks as stout as she does and doesn't have the fine detailing that Sham had."
(2) The "Lady Roxana" mold has "© 1986 Reeve Intl." engraved inside the hind leg. Evidently "Reeve" is a misspelling of "Reeves."

Lakota Pony — see under Foundation Stallion

Lamps made from Breyer models — see Lamps & Nightlights in the Appendix near the end of this book

Lapel pins — see Breyer Lapel Pins

"Legionario" — ⌘ Stallion, with brand, in the Spanish walk, neck arched, bottom half of tail attached to right hind leg. Sculpted by Chris Hess. Mold in production: pre-catalog release 1978, catalog run 1979 - current as of 1996.
Catalog-run models made from this mold:
⌘ "Legionario III" Famous Andalusian #68, alabaster; gray-shaded mane, tail, knees, and hocks; pink-gray or peach hooves; matte (pre-catalog release 1978, catalog run 1979-90). This model was also sold in "Legionario III" Gift Set #3070 [1979-81]. Though #68 does not appear in Breyer catalogs until 1979, he was sold through the 1978 Sears holiday catalog in Andalusian Stallion set with leather English saddle and bridle. This same set was offered again through the 1979, 1983, and 1984 Sears catalogs. The bridle has two reins (as on a double bridle) attached to snaffle rings. Many "Legionario IIIs" have a lot of gray shading on the body. The typical hoof color is a pink or peach tone oversprayed with gray but varies from virtually pure gray to pure pink. In March 1991, in a toy store, I found two "Legionarios" with gray dorsal stripe, and two other collectors have told me they have seen this variation as well. The real "Legionario III" was a champion Andalusian imported from Spain by Greg Garrison. The stallion stood at stud at Garrison Ranch in Thousand Oaks, California. The breed originated centuries ago in Andalusia, a region of southern Spain. (See JAH VIII/#2 1981, p. 12, and the article cited below in note 2 for this mold.) For a brief period in the late 1970s, #68 was sold in a special blister-wrapped display box that was labeled with the model number 168; this number also belonged to the black appaloosa Scratching Foal during these years (see Display Boxes above in this section for discussion). The model number 68 previously belonged to the white Poodle.
⌘ "Medieval Knight" Andalusian #880, red roan, white horse with chestnut flecks; yellow-tipped dark chestnut mane and tail; gray-shaded head, knees, and hocks; gray-brown hooves; matte (1993-94). JAH 19/#5 Winter 1992 (inside front cover) describes this horse as "white with mulberry mane, tail, and flecks."
⌘ "Promenade" Andalusian #918, liver chestnut, low blaze extending over whole muzzle, mane and tail dark chestnut that fades to white ends, black knees and hocks, 4 stockings, dark tan hooves, matte (1995 - current as of 1996). On August 18-20, 1995, the Q2 home-shopping cable TV channel offered a total of 96 "Promenades" that were ordinary regular runs but that came in boxes labeled with the special-run model number 707995 (per JAH editor Stephanie Macejko). Leftover models may have been sold on subsequent Q2 programs. In the 1996 catalog, #918's name changed to "Promenade" Lusitano.
⌘ "Spanish Pride" #851, reddish bay, solid face, black points, 1 left front stocking with gray hoof, other hooves black, semigloss (1991-92).
Set:
• "Legionario III" Gift Set #3070, alabaster horse with book The Andalusian: A Rare Breed, by Pat Garrison, owner of the real "Legionario III" (1979-81). This same model was sold separately as "Legionario III" Famous Andalusian #68 [1979-90] and through the 1983 and 1984 Sears holiday catalogs in Andalusian Stallion set with leather English saddle and bridle.
Special-run models made from this mold:
⌘ "El Campeador" SR #410395, dark dapple gray, dapples on neck and head, dappled or solid face, black points, black hooves, matte (1995). Made for the West Coast Model Horse Collector's Jamboree in Ontario, California, in August 1995. 875 models made (including an initial batch of 700 and a second batch of 175). Quantity and model

number are per Jamboree organizer Sheryl Leisure; the model number was also stamped on the large cartons in which Breyer shipped the horses. Models came with a round maroon faux-leather hang tag with a silhouette of the model and "Jamboree 1995 A.D." stamped in gold on one side; the tags were created by Sheryl Leisure. In keeping with the medieval theme of this Jamboree and the Spanish origins of the Andalusian breed represented by this mold, Sheryl named the model "El Campeador" (meaning "The Warrior"), which is one of the epithets for the eleventh-century Spanish hero Rodrigo Díaz de Vivar. Díaz, also known as El Cid ("The Lord"), fought in Castile against the Islamic Moors who had occupied Spanish territory since the eighth century. Later he conquered the kingdom of Valencia, which he ruled until his death. (*The Columbia Encyclopedia*, 5th ed.)

"Legionario" SR, chestnut, solid face, light chestnut-shaded mane and tail, 4 stockings, gray hooves, matte (1985). Sold through Horses International (a division of Atlantis International) and Bentley Sales Company. Former Breyer executive Peter Stone did not recall the quantity of this SR when I asked him about it in December 1995, but evidence indicates that about 700 models were made, perhaps more. The earliest source I have for this SR is a Bentley's sales record card for "#68 Chestnut Legionario," which shows that Bentley's received a total of about 90 models in the last two months of 1985. They appear on a Bentley's price list dated December 1985, as "68C Chestnut Legionario," for $10.49 (I don't have a Bentley's list for November 1985). They must have sold out quickly, for they are already gone from the January 1986 Bentley's list. This SR debuted on the Horses International price list dated May 20, 1986, which announced "Limited to one model per customer! / 68C Legionario—Chestnut / cost: $13.50." This price list mentions no quantity, but the Winter/Spring 1986 issue of *Model Horse World News*, which has a photo of the model, says: "New from Horses International (these have not been officially released yet) . . . Chestnut Legionario III / Special run, less than 200." Whether this projected quantity is supposed to be for the entire run or only for the models sent to Horses International is not clear, but in either case I believe it is far too low. For unlike Bentley's, Horses International kept this SR on their price lists for over two years—it is still on their price list published in the June 1988 *Model Rag*. Moreover, this list and other Horses International lists I have for 1987 and 1988 place no limit on orders. Considering that the 90 Bentley's horses sold out in under three months, the long period of unlimited sales by Horses International strongly suggests that HI had a substantial quantity of these models, considerably more than 200. Pinkham 1988 says that 700 chestnut "Legionarios" were made for Atlantis International (HI's parent company). Walerius 1991 (pp. 101-2) says that 700 went to Atlantis International in 1985 and "500 to Bentley's and Mission House" in 1986. Walerius's total may be high—at any rate, Bentley's certainly did not receive half of 500—but it is entirely possible that Mission Supply got a share of this SR. I have no 1980s price lists from this company to verify this, however. Collector Jo Kulwicki has a chestnut "Legionario" with pink hooves, which is the only specimen I've heard of like this. It may be a one-of-a-kind piece rather than a production-line variation, for the model originally belonged to Breyer consultant Marney Walerius, who painted many one-of-a-kind models at the Breyer factory.

"Legionario" SR #415091, Florentine decorator, dappled metallic gold; face, mane, and tail dappled gold; 2 hind stockings with gray hooves, front hooves gray-gold (1991). Raffle model for BreyerFest West, in Pomona, California, August 1991. 21 models made. 20 were raffled off and 1 was auctioned. The proceeds were donated to the Misty of Chincoteague Foundation and the Hooved Animal Humane Society. The model number is per a Breyer company computer printout of activity 1985-92; other information is per *JAH* 18/#2 Summer I 1991 (p. 15). The printout says only 20 pieces were made.

"Legionario" With Brenda Breyer Rider set SR, flocked white "Legionario," blue glass eyes, white synthetic hair mane and tail, painted black hooves (1985). Penney's holiday catalog. Set also includes red and white leather surcingle and bridle, red plume, and Brenda doll. Sold by Penney's for $44.99 per set. The models owned by collectors Paula DeFeyter and Heather Wells have blue glass eyes, but some models might have brown glass eyes. For details on the doll see under Brenda Breyer in the Riders - Soft Or Jointed Plastic section.

Notes:

(1) This mold has a brand—a large "H" with a small "c" perched on the crossbar—molded into the near thigh. This is the brand of the ranch in Andalusia, Spain, where the real "Legionario III" was raised (per Breyer executive Peter Stone, conversation of Mar. 1995). The brand is delicately traced in black on "Legionario III" #68 and #3070, but on models of other colors it is left the color of the horse and thus is far less visible.

(2) Chris Hess is identified as the sculptor of this mold in *JAH* Summer 1978. In creating the piece, he consulted photos and also visited the home of the real "Legionario" to observe the horse, according to Breyer executive Peter Stone (conversation of Nov. 1994). One of the photos Hess worked from, which shows the stallion performing the Spanish Walk, appears in an ad for Andalusians bred by Garrison Ranch, owners of "Legionario III." The ad was printed in a 1977-78 horse magazine along with the article "Greg Garrison—Mr. Andalusian," by Robert Dobbins. (Magazine title unknown; I have only a partial copy of the article from Mr. Stone's files.)

(3) The "Legionario" mold has the round "Breyer Molding Co." stamp. At least some early models have the "B" stamp in addition, though I'm not sure if the very earliest ones have it. Later models have only the round stamp. This mold was never given the "U.S.A." stamp.

Limited Editions — See "Precipitado Sin Par" ("Cips," 1987, see under "El Pastor"); "Breezing Dixie" (1988, see under "Lady Phase"); "Abdullah" (1989, see under Trakehner); "Dan Patch" (1990, see under Pacer); "Dream Weaver" (1991, see under "Black Beauty," stallion, cross-galloping); "Chaparral" (1992, see under Fighting Stallion); "Fugir Cacador" (1993, see under Foundation Stallion); "Starlight" (1994, see under Jumping Horse); and Princess Of Arabia (1995, see two entries under Black Stallion).

Limited Edition (LE) models, which are listed in Breyer catalogs, are produced only for one year, in quantities sufficient to fill all orders for the model. Thus the quantity is not restricted in advance to a precise number, as it is with Commemorative Editions. One LE has been issued each year since 1987. The first two—"Cips" and "Breezing Dixie"—had special hand-painted detailing: tri-color eyes, pink in the nostrils, and hand-painted hooves (though the hooves backfired in "Breezing Dixie's" case; see that entry for details). Most subsequent LEs, however, have lacked these details and any other special features that might distinguish them from ordinary catalog-run models. Even the LEs' limited period of issue does not distinguish them from ordinary catalog runs, for several of the latter have been issued for only a year or indeed for only 6 months—the Lakota Ponies and Proud Mother sets, for example. So all that really defines the 1989-94 LE models as a unique category is that their boxes have large gold stickers on them announcing that the models inside are LEs. But this failure of distinction was redressed with a vengeance by the 1995 LE, Princess Of Arabia. Although the Princess horses themselves, like their predecessor LEs, have no special paint detailing, they are spectacularly outfitted with beaded satin native costumes and ridden by dolls in gorgeous Bedouin outfits matching the horse costumes. Princess Of Arabia brought another surprise, too: the light dapple gray horse, which is the only Princess horse advertised in the 1995 catalog, was produced only for the first seven months of the year, whereafter the company decided to give the steed a completely new color, red roan, in order to stimulate sales.

Lipizzan — In the Traditionals section see "King" The Fighting Stallion Alabaster Lipizzan (under Fighting Stallion); and "Pluto." In the Classics section below see Lipizzan Stallion and Rearing Stallion "Rex" Alabaster Lipizzan.

"Lippitt Pegasus" Foundation Morgan — see under Morgan

"Little Bub," Young "Justin Morgan" — see under Running Foal

"Little Chaparral" SR — see under Rearing Stallion below in the Classics section

"Little Man" — for the horse, see Kelly Reno And "Little Man" Gift Set under Stock Horse Stallion; for the doll, see under Alec Ramsey in the Riders - Soft Or Jointed Plastic section

"Llanarth True Briton" — Stallion, trotting, looking left, large tail touching ground. Sculpted by Martha White. Mold in catalog-run production 1994 - current as of 1996.

Catalog-run models made from this mold:

"Llanarth True Briton" Champion Welsh Cob #494, dark chestnut, star, slightly darker chestnut mane and tail 1 left front and 2 hind stockings with gray-striped tan hooves, right front leg has a tan/white area above a gray hoof, slightly semigloss (1994 - current as of 1996). Models come with a small hang tag suspended from the neck by a string, which gives the name of the sculptor and tells about the real horse of which the Breyer is a portrait: "This Welsh-Cob stallion, lovingly called 'Tubby,' became a show ring superstar as a yearling. At the pinnacle of his career, he was struck by a devastating illness. His owner however never lost hope. Through his love and devotion, the long road to Tubby's recovery was gradually climbed. After recovery, the two gentlemen (Tubby and his owner) could often be seen together taking evening strolls down quiet English lanes. Llanarth True Briton continued his legacy by siring superstar offspring that have traveled to three different continents. At the announcement of his passing, over 60,000 Royal Welsh Show spectators paid silent tribute to this great stallion." The model shown in the 1994 Breyer catalog is either the original sculpture or a resin casting of it. The photo shows it to have a textured coat, but the texturing was not carried over to the metal injection mold—the plastic models produced for sale are very smooth-coated. Most models are matte/slightly semigloss, but collector Sande Schneider has seen a glossy model. The size of the light area on the right front leg varies, being nearly a stocking on some models and little more than a light area on the coronary band on others.

Notes:

(1) "Llanarth" is the second of only two Breyer molds—the first being "Lady Roxana"—that exhibit a correct trot, with only two hooves on the ground. Both molds achieve their stability via a tail that touches the ground. *JAH* editor Stephanie Macejko, in her presentation at the 1996 West Coast Model Horse Collector's Jamboree, noted that "Llanarth's" genitalia are a separately molded piece, affixed to the horse after molding.

(2) The "Llanarth True Briton" mold has the "© Reeves Breyer" stamp only.

"Lone Star" — see under Running Stallion

Lusitano Stallion — see "Fugir Cacador" (under Foundation Stallion); also see "Promenade" Andalusian (under "Legionario")

Lying Down Foal — Indeterminate gender; lying on belly, head up. Sculpted by Chris Hess. Mold in catalog-run production 1969-88, 1996 (foal mold version 1969-84, 1996; unicorn mold version 1985-88).

Catalog-run models made from this mold:

FOAL MOLD VERSION:

Lying Down Foal #165, black blanket appaloosa, bald face, unstenciled butt blanket, splashed-on black spots, black hooves, matte (1969-84). Many if not all #165s have an odd factory defect: tiny bumps or blisters all over their necks and sides, particularly on the right side. A variation #165 with no spots was offered on a sales list by collector Karen Perkins. Several pearly #165s have been found by collectors, such as Heather Wells, Lynn Isenbarger, and Jo Kulwicki. See Chalkies & Pearlies in the Appendix near the end of this book. Regarding the release date for #165, see note 1 for this mold.

Lying Down Foal #166, buckskin, bald face, black mane and tail, black or brown lower legs and hooves, matte (1969-73, 1975-76). I've seen a #166 with a dorsal stripe, but in my experience this detail is not typical. I have seen in person a model with brown lower legs and hooves, and have heard of another from collector Paula DeFeyter. Typically the lower legs are black, but only partially so; the front legs in particular are often nearly solid buckskin with just touches of black shading. Collector Linda Bell has a buckskin foal with black mane, tail, and hooves but no black at all on his buckskin legs. Regarding the release date for this model, see note 1 for this mold.

Lying Down Foal #167, red roan, tan foal with chestnut dappling, dappled face, red chestnut points, no white markings, gray hooves, matte (1969-73). The body shade under the dapples varies from dark tan to pale cream, and the dapples and points vary from a browner chestnut to red chestnut. Regarding the release date for this model, see note 1 for this mold.

UNICORN MOLD VERSION:

Lying Down Unicorn #245, alabaster; gray mane, tail, and beard; gold-and-white-striped horn; gray hooves (1985-88).

Special-run models made from this mold:

FOAL MOLD VERSION:

"Buster" SR, bay blanket appaloosa, blaze, unstenciled butt blanket with bay splashed-on spots, black points, 1 right hind stocking, hooves striped tan and gray, matte (1995). *Just About Horses* 20th anniversary subscriber special. Sold in set #400195 with SR bay blanket appy "Brandi" (Scratching Foal mold). 2,000 sets made, per *JAH* 22/#1 Jan./Feb. 1995 (back cover). This *JAH* ad refers to the set as "20th Anniversary Special Offer: Buster and Brandi Twin Appaloosa Foal set." The set commemorates the 20th year of publication of *Just About Horses*, which was first published in the fall of 1975. Both foals have "JAH '95" hand-written in black ink on the belly. Numbered certificates of authenticity, signed by Breyer executive Peter Stone and *JAH* editor Stephanie Macejko, were mailed under separate cover. The set number is per Stephanie Macejko, who also clarified for me which name belongs to which foal in this set: "Brandi," a feminine name, belongs to the Scratching Foal, which is identifiably female (according to the criteria for Breyer genders), while "Buster," a masculine name, belongs to the Lying Foal, which is physically of indeterminable gender thanks to its position. My own "Buster" and some others I know of, as well as the one pictured in *JAH*, have a right hind stocking, but collector Paula DeFeyter received a model with no stocking.

Lying Down Foal SR, buckskin, bald face, yellowish-gray points and hooves, matte (1995). Penney's holiday catalog. Sold in Serenity set #710195 with SR buckskin Grazing Mare. 5,200 sets made (per *JAH* editor Stephanie Macejko, conversation of July 2, 1996). On my own foal, the mane and tail are somewhat darker than the legs, which are a fairly light yellowy gray color. This foal's buckskin body color is quite light and yellow, whereas the old regular-run #166 buckskin Lying Down Foal is typically a darker, tanner shade. #166 also differs from the SR in having black points.

Lying Down Foal SR, chestnut, slightly lighter chestnut mane and tail, no white markings, gray-chestnut hooves, matte (1991). Penney's holiday catalog. Sold in Adorable Horse Foal Set SR #714091, with bay blanket appaloosa Grazing Foal, dark rose gray Running Foal, and alabaster Scratching Foal. 5,000 sets made. (Quantity and set number are per a Breyer company computer printout of activity 1985-92.) The name Adorable Horse Foal Set is per the Penney's catalog, but the box in which the foals were packed was marked Fun Foal Set. Some of these chestnut lying foals have tiny blisters in the plastic, chiefly on the right side. The blisters are not so extensive as those on typical #165 black appy foals.

Notes:

(1) Lying Down Foals #165, 166, and 167 are listed as "new for 1970" in the 1970 dealer catalog but were actually released in 1969—they are listed in the 1969 collector's manual and pictured in an article in *Craft Model & Hobby Industry*, which states, "The 1969 additions to the fine line of Breyer Animal Creations are ready to enhance the collections of all horse and animal fanciers." Evidently when a new dealer catalog was issued in 1970 for the first time since 1968 (there is no 1969 catalog to my knowledge), Breyer decided to list the 1969 as well as the 1970 models as "new for 1970" to bring them to the attention of dealers, who would naturally suppose that any model not listed as new was something they had seen in 1968.

(2) The Lying Down Foal mold bears quite a striking resemblance to a clay sculpture of a lying foal pictured in the January 1971 *Western Horseman* (p. 88). In color design too, Breyer's #165 appy is virtually identical to the clay foal, which is a blanket appy with bald face and no stockings. The clay foal, created by a Pueblo Indian man named Joseph Lonewolf, differs from the Breyer in some respects: its tail wraps closely around the right buttock; the legs are tucked closer to the body, and the head has a slightly more "modernistic" look. But in posture and lines, not to mention the color design, the two foals are so similar that it is hard not to think one was based on the other. I do not know which way the influence might have run, however, for I do not know which foal came first—the *Western Horseman* article does not say when Lonewolf created his clay foal. Furthermore, although Breyer sculptor Chris Hess is well known for deriving his Breyer designs from photos and other two-dimensional works, obviously he did not refer to this particular *Western Horseman* photo of Lonewolf's foal, which was printed two years after the release of the Breyer. (Thanks to Heather Wells for bringing this article to my attention.)

(3) A Lying Down Foal unusual in both color and mold was displayed at BreyerFest 1994 by collector Antina Richards, who said the model had been found at a flea market. The foal was matte palomino with a bald face, white mane and tail, vague stockings, and gray hooves. Mold-wise the foal was unusual in that its mane was basically smooth, lacking the ridges and grooves that define the "hair" of the mane on normal Lying Down Foals. Antina's foal also lacked the round Breyer stamp that is normal for this mold. This suggests that the foal is a prototype, cast before the stamp and mane detailing were added to the injection mold.

(4) To judge from models I have examined, the horn on the unicorn version of this mold is a separately molded piece glued to the foal's forehead. The beard, however, is an integral part of the mold.

(5) Early models of the Lying Down Foal mold have the round "Breyer Molding Co." stamp only, inside the right forearm. Later models have the round stamp and "U.S.A." stamp—collectors Joni Freshman and Jo Kulwicki both have #167 red roans with the "U.S.A." (I've seen Jo's in person), so it is certain that this stamp was added to the mold no later than 1973. Some "U.S.A." models also have the "B" stamp, underneath the left hock.

Lying Down Unicorn — see under Lying Down Foal

Lynn Anderson's "Lady Phase" — see under "Lady Phase"

Madame Alexander dolls and Breyer — The Madame Alexander company is a manufacturer of collectible dolls that has been in existence for many decades and enjoys a large following of collectors. In spring 1994 rumors circulated that Breyer would be issuing a special-run horse to Madame Alexander for their national doll-collectors' convention to be held in Phoenix, Arizona, in June. Galloping down the information superhighway in pursuit of further news, I contacted several Madame Alexander collectors on Prodigy computer service. Some of them were planning to attend the upcoming convention and had been to previous conventions as well—where there had been Breyer horses! After the Phoenix convention, one attendee kindly sent me photos of the horses she had received there, and another described the models she had brought home. Convention organizers had said these models were "special," but not one of them was SR: they were "Bolya" #490, Family Appaloosa Stallion #859 (bay blanket "Stud Spider" mold), and "Brighty" the burro. The models sported various items of tack crafted by convention organizers and small round medallions tied around their necks identifying them as Madame Alexander convention pieces. The photos sent to me by the collector also show a Breyer given out at a 1987 Madame Alexander convention, which horse the convention organizers had said was "special": an ordinary bay "Justin Morgan" #65 outfitted with suede saddle blanket, bedroll, and round medallion tied around the neck. Shortly after the 1994 convention, Breyer collector Cathy Hagen managed to purchase one of the #859s, which has an Indian blanket, a silver and blue medallion that says "MADCC 1994," and a "MADCC 1994" stamp on the belly. More recently I heard from Breyer collector Deanna Calder, who found yet another Breyer from the 1994 convention: a regular-run #860 Family Appaloosa Mare (leopard "Lady Phase" mold), stamped "MADCC" on the belly and tacked up with a halter and lead rope and gold "MADCC" medallion. Deanna ran across this model in a doll shop, the owner of which told her that the horse was #MA-N-002, one of 100 such horses made by Breyer to go with an Indian doll at the children's event of the Arizona Madame Alexander convention. The abbreviation "MADCC," according to the shop owner, stands for "Madame Alexander Doll Collectors' Club."

Majestic Arabian Stallion — see under Black Stallion

"Majesty" Quarter Horse — see under Quarter Horse Gelding

"Man O' War" — Stallion, standing, looking right, molded-on halter, tailtip attached to right hock. Sculpted by Chris Hess. Mold in catalog-run production 1967 - current as of 1996.

Catalog-run models made from this mold:

"Man O' War" #47, red chestnut, star, darker chestnut mane and tail, most with dark chestnut hooves, black halter with gold fittings, matte and semigloss (1967-95). In Presentation Collection mounted on American walnut wood base with brass "Man O' War" nameplate, late 1971 - 1973. The Presentation Collection is not in the 1971 manual, but "Man O' War" and five other Presentation Collection models are announced in an ad in the November 1971 *Western Horseman*. The Presentation "Man O' War" is listed as #5047 (the number later assigned to the buckskin Stablemate QH Stallion) in the 1973 price list, but previously it apparently had the same number as regular-run #47; see Presentation Collection below in this section for discussion. The name given to #47 in Breyer catalogs has changed repeatedly over the years: he is Race Horse "Man O' War" in the 1967-68 catalogs; Famous Thoroughbred "Man O' War" in 1969-74; "Man O' War" Famous Thoroughbred or simply "Man O' War" in 1975-89; "Man-o-War" or "Man-O-War" in 1990-94, and "Man-O-War" Famous Race Horse in 1995. This horse was apparently introduced to replace the old Race Horse Derby Winner, for "Man O' War" was released right after Derby Winner was discontinued. No #47s were true glossies as far as I know, but there is a glossy SR that is otherwise identical to #47 (see below). Many early "Man O' War" models have hand-painted battleship-gray hooves and black eartips; the hooves look like those on very early "Breezing Dixies." These gray-hoofed #47s come in semigloss and matte (thanks to Teresa Ward for photos of her matte model) and typically have large hand-painted eyewhites, though I've seen one that didn't have eyewhites and have heard of another like this. In 1985, #47 was sold through the Penney's catalog in a set called "Man-o-War" With Jockey And Tack, with Alec jockey doll and leather race tack. See under Alec Ramsey in the Riders - Soft Or Jointed Plastic section for details. #47 was in the Showcase Collection as #470 in 1970-72 (see Showcase Collection in this section for discussion). The model number 470 later belonged to "Misty's Twilight."

Special-run models made from this mold:

"Man O' War" SR, glossy red chestnut, star, darker chestnut mane, dark chestnut hooves, black halter with gold fittings (1990). Sears holiday catalog. Sold in Race Horse Set SR #497510, with glossy red chestnut "Secretariat" and glossy blood bay "Sham." 2,000 sets made. This SR "Man O' War" has the same color and markings as the regular-run #47, but with a high-gloss varnish coating, as on glossy Breyers from the 1950s and 1960s. The quantity and set number I've given are per a Breyer company computer printout of activity 1985-92. (A Bentley Sales list of March 15, 1993, wrongly gives the number as #713259, which is actually the number of the 1988 English Horse Collector Set SR.)

"Man O' War" SR #413091, Golden Charm decorator, solid metallic gold; white star; gold mane, tail, and halter; gray hooves; glossy (1991). Raffle model for BreyerFest in Lexington, Kentucky, August 1991. 21 models made. 20 were raffled off and 1 was auctioned. The proceeds were donated to the Misty of Chincoteague Foundation and the Hooved Animal Humane Society. The model number is per a Breyer company computer printout of activity 1985-92; other information is per *JAH* 18/#2 Summer I 1991 (p. 15). The printout says only 20 pieces were made.

Notes:

(1) *JAH* XIV/#2 1987 (p. 14) mentions specifically that Chris Hess sculpted the Man O' War mold.

(2) A test color "Man O' War" plated with sterling silver is pictured in *JAH* 17/#5 Nov./Dec. 1990 (p. 17). The blurb with the photo states, "On a number of occasions Breyer has contemplated augmenting its line with models such as this." A "Man O' War" model made from a test batch of the black plastic used for the saddle of "Tic Toc" #864 (Western Horse mold) was auctioned at BreyerFest West in Pomona, California, in 1991.

(3) Early models of the "Man O' War" mold have the round "Breyer Molding Co." stamp only. Later ones have the round stamp and the "U.S.A." stamp. Some "U.S.A." models have the "B" stamp in addition.

Mare And Foal Set SR — see Grazing Mare SR, bay blanket appaloosa; and Suckling Foal SR, red leopard appaloosa

Marguerite Henry character models — Over the years Breyer has issued numerous models representing characters in children's books by renowned author Marguerite Henry. In the Traditionals section see "Black Gold" SR (under "San Domingo"); "Hobo" #838 (under "Phar Lap"); "Justin Morgan" #65; "Lady Roxana" #425; "Little Bub" #903 (under Running Foal); "Misty" #20 and various "Misty" SRs; "Misty's Twilight" #470; "Our First Pony" set SR (under Shetland Pony); "Our First Pony" Gift Set #3066 (see under Shetland Pony in the Traditionals section and under Arabian Family Foal and Mustang Family Foal in the Classics section); "Phantom Wings" #29; "San Domingo" #67; "Sea Star" #16; "Sham" #410; and "Stormy" #19 and various "Stormy" SRs. In the Classic section see "Hobo" #625 (under "Hobo" with stand); Joey's Pony Cart #19845 (under "Merrylegs"); and King Of The Wind Gift Set #3345. In the Little Bits section see Performing "Misty" #79293. In the Donkeys And Mules section see "Brighty" #375, "Brighty" 1991 #376, and "Brown Sunshine." In the Riders - Soft Or Jointed Plastic section, see the discussion of the Paul Beebe doll in the entry for Ben Breyer #550. For a Marguerite Henry model that nearly happened, see "Grimalkin" in the Dogs & Cats section.

"Martin's Dominique" Champion Miniature Horse — see under "Merrylegs" below in the Classics section

MasterCrafters clocks — see note 1 for Western Horse; also see the Breyer Company History and MasterCrafters Clocks sections in the Appendix near the end of this book

Matte finish — see Finishes in the Appendix near the end of this book

McCormick Decanter With Old Timer set SR — see under Old Timer

"McDuff" Old Timer — see under Old Timer

Medallion Series — This is a series of five SR sets with metal "Breyer" medallion, all made exclusively for Toys R Us—three sets in 1995 and two in 1996. Two of the 1995 sets combine Classic and Traditional models: the "Buckaroo" And "Skeeter" set (see under Arabian Family Mare in the Classics section and under "Stormy" in the Traditionals section), and the "Geronimo" And "Cochise" set (see under "Kelso" in the Classics section and under "Sea Star" in the Traditionals section). The third 1995 set includes only a Traditional model: "Dustin" (see under "Phar Lap"). The two 1996 sets also include only a single Tradtional model: a bay Foundation Stallion mold named "Titan Glory" and a buckskin Black Stallion mold called "Sapphire." (These two, being 1996 releases, are not listed in this book.) The medallion is the same in all five sets in the series. It is about the size and weight of a half-dollar, with "Medallion Series," a horse head, and the Breyer logo engraved on the obverse and a larger Breyer logo and "© Reeves International, Inc." engraved on the reverse. A blue grosgrain ribbon passes through a hole near the top of the medallion, allowing the owner to wear it around his or her neck.

Medicine Hat Mare And Foal set — see under Thoroughbred Mare (ears back) and under Suckling Foal

Medicine Hat Stallion — see under "San Domingo"

"Medieval Knight" Andalusian — see under "Legionario"

"Mego" SR — see under "Adios"

"Memphis Storm" — see under Tennessee Walker

"Mesa" The Quarter Horse — see under "Adios"

"Mesteño" — see Messenger Series below in the Classics section

"Midge" — In the Traditionals section see Marguerite Henry's "Our First Pony" Gift Set and "Our First Pony" set SR (both under Shetland Pony). In the Classics section below see "Joey's Pony Cart" (under "Merrylegs").

"Midget" — see under "Kipper"

"Midnight Sun" — see under Tennessee Walker

Mid-year and summer specials — In the Traditionals section see Appaloosa Sport Horse & Canongate Saddle Set SR (1993; under "Morganglanz"); and "Domino" Gift Set SR (1994; under "Roemer"). In the Classics section see "Black Beauty" Gift Set SR (1994; under "Black Beauty"); Eagle And "Pow Wow" set SR (1995; under "Johar"); and "Riddle" SR (1995; three entries, under "Hobo").

The 1994-95 "mid-year specials" are so called because they appeared in Reeves International Mid-Year Introduction brochures, which were published for distribution to dealers of Breyers and other Reeves toy lines. 1994 was the first year in which Reeves published a Mid-Year brochure, but the precedent for the mid-year SR models had been set the previous year, with the release of the Appy Sport Horse set. This set was designated a "summer special" in *JAH* 20/#4 Fall 1993 (inside front cover), as well as in communications from the company to Breyer sales representatives and from dealers to customers.

Miniature Collection — see Miniature Collection below in the Classics section for a complete list of catalog-run and special-run flocked-horse-and-buggy sets

Miniature Horse — see "Martin's Dominique" and Miniature Horse SR, both under "Merrylegs" below in the Classics section

"Mister Mister" Champion Paint — see under "Stud Spider"

"Misty," Performing (ceramic) — see Performing "Misty" below in the Little Bits section

"Misty" — Pony mare, standing, looking right, tail attached to right buttock and leg. Sculpted by Chris Hess. Mold in catalog-run production 1972 - current as of 1996.

Catalog-run models made from this mold:

- "Misty" Of Chincoteague #20, chestnut pinto, tobiano; white mane and tail; most with pink-tan hooves, some with gray hooves; matte, semigloss, and glossy (1972 - current as of 1996). This model was also sold in various sets (see Sets following this entry). #20 is called "Misty" Of Chincoteague in catalogs 1972-75, "Misty" in catalogs 1977-80, Marguerite Henry's "Misty" in 1981-93, and "Misty" By Marguerite Henry in 1994-95. On January 21, June 1, and August 5, 1995, the QVC home-shopping cable TV channel offered a total of 1,200 "Misty" models that were ordinary regular runs but that came in boxes labeled with the special-run model number 701295 (per *JAH* editor Stephanie Macejko). The color of "Misty's" brown spots has varied over the years from tan-palomino to orangy yellow to fairly dark chestnut. The real "Misty" was one of the wild ponies that live on the island of Assateague, off the Atlantic coast of Virginia. She was captured as a foal with her dam, "The Phantom," and her sire, "The Pied Piper," and brought to live on the Beebe family farm, called Pony Ranch, on the neighboring island of Chincoteague. Her story is told in Marguerite Henry's book *Misty of Chincoteague*. For several years, Breyer has worked to benefit the foundation that is seeking to preserve the Beebe farm. Ms. Henry is the foundation's president and co-founder, and Breyer executive Peter Stone is its secretary, per a "Misty of Chincoteague Foundation" flier sent to me in March 1993. PATTERN VARIATIONS: Breyer catalogs show "Misty" models—#20 and set #2055—with a bewildering array of pinto patterns. The early 1970s catalogs and manuals show two or three different patterns apiece! Apparently two or three of these early patterns were test colors that were never produced for sale; at least, I have never heard of collector's specimens of them. A couple of the tests, shown in the 1972-74 catalogs, are similar to the test model pictured on the box of "Misty" set #2055. Another test, shown in the 1972-75 manuals and 1975 catalog, has an odd "mushroom cloud" brown spot on the right hip and flank. Of the three catalog/manual patterns that were produced for sale, one has a variation of its own which is not visible in catalogs, for a total of four regular-run patterns on #20. The first two of these patterns, which are very similar to each other, are rare. The second two, also very similar to each other, are both common. All four patterns have a round brown spot covering the right eye. In chronological order, the four are as follows: [A] The 4-eyed "Misty," probably made in 1972 only: On her left side, her head is brown with a round white spot covering the eye, echoing the round brown spot covering the right eye. The twin eye spots give the effect of silly spectacles, which is why collectors call this version "the 4-eyed Misty." Also on the left side, this pattern has a big white wiggly-edged oblong "blanket" reaching from the middle of the neck to the root of the tail, and a small white patch on the gaskin. On her right side is a large brown spot on the barrel, flank, and butt, which extends in a short, thick "finger" up over the point of the hip. 4-eyed models have gray hooves and are normally glossy, though I've seen a semigloss specimen. *JAH* 20/#3 Summer II 1993 (p. 12) reports that the 4-eyes was the first pattern, which was discontinued because Ms. Henry didn't like the white spot covering the left eye. The real "Misty" (now deceased) did not have such a spot, as can be seen in photos of her in *JAH* 19/#4 Fall 1992 (p. 15) and in a photo of her in her present taxidermied state at the Chincoteague Miniature Pony Farm, printed on the cover of *The Model Rag*, April 1989. [B] The early 3-eyed "Misty," probably made in 1972, perhaps into early 1973: This model is nearly identical to the 4-eyed "Misty," having gray hooves and the same pinto pattern on the body. The only difference is on left side of the head: early 3-eyes has no white spot covering the left eye (hence she has 2 eyes and a monocle, as Sheryl Leisure put it). Instead she has a stenciled blaze line coming nearly straight down from the ear, across the eye, and down parallel to the nasal bone; then the blaze line turns a sharp corner toward the chin, making the whole muzzle white, just as on the 4-eyed "Misty." This blaze pattern corresponds to the description in *Misty of Chincoteague*: "she had a funny white blaze that started down the left side of her face, then did a right-about and covered her whole muzzle" (p. 95). Later "Misty" patterns have a different blaze line, although they are also 3-eyed. Of the eight early-3-eyed specimens owned by collectors of my acquaintance, five are matte and three are glossy. Either the 4-eyed or the early-3-eyed is shown in the 1972 Sears catalog in a set with the *Misty* book and in the 1973-75 Breyer manuals and 1975 catalog. All these sources show the model from the right side, so you can't tell which of the two versions she is. Despite these catalogs and manuals, I do not believe that these two early versions were made after 1972 or early 1973, for the covers of the 1973 Breyer catalog feature a group photo that includes a common-pattern "Misty" (version C below). The photos of the early-pattern ponies inside the 1973-75 catalogs and manuals are for the most part the same shots recycled from year to year, which indicates that Breyer simply didn't bother to update its photos to show the common pattern that was actually in production. [C] First common "Misty," made 1973-84: On the left side, the white "blanket" is smaller and more irregular than on the A and B patterns, covering the withers and extending down in a "girth" to the belly. Pattern C also lacks the white patch on the gaskin. On the left side of the head, the blaze crosses the eye and swoops down across the cheek to the jaw. On the left front leg, some models have only a sock while others have white reaching up the back of the leg to the elbow (I have one like this). On the right side, the brown spot on the barrel, flank, and butt is bigger and rounder than on the A and B patterns and lacks the brown "finger" over the hip. Also on the right side, a short, square thumb of white pokes down into the brown in the middle of the barrel. C-pattern ponies have pink-tan hooves. These models are generally matte or semigloss, but a few are glossy (I have a glossy with a "B" stamp, which dates her to no earlier than 1979). This pattern is shown on the covers of the 1973 catalog and in catalogs 1976-84. *JAH* doesn't mention the changed body pattern introduced by the first common "Misty," but presumably this change, like that from 4-eyes to 3-eyes, was meant to improve the model's accuracy—at least, the first common pattern is closer to the real "Misty" in the photos noted above and to Wesley Dennis's illustrations in Ms. Henry's books. *Misty of Chincoteague* describes "Misty's" body pattern thus: "Like her mother she, too, wore a white map of the United States on her withers, but the outlines were softer and blended into the gold of her body" (p. 95). *The Pictorial Life Story of Misty* notes that the mare "was curiously marked. That splash of gold around one eye gave her a clownish look. Her body color was a coppery Palomino, and the white marking over her withers and down her left side took on the shape of a map of America. The map looked superimposed, like a permanent saddle pad. Her mother wore a similar map against a dark black coat" (p. 7). *Sea Star: Orphan of Chincoteague* adds that "Misty" also had a "marking on her side . . . in the shape of a plow, like the state of Virginia" (p. 39). [D] Second common "Misty," made 1985 - current as of 1996: This pattern, which is also "3-eyed," is very similar to pattern C but has slightly larger white patches on the body. On the left side, the outside of the front leg has a stenciled white patch from ankle to elbow, and the eye is covered by the white blaze. On the right side, there is no square thumb of white on the barrel but instead a wider, scalloped area of white. The second common "Misty" has pink-tan hooves and matte finish. She is shown in catalogs 1985-95. For further discussion of the real "Misty" see Performing "Misty" below in the Little Bits section.

Sets:

- Marguerite Henry's "Misty," "Stormy," And "Sea Star" Set #2169, chestnut pinto "Misty" and two foals (1983-85). These same models were sold separately as "Misty" Of Chincoteague #20 [1972 - current as of 1996], Marguerite Henry's "Stormy" #19 [1977 - current as of 1996], and Marguerite Henry's "Sea Star" #16 [1980-87]. The #2169 set plus Henry's book *Misty of Chincoteague* was offered in the 1980 Penney's holiday catalog. A set with "Misty," "Phantom Wings," "Stormy," and book was sold through the 1983 Sears holiday catalog. A set with "Misty," "Stormy," and the book was sold through the 1982 Sears holiday catalog and the 1993 Spiegel and Smithsonian holiday catalogs (the 1993 sets had the Breyer number 400293). A set with "Misty," "Stormy," book, and Paul Beebe doll (same doll and clothing as Ben Breyer #550) was sold through the fall 1993 FAO Schwarz catalog; the set's Breyer number was #700493. (Breyer numbers are per *JAH* editor Stephanie Macejko and a Breyer company computer printout of 1993 SRs.)
- "Misty" Gift Set #2055, chestnut pinto and book *Misty of Chincoteague*, by Marguerite Henry (1972-81). This same model was sold separately as "Misty" Of Chincoteague #20 [1972 - current as of 1996]. This book set was also sold through the 1972 Sears and 1985 Ward's holiday catalogs; the "Misty" shown in the 1972 Sears catalog is one of the two early pattern versions (see the entry for #20, above).

Special-run models made from this mold:

- "Misty" Of Chincoteague SR #715092, chestnut/palomino pinto, tobiano; tan hooves; matte; cold-cast porcelain (1992). Penney's holiday catalog. 1,500 models made (per the Penney's catalog). Double-numbered by hand on the belly. Sold by Penney's for $99.99. The model's box calls her "Misty Of Chincoteague / Marguerite Henry's Favorite Pony." The box also says "Made in Taiwan," and "Style No. 671-0545"; this number is a Penney's catalog number, not a Breyer model number. The Breyer number 715092 is per a Bentley Sales August 1993 price list and a Breyer company computer printout of 1992 SRs. The printout gives the full number as #7900-715092; the prefix "7900-" designates the Breyer Reeves line of cold-cast and fine porcelain models. Models came with a numbered certificate of authenticity signed by Breyer executive Peter Stone. The certificate states: "This fine Breyer model is crafted of cold-cast porcelain, and it is limited to a series of 1,500 serially numbered pieces. The cold-cast *Misty* will not be made available again and is a true collector's item." This model has basically the same pinto pattern as the regular-run "Misty" #20 except that the whole upper part of the face is brown, whereas "Misty" #20 has just a round chestnut spot covering the right eye. The cold-cast model shown in the Penney's catalog has spots dark enough to be called chestnut, but a handful of collectors' specimens I've seen have palomino spots, varying from light tan to light yellow palomino. One model I've seen had no mold stamp—the area where the stamp should have been was flattened, as though sanded off during finishing. But other specimens I've seen did have the round "Breyer Molding Co." stamp. Collector Sande Schneider discovered in March 1996 that the paint had loosened into scales on the left side of her cold-cast "Misty," which had been standing undisturbed in a china cabinet since Sande purchased her from Penney's. Some cold-cast SR "Secretariat" and "Fashionably Late" models also have developed paint-peeling problems, so it may well be that Sande's pony is not the only afflicted "Misty." The term "cold-cast porcelain" is a misnomer; the material is actually plastic resin with marble dust added to it to give the appearance of porcelain (see *JAH* 21/#4 Fall 1994, p. 3).

- "Misty" SR, flocked chestnut pinto, tobiano; painted black eyes; white synthetic hair mane and tail; painted black hooves (1984). Sears holiday catalog. Sold in SR set with flocked dark chestnut pinto "Stormy," for $29.99 per set. The pinto patterns on these two models are basically the same as the patterns on the regular-runs but less detailed. This set was flocked, haired, and detailed by the Riegseckers of Indiana (see Riegseckers Models for discussion). It is possible that some of these models have brown glass eyes, but in the sets I've seen in person, both the mare and foal had painted black eyes. Starting in January 1986, leftovers of this "Misty" SR appeared on the Bentley Sales Company price lists as #20FLK (for "flocked"), for $6.99.
- "Misty" SR #410020, Florentine decorator, dappled metallic gold; bald face; white points; pink hooves; glossy (1990). Raffle model for BreyerFest in Lexington, Kentucky. 21 models made. 20 models were raffled and 1, which was autographed on the belly by Marguerite Henry, was auctioned. The proceeds were donated to the Misty of Chincoteague Foundation. This information is per *JAH* 20/#1 Spring 1993 (pp. 15, 32). The model number is per a Breyer company computer printout of activity 1985-92. The printout says that only 20 models were made.

Note: The "Misty" mold has the round "Breyer Molding Co." stamp and the "U.S.A." stamp. The mold was evidently released with both these stamps already on it, for all the "Misty" models I've examined, including the very early pattern versions, have had them. Some models have the "B" stamp in addition, inside the right hock.

"Misty's Twilight" — Mare, in extended trot, looking right, mane braided along bottom. Sculpted by Jeanne Mellin Herrick. Mold in catalog-run production 1991 - current as of 1996.

Catalog-run models made from this mold:

- "Misty's Twilight" #470, chestnut pinto, tobiano; stripe; top of tail white, bottom of tail brown-charcoal; brown-gray hooves; matte (1991-95). This model is called "Misty's Twilight" in the 1991-92 catalogs, Marguerite Henry's "Misty's Twilight" in 1993, and "Misty's Twilight" By Marguerite Henry in 1994-95. According to the 1991 catalog, the real "Misty's Twilight" is a Thoroughbred - Chincoteague Pony cross, a registered Pinto, and a grand-daughter of "Misty." Her story is told by Marguerite Henry in the book *Misty's Twilight*. The 1991 catalog photo shows a plaster casting of Jeanne Mellin Herrick's original sculpture—the casting was painted by hobbyist Karen Gerhardt, who worked from photos of the real horse (see Production Process in the Appendix near the end of this book). The model's box sports a large round gold sticker saying, in full: "New Model! / Misty's Twilight / Not only is she a grand-daughter of Misty of Chincoteague, Twilight is also an accomplished dressage horse! She is owned by Stolen Hours Farm, Ocala, Florida." The model number 470 previously belonged to the Showcase Collection issue of "Man O' War."

Special-run models made from this mold:

- "Misty's Twilight" SR, black, stripe, black mane and tail, green and red mane ribbons, 1 left fore and 2 hind stockings with tan hooves, other hoof black, slightly semigloss (1993). Spiegel's holiday catalog. Sold in Dressage Set Of 2 Horses SR #500693, with dark bay Hanoverian. 1,130 sets made (per *JAH* editor Stephanie Macejko). The solid color of this SR "Misty's Twilight" accentuates the mold's resemblance to horses in Courier and Ives prints. The green color on the ribbons of my own models is a bright grass green. Collector Teresa Brewer wrote to me that the color is yellow on her model. The set's number is per a Breyer company computer printout of 1993 SRs.

Notes:

(1) A "Misty's Twilight" cast in an experimental plastic made from corn oil was sold at the 1993 BreyerFest auction. The model was unpainted, and its two halves were held together only by a rubber band. Breyer executive Peter Stone, who described the piece for the auction crowd, remarked that Breyer would not be making models from this plastic in the future.

(2) The "Misty's Twilight" mold has the "© Breyer Reeves" stamp only.

Model numbers — for discussion see the start of the Models By Number section near the end of this book

Mold stamps on Breyer models — see Mold Stamps in the Appendix near the end of this book

Mold variations — see Mold Variations in the Appendix near the end of this book

Money Manager — see under Breyer Company History below in the Appendix

"Moon Shadows" SR — see under Five-Gaiter

Morgan, prancing and standing — see "Sherman Morgan"; "Justin Morgan"

Morgan — Stallion, in stretched show stance, looking right. Sculpted by Chris Hess. Mold in catalog-run production 1964-95.

Catalog-run models made from this mold:

- "Lippitt Pegasus" Foundation Morgan #901, blood bay, star, black points, 1 left hind stocking with tan hoof, other hooves black, matte (1994-95). This model represents a real stallion of the Lippitt Morgan line—a family within the Morgan breed that is reputed to have "the largest percentage of Justin Morgan blood," with "no twentieth century outcrossings with other breeds" (Algarin 1994). The name "Lippitt" that prefaces the names of horses in this family derives from Robert Lippitt Knight, who in 1927 established a breeding farm with Morgans from Vermont that were believed to closely resemble "Justin Morgan," the founding stallion of the Morgan breed. "Lippitt Pegasus," born in the late 1940s or 1950, was in fact not one of Knight's foundation stallions but a later product of Knight's breeding program. The horse died at the age of about 5 years because of a scrotal hernia but was regarded as one of the finest Morgans Knight ever bred. (Information courtesy of Elizabeth Curler, director of the Justin Morgan Memorial Museum, Shelburne, Vermont.)
- Morgan #48, black; some with bald face, some with star, a few with solid face; black mane and tail; most with 4 stockings; black or gray hooves; matte and semigloss (1964-87). Some earlier models have hand-painted eyewhites. The bald face can be extensive, reaching well down the sides of the face. The main catalog listings for #48 show him with bald face and 4 stockings in 1964 and 1966-75, and with star and 4 stockings 1976-87. However, the earlier catalogs use the same old photos year after year, and it is likely that the change from bald face to star occurred before 1976—no later than 1975, for a star-faced 4-stocking #48 is shown in a group photo in the back of the 1975 catalog, and probably as early as 1970/71, when the star-faced version of bay #49 was issued (see that entry for discussion). *Breyer Collector's Video* notes that there are many stocking variations on #48, a no-stocking variation, and a variation with an "irregular star," which collector Gale Good told me is dagger shaped. Collector Judy Miller has a star-faced horse with no stockings. A 2-stocking horse, probably a star-faced version, appears in a group photo in the back of the 1974 catalog, and I saw a horse with these markings at BreyerFest 1994. Some #48s made during the 1970s oil crisis have gray stockings, owing to the gray plastic used to make the model; the video shows one of these. But some oil-crisis-era horses are solid black, with no markings and no white basecoat (see Chalkies & Pearlies in the Appendix near the end of this book). Collector Betty Mertes has a solid black #48 made of gray plastic, and Sheryl Leisure has one of purple plastic. A similar horse was advertised in the December 1978 *Model Horse Shower's Journal*: "#48 blk. Morgan stal. with a difference! He's made of red experimental plastic of several years ago & has absolutely NO white." Collector Karen Perkins told me that a small special run of solid black Morgans was issued sometime in the 1970s for the Morgan Horse Association to use as show trophies. Karen purchased one of these horses no later than the early 1980s from someone who had gotten it from a Morgan horse breeder. It seems unlikely that these horses would be distinguishable from solid-black variation #48s, which were made in the same period. #48 was in the Showcase Collection as #480 in 1970-72 (see Showcase Collection in this section for discussion). The number 480 later belonged to "Mesteño" The Messenger (Classic scale).
- Morgan #49, bay; most with bald face, 2 front stockings, and dark gray hind legs; some with star; all with black mane and tail; 4 gray hooves; matte and semigloss (1964-71). Some have hand-painted eyewhites. The bald face is typically extensive, reaching well down the sides of the face. The bald-faced version normally has 2 front stockings and gray back legs, but does come in a 4-stocking version (collector Sheryl Leisure has a model like this, which also has eyewhites). The star-faced bay Morgan also comes in two versions: one with 4 stockings and no black or gray on the legs (Sheryl and I have horses like this), and another with gray lower legs (collectors Sande Schneider, Heather Wells, and Lani Keller have this version). It is hard to say precisely when the bald-faced version was discontinued and the star was introduced. Catalogs and manuals do not show the star version—indeed only the 1964 catalog-supplement pages and the 1971 manual have any photos of #49 at all, and they show the bald-faced version (the manual has him in a herd shot on the cover). But other evidence indicates that the star debuted in 1970 or 1971, the last year of production for #49. My own star-faced bay and several others I've seen have a "U.S.A." stamp, which was put on the Morgan mold no earlier than 1970 and possibly as late as 1971. But Lani Keller's star-faced #49 has no "U.S.A.," so he could have been made as recently as early 1971, depending on when the mold got the "U.S.A." That the star version was not introduced any earlier than 1970 is indicated by a 1970 Showcase Collection brochure that shows a bald-faced Morgan, whether bay or black I'm not sure, in a Showcase box (photo reprinted in *JAH* 18/#3 Summer II 1991, p. 30, and 18/#4 Fall 1991, p. 14). The rarity of the star-faced bay also indicates a short period of production, so I seriously doubt that the star was introduced any earlier than 1970. For the solid-faced bay, see Morgan SR bay (below). #49 was in the Showcase Collection as #490 in 1970-71 (see Showcase Collection in this section for discussion). The model number 490 later belonged to "Bolya" The Freedom Horse.
- Morgan #702, light reddish bay, stripe, gray shading around eyes, black points, gray hooves, matte (1988-89). There is a beautiful buckskin variation of this model, which is a distinctly lighter, tanner color than the normal reddish bay #702s, though to judge from my own specimen, it does have a more reddish cast than a buckskin such as Mustang #87. My buckskin #702 has dorsal and ventral bands of redder color.
- Morgan #948, woodgrain, black eyes, no white markings or other color detailing, matte (1964-65).
- Show Stance Morgan #831, dark red chestnut, star, slightly lighter red mane and tail, 1 right front and 1 left hind stocking, 4 tan hooves, matte (1990-91). Typically these horses are quite dark, but I have seen one with a more medium shade and a light mane and tail with a pink cast.
- Vermont Morgan #858, chocolate sorrel, solid face, beige-flaxen mane and tail, beige lower legs, gray hooves, matte (1992-93). As is noted in *JAH* 19/#4 Fall 1992 (p. 32), a variation of this model has normal white stockings (I have one like this).

Special-run models made from this mold:

- Morgan SR, bay, solid face, no white markings, some with black-shaded muzzle and genitals, black mane and tail, dark gray or black lower legs and hooves, matte (early or mid 1970s). Made for the "Wonderful World of Horses" touring show. 1,000-2,500 models made. The models I've seen are roughly the same shade of medium reddish bay as regular-run #49, but they are more solid, having little of the light body shading that is typical of #49. Three models I know of (Sheryl Leisure's, Karen Grimm's, and a model advertised for auction in 1994) have black-shaded muzzle and genitals and dark gray lower legs and hooves. But a fourth model (Chelle Fulk's) lacks the black shading and has black legs and hooves. The date of this SR is not certain but is definitely no earlier than 1970, for the horses have the "U.S.A." stamp, which was introduced by Breyer in that year. Hollansky 1990 notes that little is known about this special; she suggests that it was made in the early 1970s for a Morgan horse show. Marney Walerius states that this special numbers about 2,500 pieces and was made in 1974-76 for John Wood's Florida-based "Wonderful World of Horses" touring exhibit featuring Morgans and Lipizzans. Marney comments that she bought one of several six-pack cartons left over from the show and that the other leftovers were sold by Bentleys Sales Company. (See Walerius 1991, p. 45.) *JAH* editor Megan Thilman, in *JAH* 19/#4 Fall 1992 (p. 31), concurring with the main part of Marney's story, says that the models were made in the early or mid 1970s and that the leftovers were sold through Breyer dealers in 1976 or 1977. Megan notes, however, that the quantity was probably only about 1,000-1,500.

Note: Early models of the Morgan mold have the round "Breyer Molding Co." stamp only. Later models have the round stamp and the "U.S.A." stamp—my own and other collectors have star-faced bay #49s with the "U.S.A.," so it is certain that this stamp was added to the mold no later than 1971, the last year of production for #49. Some "U.S.A." models might have the "B" stamp too, but I'm not sure.

"Morganglanz" — Stallion, in extended trot. Sculpted by Chris Hess. Mold in catalog-run production 1980-87 (version with brand), 1991 - current as of 1996 (version without brand).

Catalog-run models made from this mold:

MOLD VERSION WITH BRAND:

- "Morganglanz" #59, chestnut, short blaze, flaxen mane and tail, 1 left front and 2 rear stockings with gray hooves, other hoof brown, matte (1980-87). This model was also sold through the 1980 Sears, Ward's, and Penney's holiday catalogs, and the Penney's 1981, in a set with leather English saddle and bridle; the Penney's 1980 set also included three jumps and a special-run Brenda Breyer doll in hunting pink (see U.S. Equestrian Team Set SR under Brenda in the Riders - Soft Or Jointed Plastic section). #59 is a portrait of a real Trakehner stallion named "Morgenglanz" (with an "e"). The misspelling "Morganglanz" is used in all Breyer catalogs that list this model, although the *JAH* issues that mention the name use the correct spelling. The real horse, born in West Germany, was named a champion Trakehner stallion in 1967. In June 1977 he was imported to the U.S., where he continued his career as a stud and was used in eventing and dressage. (Information is per *JAH* XI/#1 1984, p. 10, and an ad flier for the real horse.) The model number 59 previously belonged to the white Western Horse.
- U.S.E.T. Traditional Assortment #6984, "Morganglanz" #59 with other models (1984). This was an assortment for dealers. I believe the packaging of the models in this assortment included a long paper strip printed with photos and various statements. See discussion under U.S.E.T. Traditional Assortment.

MOLD VERSION MAINLY WITHOUT BRAND:

- "Black Beauty 1991" #847, black, short stripe, black mane and tail, 1 right front stocking with gray hoof, 3 black hooves, semigloss (1991-95). Most of these models have no brand, but a few early specimens do have the brand (see note 2 for this mold for discussion). This is Breyer's seventh or eighth "Black Beauty." Like its precursors, this model represents the title character of the classic children's book *Black Beauty: The Autobiography of a Horse*, by the English author Anna Sewell. This was Sewell's only book; it was first published in 1877 (per *Oxford Companion to English Literature*). The box of my #847, purchased in April 1991, says "New Black Beauty" rather than "Black Beauty 1991." On July 15, 1995, the Q2 home-shopping cable TV channel offered 75 "Black Beauty 1991s" that were ordinary #847s but that came in boxes labeled with the special-run model number 704395 (per *JAH* editor Stephanie Macejko). Models that were evidently leftovers from the July program were sold on Q2 shows in November.

Special-run models made from this mold:

MOLD VERSION WITH BRAND:

- "Morganglanz" SR?, dapple gray (1985). Distributor unknown. 200 models reportedly made. This special is listed only in Gutierrez 1989 and DeFeyter and Luther 1991. I've never seen such a model and haven't heard of it outside of these two sources, so its existence seems dubious.
- "Morganglanz" SR, reddish bay, solid face, black points, 4 stockings, black hooves, matte (1989). Penney's holiday catalog. Sold in International Equestrian Collector Set SR #715963, with fleabitten gray "Halla" and dark dapple gray Hanoverian. 3,500 sets made. Quantity and set number are per a Breyer company computer printout of activity 1985-92.
- "Morganglanz" SR, unpainted white (1980). Sold through *JAH* VII/#3 1980 (p. 13). This horse and several other completely unpainted models were offered to hobbyists interested in customizing, but many collectors kept them unpainted. See Unpainted Models for a complete list.

MOLD VERSION WITHOUT BRAND:

- Appaloosa Sport Horse & Canongate Saddle Set SR #700893, chestnut leopard appaloosa, white horse with splashed-on dark brown spots; dark chestnut nose and sides of face; charcoal-chestnut and white striped mane; charcoal-chestnut tail with light streaks; shaded groin; legs charcoal-chestnut from knees and hocks down; tan hooves; matte (1993). Summer special, made for sale through model mail-order companies and toy stores. Made in open quantities for the second half of 1993; the final quantity produced was 4,260 models, per *JAH* editor Stephanie Macejko (conversation of June 1995). Set also includes Canongate Delux leather saddle and white felt saddle pad. This SR set was made as an introductory promotion for Breyer's new line of leather saddles produced by Alan Flesher Studios, of Feasterville, Pennsylvania. The set is pictured in *JAH* 20/#4 Fall 1993 (inside front cover), which refers to the set as a "summer special," as do notices I received from various Breyer dealers. The color of the horses' points varies from more red to more charcoal. Some models have appy spots on the head, others don't.
- "Morganglanz" SR, reddish bay, blaze, black points, 4 stockings, tan hooves, matte (1994). Penney's holiday catalog. Sold in Horse Salute Gift Set SR #711694, with chestnut leopard appaloosa "Lady Phase" and dark mahogany bay "Phar Lap." 2,620 sets made (per *JAH* editor Stephanie Macejko, conversations of June and Dec. 1995). In the two sets that I purchased, the "Morganglanzes" differ slightly from each other: one has a tan nose and a dark gray ventral band running from under the tail, down across groin and belly, up to the middle of the windpipe; the other has a gray nose and only a hint of ventral shading. The number for this set is per an information fax of April 11, 1994, from Breyer to dealers.
- "Pieraz" or "Cash" SR #704695, red fleabit, white horse covered with chestnut flecks; gray-shaded nose; white mane and tail; gray hooves; matte (1995). Made for the Fifth Annual IBM/USET Festival of Champions horse show and fair in Gladstone, New Jersey, held June 22-25, 1995. 1,000 models made, per the order form from the festival. The models came in a regular plastic-front yellow Breyer box labeled "No. 704695 Pieraz 'Cash.'" This SR is a portrait of the real Arabian endurance horse "Pieraz," nicknamed "Cash," who won the gold medal in the World Championship Endurance Ride at the World Equestrian Games in Holland in August 1994 (thanks to collectors Jennifer Lauermann and Alison Beniush for this information). "Pieraz" and his owner, Valerie Kanavy, were present at the IBM/USET Festival of Champions along with Breyer executive Peter Stone (per *JAH* 22/#3 May/June 1995, p. 2).

Notes:

(1) When Chris Hess was creating his original sculpture for this mold, he visited the farm where the real "Morgenglanz" lived to observe the horse, according to Breyer executive Peter Stone (conversation of Nov. 1994).

(2) Models of this mold made prior to early 1991 have a brand that looks like a pair of moose antlers engraved on the near thigh, which is like the brand on the real "Morgenglanz"as shown on a flier advertising the horse's stud services. This brand is used on all registered Trakehners. The very earliest "Black Beauty 1991" #847s, the 1989 SR reddish bay, and all earlier models have the brand. But it was removed from the mold very shortly after the first "Black Beauty 1991" #847s were issued. My own #847, purchased early in April 1991, lacks the brand, but collector Kristin McAllaster has a #847 with a brand, which she purchased new at Agway in Ithaca, New York, when the models first came out in 1991. Kristin's horse must have been from the earliest batch of #847s made. Horses without the brand have a slightly lumpy patch in the area where the brand used to be. (Thanks to Kristin for emailing me with details on her model, and to Lynn Weber for pointing out the loss of the brand to me in the first place.)

(3) Because the "Morganglanz" mold is rather unstable, some models have the toes of the near front and off rear hooves cut off to make the models stand up better. But some models have intact hooves (I think all the ones with cut hooves that I've seen have been #59s). The cut toe is not molded but sanded or pared during the model-preparation stages at the factory.

(4) The "Morganglanz" mold has the round "Breyer Molding Co." stamp. Early models have the "B" stamp as well as the round. This mold was never given the "U.S.A." stamp.

Mountain Pony — see under Haflinger

Music boxes made from Breyer models — see below in the Riders - Hard Plastic section

Mustang — Stallion, semi-rearing, nose up in the air. Sculpted by Chris Hess. Mold in catalog-run production 1961/63 - 1991, 1994 - current as of 1996.

Catalog-run models made from this mold:

- American Mustang #118, sorrel/palomino, solid or partially bald face, gray muzzle, flaxen mane and tail, 4 stockings, gray hooves, matte (1987-89). This model's face isn't visible in the 1987 catalog, but the horse in the 1988 catalog has a solid face, whereas one in the 1989 catalog is bald on the lower part of his face above the nose. On my two models, the lower three quarters of the face is baldish. One is a light sorrel, with a red body and red-shaded mane and tail; the other is a true palomino, with a golden brown body and yellow mane and tail. The model number 118 previously belonged to the black blanket appy Stock Horse Foal ("Phantom Wings" mold) as sold in blister-wrap display box.
- "Diablo" The Mustang #85, albino; gray mane and tail; reddish-brown or black eyes; gray hooves; glossy (1961/63 - 1966). This model is called "albino" in all catalogs and price lists that include him. True to this labeling, some #85s have so-called "red eyes," which are actually dark reddish-brown. Other models have black eyes. In my experience and that of other collectors, the red-eyed version is more common than the black-eyed version (this is the opposite situation from the albino Five-Gaiter, the black-eyed version of which is more common than the red-eyed). Some #85s have pink and gray stallion parts. Some models also have pink shading by the inside corners of the eyes. The model number 85 later belonged to the Dall Sheep (Bighorn Ram mold), and later still to the Azteca (Foundation Stallion mold).
- "Diablo" The Mustang #86, gray appaloosa, gray horse with black splashed-on spots, bald face, white points, pink hooves, glossy (1961/63 - 1966). The gray body color ranges from a light powder gray to dark gray. The spot pattern also varies greatly, ranging from spots only on the rump to spots all over the body. The bald face can be extensive, reaching well down the sides of the face. The model number 86 apparently was later assigned to the 1978 SR black Mustang; see that entry for discussion.
- "Diablo" The Mustang #87, buckskin, bald face, some with thin dorsal stripe, black points, black hooves, matte and semigloss (1961/63 - 1986). I have heard reports of 2 or 3 glossy buckskin Mustangs but have never seen one in person. Some #87s have a pink nose. The bald face can be extensive, reaching well down the sides of the face. A few models may have a solid face. Collector Sue Lehman told me that a few have hand-painted eyewhites; one of these was advertised in the July 1995 *Model Horse Trader*. Body color varies from flat medium buckskin to shaded dark buckskin. On #87s with a dorsal stripe, the stripe varies in length, reaching from dock to mane on some and from dock to only mid-croup on others. On most #87s, the legs are painted black only on the back and sides; the fronts are left for the most part buckskin, as shown in catalogs. Collector Joan Fauteux's dark buckskin semigloss model, which she got in 1962 or 1963, has no black at all on the legs (thanks to Joan for photos), and I've seen another model like this too. Collector Sande Schneider has seen a glossy buckskin Mustang with a lot of dark shading, a wide dorsal stripe, and a dark stripe down the throat. The horse had a "U.S.A." stamp, indicating that it was made no earlier than 1970. The piece looked and felt factory original to Sande, but we do not know whether it was a test piece or similar oddity, or perhaps a very rare variation of #87.
- "Diablo" The Mustang #88, charcoal, bald face, white points, pink hooves, glossy (1961/63 - 1970). The body color ranges from black to charcoal gray to brown, with varying degrees of body shading that makes the models appear lighter in color. Some models have hand-painted eyewhites. The bald face can be extensive, reaching well down the sides of the face. The hooves can be very pale, even white on some models. The model number 88 later belonged to Overo Paint ("Stud Spider" mold).
- "Diablo" The Mustang #985, woodgrain, solid face, black eyes, 4 painted-on stockings, black hooves, matte (1961/63 - 1965).
- "Diablo" The Mustang #1085, Copenhagen decorator, dappled blue, bald face, white points, pink hooves, glossy (1963-64). The hooves can be very pale pink or even white. For further discussion see Decorators (1960s) above in the Traditionals section.
- "Diablo" The Mustang #2085, Florentine decorator, dappled metallic gold, bald face, white points, pink hooves, glossy (1963-64). The hooves can be very pale pink or even white. The model number 2085 later belonged to the "Hobo" Of Lazy Heart Ranch Gift Set. For further discussion see Decorators (1960s) above in the Traditionals section.
- "Diablo" The Mustang #3085, Golden Charm decorator, solid metallic gold, bald face, white points, pink hooves, glossy (1963-64). The hooves can be very pale pink or even white. The gold paint on these horses can darken over time and by now often looks more like tarnished brass. For further discussion see Decorators (1960s) above in the Traditionals section. The model number 3085 later belonged to the Stablemates Stable Set.
- "Diablo" The Mustang #4085, Wedgewood Blue decorator, solid blue, bald face, white points, pink hooves, matte (1963-64). The hooves can be very pale pink or even white. For further discussion see Decorators (1960s) above in the Traditionals section.
- Paint American Mustang #828, bay paint, overo; stenciled extensive bald face; pink nose; dorsal stripe; black points; black hooves; matte (1990-91).
- "Rarin' To Go" #896, grulla, gray horse with charcoal-brown points, back, croup, and head; blaze; brown ventral band; 1 right hind stocking; 4 tan hooves; matte (1994-95).

On some models the mane and tail are darker than the other brown areas. The ventral band runs from beneath the tail, forward across the belly, to just below the chest.

Special-run models made from this mold:

- Mustang SR #410287, alabaster; soft gray mane, tail, and nose; gray hooves; matte (1988). Made for Black Horse Ranch model mail-order company. 333 models made. Sold separately or in SR set with bay blanket appaloosa, black leopard appaloosa, fleabitten gray, palomino, and red dun Mustangs. Date and quantity are per a BHR ad in the April 1988 *Model Rag* and a 1989 BHR price list. Model number is per a Breyer company computer printout of activity 1985-92. This model looks like the old #85 albino "Diablo" with black eyes, except that the SR has a matte finish and unpared left toe tip, whereas the old fellow has a glossy finish and a pared toe tip. My own SR model has a soft gray mane and tail with a tannish or golden cast, which is quite evident in the sunlight; collector Heather Wells's model has a darker gray mane a tail with a slight golden cast detectable only in the crevices.
- Mustang SR #410387, bay blanket appaloosa, bald face, unstenciled blanket covering butt and part of barrel, splashed-on bay spots, black points, black hooves, matte (1988). Made for Black Horse Ranch model mail-order company. 333 models made. Sold separately or in SR set with alabaster, black leopard appaloosa, fleabitten gray, palomino, and red dun Mustangs. Date and quantity are per a BHR ad in the April 1988 *Model Rag* and a 1989 BHR price list. Model number is per a Breyer company computer printout of activity 1985-92. *Breyer Collector's Video* shows two of these models, one a light sandy bay and the other a dark bay; in my experience the lighter color is the norm.
- Mustang SR #86, black, no white markings, black mane and tail, black hooves, semigloss (1978). Made for Bentley Sales Company. Probably about 200-250 models made. The 1978 dating is per Walerius 1991 (p. 99), Gutierrez 1986 and 1989, and Diederich 1988, Section 2. Walerius adds that Bentley's sold the models at the 1978 Model Horse Congress in Illinois (held in August, per *Model Horse Shower's Journal*, Sept. 1978). The earliest evidence I have for this SR is an old Bentley's sales record card labeled "#86 All-Black Mustang special." According to the card, Bentleys had 35 models as of February 1979 and received a shipment of 94 more in March of that year; all 129 of these pieces were sold by mid-October 1979, after which time no further shipments came in. The card does not indicate how many models might have been received in 1978 (Feb. 1979 is the earliest dating on any of the Bentley's record cards in my possession). Gutierrez and Diederich both say that a total of 200 models were made, but this figure seems a bit low if Bentley's had been selling the models since August 1978. Walerius gives the quantity as 100, but she might not have been aware of the 94 pieces received by Bentley's in 1979. A couple of collectors' sales ads for this model appear in the July 1979 *Model Horse Shower's Journal*; one ad says, "All black Mustang like Breyer #88 but in pure black matt [*sic*] finish, no wh. m/t, half-rearing, wild/glossy eyes!" The October 1979 *MHSJ* ran the following editorial item: "Contact immediately Bentley Sales Co. . . . for a new listing of what Breyers they stock as well as the specials & the discontinued in stock. They also had the all black Arab set, black Mustang #86 & others in stock. WRITE FAST! Their prices were basic Breyer prices of approx. $8 per model & postage." The number 86 previously belonged to the regular-run gray appaloosa "Diablo" Mustang.
- Mustang SR, black, solid face, black mane and tail, 1 left front stocking with tan hoof, other legs and hooves black, semigloss (1993). Penney's holiday catalog. Sold in Breyer Wild Horses Of America Set SR #710493, with red sorrel Fighting Stallion and bay blanket appaloosa Foundation Stallion. Projected quantity 1,500 sets; no final count was recorded in Breyer's computer when I spoke to *JAH* editor Stephanie Macejko in June 1995. The set's number is per a Breyer company computer printout of 1993 SRs.
- Mustang SR #410187, black leopard appaloosa, white horse with black splashed-on spots; pink nose and stallion parts; light gray mane, tail, knees, hocks, and hooves; matte (1988). Made for Black Horse Ranch model mail-order company. 333 models made. Sold separately or in SR set with alabaster, bay blanket appaloosa, fleabitten gray, palomino, and red dun Mustangs. Date and quantity are per a BHR ad in the April 1988 *Model Rag* and a 1989 BHR price list. Model number is per a Breyer company computer printout of activity 1985-92.
- Mustang SR #410487, fleabitten gray, white horse with soft gray flecks; dark gray mane and tail; pink nose and hooves; matte (1988). Made for Black Horse Ranch model mail-order company. 333 models made. Sold separately or in SR set with alabaster, bay blanket appaloosa, black leopard appaloosa, palomino, and red dun Mustangs. Date and quantity are per a BHR ad in the April 1988 *Model Rag* and a 1989 BHR price list. Model number is per a Breyer company computer printout of activity 1985-92.
- Mustang SR #410587, palomino, bald face, pink nose, white points, light gray hooves, slightly semigloss (1988). Made for Black Horse Ranch model mail-order company. 333 models made. Sold separately or in SR set with alabaster, bay blanket appaloosa, black leopard appaloosa, fleabitten gray, and red dun Mustangs. Date and quantity are per a BHR ad in the April 1988 *Model Rag* and a 1989 BHR price list. Model number is per a Breyer company computer printout of activity 1985-92.
- Mustang SR #410687, red dun, bald face, pink nose, dark brown mane and tail, dorsal stripe, 4 stockings, light dun hooves, matte (1988). Made for Black Horse Ranch model mail-order company. 333 models made. Sold separately or in SR set with alabaster, bay blanket appaloosa, black leopard appaloosa, fleabitten gray, and palomino Mustangs. Date and quantity are per a BHR ad in the April 1988 *Model Rag* and a 1989 BHR price list. Model number is per a Breyer company computer printout of activity 1985-92.
- "Rawhide" Wild Appaloosa Mustang SR #702495, chestnut roan blanket appaloosa, bald face, unstenciled blanket covering butt and part of barrel, splashed-on dark chestnut and red chestnut spots, dark chestnut points, most with 1 left hind stocking, 4 tan hooves with gray stripes, matte (1995). Breyer Tour special. 3,207 models made, per *JAH* editor Stephanie Macejko (conversation of Oct. 12 1995). The name and model number are per the model's box. Color details vary widely on these models. The basic chestnut body color, which is "roaned" with pale dappling, varies from a light tan shade to darker red chestnut to a dun color created by charcoal shading over the chestnut. Some models have a pink nose, others have gray. The sheath can be pink, whitish, chestnut, or roan. The appy spots, which are distributed over much of the body, vary greatly in size and quantity and distribution. Many "Rawhides" have a left hind stocking (as shown in *JAH* 22/#1 Jan./Feb. 1995, inside front cover), but collector Liz Strauss received a few with no stockings. The 1995 Breyer Tour was a series of about a dozen breakfast, brunch, and barbecue events with Breyer executive Peter Stone, held at toy stores, tack shops, and model-horse shows around the country; a complete list of locations was published in the *JAH* just cited (p. 3). "Rawhide" models were made available only to the participating dealers and were included in the price of admission to the events, but leftovers were sold by some of the dealers via mail order. (Mr. Stone became ill just prior to the Tour stop in Texas, so Stephanie Macejko attended this event in his place. This information is per a letter sent to mail-order purchasers by the sponsoring dealer, Jacque's Toys and Books.) The name "Rawhide" is fictitious, created by Stephanie Macejko.
- "Ruby" SR #410087, dark red roan, red chestnut with yellow dapples on chest, barrel, and rump; stripe; dark chestnut mane and tail; 1 left front and 2 hind socks; 4 reddish gray hooves; matte (1988). Made for Model Horse Collector's Supply Company. 1,000 models made. Sold in SR set with "Wildfire" red chestnut pinto ("San Domingo" mold). Quantity is per *JAH* (15/#4 Sept./Oct. 1988, inside front cover). Model number is per a Breyer company computer printout of activity 1985-92. Pay no attention to the stallion features on these models. The set represents real mares owned by Jeannie Thomas Craig, who told their story in *JAH* XII/#3 1985. The real "Ruby" was a wild Mustang mare that Jeannie bought and bred to a chestnut pinto Saddlebred stud. The filly produced was "Wildfire."
- "Turbo" The Wonder Horse SR #410592, golden palomino, stripe, white mane and tail, gray muzzle, 1 right front and 1 right hind stocking, 4 gray-brown hooves, matte (1992). Dinner/concert model for BreyerFest in Lexington, Kentucky. 1,000 models made. Quantity and model number are per a Breyer company computer printout of activity 1985-92. As noted in *JAH* 19/#2 Summer I (p. 17), this model has "just the slightest touch of metallic gold which makes him glimmer" in his palomino color. Very tiny gold flecks can be seen if the model is inspected closely in sunlight. The real "Turbo" The Wonder Horse (see photo on the cover of *JAH* 19/#2 Summer I 1992) stars in the TV show of the Riders in the Sky, a country-western band. The band played at the 1992 BreyerFest, but the real "Turbo" was not on hand. The band members autographed models for all BreyerFest attendees who wished. The models came in clear plastic bags rather than boxes.

Notes:

(1) This mold is not in the 1960 catalog; it is in the 1963. The name "Diablo," given to all early Mustangs, was dropped from catalogs after 1970/71; it was never used in manuals.

(2) Many early Mustangs have the toe of the near front hoof cut off, presumably to make the model less prone to rocking back on its tail. Later models have intact front hooves. I believe the cut-toe variation is not part of the mold but was achieved by sanding or paring during the model-preparation stages at the factory.

(3) This mold bears a considerable resemblance to the horse in a monumental bronze statue by Solon Borglum (brother of Gutzon Borglum, sculptor of Mt. Rushmore). When I asked Breyer executive Peter Stone whether Chris Hess based his design for the Mustang on this statue, he did not know but commented that it was possible—Hess often took his Breyer designs from photos and illustrations and might have seen a photo of this well-known Borglum monument in a magazine or book. The position of the Borglum horse's head and ears and his overall stance are strikingly like the Breyer Mustang's, though the leg and tail positions differ somewhat. The statue, erected in 1907 in Prescott, Arizona, is an equestrian portrait of William "Bucky" O'Neill, a Prescott native and a commanding officer of the Rough Riders who was killed in 1898 in the Spanish-American War during the battle of San Juan Hill, Cuba. An image of the statue appears on a 3¢ U.S. postage stamp issued in 1948 to commemorate the 50th anniversary of the Rough Riders, and a photo of the statue appeared in an August 1962 *Western Horseman* article titled "The Horse in Bronze" (thanks to Jo Kulwicki for the article and to Joan Berkwitz for alerting me to the stamp).

(4) At an antique mall in central California, collector Sue Lehman found a very unusual bay Mustang, which I have seen in person. His body color is dark chocolate brown, with some light shading on shoulders and flanks. He has a bald face, black mane and tail, no black on the legs, 4 stockings, gray hooves, dark shading on the genitals, and a slightly semigloss finish. He has a "U.S.A." stamp, which would date him to no earlier than 1970, but the genital shading and overall appearance would seem to date him to pre-1980. He does appear to be original factory finish, but he is the only such Mustang we know of.

(5) Early models of the Mustang mold have the round "Breyer Molding Co." stamp only. Later ones have the round stamp and the "U.S.A." stamp. Some "U.S.A." models might have the "B" stamp too, but I'm not sure.

"Mustang Lady" SR — see under Indian Pony

My Companion Rocking Horse SR — see under Saddlebred Weanling

My Favorite Rocking Horse SR — see under Saddlebred Weanling

My Own Money Manager — see Breyer Company History below in the Appendix

"Mystique" SR — see under Jumping Horse

"Native Diver" Champion Thoroughbred — see under "Phar Lap"

Neckties — see Breyer Neckties

"Nevada Star" SR — see below in the Classics section under "Hobo" (with stand)

"Night Deck" SR — see under "Lady Phase"

Nightlights made from Breyer models — see Lamps & Nightlights in the Appendix near the end of this book

"Night Vision" SR — see under Stock Horse Foal, standing

Noble Jumper — see under "Halla"

Norman Thelwell's Collection — see "Kipper"

Norwegian Fjord — see "Henry" The Norwegian Fjord

Numbers for Breyer models — for discussion see the start of the Models By Number section near the end of this book

Nursing foal — see Suckling Foal

"Ofir," Sire of "Witez II," SR — see under Black Stallion

Old Timer — Gelding, standing with left hind hoof cocked, tailtip attached to right hock, molded-on harness and bridle, glued-on blinkers, removable hat. Sculpted by Chris Hess. Mold in catalog-run production 1966-93, 1995 - current as of 1996.

Catalog-run models made from this mold:

- "McDuff" Old Timer #935, grulla blanket appaloosa, gray horse with dark gray flecks, bald face, unstenciled blanket on butt and loins, splashed-on black spots, black points, tan hooves with charcoal stripes, dark brown harness, matte; white hat with brick-red hatband (1995 - current as of 1996). Collector Karen Grimm has an unusual "McDuff" with no gray flecks on the gray areas of the horse, and I have heard of one or two other fleckless #935s as well. In the 1996 catalog, this model's name was expanded to "McDuff" Appaloosa Old Timer.
- Old Timer #200, alabaster, gray mane and tail, gray shading on body, gray hooves, dark brown or black harness, matte; yellow hat with dark green or blue hatband (1966-76). My own model has a dark brown harness, but collector Leslie Granger has one with a black harness and has seen others like this as well. *Quequechan Model Horse Collector*, August 1985, also reports the black and brown harness variations. The amount of gray body shading on #200 varies, but typically there is at least enough to make the old boy's ribs stand out. Collector Laurie Croddy wrote to me that her model is almost completely gray, with a bald face, front socks, and white hind legs. Regarding hatband color, also see note 1 for this mold. For differences between #200 and the SR alabaster Old Timer, see the entry for the SR, below. #200 was in the Showcase Collection as #2000 in 1970-72 (see Showcase Collection in this section for discussion). The number 2000 later belonged to the Classic After School Herd Assortment.
- Old Timer #205, dapple gray, typically with dapples on neck and head; bald face; gray mane and tail; 4 stockings; gray hooves; dark brown or black harness; glossy, semi-gloss, and matte; yellow hat, early ones with dark green or blue hatband, later ones with yellow hatband (1966, 1968/70 - 1987). The body color varies from dark, brightly dappled gray to a fairly light, soft dapple gray. Some models have no or very few dapples on the head and neck (thanks to Paula DeFeyter for a photo of her #205 like this). Collector Lori Ogozalek has a model with halo dapples—the larger dapples are surrounded by a haze of very minute white dots, which creates a halo effect. Regarding hatband color, see note 1 for this mold. *Production history*: This model first appears in the 1966 catalog and price list. He is in the 1967 catalog but with an announcement that he is discontinued, and the 1967 price list omits him. So far so good, but now the records get chaotic: he reappears in the 1968 catalog but not in the 1968 manual or price list; and he is in the 1969 manual but not the 1969 price list (there is evidently no 1969 catalog). Then he settles down and appears in every catalog, manual, and price list I have from 1970 through 1987. *Harness*: My own #205 has a dark brown harness; Sande Schneider's has black. Some of the glossy models have gloss varnish on the harness as well as on the horse; these are the oldest #205s, to judge from the lack of "U.S.A." stamps on specimens I've seen. But other glossies, which appear newer, have matte harnesses. On these, close inspection reveals that the whole model was varnished while the harness was still dapple gray like the horse, then the matte brown or black was painted on the harness over the layers of dapple gray and varnish. Jo Kulwicki has one of the old glossy-harness models, and she says the varnish on the harness is very bubbly. Paula DeFeyter's glossy-harness model, however, has no bubbling. #205 was in the Showcase Collection as #2050 in 1970-72 (see Showcase Collection in this section for discussion).
- Old Timer #206, bay, bald face, black points, 1 right hind stocking, 4 gray hooves, dark brown harness, matte; orangy-tan hat with red hatband (1988-90). The model in the 1988 catalog has a gray hoof only on the stockinged leg; the other hooves are black. Whether models with such hooves were actually sold in the first year I don't know. In the other catalogs, all the hooves are gray, and my own model has all gray.
- Old Timer #834, dark red roan, red chestnut with yellow flecks, dark red mane and tail, bald face, gray hooves, dark brown harness, matte; most with blue hat with red hatband (1991-93). Catalogs show this model with blue hat with red band, and most #834s I've seen have had this hat. But in January 1992, in a toy store, I saw a #834 with an orangy-tan hat with red band—a leftover, presumably, from production of #206.

Special-run models made from this mold:

- McCormick Decanter With Old Timer set SR, dapple gray, black or dark brown harness, matte; yellow hat with yellow hatband, pulling a red wooden Atlantic & Pacific Tea Co. wagon, which contains a bottle of McCormick bourbon; mounted on wood base (1984). Made for McCormick Distilling Co. of Weston, Missouri. The horse is identical to the light dapple gray, matte version of regular run #205. The date of this special is per a McCormick ad flier for the wagon. An original flier is in the archives of Reeves International; the photo from the flier is reprinted in *JAH* 17/#3 July/Aug. 1990 (p. 33). *JAH* does not give a quantity but does note: "exact production figures are uncertain, only a few are left (at press time) and can be purchased directly from McCormick." DeFeyter and Luther 1991 give the quantity as 200, but this figure seems too low if the sets were produced in 1984 yet some were left in 1990. The McCormick ad flier shows the hatband as yellow; this coloring is true of the sets I know of and is corroborated by *Quequechan Model Horse Collector*, August 1985: "The new Old Timer (SP. RN) has an all-yellow hat with no band." The McCormick flier also shows the horse with metal pins going through holes in the sides of his breast to attach him to the wagon shafts. The horses in the sets owned by collectors Sande Schneider and Lisa Whittick, however, lacks breast holes, as do two or three other sets Lisa has seen. Lisa's set, which I saw in person in October 1994, had a gold "Made in Taiwan" sticker on the bottom of the wagon. Sande's and Lisa's wagons and the others Lisa has seen, as well as the one in the McCormick flier, are painted red with a black roof, with yellow wooden shafts and gold-colored metal wheels. Collectors Gale Good and Carolyn Ruth, however, told me they have seen green wagons. The sides of the wagon are decorated with logos saying "The Great Atlantic & Pacific Tea Co. / Established 1859 / 31 Vesey St. / New York, New York." The McCormick ad flier says "McCormick Proudly Presents the A&P Cart and Horse Decanter / 1984 • McCormick Distilling Co.," and explains the piece as follows: "During James Buchanan's presidency history was made in lower Manhattan when George Huntington Hartford opened a tiny coffee, tea and spice shop on Vesey Street. A new era in shopping was launched. Red, white and blue globes hung outside, cashiers worked in Chinese pagoda-style cages, and on Saturday nights, a band played. At the turn of the century, red and gold A&P carts traveled the backroads delivering tea, baking powder and silver polish. This accurate scale model of the old A&P cart has been reproduced in honor of the A&P Stores' 125th anniversary. It is appropriate that the wagon should carry 750 ml. of our fine McCormick bourbon with a reputation of 'Superb Spirits Since 1856.'"
- Old Timer SR, alabaster, pale gray mane and tail, no body shading, gray hooves, dark brown harness, matte; yellow hat with yellow hatband (1983). Ward's holiday catalog. Collector Joy Sheesley's model has a dark brown harness; whether there is a version with black harness I don't know. In the photos of this SR in the Ward's catalog and *JAH* X/#3 1983 (p. 13), it's impossible to tell if the harness is black or dark brown, but the hat is clearly yellow with a yellow band, as on Joy's model. The old regular-run #200 alabaster had a yellow hat with dark band. The SR also has lighter mane and tail than #200, and lacks body shading, whereas #200 has gray shading on the body.

Notes:

(1) All alabaster and dapple Old Timers, whether regular run or special run, came with a yellow hat. But earlier hats have a dark green or blue band, as shown in Breyer catalogs and manuals 1966-78, whereas later hats have a yellow band, as shown in catalogs 1979-87. SRs conform to this dating too: the 1983 SR alabasters and 1984 SR dapple McCormick Decanter horses have yellow hats with yellow bands.

(2) The blinkers on this mold are separately molded pieces that are glued onto the horse. The Old Timer differs in this respect from the only other Breyer mold with blinkers, the Balking Mule, whose blinkers are an integral part of the mold.

(3) Early models of the Old Timer mold have the round "Breyer Molding Co." stamp only. Later ones have round stamp and the "U.S.A." stamp—my own alabaster #200 and others I've seen have the "U.S.A.," so it is certain that this stamp was added to the mold no later than 1976; it may have been added as early as 1970, when the "U.S.A." was first introduced into the Breyer line. Some "U.S.A." models have the "B" stamp in addition.

Open Top Buggy set — in the Traditionals section see under Proud Arabian Stallion; in the Classics section below see under "Johar"

"Our First Pony" sets — In the Traditionals section see Marguerite Henry's "Our First Pony" Gift Set and "Our First Pony" Set SR, both under Shetland Pony. In the Classics section below see Marguerite Henry's "Our First Pony" Gift Set under Arabian Family Foal and under Mustang Family Foal.

Our Rocking Horse SR — see under Saddlebred Weanling

Overo Paint — see under "Stud Spider"

Overo Paint Stock Horse Mare — see under Stock Horse Mare

"Oxidol" Rodeo Appaloosa — see under "San Domingo"

Pacer — Stallion, pacing, with molded-on halter. Sculpted by Chris Hess. Mold in catalog-run production 1967-87, 1990,1996.

Catalog-run models made from this mold:

- "Dan Patch" Famous Standardbred Pacer #819, red bay, star, black points, white right hind coronary band, 4 tan hooves, black eyes (not tri-color), red-brown halter, slightly semigloss, Limited Edition (1990). This model's box sports a large round gold sticker saying, in full: "1990 Limited Edition / Dan Patch / Champion Pacer." Limited Edition models are produced only for one year, in quantities sufficient to fill all orders for the model. The real "Dan Patch" set the world record for the mile in pacing in 1906. See the 1990 Breyer catalog for more details.
- Pacer #46, liver chestnut, solid face, liver mane and tail same color as body or darker, 3-4 stockings with gray hooves, other hoof liver-charcoal, black or red-brown halter, matte and semigloss (1967-87). Some early models have hand-painted eyewhites. Collector Paula DeFeyter sent me a photo of her glossy Pacer, which has eyewhites and 3.5 stockings (only the front of the left fore is white). The Pacer is shown with 3 stockings (1 left front and 2 hind) in catalogs and manuals for 1967-75, and with 4 stockings in 1976-81 and 1983-87 (all legs not visible in 1982), though in 1983-84 the right front stocking is so vague as almost not to count. This model is called "dark bay" in catalogs and manuals, but there is no black on the legs, and on the models I've seen, the mane and tail are not black.

Set:

- Brenda Breyer And Sulky Set #2446, alabaster Pacer; gray-shaded mane, tail, knees, and hocks; gray hooves; black halter; matte; with doll, sulky, and harness (pre-catalog release 1981, catalog run 1982-87). This set debuted in the 1981 Aldens and Ward's holiday catalogs, both of which sold the doll separately from the horse and sulky. Set #2446 is in the 1987 Breyer catalog, but with the notation "Limited quantity available in 1987." A different set, Sulky Kit #2400, containing only the sulky and harness (no doll or horse), is in the 1981 Breyer catalog and the 1981-84 Breyer price lists. For details on the doll, sulky, and tack see in the Riders - Soft Or Jointed Plastic section below.

Special-run models made from this mold:

- Brenda Breyer Harness Racing Set SR, medium bay Pacer, solid face; black mane and tail; early ones with 4 black/charcoal legs and hooves; later ones with black/charcoal knees and hocks, 4 white stockings, and gray hooves; brown halter; slightly semigloss; with doll, sulky, and harness (1981, 1982, 1983, 1984, and 1985). Sears holiday catalog. The 1981 Sears catalog shows the horse with black legs, no white stockings. The 1982-85 Sears catalogs show the 4-stocking version. Many of these horses (both versions) have the "B" stamp, but not all. Those lacking it are probably from 1984-85. For details on the doll, outfit, sulky, and tack see the Riders - Soft Or Jointed Plastic section below.
- Brenda Breyer Sulky And Pacer Set SR, light golden chestnut Pacer, solid face, lighter chestnut/flaxen mane and tail, 4 stockings, gray hooves, black halter, matte; with doll, sulky, and harness (1981, 1982, and 1983). Penney's holiday catalog. My own model and those owned by collectors Liz Strauss and Lynn Luther all have a "B" stamp, but the horses made in 1983 might not have this stamp. For details on the doll, sulky, and tack see the Riders - Soft Or Jointed Plastic section below.
- Pacer SR, dapple gray, dapples on neck, head, and face; darker gray mane, tail, knees, and hocks; 4 stockings; gray hooves; black halter; semigloss (1984). Sold separately or in set with SR dark red chestnut and palomino Pacers. Made for the Riegseckers of Indiana (per Diederich 1988, Section 2, and Walerius 1991, p. 101), but some sets were sold through other mail-order companies as well. Former Breyer executive Peter Stone did not recall the quantity of these sets when I asked him in December 1995, but judging from the apparent scarcity of these horses today, I would guess that no more than about 300-400 sets were made. Collector Gale Good got her Pacers from Riegseckers in March 1985, but I date the SR to 1984 on the basis of other evidence: all three colors are listed on a December 1984 price list from Amigo's Little Acre (business of Frank Meltzer, of Michigan), and collector Heather Wells got all three colors from Bentley Sales Company in fall 1984—her shipping label for the set is dated October 30, 1984. Bentley's sales record cards in my possession indicate that Bentley's received

only 12 pieces of each of the three colors. Oddly, the August 1983 *Quequechan Model Horse Collector* contains a list of SRs and test colors that includes a special run of "grey" Pacers, quantity 200 (no date or distributor specified). I know nothing more about such a run; to my knowledge the only gray Pacer SR is the 1984 dapple gray.

- Pacer SR, dark red chestnut, solid face, flaxen mane and tail, 1 right hind stocking with gray hoof, other hooves red-gray, black halter, matte (1984). Made for the Riegseckers of Indiana (per Diederich 1988, Section 2, and Walerius 1991, p. 101). Sold separately or in set with SR dapple gray and palomino Pacers. Some of these dark red chestnut Pacers have pale chestnut pasterns or coronary bands on the legs without stockings. See Pacer SR dapple gray for discussion of date and quantity.
- Pacer SR, light bay, solid face, black points, 1 left front and 2 hind stockings with tan hooves, other hoof black, black halter, matte (1995). Penney's holiday catalog. Sold in Race Horses Of America set SR #710295 with medium dapple gray "Phar Lap," dappled reddish chestnut Stock Horse Stallion, and one removable neck ribbon. 5,500 sets made (per *JAH* editor Stephanie Macejko, conversation of July 2, 1996). As compared to the medium bay SR Pacer with his sandy-yellow highlights, this light bay Pacer has an almost rosy cast, virtually no yellow tones. The neck ribbon is identical to the ribbon that comes with the B Ranch series horses "Cloud" and "Patches" (see in the Classics section for details).
- Pacer SR, palomino, most with bald face, white points, gray hooves, black halter, matte (1984). Made for the Riegseckers of Indiana (per Diederich 1988, Section 2, and Walerius 1991, p. 101). Sold separately or in set with SR dapple gray and dark red chestnut Pacers. The bald face and stockings on the palomino can be fairly vague, with quite a bit of palomino overspray; a model I saw at BreyerFest 1994 actually had a solid face. See Pacer SR dapple gray for discussion of date and quantity.
- Pacing Horse, Sulky And Harness set SR, black Pacer, no white markings, black mane and tail, tan hooves, brown halter, slightly semigloss (1982). Aldens holiday catalog. Probably about 700-750 models made, per former Breyer executive Peter Stone (conversation of Dec. 1995). According to Walerius 1991, who gives the undoubtedly too low quantity of 500, only half of the black Pacers were sent to Aldens before the store "declar[ed] bankruptcy in December 1982"; the rest were "distributed by Bentley Sales to sell to collectors" (p. 99). Bentley Sales Company sales record cards in my possession labeled "#46B Black Pacer" show that Bentley's received a total of 313 models, in several shipments between December 1982 and December 1985. The horses are first advertised on Bentley's price list dated January 1983, which lists them as "The Black Pacer—A 1982 Breyer Specialty Run—$9.49," and remain on Bentley's lists as late as spring 1986. Some models made their way to Horses International (a division of Atlantis International) as well; the SR black Pacer is included on their price lists, as "#46B Black Pacer" for $11, at least from 1985 through 1987. These Bentley's and Horses International models came without the blue plastic sulky and leather harness that the Aldens models came with. In the Aldens catalog, the photo shows a Brenda Breyer doll in the sulky, but according to the text, the doll was sold separately, not as part of the Pacer set. The sulky and harness are the same as in regular-run set #2446, but the SR set includes three addition items as well, according to the Aldens photo: a fuzzy blue shadow roll across the horse's nose, a small white blanket with a black "5" across the horse's back, and a tiny "head number"—a little card printed with the number 5, which attaches to the bridle's crown piece and stands up between the horse's ears. Bentley's sold leftover "head numbers" (quantity of 60) from mid-1983 through mid-1987; they appear as "Head Number—Blue and White #5," for $2.79, on Bentley's price lists of these years. Oddly, *JAH* IX/#2 1982 (p. 12), which shows all the holiday specials for that year, shows the horse alone, with no sulky or harness.

Notes:

(1) Many models of this mold have a small nub of plastic on the bottom of the left front hoof to stabilize them; it appears to be part of the mold. But some models don't have this nub; it appears to have been sanded off at the factory. Some of the models with the nub removed also had the toe of the right hind hoof cut off (I own a #46 like this), presumably to stabilize them. The toe-cutting strategy is far less effective and more defacing than the nub strategy, so why some models had their nubs sanded off in the first place I don't know.

(2) The Pacer mold has the round "Breyer Molding Co." stamp. Some models also have the "B" stamp; earlier and later ones do not. This mold was never given the "U.S.A." stamp.

Paint American Mustang — see under Mustang

Paint Horse Foal — see under Action Stock Horse Foal; Stock Horse Foal, standing; also see "Scribbles" (under "Sea Star")

Paint Horse Mare — see under Stock Horse Mare

Paint Horse Stallion — see under Stock Horse Stallion

Paint Stock Horse Foal — see under Stock Horse Foal, standing

"Pale Face" — see Prancer #P43, palomino (under "Fury" Prancer)

"Pantomime" Pony Of The Americas — see under Pony Of The Americas

Parade Of Horses Breeds set SR —see Cantering Welsh Pony SR, red roan; Proud Arabian Mare SR, bay; and Saddlebred Weanling SR, alabaster

Partially unpainted models — see Unpainted Models

Paso Fino — see all the models under "El Pastor"

Pearly models — see Chalkies & Pearlies in the Appendix near the end of this book

"Pegasus" — see "Pegasus" and Sky Blue "Pegasus" SR, both under Lipizzan Stallion in Classics section

Percheron SR — see under Belgian

Performance Horse — Stallion, standing, looking right, short tail. Sculpted by Chris Hess. Mold in catalog-run production 1974-85,1996-.

Catalog-run models made from this mold:

- Appaloosa Performance Horse #99, chestnut roan semi-leopard appaloosa, bald face, charcoal-brown mane and tail, chestnut roan forehand, white barrel and hindquarters, stenciled dark brown spots from butt to neck, 2 front stockings, 4 pink-and-gray striped hooves, matte (1974-80). The roan color on this model's forehand is brown with white dappling; the brown varies from dark to light. Some models have pink nose, others have gray nose. The model number 99 previously belonged to Quarter Horse "Two Bits," bay (Quarter Horse Gelding mold).

Set:

- Brenda Breyer Gift Set #3095, sorrel blanket appaloosa Performance Horse, solid face, flaxen mane and tail, unstenciled butt blanket, splashed-on sorrel spots, gray-brown hooves, matte; with bareback pad, bridle, and doll (1980-85). See the Riders - Soft Or Jointed Plastic section below for details on the doll and tack. The horse by itself was available in 1980, 1981, and 1982 through the Sears holiday catalog, where it was called "Sorrel Appaloosa Horse." The model number 3095 previously belonged to the Breyer Rider Gift Set with doll and palomino "Adios."

Special-run models made from this mold:

- Appaloosa Stallion With Western Tack Set SR, gray blanket appaloosa, solid face, unstenciled butt blanket, splashed-on black spots, black points, dark gray hooves, matte (1984). Penney's holiday catalog. Set includes leather Western saddle, breast collar, and bridle.
- Performance Horse SR #410199, alabaster; gray mane, tail, and hooves; matte (1989). Made for Horses International, a division of Atlantis International. 500 models made. Sold separately or in SR set with black leopard appaloosa, liver chestnut, and red roan Performance Horses. Quantity and model number are per a Breyer company computer printout of activity 1985-92.
- Performance Horse SR, black blanket appaloosa, stenciled extensive bald face, stenciled croup-and-loins blanket with black splashed-on spots, 2 hind stockings with pink hooves, front hooves black, matte (1990). Sears holiday catalog. Sold in Appaloosa-American Classic Set SR #499610, with palomino blanket appaloosa Running Stallion and blue roan semi-leopard appaloosa "Stud Spider." 2,000 sets made. (Quantity and set number are per a Breyer company computer printout of activity 1985-92.)
- Performance Horse SR #410099, black leopard appaloosa, white horse with black splashed-on spots; gray mane, tail, and hooves; matte (1989). Made for Horses International, a division of Atlantis International. 500 models made. Sold separately or in SR set with alabaster, liver chestnut, and red roan Performance Horses. The black leopard and red roan were issued first, in June; the other two became available later in the year. Quantity and model number are per a Breyer company computer printout of activity 1985-92.
- Performance Horse SR #410399, liver chestnut, solid face, chestnut-shaded flaxen mane and tail, 4 stockings, peachy tan hooves, matte (1989). Made for Horses International, a division of Atlantis International. 500 models made. Sold separately or in SR set with alabaster, black leopard appaloosa, and red roan Performance Horses. Quantity and model number are per a Breyer company computer printout of activity 1985-92.
- Performance Horse SR #410299, red roan, white horse with red chestnut flecks; chestnut mane and tail; gray-chestnut shaded knees and hocks; tan hooves; matte (1989). Made for Horses International, a division of Atlantis International. 500 models made. Sold separately or in SR set with alabaster, black leopard appaloosa, and liver chestnut Performance Horses. The black leopard and red roan were issued first, in June; the other two became available later in the year. Quantity and model number are per a Breyer company computer printout of activity 1985-92.

Notes:

(1) The 1977 Penney's holiday catalog has a photo of a Performance Horse painted in black blanket appaloosa with a star and labeled "'Stud Spider' Appaloosa." The horse was evidently a test-color piece used as a stand-in for the correct "Stud Spider" model, which was not ready at the time of the photo shoot for the Penney's catalog. Unlike normal "Stud Spiders," the Performance Horse test piece has an unstenciled blanket with splashed-on spots; it might also have striped hooves (my copy of the page is not clear). To my knowledge Penney's sold no such Performance Horses but instead ordinary "Stud Spider" models.

(2) The Performance Horse mold has the round "Breyer Molding Co." stamp and the "U.S.A." stamp. Some models also have the "B" stamp.

Performing "Misty" — see below in the Little Bits section

"Phantom Wings" — Filly, standing, looking left. Sculpted by Chris Hess. Mold in catalog-run production 1978-87, 1991-95.

Catalog-run models made from this mold:

- "Bright Socks" Pinto Foal #895, black pinto, tobiano; black face with white muzzle; white mane and tail; 4 high stockings; tan hooves; matte (1994-95). This model's pinto pattern is somewhat different from "Phantom Wings's." The foal shown in the 1994-95 catalogs is a test-color piece, with a more delicate and detailed pattern than the production-line foals have. Former Breyer employee Megan Thilman Quigley mentioned to me that the test foal's pinto pattern is based on the pattern of a "young Misty" model that Megan designed as part of a three-piece set proposed by Breyer to a department store for holiday-catalog sales (the proposal was rejected). Megan copied the pattern for that model from the markings of the real "Misty." The pattern was altered somewhat for "Bright Socks"—in particular, "young Misty's" blaze was reduced to a white muzzle and a stocking or two may have been changed.
- "Phantom Wings," "Misty's" Foal, #29, palomino pinto, tobiano; blaze; white mane; palomino tail; 4 high stockings; gray hooves; matte (1983-87). This model's pinto pattern is the same as "Rough Diamond's" except that "Phantom Wings" has a colored (palomino) tail whereas "Rough Diamond" has a white tail. My own "Phantom Wings" has a tail with white tip; the model is shown with solid palomino tail in all catalogs, however. Though no Breyer catalog mentions the fact, #29 represents a real Chincoteague pony who was "Misty's" first foal and her only colt (per *JAH* 20/#1 Spring 1993, p. 33). His sire was a Chincoteague stallion named "Wings," who also fathered "Misty's" two fillies: "Stormy" and "Wisp o' Mist." Marguerite Henry did not write a book about "Phantom Wings," nor is he mentioned in Henry's "Misty" series books (*Misty*, *Stormy*, and *Sea Star*), but he is mentioned in Henry's *Dear Marguerite Henry* and *A Pictorial Life Story of Misty*. The latter book describes him thus: "the color of a fawn, except for the white-blazed face, the beginnings of a map on his shoulder, and a perfect wing on his rump. . . . The white wing he owes to his father, who is named Wings because of this distinctive marking" (pp. 96, 101). The book also explains that "Phantom Wings" got his name—which combines the names of the colt's sire and the colt's granddam, "The Phantom," who was "Misty's" dam (p. 102)—through a contest organized by Ms. Henry. In 1983 the "Phantom Wings" model was sold through the Penney's holiday catalog as part of the Assorted Mare And Foals Stable Set SR, with

PAM SR reddish bay, PAF SR reddish bay, and Stock Horse Foal (standing) SR gray blanket appy. He was also sold through the 1983 Sears holiday catalog in a set with "Misty," "Stormy," and Marguerite Henry's book *Misty of Chincoteague*.

- "Rough Diamond" #846, dark chestnut pinto, tobiano; blaze; white mane and tail; 4 high stockings; gray hooves; matte (1991-93). This model's pinto pattern is the same as "Phantom Wings's" except that "Rough Diamond" has a white tail whereas "Phantom Wings" has a colored tail.
- Stock Horse Foal #17, chestnut blanket appaloosa, solid face, unstenciled butt blanket, splashed-on chestnut spots, darker chestnut mane and tail, no stockings, gray-brown hooves, matte (1979-82). Prior to being assigned to this foal, the model number 17 originally belonged to the "Sheik" And "Sheba" set with bay Family Arabian Stallion and Proud Arabian Mare and then belonged to the "Sheik" And "Sheba" set with bay Family Arabian Stallion and Mare.
- Stock Horse Foal #18, black blanket appaloosa, solid face, unstenciled butt blanket, splashed-on black spots, black legs and hooves, matte (1978-82). This foal is shown with gray hooves in the 1978 catalog and on the model's box; whether the earliest foals were in fact issued with gray hooves I don't know. Collector Paula Hecker's model purchased new in 1979 has black hooves. For a brief period in the late 1970s this model was sold with the model number 118 in a special blister-wrapped display carton; the number 118 was later assigned to the American Mustang (Mustang mold). For discussion see Display Boxes above in this section. The model number 18, prior to being assigned to this foal, originally belonged to the "Sheba" And "Shah" set with bay Proud Arabian Mare and Foal, and shortly thereafter was given to the "Sheba" And "Shah" set with bay Family Arabian Mare and Foal.
- "Woodsprite" Pony Foal #875, reddish bay, star, black points, black hooves, matte (1993-94).

Special-run models made from this mold:

- "Phantom Wings" SR, bay blanket appaloosa, star, unstenciled blanket covering butt and most of barrel, no appy spots, black points, 1 right front and 2 hind stockings with pink-tan hooves, other leg and hoof black, matte (1993). Penney's holiday catalog. Sold in Breyer Three Generations Appaloosa Set SR #710693, with bay blanket appy "Adios" and bay blanket appy Quarter Horse Yearling. Projected quantity 3,000 sets; no final count was recorded in Breyer's computer when I spoke to *JAH* editor Stephanie Macejko in June 1995. The set's number is per a Breyer company computer printout of 1993 SRs.

Notes:

(1) Collectors refer to #17 and #18 as "old-mold Stock Foals" because they were replaced in 1983 by the new-mold Stock Foal, that is, the standing Stock Horse Foal.

(2) The "Phantom Wings" mold has the round "Breyer Molding Co." stamp. Some early models also have a backwards (or upside-down) "B" stamp on the opposite hind leg (my #18 and Chelle Fulk's #17 and #18 are like this), though the very earliest models do not have a "B." Collector Jane Chapman wrote to me that her #18 has no "B" and has rough texturing on area where the "B" is located on other models. Thus her model must be a very early issue, for later models with no "B" are smooth in this area, presumably as a result of the removal of the "B" from the metal injection mold. This mold was never given the "U.S.A." stamp.

"Pharaoh's Horses" belt buckle — see Belt Buckles above

"Phar Lap" — Gelding, galloping on right lead. Sculpted by Chris Hess. Mold in catalog-run production 1985 - current as of 1996.

Catalog-run models made from this mold:

- Galloping Thoroughbred #803, dark dappled bay, solid face, black points, 1 left hind stocking, 4 gray hooves, slightly semigloss (1989-90). The dapples are muted, being only a shade or two lighter than the basic body color.
- "Hobo" #838, buckskin; solid face; gray muzzle; black points; gray-shaded eyes, gaskins, groin, and buttocks; tan hooves; semigloss (1991-92). This is Breyer's second portrait model of "Hobo," the real mustang saddle horse owned by "Wild Horse Annie" Johnston, the courageous defender of America's wild horses, whose story is told in Marguerite Henry's book *Mustang: Wild Spirit of the West*. "Hobo" #838 has no blaze and no brand, but Breyer's first portrait model of this horse, "Hobo" #2085 (on stand) has both of these features, as did the real horse. For further information on the real horse and on Wild Horse Annie, see "Hobo" #2085, below in the Classics section.
- "Native Diver" Champion Thoroughbred #921, black, stripe, black mane and tail, 1 right hind stocking with gray or black hoof, other hooves black, slightly semigloss (1995 - current as of 1996). The word "Champion" was dropped from this model's name in the 1996 catalog. The model shown in the 1995 and 1996 catalogs has no stocking; it is probably a test-color piece. All the regular-issue #921s I've seen have a right hind stocking, with a hoof that varies from medium gray to black. The stocking and the model's unusual blaze, an upward-pointing arrow, are true to the real horse represented by this model, "Native Diver" (born 1959), the first California-bred Thoroughbred race horse to win a million dollars. He was bred and owned by Louis Shapiro, who previously had owned the famous Standardbred pacer "Adios," also represented in plastic by Breyer. Of his 81 races, "Native Diver" won 37, including an unprecedented three Hollywood Gold Cups in a row, 1965-67. When the horse died of colic in the year of his third Gold Cup victory, he was buried at Hollywood Park. (Thanks to collector and racing fan Val Sibert for information on the real "Native Diver.") On June 1 and August 5, 1995, the QVC home-shopping cable TV channel offered a total of 1,000 "Native Divers" that were ordinary regular runs but that came in boxes labeled with the special-run model number #703395 (number is per the set's box; quantity is per *JAH* editor Stephanie Macejko).
- "Phar Lap" Famous Race Horse #90, red chestnut, S-shaped star, gray-red mane and tail, left hind stocking and right hind sock with gray hooves, front hooves gray-red, matte and semigloss (1985-88). The body color varies from a sober dark red to a lighter, bright red chestnut. The model in the 1985 catalog looks like a test color: he is dark bay, and the star looks painted on and isn't the right shape; also he has only one stocking, on the left hind leg. My own #90 and another owned by collector Jo Kulwicki have only a left hind stocking, but this is a variation; most models have a right hind sock as well. The 1986-88 catalogs show "Phar Laps" with both the stocking and the sock. The real "Phar Lap," whose name means "lightning" in Siamese, was a real Thoroughbred race horse, a gelding, foaled in New Zealand in 1925 or 1926. He was sold as a yearling and taken to Australia for training and racing. After proving hugely successful on the Australian track he was brought to race in the U.S., where he died suddenly and mysteriously in 1932. His story is told in the movie *Phar Lap*, a 1983 Australian film produced by 20th Century Fox, from whom Breyer got permission to use the name "Phar Lap." (Thanks to Debbie Vandegrift for providing me with much of the information on the real horse from the book *Julian Wilson's 100 Greatest Racehorses*.)
- Wild American Horse #881, shaded brown-gray smoke, stripe, darker brown-gray mane and tail, dorsal stripe, primitive bars on forearms, left front and left hind stockings, 4 hooves tan with brown rim at bottom, matte (1993-94). The model in the catalogs (it's the same photo) looks pure smoke gray, not at all brown; but the models produced for sale have a decidedly brown cast. As *JAH* editor Stephanie Macejko pointed out (*JAH* 22/#2 Mar./Apr. 1995, p. 25), these horses have a very subtle metallic sheen, which can best be seen in strong light.

Special-run models made from this mold:

- "Dr. Peaches" SR #410090, medium bay, broken blaze, black points, gray hooves, semigloss (1990). Dinner model for BreyerFest in Lexington, Kentucky; this was the very first BreyerFest. Approximately 1,000 models made. A Breyer company computer printout of activity 1985-92 says that 500 were made. But 1,026 were made, according to former *JAH* editor Steve Ryan at the BreyerFest West auction in Pomona, California, August 1991, where the last "Dr. Peaches" model was sold—so evidently a second batch of 526 horses was made after the initial 500 mentioned on the printout. Collector Cheryl Mundee wrote to me that 1,026 models were made but 34 defective ones were destroyed, leaving 992 models (she learned this in a discussion with Breyer executive Peter Stone and Stuart Bentley, owner of Bentley Sales Co.). This SR has ordinary monochrome eyes with no hand-painted eyewhites. The real "Dr. Peaches," owned by U.S.E.T. rider Bruce Davidson, is a 3-time winner of the Rolex Three-Day Event held at the Kentucky Horse Park (see *JAH* 17/#1 Feb./Mar. 1990, inside front cover). Steve Ryan presented Davidson with a "Dr. Peaches" model when the real horse was formally retired from competition (*JAH* 17/#3 July/Aug. 1990, inside front cover).
- "Dustin" SR #700995, red dun; short blaze; mane striped with pale dun and gray dun; tail has gray dun top, white center, and red dun tip; gray dun knees and hocks; 4 stockings; red dun hooves (1995). Comes with gold metal medallion on blue ribbon. Made for Toys R Us. 5,700 models made, per *JAH* editor Stephanie Macejko (conversation of July 2, 1996). The name and number are per the model's box. This horse-and-medallion set is one of several sets in the Medallion Series made for Toys R Us; see Medallion Series above in the Traditionals section for a full list and a description of the medallion.
- "Phar Lap" SR #410390, dark dapple gray, small dapples; no dapples on head and upper neck; blaze; dark gray mane and tail; 4 stockings; dark gray hooves; matte or semigloss (1988). Made for Your Horse Source. 500 models made. Sold separately or in SR set with liver chestnut, red bay, and sorrel "Phar Laps." Quantity is per a Your Horse Source ad flier; model number is per a Breyer company computer printout of activity 1985-92.
- "Phar Lap" SR, dark mahogany bay, solid face, black points, right front and left hind stockings with tan- gray hooves, other legs and hooves black, matte (1994). Penney's holiday catalog. Sold in Horse Salute Gift Set SR #711694, with chestnut leopard appaloosa "Lady Phase" and reddish bay "Morganglanz" with blaze. 2,620 sets made (per *JAH* editor Stephanie Macejko, conversations of June and Dec. 1995). The number for this set is per an information fax of April 11, 1994, from Breyer to dealers. A 1-stocking variation of this SR "Phar Lap" is noted by collector Meg Mac Donald in *JAH* 23/#3 May/June 1996 (p. 36).
- "Phar Lap" SR, medium dapple gray, dapples on the neck but few or none on the head; bald face; darker gray mane, tail, and front legs; darker gray shading on hindquarters; 2 hind stockings with tan hooves; front hooves gray; matte (1995). Penney's holiday catalog. Sold in Race Horses Of America set SR #710295 with light bay Pacer, dappled reddish chestnut Stock Horse Stallion, and one removable neck ribbon. 5,500 sets made (per *JAH* editor Stephanie Macejko, conversation of July 2, 1996). The neck ribbon is identical to the ribbon that comes with the B Ranch series horses "Cloud" and "Patches" (see in the Classics section for details).
- "Phar Lap" SR #410190, liver chestnut, no white markings, darker liver mane and tail, dark shading on leg joints, gray hooves, matte (1988). Made for Your Horse Source. 500 models made. Sold separately or in SR set with dark dapple gray, red bay, and sorrel "Phar Laps." Quantity is per a Your Horse Source ad flier; model number is per a Breyer company computer printout of activity 1985-92.
- "Phar Lap" SR #410490, red bay, solid face, black points, 2 hind stockings with tan hooves, gray front hooves, matte (1988). Made for Your Horse Source. 500 models made. Sold separately or in SR set with dark dapple gray, liver chestnut, and sorrel "Phar Laps." Quantity is per a Your Horse Source ad flier; model number is per a Breyer company computer printout of activity 1985-92. These bay horses are quite a bright orangy red color.
- "Phar Lap" SR #410290, sorrel, solid face, sorrel-shaded flaxen mane and tail, subtle gray shading on body and legs, 4 stockings, gray hooves, matte (1988). Made for Your Horse Source. 500 models made. Sold separately or in SR set with red bay, dark dapple gray, and liver chestnut "Phar Laps." Quantity is per a Your Horse Source ad flier; model number is per a Breyer company computer printout of activity 1985-92. The stockings on these sorrel horses can be vague and oversprayed with pale sorrel or gray.

Notes:

(1) Chris Hess is identified as the creator of this mold in *JAH* XI/#2 1984 (p. 9): "In Chris Hess' studio work has begun on a Little Bits saddlebred mare, Phar Lap the famous Australian racehouse [*sic*], and a rocking horse that will be flocked and haired." Hess took his design for the mold from a sketch by artist John Bellucci, reprinted in *JAH* 23/#1 January/February 1996 (p. 2). The sketch is signed "John Bellucci '84."

(2) For the black "Phar Lap" that almost happened, see Latigo in the Riders - Soft Or Jointed Plastic section.

(3) The "Phar Lap" mold has "© 1984 and TM 20th Century Fox" engraved inside the off gaskin; it has no other mold marks. 20th Century Fox, the film-production company that released the movie *Phar Lap*, owns the rights to the name "Phar Lap" (per *JAH* editor Stephanie Macejko).

"Pieraz" SR — see under "Morganglanz"

Pins — see Breyer Lapel Pins above

Pinto American Saddlebred — see under Five-Gaiter

Pinto Mare And Foal Set SR — see Action Stock Horse Foal SR, black paint; and Stock Horse Mare SR, black paint

Pinto Mare And Suckling Foal set SR — see Suckling Foal SR, bay pinto; and Thoroughbred Mare (ears back) SR, bay pinto

Pinto Pony — see Western Horse (#55, #56); Western Pony (#41, #42); also see note 6 for the Western Horse mold

Pinto Stock Horse Foal — see under Action Stock Horse Foal (#237); Stock Horse Foal, standing (#231)

Pinto Stock Horse Stallion, Tobiano — see under Stock Horse Stallion

"Plain Pixie" — see under Cantering Welsh Pony

"Pluto" — Stallion with no male parts, in piaffe (trotting in place). Sculpted by Jeanne Mellin Herrick. Mold in catalog-run production 1991 - current as of 1996.

Catalog-run models made from this mold:

- "Pluto" The Lipizzaner #475, alabaster; gray-shaded face, shoulders, hindquarters, knees, hocks, and tailtip; dark gray hooves; matte (1991-95). Some models have stripes of gray shading in the mane and tail. This model's alabaster color is unusual in that the white is painted on; it's not just the white plastic as on typical Breyer alabasters. The paint makes "Pluto" look like the chalkies from the 1970s (see Chalkies & Pearlies in the Appendix near the end of this book). The real "Pluto," a white horse foaled in 1765 (per Edwards 1994, p.110), was one of the six founding stallions of the Lipizzaner breed. All Lipizzaners' names include the name of one of these six stallions. The 1991 catalog photos of this model are of a plaster casting of the original sculpture. This casting, painted for Breyer by hobbyist and artist Karen Gerhardt, has very subtle dapples; but the plastic models produced for sale are not dappled (see Production Process in the Appendix near the end of this book). The model's box sports a large round gold sticker saying, in full: "New Model! / Pluto / The Lipizzaner / The Lipizzaner is a noble breed dating from 1580. Dynamic and muscular, this Lipizzan stallion epitomizes elegance." On July 15, 1995, the Q2 home-shopping cable TV channel offered 75 "Plutos" that were ordinary regular runs but that came in boxes labeled with the special-run number 703995 (per *JAH* editor Stephanie Macejko). Leftover models may have been sold on subsequent Q2 programs.

Special-run models made from this mold:

- "Favory" SR #702595, red fleabit, white or cream horse with chestnut flecks; chestnut mane; chestnut tail with lighter tip; gray-shaded muzzle, knees, and hocks; gray hooves; matte (1995). Export special, made for Modell-Pferde Versand (MPV), in Germany. 1,000 models made, per Ingrid Muensterer, owner of MVP (email of June 1995), and per *JAH* editor Stephanie Macejko (conversation of June 1995). Early MPV ad fliers announced that the quantity would be 1,100, but either this figure was in error or the order was reduced. Ingrid named this model after a real horse, "Favory," one of the six primary foundation sires of the Lipizzaner breed. "Favory" was a dun horse foaled at the Kladrub stud in 1779, according to Edwards 1994 (p. 110); *Simon & Schuster's Guide* describes "Favory" as red roan. The name is pronounced FAH-vor-ee, according to collector Carolyn Boydston, who purchased sixteen of these models from Ingrid at the Equitana horse fair in Germany in spring 1995 and had them signed and dated by Ingrid. The model number is per the model's box and per Stephanie Macejko. (The number printed on MVP ad fliers, 700195, is incorrect.) The base body color varies from stark white to cream (I've seen both in person). The mane and tail vary from red chestnut to darker brown chestnut.
- "Pluto" SR #500493, pale dapple gray; white head with gray shading on sides of nose; small dapples on body and neck; white mane with gray tips; gray tail with some white in it; gray shading in muscle grooves and on knees and hocks; 4 stockings; tan hooves; matte (1993). Spiegel holiday catalog. 1,150 models made (per *JAH* editor Stephanie Macejko). The coloring of this horse is much like that of the #839 light dapple gray Proud Arabian Stallion. This SR "Pluto" was a well-kept secret. In the Spiegel catalog, the photo shows an ordinary regular-run "Pluto," and the item description says nothing to suggest that the models in stock differed from this. Nor did Breyer mention this particular SR in its announcements to collectors about 1993 holiday specials. Consequently, most collectors simply did not know about it at the time it was available. In mid-1994 a few rumors circulated about a mysterious dapple "Pluto" that had turned up on a sales list from a hobbyist in Pennsylvania. Collector Sandy Tomezik, who ended up with this model, kindly sent me a photo of it. She had been told it was SR, but she didn't quite believe this, having never heard of other such horses. Neither she nor I nor any other collectors of my acquaintance knew that Spiegel had had such a special until I learned about it in November 1994 from *JAH* editor Stephanie Macejko, who happened to ask me why the third edition of this book (covering models through 1993) omitted the Spiegel SR "Pluto." Ha! In a letter to me confirming the news, Stephanie wrote: "The official word on the 1993 Spiegel 'Exclusive Lipizzaner' is that it was indeed produced and sold. Our special product forms indicate that special paint—a light dapple grey—was used on mold #475. The projected quantity was 1,500 pieces; however our records indicate that 1,150 were sold." As soon as I heard the news, I called Spiegel to ask if they still had any of these models in stock. They did not. I also called several Spiegel outlet stores, with no luck. Many of the models must have been purchased by families as toys for the kids. Since November 1994, three more collectors of my acquaintance have managed to locate specimens. (Thanks to Sandy Tomezik, Laura Diederich, Liz Strauss, and Robin Briscoe for photos of their models.) The model number I've given is per a Breyer company computer printout of 1993 SRs, which lists the model as "Exc Lipizzaner" ("Exc" stands for "Exclusive").

Notes:

(1) Sculptor Jeanne Mellin Herrick designed this mold's position to represent the piaffe, according to Megan Thilman Quigley, who worked at Breyer at the time "Pluto" was produced (conversation of Aug. 1995).

(2) The "Pluto" mold has the "© Breyer Reeves" stamp inside his off forearm.

Polo Pony on stand — see below in the Classics section

"Ponokah-Eemetah" The Blackfeet Indian Horse — see under Fighting Stallion

Pony Of The Americas (POA) — Mare, standing, looking right, roached mane with withers lock and forelock. Sculpted by Chris Hess. Mold in catalog-run production 1976-84, 1990-95.

Catalog-run models made from this mold:

- "Just Justin" Quarter Pony #876, dun, blaze, dorsal stripe, black points, black hooves, matte (1993-95). This model varies from a brownish lilac dun to pinkish gray dun to yellow dun. (Thanks to collectors Peri Riggins and Jennie Seaborn for these observations.)
- "Pantomime" Pony Of The Americas #884, black blanket appaloosa, stripe, large unstenciled blanket covering butt and most of barrel, black splashed-on spots, 4 stockings, tan hooves, matte (1993-94). On my own model, purchased in June 1993, the tan color on the hooves shades from pale at the top to darker at the bottom. The model in the 1993-94 catalogs, however, has uniformly tan hooves.
- Pony Of The Americas #154, bay blanket appaloosa, solid face, unstenciled butt blanket, splashed-on bay spots, black mane and tail, bay legs with no black, charcoal-brown hooves, matte and semigloss (1979-84).
- Pony Of The Americas #155, chestnut leopard appaloosa, white horse with stenciled chestnut spots, gray-shaded mane and legs, gray stripes in tail, pink-and-gray striped hooves, matte (1976-80). Despite the fact that the spots on this pony are stenciled, the number of spots varies on both sides. A well-known variation of this model is the so-called "6-spot" version, which has only 6 spots on its left side, in a cluster on the butt. This version is not shown in catalogs, so I can't be sure of the date. Collector Carol Steffus reports that she has a 5-spot variation and that she has heard of a few others like this (*The Model Trading Post*, Nov./Dec. 1993, p. 17). Evidently the 5-spot version was the first issue of #155, for it is reported in the *Model Horse Shower's Journal* issue for November 1976: "One member wrote in asking how come the new Breyer P.O.A. had spots on 1 side, but few if any on the other! Seems there was a minor slip-up in the painting areas and these 5-spotted models were produced. Now the models have been corrected, so the 5-spotted models are going to become collector's items I'm told." A *JAH* article on the POA mold says it's not certain how the spot shortage occurred, but possibly some of the holes in one of the POA paint masks got clogged (*JAH* 17/#5 Nov./Dec. 1990, p. 13). Also see the discussion of the 6-spot version in Walerius 1991 (p. 54). Diederich 1988, Section 1, mentions a variation of #155 with black spots rather than chestnut. The box in which #155 was sold has a photo of a test-color piece with splashed-on chestnut spots.
- "Rocky" Champion Connemara Stallion #821, dappled buckskin, solid face, faint dorsal band, black points, gray hooves, matte and semigloss (1990-92). Called "Rocky" Champion Connemara Stallion in the 1990 catalog, but "Rocky" Famous Connemara Stallion in 1991-92. I've seen one model with black hooves. The amount of dappling and dark shading on the body varies. Also, some models have buckskin muzzles (I got one like this in March 1990), while others have the whole muzzle shaded dark gray (I got one of these in December 1991). The real "Rocky," a stallion born in New Hampshire, was a grand champion of his breed and was also shown as a hunter and jumper (*JAH* XIV/#4 1987, p. 3).

Special-run models made from this mold:

- Pony Of The Americas SR, black blanket appaloosa, solid face, small unstenciled butt blanket, splashed-on black spots, black legs, hooves striped pale gray and black, semigloss (late 1970s or early 1980s). Made for a Pony of the Americas breeder in Illinois who was organizing a championship POA show in Mason City, Iowa. A few hundred models made. The quantity and vendor are per Breyer executive Peter Stone (conversation of Nov. 1994). The only specimen of this SR that I know of was previously owned by collector Karen Perkins, who was told by the collector she got it from that it came from a tack shop in Scottsdale, Arizona. When I asked Peter Stone about this, he definitely recalled that the models had been ordered by the POA breeder for the championships in Mason City. He surmised that some had ended up at the Scottsdale tack shop via Rudy Schorsch, of the Arizona model mail-order company Horses International, to whom Stone used to sell leftovers of various Breyer runs. I am not sure of the date of this SR, but it was evidently issued prior to 1985, for a want ad for a black blanket appy POA appears in the January 1985 *Quequechan Model Horse Collector*.
- Pony Of The Americas SR, black leopard appaloosa, white horse with splashed-on black spots, black points, black hooves, matte (1990 and 1991). Made for The Country Store, Wisconsin. Sold in Three Piece Horse Set SR #401456, with chestnut pinto Haflinger and dappled rose gray Cantering Welsh Pony. 1,000 sets made. Quantity and set number are per a Breyer company computer printout of activity 1985-92.

Note: The POA mold has the round "Breyer Molding Co." stamp. Some models also have a "B" stamp; earlier and later ones do not. This mold was never given the "U.S.A." stamp.

Porcelain models — see Ceramic Models; Cold-Cast Porcelain (Resin) Models; Fine Porcelain Models

"Prairie Flower" SR — see under "Lady Phase"

Prancer — see "Fury" Prancer; Western Prancer

Prancing Arabian Mare — see under "Lady Roxana"

Prancing Arabian Stallion — see under "Sham"

Prancing Morgan — see under "Sherman Morgan"

"Precipitado Sin Par" — see under "El Pastor"

Premier Arabian Mare — Cantering on left lead; molded-on tasseled Bedouin costume with bridle, saddle, saddle blanket, and breastcollar; raised hooves have molded frogs. Sculpted by Kathleen Moody. Mold in catalog-run production 1995.

Catalog-run models made from this mold:

- Fine Porcelain Premier Arabian Mare #79195, alabaster; brown and black eyes with white "sparkle"; light gray mane and tail; gray-shaded face, legs, and groin; charcoal hooves; black saddle and bridle with 24-karat gold trim; blanket and tassels are green, pink, and orangy-tan; matte (1995). Limited to 2,500 models, per the 1995 catalog. Numbered by hand on the belly. Models cost $160-$190 retail and came with a numbered certificate of authenticity signed by Breyer executive Peter Stone and sculptor Kathleen Moody. This mare is the first model in the Premier Fine Porcelain Series of horses in costume. That the gold detailing is real, pure gold is not mentioned in the 1995 catalog but is noted in ads for this mare in magazines such as the October 1995 *Horse Illustrated*: "Painted by hand in eight different hues and richly accent with pure 24 karat gold." The bottom of the mare's box says "Made in Taiwan." For an explanation of the model numbers of Breyer's fine porcelains, see the entry for the Icelandic Horse. On August 5, 1995, the QVC home-shopping cable TV channel offered 150 mares that were ordinary #79195s but that came in boxes labeled with the special-run model number 705595 (per *JAH* editor Stephanie Macejko).

Note: The Premier Arabian Mare mold has "© Breyer Reeves" engraved inside the right hind leg and "'95" engraved inside the left hind leg.

Premier Fine Porcelain Series — This is Breyer's second series of fine-porcelain equine figurines by sculptor Kathleen Moody, the first being the Evolution Of The Horse series of three horses. As of 1995, only one piece has been issued in this new series: the Premier Arabian Mare (released 1995). Scheduled for 1996 is a trotting palomino Saddlebred in full Western parade regalia; Moody's sketch of the piece appears in *JAH* 22/#5 Sept./Oct. 1995 (inside front cover). Future additions to the Premier series may include a Native American Horse, a Circus Horse, a Paso Fino, and others, all in costume (per the 1995 catalog). Like the Premier Arabian Mare, each of these models will be limited to 2,500 pieces (per the certificate of authenticity that came with the mare). All of Breyer's fine-porcelain horses are manufactured for Breyer by a Taiwanese firm called Everstream, which is the same firm that makes fine porcelain pieces for Franklin Mint (per Breyer executive Peter Stone, conversation of July 1995).

Presentation Collection — In the Traditionals section see "Adios"; Indian Pony (#175 chestnut pinto and #177 alabaster); "Man O' War"; Proud Arabian Stallion "Witez II"; Quarter Horse Yearling (#102); and "Yellow Mount" (under "Adios"). In the Cattle & Hogs section see Spanish Fighting Bull and Texas Longhorn. In the Wildlife section see Buffalo and Moose.

The Presentation Collection, issued in the period late 1971 - 1973, comprises 11 regular-run models (horses, bulls, and wildlife) mounted on American walnut wood bases with rectangular brass nameplates affixed to the front side. The edges of the bases, though not beveled, are not perfectly squared either in that the sides angle slightly outward. The names on the nameplates are in most cases the familiar Breyer model names ("Yellow Mount," "Texas Longhorn," "Witez II," etc.) but vary in three cases: "American Bison" appears on the Buffalo's nameplate, "Yearling" on the QH Yearling's, and "Fighting Bull" on the Spanish Fighting Bull's. The names are engraved in block letters, which are in a sans serif font in Breyer's ads for the Presentation Collection and on collector Sande Schneider's pinto Indian Pony piece, but in a serif font on Sheryl Leisure's alabaster Indian Pony.

Six of the Presentation pieces—"Adios," "Witez II," "Man O' War," alabaster Indian Pony, "Yellow Mount," and palomino QH Yearling—were announced and pictured in an ad in the November 1971 *Western Horseman*, although the 1971 Breyer manual does not mention the Presentation Collection (no 1971 price list or catalog exists to my knowledge). The 1972 manual, which shows the "Yellow Mount" piece, announces the collection without specifying the individual pieces: "The Presentation Collection, ten popular Breyer creations mounted on genuine American Walnut bases, is ideal for gifts, decorator pieces, and trophies." The 1972 Breyer catalog, which shows the "Witez II" Presentation piece on the cover, and the 1973 catalog, which shows the QH Yearling piece, both list 10 of the total 11 pieces in the collection. The one omitted in both catalogs is the alabaster Indian Pony, which stands to reason since the regular-run alabaster #177 was discontinued at the end of 1971. The alabaster is listed as such ("Indian Pony—white ... $15.00") only in the *Western Horseman* ad. It is also pictured on an undated Breyer company Presentation Collection order sheet, but the model number given on the sheet is for the pinto Indian Pony (#175), not the alabaster. The color photo from this sheet is reprinted in black and white in *JAH* 22/#4 July/Aug. 1995 (p. 15).

The model numbers given to the Presentation Collection pieces on that undated order sheet are the same as the numbers the models had as ordinary regular-runs without bases. The 1972-73 catalogs and manuals do not give any numbers at all for the Presentation Collection pieces, nor does the 1972 price list. The 1973 price list is the only Breyer publication I know of that assigns unique numbers to the ten Presentation models in production after 1971: #5050 for "Adios"; #5175 for Indian Pony; #5047 for "Man O' War"; #5102 for QH Yearling; #5212 for "Witez II"; #5051 for "Yellow Mount"; #5076 for Buffalo (called American Bison on this price list); #5079 for Moose; #5073 for Spanish Fighting Bull; and #5075 for Texas Longhorn.

On the one Presentation Collection specimen I've inspected close up—collector Sheryl Leisure's alabaster Indian Pony—the model seemed to be attached to the wooden base with both glue and screws through the bottoms of the hooves. The bottom of the base is lined with felt, so I could only feel the screws.

"Pride" — see under Family Arabian Mare; Proud Arabian Mare

"Pride And Vanity" SR — see under "Sherman Morgan"

"Prince" — see under Family Arabian Stallion above; also see under "Swaps" below in the Classics section

Princess Of Arabia — see under Black Stallion above in the Traditionals section and under Brenda Breyer in the Riders - Soft Or Jointed Plastic section

Progeny of "Wimpy P-1" — see The AQHA Ideal American Quarter Horse #497 (under Ideal Quarter Horse)

"Project Universe" — see under Five-Gaiter

"Promenade" Andalusian — see under "Legionario"

"Promises" Rearing Stallion — see under Rearing Stallion below in the Classics section

Proud Arabian Foal (PAF) — Filly, standing nearly square. Adapted by Chris Hess from Maureen Love Calvert's 7-inch "Zilla" (produced in ceramic by Hagen-Renaker). Mold in catalog-run production 1958 (possibly late 1957) - 1959, 1973-90.

Catalog-run models made from this mold:

- Arabian Foal "Joy" #9, alabaster; gray mane, tail, and muzzle; gray hooves; glossy (1958 [possibly late 1957] - 1959). During this period, "Joy" was also sold in sets #10 and #11 (see under Proud Arabian Mare, old-mold version) and in grooming-kit set #9548 (see note 3 for this mold). This mold was not called Proud Arabian Foal until 1973. The gray areas of #9 vary from light to dark. The pattern of the muzzle shading varies: Some models have a gray or charcoal lip line—on a couple of foals I've seen, the lip line went past the ends of the mouth and looked like a smile. Other foals lack the lip lines and have a gray or charcoal-shaded muzzle instead. Some models have soft gray body-shading. Collector Mary Reardon has an unusual foal (which I have seen in person) with pink muzzle and ears rather than gray. Collector Denise Chance also reports having a #9 PAF with pink nose and ears (Chance 1991). Regarding release date for this model, see note 3 for the Proud Arabian Mare mold. The model number 9 later belonged to Family Arabian Foal "Joy."
- Arabian Foal "Shah" #15, bay; long stripe that widens over the nose; black or charcoal-brown mane and tail; no black on the legs; some with 4 stockings, some with 2 hind stockings only; charcoal hooves; glossy ([possibly late 1958] - 1959). In the same period, this model was also sold in sets #16 and #18 with PAM and FAS; see under Proud Arabian Mare (old-mold version). This mold was not called Proud Arabian Foal until 1973. The color varies from caramel bay to darker bay. At least some of the old glossy models have dark gray-brown lip lines (I have a bay 4-stocking foal like this). Most do not have hand-painted eyewhites, but a few examples with eyewhites are known—collector Lani Keller owns a foal with eyewhites and 2 hind stockings only, and long-time collector Karen Perkins told me that she has heard of a few other specimens with eyewhites, all of which are the 2-hind-stocking version. A foal just like Lani's is pictured, along with the bay PAM and FAS, on an old undated Breyer company flier that was, I believe, issued to introduce the new bay color of these molds. Regarding the release date of this foal, see the note 3 for the Proud Arabian Mare mold. The model number 15 later belonged to Family Arabian Foal "Shah," and in the late 1970s was assigned to the Palomino Family Arabian Mare in a special blister-wrapped display box.
- Arabian Foal "Spot" #39, gray blanket appaloosa, bald face, black mane and tail, unstenciled blanket covering butt and much of barrel, black splashed-on spots, gray legs, black hooves, glossy (1959). This model, which is shown on *Breyer Collector's Video*, is not listed in the 1958 catalog or price list or in any other Breyer publications I know of. It is possible that Breyer didn't label her as an Arabian, but in the absence of any information, I've given her a name consistent with the names of the other old PAFs. (This mold was not called Proud Arabian Foal until 1973.) "Spot" is also omitted from September and December 1959 *Western Horseman* ads that list the bay and alabaster sets with FAS, PAM, and PAF. Nonetheless, I date her to 1959 on the basis of the dates for the mold; see note 1 for this mold and note 1 for Proud Arabian Mare. The model number 39 later belonged to Family Appaloosa Foal "Spot," gray blanket appaloosa (Family Arabian Foal mold).
- Proud Arabian Foal #218, alabaster; gray mane, tail, and hooves; matte (1973-76, 1978-81). I have seen a chalky specimen of #218, that is, a model completely covered with a basecoat of white paint, with the gray touches added over the white. See Chalkies & Pearlies in the Appendix near the end of this book.
- Proud Arabian Foal #219, mahogany bay, solid face, black points, 4 or various stockings, gray or charcoal/black hooves, matte and semigloss (1973-80). Some of the semi-glosse foals are so shiny as to appear glossy. The body color of #219 ranges from very dark chocolate or plum browns to more medium reddish-plum, sandy, and coffee-with-milk shades. The stockings can have a lot of black overspray. My photocopy of the 1974 catalog (the only catalog that pictures this model) shows her with 1 right hind sock, but Diederich 1988 (Section 1) and *Breyer Collector's Video* show her with 4 stockings. For a brief period in the late 1970s this model was sold with a different model number in a special blister-wrapped display carton; the label on the carton reads: "No. 1219 Mahogany Bay Arabian Foal." For discussion see Display Boxes above in this section.
- Proud Arabian Foal #220, dapple gray, bald or light gray face, most with gray mane and tail and 4 stockings, gray hooves, matte and semigloss (1973-88). The dapple foal came in several variations, some of which can be tracked through catalogs and manuals, although #220 is not pictured in all catalogs that list her. [A] In 1973-78 the foal is dark/medium gray with no or very few dapples on head and upper neck; dark gray mane, tail, knees, and hocks; 2 front stockings; and 1-2 hind socks or vague stockings. [B] In 1982, 1985, and 1986, she is still medium gray but with dapples on the head and neck, and 4 vague stockings. The 1981 and 1980 catalogs don't picture any dapple Proud Arabs, so the change to head/neck dapples could have occurred as early as 1980 (the mare is shown without head/neck dapples in 1979). [C] The 1983-84 catalogs show the foal with black points, black hooves, and dapples only on the butt and barrel; collector Lori Ogozalek wrote to me that her foal is like this. Some black-point foals do, however, have dapples on whole body and head, matching the black-point PAM and PAS. Black-point Proud Arabs with stockings are also known. For further discussion of the black-point horses, see Proud Arabian Mare #215. [D] The 1987-88 catalogs show the foal as soft medium gray with no dapples on the head and upper neck, slightly darker gray mane and tail, dark-shaded knees and hocks, and 4 stockings.
- Proud Arabian Foal #806, dappled rose gray; solid face; darker rose gray mane, tail, knees, hocks, and muzzle; some with dorsal stripe; dark rose gray hooves; semigloss (1989-90). The body color varies, with some models being more gray and others more rosy-orange.

Sets: see under Proud Arabian Mare (old-mold version); also see note 3 for the PAF mold.

Special-run models made from this mold:

- Proud Arabian Foal SR, pink (circa 1988). About 175-275 models made. Smuggled out of the factory. The pink color is in the plastic, not painted on. Calling these models a "special run" is stretching the definition of the term; the foals were produced not in order to be sold but in order to purge the injection molding machine of some red material that had gotten into it. The machine was repeatedly injected with clean white plastic, which mixed with the red material. The end result was a clean machine and a quantity of pink foals. Presumably the first foals made are pinker than the last ones. All information is per *JAH* 18/#1 Spring 1991 (p. 33); the article also has a picture of one of the foals. The article suggests that pinkies of molds other than the Proud Arab Foal were also smuggled out of the factory, but it doesn't say which molds. It mentions too that blue and green models (molds unspecified) have been produced under similar circumstances but that none of these seem to have sneaked out of the factory and into the collectors market. This last bit is evidently wrong, however, for collector Paula DeFeyter, who has one of the pink PAFs, wrote to me that she also has an unpainted lime green Classic Quarter Horse Foal.
- Proud Arabian Foal SR, red bay pinto, tobiano; solid face; black mane and tail; black-shaded knees and hocks; red bay front legs with red-gray hooves; 2 hind stockings with gray hooves; matte (1988). Sears holiday catalog. Sold in Arabian Mare And Foal set SR #497679, with red bay pinto Proud Arabian Mare. 3,500 sets made. (Quantity and set number are per a Breyer company computer printout of activity 1985-92.) In my experience these foals are a fairly bright red bay, but like the mare, they may vary to a sandy bay.
- Proud Arabian Foal SR, red chestnut, stripe, shaded body, black mane and tail, no black on the legs, 3 light legs with chestnut bands around fetlocks, 1 left hind stocking, gray hooves, matte (1992). Penney's holiday catalog. Sold in Frisky Foals set SR #712092, with pale yellow dun Action Stock Horse Foal, black blanket appaloosa Running Foal, and dark palomino pinto Suckling Foal. 3,000 sets made, per a Breyer company computer printout of activity 1985-92. The number for this set is per the printout and a Bentley Sales price list dated March 15, 1993.

- Proud Arabian Foal SR, reddish bay, most with long stripe that widens over the nose, black points with no stockings, gray or black hooves, matte (1983). Penney's holiday catalog. Sold in Assorted Mare And Foals Stable Set with SR reddish bay Proud Arabian Mare, SR gray blanket appaloosa standing Stock Horse Foal, and regular-run "Phantom Wings" #29. The Penney's catalog pictures this foal from the rear, thus begrudging any glimpse of facial markings. The photo in *JAH X/#3* 1983 (p. 13) shows her with a large star, teardrop-shaped with the point downward, but this is evidently a test-color model; to my knowledge none like this were issued for sale. *Breyer Collector's Video* shows this SR foal with a long stripe that widens over the nose (just as on the old #15 glossy bay foal), and I know of several collectors that have models like this. Collector Sande Schneider has two such foals, one with black hooves and one with gray, and collectors Kim Jones and Heather Wells have gray-hoofed foals identical to Sande's. The facial marking evidently does vary, however: collector Lori Ogozalek wrote to me that her SR foal has a broken stripe, and collector Paula DeFeyter sent me a photo of her foal with solid face, which she believes is an SR (rather than a regular-run #219) because of its reddish bay color and solid black legs.

Notes:

(1) The 7-inch H-R "Zilla" mold #645, from which Breyer took the design for its Proud Arabian Foal, was first introduced by Hagen-Renaker in fall 1956 (per Roller, Rose, and Berkwitz 1989, p. 22), so the PAF could not have been issued before early 1957. But I think it is highly unlikely that it was introduced that early, for all evidence is that it was released along with the Proud Arabian Mare, which debuted in late 1957 or in 1958. The earliest 1950s company publications that list the foal are the 1958 catalog and price list, which list only the alabaster, calling her Arabian Foal "Joy." Regarding the discontinuation of the PAF and PAM after 1959 see note 1 for Proud Arabian Mare. The foal, under the name Proud Arabian Foal, was reintroduced in 1973 to go with the PAM, which had been reintroduced in 1971/72, and with the PAS, which had been introduced for the first time in 1971. Some collectors call the pre-1960 PAFs "old mold" and the PAFs made from 1973 on "new mold," in parallel with the designations for PAM. In the PAM's case there was a real (if slight) alteration in the reintroduced mold; but in the PAFs case there wasn't any change, so the designations "old mold" and "new mold" for it are misleading.

(2) Regarding appaloosa #39 and bay #15 PAFs, as well as the non-existent palomino and woodgrain PAFs, see note 3 for Proud Arabian Mare.

(3) The 1958 Sears holiday catalog offered alabaster Arabian Foal "Joy" #9 in a "grooming-kit" set with girls' hair clips and a flexible vinyl "pack saddle." The ad (of which I have a Xerox) states: "Filly . . . wears cute pony tail holder and barrettes, tortoise shell color, mock pearl heart trim . . . $1.37." In the ad photo, the pony tail holder is around the filly's neck; the other barrettes are attached to the pack saddle. I first learned of these "Joy" sets at BreyerFest 1995 from collectors Kirsten, Sarah, and Ruth-Ann Wellman, who kindly allowed me to inspect a set they had recently found new in its unopened mailer carton at an antique show in Georgia. Later in the year, collector Meighan Daly got an identical set from the same Georgia vendor, who had about 10 sets, all new in unopened mailer cartons, which he said he had gotten at some old dime-store. In the Wellmans' set, the foal is a typical regular-run glossy #9. The "grooming kit" consists of a medium-blue flexible vinyl pack-saddle, two tortoiseshell barrettes, and one tortoiseshell ponytail holder. The three hair accessories are decorated with hearts made of small white "pearl" beads, as shown in the Sears ad. The pack saddle (5.25" x 1.75" overall) consists of two connected, nearly square pockets that hang down on either side of the foal. A girth of the same blue vinyl snaps under the foal's belly. The brown cardboard mailer carton is printed in red with "Breyer Molding Co. / Chicago, U.S.A.," and has the set number 9548 stamped on the top. The set is not listed in any Breyer company catalogs or price lists in my possession. For other grooming-kit sets, see Grooming Kits For People above in the Traditionals section.

(4) Most models of the Proud Arabian Foal mold have no mold stamps. Some models have the "B" stamp only (I own a #218 PAF like this, and collector Debbie Vandegrift has a #219 with a "B"). This mold was never given the round Breyer stamp or the "U.S.A."

Proud Arabian Mare (PAM) — Standing, tailtip attached to left hock. Adapted by Chris Hess from Maureen Love Calvert's 9-inch "Zara" (produced in ceramic by Hagen-Renaker). Mold in production: old-mold version, catalog run 1958 (possibly late 1957) - 1959; new-mold version, pre-catalog release 1971, catalog run 1972-92, 1996-.

Catalog-run models made from this mold:

OLD-MOLD VERSION (LEFT FRONT LEG NOT SPLAYED):

- Arabian Mare #908, woodgrain, black eyes, no white markings or other color detailing, matte (1959). This mold was not called Proud Arabian Mare until 1971. This model is not in the 1958 catalog or price list, but she appears with woodgrain Race Horse, Family Arabian Stallion, Brahma Bull, and Clydesdale Stallion in an old Ward's catalog ad that I believe dates to 1959. The ad describes the models thus: "Simulated wood grain finish figurines. Beautifully detailed Horses and Brahma Bull. Faithfully copied from original hand-carved wood pieces. Made of Tenite Acetate high quality plastic, carefully hand finished in simulated wood grain. Buy any three figurines—get free 'Album of Horses' book [by Marguerite Henry]." Since this woodgrain mare is not in the Breyer price list or other Breyer publications, I have inferred her model number from the number of the woodgrain Family Arabian Mare issued in 1960 (the FAMs in bay, alabaster, and appaloosa are known to have inherited the model numbers of the PAMs of the same colors). For full discussion of the production dates of this Proud Arab Mare, see notes 1 and 3 for this mold. The model number 908 later belonged to Family Arabian Mare, woodgrain.
- Arabian Mare "Pride" #8, alabaster; gray mane, tail, and muzzle; gray hooves; glossy (1958 [possibly late 1957] - 1959). During this period, "Pride" was also sold in sets #10, #11, and #12 (see below) and in grooming-kit set #9547 (see note 4 for this mold). This mold was not called Proud Arabian Mare until 1971. The gray parts of #8 vary from light to dark. Also the pattern of the muzzle shading varies: some models have gray or charcoal lip lines; others lack the lines and have the whole muzzle shaded gray or charcoal. Many models have some soft gray body shading. Collector Karen Perkins owns a lovely #8 with pink muzzle and ears. This is the only specimen that either of us has heard of, but conceivably there are more, for several old #9 glossy alabaster Arabian Foal "Joys" with pink nose and ears have been found (see the entry for #9 under Proud Arabian Foal). The 1958 catalog, which pictures #8 and #9 in the version with gray-shaded muzzle, comments: "The queen of the horse world and her adorable princess captured in all their loving tenderness. The china-like appearance of this majestic pair will surely be the pride and joy of all age groups. Delicate white with hand painted features." Regarding production dates for this mare, see notes 1 and 3 for this mold. The model number 8 later belonged to Family Arabian Mare "Pride," alabaster.
- Arabian Mare "Sheba" #14, bay, short blaze, black or charcoal-brown mane and tail, no black on the legs, 4 stockings, black hooves, glossy ([possibly late 1958] - 1959). In the same period, this model was also sold in sets #16, #17, and #18, with PAF and FAS; see below. Regarding the production dates of this mare, see notes 1 and 3 for this mold. This mold was not called Proud Arabian Mare until 1971. This model's color varies from caramel bay to a darker bay. Many have hand-painted eyewhites. At least some have dark gray-brown lip lines; my own #14 is like this, and she also has a brown cast to her mane and tail. Collector Karen Gerhardt's #14 has stockings only on the front legs; the back legs are solid bay. I have heard of one or two chalky #14s, which have the usual gloss finish. Collector Liz Strauss found an old glossy chestnut PAM, which has the eyewhites, short blaze, and 4 stockings that are usual for the bay mares but with grayish-chestnut mane and tail (slightly darker than the body) and gray hooves. The model number 14 later belonged to Family Arabian Mare "Sheba," bay, and in the late 1970s was assigned to the palomino Family Arabian Stallion in a special blister-wrapped display box.
- Arabian Mare "Speck" #38, gray blanket appaloosa, bald face, pink nose, unstenciled blanket covering butt and barrel, splashed-on black spots, black mane and tail, gray legs, black hooves, glossy (1959). This mold was not called Proud Arabian Mare until 1971. The three "Specks" I've seen (one in a photo in *JAH* 15/#2 May/June 1988, p. 25) have spots not only on the blanket but also on the hind legs and a few tiny spots on the front legs, shoulders, and neck. This mare is not in the 1958 catalog or price list or any other early Breyer publications that I know of, but collector Jo Kulwicki found a model new in its original cardboard mailer carton with "#38 Appaloosa" stamped on it. It is possible that Breyer didn't call this mare an Arabian, but in the absence of any information, I've given her a name consistent with the names of the other old PAMs. (This mold was not called Proud Arabian Mare until 1971.) For full discussion of production dates for this mare, see notes 1 and 3 for this mold. The model number 38 later belonged to Family Appaloosa Mare "Speck," gray blanket appaloosa (Family Arabian Mare mold).

Sets with FAS, old-mold PAM, and PAF:

- "Pride" And "Joy" Combination #10, both alabaster (1958 [possibly late 1957] - 1959). In the same period these models were also sold separately as Arabian Mare "Pride" #8 and Arabian Foal "Joy" #9. The model number 10 later belonged to the "Pride" And "Joy" set with alabaster Family Arabian Mare and Foal, and still later was assigned to Family Arabian Stallion SR black.
- "Prince" And "Pride" set #12, both alabaster (1959). These same models were also sold separately as Family Arabian Stallion "Prince" #7 [1959 {possibly late 1958} - 1973] and Arabian Mare "Pride" #8 [1958 {possibly late 1957} - 1959]. My only source for this set is an undated Breyer company flier with a photo of the alabaster Family Arabian Stallion; I date the set on the basis of the dates of the individual models. The model number 12 later belonged to the "Prince" And "Pride" set with alabaster Family Arabian Stallion and Mare, and still later was assigned to Family Arabian Foal SR black.
- "Prince," "Pride," And "Joy" set #11, all alabaster (1959). These same models were also sold separately as Family Arabian Stallion "Prince" #7 [1959 {possibly late 1958} - 1973] and Arabian Mare "Pride" #8 and Arabian Foal "Joy" #9 [both 1958 {possibly late 1957} - 1959]. My only source for this set is an undated Breyer company flier with a photo of the alabaster FAS; I date the set on the basis of the dates of the individual models. The model number 11 later belonged to the "Prince," "Pride" And "Joy" set with alabaster Family Arabian Stallion, Mare, and Foal, and still later was assigned to Family Arabian Mare SR black.
- "Sheba" And "Shah" set #18, both bay ([possibly late 1958] - 1959). In the same period, these models were also sold separately as Arabian Mare "Sheba" #14 and Arabian Foal "Shah" #15. This set is not in the 1958 catalog or price list; my only source for it is an undated Breyer company flier with a photo of the bay PAF, PAM, and FAS. I date the set on the basis of the dates of the individual models. The model number 18 later belonged to the "Sheba" And "Shah" set with bay Family Arabian Mare and Foal, and still later belonged to the black blanket appaloosa Stock Horse Foal ("Phantom Wings" mold).
- "Sheik" And "Sheba" set #17, both bay ([possibly late 1958] - 1959). These same models were also sold separately as Family Arabian Stallion "Sheik" #13 [1959 {possibly late 1958} - 1973] and Arabian Mare "Sheba" #14 [{possibly late 1958} - 1959]. My only source for this set is an undated Breyer company flier with a photo of the bay PAF, PAM, and FAS; I date the set on the basis of the dates of the individual models. The number 17 later belonged to the "Sheik" And "Sheba" set with bay Family Arabian Stallion and Mare, and still later belonged to the chestnut blanket appaloosa Stock Horse Foal ("Phantom Wings" mold).
- "Sheik," "Sheba," And "Shah" set #16, all bay ([possibly late 1958] - 1959). These same models were also sold separately as Family Arabian Stallion "Sheik" #13 [1959 {possibly late 1958} - 1973], Arabian Mare "Sheba" #14, and Arabian Foal "Shah" #15 [both {possibly late 1958} - 1959]. My only source for this set is an undated Breyer company flier with a photo of the bay PAF, PAM, and FAS; I date the set on the basis of the dates of the individual models. The model number 16 later belonged to the "Sheik," "Sheba" And "Shah" set with bay Family Arabians; still later it belonged to the palomino Family Arabian Foal in a special blister-wrapped display box and then to Marguerite Henry's "Sea Star."

NEW-MOLD VERSION (LEFT FRONT LEG SPLAYED):

- Proud Arabian Mare #215, dapple gray, most with bald or light gray face, most with gray mane and tail, most with 2 or 4 stockings, gray hooves, matte and semigloss (pre-catalog release 1971, catalog run 1972-88). This model was also sold in Proud Arabian Mare Gift Set #2155 [1972-73]; see below. Though #215 doesn't appear in catalogs and manuals until 1972, she and #327 German Shepherd were available to collectors in 1971, according to an old Breyer promotional flier of which I have a photocopy. The flier, which has photos of both models, says: "Your Model Show Sensations for 1971 / Introductory Offer!!!—Mail Order Exclusive—Has Not Been Available for Over 10 Years. Through much demand, Breyer's 'old type' Arabian Mare is being made available to collectors. This offer is being made at a substantially low introductory price—in 1972 this famous horse will be made available to the mass market at a much higher price—buy now!!!—Save!!! And be ahead." (The flier prices the mare at $3.50, the dog at $2.50, postage paid.) *Color variations*: The dapple Proud Arabs came in several variations, many of which can be tracked through catalogs and manuals, although not all family members are shown in all catalogs. The stallion isn't shown until 1982, but presumably he was similar to the mare all along. (For specifics on the foal, see Proud Arabian Foal #220.) [A] In the 1972-75 catalogs the mare is soft gray with no or very few dapples on the head and upper neck, and 2 front stockings; the back legs are soft gray. I have a mare just like this. [B] In 1976-79 the mare still has no or very few dapples on the head and upper neck, but she has 4 stockings, and varies from the same soft gray to a much darker gray with a dorsal stripe and charcoal gray shading on knees and hocks. Collector Paula DeFeyter sent me a photo of mare that is a variant of this darker version: it has a solid face and only 2 front stockings; the back "socks" are nearly obliterated with dark gray overspray. [C] In the 1982, 1985, and 1986 catalogs the whole dapple PA family is shown, in medium gray, now all with dapples on the head and neck, and with light gray lower legs or 4 white stockings. The 1980 and 1981 catalogs don't picture dapple Proud Arabs, so the change to head/neck dapples could have occurred as early as 1980. [D] The Proud Arab family with black points, black hooves, and, for the stallion and mare, dapples on the head and neck is shown in the 1983-84 catalogs. But evidently these horses were first issued in the latter part of 1982, for a black-point PAM is shown in the 1982 Aldens holiday catalog, and an item in the February 1983 *Quequechan Model Horse Collector* states: "The dapple P.A. family is now being made with black points." Confirming that the black-point horses were made into 1984 is a letter dated May 17, 1984, from Bentley Sales Company to collector Kim Jones: "The Proud Arabian Stallion, Mare and Foal have black manes, tails and legs." The black-point horses come in several variations. Some have normal dappling while others have "peacock," or "halo" dappling, as shown on *Breyer Collector's Video*: the larger dapples are surrounded by a haze of very minute white dots, which creates a halo effect. Some black-point Proud Arabs have dark gray legs and hooves rather than black; collector Teresa Ward sent me photos of her PAM like this. Still other black-points have true black coloring but with white stockings. Collector Becky Sturdy has a black-point PAF (dapples only on the butt) with 2 front stockings. At BreyerFest 1993 I saw a black-point mare with halo dapples and 3.5 stockings. Heather Wells has a whole black-point family with 4 white stockings apiece. Heather got these horses in unusual circumstances. When the black-points first appeared in the catalog, she ordered a family of them from Bentley Sales Company. But the set she received were ordinary gray-points with stockings. Heather returned the set to Bentley's and pointed out the problem. Bentleys checked their stock and found that all the horses they had in stock that were supposed to be black-point were in fact gray-point with stockings. Bentley's returned some of them to the factory for correction—Heather doesn't know whether they returned only her set or their whole inventory, though the latter seems more likely. When she finally got her replacement "black-point" set, she found that the factory had simply painted the manes, tails, knees, and hocks of the gray-point horses with black paint, leaving the white stockings intact. [E] In the 1987-88 catalogs, the family is a soft medium gray with slightly darker gray mane and tail, dark-shaded knees and hocks, 4 stockings, and, like the models from the first years, no dapples on head and neck.

- ♞ Proud Arabian Mare #216, mahogany bay, solid face, black points, various stockings, gray or charcoal/black hooves, matte and semigloss (1972-80). This model was also sold in Proud Arabian Mare Gift Set #2165 [1972-73]; see below. The body color of #216 ranges from very dark chocolate or plum browns to more medium reddish-plum, sandy, and coffee-with-milk shades. Collector Caroline Boydston found a matte model that is nearly black. There may be true glossy #216s as well as matte and semigloss. Collectors Lani Keller, Tanya Parker, and Karen Grimm, among others, have mares that look glossy (and Karen once found another in a #2165 set), but whether these models are truly glossy in the sense of having a shellac coating over the bay paint it's hard to tell. The 1972-73 catalogs (covers) show #216 with 2 hind stockings only, and collector Kay Schlumpf's mare has 2 hind stockings and gray front legs. The 1974 catalog (back page) seems to show her with 3 stockings (2 front, 1 right hind); and collector Gale Good's semigloss mare has three clear stockings. The 1975 (back pages) shows the mare with 4 stockings, though the hind ones are oversprayed; my two semigloss #216s are like this. Subsequent catalogs don't show this mare but only list her. This mare was also sold through the 1976 Sears catalog alone or in a set with leather English saddle and bridle—the blurb mentions only the saddle, but the photo shows a bridle as well, and shows the mare with 4 stockings. Collector Teresa Ward found one of these Sears sets in its original white cardboard carton, which features a line drawing of the mare wearing the tack. The printing on the box says: "Sears No. 1971 (Breyer No. 2168) / Mahogany Bay Proud Arabian Mare With English Saddle." The tack in Teresa's set does include a bridle and a fluffy saddle pad too, and the mare has four white socks. (Thanks to Teresa for a photo of the set and box.) In addition, #216 was sold through the 1980 Ward's catalog in a set with canvas stable blanket with leather surcingles; the photo shows the blanket as red and the mare as having 3.5 stockings. For a brief period in the late 1970s, #216 was sold in a special blister-wrapped display box that was probably labeled with the model number 1216. See Display Boxes above in this section for discussion.
- ♞ Proud Arabian Mare #217, alabaster; gray mane, tail, and hooves; matte (1972-76, 1978-81). This model was also sold in Proud Arabian Mare Gift Set #2175 [1972-73]; see below. On at least some #217s, the gray color is quite light and soft. I have seen a semigloss #217, whose finish looked factory original.
- ♞ Proud Arabian Mare #805, dappled rose gray; solid face; darker rose gray mane, tail, knees, hocks, and muzzle; dorsal stripe; dark rose gray hooves; semigloss (1989-90). Some of these models have rose-and-gray striped mane and tail, but most have solid rose gray mane and tail. Some of the matching stallions also have striped manes; in my experience the striped mares are less common than the striped stallions. The body color varies, with some models being more gray and others more rosy-orange. Most models have light rose lower legs, but a variation with white stockings exists (collector Gale Good has a model like this).
- ♞ Proud Arabian Mare #840, red chestnut, solid face except for small pale area just above nose, lighter chestnut mane and tail, 4 stockings, gray hooves, slightly semigloss (1991-92). This mare is redder than the SR chestnut and has a small light area above the nose that the SR lacks. The model number 840 previously belonged to the Showcase Collection issue of the chestnut Clydesdale Foal.

Sets (also see note 4 for this mold):

- Proud Arabian Mare Gift Set #2155, dapple gray, with removable blue and white yarn Arabian halter (1972-73). This same model was sold separately as Proud Arabian Mare #215 [pre-catalog release 1971, catalog run 1972-88]. Set also includes an 8.5" x 11" sheet titled "History of the Arabian Horse." The sheet begins: "'Drinkers of the Wind' is the affectionate name the Arabs have bestowed upon their magnificent horses." The halter is a simple figure-eight design with two tassels and self lead-line. Marney Walerius reports in her book (1991, p. 75) that she made the first 5,000 halters for sets #2155, #2165, and #2175, working at her home. The blue and white halter is shown on the dapple gray in the 1973 manual.
- Proud Arabian Mare Gift Set #2165, mahogany bay, with removable red and white yarn Arabian halter (1972-73). This same model was sold separately as Proud Arabian Mare #216 [1972-80]. Set also includes an 8.5" x 11" sheet titled "History of the Arabian Horse." The halter is a simple figure-eight design with two tassels and self lead-line. This set is not shown but only listed in catalogs; the halter color is per Walerius 1991 (p. 75). See PAM Gift Set #2155 for further discussion.
- Proud Arabian Mare Gift Set #2175, alabaster, with green and white yarn Arabian halter (1972-73). This same model was sold separately as Proud Arabian Mare #217 [1972-76, 1978-81]. Set also includes an 8.5" x 11" sheet titled "History of the Arabian Horse." The halter is a simple figure-eight design with two tassels and self lead-line. This set is not shown but only listed in catalogs, but I have seen collector Karen Grimm's set, which includes a green and white halter, as is also shown on the #2175 set's box. See PAM Gift Set #2155 for further discussion.

Special-run models made from this mold:

New-mold version:

- ⚇ Proud Arabian Mare SR, black, bald face, black mane and tail, 1-4 stockings, gray or black hooves, matte and semigloss (1986). Made for Breyer-sponsored model horse shows. 54-60 models made (54 per Walerius 1991, p. 102, and per a 1987 auction list of the Copper Country Model Horse Fanciers; 60 per *JAH* 15/#2 May/June 1988, p. 25). Reportedly these models were painted at the factory by Jill Göllner, who was at that time a Breyer employee though not a regular on the painting staff (per Walerius 1991, p. 102). The models came with various stockings. The CCMHF auction list describes the mare being offered at auction thus: "semi-gloss, black with white face, pink nose, and stocking." Collector Heather Wells's mare and the one shown in Diederich 1988, Section 2, have 1 right front and 2 hind stockings; a mare advertised in *Equine Miniaturist*, Mar./Apr. 1993 (p. 15), has 4 stockings. Models with 2 stockings may also exist. The width of the bald face varies too, being more of a blaze on some models, according to longtime collector Gale Good and the *JAH* cited above. Heather's model, which is very matte, has gray hooves on the legs with stockings and a black hoof on the solid leg.
- ⚇ Proud Arabian Mare SR, dark rose gray, bald face, black points, 4 stockings, matte (1986). Made for model horse shows. 5-11 models made (6, per *JAH* 15/#2 May/June 1988, p. 25). Reportedly these models were painted at the factory by Jill Göllner, who was a Breyer employee at that time though not a regular on the painting staff (per Walerius 1991, p. 102). The color description I have given is based on a mare displayed at BreyerFest 1994 by collector Pat Henry and a mare shown in Diederich 1988. Neither of these horses is dappled, but a mare described to me by collector Gale Good, which she saw at a model-horse show in Las Vegas, was subtly dappled. Gutierrez 1989 lists this SR as having dapples as well as 2 hind socks and pink nose. Walerius 1991 (p. 102) reports that these mares have various stockings and facial markings and that the mane and tail are a brown/rose color, darker than the body (no specification regarding dapples).
- ⚇ Proud Arabian Mare SR, fleabitten rose gray, white horse with light brown flecks, gray points, tan hooves, matte (1991 and 1992). Sears holiday catalog. Sold in Arabian Horses Of The World set SR #492091, with red bay Proud Arabian Stallion with blaze, and alabaster Family Arabian Stallion with black points. 4,350 sets made in all: 3,000 in 1991 and 1,350 in 1992. (Quantity and set number are per a Breyer company computer printout of activity 1985-92.) This PAM represents the Polish type Arabian, according to the 1992 Sears catalog, which states: "Set includes three types being bred internationally today: the bay American, the fleabitten grey Polish and the alabaster Spanish."
- ⚇ Proud Arabian Mare SR, light reddish chestnut, solid face, slightly lighter chestnut mane and tail, 4 stockings, gray hooves, matte (1985). Made for Bentley Sales to sell at Model Horse Congress. 288 models made, per a Bentley's price list of October 1985, which advertised leftovers of this SR: "1985 Summer Show Special / #215S—Proud Arabian Mare in Chestnut with Flaxen Mane and Tail / $11.99 each / Limited Run of 288 Models—1 per customer please." Some of these mares are a bit darker than others, but overall they are lighter and less red than regular run #840. The SRs also lack the pale area above the nose that #840 has.
- ⚇ Proud Arabian Mare SR, red bay pinto, overo; solid face; black points; 1 left hind stocking; 4 gray hooves; matte (1988). Sears holiday catalog. Sold in Arabian Mare And Foal set SR #497679, with red bay pinto Proud Arabian Foal. 3,500 sets made. (Quantity and set number are per a Breyer company computer printout of activity 1985-92.) This mare's pattern is essentially overo, though a bit of white does cross her topline, at the hips. In my experience these mares are typically a fairly bright red bay but vary to a sandy bay.
- ⚇ Proud Arabian Mare SR, reddish bay, blaze, black mane and tail, black or gray legs with no stockings, black or gray hooves, matte (1983). Penney's holiday catalog. Sold in Assorted Mare And Foals Stable Set with SR reddish bay Proud Arabian Foal, SR gray blanket appaloosa standing Stock Horse Foal, and regular-run "Phantom Wings" #29. An SR reddish bay PAS matching the PAM and PAF was also sold through this Penney's catalog but not in this mare/foal set; see Arabian Stallion With English Tack Set SR (under Proud Arabian Stallion). In my experience this mare is typically a fairly red medium bay, but collector Lani Keller's mare is a browner shade. The photo in the Penney's catalog shows the mare with a solid face, but this is probably a test color; to my knowledge none like this were sold. *JAH* X/#3 1983 (p. 13) shows her with a short blaze, black legs, and gray hooves; and the collectors' specimens known to me are all basically like this. The blaze is always wider at the top, narrowing to a stripe, but it varies somewhat in shape and varies in length from very short (actually an elongated star) to full length, stopping just above the nose. Collector Sande Schneider has had three SR mares, all with black legs, but one of these mares has black hooves, as does collector Sheryl Leisure's mare, while the other two have gray hooves, as does collector Heather Wells's specimen. Collector Kim Jones has two mares, one with black legs and hooves and one with dark gray legs and hooves, contrasting with a black mane and tail.
- ⚇ Proud Arabian Mare SR, sandy bay, solid face, black points, 1 right hind stocking with tan hoof, other hooves black, matte (1995). Made for the QVC home-shopping cable TV channel's Breyer hour aired August 5, 1995. Sold in Parade Of Horses Breeds set #705495 with bay roan Cantering Welsh Pony and alabaster Saddlebred Weanling. 1,800 sets made (per *JAH* editor Stephanie Macejko, conversation of Sept. 8, 1995). Leftovers from this batch were sold on QVC on January 20, 1996. Each model in the set came in a separate Breyer box labeled with the set's name and number.
- ⚇ Proud Arabian Mare SR #410293, "silver filigree" decorator, metallic silver horse with rather sparse, rounded white dapples; dapples on neck and head; bald face; pink nose and ears; white points; pink hooves; matte with a dull lamé sheen (1993). Volunteer special, given to the judging committee of the 1993 BreyerFest live show and perhaps to a few other volunteers who helped Breyer in 1993. 30 models made. Two of these models were sold at the 1993 BreyerFest auction (where the quantity of the run was announced), and the rest were distributed to the show judges as honoraria. At the auction, this mare's color was called "silver filigree." The model number is per a Breyer company printout of 1993 SRs.
- ⚇ Proud Arabian Mare SR, unpainted white (1980). Sold through *JAH* VII/#3 1980 (p. 13). This horse and several other completely unpainted models were offered to hobby-

ists interested in customizing, but many collectors kept them unpainted. See Unpainted Models for a complete list.

- "Steel Dust" SR #400393, pale smoke gray, shaded with darker gray; bald face; dark gray points; 1 right hind stocking with tan hoof; other hooves brownish gray; matte (1993/94). *Just About Horses* subscriber special. "JAH 1993" or "JAH '93" handwritten on the belly. 1,500 models made, per the ad for the model in *JAH* 20/#5 Winter 1993 (p. 17) and the certificate of authenticity that came with each mare. *JAH* editor Stephanie Macejko noted in a later issue that Breyer "received hundreds of requests over the limit of 1,500" (21/#2 Summer I 1994, p. 2). The certificate of authenticity, which is signed by Macejko and Breyer executive Peter Stone, states: "This limited piece is a gray Proud Arabian Mare, named Steel Dust. This horse is ______ of 1,500 produced. These models were hand-crafted at Breyer in Wayne, New Jersey at the beginning of Winter 1993." The blank is filled in by hand with the model's individual number, which is a bit confusing. My model's number, for example, is "931190." The "93" indicates the year of production, and "1190" is the number of my particular mare in the run of 1,500. Although the models were announced in *JAH* in 1993 and were, according to the certificate, manufactured then too, they were not issued to purchasers until February and March 1994; hence my dating for them. The color of these mares varies from a very pale gray with almost no shading to a darker gray with a lot of dark shading. Collector Daphne Macpherson owns a mare with no stocking and has seen another mare like this. The model number is per a Breyer company computer printout of 1993 SRs.

Notes:

(1) Mold dates: The 9-inch H-R "Zara" mold #655, from which Breyer took the design for its PAM, was first introduced by the Hagen-Renaker company, in ceramic, in spring 1957 (per Roller, Rose, and Berkwitz 1989, p. 21). So the Breyer PAM could not have been issued before late 1957. But it was certainly out in 1958, for #8 "Pride" Arabian Mare is listed and pictured, along with #9 "Joy" Arabian Foal, in the 1958 catalog and price list. It is well known among collectors that the PAM and PAF molds were produced only for a short time in the late 1950s and were then discontinued because Hagen-Renaker filed a legal complaint against Breyer for its use of the "Zara" and "Zilla" molds, sculpted by H-R employee Maureen Love Calvert. As former Breyer employee Jill Göllner stated in a letter of June 13, 1986, to collector Kim Lory Jones, "She [the old-mold mare] was discontinued in 1960 because of a claim of copyright infringement." Hagen-Renaker expert Joan Berkwitz, who is a friend of H-R founders John and Maxine Renaker, verified with them that they did take legal action against Breyer. John Renaker told Joan in March 1994 that he couldn't recall the date of the suit, but he knew that Breyer had paid $7,000 in damages, half of which went to H-R and half of which went to H-R's lawyer, a copyright specialist.) Breyer then replaced the PAM and PAF with the Family Arabian Mare and Foal molds, which were first released in 1960. 1959 was probably the last year of production for the PAM and PAF molds, though conceivably production continued into the early part of 1960. Although I know of no Breyer catalog or price list for 1959, it is virtually certain that these molds were still in production in 1959—otherwise there is no way to account for the existence of the colors other than alabaster, which are not in the 1958 catalog and price list but which were advertised in various post-1958 sources (see note 3 for the PAM mold). But the PAM and PAF molds are not in the 1960 Breyer catalog, which instead has the FAM and FAF. (For the dating of this catalog, see in the References section at the end of this book.) Oddly, the 1960 Sears holiday catalog has an ad picturing the PAM—an alabaster (presumably glossy), over whose back is slung a plastic sack of candies tied in the middle with a ribbon. (Thanks to collector Andrea Gurdon for a copy of the ad.) The ad states: "Horse with Candy. White plastic horse with 1/2 pound assorted individually wrapped hard candies in his [*sic*] 'saddle bags' . . . $1.97." Since this Sears photo could have been taken in early 1960, it raises the possibility that Breyer produced the PAM briefly into 1960 despite her omission from the 1960 Breyer catalog. But it is also possible that the Sears mares were stock remaining from 1959 production. Or again, it may be that despite the Sears photo, the mares that Breyer actually sent to Sears were alabaster FAMs. After all, the differences between the PA and FA molds, especially when the colors are the same, are so subtle that Sears probably wouldn't have objected to the switch, if they even noticed it at all. The PAM and PAF molds appear in other post-1959 sources too: the November and December 1960 and July 1961 issues of *Western Horseman* have saddlery-company ads picturing these molds with the FAS and offering the families in bay, white, and appaloosa. But it is virtually certain that these ads do not reflect late-1960 - 1961 production of the PA molds. For one thing, the photo used in all three of these ads is the same photo of the bay PAF, PAM, and FAS as in the 1959 *Western Horseman* ads mentioned above. The saddlery companies in late 1960 and 1961 might well have been selling their old stock of PA sets, or new stock of Family Arabs. In any case, to get on with the Proud Arab story, a decade later Hagen-Renaker sold Breyer a release to use the discontinued PA molds. (A release is a grant of permission secured through a one-time payment, as opposed to a lease, which is secured through annual payment. Joan Berkwitz learned about this arrangement concerning the PAM and PAF molds from H-R founder John Renaker in March 1994.) Breyer wished to use these molds to go with the PAS, an original Breyer mold that had been introduced in the 1971 Breyer collector's manual. The mare was reintroduced in a 1971 pre-catalog exclusive (see entry for #215, above) and in the 1972 catalog. The PAF followed in 1973. With these reintroductions, the mare and foal were called Proud Arabians for the first time. For comparison views of the Breyers and Hagen-Renakers see *Breyer Collector's Video*.

(2) Mold variations: Collectors call the pre-1960 PAMs "old mold," and the PAMs produced from 1971 on "new mold." The difference is in the left front leg, viewed from the front: on the old mold, the leg angles slightly in from chest to fetlock, while on the new mold, the leg hangs straight down from chest to knee and splays out rather unnaturally from knee to hoof. Reportedly, a piece of the mold got lost during storage after the PAM was discontinued at the end of 1959, so it had to be recast and a new cooling board made for the reissue of the mold in 1972. This new equipment wasn't shaped quite right, and the splayed-out left foreleg is the result. (See Walerius 1985 and 1991, p. 5; and *JAH* 15/#2 May/June 1988, p. 25). Collector Eleanor Harvey brought to my attention another, smaller change in this mold: the development of a small bump at the back of the right foreleg, probably the result of pitting or wear in the metal injection mold. Old-mold mares do not have the bump. It developed in the new-mold mares sometime in the mid to late 1970s or very early 1980s, to judge from my own mares: my old mahogany bays and dapple grays don't have the bump but only a slight rough spot in that area, but my black-point mare from 1982-84 has a full-blown bump, as do all my later new-mold mares.

(3) Colors: Old-mold PAMs come in 4 regular-run colors—alabaster, bay, gray blanket appaloosa, and woodgrain. Old PAFs come only in the first three colors, not in woodgrain. The alabasters were issued first and were made for the longest time, and are accordingly the most common. The 1958 catalog and price list include the alabaster mare and foal but none of the other colors. The bay PAM and PAF were certainly out by 1959, for they and their matching Family Arabian Stallion are advertised, along with the alabasters, in the September and December 1959 issues of *Western Horseman* (it's the same ad in both issues). The bays might have been released in late 1958, but in any event it is quite certain that they were introduced before the appy and woodgrain colors. For one thing, bay is the second most common of the four PAM/PAF colors, which suggests a longer production period for them than for the last two colors. Further, the bay mare and foal are advertised, along with the bay FAS, on an undated Breyer company flier that advertises the alabasters on the reverse side (I have seen the original flier in the archives of Reeves International)—and the flier does not mention the appy and woodgrain colors, which suggests that they did not yet exist. The photo on the side of the flier with the bays shows the whole family, while the photo on the alabaster side shows only the stallion—an arrangement suggesting that this flier was designed to introduce the new FAS mold and the new bay color for the mare and foal. The flier may have been issued along with an undated news release from Eastman Chemical Products, Inc.—manufacturer of Breyer's Tenite plastic—that announces the bay family. (The last line on the release says: "Material: Tenite acetate supplied by Eastman.") The last two old-mold colors—gray blanket appy and woodgrain—in all likelihood were introduced in 1959, perhaps in the latter part of the year. They are not listed in any Breyer catalog or price list known to me, but the woodgrain PAM is advertised on an old Ward's catalog ad featuring 5 Breyer woodgrains, which I believe dates to 1959. (For discussion of this 1959 dating, see under Woodgrains below in this section.) *Breyer Collector's Video* and Diederich 1988 (Section 1) say that there is no record of a woodgrain PAF and that none are known to exist. Walerius 1985 agrees with this; but Walerius 1991 does list woodgrain PAF (pp. 35 and 71). Walerius (1985; 1991, pp. 22 and 40-41) and DeFeyter and Luther 1991 also list glossy palomino PAF and old-mold PAM, but I believe these reports too are apocryphal. To my knowledge no Breyer records or other solid evidence of regular-run palomino models exist. Longtime collector Gale Good told me she knows of one test color glossy palomino PAM but otherwise has never heard of such models either. A black-and-white photo showing what seems to be a palomino old-mold PAM appears in the March./April 1994 *Model Horse Gazette*; perhaps this is the test mare in question. (The photo is of the first-place exhibit in the collector's class of the 1993 Northwest Expo.) The idea that there are regular-run palomino PAMs and PAFs from the old-mold era may have been started through a misunderstanding of the well-known fact that the earliest FAMs and FAFs were issued in all the colors that the late-1950s Proud Arabs had been issued in. The FAM and FAF were issued in palomino in the early 1960s; so, the reasoning goes, there must have been a palomino PAM and PAF. The trouble with this is that the rule "early FAs are the same colors as the preceding PAs" is true only with respect to the *first* FAMs and FAFs, namely, those introduced in 1960. The only colors for these molds listed in the 1960 catalog are alabaster, bay, gray blanket appaloosa, and woodgrain. The palomino and also charcoal Family Arabs were a second wave, introduced in 1961 or 1962. It is interesting in this regard that there seem to be no rumors of charcoal PAMs and PAFs.

(4) The 1958 Sears holiday catalog offered alabaster Arabian Mare "Pride" #8 in a "grooming-kit" set with a flexible vinyl "pack saddle." The ad (of which I have a Xerox) states: "Arabian Horse, life-like, white plastic. Holds comb, note book, ball point pen, nail clipper. Personalized with gold leaf incl. . . . $2.97." Collectors Kirsten, Sarah, and Ruth-Ann Wellman found one of these "Pride" kits new in its unopened mailer carton at an antique show in Georgia in 1995. According to the photo and description that the Wellmans kindly gave me, the mare is a typical regular-run #8. Her "grooming kit" consists of a medium-blue, smooth, flexible vinyl "pack saddle" holding a white plastic comb, metal nail file, nail clippers, small white note pad, and a small rectangle of 24-carat gold leaf with which the owner can transfer her signature or monogram onto something, presumably the saddle (or the mare?). The saddle (8" x 3.5" overall) consists of two connected trapezoidal pockets (one is divided into three compartments) that hang down on either side of the mare. A girth of the same blue vinyl snaps under the mare's belly. The brown Breyer Molding Co. cardboard mailer carton has the set number 9547 stamped on it. This set is not listed in any Breyer company catalogs or price lists known to me. For other grooming-kit sets, see Grooming Kits For People above in the Traditionals section.

(5) The old-mold Proud Arabian Mare models have no mold marks. New-mold models have both the round "Breyer Molding Co." stamp and the "U.S.A." stamp. Some new-mold models also have the "B" stamp. On the very earliest new-mold mares, the "U.S.A." stamp may be very faint. I had an early new-mold mare that had been painted gloss alabaster in the factory by Marney Walerius, and its "U.S.A." was so faint as to be invisible except in bright sunshine, and even then only parts of it could be made out. Sande Schneider likewise has an early test-run new-mold mare whose "U.S.A." is faint. On most new-mold mares however the "U.S.A." stamp is clear and distinct.

Proud Arabian Stallion (PAS) — Standing, looking left, bits of tail attached to both buttocks. Sculpted by Chris Hess. Mold in catalog-run production 1971 - current as of 1996.

Catalog-run models made from this mold:

- Proud Arabian Stallion #211, alabaster, gray-striped mane and tail, gray hooves, matte (1971-76, 1978-81). The mane and tail stripes are dimly visible in catalogs for several years; they are bright and clear in the 1976 catalog. Some models have gray shading on the forearms (per Paula DeFeyter). #211 was in the Showcase Collection as #2110 in 1971-72 (see Showcase Collection in this section for discussion).
- Proud Arabian Stallion #213, dapple gray, bald or light gray face, most with gray mane and tail and 4 white stockings, gray hooves, matte and semigloss (1972-88). For color variations of this horse, including the black-point, see Proud Arabian Mare #215. This stallion was sold through the 1977 Penney's holiday catalog in Arabian Stallion And Tack Set with leather English saddle and bridle. The model number 213 previously belonged to the set "Hickory," "Dickory," And "Doc," charcoal (Family Arabian Stallion, Mare, and Foal molds).
- Proud Arabian Stallion #804, dappled rose gray; solid face; gray-shaded mane, tail, knees, hocks, and muzzle; many with dorsal stripe; dark rose gray hooves; semigloss (1989-90). Some of these models have rose-and-gray striped mane and tail, but most have solid rose gray mane and tail. Some of the matching mares also have striped manes, but in my experience the striped stallions are more common than the striped mares. The body color varies from a gray shade with almost no rose tone to a rosy orange with virtually no gray tone. The dappling is typically very subtle. Most models have light rose lower legs, but a variation with white stockings exists (collector Gale Good has a model like this).
- Proud Arabian Stallion #839, light dapple gray; white head with gray shading on sides of nose; white mane with gray tips; gray tail with some white in it; darker gray shading in muscle grooves and on knees and hocks; 4 stockings; tan hooves; matte (1991-94). The size and quantity of dapples vary considerably, as does the amount of gray wash on the body—some horses are very pale, while others approach medium gray. In the 1991-92 catalogs, #839's tail appears solid gray. My model purchased in January 1991 has the top half of his tail gray and the bottom half white. The 1993-94 catalogs show the tail as gray with large vertical white areas on the sides, and my model pur-

chased in 1994 is like this.

- Proud Arabian Stallion "Witez II" #212, mahogany bay, blaze, black points, most with either 4 stockings or 2 hind stockings, gray or charcoal/black hooves, matte and semigloss (1971-80). In Presentation Collection mounted on American walnut wood base with brass "Witez II" nameplate, late 1971 - 1973. The Presentation Collection is not in the 1971 manual, but "Witez II" and five other Presentation models are announced in an ad in the November 1971 *Western Horseman*. The Presentation "Witez II" is listed as #5212 in the 1973 price list, but previously it apparently had the same number as regular-run #212. A Presentation "Witez II" is shown in the 1972 catalog, and one owned by collector Teresa Ward appears in *The Hobby Horse News* (Oct./Nov. 1995, p. 39). See Presentation Collection above in this section for further discussion. The name "Witez II" for #212 was dropped from catalogs after 1975 (it was never used in manuals). #212s come in textured-coat and smooth-coat versions, both of which occur in matte and semigloss finishes. The smooth-coated semigloss models can be so shiny as to appear glossy (collector Lani Keller's has a stallion like this). The body color of #212 ranges from very dark chocolate or plum browns to more medium reddish-plum, golden, and coffee-with-milk shades. #212's blaze is to my knowledge always wider at the top, narrowing to a stripe down the face—it is this way in every catalog in which the blaze is visible. The blaze does however vary somewhat in length, ending anywhere from nostril level to well above the nostrils; and the wide area at the top can fan out asymmetrically to either the right or the left of the forelock (I have one of each) or symmetrically around or just below the forelock. Collectors sometimes say that 2-stocking #212s are earlier ("Witez IIs") and the 4-stocking horses later, but this is oversimplified. The earliest documentation I know of for this model, a November 1971 *Western Horseman* ad with the Presentation Collection "Witez II," shows him with 4 stockings. The 1972 Breyer catalog and an undated Breyer order sheet with the Presentation Collection do show "Witez II" with 2 hind stockings only, but the 1975 catalog, which still calls the model "Witez II," has a herd shot that shows him with 3 stockings: 1 right hind and 2 front. ("Witez II" is listed but not pictured in the 1973-74 and 1976 catalogs.) In the 1977-79 catalogs, which omit the name "Witez II," #212 again has 4 stockings. Collector Kim Jones has a 4-stocking horse with oddly painted front legs: the cannons and hooves are white, while the pasterns and fetlocks are black. She got the horse at a toy shop in southern California, which had several others like hers. The real "Witez II" was a famous Polish Arabian stallion sired by "Ofir" and imported to the U.S. from Germany after World War II. A photo of him in *JAH* 20/#5 Winter 1993 (p. 9, shows that he had at least 3 socks (2 front and 1 left hind; the other hind is hidden) and a star and snip, not a blaze. #212 was sold through the 1978 Sears holiday catalog in a set with leather halter and lead, leather fly mask, and canvas stable blanket with leather surcingles (the photo shows the blanket as blue). #212 was in the Showcase Collection as #2120 in 1971-72 (see Showcase Collection in this section for discussion). The number 2120 previously belonged to the Florentine decorator Running Mare.
- "Sundown" Proud Arabian Stallion #933, light reddish chestnut, snip, flaxen mane and tail, 4 stockings, tan hooves, matte (1995 - current as of 1996). On August 18-20, 1995, the Q2 home-shopping cable TV channel offered a total of 96 "Sundowns" that were ordinary regular runs but that came in boxes labeled with the special-run model number 708195 (per *JAH* editor Stephanie Macejko). Leftover models may have been sold on subsequent Q2 programs. In the 1996 catalog, #933's name was shortened to "Sundown" Arabian.

Sets:

- Open Top Buggy #19841, flocked chestnut Proud Arabian Stallion, blaze, painted black eyes, chestnut synthetic hair mane and tail same color as body or darker, 1 right hind and 2 front stockings, 4 painted black hooves, in the Miniature Collection (1984). Set also includes authentic black leather harness; Brenda doll; and metal and wood buggy in black with green upholstery and black wheels with yellow spokes and rims. Set is mounted on a rectangular wood base with green inset and has a clear Plexiglas display cover. Signed and numbered on the underside of the buggy. The Ward's 1983 holiday catalog offered this set, minus the doll, as a special run for $154.97; it also offered the buggy, horse, and display case (base and cover) as separate items (see Proud Arabian Stallion SR flocked chestnut). *JAH* 20/#3 Summer II 1993 (p. 15) states that about 350 of the Ward's sets and fewer than 30 of the regular-run sets were made. The regular-run set with PAS and Brenda is shown only in the 1984 catalog. The 1984 manual and later manuals and catalogs feature a similar set that has the same model number but a different name (Drive On A Sunny Day), a slightly smaller version of what is otherwise the same buggy, a flocked Classic "Johar" (rather than the PAS), and a ceramic doll. Diederich 1988 (Section 3) and the *JAH* cited above confirm that the set with PAS was actually sold as a regular run in 1984, but evidently only for a limited time, to judge from the small quantity noted by *JAH*. The April 1984 Bentley Sales Company price list offered #19841 for $199.00; whether this was the PAS or "Johar" version is not clear. The Miniature Collection series of horse-and-buggy models was made for Breyer by the Riegseckers of Indiana (see Riegseckers Models for discussion). Collector Cathy Hagen sent me photos of the buggy she purchased from Ward's, showing the inscription in yellow paint on the bottom of the buggy: "Made By: / The Riegseckers / Nov. 1983 / #38." Collector Heather Wells's Ward's set is similarly inscribed in yellow paint on the bottom of the buggy: "Made By: / The Riegseckers / Dec. 1983 / #61." The horse in Heather's set has painted black eyes, as did the horse in a similar set on display at BreyerFest 1994; but some models might have brown glass eyes. Collector Teresa Ward purchased a set with a flocked bay PAS rather than chestnut; the bottom of her buggy is inscribed "Made By / The Riegseckers / Jan. 1984 / #278." Teresa got the set second hand, so we can't be positive that a prior owner didn't substitute the bay for a chestnut; but since the Riegseckers were also manufacturing the SR flocked bay PAS with halter in 1984, it is entirely possible that they put the bay in Teresa's set. For details on the harness and buggy see Drive On A Sunny Day, under "Johar" below in the Classics section. For details on the doll see Open Top Buggy under Brenda Breyer in the Riders - Soft Or Jointed Plastic section.

Special-run models made from this mold:

- Arabian Stallion With English Tack Set SR, reddish bay; low blaze, solid face, star, or stripe; black points; 4 or various stockings or no stockings; gray or black hooves; matte (1983 and 1984). Penney's holiday catalog. Set includes leather English saddle and bridle. A matching PAM and PAF were also sold through this Penney's catalog but in a different set; see Proud Arabian Mare SR, reddish bay. This SR stallion is one of the most maddeningly variable models in Breyer Land. In body color he is typically a smooth, fairly matte bay, somewhat lighter and redder and more flatly colored (unshaded) than the regular-run #212 mahogany, which was discontinued a couple of years before the SR appeared. However, collector Kim Jones's SR stallion, which she got straight from Penney's in the tack set, is a brown bay, very much like a #212 except for the extreme flatness of his coloring. The SR's white markings vary crazily. The 1983 Penney's catalog shows a model that is virtually indistinguishable from the 4-stocking version of #212: he has a blaze that widens at the top, black knees and hocks, 4 stockings, and gray hooves. The 1984 Penney's catalog too shows a 4-stocking stallion, but the face is hidden. *JAH* X/#3 1983 (p. 13) also shows this SR with a blaze that widens at the top, but he has solid black hind legs with gray hooves (front legs not visible). Collector Sande Schneider has a model with a blaze that widens at the top and 4 solid black legs. Sande is not positive it is a Penney's SR, but its smooth, matte red bay finish and its markings like those in *JAH* indicate that it is. A model like Sande's is shown in the January/February 1987 *American Model Horse Journal*, which identifies the horse as a 1984 Penney's SR with "a wide blaze on its face, no socks at all" (p. 3). Collector Gale Good's stallion has a solid face, gray-brown knees and hocks, 4 stockings, and gray hooves. One of collector Lani Keller's models (purchased from another collector) is a smooth red bay with solid face, 1 left hind stocking, 3 black legs, and 4 gray hooves. Lani's second horse (which she got from Penney's) has a stripe that widens only slightly at the top, 4 black legs, and gray hooves. Collector Heather Wells's model (ordered directly from Breyer in 1983) is like Lani's but with charcoal legs and hooves. Collector Sheryl Leisure's stallion (purchased from another collector, who said it was a Penney's SR) has a similar stripe, black knees and hocks, 4 stockings, and gray hooves. Kim Jones's brown-bay model mentioned above also has the stripe, black knees and hocks, 3 stockings, a white left hind fetlock, and gray hooves. Collector Karen Grimm has a model, shown on *Breyer Collector's Video*, with a small low star, black knees and hocks, 4 stockings, and gray hooves; this horse came from another collector, who said she got it from Penney's.
- Proud Arabian Stallion SR #412213, black, solid face, black mane and tail, 4 stockings, gray hooves, matte (1987). Made for Black Horse Ranch (BHR). 500 models made, per BHR's *Breyer Collector's Video*. Sold separately or in SR set with light red chestnut PAS and red bay PAS with solid face. An early BHR ad for these three horses in the May 1987 *Model Rag* states that only 333 of each color were made. Collector Heather Wells, BHR's customer service representative, explained to me that although BHR ordered this smaller quantity of horses, which they thought would be exclusive to BHR, Breyer decided to run additional pieces of each color to be sold through other model mail-order companies. And then, many models proved to be defective and had to be returned to the factory. Leonard Huffman, of Model Horse Collector's Supply, told me in May 1992 that in his shipments of these three SRs, which he received a couple months after BHR got theirs, many pieces were so flawed that he had to returned them to Breyer. A BHR ad in the November 1987 *Model Rag* also mentions that many of their horses were defective and had been returned; a replacement order was expected later that month. Bentley Sales Company too got some defective pieces in their shipments, according to Bentley's sales record cards in my possession. These cards show that Bentley's received 300 of the black horses and 200 of the chestnuts in July 1987. I lack the record card for the bay SR, but Bentley's did receive this too—it is included on their price lists of that time. Horses International, a division of Atlantis International, also got shipments of all three colors, and other companies may have received them as well. In view of this chaos of shipments to various companies and returns and replacements of defective models, undoubtedly the "final" figure of 500 pieces of each color is an approximation. The model number 412213 for the black model is per a Breyer company computer printout of activity 1985-92 and the Bentley's record cards.
- Proud Arabian Stallion SR, flocked bay, blaze, brown glass eyes, black synthetic hair mane and tail, 1 right hind and 2 front stockings, painted black hooves (1984). Ward's holiday catalog. Sold in SR set with white leather halter and lead, for $27.00. Some models may have painted black eyes, but a horse on display at BreyerFest 1995 had brown glass eyes, as does the model shown in *JAH* XI/#3 1984 (p. 9). Flocking, hairing, and tack by the Riegseckers of Indiana; the Ward's catalog states, "Expertly handcrafted in Amish country of northern Indiana. See Riegseckers Models for discussion. The horses shown in the Ward's catalog and in *JAH* have a bit of black shading on the knees and hocks, as did the BreyerFest specimen. Starting in January 1986, leftovers of this SR appeared on Bentley Sales Company price lists as "211FLK Proud Arabian Stallion, flocked chestnut, black hair mane and tail, halter," for $9.99.
- Proud Arabian Stallion SR, flocked chestnut, blaze, painted black eyes, chestnut synthetic hair mane and tail same color as body or slightly darker, 1 right hind and 2 front stockings, painted black hooves (1983). Ward's holiday catalog. Flocking and hairing by the Riegseckers of Indiana; the Ward's catalog states, "Expertly handcrafted in the Indiana Amish community, shipped from factory in Middleburg [*sic*], IN." The name of the town is actually Middlebury. See Riegseckers Models for further discussion. This Ward's catalog offered the horse both separately for $24.99 and in a set with black leather harness, wood and metal buggy, and a display case consisting of a clear acrylic cover and a wood base topped with "Brewster green felt," all for $154.97. (The buggy and display case could also be purchased separately.) The set with buggy was the same as the Open Top Buggy set sold as a regular run in 1984 (see above, under Sets for PAS), except that the regular-run set included a Brenda doll whereas the Ward's set had no doll. About 350 of the buggy sets were made for Ward's (per *JAH* 20/#3 Summer II 1993, p. 15). The horse in collector Heather Wells's buggy set has painted black eyes, as did the horse in a similar set on display at BreyerFest 1994; but some models might possibly have brown glass eyes.
- Proud Arabian Stallion SR #413213, light red chestnut, solid face, flaxen mane and tail oversprayed with reddish chestnut, no stockings, gray hooves, matte (1987). Made for Black Horse Ranch. 500 models made, per *Breyer Collector's Video*. Sold separately or in SR set with black PAS and red bay PAS with solid face. This model is quite a bright orangy shade. The model number is per a Breyer company computer printout of activity 1985-92. For discussion of this SR see Proud Arabian Stallion SR, black. Gutierrez 1985 and 1989 list a small special run of 5 chestnut Proud Arab Stallions made in 1982 for Model Horse Congress; these are the only sources I know of that mention this earlier chestnut SR.
- Proud Arabian Stallion SR, red bay, blaze, pink nose, black points, 1 left front and 2 hind stockings with tan hooves, other leg and hoof black, semigloss (1991 and 1992). Sears holiday catalog. Sold in Arabian Horses Of The World set SR #492091, with fleabitten rose gray Proud Arabian Mare and alabaster Family Arabian Stallion with black points. 4,350 sets made in all: 3,000 in 1991 and 1,350 in 1992. (Quantity and set number are per a Breyer company computer printout of activity 1985-92.) This PAS represents the American type Arabian, according to the 1992 Sears catalog, which states: "Set includes three types being bred internationally today: the bay American, the fleabitten grey Polish and the alabaster Spanish."
- Proud Arabian Stallion SR #411213, red bay, solid face, black points, black hooves, matte (1987). Made for Black Horse Ranch. 500 models made, per *Breyer Collector's Video*. Sold separately or in SR set with black and light red chestnut PASs. The model number is per a Breyer company computer printout of activity 1985-92. For discussion

see Proud Arabian Stallion SR, black.

⊛ Proud Arabian Stallion SR, unpainted white (1980). Sold through *JAH* VII/#3 1980 (p. 13). This horse and several other completely unpainted models were offered to hobbyists interested in customizing, but many collectors kept them unpainted. See Unpainted Models for a complete list.

Notes:

(1) Collector Sande Schneider wrote to me that she has three mahogany Proud Arab Stallions all of different sizes. The smallest is about an inch shorter than the tallest, and is "visibly narrower and smaller all over." For discussion of this phenomenon, see Mold Variations in the Appendix near the end of this book.

(2) The Proud Arabian Stallion mold has the round "Breyer Molding Co." stamp and the "U.S.A." stamp. Some models also have the "B" stamp; earlier and later ones do not.

Proud Mother And Newborn Foal sets #3160 and #3161 — see under "Lady Roxana" in the Traditionals section and under Andalusian Family Foal below in the Classics section

"Pumpkin" — see under "Kipper"

Quarter Horse Foal — see under Action Stock Horse Foal; "Phantom Wings"; and Stock Horse Foal (standing)

Quarter Horse Gelding — ♞ No male parts, walking, molded-on halter. Sculpted by Chris Hess. Mold in catalog-run production 1960-80, 1995 - current as of 1996.

Catalog-run models made from this mold:

♞ Appaloosa Gelding #97, sorrel blanket appaloosa; most with broken blaze; darker grayed-sorrel mane and tail; unstenciled butt blanket with splashed-on sorrel spots; most with 2 front stockings; 4 gray hooves; black or dark brown halter; matte (1971-80). The broken blaze is the same as that on #99 bay and #999 woodgrain. Collector Robin Briscoe kindly sent me photos of a #97 with unstenciled bald face. I've seen a variation of #97 with black spots on the blanket. There is also a variation of #97 with no stockings and 4 dark gray-sorrel hooves, shown in the 1979 catalog. All other catalogs with #97 show him with 2 front stockings. Collector Kim Jones has a #97 with 4 stockings, which she purchased later than her #97 with 2 stockings. #97 was in the Showcase Collection as #970 in 1971-72 (see Showcase Collection in this section for discussion). The model number 970 previously belonged to the woodgrain Brahma Bull.

♞ "Majesty" Quarter Horse #924, light dapple gray, head mostly white, white mane and tail touched with gray shading, 4 stockings, tan hooves, dark brown halter, matte (1995 - current as of 1996). The dapples on this horse are sparse and round, tending to look like polka dots. The body color varies from soft medium gray to nearly white. In the 1996 catalog, #924's name was expanded to "Majesty" American Quarter Horse.

♞ Quarter Horse "Two Bits" #98, buckskin, bald face, some with dorsal stripe, black mane and tail, most with black-shaded lower legs, black hooves, most with black or dark brown halter, matte (1961/63 - 1980). Some have hand-painted eyewhites. On many if not all #98s, and in catalog photos, the legs are painted black only on the backs and sides, with the fronts left buckskin. The buckskin color on #98 ranges from pale to dark. Collector Liz Strauss showed me a very dark one with short brown (not black) stockings; and collector Gale Good told me of a #98 with a broken blaze, like that normally found only on the bay #99, appy #97, and woodgrain #999. The halter color also varies; black and dark brown are the most common, but brick red also occurs. *JAH* XIV/#1 1987 (p. 13) reports that #98 was made in glossy finish 1961-64. If there are such models, I have never seen one. #98 was in the Showcase Collection as #980 in 1970-72 (see Showcase Collection in this section for discussion). The model number 980 previously belonged to the woodgrain Clydesdale (Clydesdale Stallion mold).

♞ Quarter Horse "Two Bits" #99, bay, broken blaze, black mane and tail, no black on the legs, 4 stockings, black hooves, black halter, glossy (1960-66). The blaze is the same as that on #97 appy and #999 woodgrain. Many #99s have hand-painted eyewhites. Most are a medium reddish or caramel bay, but can vary to dark chocolate bay and a very dark mahogany brown bay (per collectors Gale Good and Paula DeFeyter; thanks to Paula for sharing a photo of her dark chocolate bay). I have heard of one or two #99s with hoof pads, such as the Breyer factory used to put on quite a lot of Fighting Stallions in the 1960s (see note 2 for the Fighting Stallion mold). The extreme scarcity of such QH Gelding specimens, however, raises the possibility that they got their pads from a previous owner rather than the factory. Regarding the release date of #99, see note 2 for this mold. The model number 99 later belonged to the Appaloosa Performance Horse.

♞ Quarter Horse "Two Bits" #999, woodgrain, painted-on broken blaze, 4 painted-on stockings, black hooves, black halter, matte (1960-64). The blaze is the same as that on #97 appy and #99 bay. Regarding release date, see note 2 for this mold.

Special-run models made from this mold:

⊛ Quarter Horse Gelding SR, bay, broken blaze, black mane and tail, no black on the legs, 4 stockings, black hooves, black halter, matte (1984). Sold through Eighmey's Wagon Shop in Waterloo, Iowa, and possibly other companies as well. Breyer executive Peter Stone did not recall this SR when I asked him about it in November 1994. When I wrote to Mr. Dick Eighmey about it in October 1995, he replied that he did not know the total quantity made by Breyer, but he did recall that they were made in 1984 and that he had received 300 of them, about 250 of which he flocked and made into mules for his hand-crafted miniature vehicle sets—thus he kept only about 50 of the horses in their original factory condition for sale to collectors. When collector Sheryl Leisure ordered her model from Eighmey's in April 1987, Mr. Eighmey commented to her that he had only a couple left. What other dealers might have gotten these models from Breyer too I don't know, but Diederich 1988 notes that this SR was "sold through a distributor in Nebraska in 1984." These models are very similar to the glossy bay regular runs except that the SRs are matte. Also the SRs have no hand-painted eyewhites, whereas many of the regular runs do. Sheryl's SR has stockings that come to the middle of the knees and hocks, as does collector Joy Sheesley's, but the SR shown in Diederich 1988 appears to have lower stockings.

⊛ Quarter Horse Gelding SR, palomino, bald face, pink nose, 4 stockings, pink hooves, brown halter, matte (1990). Penney's holiday catalog. Sold in Breyer Traditional Horse Set SR #717450, with red chestnut "Rugged Lark" and dapple gray "Lady Phase." 3,500 sets made. (Quantity and set number are per a Breyer company computer printout of activity 1985-92.) The Penney's catalog says this set represents "the evolution of the American Quarter Horse": the palomino QH Gelding is an "early style" Quarter Horse, the dapple gray "Lady Phase" represents the "middle style," and the red chestnut "Rugged Lark" is the "modern style."

⊛ Quarter Horse Gelding SR, red chestnut, long star, slightly darker chestnut mane and tail, 4 stockings, gray hooves, black halter, matte (1986/87). Made for Eighmey's Wagon Shop in Waterloo, Iowa, and other model mail-order companies. 1,400 models made, per a Breyer company computer printout of activity 1985-92, but considerably fewer than that exist today: in a letter of October 1995, Mr. Eighmey told me that he got 700 of these horses but made nearly all of them into flocked mules for his hand-crafted miniature vehicle sets. The Breyer company printout dates this special to 1986, but Mr. Eighmey did not receive his allotment until January 1987, nor did other companies receive theirs until 1987: the January 1987 Bentley Sales Company price list says this SR is "for January delivery"; also a Model Horse Collector's Supply price list dated December 22, 1986, states that it "will have" this SR. A Horses International price list dated January 2, 1987, also lists this SR. The Breyer printout gives the model number for this special as #98CH (for "chestnut"). The star on this horse's face is a long diamond, much like the top portion of the broken blaze on the old bay #99.

⊛ "Silver" Quarter Horse SR #700097, steel gray, solid face, tri-color eyes, pink in nostrils, black points, brownish-gray hooves, black halter, matte, Commemorative Edition (1989). 5,000 models made, numbered by hand on the belly. "Silver" was Breyer's first Commemorative Edition. Strictly speaking he is a special run since he did not appear in the 1989 catalog but was marketed as a special through model mail-order companies. All subsequent Commemorative Editions have appeared in catalogs, however. The model's box bears a large round gold sticker saying, in full: "1989 'Commemorative Edition' / Silver Quarter Horse / Limited to 5000 pieces / No. 700097." A Breyer company computer printout of activity 1985-92 lists this model's color as "grulla." I have seen and heard of models with a distinctive pinkish opalescent sheen, which is very noticeable in sunlight. The "Silver" shown in the 1989 Your Horse Source brochure has a striking tannish opalescence. My own model is quite a flat gray, with only slight tannish highlights visible in the sun.

Notes:

(1) "Quarter Horse Gelding" is the collectors' name for this mold; Breyer catalogs use the word "Gelding" only for #97. The name "Two Bits" was dropped from catalogs after 1970/71; it was never used in manuals.

(2) Chris Hess is identified as the sculptor of the Quarter Horse Gelding in *JAH* XIV/#1 1987 (p. 13). The mold first appears in the 1960 catalog, and I believe this was the first year the mold was issued, although to my knowledge no 1959 catalog or price list exists to verify this. All models of this mold that I've checked, including numerous early ones, have the round "Breyer Molding Co." stamp, which was first issued in 1960 (see Mold Marks in the Appendix near the end of this book). Further, I know of no 1959 magazine ads or department-store catalog ads for the Quarter Horse Gelding. The only smidgen of evidence I have for a 1959 dating is a July 1989 Mission Supply House ad for the SR "Silver" Quarter Horse Commemorative Edition, which states "Introduced 30 years ago in 1959." If this is true, then the models made in that year would have no mold stamps; but I have never seen a stampless model of this mold.

(3) As just mentioned, to my knowledge all models of the QH Gelding mold have the round "Breyer Molding Co." stamp. Later models have the "U.S.A." stamp in addition—I have a buckskin #98 and a sorrel appy #97 with the "U.S.A.," so the mold had certainly received this stamp by 1980; it may have received it as early as 1970. Some "U.S.A." models also have the "B" stamp.

Quarter Horse Mare And Foal Set SR — see "Lady Phase" SR, buckskin; standing Stock Foal SR, buckskin

Quarter Horse Stallion — see under "Adios" (#830); Stock Horse Stallion (#226)

Quarter Horse Stock Foal — see under Stock Horse Foal, standing (#228)

Quarter Horse Stock Mare — see under Stock Horse Mare (#227)

Quarter Horse Stock Stallion — see under Stock Horse Stallion (#226)

Quarter Horse Yearling — ♞ Filly, standing, looking left, tail attached to right buttock and hock. Sculpted by Chris Hess. Mold in catalog-run production 1970-88, 1995 - current as of 1996.

Catalog-run models made from this mold:

♞ Appaloosa Yearling #103, sandy bay blanket appaloosa, blaze, unstenciled blanket usually confined to the butt, splashed-on bay spots, black mane and tail, most with solid bay legs (no black), dark brown hooves, matte and semigloss (1971-88). For blaze variations see note 1 for this mold. #103 is called "sandy bay" in Breyer catalogs, but the color varies from light sandy bay to a darker brown bay. In all catalogs and manuals but 1976 this model is shown with bay legs and no stockings, but I've seen variations with 2 front stockings and 4 stockings. In the 1976 catalog the legs and hooves are black with no stockings. A no-stocking #103 was also advertised in the 1976 Sears holiday catalog in a set with tooled leather Western saddle, breastcollar, and bridle with curb-bit cheekpieces. Collector Teresa Ward found one of these Sears sets in its original white cardboard carton, which features a line drawing of the Yearling wearing the tack, minus the breastcollar (which is shown in the Sears catalog photo). The printing on the box says: "Sears No. 1984 (Breyer No. 1036) / Sandy Bay Appaloosa with Western Saddle and Western Tack." The tack in Teresa's set included a blue and white cloth saddle blanket and a white string lariat tied to the saddle, as well as the bridle and breastcollar. Her Yearling has dark brown legs with no socks. (Thanks to Teresa for a photo of the set and box.) Yet another variation of #103 that I have seen has black spots on the white blanket rather than bay spots. Typically #103's blanket is confined to the hindquarters, perhaps shading a bit onto the back or barrel, but catalogs and manuals 1971-75 show her with a blanket extending well forward of the hips and stifles onto the barrel (the same 1971 photo is used in all these publications, but the 1974 catalog has a new group photo in the back which includes a #103 with the extended blanket). Collector Paula DeFeyter wrote to me that has seen a model with the white blanket extending all the way to the withers, and this variation is shown on the picture box in which #103 was originally sold, according to collector Sandy Bellavia (*The Model Trading Post*, Jan./Feb. 1996, p. 11). #103 was in the Showcase Collection as #1030 in 1971-72 (see Showcase Collection in this section for discussion).

♞ "Calypso" Quarter Horse #937, tan dun, blaze, dark chestnut mane and tail, ruddy shading on cheeks and body, chestnut knees and hocks, 1 left hind stocking with tan hoof; other legs pale tan with chestnut fetlocks and brownish-gray hooves; matte (1995 - current as of 1996). The dark shading on the joints makes this young mare's legs look striped. In spring 1995 at a toy shop, I saw a "Calypso" with no stocking. In the 1996 catalog, #937's name was expanded to "Calypso" Quarter Horse Yearling.

● Quarter Horse Yearling #101, <u>liver chestnut</u>; blaze; black mane and tail; some with 2 hind stockings, some with 4 stockings; 4 gray hooves; matte (1970-80). The catalogs call this model liver chestnut. For blaze variations see note 1 for this mold. Evidently the 2-stocking version came first: promotional materials from late 1969 and catalogs and manuals 1970-75 show #101 with 2 hind stockings only. Collector Gale Good got a 4-stocking horse in November 1975, and the 1976-79 catalogs show 4-stocking models. (#101 is listed but not shown in 1980.) #101 was the focus of Breyer's "Name The Yearling" contest, held in celebration of the company's twentieth year (1970) of production of model animals. The contest was launched in November 1969 and closed in March 1970. First prize, according to contest ads in periodicals such as *Western Horseman* and *Western Wear and Equipment Magazine*, was a live "registered quarter horse yearling sired by Roy Deck—sire of the first AQHA supreme champion mare, Miss Roy Deck." A couple of ads have photos of the stallion Roy Deck, which show him to be colored like #101: dark chestnut, a blaze that goes over his nose, and 2 hind stockings. So evidently #101 is a portrait of "Roy Deck," except with the gender altered. In any case, contest entrants, according to the ads, were to submit names for Breyer's Quarter Horse Yearling model: "Contest Rules . . . 1. Simply fill in the entry form including your name, address, zip code, and name for Breyer's 1970 Quarter Horse Model 'Yearling.' The model is a filly" (ad in *Western Horseman*, Dec. 1969, p. 171). The model's color isn't mentioned, but one of the ads has a photo of liver #101. Also according to the contest rules, the "first prize name will be used in our advertising" (ibid.). Now things get confusing. First off, no name other than "Quarter Horse Yearling" ever subsequently appeared in Breyer catalogs, manuals, or other materials that I know of—so what became of the contest name? According to *JAH* X/#4 1983 (p. 8), the contest was won by a young woman named Sherri Buck. The photo in the *JAH* article shows her with her contest prize, a real palomino yearling colt. The article states: "Way back in 1970, Sherri Buck won our Name the Yearling Contest. She named the 15.1 hands, palomino colt, Sandy Gold Deck." So Sherri won the contest by naming the live palomino colt, not the model liver chestnut filly? Not so, according to collector Paula Reeves, who wrote to me that she received a flier back in 1970 announcing that Sherri had won the contest by naming the model filly "Miss Top Tenite." Why this name was not subsequently used in Breyer advertising remains a mystery; when I asked former Breyer executive Peter Stone about it in December 1995, he could not recall. #101 was in the Showcase Collection as #1010 in 1971-72 (see Showcase Collection in this section for discussion). The number 1010 later belonged to a Dealer Starter Assortment, and after that to the Little Bits Bitsy Breyer and Thoroughbred Jockey Set. The model number 101 belonged to the Golden Buck (see Wildlife section) before being assigned to this liver QH Yearling.

● Quarter Horse Yearling #102, <u>palomino</u>, blaze, light palomino mane and tail, 4 stockings, gray hooves, matte and semigloss (1970-80). In Presentation Collection mounted on American walnut wood base with brass "Yearling" nameplate, late 1971 - 1973. The Presentation Collection is not in the 1971 manual, but the palomino Yearling and five other Presentation Collection models are announced in an ad in the November 1971 *Western Horseman*. This Presentation Yearling is listed as #5102 in the 1973 price list, but previously it apparently had the same number as regular-run #102; see Presentation Collection above in this section for discussion. The color of #102 varies from light tan palomino to dark orangy palomino to medium/light chestnut. A variation of this model has a bald face (as pictured in *Quequechan Model Horse Collector*, Nov. 1985), but most have a blaze. For blaze variations see note 1 for this mold. #102 is pictured only in the 1980 catalog, where she appears to have light palomino mane and tail; this is the normal coloring in my experience. I have seen and heard of some models with true white areas on the mane and tail, but most models have manes and tails completely covered with palomino overspray. #102 was also offered through the 1980 Ward's catalog in a set with canvas and leather bareback pad and leather bridle. #102 was in the Showcase Collection as #1020 in 1971-72 (see Showcase Collection in this section for discussion). The model number 102 previously belonged to the Golden Doe (see in the Wildlife section).

● "Thunder Bay" Quarter Horse #927, <u>dark mahogany bay</u>, diamond star, black points, 4 stockings, tan hooves striped with dark gray, slightly semigloss (1995). The color ranges from a rich deep bay, as shown in the 1995 catalog, to nearly black.

Special-run models made from this mold:

⊛ Quarter Horse Yearling SR, <u>bay blanket appaloosa</u>, blaze, unstenciled blanket covering butt and much of barrel, splashed-on bay spots, black points, 2 hind stockings with pink-tan hooves, front hooves black, matte (1993). Penney's holiday catalog. Sold in Breyer Three Generations Appaloosa Set SR #710693, with bay blanket appy "Adios" and bay blanket appy "Phantom Wings." Projected quantity 3,000 sets; no final count was recorded in Breyer's computer when I spoke to *JAH* editor Stephanie Macejko in June 1995. This SR Yearling is a redder bay than the old sandy bay #103, and has a much larger blanket. The SR's blaze is different from any of the blazes I know of on regular-run Yearlings; it is shaped like a dog bone or a barbell, with a long straight stripe connecting two white rounds. I have heard of a variant model with 4 stockings and 4 tan hooves. The set's number is per a Breyer company computer printout of 1993 SRs.

⊛ Quarter Horse Yearling SR #400101, <u>blue roan</u>, white horse with gray flecks, pink nose and ears, black points, black hooves, matte (1989). *Just About Horses* subscriber special. 1,500 models made (per *JAH* 16/#3 July Aug. 1989, p. 14), numbered by hand on the belly. The model number is per a Breyer company computer printout of activity 1985-92.

⊛ Quarter Horse Yearling SR #410492, <u>buckskin</u>, solid face, dorsal stripe, black points, 1 left hind stocking with tan hoof, other legs and hooves black, matte (1992). Raffle model for BreyerFest in Lexington, Kentucky. 20 models made. Breyer chose the color scheme for these models as a tribute to Marney Walerius, a long-time hobbyist and consultant to Breyer, who died in April 1992. Marney had suggested this color for the QH Yearling mold prior to its release in 1970 (but Breyer picked other colors instead; see Walerius 1991, p. 20). The proceeds from the raffle were donated in Marney's name to the American Diabetes Association (per *JAH* 19/#2 Summer I 1992, pp. 9, 16). The model number for this SR is per a Breyer company computer printout of activity 1985-92.

Notes:

(1) The blazes on #101, #102, and #103 vary; I've seen at least four different styles. On all three models, the earliest blaze, shown in catalogs and manuals through 1975, is an irregular, long blaze that runs wide over the nose and onto the chin (I have a liver #101 like this). The white on the nose is widest on some liver #101s; catalogs 1970 and 1975, and promotional materials from late 1969, show her nostrils as completely white. A second style of blaze, which I've seen on all three models, is a shorter, irregular blaze that ends in a point over the right nostril. A third style of blaze has a keyhole shape: a round star connecting to a long, straight, narrow stem that runs down between the nostrils (I have

a #101 like this). Finally, a fourth style of blaze has a diamond star connecting to a long, straight, somewhat wider stem that runs down between the nostrils (I have another #101 like this).

(2) Several collectors have found MasterCrafters clocks featuring a bas-relief horse very similar in design to the QH Yearling mold. Evidence indicates that the clock preceded the Breyer by several years and thus could not have been copied from it. I do not know whether the resemblance is purely coincidental or whether Chris Hess took his design for the Yearling from this clock or from some other prototype from which the clock may also have been copied. See MasterCrafters Clocks in the Appendix near the end of this book.

(3) The very earliest models of the Quarter Horse Yearling mold have the round "Breyer Molding Co." stamp only (collectors Liz Strauss and Lynn Isenbarger have palominos like this). Later models have the round stamp and the "U.S.A." stamp. The "U.S.A." must have been added to the mold in 1971 or 1972 at the latest—for models without this stamp are scarce, which means they weren't issued for long; also, I have "U.S.A." models of every blaze version, including the oldest (see note 1 for this mold). Some "U.S.A." models also have a "B" stamp.

Quarter Pony — see "Just Justin" Quarter Pony (under Pony Of The Americas)

Quiet Foxhunters set SR — see "John Henry" SR, liver chestnut; "Roemer" SR, seal brown; and "Rugged Lark" SR, dapple gray

QVC and Q2 Specials — See Cantering Welsh Pony SR, bay roan; Ideal Quarter Horse SR, red chestnut; Jumping "Gem Twist" SR (under Jumping Horse); Proud Arabian Mare SR, sandy bay; Saddlebred Weanling SR, alabaster; "Sham" SR blood bay with date stamp; and Western Horse SR palomino with date stamp.

QVC is a home-shopping TV channel available on cable across the nation. Q2, also on cable, is a sister channel to QVC. A selection of Breyer models—including two SRs: the "Sham" and Western Horse—were sold on QVC for the first time ever on the "Collector's Day" show on January 21, 1995, with QVC hostess Judy Crowell. The show was such a success that QVC aired further Breyer hours on June 1, with Jumping "Gem Twist" SR, and August 5, 1995, with the Parade Of Horses Breeds SR set. Q2 had its first Breyer program on July 15, 1995, with no SRs, and another show on August 18-20, 1995, with the SR Ideal QH. Leftover regular-run models were sold on Q2 programs in November. Breyer executive Peter Stone appeared on all of the pre-November programs, chatting throughout the hour with the show hostess about the particular models being sold on the show and about Breyer history and current events. On the June 1 show, Ms. Crowell remarked that QVC began selling Breyers at the instigation of a QVC purchasing agent's daughter, who is a horsewoman and Breyer collector.

Confusingly, the regular-run models sold on QVC and Q2 come in Breyer boxes labeled with special-run model numbers. This numbering system helps Breyer keep track of the large shipments of models headed for these TV programs, according to *JAH* editor Stephanie Macejko. My listings for all the regular-run models in question mention the SR numbers as well as the regular-run numbers. Stephanie also mentioned to me (conversation of Nov. 1995) that Breyer had canceled a QVC show planned for January 1996 and had decided not to sell through the Q shows again. QVC, she explained, has a lot of rules—such as packaging restrictions that prohibit brochures in the boxes—up with which Breyer prefers not to put (to borrow Winston Churchill's turn of phrase).

Race Horse — ▲ Small genderless horse, standing, molded-on halter, some with snap-on plastic race saddle. Evidently copied from an original wooden sculpture produced by Grand Wood Carving, of Chicago. Mold in catalog-run production ca.1954 - 1966.
Catalog-run models made from this mold:

▲ Race Horse, Derby Winner #36, <u>chestnut</u>, bald face, mane and tail same chestnut as body, various stockings, gray or black hooves, glossy (ca.1954 - 1966). Called Derby Winner in the ca.1954 catalog and 1958 catalog and price list; called Race Horse in catalogs and price lists 1960-66. The ca.1954 catalog shows this model without a saddle, as does an ad for him in the October/November 1954 *Horse Lover's Magazine* (the ad is by the "little joe" Wiesenfeld Co. and calls the horse "Turf Queen"). He is shown with the race saddle in an old Breyer company sheet that probably dates to 1955/57 and in the 1958, 1960, and 1963 catalogs. For a description of the saddle, see note 3 for this mold. Walerius 1991 observes that some #36s were sold with a little "hang tag" suspended from the neck on a string; the tag says "Derby Winner" on one side, and on the other "This reproduction of an authentic derby winner is made of durable Tenite" (per a photo of the tag, in Walerius 1991, p. 12). Race Horse's color varies from light caramel to dark red sorrel. Breyer catalogs call him "bay," though his mane and tail are chestnut. Some do, however, have a charcoal forelock. The ca. 1954 and 1963 catalogs show #36 with 4 stockings and black hooves; the 1955/57 sheet and 1958 and 1960 catalogs show him with 2 front stockings, solid hind legs, and black hooves (such a model is also shown in *JAH* XIII/#4 1986, p. 13). Collector Karen Oelkers wrote to me that some of the 2-stocking models have charcoal hind lower legs. My own Race Horse from childhood has chestnut forelock, 2 front stockings, chestnut hind legs, and gray hooves. The width of the bald face varies too, being as narrow as a blaze on some and extending down the sides of the face on others.

▲ Race Horse, Derby Winner #936, <u>woodgrain</u>, painted-on diamond star, black eyes, black halter, 4 painted-on stockings, black hooves, matte (1959-65). The woodgrain Race Horse first appears with woodgrain Brahma Bull, Family Arabian Stallion, Proud Arabian Mare, and Clydesdale Stallion in an old Ward's catalog ad that I believe dates to 1959. (For discussion of this dating, see under Woodgrains below in this section.) The ad describes the models thus: "Simulated wood grain finish figurines. Beautifully detailed Horses and Brahma Bull. Faithfully copied from original hand-carved wood pieces. Made of Tenite Acetate high quality plastic, carefully hand finished in simulated wood grain. Buy any three figurines—get free 'Album of Horses' book [by Marguerite Henry]." The woodgrain Race Horse was offered again in the 1962 Ward's holiday catalog. Both of these sources and all Breyer catalogs and price lists that picture this model show him without a saddle.

Notes:

(1) If you didn't know about this mold, you wouldn't guess it was a Breyer. It is strange looking. Evidently Breyer thought so too, for they replaced it with the much more realistic "Man O' War" #47 in 1967. Race Horse is small, delicate, and deerlike, but also vague and abstract, with flat, empty-looking eyes and no detailing of muscles, bones, or veins. Some collectors find it ugly, but others (among them *moi*) are charmed by it, perhaps sensing in those smooth lines the piece's origins in a nobler medium. For the Race Horse mold, although identified as the creation of Chris Hess in *JAH* XIII/#4 1986 (p. 13), evidently was copied from a mahogany sculpture of the famous race horse "Whirlaway" produced by Grand Wood Carving company, of Chicago. Grand Wood issued many horse figurines carved from Honduras mahogany and accented with painted details, with

the body of the horse often left in the natural wood color. "Whirlaway," first released in 1943 as part of Grand Wood's Named Race Horse Series of 8-inch models, bears an unmistakable resemblance to Breyer's Race Horse, even down to the halter, which is part of the carving on the Grand Wood piece. "Whirlaway" also has 4 stockings, as does one version of the Race Horse. But there are slight differences: "Whirlaway's" ears are a bit more upright, his left rear leg is a bit further back than the Breyer's, and his tail is a bit thicker than the Breyer's. (Information on "Whirlaway" is per Grand Wood catalogs and Berkwitz 1993.)

(2) Collector and former Breyer employee Megan Thilman Quigley told me about two matte dapple gray test-color Race Horse models made in 1991 or 1992, when she was at Breyer. A photo of one of these models shows him as a medium gray shade with virtually no dapples on the upper neck and head, a bald face, brown halter, and black points and hooves. According to Megan, several pieces of the Race Horse mold's production equipment—its cooling board and its soaking and press fixtures (for bonding together the molded halves)—have been lost, so that the two test models had to be assembled by hand. The loss of this equipment makes it unlikely that the Race Horse will be issued for sale again.

(3) The race saddle that came with many #36s is identical to the saddle that came with the Canadian Mountie rider model sets and with some "Fury" Prancers without riders (see note 6 for the "Fury" Prancer mold). But the Mountie sets and riderless Prancers had separate plastic saddle blankets as well, whereas the Race Horses with saddles have no blanket. The saddle is cast in hard brown plastic and has light gray hard-plastic stirrups. The stirrup leathers and girth are dark brown flexible vinyl and are attached to the saddle with grommets. The two halves of the girth fasten together with a snap under the horse's belly.

(4) Early Race Horses, and probably all models of this mold, have no mold marks. Later models might have the round Breyer stamp, but I've never heard of one like this. The saddle has no mold stamps either.

Race Horse Set SR — see "Man O' War" SR, glossy red chestnut; "Secretariat" SR, glossy red chestnut; and "Sham" SR, glossy blood bay

Race Horses Of America set SR — see Pacer SR, light bay; "Phar Lap" SR, medium dapple gray; and Stock Horse Stallion SR, dappled reddish chestnut

"Rana" The Arab Stallion — see under "Sham"

"Ranger" Cow Pony — see under Western Prancer

"Rarin' To Go" — see under Mustang

"Raven" SR — see under Saddlebred Weanling

"Rawhide" SR — see under Mustang

Rearing Circus Stallion With Ringmaster Set SR — see under Fighting Stallion for the horse and under Alec Ramsey (in the Riders - Soft Or Jointed Plastic section) for the doll and tack

Rearing Stallion — see below in the Classics section

Reeves International — Reeves is the company of which Breyer Animal Creations has been a division since late 1984. For discussion see Breyer Company History in the Appendix near the end of this book.

Resin models — see Cold-Cast Porcelain (Resin) Models

"Rex" — see Rearing Stallion below in the Classics section

Riegseckers models — The Riegseckers are an Amish family that lived and worked in Middlebury, Indiana, in the early 1980s and established the Shipshewana Craft Barn in Shipshewana, Indiana, in 1985. (See the article on Mel Riegsecker in *JAH* XI/#5 1985, p. 5.) This still-flourishing business produces, among many other craft items, beautiful handmade model-horse vehicles pulled by flocked and haired Breyer models with handmade leather harnesses. Although collectors do not generally regard models finished by anyone other than Breyer as being "real Breyers," that is, true original-finish models, many do accept into this sanctified category a select group of Riegsecker pieces commissioned by the Breyer company during the 1980s. Some of these pieces appeared as regular runs in Breyer catalogs; others were marketed by Breyer as special runs through department-store holiday catalogs. Most of these horses were flocked and haired, and many came with vehicles, tack, ceramic dolls, bases, and Plexiglass display covers, all made by the Riegseckers. Breyer had the Riegseckers make two non-flocked models during this period as well, both from Little Bits molds: the SR Merry-Go-Round Horse in mauve (LB Morgan Stallion mold) and the SR Unicorn in white with blue mane and tail, both mounted on wood bases with brass carousel poles. The Riegseckers also made a canopied carousel to go with the SR Unicorn and was supposed to make several additional models to complete the carousel set, but the project was canceled (see SR Unicorn below in the Little Bits section for discussion). For a list of Breyer's Riegsecker flockies see Flocked Models above.

Not only have the Riegseckers made horses for Breyer; Breyer has also made horses (special runs) for the Riegseckers. In the Traditionals section, see Pacer SRs, dapple gray, dark red chestnut, and palomino; and Shire SRs, black, palomino with bald face, reddish bay, and smoke gray. In the Stablemates section see Draft Horse SRs, black, chestnut, palomino, red sorrel, smoke gray, red roan, and unpainted white.

Roan Belgian Brabant — see under "Roy"

Rocking Horse — see Collector's Rocking Horse, My Companion Rocking Horse SR, My Favorite Rocking Horse SR, and Our Rocking Horse SR, all under Saddlebred Weanling

"Rocky" — see under Pony Of The Americas (POA)

Rocky Mountain Horse — see "Tobe" (under "El Pastor")

"Roemer" — Stallion, with brand, cantering, slightly crouched on the hind legs, braided mane. Sculpted by Jeanne Mellin Herrick. Mold in catalog-run production 1990-95.

Catalog-run models made from this mold:

- "Roemer" Champion Dutch Warmblood #465, dark chestnut, blaze, pink chin, 4 stockings, tan hooves, matte (1990-93). The photos of this model in the 1990 catalog show either Jeanne Mellin Herrick's original sculpture or a plaster casting of it. "Roemer's" box sports a large round gold sticker saying, in full: "New Model! / Roemer / International Grand Prix Jumping and Dressage Champion Dutch warmblood. Owned by Iron Spring Farm." The real "Roemer" was awarded the prestigious status of Keur Stallion by the Royal Warmblood Studbook of the Netherlands. He was born in Germany but now lives in Pennsylvania. See the 1990 catalog for more details and a photo of the real horse.
- "Vandergelder" Dutch Warmblood #900, dappled bay, no white markings, pale bay belly, black points, gray-brown hooves, matte (1994-95). The dapples on this model are very muted, being only slightly lighter than the body.

Special-run models made from this mold:

- "Domino" Gift Set SR #700994, black pinto, tobiano; low stripe and snip; tail black on the outside, white on the underside; pink fundament; 4 high stockings; tan hooves; matte (1994). Mid-year special, made for sale through model mail-order companies and toy stores. 5,000 sets made. Set also includes black leather Stoneleigh dressage saddle and white quilted cloth saddle pad with black edging and a small cloth "Breyer" emblem in each rear corner. The model number is per the set's box. The quantity is per *JAH* editor Stephanie Macejko (conversation of June 1995) and per a Reeves International memo of June 24, 1994, to sales representatives, subject "1994 Breyer Summer Specials." The "Domino" set is also advertised in the Reeves International 1994 Mid-Year Introduction brochure, which does not designate the set as "summer special." The model is a portrait of a real horse named "Domino," a Dutch Warmblood stallion used for dressage, jumping, and breeding (see *JAH* 21/#3 Summer II 1994, pp. 8-9). This SR set introduces the dressage saddle and pad, the latest additions to Breyer's regular-run line of tack produced by Alan Flesher Studios, of Feasterville, Pennsylvania. Although the 1994 promotional materials for the set do not give the saddle a name, it is called the Stoneleigh Dressage Saddle in the 1995 and 1996 catalogs. "Domino" also appears in these catalogs, modeling the saddle, but in fact he was not available in these years.
- "Roemer" SR, seal brown, star, lighter areas at elbows and stifles, black points, 1 right fore and 2 hind stockings with tan hooves, other hoof black, semigloss (1992). Sears holiday catalog. Sold in Quiet Foxhunters set SR #491192, with liver chestnut "John Henry" and dapple gray "Rugged Lark." 1,800 sets made. Quantity and set number are per a Breyer company computer printout of activity 1985-92. (The number 11218, given for this set on the Bentley Sales price list of March 15, 1993, is the Sears number, not the Breyer number.)

Notes:

(1) This mold has a brand—a "W" inside a diamond shape—engraved on the near thigh. This is the Westphalian brand, indicating the region of Germany where the real horse "Roemer" was foaled (see the 1990 Breyer catalog and *JAH* 23/#3 May/June 1996, p. 23).

(2) In an interview published in the December 1990 issue of *Horse Illustrated*, sculptor Jeanne Herrick commented on the gait of this mold: "Roemer [the real horse] is a beautiful mover, and I didn't want to show him in anything but a perfectly correct dressage pose. A piaffe or a passage (the most difficult moves) would have been my first choices. But because all Breyers are free-standing without a base, they need at least three points of support. And only two feet would be touching the ground if you were to freeze an ideal moment of a piaffe or a passage. So I settled on a collected canter. . . . I chose a particular phase of the canter, with the left leg leading."

(3) The "Roemer" mold has the "© Breyer Reeves" stamp only.

"Rough Diamond" — see under "Phantom Wings"

"Rough 'N' Ready" Quarter Horse — see under "Adios"

"Roy" — Gelding, jogging, looking slightly left, bundled tail, molded-on "shoes." Sculpted by Francis Eustis. Mold in catalog-run production 1989-93, 1996-.

Catalog-run models made from this mold:

- Belgian Brabant #837, tan dun, solid face, rust shading on sides of face and body, charcoal belly and muzzle, black points, tan hooves, matte (1991-93). The color varies subtly, with some models emphasizing the red shading and others emphasizing tan tones. Three sources on horse breeds—*The Ultimate Horse Book*, by E. H. Edwards; *The World's Finest Horses and Ponies*, by R. Glyn; and *Simon & Schuster's Guide to Horses and Ponies of the World*—identify the Brabant and the Belgian draft horse as the same breed. "Brabant" is the name of the province in Belgium where the breed was principally developed. Colors of the real horses include bay, dun, gray, sorrel, chestnut, and roan. All three books have photos of red roan horses with black points, which look remarkably like Breyer's Brabant.
- "Roy" Belgian Drafter #455, light sorrel, solid face, flaxen mane and tail, light tan patches on flanks, gray muzzle and hooves, matte (1989-90). The color varies from a rich red sorrel to a golden palomino color. The flank patches, which represent coloration typical of sorrel Belgians, vary from overly distinct to nearly nonexistent. "Roy's" box sports a large round gold sticker saying, in full: "Belgian Draft Horse / Roy / by Francis Eustis, famous horse sculptor, judge and breeder of outstanding draft horses." See Belgian Brabant #837 for discussion of breed.

Special-run models made from this mold:

- "Roy" SR, liver chestnut, blaze, light chestnut mane and tail, green tail ribbon, light chestnut lower legs, gray hooves, slightly semigloss (1992). Sears holiday catalog. Sold in Drafters Set SR #497092, with alabaster Belgian and palomino Shire with stripe. 2,250 sets made. Quantity and set number are per a Breyer company computer printout of activity 1985-92. (The number 11216, given for this set on the Bentley Sales price list of March 15, 1993, is the Sears number, not the Breyer number.) This is the first model from the "Roy" mold to have a tail ribbon; it is painted around the tail's topknot. The model's color is called "liver chestnut" in the Sears catalog, though it might be more accurately described as chocolate sorrel. Collector Liz Strauss got a model with the tail the same color as the body and the mane heavily shaded with the body color.

Notes:

(1) Francis Eustis is identified as the sculptor of this mold in the 1989 catalog and on the box of "Roy" Belgian Drafter #455. Shortly after "Roy" was released in 1989, rumors spread that Mr. Eustis was having a dispute with Breyer about "Roy" and that the model might be withdrawn from the Breyer line. I asked Breyer executive Peter Stone about this in October 1995. He recalled that when he and other Breyer personnel had met with Eustis at his farm to discuss the model, Eustis said he disliked the model's color and wanted to alter the flank patches in some way, and in general felt frustrated by Breyer's art-by-committee approach.

(2) The "Roy" mold has the "© Breyer Reeves" stamp only, inside the right gaskin. On some models the stamp can be so faint and blurry that it may be overlooked, but to my knowledge no "Roys" were issued without the stamp. The "Roy" I purchased in September

1989 has the stamp, as do all other models of this mold that I've checked.

"Ruby" SR — see under Mustang

"Rugged Lark" — Stallion, walking or backing, looking right. Sculpted by Pam Talley Stoneburner. Mold in catalog-run production 1989 - current as of 1996.

Catalog-run models made from this mold:

- "Rugged Lark" Champion American Quarter Horse Stallion #450, bay, no white markings, black points, black or gray hooves, slightly semigloss (1989-95). My own model, purchased new in September 1989, has black hooves, and black hooves are shown in all catalogs that have #450 (though the 1993-95 catalogs all use the same photo). Collector Laurie Croddy wrote to me that her model has gray hooves. The 1989 catalog says that the real "Rugged Lark" was the only two-time winner of the Superhorse title, which is awarded at the World Championship Horse Show to the top horse excelling at three or more events. The model's box sports a large round gold sticker saying, in full: "1985 and 1987 American Quarter Horse Association Superhorse / Rugged Lark / Owned by Roger and Carol Parker / by Pam Talley Stoneburner." The model number 450 previously belonged to the Showcase Collection issue of the white Western Pony.

Special-run models made from this mold:

- "Rugged Lark" SR, dapple gray, shaded gray forehand and hindquarters with very subtle dappling confined mainly to shoulders and butt; baldish face; white barrel; gray points; tan hooves; matte (1992). Sears holiday catalog. Sold in Quiet Foxhunters set SR #491192, with liver chestnut "John Henry" and seal brown "Roemer." 1,800 sets made. Quantity and set number are per a Breyer company computer printout of activity 1985-92. (The number 11218, given for this set on the Bentley Sales price list of March 15, 1993, is the Sears number, not the Breyer number.) The coloring of this horse is a new style of dapple gray for Breyer.
- "Rugged Lark" SR, red chestnut, blaze, darker chestnut mane and tail, gray nose and hooves, 1 left hind stocking, semigloss (1990). Penney's holiday catalog. Sold in Breyer Traditional Horse Set SR #717450, with dapple gray "Lady Phase" and palomino Quarter Horse Gelding. 3,500 sets made. Quantity and set number are per a Breyer company computer printout of activity 1985-92. The Penney's catalog says this set represents "the evolution of the American Quarter Horse": the palomino QH Gelding is an "early style" Quarter Horse, the dapple gray "Lady Phase" represents the "middle style," and the red chestnut "Rugged Lark" is the "modern style."

Notes:

(1) The original unpainted clay sculpture of this mold is pictured in *JAH* 16/#2 May/June 1989 (p. 14). On the next page of the same issue is a photo of the real "Rugged Lark" in the show arena during the Superhorse awards ceremony in 1987 (per p. 7), being ridden with no bridle but only a garland of roses around his neck. He is pictured at a somewhat awkward phase of movement; perhaps he is in transition between movements. In any case he is in nearly the same pose as the Breyer mold, except that the positions of the hind legs are switched.

(2) The earliest models of the "Rugged Lark" mold have no mold marks (my own and Debbie Vandegrift's #450s, both purchased in fall 1989, are like this). Later ones have the "© Breyer Reeves" stamp inside the near gaskin. My SR red chestnut has the stamp, so evidently it was added to the mold sometime in late 1989 or in 1990. The stamp can be faint on some models.

"Rumbling Thunder" — see under Running Stallion

Running Appaloosa Stallion — see "Donovan," under "Black Beauty" (stallion, cross-galloping)

Running Arabian Foal — see note 1 for the Running Foal mold

Running Arabian Mare — see note 1 for the Running Mare mold

Running Foal — Colt, trotting, looking right. Sculpted by Chris Hess. Mold in catalog-run production 1961/63 - 1987, 1991 - current as of 1996.

Catalog-run models made from this mold:

- Bluegrass Foal #865, blue roan, blue-gray foal with tiny dark gray flecks, solid face, black points, black hooves, matte (1992-94).
- "Little Bub," Young "Justin Morgan," #903, red bay, no white markings, black points, black hooves, matte (1994-95). This model is quite similar to the 1984 SR bay Running Foal, but there are differences: "Little Bub" is a redder shade, while the SR foal is browner; also "Little Bub" has black hooves, whereas the SR typically has dark gray hooves. The "Little Bub" model represents the real horse "Justin Morgan," foundation stallion of the Morgan breed, as a foal. The name "Little Bub" is used for the young "Justin Morgan" in Marguerite Henry's book *Justin Morgan Had a Horse*; it is a fictional name, or at best a speculative one, for in fact little is known about the parents of "Justin Morgan" (see Beard 1992).
- Running Foal #849, dark chestnut pinto, star, beige mane, beige tail with chestnut tip, 2 left stockings with gray hooves, right legs chestnut with brown hooves, matte (1991-93).
- Running Foal #1130, Copenhagen decorator, dappled blue, bald face, white points, pink hooves, glossy (1963-64). In the same year, this model was also sold in set #1351; see under Running Mare. The hooves can be very pale pink or even white. For further discussion see Decorators (1960s) above in the Traditionals section.
- Running Foal #2130, Florentine decorator, dappled metallic gold, bald face, white points, pink hooves, glossy (1963-64). In the same year, this model was also sold in set #2351; see under Running Mare. The hooves can be very pale pink or even white. For further discussion see Decorators (1960s) above in the Traditionals section.
- Running Foal #3130, Golden Charm decorator, solid metallic gold, bald face, white points, pink hooves, glossy (1963-64). In the same year, this model was also sold in set #3351; see under Running Mare. The hooves can be very pale pink or even white. The gold paint on these foals can darken over time and by now often looks more like tarnished brass. For further discussion see Decorators (1960s) above in the Traditionals section.
- Running Foal #4130, Wedgewood Blue decorator, solid blue, bald face, white points, pink hooves, matte (1963-64). In the same year, this model was also sold in set #4351; see under Running Mare. The hooves can be very pale pink or even white. For further discussion see Decorators (1960s) above in the Traditionals section.
- Running Foal "Spice" #130, alabaster, solid gray mane and tail, gray hooves, matte (1961/63 - 1971). This model was also sold in "Sugar" And "Spice" set #352 [1961/63 - 1964]; see under Running Mare. #130 was in the Showcase Collection as #1300 in 1970-71 (see Showcase Collection in this section for discussion). Regarding gloss finish, see Running Mare "Sugar" #120.
- Running Foal "Spice" #131, smoke (solid gray), bald face, white points, gray hooves, matte (1961/63 - 1970). This model was also sold in "Sugar" And "Spice" set #351 [1961/63 - 1964]; see under Running Mare. The body color ranges from light gray to charcoal gray. The bald face can be extensive, reaching well down the sides of the face. At a flea market in 1994, collector Sheryl Leisure found two unusual specimens that appear to be variation #131s: they are a fairly light smoke gray with matching smoke mane and tail. They have "U.S.A." stamps, which date the foals to 1970 or later. Regarding gloss finish, see Running Mare "Sugar" #120. #131 was in the Showcase Collection as #1310 in 1970 (see Showcase Collection in this section for discussion).
- Running Foal "Spice" #133, dapple gray, bald face, gray mane and tail, 4 stockings, gray hooves, glossy (1961/63 - 1973). The bald face can be extensive, reaching well down the sides of the face. Many #133s look like snowflake appaloosas in that they have dappling only on the rump and flanks, as shown in the 1963 catalog (the only catalog that pictures this foal). There are variations, however. Collector Gale Good's model has dapples nearly to the withers, and collector Tanya Parker's foal has dapples up onto the neck. Another variation, shown on *Breyer Collector's Video*, has dapples all over, even on the head. Collector Lani Keller's fully dappled foal has a "U.S.A." stamp (dating the foal to no earlier than 1970), but collector Joan Fauteux's fully dappled foal has no "U.S.A.," so apparently this version was not made all at one time. Collector Karen Perkins told me that a batch of 6 fully dappled foals were found by collector Marney Walerius in the Breyer factory in Chicago when it closed in 1985. Collector Paula DeFeyter has a fully dappled foal with a matching fully dappled Running Mare, both of which are very glossy with dark gray mane, tail, and hooves; bright pink nose; and "U.S.A." stamp. Paula purchased the pair from a Nebraska collector who had bought them new from a tack store in Nebraska no later than about 1978. Whether these pieces are part of a small special run or just variations of the regular run dapple Running Mare and Foal is not known. #133 was in the Showcase Collection as #1330 in 1970-72 (see Showcase Collection in this section for discussion).
- Running Foal "Spice" #134, bay, bald face, black mane and tail, no black on the legs, 4 stockings, black hooves, matte and semigloss (1961/63 - 1987). Catalogs from 1970 back and manuals from 1975 back call this foal "chestnut"; subsequent catalogs and manuals call him "bay." Despite the change in color label, however, all the foals have the same basic pattern of coloring, with black mane, tail, and hooves but no black on the legs. For color and finish variations, see the entry for bay Running Mare #124. The bald face on this foal can be extensive, reaching well down the sides of the face. #134 was in the Showcase Collection as #1340 in 1970-72 (see Showcase Collection in this section for discussion). She was also sold in the late 1970s in a blister-wrapped display carton with the model number 1134 (see Display Boxes above in this section).
- Running Foal "Spice" #930, woodgrain; black eyes; black hooves; no white markings or other color detailing; most matte, some glossy (1961/63 - 1965). For discussion of glossy woodgrain Running Foals and Mares see Running Mare "Sugar" #920.

Sets: see under Running Mare.

Special-run models made from this mold:

- Running Foal SR, alabaster; striped gray mane and tail; gray-shaded knees, hocks, and fetlocks; gray hooves; matte (1994). Penney's holiday catalog. Sold in Spirit Of The East Gift Set SR #710294, with matching alabaster Running Mare. 4,400 sets made (per *JAH* editor Stephanie Macejko, conversation of June 1995). On the sets I've seen, the striping in the mane and tail is soft and pale on the mare, and darker and crisper on the foal. The number for this set is per an information fax of April 11, 1994, from Breyer to dealers.
- Running Foal SR, bay, no white markings, black points, dark gray hooves, matte (1984). Sears holiday catalog. Sold in Running Horse Family set SR with bay Running Mare and bay "Black Beauty" (stallion, cross-galloping). The Sears catalog and *JAH* XI/#3 1984 (p. 20) seem to show this foal's hooves as black, but my own and collectors' specimens I know of have gray hooves. For differences between this model and regular-run "Little Bub," see the entry for the latter.
- Running Foal SR, black blanket appaloosa, thin star, diamond snip, unstenciled butt blanket, splashed-on black spots, 4 stockings, gray hooves, matte (1992). Penney's holiday catalog. Sold in Frisky Foals set SR #712092, with pale yellow dun Action Stock Horse Foal, red chestnut Proud Arabian Foal, and dark palomino pinto Suckling Foal. 3,000 sets made, per a Breyer company computer printout of activity 1985-92. The number for this set is per the printout and a Bentley Sales price list dated March 15, 1993.
- Running Foal SR?, buckskin, bald face, black mane and tail, black-shaded lower legs with some areas left buckskin, black hooves, matte (1960s). Only two of these models are known to me, one of which has the additional detail of a short dorsal stripe coming up from the dock. These foals are datable to the 1960s by the fact that they have the round "Breyer Molding Co." stamp but no "U.S.A." stamp, unlike the SR buckskin foal from 1983 (see next entry). For further discussion see the entry for the 1960s Running Mare SR buckskin.
- Running Foal SR, buckskin, bald face, black mane and tail, black lower legs with some areas left buckskin on most models, black hooves, matte (1983). Made for Bentley Sales Company. 32 models made. These foals, unlike the 1960s foals (see preceding entry), have a "U.S.A." stamp. The 1983 date is per Walerius 1991 (p.100); Diederich 1988 Section 2; and collector Heather Wells. Heather is responsible for the existence of this 1983 special. The story as she told it to me is as follows. Breyer had made two buckskin test-color sets for Penney's to consider for its 1983 holiday catalog: a Running Mare and Running Foal set and a "Lady Phase" and standing Stock Foal set. Penney's chose the standing set, but somehow got the foals scrambled for the photo for their catalog—the 1983 Penney's catalog erroneously shows the buckskin Running Foal with the "Lady Phase." The foal that was actually sold in the set was the standing Stock Horse Foal. When Heather got her set, complete with Stock Foal, she returned it and reordered, hoping to get the Running Foal as shown in the catalog. When her second set arrived complete with Stock Foal, she told Penney's that she wasn't satisfied, she wanted the advertised foal. The Penney's people contacted Breyer about the problem. Breyer then contacted Heather and obligingly asked her how many buckskin Running Foals she would like to order. "Just one," Heather replied—an answer she would kick herself for in later years. The company decided to paint some extras while they were painting Heather's order. Heather got her one foal from the Breyer company in late fall 1983, and Bentley Sales received 24 others, undoubtedly about the same time. No Bentley's sales lists in my possession include this SR, so I would guess that the foals sold out by word of mouth before Bentley's had time to advertise them. The only written record I have for them is an old undated sales record card from Bentley's (sent to me by Stuart

Bentley in Feb. 1996), which lists "#134 buckskin—24," where the "24" indicates the quantity of models received. Marney Walerius comments in her book (p. 100) that she found about 10 additional foals in the "destroy bin" at the Breyer factory, which had been discarded "because the black stockings were not completely painted on the inside curve of the legs under the foal." Marney took 6 of these foals and "released them to collectors who did not get one of the original 24" but left the others in the trash since they "had too much body damage to be sold." Heather's foal has solid black legs, but at least some of the Bentley's foals—such as one previously owned by collector Lani Keller, which she got straight from Bentley's—do have the fronts or the backs of some of their lower legs left buckskin. (This is typical of many old buckskin Mustangs and QH Geldings of that era as well.) So perhaps the foals Marney rescued from the trash had been put there because they were worse than normal in this respect or had other flaws. In any case, Heather's foal, the Bentley's two dozen, the test piece shown in the Penney's catalog, and Marney's half-dozen rescuees total 32 foals. Conceivably other test pieces were made, but I don't know this for certain. I should mention here that the "235BU Buckskin Running Foal" listed on Horses International (HI) 1992 price lists was actually the SR buckskin Action Stock Horse Foal, leftover from the 1984 Sears buckskin Stock Horse family. I called HI in 1992 to check on this mysterious listing, and asked the HI representative who took my call to look at the Running Foal and Action Foal molds in the 1992 catalog to make sure of her identification. She said that the SR buckskin foal in stock at HI was the Action Foal mold. So "Running" on the 1992 HI lists was an error. This is corroborated by other facts too. This foal had been listed on HI price lists at least since 1988 under the name "Buckskin Foal" (no mention of "Action" or "Running"), always with the same number, 235BU, "235" indicating the mold by reference to a regular-run model and "BU" indicating the special-run color. But there is no regular-run Running or Action Foal or any other Breyer model to date with the number 235. Thus on HI's lists the "235" too was an error. I believe it was a typo for #236—the number of the regular-run sorrel Action Foal—for HI's 1991 Christmas Sale price list includes, along with "235BU Buckskin Foal," the item "227BU Buckskin Mare" (no mention of "Stock Horse" or "Running"), and #227 is the number of the regular-run sorrel Stock Horse Mare.

- Running Foal SR, dapple gray, dappling on neck and head; bald face; darker gray mane and tail; 4 stockings; gray hooves; matte (1982/83). Sold through a Nebraska distributor. About 200 models made, according to rumor (per *Breyer Collector's Video*). Sold in SR set with matching dapple gray Running Mare. The paint finish on some of these models tends to look scruffy in spots. The dappling on the foal's neck and head can be sparse. For further discussion, see the entry for the 1982/83 SR dapple gray Running Mare.
- Running Foal SR, dapple gray, most with no dapples on neck and head; bald face; white mane and tail; 4 stockings; pink hooves; matte (1987). Sears holiday catalog. Sold in SR set #491212, with matching dapple gray Running Mare. The set number is per a Breyer company computer printout of activity 1985-92; no quantity given. Collector Mel Price's foal does have dapples on its neck and a few on the head. Mel has another foal that has gray hooves rather than pink; this is the only gray-hoof specimen I know of.
- Running Foal SR, dark rose gray, no dapples; darker gray mane, tail, and hooves; no white markings; matte (1991). Penney's holiday catalog. Sold in Adorable Horse Foal Set SR #714091, with bay blanket appaloosa Grazing Foal, chestnut Lying Down Foal, and alabaster Scratching Foal. 5,000 sets made. Quantity and set number are per a Breyer company computer printout of activity 1985-92. The name Adorable Horse Foal Set is per the Penney's catalog, but the box in which the foals were packed was marked Fun Foal Set.
- Running Foal SR, flocked palomino; blaze; some with painted black eyes, some with brown glass eyes; white synthetic hair mane and tail; 4 stockings; painted black hooves (1984). Penney's holiday catalog. Sold in Collector's Mare And Foal Set SR with flocked palomino Running Mare, for $29.99 per set. Flocking and hairing by the Riegseckers of Indiana (see Riegseckers Models for discussion). A mare and foal displayed at BreyerFest 1995 both had brown glass eyes, but collector Heather Wells's models and a couple of other sets I have seen have painted black eyes. Collectors Robin Briscoe, Lillian Sutphin, and Kitty Anderson told me that their mares and foals are also the painted-eye version. Leftovers of this SR foal appeared on the Bentley Sales Company price list of January 1986 as #130FLK (for "flocked"), for $5.99. Old Bentley's sales record cards in my possession show that Bentley's received a quantity of 144 foals.
- Running Foal SR, flocked white, blue glass eyes, pink synthetic hair mane and tail, painted hot-pink hooves (1985). Penney's holiday catalog. Sold in Fanciful Mare And Pony Set SR with matching flocked white Running Mare and plastic brush and comb for the manes and tails, for $29.99 per set. The foals owned by collectors Heather Wells, Paula DeFeyter, and Sande Schneider all have blue glass eyes. Heather's mare and foal set came with both brush and comb, although the Penney's catalog mentions only a brush ("mane brush included").
- Running Foal SR, red roan, yellowish-tan foal with red chestnut dappling, dappled face, red chestnut points, no white markings, gray hooves, matte (1982). Made for Bentley Sales Company to sell at Model Horse Congress and via mail order. 315-344 foals made, per old Bentley's sales record cards in my possession. Sold separately or in set with SR red roan Running Mare. Regarding the date and quantity of this special, see Running Mare SR, red roan. Collector Kim Jones's foal, which she purchased from Bentley's, has its legs dappled down to the hooves, with no chestnut shading; its mane and tail are a light rusty-tan color, matching the dapples.

Notes:

(1) This mold is not in the 1960 catalog; she first appears in the 1963 catalog and price list. She is called Running Arabian Foal on the 1963 price list, Running Foal "Spice" in the 1963-70 catalogs, and Running Foal thereafter. The name "Spice" was dropped from catalogs after 1970; it was never used in manuals.

(2) Chris Hess is identified as the sculptor of the Running Foal in *JAH* XIV/#2 1987 (p. 13).

(3) Some old Running Foals come with the toe pared off of the right hind hoof. This alteration was undoubtedly made at the factory after molding, probably in an effort to improve the models' balance. Several other molds, such as the Stock Horse Stallion and Mustang, underwent similar surgery early in their histories.

(4) Collector Sheryl Leisure found two unusual solid smoke gray Running Foals amidst a collection of Breyers at a flea market in Southern California in the fall of 1994. The seller was a Mexican man who said his family had bought all their Breyers at toy stores many years ago. The foals are a fairly light smoke gray, like the lighter version of regular-run smoke Running Foal #131, with slightly darker gray mane, tail, and hooves, and no white markings. Being solid and a fairly light shade, they bear a decided resemblance to the 1991 SR dark rose gray Running Foal, but they lack the rose-brown tone of the SR and look significantly older than the SR. Both of Sheryl's foals have the "U.S.A." stamp, which dates them to no earlier than 1970. Regular-run #131 was made in 1970 (this was its last year), so it is possible that Sheryl's foals are variant #131s made in that year. But it is also conceivable that they are specimens of an obscure special run made in the 1970s or 1980s.

(5) Early models of the Running Foal mold have the round "Breyer Molding Co." stamp only. Later models have round stamp and the "U.S.A." stamp—I have seen glossy dapple gray #133s with the "U.S.A.," so we know this stamp was added to the mold no later than 1973. Some "U.S.A." models have the "B" stamp in addition. On some models, both older and newer, the round stamp is partially effaced: the outer circle is present but not the words. I think this must be caused by a leakage problem or some similar problem with the injection mold.

Running Horse Family SR — see "Black Beauty" (stallion, cross-galloping) SR, bay; Running Foal SR, bay; Running Mare SR, bay; Running Stallion SR, bay

Running Mare — Trotting, looking left. Sculpted by Chris Hess. Mold in catalog-run production 1961/63 - 1987, 1991 - current as of 1996.

Catalog-run models made from this mold:

- Running Mare #119, red roan, tan horse with brown-chestnut dappling, dappled face, red chestnut points, no white markings, gray hooves, matte (1971-73). The body shade under the dapples varies from dark tan to pale cream, and the dapples and points vary from a brown chestnut to red chestnut. Breyer issued no regular-run Running Foal to match this mare but did produce an SR red roan foal, with matching SR mare, in 1982. The regular-run and SR mares are very similar, but there are subtle differences. Generally speaking #119 has a more tan body tone with browner dapples, while the SR has a more yellowish or orangy body tone with red dapples. Another difference is in the contours of the right eyeball: #119's eyeball is round and normal looking (like the eye on Running Mares from the 1960s), but the SR's eyeball is typically flat on the inner half. See note 3 for this mold for a full discussion of the Running Mare's ophthalmic problems. #119 was in the Showcase Collection as #1190 in 1971-72 (see Showcase Collection in this section for discussion). The number 119 later belonged to Marguerite henry's "Stormy" as sold in a special blister-wrapped display box.
- Running Mare #848, dark chestnut pinto, solid face, beige mane, beige tail with chestnut tip, 1 right hind and 2 front stockings with gray hooves, other leg chestnut with brown hoof, matte (1991-93). Collector Heather Wells mentioned to me that the earliest #848s produced are a lighter color than later ones. The 1991 catalog has 2 photos of this model (inside front cover and p. 8), which show slightly different pinto patterns. The model on which the white belly patch ends in a scallop pattern high on the barrel is the regular run. The other, on which the belly patch continues up the barrel and over the back in a narrow band, is a test color model, which was sold at the BreyerFest West auction in Pomona, California, in 1991. At the auction, then-Breyer-employee Steve Ryan commented that the engineer who makes the painting masks for the company insisted that a mask couldn't be made to duplicate the test mare's markings.
- Running Mare #1120, Copenhagen decorator, dappled blue, bald face, white points, pink hooves, glossy (1963-64). In the same year, this model was also sold in set #1351; see below. The hooves can be very pale pink or even white. The model number 1120 later belonged to the Showcase Collection issue of the palomino Western Prancer, and after that to the Brenda Western Gift Set with chestnut pinto Western Prancer. For further discussion see Decorators (1960s) above in the Traditionals section.
- Running Mare #2120, Florentine decorator, dappled metallic gold, bald face, white points, pink hooves, glossy (1963-64). In the same year, this model was also sold in set #2351; see below. The hooves can be very pale pink or even white. The model number 2120 later belonged to the Showcase Collection issue of the mahogany bay Proud Arabian Stallion. For further discussion see Decorators (1960s) above in the Traditionals section.
- Running Mare #3120, Golden Charm decorator, solid metallic gold, bald face, white points, pink hooves, glossy (1963-64). In the same year, this model was also sold in set #3351; see below. The hooves can be very pale pink or even white. The gold paint on these mares can darken over time and by now often looks more like tarnished brass. For further discussion see Decorators (1960s) above in the Traditionals section.
- Running Mare #4120, Wedgewood Blue decorator, solid blue, bald face, white points, pink hooves, matte (1963-64). In the same year, this model was also sold in set #4351; see below. The hooves can be very pale pink or even white. For further discussion see Decorators (1960s) above in the Traditionals section.
- Running Mare "Sugar" #120, alabaster, solid gray mane and tail, gray hooves, matte (1961/63 - 1971). This model was also sold in "Sugar" And "Spice" set #351 [1961/63 - 1964]; see below. Walerius 1991 (pp. 52-53) says the alabaster and smoke Running Mares and Foals were made in glossy finish in 1961-65, but I believe this is wrong. I've never seen such horses, and my own #120, which I got sometime in 1961-63, is very matte. Collector Sande Schneider reported to me that she knows of a collector with a glossy alabaster mare and foal, but this is the only set I've heard of; possibly they are tests. If glossies were made as normal production runs, they are very extremely rare, and it is highly unlikely that they would have been in production for as long as five years. #120 was in the Showcase Collection as #1200 in 1970-71 (see Showcase Collection in this section for discussion).
- Running Mare "Sugar" #121, smoke (solid gray), bald face, white points, pink nose and ears, gray hooves, matte (1961/63 - 1970). This model was also sold in "Sugar" And "Spice" set #352 [1961/63 - 1964]; see below. The body color ranges from light gray to charcoal gray, nearly black. The bald face can be extensive, reaching well down the sides of the face. Regarding gloss finish, see Running Mare "Sugar" #120. Smoke #121 was in the Showcase Collection as #1210 in 1970 (see Showcase Collection in this section for discussion).
- Running Mare "Sugar" #123, dapple gray, bald face, gray mane and tail, 4 stockings, gray hooves, glossy (1961/63 - 1973). The most common version of this mare looks like a snowflake appaloosa because she has dapples only on the rump and flanks, as shown in the 1963 and 1972-73 catalogs (the only three catalogs in which #123 is pictured). Some models, however, are more fully dappled. Collector Sande Schneider has a mare with dapples up to the withers; the model must date to pre-1970 since it has no "U.S.A." stamp. Collectors Lynn Isenbarger and Tanya Parker have #123s with tiny dapples even on the shoulders and neck; both models lack the "U.S.A." Collector Paula DeFeyter has a mare with dapples all over, even on the head; for discussion see Running Foal "Spice" #133 dapple gray. The bald face on #123 can be extensive, reaching well down the sides of the face. #123 was in the Showcase Collection as #1230 in 1970-72 (see Showcase Collection in this section for discussion). The number 123 later belonged to the bay Shetland Pony in a special blister-wrapped display box.

- Running Mare "Sugar" #124, bay, bald face, black mane and tail, no black on the legs, 4 stockings, black hooves, matte and semigloss (1961/63 - 1987). Some early mares have hand-painted eyewhites. Catalogs from 1970 back and manuals from 1975 back call this mare and the matching #134 foal "chestnut"; subsequent catalogs and manuals call them "bay." Despite the change in color description, however, all the mares and foals have the same basic pattern of coloring, with black mane, tail, and hooves but no black on the legs. Earlier models are often a darker shiny semigloss bay; later ones are typically medium matte bay. The color varies from brown bay with very little red tone to rich reddish bay. Collector Karen Grimm has an unusual reddish bay mare with the usual bald face but with no stockings—the legs are solid bay with dark gray shading and dark gray hooves (this version is not shown in catalogs). I have heard reports of mares and foals in glossy finish, and certainly such specimens may exist, but I have not seen one that convinced me. The old semigloss models can be deceptively shiny—my own semigloss mare fooled me into thinking she was glossy until I compared her to an old glossy bay PAM. The bald face on #124 can be extensive, reaching well down the sides of the face. #124 was in the Showcase Collection as #1240 in 1970-72 (see Showcase Collection in this section for discussion). She was also sold in the late 1970s in a blister-wrapped display box with the model number 1124 (see Display Boxes above in this section).
- Running Mare "Sugar" #920, woodgrain; black eyes; black hooves; no white markings or other color detailing; most matte, some glossy (1961/63 - 1965). Most woodgrain Running Mares and the matching Running Foals have the matte finish that is normal for woodgrains, but glossy specimens do exist. Collector Judy Davinich owns a glossy foal, of which she kindly sent me a photo. Diederich 1988, Section 1 (p. 96), notes the existence of glossy mares and foals, commenting that these were meant to be mounted on lamps. Sande Schneider, however, does have a lamp with matte woodgrain Running Mare and Foal. (For further discussion see the Lamps & Nightlights section in the Appendix near the end of this book.) These glossy mares and foals and the glossy woodgrain Clydesdale Stallions mentioned on the video are the only glossy woodgrains I have heard of. The number 123 belonged to the Bay Shetland Pony in a special blister-wrapped display box.
- "Wild Diamond," "Justin Morgan's" Dam, #902, sandy bay, solid face, black points, 2 hind stockings with tan hooves, front hooves black, matte (1994-95). This model represents the mother of the real horse "Justin Morgan," founding stallion of the Morgan breed. The name and coloration of the model are speculative, for little is known of "Justin Morgan's" background; but according to one theory, his dam was a light bay mare sired by a horse named "Diamond," who was himself sired by "Wildair." (Information per Beard 1992 and Self 1946.) Marguerite Henry's book *Justin Morgan Had a Horse*, on which Breyer's model "Little Bub," Young "Justin Morgan," is based, does not speculate on the name of "Justin Morgan's" dam: "Likely nobody will ever know who was this fellow's sire and who was his dam. He was just a little work horse that cleared the fields and did what was asked of him" (Henry 1954, p.170).

Sets:

- Running Mare And Foal set #1351, both Copenhagen decorator, dappled blue (1963-64). In the same years, these models were also sold separately as Running Mare #1120 and Running Foal #1130.
- Running Mare And Foal set #2351, both Florentine decorator, dappled metallic gold (1963-64). In the same years, these models were also sold separately as Running Mare #2120 and Running Foal #2130.
- Running Mare And Foal set #3351, both Golden Charm decorator, solid metallic gold (1963-64). In the same years, these models were also sold separately as Running Mare #3120 and Running Foal #3130.
- Running Mare And Foal set #4351, both Wedgewood Blue decorator, solid blue (1963-64). In the same years, these models were also sold separately as Running Mare #4120 and Running Foal #4130.
- "Sugar" And "Spice" set #351, alabaster Running Mare and smoke Running Foal (1961/63 - 1964). These same models were also sold separately as Running Mare "Sugar" #120 and Running Foal "Spice" #131 [1961/63 - 1970]. The model number 351 later belonged to the Brown Swiss Calf.
- "Sugar" And "Spice" set #352, smoke Running Mare and alabaster Running Foal (1961/63 - 1964). These same models were also sold separately as Running Mare "Sugar" #121 and Running Foal "Spice" #130 [1961/63 - 1971]. The nimber 352 was later assigned to the Black Angus Calf SR.

Special-run models made from this mold:

- Running Mare SR, alabaster; striped gray mane and tail; gray-shaded knees, hocks, and fetlocks; gray hooves; matte (1994). Penney's holiday catalog. Sold in Spirit Of The East Gift Set SR #710294, with matching alabaster Running Foal. 4,400 sets made (per *JAH* editor Stephanie Macejko, conversation of June 1995). On the sets I've seen, the striping in the mane and tail is soft and pale on the mare, and darker and crisper on the foal. The number for this set is per an information fax of April 11, 1994, from Breyer to dealers.
- Running Mare SR, bay, no white markings, black points, black hooves, matte (1984). Sears holiday catalog. Sold in Running Horse Family set SR with bay Running Foal and bay "Black Beauty" (stallion, cross-galloping). The Sears catalog and *JAH* XI/#3 1984 (p. 20) seem to show this mare's hooves as black, and my own and other collectors' specimens I know of are like this. However, the matching SR bay foals and stallions I know of have gray hooves.
- Running Mare SR?, buckskin, bald face, black mane and tail, black-shaded lower legs with some areas left buckskin, black hooves, matte (1960s). A buckskin Running Mare and Foal, found by collector Lisa Rowland at a flea market or antique shop, were sold at BreyerFest 1995 to collectors Mary Ann and Dave Snyder (thanks to Dave for reference photos). The models are datable to the 1960s by the fact that they have the round "Breyer Molding Co." stamp but no "U.S.A." stamp. I know of two other models like Mary Ann's: a mare, owned by collector Laura Behning, who got it from another collector (who had found it at a flea market), and a foal, owned by Chris Wilder. Both of these models, like Mary Ann's have bald faces, black points, and no "U.S.A." Mary Ann's models both have the additional detail of a short dorsal stripe coming up from the dock. Conceivably these four 1960s pieces represent a small special run issued at that time, but I have no further evidence of this.
- Running Mare SR?, buckskin (1979). Evidently never produced as a full-blown SR, but a few pieces are known. Published hobby sources conflict about the date and the very existence of a buckskin Running Mare SR. The sources that say such an SR was produced in 1979 for J.C. Penney are *JAH* XIII/#1 1985 (p. 13), Walerius 1991 (p. 99), and Gutierrez 1989. But I have copies of the 1979 Penney's holiday catalog Breyer pages, and there is no buckskin Running Mare or any other SR on them. Nor is this mare in the Aldens, Ward's, or Sears holiday catalogs for that year (though the Aldens does have a regular-run #124 bay Running Mare). If a buckskin Running Mare SR had been issued through such catalogs, you would expect a significant number of models to be around today, but to my knowledge only a few specimens exist. One of these mares, which has a solid face, black points, and gray hooves, was owned by collector Karen Perkins, who told me she got it from longtime collector and Breyer consultant Marney Walerius. Marney had told Karen that this mare was one of about a half dozen sold by Bentley Sales Company at the 1979 Model Horse Congress. When I asked Stuart Bentley, owner of Bentley Sales, about this in December 1995, he said he recalled getting "a couple dozen" buckskin Running Mares on a trip to the Breyer factory in Chicago to pick up odds and ends; he was not sure of the year. Apparently there are a couple more buckskin Running Mares of a slightly later vintage as well. *Breyer Collector's Video* and collectors Sheryl Leisure and Gale Good, among others, say that one or two buckskin test-color Running Mares were made in 1983, when Breyer created two test-color buckskin sets of different molds for Penney's to consider for its 1983 holiday catalog. The sets were a Running Mare and Running Foal set and the "Lady Phase" and standing Stock Foal set. Penney's chose the standing set, and consequently the buckskin Running Mare was not produced. This story seems highly credible in view of the fact that a buckskin Running Foal appears, by mistake, with the buckskin "Lady Phase" in the 1983 Penney's catalog photo (the foal actually issued was a buckskin standing Stock Horse Foal). This mistake led subsequently to the creation of a small special run of buckskin Running Foals; for details see the entry for the 1983 Running Foal SR buckskin.
- Running Mare SR, dapple gray, dapples on neck and head; bald face; darker gray mane and tail; 4 stockings; gray hooves; matte (1982/83). Sold through a Nebraska distributor. No more than 200 models made, according to rumor (per *Breyer Collector's Video*). Sold in SR set with matching dapple gray Running Foal. The dappling on the neck and head can be sparse. The paint finish on some of these models tends to look scruffy in spots. The "grapevine" story on these sets is that they were an unauthorized run, made on the sly at the Breyer factory and smuggled out. Whether this is true I have no idea. *Breyer Collector's Video* and Diederich 1988, Section 2, both give the date of the SR mare and foal set as 1983. Contemporary evidence indicates that the set was indeed out no later than that year: the mare is included on a list of test and SR models in the August 1983 *Quequechan Model Horse Collector* (the list gives no date, quantity, or distributor, and oddly omits mention of the foal.), and both mare and foal are listed in a collector's want ad in the same issue. (The June 1985 issue has a photo of the mare.) However, I suspect that these horses were made earlier, at least by early 1982, for on the mares I have examined, the right eye is normal. See note 3 for this mold for full discussion of the Running Mare's eye deformities.
- Running Mare SR, dapple gray, no or very few dapples on head and upper neck; bald face; white mane and tail; 4 stockings; pink hooves; matte (1987). Sears holiday catalog. Sold in SR set #491212, with matching dapple gray Running Foal. I've heard a rumor that some of these mares have gray mane and tail, but I suspect that this rumor stems from confusion about the 1983 SR dapple gray. The set number is per a Breyer company computer printout of activity 1985-92; no quantity given. The dappling on these mares and the matching foals can be a bit messy, with occasional oversized dapples or clumps of dapples run together.
- Running Mare SR, flocked palomino; blaze; some with painted black eyes, some with brown glass eyes; white synthetic hair mane and tail; 4 stockings; painted black hooves (1984). Penney's holiday catalog. Sold in Collector's Mare And Foal Set SR with flocked palomino Running Foal, for $29.99 per set. Flocking and hairing by the Riegseckers of Indiana (see Riegseckers Models for discussion). A mare and foal displayed at BreyerFest 1995 both had brown glass eyes, but collector Heather Wells's models and a couple of other sets I have seen have painted black eyes. Collectors Robin Briscoe, Lillian Sutphin, and Kitty Anderson told me that their mares and foals are also the painted-eye version. Starting in January 1986, leftovers of this SR mare appeared on the Bentley Sales Company price lists as #120FLK (for "flocked"), for $9.99. Old Bentley's sales record cards in my possession show that Bentley's received a quantity of 144 mares.
- Running Mare SR, flocked white, blue glass eyes, pink synthetic hair mane and tail, painted hot-pink hooves (1985). Penney's holiday catalog. Sold in Fanciful Mare And Pony Set SR with matching flocked Running Foal and plastic brush and comb for the manes and tails, for $29.99 per set. The mares owned by collectors Heather Wells, Paula DeFeyter, and Sande Schneider all have blue glass eyes. Heather's set came with both brush and comb, although the Penney's catalog mentions only a brush ("mane brush included").
- Running Mare SR, palomino (not flocked), bald face, white points, gray hooves, matte (1982). Ward's holiday catalog. Sold in SR set with leather English saddle and bridle. The bridle has two reins (as on a double bridle) attached to snaffle rings. The color of this mare ranges from a light yellowy to dark tan palomino (thanks to collector Sande Schneider for a photo of her 4 mares illustrating the color gamut).
- Running Mare SR, red roan, yellowish tan horse with red-chestnut dappling, dappled face, red chestnut points, no white markings, gray hooves, matte (1982). Made for Bentley Sales Company to sell at Model Horse Congress in summer 1982 and via mail order. 300-330 mares made, per old Bentley's sales record cards in my possession. Sold separately or in set with SR red roan Running Foal. The Bentley's record cards are variously labeled "#124 Red Roan Mare," "#134 Red Roan Foal, "#124/119R Red Roan mare," and "#119R—Red Roan Running Mare—Cong. Spec. 1982." Bentley's price lists, starting in September 1982, advertised these models as "119R $9.95 Red Roan Running Mare" and "134R $7.95 Red Roan Running Foal." For the differences between this SR mare and the regular-run #119, see the entry for #119 above.
- State Line Tack '95 "Special Delivery" SR #702295, dark plum bay, low blaze, white "SLT" brand hand-painted on left hip, black mane and tail, charcoal-shaded knees and hocks, 4 stockings, gray hooves, matte (1995). Made for State Line Tack, in Plaistow, New Hampshire. 1,510 models made (per *JAH* editor Stephanie Macejko, conversation of Dec. 1995). These mares came in Breyer boxes with the label "No. 702295 State Line Tack '95." State Line's *1995-96 Annual Discount Catalog*, where this SR was first advertised, states: "Unlike any other Breyer horse, it carries the State Line brand and is available only here. But our proud new horse needs a name. Send your suggestions ... The winning name will appear in our Fall, 1995 catalog." The winning name announced in State Line's fall/winter 1995- 96 supplemental catalog is "Special Delivery," submitted by Kathryn Yurkonis. Collector Robin Briscoe heard from a friend who works at State Line that the store selected the Running Mare mold for this special because it resembles one of their logos.

Notes:

(1) This mold is not in the 1960 catalog; she appears first in the 1963 catalog and price list. She is called Running Arabian Mare on the 1963 price list, Running Mare "Sugar" in the 1963-70 catalogs, and Running Mare thereafter. The name "Sugar" was dropped

from catalogs after 1970; it was never used in manuals.

(2) Chris Hess is identified as the sculptor of the Running Mare in *JAH* XIII/#1 1985 (p. 13).

(3) On my own Running Mares and many others I've examined, I've noticed a series of changes in the mold in the area of the right eye. On mares from the 1960s, the area is subtly but sharply detailed: the upper part of the eyeball curves neatly in under the upper eyelid; the upper eyelid has two distinct folds; and the supraorbital area has distinct valleys and ridges, very normal and realistic looking. Mares of the 1970s too usually have a normal eye, although collector Joy Sheesley has a couple of red roans, apparently #119s, with a slight defect on the inner half of the eyeball. On the 1982 SR red roan mares, the eye area is still basically normal except for the inner half of the eyeball, which is decidedly flat, as though someone had whacked it with the bottom of a tiny cast-iron frying pan. Several of the 1982 SR palomino mares I've seen have a normal eye, suggesting that they were molded prior to the SR red roans, but collectors Jo Kulwicki and Sue Lehman have palominos that do have the flattened eyeball. I'm not sure about 1983, but something nasty happened to the mold by 1984. Mares made in that year and in the following years through 1993 look as if they've been punched in the right eye by a prize fighter—the whole eye area is swollen looking; the eyeball merges straight into the bulging upper eyelid; the two folds of the upper lid are virtually gone; the supraorbital area is puffy and ill-defined; and there is a "bag" or blister, shaped like a sideways teardrop, just below the lower eyelid. The corner of the cheekbone too has lost its sharp definition. This swollen condition is present on 1984 SR bay, on all the #848s I've seen (including the one in the 1993 catalog), and on all mares produced in the years between. As of 1994, the mold has been retooled and the eye restored to quasi-normalcy: the 1994 models, "Wild Diamond" #902 and SR alabaster Running Mare, have well-defined eyeball and eyelids, as do all subsequent mares. However, this retooled eyeball is a bit strange—it is larger and more protrusive than the 1960s-70s normal eyeball and is slightly pointed and faceted; the supraorbital area is still puffy; and the bag still adorns the lower lid. Nonetheless, the improvement is great.

(4) Some Running Mares are noticeably smaller than others. For discussion of this phenomenon, see Mold Variations in the Appendix near the end of this book.

(5) Longtime collector Karen Perkins mentioned to me that she has heard of a very small special run of solid black Running Mares, made in the 1970s or possibly the early 1980s. I have not seen or heard of such mares outside this report.

(6) Early models of the Running Mare mold have the round "Breyer Molding Co." stamp only. Later models have the round stamp and the "U.S.A." stamp—I have seen a smoke #121 with the "U.S.A.," so it is certain that this stamp was added to the mold in 1970, when the "U.S.A." was introduced into the Breyer line. Some "U.S.A." models have the "B" stamp in addition (collector Chelle Fulk has a bay #124 like this).

Running Stallion — Cross-galloping, looking right. Sculpted by Chris Hess. Mold in catalog-run production 1968-88, 1993 - current as of 1996 (horse mold version 1968-81, 1993 - current as of 1996; unicorn mold version 1982-88)

Catalog-run models made from this mold:

Horse mold version:

- "Lone Star" #928, rose gray snowflake appaloosa, with white spotting concentrated on hindquarters, shoulders, and nose; solid or snowflaked face; darker rose gray mane, tail, knees, and hocks; 4 stockings; tan hooves; matte (1995 - current as of 1996). In the 1996 catalog, this model's name was expanded to "Lone Star" Appaloosa. The body color varies from a distinctly rosy gray to a dove gray with virtually no rose tone. On August 18-20, 1995, the Q2 home-shopping cable TV channel offered a total of 96 "Lone Stars" that were ordinary regular runs but that came in boxes labeled with the special-run model number 708095 (per *JAH* editor Stephanie Macejko). Leftover models may have been sold on subsequent Q2 programs.
- "Rumbling Thunder" #879, dark dapple gray, charcoal horse with lighter gray dapples, solid face, black points, black hooves, semigloss and matte (1993-94). These models vary both in color and in finish. In my experience, the models issued in the first few months of 1993 are a medium/dark gray with a shiny semigloss finish and a lot of body shading. Next came models in the same gray color but with a matte finish and less shading. Then in 1994, the semigloss finish reappeared on a nearly black body color.
- Running Stallion #125, alabaster; white mane and tail; most with either pink or white nose; gray hooves; matte (1968-71). Some models have gray or pink and gray stallion parts. A couple of collectors have told me of #125s with gray noses.
- Running Stallion #126, charcoal, bald face, white points, pink hooves, glossy (1968-70). The body color ranges from black to deep brown. The bald face often starts below the level of the eyes, with the forehead charcoal. Also the width of the bald face varies, reaching down the sides of the face on some and being confined to the front of the face on others. The pink on the hooves can be very pale. Most #126s have white mane and tail, but I've seen a color photo of one with black mane and tail, and there is a photo of another like this in the August 1985 *Quequechan Model Horse Collector*.
- Running Stallion #127, black blanket appaloosa, bald face, unstenciled butt blanket, splashed-on black spots, gray or black hooves, matte (1968-81). In the 1969-75 manuals and 1975 catalog this model is shown with an extensive bald face, with the white covering the eyes and running over the muzzle and well down both sides of the face. But in my experience this version is rarer than the catalogs would indicate; I have seen only a couple of #127s like this—my own, which has gray hooves, no socks, and no "U.S.A." stamp; another one I have seen in person with gray hooves and 1 right front sock; and another with no socks in a photo in *Model Horse Gazette* (Mar./Apr. 1991, p. 15). Later catalogs and manuals that picture #127 show him with the white restricted for the most part to the front of his face, and this is the pattern commonly seen. No catalogs or manuals show #127 with any stockings, but as just mentioned, I have seen one with 1 sock. Collector Linda Bell wrote to me that she has a #127 with no spots on his blanket. On many #127s the left ear is partially bald; catalogs and manuals do show this feature. Some #127s were sold with grooming kits for human beings, with a flat, flexible brown vinyl "pack saddle" containing a comb, toothbrush, nail file, and nail clipper. Similar kits with Western Ponies were sold for many years and are comparatively common. I have never seen one of the Running Stallion kits in person, but they are advertised in the 1969 Gamble-Aldens Christmas catalog. As shown in the photo, the Running Stallion's "pack saddle" is very similar to the Western Pony's but slightly larger. I can't tell if it is tooled, as are some Western Pony "pack saddles." See note 4 for the Western Pony mold for further discussion, and for other grooming-kit sets, see Grooming Kits For People above in the Traditionals section.
- Running Stallion #128, red roan, tan horse with chestnut dappling, dappled face, red chestnut points, no white markings, most with gray hooves, matte (1968-74). The body shade under the dapples varies from dark tan to pale cream, and the dapples and points vary from a browner chestnut to red chestnut. Some models have gray-shaded stallion parts. Some have a pink-shaded muzzle. Collector Val Sibert has a model with red chestnut hooves.
- Running Stallion #129, bay, bald face, black mane and tail, no black on the legs, 4 stockings, black or gray hooves, matte and semigloss (1971-76, 1978-80). The gray-hoofed version of #129 was brought to my attention by collector Denise Deen, who owns such a model. In my experience the black-hoofed version is more common. Some #129s, like many #127 black appaloosas, have a partially bald (white) left ear.

Unicorn mold version:

- Unicorn #210, alabaster; pink nose; gray mane, tail, and beard; gold-and-white-striped horn; gray hooves; matte (1982-88). See note 1 for this mold.

Special-run models made from this mold:

Horse mold version:

- Running Stallion SR #410212, bay, subtly dark-shaded; solid face; black mane and tail; no black on the legs; cream lower legs; gray-shaded knees and hocks; most with gray hooves, a few with black hooves; matte (1989). Made for Black Horse Ranch. 146 models made, per the BHR notice enclosed with the horses shipped in January 1989; a BHR newsletter of December 1989 says 147. The model number and date are per a Breyer company computer printout of activity 1985-92. Except for their black manes and tails, these models are the same color as the *JAH* SR chestnut Running Stallions and were in fact made from some of the leftovers of that run, according to a December 1988 BHR newsletter: "We will be getting in shortly a small overrun of the Just About Horses special run running stallion in chestnut, but will have black mane, tail & legs added to make it bay. We are waiting for an exact count from Breyer, and costs. . . . They were replacing defective & damaged models, so when they have gotten all of them replaced, we will get the remainder." The black was not added to the legs as BHR expected, but only to the mane and tail. The Breyer printout states: "paint same as item #400212 [the *JAH* SR chestnut], only add a little black to mane & tail." This statement from a Breyer company document verifies that the black mane and tail were painted by the factory, not by Black Horse Ranch as has been rumored. (On this issue also see BHR owner Karen Grimm's comment to the editor in *Model Trading Post*, Sept./Oct. 1992, p. 3.) The bays do not have belly numbers, whereas most of the *JAH* chestnuts do.
- Running Stallion SR #400212, chestnut, subtly dark-shaded; solid face; cream mane, tail and lower legs; gray-shaded knees and hocks; gray hooves; matte (1988). *Just About Horses* subscriber special. 1,500 models made (per *JAH* 15/#3 July/Aug. 1988, p. 12). The model number is per a Breyer company computer printout of activity 1985-92. The models sold through *JAH* are numbered by hand on the belly. Collector Sue Lehman brought it to my attention that some leftover models without belly numbers were sold through Black Horse Ranch mail-order company. Sue purchased one of these models from BHR, and they are listed on a 1991 BHR ad flier in my possession. (These are not the SR bays made for BHR in 1989 but the original chestnuts.) Leftover unnumbered chestnuts were also sold through Bentley Sales Company, according to collector Georgeanne Wilcox, who purchased one from another collector who got it from Bentley's; these were undoubtedly the models listed on the May 1991 Bentley's price list as "127C Dark Chestnut Running Stallion." When I asked Breyer executive Peter Stone about these unnumbered chestnuts in March 1995, he replied that they were from the 1,500-piece run, not additional to that run. On my own belly-numbered chestnut from *JAH*, the facial seam along the nose looks like a hairline fissure about to split. I learned from collector Liz Strauss that a number of these models do have a split seam in this area.
- Running Stallion SR, palomino blanket appaloosa, blaze, stenciled blanket on upper butt and loins, stenciled palomino spots, white points, tan hooves, matte (1990). Sears holiday catalog. Sold in Appaloosa-American Classic Set SR #499610, with black blanket appaloosa Performance Horse and blue roan semi-leopard appaloosa "Stud Spider." 2,000 sets made. Quantity and set number are per a Breyer company computer printout of activity 1985-92.

Unicorn mold version:

- Sky Blue Unicorn SR, flocked sky blue; solid face; brown or blue glass eyes; darker blue synthetic hair mane, tail, and beard; gold-and-white striped horn; painted silver or pearly white hooves (1985). Penney's holiday catalog. Sold in set with plastic brush and comb for the mane and tail, for $25.99. In the Penney's catalog, the photo shows this horse as white with medium blue mane and tail, while the description says "bluish toned white body with sparkles and baby blue hair." But the collectors' specimens known to me, several of which I have seen in person, are quite different, being sky blue, close to a turquoise shade. Some have sparkly flecks sprinkled over the body, as on collector Sande Schneider's model. Most of the models I know of have brown glass eyes, but collector Sue Lehman's model, which I have seen in person, has blue glass eyes, as well as silver hooves and an unsparkly body. On the models I have seen, silver hooves are the norm. Collector Heather Wells's model came with both brush and comb, although the Penney's catalog mentions only a brush ("mane brush included").
- Unicorn SR #700394, alabaster, gray nose, gray mane and tail, pale gray beard, silver-and-white striped horn, gray hooves, matte (1994). Made for Toys R Us. 13,500 models made (per *JAH* editor Stephanie Macejko, conversation of June 1995). The model name and number are per the model's box. The box is decorated with a large round gold sticker saying, in full: "1994 Special Collector Edition / (Limited Production) / Unicorn / Legendary and elusive, this Breyer Creature is a highly collectible edition of a 1980's Classic." The latter reference is to the regular-run Unicorn #210, which is very similar to this SR but has a horn striped with gold rather than silver. See note 1 for this mold.
- Unicorn II SR #700595, black, no white markings, black mane and tail with gold accent lines, black beard with gold tip, gold-and-black-striped horn, black hooves, gold band around top of right front hoof, glossy (1995). Made for Toys R Us. 10,500 models made, per *JAH* editor Stephanie Macejko (conversation of July 2, 1996). The model name and number are per the model's box. The box is decorated with a large round gold sticker saying, in full: "1995 Special Collector Edition / (Limited Production) / Unicorn II / Mysterious, this Breyer inspiration in black, captivates the beholder with his wariness and guile." The gold accent line in the tail runs halfway down the tail from the top of the dock. The line in the mane runs up the from the center of the crest on the right side and down the top of the mane to the withers. See note 1 for this mold.

Notes:

(1) On the unicorn version of this mold, the horn is a separately molded piece with a peg on the wide end, which is glued into a hole drilled (not molded) in the horse's forehead, according to former Breyer executive Peter Stone (conversations of Nov. 1994 and Dec. 1995). But the Unicorn beard, Stone confirmed, is an integral part of the mold. The beard was added to the metal injection mold at the end of 1981 in preparation for production of #210 Unicorn. When #210 was discontinued at the end of 1988, the beard portion of the injection mold was sealed off for the production of the 1989 SR chestnut Running Stallion. This SR and Running Stallion models issued subsequently often have a

scar at the site where the beard once was, caused by the seal in the injection mold (the scar is sometimes effaced by the sander after molding). The seal was removed and reinstalled with some frequency in 1994 and 1995 for the production of the SR Unicorns and regular-run "Rumbling Thunder" and "Lone Star"; according to Stone, unplugging and replugging such areas in an injection mold is not difficult. Evidently the beard itself was also retooled for the 1994-95 SR Unicorns, for their beard is slightly larger than the old #210 beard and somewhat differently shaped.

(2) The earliest models of the Running Stallion mold have the round "Breyer Molding Co." stamp only. Later ones have the round stamp and the "U.S.A." stamp—I have seen a couple charcoal #126s with the "U.S.A.," so it is certain that this stamp was added to the mold in 1970, when the "U.S.A." was introduced into the Breyer line. Some "U.S.A." models also have a backwards (or upside-down) "B" stamp on the opposite hind leg (collector Linda Bell and I both have #127s like this).

Running Stock Horse Foal — see Action Stock Horse Foal

Saddlebred — See Five-Gaiter; Saddlebred Weanling. Also see Premier Fine Porcelain Series for discussion of the porcelain Saddlebred in parade tack scheduled for 1996.

Saddlebred Weanling — ♞ Filly, in show stance, looking right, roached mane. Sculpted by Marvin Morin. Mold in catalog-run production: tailtip-attached mold version 1973-80, haired version 1985-87, tailtip-unattached mold version 1990, 1995 - current as of 1996. Catalog-run models made from this mold:

TAILTIP-ATTACHED MOLD VERSION:

♞ Saddlebred Weanling #62, dark chestnut, blaze, same color or slightly darker chestnut mane and tail, most with 1 left hind and 2 front stockings with gray hooves, other hoof dark brown, matte and semigloss (1973-80). The color of #62 varies from liver to dark and medium red chestnut to medium sandy chestnut; the darker colors are more common in my experience. The 1973-79 catalogs and manuals show this model with 1 left hind and 2 front stockings, and this is the most common version among models I've seen. Collector Delana Metcalf kindly sent me a photo of her 4-stocking #62; this variation is also noted by *Breyer Collector's Video* and *The Model Trading Post* May/June 1994 (p. 4). Collector Leslie Granger sent me a photo of her model with 2 stockings (right front and left hind). A variation with 1 stocking was offered on a sales list by collector Karen Perkins. In 1980, the final year for #62, she is shown in the catalog with no stockings, but I'm not sure if this version was actually produced for sale. The shape of the blaze on this model also varies: four different blazes are shown in *JAH* 20/#3 Summer II 1993 (p. 30), and five are shown on *Breyer Collector's Video*. Photos in catalogs and manuals are too dim to divulge the chronology of the blazes precisely, but they do indicate that the blazes that came down between the nostrils to cover the whole upper lip were earlier (1973-75), and the blazes that ended at or just below the nostrils were later (1975-76). A wide, nearly rectangular blaze is clearly shown in the 1980 catalog.

HAIRED VERSION:

♞ Collector's Rocking Horse #701, flocked chestnut; blaze; brown or blue glass eyes; chestnut synthetic hair mane and tail same color as body or slightly lighter; 4 stockings; painted black hooves; snaffle bit with tan leather reins; tan leather saddle; yellow felt saddle pad; yellow or dark brown plastic rockers (1985-87). This model was flocked, haired, and outfitted by the Riegseckers of Indiana (see Riegseckers Models for discussion). The suggested retail price for #701 was $37.50 on the Breyer company's 1985-86 price lists and went to $40.00 on the 1987 price list. The 1985 catalog shows this model with snaffle bridle but no saddle; the 1986-87 catalogs show it with English saddle and snaffle bit with reins but no headstall. I believe the 1985 photo shows prototype tack that was not issued for sale, for my own #701 and all others I've seen have the 1986-87 tack. The bit goes through small holes in the sides of the mouth. My own model, collector Sande Schneider's, and all those shown in Breyer catalogs have brown glass eyes, but the models owned by collectors Robin Briscoe, Sue Lehman, and Heather Wells have blue glass eyes, as does the one shown in *JAH* 20/#3 Summer II 1993 (p. 31). In the 1985-86 catalogs, the rockers are yellow, as on Heather's and Robin's models. But in the 1987 catalog the rockers are either dark brown or black (it's hard to tell); my own and Sande's models both have dark brown rockers.

TAILTIP-UNATTACHED MOLD VERSION:

♞ "Kentuckiana" Saddlebred Weanling #915, dappled liver chestnut, blaze that goes over the muzzle, darker liver mane and tail, 1 left hind and 2 front stockings, 4 tan hooves with charcoal stripes, matte (1995 - current as of 1996). The dapples are very muted, being only a slight shade lighter than the basic body color. The stockings, which are stenciled, extend onto the knees and hock. In the 1996 catalog, this model's name was changed to "Kentuckiana" American Saddlebred.

♞ Saddlebred Weanling #818, caramel pinto, tobiano; narrow blaze; tri-color eyes; pink in nostrils; white tail; tan hooves; matte; Commemorative Edition (1990). 5,000 models made. Most double-numbered by hand on belly. The numbering on these fillies typically has the run-total number first (e.g., my model is numbered "5000/2749"). Collector Elaine Lindelef found a filly with no belly numbers at a toy store. #818's box features a large round gold sticker saying, in full: "1990 Commemorative Edition / Saddlebred Weanling / Limited to 5,000 models." A one-of-a-kind black pinto Weanling with the same pinto pattern as #818 (except with black tail) was awarded by Breyer to collector Marney J. Walerius (b.1948, d.1992) at BreyerFest 1990 in recognition of her years of promotional activity in the hobby and consulting service to the company. The black pinto Weanling is pictured in *JAH* 19/#2 Summer I 1992 (p. 6) and in Walerius 1991 (p. i). See Future Champion Show Set SR, bay pinto, for the slight differences in pattern between the bay and caramel pintos.

Special-run models made from this mold:

TAILTIP-ATTACHED MOLD VERSION:

♘ Saddlebred Weanling SR, chestnut, star, flaxen mane and tail, 4 stockings, gray hooves, matte (1984). *Just About Horses* subscriber special. 1,000 models made (per *JAH* XI/#2 1984, pp. 14-15). Double-numbered and dated "1984" by hand on the belly. My own model's belly appears to have been hit by a graffiti vandal: it has "1984," Peter Stone's signature, and the double number "000466/1000." (Evidently whoever put the numbers on thought that since the first number of the series needs three zeros [0001], all the rest must likewise need three. I'm glad I didn't get the thousandth horse.) Collector Debbie Vandegrift's and Sande Schneider's models are also double-numbered and dated. Sheryl Leisure's model, however, has no numbers or date. The *JAH* SR Weanling was the last model of this mold to be produced with the tip of the tail attached to the buttock. The *JAH* ad for this special states: "This mold will be destroyed as you know it."

♘ Saddlebred Weanling SR, unpainted white (1980). Sold through *JAH* VII/#3 1980 (p. 13). This horse and several other completely unpainted models were offered to hobbyists interested in customizing, but many collectors kept them unpainted. See Unpainted Models for a complete list.

HAIRED VERSION:

♘ My Companion Rocking Horse SR, flocked white, blue glass eyes, pink synthetic hair mane and tail, painted pink hooves, pink suede leather English saddle and reins, pink plastic rockers (1985). Penney's holiday catalog. Sold in SR set with brush for mane and tail, for $25.99. This SR was flocked, haired, and outfitted by the Riegseckers of Indiana (see Riegseckers Models for discussion). The reins attach to a wire bit that goes through small holes in the sides of the mouth; there is no headstall. The Penney's catalog notes: "Femininity abounds with the flocked white and pink mane and tail made of life-like hair." Quite a role model here, gals.

♘ My Favorite Rocking Horse SR, most flocked mauve (grayish lavender), solid face, most with blue glass eyes, lavender synthetic hair mane and tail, painted dark purple or bright pink hooves, dark purple suede leather English saddle and reins, medium purple plastic rockers (1985). Penney's holiday catalog. Sold in SR set with brush for mane and tail, for $25.99. This SR was flocked, haired, and outfitted by the Riegseckers of Indiana (see Riegseckers Models for discussion). The reins attach to a wire bit that goes through small holes in the sides of the mouth; there is no headstall. This model varies quite a bit in color scheme, to judge from the few specimens I know of. The one shown in the Penney's catalog has a mauve body, lighter pinky lavender mane and tail, fairly dark purple hooves and rockers, and dark purple tack. (The description in the Penney's catalog reads: "mauve body, lavender hair mane and deep lavender leather accessories.") Collector Heather Wells's model and one that was displayed at the 1994 BreyerFest live show have mauve body, medium purple mane and tail, bright pink hooves, medium purple rockers, and dark purple tack. Collector Sande Schneider's horse is like this but has a lighter, pinker mane and tail. One of collector Paula DeFeyter's two horses is also like the preceding but has a strawberry blonde mane and tail that are lighter than the body. Her other horse has a medium purple body and dark purple mane and tail. Another model at the 1994 BreyerFest show, which was labeled by the exhibitor as a 1985 Penney's SR, was very different, having a dark purple body, brown glass eyes, pale lavender mane and tail, black hooves, bright pink suede leather tack, and bright pink rockers. All the other specimens have blue glass eyes. I do not know for a fact that all the variant specimens just listed are from the 1985 Penney's run; conceivably some were made and sold independently by the Riegseckers.

♘ Our Rocking Horse SR, flocked black blanket appaloosa, bald face with white muzzle, blue glass eyes, black synthetic hair mane and tail, 4 stockings, painted black hooves, black leather English saddle and reins, red felt saddle blanket, most with red plastic rockers (1985). Sears holiday catalog. The Sears catalog, which prices the model at $24.99, does not indicate whether she came with a plastic brush, as did the SR flocked rocking horses from Penney's. This SR, like other Breyer flockies, was flocked, haired, and outfitted by the Riegseckers of Indiana (see Riegseckers Models for discussion). The reins attach to a wire bit that goes through small holes in the sides of the mouth; there is no headstall. Although red rockers are the norm, Diederich 1988, Section 3, notes that some models have black rockers. Collector Lani Keller's former model and others I've seen have red in the nostrils, but collector Sande Schneider's model lacks this detail.

TAILTIP-UNATTACHED MOLD VERSION:

♘ Future Champion Show Set SR #494092, bay pinto Saddlebred Weanling, tobiano; solid face; mane mostly white; black tail with white streaks; legs have high white with no black; tan hooves; matte (1992). Sears holiday catalog. Set also includes Brenda doll and removable leather show halter and lead. 2,250 sets made. Quantity and set number are per a Breyer company computer printout of activity 1985-92. For details on the doll and tack, see under Brenda Breyer in the Riders - Soft Or Jointed Plastic section. Her pinto pattern is very similar to the caramel pinto Weanling's (#818), but there are differences. On her left side, the caramel pinto has a long finger of color across her barrel and a finger of white across the top of the neck; the bay pinto lacks these fingers. The caramel pinto has more white on the forehand than does the bay pinto. The caramel pinto's crest is all white, whereas the bay pinto's crest is black at the top. The caramel pinto has a white tail and a stripe on her face; the bay pinto has a black tail and solid face. Former *JAH* editor Megan Thilman told me (in Dec. 1993) that she instigated the pattern changes; she particularly disliked the "fingers" on the caramel pinto's left side.

♘ "Raven" SR #701091, plum black, star, no stockings, black mane and tail, black hooves, semigloss (1991). Made for signing parties and toy store promotional events. 8,000 models made (per a Breyer company computer printout of activity 1985-92). The model's number is given on her box. Each model came with a certificate of authenticity signed by Breyer executive Peter Stone. The model's name is taken from her color, as the certificate indicates: "The color Raven Black is characterized by a deep purple sheen, highlighting the rich black coat. This Special Run model was produced in the year 1991 for nationwide Breyer Special Events. It will not be made available again and is a true collector's item." The color was created by applying three layers of paint: red, blue, and black (per Breyer's Steve Ryan in his 1991 BreyerFest West presentation). In my experience the earlier models tend to be more plum-colored, being a deep plum brown-black; later ones are stark black. I believe most models have a diamond star, as shown in the announcement of "Raven" in *JAH* 18/#2 Summer I 1991, though it can be vague from overspray. Collector Andrea Westedt's model has a solid face.

♘ Saddlebred Weanling SR, alabaster, soft gray mane and tail, subtle gray shading over most of the body, gray or charcoal hooves, matte (1995). Made for the QVC home-shopping cable TV channel's Breyer hour aired August 5, 1995. Sold in Parade Of Horses Breeds set #705495 with bay roan Cantering Welsh Pony and sandy bay Proud Arabian Mare. 1,800 sets made (per *JAH* editor Stephanie Macejko, conversation of Sept. 8, 1995). Leftovers from this batch were sold on QVC on January 20, 1996. Each model in the set came in a separate Breyer box labeled with the set's name and number. The intensity of the gray body shading on the Weanling varies—some models are almost pure white while others have a definite smoky cast.

Notes:

(1) Prior to 1985, this mold had the tip of the tail molded to the right buttock. The metal injection-mold was retooled to remove the tail and to add molded-on pegs to the bottoms of the hooves, in preparation for production of Collector's Rocking Horse #701 and the three 1985 SR rocking horses. All of these horses have a hair tail glued on, and at least some of them are attached to their rockers by means of the plastic hoof-pegs, which fit into holes molded into the crosspieces on the rockers. My own #701 can be removed from her rockers simply by pulling her pegs out of the holes; her hooves are not glued down. I have however seen at least one flocked black appy and one flocked mauve rocking horse attached to their rockers by means of screws through the hooves; whether this means that their pegs had been accidentally broken off or instead that the hoof pegs were added to

the injection mold sometime after the tail was removed (so that all early rocking horses have screws rather than pegs) I don't know. Collector Ida Santana found an unflocked, unhaired, unpainted rocking horse, which I saw in person in July 1994; the horse has molded-on hoof pegs, and her dock area is molded completely smooth, with no hole or other sign of where the plastic tail once was. Prior to the release of #818 in 1990, the injection mold was again retooled to remove the hoof pegs and restore the plastic tail. The restored tail is nearly identical to the original one except that the tip stands free from the buttock.

(2) At a signing party in 1988, Breyer executive Peter Stone told me that the Saddlebred Weanling was sculpted for Breyer by an American Indian man from Montana. Mr. Stone repeated this statement about the Weanling at BreyerFest 1990, specifying that it was sculpted by a Crow artist named Marvin Morin (spelling per Mac Donald 1993 and *JAH* 21/#1 Spring 1994, p. 15).

(3) The Saddlebred Weanling mold has the round "Breyer Molding Co." stamp and the "U.S.A." stamp. Later models of the tailtip-attached mold version might also have the "B" stamp, but I'm not sure. The Rocking Horse models' rockers, which are also molded by Breyer (per Breyer executive Peter Stone, conversation of Nov. 1994), have no mold stamps.

Saddle Club horses — In the Traditionals section see "Starlight" (under Jumping Horse). In the Little Bits section see Saddle Club Collection and Saddle Club Series. In the Stablemates Section see Saddle Club Collection. All of these horses and sets are based on the Saddle Club series of books by author Bonnie Bryant, published by Bantam.

"Sam I Am" SR — see under Stock Horse Stallion

"San Domingo" — ♞ Stallion, walking, looking left. Sculpted by Chris Hess. Mold in catalog-run production 1978-93, 1995 - current as of 1996.

Catalog-run models made from this mold:

♞ Blanket Appaloosa #703, dark gray blanket appaloosa, solid upper face, bald above nose, unstenciled blanket covering butt and half of barrel, dark gray splashed-on spots, black points, black hooves, matte (1988-89). My own model and those in the 1988-89 catalogs are bald only on the lower part of the face, but collector Sande Schneider's model is baldish on the whole face.

♞ Comanche Pony #829, dark palomino, solid face, white points, gray-shaded muzzle and eyes, tan hooves, slightly semigloss (1990-92).

♞ "Domino" The Happy Canyon Trail Horse #871, dark olive-brown paint, overo; black mane and tail; white head; pink nose; right eye blue with pink shading around it; left eye tri-color; tan hooves; matte, Commemorative Edition (1993). 7,500 models made, most double numbered by hand on the belly (I have heard of an unnumbered model, sent to a collector by the factory to replace a damaged piece). Some models have a lot of gray shading around the tri-color eye. The body color varies from chocolate-charcoal to a lighter olive brown, the latter being more common among models I've seen. Photos I've seen of the real "Domino" make him look like a black and white pinto, but collector Rusty Black, the horse's owner, told me that his "black" spots were actually roaned. The model's unusual olive color is an attempt to capture the roan effect, according Megan Thilman Quigley, who worked at Breyer when this model was produced. *JAH* 19/#5 Winter 1992 (inside front cover) says the spots on these models are airbrushed free-hand rather than with a paint mask. The test-color models pictured in *JAH* and the catalog do look this way, but the models produced for sale do not—their spots have the characteristic stenciled look of patterns painted with masks, and the patterns are consistent from model to model even in subtle details of the shapes of the spots. Collector Peri Riggins did note a spot variation on the horses in the toy shop where she works: on some models, the dark spot on the left front cannon covered the front of the leg as well as the sides, while on others the front of the leg was white, with dark only on the sides. The real "Domino," a gelding with one blue eye, was an equine actor of sorts. Nearly every year from 1956 to 1973 he performed in the Happy Canyon Pageant, in Pendleton, Oregon. This pageant, which is still performed today, is an annual outdoor drama portraying the old West. "Domino" was destroyed in 1975, at the age of 25, because he had developed bone cancer. (Information per the 1993 catalog and Beard 1993.) The model's box bears a large round gold sticker saying, in full: "1993 Commemorative Edition / (Limited to 7,500 pieces serially numbered by hand) / Domino / The Happy Canyon Trail Horse / From the Happy Canyon Western Pageant in Pendleton, Oregon." Owner Rusty Black offered a collector's package of a "Domino" model, photo plaque of the real horse, and a short history of the horse (advertised in Paula Beard's *Traveler's Rest Ranch Newsletter*, March 1, 1993).

♞ Marguerite Henry's "San Domingo" #67, chestnut pinto, with medicine hat pattern; white mane and tail; tan hooves; matte (1978-87). This model is called Marguerite Henry's "San Domingo" only in the 1987 catalog; in all previous years he is called simply "San Domingo," though the 1978 catalog notes in small print that he is "Marguerite Henry's Famous Medicine Hat Stallion." The medicine-hat pattern, which was sacred to the Plains Indians, is a pattern in which the horse is mainly white with a characteristic patch or "bonnet" of color remaining over the ears, as well as colored spots, called "war shields," on the chest, flanks, and base of the tail (see *JAH* VIII/#2 1981, p. 12, and Sponenberg and Beaver 1983). The color on #67 varies from fairly dark chestnut on earlier models to light chestnut on later ones. Many models have a pink nose. Collector Sheryl Leisure found a model whose chestnut spots, unlike those on normal #67s, are unstenciled, slightly mottled in color, and somewhat different in shape from normal #67s' spots. The horse also has gray-tan hooves rather than the pure tan of normal #67s. Sheryl got the model in an old collection from the 1970s, so we surmise that he was one of the first #67s made and that Breyer issued these earliest horses before it had the paint mask (stencil) for the normal pinto pattern ready. The #67 in the 1978 catalog also has a slightly deviant pattern and is probably an unstenciled test piece. The normal, stenciled pattern debuted in the 1979 catalog. #67 represents the title character in M. Henry's book *San Domingo, The Medicine Hat Stallion*, a story about a boy named Peter Lundy, who became a Pony Express rider at the age of 15 in the year 1860, the year the Express began (it existed only for a few years). In the story, the boy acquires a medicine hat Indian pony colt, which he names "San Domingo," and later becomes friends with a government surveyor named Robert Brislawn ("Brisley"), who identifies the pony as a pure Spanish Barb. The "Brisley" and "San Domingo" characters in the book are fictitious but based on real, 20th-century figures. The real Robert E. Brislawn, Sr., with his children and a colleague, founded the Spanish Mustang Registry in 1957; the first horse registered was "Buckshot" (see *JAH* XII/#2 1985, pp. 12-13). The cover of *JAH* VIII/#1 (1981) features a color photo Brislawn astride the real medicine hat stallion "San Domingo." This model was sold through the 1979 Sears holiday catalog in a set with leather Western saddle, bridle, and breastcollar. The model number 67 previously belonged to the black Poodle.

♞ "Oxidol" Rodeo Appaloosa #917, no-spot white with light tan body shading, pink and gray mottling on muzzle and sides of face, light tan mane, tail streaked pale tan and white, tan hooves, matte (1995 - current as of 1996). The quantity and vividness of the pink and gray facial mottling vary considerably, and the pink shade varies to a peach tone. This model is a portrait of the real appaloosa gelding "Oxidol," a trick horse owned by professional rodeo clown Bob Courtney (per *JAH* 22/#2 Mar./Apr. 1995, p. 14; photo on p. 18). On August 5, 1995, the QVC home-shopping cable TV channel offered 1,000 "Oxidols" that were ordinary regular runs but that came in boxes labeled with the special-run model number 705295 (per *JAH* editor Stephanie Macejko). In the 1996 catalog, #917's name was shortened to "Oxidol" Appalossa.

Special-run models made from this mold:

♘ "Black Gold" SR, black, no white markings, black mane and tail, tan hooves, slightly semigloss (1985). Ward's holiday catalog. Sold in SR set with Marguerite Henry's book *Black Gold*. At least several hundred models made. Leftovers of this SR were sold through Bentley Sales Company; the model is on Bentley's price lists for March-August 1986, as "#67BG Black Gold from Ward's catalog," for $10.49. (Ward's had offered the horse with the book for $12.99.) Old Bentley's sales record cards sent to me by Stuart Bentley in February 1996 show that Bentley's received 334 models at the start of March 1986. Presumably at least a couple hundred pieces would have been sold through Ward's the previous holiday season as well. This model represents the title character in *Black Gold*, the story of a real Thoroughbred race horse so named because the owners of his dam got the money to have her bred from the discovery of a vast field of oil on the Osage Indian lands where they lived. The Osages called oil "black gold" (*Black Gold*, p. 88). After winning the 50th Kentucky Derby (1924), "Black Gold" stood at stud but proved to be nearly sterile—he sired only one foal (p. 159)—so he was put back on the track. In 1927 he broke a leg during the Salome Purse race in New Orleans and was destroyed. Marguerite Henry's book describes the scene thus: "Black Gold's leg . . . snapped above the ankle. His bandage was all that held it together. But he finished his race" (p. 168). According to Henry, the horse was solid black except for a small heart-shaped star (p. 84). The Breyer model shown in the 1985 Ward's holiday catalog has a small star, but apparently this photo model was a test piece, for all the models I know of have a solid face. Some "Black Golds" do however have white coronary bands because the black paint of the legs was not brought quite far enough down to meet the tan of the hooves.

♘ "Bright Zip" SR #700794, chestnut roan blanket appaloosa; blaze; hand-painted eyewhites; chestnut mane and tail, some tails have light streaks; unstenciled blanket covering butt and much of barrel, splashed-on chestnut spots; pale "roaning" (dappling) concentrated on flanks, shoulders, and sides of face; white brand on left shoulder; hooves striped chestnut and gray; matte (1994). Dinner model for BreyerFest in Lexington, Kentucky. 2,244 models made, per *JAH* editor Stephanie Macejko (conversation of June 1995). The extent of the roaning and the size of the white blanket vary, as do the occurrence and brightness of the light streaks in the tail. At least one model came without a shoulder brand (see *JAH* 22/#3 May/June 1995, p. 3). The brand, called the "Bar Y" (per *JAH* 21/#3 Summer II 1994, p. 13), is a "Y" with a horizontal line extending out from the top of its left arm. John Lyons, owner and trainer of the real appy stallion "Bright Zip," commented at BreyerFest that this is the brand of his ranch. Mr. Lyons is an internationally renowned horse trainer. He and "Zip" were present at the Kentucky Horse Park during BreyerFest 1994 and put on exhibitions of riding without a bridle and riding with bridle but without leg and seat aids. For all BreyerFest attendees who wished, Mr. Lyons also autographed "Bright Zip" models on the belly in silver ink, typically with the inscription "John Lyons & Zip 94." The models came in a regular Breyer box (yellow backing, clear plastic front) labeled "No. 700794 BreyerFest 1994 Bright Zip." The numerous steps in the painting of the "Bright Zip" models are illustrated in *JAH* 21/#3 Summer II 1994 (p. 17).

♘ "San Domingo" SR #416091, Copenhagen decorator, dappled blue; dappled blue face; solid blue points; gray hooves; semigloss (1991). Raffle model for BreyerFest Northwest, in Redmond/Bend, Oregon, June 1991. 21 models made. 20 were raffled off and 1 was auctioned. The proceeds were donated to the Misty of Chincoteague Foundation and the Hooved Animal Humane Society. (Model number is per a Breyer company computer printout of activity 1985-92; other information is per *JAH* 18/#2 Summer I 1991, p. 15. The printout says only 20 pieces were made.) These SRs are more turquoise in color than the old Copenhagen blue regular-run decorators. Some of these SRs might have dapples on the mane and tail—the one pictured in *JAH* looks that way—but the one I've seen in person had solid blue mane and tail.

♘ "San Domingo" SR, red bay, solid face, black mane and tail, black-shaded knees and hocks, most with bay front lower legs with brown-gray hooves, white hind stockings with gray hooves, matte (1987). Penney's holiday catalog. Sold in Breyer Traditional Western Horse Collector Set SR #712848, with red dun semi-leopard appaloosa "Adios" and liver-charcoal Foundation Stallion. 3,800 sets made. Quantity and set number are per a Breyer company computer printout of activity 1985-92. The Penney's catalog describes the horses as representing particular breeds: "the Appaloosa (speckled horse). The Quarter-horse (brown with white hind legs), and the Mustang (the charcoal brown horse)." So the "Adios" is an appaloosa, the "San Domingo" a quarter horse, and the Foundation Stallion a mustang. The "San Domingos" can have quite a bit of sandy/gold undertone that gives them an orangish cast. Collector Deanna Schane has a model that is nearly a golden bay, which also has no dark shading on the knees and only a touch of gray on the hocks. Collector Meg Mac Donald wrote to me that some of the "San Domingos" have black front legs rather than brown; she has seen a photo of one like this.

♘ "Spotted Bear" Indian Pony SR #490465, black pinto, with medicine hat pattern; tan nose; white mane and tail; tan hooves; matte; cold-cast porcelain (1991). Sears holiday catalog. 1,000 models were made, but fewer survived. Double-numbered by hand on the belly. Made for Breyer in Taiwan. Models cost $95 new from Sears and came with numbered certificate of authenticity signed by Breyer executive Peter Stone. The certificate states: "This fine Breyer model is crafted of cold-cast porcelain, and it is limited to a series of 1,000 serially numbered pieces. Native Americans cherished this type of horse, saying they possessed mystical powers. *Spotted Bear* will not be made available again and is a true collector's item." Some models came with a tiny gold "Made in Taiwan" sticker on the bottom of one hoof. This SR's pinto pattern is the same as that on "San Domingo" #67, except that the outlines of the colored spots are blunter and less detailed. (See #67 for discussion of the medicine hat pattern.) Some "Spotted Bears" are hand-painted, with hard-edged spots, as shown in the Sears catalog; others are airbrushed, with softer-edged spots. The painting on a few of the hand-painted models I have seen is messy, with crude streaks and outlining around the black spots. Collector Megan Thilman Quigley, who worked at Breyer when this SR was issued, told me that "Spotted Bear" was originally painted as well as cast in Taiwan, but the painting was so unsatisfactory on some models that Breyer washed them off and repainted them at the Breyer factory. There may now be considerably fewer that 1,000 "Spotted Bears," to judge from Lynn Isenbarger's tale as reported in *The Small Horse* (#3, Oct. 1992). Lynn ordered 3 of these models from Sears. When she returned 2 of them that had arrived with flaws, the clerk told her that Sears was destroying the returned defective ones and submitting forms to Breyer for reimbursement. I have also heard of other collectors returning models with warped legs, breaks, and other defects. The Sears catalog says this horse is a "limited edition porcelain pony. . . . It has been cold cast in porcelain." He is in fact not porcelain but cold-cast porcelain, which is plastic resin with marble dust added to it to give the appearance of porcelain (see *JAH* 21/#4 Fall 1994, p. 3). "Spotted Bear" has the round "Breyer Molding Co." stamp, as do all the plastic models of this mold. The model number is per a Breyer company computer printout of 1991 SRs.

- "Wildfire" SR #410067, red chestnut pinto, tobiano; stenciled bald face; white mane; dark red chestnut tail; grayish tan hooves; matte (1988). Made for Model Horse Collector's Supply Company. 1,000 models made. Sold in SR set with "Ruby" red roan (Mustang mold). Quantity is per *JAH* 15/#4 Sept./Oct. 1988 (inside front cover); model number is per a Breyer company computer printout of activity 1985-92. Nevermind the stallion parts on the "Wildfire" and "Ruby" models. They represent real mares owned by Jeannie Thomas Craig, who told their story in *JAH* XII/#3 1985. The real "Ruby" was a wild Mustang mare that Jeannie bought and bred to a chestnut pinto Saddlebred stud. The filly produced was "Wildfire."

Notes:

(1) Regarding the test color "San Domingos" standing proxy for Stock Stallions in the 1981 dealer catalog, see note 1 under Stock Horse Stallion.

(2) Chris Hess is identified as the sculptor of this mold in *JAH* Fall 1977. This issue also has a photo of an unpainted plaster casting of the sculpture.

(3) The "San Domingo" mold has the round "Breyer Molding Co." stamp. Some models of this mold also have the "B" stamp; later ones, and possibly the very earliest ones, do not. This mold was never given the "U.S.A." stamp.

"Sargent Pepper" Appaloosa Pony — see under Haflinger

"Satin Star" Drafter Foal — see under Clydesdale Foal

"Scamper" — In a 1987 newsletter, Small World toy company announced: "Preview of '88 Plans . . . There will be two new Artist Series molds: 'John Henry' richest ever thoroughbred gelding and 'Scamper' barrel racer nonpareil." But Breyer's plans for a portrait model of "Scamper," the famous champion barrel racer, were never completed. "Scampers's" owners agreed to let Breyer create a model of him, and the project got as far as the creation of a sculpture by artist Chuck DeHaan. But the sculpture—evidently one of the artist's first attempts at a 3-dimensional work—was awful, so Breyer executive Peter Stone rejected it. "Scamper's" owners resented the collapse of the project and refused ever to cooperate with Breyer again. Stone has told this story at many model-horse events, such as the West Coast Model Horse Collector's Jamboree in August 1993. Stone told me in March 1995 that he had met DeHaan in 1986 through the Potts-Longhorn Leather company, for which DeHaan created ad art and to which Stone sold a special run (see "Adios" SR, chestnut). The "Scamper" model was to be #440, according to an item in the Small World brochure of Fall/Winter 1988. The item continues: "Although it appears there won't be a Breyer model—Scamper IS a champion barrel racing quarter horse. Along with his teenaged female rider/handler he's amassed quite a record in the southwest at barrel racing events. We saw a video in which his bridle broke midway and he completed the course on his own!"

"Scat Cat" Children's Pony — see under Haflinger

Scratching Foal — Filly, standing with legs braced, scratching chin with left hind hoof. Sculpted by Chris Hess. Mold in catalog-run production 1970-86.

Catalog-run models made from this mold:

- Scratching Foal #168, black blanket appaloosa, bald face, unstenciled butt blanket, splashed-on black spots, early ones have 4 stockings, later ones have black legs, black hooves, matte (1970-86). The models with 4 stockings are pictured in the 1970 and 1974 catalogs (catalogs 1972-73 and manuals 1970-73 list but do not picture #168). The version with black legs is shown in the 1974 manual and all subsequent catalogs and manuals through 1986. Some early models might have gray hooves, but I am not sure. The bald face varies in size from very large, covering the forehead and extending down over the sides of the face, to small, just an unstenciled blaze below a black forehead. The model number 168 belonged not only to the appy Scratching Foal but also to the alabaster "Legionario III" as sold in a special blister-wrapped display box during the late 1970s.
- Scratching Foal #169, liver chestnut, bald face, pink nose, black mane and tail, 1-4 stockings, gray hooves on stockinged legs, other hooves dark gray-brown, matte (1970-71). This model is listed but not pictured in any Breyer manual or catalog, so it's impossible to say what assortment of stockings it was "supposed" to have. One of my own models and a few others I've seen have 2 stockings (right hind and right front). Schneider 1992b lists a version with 4 stockings, and collectors Robin Briscoe and Kim Lory Jones own 4-stocking models. I've seen a foal with 1 right hind and 2 front stockings, and I own a model with 1 stocking (right front) and 2 pale chestnut pasterns (right hind and left front).
- Scratching Foal #170, red roan, tan foal with chestnut dappling, dappled face, red chestnut points, no white markings, gray-brown hooves, matte (1970-73). The body shade under the dapples varies from dark tan to pale cream, and the dapples and points vary from a browner chestnut to red chestnut.

Special-run models made from this mold:

- "Brandi" SR, bay blanket appaloosa, blaze, unstenciled blanket covering whole butt and barrel, bay splashed-on spots, black points, 1 right hind stocking, right hind and both front hooves striped tan and gray, left hind hoof brown-charcoal, matte (1995). *Just About Horses* 20th anniversary subscriber special. Sold in set #400195 with SR bay blanket appy "Buster" (Lying Down Foal mold). 2,000 sets made, per *JAH* 22/#1 Jan./Feb. 1995 (back cover). This *JAH* ad refers to the set as "20th Anniversary Special Offer: Buster and Brandi Twin Appaloosa Foal set." The set commemorates the 20th year of publication of *Just About Horses*, which was first published in the fall of 1975. Both foals have "JAH '95" hand-written in black ink on the belly. Numbered certificates of authenticity, signed by Breyer executive Peter Stone and *JAH* editor Stephanie Macejko, were mailed under separate cover. The set number is per Stephanie Macejko, who also clarified for me which foal has which name in this set. "Brandi," a feminine name, belongs to the Scratching Foal, which is identifiably female (according to the criteria for Breyer genders), while "Buster," a masculine name, belongs to the Lying Foal, which is physically of indeterminable gender thanks to its position. The "Brandi" shown in *JAH* has two hind stockings, but my own and Jo Kulwicki's specimens have only a right hind stocking.
- Scratching Foal SR, alabaster; gray mane, tail, and joints; gray hooves; matte (1991). Penney's holiday catalog. Sold in Adorable Horse Foal Set SR #714091, with bay blanket appaloosa Grazing Foal, chestnut Lying Down Foal, and dark rose gray Running Foal. 5,000 sets made. Quantity and set number are per a Breyer company computer printout of activity 1985-92. The name Adorable Horse Foal Set is per the Penney's catalog, but the box in which the foals were packed was marked Fun Foal Set.

Note: The earliest models of the Scratching Foal mold have the round "Breyer Molding Co." stamp only; I own a #169 liver foal like this and have seen others. Later ones have the round stamp and the "U.S.A." stamp—the "U.S.A." must have been added to the mold by 1971, for I own another liver #169 that does have this stamp. Some "U.S.A." models might have the "B" stamp too, but I'm not sure.

"Scribbles" Paint Horse Foal — see under "Sea Star"

Sculptors of Breyer molds — see Sculptors in the Appendix near the end of this book

"Sea Star" — Pony stud colt with no stud colt parts, standing/walking. Sculpted by Chris Hess, design apparently based on a painting by Wesley Dennis. Mold in catalog-run production 1980-87, 1991-95.

Catalog-run models made from this mold:

- Chincoteague Foal #845, buckskin, star, primitive stripes on upper legs, black points, tan hooves, matte (1991-93).
- Marguerite Henry's "Sea Star" #16, red chestnut; star; darker chestnut mane, tail, and hooves; matte (1980-87). This model was also sold in Marguerite Henry's "Misty," "Stormy," And "Sea Star" Set #2169 [1983-85]. Collector Chelle Fulk has a bay "Sea Star"; the model has a "B" stamp, which would date it to the early years of release. Breyer's "Sea Star" represents a real Assateague/Chincoteague pony foal whose story is told by Marguerite Henry in her book *Sea Star: Orphan of Chincoteague*. The book describes "Sea Star" as "a tiny brown colt" (p. 117) with a curly mane and tail (p. 114) and "a crooked star on his forehead" (p. 106). The model number 16 originally belonged to a set with bay Family Arabian Stallion, Proud Arabian Mare, and Proud Arabian Foal; then it belonged to the set with bay Family Arabian Stallion, Mare, and Foal; and next it went to the palomino Family Arabian Foal as sold in a special blister-wrapped display box—all before it was assigned to "Sea Star."
- "Scribbles" Paint Horse Foal #893, chestnut paint, tobiano; stripe; chestnut mane and tail slightly darker than body; 4 stockings; tan hooves; matte (1994-95).

Set: see under "Misty."

Special-run models made from this mold:

- "Cochise" SR, chestnut blanket appaloosa, solid face, dark chestnut mane, dark chestnut tail with light tip, unstenciled butt blanket, splashed-on chestnut spots, dark-shaded knees and hocks, 4 stockings, tan hooves, matte (1995). Made for Toys R Us. Sold in "Geronimo" And "Cochise" set #700695 with SR chestnut blanket appaloosa "Geronimo" (Classic "Kelso" mold) and gold metal medallion on blue ribbon. 4,300 sets made, per *JAH* editor Stephanie Macejko (conversation of July 2, 1996). Stephanie also clarified which model has which name: the foal's name comes second in the set name. The set name and number are per the set's box. The shading on the mane, tail, and legs can be so dark on some models as to make them nearly bay. This set is one of several in the Medallion Series made for Toys R Us; see Medallion Series above in the Traditionals section for a full list and a description of the medallion.

Notes:

(1) Chris Hess took the designs for many of his Breyer sculptures from illustrations and photographs (see the entry for Hess in the Sculptors section of the Appendix near the end of this book). To judge from appearances, I would say that he based the "Sea Star" mold on Wesley Dennis's painting of the foal on the cover of Marguerite Henry's *Sea Star: Orphan of Chincoteague*. Viewed from the left three-quarters angle, Hess's mold looks very much like the illustration, notably the shape and position of the legs, the jug head, the flipped-up tail, and the overall gawky look.

(2) The "Sea Star" mold has the round "Breyer Molding Co." stamp. At least some early models have the "B" stamp in addition, though I do not know whether the very earliest ones do. This mold was never given the "U.S.A." stamp.

"Secretariat" — Stallion, standing, looking left. Sculpted by Chris Hess. Mold in catalog-run production 1987-95.

Catalog-run models made from this mold:

- "Secretariat" Famous Race Horse #435, red chestnut, stripe, slightly darker chestnut mane and tail, 1 right front and 2 hind stockings, 4 gray hooves, matte, Artist Series (1987-95). The models came with a small "Artist Series" brochure telling about sculptor Chris Hess and the real "Secretariat," a famous Thoroughbred racehorse who won the Triple Crown in 1973. The color of #435 varies from medium red chestnut to sandier and browner shades, as on collector Jo Kulwicki's reddish dun model. A variation of #435 has 4 stockings; collectors Heather Hagerstrand and Paula DeFeyter both wrote to me that they have such models. The fourth "stocking," on the left front leg, is typically just a sock. For the origins of #435 see note 1 for this mold.

Special-run models made from this mold:

- "Burmese" Her Majesty The Queen's Horse SR #700435, black, no white markings, black mane and tail, black hooves, semigloss (1990-91). Export special, made for European companies. 500 models made, per Ingrid Muensterer, owner of the German company Modell-Pferde Versand (email of June 1995). A Breyer company computer printout of activity 1985-92 states that this model was "in line 1990-1991," and lists one batch of 144 models, produced in 1990. Other batches must have been made subsequently and omitted from the computer records. The model's box is labeled "No. 700435 Burmese" and sports a large round gold sticker with phrases in English, French, and German (I quote in full): "Let your imagination play! / Laizzez-jouer votre imagination! / Lassen Sie ihrer Phantasie freien lauf! / Burmese / Her Majesty the Queen's Horse." This special was announced in *JAH* 17/#4 Sept./Oct. 1990 (p. 31); the article states that the model represents the real horse "Burmese," a jet black mare given to Queen Elizabeth II by the Canadian Mounted Police. The Queen used to ride the horse when she reviewed her troops. The mare died in July 1990, at the age of 28. Although "Burmese" was a mare, her portrait model is a stallion mold.
- "Secretariat" SR, glossy red chestnut, stripe, slightly darker chestnut mane and tail, 1 right front and 2 hind stockings, 4 gray hooves (1990). Sears holiday catalog. Sold in

Race Horse Set SR #497510, with glossy red chestnut "Man O' War" and glossy blood bay "Sham." 2,000 sets made. This SR "Secretariat" has the same color and markings as the regular-run #435, but with a high-gloss varnish coating, as on glossy Breyers from the 1950s and 1960s. Collector Jo Kulwicki has a variation with the front stocking on the left leg, and another such horse was offered on a sales list by collector Karen Perkins. Megan Thilman Quigley, who worked at Breyer when this SR was issued, mentioned to me that some models are a pale pinkish "hot dog or baloney color"; some of these pinkies were sold at a Breyer warehouse sale. Quantity and set number are per a Breyer company computer printout of activity 1985-92. (A Bentley Sales list of March 15, 1993, wrongly gives the number as #713259, which is actually the number of the 1988 English Horse Collector Set SR.)

- "Secretariat" SR #410435, Golden Charm decorator, solid metallic gold, stripe, gold mane and tail, 1 front and 2 hind stockings, 4 tan hooves, semigloss (1990). Made for signing parties. 3,500 models made. Quantity and model number are per a Breyer company computer printout of activity 1985-92. This model was the first revival of the decorator colors that were issued in the mid-1960s. Unlike the old decorators, which had white manes and tails, the Golden Charm "Secretariat" has a gold mane and tail. I have heard reports that some Golden Charm "Secretariats" have tarnished. The model number for this horse is per price lists from Bentley Sales Co., Mission Supply House, and the German model mail-order company Modell-Pferde Versand.
- "Secretariat" SR #491292, red chestnut, stripe, slightly darker chestnut mane and tail, 1 right front and 2 hind stockings, 4 gray hooves, matte, cold-cast porcelain (1992). Sears holiday catalog. 1,000 models made, but breakage may have reduced this quantity. Numbered by hand on the belly. Models cost $119.00 new from Sears and came with numbered certificate of authenticity signed by Breyer executive Peter Stone. The certificate states: "This fine Breyer model is crafted of cold-cast porcelain, and it is limited to a series of 1,000 serially numbered pieces. The cold-cast *Secretariat* will not be made available again and is a true collector's item." This SR is the same as the regular-run "Secretariat" except for the medium. The term "cold-cast porcelain" is a misnomer; the material is actually plastic resin with marble dust added to it to give the appearance of porcelain (see *JAH* 21/#4 Fall 1994, p. 3). I don't own one of these models, but I received a sales list offering one with cracks in the paint on the face, neck, and crest; the seller commented that she had heard that this cracked-paint condition was common among resin "Secretariats." The model's box says "Made in Taiwan." It also says "Style No. 349-11215"; this is a Sears catalog number, not a Breyer model number. The Breyer number I've given is per *JAH* editor Stephanie Macejko and per a Breyer company computer printout of 1992 SR models.

Notes:

(1) The "Secretariat" mold was sculptor Christian Hess's final contribution to the Breyer line. Hess took his design for this sculpture from a photo of the real "Secretariat" (per Walerius 1991, p. 17, and per former *JAH* editor Megan Thilman Quigley). I do not know the location of the photo in question. Breyer executive Peter Stone commented to me in May 1994 that "Secretariat's" owners were somewhat reluctant to authorize the Breyer model, but Stone persuaded them with an appeal he had found useful in similar situations: "But what about the children?"

(2) The "Secretariat" mold has the "© Breyer Reeves" stamp only.

Selle Français — see under "Touch Of Class"

Semigloss finish — see Finishes in the Appendix near the end of this book

Serenity set SR — see Grazing Mare SR, buckskin; and Lying Down Foal SR, buckskin

"Shah" — see under Family Arabian Foal; Proud Arabian Foal

"Sham" — Stallion, prancing, looking left; mold versions with and without molded-in wheat ear. Sculpted by Rich Rudish. Mold in catalog-run production 1984-94.

Catalog-run models made from this mold:

WHEAT-EAR AND NO-WHEAT-EAR MOLD VERSIONS:

- Marguerite Henry's "Sham" The Godolphin Arabian #410, blood bay; solid face; black points; white spot on back of right hind fetlock; some with wheat ear; most earlier ones with gray hooves, later ones with black hooves; matte and semigloss; Artist Series (1984-88). The models came with a small "Artist Series" brochure telling about sculptor Rich Rudish and the real "Sham," known as the Godolphin Arabian, one of the three foundation stallions of the Thoroughbred breed. His story is told by Marguerite Henry in her book *King of the Wind*, which was sold in a set with #410 through the 1984-85 Penney's and Ward's holiday catalogs. In this book, "Sham" is "red gold" (p. 32) with a white spot on the right hind heel; the spot was "no bigger than an almond" and was regarded as "the emblem of swiftness" (p. 32) by the eighteenth-century Islamic Moroccans who bred him. "Sham" in Henry's story also has a "wheat ear" cowlick on the chest, which was believed to be an ill omen ("It foretells evil," p. 35). Earlier "Sham" models indeed have a wheat ear, but later "Shams" do not (see notes 2 and 3 for this mold). Typical early models also have gray hooves and body color ranging from a deep brownish bay to bright blood bay. Typical later models have black hooves and color ranging from bright blood bay to a bright orange bay (collector Georgeanne Wilcox has one of these, and I have seen others). "Sham" is shown with gray hooves in the 1985-87 catalogs and black hooves only in 1988. However, some black-hoofed models were issued prior to 1988 (collectors Laura Whitney and Colleen Henry got such models new at Christmastime in 1985 and 1986 respectively). Some pre-1988 models have a mixture of black and gray hooves (collector Paula Hecker has such a model). Georgeanne Wilcox's and Jennifer Barnas's non-wheat-ear, black-hoofed models have no white spot on the fetlock, and my wheat-ear, gray-hoofed model has only a very dim gray fetlock spot. Since the white spot is a very small area created by freehand airbrushing, undoubtedly more than a few models have dim or nonexistent spots. Collector Alicia Isicson wrote to me that she has a "Sham" with 4 socks, which she bought new. The 1984 catalog has photos of both the unpainted original clay sculpture of this mold and a painted piece that is either the original clay sculpture or a plaster casting of it. The lore about "three foundation stallions" is oversimplified, according to animal geneticist Patrick Cunningham. He states (1991, pp. 80-81) that 80 foundation animals—stallions and mares—are recognized in the Thoroughbred Stud Book, compiled in 1791. Among these were 10 foundation stallions who together contributed half the genetic makeup of the current population of Thoroughbreds. Among these 10 were the 3 celebrated "pillars of the *Stud Book*": "the Godolphin Arabian (born about 1725), the Darley Arabian (born about 1688), and the Byerley Turk (born about 1690)." These 3 are famous because they "appear in the pedigrees of a remarkably large proportion of the Thoroughbred population." However, continues Cunningham, "a fourth stallion—the Curwen Bay Barb [born about 1699]—should have a place with this famous trio because his genetic contribution is slightly higher than that of the Byerley Turk. . . . These four top stallions donated about one third of the genes in the current population." For a Breyer companion piece to "Sham" that almost happened, see "Grimalkin" in the Dogs & Cats section below. The model number 410 previously belonged to the Showcase Collection issue of the black pinto Western Pony.
- Prancing Arabian Stallion #411, fleabitten gray, white horse with gray flecks, gray mane and tail, pink hooves, matte (1988-90). Typically, earlier models have larger, wilder gray flecks, slightly yellow plastic, and a gray nose. Later models have tiny, delicate flecking, very white plastic, and usually a pink nose (but occasionally white, as on collector Paula DeFeyter's model). Surprisingly, some early #411s have the wheat-ear mold marking on the chest. I have a model like this and have seen several others. See notes 2 and 3 for this mold for discussion.

NO-WHEAT-EAR MOLD VERSION ONLY:

- Prancing Arabian Stallion #812, dark palomino, solid face, white mane and tail, 1 right hind and 2 front stockings, gray hooves, matte (1989-91). The color ranges from a deep golden palomino on earlier models to a bright orangy shade on later models.
- "Rana" The Arab Stallion #863, blue chocolate, solid face, gray- gold mane and tail, 4 stockings, gray hooves, slightly semigloss (1992-93). Called "Rana" The Arab Stallion in the 1992 catalog, "Rana" The Arabian Stallion in the 1993 catalog. The model in the 1992 catalog has gray hooves, and my own model is like this; the one in the 1993 catalog however appears to have brown-gray hooves. This model's body color, which is very dark and rather bizarre, isn't named in the catalogs but is called "slate grey" on a Breyer company computer printout of activity 1985-92.

Sets:

- Arabian Stallion And Frisky Foal set #3162, dappled bay Arabian Stallion, solid face, lighter bay belly, black points, black hooves, matte (Jan. 1 - June 30, 1994). Set also includes gray dun Frisky Foal (Classic-scale Arabian Family Foal mold). Production dates are per the 1994 catalog. The stallion's dapples are muted, being only slightly lighter than the basic body color.
- Arabian Stallion And Frisky Foal set #3163, dappled dark yellow-gray dun Arabian Stallion, solid face, lighter yellow dun belly, black points, gray hooves, matte (July 1 - Dec. 31, 1994). Set also includes light sandy bay Frisky Foal (Classic-scale Arabian Family Foal mold). Production dates are per the 1994 catalog. The stallion's dapples are muted, being a pure gray tone only slightly lighter than the basic body color. On many models I've seen, the color has a green cast, which is not evident on the model in the 1994 catalog. I have heard of a variation with a dappled golden buckskin color and another variation with a blue cast; no such models have crossed my path, however.

Special-run models made from this mold:

WHEAT-EAR MOLD VERSION ONLY:

- "Sham" SR, golden bay, solid face, black points, white spot on back of right hind fetlock, gray hooves, matte (1984). Made for the Heart of America model-horse show in Kansas City, held in June 1984. 24 models made; no more than 23 still exist. I first heard about this SR from a sales ad for one of these "Shams" in *The Hobby Horse News* (Feb./Mar. 1992, p. 45). More recently, model-horse artist Chris Nandell (formerly Cook), who organized the 1984 show where these horses were sold, kindly wrote to me with the story of their origin. "Sham" sculptor Rich Rudish, who was a good friend of Chris's and very interested in the model-horse hobby, planned to attend the show as guest judge of a small all-Arab model event to be held prior to the regular classes. (A photo of Rudish judging at the show is printed in *JAH* XI/#3 1984, p. 12.) About a week before the show, out of the blue, Chris received a box from Breyer containing 24 golden bay "Shams." She had not ordered these pieces and knew nothing about them. An invoice in the box stated, according to Chris, "that this was a no-charge shipment for a 'signing party' with Rich Rudish to be held in conjunction with my show." When she called Rich about the models, they were news to him too, but he noted that he had "been after" Breyer executive Peter Stone to change the red bay color that Breyer had been issuing on "Sham" #410 to the correct golden bay. "Sham" #410 was supposed to be the color of the golden bay "Sham" in Wesley Dennis's original oil painting used for the cover of Marguerite Henry's *King of the Wind*, which painting Rich owned. In this light, the surprise shipment of golden bays naturally led Chris to think that Breyer had heeded Rich's request and that the 24 models were examples of the new regular-issue #410 color. Subsequently it became clear that Breyer had in fact not changed #410, and in retrospect, Chris believes that Peter Stone had the 24 horses specially painted just as a favor to Rich. In any case, at the show, a number of people purchased the golden bays and had Rich sign them on the belly, but not all 24 were sold. Chris knows that at least one of the leftovers was customized—an understandable sacrifice given that show participants believed "Sham" #410 would henceforth be readily available in golden bay. The color description I've given is based on specimens I have seen in person, owned by collectors Connie Bryan, Lani Keller, and Sue Lehman. These horses are not dramatically different from regular-run "Shams" but are definitely a lighter, browner shade of bay.

NO-WHEAT-EAR MOLD VERSION ONLY:

- "Galaxias" SR #710410, dapple gray, star, black points, 2 hind stockings, 4 black hooves, matte, cold-cast porcelain (1991). Penney's holiday catalog. 3,000 models made (per the Penney's catalog and the model's certificate of authenticity). Numbered by hand on the belly. Models cost $99.99 new from Penney's and came with numbered certificate of authenticity signed by Breyer executive Peter Stone. The certificate explains the model's name: "This fine Breyer model is crafted of cold-cast porcelain, and it is limited to a series of 3,000 serially numbered pieces. Dapple grey in color, this Prancing Arabian Stallion embodies the heavens for which he was named: the Galaxy. *Galaxias* will not be made available again and is a true collector's item." The dapples on this model are white paint splashed on over the gray body color. Some models have dapples on the neck and head; others don't. Some models have hand-painted manes and leg markings and others are air-brushed; the hand-painted portions are more sharply outlined. Some models came with a tiny gold "Made in Taiwan" sticker on the bottom of one hoof. Collector Megan Thilman Quigley, who worked at Breyer when this SR was issued, told me that at least some and possibly all of the models were originally painted as well as cast in Taiwan, but the painting was so unsatisfactory that Breyer washed it off and repainted the models at the Breyer factory. The Penney's catalog says this horse is "an authentic hand-painted porcelain horse," but he is not porcelain—he is cold-cast porcelain. This term is itself a misnomer since the material is actually plastic resin with marble dust added to it to give the appearance of porcelain (see *JAH* 21/#4 Fall 1994, p. 3). "Galaxias," like all the plastic models of this mold, has the round "Breyer Molding Co." stamp. The model number for this horse is per a January 1993 price list from Leonard Huffman, of Model Horse Collector's Supply, and per a Breyer company computer printout of 1991 SRs.

"Sham" The Godolphin Arabian Horse SR #701595, blood bay, most with "'95" date stamp molded inside right hind leg; solid face, black points, white spot on back of right hind fetlock, black hooves, matte (1995). Made for the QVC home-shopping cable TV channel's Breyer hour aired January 21, 1995. 1,300 models made (per *JAH* editor Stephanie Macejko, conversation of June 1995). The model's name and number are per the model's box. These horses are colored much the same as some regular-run "Sham" #410s (the #410s varied quite a bit in body color) and, like many #410s, lack the wheat-ear marking. Consequently, the only definite distinction between them is the "'95" date stamp, which is not present on any #410s but is present on most of the SRs. Oddly, some of the SRs lack the date stamp and are thus not physically distinguishable from black-hoofed, non-wheat-ear #410s. Jo Kulwicki and Tanya Parker, among other collectors of my acquaintance, both received SR "Shams" with no date stamp and reported this fact to the model-horse group on Prodigy computer service as soon as they received the models, within a week or two of the QVC show. Jo and some other collectors also got SR palomino Western Horses from this QVC show that likewise did not have a "'95" date stamp as they were supposed to have. When I asked Breyer executive Peter Stone about the situation, he had no idea how the stampless horses could have been issued. The absence of the stamp is perplexing because mold stamps are engraved into the metal injection-molds in which the plastic horses are formed. Unlike a hand-painted detail, which might accidentally be omitted on a model here and there owing to inattention of the painter, a molded-in feature should be present on every single horse. The only plausible explanation, it seems to me, is that some of the SR "Shams" and Western Horses were molded before the date stamp was added to the metal injection-molds. Conceivably some were leftover unpainted pieces of the Arabian Stallion ("Sham") and "Tic Toc" (Western Horse) runs produced in 1994, which inadvertently got mixed in with the horses molded for QVC. This is purely speculation on my part, however.

"Sham" SR, glossy blood bay, solid face, black points, white spot on back of right hind fetlock, black hooves (1990). Sears holiday catalog. Sold in Race Horse Set SR #497510, with glossy red chestnut "Secretariat" and glossy red chestnut "Man O' War." 2,000 sets made. This SR "Sham" has the same color and markings as the regular-run #410 but with a high-gloss varnish coating. As with #410, there is a bright orange bay variation of the glossy SR; I call this the Halloween Sham in honor of his festive orange and black coloration (I own one of these, as do collectors Jo Kulwicki and Linda Bell). Collector Megan Thilman Quigley, who worked at Breyer when this SR was produced, mentioned to me that at least 100-200 of the models lack the white spot on the fetlock. The quantity and set number I've given are per a Breyer company computer printout of activity 1985-92. (A Bentley Sales price list of March 15, 1993, wrongly gives the number as #713259, which is actually the number of the 1988 English Horse Collector Set SR.)

"Sham" SR #410994, liver chestnut, solid face, flaxen mane and tail, 2 hind stockings with gray hooves, front legs liver with darker liver hooves, matte (1994). Made for the West Coast Model Horse Collector's Jamboree in Ontario, California, in August 1994. 550 models made. Quantity and model number are per Jamboree organizer Sheryl Leisure. Many of these horses have dark gray-shaded muzzle, knees, and hocks. The flaxen mane and tail vary from pale towhead to reddish yellow-blond.

"Sham" SR #414091, Wedgewood Blue decorator, solid blue; solid face; white points; gray hooves; matte (1991). Raffle model for BreyerFest East, in York, Pennsylvania, July 1991. 21 models made. 20 were raffled off and 1 was auctioned. The proceeds were donated to the Misty of Chincoteague Foundation and the Hooved Animal Humane Society. (Model number is per a Breyer company computer printout of activity 1985-92; other information is per *JAH* 18/#2 Summer I 1991, p. 15. The printout says only 20 pieces were made.) This model is more turquoise in color than the old Wedgewood Blue decorator regular runs.

Notes:

(1) There is a big photo of the unpainted original clay sculpture of this mold, with unfinished tail, in the 1984 catalog and a smaller photo in the 1985 catalog.

(2) The "wheat ear" on early "Sham" #410s, representing the sinister cowlick on the breast of "Sham" in Marguerite Henry's *King of the Wind*, is located high on the mold's chest, just below and slightly to the right of the windpipe. It is a small engraved design in the shape of an ear of wheat, molded into the plastic. Later "Sham" #410s do not have the wheat ear. An article on "Sham" #410 in *JAH* 20/#5 Winter 1993 (p. 15), which has a close-up photo of the marking, explains why it was eliminated: "The wheat ear was soon removed from the mold—consumers thought it was a flaw in the mold, and in production, workers who thought the same thing tried to smooth out the area." It is not clear just when the marking was removed. The *JAH* quotation says it happened "soon" after the introduction of "Sham" in 1984. But the fact that early Prancing Arabian Stallion #411s (introduced in 1988) have the wheat ear suggests that the marking was removed some months into 1988, the last year of issue for "Sham" #410. However, there is another possible explanation for the wheat-ear #411s: if indeed the wheat ear was removed from the mold prior to 1988, the wheat-ear #411s could have been made from a leftover batch of unpainted "Shams" molded prior to the removal of the wheat ear. As former *JAH* editor Megan Thilman explained to me, because a lot of labor and material are required to start up the injection molding equipment, the company sometimes molds more pieces than are needed for a specific order. Such a batch of excess unpainted wheat-ear "Shams," Megan noted, could have been stored and overlooked for some time in the warehouse, then discovered and turned into #411s in early 1988.

(3) Sculptor Rich Rudish got the idea for "Sham's" pose as he was watching his own 3-year-old chestnut Arab gelding, "Lippy," frisking in the pasture one windy fall day: "Just as he stopped at the fence line, he woofed out a big snort and started to whirl to the left. The wind blew his mane over his neck and his tail over his hip. . . . I knew then that was the way I wanted Sham to look ... challenging, full of life, almost windborne. . . . We know through historical research that Sham was only 14.2 hands high. He was a bay and of the muscular body type that comes through the ancient Kuhaylan strain of Arabian horses. He was referred to as being 'cresty' so I accentuated the arch in his neck and gave him a short back and a compact body. The 'Wheat Ear' hair on his chest, a sign of misfortune, was difficult to duplicate. The white spot on his heel, a sign of speed, is more apparent. I didn't make him too fat since he grew up in the desert and led a rather hard life." (Rudish 1984, pp. 3-4.)

(4) The "Sham" mold has the round "Breyer Molding Co." stamp. It was never given the "U.S.A." stamp. In 1995, a "'95" mold stamp was added to the mold's right hind leg for the production of the only "Sham" model issued that year, namely the SR "Sham" The Godolphin Arabian Horse in blood bay made for QVC TV (see the entry for this model above). This stamp should have been removed from the mold before any further models were issued, but it turned up on some specimens of the bay pinto "Tseminole Wind" SR, the 1996 BreyerFest dinner model (not listed in this book). Undoubtedly these pieces were made from unpainted leftovers of the 1995 run.

"Shane" American Ranch Horse — see under Stock Horse Stallion

"Sheba" — see under Family Arabian Mare; Proud Arabian Mare

"Sheik" — see under Family Arabian Stallion

"Sherman Morgan" — Stallion, prancing, neck arched. Sculpted by Jeanne Mellin Herrick. Mold in catalog-run production 1987-92.

Catalog-run models made from this mold:

Prancing Morgan #835, black, low blaze, black mane and tail, 1 left hind and 2 front stockings, 4 gray hooves, matte (1991-92). Collector Chris Wilder found a 4-stocking variation of this model. The blaze on #835 is identical to that on chestnut #430.

"Sherman Morgan," Son Of "Justin Morgan," #430, red chestnut, low blaze, darker chestnut mane and tail, 1 right hind stocking with gray hoof, other hooves dark gray-chestnut, matte, Artist Series (1987-90). The models came with a small "Artist Series" brochure telling about sculptor Jeanne Herrick and the real "Sherman Morgan," a son of "Justin Morgan," the founding sire of the Morgan breed. *JAH* XIV/#4 1987 (p. 14) states: "Breyer's model of Sherman Morgan, created by Jeanne Herrick, is authorized to be the accepted 'ideal type' Morgan horse by the American Morgan Horse Association," whatever that means (surely the AMHA isn't asking Morgan owners to refer to a plastic model for conformation standards?). This model's blaze is identical to that on #835 black. Collector Blain Kukevitch kindly sent me photos of his #430 "Sherman Morgan" variation with two hind stockings with gray hooves—the stocking on the left hind is short, reaching only to the middle of the fetlock. The model also has an unusually bright red body color that shades to a pale belly. The model number 430 previously belonged to the Showcase Collection issue of the palomino Western Pony.

Special-run models made from this mold:

"Fashionably Late" SR #498092, chocolate sorrel; solid face; flaxen mane, tail, and lower legs; gray hooves; matte and semigloss, cold-cast porcelain (1992). Sears holiday catalog. 1,000 models made. Numbered by hand on the belly. Models cost $119.00 new from Sears and came with numbered certificate of authenticity signed by Breyer executive Peter Stone. The certificate states: "This fine Breyer model is crafted of cold-cast porcelain, and it is limited to a series of 1,000 serially numbered pieces. The cold-cast *Fashionably Late* will not be made available again and is a true collector's item." The Sears holiday catalog calls this model's color "chocolate sorrel, a color uncommon to the Morgan breed." I have seen two variations of this model. One, which Sheryl Leisure told me is the earlier, has a slightly lighter body color, matte finish, and beige mane, tail, and lower legs. The other has a darker color, semigloss finish, and yellow mane, tail, and lower legs. Former *JAH* editor Megan Thilman Quigley mentioned to me that she knows of some models on which the paint is lifting from the left hock. The term "cold-cast porcelain" is a misnomer; the material is actually plastic resin with marble dust added to it to give the appearance of porcelain (see *JAH* 21/#4 Fall 1994, p. 3). The model's box says "Made in Taiwan." It also says "Style No. 349-11221"; this is a Sears catalog number, not a Breyer model number. The Breyer number I've given is per *JAH* editor Stephanie Macejko and per a Breyer company computer printout of 1992 SR models.

"Pride And Vanity" SR #400192, alabaster; mane streaked with pale gray; lower part of tail pale gray; gray-shaded nose, eyes, knees, and hocks; gray hooves (1992/93). *Just About Horses* subscriber special. 1,500 models made (per *JAH* 19/#4 Fall 1992, p. 16). Most have "JAH 1992" written by hand on the belly. (Collector Lynn Isenbarger's model came with a blank belly, apparently an oversight at the factory.) Models came with a numbered certificate of authenticity signed by Breyer executive Peter Stone and *JAH* editor Megan Thilman. The certificate also bears the particular model's registration number (my certificate, e.g., says "This horse is 0094 of 1,500 produced"), and states: "These models were hand-crafted at Breyer in Wayne, New Jersey at the end of Winter 1992." This SR was announced in *JAH* in 1992 but not distributed until early 1993; hence my dating for it. "Pride And Vanity" is the last model that will ever be made from this mold, according to the same *JAH* issue; see note 2 for this mold for details. Only 255 gray Morgans have ever been registered by the American Morgan Horse Association (see *JAH* 20/#1 Spring 1993, p. 5). I've heard a third-hand report of a "Pride And Vanity" with gray fleabites. The model number is per a Breyer company computer printout of activity 1985-92.

Notes:

(1) There are photos of Jeanne Mellin Herrick with either the unpainted original clay sculpture of this mold or plaster casting of it in the 1987 catalog and in *JAH* XIV/#4 1987 (p. 14).

(2) This mold was discontinued after the release of the 1992/93 SR "Pride and Vanity" because of "irreparable damage" to the injection mold (*JAH* 19/#4 Fall 1992, p. 16). Megan Thilman Quigley, who was editor of *JAH* when this SR was produced, told me that the mold suffered from a thinning and collapsing in the throatlatch area, which caused problems in production. Breyer repaired the metal injection-mold several times before deciding for physical and economic reasons to retire the mold. (See Quigley 1995). The thinning is noticeable on the right side of the throatlatch if one compares an early "Sherman Morgan" model with an SR "Pride and Vanity."

(3) The "Sherman Morgan" mold has the "© Breyer Reeves" stamp only.

"Shetan" — see Walter Farley's Black Stallion (under Black Stallion)

Shetland Pony — Mare, standing, tailtip attached to left hock. Sculpted by Chris Hess. Mold in catalog-run production 1960 - current as of 1996.

Catalog-run models made from this mold:

Shetland Pony #21, black pinto, tobiano; bald face; white mane; black tail with white tip; 4 stockings; pink hooves; earlier ones glossy, later ones matte or semigloss (1960-73, 1976). Same pattern as #22 brown pinto. Regarding release date, see note 3 for this mold. Most #21s lack hand-painted eyewhites, but a few glossies with eyewhites are known—collectors Sande Schneider, Heather Hagerstrand, and Sue Lehman have such models. A Breyer price sheet dated November 18, 1968, lists #21 and alabaster #25 with "the attractive matte" finish new for these items. This implies that matte #21 was made for years and thus should be quite common, as is matte #25. But in my experience matte #21 is quite rare, like matte #22. Perhaps Breyer changed its mind in 1968 and issued #21 in matte only later. The black pinto Shetland was reintroduced with a modified pinto pattern as "Midge" in "Our First Pony" set [1984 and 1985] and in Marguerite Henry's "Our First Pony" Gift Set #3066 [1987 - current as of 1996]. One distinctive pattern difference between #21 and the "Our First Pony" models is that the latter have stenciled blazes whereas #21 has an unstenciled bald face, which on earlier models can be extensive. For further details see Marguerite Henry's "Our First Pony" Gift Set #3066, below.

♞ Shetland Pony #22, brown pinto, tobiano; bald face; white mane; brown tail with white tip; 4 stockings; pink hooves; glossy, matte, and semigloss (1960-66, 1970-73). Same pattern as #21 black pinto. Regarding the release date for #22, see note 3 for this mold. Brown pinto #22 is not in the 1970 dealer catalog, but I assume this omission was an error since #22 is in both the price list and the collector's manual for that year. Most #22s are glossy, but mattes do exist—collector Lani Keller has two of them and collector Judy Davinich has one—which undoubtedly date to the early 1970s. Collector Sheryl Leisure told me she has seen semigloss #22s. Catalogs call this model "brown pinto," but the color is lighter than this may suggest, ranging from pale honey palomino to peachy or orangy tan to caramel to medium brown chestnut. The bald face can be extensive, reaching well down the sides of the face. I have heard rumors of a specimen with hand-painted eyewhites but have not actually seen such a model.

♞ Shetland Pony #23, bay, bald face, black points, black hooves, matte (1973-88). It appears from catalogs that models from the first couple of years have dark brown legs and possibly even dark brown mane and tail, but I haven't seen a model like this. For a brief period in the late 1970s #23 was sold in a special blister-wrapped display box with the model number 123 (see Display Boxes above in this section for discussion). The number 123 had previously belonged to the dapple gray Running Mare.

♞ Shetland Pony #25, alabaster; gray mane and tail; pink hooves; earlier ones glossy, later ones matte (1960-72). Regarding release date, see note 3 for this mold. Apparently the matte finish was introduced in 1968: I have a Breyer price sheet dated November 18, 1968, that lists #21 and #25 with an asterisk, which, as a footnote explains, "denotes the attractive matte finish new for these items." The 1968 catalog doesn't mention this however, although it does mention the new matte finish for the Family Arabians.

♞ Shetland Pony #801, bay pinto, tobiano; blaze with pink nose; black mane and tail; legs have high white with no black; pink hooves; matte (1989-91). The models shown in the 1989 catalog and manual have a jagged band of white on the right side between the black mane and brown body color. This band is not present in the 1990-91 catalogs; instead the black and brown meet. Whether any models with the band were actually produced for sale I don't know. If they were, it was only for a few months, for my own model, purchased in September 1989, does not have the band. This model's pinto pattern differs from that of all other pinto Shetlands.

♞ Shetland Pony #857, dark red chestnut, stripe, flaxen mane and tail, 1 left front and 2 hind stockings with tan hooves, other hoof brown, slightly semigloss (1992-94).

♞ Shetland Pony #925, woodgrain, black eyes, no white markings or other color detailing, matte (1960-64). Regarding release date, see note 3 for this mold.

Set:

♞ Marguerite Henry's "Our First Pony" Gift Set #3066, black pinto mare "Midge" (or "Midget"), tobiano; blaze; white mane; black tail with white tip; 4 stockings; pink hooves; matte (1987 - current as of 1996). Set also includes twin foals "Teeny" (black pinto Classic Mustang Family Foal) and "Friday" (bay pinto Classic Arabian Family Foal), and pale tan leather halter and lead for "Midge." The name of the set changed to "Our First Pony" By Marguerite Henry in the 1994-95 catalogs. "Midge's" tack is made in Taiwan, according to the packet that came in my set. Collector Karen Crossley pointed out to me that the halter and lead shown in the 1987 catalog are medium brown. These may be test pieces, for pale tan tack is shown in all subsequent catalogs. This set represents the equine characters in Marguerite Henry's book *Our First Pony*, which is based on real ponies and people, as Ms. Henry discussed in an article in *JAH* (XI/#3 1984, p. 3). Though her article doesn't mention so, the real people in question are Breyer executive Peter Stone and his family, who lived on a farm in Wisconsin at that time. When Ms. Henry heard how Stone's son Paul had replied to an ad in a local paper and ended up with a free pony, she and illustrator Rich Rudish created the book without telling Mr. Stone—so it was a surprise to him when it was published. The photo on the cover of that *JAH* issue shows Paul riding the pony (at full tilt, quirt flailing) in front of the Stones' Wisconsin farmhouse. Mr. Stone told this story during the Breyer hour on the QVC home-shopping cable TV channel on January 21, 1995. During the show, QVC also sold 600 "Our First Pony" sets that were ordinary regular runs but that came in boxes labeled with the special-run number 701695 (per *JAH* editor Stephanie Macejko). Breyer catalogs call this Shetland model "Midget," but the book refers to the pony only as "Midge." The book is not included in set #3066 but was part of the SR "Our First Pony" set sold in 1984 and 1985 (see below). The #3066 "Midge" has the same pinto pattern as the SR "Midge"; the only difference between them is that #3066 has pink hooves whereas the SR has gray-brown hooves, as collector Gale Good pointed out to me. *Pattern variations*: The pinto pattern of #3066 and the SR differs from the pattern of #21. #21 has an unstenciled bald face; a white spot low on the left shoulder, reaching a bit onto the neck; a white spot on the right shoulder that reaches only a short way down the front of the forearm; and a white patch on the hindquarters that remains wide over the croup. #3066 and the SR have a stenciled blaze; a white patch on the left side of the neck coming down from the crest and down the girth in a thin spear; a white patch on the right shoulder that reaches in a long tail down the outside of the forearm; and a white patch on the hindquarters that narrows over the croup and has a thin "spur" on the left hip. On some #3066 and SR mares, the blaze stays wide all the way up to the forelock, as shown in the 1988-89 catalogs; on others, the blaze narrows to a point just below the forelock, as shown in the 1990 and 1993-95 catalogs. Collector Sande Schneider has a matte, pink-hoofed black pinto Shetland with several pattern differences from all the ponies just described. It has a solid black face with white nose, a white patch on the hindquarters that is very wide across the croup and loins, and a white spot on the left shoulder that reaches down the outside of the left forearm. We don't know if this pony is a #3066 variation or something else.

Special-run models made from this mold:

♘ "Our First Pony" set SR, black pinto mare "Midge," tobiano; blaze; white mane; black tail with white tip; 4 stockings; gray-brown hooves; matte (1984 and 1985). Sears holiday catalog. Set also includes pale tan leather halter and lead and Marguerite Henry's book *Our First Pony*. This set does not include the foals that are part of the regular-run Marguerite Henry's "Our First Pony" Gift Set #3066 (see above). The SR "Midge" has the same pinto pattern as the #3066 "Midge" and differs from her only in hoof color, the SR having gray-brown hooves while #3066 has pink. My own SR, which was purchased from Sears in 1984 by collector Becky Brooks, has small, rather dim, oversprayed socks, while many #3066s have higher, clean white stockings. I believe the pony shown in the 1984 Sears catalog is a test color; it differs in pattern from the pony in the 1985 Sears catalog and from my own model and others I've seen.

• Shetland SR?, chestnut (1985). My only source for this pony is Gutierrez 1989, which says about 20-30 models were made for Model Horse Congress in Chicago in 1985. I am skeptical of the existence of this SR; no specimens are known to me. The company that sold special models at the congress shows around that time was Bentley Sales, so I asked company owner Stuart Bentley about chestnut Shetlands. He had no memory of such a model (conversation of Dec. 1995).

Notes:

(1) *JAH* XV/#1 Feb./Mar. 1988 (p. 25) states that there was a palomino Shetland #24, introduced one year after #21, #22, and #25. This information is evidently wrong—there is no such model or model number listed in any Breyer catalog or price list known to me. Some collectors have suggested the #24 was the palomino pinto Shetland, as distinct from the darker shades of #22 brown pinto. But again I find no evidence for this in Breyer catalogs, manuals, and price lists, which do not list a number 24; so I count the palomino pinto as a color variation of #22. It is odd, though, that the Shetland's model numbers jump from #23 to #25. No other Breyer model ever had #24. So what happened to this number?

(2) A glossy black-point gray appaloosa Shetland Pony was discovered by Northern California collector Deb Buckler at an antique shop. Deb brought the pony to the West Coast Model Horse Collector's Jamboree in August 1995, where she kindly allowed me to inspect it. Like the "belly stripe" version of the glossy gray appy Family Arabs of the 1960s, this bald-faced pony has a white belly and gray-shaded forehand and hindquarters, with black spots splashed onto the hindquarters. He has the mold stamps typical of the earliest Shetlands made: a round Breyer stamp and a "CHess" engraving (see note 4 for this mold). A second such pony turned up in 1996, found by the father of another Northern California collector at an antique store in Southern California. I have not seen this second specimen, but reportedly Deb said it was just like hers. Conceivably these two ponies represent a small special run or test run from the early 1960s.

(3) Chris Hess is identified as the sculptor of the Shetland Pony not only in *JAH* XV/#1 Jan./Feb. 1988 (p. 25) but also by a mark on early models of the mold (see note 4 for this mold). The Shetland first appears in the 1960 catalog, and I believe this was the first year the mold was issued, although to my knowledge no 1959 catalog or price list exists to verify this. All Shetland models I've checked, including numerous early ones, have the round "Breyer Molding Co." stamp, which was first issued in 1960 (see Mold Marks in the Appendix near the end of this book). Further, I know of no 1959 magazine ads or department-store catalog ads for the Shetland. Aside from the 1960 catalog, the earliest ads that I know of for the Shetland appear in the May 1961 *Western Horseman* (p. 160), which offered the ponies and other Breyers in "Natural or Wood Grains," and the 1962 Ward's holiday catalog, which sold the ponies in alabaster and woodgrain.

(4) The Shetland Pony mold has the usual round "Breyer Molding Co." stamp but in an unusual place—on the belly. In addition to the round stamp, some early Shetlands have a "CHess" engraving (a mark of sculptor Chris Hess), located inside the right thigh. I believe these models are the earliest ones—a brown pinto that I got in the very early 1960s has the engraving, as does collector Joan Fauteux's brown pinto, which she bought in 1963. Collector Denise Deen's woodgrain Shetland also has the engraving. But the engraving was removed from the mold sometime in the mid to late 1960s—there are models with the round stamp only, and no "CHess" or "U.S.A." I've seen a #21 black pinto like this, and Joan has an alabaster. Next came models that have the round stamp on the belly and the "U.S.A." inside the left thigh—I have a matte alabaster #25 with the "U.S.A.," so we know this stamp was added to the mold no later than 1972. Still later models have the round, the "U.S.A.," and a "B" stamp—collector Lillian Sutphin has a bay #23 with this assortment of stamps, and indeed all models with this assortment should be #23s, for this was the only color made during the "B"-stamp period of 1979-83. Then the "B" was removed from the mold, and models made since then, like the models made just before the "B," have the round and "U.S.A." only.

Shire — ♞ Mare, walking placidly, looking very slightly left. Sculpted by Chris Hess. Mold in catalog-run production 1972-76, 1978-80.

Catalog-run models made from this mold:

♞ Shire #95, dapple gray, no or very few dapples on head and upper neck; bald face; gray nose and ears; gray mane and tail darker than the body; wide dorsal stripe; dark gray knees and hocks; white feathers and hooves; matte and slightly semigloss (1972-73, 1975-76). The bald face can be vague and oversprayed to a pale gray. Many of these models have dark gray shading on the hindquarters and shoulders. Collector Karen Perkins has a glossy dapple Shire which she told me is one of six such mares found by long-time collector and Breyer consultant Marney Walerius at the Breyer factory in Chicago when it closed in 1985. Karen's mare, which I saw at BreyerFest 1995, is a chalky, with painted-on stockings and evidently a white paint basecoat under the gray paint and gloss finish. In color scheme, aside from having a pale gray face rather than bald white, she is quite similar to normal #95s, with a medium gray body color, no or very few dapples on the head and neck, darker gray mane and tail, and dorsal stripe.

♞ Shire #96, honey sorrel; bald face, stenciled and unstenciled versions; brown mane and tail darker than body; white feathers and hooves; matte and semigloss (1972-76, 1978-80). This model's facial pattern comes in two basic versions, which are discernible in catalogs: models produced 1972-76 and 1978 have a big stenciled bald face; models produced 1979-80 have unstenciled bald face. The stenciled face itself comes in two versions: One has a sharp, stenciled jag of brown cutting into the white on the left side of the mare's face and has the white covering the eye on the right side. The other version has no jag on the left side but just a more or less straight line that tends to look unstenciled and has the white only touching the inner corner of the eye on the right. These two stenciled versions cannot be distinguished in catalog photos. The unstenciled bald faces have the same general shape as the stenciled ones, with the white at least partially covering the right eye. The color description "honey sorrel" is from Breyer catalogs and manuals. The body color of #96 varies from dark chestnut, which is more typical of the stenciled-face mares, to a medium/light cinnamon shade, more typical of the newer, unstenciled mares. The mane and tail are always darker than the body but range in shade from charcoal-brown to medium chestnut.

Special-run models made from this mold:

♘ Shire SR, black, bald face, black mane and tail, white feathers, gray hooves, slightly semigloss (1985). Made for the Riegseckers of Indiana. Sold in SR set with reddish bay, palomino with bald face, and smoke gray Shires. 300 sets made, per an announcement for this set in the 1985 Results Program of the IMHCC (International Model Horse Collector's Congress). Collector Heather Wells has a Riegseckers receipt for this set dated November 1985. Some of these horses might have white hooves, but I've seen one with dark gray hooves.

♘ Shire SR, dapple gray, dapples on head and neck; bald face; pink-gray nose and ears; gray mane and tail darker than the body; no dorsal stripe; dark gray knees and hocks; white feathers and hooves; semigloss (1982 and 1983). Ward's holiday catalog. Sold in SR set with black Percheron (Belgian mold). This set is shown not only in the Ward's catalogs but also in *JAH* IX/#2 1982 (p. 13) among the holiday specials for that year.

⊕ Shire SR, palomino, bald face, light yellow mane and tail, white feathers, gray hooves, slightly semigloss (1985). Made for the Riegseckers of Indiana. Sold in SR set with black, reddish bay, and smoke gray Shires. 300 sets made, per an announcement for this set in the 1985 Results Program of the IMHCC (International Model Horse Collector's Congress). Collector Heather Wells has a Riegseckers receipt for this set dated November 1985. This palomino model is an unrealistic bright yellow color.

⊕ Shire SR, palomino, stripe, gray-shaded muzzle, white mane and tail, white feathers, gray hooves, matte (1992). Sears holiday catalog. Sold in Drafters Set SR #497092, with liver chestnut "Roy" and alabaster Belgian. 2,250 sets made. Quantity and set number are per a Breyer company computer printout of activity 1985-92. (The number 11216, given for this set on the Bentley Sales price list of March 15, 1993, is the Sears number, not the Breyer number.) This Shire is a realistic, deep golden palomino color—that is, the color is a realistic shade of palomino, though palomino is not a realistic color for a Shire.

⊕ Shire SR, reddish bay, bald face, black points, white feathers, white hooves, slightly semigloss (1985). Made for the Riegseckers of Indiana. Sold in SR set with black, palomino with bald face, and smoke gray Shires. 300 sets made, per an announcement for this set in the 1985 Results Program of the IMHCC (International Model Horse Collector's Congress). Collector Heather Wells has a Riegseckers receipt for this set dated November 1985. The Results Program incorrectly lists this horse as "red sorrel chestnut" and the gray horse as "dapple Gray." The program was probably published before the horses were actually produced, and it may well list the colors initially ordered by Riegseckers but subsequently changed.

⊕ Shire SR, smoke gray, bald face, darker gray mane and tail, white feathers, gray hooves, slightly semigloss (1985). Made for the Riegseckers of Indiana. Sold in SR set with black, reddish bay, and palomino with bald face Shires. 300 sets made, per an announcement for this set in the 1985 Results Program of the IMHCC (International Model Horse Collector's Congress). Collector Heather Wells has a Riegseckers receipt for this set dated November 1985. The Results Program incorrectly lists this horse as "dapple Grey"; see Shire SR reddish by for discussion.

Notes:

(1) The Shire is an unusually heavy mold because of her large size and her magnificently feathered legs, which are solid plastic. Her heftiness got her discontinued as an economy measure for a year during the oil-crisis era of the 1970s. Breyer's cellulose acetate plastic is not a petroleum product but did become scare during that period. For discussion see the Breyer Company History section below in the Appendix.

(2) The Shire mold has "C.HESS .71" (referring to sculptor Chris Hess and the year he created this mold) stamped inside the off stifle above the round "Breyer Molding Co." and "U.S.A." stamps. Some models have the "B" stamp in addition (my #96 with unstenciled bald face has a "B").

Shire Horse — ♞ Mare, prancing, tail swung out, neck arched, head tucked, looking left; raised hooves have molded frogs. Sculpted by Kathleen Moody. Mold in catalog-run production 1993-95.

Catalog-run models made from this mold:

♞ Fine Porcelain Shire Horse #79193, dark dappled bay, blaze that goes wide over the muzzle, tri-color eyes with white "sparkle," black points, 1 right front and 2 hind stockings with brown hooves, other hoof black, painted-on silver shoes, matte (1993-95). Models cost $140-$185 retail and came with numbered certificate of authenticity signed by Breyer executive Peter Stone and sculptor Kathleen Moody. These horses were not limited to a designated quantity in advance, but the final quantity made was approximately 2,200 models, per Breyer executive Peter Stone (conversation of July 1995). The Shire is the second model in the Evolution Of The Horse series of fine porcelain horses; for discussion, see Evolution Of The Horse series above in the Traditionals section. The Shire's dapples are muted, being nearly the same color as the body. The bottom of the Shire's box says "Made in Taiwan," and many models come with a small white "Made in Taiwan" sticker on the body or hoof. The hoof color may vary, but I have seen a model with hooves as described above. For an explanation of the model numbers of Breyer's fine porcelains, see the entry for the Icelandic Horse.

Notes:

(1) The 1993 catalog calls this mold "he," but *JAH* 20/#4 Fall 1993 (p. 11) calls it a mare. In person, it looks like a mare: what bulge there is on the mold's underside is situated and shaped like a mare's udder, not a gelding's or stallion's sheath.

(2) The Shire Horse mold has a "© Breyer Reeves" engraving inside the right hind leg and a "'93" engraving inside the left hind leg.

Shire Mare, standing — see under Clydesdale Mare

Showcase Collection — This series, produced 1970-72, comprised a large number of ordinary regular-run Traditional horse models, 54 in all, packaged in special carrying-case boxes made of "sparkling clear plastic—clean, pilferage free, and eye appealing," according to 1970-72 Breyer Showcase Collection brochures. This packaging allowed the discriminating customer (and wary shopkeeper) to view the models in the store and provided the purchaser with a convenient case "for stabling or hauling" (1971-72 manuals). Each carrying case has a molded-in handle and self hinges along the bottom. The word "Breyer" is molded into the side in large letters. To judge from the photos in the publications cited above, the earliest cases were decorated with a blue-ribbon sticker and had nothing in the case to keep the horse from rattling around at liberty. By 1971, the cases featured a rectangular sticker containing the blue-ribbon logo and the words "Showcase Collection by Breyer / made in USA" and had a Styrofoam insert in the bottom of the case to minimize the model's rattling room. In 1995, collector Sande Schneider purchased a buckskin Western Prancer in unopened Showcase Collection box, which she kindly allowed me to inspect. The case had a thick Styrofoam insert in the bottom and contained a 1971 Breyer collector's manual. Not surprisingly, the "sparkling clear plastic" had yellowed over the decades. What did surprise me, however, was its flimsiness. The brochures' lovely photos and enticing talk of "stabling or hauling," "play and transport" had led me to expect something sturdy, a thin Plexiglas perhaps. But the reality, as Sande observed, fell more into the genre of the molded-plastic trays in cookie packages that keep the marshmallow pinwheels from sticking together.

The models in the Showcase Collection were assigned special numbers, which generally consisted of the model's normal number with either one or two zeros added on the right—thus all Showcase Collection numbers had either three or four digits. For instance, the palomino Family Arabian Mare, whose usual number was #5, became #500 as a Showcase model; black pinto Western Pony #41 became #410; buckskin Indian Pony #176 became #1760; "Adios" #50 became #5000; alabaster Running Foal #130 became #1300. Sande's buckskin Western Prancer #111 has the number #1110 stamped on the Styrofoam base inside his Showcase carrying case. The only exceptions to this numbering system were the bay Family Arabian Stallion #13 and alabaster Family Arabian Mare #8, whose Showcase Collection numbers had zeros to the left as well as to the right: #0130 and #0800. All numbers in the series are mentioned in this book's entries for the particular models and are listed in the Models By Number section at the end of the book.

The Showcase Collection is not mentioned in the 1970 catalog, manual, or regular price list but is announced in a separate brochure dated 1970, as noted above. (A photo from this brochure is reprinted in *JAH* 18/#3 Summer II 1991, p. 30, and 18/#4 Fall 1991, p. 14.) The series is advertised in the 1972 catalog and 1971-72 manuals and in Showcase Collection brochures (see photo reprinted in *JAH* 22/#6 Nov./Dec. 1995, p. 24), but no trace of it is to be found in the 1973 or subsequent catalogs and manuals. According to Breyer executive Peter Stone, the Showcase packaging was discontinued because it cost too much and thus didn't sell well and was not worth the bother of having to keep two separate inventories of model (conversation of Oct. 4, 1995). For other types of display packaging used by Breyer, see Display Boxes above in the Traditionals section.

Show specials — see Signing Party Specials

Show Stance Morgan — see under Morgan, stretched

"Sierra" SR — see under Fighting Stallion

Signing Party Specials / Breyer Show Specials — In the Traditionals section see "Lady Phase" SR, red roan (1989); "Secretariat" SR, Golden Charm (1990); and "Raven" SR (1991; under Saddlebred Weanling); and "Kaleidoscope" SR (1995; under Trakehner). In the Classics section below see Arabian Family Foal SR, dark shaded chestnut (1988); "Johar" SR, rose alabaster (1988); Bucking Bronco SR, black paint (1992); "Little Chaparral" SR (1993, see under Rearing Stallion); and "Silver Comet" SR (1994, see under Polo Pony).

Signing parties were Breyer promotional events held at toy stores and tack shops across the nation. At these events, Breyer executive Peter Stone, son of one of the founders of Breyer Animal Creations, met with collectors and autographed their models on the belly. Signing parties were first held in 1983 and became hugely popular in the following years. Starting in 1988, Breyer produced a "signing party special" model each year, which was available only at these events and via mail order from the dealers sponsoring the events. After 1990, which was the busiest ever signing-party year, with about 95 parties, symptoms of carpel tunnel syndrome forced Stone to stop attending these events for the most part. (Information per a 1990 Breyer company "Signing Party Tour" news release and *JAH* 20/#3 Summer II 1993, p. 13; also see *JAH* XIII/#2 1985, pp. 11, 12.) However, Breyer has continued to make a "show special" model each year that is available to toy stores, mail-order companies, and model-horse shows for promotional purposes.

Also in 1990 Mr. Stone launched the "Breakfast with Peter Stone" events, which had their own SR models. The first of these events to my knowledge was a breakfast held in October 1990 at Hobby Center Toys in Ohio, where attendees received leftover 1985 SR red sorrel Little Bits American Saddlebreds. This same SR was given out at 1992 Breakfast events in San Antonio and at the Spokane, Washington, Bon Marché store. Whether other Breakfasts took place in 1990-92 I am not sure, but at least two were held in 1993, at toy stores in Ramsey, New Jersey, and Seattle, Washington. Most attendees of the 1993 events received an SR light bay Little Bits Morgan Stallion, but a few people at the Seattle event got a 1989 SR reddish bay Little Bits Thoroughbred Stallion owing to short supplies of the Morgan Stallion.

Mr. Stone enlarged upon the "Breakfast" idea with his "Breyer Tour," a series of breakfast, brunch, and barbecue events around the country. On Stone's first Breyer Tour, which took place in 1994, attendees received "Ofir" SR (Traditional Black Stallion mold); on the 1995 Breyer Tour, attendees received "Rawhide" SR (Mustang mold).

"Silver Comet" SR — see under Polo Pony below in the Classics section

"Silver" Quarter Horse SR — see under Quarter Horse Gelding

Six-month catalog runs — see Half-Year Catalog Runs

"Skeeter" SR — see under "Stormy"

"Skipster's Chief" — see under Stock Horse Stallion

Sky Blue Unicorn SR — see under Running Stallion

"Smoky" — ♞ Gelding, with brand, looking left, legs all braced out, mane and tail flying. Sculpted by Chris Hess, design based on a drawing by Will James. Mold in catalog-run production 1981-85.

Catalog-run models made from this mold:

♞ "Smoky" The Cow Horse #69, steel gray, blaze, black mane and tail, most with 4 stockings and gray hooves, matte (1981-85). In the same years, this horse was also sold in "Smoky" The Cow Horse Gift Set #2090. The blaze is sometime faint. Most "Smokys" have 4 stockings and gray hooves, as shown in the 1981-84 catalogs. The latest ones, however, have 1 stocking (left hind), 3 black legs, and 4 tan hooves, as shown in the 1985 catalog. This model represents the title character in a book by cowboy writer and artist Will James, *Smoky, the Cow Horse*, published in 1926. In the book, "Smoky" is a range horse of mainly mustang heritage, belonging to the Rocking R cattle ranch. He was born black but by the time he was 3 had a coat like "fine mouse colored silk" (p. 47). He had a blaze and some stockings; the book isn't clear on this point. The text just says "His blazed face loomed up snow white and to match his trim ankles" (p. 47), and the illustrations show him sometimes with 4 stockings and sometimes with fewer. Three movies entitled *Smoky* have been made from James's book; the first was released in 1933 (I don't know who was in it), the next in 1946 (starring Louis Kind and Fred MacMurray), and the last in 1966 (starring George Sherman and Fess Parker). The model number 69 previously belonged to the silver gray Poodle.

Set:

• "Smoky" The Cow Horse Gift Set #2090, steel gray horse and book *Smoky, the Cow Horse*, by Will James (1981-85). In the same years, this model was also sold separately as "Smoky" The Cow Horse #69. The 1981 Ward's and Penney's holiday catalogs offered a similar set, which included the horse, book, and a cloth bareback pad with leather surcingle. The Ward's catalog shows the pad as red. The Penney's photo shows the horse wearing a leather bridle as well as the bareback pad, but the item description mentions only the pad, so the bridle might not have been included.

Special-run models made from this mold:

- Collector's Unicorn SR, flocked white; painted black eyes; red in nostrils; powder-gray synthetic hair mane, tail, and beard; gold and white striped unicorn horn; painted black hooves (1984). Penney's holiday catalog. Flocking and hairing by the Riegseckers of Indiana (see Riegseckers Models for discussion). The horn was undoubtedly added by the Riegseckers too, so I don't regard it as a true Breyer mold variation. The specimens I have seen in person all had painted black eyes, but some may have brown glass eyes, as the model shown in *JAH* XI/#3 1984 (p. 19) appears to have. Penney's priced this SR Unicorn at $25.99. Starting in January 1986, leftovers appeared on Bentley Sales Company price lists as #69FLK (for "flocked"), for $3.99 each, "no limit—at this low price, all sales final." Old Bentley's sales record cards in my possession reveal the reason for the big sale: Bentley's received 588 of these models—a grand quantity for leftovers.

Notes:

(1) To judge from appearances, sculptor Chris Hess took his design for this mold from Will James's drawing of "Smoky" in James's book *Smoky, the Cow Horse* (1926, p. 235). The poses are quite similar, even to the arrangement of the mane and tail. The chief difference between them is that James's horse has his hind legs more under him, in a somewhat of a squat.

(2) This mold has a Rocking R brand engraved on the near shoulder. This is the brand of the Rocking R Ranch, "Smoky's" home in Will James's book.

(3) The "Smoky" mold has the round "Breyer Molding Co." stamp. Some models also have the "B" stamp, on the same leg as the round stamp. This mold was never given the "U.S.A." stamp.

Sorrel Appaloosa Horse SR — see under Performance Horse

Sorrel Quarter Horse Stock Mare — see under Stock Horse Mare

Spanish Barb — see under "Buckshot"; also see next entry

Spanish Barb — Stallion, walking, looking left, one ear forward and one back; raised hooves have molded frogs. Sculpted by Kathleen Moody. Mold in catalog-run production 1994-95.

Catalog-run models made from this mold:

- Fine Porcelain Spanish Barb #79194, pale tan dun, broken stripe, gray shading on head, brown and black eyes with white "sparkle" and pink corners, dark chestnut points, primitive stripes on forearms and gaskins, 1 right front stocking, right front hoof is pink-tan with a black stripe, other hooves gray, matte (1994-95). Models cost $105-$130 retail and came with numbered certificate of authenticity signed by Breyer executive Peter Stone and sculptor Kathleen Moody. These horses were not limited to a designated quantity in advance, but the final quantity made was approximately 2,200 models, per Breyer executive Peter Stone (conversation of July 1995). This is the third and last model in the Evolution Of The Horse series of fine porcelains; for discussion, see Evolution Of The Horse series above in the Traditionals section. The Barb's color is called "slate grullo" in *JAH* 21/#1 Spring 1994 (inside front cover). The bottom of the Barb's box says "Made in Taiwan," and at least some models come with a small white "Made in Taiwan" sticker on the body or hoof. For an explanation of the model numbers of Breyer's fine porcelains, see the entry for the Icelandic Horse.

Note: The Spanish Barb mold has "© Breyer Reeves" engraved inside the right thigh and "'94" engraved inside the left thigh.

"Spanish Pride" — see under "Legionario"

"Special Delivery" SR — see State Line Tack '95 "Special Delivery" SR (under Running Mare)

Special runs (SRs) — See the Special Run listings for each mold. For listings and further discussion of particular categories of SRs, see "Breakfast with Peter Stone" Specials (in the Little Bits section); BreyerFest SR Models; Cold-Cast Porcelain (Resin) Models; Decorators (1960s); Decorators (post-1960s); Export Specials; Flocked Models; Jamboree Specials; *Just About Horses* Subscriber Specials; Mid-Year And Summer Specials; QVC And Q2 Specials; Signing Party Specials; and Toys R Us Specials.

Special runs are batches of models painted in a special-order color for sale at events and through mail-order companies, toy stores, department store holiday catalogs, livestock associations, and tack shops. These models are produced in limited quantities—from a dozen or two to several thousand—and are not listed in Breyer catalogs or manuals.

It is impossible to say for sure what the very first special run was since contemporary documentation on early specials is extremely scarce and hobby sources conflict about them. Some special runs were apparently made in the late 1950s and early 1960s. The white Boxer, although his status as SR is uncertain, was issued in the 1950s (see in the Dogs & Cats section). Also early are a few woodgrain models that I categorize as SRs because they are not in Breyer catalogs or price lists: the woodgrain Black Angus Bull (polled, walking) and Elephant, both of which probably came out in 1959 or the early 1960s, and the woodgrain Buffalo, which followed shortly thereafter (see in the Wildlife section). The SR matte medium chestnut Family Arabians and the SR Wedgewood Blue "Fury" Prancer were all 1960s SRs. Even the 20 original decorator horses from the 1960s might have been released as SRs (see Decorators [1960s]). The SR "white" (actually light smoke gray) Buffalo probably appeared in about the mid-1970s. The bay Morgan with solid face is another early special, having been produced in the early or mid 1970s. The first SR Stablemate known to me, a palomino Arabian Stallion called "Emperor's Gold Bar," was made sometime in the period 1975-80. The SR black Family Arabian Stallion, Mare, and Foal were produced in 1977 and distributed to retail shops nationally as a promotion. The black blanket appy Pony Of The Americas SR also probably appeared in the late 1970s. SR hogs painted on the "Jasper" mold came out in 1979 or a year or two thereafter. The specials just mentioned were issued to persons or businesses having nothing in particular to do with the model-horse hobby community. The production of specials made specifically for sale to Breyer collectors came into its own in the later 1970s thanks to the growth of model-horse shows, particularly the Model Horse Congresses held in the Midwest in that period (see Walerius 1991, p. i). The SR Black Angus Calf was sold at the Congress in 1977. The SR solid black Mustang was issued in 1978 for Congress, where leftover black Family Arab sets were also sold. In 1979 the first SR buckskin "Lady Phase" was made for the model mail-order company VaLes Bead Trailor of Arizona to sell at the ValSun live show in Arizona, and three special-run dapple gray draft models, made for Bentley's to sell at Congress: Belgian, Clydesdale Stallion, and Clydesdale Mare. The first SR dapple Clydesdale Foal, and other SRs as well, appeared in 1980.

Department store holiday catalogs—Sears, Penney's, Montgomery Ward, and Aldens—carried Breyer regular runs as early as the 1950s. It is possible that the first specials sold through such catalogs were the original decorator horses, which evidently debuted in a Ward's holiday catalog of the early 1960s. Aside from this, to my knowledge the first specials sold through such catalogs were the 1981 sets with SR Pacers and sulkies: the Sears set had a bay Pacer, the Penney's set a light golden chestnut. The following year brought an avalanche of holiday catalog SRs from Sears, Penney's, Aldens, and Ward's. That year, 1982, was not only the first but the last for Aldens SRs, for the store declared bankruptcy in the midst of the 1982 holiday season (per Walerius 1991, p. 99). Ward's continued to offer Breyer SRs through 1985, after which time its mail-order catalog went out of business too. Sears sold SRs through 1992, then closed down most of its catalog business—although in 1995 Sears issued a holiday catalog once again, albeit with nary a Breyer (per collector Georgeanne Wilcox's Haynet report of Sept. 1995). The Penney's holiday catalog is still going strong, with a generous annual offering of Breyer specials. The Spiegel holiday catalog offered Breyer SRs—among them the "stealth" pale dapple gray "Pluto"—for the first time in 1993 but has carried only regular runs since then.

Three other large-scale retailers have offered Breyer SRs in recent years. The U.S.-based international chain store Toys R Us has carried regular runs for years but got its first SR, the Classic SR Lipizzaner #620, in 1992. American Toys R Us stores sold their first SRs in 1993 and have had several more since then. (See Toys R Us Specials for a complete list.) The QVC home-shopping cable TV channel sold Breyers for the first time ever on a "Collector's Day" show in January 1995, offering two SRs: blood bay "Sham" and palomino Western Horse, both with molded-in date stamp. The Q2 home-shopping channel, sister channel to QVC, sold Breyers in July and August 1995 (a couple of shows in November sold leftover models). See QVC And Q2 Specials for a complete list and further discussion.

"Speck" — see under Family Arabian Mare; Proud Arabian Mare

"Spice" — see under Running Foal

Spirit Of The East Gift Set SR — see Running Foal SR, alabaster; Running Mare SR, alabaster

Spirit Of The West set SR — see "Lady Phase" SR, bay paint; Stock Horse Foal, standing, SR, bay paint

Spirit Of The Wind Mare And Foal Set SR — see Family Arabian Mare SR, dapple gray; and Family Arabian Foal SR, dapple gray

Sport Horse & Canongate Saddle Set SR — see under "Morganglanz"

"Spot" — see under Family Arabian Foal; Proud Arabian Foal

"Spotted Bear" Indian Pony SR — see under "San Domingo"

Stallion Mare (*sic*) And Foal Set SR — see Action Stock Horse Foal SR, bay; and Stock Horse Stallion SR, rose alabaster

Standing Quarter Horse Stallion — see under "Adios"

Standing Stock Horse Foal — see Stock Horse Foal, standing; also see under "Phantom Wings"

"Starlight" — see under Jumping Horse

State Line Tack '95 "Special Delivery" SR — see under Running Mare

"Steel Dust" SR — see under Proud Arabian Mare

Stickers — For stickers affixed to older Breyer models, see Stickers & Hang Tags in the Appendix near the end of this book. For puffy and other play stickers, see Brenda Breyer Horse Stickers above in this section and Dapples Deluxe Rider Set (under "Amazement") in the Dapples section.

Stock Horse Foal, old mold — see under "Phantom Wings"

Stock Horse Foal (SHF) — Standing square, colt, looking left. Sculpted by Chris Hess. Mold in catalog-run production 1983-94.

Catalog-run models made from this mold:

- American Buckskin Stock Horse Foal #224, buckskin, solid face, charcoal/gray nose, black points, black hooves, matte (1987-88). This foal is indistinguishable from the solid-faced version of the Penney's 1983-84 SR buckskin SHF.
- Appaloosa Stock Horse Foal #234, gray blanket appaloosa, most with bald face, unstenciled butt blanket, black splashed-on spots, black points, most with black hooves, matte and semigloss (1983-86). Three black-legged gray appy SHF versions with different facial markings are known: [A] Star and gray or black hooves. A foal with star and gray hooves is shown on the back cover of the 1983 catalog; this version is identical to the 1983 Sears SR, but evidently some were sold as regular runs in toy shops, for collector Alicia Coolidge got one at a Circus World Toys. Collector Linda Bell has a star-faced model with black hooves. [B] Bald face and black hooves, shown in the 1985-86 Breyer catalogs. Identical foals were sold through the 1983 Penney's holiday catalog. [C] Solid face and black hooves, not shown in any catalog; I own this version. Maestas 1987c notes the solid-faced foal as a regular-run variation, but possibly some were also sold as a variation of the 1983 Sears or Penney's SR. Collectors Lillian Sutphin and Sande Schneider wrote to me that their solid-faced foals have medium gray spots on the blanket rather than black spots; this variation does not appear in catalogs. The 1983-84 catalogs show a foal with a star, 4 stockings, and gray hooves (it's the same photo in both catalogs), but evidently this is a test color; to my knowledge models with stockings were not produced for sale. *Breyer Collector's Video* shows only black-legged foals, and long-time collector Gale Good told me that she has never heard of one with stockings.
- Bay Quarter Horse Stock Foal #228, bay, solid face, black points, 2 hind stockings or 4 stockings, gray hooves on stockinged legs, other hooves black, matte (1983-88). Called Bay Quarter Horse Stock Foal in the 1983-86 catalogs, American Quarter Horse Foal in 1987-88. The body color ranges from dark/medium brown bay to fairly light

sandy bay and can have a lot of nice shading; my own 2-stocking foal is a shaded sandy bay-buckskin color. #228 is shown with only 2 hind stockings on the cover of the 1983 catalog, with 4 stockings inside the 1983-84 catalogs, and again with 2 hind stockings inside the 1985-88. A variation with no stockings is shown in Diederich 1988, Section 1. I have seen a 2-stocking foal with black hooves rather than gray on the stockinged legs.

- Family Appaloosa Foal #861, bay blanket appaloosa, stripe, unstenciled butt blanket, bay splashed-on spots, black points, 1 right front and 2 hind stockings with tan hooves, other hoof black, matte (1992-94).
- Paint Horse Foal #809, liver chestnut paint, overo; stripe with pink nose; slightly darker liver mane and tail; 2 hind stockings with gray hooves; front hooves dark brown; matte (1989-90). Same pinto pattern as Paint Horse Foal #844.
- Paint Horse Foal #844, light chestnut paint, overo; stripe with pink nose; slightly darker chestnut mane and tail; 2 hind stockings with gray hooves; front hooves gray-brown; matte (1991-92). Same pinto pattern as Paint Horse Foal #809.
- Pinto Stock Horse Foal #231, black paint, tobiano; stripe; 4 stockings; gray hooves; matte (1983-88). Called Pinto Stock Horse Foal in the 1983 catalog, Paint Stock Horse Foal in 1984-86, American Paint Horse Foal in 1987-88.

Special-run models made from this mold:

- "Night Vision" SR, bay snowflake leopard appaloosa, dark bay foal with small, light gray splashed-on spots; solid face; black points; 2 hind socks with tan hooves; front hooves tan with gray stripes; slightly semigloss (1992). Made for Black Horse Ranch. Sold in SR set #410392 with black "Night Deck" ("Lady Phase" mold). 1,500 sets made. Most sets came with a numbered certificate of ownership signed "Karen Grimm" either personally by Karen Grimm, of Black Horse Ranch, owner of the real horses represented by this set, or by BHR employees (employee initials appear on at least some of the latter certificates). Most of the models are numbered in gold on the belly by BHR (per BHR employee Heather Wells). The style of numbering varies on both the mares and the foals: many are double-numbered, with the particular set's number followed by a slash and the run total (the abbreviation "S/N," for "set number," is sometimes present and sometimes not); but some are single-numbered, having only the set's number and no run total (e.g., collector Karen Crossley's "Night Vision" is numbered simply "S/N 884"). Approximately 20-30 unnumbered sets and a few sets with mismatched numbers, all without certificates, were sold in the mid-1990s; these were the last of the 1,500-set run (per Heather Wells). The real "Night Vision" was named world champion appaloosa filly in 1991, and in the same year her dam, "Night Deck," was named world champion appaloosa broodmare. "Night Vision's" sire is world and national champion stallion "Dreamfinder." Information is per the certificate of ownership and a BHR ad in *Model Horse Trader*, May 1992. The set number is per a Breyer company computer printout of activity 1985-92.
- Stock Horse Foal SR, bay paint, overo; stenciled wide blaze covering muzzle; black points; 1 right front and 2 hind stockings with tan hooves; other hoof black; matte (1992). Sears holiday catalog. Sold in Spirit Of The West set SR #492092, with bay paint "Lady Phase." 4,500 sets made. Quantity and set number are per a Breyer company computer printout of activity 1985-92. The foal shown in the Sears catalog must be a test color; it has a stenciled extensive bald face, while the foals actually produced have only a wide blaze.
- Stock Horse Foal SR, buckskin, bald or solid face, charcoal/gray nose, black points, black hooves; matte (1983 and 1984). Penney's holiday catalog. Sold in Quarter Horse Mare And Foal Set SR with matching buckskin "Lady Phase." Collectors Sheryl Leisure and Karen Malcor got the solid-faced version of this SR mare and foal set. The foal is indistinguishable from regular run #224 solid-faced buckskin foal. The bald-faced mare and foal set is pictured in *JAH* X/#3 1983 (p. 13) and possibly in the 1984 Penney's holiday catalog (the photo is a dismally small, side-view shot). The set pictured in the 1983 Penney's holiday catalog shows a star-faced "Lady Phase" and a solid-faced buckskin Running Foal. The standing SHS was the foal actually sold in the set. See "Lady Phase" SR buckskin (1983 and 1984), Running Mare SR buckskin, and Running Foal SR buckskin for further discussion.
- Stock Horse Foal SR, gray blanket appaloosa; some with star and gray hooves, some with bald face and black hooves; black points; unstenciled butt blanket; black splashed-on spots; black hooves; matte and semigloss (1983). Sears and Penney's holiday catalogs. Sears sold the star-faced foal in a set with SR gray blanket appaloosa Stock Horse Mare and Stock Horse Stallion. Penney's sold the bald-faced foal in the Assorted Mare And Foals Stable Set with SR reddish bay Proud Arabian Mare, SR reddish bay Proud Arabian Foal, and regular-run "Phantom Wings" #29. The Sears catalog shows this appy foal with a star, and collector Gale Good's model that she got from Sears is like this. The Penney's catalog picture is small and dim, but the foal seems to have a bald face, and Gale's foal from Penney's does have a bald face. Both the star and bald versions are indistinguishable from the star and bald versions of regular-run #234. The Sears catalog shows the star-faced foal with black hooves, but to my knowledge they came with gray hooves. See the entry for #234 for further discussion of gray appy SHF variations.
- Stock Horse Foal SR, pale smoke gray, bald face, mane and tail striped with medium and light gray, pink ears and nose, medium gray legs and hooves, matte (1993). Made for Toys R Us in the U.S. Sold in The Watchful Mare And Foal set SR #700593, with alabaster "Lady Phase." 18,000 sets made (per Breyer executive Peter Stone, cònversation of Aug. 24, 1995). This set was sold in a normal plastic-front Breyer box with a large round gold sticker on front saying, in full: "1993 Special Collector Edition / Limited Production / The Watchful Mare & Foal / This highly collectible edition represents the ideal type American Quarter Horse." The stripes on the foal's tail are horizontal; the stripes on the mare's tail are vertical. On the several dozen sets I've seen, the foal is typically darker than the mare, I have seen one or two of these foals that are the same alabaster color as the mare. The intensity of the foal's mane and tail striping also varies, and some models lack it altogether.
- Stock Horse Foal SR, palomino, bald face, white points, gray hooves, matte (1983). Ward's holiday catalog. Sold in Palomino Horse And Foal Set SR with palomino Foundation Stallion. The bald face isn't shown clearly in the Ward's catalog photo, but it is clear in *JAH* X/#3 1983 (p. 12), and collector Karen Malcor's foal has a bald face, which is slightly off-center. Bentley Sales Company sold leftovers of these models in 1985: 25 foals and 29 stallions, per Bentley's sales record cards in my possession.

Notes:

(1) This mold is sometimes called the "new mold" Stock Horse Foal because it replaced the "old mold" Stock Horse Foals made from the "Phantom Wings" mold (see Stock Horse Foal #17 and #18, under "Phantom Wings"). More typically, collectors refer to this mold as the "standing" Stock Horse Foal to distinguish it from the Action Stock Horse Foal.

(2) The Stock Horse Foal mold has the round "Breyer Molding Co." stamp. The mold debuted at the very end of the "B" stamp era , so it is virtually certain that he was never given this stamp. This mold was never given the "U.S.A." stamp, either.

Stock Horse Foal, running — see Action Stock Horse Foal

Stock Horse Mare (SHM) — Jogging, looking right. Sculpted by Chris Hess. Mold in catalog-run production 1982-92, 1996- (foreleg-raised mold version 1982; foreleg-down mold version 1983-92, 1996-).

Catalog-run models made from this mold:

FORELEG-RAISED AND FORELEG-DOWN MOLD VERSIONS:

- Appaloosa Stock Horse Mare #233, black blanket appaloosa, short blaze, stenciled blanket covering butt and part of barrel, black splashed-on spots, 4 stockings, gray hooves, matte (1982-88). Called Appaloosa Stock Horse Mare in the 1982-86 catalogs, American Appaloosa Stock Horse Mare in 1987-88. *Breyer Collector's Video* notes that a few #233s without spots on the blanket have been found. The mare in the 1982 catalog, in addition to having her foreleg raised, has only 2 stockings (hind). This could be a test-color piece, however, for my own foreleg-raised #233 has four stockings, as do those shown in Diederich 1988, Section 1, and the Penney's and Sears holiday catalogs for 1982. Penney's sold the foreleg-raised mare in a set with leather English saddle and bridle, and Sears sold her with leather Western saddle, bridle, roping rein, and breastcollar. The 1983-88 Breyer catalogs all show the foreleg-down mare with 4 stockings.
- Overo Paint Stock Horse Mare #230, bay paint, solid upper face, stenciled white muzzle, black mane and tail, black or gray knees and hocks, 4 stockings, gray hooves, matte (1982-88). Called Overo Paint Stock Horse Mare in the 1982-86 catalogs, American Paint Horse Mare in 1987-88. Same pinto pattern as the SR black paint SHM. The mare in the 1982 catalog, in addition to having her foreleg raised, has a very dark bay color with 2 front stockings and solid bay hind legs. I believe this is a test color, for my own foreleg-raised #230 is a medium bay with 4 stockings; Diederich 1988, Section 1, and the 1982 Penney's holiday catalog also show 4 stockings on the foreleg-raised mare. Penney's sold her in a set with leather Western saddle, bridle, and breastcollar. The 1983-88 Breyer catalogs show foreleg-down #230s as medium to light bay with 4 stockings, broadly speaking (in the early years the stockings are sometimes so oversprayed as to disappear). A variation of foreleg-down #230 is a very distinctive pale peach color—I own one and have seen a couple others.
- Sorrel Quarter Horse Stock Mare #227, deep red sorrel, blaze, flaxen mane and tail, 1 left hind stocking, 4 reddish-charcoal hooves, matte and semigloss (1982-86). The stocking can be very vague. The 1983-84 catalogs, which show the foreleg-down mare, show the stocking as high, reaching to the hock. Foreleg-raised #227 was sold through the 1982 Sears holiday catalog in a set called Bay [*sic*; the horse shown is sorrel] Quarter Horse With English Tack, with leather English saddle and bridle, and through the 1982 Ward's holiday catalog in a set called Chestnut Stock Horse Mare With Authentic Leather Tack, with leather Western saddle, bridle, and breastcollar.

FORELEG-DOWN MOLD VERSION ONLY:

- American Buckskin Stock Horse Mare #222, buckskin, solid face, gray nose, black points, black hooves, matte (1987-88). This model is typically a bit darker than the SR buckskin Stock Horse Mare but is otherwise indistinguishable from the black-hoofed version of the SR.
- Appy Mare #852, red roan leopard appaloosa, white horse with tiny splashed-on red chestnut flecks and spots, chestnut mane and tail, gray-shaded muzzle and joints, gray hooves, matte (1991-92).
- Paint Horse Mare #808, liver chestnut paint, overo; star; slightly darker liver mane and tail; 2 hind stockings with gray hooves; front hooves dark brown; matte (1989-90).

Special-run models made from this mold:

Foreleg-down mold version only:

- Stock Horse Mare SR, bay peppercorn leopard appaloosa, bay horse with darker brown splashed-on spots, star, red shading on face, black points, gray hooves, matte (1986). Penney's holiday catalog. Sold in Breyer Traditional Collector's Family Set SR #712459, with bay peppercorn appaloosa Stock Horse Stallion and Action Stock Horse Foal. On some mares the red facial shading is a bright orangy hue. The Penney's catalog shows this mare with 1 left hind sock; her face is turned away, so any white markings there aren't visible. The number for this set is per a Breyer company computer printout of activity 1985-92 and a Model Horse Collectors Supply price list of July 1987.
- Stock Horse Mare SR, black paint, overo; solid upper face; stenciled white muzzle; black mane and tail; 4 stockings; gray hooves; matte (1984 and 1985). Penney's holiday catalog. Sold in Pinto Mare And Foal Set SR with black paint Action Stock Horse Foal.
- Stock Horse Mare SR, buckskin, solid face, gray nose, black points, black or gray hooves, matte (1984). Sears holiday catalog. Sold in Collectible Stock Horse Family set SR with buckskin Stock Horse Stallion and buckskin Action Stock Horse Foal. This mare is typically paler and creamier in color than the regular-run buckskin Stock Horse Mare. Also, although many of the SR models have black hooves as shown in the Sears catalog and in *JAH* XI/#3 1984 (p. 20), a variation of the SR has gray hooves (collector Heather Wells has a specimen like this), whereas to my knowledge all the regular runs have black hooves, as shown in the 1987-88 Breyer catalogs.
- Stock Horse Mare SR, gray blanket appaloosa, bald face, pink ears and nose, unstenciled butt blanket, splashed-on black spots, black points, black hooves, matte (1983). Sears holiday catalog. Sold in SR set with gray blanket appaloosa Stock Horse Foal and Stock Horse Stallion.

Notes:

(1) In 1982, when this mold was introduced, she had her left front leg raised high enough that the tip of the toe was roughly half an inch above the ground. All three SHM colors issued that year have the raised foreleg, as shown in the 1982 catalog: the black appy #233, sorrel #227, and bay overo paint #230. But the mold was very unstable—these early mares fall over if you wink at them. Thus the mold was altered to lower the leg so that the tip of the toe touches the ground and stabilizes the mare. The leg-down version is shown in catalogs from 1983 on. Oddly, I have seen a couple of mares that were actually the leg-down version but nonetheless had the left front toe off the ground because of warping of the hind legs. Such "faux leg-raised" mares look deceptively like true leg-raised ones but can be distinguished from them. For one thing, the "faux" mares I have seen can be made to stand on the raised toe (a hind leg leaves the ground), whereas the true leg-raised version falls over if she is tipped to the left in an attempt to make her stand on the raised toe. There are also differences in the molds. On the "faux" mares, as on all normal, unwarped leg-down mares, the forearm is more vertical than the head, forms a more open angle with the front of the shoulder, and, on the inside, curves smoothly into the breast. But on the true leg-raised mares, the forearm is very nearly parallel with the

head, forms a more acute angle with the front of the shoulder, and, on the inside, meets the breast in a rather sharp groove. Both the leg-raised and the leg-down versions have an oversized, elongated right hind hoof—the mold must have been sculpted this way to get the leg-raised mares, which were the original version, to stand up at all.

(2) The Stock Horse Mare mold has the round "Breyer Molding Co." stamp. The mold never had the "B" stamp, to judge from the fact that my two foreleg-raised SHMs (1982) and my SR gray appy SHM (1983) do not have it (1983 was the last gasp of the "B" stamp era). This mold was never given the "U.S.A." stamp either.

Stock Horse Stallion (SHS) — ♞ Walking, looking left. Sculpted by Chris Hess. Mold in catalog-run production 1981-92, 1995 - current as of 1996.

Catalog-run models made from this mold:

♞ American Buckskin Stock Horse Stallion #221, buckskin, solid face, gray nose, black points, black hooves, matte (1987-88). This model is typically a bit darker than the SR buckskin Stock Horse Stallion but is otherwise indistinguishable from the black-hoofed version of the SR.

♞ Appaloosa Stock Horse Stallion #232, bay blanket appaloosa; solid face; stenciled blanket covering butt and most of barrel; stenciled bay spots; black mane and tail; black or gray-shaded knees and hocks; most with 4 stockings, some with 4 brown lower legs; gray or brown-gray hooves; matte (1981-86). The body color ranges from buckskin to dark red bay. The 1981 catalog shows "San Domingos" standing proxy for the Stock Horse Stallions (see note 1 for this mold), and scrambles the names of #229 and #232, calling them "No. 229 Pinto Stock Horse Stallion" and "No. 232 Tobiano Appaloosa Stock Horse Stallion." The 1981 collector's manual has the correct SHS mold and names, but shows a bay appy #232 with splashed-on spots and an unstenciled blanket, as well as black hind legs and hooves and front white stockings with gray hooves. The 1981 Ward's holiday catalog, which offered #232 in a set with leather English saddle and bridle, also shows the model with splashed-on spots and, I think, an unstenciled blanket (the gargantuan saddle flap obscures the view), but he appears to have no stockings. *Breyer Collector's Video* states that the 1981 splash-spot model was a test color never produced for sale; but Walerius 1991 (p. 57) and Maestas 1987b say he was produced for the first part of 1981. I have heard of only one or two splash-spot horses in collections. The 1982-86 catalogs and manuals show the model with normal stenciled blanket and spots, and with 4 (sometimes vague) stockings and gray hooves. Some models however were issued with no stockings but instead brown lower legs (as shown in Diederich 1988, Section 1). The box in which at least some #232s were sold has a photo of him in chestnut appy, with slightly darker chestnut mane and tail, unstenciled blanket, splashed-on spots, and 2 front stockings. This is undoubtedly a test-color model.

♞ Bay Quarter Horse Stock Stallion #226, bay, no white markings, black points, black hooves, matte (1981-88). Called Bay Quarter Horse Stock Stallion in the 1981-84 catalogs, Bay Quarter Horse Stallion in 1985-86, American Quarter Horse Stallion in 1987-88. The color varies from a fairly dark brown bay to a medium reddish bay to a golden bay that is nearly dark buckskin. Earlier models have nice shading on them; later models tend to be flatter in tone. #226 was sold through the 1981 Sears holiday catalog in a set with leather English saddle and bridle.

♞ Paint Horse Stallion #807, liver chestnut paint, overo; solid face with pink nose; slightly darker liver mane and tail; 2 hind stockings with gray hooves; front hooves dark brown; matte (1989-90).

♞ "Shane" American Ranch Horse #938, blue roan, light bluish-gray horse with darker gray flecks; black head with blaze; white rocking-B brand painted on left shoulder; black points; 2 hind stockings with tan hooves; other hooves black; matte (1995 - current as of 1996). Many of these models have a greenish cast. Collector Peri Riggins purchased a "Shane" with no brand.

♞ "Skipster's Chief" Famous Therapeutic Riding Horse #842, sorrel, blaze, pink nose, gray shading on sides of face, flaxen mane and tail, 4 stockings, gray hooves, matte (1991-92). Presumably this model represents a real horse, though the catalogs don't specifically say so. Next to the photo of the model, the 1991-92 catalogs give the address of the North American Riding for the Handicapped Association, for collectors who wish to inquire about therapeutic riding programs: NARHA, P.O. Box 33150, Dept. BC, Denver, CO 80233.

♞ Tobiano Pinto Stock Horse Stallion #229, black paint; solid face; black mane and tail; most with 4 stockings and gray hooves, some with 1 left front stocking and 4 black or gray hooves; matte (1981-88). Called Tobiano Pinto Stock Horse Stallion in the 1981 manual and 1982-86 manuals and catalogs, American Paint Horse Stallion in 1987-88. The 1-stocking and 4-stocking versions and the SR bay paint SHS all have the same tobiano body pattern. (shown in the 1982-88 catalogs). I own a 1-stocking horse with black hooves, as does collector Delana Metcalf, but I have seen other 1-stocking horses with gray hooves. The 1-stocking stallion was the first version, issued in 1981 and perhaps into 1982. The 1981 catalog shows a 1-stocking horse, but it is a "San Domingo" test piece standing proxy for the Stock Horse Stallion (see note 1 for this mold). This catalog also scrambles the names of #229 and #232, calling them "No. 229 Pinto Stock Horse Stallion" and "No. 232 Tobiano Appaloosa Stock Horse Stallion." The correct SHS mold and names appear in the 1981 manual, but the #229 black paint appears to be a test color: he is overo rather than tobiano, and his 1 stocking (left front) goes up the front of the leg onto the knee. The 1981 Penney's, Sears, and Ward's holiday catalogs—which all offered #229 in a set with leather Western saddle, bridle, and breastcollar (the Sears set also included a "roping rein")—and the 1981 Alden's holiday catalog (which sold the horse alone) also show 1-stocking horses that appear to be test colors: the Penney's, Ward's, and Alden's horses have odd body patterns, and the Sears horse, although his body pattern looks normal, has a long star. The 1982 Penney's holiday catalog also shows the 1-stocking horse (for sale without tack), though the 1982 Breyer catalog has the 4-stocking version, as do subsequent catalogs through 1988. The 1983 Penney's holiday catalog offered a 4-stocking #229 in a set with leather Western saddle and bridle. Collector Kim Jones showed me an early box for #229, which oddly enough pictures a *chestnut* paint SHS with only a couple of small white spots; this was undoubtedly a test-color piece.

Set:

♞ Kelly Reno And "Little Man" Gift Set #3096, palomino "Little Man," blaze, white points, gray hooves, matte (1984-85). Set also includes bareback pad, bridle, and Kelly Reno rider doll. For details on the doll and tack see under Alec Ramsey in the Riders - Soft Or Jointed Plastic section. All #3096 horses I've seen have the right hind toe pared off (see note 2 for this mold). The real "Little Man" is a palomino owned by actor Kelly Reno, the boy who starred in the Black Stallion movies (per the 1984 catalog and *JAH* VIII/#2 1981, p. 2). The *JAH* article has two photos of the real "Little Man."

Special-run models made from this mold:

♘ "Sam I Am" SR, dark bay paint, overo with "solar eclipse" pattern on left side of barrel; stenciled extensive bald face; pink nose; black points; 1 left hind stocking; 4 dark gray hooves; matte (1984). Made for Sam & Co., Henderson Farms, Jackson, Ohio. 1,200-1,600 models made (per *JAH* 18/#5 Winter 1991, p. 33). This model represents a real registered Paint Horse owned by Beverly and Jerry Henderson. The models were sold by the Hendersons through an ad in *JAH* (XI/#3 1984, p. 6) and through retail stores (see *JAH* XI/#4 1985, p. 16). The models came in a special "Sam I Am" box, along with a large color photo of the real horse and an "Application For Certificate of Ownership," which the purchaser of the model could submit to the Hendersons to become a "recorded owner of an undivided one-millionth share or interest" in the real "Sam I Am." The certificate stipulates that "the total consideration for the one-millionth share in said horse is one cent." A test color chestnut overo "Sam I Am" is shown in *JAH* 21/#3 Summer II 1994 (p. 33). *JAH* editor Stephanie Macejko, who told me that this piece is in the sample room at the Breyer factory, had also heard from a collector who claimed to have a chestnut overo "Sam I Am." How many such pieces without black points might have been inadvertently issued we don't know.

♘ Stock Horse Stallion SR, bay paint, tobiano; solid face; black points; 4 stockings; gray hooves; matte (1984). Penney's holiday catalog. This bay paint SHS has the same pinto pattern as regular-run black paint SHS #229. The stockings can be vague from overspray.

♘ Stock Horse Stallion SR, bay peppercorn leopard appaloosa, bay horse with darker brown splashed-on spots, long star, black points, black hooves, matte (1986). Penney's holiday catalog. Sold in Breyer Traditional Collector's Family Set SR #712459, with bay peppercorn appaloosa Stock Horse Mare and Action Stock Horse Foal. The Penney's catalog shows the stallion with 1 right front sock, but this may be a test-color horse. My own specimen has no socks. The number for this set is per a Breyer company computer printout of activity 1985-92 and a Model Horse Collectors Supply price list of July 1987.

♘ Stock Horse Stallion SR, buckskin, solid face, gray nose, black points, black or gray hooves, matte (1984). Sears holiday catalog. Sold in Collectible Stock Horse Family set SR with buckskin Stock Horse Mare and buckskin Action Stock Horse Foal. This stallion is typically somewhat paler and creamier in color than the regular-run buckskin Stock Horse Stallion. Also, although many of the SR models have black hooves as shown in the Sears catalog and in *JAH* XI/#3 1984 (p. 20), a variation of the SR has gray hooves (collectors Heather Wells, Karen Grimm, and Karen Malcor have specimens like this), whereas to my knowledge all the regular runs have black hooves, as shown in the 1987 Breyer catalog (the stallion's hooves are hidden in the 1988 catalog, but the mare and foal there have black hooves, as in 1987).

♘ Stock Horse Stallion SR, dappled reddish chestnut; blaze; subtle gray shading on breast, shoulders, and hindquarters; slightly darker red chestnut mane and tail; 1 right front and 2 hind stockings with gray hooves; other hoof chestnut-gray; matte (1995). Penney's holiday catalog. Sold in Race Horses Of America set SR #710295 with light bay Pacer, medium dapple gray "Phar Lap," and one removable neck ribbon. 5,500 sets made (per *JAH* editor Stephanie Macejko, conversation of July 1996). The dapples on this Stock Stallion are muted, being only a shade lighter than the basic body color. The neck ribbon is identical to the ribbon that comes with the B Ranch series horses "Cloud" and "Patches" (see in the Classics section for details).

♘ Stock Horse Stallion SR, gray blanket appaloosa, bald face, pink ears and nose, unstenciled butt blanket, splashed-on black spots, black points, black hooves, matte (1983). Sears holiday catalog. Sold in SR set with gray blanket appaloosa Stock Horse Foal and Stock Horse Mare. The stallion in the Sears catalog photo has a long star, but this must be a test color. The horses produced for sale have a bald face.

♘ Stock Horse Stallion SR, rose alabaster, white horse with soft gray and orangy shadings; mane pale rose along the crest and gray on the ends; tail subtly streaked with pale orange and gray; gray nose, knees, hocks, and hooves; matte (1984). Penney's holiday catalog. Sold in SR "Stallion Mare And Foal Set" (yes, that's how the Penney's catalog reads) with bay Action Stock Horse Foal. The catalog description says the set "includes stock horse mare and foal." Evidently no one checked the candidate "mare" mold for serviceability, so to speak.

Notes:

(1) The 1981 dealer catalog shows test run "San Domingo" models in place of SHSs for #226 bay, #229 black paint, and #232 bay blanket appy. The October 1985 *Quequechan Model Horse Collector* printed the following letter from Patty Bramman concerning these test pieces: "The San Domingo models are one-of-a-kind models painted solely for the 1981 dealer's catalog as the proposed and current Stock Horse stallion was not completed in time for the photography session. (The dealer's catalogs are printed much earlier than the collector's catalogs.) After Breyer took that picture, they shipped the three horses to the Breyer importer in England who gave them to the British Model Horse Club. The President of the club sold the models to three club members in order to raise funds for the treasury. There they remain and will, most likely, continue to remain as many offers have been made to buy them." The 1981 collector's manual shows the correct SHS mold, but the models shown are test colors that differ greatly from the models actually produced for sale (see #229 and #232 for discussion).

(2) Because this mold is rather unstable, the factory sometimes used to cut down the toe of the off hind hoof after molding in an effort to make the models stand up better. In some cases the cutting was so extreme as to make the hoof look deformed. All #3096 "Little Man" models I've ever seen have cut toes; with other SHS models, some individuals have the cut and others have intact hooves. In my experience, the cut models are no more stable than the uncut ones. Breyer must have realized this too, for recent models do not have cut toes.

(3) The Stock Horse Stallion mold has the round "Breyer Molding Co." stamp. The early models also have a backwards (or upside-down) "B" stamp (Chelle Fulk's, Linda Bell's, and my own one-sock #229s have it, as do other early models). This mold was never given the "U.S.A." stamp.

"Stonewall" — see Jumping Horse

"Stormy" — ♞ Pony filly, standing, looking right, ears back. Sculpted by Chris Hess. Mold in catalog-run production 1977 - current as of 1996.

Catalog-run models made from this mold:

♞ Marguerite Henry's "Stormy" #19, chestnut pinto, tobiano; crescent-moon star; white mane and tail; 4 high stockings; gray hooves; matte (1977 - current as of 1996). #19 is called simply "Stormy" in catalogs 1977-80, Marguerite Henry's "Stormy" in 1981-93, and "Stormy" By Marguerite Henry in 1994-95. This same model was sold in Marguerite Henry's "Misty," "Stormy," And "Sea Star" Set #2169 [1983-85] and in similar sets through store holiday catalogs in 1982, 1983, and 1993 (see Sets under "Misty"). The color of the chestnut spots varies from dark palomino to deep reddish chestnut. The "Stormy" model represents a real Chincoteague filly named "Stormy," whose dam was "Misty" and whose sire was "Wings." "Stormy" was born on the island of Chincoteague in the kitchen of the Beebe family (owners of "Misty" and "Wings") during a terrible storm in which the island was nearly inundated by the Atlantic Ocean. The story is told by Marguerite Henry in her book *Stormy: Misty's Foal*. According to the book, "Stormy" was a sorrel pinto with 4 stockings and a "strange marking on her forehead . . . in the shape of a new sickle moon" (p. 176). The color pattern on the Breyer model accurately reflects this description and looks pretty much like the color pattern in Wesley Dennis's illustrations for the book, except that Dennis gives "Stormy" a white muzzle and a tail with a brown lower half. (The pinto pattern is the same as on "Skeeter" SR, except for the stockings.) "Stormy," who died in November 1993 at age 31, was actually "Misty's" third foal, according to *JAH* 20/#1 Spring 1993 (p. 33). For a brief period in the late 1970s the regular-run "Stormy" model was sold in a special blister-wrapped display box that probably was labeled with the model number 119, which had previously belonged to the regular-run red roan Running Mare. (See Display Boxes above in this section.) On January 21 and August 5, 1995, the QVC home-shopping cable TV channel offered a total of 1,200 "Stormy" models that were also ordinary regular runs but that came in boxes labeled with the special-run model number 701495 (per *JAH* editor Stephanie Macejko).

Sets: see under "Misty."

Special-run models made from this mold:

- "Skeeter" SR, dark bay pinto, star, black points, 1 left front and 2 hind stockings with tan hooves, right front hoof tan with charcoal stripes (1995). Made for Toys R Us. Sold in "Buckaroo" And "Skeeter" set #700795 with SR red dun "Buckaroo" (Classic Arabian Family Mare mold) and gold metal medallion on blue ribbon. 4,200 sets made, per *JAH* editor Stephanie Macejko (conversation of July 1996). Stephanie also clarified which model has which name: the foal's name comes first in the set name. The set name and number are per the set's box. This set is one of several in the Medallion Series made for Toys R Us; see Medallion Series above in the Traditionals section for a full list and a description of the medallion. Except for her stockings, "Skeeter" has the same pinto pattern as regular-run "Stormy."
- "Stormy" SR, flocked dark chestnut pinto, tobiano; star; painted black eyes; white synthetic hair mane and tail; 4 high stockings; painted black hooves (1984). Sears holiday catalog. Sold in SR set with flocked chestnut pinto "Misty," for $29.99 per set. The pinto patterns on these two models are basically the same as the patterns on the regular-runs but less detailed. This set was flocked, haired, and detailed by the Riegseckers of Indiana (see Riegseckers Models for discussion). It is possible that some of these models have brown glass eyes, but in the sets I've seen in person, both the mare and foal had painted black eyes. Starting in January 1986, leftovers of this SR foal appeared on Bentley Sales Company price lists of January 1986 as #19FLK (for "flocked"), for $4.99.

Notes:

(1) Chris Hess took the design for this mold from a photo of the real foal "Stormy." The photo is printed in JAH 23/#3 May/June 1996 (p. 4).

(2) The "Stormy" mold has the round "Breyer Molding Co." stamp. Some early models probably have the "B" stamp too, but I'm not sure. This mold was never given the "U.S.A." stamp.

Stretched Morgan — see Morgan, stallion, in stretched show stance

"Stud Spider" — Stallion, standing, looking right. Sculpted by Chris Hess. Mold in catalog-run production late 1977 - current as of 1996.

Catalog-run models made from this mold:

- Blanket Appaloosa #823, red bay blanket appaloosa, stripe, stenciled butt blanket that comes forward over the loins, splashed-on red bay spots, black mane and tail, no black on the legs, 4 stockings, pale tan hooves, matte (1990-91). This model's blanket is rather unnatural looking—its edge is a slightly wavy diagonal line cutting straight upward from the lower buttock to the loins, as though the butt had been masked with a fluted custard cup.
- Family Appaloosa Stallion #859, bay blanket appaloosa, star, stenciled blanket covering butt and half of barrel, stenciled bay spots, black points, 2 hind stockings with tan hooves, front hooves black, matte (1992-94). This model's stenciled blanket and spots are the same pattern as on "Stud Spider" #66, but the star and stockings are different.
- "Mister Mister" Champion Paint #916, medium chestnut paint, overo; head mostly white; black spot on right side of nose; medium chestnut mane and tail; white left front leg and hind stockings with tan hooves; other hoof brownish-gray; matte (1995 - current as of 1996). This model represents the real paint gelding "Mister Mister," owned and shown by J. W. Christensen, of Utah. The horse has won numerous awards, including the 1994 American Paint Horse Association All-Around World Championship and the 1994 APHA Super Gelding Award. (Information on is per *JAH* 22/#2 Mar./Apr. 1995, p. 14). As the photo in *JAH* shows, the real horse has a black spot on the side of his nose, as represented on the model. Such spots are not uncommon on chestnut paints, for the skin from which the chestnut hair grows is typically black and shows through on relatively hairless areas such as the muzzle and groin. Collector Karen Grimm and Heather Wells have "Mister Mister" models from which the black spot was omitted, so that the whole muzzle is white. The cover of the 1995 catalog shows a test-color "Mister Mister" with no white spot on the neck. On August 5, 1995, the QVC home-shopping cable TV channel offered 800 "Mister Misters" that were ordinary regular runs but that came in boxes labeled with the special-run model number 705195 (per *JAH* editor Stephanie Macejko). In the 1996 Breyer catalog, #916's name was changed to "Mister Mister" American Paint.
- Overo Paint #88, dark chestnut paint, bald face, slightly darker chestnut mane and tail, 4 stockings, gray hooves, matte and semigloss (1979-81). The color varies from dark to medium brown chestnut. Catalog pictures show a different pinto pattern in each of the three years of this model's production. And in fact three patterns are known to exist on models produced for sale—but only one of them precisely matches one of the catalog patterns, namely, the 1981. The models in the 1979 and 1980 catalogs look like test pieces in that their white spots have sharp, clean edges. The patterns produced for sale all have 4 stockings and bald face; on the right side, all have a large white "maple leaf" on the belly and a long, jagged white spot on neck and shoulder (the shape of these spots varies among the patterns); and on the left side, all have a large white belly/flank spot, a low shoulder spot, a high shoulder spot, and a windpipe spot. Key differences between the patterns are as follows (all spots mentioned are white): [A] The no-forearm-spots pattern: This pattern has solid chestnut forearms. On the right side of the back just below the withers are 2 very small spots and 1 a bit bigger; on some models the 2 small spots blur together. On the left side, this pattern has no spots on the upper neck, as the other patterns have. Pattern A corresponds most to the 1979 catalog, though the match is not exact. [B] The spot-and-crescent pattern: This pattern takes its name from the striking white markings on the right side of the back just below the withers—a spot over a smiling crescent. This pattern also has a spot on each forearm. On the left side it has 2 small spots on upper neck. Pattern B corresponds most to the 1980 catalog (though the match is not exact), but the horse was released earlier, in 1979. Collector Gale Good's records show that she got her spot-and-crescent horse in May 1979, and this version is shown in the 1979 Penney's holiday catalog. So if pattern A was the first Overo Paint made, it was issued only for a short time in 1979, being replaced within a few months by the spot-and-crescent, which was then produced through part of 1980. [C] The one-forearm-spot pattern: This pattern has a spot on the left forearm but none on the right forearm. On the right side of the back just below the withers are 3 small spots, a bit bigger than those on pattern A but similar in shape and configuration. On the left side, pattern C is identical to the spot-and-crescent version, with two small spots on the upper neck. Pattern C precisely matches the 1981 catalog but was introduced late in 1980: he was offered through the 1980 Sears holiday catalog in a set with leather Western saddle, breastcollar, bridle, and "roping rein." The horse in the Sears photo has a saddle on, so his back spots are not visible, but it's clear that he has no spot on the right forearm and has a right-side neck/shoulder spot matching that on pattern C. For a brief period in the late 1970s, Overo Paint #88 was sold in a special blister-wrapped display box that was labeled with the model number 188. See Display Boxes above in this section for discussion. The model number 88 previously belonged to "Diablo" The Mustang, charcoal (Mustang mold).
- "Stud Spider" Appaloosa #66, black blanket appaloosa; S-shaped star; stenciled blanket covering butt and half of barrel; stenciled black spots; various stockings; black, gray, or brownish-gray hooves; matte (1978-89). This model was also sold in "Stud Spider" Gift Set #3080 [late 1977 - 1983]. "Stud Spider's" blanket and spots are the same pattern as on Family Appaloosa Stallion #859, but the star and stockings are different. The real "Stud Spider" was a racing appaloosa stallion owned by actor James Brolin, star of the movie *Lombard and Gable* and co-star of the TV show *Marcus Welby, M.D.* (per an ad in a 1975 *Western Horseman*; also see *JAH* VIII/#2 1981, p. 12). The horse was named after a song (see Mac Donald 1993). The name "Stud Spider" was dropped from Breyer catalogs after 1984, reportedly because "the terms of the license to the name expired" (Mac Donald 1993); and from 1985 on the model was called simply Appaloosa. *Stocking variations:* The 1978-88 catalogs show 1 right front stocking only (on both #66 and, in 1978-83, the #3080 gift set horse); my own two models are like this, but one has 4 gray hooves while the other has a gray hoof on the stockinged leg and the other hooves black. The 1989 catalog shows 1 left front stocking only; collector Jo Kulwicki has a horse like this. She also has one with 4 stockings and one with no stockings, neither of which variations is shown in catalogs. *Sears sets:* The Sears holiday catalogs for 1978, 1979, and 1983 offered "Stud Spider" with leather Western saddle, bridle, breastcollar, and, at least in 1978 and 1983, a "roping rein." The horse in all three years is shown with 1 right front stocking only. The 1978 Sears catalog also shows a braided leather item coiled on the ground beneath the tacked-up horse, which is perhaps meant to be a reata. In 1981 the Sears holiday catalog offered "Stud Spider" in a set with Jim Brolin's book *Let's Go to the Races with the Appaloosa*, plus leather racing saddle, leather bridle, and saddle pad with elastic girth and number "3" in the corner. My copy of this Sears page is blurry, but I would guess the tack is the same as in the Black Stallion And Alec Set #3000. For the Penney's 1977 set with book and leg wraps, see "Stud Spider" Gift Set #3080 below. The number 66 previously belonged to the Boxer dog model (see below in the Dogs And Cats section).

Set:

- "Stud Spider" Gift Set #3080, black blanket appaloosa horse and book *Let's Go to the Races with the Appaloosa*, by Jim Brolin (late 1977 - 1983). This same model was sold separately as "Stud Spider" Appaloosa #66 [1978-89]. Set #3080 is not in the 1977 catalog or manual but is in a Breyer company price list issued late in 1977. *JAH* Spring 1977 announced that set #3080 would include leg wraps for the horse, and apparently the sets issued in late 1977 did come with the wraps—at least, a set with book and 4 red leg wraps was advertised in the 1977 Penney's holiday catalog. But the wraps were subsequently omitted from the #3080 set: they are not part of the set as advertised in Breyer catalogs 1978-83. Oddly enough, Bentley Sales Company price lists offered "Leg Wraps—1 set of 4—Red only" from January 1983 through mid-1987 (for $1-$1.29); these were undoubtedly leftovers from 1977. Another oddity is that the model shown in the 1977 Penney's catalog photo is not a "Stud Spider" but a Performance Horse painted somewhat like a "Stud Spider." It is a black blanket appy with unstenciled blanket and splashed-on spots; it might also have striped hooves, but I'm not sure (my copy of the page is unclear). Undoubtedly this is a test piece standing proxy because the correct "Stud Spider" models were not ready at the time of the Penney's photo shoot. A "Stud Spider" set with book and race tack was offered by Sears in 1981; see the entry for #66 for details.

Special-run models made from this mold:

- Bay Stock Horse SR, bay; solid face; black mane and tail; most with no black on legs; front legs and hooves are gray-brown; hind legs have gray-brown hocks, white stockings, and gray hooves; matte (1986). Made for Your Horse Source. 1,000 models made. Quantity and model name are per a 1986 Your Horse Source brochure. According to the brochure, YHS initially used this model as a promotional gift: "Free special edition bay stock horse limited to 1000. Order $30.00 of merchandise now and receive free the BAY STOCK HORSE pictured on cover. HURRY this horse will not be available again." Later YHS brochures offer the horse for sale. Some models may have a bit of black on the legs; I've seen a photo of one that appeared to have black front socks and hooves. Reportedly, some models have front legs the same color as the body, with dark shading only on the front hooves and the hocks (see Mac Donald 1993). The 1986 YHS brochure gives this SR the number 700, but later YHS brochures list him as #8066. Apparently neither of these numbers is an actual Breyer number, for this SR is numbered 66BY (for "bay") in a Breyer company computer printout of activity 1985-92.
- "Stud Spider" SR, blue roan semi-leopard appaloosa, blue-gray horse, solid face, unstenciled croup blanket, black splashed-on spots from butt to shoulders, black points, 1 left hind stocking, 4 tan hooves, matte (1990). Sears holiday catalog. Sold in Appaloosa-American Classic Set SR #499610, with palomino blanket appaloosa Running Stallion and black blanket appaloosa Performance Horse. 2,000 sets made. Quantity and set number are per a Breyer company computer printout of activity 1985-92. Mac Donald 1993 says that 5,119 of these SR "Stud Spiders" were made. Perhaps 3,119 further models (or full sets) were produced after the 2,000 indicated on the printout; I don't know.
- "Stud Spider" SR, unpainted white (1980). Sold through *JAH* VII/#3 1980 (p. 13). This

horse and several other completely unpainted models were offered to hobbyists interested in customizing, but many collectors kept them unpainted. See Unpainted Models for a complete list.

Notes:

(1) The Spring 1977 *JAH* identifies Chris Hess as the sculptor of this mold, and has a photo of him working on the original clay sculpture. Though the article doesn't explicitly state that Hess created his "Stud Spider" from photos, it does say "Chris usually works from photographs." Regarding the release of this mold late in 1977, see the entry for "Stud Spider" Gift Set #3080.

(2) The "Stud Spider" mold has the round "Breyer Molding Co." stamp. Some early models also have the "B" stamp—collector Chelle Fulk's spot-and-crescent #88 has this stamp, and I have seen version C #88s and also an unpainted model with it—but the very earliest models probably do not have the "B." This mold was never given the "U.S.A." stamp.

Suckling Foal — Filly, standing, head and neck stretched to right in nursing posture. Sculpted by Chris Hess. Mold in catalog-run production 1973-84, 1994 - current as of 1996.

Catalog-run models made from this mold:

- Medicine Hat Mare And Foal set #3180, chestnut pinto foal, tobiano; white body with dark chestnut head and lighter chestnut patch on left hindquarter; tan hooves; matte (1994 - current as of 1996). Set also includes chestnut pinto Medicine Hat Mare (Thoroughbred Mare mold). Although the mare's pattern is medicine hat (see the entry for #3180 under Thoroughbred Mare for discussion), the foal's is not, for her entire head is chestnut except for a bald area above the nose.
- Thoroughbred Mare And Suckling Foal set #3155, chestnut foal; no white markings; darker chestnut mane, tail, and hooves; matte (1973-84). Set also includes bay ears-back Thoroughbred Mare. The 1974-75 catalogs list this set as "Family Of The Bluegrass, Thoroughbred Mare And Suckling Foal." The 1973-75 manuals call it "Thoroughbred Mare And Foal Gift Set." The 1976-84 catalogs and manuals list it simply as "Thoroughbred Set." I have two of these foals, which are very different from each other. One is a rich red chestnut with slightly darker chestnut mane, tail, and hooves. The other is a lighter, sandy "bay" color with brownish-charcoal mane, tail, and hooves (no black or charcoal on the legs). Evidently the sandy version is earlier, for collector Tanya Harding got her foal of this version in the first year the set was released. The sandy version is also shown on the set's box. Collector Heather Wells found a pearly specimen of the chestnut version. See Chalkies & Pearlies in the Appendix near the end of this book.

Special-run models made from this mold:

- Suckling Foal SR, bay pinto, tobiano; solid face; black mane and tail; leg coloring and stockings vary; various black and gray hooves; matte (1982 and 1983). Sears holiday catalog. Sold in Pinto Mare And Suckling Foal set SR with bay pinto Thoroughbred Mare (ears back). The 1982 Sears catalog shows the foal with 1 right hind stocking. *JAH* IX/#2 1982 (p. 13) shows her with 1 left hind stocking. The 1983 Sears catalog shows her with left hind and right front stockings, and my own model is like this. Collector Sande Schneider has a foal with right hind and left front stockings. Collector Laurie Croddy has a foal with no stockings; its right lower legs are chestnut and its left lower legs are black.
- Suckling Foal SR, dark palomino pinto, overo; blaze and white muzzle; white mane and tail; right hind leg and both front legs white with gray hooves; other leg palomino with hoof brown; matte (1992). Penney's holiday catalog. Sold in Frisky Foals set SR #712092, with pale yellow dun Action Stock Horse Foal, red chestnut Proud Arabian Foal, and black blanket appaloosa Running Foal. 3,000 sets made, per a Breyer company computer printout of activity 1985-92. The number for this set is per the printout and a Bentley Sales price list dated March 15, 1993. The Suckling Foal shown in the Penney's holiday catalog is a test color, to judge from the hard edges of its pinto spots.
- Suckling Foal SR, red leopard appaloosa, white foal with red chestnut splashed-on spots, red chestnut mane and tail, red-gray shaded joints and muzzle, gray hooves, matte (1989 and 1990). Sears holiday catalog. Sold in Mare And Foal Set SR #494155, with red bay blanket appaloosa Grazing Mare. 11,000 sets made (1,000 of them for Sears in Canada). Quantity and set number are per a Breyer company computer printout of activity 1985-92.

Note: The Suckling Foal mold has the round "Breyer Molding Co." stamp and the "U.S.A." stamp. Some models might also have the "B" stamp, but I'm not sure.

"Sugar" — see Running Mare

Sulky sets — For details on the horses in these sets see the following entries under Pacer: Brenda Breyer And Sulky Set #2446, Brenda Breyer Harness Racing Set SR, and Brenda Breyer Sulky And Pacer Set SR. For details on the dolls and accessories in these sets, and for Sulky Kit #2400, see under Brenda Breyer in the Riders - Soft Or Jointed Plastic section.

Summer specials — see Mid-Year And Summer Specials

"Sundown" Proud Arabian Stallion — see under Proud Arabian Stallion

"Sunny" Action Foal — see under Action Stock Horse Foal; also see "Sunny" in the Dapples section below

"Tara" Welsh Pony — see under Cantering Welsh Pony

Tennessee Walker — Gelding, in the running walk, "built-up" front hooves, molded-on ribbons in mane and forelock. Sculpted by Chris Hess. Mold in catalog-run production 1972-89, 1992, 1995 - current as of 1996.

Catalog-run models made from this mold:

- "High Flyer" Tennessee Walker #913, chestnut pinto, tobiano; stenciled bald face; mane white up to the roach; blue mane ribbons with white designs; white tail; 2 high front stockings; back legs mostly white; tan-gray or pure gray hooves; matte (1995 - current as of 1996). The model in the 1995 catalog has tan-gray hooves, and this is the more prevalent color on the models I've seen.
- "Memphis Storm" Tennessee Walking Horse #854, charcoal-brown, bald face, tri-color eyes, white points, yellow mane ribbons with red designs, pink hooves, glossy, Commemorative Edition (1992). 7,500 models made, numbered by hand on the belly. It's hard to read the black numbers on the charcoal bellies of these horses. Collector Thea Ryan got a specimen with no eye detailing; he has normal monochrome black eyes. "Memphis Storm's" box sports a large round gold sticker saying, in full: "1992 Commemorative Edition (Production limited to 7,500 pieces, serially numbered by hand) / Memphis Storm / A regal Tennessee Walker with the collectible, Glossy Charcoal finish. A new classic!"
- "Midnight Sun" Famous Tennessee Walker #60, black; no white markings; black mane and tail; red mane ribbons with white designs; black, brown, or gray hooves; semigloss (1972-87). This model is on the 1988 price list, but I believe this inclusion is an error, for #60 is not in the 1988 catalog or manual. The word "Famous" is part of this model's name in the 1972-75 catalogs but is omitted from the name in catalogs 1976-87. The photos in catalogs and manuals are often too small to show hoof color clearly, but the hooves look black in the 1972 manual (the model here could be a test color), decidedly brown in the 1973-75 manuals, and black again from 1976 on. Probably the gray-hoofed models, like the brown-hoofed, were made in the early years; I own one of each and have seen others, so it is certain that they were produced. A black-hoofed #60, in a set with leather English saddle and bridle (with double reins attached to snaffle rings), was advertised in the 1979 Ward's catalog. I have seen a chalky "Midnight Sun" with 4 socks. Not all chalky #60s are like this, however; collector Sande Schneider's chalky, which is made of purple plastic, has no white markings aside from the mane ribbons. #60 is a portrait of the real Tennessee Walker stallion "Midnight Sun," a celebrated show horse who earned the title World Grand Champion in 1945 and 1946. Although he died in 1965, he remains an important influence in the breed today through the 2,000-plus foals that he sired. The Breyer model, with its built-up shoes and brilliant "big lick" gait, misrepresents the real "Midnight Sun," who, like typical Tennessee Walkers of his time, went flat-shod and did not have the extreme action displayed by show-ring Tennessee Walkers of later generations. When I asked Breyer executive Peter Stone about this in July 1995, he said that at the time Breyer created the "Midnight Sun" model, several years after the death of the real horse, all that he and sculptor Chris Hess knew about the horse was that he had been black. Stone recalled that Hess had actually created the mold as a generic Tennessee Walker, working from photos in a Tennessee Walker breed magazine. Undoubtedly these photos showed horses conforming to the "big lick" show-ring style that had become prevalent by then, and Hess would have followed their lines with his characteristic attention to detail. When the mold was complete, Stone contacted the Tennessee Walking Horse association in Shelbyville, Tennessee, to ask for suggestions about what particular Tennessee Walker Breyer might portray with its model. The association recommended Midnight Sun. Breyer then approached the former owners of this horse for permission to do the portrait model. At BreyerFest 1995 I happened to meet the former Breyer representative, Mr. Taylor, who had paid that visit to "Midnight Sun's" owners. According to Mr. Taylor, the owners were delighted to have their horse portrayed by Breyer but did not inspect the model to approve it prior to release. (Thanks to collectors Kristi Hale and Melinda Arnold for information about the real "Midnight Sun"; Melinda also kindly sent me a photo of him in action.)
- Tennessee Walking Horse #704, red bay, no white markings, pale gray mane ribbons with red designs, black points, gray hooves, matte (1988-89). The body color of this model varies from a darker, browner bay to a light, bright orange shade. Collector Peri Riggins has a bright orange model—it really must be seen to be believed (my retinas are still smarting)—with yellow highlights in the shaded areas. Collector Megan Thilman Quigley has a specimen at the other extreme, a dark brownish bay.

Special-run models made from this mold:

- Tennessee Walker SR, light/medium sorrel, no white markings, dark flaxen mane and tail, gray-shaded nose, red mane ribbons with black designs, gray-sorrel hooves, matte (1984). Made for Bentley Sales to sell at Model Horse Congress. 240 models made, per an August 1984 Bentley Sales price list that announces this special. This price list describes the model thus: "Congress Special #60S—Light cream chestnut with flaxen mane and tail . . . Limited run of 240 pieces—One model per customer."

Notes:

(1) The odd elongation of this model's front hooves represents the built-up shoes used on real show Tennessee Walkers to get them to execute their characteristic, highly animated and exaggerated "big lick" gait. A stack of leather or plastic pads is nailed to each front hoof, and a special type of metal shoe is nailed to the bottom of the stack. (Information per Robinson 1993.)

(2) At some point along the line, the Tennessee Walker mold developed an odd flaw: a small round "plug" high in the left corner of the mouth. It looks like the end of a bit with no rings. The "plug" is present on my red bay #704 (1988-89) and on all of my later models of this mold. It is not present on any of my "Midnight Sun" #60s but could easily have been added to the mold during the later years of #60's production.

(3) The Tennessee Walker mold has the round "Breyer Molding Co." stamp and the "U.S.A." stamp. Some models might have the "B" stamp too, but I'm not sure.

"Tesoro" Paso Fino — see under "El Pastor"

Thelwell's Collection — see "Kipper"

Thoroughbred Foal — see Suckling Foal

Thoroughbred Mare — Ears back, standing, looking right, tailtip attached to right hock. Sculpted by Chris Hess. Mold in catalog-run production 1973-84, 1994 - current as of 1996.

Catalog-run models made from this mold:

- Medicine Hat Mare And Foal set #3180, chestnut pinto mare with medicine-hat pattern; tan hooves; matte (1994 - current as of 1996). Set also includes chestnut pinto foal (Suckling Foal mold). Horses with the medicine-hat pattern, which were sacred to the Plains Indians, are mainly white with a characteristic patch or "bonnet" of color remaining over the ears, as well as colored spots, called "war shields," on the chest, flanks, and base of the tail (see *JAH* VIII/#2 1981, p. 12, and Sponenberg and Beaver 1983).
- Thoroughbred Mare And Suckling Foal set #3155, bay mare, no white markings, black mane and tail, no black on the legs, black hooves, matte (1973-84). Set also includes chestnut Suckling Foal. See #3155 under Suckling Foal for discussion.

Special-run models made from this mold:

- Thoroughbred Mare SR, bay pinto, tobiano; solid face; black mane and tail; leg coloring and stockings vary; gray hooves and possibly some black hooves; matte (1982 and 1983). Sears holiday catalog. Sold in Pinto Mare And Suckling Foal set SR with bay pinto Suckling Foal. A mare with 2 stockings, right front and left hind, is shown in *JAH* IX/#2 1982 (p. 13). The 1982 Sears holiday catalog too shows the right front stocking but the left hind leg is hidden. The 1983 Sears catalog shows the mare with a right hind stocking only. In all these photos, the non-stockinged legs and hooves appear black.

My own mare has 2 vague stockings (right front and left hind), the other legs charcoal gray, and 4 gray hooves. Collector Paula DeFeyter sent me a photo of her mare with 4 stockings, gray hooves, and no gray or black on the legs.

Notes:

(1) *Breyer Collector's Video* points out that the Thoroughbred Mare mold's ears are reversed: her eartips point inward even though her ears are back. When a real horse's ears are back, the tips point outward.

(2) The Thoroughbred Mare mold has the round "Breyer Molding Co." stamp and the "U.S.A." stamp. Some models might have the "B" stamp too, but I'm not sure.

Thoroughbred Mare, ears forward — see "Touch Of Class"

Three Generations Appaloosa Set SR — see Breyer Three Generations Appaloosa Set SR

Three Piece Horse Set SR — see Cantering Welsh Pony SR, dappled rose gray; Haflinger SR, chestnut pinto; and Pony Of The Americas SR, black leopard appaloosa

"Thunder Bay" Quarter Horse — see under Quarter Horse Yearling

"Tic Toc" — see under Western Horse

Ties — see Breyer Neckties

"Tobe" Rocky Mountain Horse — see under "El Pastor"

Tobiano Pinto Stock Horse Stallion — see under Stock Horse Stallion

"Touch Of Class" — ♞ Mare, standing/walking, ears forward, looking left. Sculpted by Chris Hess. Mold in catalog-run production 1986-94, 1996-.

Catalog-run models made from this mold:

♞ "Guinevere" English Hack #877, red bay, crescent star, black points, black hooves, slightly semigloss (1993-94).

♞ Selle Français #843, shaded liver chestnut, blaze, 4 stockings, gray hooves, slightly semigloss (1991-92). The blaze is the same as that on "Touch Of Class." The Selle Français ("cell fron-SAY") is a French warmblood breed used for jumping, eventing, and dressage (*Simon & Schuster's Guide*).

♞ Thoroughbred Mare #813, black, blaze, black mane and tail, 4 stockings, gray hooves, matte (1989-90). The blaze is the same as that on "Touch Of Class."

♞ "Touch Of Class" Olympic Champion #420, medium/light bay; blaze; some with dorsal stripe; black points; gray-brown, gray, or black hooves; matte; Artist Series (1986-88). The blaze is the same as that on the Selle Français and the black Thoroughbred Mare #813. My own "Touch Of Class" has a dorsal stripe, but collector Laurie Croddy wrote to me that her model lacks this detail. Laurie's model also has black hooves, as are shown in the 1988 catalog. Catalogs 1986-87 show the mare with gray hooves, and my own model, purchased new in February 1988, has brownish-gray hooves. #420 came with a small "Artist Series" brochure telling about sculptor Chris Hess and about the real horse "Touch Of Class," a Thoroughbred mare who won the 1984 Olympic gold medals in team and individual jumping. See the 1986-87 catalogs for further details. Regarding the origins of this model, see note 1 for this mold.

Notes:

(1) Breyer executive Peter Stone, in an item in *JAH* XII/#4 1985 (p. 12), tells about the visit he made with sculptor Chris Hess to the Long Island home of the real "Touch Of Class" so that Hess could study the mare for his Breyer portrait. Hess also used photos as he created the sculpture; former *JAH* editor Megan Thilman Quigley told me that the mold looks just like a photo of the real mare that may still be on file at Breyer. A photo of Hess with his unpainted original clay sculpture appears in the 1986-87 catalogs.

(2) The "Touch Of Class" mold has "©1985" engraved inside the near gaskin; it has no other mold marks.

Toys R Us Specials — Toys R Us is a U.S.-based international chain store that has carried Breyer regular runs for some years but has offered SRs only since 1992, when a special Classic Lipizzaner was made for Toys R Us in Germany. Toys R Us first sold SRs in its U.S. stores in 1993 and has carried several since then. In 1995 and 1996, Toys R Us offered, among other SRs, the Medallion Series of SR sets with metal medallion. See under Medallion Series above in this section for discussion and a full list.

For Toys R Us SRs other than the Medallion Series, in the Traditionals section, see Bay Fighting Stallion SR (1993; under Fighting Stallion); "Lady Phase" SR, alabaster (1993); Stock Horse Foal SR, pale smoke gray (1993); Unicorn SR, alabaster (1994; under Running Stallion); "Cochise" SR (1995; under "Sea Star); "Dustin" SR (1995; under "Phar Lap"); "Skeeter" SR (1995; under "Stormy"); Unicorn II SR, black (1995; under Running Stallion). In the Classics section, see Lipizzaner SR #620 (1992; under Lipizzan); Drinkers Of The Wind Set SR (1993); Spanish-Norman Family Set SR (1994); "Buckaroo" SR (1995; under Arabian Family Mare); and "Geronimo" SR (1995; under "Kelso"). In 1996, Toys R Us offered two more SRs (in addition to the Medallion Series models), both made from the Classic Lipizzan mold with an added unicorn horn: a glossy black model called Unicorn III Black Pearl and an iridescent white model called Unicorn III White Pearl. (These two, being 1996 releases, are not listed in this book.)

Traditional scale — Breyer's largest scale of models. For discussion see the General Note at the start of the Traditionals section.

Trakehner — ♞ Stallion, with brand (prior to spring 1996), standing. Sculpted by Chris Hess. Mold in catalog-run production 1979-84, 1989, 1995 - current as of 1996.

Catalog-run models made from this mold:

♞ "Abdullah" Champion Trakehner #817, pale dapple gray; nearly white upper neck and head with no dapples; 2 gray birthmarks on neck (right side); black eyes; white points; streaks of gray shading in muscle grooves, along ribs, and across knees and hocks; gray hooves; matte; Limited Edition (1989). On some models the elaborate gray shading is so stripy as to give the effect of a skeleton in a cartoon x-ray. All the shading was done freehand, without a mask, according to former Breyer employee Steve Ryan in his talk at BreyerFest West 1991. This model's box sports a large round gold sticker saying, in full: "1989 Limited Edition / Abdullah / Famous Trakehner / Olympic Gold Medal Winner Owned by Terry and Sue Williams." Limited Edition models are produced only for one year, in quantities sufficient to fill all orders for the model. The real "Abdullah" is a Trakehner stallion who was the first horse ever to win all three of the highest awards in show jumping. He won Olympic gold and silver medals in 1984, the World Cup Finals in West Germany in 1985, and the World Championships in Aachen, West Germany, in 1986. See the 1989 catalog for more details.

♞ "Hanover" Trakehner #912, liver chestnut, blaze, lighter chestnut mane and tail, front lower legs light chestnut with chestnut-gray hooves, 2 hind white stockings with tan hooves, matte (1995 - current as of 1996). On the "Hanovers" I have seen, the lower legs vary from a very pale tan to a chestnut shade nearly as dark as the body; one specimen had gray lower legs and hooves.

♞ Trakehner #54, bay, no white markings, black points, gray hooves, matte and semigloss (1979-84). The color ranges from a medium reddish or sandy bay, with the black on the legs reaching just over the knees and hocks, to a dark seal bay with the black on the legs extending all the way up to the body. My own seal bay has a faint black dorsal stripe as well. Catalogs show that the darker horses were earlier. The color difference between the medium and seal versions is striking; in fact the medium #54 is considerably closer in body color to the SR bay Trakehner with star than to the seal bay #54. My medium #54 is just a slight shade darker than my SR bay. #54 was also sold through the 1979 Sears holiday catalog in a set with leather English saddle and bridle; the bridle is shown with two reins (as on a double bridle) attached to snaffle rings. The word "Trakehner," according to the *Oxford English Dictionary* (the only dictionary in which I could find this word), is pronounced trä (as in "tralala") - KAY - ner.

• U.S.E.T. Traditional Assortment #6984, Trakehner #54, with other models (1984). This was an assortment for dealers. I believe the packaging of the models in this assortment included a long paper strip printed with photos and various statements. See discussion under U.S.E.T. Traditional Assortment.

Special-run models made from this mold:

♘ "Kaleidoscope" SR #702395, light bay pinto, tobiano; blaze; gray-shaded muzzle; black and white mane; black tail; white legs; gray or charcoal hooves; matte (1995). Breyer show special, made for shows and parties sponsored by Breyer dealers. 7,286-7,700 models made, per *JAH* editor Stephanie Macejko. (7,286 had been produced as of our conversation of Oct. 13, 1995; Breyer's computer records were unclear as to a final figure during our conversation of July 1996 but indicated that as many as 7,700 may have been produced.) Models came with a certificate of authenticity signed by Breyer executive Peter Stone. The certificate states: "This bay pinto Trakehner sport horse was hand painted at Breyer in Wayne, New Jersey. Available only in 1995 and produced exclusively for Breyer Special Events nationwide, Kaleidoscope [*sic*] is a true collector's item." The model number is per the certificate and the model's box. The bay color is rather orangy. Some models have gray shading around the eyes, but others lack this detail. The name "Kaleidoscope" is fictitious, created by Stephanie Macejko.

♘ Trakehner SR, chestnut, star, slightly darker chestnut mane and tail, 4 stockings, gray hooves, matte (1987). *Just About Horses* subscriber special. 1,500 models made (per *JAH* XIV/#1, 1987, p. 14), all or most of them numbered by hand on the belly. A Breyer company computer printout of activity 1985-92 gives the model number of this SR as #54CH (for "chestnut"). See Trakehner SR bay for further discussion.

♘ Trakehner SR #400154, golden bay, star, black points, 4 stockings, gray hooves, matte (1987). Made for Small World. Approximately 467 models made. This quantity is per two sources: an ad for the horse in a 1987 newsletter from Small World in New Jersey, which says "Only 367 models available," and a handwritten note from Small World jotted by an employee on the form on which collector Kim Lory Jones ordered her golden bay Trakehner in February 1988. On her order, Kim had asked, "How many Golden Bay Trakehners were made? Were they made special for you?" The handwritten reply she got back was this: "Overrun of JAH chestnut overpainted / we got 367 / another 'Small World' retail store in N.Y. got » 100." As this note indicates, the black mane, tail, and leg joints were added by the Breyer factory to excess models from the *JAH* SR chestnut Trakehner made in 1987. The SR golden bays do not have belly numbers, whereas all or most of the SR chestnuts do. The model number for the golden bay special is per the Small World ad and a Breyer company computer printout of activity 1985-92.

♘ Trakehner SR, unpainted white (1980). Sold through *JAH* VII/#3 1980 (p. 13). This horse and several other completely unpainted models were offered to hobbyists interested in customizing, but many collectors kept them unpainted. See Unpainted Models for a complete list.

Notes:

(1) Prior to spring 1996, the Trakehner mold had a brand that looks like a pair of moose antlers engraved on the near thigh. This is the brand used on real Trakehners (*Dressage Today*, Jan. 1997, p.119). Breyer removed the brand from the mold in spring 1996, however, in order to produce the 1996 special-run "Calypso" #701696 (not listed in this book) for the U.S.E.T. Festival of Champions. The real horse "Calypso," a show jumper who won a gold medal at the 1984 Olympics, does not have the brand, so the brand had to be omitted from the portrait model. This information is per *JAH* editor Stephanie Macejko (conversation of July 2, 1996). According to Stephanie, it is possible that the brand will be restored to the mold later on.

(2) Breyer sculptor Chris Hess took his design for the Trakehner mold from a photograph or illustration, not from a real horse observed live, according to Breyer executive Peter Stone (conversation of Nov. 1994).

(3) The Trakehner mold has the round "Breyer Molding Co." stamp. Early models might have the "B" stamp too, but I'm not sure. This mold was never given the "U.S.A." stamp.

"Trouble" — A large rearing horse by Breyer sculptor Chris Hess; not a Breyer product. For discussion see the entry on Christian Hess, under Sculptors in the Appendix near the end of this book.

Truck — see Breyer Anniversary Truck

"Turbo" The Wonder Horse SR — see under Mustang

"Turf Queen" — see Race Horse, Derby Winner #36

T.V.'s "Fury" — see under "Fury" Prancer

"Two Bits" — see under Quarter Horse Gelding

Unicorn — In the Traditionals section see Collector's Unicorn SR (under "Smoky"); Lying Down Unicorn (under Lying Down Foal); Sky Blue Unicorn SR (under Running Stallion); Unicorn #210 (under Running Stallion); Unicorn SR (under Running Stallion); and Unicorn II SR (under Running Stallion). In the Little Bits section below see Unicorn.

Unpainted models — In the Traditionals section see "SR unpainted white" under "Adios"; Belgian; "Black Beauty," stallion, cross-galloping; Cantering Welsh Pony; Clydesdale Mare; Five-Gaiter; Foundation Stallion; Hanoverian; Indian Pony; "Lady Phase"; "Morganglanz";

Proud Arabian Mare; Proud Arabian Stallion; Saddlebred Weanling; "Stud Spider"; and Trakehner. In the Stablemates section see SR unpainted white Draft Horse. In the Cattle & Hogs section see SR unpainted white Calf.

These models are completely unpainted white plastic. All the Traditional horses just listed except for the Belgian were offered to hobbyists interested in model-horse customizing through *JAH* VII/#3 1980 (p. 13; see *Just About Horses* Subscriber Specials above in this section for discussion). These and the Belgian (1986), Stablemate Draft Horse (1984), and Calf (1987) are to my knowledge the only unpainted Breyers that have been offered as SRs to collectors. But as experienced collectors know, many other unpainted models have found their way into the hobby market. Some of these may be unauthorized factory escapees, but others have undoubtedly come through legitimate channels. A Breyer company computer printout of activity 1985-92 lists numerous orders for unpainted models—Clydesdale Stallion, FAF, FAS, "Lady Roxana," "Man O' War" (Traditional), "Roy," "Sham," Stock Horse Stallion and Mare, "Stormy," and others—sent to companies such as Greiman Supply, Turnamics Inc., and Decorative Creations. Presumably these companies and others that ordered unfinished models intended to finish the pieces themselves, but they might easily have sold raw specimens to collectors.

Experienced collectors also know that in 1990 or thereabouts, a large number of partially painted and otherwise defective models turned up at flea markets and soon thereafter on hobbyists' sales lists. These models typically have unpainted eyes and/or hooves, among other shortcomings. According to Breyer executive Peter Stone (conversation of Nov. 1994), a recycler of painted acetate purchased from Breyer-Reeves a large truckload of partially painted Breyers that had been rejected by the factory for quality-control reasons. The load consisted of an entire year's accumulation of reject models. Rather than taking the models for recycling as agreed, the recycler sold the models to flea-market dealers.

U.S. Equestrian Team Set with SR Brenda Breyer — see under Brenda in the Riders - Soft Or Jointed Plastic section

U.S.E.T. Traditional Assortment #6984 — This was a dealer package containing regular-run "Halla" #63; Hanoverian #58; two Jumping Horse #300s; "Morganglanz" #59; and Trakehner #54. This assortment is advertised only in the 1984 dealer catalog, which states, "This 6 piece assortment features the special types and breeds of horses used in International Equestrian Competition such as the 1984 Olympics." The horses were ordinary regular runs but came with "Special packaging," as the catalog calls it, consisting of a long paper strip printed with photos of a cross-country rider on a gray horse. (The catalog does not picture the "special packaging," but I saw an original strip in the Reeves International archives in Wayne, New Jersey.) The strip states, "This model horse is representative of the horses used by the USET Team" and "Breyer Animal Creations is proud to be an official supplier to the United States Equestrian Team." A bay Trakehner from this assortment, purchased by collector Robin Lee in 1984, came in a regular cardboard picture-box with the paper strip wrapped around it underneath the box's cellophane wrap.

"Vandergelder" Dutch Warmblood — see under "Roemer"

Vaulting Horse SR — see under Hanoverian

Vehicle sets — see Miniature Collection below in the Classics section for a full list

Vermont Morgan — see under Morgan, stretched

Voltigier-Pferd SR — see Vaulting Horse SR (under Hanoverian)

Volunteer specials — These are SR models made as honoraria for hobbyists who help Breyer with important functions. Most of these models have been given to BreyerFest show judges and seminar leaders. See under BreyerFest SR Models for a complete list.

Walter Farley's Black Stallion — see under Black Stallion

Warpaint Indian ponies — In the Traditionals section see "Ichilay" The Crow Horse (under Indian Pony); Indian Pony (#175 chestnut pinto, #176 buckskin, and #177 alabaster); Lakota Pony (under Foundation Stallion); and "Ponokah-Eemetah" The Blackfeet Indian Horse (under Fighting Stallion). In the Classics section see Willow And "Shining Star" set SR (under Rearing Stallion).

Watchful Mare And Foal set SR — see "Lady Phase" SR, alabaster; and Stock Horse Foal, standing, SR, pale smoke gray

Weanling — see Saddlebred Weanling

Welsh Cob — see "Llanarth True Briton"

Welsh Pony — see Cantering Welsh Pony

West Coast Model Horse Collector's Jamboree SRs — see Jamboree Specials above in the Traditionals section

Western Horse — Large genderless horse, standing square, mane on left side of neck, molded-on bridle and breast collar, gold metal chain reins, removable plastic Western saddle. Apparently adapted by Chris Hess from Hartland's Large Western Champ, sculpted by Roger Williams. Mold in production 1950-94, 1996- (diamond-conchas mold version 1950; normal mold version 1951-94, 1996-).

Catalog-run models made from this mold:

DIAMOND-CONCHAS AND NORMAL MOLD VERSIONS:

- Western Horse #59, white, most with white mane and tail, gray hooves, solid gold bridle, most with white breastcollar with gold studs and upper straps, glossy and semigloss; most with black old-style Western saddle with gold trim (1950 - 1960/62). Called Western Mount Horse in the ca.1954 catalog; called Western Horse subsequently. Some horses have a solid gold breastcollar, as collector Sande Schneider brought to my attention. Western Horse #59 is Breyer's very first model, and comes in several versions. [A] The earliest ones, made in 1950 and possibly into the first part of 1951, are the diamond-conchas mold version (see note 3 for this mold). Most of the Western Horses on the horse-over-the-clock style MasterCrafters clocks (see notes 1 and 2) that I've seen, and some free-standing horses too, are white or cream-colored horses of this mold version. These earliest horses typically have "antique" brown-shaded mane and tail, but sometimes white; charcoal-brown or black hooves; semigloss finish; gold only on the studs of the bridle and breastcollar; o-link reins (see note 8); and brown old-style saddle with "antique" whitewashing on skirts and fenders and with either no cinch or a cinch with slide-through buckle (see note 7). Ads for free-standing horses of this earliest version, apparently with brown-shaded mane and tail, appear in the November 1950 and November 1951 issues of *Western Horseman* (though the mold had been changed to the normal version no later than September 1951; see note 3). These ads, by the "little joe" Wiesenfeld Co. of Baltimore, Maryland, dub the horse "Cream Puff" and do not mention Breyer. But the horse is clearly a Breyer, to judge from the pictures and the description: "Here's a handsome Western horse model, about 10 inches high. 'Cream Puff' is complete with a bridle and chain rein, martingale [the photo shows no martingale; this must refer to the breastcollar], and a saddle you can take off to show every inch of his perfect conformation. Beautifully made of strong, but light weight, unbreakable, cream colored plastic." This contemporary description of the horses as cream colored indicates that the creamy off-white shade of many of these horses today is not simply a result of age-related yellowing. Collector Paula DeFeyter, who kindly sent me copies of the ads, found one of these early free-standing horses in original box (a mailing carton with Breyer's name and address but no model number or name); he has brown-shaded mane and tail, and his brown old-style saddle has the usual whitewashing and a cinch with slide-through buckle. [B] Slightly later #59s are normal-mold, round-concha horses (see note 3), with the same coloring and tack as the earliest #59s—"antique" brown-shaded or white mane and tail, dark brown or black hooves, gold only on the studs of the bridle and breastcollar, o-link reins, and brown old-style saddle—except that the saddle typically has goldwashing on skirts and fenders and a snap-on cinch (see note 7). Most horses of this version that I have seen have been on beside-the-clock style MasterCrafters clocks, but at BreyerFest 1996 I saw a couple of free-standing ones, one with brown-shaded mane and tail and another with white mane and tail. The latter horse also had a cylinder bit with "safety pin" hooks (see note 8), which in my experience is far more typical of version A horses. An ad in the January 1952 *Western Horseman* shows a free-standing white horse that appears to be a version B (normal mold with gold only on the studs) with white mane and tail, but his saddle appears to have gold-touched tooling rather than goldwashing and could be black rather than brown (the ad is black and white). [C] Ads in the March and November 1952 issues of *Playthings* magazine again show the normal mold version free-standing, with white mane and tail, black hooves, and o-link reins, but he now has a solid gold bridle, gold on the upper straps as well as the studs of the breastcollar, and a black old-style saddle with gold-touched tooling. The same version is shown in the October/November 1952 *Horse Lover's Magazine* except that the horse here seems to have the gray hooves that #59 would have for the rest of his years of production. Some #59s of both versions B and C have a chalky appearance, which is a quality of the plastic though it looks like paint; typically these horses are stark white, but collector Jo Kulwicki has a pinkish one. I've seen such chalky-looking version B horses on beside-the-clock MasterCrafters clocks, and I have a free-standing chalky-looking version C. [D] #59 is listed but not shown in the ca.1954 catalog, but the Western Horses that are pictured there indicate that white #59 had by this time acquired normal, twisted-link reins. As collector's specimens indicate, this twisted-link model has white mane and tail, gray hooves, solid gold bridle, gold on studs and upper straps of the breastcollar, and black saddle with gold-touched tooling. He would remain like this for the rest of his years in production and thus is the most common version of #59. The #59 I got in about 1959-60 has all of these features. The model number 59 later belonged to chestnut "Morganglanz."

NORMAL MOLD VERSION ONLY:

- "Tic Toc" #864, alabaster; gray-shaded mane, tail, knees, and hocks; pink nose and ears; gray hooves; gold bridle; breastcollar white with gold studs and upper straps; matte; black new-style Western saddle with gold trim (1992-94). This model's name is spelled without a space ("TicToc") in the 1992 catalog but with a space in 1993-94. The catalogs don't say so, but I suspect the company named this model in commemoration of the Western Horses made for MasterCrafters clocks in 1950-51, the oldest of which horses were white (see notes 1 and 2 for this mold). "Tic Toc's" new-style saddle (see note 7 for this mold) is molded in black plastic with the gold trim painted on.
- Western Horse #50, black, bald face and muzzle, black mane, black tail with white tailtip, 4 stockings, gray hooves, solid silver bridle, black breastcollar with silver studs and upper straps, glossy; black old-style Western saddle with silver trim (1959/60 - 1960/62). This horse is cast in white plastic, and his unstenciled bald face, which extends down over the whole muzzle, is the unpainted natural plastic. The stockings on #50 come in two variations: some are natural white plastic and some are painted on over the painted black legs. The specimens that I know of have low-grommet old-style saddles (see note 7 for this mold). One of my own two models has a pink nose and inner ears; the other has white in these areas. Three specimens of a variation of #50 with a stenciled blaze have come to my attention. The first was reported to me by collector Daphne Macpherson. In the photo she sent me, the stenciling is clear; the sharp-edged blaze makes a hard right-angle turn above the nostrils, so that the muzzle is stenciled white. I believe the blaze is unpainted plastic, but I am not sure. The second specimen, owned by collector Joy Sheesley, has a painted-on stenciled blaze, and also eyewhites. The third specimen, found by collector Ida Santana, has a stenciled blaze that widens over the eyes, a white forelock, and pink inner ears. In all other respects these stenciled-blaze models are like normal unstenciled #50s with painted-on stockings and tailtip, silver bridle, etc.; Ida's horse even has the bump on its back that is characteristic of many old Western Horses, though it does not have ear pits (see note 3 for this mold). To my knowledge the reins on #50 are the same gold metal chains as were used on other Western Horses and Ponies; my own #50's bit and rein remnants (a few links on each side) are gold, heavily tarnished of course. See Western Mount Horse "Black Beauty" #58 for discussion of dates and model numbers of black Western Horses. The model number 50 later belonged to "Adios" Famous Standardbred.
- Western Horse #55, black pinto, bald face, white mane, black tail with white tip, 4 stockings, gray hooves, gold bridle, breastcollar black with gold studs and upper straps, glossy, semigloss, and matte; Western saddle (ca.1954 - 1973, 1975-76). There may be a variation with solid gold breastcollar. This model was called Pinto Pony in the ca.1954 catalog, but called Western Horse subsequently. Same pinto pattern as #56. The pattern is nearly identical to that on most pinto Western Ponies. Early #55s are glossy and have an extensive bald face that goes over the whole nose and onto the cheeks. Later ones have a blaze-style bald face that doesn't cover the nostrils. Early #55s also have black old-style Western saddles with gold trim. In 1968, #55 acquired the new-style saddle of white plastic with black shading. (Regarding saddle styles, see note 7 for this mold.) #55 was in the Showcase Collection as #550 in 1970-72 (see Showcase Collection in this section for discussion). The model number 550 later be-

longed to the Ben Breyer doll.

- Western Horse #56, brown pinto, bald face, white mane, many with gray forelock, brown tail with white tip, 4 stockings, gray hooves, gold bridle, breastcollar same brown as horse with gold studs and upper straps, glossy and matte; brown old-style Western saddle with gold trim (ca.1954 - 1966). Called Pinto Pony in the ca.1954 catalog; called Western Horse subsequently. Same pinto pattern as #55. The pattern is nearly identical to that on pinto Western Ponies. Western Horse #56 is called "brown pinto" in catalogs, but the color is lighter than this may suggest, varying from light tan palomino to peach to caramel to deep red sorrel. Many #56s are glossy, but collector Jo Kulwicki's deep sorrel version is matte or slightly semigloss, and I have heard of another matte #56. There is a variation with solid gold breastcollar (collector Karen Grimm has one like this). *Breyer Collector's Video* notes that there are black-eyed and gold-eyed #56s. On older #56s the bald face is extensive, going over the whole nose and onto the cheeks. More recent #56s have a blaze-style bald face that doesn't cover the nostrils. Regarding saddle style, see note 7 for this mold. Regarding differences between #56 and the SR caramel pinto, see the entry for the SR, below.
- Western Horse #57, palomino; bald face; white or light palomino mane and tail; 4 stockings; most with gray hooves, some with black; most with solid gold bridle and palomino breastcollar with gold studs and upper straps; glossy, semigloss, and matte; Western saddle (1951-91). Called Western Mount Horse in the ca.1954 catalog; called Western Horse subsequently. #57 is Breyer's second model, the white Western Horse alone having preceded him. To my knowledge all #57s are of the normal mold version (see note 3 for this mold). For this reason, and because the earliest documentation I have found on #57 is an ad in the September 1951 *Western Horseman*, I date him to 1951 rather than to 1950. However, I know of a handful of bizarre, bile yellow-charcoal Western Horses of the diamond-conchas mold version, most of them on MasterCrafters clocks of the horse-over-the-clock style made in 1950, whose authenticity is not absolutely certain but which could conceivably be precursors to #57. For details see MasterCrafters Clocks in the Appendix near the end of this book. *Color and tack variations*: The color of #57 varies from dark palomino-sorrel to light honey-tan to yellow palomino. Many #57s from the early years have gold eyes, which are now often tarnished; others have charcoal eyes. Some old #57s, as collector Sande Schneider has observed, have oddly rough-textured bellies with no gloss, while others have bellies as smooth and glossy as the rest of the horse. The earliest #57s I know of, including most of those on horse-beside-the-clock MasterCrafters clocks (see notes 1 and 2 for this mold), have black or nearly black hooves, o-link chain reins (see note 8), and brown old-style Western saddle (see note 7). Most of these black-hoofed horses have a solid gold bridle, but some have a palomino bridle with gold buckles and studs, matching the breastcollar (collectors Sande Schneider, Lorraine Mavrogeorge, and Karen Grimm have such specimens, and one on a MasterCrafters clock was displayed at BreyerFest 1994). As Sande pointed out to me, the breastcollar sometimes has palomino upper straps rather than gold. Collector Sheryl Leisure has a black-hoofed model that appears to be chalky (see Chalkies & Pearlies in the Appendix near the end of this book), though it is hard to tell whether it has a white paint basecoat or is just made of an opaque, chalky-looking plastic. The black-hoofed #57 dates to 1951: there is a photo of him as a free-standing horse (not on a clock) in the September and November 1951 issues of *Western Horseman* and the February and March 1952 issues of *Playthings* magazine. (Oddly, this same old photo was used again in the 1958 catalog, though it was several years out of date by then.) #57 with medium gray hooves, which would persist through 1991, evidently began in 1951, for a couple of #57s I have seen on MasterCrafters clocks (such as collector Heather Wells's) have gray hooves. The #57 in the ca.1954 catalog also has gray hooves, as well as the old-style saddle, but he has acquired the normal twisted-link reins that #57 would retain through 1991. A variation of this early gray-hoofed horse has a solid gold breastcollar to match his gold bridle (collector Karen Grimm has one like this). In 1968, as shown in the catalog for that year, #57 acquired the new-style saddle of white plastic with tan shading that he would wear for the rest of his years. *Grooming-kit horses*: The 1956 and 1957 Sears holiday catalogs offered #57 in a grooming kit for human beings. Instead of a normal hard-plastic Western saddle, this "Giant Palomino Groomer," priced at $4.98 in 1956 but a mere $3.97 in 1957, came with a flat, flexible vinyl "pack saddle," described as "tan" in the 1956 Sears ad. Tucked into the saddle's pockets were a nail file, nail clipper, toothbrush, and comb. This saddle is a larger version of the pack saddles that came with Western Pony grooming kits sold in the 1950s and 1960s (see note 4 for the Western Pony mold). Collector Paula DeFeyter found a Giant Palomino Groomer, with a glossy palomino Western Horse and a pack saddle covered with embossed "tooled" designs, as on many of the Western Pony pack saddles. For grooming-kit sets with other Breyer molds, see Grooming Kits For People above in the Traditionals section. #57 was in the Showcase Collection as #570 in 1970-72 (see Showcase Collection in this section for discussion).
- Western Mount Horse "Black Beauty" #58, black, no white markings, black mane and tail, gold hooves, gold bridle, black breastcollar with gold studs and upper straps, glossy; black old-style Western saddle with gold trim (ca.1954 - pre-1958). There are two basic versions of black Western Horses. The rarer one, according to *Breyer Collector's Video*, is the solid black with gold hooves, which is cast in black plastic. The more common one is the black with bald face and 4 stockings, listed above as Western Horse #50. My assignment of model numbers and dates to these two versions is speculative, for no old Breyer catalogs have photos of black Western Horses; nor do any magazine ads I know of from the 1950s picture or even mention a black. The Western Horse in black is first listed in the ca.1954 catalog, where he is called Western Mount Horse "Black Beauty" #58 (on this early name, see note 6 for this mold). An old Breyer company sheet that probably dates to 1955/57 also mentions a "Black Beauty" Western Horse (no number is given), and the 1960 catalog lists a black Western Horse #50 (with no reference to "Black Beauty"). I identify the solid black gold-hoofed horse as the early one, #58 in the ca.1954 catalog, on the basis of his close resemblance to the solid black gold-hoofed Western Pony, which is also listed in the ca.1954 catalog and whose identity is confirmed by good evidence (see Western Mount Horse "Black Beauty" #44, under Western Pony). It stands to reason that Breyer would issue matching color versions on the Western Horse and Pony molds at the same time. The model number 58 later belonged to the bay Hanoverian.

Special-run models made from this mold:

- Western Horse SR #400057, caramel pinto, bald face, white mane, gray forelock, palomino-shaded tail with white tip, 4 stockings, gray hooves, solid gold bridle, caramel breastcollar with gold studs and upper straps, glossy; "antique" brown new-style Western saddle (1990). *Just About Horses* subscriber special. 1,525 models made. "*JAH* 1990" written by hand on the belly. Models came with numbered certificate of authenticity signed by Breyer executive Peter Stone and then-Breyer-employee Steven Ryan. The quantity I've given, as well as the model number, is per a Breyer company computer printout of activity 1985-92. However, the *JAH* issue that offers this SR says "limited to 1,500," a quantity also noted on the model's certificate (my certificate says "This horse is number 0399 of 1,500 produced"). Undoubtedly an overrun of 25 models was produced to cover damage and loss in the mail. The certificate also notes: "Models were made at the Breyer facility in Wayne, New Jersey at the end of Summer 1990." This model has the same pinto pattern as the old regular-run black pinto #55 and brown pinto #56. This SR differs from the caramel version of the old regular-run #56 chiefly in the saddle mold (all #56s came with old-style saddles) and the tail color: #56s have darker, thoroughly painted tails, not just lightly oversprayed ones as on the SRs. Regarding saddle styles, see note 7 for this mold.
- Western Horse SR #701895, palomino, most with "'95" date stamp molded inside right hind leg; light palomino mane and tail; 4 stockings; gray hooves; solid gold bridle; palomino breastcollar with gold studs and upper straps; matte; tan-shaded new-style Western saddle (1995). Made for the QVC home-shopping cable TV channel's Breyer hours aired January 21, June 1, and August 5, 1995. 3,678 models made (per *JAH* editor Stephanie Macejko). The model's number is per the model's box. This SR and the most recent version of regular-run palomino #57 are identical in color, and both have "© Breyer Reeves" copyright stamp as well as the "U.S.A." stamp. Thus the only definite distinction between them is the "'95" date stamp, which is not present on any #57s but is present on most of the SRs. Oddly, some of the SRs lack the date stamp and are thus not physically distinguishable from recent #57s. Jo Kulwicki and Thea Ryan, among other collectors of my acquaintance, both received SR Western Horses with no date stamp and reported this fact to the model-horse groups on the Internet and Prodigy computer service as soon as they received the models, within a week or two of the January QVC show. From this same show Jo and some other collectors also got SR "Shams" that likewise did not have a "'95" date stamp as they were supposed to have. For further discussion, see "Sham" The Godolphin Arabian SR blood bay.

Notes:

(1) Dating: Breyer company literature tells that the Western Horse was the company's first animal mold, created in 1950 as a custom order for MasterCrafters Clock Company, which mounted the horses on mantel clocks. But free-standing Western Horses, that is, horses not on clocks, were also sold in 1950: an ad for a white/cream free-standing horse, exactly like the horses on the older style of MasterCrafters clocks, appears in the November 1950 *Western Horseman* (see entry for white #59 above). Ads for the free-standing palomino Western Horse appear as early as September 1951 (see entry for #57 above). For details, see Breyer Company History in the Appendix near the end of this book; also see MasterCrafters Clocks in the Appendix.

(2) Sculptor: Chris Hess is identified as the sculptor of the Western Horse by *JAH* 16/#1 Feb./Mar. 1989 (p. 12). Quite evidently, however, the designs for this horse and for the Western Pony were not Hess originals but adaptations from Hartland's Large and Small Western Champs, which were sculpted by Roger Williams (per Fitch 1993, 2: 4, 6). According to Fitch, the Large Champ was released in 1946 or 1947 and the Small Champ no later than 1952. The Breyers are very similar to the Hartlands, though there are differences, the most obvious being that the Breyers have their manes on the left and have relatively smooth tails, while the Hartlands have manes on the right and have deeply grooved tails. It is not an accident that Breyer looked to Hartland for its designs. Three hobby sources—Fitch 1993, English 1989, and Walerius 1991 (p. 1)—tell how the two companies crossed paths via the MasterCrafters Clock Company. Before Breyer made Western Horses for MasterCrafters' mantel clocks (see note 1 for this mold), Hartland had provided large Western Champs to the same clock company for use on the same mantel clocks. Hartland subsequently stopped supplying MasterCrafters, and the clock company then approached Breyer. Undoubtedly MasterCrafters showed the Hartland Western Champ to Breyer to explain what was needed (see Walerius 1991, p. 1). Fitch comments, "The Breyer clock horse was a copy of the Hartland clock horse, and Hartland was angry about it, according to Thomas Caestecker, whose father owned both Hartland and interest in Master Crafters" (Fitch 1995b, 2: 123). Indeed, the clocks with Hartland Champs and some of the earliest clocks with Breyers (with white horse standing over the clock) are virtual mirror images—nearly identical except that the horses face opposite directions, so that the mane sides always face the front. The Breyer and Hartland horses on these clocks resemble each other even more closely than later Western Horses and Champs resemble each other: these early clock Breyers and the clock Hartlands have diamond-shaped conchas (see note 3 for this mold), creamy white bodies, brown-shaded manes and tails, and brown/black hooves. See MasterCrafters Clocks below in the Appendix for further details.

(3) Mold variations: There are two basic mold versions of the Western Horse—the early version, which I call the "diamond conchas" (DC) mold, made in 1950 and possibly into early 1951, and the normal version, which replaced the diamond-conchas horse and is still produced today. *Basic differences between the DC and normal molds*: On DC's bridle nearly all the conchas are molded in a diamond shape; only the center concha on each side is rounded. On his breastcollar, the top concha on each side is diamond shaped, and all the rest are rounded. On the normal mold, all the conchas on bridle and breast-collar are rounded. The studs in the centers of DC's conchas are larger than the normal mold's studs. On the left side of DC's brow band are four studs, whereas the normal mold has three. The chest placket on DC's breastcollar is narrower than normal mold's placket. DC's mane, forelock, and tail have slightly different contours than normal mold's. Most of the Western Horses that I have seen on the horse-over-the-clock style of MasterCrafters clocks are white/cream horses of the DC mold (for the exceptions, including DC horses of a somewhat dubious bile yellow-charcoal coloring, see MasterCrafters Clocks in the Appendix near the end of this book). All the horses I have seen on the horse-beside-the-clock style of clock are the normal-mold version, either white or palomino. There are also free-standing DC horses, all of them that I have seen being white except for one (a bile yellow-charcoal). Some if not all DC horses were molded with plastic pegs coming out of the bottoms of their hooves, which were used to attach the horses to the clock bases (thanks to Donna Schildberg for pointing this out to me). I have seen these pegs on a couple of clock horses, and Paula DeFeyter's free-standing DC horse and my own two such horses have round areas on the bottoms of their hooves that look like the remnants of amputated pegs. (Some horse-over-the-clock horses, however, are attached to the base with screws; see MasterCrafters Clocks in the Appendix.) An ad for the free-standing DC horses appears in the November 1950 *Western Horseman*. This ad appears again in the November 1951 issue but must be for leftover stock, for by this time the mold had been changed to the normal version: an ad for free-standing palomino normal mold horses appears in the September 1951 *Western Horseman*. *DC mold sub-variations*: Collector Sande Schneider discovered a couple of mold variations among DC horses. First, a few have an indentation on the underside of the lower part of the tail, which is visible from the side. It looks as though someone had pressed a thumb into the hot plastic. Sande owns a free-standing DC horse like this, and the over-the-clock style MasterCrafters on *Breyer Collector's Video*

seems to sport such a horse. Second, Sande's indented-tail horse has no bit holes; there is solid plastic inside the bit rings, as though you were seeing the sides of the horse's face. This suggests that the bit holes on DC horses were drilled rather than molded in. *Normal mold sub-variations*: There are two slight mold sub-variations among old normal-mold horses. Some have a pit near the base of each ear on the poll side. Collector Liz Strauss's white horse on her horse-beside-the-clock MasterCrafters clock has ear pits, and I've seen the pits on palomino and white free-standing horses, which also had o-link reins (see note 8 for this mold) and thus must be among the earliest of the normal-mold horses. I've never noticed ear pits on later horses. A second sub-variation was pointed out to me by Sande Schneider: some old Western Horses have a small bump on their back, which looks proportionally like a large boil. Sande has a couple of old white normal-molds with brown-shaded mane and tail, each with a boil. My old ear-pit horse has such a bump too, and my somewhat newer black pinto has a slightly smaller bump.

(4) Horse versus Pony: Western Horse is large and Western Pony is small. Other than this, the molds are nearly identical. There are two slight differences that can help you tell one mold from the other in photos. First, the normal-mold Western Horse's browband has three studs on each side, while Western Pony's browband has four studs on each side. Second, the bottom lines of the manes (left side of neck) differ slightly: both molds have a gap between locks of mane just above the shoulder, but Western Horse's gap falls below the breastcollar strap so that the strap is not visible there, whereas Western Pony's gap crosses the strap so that the strap is visible.

(5) Copies of the Western Horse: There are two molds that look very much like Breyer Western Horses but that I believe are copies. Both of these molds are old, dating probably to the 1950s, and are, like Breyers, made of nice-quality plastic. I have seen both of these molds on MasterCrafters clocks as well as free-standing (see MasterCrafters Clocks in the Appendix near the end of this book). Neither mold has any identifying mold stamps. They are not Hartland Champs, for they both have their manes on the left side. The two molds are as follows. *Scooper-eared horse*: This horse particularly resembles the diamond-conchas version of the Breyer Western Horse in that he has similar diamond-shaped conchas on his bridle. But he differs from the Breyer in several ways. His most distinctive feature is his absurd ears, which look like slippers or scoopers, wider near the top than at the bottom. Unlike a Breyer, he has no facial veins. He is everywhere narrower than a Breyer: his tail, body, neck, forelock, and head are all thin. His saucerlike nostrils are more vague and sloppily formed, and his right nostril is much larger than his left. His bridle straps are narrower and his buckles smaller than the Breyer's. The center placket on his breastcollar has two studs rather than three. His hooves are blobby and lack coronary bands. His reins are soft plastic lace, and his Western saddle is semi-soft plastic with no cinch. The scooper-ears mold comes in several colors. Two colors of which I've seen several specimens are black with gold bridle and breastcollar and gold hooves, mane, and tail; and dark brown with gold bridle and breastcollar and copper hooves, mane, tail, and body highlights. (This dark brown horse may be the model referred to as a Breyer Western Horse by Walerius 1991, p. 22.) My own dark brown specimen is cast in red plastic, to judge from a sizable red wound on his stifle where the brown paint is rubbed off. A palomino horse of what I believe is the same scooper-ears mold was found new in unopened cellophane "window" package by collector Sheryl Leisure in spring 1996. Aside from his dark brown bridle and breastcollar, Sheryl's horse is strikingly similar to #57 Breyer Western Horses of the 1950s and 1960s, with a rich, slightly orangish body color and oversprayed lighter palomino mane and tail. Sheryl has not removed him from his packaging, but he appears to be made of nice-quality plastic, like most other scooper-ears horses. (Sheryl subsequently came upon another palomino virtually identical to her own but made of poor-quality styrene.) The flexible brown plastic Western saddle on Sheryl's horse is like the saddle of a dark brown scooper-ears horse found by collector Sande Schneider, but the palomino's plastic lace reins are a bit wider than those on Sande's horse and my own. Although the palomino's ears and hooves are hidden in the cardboard frame of the window package, the rest of him can readily be seen to be identical in mold to the black and dark brown horses, with one exception: the breastcollar and bridle of Sheryl's horse have stars molded onto the centers of the conchas and other little raised designs molded onto the straps. The black and dark brown horses known to me have simple rounded nubs on the conchas and no designwork on the straps. As noted above, these horses have no mold stamps on them, but the packaging of Sheryl's palomino identifies the manufacturer as The Ohio Plastic Company, of Frazeysburg, Ohio. The Payless pricetag on the package offers him at $1.69, reduced from $2.00. A sticker on the front proclaims, "Famous TV Horses," and tells that the model is available in black, white, red, tan, and palomino. One wonders what the red horse might look like (is he the same red as the wound on my dark brown horse?) and what the difference is between the tan and the palomino. Be that as it may, another label on the package implies that Sheryl's horse must date to about 1964. This label advertises a "win this beautiful live pony" contest (there's a photo showing a real pony), "courtesy Ohio Plastic Co.," and mentions the "1963 winner / Cathy Mehner / Cape Girardeau MO." Presumably 1963 was in the recent past at the time this new contest was advertised. However, the dark brown horses and some of the black ones may be earlier than the mid-1960s; at least, this is suggested by the fact that the black scooper-ears horse has been found on a MasterCrafters clock very similar in design to the early-1950s horse-beside-the-clock style of MasterCrafters with Breyer Western Horses. *Textured-tack horse and pony*: The textured-tack horse, like the Breyer normal-mold Western Horse, has round conchas on his bridle. His most distinctive difference from the Breyer is that he has texturing on his bridle and breastcollar: it looks as though there were tiny chicken wire embedded in the plastic. The saddle of one specimen I've seen had an oval of matching texture on each side of the seat. This mold also has smaller ears than a Breyer, and his left ear is rotated out. He has noticeably thinner legs and bigger hooves than a Breyer; the hooves look ridiculously oversized for the horse. The reins are metal bead-chain, such as you'd hang car keys on. Three of these horses that I've seen are white with white mane and tail, gray hooves, and black Western saddle. Two of the three had solid gold bridle and breastcollar, the other had black with silver studs. A fourth specimen, which I've seen photos of, is a black pinto, owned by collector Karen Lebeda's mother. Mrs. Lebeda got the horse new in the 1950s. Like the black pinto Breyer Western Horse, he has a bald face, gold on the bridle and breastcollar, 4 stockings, gray hooves, and white mane. But unlike the Breyer, he has an all-white tail, he has no white shoulder spots, and his white butt/croup patch ends well above the leg. Collector Arlene Winter has a brown pinto version of this horse, which has a brown bridle and breastcollar and the same pinto pattern as Mrs. Lebeda's black pinto. Arlene also has a black textured-tack pony, which is very similar in mold to Breyer's Western Pony except that the textured-tack pony's tail is much thinner and more pointed. This black pony has a solid-faced, painted-on white stockings, gray hooves, silver bridle and breastcollar with red-dot conchas, and twisted-link chain reins like those on a Breyer Western Pony. Collector Sande Schneider too has a textured-tack pony, which is ivory colored, with bead-chain reins like those on textured-tack horses, and a brown Western saddle with areas of texturing on either side. Unlike Arlene's pony, Sande's is made of styrene. I have also seen a palomino textured-tack pony made of styrene, with bead-chain reins and black Western saddle. On the pieces I've inspected, neither the ponies nor the larger horses have any identifying mold stamps.

(6) Names: The names "Western Horse" and "Western Pony," which designate the large and small molds respectively, do not appear in the ca.1954 catalog, the earliest Breyer catalog known to me. The names that do appear there designate the models by color type rather than by size: the solid colors of both sizes are called "Western Mount Horses," and the pintos of both sizes are called "Pinto Ponies." Under these names, inch dimensions are given to distinguish the two sizes, and the two sizes of the same color are given different model numbers (numbers in the 50s for the large size, in the 40s for the small). Ads for the white and palomino Western Horses placed by the Breyer company in the February and March 1952 issues of *Playthings* magazine also refer to the horses as "Western Mount." (Earlier ads that I know of for Western Horses were placed by saddlery companies and similar retailers, and refer to the horses in various ways.) In the 1958 Breyer catalog and price list and in an old Breyer sheet that probably dates to 1955/57 (partially reprinted in Walerius 1991, p. 25), the color-type names are gone and the names "Western Horse" and "Western Pony" appear, referring in the familiar way to the two sizes.

(7) Saddles: The Western Horse has come with at least two different basic styles of Western saddle over the years—three if you count the Western Prancer saddle, with which Western Horse was advertised and apparently sold for a brief period in the mid-1970s. All of these saddles were manufactured by Breyer, according to Breyer executive Peter Stone (conversation of Nov. 1994). *Old style Western saddle*: This is the original Western Horse saddle. It came with the horses on MasterCrafters clocks of both types (horse standing over the clock and horse standing beside the clock); it appears in ads for the Western Horse in 1950-52 issues of *Western Horseman* and *Playthings* magazine; and it is shown in Breyer catalogs from ca.1954 through 1967. It is a hard-plastic saddle with tapaderos (pointed stirrup-covers). It has no molded-on blanket, as the post-1967 saddle has. It comes in black or brown, with the brown ones ranging from dark chocolate brown to brick red. (For an unusual white version with yellow-charcoal shading, found on strange, bile yellow-charcoal diamond-conchas horses, see MasterCrafters Clocks in the Appendix near the end of this book.) Typically the color is in the plastic, not painted on. Collector Sande Schneider has pointed out that the old-style saddle comes in four versions: one without a cinch and three with a flexible vinyl cinch (see Schneider 1992a). In likely chronological order (though versions A and B may be contemporaneous), the versions are as follows: [A] Saddle with no cinch and no grommet holes in the fender where a cinch might have been attached. These saddles are brown and have whitewashed skirts and fenders. They have been found on the earliest Western Horses, that is to say the diamond-conchas mold version, both on horse-over-the-clock style clocks and free-standing. Horses with these saddles often have red or yellow stains on their backs, apparently owing to bleeding of the color out of the saddles. [B] Cinch saddle with slip-through buckle on the cinch and high-set grommets holding the cinch to the saddle. The grommets are near the top of the fenders, and look like nail heads, with a solid surface. These saddles are brown with whitewashed skirts and fenders. These saddles, too, have been found on diamond-conchas horses, both on over-the-clock MasterCrafters and free-standing, but could possibly have been issued on some very early normal-mold horses as well. Collector Paula DeFeyter's old free-standing horse, which she found in his original box, came with this type of saddle. Ads for these old free-standing diamond-concha horses in the November 1950 and November 1951 *Western Horseman* seem to show the whitewashing on the saddle, but it's not clear whether there's a cinch. These saddles too can stain the horse's back, to judge from my own specimen. [C] This saddle and version D are often called "snap saddles" or "snap-on saddles" because their cinches snap together under the horse's belly. Version C has high-set grommets holding the cinch to the saddle. The grommets have holes in the middle, like donuts. These saddles are found on normal-mold horses—both later (horse-beside-the-clock style) MasterCrafters clock horses and free-standing horses. In my experience the saddles on the beside-the-clock horses, both white and palomino, are always brown, though typically they have goldwashed skirts and fenders on the white horses and gold-touched tooling on the palominos (though collector Sheryl Leisure found an old black-hoofed #57 palomino with goldwashed saddle). The brown, gold-washed, high-grommet saddle on collector Liz Strauss's white horse-beside-the-clock horse is, as she wrote to me, a little softer in consistency than later saddles, and its girth straps "are a very wimpy brown vinyl with darker brown flecks on it." I've seen several of the white clock horses with a felt saddle blanket (white), but only one palomino, which had a red felt blanket and was mounted on an unusual metal clock base, not the normal plastic base. Version-C saddles on free-standing horses come in black and brown, in both cases with gold on the tooled designs. Some version-C saddles have a little pad of felt over the inside of each grommet, and some have the cinch strap doubled over the grommet (Kay Schlumpf has one like this), both designs aimed apparently at protecting the horse's finish from the grommets. Gold-touched, high-grommet saddles are visible in ads for Western Horses in 1952 issues of *Playthings* and *Horse Lover's Magazine* and in the ca.1954 Breyer catalog. The palomino Western Horses in ads in the September and December 1951 *Western Horseman* issues also appear to have gold-touched high-grommet saddles, but the photos are not too clear. [D] Cinch saddle with a snap on the cinch and low-set grommets holding the cinch to the saddle. The grommets are donut style and are near the bottom of the fenders. These saddles come in black touched with gold or silver and in brown touched with gold. Low-grommet saddles are visible in the 1960-67 catalogs, and were evidently introduced sometime between 1955 and 1958/59. Finally, Sande observed that versions C and D each come in two sub-versions. On one sub-version, the pinwheel designs on the two fenders both swirl clockwise, while on the other sub-version, the pinwheels swirl in different directions. These swirl differences are accompanied by slight differences in the floral decorations on the fenders and skirts. As if this weren't enough, collector Kay Schlumpf noticed that some old-style saddles have the fender and stirrup angled further forward than others do. *New-style Western saddle*: This saddle is shown in catalogs 1968 - 1973/74 and 1976-94 and was also issued on the 1995 SR horse. It is a hard-plastic cinchless saddle with tapaderos and molded-on blanket. New-style saddles sold with "Tic Toc" #864 are molded in black plastic, but all previous ones have been molded in white plastic and colored with paint. *Western Prancer saddle*: The 1974 manual and 1975 catalog and manual show the Western Horse wearing a Western Prancer saddle (uncovered stirrups), which looks uncomfortably small for him. One would suppose that this was just an error, that the photographer managed to grab the wrong saddle for the horse. But collector Betty Mertes wrote to me that she got a Western Horse new in box years ago that did indeed come with the Western Prancer saddle. Perhaps Breyer briefly experimented with paring down its line of accessories.

(8) Reins and bits: The Western Horse has come with two different types of reins over the years, both of them gold metal chain. *O-link reins*: The o-link reins, as I call them, were the first reins used on the Western Horse, and he was the only Breyer mold ever to have this type of reins to my knowledge. These reins are gold-colored metal (usually heavily tar-

nished by now), with links shaped like tiny wedding bands: beefy little circles that are flat on the inside, gently convex on the outside. These reins came on Breyer Western Horses on MasterCrafters clocks (over-the-clock and beside-the-clock styles) and on early free-standing Western Horses of both mold versions (see note 3 for this mold). O-link reins are shown in ads for white and palomino Western Horses in 1950-52 magazines, but they are gone by the ca.1954 Breyer catalog, which shows normal (twisted-link) reins. O-link reins are attached to the horse in several different ways. On some models, there is a bit which is a metal cylinder with a hole drilled through each end, to which the reins are attached either with large round wire links or with hooks that look a little like miniature safety pins. I have seen the cylinder-bit-with-safety-pin arrangement on diamond-conchas horses on over-the-clock style clocks (as shown in *JAH* 16/#1 Feb./Mar. 1989, p. 29), and on one very early free-standing normal-mold #59 white Western Horse. Both the white and palomino free-standing Western Horses in the March 1952 *Playthings* ad also have the safety pins; the bits aren't clear in the ad photo, but they are probably cylinders. On other models, there is no bit; instead the chain runs through the horse's mouth and the chain ends are fastened together with one large round wire link. I've seen this arrangement on both styles of clocks and on free-standing horses of both mold versions. On still other models, there is a wire bit as on recent Western Horses, to which the o-link reins are attached either with a large round wire link on each side or with a large link only on one side and the rein attached directly to the bit loop on the other side. I've seen this bit style on over-the-clock and beside-the-clock horses and on free-standing horses of both mold versions. An ad in the October/November 1952 *Horse Lover's Magazine* shows a round wire link attachment, but it's not clear which bit the horse has. *Twisted-link reins*: This type of chain is still used for reins on Western Horses, Western Ponies, and Western Prancers today, and was used in earlier years for reins on "Fury" Prancers and for collars of some Boxers. These reins first appear in the ca.1954 catalog, but I believe they were introduced in 1953, for this is the year in which the Western Pony mold was introduced (per an ad for a black Western Pony in the Sept. 1953 *Western Horseman*), and to my knowledge no Western Pony was ever issued with reins other than these. The links are ovals made of heavy, gold-colored wire, and each link is twisted so that the chain as a whole lies flat. The reins are attached to a gold-colored wire bit by means of round wire rings. According to Breyer executive Peter Stone (conversation of Nov. 1994), these reins used to be supplied to Breyer by two companies, Dudek & Bock of Chicago and Clover Bead & Chain of Rhode Island; he was not certain who supplies the reins now. *A note on bead-chain reins*: Some old Western Horses, including clock horses, have been found with bead chains (sometimes called ball chains) of the type you put car keys on. Some free-standing Hartland Western Champs were issued with this type of reins, but to my knowledge such reins were never put on Western Horses by the Breyer factory.

(9) Early models of the Western Horse mold have no mold marks. Later ones have a "U.S.A." stamp inside the right hind leg. Collector Sande Schneider has a couple of matte black pinto #55s with the "U.S.A," so it is certain that this stamp was added to the mold no later than 1976, the last year of production for #55; it may have been added as early as 1970, when the "U.S.A." was introduced into the Breyer line. Some "U.S.A." models also have a backwards (or upside-down) "B" stamp, located on the same leg as the "U.S.A." (collector Mel Price has a model like this). This mold was never given the round "Breyer Molding Co." copyright stamp, perhaps because MasterCrafters Clock Company held copyright to the Western Horse as part of its clocks (see Walerius 1991, pp. 3, 12). However, since 1991, this mold has had a "© Breyer Reeves" copyright stamp (inside the left hind leg) as well as the "U.S.A." We can be sure of the 1991 introduction date because this copyright stamp is not on the *JAH* SR caramel pinto issued in 1990 but is on a #57 palomino with a 1991 manual in its box that I bought new from Mission Supply House in June 1992. The #57s made in 1991 are thus rather special despite their too familiar, plain-Jane appearance, for they were not only the last pieces made of #57, Breyer's all-time longest-running model, but also the first copyright-stamped pieces of Breyer's oldest mold. In 1995, a "'95" mold stamp was added to the mold's right hind leg for the production of the only Western Horse model issued that year, the SR palomino Western Horse made for QVC TV (see the entry for this model above). This "'95" stamp was removed from the mold, or rather, partially removed—the apostrophe is still present—in preparation for the 1996 release of #960 "Royal Te" Appaloosa (not listed in this book). It is not impossible that a few "Royal Te's" were made before the "95" was removed, but I have not heard of such specimens, and my own very early specimen (purchased in March 1996) has only the apostrophe. No Western Horse saddle I've ever seen, whether old or new, has any mold stamps.

Western Mount Horse — see under Western Horse (#57, #58, #59); Western Pony (#43, #44, #45); also see note 6 for the Western Horse mold

Western Pony — Small genderless horse, standing square, mane on left side of neck, molded-on bridle and breastcollar, gold metal chain reins, removable plastic Western saddle. Adapted by Chris Hess from Hartland's Small Western Champ, sculpted by Roger Williams. Mold in catalog-run production 1953-76, 1995 - current as of 1996.

Catalog-run models made from this mold:

- "Cisco" Western Pony With Saddle #910, buckskin; bald face; black mane, tail, knees, and hocks; 4 stockings; gray hooves; solid gold bridle; buckskin breastcollar with gold conchas and upper straps; matte; new-style black Western saddle with gold detailing (1995 - current as of 1996). This pony has the same wire bit and twisted-link gold-colored chain reins as Western Ponies of earlier decades. The saddle is the same mold as the new-style Western saddle issued in the 1960s and 1970s but is molded in black plastic. The 1995 and 1996 catalogs show the saddle with several gold stripes, including one down the back edge of the stirrup leather. My own "Cisco" saddle and others I've seen lack this stirrup-leather stripe. In the 1996 catalog, the phrase "With Saddle" was dropped from #910's name.
- Western Mount Horse "Black Beauty" #44, black, no white markings, black mane and tail, gold hooves, solid gold bridle and breastcollar, glossy; black old-style Western saddle with gold trim (1953 - 1955/57). This pony is cast in black plastic. He is the earliest of three distinct versions of black Western Ponies known to exist, the other two versions being #40 with bald face and #40 with diamond star. The earliest documentation for him (and for the mold) that I know of is an ad by the "little joe" Wiesenfeld Company in the September 1953 *Western Horseman*, of which collector Paula DeFeyter kindly sent me a copy. The ad has a picture of the model and give this description: "a stunning plastic model of Black Beauty, with shiny black coat and gold hoofs." This pony is also listed in the ca.1954 catalog—the earliest Breyer catalog I know of—under the name Western Mount Horse "Black Beauty" #44 (regarding this early name, see note 6 for Western Horse). Although this catalog does not show the pony, a model found by collector Sande Schneider confirms that #44 is the solid black with gold hooves. Sande purchased a solid black, gold-hoofed pony in what she feels certain is its original box, on which is stamped "#44," the number in the ca.1954 catalog. The box has no picture of the model, but the pony inside was brand new in appearance and was wrapped in what seemed to be the original tissue paper. The collector who sold it to Sande had several identically boxed and tissue-wrapped models. Collector Rebecca Splan also got one of these mint-in-original-box gold-hoof #44's.
- Western Pony "Black Beauty" #40, black; some with bald face and silver bridle and breastcollar; some with diamond star and gold bridle and breastcollar; most with 4 stockings; glossy; old-style Western saddle (1955/58 - 1960/62). There are two distinct versions of black #40: [A] The bald-faced version has black mane, black tail with white tip, 4 stockings, gray hooves, and silver bridle and breastcollar. His saddle is black with silver trim to match the bridle and breastcollar, but the reins are the same gold metal chains as on other Western Ponies. Some specimens have hand-painted eyewhites (collector Sheryl Leisure's has eyewhites; my own two do not). The stockings on some specimens are the natural white plastic, but on others the stockings are painted on over painted black legs (the models are cast in white plastic). [B] The diamond-star version has solid black mane and tail, usually 4 stockings, black hooves, and gold bridle and breastcollar. His saddle is brown or black with gold trim. Some diamond-star ponies are white plastic painted black, with either all the white markings painted over the black (as on Sheryl Leisure's pony) or only the star painted over the black while the stockings are the natural white plastic (one of collector Liz Strauss's ponies is like this). Other diamond-star ponies are black plastic with the white markings painted on (as with Sande Schneider's model). Liz Strauss also has a diamond-star pony with solid black legs, no stockings, and I have heard of one or two others like this. A 4-stocking diamond-star "Black Beauty" is pictured in the 1958 catalog in the #240 Indian Warrior and #540 Kit Carson sets and is listed in the catalog individually as Western Pony "Black Beauty" #40. An old Breyer company sheet that probably dates to 1955/57 also mentions a "Black Beauty" Western Pony (no number is given), and the 1960 catalog lists a black Western Pony #40 (with no reference to "Black Beauty"). But neither of these publications has a picture of the pony, so it is impossible to be sure whether the bald-faced version preceded or followed the diamond-star version. However, the eyewhites that sometimes occur on the bald-faced version suggest that he followed the diamond-star pony, for eyewhites are not typical of mid-1950s models but appear commonly on models of the late 1950s and the 1960s. A post-1958 dating for the bald-faced pony also coincides with my dating for black Western Horse #50 with bald face and silver trim, and it does make sense to think that Breyer issued these matching Horses and Ponies at the same time. The model number 40 was later assigned to Lynn Anderson's "Lady Phase."
- Western Pony #40, dark brown, diamond star, dark brown mane and tail, 4 stockings, black hooves, gold bridle and breastcollar, glossy; brown or black old-style Western saddle with gold trim (sometime in the period 1955-57). My description of this model's white markings is per my own model and those owned by collectors Heather Wells, Joy Sheesley, Sande Schneider, and Becky Brooks. These ponies are made of dark brown plastic with the white markings and black hoof color painted on. The markings are the same as on the diamond-star version of the black Western Pony (see preceding entry). Sande and Joy's brown ponies came with brown saddles, but Becky's came with a black saddle. This brown model is listed only on an old undated Breyer company sheet that probably dates to 1955/57, and which describes the model simply as "dark brown." The model is not in the ca. 1954 or 1958 catalogs. The model number 40 later belonged to Western Pony "Black Beauty," black with bald face, and much later was assigned to Lynn Anderson's "Lady Phase."
- Western Pony #41, black pinto, tobiano; bald face; white mane; black tail with white tip; 4 stockings; gray hooves; solid gold bridle and breastcollar; glossy and matte/semigloss; Western saddle (ca.1954 - 1976). Called Pinto Pony in the ca.1954 catalog; called Western Pony subsequently. This same model was also sold in the mid-1950s in Cowboy & Pinto #341, Indian & Pinto #241, and Lucky Ranger #341 sets. Western Pony #41 came with a black plastic old-style saddle with gold trim through 1967, and a charcoal-shaded new-style saddle from 1968 on (see note 3 for this mold). There are three variations that I know of on the pinto pattern of #41. Their defining characteristics are as follows: [A] Low-spot pattern: The white spot on the right shoulder is low on the shoulder, reaching onto the elbow and upper forearm. This pattern is nearly identical to that on pinto Western Horses and is the same pattern as on brown pinto Western Pony #42. Because of this match with #42, which is an early model, I believe the low-spot #41s are also early, dating to the 1950s and 1960s. The 1960s dating is borne out by the 1961 and 1962 Sears holiday catalogs, which show low-spot #41s in "grooming kit" sets (see note 4 for this mold). [B] No-spot pattern: There is no white spot on the right shoulder. This pattern seems to have been produced at various times: a no-spot pony was included in a #241 Indian set, dating to about 1954, found in original box by collector Paula DeFeyter; and a pony dating to no earlier than the late 1960s, to judge from his matte finish and new-style saddle, was found by Sande Schneider at an antique shop. [C] High-spot pattern: There is a white spot on the right shoulder, but it is decidedly higher and further back than on the low-spot pony; it lies below the withers and reaches onto the barrel. This pattern is visible in catalogs 1975-76, the last years that #41 was made. These catalogs (and the 1976 manual) are the only ones that show #41 from the right side. #41 was in the Showcase Collection as #410 in 1970-72 (see Showcase Collection in this section for discussion). The model number 410 later belonged to Marguerite Henry's "Sham."
- Western Pony #42, brown pinto, tobiano; bald face; white mane; brown tail with white tip; 4 stockings; gray hooves; solid gold bridle and breastcollar; glossy; brown old-style Western saddle with gold trim (ca.1954 - 1966). Called Pinto Pony in the ca.1954 catalog; called Western Pony subsequently. This same model was also sold in the mid-1950s in Kit Carson #542, Cowboy & Pinto #342, and Indian & Pinto #242, and Lucky Ranger #342 sets. This pony has the same pinto pattern as early #41s (low-spot pattern); the pattern is nearly identical to that on pinto Western Horses. Catalogs refer to #42 as "brown pinto," but the color is lighter than this may suggest, ranging from light honey palomino to red sorrel. Some models have gray eyes, others have gold eyes, which are now often tarnished. Possibly the latest #42s came with a new-style Western saddle; see note 3 for this mold.
- Western Pony #43, palomino, bald face, palomino-shaded mane and tail, 4 stockings, gray hooves, solid gold bridle and breastcollar, glossy and matte; Western saddle (ca.1954 - 1973). Called Western Mount Horse in the ca.1954 catalog; called Western Pony subsequently. This pony was also sold in Cowboy #343 and Lucky Ranger #343 sets in the mid-1950s. #43 came with a brown old-style saddle with gold trim through 1967, and with a tan-shaded new-style saddle subsequently (see note 3 for this mold). On some models the stockings are vague or nearly nonexistent. Some models have gray eyes, others have gold eyes, which are now typically tarnished. Some of these gold-eyed palominos came with grooming kits for human beings; for discussion see

note 4 for this mold. #43 was in the Showcase Collection as #430 in 1970-72 (see Showcase Collection in this section for discussion). The model number 430 later belonged to "Sherman Morgan."

- Western Pony #45, white; white mane and tail; gray eyes, ears, and hooves; solid gold bridle and breastcollar; glossy; Western saddle (ca.1954 - 1970). Called Western Mount Horse in the ca.1954 catalog; called Western Pony subsequently. This pony was also sold in Lucky Ranger #345 set in the late 1950s. #45 is not pictured in any of the catalogs that list him, but I believe he came with a black old-style saddle with gold trim through 1967, and with charcoal-shaded new-style saddle from 1968 on (see note 3 for this mold). Some white Western Ponies were sold with grooming kits for people; for discussion see note 4 for this mold. #45 was in the Showcase Collection as #450 in 1970 (see Showcase Collection in this section for discussion). The model number 450 later belonged to "Rugged Lark."
- Western Pony #945, woodgrain, black eyes, no white markings or other color detailing, matte (1959/60 - 1964). The 1960 catalog, which is the only catalog that pictures this model, shows him with no reins or saddle. Collector Sande Schneider has a #945 that was certainly issued without reins, for he has a thin sheet of woodgrain finish plugging one of his bit holes; she has seen another like this as well. A #945 with reins is shown in Diederich 1988, Section 1, and one with a saddle is shown on *Breyer Collector's Video*; but these tack items could have been added by previous owners.

Sets:

- Cowboy & Pinto set #341, rider on black pinto Western Pony (ca.1954 - pre-1958). This pony was also sold separately as Western Pony #41 [ca.1954 - 1976]. For discussion of dates and details see the Riders - Hard Plastic section. The model number 341 later belonged to the regular-run horned Holstein Cow.
- Cowboy & Pinto set #342, rider on brown pinto Western Pony (ca.1954 - pre-1958). This pony was also sold separately as Western Pony #42 [ca.1954 - 1966]. For discussion see the Riders - Hard Plastic section. The model number 342 later belonged to the regular-run horned Guernsey Cow.
- Cowboy set #343, rider on palomino Western Pony (ca.1954 - pre-1958). This pony was also sold separately as Western Pony #43 [ca.1954 - 1973]. For discussion see the Riders - Hard Plastic section. The model number 343 later belonged to the regular-run horned Jersey Cow.
- Indian & Pinto set #241, rider on black pinto Western Pony (ca.1954 - pre-1958). This pony was also sold separately as Western Pony #41 [ca.1954 - 1976]. The black pinto pony that came in collector Paula DeFeyter's set is the no-spot version (see Western Pony #41 above). For further discussion see the Riders - Hard Plastic section.
- Indian & Pinto set #242, rider on brown pinto Western Pony (ca.1954 - pre-1958). This pony was also sold separately as Western Pony #42 [ca.1954 - 1966]. For discussion see the Riders - Hard Plastic section.
- Indian Warrior set #240, rider on black Western Pony with diamond star (1958 [maybe earlier] - 1958/59). This pony was also sold separately as Western Pony "Black Beauty" #40 [1955/58 - 1960/62]. For discussion see the Riders - Hard Plastic section.
- Kit Carson set #540, rider on black Western Pony with diamond star (1957/58 - 1958/59). This pony was also sold separately as Western Pony "Black Beauty" #40 [1955/58 - 1960/62]. For discussion see the Riders - Hard Plastic section.
- Kit Carson set #542, rider on brown pinto Western Pony (sometime in the period 1956-57). This pony was also sold separately as Western Pony #42 [ca.1954 - 1966]. For discussion see the Riders - Hard Plastic section.
- Lucky Ranger set #341, rider on black pinto Western Pony (1955/56 - 1957). This pony was also sold separately as Western Pony #41 [ca.1954 - 1976]. For discussion see the Riders - Hard Plastic section.
- Lucky Ranger set #342, rider on brown pinto Western Pony (1955/56 - 1957). This pony was also sold separately as Western Pony #42 [ca.1954 - 1966]. For discussion see the Riders - Hard Plastic section.
- Lucky Ranger set #343, rider on palomino Western Pony (1955/56 - 1957). This pony was also sold separately as Western Pony #43 [ca.1954 - 1973]. For discussion see the Riders - Hard Plastic section.
- Lucky Ranger set #345, rider on white Western Pony (1957/58 - 1958/59). This pony was also sold separately as Western Pony #45 [ca.1954 - 1970]. For discussion see the Riders - Hard Plastic section. The model number 345 later belonged to the regular-run horned Brown Swiss Cow.

Notes:

(1) Regarding the release date of this mold, see the entry above for the #44 black pony. Regarding the sculptor of the Western Pony, see note 2 for Western Horse. For discussion of the names of the Western Pony, see note 6 for Western Horse. Regarding copies of the Western Pony, see note 5 for Western Horse.

(2) Western Pony is small and Western Horse is large. Other than this, the molds are almost identical. For the slight mold differences other than size, see note 4 for Western Horse.

(3) To the best of my knowledge, all the Western Ponies that came with reins were issued with the twisted-link style of gold-colored metal chain reins with a gold wire bit, as on "Fury" Prancers, Western Prancers, and most Western Horses. (For the history of these reins, see note 8 for the Western Horse mold.) But Western Ponies came with two different types of Western saddle over the years. *Old-style hard plastic saddle* with tapaderos (pointed stirrup-covers) and no molded-on blanket. This saddle is very similar to the Western Horse's old-style saddle except in size, the pony's being of course smaller. It comes in black or brown, the brown ones ranging in color from dark chocolate brown to brick red. This saddle is shown on the Western Pony in an ad in the September 1953 *Western Horseman* and in the ca.1954 - 1967 catalogs. It came in three variations, as discussed by collector Sande Schneider in one of her articles (1992a). One variation, shown in the ca.1954 catalog on ponies without riders, has long fenders and a vinyl snap-on cinch attached to the saddle by grommets placed high on the fenders. (The saddle in the 1953 *Western Horseman* ad too has a snap-on cinch saddle, but the grommets aren't clear.) A second variation, shown in the ca.1954 catalog with the Cowboy rider and pony set, has no cinch and no grommet hole on the fenders; I can't tell about fender length. The third variation, shown in catalogs 1960-67, has short fenders and a vinyl snap-on cinch attached to the saddle by grommets placed low on the fenders. (Western Horse old-style saddles also had high- and low-grommet variations, but the fender length didn't vary.) Collector Heather Wells found an unusual black saddle of this short-fender version on a black pinto Western Pony #41, at a flea market. The saddle is normal in all respects except that is has a tiny, in-scale nameplate located on the saddle skirt just behind the cantle. The nameplate is plastic, of a color like tarnished brass, and says "Kentucky Dam." It looks professionally made, and is apparently glued onto the saddle rather than molded on. Heather's is the only saddle I know of with a nameplate. *New-style hard plastic saddle* with tapaderos and molded-on blanket, no cinch. Collectors often refer to this as the slip-on saddle. It is virtually identical to the Western Horse's new-style saddle except in size. Prior to 1995, the saddle was molded in white plastic and shaded with tan or charcoal paint. Western Pony is shown with this saddle in the 1968-76 catalogs. However, the saddle was evidently issued earlier than 1968, for I have heard of a brown pinto Western Pony (last produced in 1966) that was found in its box with a new-style saddle.

(4) In the 1950s and 1960s, some black pinto #41s, palomino #43s, and white #45s were offered through department-store catalogs in various sets. Although some sets included such exotica as astronaut watches, rifle-shaped pens, and candies (as I'll discuss below), by far the most common sets were the so-called "groomers" or "grooming kits" for human children, which included, in lieu of normal Western saddles, flexible vinyl "pack saddles" that held various hygiene and beauty aids such as combs, nail files, hair barrettes, toothbrushes, and tie clips. Two different basic types of "pack saddle" are known to me, one quite large, which might more precisely be called a "pack saddle-blanket," and one smaller. The smaller type itself comes in different versions, as I'll discuss in a moment. *Large "pack saddle-blanket" grooming kit:* This set, featuring a bizarre houndstooth-checked vinyl "saddle blanket complete with stirrups," was sold through the 1958 and 1959 Sears holiday catalogs, where it is labeled "Palomino Groomer" and credited with supernatural powers: "See tiny cowhands rush to clean up." (Thanks to collector Andrea Gurdon for Xeroxes of the Sears pages.) In the 1958 set, priced at $2.77, the saddle blanket "holds ball point pen, nail file, toothbrush and comb." The 1959 set, which cost a dime less, was the same except that it included a nail clipper instead of a pen. One of the 1958 sets, new in unopened cardboard mailer carton, turned up in 1995 at an antique show in Georgia, where it was lassoed by collectors Kirsten, Sarah, and Ruth-Ann Wellman. According to the photo and description the Wellmans kindly gave me, the pony is a glossy palomino #43 with the usual gold chain reins, and the grooming articles include a white plastic comb, metal nail file, transparent red plastic toothbrush, and ball-point pen (the pen dates the set to 1958). The "saddle blanket," which looks just like those in the Sears catalogs, consists mainly of a flexible vinyl "blanket"—the size of a stable blanket relative to the Western Pony—printed with brown and white houndstooth checks, with a girth of the same material that snaps under the pony's belly. Sewn atop this blanket is a flat, solid-brown vinyl "saddle," whose "stirrup leathers" are stitched onto the blanket in such a way as to bulge out in 4 loops (2 on each side) to hold the grooming articles. Rectangular brass stirrups dangle from the ends of the stirrup leathers. The brown cardboard mailer carton in which the Wellmans' set came is printed with a green line drawing of the Western Pony in a normal old-style Western Saddle and the words "Breyer Molding Co. / Chicago, U.S.A." The top of the carton is stamped with the set number 9549. This set is not listed in any Breyer company catalogs or price lists known to me. *Small-saddle grooming kits:* Sold through department-store catalogs from the mid-1950s through the 1960s, these Western Pony grooming sets included a flat, flexible vinyl "pack saddle" with two rectangular pockets hanging down on either side of the pony and a self girth that snaps under the pony's belly. To my knowledge, the pack saddle came in three different versions: one made of smooth black vinyl (this is rare; no collectors' specimens are known to me), one made of smooth tan or brown vinyl, and one made of brown vinyl with embossed with "tooling." My own tooled saddle, which came on a glossy palomino Western Pony, is a dark reddish-brown vinyl embossed with a random scattering of nifty designs such as a cowboy in old-fashioned fleece chaps, a Western saddle, and a calf's head. Collector Kim Jones's tooled saddle, which also came on a palomino pony, is light tan vinyl embossed with, among other designs, a standing horse mounted by a cowboy and a bucking horse parting company with another cowboy. On my saddle, the two layers of vinyl that make the pockets are sewn together; on Kim's they are heat bonded. The earliest Western Pony set I know of, a "Palomino Groomer" advertised in the 1954 and 1955 Sears holiday catalogs, includes a palomino pony with a small pack-saddle that the ad calls "tan" and that appears in my Xerox copies to be smooth. A "nail clipper, nail file, Sears approved toothbrush, comb" fill the saddle's pockets. This set cost $3.95 in 1954 but was "now $2.98" in the 1955 Sears catalog, which attempts to stimulate sales by alleging that the kit "spurs youngsters to tidy up." Identical smooth-saddle Palomino Groomers appear in other department-store holiday catalogs: Ward's 1962 ($2.69; the Ward's photo shows a smooth pack-saddle, although the text says "richly embossed vinyl saddle bags"), Ward's 1964 ($2.69), and Aldens 1969 ($2.64). The other two versions of the small pack-saddle both appear for the first time to my knowledge in the 1956 Sears holiday catalog. Here the black pack-saddle is offered on a white Western Pony in a set called "'My Fair Lady' Horse," "an easy answer to the problem of rounding up would-be 'cowgirls' at tidy-up time," for $2.98. The ad text describes the saddle as black, and the photo seems to show it as smooth. It holds "six gold-color barrettes (three pairs in various designs) and a white nylon comb." The same catalog offers a pack saddle with embossed "tooling" in a "Palomino Groomer" set ($2.98) that is otherwise identical to the 1954-55 Palomino Groomer. The 1956 text, which says the saddle is "tan," doesn't mention the embossed designs, but the embossing is evident in the photo. Sears offered these same two sets again in 1957, with the girls' "My Fair Lady" kit reduced to $2.27 and the boys' Palomino Groomer, less generously, to $2.97 (a big one-cent savings). More Western Pony groomer kits appear in Sears holiday catalogs of the 1960s. In 1960, Sears offered two such sets: a "Girls' Grooming Horse" with white pony, embossed pack saddle (color not mentioned), "hand mirror, comb, nail file, tooth brush," for $2.29; and a "Boys' Palomino Grooming Horse" with palomino pony, embossed saddle (color not mentioned), nail clip, file, comb, and "gunholster tie-clip with removable gun," for $2.67. I would guess from the photo that the tie clip is metal, but the ad text doesn't say. A black pinto Western Pony turns up in a "Pinto Groomer Set" for $2.47 in the 1961 and 1962 Sears holiday catalogs, with the usual four articles (nail file, nail clipper, toothbrush, and comb); the 1961 set, "for your cowboy or cowgirl," has an embossed pack-saddle, but the 1962 set, "for neat little boys and girls," appears in the photo to have a smooth pack-saddle (color not mentioned for either saddle). The 1962 and 1968 Sears catalogs also offer white Western Pony pack-saddle sets, but my copies of these pages are too obscure to reveal the details. Another white Western Pony kit appears in the Sears 1963 holiday catalog: a "Groomer Set" whose apparently smooth "brown saddlebags hold implements to keep little boys and girls neat. Nail clipper, file, toothbrush and comb," for $1.98. Please wake me up when the excitement is over. The latter set crops up again in the 1964 and 1966 Sears catalogs, although the price has been raised two cents (to $2.00) and the target audience has been reassessed: "Everything a young man needs to look his best." Collector Paula DeFeyter has a 1969 Sears holiday catalog that offers apparently the same white Western Pony grooming kit, including the smooth pack-saddle and the usual grooming articles, for $2.50. Finally, I have a copy of a Mission Supply House ad flier showing same smooth-saddle, white-pony kit, for $4.90. The flier has no printed date but must be from the early 1970s since it also features #327 German Shepherd (not with a grooming kit!), which was first released in late 1971. But these Mission Supply kits must have been leftovers of earlier stock, for the white Western Pony was discontinued after 1970. *Sets with other types of items:* Not all Western Pony sets were grooming kits. The 1954 Sears catalog featured, in addition to the above-mentioned

groomers, a "Special Christmas Gift Combination . . . for that special man or boy," consisting of a palomino Western Pony with normal plastic old-style Western saddle, a pocket knife with multiple utility blades and "simulated bone" handle, and a compass, connected to the knife by a long chain, all for $4.95. The Sears 1956 catalog sold "Steed 'N Sweets," a palomino ("taffy-colored") Western Pony with Western saddle and a pair of "saddle bags" holding a "gay one-half pound assortment of delicious, wrapped candies," for $1.98. It's impossible to be sure from my Xerox, but I would guess that the saddle bags are merely cellophane. Another novel Western Pony set turns up in the 1962 Ward's holiday catalog: "Pinto Pony with Boy's Astronaut Watch," for $9.97. The photo shows a pinto, color not identified, wearing a normal old-style Western saddle with a wristwatch placed around it like a surcingle. The description asserts with tortured syntax that the watch "tells our time and in far away places—Rome, Hong Kong, others." One might have expected locales such as Mars and Venus for an astronaut watch, but who's complaining? The Sears 1963 holiday catalog sold a set misleadingly labeled "Cowboy Groomer with school kit," which included nary a grooming article but only a "ball-point pen, eraser, 6-inch plastic ruler" in what appears to be a smooth pack-saddle (no color mentioned), for $1.87. The photo seems to show the pen as being rifle-shaped, like the "rifle ball-point pen" sold in a Rearing Stallion "Desk Set" by Sears in 1963 (see Rearing Stallion "Rex" #185 below in the Classics section). For grooming kits and similar sets with other Breyer molds, see Grooming Kits For People above in the Traditionals section.

(5) The Western Pony mold has never had any mold marks. Nor has any Western Pony saddle I've seen, whether old-style or new-style, had any mold marks.

Western Prancer — Stallion, prancing, looking slightly right, tailtip attached to right hock, molded-on bridle, gold metal chain reins, removable plastic Western saddle with uncovered stirrups. Sculpted by Chris Hess. Mold in catalog-run production 1961/63 - 1985, 1994 - current as of 1996.

Catalog-run models made from this mold:

- "Ranger" Cow Pony #889, red dun, blaze, dark red dun mane and tail, chestnut-charcoal knees and hocks, 4 stockings, tan hooves, dark reddish brown bridle, matte; dark reddish brown plastic saddle (1994-95).
- Western Prancing Horse "Cheyenne" #110, smoke (solid gray), bald face, white points, gray/charcoal hooves, gold bridle, matte; black-shaded white plastic saddle (1961/63 - 1976). Some have hand-painted eyewhites. Body color ranges from medium gray to charcoal gray. The bald face can be extensive, reaching well down the sides of the face. #110 was in the Showcase Collection as #1100 in 1970-72 (see Showcase Collection in this section for discussion).
- Western Prancing Horse "Cheyenne" #111, buckskin, bald face, black points, black hooves, gold bridle, matte; black-shaded or tan-shaded white plastic saddle (1961/63 - 1973). Some have hand-painted eyewhites. Some have a thin dorsal stripe. The bald face can be extensive, reaching well down the sides of the face. Many of these models have a couple of buckskin shins on their otherwise black lower legs, as also occurred on buckskin QH Geldings and Mustangs. It is certain that at least some buckskin Western Prancers came with a black-shaded saddle, for collector Sande Schneider found a Showcase Collection buckskin still sealed in his box with such a saddle. But some buckskins came with tan-shaded saddles, according to Diederich 1988, Section 1 (p. 130). Which of the two saddle colors was the norm for this horse is hard to say since the only Breyer catalogs that show the buckskin Western Prancer (1972-73) are printed in black and white. #111 was in the Showcase Collection as #1110 in 1970-72 (see Showcase Collection in this section for discussion).
- Western Prancing Horse "Cheyenne" #112, palomino, bald face, white points, gray hooves, gold bridle, matte; tan-shaded white plastic saddle (1961/63 - 1985). Some have hand-painted eyewhites. The bald face can be extensive, reaching well down the sides of the face. Collector Linda Bell kindly sent me a photo of her #112 that has a solid face with only a bald white nose. The color of #112 varies from golden tan on older models to lemony yellow or orangy on newer ones. #112 was in the Showcase Collection as #1120 in 1970-72 (see Showcase Collection in this section for discussion). The number 1120 previously belonged to the Copenhagen decorator Running Mare, and later belonged to the Brenda Western Gift Set (Western Prancer mold).
- Western Prancing Horse "Cheyenne" #113, black pinto, bald face, white points, gray hooves, gold bridle, glossy; black-shaded white plastic saddle (1961/63 - 1966). Some have hand-painted eyewhites. The bald face can be extensive, reaching well down the sides of the face. This model has the same pinto pattern as the horse in Brenda Western Gift Set #1120.
- Western Prancing Horse "Cheyenne" #114, bay, bald face, black or dark brown mane and tail, no black on the legs, 4 stockings, gray hooves, gold bridle, matte; brown-shaded white plastic saddle (1961/63 - 1971). Some have hand-painted eyewhites. Since #114 has no black on the legs, the models with dark brown mane and tail might well be called chestnut. The bald face on #114 can be extensive, reaching well down the sides of the face. I have seen models that vary in body color from dark to medium/light shades and from reddish bay to coffee brown to sandy bay. #114 was in the Showcase Collection as #1140 in 1970-71 (see Showcase Collection in this section for discussion).
- Western Prancing Horse "Cheyenne" #115, black leopard appaloosa, white horse with black splashed-on spots, black points, black hooves, gold bridle, semigloss; black-shaded white plastic saddle (1961/63 - 1973). Some have hand-painted eyewhites. Typically #115s have black-shaded genitals, pink nose and ears, and gray shading along the crest on the non-mane side; some also have a touch of gray shading along the buttocks. The spotting on the body and neck varies from sparse to heavy. Even on the heavily spotted models, there are no or very few spots on the head, windpipe, and chest. Oddly, although this model was discontinued after 1973, he is pictured in an ad in the October 1978 issue of *Horse of Course!* (p. 73), along with a mahogany PAS and alabaster PAM. The ad is for a wooden "Show Farm Box Stall" ("horses not included"), made by Jan Legere Studios, of Youngsville, Pennsylvania. Presumably the Western Prancer was grabbed from somebody's collection as a handsome prop. #115 was in the Showcase Collection as #1150 in 1970-72 (see Showcase Collection in this section for discussion).

Set:

- Brenda Western Gift Set #1120, chestnut pinto Western Prancer, bald face, white points, gray hooves, gold bridle, matte; brown-shaded plastic saddle (1983-85). Set also includes Brenda Western rider doll. This horse has the same pinto pattern as Western Prancer #113. The color is typically a dark tan palomino shade with no red tones. The saddle in this set is the normal Western Prancer saddle, as is shown with the set in Breyer catalogs and in the 1983 Ward's and Sears holiday catalogs. Collectors Ali Willis and Betty Mertes have told me that their sets came new with the saddle. For details on the doll, see under Brenda Breyer in the Riders - Soft Or Jointed Plastic section below. The model number 1120 originally belonged to the Copenhagen decorator Running Mare and next belonged to the Showcase Collection issue of the palomino Western Prancer, before being assigned to the Brenda Western set.

Special-run models made from this mold:

- Western Prancer SR, brown pinto, solid face, black mane and tail, 4 stockings, gray hooves, glossy (1963). Made as gifts for collectors who assisted Breyer and possibly also for Breyer employees. About 4-5 models made. The pinto pattern is the same as on black pinto #113 and chestnut pinto #1120, except that the SR is solid faced while the regular runs are bald faced. The date and quantity I've given are per long-time collector Judy Davinich, who kindly sent me photos of her own SR glossy brown pinto. According to Judy, 4 or 5 of these horses were made in 1963 as gifts to collector Ellen Hitchens and her friends. Judy purchased her horse from Ellen in the late 1960s. In Judy's photos, the horse has no reins or saddle and no painted eyewhites; his molded-on bridle appears to be brown, just a shade darker than his medium brown body color. The quantity of about 5 models is also suggested by Sande Schneider 1992b. Sande wrote to me that she had learned of this special from a collector who got one from a former Breyer employee. Diederich 1988, Section 1 (p. 129), mentions this model too and says it is glossy, and collector Gale Good, who told me she had seen one of these models, recalled it as being glossy. The date is given as 1970 by Gutierrez 1986 and as 1981 by Gutierrez 1989 and by a list of SRs and test colors in the August 1983 *Quequechan Model Horse Collector*; I think these sources are probably wrong.
- Western Prancer SR, sorrel, solid upper face, baldish lower face, light yellow-sorrel mane and tail, 4 stockings, gray hooves, gold bridle, matte, (probably sometime in the period 1979-83). I learned about this model from Sheryl Leisure, who got one from another collector who did not know where it came from. None of my published sources mentions this horse. I've seen a photo of another model just like Sheryl's, and Sheryl has seen a third. These horses are probably not just color variations of the regular-run palomino since they are too red and their manes and tails are colored; hence I list it as an SR, though I have no information on such a special. My dating of these models is based on the fact that Sheryl's has a "B" stamp.

Notes:

(1) This mold replaced the less realistic "Fury" Prancers, all of which except "Fury" #27 were discontinued when the Western Prancer mold debuted in the early 1960s. The name "Cheyenne" was dropped from catalogs after 1970/71; it was never used in manuals. All catalogs and manuals and many price lists that list this mold call him Western Prancing Horse, but some later price lists call him simply Western Prancer, which is also the collector's name for him.

(2) All Western Prancers came with gold twisted-link type reins with a gold wire bit, as on "Fury" Prancers, Western Ponies, and most Western Horses. (For the history of these reins, see note 8 for the Western Horse mold.) The Western Prancer's hard-plastic cinchless saddle is a different mold from the cinchless saddles sold with later Western Horses and Western Ponies. The most obvious difference is that the Western Prancer saddle has uncovered stirrups, whereas the Western Horse and Western Pony saddles have tapaderos (pointed covers over the stirrups).

(3) Early models of the Western Prancer mold have the round "Breyer Molding Co." stamp only. Later ones have the round stamp and the "U.S.A." stamp. The "U.S.A." was definitely on the mold by 1973, for I have seen buckskin #111s with this stamp, and collector Sande Schneider has a leopard appy #115 with the "U.S.A."; but it was apparently not added before late 1971 or 1972, for Sande's buckskin that she got new in sealed Showcase box with 1971 manual has no "U.S.A." Some "U.S.A." models also have the "B" stamp. Early Western Prancer saddles have no mold stamps, but later ones have a "P^P" stamp underneath the seat. Some with the "P^P" stamp also have a "B" stamp, inside the fender, but more recent ones lack the "B."

Wild American Horse — see under "Phar Lap"

"Wild Diamond," "Justin Morgan's" Dam — see under Running Mare

"Wildfire" SR — see under "San Domingo"

Wild Horses Of America Set SR — see Breyer Wild Horses Of America Set SR

"Wimpy P-1" — see The AQHA Ideal American Quarter Horse #497 (under Ideal Quarter Horse)

"Winchester" SR — see under "Buckshot"

"Wing Commander" — see under Five-Gaiter

"Witez II" — see Proud Arabian Stallion #212

Woodgrains — In the Traditionals section see under Belgian; Clydesdale Stallion; Family Arabian Foal; Family Arabian Mare; Family Arabian Stallion; Fighting Stallion; Five-Gaiter; "Fury" Prancer; Morgan, stretched; Mustang; Proud Arabian Mare; Quarter Horse Gelding; Race Horse; Running Foal; Running Mare; Shetland Pony; and Western Pony. In the Cattle & Hogs section see under Black Angus Bull, polled, walking, SR; Brahma Bull; Cow (see note 2 for this mold); Hereford Bull, horned, walking; Polled Hereford Bull, standing, large (see note 1 for this mold); and Texas Longhorn Bull. In the Dogs & Cats section see under Boxer and Poodle. In the Wildlife section see Buffalo SR and Elephant SR.

Woodgrain models are made of Breyer's usual cellulose acetate plastic but are finished with brown paint applied in a way that imitates the streaks and swirls of carved, polished wood. Several of them, but not all, have a hand-painted details such as black hooves and white facial markings. Most woodgrains are matte or slightly semigloss, but *Breyer Collector's Video* mentions that a few glossy woodgrain Clydesdales are known, and Diederich 1988, Section 1, notes the existence of glossy woodgrain Running Mares and Foals. Early woodgrains often came with a gold foil sticker glued somewhere on their body (see Stickers & Hang Tags in the Appendix near the end of this book). Many old woodgrain models today suffer from bubbling of the paint surface. On models I have seen with this condition, the bubbles are tiny and numerous, giving the paint surface a scabby appearance.

All the woodgrains have three-digit model numbers beginning with 9. In most cases the 9 is followed by the number of one of the realistically colored models of the mold; for example, the woodgrain Belgian is #992, with 92 being the number of the smoke gray Belgian model. The numbers for the woodgrain Running Mare #920 and Running Foal #930 are exceptions since they include only partial numbers for realistic models—alabaster Running Mare #120 and Running Foal #130—presumably so that the woodgrain numbers would be three digits long like all the others. The number of the woodgrain

Fighting Stallion #931 is an exception too since there never was any Fighting Stallion #31 (see note 5 for the Fighting Stallion mold for discussion).

The woodgrains were evidently first issued in 1959 and were in their heyday in the early to mid 1960s. All but one of the woodgrain catalog runs had been discontinued by the start of 1967; the one remaining, the Fighting Stallion, was produced through 1973. As Berkwitz 1993 suggests, Breyer might have gotten the idea for woodgrain-finish models from the real wooden horse sculptures made chiefly in the 1940s through 1960s by the Grand Wood company of Chicago, from one of whose pieces Breyer had earlier taken the design for the Race Horse mold. (The woodgrain idea could not have come from the Hartland company, for Hartland did not issue woodgrain or woodcut models until 1965, per Fitch 1993, 2: 38.) With this in mind it is interesting to note that the earliest evidence I have of Breyer woodgrains—an old Montgomery Ward catalog ad offering the woodgrain Race Horse as well as woodgrain Brahma Bull, Family Arabian Stallion, Proud Arabian Mare, and Clydesdale Stallion (the horses were $3.98, the bull $4.98)—touts the models as "Faithfully copied from original hand-carved wood pieces." For a couple of reasons, I believe this Ward's ad dates to 1959. For one thing, all the molds shown in the ad were introduced in the 1950s; if the ad dated to 1960-61 you would expect it to include some of the woodgrains in new molds introduced in those years. Further, the fact that the ad has the PAM suggests that it is no later than 1959, and the fact that it has the FAS suggests that it is no earlier than 1959. Ward's again offered a bounty of woodgrain models through its 1962 holiday catalog—Clydesdale Stallion, Fighting Stallion, Five-Gaiter, Race Horse, Shetland Pony, Brahma Bull, and the Family Arabian Foal, Mare, and Stallion. In the Ward's 1964 holiday catalog, the selection of woodgrains has dwindled to a meager two, the Fighting Stallion and Five-Gaiter.

In 1990, Breyer's magazine, *Just About Horses*, announced that four woodgrain pieces, each of a different mold, would be made as prizes for a "Win a Limited Edition Woodgrain" subscription contest (see *JAH* 17/#1 Feb./Mar. 1990, p. 19; 17/#2 May/June 1990, p. 18). But the contest was repeatedly delayed, and finally Peter Stone of Breyer announced in his presentation at the July 1992 West Coast Model Horse Collector's Jamboree that the contest had become impossible because the last Breyer employee who knew how to paint the woodgrain finish had quit.

"Woodsprite" Pony Foal — see under "Phantom Wings"

"Yellow Mount" — see under "Adios"

Classics

General note: The Classic scale, the second largest of Breyer's four scales of realistic models, ranges from about 5.5 inches to 7 inches at the eartips for the standing adult molds. Like the Traditional scale, the Classic is far from consistent; the U.S.E.T. horses and the Classic Arabian Family, for example, tower over the race horses and the Quarter Horse Family. The first Classic-scale models that were designated as Classics in Breyer catalogs were the stallion, mare, and foal of the Classic Arabian Family Gift Set #3055, introduced by Breyer in 1973. But two molds of this scale had been introduced into the Breyer line in the 1960s: Bucking Bronco and Rearing Stallion. These two, as well as several more recent molds—"Hobo" on stand, Polo Pony, and the Kiger Mustangs of the Messenger Series—are listed among the Traditionals in Breyer catalogs but are actually Classic scale and are therefore listed below with the other Classics.

The Classic scale in general should not be confused with the "Classic Series," a label that Breyer catalogs have used only in reference to particular groups of Classic-scale horses over the years. The first such group comprised the six race horses plus the Lipizzan, which were designated as "Classic Series" from 1975, when this group was introduced, through 1990, the last year of production for the race horses. (See Classic Series below for a complete list. The race horses, in addition to being in the Classic Series, were also offered as Race Horse Assortment #6750 in dealer catalogs 1977-90.) The 1991-94 catalogs use the label "Classic Series" to refer exclusively to The After School Herd Assortments #2000 and #2001. Aside from these Classic Series and the Classic Arabian Family noted above, only a few Classic-scale models and sets have names that actually included the term "Classic" in Breyer catalogs—and they included it only for a few years. These are the #3060 Classic Andalusian Family set, the #4000 Classic Arabian Foal in assorted colors, and the #4001 Classic Quarter Horse Foal in assorted colors (designated as "Classic" only for one year). The 1995 catalog omits the terms "Classic Series" and "Classic" altogether, instead designating the race horse molds in new colors as #2002 B Ranch Series Assortment.

Of the many Classic-scale molds, 15 were sculpted by Christian Hess, Breyer's main sculptor from 1950 to 1987; 14 by Maureen Love Calvert, an employee of the Hagen-Renaker company; and the remainder, all of them recent molds, by Rowland Cheney. The molds by Calvert were produced in ceramic by Hagen-Renaker prior to their production in plastic by Breyer starting in 1973. The first Breyer catalog ever to mention the source of these Calvert molds is the 1995, which states "A Hagen-Renaker Design" in a footnote on each page that features these molds. These footnote acknowledgments reflect a refurbished licensing agreement worked out between the two companies in 1994 (per Breyer executive Peter Stone, conversation of Mar. 1995).

Nearly all Classic horses are matte or semigloss finish. The few exceptions—the flocked models and one or two glossies—are noted in the entries below.

"Affirmed" SR — see under "Man-O-War"

After School Herd Assortment #2000 — This assortment consists of six horse models, all sold separately. See "Gaucho" (under "Terrang"); "Hawk" (under "Swaps"); "Lula" (under "Ruffian"); "Norita" (under "Kelso"); "Pepe" (under "Man-O-War"); and "T-Bone" (under "Silky Sullivan"). The number 2000 previously belonged to the Showcase Collection issue of the alabaster Old Timer (Traditional). The boxes of the #2000 models typically came with a large round blue sticker saying "New! The After School Herd," but I've seen numerous boxes without the sticker.

After School Herd #2001 — This assortment, like the earlier After School Herd Assortment #2000, comprises six horse models, all sold separately. See "Andrew" (under "Silky Sullivan"); "Colleen" (under "Ruffian"); "Jeremy" (under "Kelso"); "King" (under "Man-O-War"); "Prince" (under "Swaps"); and "Ten Gallon" (under "Terrang"). The boxes of the #2001 models typically came with a large round blue sticker saying "New! The After School Herd," but I've seen numerous boxes without the sticker. The sticker is identical to the one that came on the #2000 After School Herd boxes.

"Ahlerich" SR — see under "Keen"

Alabaster Lipizzan — in the Classic section see Lipizzan and Rearing Stallion "Rex" #180; in the Traditionals section see "King" The Fighting Stallion #30 (under Fighting Stallion) and "Pluto"

Andalusian Family Foal — Colt, prancing, looking right. Sculpted by Chris Hess. Mold in production: pre-catalog release 1978, catalog run 1979-93, 1996-.

Catalog-run models made from this mold:

- Andalusian Family Gift Set #3060, chestnut foal, bald face, darker chestnut mane and tail, 3-4 stockings, gray hooves (pre-catalog release 1978, catalog run 1979-93). Set also includes dapple gray Andalusian Family Mare and alabaster Andalusian Family Stallion. The set did not appear in Breyer catalogs until 1979 but was issued earlier through the 1978 Penney's, Gemco, and Ward's holiday catalogs. The set's name included the term "Classic" (Classic Andalusian Family) in the 1979-86 Breyer catalogs but omitted this term in the 1987-93 catalogs. In most Breyer catalogs the foal has 4 stockings, some occasionally vague; but the 1985-87 catalogs show the raised front leg as solid chestnut.
- Hanoverian Family set #3346, bay foal, no white markings, black points, black hooves (1992-93). Set also includes light sandy bay Hanoverian Family Mare ("Ginger" mold) and black Hanoverian Family Stallion ("Keen" mold). This foal is very similar to the 1984 SR red bay foal—both are black-point solid bays of a medium/dark tone. To judge from my own specimens and others I have seen, the only difference is that the #3346 foal is a browner, less red shade of bay whereas the SR foal is quite red.
- Proud Mother And Newborn Foal set #3160, tan dun foal, bald face, slightly darker dun mane and tail, 1 left hind stocking, dun hooves (Jan. 1 - June 30, 1993). Set also includes chocolate sorrel Proud Mother (Traditional-scale "Lady Roxana" mold). Production dates are per the 1993 catalog.
- Proud Mother And Newborn Foal set #3161, dark bay foal, solid face, black points, 1 left hind stocking with tan hoof, other legs and hooves black (July 1 - Dec. 31, 1993). Set also includes tan dun Proud Mother (Traditional-scale "Lady Roxana" mold). Production dates are per the 1993 catalog.

Special-run models made from this mold:

- Andalusian Family Foal SR, red bay, no white markings, black points, black hooves (1984). Sears holiday catalog. Sold in SR set with alabaster Andalusian Family Mare and dapple gray Andalusian Family Stallion. For the difference between this SR foal and the #3346 Hanoverian Family foal, see the entry for the latter model.
- Spanish-Norman Family Foal SR, steel gray, solid face, black points, black hooves (1994). Made for Toys R Us. Sold in Spanish-Norman Family SR set #700294 with red roan stallion (Andalusian Family Stallion mold) and alabaster mare with white mane and tail ("Ginger" mold). 6,300 sets made (per *JAH* editor Stephanie Macejko, conversation of June 1995). The model number is per the set's box, which also sports a large round gold sticker saying, in full: "1994 Special Collector Edition / (Limited Production) / The Spanish-Norman Family / This highly collectible edition represents a unique breed, the blending of the Andalusian of Spain and the Percheron of France." The foal has a slight metallic shimmer to his finish.

Notes:

(1) Chris Hess is identified as the sculptor of this mold in *JAH* Summer 1978.

(2) The Andalusian Family Foal mold has the round "Breyer Molding Co." stamp. I believe the earliest models have the round stamp only, with no "B" stamp, but slightly later models do have a "B" stamp (I own a #3060 foal like this, as does Chelle Fulk). This mold was never given the "U.S.A." stamp.

Andalusian Family Mare — Walking, looking slightly right, long mane swinging. Sculpted by Chris Hess. Mold in production: pre-catalog release 1978, catalog run 1979-93.

Catalog-run models made from this mold:

- Andalusian Family Gift Set #3060, dapple gray mare, bald face, gray mane and tail, most with 4 stockings, gray hooves (pre-catalog release 1978, catalog run 1979-93). Set also includes chestnut Andalusian Family Foal and alabaster Andalusian Family Stallion. The set did not appear in Breyer catalogs until 1979 but was issued earlier through the 1978 Penney's, Gemco, and Ward's holiday catalogs. The set's name included the term "Classic" (Classic Andalusian Family) in the 1979-86 Breyer catalogs but omitted this term in the 1987-93 catalogs. Breyer catalogs show the mare as varying in depth of color: early ones have washed-out body and dark gray mane and tail; later models are dark or medium gray all over and have shaded hindquarters. Most catalogs show the mare with roughly 4 stockings, but they get pretty vague here and there. Collector Linda Bell has a mare with no stockings. Set #3060 was also sold through the Penney's 1979 and Sears 1979-81 holiday catalogs; the mares in the photos look very dark except on the barrel and have solid dark gray legs. My own mare, which is dark with solid legs, has dapples on neck and head.

Special-run models made from this mold:

- Andalusian Family Mare SR, alabaster, gray mane, tail, and hooves (1984). Sears holiday catalog. Sold in SR set with red bay Andalusian Family Foal and dapple gray Andalusian Family Stallion.

Notes:

(1) Chris Hess is identified as the sculptor of this mold in *JAH* Summer 1978. Hess took his design for this piece from a photo of a real dapple gray mare being shown in hand. I am not sure where the photo came from, but it is in the files of former Breyer executive Peter Stone. The Breyer mold's resemblance to the mare in the photo is extremely close, even down to the precise swing of her mane and tail. The jottings on the photo say "Scottish bred mare without halter (please) prancing nervously along."

(2) The Andalusian Family Mare mold has the round "Breyer Molding Co." stamp. The earliest models have the round stamp only, with no "B" stamp (collector Lori Ogozalek's #3060 mare from the first year of issue is like this), but slightly later models do have a backwards (or upside-down) "B" stamp (collectors Chelle Fulk and Linda Bell both have #3060 mares like this, and I have seen another in person). This mold was never given the "U.S.A." stamp.

Andalusian Family Stallion — Cantering on right lead, looking right, mane and tail flying. Sculpted by Chris Hess. Mold in production: pre-catalog release 1978, catalog run 1979-93.

Catalog-run models made from this mold:

- Andalusian Family Gift Set #3060, alabaster stallion; gray-shaded mane, tail, knees, and hocks; gray or pink-gray hooves (pre-catalog release 1978, catalog run 1979-93). Set also includes dapple gray Andalusian Family Mare and chestnut Andalusian Family Foal. The set did not appear in Breyer catalogs until 1979 but was issued earlier through the 1978 Penney's, Gemco, and Ward's holiday catalogs. The set's name included the term "Classic" (Classic Andalusian Family) in the 1979-86 Breyer catalogs but omitted this term in the 1987-93 catalogs. My own stallion, which is fairly old, has pink-gray hooves, but many catalogs show the stallion with plain gray hooves.

Special-run models made from this mold:

- Andalusian Family Stallion SR, dapple gray, dapples on hindquarters and forequarters, including neck and head, but no dapples on barrel; baldish face; gray mane and tail; 4 stockings; gray hooves (1984). Sears holiday catalog. Sold in SR set with alabaster Andalusian Family Mare and red bay Andalusian Family Foal. This stallion has an unusual pattern of dappling, with dapples everywhere but the main part of his barrel.
- Spanish-Norman Family Stallion SR, red roan, tan horse covered with tiny red chestnut flecks, darker shading on hindquarters and shoulders, solid face, dark chestnut points, gray hooves (1994). Made for Toys R Us. Sold in Spanish-Norman Family SR set #700294 with steel gray foal (Andalusian Family Foal mold) and alabaster mare with white mane and tail ("Ginger" mold). 6,300 sets made (per *JAH* editor Stephanie Macejko, conversation of June 1995). The model number is per the set's box, which also sports a large round gold sticker saying, in full: "1994 Special Collector Edition (Limited Production) / The Spanish-Norman Family / This highly collectible edition represents a unique breed, the blending of the Andalusian of Spain and the Percheron of France."

Notes:

(1) Chris Hess is identified as the sculptor of this mold in *JAH* Summer 1978.

(2) The Andalusian Family Stallion mold has the round "Breyer Molding Co." stamp. The earliest models have the round stamp only, with no "B" stamp (collector Lori Ogozalek's #3060 stallion from the first year of issue is like this), but slightly later models do have the "B" stamp (Chelle Fulk's #3060 stallion is like this). This mold was never given the "U.S.A." stamp.

"Andrew" — see under "Silky Sullivan"

"Another" — see "A Pony For Keeps" Gift Set, under "Might Tango"

"Apache" — see under "Man-O-War"

Appaloosa Family set SRs — see SR black blanket appaloosa and SR chestnut blanket appaloosa under Quarter Horse Family Foal, Mare, and Stallion

Appaloosa Mustang Family Gift Set — see under Mustang Family Foal, Mustang Family Mare, and Mustang Family Stallion

Arabian Family Foal — Filly, standing/walking, neck arched, tail up. Sculpted by Maureen Love Calvert. Mold in catalog-run production 1973 - current as of 1996.

Catalog-run models made from this mold:

- Classic Arabian Foal #4000, alabaster, gray mane, tail, and hooves (1973 - 1982/83). This foal is not pictured in any Breyer catalogs or manuals. See Classic Arabian Foal #4000, chestnut, for discussion.
- Classic Arabian Foal #4000, black; most with bald face; black mane and tail; 4 stockings; gray or charcoal hooves (1973 - 1982/83). This foal is shown in the 1973 manual. Collector Sande Schneider has a solid-faced #4000 black foal (purchased at a flea market on March 11, 1990), which is indistinguishable from the black SR foal issued in the fall of 1990. See classic Arabian Foal #4000, chestnut, for further discussion.
- Classic Arabian Foal #4000, chestnut; most with bald face; mane and tail same color as body or darker; 4 stockings; gray hooves (1973 - 1982/83). This foal was also sold in the Arabian Family Gift Set #3055 [1973-91]; see that entry for the solid-faced variation. The alabaster, black, chestnut, palomino, and smoke gray foals, sold individually in blister packs, all had the model number 4000. Catalogs and manuals don't list the #4000 colors separately but just say "assorted colors"; my information on specific colors comes from *Breyer Collector's Video*, Diederich 1988 (Section 3), collector Gale Good, and my own observations. Diederich is the only one who lists bay among the #4000 colors; I believe she counts as bay the version of the chestnut #4000 shown in its blister pack in the 1976 catalog: it is dark chestnut with black mane and tail, no black on the legs, 4 stockings, and gray hooves. The chestnut foal is also shown in the 1977-82 manuals and catalogs. Her body color ranges from dark reddish chestnut to light chestnut. #4000 assorted colors is listed in the 1983 price list but not in the 1983 catalog or manual, so I am not sure if these foals were produced that year.
- Classic Arabian Foal #4000, palomino, bald face, palomino mane and tail, 4 stockings, gray hooves (1973 - 1982/83). This color is not pictured in catalogs or manuals, but does certainly exist. Collector Gale Good has one that she got new in a blister pack in April 1973. I got a palomino foal in a #3055 Arabian Family Gift Set from another collector. The color is a medium tan palomino, not at all yellow. See Classic Arabian Foal #4000, chestnut, for further discussion.
- Classic Arabian Foal #4000, smoke gray, bald face, dark gray mane and tail, 4 or various stockings, gray hooves (1973 - 1982/83). This foal is pictured in the 1974-75 catalogs and manuals. See Classic Arabian Foal #4000, chestnut, for further discussion.

Sets:

- Arabian Family Gift Set #3055, chestnut foal, most with bald face, mane and tail same color as body or darker, 4 stockings, gray hooves (1973-91). Set also includes chestnut Arabian Family Mare and chestnut Arabian Family Stallion. The set's name included the term "Classic" (Classic Arabian Family) in the 1973-86 catalogs but omitted this term in the 1987-91 catalogs. This foal was also sold separately as #4000 [1973 - 1982/83]. A variation of this foal with solid face was reported in the January 1979 *Model Horse Shower's Journal*: "Have you noticed that all the new Breyer Clas. Arab stallions coming out lack stars or blotches on their foreheads? I've seen it in most of the stores which have just got new shipments in. And a few of the foals have no white faces." Catalogs show this foal as ranging from a dark chestnut to medium red chestnut, but the color varies even more than this. The foal in a family set I got from another collector is actually palomino. Collector Gale Good got a dark red chestnut Arab Family Foal new in a Classic Mustang Family Gift Set; presumably this was just a factory mix-up. Gale's foal has a bald face, very dark red-brown mane and tail, 4 stockings, and gray hooves.
- Arabian Stallion And Frisky Foal set #3162, gray dun foal; solid face; mottled gray dun mane and tail; darker gray front legs, front hooves, and hocks; 2 hind stockings with tan or tan-gray hooves (Jan. 1 - June 30, 1994). Set also includes dappled bay Arabian Stallion (Traditional-scale "Sham" mold). Production dates are per the 1994 catalog. My own foal has tan-gray hind hooves, but others I've seen have tan.
- Arabian Stallion And Frisky Foal set #3163, light sandy bay foal, no white markings, black points, black hooves (July 1 - Dec. 31, 1994). Set also includes dappled dark yellow-gray dun Arabian Stallion (Traditional-scale "Sham" mold). Production dates are per the 1994 catalog.
- Bedouin Family Gift Set #3057, chestnut foal, low blaze that covers whole muzzle, mane striped with white and dark chestnut, tail dark chestnut at the top and white on the bottom, dorsal stripe, black-shaded legs, right front and left hind stockings, white spot on right hind fetlock, 4 tan hooves (1995 - current as of 1996). Set also includes black mare with mottled mane (Arabian Family Mare mold) and dark chestnut stallion with partially striped mane (Arabian Family Stallion mold). The white spot on the foal's right hind fetlock may disappear on some models owing to overspray. White coronary bands on that leg and the left front may also occur as a result of imprecise painting.
- Desert Arabian Family set #3056, bay foal, solid face, charcoal-shaded muzzle, black points, 1 right hind stocking with tan hoof, other hooves black (1992-94). Set also includes dark bay Desert Arabian Family Mare (Arabian Family Mare mold) and bay Desert Arabian Family Stallion (Arabian Family Stallion mold). This foal has a medium/dark reddish bay color, about like the SR bay foal made 1984-85.
- Marguerite Henry's "Our First Pony" Gift Set #3066, bay pinto foal "Friday," tobiano; big blaze; black and white mane and tail; black on upper legs; 4 stockings; pink hooves (1987 - current as of 1996). See next entry for the black pinto version of "Friday." The set also includes black pinto "Teeny" (Mustang Family Foal mold), black pinto "Midge" (Shetland Pony mold, Traditional), and leather halter and lead for "Midge." This set represents the characters in Marguerite Henry's book *Our First Pony*, which is based on real ponies and people (see under Shetland Pony for discussion). Although this mold is a filly, "Friday" is a colt in the book. For discussion of the names of the foals in this set, see under Mustang Family Foal.
- Marguerite Henry's "Our First Pony" Gift Set #3066, black pinto foal "Friday," tobiano; big blaze; 4 stockings; gray hooves (foal early 1987 only). The 1987 catalog and manual, and 1987 Your Horse Source brochures, show the Arabian Family Foal in this set as black pinto; all subsequent Breyer catalogs show it as a bay pinto with the same pinto pattern. Collector Heather Wells told me the following story about the situation. In 1987, when the "Our First Pony" set was first released, Heather noticed that the sets being sent to retail outlets contained bay pinto "Fridays" even though the foal shown in the catalog was black pinto. She called Breyer employee Jill Göllner to ask whether any black pinto "Fridays" had actually been produced. Jill believed that the first batch of 200 or so sets had been made with black pinto "Fridays." But when she checked the warehouse to see if any were left, she learned that the first batch had already been sent out (to Japan, Germany, and the U.S.), so she couldn't be absolutely sure that black pintos had indeed been produced. Whether the set with black pinto "Friday" pictured in the Your Horse Source brochures is a test-color set or a set from that first batch of production-line issues I do not know.

Special-run models made from this mold:

- Arabian Family Foal SR, bay; solid face, bald face, or star; black points; no or various stockings; gray hooves on stockinged legs, other hooves black (1984 and 1985). Sears holiday catalog. Sold in SR set #21058, with rose alabaster Arabian Family Mare and bay Arabian Family Stallion. This foal has a medium/dark reddish bay color, about like the foal in the #3056 Desert Arabian Family set. Her white markings vary chaotically. According to collector Heather Wells, some of these SR foals have a star. One of my own foals and those owned by collectors Sheryl Leisure, Gale Good, Ida Santana, and Lynn Luther are all solid bay with black points and hooves, no white markings. Gale told me of a version with bald face and 1 hind stocking. My other foal is bald-faced with black points and hooves (no stockings), just like the model pictured in the 1985 Sears holiday catalog. The 1984 Sears catalog shows a foal with right hind and left front stockings, but the face isn't visible. *JAH* XI/#3 1984, which pictures the holiday SRs for that year (p. 20), shows a foal with at least a right hind stocking (left front isn't visible) and a solid face. The set number is per a Breyer company computer printout of activity 1985-92.
- Arabian Family Foal SR, black, most with solid face, some with gray muzzle, black mane and tail, 4 stockings, gray or black hooves (1990). Penney's holiday catalog. Sold in Breyer Classic Collector's Arabian Family Set SR #713055, with black Arabian Family Mare and black Arabian Family Stallion. 3,000 sets made. Quantity and set number are per a Breyer company computer printout of activity 1985-92. The Penney's catalog shows this foal from the side, hiding whatever facial markings she may have, but it clearly shows the hooves as gray. My own foal and those owned by collectors Sheryl Leisure, Kay Schlumpf, and Ida Santana are gray-hoofed, but collector Gale Good's foal has black hooves. Kay's and my models also have gray muzzles, but Ida's foal is completely solid-faced. Collector Sande Schneider's model, which she got in the family set directly from Penney's, has a gray face.
- Arabian Family Foal SR #413155, dapple gray, no dapples on neck and head; bald face; gray mane and tail; 4 stockings; pink-tan hooves (1987 and 1988). Export special, made for the English company Equorum, a division of House of Nisbet. Sold in SR set with dapple gray Arabian Family Mare and dapple gray Arabian Family Stallion. 550 sets made (300 in 1987; 250 in 1988). See Arabian Family Mare SR dapple gray for discussion.
- Arabian Family Foal SR, dark rose gray, solid face, dark brown-gray points and hooves, 1 right hind stocking (1993). Made for Toys R Us. Sold in Drinkers Of The Wind set SR #700693 with smoke gray Arabian Family Stallion and fleabitten rose gray "Johar." 18,000 sets made (per Breyer executive Peter Stone, conversation of Aug. 24, 1995). This set was sold in a regular plastic-front Breyer box with a large round gold sticker on the front saying, in full: "1993 Special Collector Edition / Limited Production / Drinkers of the Wind / This highly collectible edition represents the Arabian Family—Stallion, Mare and Foal." The phrase "drinkers of the wind" is, as I understand, a traditional Arabic reference to the horses of the desert. For an earlier Breyer reference to "drinkers of the wind," see above in the Traditionals section, Proud Arabian Mare Gift Set #2155.
- Arabian Family Foal SR, dark shaded chestnut; face solid with light area above the nose; dorsal stripe; dark mane, knees, and hocks; dark tail with light tip; 4 stockings; gray hooves (1988). Sold at signing parties at Black Horse Ranch and other retailers, in SR set #413550, with rose alabaster "Johar." Also sold in 1988 by Enchanted Doll House in a set called "Foal's First Day," #403755. See "Johar," SR rose gray, for discussion of quantity. The color description I've given is based on my own foal, which I got at the BHR signing party; details may vary on other foals. Collector Heather Wells's BHR foal is heavily shaded like mine, with a dark chestnut forehand and lighter barrel and hindquarters, but its tail is light on the underside rather than on the tip. Her foal from the Enchanted Doll house has a light tail tip, as on my BHR foal, but a less shaded body and only a hint of a dorsal stripe. Some foals may have a completely solid face with no light area.

Notes:

(1) A pearly version of the chestnut #4000 foal is shown on *Breyer Collector's Video*. See Chalkies & Pearlies in the Appendix near the end of this book.

(2) This mold was created by Maureen Love Calvert for the Hagen-Renaker company, which produced it in ceramic under the name "Sherif" Arabian Foal #658 (see Roller, Rose, and Berkwitz 1989, p. 22).

(3) Most models of the Arabian Family Foal mold have no mold stamps. Some models have a "B" stamp only (collectors Kay Schlumpf and Joan Fauteux have regular-run chestnuts like this).

Arabian Family Mare — ♞ Prancing/balking, looking right, tail tip attached to right buttock. Sculpted by Maureen Love Calvert. Mold in catalog-run production 1973 - current as of 1996.

Catalog-run models made from this mold:

♞ Arabian Family Gift Set #3055, chestnut mare, blaze, darker chestnut mane and tail, most with 4 stockings, early ones with tan hooves, later ones with gray hooves (1973-91). Set also includes chestnut Arabian Family Foal and chestnut Arabian Family Stallion. The set's name included the term "Classic" (Classic Arabian Family) in the 1973-86 catalogs but omitted this term in the 1987-91 catalogs. Mares that I have seen vary in body color from dark brown chestnut to medium red chestnut. This mare is shown with tan hooves in the 1973-82 catalogs (my own model is like this) and with gray hooves in 1983-91. She is shown with 2 hind stockings and solid chestnut front legs in the 1973 catalog and on the cover of the 1974; inside the 1974 and in all subsequent catalogs she has 4 stockings. The 2-stocking horse was produced for sale—collector Linda Bell sent me a photo of hers. The 1991 catalog and manual, the last in which this long-running mare appears, mix her up with the Quarter Horse Family Mare.

♞ Bedouin Family Gift Set #3057, black mare, irregular blaze that covers left eye and whole muzzle, mane and tail mottled with black and light gray, 1 right hind and two front stockings, white spot on front of left hind fetlock, 4 tan hooves (1995 - current as of 1996). Set also includes chestnut foal with striped mane (Arabian Family Foal mold) and dark chestnut stallion with partially striped mane (Arabian Family Stallion mold). The mare's two front stockings are only partial—the fronts of these legs are black to the hooves. The white spot on the left hind fetlock may disappear on some models owing to overspray. On my own mare, the mane has a lot of light gray and even a bit of white, while the tail is mostly black with just a few gray streaks.

♞ Desert Arabian Family set #3056, dark bay mare, stripe that widens at the nose, black points, 2 hind stockings with tan hooves, front hooves black (1992-94). Set also includes bay Desert Arabian Family Foal (Arabian Family Foal mold) and bay Desert Arabian Family Stallion (Arabian Family Stallion mold).

Special-run models made from this mold:

♘ Arabian Family Mare SR, black, blaze, black mane and tail, 2 front stockings with gray hooves, hind hooves gray or black (1990). Penney's holiday catalog. Sold in Breyer Classic Collector's Arabian Family Set SR #713055, with black Arabian Family Foal and black Arabian Family Stallion. 3,000 sets made. Quantity and set number are per a Breyer company computer printout of activity 1985-92. The Penney's catalog shows all 4 hooves as gray, and my own model and those owned by collectors Sheryl Leisure, Kay Schlumpf and Ida Santana are like this, but I have seen other mares with black hind hooves.

♘ Arabian Family Mare SR #413255, dapple gray, no dapples on neck and head; bald face; gray mane and tail; 4 stockings; pink-tan hooves (1987 and 1988). Export special, made for the English company Equorum, a division of House of Nisbet. Sold in SR set with dapple gray Arabian Family Foal and dapple gray Arabian Family Stallion. 550 sets made (300 in 1987, 250 in 1988). Dates, dealer, and quantities are per a Breyer company computer printout of activity 1985-92. The printout lists the 1987 horses in three separate entries for the customer Equorum Hobbies & Crafts (foal #413155, mare #413255, and stallion #413355) and the 1988 horses in one entry for the customer House of Nisbet (#413455 for the full set). Collector Heather Wells got her sets from Equorum; in speaking with them she learned that Equorum is a division of House of Nisbet (whose name was on the customs declaration on Heather's shipment). Some sets were also sold through various U.S. model mail-order companies and at a signing party or two with Breyer executive Peter Stone in 1988 (per *Model Rag,* Aug. 1988, p. 58; Diederich's Section 2; and Walerius 1991, p. 104).

♘ Arabian Family Mare SR, rose alabaster, white horse with soft gray and orangy shadings, soft gray mane and tail, gray hooves (1984 and 1985). Sears holiday catalog. Sold in SR set #21058, with bay Arabian Family Foal and bay Arabian Family Stallion. The amount of shading varies on this mare, and the rose/orange can be faint, even nonexistent on some models. The set number is per a Breyer company computer printout of activity 1985-92.

♘ "Buckaroo" SR, red dun, white nose, black forelock, mane and tail pale dun with charcoal-black stripe, black knees and hocks, 4 stockings, tan hooves (1995). Made for Toys R Us. Sold in "Buckaroo" And "Skeeter" set #700795 with SR dark bay pinto "Skeeter" (Traditional "Stormy" mold) and gold metal medallion on blue ribbon. 4,200 sets made, per *JAH* editor Stephanie Macejko (conversation of July 1996). Stephanie also clarified which model has which name: the adult horse's name comes first in the set name. The set name and number are per the set's box. This set is one of several in the Medallion Series made for Toys R Us; see Medallion Series above in the Traditionals section for a full list and a description of the medallion.

Notes:

(1) This mold was created by Maureen Love Calvert for the Hagen-Renaker company, which produced it in ceramic under the name "Sheba" Arabian Mare #698 (see Roller, Rose, and Berkwitz 1989, p. 22).

(2) The Arabian Family Mare mold has the round "Breyer Molding Co." stamp and the "U.S.A." stamp. Some models have the "B" stamp in addition.

Arabian Family Stallion — ♞ Prancing/walking, looking right, tail tip attached to right hock. Sculpted by Maureen Love Calvert. Mold in catalog-run production 1973 - current as of 1996.

Catalog-run models made from this mold:

♞ Arabian Family Gift Set #3055, chestnut stallion; early ones with large star, later ones with solid face; flaxen mane and tail; 4 stockings; tan or gray hooves (1973-91). Set also includes chestnut Arabian Family Mare and chestnut Arabian Family Foal. The set's name included the term "Classic" (Classic Arabian Family) in the 1973-86 catalogs but omitted this term in the 1987-91 catalogs. Stallions that I have seen vary in body color from dark brown chestnut to red sorrel to tan palomino. The stallion is shown with a large star and tan hooves in the 1973-78 catalogs, with solid face and tan hooves in 1979-81, and with solid face and gray hooves in 1982-91; all three versions were produced for sale. An item in the January 1979 *Model Horse Shower's Journal* remarks: "Have you noticed that all the new Breyer Clas. Arab stallions coming out lack stars or blotches on their foreheads? I've seen it in most of the stores which have just got new shipments in."

♞ Bedouin Family Gift Set #3057, dark chestnut stallion, low blaze that covers muzzle, dark chestnut mane with tips striped white and dark chestnut, dark chestnut tail with white tip, dorsal stripe, black-shaded legs, 4 stockings, 4 tan hooves (1995 - current as of 1996). Set also includes chestnut foal with striped mane (Arabian Family Foal mold) and black mare with mottled mane (Arabian Family Mare mold). The stallion's right hind stocking is only partial in that the black leg-shading comes down the front of the leg to the hoof. The "white" stripes on the tips of the mane may be pale tan from overspray.

♞ Desert Arabian Family set #3056, bay stallion, star, charcoal-shaded nose, black points, 1 left hind stocking with tan hoof, other hooves black (1992-94). Set also includes dark bay Desert Arabian Family Mare (Arabian Mare mold) and bay Desert Arabian Family Foal (Arabian Family Foal mold).

Special-run models made from this mold:

♘ Arabian Family Stallion SR, bay, star; some with unstenciled snip, some with dark nose; black points; 3-4 stockings; charcoal-gray hooves (1984 and 1985). Sears holiday catalog. Sold in SR set #21058, with bay Arabian Family Foal and rose alabaster Arabian Family Mare. The 1984 Sears catalog and *JAH* XI/#3 1984 show this stallion with a small star, small snip, and right front stocking (the back legs are hidden). I do not know if models with the small star were issued for sale; in my experience all have a large star. The 1985 Sears catalog shows the stallion with a large star and a large, vivid snip. The model on *Breyer Collector's Video* has a large star, dark nose, and 4 stockings. My own horse and a number of others I've seen, such as Sheryl Leisure's, Lynn Luther's and Ida Santana's, have a large star, fairly large but sometimes vague unstenciled snip, and 3 stockings (1 right front and 2 hind). The set number is per a Breyer company computer printout of activity 1985-92.

♘ Arabian Family Stallion SR, black, solid face with white or gray muzzle, black mane and tail, 4 stockings, gray hooves (1990). Penney's holiday catalog. Sold in Breyer Classic Collector's Arabian Family Set SR #713055, with black Arabian Family Mare and black Arabian Family Foal. 3,000 sets made. Quantity and set number are per a Breyer company computer printout of activity 1985-92. The model in the Penney's catalog has only a vague light spot on the tip of the nose, but the muzzle of collector Ida Santana's horse is largely white. My own model and those of collectors Kay Schlumpf and Sheryl Leisure have gray muzzles.

♘ Arabian Family Stallion SR #413355, dapple gray, no dapples on neck and head; bald face; gray mane and tail; 4 stockings; pink-tan hooves (1987 and 1988). Export special, made for the English company Equorum, a division of House of Nisbet. Sold in SR set with dapple gray Arabian Family Mare and dapple gray Arabian Family Foal. 550 sets made (300 in 1987; 250 in 1988). See Arabian Family Mare SR dapple gray for discussion.

♘ Arabian Family Stallion SR, smoke gray, solid; solid face; black mane, tail, knees, and hocks; 4 stockings; tan hooves (1993). Made for Toys R Us. Sold in Drinkers Of The Wind set SR #700693 with dark rose gray Arabian Family Foal and fleabitten rose gray "Johar." 18,000 sets made (per Breyer executive Peter Stone, conversation of Aug. 24, 1995). This set was sold in a regular plastic-front Breyer box with a large round gold sticker on the front saying, in full: "1993 Special Collector Edition / Limited Production / Drinkers of the Wind / This highly collectible edition represents the Arabian Family—Stallion, Mare and Foal." The phrase "drinkers of the wind" is, as I understand, a traditional Arabic reference to the horses of the desert. For an earlier Breyer reference to "drinkers of the wind," see above in the Traditionals section, Proud Arabian Mare Gift Set #2155. The stallion's gray coat has a slight metallic shimmer in bright light. In many sets I've seen, the stallion has given new meaning to the set's name, being slightly heat-bloated, most noticeably in the girth and upper neck. Evidently the stallions came from the factory that way, for the mares and foals in the same boxes are not bloated, which they would be if the problem had occurred during shipping.

Notes:

(1) This mold was created by Maureen Love Calvert, of the Hagen-Renaker company, as a portrait of the real Arabian stallion "Ferseyn." H-R produced it in ceramic under the name "Ferseyn" Arabian Stallion #697 (see Roller, Rose, and Berkwitz 1989, p. 22).

(2) A one-of-a-kind pale smoke gray Classic Arab Stallion and a one-of-a-kind chocolate sorrel Classic "Black Beauty," both in original Breyer boxes, are pictured in an auction ad in *The Hobby Horse News* (Feb./Mar. 1995, p. 12). These horses are from a group of approximately 30 one-of-a-kind models that were presented by Breyer to their sales representatives at a meeting in December 1993. Each horse came in a Breyer box with the label "Unique Breyer Model." The photo in the auction ad shows the Arab Stallion to have solid dark front legs (the back legs are hidden) and to be paler than the 1993 Toys R Us SR smoke gray stallion, which has 4 stockings. (Information is from the auction ad and Daphne Macpherson, of Cascade Models, who asked her Breyer sales representative about these horses.)

(3) The Arabian Family Stallion mold has the round "Breyer Molding Co." stamp and the "U.S.A." stamp. Some models have the "B" stamp in addition (I have seen a solid-faced, gray-hoofed sorrel #3055 with the "B").

Arabian Stallion And Frisky Foal sets #3162 and #3163 — see under Arabian Family Foal in the Classics section and under "Sham" in the Traditionals section

"Azul" — see under "Terrang"

Bedouin Family Gift Set — see under Arabian Family Foal, Arabian Family Mare, and Arabian Family Stallion

"Black Beauty" — ♞ Gelding, cantering?, head up, looking left. Sculpted by Chris Hess. Mold in catalog-run production 1980-93.

Catalog-run models made from this mold:

♞ "Black Beauty" Family set #3040, black "Black Beauty," tiny star or long star, black mane and tail, 1 right front stocking with gray hoof, other legs and hooves black, matte or semigloss (1980-93). Set also includes bay "Duchess," chestnut "Ginger," and dapple gray "Merrylegs." Called "Black Beauty" Family And Friends Gift Set in the front of the 1980 catalog but "Black Beauty" Family in the back pages and in all subsequent catalogs. "Black Beauty" is shown with a tiny diamond star in the 1980-84 and 1988 catalogs (face not visible 1985-87), and collector Kay Schlumpf's and Mel Price's models have models like this. The horse is shown with a larger, long star in the 1989-93 catalogs; my own model is like this. Collector Chelle Fulk has a variation tiny-star

"Black Beauty" with no stockings. Set #3040 represents the characters of the children's book *Black Beauty*, by the English author Anna Sewell, first published in 1877. It was Sewell's only book (see *Oxford Companion to English Literature*). The 1982 Penney's holiday catalog offered a set called "Black Beauty" And Friends, which was just the #3040 set minus "Duchess" ("Black Beauty's" dam). In 1989 "Black Beauty" was issued by himself to European companies; his individual model number is given as #703540 in a Breyer company computer printout of activity 1985-92 and as #3540 in the German edition of the 1989 Breyer collector's manual. This German manual shows the horse to be the large-star version "Black Beauty" from set #3040.

- "King Of The Wind" Gift Set #3345, golden bay "Lath," no white markings, black points, black hooves (1990-93). Set also includes blood bay "Sham" (Black Stallion mold) and alabaster "Lady Roxana" ("Duchess" mold). This model represents "Lath," the son of "Sham" and "Lady Roxana," in Marguerite Henry's book *King of the Wind*. These equine characters are based on real horses: the Godolphin Arabian; "Roxana," a mare to whom he was bred several times; and "Lath," the first of their offspring. According to *King of the Wind*, the colt was named "Lath" because he was so skinny (p. 149). "Lath's" color is not mentioned explicitly in the book, but it is indicated by a character who says to Agba, "Sham's" guardian, "that little c-c-colt was the spit image o' your horse" (p. 149). "Sham's" color is said to be "red gold" (p. 32). The 1990 Breyer catalog states that the models in the #3345 set represent "Sham," "Lady Roxana," and "Lath" but does not indicate which model is which. The models are identified, however, in a Breyer company computer printout of activity 1985-92: "'King of the Wind' Gift Set. Mold #3030ST (Sham/red bay), #3040BB (Lath/light bay), #3040DU (Lady Roxana/alabaster)."

Special-run models made from this mold:

- "Black Beauty" Gift Set SR #700894, black horse, star, black mane and tail, 1 right front stocking with gray hoof, other legs and hooves black, glossy (1994). Mid-year special, made for sale through model mail-order companies and toy stores. 7,375 sets made (per *JAH* editor Stephanie Macejko, conversation of June 1995). The set also includes leather show halter and lead, Brenda doll, and a small paperback edition of Anna Sewell's book *Black Beauty*, adapted by Cathy East Dubowski and illustrated by Domenick D'Andrea (Bullseye Step Into Classics series by Random House publishers). The release of the set was timed to coincide with the summer 1994 release of the movie remake of *Black Beauty*. This SR is Breyer's first Classic-scale model to be issued in glossy finish. Except for the finish, it is identical to the regular-run "Black Beauty" in set #3040. For details on the doll and tack, see under Brenda Breyer in the Riders - Soft Or Jointed Plastic section below. The set number is per the set's box and a Reeves International memo of June 24, 1994, to sales representatives, subject "1994 Breyer Summer Specials." The Reeves International 1994 Mid-Year Introduction brochure also features this set but does not refer to it as a "summer special."
- Collector's One Horse Open Sleigh set SR, flocked dapple gray horse, bald face, painted black eyes, gray synthetic hair mane and tail, painted black hooves (1984). Penney's holiday catalog. 1,500 or fewer sets made. Set also includes authentic black leather harness; black wooden sleigh with red seat and red metal runners; and two porcelain dolls, a man and a woman, with cloth clothing. Set is mounted on a rectangular wood base with a white inset that looks like snow and has a clear Plexiglas display cover. Signed and numbered by the maker, the Riegseckers of Indiana. Sets also came with certificate of authenticity signed by Mel Riegsecker (per *JAH* XI/#3 1984, p. 19). The Penney's catalog, which priced the set at $220.00, comments: "Production will not exceed 1500. . . . Produced individually with great care by Amish craftsmen. . . . Shipped from a factory near Middlebury, Indiana." See Miniature Collection for further discussion of the Riegseckers. This set is pictured not only in the Penney's catalog, which calls it "Collector's One Horse Open Sleigh," but also in *JAH* XI/#3 1984 (p. 19), where it is called "Those Wonderful Wintry Rides." The woman doll has a red cap with white pompom on top, a red coat, dark green neck scarf, and fluffy white muff. The man has an identical red cap, a dark green coat, and red neck scarf. A plaid blanket covers the dolls' laps. The horse in collector Heather Wells's set has brown dapples, although the steeds in *JAH* and the Penney's catalog appear to have gray dapples. See Miniature Collection for further discussion.
- "Iltschi" SR #703440, black, long star, black mane and tail, 4 stockings, charcoal/black hooves (1989 and 1990). Export special. Sold separately or in Karl May set with bay "Hatatitla" ("Ginger" mold). The model number is per a Breyer photo sheet entitled "Breyer's 1990 Export Offerings" and a Breyer company computer printout of activity 1985-92. (The German edition of the 1989 Breyer collector's manual gives a shortened number: #3440.) The printout lists the following batches of these SRs made in 1989: 144 "Hatatitlas" and 144 "Iltschis" for European customers, and 500 sets (listed as #403640) to a German company called Siwek GMBH. The Karl May special is also mentioned in *JAH* 16/#4 Sept./Oct. 1989 (p. 28). Ingrid Muensterer, owner of the German model mail-order company Modell-Pferde Versand, told me that Karl May (pronounced "my") was a German author who wrote a large number of Western stories for German children—that's Western as in cowboys and Indians—though he apparently never even visited the western United States. The horses "Hatatitla" and "Iltschi" were two of his characters. May's stories, Ingrid said, became hugely popular among Germans of her generation (she was 50ish in 1993). Collector Liz Strauss's two models came in ordinary plastic-fronted yellow Breyer boxes with no model numbers but decorated with large round gold-foil stickers with German print. "Iltschi's" sticker says: "Modellpferde / Iltschi / Winnetou's Pferde / Weltberühmte Karl May Figur / Zum Spielen & Sammeln / Naturgetreu - Handbemalt."

Notes:

(1) Regarding a one-of-a-kind chocolate sorrel "Black Beauty" see note 2 for the Classic Arabian Family Stallion mold.

(2) The "Black Beauty" mold has the round "Breyer Molding Co." stamp. The earliest models have the round stamp only, with no "B" stamp (collector Lori Ogozalek's model from the first year of issue is like this); but slightly later models do have the "B" stamp. This mold was never given the "U.S.A." stamp.

"Black Beauty" Family set — The horses in this set are "Black Beauty," "Duchess," "Ginger," and "Merrylegs." See "Black Beauty" Family set under those mold names for details.

"Black Beauty" Gift Set SR — see under "Black Beauty"

"Blackjack" — see under "Kelso"

Black Stallion — Standing, head up, nose poked out, lower part of tail attached to right buttock. Sculpted by Chris Hess. Mold in catalog-run production 1983-93.

Catalog-run models made from this mold:

- "The Black Stallion Returns" Set #3030, black Black Stallion, no white markings, black mane and tail, tan hooves (1983-93). Set also includes alabaster "Johar" and red chestnut "Sagr." This set represents the characters in Walter Farley's book *The Black Stallion Returns*, the second book of the Black Stallion series. In this book, the Black Stallion's proper name is identified as "Shetan" (thanks to Karen Crossley for this information; also see *JAH* IX/#4 1982, p. 8).
- The Doctor's Buggy set #19842, flocked bay horse, blaze, black synthetic hair mane and tail, 1 left hind and 2 front stockings, 4 painted black hooves, in the Miniature Collection (1984-87). Set also includes authentic black leather harness, wood and metal buggy in black with red upholstery, and ceramic doctor doll with cloth clothing. Set is mounted on wood base with a red inset and has a clear Plexiglas display cover. Signed and numbered. Bentley Sales Company price lists for April 1984 and April 1985 offered the #19842 set for $219.00, but the price jumped to $349.00 on the August 1985 through August 1986 Bentley's lists and to $374.99 on the February 1987 list, both increases corresponding to hikes in suggested retail prices on Breyer company price lists for those years. This set is called The Country Doctor in some catalogs and manuals, The Doctor's Buggy in others. (Oddly, the set is not in the 1987 manual, though it is in that year's catalog.) The doll driver is not pictured in any Breyer catalogs or manuals, but the photo captions in the 1985-87 catalogs state, "The Doctor's Buggy comes with the Doctor Doll (not shown)." Collector Sandy Tomezik wrote to me that the doctor in her Doctor's Buggy set has painted gray hair and a beard and is dressed like the father doll in the Family To Church On Sunday set #19843 (see that entry under "Duchess" for description). The 1987 catalog offers this further description of the set: "The Doctor's Buggy is handcrafted of wood and metal and takes one back in time. Beautifully crafted with a leatherette top[,] pin striping on the wheels and carriage, and red upholstery. It's the Model T of carriages used to make housecalls." The Miniature Collection series of horse-and-buggy models was made for Breyer by the Riegseckers of Indiana. See Miniature Collection for further discussion.
- "King Of The Wind" Gift Set #3345, blood bay "Sham," solid face, black points, white spot on back of right hind fetlock, black hooves (1990-93). Set also includes golden bay "Lath" ("Black Beauty" mold) and alabaster "Lady Roxana" ("Duchess" mold). This set represents the characters in Marguerite Henry's book *King of the Wind*. These equine characters are based on real horses: the Godolphin Arabian; "Roxana," a mare to whom he was bred several times; and "Lath," the first of their offspring. The 1990 Breyer catalog states that the models in the #3345 set represent "Sham," "Lady Roxana," and "Lath" but does not indicate which model is which. The models are identified, however, in a Breyer company computer printout of activity 1985-92: "'King of the Wind' Gift Set. Mold #3030ST (Sham/red bay), #3040BB (Lath/light bay), #3040DU (Lady Roxana/alabaster)." For further discussion see "Sham" and "Lady Roxana" above in the Traditionals section.

Note: The Black Stallion mold has the round "Breyer Molding Co." stamp. The mold debuted at the very end of the "B" stamp era, so it is virtually certain that he was never given this stamp. This mold was never given the "U.S.A." stamp, either.

"Black Stallion Returns" Set — The horses in this set are The Black Stallion, "Johar," and "Sagr." See "Black Stallion Returns" Set under those mold names for details.

"Blaze" SR — see under Quarter Horse Family Foal

"Blue" — see "A Pony For Keeps" Gift Set, under "Ginger"

Bolo Tie — see below in the Wildlife section

B Ranch Series — Designed to appeal to youngsters, this series was introduced by Breyer in 1995. The series includes Classic-scale horses, dolls, tack (English and Western saddles and bridles), jumps (roll-top, panel, and plank jumps), three different neck ribbons, and a wooden carrying case that accommodates one horse, a doll, and various tack. The horses all have their own model numbers, but the six B Ranch horses that used to be the After School Herd (and before that the race horses of the Classic Series) are also available to dealers in B Ranch Series Assortment #2002. For the horses, see "Apache" (under "Man-O-War"); "Azul" (under "Terrang"); "Blackjack" (under "Kelso"); "Buck" And Hillary Gift Set (under "Silky Sullivan"); "Cloud" (under "Swaps"); "Glory" And Plank Jump Gift Set (under "Ruffian"); "Patches" (under "Ruffian"); and "Spice" (under "Silky Sullivan"). For the dolls, see all entries for Hillary in the Riders - Soft Or Jointed Plastic section. The boxes in which all these horses and sets are packaged are decorated with a big gold sticker (shaped somewhat like a shooting star) that says "B°Ranch / Horse Kids Headquarters."

Breyer Classic Collector's Arabian Family Set SR — see Arabian Family Foal SR, black; Arabian Family Mare SR, black; and Arabian Family Stallion SR, black

Brown Pinto Mare SR — see under Quarter Horse Family Mare

"Buck" And Hillary Gift Set — for the horse, see under "Silky Sullivan"; for the doll, see under Hillary in the Riders - Soft Or Jointed Plastic section

"Buckaroo" And "Skeeter" set SR — in the Classics section see "Buckaroo" (under Arabian Family Mare); in the Traditionals sections see "Skeeter" (under "Stormy")

Bucking Bronco — Small bucking stallion, tail looped over back. Sculpted by Chris Hess. Mold in catalog-run production 1966-73, 1975-76, 1995 - current as of 1996.

Catalog-run models made from this mold:

- Bucking Bronco #190, black, bald face, black mane and tail, 4 stockings, gray hooves, matte (1966-73, 1975-76). On earlier models the bald face is larger and often extensive, reaching well down the sides of the face. Later models have the white restricted to the front of the face. On some models the face can be quite oversprayed, and collector Sue Lehman found a #190 with solid face, but with the usual stockings and gray hooves.
- Bucking Bronco #191, steel gray, bald face, mane and tail same color as body or slightly darker, 4 stockings, gray hooves, matte (1966). The catalog shows this model with an extensive bald face, reaching well down the sides of the face, and specimens that I've seen are like this.
- Bucking Bronco #192, bay, bald face, black mane and tail, no black on the legs, 4 stockings, most with gray hooves, matte (1967/68 - 1970). This model is in the 1967 price list but not in the 1967 catalog. It is in the 1968 price list, catalog, and manual. The bald face on this model can be extensive, reaching well down the sides of the face. Collector Val Sibert has a model with black hooves. Gutierrez 1989 reports a variation with no black on the mane and tail.
- "Dakota" Bucking Bronco #932, dappled palomino, bald face, white mane and tail, 2

hind stockings with tan hooves, front hooves dark palomino, matte (1995 - current as of 1996). The sparse, round dapples are muted, being only a shade lighter than the basic dark golden-tan color. In the 1996 catalog, #932's name changed to "Dakota" Ranch Horse.

Special-run models made from this mold:

- Bucking Bronco SR #413190, black leopard appaloosa, white horse with black splashed-on spots; mane and tail part gray and part white; gray knees and hocks; gray hooves; matte (1988). Made for Bentley Sales Company. Probably 400 models made. Sold separately or in SR set with chestnut, steel gray, and red roan Bucking Broncos. The model number I've given is per a Breyer company computer printout of activity 1985-92; Bentley's price lists give the number as #190A. See Bucking Bronco SR steel gray for discussion of date and quantity.
- Bucking Bronco SR #701092, black paint, overo; head white up to forelock and throatlatch; pink nose with gray nostrils; 1 right front stocking (goes over knee) and 2 hind; stockinged legs have tan hooves; other hoof black; semigloss (1992). Breyer show special, made for shows and parties sponsored by Breyer dealers. 9,000 models made (per a Breyer company computer printout of activity 1985-92). This model came in a regular Breyer box, printed with the model's number, and with a certificate of authenticity signed by Breyer executive Peter Stone. The certificate states: "The spirit of the American West lives on in this wild black and white pinto. This Special Run model was produced in the year 1992 for Breyer Special Events nationwide. It will not be made available again and is a true collector's item." The left hind stocking varies: on some models it comes up to the middle of the hock, bisecting the hock with an unnatural straight line; on others the stocking ends below the hock.
- Bucking Bronco SR #412190, chestnut, slightly darker mane and tail, bald lower face, 4 stockings, gray hooves, matte (1988). Made for Bentley Sales Company. Probably 400 models made. Sold separately or in SR set with black leopard appaloosa, steel gray, and red roan Bucking Broncos. At least some models have gray shading on knees and hocks. The model number I've given is per a Breyer company computer printout of activity 1985-92; Bentley's price lists give the number as #190C. See Bucking Bronco SR steel gray for discussion of date and quantity.
- Bucking Bronco SR #411190, red roan, white horse with red chestnut flecks; red chestnut mane, tail, knees and hocks; tan hooves; matte (1988). Made for Bentley Sales Company. Probably 400 models made. Sold separately or in SR set with black leopard appaloosa, chestnut, and steel gray Bucking Broncos. The model number I've given is per a Breyer company computer printout of activity 1985-92; Bentley's price lists give the number as #190RR. See Bucking Bronco SR steel gray for discussion of date and quantity.
- Bucking Bronco SR #414190, steel gray, solid face, black mane and tail, 4 stockings, gray hooves, semigloss (1988). Made for Bentley Sales Company. 400 models made. Sold separately or in SR set with black leopard appaloosa, chestnut, and red roan Bucking Broncos. The January 1988 Bentley's price list advertising this set says the steel gray has "hind socks," but my own specimen and others I've seen have front socks as well as hind. The model number I've given is per a Breyer company computer printout of activity 1985-92; Bentley's price lists give the number as #190G. The printout also gives the quantity for the gray Bronco. It does not give the quantity for the other three colors, but I assume they were made in the same quantities as the steel gray. All the models in the set were made in 1987 according to the printout, but they didn't become available until the start of 1988: Bentley's January 1988 price list is the first list on which these horses are advertised, and it says "We are taking orders now for late February delivery."

Notes:

(1) This mold is Classic size, but in catalogs it was always listed with the Traditionals. It can stand either on its head and front legs or on three legs.

(2) This mold is called "Bucking Horse" in the 1966-70 catalogs, though the price lists for those years call him "Bucking Bronco," as do catalogs after 1970.

(3) The Bucking Bronco mold has the round "Breyer Molding Co." stamp only. It was never given the "U.S.A." stamp. Nor, I believe, did it ever have the "B" stamp, for the mold was not in production during the "B" stamp era.

The Challenger Gift Set, "Mesteño" And "Sombra" — see both entries under "Mesteño" Challenger; also see Messenger Series Of Kiger Mustangs

"Citation" SR — see under "Kelso"

Classic Series — This series consists of seven horse models, all sold separately. See "Kelso"; Lipizzan; "Man-O-War"; "Ruffian"; "Silky Sullivan"; "Swaps"; and "Terrang." For further discussion of this series, see the General Note at the start of the Classics section.

"Cloud" — see under "Swaps"

Collector's One Horse Open Sleigh set SR — see under "Black Beauty"

"Colleen" — see under "Ruffian"

"Count Fleet" SR — see under "Terrang"

Country Doctor set — see The Doctor's Buggy set, under Black Stallion

"Dakota" Bucking Bronco — see under Bucking Bronco

The Dawning Gift Set, "Mesteño" And His Mother — see under "Mesteño" Dawning and under "Mesteño's" Mother; also see Messenger Series Of Kiger Mustangs

Delivery Wagon (or Delivering The Goods) set — see under "Keen"

"Denver" SR — see under "Kelso"

Desert Arabian Family set — see under Arabian Family Foal, Arabian Family Mare, and Arabian Family Stallion

Doctor's Buggy set — see under Black Stallion

Drinkers Of The Wind set SR — see Arabian Family Foal SR, dark rose gray; Arabian Family Stallion SR, smoke gray; and "Johar" SR, fleabitten rose gray

Drive On A Sunny Day set — see under "Johar"

"Duchess" — Mare, standing, looking left. Sculpted by Chris Hess. Mold in catalog-run production 1980-94.

Catalog-run models made from this mold:

- "Black Beauty" Family set #3040, bay "Duchess," no white markings, black points, black hooves (1980-93). Set also includes black "Black Beauty," chestnut "Ginger," and dapple gray "Merrylegs." Set #3040 represents the characters of the children's book *Black Beauty*, by the English author Anna Sewell, first published in 1877. It was Sewell's only book (see *Oxford Companion to English Literature*). Breyer catalogs list the names of the models in this set but omit to indicate which model is which—leaving it unclear which mare mold is "Duchess" and which "Ginger." The models are individually labeled, however, in *JAH* IX/#1 1981 [1982], p. 12.
- Family To Church On Sunday set #19843, flocked bay mare, blaze, black synthetic hair mane and tail, 1 left hind and 2 front stockings, 4 painted black hooves, in the Miniature Collection (1984-87). Set also includes flocked bay "Jet Run," authentic black leather harness, wood and metal surrey with maroon/ruby upholstery, and ceramic 4-doll family with cloth clothing. Set is mounted on wood base with maroon/ruby inset and has a clear Plexiglas display cover. Signed and numbered. Bentley Sales Company price lists for April 1984 and April 1985 offered the #19843 set for $299.00, but the price jumped to $499.00 on the August 1985 through August 1986 Bentley's lists and to $549.99 on the February 1987 list, both increases corresponding to hikes in suggested retail prices on Breyer company price lists for those years. Some catalogs and manuals call this model Surrey To Church On Sunday; others call it Surrey With The Fringe On Top. (Oddly, the set is not in the 1987 manual, although it is in the catalog.) The 1985 catalog offers this description of the set: "Dressed in their Sunday best, with a fringed top surrey and beautiful haired and flocked matched team, Family to Church on Sunday is a must for any serious miniature collector. The 'family' are authentically costumed ceramic dolls. With genuine leather tack and handcrafted surrey, Family to Church on Sunday is a signed and numbered edition complete with wood base and clear plastic display case." As shown in catalogs, the dolls are as follows: Father doll with painted light brown hair and mustache, long-sleeved white cloth shirt, dark pants, and dark vest. Boy doll with painted blond hair, long-sleeved white cloth shirt, blue pants, and blue vest. Girl doll with painted light brown hair, clothing not visible except for a light-colored, high-collar top. Mother doll with painted light brown hair and long-sleeved, ankle-length dress of calico-type cloth (white covered with a tiny red print), with high collar and lace hem. Collector Mardi Banks told me that the two horses in her set do not have glass eyes but have the normal molded plastic eyes, which are painted glossy black. The Miniature Collection series of horse-and-buggy models was made for Breyer by the Riegseckers of Indiana. See Miniature Collection for further discussion.
- "King Of The Wind" Gift Set #3345, alabaster "Lady Roxana," gray mane and tail, gray hooves (1990-93). Set also includes golden bay "Lath" ("Black Beauty" mold) and blood bay "Sham" (Black Stallion mold). This model represents "Lady Roxana," the mate of "Sham" and dam of "Lath" in Marguerite Henry's book *King of the Wind*. These equine characters are based on real horses: the Godolphin Arabian; "Roxana," a mare to whom he was bred several times; and "Lath," the first of their offspring. *King of the Wind* says of the mare, "Except for her tail, which was a smoky plume, Roxana was the shininess of white marble in the sun" (p. 138).
- Trakehner Family set #3347, pale dapple gray mare, bald face, gray-shaded mane and tail, 4 stockings, tan hooves (1992-94). Set also includes dark chestnut Trakehner Family Stallion ("Jet Run" mold) and bay Trakehner Family Foal (Mustang Family Foal mold). Breyer catalogs omit to indicate which of the two adult molds in this set is supposed to be the mare, thus leaving us in a quandary since both are mare molds. However, the models in the set are individually identified in a Breyer company computer printout of activity 1985-92: "7000-3347...Trakehner Fam...Mold #3035JR (stallion/liver chestnut), #3040DU (mare/dapple gray), #3065FO (foal/bright bay)." My own mare has a soft gray mane and a white tail with vertical gray stripes.

Note: The "Duchess' mold has the round "Breyer Molding Co." stamp. The earliest models have the round stamp only, with no "B" stamp (collector Lori Ogozalek's model from the first year of issue is like this); but slightly later models do have the "B" stamp. This mold was never given the "U.S.A." stamp.

Eagle And "Pow Wow" set SR — for the horse see under "Johar"; for the doll see under Eagle in the Riders - Soft Or Jointed Plastic section

Export specials — for a complete listing of these SRs, see Export Specials above in the Traditionals section

Family To Church On Sunday surrey set — see under "Duchess" and under "Jet Run"

Fine Horse Family set — see under "Kelso," Mustang Family Foal, and "Silky Sullivan"

Flocked Classic-size models — see Sky Blue "Pegasus" SR (under Lipizzan), and see Miniature Collection for a complete list of catalog-run and special-run sets with vehicles and flocked horses

Foal's First Day set SR — see Arabian Family Foal SR, dark shaded chestnut; and "Johar" SR, rose alabaster

"Friday" — see the two entries for Marguerite Henry's "Our First Pony" Gift Set, under Arabian Family Foal

"Gaucho" — see under "Terrang"

German Olympic Team Set SR — see "Ahlerich" SR (under "Keen"), "Orchidee" SR (under "Might Tango"), and "Rembrandt" SR (under "Jet Run")

"Geronimo" And "Cochise" set SR — in the Classics section see "Geronimo" SR (under "Kelso); in the Traditionals section see "Cochise" SR (under "Sea Star")

"Ginger" — Mare, cross-cantering, looking left. Sculpted by Chris Hess. Mold in catalog-run production 1980-93, 1996-.

Catalog-run models made from this mold:

- "Black Beauty" Family set #3040, chestnut "Ginger," blaze, darker chestnut mane and tail, chestnut-gray hooves (1980-93). Set also includes black "Black Beauty," bay "Duchess," and dapple gray "Merrylegs." This set represents the characters of the children's book *Black Beauty*, by the English author Anna Sewell, first published in 1877. It was Sewell's only book (see *Oxford Companion to English Literature*). Breyer catalogs list the names of the models in this set but omit to indicate which model is which—leaving it unclear which mare mold is "Duchess" and which "Ginger." The models are individually labeled, however, in *JAH* IX/#1 1981 [1982], p. 12. Also, Sewell's book describes "Ginger" as "a tall chestnut mare" (p. 22). The 1982 catalog shows "Ginger" with just a vague half-blaze on the lower part of her face; whether this variation was produced for sale I don't know. "Ginger's" usual blaze is the same as that on the Hanoverian Family mare.

♞ Hanoverian Family set #3346, light sandy bay mare, blaze, some with dorsal stripe, black points, 4 stockings, tan hooves (1992-93). Set also includes black Hanoverian Family Stallion ("Keen" mold) and bay Hanoverian Family Foal (Andalusian Family Foal mold). This mare's blaze is the same as that on "Ginger" in the "Black Beauty" Family set. Collector Sande Schneider's #3346 mare and some others I have seen have a dorsal stripe, but my own mare lacks this detail.

♞ "A Pony For Keeps" Gift Set #3234, alabaster "Blue," gray mane and tail, gray hooves (1990-91). Set also includes light dapple gray "Another" ("Might Tango" mold); chestnut "Jefferson" (Mustang Family Stallion mold); and white "Lady Jane Grey" ("Merrylegs" mold). The "Blue" model in this set represents the real white-gray purebred Section B Welsh Mountain Pony gelding—not a mare, as his portrait on the "Ginger" mold would suggest—owned by a son of Beth Sutton, author of children's books and founder of the Children's Pony Program (see *JAH* 16/#5 Nov./Dec. 1989, p. 3). "Blue," whose full name is "Dixie Blue Devil," is featured in Sutton's book *The Pony Champions* but is not mentioned in *A Pony for Keeps*. The 1990 Breyer catalog lists the names of the models in this set but does not indicate which model is which. The models are identified individually, however, in a Breyer company computer printout of activity 1985-92: "7000-3234...A Pony For Keeps...Mold #3035MT (Another/light dapple grey), #3040GI (Blue/alabaster), #3040ML (Lady Jane Grey/alabaster), #3065ST (Jefferson/sorrel)." Also the book *The Pony Champions* identifies "Another" as a gray and "Blue" as white. The *JAH* issue cited above gives the names but mixes up two of them, calling the white "Ginger" mold "Another" and the dapple gray "Might Tango" mold "Blue." The real "Blue" in all his whiteness is shown on the cover of *JAH* 19/#5 Winter 1992. For further discussion see the entry for "Lady Jane Grey" or "Jefferson."

Special-run models made from this mold:

♘ "Hatatitla" SR #703240, medium bay, no white markings, black points, black hooves (1989 and 1990). Export special. Sold separately or in Karl May set with black "Iltschi" ("Black Beauty" mold). The model number is per a Breyer photo sheet titled "Breyer's 1990 Export Offerings" and a Breyer company computer printout of activity 1985-92. (The German edition of the 1989 Breyer collector's manual gives a shortened number: #3240.) The printout lists the following batches of these SRs made in 1989: 144 "Hatatitlas" and 144 "Iltschis" for European customers, and 500 sets (listed as #403640) to a German company called Siwek GMBH. The Karl May special is also mentioned in *JAH* 16/#4 Sept./Oct. 1989 (p. 28). Collector Liz Strauss's two models came in ordinary plastic-fronted yellow Breyer boxes with no model numbers but decorated with large round gold-foil stickers with German print. "Hatatitla's" sticker says: "Modellpferde / Hatatitla / Old Shatterhand's Pferd / Weltberühmte Karl May Figur / Zum Spielen & Sammeln / Naturgetreu - Handbemalt." For discussion of Karl May, see "Iltschi" SR.

♘ Spanish-Norman Family Mare SR, alabaster, white mane and tail, gray hooves (1994). Made for Toys R Us. Sold in Spanish-Norman Family SR set #700294 with steel gray foal (Andalusian Family Foal mold) and red roan stallion (Andalusian Family Stallion mold). 6,300 sets made (per *JAH* editor Stephanie Macejko, conversation of June 1995). The model number is per the set's box, which also sports a large round gold sticker saying, in full: "1994 Special Collector Edition (Limited Production) / The Spanish-Norman Family / This highly collectible edition represents a unique breed, the blending of the Andalusian of Spain and the Percheron of France."

Note: The "Ginger" mold has the round "Breyer Molding Co." stamp. The earliest models have the round stamp only, with no "B" stamp (collector Lori Ogozalek's model from the first year of issue is like this); but slightly later models do have the "B" stamp. This mold was never given the "U.S.A." stamp.

"Glory" And Plank Jump Gift Set — see under "Ruffian"

Hanoverian Family set — see under Andalusian Family Foal, "Ginger," and "Keen"

"Hatatitla" SR — see under "Ginger"

"Hawk" — see under "Swaps"

"Hobo" — ♞ On removable stand; stallion, galloping; versions with and without molded-in brand on horse and writing on stand. Sculpted by Chris Hess. Mold in catalog-run production 1975-81 (all with brand and writing).

Catalog-run models made from this mold:

MOLD VERSION WITH HIP BRAND:

♞ "Hobo" The Mustang Of Lazy Heart Ranch #625, buckskin, blaze, black points, gray-brown hooves, matte; stand painted brown, with molded-on sign saying "Hobo of the ♡ ♡ Ranch" (1975-80). (The hearts actually lay sideways, with their lobed ends toward each other.) This same model was sold in "Hobo" Of Lazy Heart Ranch Gift Set #2085 [1975-81]; see below. Called "Hobo" The Mustang Of Lazy Heart Ranch in the 1975 catalog; called simply "Hobo" Mustang in the 1976-80 catalogs. Some models have gray body shading and a gray ventral stripe running from the upper lip, down the throat, windpipe, chest, and belly, to the groin. Other models are a solid buckskin with no gray shading or stripe. This model represents a real horse, the blaze-faced buckskin mustang gelding owned by "Wild Horse Annie" (Velma B. Johnston), the Nevada rancher's wife who led the successful fight to protect the wild mustangs of America. Outraged by the cruel roundups of mustangs for slaughter and grinding into pet food—a practice that had decimated the nation's wild horse population—Annie Johnston wrote and campaigned for a federal bill to prevent all hunting of mustangs by means of aircraft and motorized land vehicles. Her bill was signed into law by President Eisenhower in 1959. In 1973 Annie founded Wild Horse Organized Assistance, Inc. (WHOA), to further the preservation of wild horses and burros and to defend the mustang protection law against efforts to undermine it through amendment. Annie's story is told in Marguerite Henry's book *Mustang: Wild Spirit of the West*. As a child, Annie lived with her parents, the Bronns, on the Lazy Heart Ranch, near Reno, Nevada. Her father gave "Hobo" to her. Later she married a neighbor boy, Charlie Johnston, and the newlyweds bought the Lazy Heart from the Bronns, and changed the name and the brand to the Double Lazy Heart. Annie died in 1976. (Additional information per *JAH* VII/#4 [1980], p. 13, and Henry 1969, pp. 141-152). Regarding the model's brand and the writing on his stand, see note 1 for this mold.

Set:

• "Hobo" Of Lazy Heart Ranch Gift Set #2085, buckskin horse and Marguerite Henry's book *Mustang: Wild Spirit of the West* (1975-81). Called "Hobo" Of Lazy Heart Ranch Gift Set in the 1975 catalog; called simply "Hobo" Gift Set in the 1976-81 catalogs. This same model was sold separately as "Hobo" The Mustang Of Lazy Heart Ranch #625 [1975-80]. The model number 2085 previously belonged to "Diablo" The Mustang, Florentine decorator (Mustang mold).

Special-run models made from this mold:

MOLD VERSION WITHOUT HIP BRAND:

♘ "Nevada Star" SR #410493, smoke gray, solid light gray face, charcoal-brown primitive stripes above knees and hocks, charcoal-brown dorsal stripe, black points, black hooves, matte; stand painted light tan in the center, shading to darker brown on the perimeter, with molded-on sign with no writing (1993). Raffle model for BreyerFest in Lexington, Kentucky, July 30-31, 1993. 21 models made. 20 models were raffled off and 1 auctioned. Proceeds were donated to the Misty of Chincoteague Foundation. (Information per *JAH* 20/#2 Summer I 1993, p. 16.) This model's name was announced at the BreyerFest raffle. Two models I have seen, owned by collector Sheryl Leisure and by collector Julie Harris's husband, have no writing at all on the sign that is molded onto the base; the sign is smooth and blank. But a "Nevada Star" in the collector's class at BreyerFest 1995 had "Nevada Star" written on the sign in black. I do not believe the words were molded in as well; they were only written on. Possibly the owner had Breyer executive Peter Stone add this to the sign. The model number for this special is per a Breyer company computer printout of 1993 SRs.

♘ "Riddle" Passing Through Time, Phase One, SR #703595, bay blanket appaloosa, solid face, unstenciled blanket covering butt and part of barrel, splashed-on bay spots, black points, 2 hind stockings with tan hooves, front hooves black, matte; stand painted medium/light red-brown, with molded-on sign saying "Passing Through Time" (1995). Mid-year special; made for sale through model mail-order companies and toy stores. Sold in Passing Through Time set SR #703595, with chestnut-point leopard appaloosa and gray-point leopard appaloosa "Riddles" (both "Hobo" mold). About 3,800 sets made, per *JAH* editor Stephanie Macejko (conversation of July 1996). Each of the three horses comes in a separate box with the model name and number. This set was advertised in the Reeves International 1995 Mid-Year Introduction brochure, which states: "Riddle / Limited to production in the second half of 1995. Experience the 'PASSING' ... Riddle ... as he matures and ages! Collectors will want all three Riddles as each model represents the phases of changing coat patterns so typical of the Appaloosa breed of horse" (ellipses in the original).

♘ "Riddle" Passing Through Time, Phase Two, SR #703595, chestnut-point leopard appaloosa, white horse with splashed-on chestnut spots, chestnut points, light tan hooves, matte; stand painted milk-chocolate brown, with molded-on sign saying "Passing Through Time" (1995). Mid-year special; made for sale through model mail-order companies and toy stores. Sold in Passing Through Time set SR #703595, with bay blanket appaloosa and gray-point leopard appaloosa "Riddles" (both "Hobo" mold). About 3,800 sets made, per *JAH* editor Stephanie Macejko (conversation of July 1996). This leopard appy's chestnut mane and tail are mottled—on my own horses, the mane is prominently mottled with dark gray while the tail is quietly mottled in chestnut shades. My model also has soft gray shading on the sides of the face, although the ones on display at BreyerFest 1995 and in the Reeves 1995 Mid-Year brochure had dark chestnut shading. For further discussion see "Riddle" SR bay blanket appaloosa.

♘ "Riddle" Passing Through Time, Phase Three, SR #703595, gray-point leopard appaloosa, white horse with splashed-on chestnut spots, mane mottled gray and white, gray tail with tan tip, white legs with appy spots, gray-tan hooves, matte; stand painted dark-chocolate brown, with molded-on sign saying "Passing Through Time" (1995). Mid-year special; made for sale through model mail-order companies and toy stores. Sold in Passing Through Time set SR #703595, with bay blanket appaloosa and chestnut-point leopard appaloosa "Riddles" (both "Hobo" mold). About 3,800 sets made, per *JAH* editor Stephanie Macejko (conversation of July 1996). My own Phase Three model has soft red-gray shading on the sides of his face. For further discussion see "Riddle" SR bay blanket appaloosa.

Notes:

(1) For all its years in production as buckskin "Hobo" #625 and #2085, this mold had a double-heart brand molded into the near hip and delicately traced in black paint. (See entry for #625 for an explanation of this brand.) The stand with #625 and #2085 is molded to look like rough earth and has a little molded-on "wooden" sign on the right side that says "Hobo of the ♡ ♡ Ranch" (the hearts lie sideways with their lobes toward each other). In 1993, for the production of SR "Nevada Star," both the horse and stand were modified: the brand was removed from the horse mold, and the molded-in writing was removed from the stand's sign. In 1995, for the production of the SR "Riddle" horses, the stand was modified again, this time in two ways: the series name "Passing Through Time" was molded into the sign, and two long ridges were added to the underside of the stand to help it resist warping. All horses of this mold have a small inverted pyramid of plastic molded to the bottom of one front hoof, which fits into a hole in the stand.

(2) Sculptor Chris Hess may well have taken his concept for this mold from a drawing by illustrator Robert Lougheed in Marguerite Henry's book *Mustang: Wild Sprit of the West* (p. 3; image reversed on p. 214). The drawing shows a horse in precisely the same phase of the gallop as Hess's mold. (Thanks to collector Karen Crossley for bringing this to my attention.)

(3) The "Hobo" mold is Classic size, but in catalogs it was always listed with the Traditionals.

(4) The "Hobo" mold has the round "Breyer Molding Co." stamp inside one hock. Some "Hobo" models might have the "B" stamp too, but I've never seen one like this. This mold was never given the "U.S.A." stamp. The stand has never had any stamps to my knowledge, though conceivably it had a "B" for a brief time.

Horse Set SR (1987) — see "Jet Run" SR, chestnut; "Keen" SR, steel gray; and "Might Tango" SR, reddish bay with solid face

"Iltschi" SR — see under "Black Beauty"

"Jefferson" — see "A Pony For Keeps" Gift Set, under Mustang Family Stallion

"Jeremy" — see under "Kelso"

"Jet Run" — ♞ Gelding with no genitalia, standing/walking, braided mane. Sculpted by Chris Hess. Mold in catalog-run production 1980-94.

Catalog-run models made from this mold:

♞ Family To Church On Sunday set #19843, flocked bay horse, blaze, black synthetic hair mane and tail, 1 right hind and 2 front stockings, 4 painted black hooves, in the Miniature Collection (1984-87). Set also includes flocked bay "Duchess," surrey, and ceramic doll family. For details see Family To Church On Sunday (under "Duchess").

- Trakehner Family set #3347, dark chestnut stallion, star, slightly lighter chestnut mane and tail, 1 right hind stocking with tan hoof, other hooves dark brown (1992-94). Set also includes pale dapple gray Trakehner Family Mare ("Duchess" mold) and bay Trakehner Family Foal (Mustang Family Foal mold). Breyer catalogs omit to indicate which of the two adult molds in this set is supposed to be the stallion, thus leaving us in a quandary since both look like mare molds. However, the models in the set are individually identified in a Breyer company computer printout of activity 1985-92: "7000-3347...Trakehner Fam...Mold #3035JR (stallion/liver chestnut), #3040DU (mare/dapple gray), #3065FO (foal/bright bay)."
- U.S. Equestrian Team Gift Set #3035, bay "Jet Run," star, black points, black hooves (1980-93). Set also includes red chestnut "Keen" and medium dapple gray "Might Tango." All three models in this set are portraits of real U.S.E.T. horses. The real bay gelding "Jet Run" was a 16.2-hand jumper ridden by Michael Matz; the pair won many international show-jumping awards (per the set's box and *JAH* 22/#3 May/June 1995, p. 33).The Breyer set was not released until late in 1980. The 1980 manual neither pictures nor mentions the set, and the catalog for that year has no picture of the set but only a notice saying "available summer 1980." And 1980 department-store holiday catalogs purporting to sell this set don't show the proper U.S.E.T. molds but instead test-color proxies (see "Kelso" SR light reddish chestnut, "Ruffian" SR dapple gray, and "Swaps" SR bay). Bentley Sales Company record cards in my possession show that Bentley's didn't receive their first shipment of #3035 sets until mid-September 1980. Breyer catalogs don't clearly identify which horse has which name in set #3035, but the set's box and *JAH* IX/#1 1981 (p. 13) picture the three models and label each separately with its proper name. Most Breyer catalogs show "Jet Run" with a small star and dark to medium bay color, but two show him with variations: in 1986 he is dark buckskin rather than bay, and in 1989 his star is three times its normal size. Also the 1981 Ward's holiday catalog, which offered the regular #3035 set, shows "Jet Run" with a solid face. Whether models with any of these variations were produced for sale I don't know. The 1981 Sears holiday catalog sold a "2-horse U.S. Equestrian Team Special Set" with the regular-run "Keen" and "Jet Run," but the "Jet Run" has a normal star.

Special-run models made from this mold:

- "Jet Run" SR, medium/light chestnut, blaze, darker chestnut mane and tail, 2 front stockings with gray hooves, hind hooves brown-gray (1987). Sears holiday catalog. Sold in Horse Set SR #493035, with steel gray "Keen" and reddish bay "Might Tango" with solid face. The set number is per a Breyer company computer printout of activity 1985-92; no quantity given. To my knowledge this set does not portray any particular real horses. The Sears catalog doesn't give this set any definite name but simply describes it thus: "Horse set portrays 2 horses performing the canter and 1, the halt." My own "Jet Run" from this set is a normal medium reddish chestnut, but a model I saw at BreyerFest 1996 was very light, actually a light red dun rather than chestnut, with a dark red mane and tail.
- "Rembrandt" SR #703235, reddish bay, solid face, black points, 1 left hind sock, 4 tan hooves (1989 and 1990). Export special; also sold through the 1989 and 1990 Sears holiday catalogs. Sold in German Olympic Team set with reddish bay "Ahlerich" ("Keen" mold) and reddish bay "Orchidee" ("Might Tango" mold). About 5,144 sets produced, per a Breyer company computer printout of activity 1985-92. The printout lists several batches of these SRs: 178 "Ahlerichs," 144 "Rembrandts," and 144 "Orchidees" for European customers; 500 sets (listed as #403535) for a German company called Siwek GMBH; and 4,500 sets (listed as #493535) for Sears in the U.S. The set is also announced and pictured in *JAH* 16/#4 Sept./Oct. 1989 (p. 3). The model number for "Rembrandt" is per the printout and a Breyer photo sheet titled "Breyer's 1990 Export Offerings." (The German edition of the 1989 Breyer collector's manual gives "Rembrandt" a shortened number: #3235.) The three models in this set represent real horses of the German Olympic team. *JAH* 19/#4 Fall 1992 (p. 3) mentioned that the "Rembrandt" model alone might be reissued in honor of the real horse's recent win of Olympic gold in dressage; but to my knowledge the model was not reissued. My own "Rembrandt" has nearly white hooves, though the "Export Offerings" sheet shows the hooves as tan.

Note: The "Jet Run" mold has the round "Breyer Molding Co." stamp. Early models have the "B" stamp as well as the round. This mold was never given the "U.S.A." stamp.

Joey's Pony Cart set — see under "Merrylegs"

"Johar" — Mare, pawing, neck gently arched, tail tip attached to right hock. Sculpted by Chris Hess. Mold in catalog-run production 1983-93.

Catalog-run models made from this mold:

- "The Black Stallion Returns" Set #3030, alabaster "Johar," gray mane, tail, and hooves (1983-93). Set also includes black Black Stallion and red chestnut "Sagr." This set represents the characters in Walter Farley's book *The Black Stallion Returns*.
- Drive On A Sunny Day set #19841, flocked chestnut mare, blaze, painted black eyes, chestnut synthetic hair mane and tail same color as body or darker, 1 right hind and 2 front stockings, 4 painted black hooves, in the Miniature Collection (1984-87). Set also includes authentic black leather harness, ceramic woman doll with painted blond hair and green cloth dress, metal and wood buggy in black with green upholstery, black wheels with yellow spokes and rims. Set is mounted on wood base with green inset and has clear Plexiglas display cover. Signed and numbered. As shown in catalogs, the doll's dress, made of green floral-print cloth, is an old-fashioned ankle-length gown with long sleeves, high collar, and lace trim. In a set that was on display at BreyerFest 1994, the doll had a green dress as shown in the catalogs, and the horse had painted black eyes. The 1987 catalog offers this description of the set: "Drive On A Sunny Day . . . features a genuine leather harness, a beautiful doll with an authentic costume. Also pin striping on the wheels and carriage, and a cushioned seat for the leisurely afternoon drive." The 1984 catalog shows a somewhat different set with the same number and the same buggy on a slightly larger scale; this set is called Open Top Buggy, and has a flocked chestnut Proud Arab Stallion and Brenda doll in period costume. (See under Proud Arabian Stallion above in the Traditionals section for details.) The 1984 collector's manual, however, shows the "Johar" and ceramic doll version of the set and calls it Drive On A Sunny Day, as do the 1985-86 manuals and catalogs. The "Johar" version is also in the 1987 catalog but not the 1987 manual. The April 1984 and April 1985 Bentley Sales Company price lists offered #19841 for $199.00 (whether the 1984 set was the PAS or "Johar" version is not clear). The price jumped to $299.00 on the August 1985 Bentley's list and to $349.99 on the February 1987 list, both increases corresponding to hikes in suggested retail prices on Breyer company price lists for those years. The Miniature Collection series of horse-and-buggy models was made for Breyer by the Riegseckers of Indiana. See Miniature Collection for further discussion.

Special-run models made from this mold:

- Eagle And "Pow Wow" set SR #705095, black pinto "Pow Wow," black horse with white nose, breast, belly, and legs; black mane and tail; tan hooves (1995). Mid-year special; made for sale through model mail-order companies and toy stores. Set also includes a Native American girl doll named Eagle, cloth riding blanket, and tan leather halter and lead. About 4,000 sets made, per *JAH* editor Stephanie Macejko (conversation of July 2, 1996). This set was advertised in the Reeves International 1995 Mid-Year Introduction brochure. The brochure clarifies which piece has which name in this set: "Enjoy this little indian [*sic*] maid, Eagle, and her favorite free-spirited mount, Pow Wow." The mare's unusual pinto pattern is of the type called "splash white" or "splash marked" (per Kathman 1993). For details on the doll and tack, see under Eagle in the Riders - Soft Or Jointed Plastic section.
- "Johar" SR, fleabitten rose gray, white horse with splashed-on chestnut freckles; gray-shaded mane, tail, knees, and hocks; gray-brown hooves (1993). Made for Toys R Us. Sold in Drinkers Of The Wind set SR #700693 with dark rose gray Arabian Family Foal and smoke gray Arabian Family Stallion. 18,000 sets made (per Breyer executive Peter Stone, conversation of Aug. 24, 1995). This set was sold in a regular plastic-front Breyer box with a large round gold sticker on the front saying, in full: "1993 Special Collector Edition / Limited Production / Drinkers of the Wind / This highly collectible edition represents the Arabian Family—Stallion, Mare and Foal." The phrase "drinkers of the wind" is, as I understand, a traditional Arabic reference to the horses of the desert. For an earlier Breyer reference to "drinkers of the wind," see above in the Traditionals section, Proud Arabian Mare Gift Set #2155.
- "Johar" SR, rose alabaster, white horse with soft gray and orangy shadings; gray mane, tail, knees, and hocks; gray hooves (1988). Sold in set with dark shaded chestnut Arabian Family Foal. These sets were made in two batches. One batch was made for signing parties at Black Horse Ranch (BHR) and other retailers and included 408 sets with the set number 413550, according to a Breyer company computer printout of activity 1985-92. Another batch was made for Enchanted Doll House and included an unspecified quantity of sets numbered 403755 and named "Foal's First Day." These latter sets came with a 2-gallon metal pail with paintings by Sam Savitt on the lid and sides. The Breyer printout lists the two batches separately and describes the horses differently (the BHR mare and foal are called "rose smoke" and "light brown" respectively, the Doll House mare and foal "alabaster" and "bay"), but in fact the two batches are virtually identical. Collector Heather Wells has sets from both the BHR signing party and the Doll House, and the models in them differ from each other no more than models in a single run typically vary. Her Doll House mare has a heavier dose of rose shading than her and my own BHR mares but is otherwise identical to them. For comparison of the foals, see that entry.

Note: The "Johar" mold has the round "Breyer Molding Co." stamp. The mold debuted at the very end of the "B" stamp era, so it is virtually certain that she was never given the "B" stamp. This mold was never given the "U.S.A." stamp, either

Karl May set SR — see "Iltschi" SR (under "Black Beauty"), and "Hatatitla" SR (under "Ginger")

"Keen" — Gelding, in the canter (left lead) or extended walk, right hind hoof cocked back, neck and tail arched, braided mane. Sculpted by Chris Hess. Mold in catalog-run production 1980-93.

Catalog-run models made from this mold:

- Delivery Wagon set #19846, flocked chestnut horse, blaze, flaxen synthetic hair mane and tail, 1 right hind and 2 front stockings, 4 painted black hooves, in the Miniature Collection (1987). Set also includes black leather harness; wood and metal wagon painted green and trimmed with white lines, with red wheels; and ceramic man doll driver with cloth clothing (white shirt, black pants, gray apron) and yellow hat. Set is mounted on wood base with white inset and has clear Plexiglas display cover. Signed and numbered. The suggested retail price for this set on the 1987 Breyer company price list was $350.00. This set is not in the 1987 manual but is in the 1987 catalog, which states: "It's a sturdy, utilitarian rig to deliver goods over cobblestone and dusty trackless expanses. Known as express wagons, delivery goods or spring wagons, they are the pickup trucks of the old days. This finely crafted model is made of metal and hard maple." A nearly identical set was issued through Ward's as a special run in 1984 under the name Montgomery Ward Delivery Wagon (see below). The Miniature Collection series of horse-and-buggy models was made for Breyer by the Riegseckers of Indiana. See Miniature Collection for further discussion.
- Hanoverian Family set #3346, black stallion, blaze, black mane and tail, 1 right hind and 2 front stockings with tan hooves, other hoof black (1992-93). Set also includes light sandy bay Hanoverian Family Mare ("Ginger" mold) and bay Hanoverian Family Foal (Andalusian Family Foal mold). This stallion's blaze is the same as that on #3035 "Keen" and SR "Ahlerich."
- U.S. Equestrian Team Gift Set #3035, red chestnut "Keen," blaze, darker chestnut mane and tail, 1 right hind stocking with gray hoof, other hooves red-gray (1980-93). Set also includes bay "Jet Run" with star and medium dapple gray "Might Tango." For discussion of release date of this set, the names of the individual horses, and holiday catalog offerings of the set, see under "Jet Run," above. "Keen's" blaze is the same as that on the Hanoverian Family stallion and SR "Ahlerich." The real "Keen," a dressage champion, is a 17.1-hand chestnut Thoroughbred gelding owned and ridden by Hilda Gurney. The pair were members of the bronze-medal-winning U.S. dressage team at the Montreal Olympics (per the set's box and *JAH* VIII/#3 1981, p. 4).

Special-run models made from this mold:

- "Ahlerich" SR #703135, reddish bay, blaze, black points, 2 hind stockings, 4 dark tan hooves (1989 and 1990). Export special; also sold through the 1989 and 1990 Sears holiday catalogs. Sold separately or in German Olympic Team set with reddish bay "Orchidee" ("Might Tango" mold) and reddish bay "Rembrandt" ("Jet Run" mold). About 5,144 sets produced (for discussion of quantity, see "Rembrandt" SR, under "Jet Run"). The model number for "Ahlerich" is per a Breyer photo sheet titled "Breyer's 1990 Export Offerings" and a Breyer company computer printout of activity 1985-92. (The German edition of the 1989 Breyer collector's manual gives "Ahlerich" a shortened number: #3135.) The three models in this set represent real horses of the German Olympic team. The real "Ahlerich" was an Olympic dressage horse owned by Reiner Klimke. The death of the horse was announced in *JAH* 20/#1 Spring 1993 (p. 2). The blaze on the "Ahlerich" model is the same as that on "Keen" #3035 and Hanoverian Family stallion #3346.
- "Keen" SR, steel gray, solid face, mane and tail same color as body or slightly darker, 4 stockings, gray hooves (1987). Sears holiday catalog. Sold in Horse Set SR #493035, with medium/light chestnut "Jet Run" and reddish bay "Might Tango" with solid face. The set number is per a Breyer company computer printout of activity 1985-92; no

quantity given. To my knowledge this set does not portray any particular real horses. The Sears catalog doesn't give this set any definite name but simply describes it thus: "Horse set portrays 2 horses performing the canter and 1, the halt." My own "Keen" from this set has dark gray shading on his croup and back.

- Montgomery Ward Delivery Wagon set SR, flocked chestnut horse, blaze, flaxen synthetic hair mane and tail, 3 or 4 stockings, 4 painted black hooves (1984). Ward's holiday catalog. Set also includes authentic black leather harness, red-wheeled wood and metal wagon painted green and trimmed with gold lines, and ceramic man doll driver with cloth clothing. Set is mounted on a rectangular wood base with tan inset and has a clear Plexiglas display cover. Signed and numbered by the maker, the Riegseckers of Indiana. Sets came with certificate of authenticity signed by the maker (per *JAH* XI/ #3 1984, p. 9), and were priced at $260.00. The Ward's catalog states: "Expertly hand-crafted in Amish country of Northern Indiana. Shipped from factory." See Miniature Collection for further discussion of the Riegseckers. The doll is wearing a white shirt, black pants, gray apron, and black cap. "Montgomery Ward & Co" is painted on the side of the wagon. The set pictured in the *JAH* cited above differs somewhat from the one in the Ward's catalog. In *JAH*, the set is called Delivering The Goods; the "Montgomery Ward" sign painted on the wagon is white; and the horse has three stockings (1 right hind and 2 front). In the Ward's catalog, the set is called The Montgomery Ward Delivery Wagon; the "Montgomery Ward" sign on the wagon is gold; and the horse has 4 stockings. In 1987 a third version was issued as a regular-run set with the name Delivery Wagon #19846 (see above); the horse in this set is the 3-stocking version as shown in the 1984 *JAH*, but the wagon has no sign and the driver has a yellow "straw" sun hat.

Note: The "Keen" mold has the round "Breyer Molding Co." stamp. Early models have the "B" stamp as well as the round. This mold was never given the "U.S.A." stamp.

"Kelso" — "Gelding" with no genitalia, prancing, looking right. Sculpted by Maureen Love Calvert. Mold in catalog-run production 1975 - current as of 1996.

Catalog-run models made from this mold:

- "Blackjack" #263, black pinto, tobiano; irregular blaze; white mane and tail; 4 tan hooves; with neck ribbon (1995 - current as of 1996). In the B Ranch series. The removable neck ribbon, with blue rosette and red, yellow, and blue streamers, attaches around the horse's neck with a Velcro closure. It is identical to the ribbons that come with the B Ranch series horses "Spice" and "Buck."
- "Jeremy" #257, liver chestnut with red shading, long star, reddish chestnut mane and tail slightly lighter than body, 4 stockings, tan hooves (1993-94). Part of The After School Herd Assortment #2001. "Jeremy" is not named for any real horse; the name is a Breyer invention (per Breyer executive Peter Stone).
- "Kelso" #601, dark bay, solid face, black points, most with 1 or 2 hind stockings with gray hooves, other hooves black (1975-90). In the Classic Series and in Race Horse Assortment #6750 (see general note at the start of the Classics section). This model is shown in the 1975-79 catalogs with 2 hind stockings; in 1980-84 apparently with only a right hind stocking (the photos are dim), as on my own model; in 1985-88 with 2 hind stockings again; and in 1989-90 with no stockings. Collector Delana Metcalf wrote to me that she has a #601 with 4 stockings; the horse's lovely shading and lack of mold stamps indicate that it is a very early piece. The 1982 Sears holiday catalog offered "Kelso" with racing tack, described thus: "Classic-size Race Tack. Genuine leather tack fits classic-size horse, 7 x 7 inches high. Includes racing saddle, numbered saddle pad and elastic girth with bridle [*sic*]." This tack must be SR, for no Classic-scale tack was offered in Breyer catalogs of the early 1980s. The Sears photo shows the bridle and saddle but not the saddle pad. The horse in the photo appears to have no stockings, but it is quite certainly just a variation #601, not an SR, for it is the normal dark bay color of #601 and is called "Kelso" in the Sears catalog text. #601 is a portrait of the real Thoroughbred race horse "Kelso," born in 1957. Because he was rather scrawny as a foal, "Kelso" was gelded early "to aid in growth" (per the biography on the Breyer box). In his 8-year racing career, he was voted Horse of the Year five times and set several speed records. The model number 601 previously belonged to the set Circus Boy Corky On "Bimbo" (rider with gray Elephant).
- "Norita" #251, dapple gray, no or very few dapples on head and upper neck; bald face; darker gray mane and tail; hindquarters shaded with darker gray, 4 stockings; gray hooves (1991-92). Part of The After School Herd Assortment #2000. "Norita" is not named for any real horse; the name is a Breyer invention (per Breyer executive Peter Stone).

Set:

- Fine Horse Family set #3348, red roan mare, off-white horse with tiny pale-chestnut flecks, chestnut head with low blaze, chestnut points, gray hooves (1994 - current as of 1996). Set also includes chestnut blanket appaloosa foal (Mustang Family Foal mold) and liver chestnut stallion ("Silky Sullivan" mold). Presumably the roan "Kelso" is meant to be the mare of this family in that the mold is "female" by the principles of Breyer anatomy: mares are the horses with no genitalia represented.

Special-run models made from this mold:

- "Citation" SR, medium reddish bay, solid face, black mane and tail, no black on the legs, 2 hind socks with gray hooves, bay front legs with brown-charcoal hooves (1987). Made for Hobby Center Toys, Ohio. Sold in Triple Crown Winners I set SR #406135, with dark olive chestnut "Count Fleet" ("Terrang" mold) and medium/light red chestnut "Whirlaway" ("Silky Sullivan" mold). The set's number is per a Breyer company computer printout of activity 1985-92. 1,000 sets were made, according to the printed paper slip that came in the set's box and an article on Hobby Center Toys in *JAH* 16/#1 Feb./Mar. 1989 (p. 28). However, additional pieces of "Citation" and "Count Fleet" may have been made, for shipments of these models to Bentley Sales Company in 1988 are listed in the Breyer printout. These listings, which specify no quantities, assign "Citation" the individual model number 410601 and "Count Fleet" the number 410605. The slip in the set's box clarifies which model is which by identifying the color: "Whirlaway—chestnut stallion / Count Fleet—brown stallion / Citation—bay stallion." The printout confirms these identifications by cross-referencing the SR names to the regular-run mold numbers as well as to the SR set number: "Citation . . . mold #601 (FM 7000-406135). . . . Count Fleet . . . mold #605 (FM 7000-406135)." On my own and collector Heather Wells's "Citations," the neck and head are a darker bay than the body, but I've seen another "Citation" with even coloring. The socks can be rather vague. The real "Citation" was a Thoroughbred race horse who won the Triple Crown (Kentucky Derby, Preakness, and Belmont Stakes) in 1948.
- "Denver" SR, dark bay, blaze, black points, black hooves (1994). Made for Aristoplay Ltd., an educational toy company in Ann Arbor, Michigan, which sold the sets direct and also distributed them to toy stores and mail-order businesses. Sold in SR set #410194 with dark bay "Blaze" (Quarter Horse Family Foal mold); the set number is per *JAH* editor Stephanie Macejko. 4,000 sets made (per Vicky at Aristoplay and per various mail-order catalogs). The set also came with a small poster and a numbered certificate of authenticity. According to the certificate, the Breyer issued the models "in honor of the introduction of the game know as *Herd Your Horses!*," manufactured by Aristoplay. The models represent two equine characters in the game, which includes 55 horse cards with illustrations and breed descriptions. The card for "Denver" and "Blaze" identifies their color as mahogany bay, their breed type as warmblood, and their breed as Dutch Warmblood. It also clarifies which horse is which: "Denver and her foal Blaze are Warm Bloods." (Thanks to Kay Schlumpf for a copy of her card.) Drawings of many other horses in the game appear on the small poster included with the set.
- "Geronimo" SR, chestnut blanket appaloosa, solid face, dark chestnut mane, dark chestnut tail with light tip, unstenciled blanket covering butt and part of barrel, splashed-on chestnut spots, charcoal knees and hocks, 1 right front and 2 hind stockings with tan hooves, left front lower leg charcoal with tan-and-charcoal striped hoof (1995). Made for Toys R Us. Sold in "Geronimo" And "Cochise" set #700695 with SR chestnut blanket appaloosa "Cochise" (Traditional "Sea Star" mold) and gold metal medallion on blue ribbon. 4,300 sets made, per *JAH* editor Stephanie Macejko (conversation of July 1996). Stephanie also clarified which model has which name: the adult horse's name comes first in the set name. The set name and number are per the set's box. The shading on the mane, tail, and legs can be so dark on some models as to make them nearly bay. This set is one of several in the Medallion Series made for Toys R Us; see Medallion Series above in the Traditionals section for a full list and a description of the medallion.
- "Kelso" SR?, light reddish chestnut, blaze, slightly darker chestnut mane and tail, 1 right hind stocking with gray hoof, other hooves dark chestnut-gray (1980). Probably never released. Ward's and Sears holiday catalogs. In the Ward's catalog this "Kelso" is shown as part of a 3-horse set called U.S. Equestrian Team, which also includes dapple gray "Ruffian" and bay "Swaps." In the Sears catalog the same "Kelso" is shown as part of a 2-horse set called U.S. Equestrian Team Special Set, with the same dark bay "Swaps." Several hobby sources list one or more of these three models as existing SRs, but other evidence indicates that these horses were never produced (see "Ruffian" SR dapple gray for discussion). Surprisingly, collector Lisa Esping did find a chestnut "Kelso" at a flea market in Illinois. In the photo Lisa sent me, her horse looks exactly like the photo models in the Ward's and Sears catalogs. (Lisa said the model also has the round Breyer stamp only, as is normal for this mold.) Evidently Lisa had the good fortune to find a test model. Collector Karen Perkins too has a chestnut "Kelso," which she advertised on a sales list as a test piece for a 1980 Christmas catalog.
- "Kelso" SR, medium reddish bay, large star, black points, 4 stockings, tan hooves (1992). Sears holiday catalog. Sold in SR set #493092, with the book *Draw Horses with Sam Savitt*. 900 models made. Quantity and set number are per a Breyer company computer printout of activity 1985-92.

Notes:

(1) This mold was created by Maureen Love Calvert, of the Hagen-Renaker company, as a portrait of the real Thoroughbred race horse "Kelso," and H-R produced it in ceramic as "Kelso" #772 (see Roller, Rose, and Berkwitz 1989, p. 23). The real "Kelso" was in fact a gelding, not a mare as Love's sculpture would imply (thanks to collector Nancy Timm for this information). Genitalia are lacking on the H-R ceramic "Kelso" as well as on the Breyer.

(2) Some models of the "Kelso" mold have no mold marks; I believe these are the earliest models made. All other models of this mold have the round "Breyer Molding Co." stamp. Some models with the round stamp might have the "B" stamp too, but I'm not sure. This mold was never given the "U.S.A." stamp.

Kiger Mustangs — see Messenger Series Of Kiger Mustangs

"King" — see under "Man-O-War"

"King Of The Wind" Gift Set — The horses in this set are "Lath" ("Black Beauty" mold), "Sham" (Black Stallion mold), and "Lady Roxana" ("Duchess" mold). See "King Of The Wind" Gift Set under those mold names for details.

"Lady Jane Grey" — see "A Pony For Keeps" Gift Set, under "Merrylegs"

"Lady Roxana" — see "King Of The Wind" Gift Set, under "Duchess"

"Lath" — see "King Of The Wind" Gift Set, under "Black Beauty"

Lipizzan — Gelding, in the levade (controlled rearing), ears back. Sculpted by Chris Hess. Mold in catalog-run production 1975-80 (Lipizzan mold version) and mid-1983 - 1987 ("Pegasus" mold version).

Catalog-run models made from this mold:

LIPIZZAN MOLD VERSION:

- Lipizzan Stallion #620, alabaster; white mane and tail touched with gray shading; grayish pink muzzle; gray-shaded eyes, inner ears, and knees; many with gray ventral stripe; pink or grayish pink hooves (1975-80). In the Classic Series. The ventral stripe runs from the throat, down the windpipe, chest, and belly, to the genitals. Many #620s have pink genitals. #620 came in an especially pretty cardboard picture box with a photo of the model superimposed on a watercolor sketch of the magnificent arena of the Spanish Riding School in Vienna, home of the original performing Lipizzaners. The model number 620 was later assigned to the 1992 alabaster Lipizzaner SR made for Toys R Us in Germany (see below).

"PEGASUS" MOLD VERSION:

- "Pegasus" #209, alabaster with white wings, white mane and tail, white body with no shading, pink-tan hooves (mid-1983 - 1987). The removable wings, which fit into slots on the horse's sides, are made of the same plastic as the horse and are molded with elaborate "feathers." This model is not in the 1983 catalog or price list but is in the 1983 Penney's holiday catalog, in a version with what the catalog text describes as "flexible wings"! A 1983 flyer from Bentley Sales also announces the 1983 summer release of #209 but doesn't mention whether the wings were flexible. The wings on the model shown in the Penney's catalog photo appear slightly thinner and more vertical than #209's normal rigid plastic wings. I have never seen a flexible-winged model, and when I asked Breyer executive Peter Stone about it (conversation of May 1994), he not only had no memory of such wings but was flatly incredulous. Nonetheless, collector Tanya Parker distinctly recalls that some friends of hers had one. Its wings, according to Tanya, "were a rubbery type material, very different from what the horse itself was made of. They were also removable." If Tanya is correct, I would guess that the injection mold for #209's wings had not been finished in time for the 1983 holiday order, so some flexible wings were concocted to fill in. "Pegasus" was also in the 1984 Penney's holiday catalog, and the description still said "flexible wings," but the wings shown in the photo are the normal rigid plastic wings, to judge from their shape and angle.

Special-run models made from this mold:

LIPIZZAN MOLD VERSION:

- Lipizzaner SR #620, alabaster; white mane with pale gray shading; tail white on top half, gray on the bottom; gray muzzle with pink between nostrils; ears gray inside and out; gray-shaded neck, shoulders, butt, knees and hocks; gray hooves (1992). Export special, made for Toys R Us in Germany. 900 models made (per Breyer dealer Lynn Luther, who got the information from Breyer executive Peter Stone in 1993). This SR came in a normal plastic-fronted Breyer box with yellow backing, labeled "#620—Lipizzaner"; this is the same model number that the old regular run Lipizzan Stallion had. However, a Breyer company computer printout of activity 1985-92 lists this 1992 issue by the SR #700192. The model's box also sports a large round gold sticker that says "Lipizzaner / Zum Spielen & Sammeln / Naturgetreu / Handbemalt" (translation: "Lipizzaner / For Play & Collecting / Lifelike / Handpainted"). I purchased one of these horses in 1993 from the model mail-order company Modell-Pferde Versand, owned by Ingrid Muensterer. When I first spoke to Ingrid about this SR in spring 1993, she knew that the models had been available for some time at German Toys R Us but hadn't realized they were SR. She was able to buy up only a few for resale to overseas collectors. Unless it is kept in its box, this German SR is indistinguishable from the Lipizzaner SR sold by Entertainment Specialists in Florida (see next entry). Both SRs are essentially reissues of the old regular-run #620, but there are differences. The SRs have gray hooves, a predominantly gray muzzle, body shading that tends to follow the muscle grooves in streaks and spots, and no ventral stripe. The old regular run has pink or gray-pink hooves, a predominantly pink muzzle, body shading that is vague (if it is present at all), and a ventral stripe. There is also a slight mold difference; see note 1 for this mold for discussion.
- Lipizzaner SR #700393, alabaster; white mane with pale gray shading; tail white on top half, gray on the bottom; gray muzzle with pink between nostrils; ears gray inside and out; gray-shaded neck, shoulders, butt, knees and hocks; gray hooves (1993 - current as of 1996). Made for "The Wonderful World of Horses" touring show starring the Royal Lipizzaner Stallions, in celebration of the show's 25th anniversary. About 5,000 models made as of July 1996, and more may be ordered in the future by Entertainment Specialists. (About 4,000 had been made as of my conversation with Breyer executive Peter Stone on Oct. 3, 1995; 1,000 more had been made as of my conversation with *JAH* editor Stephanie Macejko on July 2, 1996.) These SR Lipizzans come in normal plastic-fronted Breyer boxes with yellow backing. The box bears the model number 700393 and is decorated with a large round gold sticker that says "Exclusive 25th Anniversary Edition for the Wonderful World of Horses ® Starring the 'World Famous' Royal Lipizzaner Stallions." Unless it is kept in its box, this model is indistinguishable from the 1992 German SR Lipizanner (see preceding entry).

"PEGASUS" MOLD VERSION:

- Sky Blue "Pegasus" SR, flocked sky blue, solid face, brown or blue glass eyes, darker blue synthetic hair mane and tail, flocked white wings with sparkles, painted sky-blue hooves (1985). Penney's holiday catalog. Sold for $25.99 in SR set with brush and comb for mane and tail—the Penney's catalog mentions only the brush, but collector Heather Wells's model came with a comb as well. The model shown in the Penney's catalog has a whiter body than the models that were actually sold, which are definitely blue, almost turquoise in shade. The wings are removable. Of the several collectors' specimens I know of, most have brown glass eyes, but collector Sue Lehman's "Pegasus" has blue glass eyes.

Notes:

(1) This mold comes in two different versions: Lipizzan and "Pegasus." The Lipizzan version, which was issued first, is an ordinary horse mold with a smooth barrel. Later, the mold was retooled to create slots high on the barrel to accommodate the removable plastic wings of the "Pegasus" models. After "Pegasus" was discontinued, the mold was again retooled, this time to close the slots and restore the mold to its original Lipizzan form. However, the retooled Lipizzan mold can be distinguished from original Lipizzan. Models made from the retooled mold (starting with the SRs issued in 1992 and 1993) have subtle, shallow grooves on their backs where the wing slots used to be, about a half inch down from the spine and parallel to it. The groove on the right side is nearly undetectable, but the one on the left can be felt quite easily.

(2) Hobbyists typically identify the *haute école* movement represented by this mold as the levade, and I have followed this precedent in my description of the model. But collector Sue Stewart mentioned to me that in an accurate levade, which is an extremely difficult movement, the angle of the horse's body to the ground is under 45 degrees. The angle of the Breyer Lipizzan is considerably greater and is much more characteristic of the easier movement called pesade.

(3) The Lipizzan mold has the round "Breyer Molding Co." stamp. Some models also have the "B" stamp. This mold was never given the "U.S.A." stamp. The wings that came with the "Pegasus" mold version vary: Some have no stamps at all; the wings on my own and collector Delana Metcalf's pegasi are like this. Others have "L" and "R"—actually sort of a double "L" and double "R"—stamped on the tabs that fit into the slots on the horse's back; Jo Kulwicki's "Pegasus" and others I have seen have wings with these stamps. Presumably the "L" and "R" stand for "Left" and "Right." The mystery is why Breyer thought its customers needed help with the profoundly complicated task of sticking two wings into two slots. I am not certain which models came first, but I would guess that the models without wing stamps did.

"Little Chaparral" SR — see under Rearing Stallion

"Lula" — see under "Ruffian"

"Man-O-War" — Stallion, standing, head up, all of tail but tip attached to left buttock and leg. Sculpted by Maureen Love Calvert. Mold in catalog-run production 1975 - current as of 1996.

Catalog-run models made from this mold:

- "Apache" #264, pale grulla, very pale gray horse with medium-gray head; blaze; medium-gray points; 4 tan hooves; with neck ribbon (1995 - current as of 1996). In the B Ranch series. The removable neck ribbon, with red rosette and red, yellow, and blue streamers, attaches around the horse's neck with a Velcro closure. It is identical to the ribbons that come with the B Ranch series horses "Glory" and "Azul." Many "Apaches" have a virtually white body touched with soft gray shading on the shoulders and hindquarters, but a model I found at a toy shop in March 1995 is a nearly solid light smoke gray, with the head just a shade darker than the body.
- "King" #258, dark mahogany brown, solid face, black points, 1 left hind stocking with tan hoof, other hooves black (1993-94). Part of The After School Herd Assortment #2001. Some of these models are virtually black, with just the slightest glow of brown here and there. "King" is not named for any real horse; the name is a Breyer invention (per Breyer executive Peter Stone).
- "Man-O-War" #602, red chestnut; early ones with broken stripe, later ones with roundish star; darker chestnut mane and tail; no stockings; chestnut-gray hooves (1975-90). In the Classic Series and in Race Horse Assortment #6750 (see general note at the start of the Classics section). The color of this model ranges from bright red to a darker, browner shade. Early models often have charcoal eartips. Catalogs indicate that the broken-stripe version of #602 was made 1975-87 (the face is shown clearly in the 1975 and 1980-87 catalogs, though not in 1976-79) and the star version 1988-90 (the star is shown clearly in the catalogs for these years). The star version is easy to confuse with SR "Affirmed"; see that entry for differences. At BreyerFest 1996 I saw a very old model (he had no mold stamps) with an unbroken stipe. The names of this model and "Terrang" are switched in the 1985-86 catalogs and the 1985-87 manuals. "Man-O-War" #602 was sold in a "2-horse Thoroughbred Set" with regular-run "Silky Sullivan" #603 through the 1981 Sears holiday catalog. The "Man-O-War" model is a portrait of the famous Thoroughbred race horse, who was born in March 1917. "Big Red," as the stallion was nicknamed, set a world record for the mile and three eighths and stood at stud for 25 years. (Information is per the biography printed on the model's box.)
- "Pepe" #252, reddish chestnut, solid face, darker chestnut mane and tail, 4 stockings, tan hooves (1991-92). Part of The After School Herd Assortment #2000. "Pepe" is not named for any real horse; the name is a Breyer invention (per Breyer executive Peter Stone).

Special-run models made from this mold:

- "Affirmed" SR, reddish chestnut, long star, darker chestnut mane and tail, no stockings, chestnut-gray hooves (1988). Made for Hobby Center Toys, Ohio. Sold in Triple Crown Winners II set SR #406254, with medium/dark chestnut "Seattle Slew" ("Swaps" mold) and red chestnut "Secretariat" ("Terrang" mold). The set's number is per a Breyer company computer printout of activity 1985-92 and per a flyer that came attached to the boxes of some sets. The flyer also clarifies which name belongs to which model in the set. 1,000 sets were made, according to the printed card that came with the set and an article on Hobby Center Toys in *JAH* 16/#1 Feb./Mar. 1989 (p. 28). The real "Affirmed" was Thoroughbred race horse who won the Triple Crown (Kentucky Derby, Preakness, and Belmont Stakes) in 1978. The "Affirmed" model is similar to the star-faced version of "Man-O-War" #602, but there are differences: "Affirmed's" star is a big, long diamond starting up by the forelock and reaching down halfway to the nose, while #602's star is more or less round, though irregular in outline and slightly longer than it is wide. Also, "Affirmed" is a somewhat lighter, more golden or orangy shade of chestnut, whereas "Man-O-War" #602 is a deeper, more blood-red shade.

Notes:

(1) This mold was created by Maureen Love Calvert, of the Hagen-Renaker company, as a portrait of the real Thoroughbred race horse "Man-O-War." H-R produced it in ceramic under the name "Man O' War" #742 (see Roller, Rose, and Berkwitz 1989, p. 23).

(2) Some models of the "Man-O-War" mold have no round stamp or other mold marks; I believe these are the earliest models. All others have the round "Breyer Molding Co." stamp. Some models with the round might have the "B" stamp too, but I'm not sure. This mold was never given the "U.S.A." stamp.

Marguerite Henry's "Our First Pony" Gift Set — The ponies in this set are "Midge" (Traditional Shetland Pony mold), "Friday" (Classic Arabian Family Foal mold), and "Teeny" (Classic Mustang Family Foal mold). See Marguerite Henry's "Our First Pony" Gift Set under those mold names for details.

"Martin's Dominique" Champion Miniature Horse — see under "Merrylegs"

Medallion Series — For discussion see Medallion Series above in the Traditionals section. For the horses, in the Classics section see "Buckaroo" (under Arabian Family Mare), and "Geronimo" (under Classic "Kelso"). In the Traditionals section see "Cochise" (under "Sea Star"), "Dustin" (under "Phar Lap"), and "Skeeter" (under "Stormy").

"Merrylegs" — Pony mare, walking, tail tip attached to left hock. Sculpted by Chris Hess. Mold in catalog-run production 1980 - current as of 1996.

Catalog-run models made from this mold:

- "Martin's Dominique" Champion Miniature Horse #898, black, solid face, black mane and tail, 1 right front and 2 hind stockings, 4 tan hooves, right front hoof striped with gray (1994-95). This model represents a real miniature horse mare, the 29-inch-high "Martin's Dominique," winner of 4 national championship titles. A photo of her appears in *JAH* 21/#2 Summer I 1994 (inside front cover).

Sets:

- "Black Beauty" Family set #3040, dapple gray "Merrylegs," bald face, white mane and tail, various stockings, gray hooves (1980-93). Set also includes black "Black Beauty," bay "Duchess," and chestnut "Ginger." Set #3040 represents the characters of the children's book *Black Beauty*, by the English author Anna Sewell, first published in 1877. It was Sewell's only book (see *Oxford Companion to English Literature*). "Merrylegs's" gray color varies from dark with loud dappling to medium with soft dappling. Catalogs show that the model had dapples on neck and head 1980-87, no dapples on neck and head 1988-93. Collector Paula DeFeyter kindly sent me a photo of her variation "Merrylegs" with gray mane and tail; he is a fairly pale gray with 4 vague stockings. Set #3040 represents the characters of the children's book *Black Beauty*, by the English author Anna Sewell, first published in 1877. It was Sewell's only book (see *Oxford Companion to English Literature*). In the book, "Merrylegs," "a little fat gray pony" (p. 21), is said to be a "he" (p. 22), but the Breyer mold omits all male parts.
- Joey's Pony Cart set #19845, flocked black pinto "Midge," tobiano; blaze; inset black plastic eyes; white synthetic hair mane and tail; 4 stockings; painted black hooves; in the Miniature Collection (1987). Set also includes authentic black leather harness, wood and metal 2-wheeled cart, and ceramic boy doll with painted blond hair, cloth bluejeans, and long-sleeved red-and-white checked cloth shirt. The set is mounted on a wood base with a green inset and has a clear Plexiglas display cover. Signed and numbered. The suggested retail price for this set on the 1987 Breyer company price list was $165.00. This set is not in the 1987 manual but is in the 1987 catalog, which states: "There goes little Joey, the central character of Marguerite Henry's 'Our First Pony' story. The cart is hand crafted, and comes with rigging, doll and pony." Henry's book *Our First Pony*, about the boy Joey and his pony "Midge," is based on the real-life family of Breyer

executive Peter Stone; for discussion, see Marguerite Henry's "Our First Pony" Gift Set #3066, under Shetland Pony above in the Traditionals section. An identical Pony Cart set was sold through the Ward's holiday catalog in 1985 as a special run (see below). In the one pony cart set I have inspected, owned by collector Heather Wells, the pony's eyes are not the model's own molded-on eyes but inset black plastic "beads." The model in the 1987 Breyer catalog too seems to have these eyes. The Miniature Collection series of horse-and-buggy models was made for Breyer by the Riegseckers of Indiana. See Miniature Collection for further discussion.

♞ "A Pony For Keeps" Gift Set #3234, white "Lady Jane Grey," white mane and tail, gray nose and hooves (1990-91). Set also includes light dapple gray "Another" ("Might Tango" mold); alabaster "Blue" ("Ginger" mold); and chestnut "Jefferson" (Mustang Family Stallion mold). The "Jefferson" and "Lady Jane Grey" models in this set represent equine characters in the book *A Pony for Keeps*, by Beth Sutton, founder of the Children's Pony Program (see *JAH* 16/#5 Nov./Dec. 1989, p. 3). The book is about Sutton's daughter Meg, who took riding lessons on a tiny sorrel pony named "Jefferson" and then became the owner of a little white pony which was hers to keep, "Lady Jane." The full name "Lady Jane Grey" is not used in the book but does appear in the 1990 Breyer catalog and in Sutton's *JAH* article—although Sutton uses the spelling "Gray." I have followed the Breyer catalog spelling for this model's name. See the entries for "Another" and "Blue" for further discussion.

Special-run models made from this mold:

♘ Miniature Horse SR, palomino, solid face, white mane and tail shaded with palomino, 4 stockings, gray hooves (1992). Sears holiday catalog. Sold in Horses Great And Small set SR #496092, with Traditional-scale black Cantering Welsh Pony and grulla Clydesdale Stallion. 2,250 sets made. Quantity and set number are per a Breyer company computer printout of activity 1985-92. (The number 11217, given for this set on the Bentley Sales price list of March 15, 1993, is the Sears number, not the Breyer number.) The Sears catalog calls this model a Miniature Horse.

• Pony Cart And Driver set SR, flocked black pinto "Midge," tobiano; blaze; inset black plastic eyes; white synthetic hair mane and tail; 4 stockings; painted black hooves (1985). Ward's holiday catalog. Set also includes authentic black leather harness, 2-wheeled cart, and ceramic boy doll with cloth clothing, for $100.00 per set. The set is mounted on a rectangular wood base with a green inset and has a clear Plexiglas display cover. Cart is signed and numbered by the maker, the Riegseckers of Indiana. Sets also came with certificate of authenticity signed by the maker (per the Ward's catalog). The Ward's catalog states: "Hand-crafted in Amish country of Northern Indiana. . . . Shipped from factory." See Miniature Collection for further discussion of the Riegseckers. This SR is the same as the regular-run set released in 1987; see Joey's Pony Cart #19845 for details.

Note: The "Merrylegs" mold has the round "Breyer Molding Co." stamp. The earliest models have the round stamp only, with no "B" stamp (collector Lori Ogozalek's model from the first year of issue is like this); but slightly later models do have the "B" stamp. This mold was never given the "U.S.A." stamp.

Messenger Series Of Kiger Mustangs — This is a series in five installments—one single horse and four sets of horses—which reproduce in plastic the figures in five water-color paintings by artist and conservationist Rowland Cheney. The paintings are reproduced in Breyer catalogs 1992-95. All the pieces in the Breyer series are sculpted by Cheney, as is noted in Breyer catalogs and on the models' boxes and hang tags. The models and the paintings all celebrate the Kiger Mustangs of Oregon, focusing on one particular horse, "Mesteño," the dominant stallion of the herd. These wild horses, derived from the Spanish Barbs brought by the Conquistadors to the New World during the Renaissance, are a distinct type of mustang from the Kiger Pass area of the Steens Mountains in southeastern Oregon. They were discovered there in 1974, when the government was searching for wild horses to rescue from a drought. The Kigers are now recognized as a separate breed of horse, registered by the Kiger Mesteño Association of Oregon. As the Breyer series depicts, Kiger Mustangs are dun-factor horses, meaning that their coloration is always some shade of dun—most typically red or claybank dun but varying to grulla, or gray dun, and other shades—punctuated by a dorsal stripe and primitive striping on the legs. (Information is from the 1992-95 catalogs, *JAH* 18/#4 Fall 1991, p. 15, and *JAH* 19/#3 Summer I 1992, p. 31.)

The first installment of the Breyer series—"Mesteño" The Messenger—is a portrait of the mature stallion. The other installments present him in four stages of his long life: The Dawning Gift Set, "Mesteño" And His Mother (see under "Mesteño" Dawning and under "Mesteño's" Mother); The Challenger Gift Set, "Mesteño" And "Sombra" (for both horses see under "Mesteño" Challenger); The Progeny Gift Set, "Mesteño" And "Rojo" (see under "Mesteño" Progeny and under "Rojo"); and Reflections (to be released in 1996). Prints of Cheney's five paintings are available from Western Heritage Enterprise (see the 1992-96 Breyer catalogs).

"Mesteño" Challenger — ♞ Stallion, rearing, ears back. Sculpted by Rowland Cheney. Mold in catalog-run production 1994 - current as of 1996 ("Mesteño" mold version with hind hooves flat on the ground, 1994 - current as of 1996; "Sombra" mold version with left hind hoof cocked, 1994 - current as of 1996).

Catalog-run models made from this mold:

"MESTEÑO" CHALLENGER MOLD VERSION:

♞ The Challenger Gift Set, "Mesteño" And "Sombra" #4811, reddish dun "Mesteño," charcoal mane and tail streaked with reddish dun, no white markings, dorsal stripe, primitive bars on knees and hocks, black lower legs and hooves (1994 - current as of 1996). Set also includes grulla "Sombra." This set is the third installment in the Messenger Series Of Kiger Mustangs (see Messenger Series for discussion and a full list). The "Mesteño" piece in the Challenger set comes with a small hang tag suspended from his neck on a string, giving the sculptor's name and telling about the horses: "Young Mesteño must meet the challenges of his peers to achieve dominance as the herd stallion of the Kiger Mustangs. He will do battle many times to maintain his status. Sombra is also a young and strong stallion seeking status within the wild herd. . . . Mesteño represents the most common dun color phase in the wild; while Sombra offers one of the rare color factors, the grulla (pronounced gruya), of the Kiger Mustangs. His slate grey coat casts many hues in the desert sun." The Challenger horses shown in the 1994-95 catalogs are hand-painted resin castings of the original sculptures (per *JAH* editor Stephanie Macejko). The Penney's 1994 holiday catalog sold the Challenger set together with a watercolor print of "The Challenger" by Rowland Cheney; this set is listed by the Breyer number #710694 in an information fax of April 11, 1994, from Breyer to dealers. On January 21 and June 1, 1995, the QVC home-shopping cable TV channel offered a total of 504 Challenger sets that were ordinary regular-run sets but that came in boxes labeled with the special-run number 701195. On July 15, 1995, the Q2 home-shopping channel offered 50 Challenger sets in boxes labeled with the number 703795. (Information is per *JAH* editor Stephanie Macejko.) Leftover models may have been sold on subsequent Q2 programs.

"SOMBRA" MOLD VERSION:

♞ The Challenger Gift Set, "Mesteño" And "Sombra" #4811, grulla "Sombra," dark yellowish gray horse with charcoal mane and tail streaked with yellow dun, no white markings, dorsal stripe, primitive bars on knees and hocks, black lower legs and hooves (1994 - current as of 1996). Set also includes reddish dun "Mesteño." Collector Donna Alexander-Collins got a Challenger set in which the grulla "Sombra" was identical in mold to the "Mesteño," with both hind hooves flat on the ground and no bend in the front legs. See preceding entry for further discussion.

Notes:

(1) The two stallions in The Challenger set are made from the same metal injection-mold. The "Mesteño" mold version, which has both hind hooves flat on the ground and front legs raised to roughly equal height, is the basic version. The "Sombra" mold version, which has its right hind hoof cocked and its front legs raised to unequal heights (the right front is slightly higher than "Mesteño's" and his left front is slightly lower than "Mesteño's"), acquires these variations in two stages, as I learned during a tour of the Breyer factory in November 1994. "Sombra's" cocked hind hoof is actually molded that way, by means of a small metal mold of the cocked hoof (starting from just above the fetlock) which is inserted into the main metal mold in a way that blocks off the "Mesteño" version of the hoof. "Sombra's" front legs are bent after molding, while still warm from the machinery, on cooling boards equipped with special attachments. By using these attachments, factory workers can get the leg bends to come out the same on each "Sombra." *JAH* editor Stephanie Macejko, in her presentation at the 1996 West Coast Model Horse Collector's Jamboree, noted that the genitalia on this mold are a separately molded piece affixed to each model after molding.

(2) The "Mesteño" Challenger mold (both versions) has the "© Breyer Reeves" stamp only.

"Mesteño" Dawning — ♞ Foal, standing, head up, looking slightly left, minuscule ears, tail attached to right buttock. Sculpted by Rowland Cheney. Mold in catalog-run production 1993 - current as of 1996.

Catalog-run models made from this mold:

♞ The Dawning Gift Set, "Mesteño" And His Mother #4810, light red dun foal "Mesteño," solid or semi-bald face, dark red dun mane, light red dun tail, dorsal stripe from withers to tail tip, white underbelly, white front cannons, gray hooves (1993 - current as of 1996). Set also includes pale buckskin mare (see under "Mesteño's" Mother). This set is the second installment in the Messenger Series Of Kiger Mustangs (see Messenger Series for discussion and a full list). As shown in the 1993 catalog, the mare and foal in this set were designed to stand facing each other, sniffing noses. The foal comes with a small hang tag suspended from the neck with a string, which gives the sculptor's name and tells about the Kiger breed and their dominant stallion, "Mesteño": "The Dawning marks the beginning of Mesteño's life. . . . Through the years, he will grow strong and wise, becoming the patriarch of the Steens Mountains." On July 15, 1995, the Q2 home-shopping cable TV channel offered 75 Dawning sets that were ordinary regular runs but that came in boxes labeled with the special-run model number 703695 (per *JAH* editor Stephanie Macejko). Leftover models may have been sold on subsequent Q2 programs. See "Mesteño's" Mother for further discussion.

Notes:

(1) Photos of the unpainted original sculptures of the two Dawning molds, or plaster castings of them, appear inside the front covers of *JAH* 18/#5 Winter 1991 and 19/#2 Summer I 1992.

(2) This foal appears to be solid plastic, to judge from his remarkable heft. If he is solid, he is the only non-Stablemate Breyer to be so; all others, even the Classic foals and Little Bits, are hollow in the body.

(3) The "Mesteño" Dawning foal mold has the "© Breyer Reeves" stamp only, on the belly.

"Mesteño" Messenger — ♞ Stallion, standing/walking, looking left, mane reaches to fore-arm on right side, center of tail attached to right hock. Sculpted by Rowland Cheney. Mold in catalog-run production 1992 - current as of 1996.

Catalog-run models made from this mold:

♞ "Mesteño" The Messenger #480, reddish dun, charcoal mane and tail streaked with reddish dun, no white markings, dorsal stripe, primitive bars on knees and hocks, brown-black lower legs and hooves (1992 - current as of 1996). This model was the first piece in the Messenger Series Of Kiger Mustangs (see Messenger Series for discussion and a full list). The #480 model represents a real horse, "Mesteño" (pronounced "must-ANN-yo"), the dominant stallion of the Kiger Mustangs. His name is the Spanish term for the wild horses of America, as Marguerite Henry explains in her book *Mustang: Wild Spirit of the West:* "The Spaniards call those wild ones mesteños, . . . meaning strayed or running free, but the English-speaking settlers changed it to mustang" (Henry 1966, p. 208). The stallion "Mesteño," according to Ryan 1992, "is called 'the messenger' because, through him, we learn of a marvelous, untouched part of our great American frontier. Through him, we know that we must preserve the wild creatures and places on this earth, lest they disappear forever." "Mesteño" models come with a small hang tag suspended from the neck with a string; the tag gives the sculptor's name and tells about the real "Mesteño" and the Kiger breed. On January 21, 1995, the QVC home-shopping cable TV channel sold 1,000 "Mesteño" The Messenger models that were ordinary regular runs but that came in boxes labeled with the special-run model number 701095. On July 15, 1995, the Q2 home-shopping channel offered 100 "Mesteños" in boxes labeled with the number 703895. (Information is per *JAH* editor Stephanie Macejko.) Leftover models may have been sold on subsequent Q2 programs. For the video tape *The Kiger Mustang Story* see *JAH* 19/#5 Winter 1992 (p. 23). For the "Mesteño The Messenger Limited Premium Gift Set" with "Mesteño" model and signed watercolor print by Rowland Cheney, see *JAH* 19/#5 Winter 1992 (p. 23) and 20/#1 Spring 1993 (p. 21). The model number 480 previously belonged to the Showcase Collection issue of the black Morgan (Traditional).

Note: The "Mesteño" Messenger mold has the "© Breyer Reeves" stamp only.

"Mesteño" Progeny — ♞ Stallion, charging, head tucked. Sculpted by Rowland Cheney. Mold in catalog-run production 1995 - current as of 1996.

Catalog-run models made from this mold:

♞ The Progeny Gift Set, "Mesteño" And "Rojo" #4812, reddish dun "Mesteño," charcoal mane and tail streaked with reddish dun, no white markings, dorsal stripe, primitive bars above knees and hocks, black lower legs and hooves (1995 - current as of 1996). Set also includes light red dun "Rojo." This set is the fourth installment in the Messenger Series Of Kiger Mustangs (see Messenger Series for discussion). The "Mesteño" in the

Progeny set comes with a hang tag suspended from his neck on a string, giving the sculptor's name and telling about the real Kiger Mustangs "Mesteño" and "Rojo." The adult model in this set depicts "Mesteño" charging a predator that is threatening his yearling son "Rojo," as the hang tag suggests: "Established as herd stallion, Mesteño must protect his band from intruders and predators." The original sculptures proposed for The Progeny set, displayed at The Event model horse show in New York state in April 1994, included a cougar as well, but it was omitted from the set because it proved difficult to fit into the packaging, according to Breyer executive Peter Stone (conversation of Oct. 1995). The Progeny horses shown in the 1995 catalog are hand-painted resin castings of the original sculpture (per *JAH* editor Stephanie Macejko). On June 1, 1995, the QVC home-shopping TV channel offered 1,000 Progeny sets that were ordinary regular runs but that came in boxes labeled with the special-run number 702995 (per Stephanie)

Note: The "Mesteño" Progeny stallion mold has the "© Breyer Reeves" stamp inside the hind leg, and a tiney "JEH" stamp in the mane on the right side, which gives the initials of John E. Harrold, maker of the metal injection-mold (Kathleen Moody, Haynet email, Dec. 11, 1996).

"Mesteño's" Mother — Mare, standing/pacing, looking right, tail flipped out to right. Sculpted by Rowland Cheney. Mold in catalog-run production 1993 - current as of 1996.

Catalog-run models made from this mold:

- The Dawning Gift Set, "Mesteño" And His Mother #4810, pale buckskin "Mesteño's" Mother, baldish face; primitive stripes above knees and hocks; dorsal stripe; most with black points and hooves, some with gray points and hooves (1993 - current as of 1996). Set also includes light red dun foal (see under "Mesteño" Dawning). This set is the second installment in the Messenger Series Of Kiger Mustangs (see Messenger Series for a full list). As shown in the 1993 catalog, the mare and foal in this set were designed to stand facing each other, sniffing noses. This catalog refers to the mare's color as "claybank." The mare shown in the catalog has grayish chocolate points, with light areas variegating the mane and tail; this may be a test-color piece. The first mares produced for sale have soft ash-gray points, with the wispy-looking mane delicately painted in stripes and with lots of buckskin variegation in the tail. After only a couple of months, this coloring was discontinued and the mares were issued with black points, typically with little striping or variegation in the mane and tail. I asked sculptor Rowland Cheney at the West Coast Model Horse Collector's Jamboree in August 1993 whether he had had anything to do with the change. He said yes, that after the first batch was run with the gray points, he requested the change for the sake of realism. The real Kiger Mustangs, he explained, have very dark points, typically black, and the manes and tails are dense and heavy. He also mentioned that the real "Mesteño's" mother had no name. On July 15, 1995, the Q2 home-shopping cable TV channel offered 75 Dawning sets that were ordinary regular runs but that came in boxes labeled with the special-run model number 703695 (per *JAH* editor Stephanie Macejko). Leftover models may have been sold on subsequent Q2 programs. For the "The Dawning Limited Premium Gift Set" with "The Dawning" models and signed watercolor print by Rowland Cheney, see *JAH* 20/#1 Spring 1993 (p. 21).

Notes:

(1) Photos of the unpainted original sculptures of the two Dawning molds, or plaster castings of them, appear inside the front covers of *JAH* 18/#5 Winter 1991 and 19/#2 Summer I 1992.

(2) The "Mesteño's" Mother mold has the "© Breyer Reeves" stamp only.

Mid-Year Specials — see Mid-Year And Summer Specials above in the Traditionals section for a full list

"Might Tango" — Gelding with no genitalia, looking slightly left, cantering slowly on right lead, left hind hoof cocked back, braided mane. Sculpted by Chris Hess. Mold in catalog-run production 1980-93.

Catalog-run models made from this mold:

- "A Pony For Keeps" Gift Set #3234, light dapple gray "Another," no dapples on head and upper neck; bald face; gray mane; white tail; 4 stockings; gray hooves (1990-91). Set also includes alabaster "Blue" ("Ginger" mold); chestnut "Jefferson" (Mustang Family Stallion mold); and white "Lady Jane Grey" ("Merrylegs" mold). The "Another" model in this set represents the real dapple gray hunter gelding owned by Beth Sutton, author of children's books and founder of the Children's Pony Program (see *JAH* 16/#5 Nov./Dec. 1989, p. 3). "Another" is mentioned in Sutton's book *The Pony Champions* but not in *A Pony for Keeps*. The 1990 Breyer catalog lists the names of the models in this set but does not indicate which model is which. The models are identified individually, however, in a Breyer company computer printout of activity 1985-92: "7000-3234...A Pony For Keeps...Mold #3035MT (Another/light dapple grey), #3040GI (Blue/alabaster), #3040ML (Lady Jane Grey/alabaster), #3065ST (Jefferson/sorrel)." Also the book *The Pony Champions* identifies "Another" as a gray and "Blue" as white. The *JAH* issue cited above too gives the names but mixes up two of them, calling the alabaster "Ginger" mold "Another" and the dapple gray "Might Tango" mold "Blue." The real "Blue" in all his white glory is shown on the cover of *JAH* 19/#5 Winter 1992. For further discussion see the entry for "Lady Jane Grey" or "Jefferson."
- U.S. Equestrian Team Gift Set #3035, medium dapple gray "Might Tango," no dapples on head; early ones with solid gray face, later ones with bald face; darker gray shading on head and butt; dark gray mane and tail; 4 stockings; gray hooves (1980-93). Set also includes red chestnut "Keen" and bay "Jet Run" with star. For discussion of release date and the names of the horses in this set, see "Jet Run," above. The 1981-84 Breyer catalogs show "Might Tango" with solid gray face and dapples on the whole neck (my own model is like this); in 1985-93 he's shown with a bald face and no dapples on the upper neck. The real "Might Tango" was a 17-hand dapple gray gelding ridden by Bruce Davidson. The pair participated in the Olympics and won many international championships in 3-day events (per the set's box and *JAH* VII/#4 [1980], p. 10).

Special-run models made from this mold:

- "Might Tango" SR, reddish bay, solid face, 2 hind stockings with gray hooves, front hooves black (1987). Sears holiday catalog. Sold in Horse Set SR #493035, with medium/light chestnut "Jet Run" and steel gray "Keen." The set number is per a Breyer company computer printout of activity 1985-92; no quantity given. To my knowledge this set does not portray any particular real horses. The Sears catalog doesn't give this set any definite name but simply describes it thus: "Horse set portrays 2 horses performing the canter and 1, the halt."
- "Orchidee" SR #703335, reddish bay; large star; gray-shaded muzzle; black mane, tail, and front legs; no black on the hind legs; 1 right hind sock; 4 black hooves (1989 and 1990). Export special; also sold through the 1989 and 1990 Sears holiday catalogs. Sold separately or in German Olympic Team set with reddish bay "Ahlerich" ("Keen" mold) and reddish bay "Rembrandt" ("Jet Run" mold). About 5,144 sets produced (for discussion of quantity, see "Rembrandt" SR, under "Jet Run"). The model number for "Orchidee" is per a Breyer photo sheet titled "Breyer's 1990 Export Offerings" and a Breyer company computer printout of activity 1985-92. (The German edition of the 1989 Breyer collector's manual gives "Orchidee" a shortened number: #3335.) The three models in this set represent real horses on the German Olympic team.

Note: The "Might Tango" mold has the round "Breyer Molding Co." stamp. Early models have the "B" stamp as well as the round. This mold was never given the "U.S.A." stamp.

Miniature Collection — The Miniature Collection strictly so-called, issued in the period 1984-87, is a series of catalog-run horse-and-vehicle sets that use flocked Breyer models with synthetic hair manes and tails. Several similar sets were issued as special runs in the 1980s, and although these were not advertised specifically as Miniature Collection pieces, collectors generally regard them as forming a group with the catalog-run sets. The horses in all these catalog-run and SR sets are outfitted with realistic leather harnesses and pull hand-crafted vehicles. Several sets include ceramic dolls with "period" costumes made of cloth, and one set came with a Brenda Breyer doll in period costume. All the sets were manufactured under contract with Breyer by Mel Riegsecker and his family, who lived and worked in Middlebury, Indiana, in the early 1980s and established the Shipshewana Craft Barn in Shipshewana, Indiana, in the mid-1980s. The 1984 Breyer catalog introduces the Miniature Collection as follows: "A totally new collection from Breyer for the discriminating 'miniature' collector. Each piece is a limited edition, designed by the Riegsecker Family and handcrafted in the Amish Colonies of Indiana. . . . All harnesses are genuine leather and the horses are flocked, with lifelike hair mane and tail. The buggies are metal and wood. Each piece comes with wood base and clear plastic display cover. These collectors pieces, with their unusual detail are a delight to the eye, and each will be individually signed and numbered; the true mark of a limited, handcrafted piece." The 1986-87 catalogs add that the wood bases are felt covered and the plastic covers are Plexiglas. For further discussion see Flocked Models and Riegseckers Models above in the Traditionals section; also see the article on Mel Riegsecker in *JAH* XI/#5 1985 (p. 5).

For the individual Miniature Collection sets see Delivery Wagon (under "Keen"); The Doctor's Buggy (under Black Stallion); Drive On A Sunny Day (under "Johar"); Family To Church On Sunday (under "Duchess" and under "Jet Run"); Joey's Pony Cart (under "Merrylegs"); and Open Top Buggy (under Proud Arabian Stallion, above in the Traditionals section). For SR flocked-horse-and-buggy sets that were not advertised as Miniature Collection pieces, see Collector's One Horse Open Sleigh SR (under "Black Beauty"); Montgomery Ward Delivery Wagon SR (under "Keen"); Pony Cart And Driver SR (under "Merrylegs"); and, in the Traditionals section, Proud Arabian Stallion SR, flocked chestnut (sold separately or with buggy).

Miniature Horse — see "Martin's Dominique" and Miniature Horse SR, both under "Merrylegs"

"Misty," Performing (ceramic) — see Performing "Misty" below in the Little Bits section

Montgomery Ward Delivery Wagon SR — see under "Keen"

Mustang Family Foal — Filly, standing, looking right. Sculpted by Maureen Love Calvert. Mold in catalog-run production 1976 - current as of 1996.

Catalog-run models made from this mold:

- Appaloosa Mustang Family Gift Set #3349, chestnut blanket appaloosa foal, stripe, charcoal mane and tail, unstenciled blanket covering butt and barrel, splashed-on chestnut spots, 1 right front and 2 hind stockings with tan hooves, other hoof chestnut (1995 - current as of 1996). Set also includes black blanket appaloosa mare (Mustang Family Mare mold) and rose dun blanket appaloosa stallion (Mustang Family Stallion mold).
- Fine Horse Family set #3348, chestnut blanket appaloosa foal, blaze, chestnut mane slightly darker than body, white tail with chestnut tip, unstenciled blanket covering butt and barrel, no spots, 2 hind stockings, 4 tan hooves (1994 - current as of 1996). Set also includes red roan mare ("Kelso" mold) and liver chestnut stallion ("Silky Sullivan" mold).
- Marguerite Henry's "Our First Pony" Gift Set #3066, black pinto foal "Teeny," tobiano; blaze; mostly white mane; white tail tip; 4 stockings; most with pink hooves (1987 - current as of 1996). Set also includes bay pinto "Friday" (Classic Arabian Family Foal mold), black pinto "Midge" (Shetland Pony mold, Traditional), and leather halter and lead for "Midge." "Teeny" has the same pinto pattern as the SR chestnut Mustang Family Foal. "Teeny" is shown with gray hooves in the 1987 catalog only, and evidently models like this were produced for sale, for collector Lillian Sutphin wrote to me that she now owns one, having expropriated it from her toddler when she realized that it was rare. This set represents the characters in Henry's book *Our First Pony*, which is based on real ponies and people (see under Shetland Pony for discussion). The two foals are named for the day they were born: Friday the Thirteenth ("Teeny" is short for "Thirteenth"). It took some sleuthing to figure out which foal in the Breyer set is supposed to be "Friday" and which "Teeny." Breyer catalogs just say "twin foals 'Friday' and 'Teeny'" without clarifying which is which, and the set's box doesn't help either. Fortunately the book *Our First Pony* gives two clues. First, the text, though it doesn't mention the foals' colors, does note their sizes: "Friday's the big colt, and his twin is 'The Thirteenth.'" Second, the illustrations show the big colt as bay pinto and the small weakling filly as black pinto. In the Breyer set, the Arab Family Foal is a bay pinto and is bigger than the black pinto Mustang Family Foal. Final confirmation is offered by a Breyer company computer printout of activity 1985-92, which, in an entry for an order of #3066 sets, identifies the foals by mold and color: "#3055FO [i.e., foal] (Friday/brown-black pinto) / #3065fo (Teeny/black pinto)."
- Mustang Family Gift Set #3065, chestnut foal, bald face, darker chestnut mane and tail, 4 stockings, gray hooves (1976-90). Set also includes chestnut pinto Mustang Family Mare and chestnut Mustang Family Stallion. The set was sold with Marguerite Henry's book *Mustang: Wild Spirit of the West* through the 1981 Penney's holiday catalog.
- Trakehner Family set #3347, bay foal, solid face, black points, 1 right hind stocking with tan hoof, other hooves black (1992-94). Set also includes dark chestnut Trakehner Family Stallion ("Jet Run" mold) and pale dapple gray Trakehner Family Mare ("Duchess" mold).

Special-run models made from this mold:

- Mustang Family Foal SR, chestnut pinto, tobiano; blaze; mostly white mane; white tail tip; 4 stockings; gray hooves (1985). Sears holiday catalog. Sold in SR set #21025, with bay Mustang Family Mare and buckskin Mustang Family Stallion. This SR foal has the same pinto pattern as "Teeny," the black pinto Mustang Family Foal in "Our First Pony" Gift Set #3066. The SR foal as shown in the Sears catalog has a very dark, possibly black mane, but collector Sheryl Leisure's model has a white mane like "Teeny's," as do the foals shown in *The Model Trading Post* (Nov./Dec. 1993, p. 11), *Breyer Collector's Video*, and *JAH* 22/#6 Nov./Dec. 1995 (p. 17). The Sears catalog model may be a test color. The number for this set is per a Breyer company computer printout of activity 1985-92, which also specifies that the foal is chestnut pinto.

Mustang Family Foal SR, lilac grulla, solid face, red chestnut mane and tail, primitive stripes on knees and hocks, 4 stockings, pink-tan hooves (1992). Penney's holiday catalog. Sold in Mustang Family set SR #713092, with dark bay Mustang Family Mare and buckskin Mustang Family Stallion with primitive stripes. 5,000 sets made. Quantity and set number are per a Breyer company computer printout of activity 1985-92. The description of this foal as "grulla" is in the Penney's catalog; the Breyer printout calls it "light grulla."

Notes:

(1) This mold was created by Maureen Love Calvert for the Hagen-Renaker company, which produced it in ceramic under the name "Butch" Mustang Foal #732 (see Roller, Rose, and Berkwitz 1989, p. 23).

(2) Most models of the Mustang Family Foal mold have no Breyer stamp or other mold marks. The only models with any mark at all are those with the "B" stamp, as on collector Marie Kelly's foal.

Mustang Family Mare — Standing, ears back, looking right, tail attached to right buttock and hock. Sculpted by Maureen Love Calvert. Mold in catalog-run production 1976-90, 1995 - current as of 1996.

Catalog-run models made from this mold:

Appaloosa Mustang Family Gift Set #3349, black blanket appaloosa mare, stripe, black mane and tail, unstenciled butt blanket, splashed-on black spots, 1 left hind stocking, 4 tan hooves (1995 - current as of 1996). Set also includes chestnut blanket appaloosa filly (Mustang Family Foal mold) and rose dun blanket appaloosa stallion (Mustang Family Stallion mold).

Mustang Family Gift Set #3065, chestnut pinto mare, tobiano; darker chestnut mane and tail; gray hooves (1976-90). Set also includes chestnut Mustang Family Foal and chestnut Mustang Family Stallion. The mare pictured on the box (shown in catalogs) appears to be a test color, for she has a different pinto pattern and darker chestnut spots than normal. As shown in catalogs, this mare had unstenciled chestnut areas on the neck and sides of the face for all her years of production except the last. In the catalog for 1990, her final year, she is shown from the right side with a stark white neck and head, as well as unusually clean-edged spots with virtually no overspray. Collector Paula DeFeyter's model of this version has a single chestnut spot on the left cheek; the rest of the head and neck is stark white (thanks to Paula for photos of this model). The set was sold with Marguerite Henry's book *Mustang: Wild Spirit of the West* through the 1981 Penney's holiday catalog.

Special-run models made from this mold:

Mustang Family Mare SR, bay, solid face, black mane and tail, no black on the legs, 4 vague stockings, gray or black hooves (1985). Sears holiday catalog. Sold in SR set #21025, with chestnut pinto Mustang Family Foal and buckskin Mustang Family Stallion. The set number is per a Breyer company computer printout of activity 1985-92. My own and collector Kim Jones's mares have gray hooves, but Kim has seen a black-hoofed model as well.

Mustang Family Mare SR, dark bay, solid face, faint dorsal stripe, black points, 1 right hind stocking with pink-tan hoof, other hooves black (1992). Penney's holiday catalog. Sold in Mustang Family set SR #713092, with lilac grulla Mustang Family Foal and buckskin Mustang Family Stallion with primitive stripes. 5,000 sets made. Quantity and set number are per a Breyer company computer printout of activity 1985-92.

Notes:

(1) This mold was created by Maureen Love Calvert for the Hagen-Renaker company, which produced it in ceramic under the name "Daisy" Mustang Mare #731 (see Roller, Rose, and Berkwitz 1989, p. 23).

(2) Early models of the Mustang Family Mare mold have no mold marks. Later ones have the round "Breyer Molding Co." stamp. Some models might have the "B" stamp as well as the round, but I'm not sure. This mold was never given the "U.S.A." stamp.

Mustang Family Stallion — Standing, looking left, tail attached to right buttock and leg. Sculpted by Maureen Love Calvert. Mold in catalog-run production 1976-91, 1995 - current as of 1996.

Catalog-run models made from this mold:

Appaloosa Mustang Family Gift Set #3349, rose dun blanket appaloosa stallion, baldish face, gray mane, tail striped with gray and pale rose, unstenciled "blanket" covering butt and barrel, gray-shaded legs, 1 left hind stocking, 4 tan hooves (1995 - current as of 1996). Set also includes chestnut blanket appaloosa filly (Mustang Family Foal mold) and black blanket appaloosa stallion (Mustang Family Stallion mold). This stallion might be called a semi-leopard in that his "blanket" has no definite edges but simply melts into the softly shaded rose dun forehand. The model in the 1995 catalog has black-shaded legs, but this may be a test-color piece; my own stallion and others I've seen have gray-shaded legs. The gray mane is slightly mottled with lighter areas.

Mustang Family Gift Set #3065, chestnut stallion, solid face, light chestnut or flaxen mane and tail, 4 or various stockings, gray hooves (1976-90). Set also includes chestnut pinto Mustang Family Mare and chestnut Mustang Family Foal. The stockings on the stallion can be very vague. His body color varies from dark to medium/light chestnut. This set was also sold with Marguerite Henry's book *Mustang: Wild Spirit of the West* through the 1981 Penney's holiday catalog.

"A Pony For Keeps" Gift Set #3234, chestnut "Jefferson," solid face, flaxen mane and tail, charcoal legs and hooves (1990-91). Set also includes light dapple gray "Another" ("Might Tango" mold); alabaster "Blue" ("Ginger" mold); and white "Lady Jane Grey" ("Merrylegs" mold). "Jefferson" and "Lady Jane" in set #3234 represent equine characters in the book *A Pony for Keeps*, by Beth Sutton, founder of the Children's Pony Program (see *JAH* 16/#5 Nov./Dec. 1989, p. 3). The book is about Sutton's daughter Meg, who took riding lessons on a tiny sorrel pony named "Jefferson" and then became the owner of a little white pony, "Lady Jane." See the entries for "Another" and "Blue" for further discussion.

Special-run models made from this mold:

Mustang Family Stallion SR, buckskin, no white markings, black points, gray or black hooves (1985). Sears holiday catalog. Sold in SR set #21025, with bay Mustang Family Mare and chestnut pinto Mustang Family Foal. Gutierrez 1989 lists a variation of this stallion with 4 socks. The set number is per a Breyer company computer printout of activity 1985-92. My own and collector Kim Jones's stallions have gray hooves, but Kim has seen a black-hoofed model as well.

Mustang Family Stallion SR, buckskin, primitive stripes on forearms and across withers, dorsal stripe, no white markings, black points, gray hooves (1992). Penney's holiday catalog. Sold in Mustang Family set SR #713092, with dark bay Mustang Family Mare and lilac grulla Mustang Family Foal. 5,000 sets made. Quantity and set number are per a Breyer company computer printout of activity 1985-92.

Notes:

(1) This mold was created by Maureen Love Calvert for the Hagen-Renaker company, which produced it in ceramic under the name "Comanche" Mustang Stallion #730 (see Roller, Rose, and Berkwitz 1989, p. 23).

(2) Early models of the Mustang Family Stallion mold have no mold marks. Later ones have the round "Breyer Molding Co." stamp. Some models might have the "B" stamp as well as the round, but I'm not sure. This mold was never given the "U.S.A." stamp.

"Nevada Star" SR — see under "Hobo"

"Norita" — see under "Kelso"

Olympic Team sets — see U.S. Equestrian Team Gift Set #3035; German Olympic Team set SR; and Horse Set SR

One Horse Open Sleigh set SR — see Collector's One Horse Open Sleigh set SR, under "Black Beauty"

Open Top Buggy set — see Drive On A Sunny Day set, under "Johar"

"Orchidee" SR — see under "Might Tango"

"Our First Pony" Gift Set — see Marguerite Henry's "Our First Pony" Gift Set

Passing Through Time set SR — see the three entries for "Riddle" SR, under "Hobo" (with stand)

"Patches" — see under "Ruffian"

"Pegasus" — see "Pegasus" #209, "Pegasus" SR, and Sky Blue "Pegasus" SR, all under Lipizzan

"Pepe" — see under "Man-O-War"

Performing "Misty" — see below in the Little Bits section

Pinto Mare — see Brown Pinto Mare SR, under Quarter Horse Family Mare

Polo Pony — On removable stand; mare, galloping, roached mane, bundled tail. Sculpted by Chris Hess. Mold in catalog-run production 1976-82 (original version of the stand 1976-82).

Catalog-run models made from this mold:

ORIGINAL-STAND MOLD VERSION:

Polo Pony #626, bay, solid face; many with gray ventral stripe; black points; most with 4 stockings, some with no stockings; gray hooves; matte and semigloss; stand painted brown (1976-82). This model is shown with 4 socks in the 1976-81 catalogs and with no socks in 1982. The no-stocking version was produced for sale; collector Paula DeFeyter sent me a photo of hers, which has solid black legs. On some models the black on the legs above the stockings goes nearly up to the body. The ventral stripe on some models runs from the throatlatch down the windpipe to the breast.

Special-run models made from this mold:

NEW-STAND MOLD VERSION:

"Silver Comet" SR #700594, dapple gray, no or very few dapples on upper neck and head, bald face or all-white head, dark gray knees and hocks, white tail with 1 blue upper band and red lower band, 4 stockings, tan hooves, matte; stand painted brown (1994). Breyer show special, made for shows and parties sponsored by Breyer dealers. Open quantities made throughout the year; the final count was 9,300 models, according to *JAH* editor Stephanie Macejko (conversation of June 1995). This model came with a certificate of authenticity signed by Breyer executive Peter Stone. The certificate states: "This mold has not been used by Breyer in twelve years. The Dappled Grey colored polo pony captures the action of the sport in the Breyer tradition. This Special Run model was produced in the year 1994 for Breyer Special Events nationwide. It will not be made available again and is a true collector's item." The label on the model's box says "No. 700594 Silver Comet / Breyer Show Special 1994." The dappling on this model is quite sparse, and the color, which varies from a shaded medium gray to very pale gray, has the delicate appearance of a watercolor wash. The medium grays are bald-faced, but the pale ones have virtually the whole head white except for gray shading on the nose.

Notes:

(1) The Polo Pony mold is Classic size, although in catalogs it was always listed with the Traditionals.

(2) The plastic stand comes in two mold versions. In both, the stand is molded to look like carved wood and has a triangular hole near the center to hold the small pyramid of plastic that is molded to the bottom of the pony's left front toe. The new version of the stand, issued for the first time in 1994 with SR "Silver Comet," has a slightly larger hole than the old version, has a different pattern to the "woodgrain" texturing molded into the surface, and has six small plastic "studs" molded around the edges on the underside (the old version has no studs). According to former *JAH* editor Megan Thilman, the new stand was created because the metal injection mold for the old stand was lost. Many of the original stands have warped over time.

(3) Many and perhaps all models of the Polo Pony mold have no mold stamps. The only possible exception is that some #626s might have the "B" stamp only, but I have not actually found one like this. Neither version of the stand has any stamps either.

Pony Cart And Driver set — see Joey's Pony Cart set #19845 and Pony Cart And Driver set SR, both under "Merrylegs"

"A Pony For Keeps" Gift Set — The horses in this set are "Another" ("Might Tango" mold), "Blue" ("Ginger" mold), "Jefferson" (Mustang Family Stallion mold), and "Lady Jane Grey" ("Merrylegs" mold). See "A Pony For Keeps" Gift Set under those mold names for details.

"Pow Wow" SR — see Eagle And "Pow Wow" set SR, under "Johar"

"Prince" — see under "Swaps"

The Progeny Gift Set, "Mesteño" And "Rojo" — see under "Mesteño" Progeny and under "Rojo"; also see Messenger Series Of Kiger Mustangs

"Promises" Rearing Stallion — see under Rearing Stallion

Proud Mother And Newborn Foal sets #3160 and #3161 — see under Andalusian Family Foal in the Classics section and under "Lady Roxana" above in the Traditionals section

Quarter Horse Family Foal — ♞ Colt, standing/walking, looking left. Sculpted by Maureen Love Calvert. Mold in catalog-run production 1974-93.

Catalog-run models made from this mold:

- ♞ Quarter Horse Foal #4001, bay, solid face, black points, 4 stockings, most with gray hooves (1974-82). This model was also sold in Quarter Horse Family Gift Set #3045 [1974-93]. The bay, black, chestnut, and palomino foals, sold individually in blister packs, all had the model number 4001. Catalogs and manuals don't list the #4001 colors separately but just say "assorted colors"; my information on the specific colors is from *Breyer Collector's Video;* Diederich 1988, Section 2; and my own observations. #4001 is called Quarter Horse Foal Assortment in the 1974-75 catalogs, Classic Quarter Horse Foal in 1976, and Quarter Horse Foal in 1977-79 and 1982; no name but only the number appears in 1980-81. A bay foal is shown in the #4001 blister pack in the 1974-75 catalogs and manuals. Regarding variations of the bay foal see Quarter Horse Family Gift Set #3045, bay foal.
- ♞ Quarter Horse Foal #4001, black, bald face, black mane and tail, 4 stockings, gray hooves (1974-82). This foal is shown in the 1982 catalog. Some may have a solid face, but I'm not sure. See Quarter Horse Foal #4001, bay, for further discussion.
- ♞ Quarter Horse Foal #4001, chestnut, bald face, slightly lighter or darker chestnut mane and tail, 4 stockings, gray hooves (1974-82). This foal is shown in the 1976 and 1980-81 catalogs. See Quarter Horse Foal #4001, bay, for further discussion.
- ♞ Quarter Horse Foal #4001, palomino, bald face, light palomino mane and tail, 4 stockings, gray hooves (1974-82). This foal is shown in the 1977-79 manuals and catalogs. See Quarter Horse Foal #4001, bay, for discussion.

Set:

- Quarter Horse Family Gift Set #3045, bay foal, most with solid face, black points, 4 stockings, most with gray hooves (1974-93). Set also includes bay Quarter Horse Family Mare and palomino Quarter Horse Family Stallion. This same foal was also sold separately as Quarter Horse Foal #4001 bay [1974-82]. The color varies from medium brownish bay to red bay to light sandy bay to true buckskin. Collector Paula DeFeyter sent me a photo of her buckskin foal, which has charcoal/black legs with no stockings. Collector Tracy Phillips reports that she has a pale honey bay foal, nearly buckskin, with a small star, 4 clear socks, and pink hooves, and she saw another like it at BreyerFest (Phillips 1993). Evidently these star-faced foals are the earliest made, for the #3045 foals shown in the 1974 Breyer manual and the 1974 Sears holiday catalog fit Tracy's description: they have a nearly buckskin body color, light hooves which could be pink (the photos are not too clear), and a tiny, round star. The star is visible as well in the 1974 Breyer dealer catalog (which is printed in black and white). Collector Lori Ogozalek wrote to me that in her old #3045 set, the foal, mare, and stallion all have stars. Collector Sheryl Leisure found such a set as well; her foal is a normal bay color with gray knees and hocks, 4 stockings, and pale tan hooves. The #3045 set was announced in the May 1974 *Western Horseman* in a short article (p. 62).

Special-run models made from this mold:

- "Blaze" SR, dark bay, blaze, black points, black hooves (1994). Made for Aristoplay Ltd., an educational toy company in Ann Arbor, Michigan. Sold in SR set #410194 with dark bay "Denver" ("Kelso" mold); the set number is per *JAH* editor Stephanie Macejko. 4,000 sets made (per Vicky at Aristoplay and various mail-order catalog ads). The set also includes a small poster and a numbered certificate of authenticity. For discussion see "Denver" SR.
- Quarter Horse Family Foal SR, alabaster; gray mane, tail, and hooves (1991). Penney's holiday catalog. Sold in Quarter Horse Family set SR #716091, with liver chestnut Quarter Horse Family Mare and liver chestnut Quarter Horse Family Stallion. 6,000 sets made. Quantity and set number are per a Breyer company computer printout of activity 1985-92.
- Quarter Horse Family Foal SR, black blanket appaloosa, solid face, unstenciled butt blanket, splashed-on black spots, black legs and hooves (1984). Ward's holiday catalog. Sold in Appaloosa Family set SR, with black blanket appaloosa Quarter Horse Family Mare and Stallion. The picture of this set in *JAH* XI/#3 1984 (p. 9) shows the foal with 2 front stockings; I don't believe foals like this were produced for sale. The picture in the Ward's catalog shows the foal with no stockings, and to my knowledge all the models sold were like this, as are the ones shown in Diederich 1988 (Section 3) and on *Breyer Collectors Video.*
- Quarter Horse Family Foal SR, chestnut blanket appaloosa, solid face, dark chestnut mane and tail, unstenciled butt blanket, splashed-on chestnut spots, chestnut legs, dark hooves (1986). Sears holiday catalog. Sold in Appaloosa Family set SR #21061, with chestnut blanket appaloosa Quarter Horse Family Mare and Stallion. The set number is per a Breyer company computer printout of activity 1985-92.

Notes:

(1) A pearly version of the bay or chestnut #4001 is shown on *Breyer Collector's Video,* and collector Gale Good has found pearlies in both chestnut and palomino. See Chalkies & Pearlies in the Appendix near the end of this book. For the lime green plastic Classic QH Foal, see Proud Arabian Foal SR, pink, above in the Traditionals section.

(2) This mold was created by Maureen Love Calvert for the Hagen-Renaker company, which produced it in ceramic under the name "Shamrock" Quarter Horse Foal #756 (see Roller, Rose, and Berkwitz 1989, p. 24).

(3) Most models of the Quarter Horse Family Foal mold have no Breyer stamp or other mold marks. Some models have the "B" stamp only (Sande Schneider has a black and a palomino with this stamp).

Quarter Horse Family Mare — ♞ Standing, looking slightly left, tail attached to right buttock and leg. Sculpted by Maureen Love Calvert. Mold in catalog-run production 1974-93.

Catalog-run models made from this mold:

- ♞ Quarter Horse Family Gift Set #3045, bay mare, most with solid face, black points, most with 1 left front and 2 hind stockings with gray hooves, other hoof black (1974-93). Set also includes bay Quarter Horse Family Foal and palomino Quarter Horse Family Stallion. The set was announced in the May 1974 *Western Horseman* in a short article (p. 62). The mare shown in the 1974 Breyer manual has 4 stockings and pale tan hooves (face not visible). Collector Sheryl Leisure found such a mare, which also has a star, in an old #3045 set; the stallion and foal in the set have stars as well. Another #3045 set with stars was found by collector Lori Ogozalek. Sheryl's star-faced mare actually has only one or two pale tan hooves; the other hooves are unpainted white.

Special-run models made from this mold:

- Brown Pinto Mare SR #703245, dark chestnut paint, tobiano; solid face; darker chestnut mane and tail; 4 stockings; gray hooves (1989). Export special; made for House of Nisbet, a British company. 2,500 models made. Dealer and quantity are per a Breyer company computer printout of activity 1985-92. This mare was also sold through the German mail-order company Modell-Pferde Versand, owned by Ingrid and Andrea Muensterer (per *JAH* 16/#4 Sept./Oct. 1989, p. 28). The model became available through U.S. model mail-order companies as well; I got my mare from Bentley Sales in July 1990. The model's box is labeled "No. 703245—Brown Pinto Mare." The German edition of the 1989 Breyer collector's manual gives a shortened number for this model: #3245.
- Quarter Horse Family Mare SR, black blanket appaloosa, solid face, unstenciled butt blanket, splashed-on black spots, black legs and hooves (1984). Ward's holiday catalog. Sold in Appaloosa Family set SR, with black blanket appaloosa Quarter Horse Family Foal and Stallion. The picture of this set in the Ward's catalog shows the mare with 2 hind stockings and a large blanket extending from the butt well up onto the back and barrel. The picture in *JAH* XI/#3 1984 (p. 9) also shows the mare with 2 hind stockings, but the blanket is confined to the butt, as on the stallion and foal. To my knowledge no 2-stocking or large-blanket versions were produced for sale; the mares all had black legs and blanket only on the butt, as shown on *Breyer Collectors Video* and in Diederich 1988, Section 3.
- Quarter Horse Family Mare SR, chestnut blanket appaloosa, solid face, dark chestnut mane and tail, unstenciled butt blanket, splashed-on chestnut spots, chestnut legs, dark hooves (1986). Sears holiday catalog. Sold in Appaloosa Family set SR #21061, with chestnut blanket appaloosa Quarter Horse Family Foal and Stallion. The set number is per a Breyer company computer printout of activity 1985-92.
- Quarter Horse Family Mare SR, liver chestnut, solid face, darker liver mane and tail, 2 hind stockings with gray hooves, front hooves liver (1991). Penney's holiday catalog. Sold in Quarter Horse Family set SR #716091, with alabaster Quarter Horse Family Foal and liver chestnut Quarter Horse Family Stallion. 6,000 sets made. Quantity and set number are per a Breyer company computer printout of activity 1985-92. The mare is a just a bit darker and less shaded than the stallion.

Notes:

(1) This mold was created by Maureen Love Calvert for the Hagen-Renaker company, which produced it in ceramic under the name "Erin" Quarter Horse Mare #755 (see Roller, Rose, and Berkwitz 1989, p. 24).

(2) The Quarter Horse Family Mare mold has the round "Breyer Molding Co." stamp and the "U.S.A." stamp. Unlike the QH Family Stallion, the mare seems to have had these mold stamps from the very beginning—for I have never found a mare without stamps, and the star-faced mare in a very early #3045 set found in box by collector Sheryl Leisure does have stamps, although the stallion does not. Some later mares might have the "B" stamp in addition, but I'm not sure.

Quarter Horse Family Stallion — ♞ Standing, looking right. Sculpted by Maureen Love Calvert. Mold in catalog-run production 1974-93.

Catalog-run models made from this mold:

- ♞ Quarter Horse Family Gift Set #3045, palomino stallion, most with solid face, white or palomino mane and tail, various stockings, gray or palomino-gray hooves (1974-93). This set also includes bay Quarter Horse Family Foal and bay Quarter Horse Family Mare. The set was announced in the May 1974 *Western Horseman* in a short article (p. 62). The stallion has varied in color and markings over the years, according to the photos in Breyer catalogs and manuals. In the 1974 manual and on the cover of the 1995 he is palomino with vague right front and left hind stockings, and a small star. Some star-faced stallions were released for sale—collector Tracy Phillips reports having seen one at a flea market (Phillips 1993), and collector Lori Ogozalek wrote to me that in her old #3045 set, the foal, mare, and stallion all have stars. Collector Sheryl Leisure also found such a set, which I have seen in person; her stallion is tan palomino with tan palomino mane and tail, right front and left hind stockings, and a small teardrop star with the point down. The stallion inside the 1975 catalog and those in all subsequent catalogs have a solid face. In the 1975-78 catalogs it's hard to tell about the mane and tail, but the model seems to have various vague stockings. In 1979-84 he is dusky yellow dun with yellow mane and tail, and various legs: 1-2 vague front stockings (1979), 1 vague hind stocking (1980-81), or no stockings (1982-84). In 1985-87 he's palomino with white mane and tail, no stockings. In 1988-91 he is light sorrel/dusky dun with yellow mane and tail, no stockings. In 1992-93 he is palomino with crisp white mane and tail, no stockings. Production-line models can of course vary from the pieces shown in the catalogs, as does collector Lynn Weber's post-1987 stallion with right front and left hind socks.

Special-run models made from this mold:

- Quarter Horse Family Stallion SR #703145, black blanket appaloosa, solid face, large unstenciled blanket covering butt and barrel, splashed-on black spots, 2 front stockings, 4 black hooves (1989). Export special; made for the British company House of Nisbet. 2,500 models made. The model number, customer, and quantity are per a Breyer company computer printout of activity 1985-92. (The German edition of the 1989 Breyer collector's manual gives a shortened number for this model: #3145.) This horse was also sold through the German mail-order company Modell-Pferde Versand, owned by Ingrid and Andrea Muensterer (see *JAH* 16/#4 Sept./Oct. 1989, p. 28); I purchased one from them in 1993.
- Quarter Horse Family Stallion SR, black blanket appaloosa, solid face, unstenciled butt blanket, splashed-on black spots, black legs and hooves (1984). Ward's holiday catalog. Sold in Appaloosa Family set SR, with black blanket appaloosa Quarter Horse Family Mare and Foal.
- Quarter Horse Family Stallion SR, chestnut blanket appaloosa, solid face, darker chestnut mane and tail, unstenciled butt blanket, splashed-on chestnut spots, chestnut legs, dark hooves (1986). Sears holiday catalog. Sold in Appaloosa Family set SR #21061, with chestnut blanket appaloosa Quarter Horse Family Mare and Foal. The set number is per a Breyer company computer printout of activity 1985-92.
- Quarter Horse Family Stallion SR, liver chestnut, solid face, slightly darker liver mane and tail, light tan nose, 1 right hind stocking with gray hoof, other hooves liver (1991).

Penney's holiday catalog. Sold in Quarter Horse Family set SR #716091, with alabaster Quarter Horse Family Foal and liver chestnut Quarter Horse Family Mare. 6,000 sets made. Quantity and set number are per a Breyer company computer printout of activity 1985-92. The stallion is just slightly lighter and more shaded than the mare.

Notes:

(1) This mold was created by Maureen Love Calvert for the Hagen-Renaker company, which produced it in ceramic under the name "Two Bits" Quarter Horse Stallion #712 (see Roller, Rose, and Berkwitz 1989, p. 24).

(2) Some models of the Quarter Horse Family Stallion mold have no mold stamps; I believe these are the earliest ones, for the star-faced palomino stallion in a very early #3045 set found in box by collector Sheryl Leisure has no stamps. Collector Caroline Boydston found a solid-faced chalky #3045 stallion with no stamps. But most models have the round "Breyer Molding Co." stamp. Some models with the round stamp might also have the "B" stamp, but I'm not sure. This mold was never given the "U.S.A." stamp—oddly, since the QH Family Mare does have this stamp.

Race Horse Assortment #6750 — This assortment consists of six horse models, all sold separately. See "Kelso"; "Man-O-War"; "Ruffian"; "Silky Sullivan"; "Swaps"; and "Terrang"

Rearing Stallion — Rearing horse, left hind leg further forward than right hind leg. Sculpted by Chris Hess. Mold in catalog-run production 1965-85, 1994 - current as of 1996.

Catalog-run models made from this mold:

- "Promises" Rearing Stallion #890, dark chestnut pinto, tobiano; solid dark chestnut face; black mane and knees; charcoal-chestnut tail; 2 front stockings; back legs white; 4 tan hooves with gray bands around the tops; matte (1994-95). This model has the same pinto pattern as the SR buckskin pinto "Little Chaparral." Some might prefer to call this model a bay pinto in view of his black mane and knees, but the chestnut tail runs afoul of that description.
- Rearing Stallion "Rex," Alabaster Lipizzan, #180, alabaster, white mane and tail, gray hooves, matte (1965-76, 1978-85). Some of these models have pink and gray stallion parts, and many have pink noses. This horse is called Alabaster Lipizzan in catalogs through 1970; thereafter he is called simply Alabaster.
- Rearing Stallion "Rex" #183, palomino; bald face, white points; most with pink-tan hooves, some with gray hooves; matte (1965-85). The palomino color ranges from light golden tan to lemon yellow to vivid orangy to dark tan. At least some of the loud ones are late—collector Kay Schlumpf's specimen, which she described to me as "bright florescent orange palomino," came new in box with a 1985 manual. Kay's model and collector Sande Schneider's both have gray hooves; in my experience these are less common than pink-tan hooves. On earlier models the bald face can be extensive, reaching well down the sides of the face. Many #183s have pink noses. I have heard of a couple of glossy #183s, one owned by collector Chris Wilder and another, of which I've seen photos, owned by Jennifer Fleischman. Jennifer's horse has a "U.S.A." stamp, which dates the model to no earlier than 1970. Both horses were obtained second-hand, so we can't be positive that the gloss is original finish. Some #183s are pearlies; see note 3 for this mold.
- Rearing Stallion "Rex" #185, bay, bald face, black mane and tail, many with no black on the legs, 4 stockings, black hooves, matte (1965-80). On earlier models the bald face can be extensive, reaching well down the sides of the face. Many #185s have pink noses. Collector Paula DeFeyter sent me a photo of her #185 with black legs, no white stockings. Catalogs do not indicate when this black-legged version was made—catalogs 1966-70 show #185 with 4 stockings and no black on the legs, and most catalogs after 1970 list but do not show this model. Some #185s are pearlies; see note 3 for this mold. The 1966 Sears holiday catalog offered the bay Rearing Stallion in a "Desk Set," "a study aid that makes homework almost fun," for $2.47. The set consists of a #185 wearing a "plastic pack with rifle ball-point pen, 6-inch ruler, eraser." The photo in my Xerox of this Sears page is obscure, but the "pack," with ruler and rifle-shaped pen sticking out of it, appears to be a flat, flexible vinyl "saddle" with pockets, similar to the pack saddles that came with many so-called "grooming kits" with Breyers throughout the 1950s and 1960s. For other grooming-kit sets, see Grooming Kits For People above in the Traditionals section.

Special-run models made from this mold:

- "Little Chaparral" SR #700293, buckskin pinto, tobiano; blaze; black tail with white streaks; mane half black and half white; black eyes; black knees; tan hooves; matte (1993). Breyer show special, made for shows and parties sponsored by Breyer dealers. Open quantities made throughout the year. According to *JAH* editor Stephanie Macejko (conversation of June 1995), 7,050 had been made by November 1993; more could have been made in December but her computer showed no further figures. This model came with a certificate of authenticity signed by Breyer executive Peter Stone. The label on the model's box says "No. 700293 Little Chaparral / Breyer Show Special." This model's color and pinto pattern are virtually identical to "Chaparral's" (see under Fighting Stallion), and the pattern is also the same as on regular-run "Promises" Rearing Stallion.
- Rearing Stallion SR #410593, buckskin, solid face, black points, black hooves, matte (1993). Made for the West Coast Model Horse Collector's Jamboree in Ontario, California, in August 1993. 400 models made. Quantity is per Sheryl Leisure, organizer of the Jamboree; model number is per Sheryl and a Breyer company computer printout of 1993 SRs. The buckskin color is fairly light.
- Willow And "Shining Star" set SR #703495, dark bay blanket appaloosa "Shining Star," solid face with light brown area above nose, unstenciled blanket covering butt and part of barrel, splashed-on black spots, black points, gray hooves, Indian symbol on neck, matte (1995). *Just About Horses* Retail Set for subscribers only. 5,000 sets made. Set also includes a Native American doll named Willow and leather halter and lead. To receive a set, subscribers had to submit to their Breyer retailer a coupon that came with *JAH* 22/#4 July/Aug. 1995. The horse is double numbered in bronze ink on the belly. The set is advertised in the Reeves International 1995 Mid-Year Introduction brochure, which clarifies which piece has which name in this set: "This colorful Native American doll, Willow, is luxuriously dressed in a hand-beaded costume. Her spirited Cayuse pony, Shining Star, comes complete with a hand-painted design and leather halter." The horse in this set is a miniature version of "Ponokah-Eemetah" (Traditional-scale Fighting Stallion mold), but with a different Indian symbol, located on the right side of the neck: a white dandelion shape with a yellow line running through and below it; the lower part of the line is decorated with blue and red dots. For details on the doll and tack, see under Eagle in the Riders - Soft Or Jointed Plastic section.

Notes:

(1) The name "Rex" was dropped from catalogs after 1970/71; it was never used in manuals.

(2) Rearing Stallion and Fighting Stallion molds are nearly identical to each other except that Rearing Stallion is small and Fighting Stallion large. Also the Rearing Stallion's face is slightly dished while the Fighting Stallion's is straight. The Rearing Stallion is actually Classic size, but catalogs always list him with the Traditionals.

(3) Some Rearing Stallions from the early/mid 1970s are made of pearly plastic. All of these that I know of are either #183 palomino, such as the one shown on *Breyer Collector's Video*, or #185 bay, such as my own and collector Sheryl Leisure's specimens. I have not heard of a #180 alabaster in pearly, but they could exist. See Chalkies & Pearlies in the Appendix near the end of this book for further discussion.

(4) Earlier models of the Rearing Stallion mold have the round "Breyer Molding Co." stamp only. Later ones have the round stamp and the "U.S.A." stamp—I have a chalky alabaster #180 and a bay pearly #185 with "U.S.A.," so it is virtually certain that the mold got this stamp in the 1970s; it may have gotten it as early as 1970. Still later Rearing Stallions also have a "B" stamp, inside the right hock. This mold carries the "B" stamp to the present day; it was never removed from him, as it was from most other molds that received this stamp.

Reflections — see Messenger Series Of Kiger Mustangs

"Rembrandt" SR — see under "Jet Run"

"Rex" — see under Rearing Stallion

"Riddle" SR — see the three "Riddle" SR entries under "Hobo" (with stand)

Riegseckers — see Riegseckers Models above in the Traditionals section; also see Miniature Collection in the Classics section

"Rojo" — Yearling studcolt with no genitalia, grazing. Sculpted by Rowland Cheney. Mold in catalog-run production 1995 - current as of 1996.

Catalog-run models made from this mold:

- The Progeny Gift Set, "Mesteño" And "Rojo" #4812, light red dun yearling "Rojo," solid or semi-bald face, darker red dun mane and tail, dorsal stripe, gray-shaded underbelly and leg joints, primitive bars above knees and hocks, white front cannons, gray hooves (1995 - current as of 1996). Set also includes reddish dun charging stallion "Mesteño" (see under "Mesteño" Progeny). This set is the fourth installment in the Messenger Series Of Kiger Mustangs (see Messenger Series for discussion and a full list). The "Mesteño" piece in the Progeny set comes with a small hang tag suspended from his neck on a string, giving the sculptor's name and telling about the real Kiger Mustangs "Mesteño" and "Rojo." According to the tag, the name "Rojo" means "newcomer." I have seen "Rojo" models with gray shading on the tail tip as well as the leg joints. On June 1, 1995, the QVC home-shopping cable TV channel offered 1,000 Progeny sets that were ordinary regular runs but that came in boxes labeled with the special-run model number 702995 (per *JAH* editor Stephanie Macejko).

Note: The "Rojo" mold has the "© Breyer Reeves" stamp only.

"Ruffian" — Mare, in extended walk, looking right. Sculpted by Chris Hess. Mold in catalog-run production 1977 - current as of 1996.

Catalog-run models made from this mold:

- "Colleen" #262, red sorrel, blaze, flaxen/light sorrel mane and tail, 1 left front and 2 hind stockings with tan hooves, other hoof dark red-gray (1993-94). Part of The After School Herd Assortment #2001. "Colleen" is not named for any real horse; the name is a Breyer invention (per Breyer executive Peter Stone).
- "Lula" #256, medium reddish bay, solid face, black points, 2 hind stockings with black or gray hooves, front hooves black (1991-92). Part of The After School Herd Assortment #2000. "Lula" is not named for any real horse; the name is a Breyer invention (per Breyer executive Peter Stone). My own mare and some others I've seen have gray hind hooves, but I've seen still others with black hind hooves.
- "Patches" #268, dark chestnut pinto, tobiano; small blaze; white mane; white tail with gray-brown tip; black shading on right hock; all hooves striped tan and gray; with neck ribbon (1995 - current as of 1996). In the B Ranch series. The removable ribbon has red, yellow, and blue streamers; a blue rosette at the breast; and 6 small red rosettes on the ribbon going around the horse's neck. It is identical to the ribbon that come with the B Ranch series horse "Cloud."
- "Ruffian" #606, dark brown bay, small star, black points, 1 left hind stocking with gray hoof, other hooves black (1977-90). In the Classic Series and in Race Horse Assortment #6750 (see general note at the start of the Classics section). In catalogs for the first several years, the model has a tiny star and a stocking that is just a half sock covering the back part of the ankle and hoof for the first few years (my own model is like this), but in 1985-90 she is shown with a larger diamond star and a normal stocking. Collector Kay Schlumpf found a Ruffian with star but no socks at all; it also has a "B" stamp, which dates the model to the period 1979-83. Maestas 1987c has a photo of 4 "Ruffians" with different facial markings, including a tiny round spot, a slightly larger diamond, an ill-defined "splotch," and a fairly large roundish star. The real "Ruffian," born in April 1972, was a Thoroughbred filly who was undefeated prior to her match race with "Foolish Pleasure," held on July 6, 1975, at the Belmont race track. She never finished the match, for just as she began to take the lead over "Foolish Pleasure," "Ruffian's" ankle shattered. Surgery was performed to repair the broken leg, but afterward "Ruffian" became unruly and kicked her cast off. Consequently, she had to be destroyed. (Information per Nack and Munson 1993, collector Nancy Timm, and the model's box.)

Set:

- "Glory" And Plank Jump Gift Set #2003, buckskin "Glory"; blaze; black mane, tail, knees, and hocks; 4 stockings; tan hooves; with plank jump and neck ribbon (1995 - current as of 1996). In the B Ranch series. The horse is a tan buckskin, not at all yellow. The removable neck ribbon, with red rosette and red, yellow, and blue streamers, attaches around the horse's neck with a Velcro closure. It is identical to the ribbons that come with the B Ranch series horses "Apache" and "Azul." The jump is all painted wood, and consists of two white standards with yellow bases, joined by three planks and a round rail on top. The rail and bottom plank are white, the two center planks dark blue. A metal "Breyer" cartouche logo is glued to the lower blue plank.

Special-run models made from this mold:

- "Ruffian" SR?, dapple gray, dapples on neck and head; bald face; darker gray mane and tail; 4 stockings; gray hooves (1980). Probably never released. Ward's holiday catalog. In U.S. Equestrian Team set with light reddish chestnut "Kelso" and bay "Swaps." In the same year (1980), the Sears holiday catalog advertised a two-horse U.S.E.T. set with the same light reddish chestnut "Kelso" and bay "Swaps" as in the Ward's set, but with no "Ruffian." I seriously doubt that these SRs were ever issued. I know of no such "Swaps" models in collections. I am aware of one specimen of a light reddish chestnut "Kelso" (see under "Kelso" for discussion) and one dapple "Ruffian," pictured in a mid-1980s issue of *Collector's Journal*—but one specimen does not a special run make, and both of these pieces could be tests or factory oddities. Furthermore, in perusing model-horse magazines from the 1970s and 1980s, I noticed no sales ads listing such horses. When I asked Breyer executive Peter Stone about these horses in March 1995, he said that the sets pictured in the Ward's and Sears catalogs were test-color proxies for the regular-run U.S.E.T. set horses, which were not ready at the time of the photo shoot for these catalogs but which were the models actually sold when the catalogs were issued. His statement is corroborated by the fact that the regular-run set is not pictured in the 1980 Breyer catalog either, although it is announced there. The fact that the "Kelso," "Ruffian," and "Swaps" in the Ward's and Sears catalogs are painted nearly identically to the regular U.S.E.T. horses also supports Stone's statement: the light reddish chestnut "Kelso" is painted like chestnut "Keen," the bay "Swaps" like bay "Jet Run" (though the "Swaps" lacks a star), and the dapple "Ruffian" like dapple "Might Tango." Oddly enough, several hobby sources report a dapple "Ruffian" SR made prior to 1980. A list of test colors and SRs printed in the June 1983 *Quequechan Model Horse Collector* reports a 1979 dapple "Ruffian" SR of 500 quantity, store unspecified, as well as an SR bay "Swaps" with no white and an SR bright chestnut "Kelso" (no date, store, or quantity given for either horse). Gutierrez 1989 lists two dapple gray "Ruffian" SRs a 1978 Sears special of 500 and a 1979 special of 500, store unspecified—as well as an SR bright chestnut "Kelso" (no date, store, or quantity). She also lists a bay "Swaps" with no white, but in a quantity of 1 (no date). Walerius 1991 says a dapple gray "Ruffian" special of 500 was made in 1977; she says on p. 19 that it was sold by Penney's and on p. 99 that it was sold by Sears. Hollansky 1990 also mentions a 1977 dapple gray "Ruffian" SR of 500, commenting "There is proof of this release in a catalog back in the Midwest. Sears in California only offered a two horse USET Team." But then she sounds a note of skepticism: "If so there should be a lot more out there than have ever shown up in known collections." She is wise to be skeptical. I think what we have in all these reports is a lot of rumors and misinformation, perhaps based on faulty memories of the 1980 Ward's and Sears photos. I have copies of the Breyer pages from several department store holiday catalogs in addition to these two from 1980—Sears 1978-79, Aldens 1979-80, Penney's 1977-80, and Ward's 1977-79—and there are no dapple "Ruffians" or other SRs of any kind on them. Certainly my archives are missing some crucial years, such as Sears 1977; but nonetheless, in view of the evident non-existence of such models today, it is unlikely that the alleged SRs were ever produced.

Note: The "Ruffian" mold has the round "Breyer Molding Co." stamp. Some models also have the "B" stamp. This mold was never given the "U.S.A." stamp.

"Sagr" — ♞ Stallion, walking, nose poked down and out to the right. Sculpted by Chris Hess. Mold in catalog-run production 1983-93.

Catalog-run models made from this mold:

♞ "The Black Stallion Returns" Set #3030, red chestnut "Sagr," solid face, flaxen mane and tail, 4 stockings, gray hooves (1983-93). Set also includes black Black Stallion and alabaster "Johar." This set represents the characters in Walter Farley's book *The Black Stallion Returns*. The "Sagr" model tends to be quite vividly colored, with shades ranging from catsup red (as on my own model) to retina-searing orange. Collector Lori Ogozalek wrote to me that her "Sagr" from the last year of issue is *"ugly* bright orange—hideous!"

Note: The "Sagr" mold has the round "Breyer Molding Co." stamp. This mold debuted at the very end of the "B" stamp era, so it is virtually certain that he was never given the "B" stamp. This mold was never given the "U.S.A." stamp, either.

"Seattle Slew" SR — see under "Swaps"

"Secretariat" SR — see under "Terrang"

"Sham" — see under Black Stallion

"Shetan" — see "The Black Stallion Returns" Set (under Black Stallion)

"Shining Star" SR — see Willow And "Shining Star" set SR (under Rearing Stallion)

"Silky Sullivan" — ♞ Stallion, standing/walking, looking left, tail tip attached to left hock. Sculpted by Maureen Love Calvert. Mold in catalog-run production 1975 - current as of 1996.

Catalog-run models made from this mold:

♞ "Andrew" #259, shaded smoke gray, bald face, darker gray mane and tail, dorsal stripe, 2 hind stockings, 4 gray hooves (1993-94). Part of The After School Herd Assortment #2001. "Andrew" is not named for any real horse; the name is a Breyer invention (per Breyer executive Peter Stone).

♞ "Silky Sullivan" #603, medium/dark chestnut, star, slightly darker chestnut mane and tail, most with 1 left front stocking with gray hoof, other hooves dark chestnut-gray (1975-90). In the Classic Series and in Race Horse Assortment #6750 (see general note at the start of the Classics section). This model's stocking is on the left front in the 1975-76 and 1985-90 catalogs; in 1977-84 the stocking is sometimes on the right front and sometimes not present at all (collector Lori Archer wrote to me that she has one of these no-stocking models). Collector Lori Ogozalek pointed out to me that the star on "Silky Sullivan" varies from a small straight-edged diamond to a larger irregular shape with wiggly outlines. The photos in the 1975-80 catalogs are not clear, but the 1981-84 catalogs plainly show the diamond version. I believe the 1975-80 horses were the diamond version, for my own #603 with a small diamond is a very early model with no mold stamps. The 1985-90 catalogs clearly show the version with an irregular star. "Silky Sullivan" #603 was sold in a "2-horse Thoroughbred Set" with regular-run #602 "Man-O-War" through the 1981 Sears holiday catalog. The real "Silky Sullivan," according to the model's box, was a race horse born in California in 1955, who ran all his races in that state. Though his record of wins was not outstanding, he gained fame for his running style: he would stay at the back of the pack until the final quarter mile, then he would race forward past the pack with an astounding burst of speed.

♞ "Spice" #265, bay blanket appaloosa, star, unstenciled butt blanket, splashed-on bay spots, black points, 2 hind stockings, 4 tan hooves; with neck ribbon (1995 - current as of 1996). In the B Ranch series. The removable ribbon, with red, yellow, and blue streamers and a blue rosette, attaches around the horse's neck with a Velcro closure. It is identical to the ribbons that come with the B Ranch series horses "Blackjack" and "Buck."

♞ "T-Bone" #253, fleabitten gray, white horse with gray flecks, black points, black hooves (1991-92). Part of The After School Herd Assortment #2000. "T-Bone" is not named for any real horse; the name is a Breyer invention (per Breyer executive Peter Stone). The model's box describes his color as "fleabitten grey."

Sets:

♞ "Buck" And Hillary Gift Set #2004, pale buckskin horse "Buck," blaze, black mane and tail, pale buckskin legs with soft gray shading on the joints, grayish-tan hooves; with Hillary doll, blue leather saddle and bridle, roll-top jump, and neck ribbon for "Buck" (1995 - current as of 1996). In the B Ranch series. The removable neck ribbon, with blue rosette and red, yellow, and blue streamers, attaches around the horse's neck with a Velcro closure. It is identical to the ribbons that come with the B Ranch series horses "Spice" and "Blackjack." For details on the doll, tack, and jump, see under Hillary in the Riders - Soft Or Jointed Plastic section.

♞ Fine Horse Family set #3348, liver chestnut stallion, diamond star, 1 right front and 2 hind stockings, 4 tan hooves (1994 - current as of 1996). Set also includes red roan mare ("Kelso" mold) and chestnut blanket appaloosa foal (Mustang Family Foal mold). Some of these liver stallions may have a bit of white above the left front hoof in addition to the stockings on the other three legs.

Special-run models made from this mold:

♘ "Whirlaway" SR, medium/light red chestnut, star, dark chestnut mane and tail, 1 left hind stocking with gray hoof, right front and hind socks with gray hooves, other hoof dark chestnut (1987). Made for Hobby Center Toys, Ohio. Sold in Triple Crown Winners I set SR #406135, with dark olive chestnut "Count Fleet" ("Terrang" mold) and medium reddish bay "Citation" ("Kelso" mold). The set number is per a Breyer company computer printout of activity 1985-92. 1,000 sets were made, according to the printed slip that came in the set's box and an article on Hobby Center Toys in *JAH* 16/#1 Feb./Mar. 1989 (p. 28). The right socks on "Whirlaway" are quite vague on my own model and others I've seen. The star on this SR is the same as the irregular-shaped star version on "Silky Sullivan" #603. The real "Whirlaway" was a Thoroughbred race horse who won the Triple Crown (Kentucky Derby, Preakness, and Belmont Stakes) in 1941. For discussion of which model is which in this set, see "Citation" SR (under "Kelso").

Notes:

(1) This mold was created by Maureen Love Calvert, of the Hagen-Renaker company, as a portrait of the real Thoroughbred race horse "Silky Sullivan." H-R produced it in ceramic under the name "Silky Sullivan" #770 (see Roller, Rose, and Berkwitz 1989, p. 23).

(2) Some models of the "Silky Sullivan" mold have no mold stamps; I believe these are the earliest models. Most models have the round "Breyer Molding Co." stamp. Some models might have the "B" stamp as well as the round, but I'm not sure. This mold was never given the "U.S.A." stamp.

"Silver Comet" SR — see under Polo Pony

Sky Blue "Pegasus" SR — see under Lipizzan

"Sombra" — see under "Mesteño" Challenger; also see Messenger Series Of Kiger Mustangs

Spanish-Norman Family set SR — see under Andalusian Family Foal, Andalusian Family Stallion, and "Ginger"

"Spice" — see under "Silky Sullivan"

Surrey With The Fringe On Top (or Surrey To Church On Sunday) set — see Family To Church On Sunday set, under "Duchess " and under "Jet Run"

"Swaps" — ♞ Stallion, standing, head up, looking right, tail tip attached to right hock. Sculpted by Maureen Love Calvert. Mold in catalog-run production 1975 - current as of 1996.

Catalog-run models made from this mold:

♞ "Cloud" #266, dark candy-spot gray, with white dapples on the barrel and light gray dapples on the forehand and hindquarters; bald face with gray band over the nose; rose gray mane and tail; charcoal knees and hocks; 1 right front and 2 hind socks; 4 tan hooves; with neck ribbon (1995 - current as of 1996). In the B Ranch series. The number of socks may vary; my own "Cloud" has three, but the one in the 1995 catalog has two, on the right front and left hind legs. The dappling on this horse is new style for Breyer. The dapples, which are made by hand (per *JAH* editor Stephanie Macejko), are large and squarish, like confetti, and quite widely spaced, set out almost in rows. "Cloud" looks like an extreme example of what is called "chubari gray" or "candy-spot gray" in real horses, according to collector and horse-color expert Lesli Kathman (Haynet email of May 1996). The model's removable ribbon has red, yellow, and blue streamers; a blue rosette at the breast; and 6 small red rosettes on the ribbon going around the horse's neck. It is identical to the ribbon that comes with the B Ranch series horse "Patches."

♞ "Hawk" #254, black, crescent star, black mane and tail, 4 stockings, gray hooves (1991-92). Part of The After School Herd Assortment #2000. "Hawk" is not named for any real horse; the name is a Breyer invention (per Breyer executive Peter Stone).

♞ "Prince" #260, rose alabaster, white horse shaded with pale gray; some also shaded with orangy-tan; soft gray mane and tail with touches of orangy-tan; dorsal stripe; gray knees and hocks; 4 stockings; tan hooves (1993-94). Part of The After School Herd Assortment #2001. Some of these horses have no orangy-tan shading and thus are more properly called alabaster rather than rose alabaster. On the true rose alabasters, the rose shading varies from soft tan to a more orange shade. On some models the dorsal stripe is very faint or even nonexistent. "Prince" is not named for any real horse; the name is a Breyer invention (per Breyer executive Peter Stone).

♞ "Swaps" #604, medium chestnut, star, darker chestnut mane and tail, 1 or 2 stockings with gray hooves, other hooves chestnut-gray (1975-90). In the Classic Series and in Race Horse Assortment #6750 (see general note at the start of the Classics section). The body color ranges from browner shades to plum-pink shades. In catalogs 1975-88 this model has left front and right hind stockings, but in 1989-90 he is shown with only a right hind stocking. However, this 1-stocking version may have debuted in late 1987 or early 1988, for my own 1-stocking, plum-pink "Swaps" came new in box with a 1987 manual enclosed (the manual for a given year is often enclosed with the first releases of the following year since the new manuals aren't ready until the spring).

Collector Sheryl Leisure has a variation with only a left hind stocking. The star on "Swap's" forehead also varies. Early models have a fairly large diamond star; this is clearly visible in the 1976 catalog and is present on my very early brown/olive chestnut "Swaps" with no mold stamps. Later models have a smaller, teardrop-shaped star, as on my plum-pink horse. Catalog photos are not entirely clear about when the star changed, but I believe the 1980 catalog shows a diamond and 1981 and subsequent catalogs show the teardrop. Many models, both early and late, have dark shading on the face. My early olive horse has black on and above his nose, while my later, plum-pink horse has a dark plum-gray face. The 1982 Sears holiday catalog offered "Swaps" with racing tack, described thus: "Classic-size Race Tack. Genuine leather tack fits classic-size horse, 7 x 7 inches high. Includes racing saddle, numbered saddle pad and elastic girth with bridle [sic]." This tack must be SR, for no Classic-scale tack was offered in Breyer catalogs of the early 1980s. The Sears photo shows the bridle and saddle but not the saddle pad. #604 is a portrait of the real Thoroughbred race horse "Swaps," a beautifully built chestnut stallion with a small star and two socks (left front and right hind), foaled in California in 1952. "Swaps" not only won the Kentucky Derby in 1955 but also set several records during his career, among them world records for the mile and the mile and five eighths. (Information per the biography printed on the model's box and per Beard 1994.)

Special-run models made from this mold:
- ⚘ "Seattle Slew" SR, medium/dark chestnut, stripe, darker chestnut mane and tail, no stockings, no white markings, black points, dark gray hooves (1988). Made for Hobby Center Toys, Ohio. Sold in Triple Crown Winners II set SR #406254, with reddish chestnut "Affirmed" ("Man-O-War" mold) and red chestnut "Secretariat" ("Terrang" mold). The set's number is per a Breyer company computer printout of activity 1985-92 and per a flyer that came attached to the boxes of some sets. The flyer also clarifies which name belongs to which model in the set. 1,000 sets were made, according to the printed card that came in the set's box and an article on Hobby Center Toys in JAH 16/#1 Feb./Mar. 1989 (p. 28). The real "Seattle Slew" was a Thoroughbred race horse who won the Triple Crown (Kentucky Derby, Preakness, and Belmont Stakes) in 1977.
- • "Swaps" SR?, bay, no white markings, black points, dark gray hooves (1980). Probably never released. Ward's and Sears holiday catalogs. In the Ward's catalog this horse is shown as part of a 3-horse set called U.S. Equestrian Team, which also included light reddish chestnut "Kelso" and dapple gray "Ruffian." In the Sears catalog the same "Swaps" is shown as part of a 2-horse set called U.S. Equestrian Team Special Set, with the same light reddish chestnut "Kelso." Several hobby sources list one or more of these three models as existing SRs, but other evidence indicates that these horses were never produced. See "Ruffian" SR dapple gray for further discussion.

Notes:
(1) This mold was created by Maureen Love Calvert, of the Hagen-Renaker company, as a portrait of the famous Thoroughbred race horse "Swaps" (see "Swaps" #604 for discussion). Hagen-Renaker produced the mold in ceramic under the name "Swaps" #671 (see Roller, Rose, and Berkwitz 1989, p. 23).
(2) Except in size, this mold is nearly identical to the Stablemate "Swaps" mold, which was also sculpted by Maureen Love Calvert.
(3) Some models of the "Swaps" mold have no mold marks; I believe these are the earliest models (Kay Schlumpf has a 2-stocking "Swaps" #604 with no stamps). All other models of this mold have the round "Breyer Molding Co." stamp. Some models with the round stamp have the "B" stamp in addition (Chelle Fulk's #604 is like this). This mold was never given the "U.S.A." stamp.

"T-Bone" — see under "Silky Sullivan"

"Teeny" — see Marguerite Henry's "Our First Pony" Gift Set #3066, under Mustang Family Foal

"Ten Gallon" — see under "Terrang"

"Terrang" — 🐎 Stallion, standing, looking right, tail just above the tip is attached to left hock. Sculpted by Maureen Love Calvert. Mold in catalog-run production 1975 - current as of 1996.

Catalog-run models made from this mold:
- 🐎 "Azul" #267, blue-bay roan, pale bluish-gray horse with darker gray flecks, brown head with solid face, black points, 2 hind stockings with tan hooves, front hooves striped tan and black; with neck ribbon (1995 - current as of 1996). In the B Ranch series. The removable neck ribbon, with red rosette and red, yellow, and blue streamers, attaches around the horse's neck with a Velcro closure. It is identical to the ribbons that come with the B Ranch series horses "Glory" and "Apache." Most "Azul's" I have seen have a bay-brown head, but I own one whose head is nearly black.
- 🐎 "Gaucho" #255, red roan, white horse with chestnut flecks, chestnut mane and tail, red-gray knees and hocks, tan hooves (1991-92). Part of The After School Herd Assortment #2000. "Gaucho" is not named for any real horse; the name is a Breyer invention (per Breyer executive Peter Stone). The model's box describes his color as "fleabitten red roan."
- 🐎 "Ten Gallon" #261, pale tan dun, bald face, mane and tail dark gray dun touched with pale tan dun, 1 left hind stocking with tan hoof, other legs dark gray dun with tan or tan-gray hooves (1993-94). Part of The After School Herd Assortment #2001. In my experience #261 is typically a light/medium tan on the forehand adn pale cream or even white on the barrel and butt. "Ten Gallon" is not named for any real horse; the name is a Breyer invention (per Breyer executive Peter Stone).
- 🐎 "Terrang" #605, dark/medium bay, no white markings, black points, black hooves (1975-90). In the Classic Series and in Race Horse Assortment #6750 (see general note at the start of the Classics section). The names of this model and "Man-O-War" are switched in the 1985-86 catalogs and the 1985-87 manuals. The color varies from medium to dark brown-bay, with varying amounts of shading. Some models have a pale belly; my own and collector Lori Ogozalek's models are like this. Collector Kelly O'Connor has a "Terrang" with 4 gray hooves and partially oversprayed white markings on the hind legs—a stocking on the right and a sock on the left. Catalogs do not show a variation with stockings, but the early catalogs may show gray hooves; it's hard to tell. The real "Terrang" was a Thoroughbred race horse born in 1953, who placed in 36 of the 66 races in which he started during his 5-year racing career. (Information is per the biography printed on the model's box.)

Special-run models made from this mold:
- ⚘ "Count Fleet" SR, dark olive chestnut, solid face, charcoal-brown mane and tail, 1 left hind stocking with gray hoof, other hooves charcoal-brown (1987). Made for Hobby Center Toys, Ohio. Sold in Triple Crown Winners I set SR #406135 with medium red-

dish bay "Citation" ("Kelso" mold) and medium/light red chestnut "Whirlaway" ("Silky Sullivan" mold). The set's number is per a Breyer company computer printout of activity 1985-92. 1,000 sets were made, according to the printed slip that came in the set's box and an article on Hobby Center Toys in JAH 16/#1 Feb./Mar. 1989 (p. 28). However, additional pieces of "Citation" and "Count Fleet" may have been made, for shipments of these models to Bentley Sales Company in 1988 are listed in the Breyer printout. These listings, which specify no quantities, assign "Citation" the individual model number 410601 and "Count Fleet" the number 410605. For discussion of which model is which in this set, see "Citation" SR (under "Kelso"). "Count Fleet" is a fairly dark chestnut that is sometimes called liver, but he lacks the red tone that that term may suggest, so I use "olive" to indicate an un-red shade. The real "Count Fleet" was a Thoroughbred race horse who won the Triple Crown (Kentucky Derby, Preakness, and Belmont Stakes) in 1943.
- ⚘ "Secretariat" SR, red chestnut, stripe, darker chestnut mane and tail, 1 right front and 2 hind stockings, 4 gray hooves (1988). Made for Hobby Center Toys, Ohio. Sold in Triple Crown Winners II set SR #406254, with reddish chestnut "Affirmed" ("Man-O-War" mold) and medium/dark chestnut "Seattle Slew" ("Swaps" mold). The set's number is per a Breyer company computer printout of activity 1985-92 and per a flyer that came attached to the boxes of some sets. The flyer also clarifies which name belongs to which model in the set. 1,000 sets were made, according to the printed card that came in the set's box and an article on Hobby Center Toys in JAH 16/#1 Feb./Mar. 1989 (p. 28). The real "Secretariat" was a Thoroughbred race horse who won the Triple Crown (Kentucky Derby, Preakness, and Belmont Stakes) in 1973.

Notes:
(1) This mold was created by Maureen Love Calvert, of the Hagen-Renaker company, as a portrait of the real Thoroughbred race horse "Terrang." H-R produced it in ceramic under the name "Terrang" #741 (see Roller, Rose, and Berkwitz 1989, p. 23).
(2) Some models of the "Terrang" mold have no mold stamps; I believe these are the earliest models made (collector Sheryl Leisure has an old shaded dark bay #605 with no stamp). But most models have the round "Breyer Molding Co." stamp. Some models with the round stamp also have a "B" stamp (collector Kelly O'Connor has two #605s like this). This mold was never given the "U.S.A." stamp.

Those Wonderful Wintry Rides set SR — see Collector's One Horse Open Sleigh set SR, under "Black Beauty"

Trakehner Family set — see under "Duchess," "Jet Run," and Mustang Family Foal

Triple Crown Winners I set SR (1987) — see "Citation" SR, medium reddish bay (under "Kelso"); "Count Fleet" SR, dark olive chestnut (under "Terrang"); and "Whirlaway" SR, medium/light red chestnut (under "Silky Sullivan")

Triple Crown Winners II set SR (1988) — see "Affirmed" SR, reddish chestnut (under "Man-O-War"); "Seattle Slew" SR, medium/dark chestnut (under "Swaps"); and "Secretariat" SR, red chestnut (under "Terrang")

U.S. Equestrian Team Gift Set #3035 — The horses in this set are "Jet Run," "Keen," and "Might Tango." See U.S. Equestrian Team Gift Set under those mold names for details.

U.S. Equestrian Team set SR (1980) — see "Kelso" SR, light reddish chestnut; "Ruffian" SR, dapple gray; and "Swaps" SR, bay

U.S. Equestrian Team Special Set SR (1980) — see "Kelso" SR, light reddish chestnut; and "Swaps" SR, bay

U.S. Equestrian Team Special Set (1981) — see U.S. Equestrian Team Gift Set #3035, under "Keen" and under "Jet Run"

U. S. Equestrian Team SR set called Horse Set SR (1987) — see "Jet Run" SR, chestnut; "Keen" SR, steel gray; and "Might Tango" SR, reddish bay with solid face

"Whirlaway" SR — see under "Silky Sullivan"

Willow And "Shining Star" set SR — for the horse, see Willow And "Shining Star" set SR, under Rearing Stallion; for the doll, see under Eagle in the Riders - Soft Or Jointed Plastic section

Little Bits

General note: The Little Bits scale, with molds averaging about 4.5 inches to 5 inches tall at the eartips, is the third largest of Breyer's four sizes of realistic models. The seven plastic Little Bits molds belong to a group that was called the Little Bits Series from late 1983, when the first four molds debuted, through 1994. Two more of the seven Little Bits Series molds appeared in 1984, and the last one, the American Saddlebred, in 1985. In the 1995 catalog, the name Little Bits is nowhere to be found but has been supplanted by the name Saddle Club Series. The name change coincided with the discontinuation of all the older colors and the introduction of several new colors and names on the same molds.

Six of the seven plastic molds were originally sculpted by Christian Hess and one was apparently adapted by him from a piece sculpted by Maureen Love Calvert (for details see the notes for the molds listed below). Calvert also sculpted the eighth mold of this scale, the ceramic Performing "Misty." This piece is not listed as a Little Bit in the one Breyer catalog in which she appeared, but she is of this scale nonetheless.

Sometime in the period 1985-87, at least some Little Bits horses had their packaging adorned with a red, sun-shaped sticker advertising the "Free Bitsy Breyer Offer," whereby collectors could get a free Little Bits Bitsy doll (mold version unspecified) plus accessories. All one had to do was send the model-number labels from the packets of any two LB horses to Reeves International, the company that purchased Breyer Animal Creations in late 1984. My bay #9030 American Saddlebred came with this sticker on his packet. The sticker does not appear in any Breyer catalogs, so I can't be sure precisely when the offer was in effect, but presumably it lasted no longer than Bitsy, who was discontinued in all of her versions by the end of 1987.

The Little Bits have individual model numbers, as listed below. They have also had two different dealer-assortment group numbers over the years: #9000 from 1983 to 1988, and #9100 from 1989 to 1994. The change in group number coincided with a change of colors on all the Little Bits molds in 1989. No new group number was assigned to the Saddle Club Series models that debuted in the 1995 catalog.

All plastic Little Bits are matte or semigloss finish. Many have factory-glossed eyes. Prior to 1996, the Little Bits-scale plastic horses were made in the United States at the Breyer factory. At the end of 1995 or start of 1996, production of these little horses—the molding and the painting—was exported to China, according to *JAH* editor Stephanie Macejko (conversation of May 1996). But unlike the Stablemates models, which have been produced in China from a material called ABS plastic since 1992, the Little Bits are still made from high-quality cellulose acetate plastic, which Breyer supplies to the Chinese manufacturer.

Action Drafters, Big And Small set — see under Clydesdale in the Little Bits section and under Friesian in the Traditionals section

American Saddlebred — Mare, trotting (right front leg up), looking left. Sculpted by Chris Hess. Mold in catalog-run production 1985 - current as of 1996.

Catalog-run models made from this mold:

- American Saddlebred #9030, medium bay, star or solid face, black points, black hooves (1985-88). The medium bay, palomino, and red chestnut regular runs all have the model number 9030. The star on the bay and the red chestnut #9030s is a pointy, asymmetrical hexagram. The star-faced version of the bay is shown in all the catalogs that list #9030, but the solid-faced version is not rare—I own one (which was still sealed in its original package when I got it) and have seen numerous others. The body color, which does not have much red tone, varies from medium/dark brown bay to lighter sandy bay.
- American Saddlebred #9030, palomino, solid face, white points, gray hooves (1985-88). The medium bay, palomino, and red chestnut regular runs all have the model number 9030. The body color of the palominos varies from sober tan shades to bright yellow-orange. The stockings can be very vague.
- American Saddlebred #9030, red chestnut, star, chestnut mane and tail same color as body or darker, chestnut-gray hooves (1985-88). The medium bay, palomino, and red chestnut regular runs all have the model number 9030. The star, which is shown in all the catalogs that list #9030 chestnut, is a pointy, asymmetrical hexagram.
- American Saddlebred #9070, black pinto, tobiano; long star; white mane and tail; pink hooves (1989-94). This model has the same pinto pattern as the SR dark chestnut pinto and SR palomino pinto American Saddlebreds. The star is a long thin streak, which may be vague owing to overspray. Collector Sande Schneider's model is actually solid faced.
- "Belle" #1021, reddish bay, double star, black points, 4 stockings, pink-tan hooves (1995 - current as of 1996). Part of The Saddle Club Collection. For a full list of the horses in this group, see Saddle Club Collection. "Belle's" facial marking consists of a small round star between the eyes with a larger, oblong star just below it. Only a small isthmus of bay paint separates the two stars, so the two may merge into one snowman-shaped star on some models owing to hasty work at the factory. In The Saddle Club series of books by author Bonnie Bryant, "Belle" is "a feisty, spirited Saddlebred Arabian mix" owned by a girl named Stevie Lake (per the 1995 Breyer catalog).

Special-run models made from this mold:

- American Saddlebred SR, dark chestnut pinto, tobiano; long star; white mane and tail; pink hooves (1988). Penney's holiday catalog. Sold in Parade Of Breeds Collector Assortment I set SR #713267. The set number is per a Breyer company computer printout of activity 1985-92. See Parade Of Breeds Collector Assortment I for a complete list of this set. This dark chestnut pinto special has the same pinto pattern as the SR palomino pinto and regular-run black pinto #9070.
- American Saddlebred SR, palomino pinto, tobiano; long star; white mane and tail; pink hooves (1989). Penney's holiday catalog. Sold in Parade Of Breeds Collector Assortment II set SR #719051. 10,000 sets made. Quantity and set number are per a Breyer company computer printout of activity 1985-92. See Parade Of Breeds Collector Assortment II for a complete list of this set. This palomino pinto special has same pinto pattern as the SR dark chestnut pinto and regular-run #9070 black pinto. The star can be so oversprayed as to nearly disappear.
- American Saddlebred SR, red sorrel, solid face, flaxen/pale sorrel mane and tail, 1 left front and 2 hind stockings with gray hooves, other hoof dark red-gray (1985). Made for distribution by Breyer employees in celebration of Reeves International's first year of ownership of Breyer Animal Creations. Some models were also distributed at "Breakfast with Peter Stone" events 1990-92. 5,000 models made, per Breyer executive Peter Stone (conversation of Mar. 1995). Many models came with a hang tag suspended from the neck on a string, which says on the outside "a special edition for a special year!" and on the inside "1985, a special year for Breyer Animal Creations . . . the year the tradition of Breyer creativity and quality is joined with the strength and marketing diversity of Reeves International, Inc. Let this limited edition of Breyer's Little Bits Series remind you of a very special year and a very special company . . . Breyer Animal Creations, now a division of Reeves International, Inc.!" (Thanks to collector Robin Briscoe for a photocopy of the tag on her model, which she purchased from another collector.) Collector Sande Schneider learned that these models were given to attendees of a "Breakfast with Peter Stone" event held at Hobby Center Toys in Ohio in October 1990, and collector Denise Gregoire went to a Breakfast event in San Antonio, in 1992 as she recalls, where attendees received these red sorrel Saddlebreds. Peter Stone told me that some were also given out at a Breakfast event at the Bon Marché store in Spokane, Washington, in 1992.
- American Saddlebred SR, seal brown, solid face, charcoal-brown points, 4 stockings, gray hooves (1990). Penney's holiday catalog. Sold in Parade Of Breeds Collector Assortment III set SR #711090. 8,500 sets made. Quantity and set number are per a Breyer company computer printout of activity 1985-92. See Parade Of Breeds Collector Assortment III for a complete list of this set. Some models may have a true black mane, tail, knees, and hocks, as shown in the Penney's catalog photo, but specimens I know of, including my own, have a definite brown cast in these areas.

Notes:

(1) Chris Hess is identified as the sculptor of this mold in *JAH* XI/#2 1984 (p. 9), and XI/#3 1984 (p. 11). The latter issue shows him consulting with an official of the American Saddlebred Association on the accuracy of the original clay sculpture.

(2) The American Saddlebred mold has the round "Breyer Molding Co." stamp only. It is the only Little Bits mold with this stamp, and was the last Breyer mold of any size to receive it. The stamp was discontinued after this, owing to the acquisition of the Breyer company by Reeves International. (See Breyer Company History in the Appendix near the end of this book.)

Appaloosa — see under Quarter Horse Stallion

Arabian Stallion — Standing/walking, head up, looking right. Sculpted by Chris Hess. Mold in catalog-run production late 1983 - current as of 1996.

Catalog-run models made from this mold:

- Arabian Stallion #9001, chestnut; no white markings; darker chestnut mane, tail, and hooves (late 1983 - 1988). The chestnut, medium bay, and smoke regular runs all have the model number 9001. All three colors were also sold in Bitsy Breyer And Arabian Stallion Beach Set #1001 [late 1983 - 1985]. For discussion of release date, see the entry for #9001 medium bay. The body color of the chestnut varies from medium/dark brown chestnut to lighter golden chestnut. Oddly, a horse that appears to be a variation #9001 chestnut with two hind stockings appears on the back cover of the 1994-95 catalogs, several years after the discontinuation of #9001. He may be a test piece; to my knowledge such horses were not produced for sale.
- Arabian Stallion #9001, medium bay, no white markings, black points, black hooves (late 1983 - 1988). The chestnut, medium bay, and smoke regular-runs all have the model number 9001. All three colors were also sold in Bitsy Breyer And Arabian Stallion Beach Set #1001 [late 1983 - 1985]. These horses are not in the 1983 catalog or manual, but they were evidently released late in that year, for #9001 in "assorted colors" is on the 1983 price list, and a bay #9001 is pictured in various 1983 holiday catalog sets. The Sears 1983 holiday catalog sold it in a set called Breyer And The Little Bits, which also included chestnut Thoroughbred Stallion #9010, black Morgan Stallion #9005, and Bitsy Breyer And Quarter Horse Western Set #1015 with buckskin Quarter Horse Stallion. The Ward's 1983 holiday catalog sold it in a set called New Collector Series...The Little Bits, which also included palomino Quarter Horse Stallion #9015 and Bitsy Breyer And Thoroughbred Jockey Set #1010 with black Thoroughbred Stallion. (My description of this set is based on the Ward's photo, not their description, which is garbled and has little in common with the photo: "grey Arab, bay Morgan thoroughbred and palomino quarter horse.") The 1983 Penney's catalog may have sold it in a set called Bitsy Breyer English Rider Set, with English Bitsy Breyer and brown rubber English saddle and bridle. The Penney's photo does show the bay Arab, but the accompanying description of the set says the horse is a Morgan.
- Arabian Stallion #9001, smoke gray, no white markings, black points, black hooves (late 1983 - 1988). The chestnut, medium bay, and smoke regular-runs all have the model number 9001. All three colors were also sold in Bitsy Breyer And Arabian Stallion Beach Set #1001 [late 1983 - 1985]. For discussion of release date, see the entry for #9001 medium bay. Collector Paula DeFeyter has a smoke stallion whose lower legs are not black but just slightly darker gray than the body.
- Arabian Stallion #9045, alabaster; pink nose and inner ears; gray mane, tail, and hooves (1989-94). This horse was also part of the Parade Of Breeds Collector Assortment III set SR #711090, sold through the Penney's holiday catalog in 1990—see Parade Of Breeds Collector Assortment III for a complete list of this set. I own both an alabaster Arab from the Parade of Breeds set and a regular #9045 (purchased new in November 1994), and they are identical in coloring. The #9045 shown in the 1993-94 Breyer catalogs has a striped effect in the mane and tail; I am not sure whether this variation was issued for sale. The specimens in previous catalogs have solid gray mane and tail, as on my own models.

Sets:

- Bitsy Breyer And Arabian Stallion Beach Set #1001, horse, Bitsy rider, tack, and accessories (late 1983 - 1985). Per a 1984 ad flier from Bentley Sales Company, the horse in the #1001 set came in the same three colors as the #9001 horses sold in 1983-88. This set is not in the 1983 catalog or manual, but evidently it was released late in that year, for it is on the 1983 price list. A similar beach set with an SR black Arabian Stallion and slightly different Beach Bitsy is shown in the 1983 Penney's holiday catalog; see Bitsy Breyer Beachcomber Set SR, below. See under Bitsy Breyer in the Riders - Soft Or Jointed Plastic section for the dolls, tack, and accessories in both sets.
- "Starlight" And Carol, Cross Country Set #1016, dark mahogany bay "Starlight," star, black points, black hooves, with Bitsy-mold rider and tack (1994 - current as of 1996). In the Saddle Club Series. The star is shaped like a fat X. For discussion and details on the doll and tack, see Saddle Club Series in this section and the entries for these sets under Bitsy Breyer in the Riders - Soft Or Jointed Plastic section.

Special-run models made from this mold:

- Arabian Stallion SR, black, no white markings, black mane and tail, tan hooves (1988). Penney's holiday catalog. Sold in Parade Of Breeds Collector Assortment I set SR #713267. The set number is per a Breyer company computer printout of activity 1985-92. See Parade Of Breeds Collector Assortment I for a complete list of this set. In the 1988 Penney's catalog, only a tiny tip of one toe is visible on this black Arab, but it looks tan. The models owned by collectors Robin Briscoe and Kim Jones also have tan hooves.

- Arabian Stallion SR, dapple gray, no or very few dapples on head and upper neck; solid face; dark gray or charcoal points; 4 stockings; gray/charcoal hooves (1989). Penney's holiday catalog. Sold in Parade Of Breeds Collector Assortment II set SR #719051. 10,000 sets made. Quantity and set number are per a Breyer company computer printout of activity 1985-92. See Parade Of Breeds Collector Assortment II for a complete list of this set. The model shown in the Penney's catalog has a few dapples on the head and upper neck, and collector Ingrid Parker has one like this; but Ingrid's second specimen and the horses owned by collector Jo Kulwicki and Heather Wells have no dapples in these areas.
- Bitsy Breyer Beachcomber Set SR, black horse, no white markings, black mane and tail, black hooves; Bitsy beach set doll, bridle, and accessories (1983). Penney's holiday catalog. This set is similar to the Bitsy Breyer And Arabian Stallion Beach Set #1001 sold 1983-85, except that in the SR set, as shown in the Penney's catalog, the horse is apparently solid black and the doll has a different T-shirt than usual. Both the doll and the horse shown in the Penney's catalog could be test pieces; whether the sets actually sold were like this or were instead regular-run #1001 sets I do not know. See under Bitsy Breyer in the Riders - Soft Or Jointed Plastic section for details on the doll, tack, and accessories.

Note: The Arabian Stallion mold has a small "© B.M.C." stamp only.

Bay Pinto — see under Quarter Horse Stallion

"Belle" — see under American Saddlebred

Bitsy Breyer sets — For the horses, see regular run and SR entries under Arabian Stallion, Morgan Stallion, Quarter Horse Stallion, and Thoroughbred Stallion in this section. For the dolls and tack, see under Bitsy Breyer in the Riders - Soft Or Jointed Plastic section.

"Breakfast with Peter Stone" Specials — See Morgan Stallion SR, light sandy bay (1993); also see American Saddlebred SR, red sorrel (1985), and Thoroughbred Stallion SR, reddish bay (1989). For discussion see Signing Party Specials / Breyer Show Specials above in the Traditionals section.

Carousel Horse SR — see under Morgan Stallion

Charger, The Great Horse, SR — see under Clydesdale

Circus Extravaganza set — see under Clydesdale in the Little Bits section and under Clydesdale Stallion in the Traditionals section

Clydesdale — Gelding, cantering on left lead. Sculpted by Chris Hess. Mold in catalog-run production 1984-95.
Catalog-run models made from this mold:
- Clydesdale #9025, bay, solid face, black mane and tail, no black on the legs, 4 stockings, gray hooves (1984-88). The 1984 catalog shows this model with a bald face, but this could be a test color; to my knowledge such horses were not produced for sale. Collector Gale good purchased her solid-faced model in August 1984, and catalogs 1985-88 show #9025 with solid face.
- Shire #9065, black, solid face, gray nose, black mane and tail, 4 stockings, pink hooves (1989-94).
Sets:
- Action Drafters Big And Small set #3175, gray dun small drafter, solid face, rust shading on sides of face and body, charcoal belly and muzzle, black points, black hooves, matte (1994-95). Set also includes dark dappled bay large drafter (Traditional-scale Friesian mold). This small drafter's body coloring is similar to that of the Traditional-scale Belgian Brabant.
- Circus Extravaganza set #3170, dark dappled bay small horse, solid face, black points, some with a small right front sock, gray hooves, matte (1994-95). Set also includes grulla large horse (Traditional-scale Clydesdale Stallion mold). The dapples on this small drafter are very muted, being only slightly lighter than the basic body color. The small horse shown in the 1994-95 catalogs, which may be a test piece, is a very shaded medium sandy bay with a small right front sock. All the models I have seen in person are a quite unshaded dark dappled bay, and only a couple of them, which I found at a tack store in 1996, have the sock. The model I got in 1994 and others I saw at that time have no socks.
Special-run models made from this mold:
- Charger, The Great Horse, SR #419025, dapple gray, no or very few dapples on head and upper neck; baldish face; darker gray mane and tail; 4 stockings; gray hooves (1989). Made for Hobby Center Toys. 1,000 models made. Models came with a Hobby Center Toys certificate of authenticity, with the model's number in the run handwritten on it in calligraphic letters in the blank: "This is to certify that 'Charger' is one of a limited edition of 1000 Shire horses created exclusively for Hobby Center Toys by Breyer Animal Creations." In my experience, this SR Charger generally has rather sparse dappling and a very matte, powdery-looking finish, while the 1990 SR dapple gray Clydesdale tends to have heavier dappling and a semigloss finish. However, both the Charger and the 1990 SR vary in shade, quantity of dappling, and other details, so one run cannot be firmly distinguished from the other. Collector Heather Wells's three Chargers demonstrate the problem: two have the typical soft powdery appearance (one has a pink nose, the other gray); but the third is medium/dark gray with a more semigloss finish (and gray nose), similar to a typical 1990 SR. One of Heather's powder gray horses is mounted on a wooden desk plaque with a metal plate saying "'Charger' Award 1989." These plaque horses, according to Heather, were presented by the Breyer company to Breyer sales representatives. Model number is per a Breyer company computer printout of activity 1985-92. Quantity is per the printout, a Hobby Center Toys price list, and the certificate of authenticity.
- Clydesdale SR, dapple gray, dappling on head and upper neck varies; bald face; darker gray mane and tail; 4 stockings; gray hooves (1990). Penney's holiday catalog. Sold in Parade Of Breeds Collector Assortment III set SR #711090. 8,500 sets made. Quantity and set number are per a Breyer company computer printout of activity 1985-92. See Parade Of Breeds Collector Assortment III for a complete list of this set. Some 1990 dapple Clydesdales I've seen have no or very few dapples on the head and upper neck, but my own specimen and collector Kim Jones's are as heavily dappled in these areas as on the body. These 1990 horses in my experience have a semigloss finish, fairly heavy dappling, and a pink nose, but some specimens may well vary from this. See Charger SR dapple gray for further discussion.
- Clydesdale SR, golden sorrel, solid face, flaxen/light sorrel mane and tail, 4 stockings, gray hooves (1989). Penney's holiday catalog. Sold in Parade Of Breeds Collector

Assortment II set SR #719051. 10,000 sets made. Quantity and set number are per a Breyer company computer printout of activity 1985-92. See Parade Of Breeds Collector Assortment II for a complete list of this set.
Note: The Clydesdale mold has a large "© B.M.C." stamp only.

"Cobalt" And Veronica, Hunter/Jumper Set — see under Thoroughbred Stallion

"Delilah" — see under Morgan Stallion

Little Bits set (1985) — This set is advertised in the 1985 Sears holiday catalog as "A Sears Exclusive," which phrase usually indicates a special run. None of the horses shown, however, are SR colors; they are all identical to regular-run horses in the 1985 Breyer catalog. This set, as shown in the Sears catalog photo, includes palomino American Saddlebred #9030, bay Clydesdale #9025, Appaloosa #9040 (black appy QH Stallion), Bay Pinto #9035 (QH Stallion), and alabaster Unicorn #9020. Sears's description of this set is a tad incoherent: "Set includes a Clydesdale, unicorn, Morgan, quarterhorse and stallion."

Merry-Go-Round Horse SR — see under Morgan Stallion

"Moonglow" — see under Quarter Horse Stallion

Morgan Stallion — Trotting/prancing (left front leg up), head up. Sculpted by Chris Hess. Mold in catalog-run production late 1983 - current as of 1996.
Catalog-run models made from this mold:
- "Delilah" #1024, palomino, solid face, white mane and tail, 4 stockings, pink-tan hooves (1995 - current as of 1996). Part of The Saddle Club Collection. For a full list of the horses in this group, see Saddle Club Collection. The mane and tail on this model are cleanly white, with virtually no overspray, for they are masked off during the painting of the palomino body. In The Saddle Club series of books by author Bonnie Bryant, "Delilah" is a palomino horse favored by the girls at Pine Hollow riding academy for her gentle disposition (per the 1995 Breyer catalog).
- Morgan Stallion #9005, dark/medium bay, no white markings, black mane and tail, black or bay lower legs, black hooves (late 1983 - 1988). The bay, black, and chestnut regular-run Morgan Stallions all have the model number 9005. All three colors were also sold in Bitsy Breyer And Morgan English Set #1005 [late 1983 - 1987] and Bitsy Breyer Stable Set #9950 [1986-87]. For discussion of release date, see the entry for #9005 black. The bays owned by collectors Sheryl Leisure, Kim Jones, and Sande Schneider have black lower legs. My own horse and collector Robin Briscoe's, however, have black hooves but no black on the legs, as also seems to be the case on the bay in the 1984 Breyer catalog. These brown-legged bays are hard to distinguish from #9005 chestnuts, which can have a very dark, brown-black mane, tail, and hooves. But the bays have a browner, less red body color than the chestnuts, and a true black mane and tail. Robin also brought it to my attention that the blister-packs of some #9005s came adorned with a round sticker, an inch and a half in diameter, identifying the model as the "Official Youth Model" of the American Morgan Horse Association. The sticker that came on Robin's bay #9005, which she purchased new in 1988, is white with black type and has the AMHA's "coat of arms" printed in color in the center. On the coat of arms, a banner at the top says "American Morgan Horse Association" and a banner at the bottom says "The Morgan Horse—Pride & Product of America." (Thanks to Robin for sending me her sticker and other materials.) All three colors of #9005 (bay, black, and chestnut) came with this endorsement, according to the 1988 AMHA Gift Collection catalog. Apparently the endorsement lasted for three years, for the sticker is shown on the Morgan's packet in photos of Little Bits packaging in Breyer catalogs 1986-88.
- Morgan Stallion #9005, black; solid face; black mane and tail; 1 left hind stocking with gray, pink, or tan hoof; other legs and hooves black (late 1983 - 1988). The bay, black, and chestnut regular-run Morgan Stallions all have the model number 9005. All three colors were also sold in Bitsy Breyer And Morgan English Set #1005 [late 1983 - 1987] and Bitsy Breyer Stable Set #9950 [1986-87]. These horses are not in the 1983 catalog or manual, but evidently they were released late in that year, for #9005 in "assorted colors" is listed on the 1983 price list, and the black horse appears in the 1983 Sears holiday catalog in a set called Breyer And The Little Bits, which also included bay Arabian Stallion #9001, chestnut Thoroughbred Stallion #9010, and Bitsy Breyer And Quarter Horse Western Set #1015 with buckskin Quarter Horse Stallion. The Morgan in the Sears catalog photo is like the black #9005 in the 1984-88 Breyer catalogs except that the Sears model's stocking is on the right hind leg rather than the left hind. This photo model could be a test color; whether horses like it were actually sold I don't know. The 1984 Breyer catalog shows black #9005's left hind hoof as gray, and the black Morgan that came in my #1005 Bitsy Breyer English set has a gray hoof. In catalogs after 1984, the left hind hoof is tan; collector Kim Jones has one model like this and another model with a pink hoof, as on collector Sheryl Leisure's horse. Regarding the American Morgan Horse Association endorsement of this model, see the entry for #9005 dark/medium bay.
- Morgan Stallion #9005, dark/medium chestnut; no white markings; dark brown mane, tail, and hooves (late 1983 - 1988). The bay, black, and chestnut regular runs all have the model number 9005. All three colors were also sold in Bitsy Breyer And Morgan English Set #1005 [late 1983 - 1987] and Bitsy Breyer Stable Set #9950 [1986-87]. For discussion of release date, see the entry for #9005 black. Regarding the American Morgan Horse Association endorsement of this model, see the entry for #9005 dark/medium bay.
- Morgan Stallion #9050, golden sorrel/palomino, solid face, oversprayed flaxen mane and tail, 4 stockings, gray hooves (1989-94). The body color varies from a reddish-golden sorrel to tan palomino. The model shown in the 1989-92 catalogs (it's the same photo in all of them) appears to have a pure white mane and tail; I'm not sure if horses like this were produced for sale. My own horse and others I have seen in person, as well the one in the 1993-94 catalogs, have the mane and tail lightly oversprayed with the body color, creating a flaxen effect, with the bottom half of the tail white. #9050 was issued in some Parade Of Breeds II sets in 1989; see Morgan Stallion SR rose chestnut for discussion.
Sets:
- Bitsy Breyer And Morgan English Set #1005, horse, Bitsy rider, and tack (late 1983 - 1987). Per a 1984 ad flier from Bentley Sales Company, the horse in this set came in the same three colors as the #9005 horses sold in 1983-88. This set is not in the 1983 catalog or manual, but evidently it was released late in that year, for it is on the 1983 price list. This set or a version of it was sold through the 1983 Penney's catalog as the Bitsy Breyer English Rider Set. This early set has the same doll and tack as #1005, but it's not clear what horse came with it—the Penney's catalog photo shows a bay Arabian

Stallion #9001, but the accompanying description says the horse is a Morgan. See the Riders - Soft Or Jointed Plastic section for the doll and tack in these sets.

- Bitsy Breyer Stable Set #9950, cardboard stable covered with clear vinyl, Morgan Stallion, English Bitsy rider, comb for Bitsy, and English tack (1986-87). This set is just the Bitsy Breyer And Morgan English Set #1005 plus a stable, according to Breyer catalogs and the list of included items printed on the stable itself. An integral vinyl-covered cardboard yard or riding area extends out from the bottom of the stable and folds up over the stable to form a carrying case with a plastic handle on top. Evidently the horse in #9950 sets came with any of the three #9005 colors: Breyer catalogs show the model as bay; the photo on the stable shows him as black; and collector Kay Schlumpf's set, still sealed in its original shrink-wrap when she purchased it, contained a dark/medium chestnut. The list of included items printed on the stable lists only the Morgan Stallion, and Breyer catalog photos show only him in the #9950 set, but Kay's set contained a #9035 bay paint Quarter Horse Stallion in addition to the Morgan.

♞ "Pepper" And Lisa, Hunter/Jumper Set #1018, dapple gray "Pepper," solid face, black points, black hooves, with Bitsy-mold rider and tack (1994 - current as of 1996). In the Saddle Club Series. For discussion and details on the doll and tack, see Saddle Club Series in this section and the entries for these sets under Bitsy Breyer in the Riders - Soft Or Jointed Plastic section.

Special-run models made from this mold:

♘ Merry-Go-Round Horse SR, mauve (grayish lavender); solid face; pink mane, tail, and hooves; some are carousel horses with a brass pole passing through back and belly, pink suede leather saddle and reins and wire bit, mounted on a rectangular wood base painted pinkish or lavender (1985). Carousel version (with tack, pole, and base) made for Penney's holiday catalog. These models are painted, not flocked. The carousel horses, which Penney's priced at $14.99, were outfitted with their tack, pole, and base by Riegseckers of Indiana (see Riegseckers Models above in the Traditionals section), but I am not sure whether Breyer or Riegseckers painted the horses—former Breyer executive Peter Stone could not recall who did the painting when I asked him in December 1995. Models without the pole and base were sold by Riegseckers; collector Ida Santana found a barrel full of these SR Morgans and SR LB Unicorns with blue mane and tail at the Riegseckers' store in the early 1990s. Some of these free-standing Morgans came with the pink tack and others came without tack (per Black Horse Ranch employee Heather Wells, conversation of Nov. 1995). The Penney's catalog and Diederich 1988 (Section 3) describe the mane and tail as lavender, though the Penney's photo shows them as pink. The free-standing horses owned by Jo Kulwicki, Kim Jones, and other collectors I know of have pink mane and tail, as did a carousel version on display at BreyerFest 1994.

♘ Morgan Stallion SR, dark shaded bay, no white markings, black points, gray hooves (1988). Penney's holiday catalog. Sold in Parade Of Breeds Collector Assortment I set SR #713267. The set number is per a Breyer company computer printout of activity 1985-92. See Parade Of Breeds Collector Assortment I for a complete list of this set. This model is dark bay with subtle areas of lighter, sandy shading. He is very similar to darker specimens of the old #9005 bay, but the SR tends to have more body shading and has medium to light gray hooves, whereas #9005 has black hooves.

♘ Morgan Stallion SR, light sandy bay, solid face, black points, 2 hind stockings with pink-tan hooves, front hooves black (1993). Made for two "Breakfast with Peter Stone" promotional events in September 1993, one hosted by Hi-Way Hobby House of Ramsey, New Jersey (the event was held at Ramada Inn in Mahway, N.J.), the other at Bon Marché in Seattle, Washington. 500 models made, per Breyer executive Peter Stone at the New Jersey event (information provided to me by Robin Briscoe, who attended this event). This horse's light sandy bay color could be described alternatively as cinnamon buckskin. Collector Nancy Timm's daughter got a model with a dorsal stripe (at the New Jersey event), though the other models they saw at the event lacked this detail. Collector Jennifer Pegg's model, which she got at the Seattle event, is identical to the models from the New Jersey event, as is collector Heather Wells's horse, which she got in late September 1993 from another collector who attended the Seattle event.

♘ Morgan Stallion SR, medium bay, solid face, black points, 2 hind stockings, 4 black hooves (1990). Penney's holiday catalog. Sold in Parade Of Breeds Collector Assortment III set SR #711090. 8,500 sets made. Quantity and set number are per a Breyer company computer printout of activity 1985-92. See Parade Of Breeds Collector Assortment III for a complete list of this set. Collector Heather Wells's horse is a medium/light brown bay with no red cast.

♘ Morgan Stallion SR, rose chestnut, solid face, darker chestnut mane and tail, 4 stockings, gray hooves (1989). Penney's holiday catalog. Sold in Parade Of Breeds Collector Assortment II set SR #719051. 10,000 sets made. Quantity and set number are per a Breyer company computer printout of activity 1985-92. See Parade Of Breeds Collector Assortment II for a complete list of this set. This Morgan Stallion has a rosy hue reminiscent of the color of cooked salmon. My own horse (purchased from another collector) is a medium/light brownish salmon; collector Robin Briscoe's (purchased at a Breyer warehouse sale in 1993) is slightly brighter red; and collector Kim Jones's is a light soft salmon shade. The horse shown in the Penney's catalog appears a bit darker and more soberly colored, more of a true red chestnut, as is collector Sheryl Leisure's horse. This SR horse came with only some Penney's sets. Other sets came with regular-run #9050 golden sorrel/palomino. I learned about this confusing situation from collector Sande Schneider (1992b and letter to me). When the Penney's catalog came out in 1989, Sande ordered two of the LB sets, both of which contained the regular-run #9050. A short while later, when she heard that a friend had gotten a set with a true SR chestnut Morgan, Sande sent off to Penney's for two additional sets, which turned out to have the SR Morgan. Possibly the inclusion of regular-run #9050 in some sets was just a mix-up at the factory, caused perhaps by the fact that #9050 was a new release in that same year.

Notes:

(1) This mold is labeled Morgan Horse Stallion on the 1983 price list and in the 1984-87 catalogs, but simply Morgan Stallion in the 1988 catalog.

(2) Chris Hess is identified as the sculptor of the Morgan Stallion mold in *JAH* X/#2 1982 (p. 9). The article shows Hess working on the original clay sculpture of the mold.

(3) The Morgan Stallion mold has a small "© B.M.C." stamp only.

Paint — see under Quarter Horse Stallion

Parade Of Breeds Collector Assortment I SR #713267 (1988) — See American Saddlebred SR, dark chestnut pinto; Arabian Stallion SR, black; Morgan Stallion SR, dark shaded bay; Quarter Horse Stallion SR, red leopard appaloosa; Quarter Horse Stallion SR, smoke gray; and Thoroughbred Stallion SR, dark bay with baldish face.

Parade Of Breeds Collector Assortment II SR #719051 (1989) — see American Saddlebred SR, palomino pinto; Arabian Stallion SR, dapple gray; Clydesdale SR, golden sorrel; Morgan Stallion SR, rose chestnut (some sets came with regular-run #9050 golden sorrel/palomino Morgan Stallion instead of the SR rose chestnut); Quarter Horse Stallion SR, black; and Thoroughbred Stallion SR, reddish bay.

Parade Of Breeds Collector Assortment III SR #711090 (1990) — Only 5 of the 6 horses in this set are SR. See American Saddlebred SR, seal brown; Arabian Stallion #9045, alabaster; Clydesdale SR, dapple gray; Morgan Stallion SR, medium bay; Quarter Horse Stallion SR, black leopard appaloosa; and Thoroughbred Stallion SR, dappled rose gray.

"Pepper" And Lisa, Hunter/Jumper Set — see under Morgan Stallion

Performing "Misty" — ♞ Pony, standing with one front leg raised and the other on a stool; version with stool attached to the hoof and version with stool separate. Sculpted by Maureen Love Calvert. Mold in catalog-run production 1993.

Catalog-run models made from this mold:

♞ Performing "Misty" #79293, ceramic, light chestnut pinto, tobiano; bald face; 4 stockings; tan or dark brown hooves; glossy; small brown 4-legged ceramic stool (1993). This model was commissioned by Breyer from the Hagen-Renaker company of San Dimas, California. Hagen-Renaker produced and boxed the models (some of which came with Hagen-Renaker stickers on them while others did not), and Breyer marketed them through the 1993 catalog. The retail price was about $30-$35. The model represents the real Assateague/Chincoteague pony "Misty," whose story is told by Marguerite Henry in *Misty of Chincoteague*. The model portrays "Misty" in what might be called her signature pose: the real "Misty" would perform by putting her front hooves on a stool and "shaking hands" with people. This trick is mentioned in Henry's books *Stormy: Misty's Foal* (pp. 200, 212-13) and *Sea Star: Orphan of Chincoteague* (p. 19); the latter book also has a Wesley Dennis drawing of Misty shaking hands. A photo of "Misty" shaking hands with Ms. Henry herself is printed in *JAH* XII/#3 1985 (p. 21), and Wesley Dennis's painting of "Misty" in Henry's *Album of Horses* shows the pony with both front hooves on a stool. The 1993 Breyer catalog states, "A share of the proceeds from the sales of Performing Misty will be donated to The Misty of Chincoteague Foundation." For further discussion see the entry for "Misty" Of Chincoteague #20 (under "Misty" above in the Traditionals section).

Notes:

(1) The first batch of about 200 Performing "Misty" models had the stool factory-glued to the pony's hoof. But according to Hagen-Renaker president Susan Renaker Nikas, in her presentation at the August 1993 West Coast Model Horse Collector's Jamboree, about 30 models suffered leg and stool breaks in shipping as a result of the gluing, so thereafter the pony and stool were packaged as separate pieces, with gluing instructions included. The stool-separate models were available by April 1993. H-R expert Joan Berkwitz told me that the glue used by the factory on the stool-attached pieces was ordinary epoxy.

(2) The sculptor of this mold is identified in the 1993 catalog: "Misty, the beloved Chincoteague Pony of Marguerite Henry's book, has been created in ceramic by renowned artist Maureen Love Calvert."

(3) The Performing "Misty" mold has no mold stamps.

"Prancer" — see under Thoroughbred Stallion

Quarter Horse Stallion — ♞ Standing/walking, looking slightly left. Sculpted by Chris Hess. Mold in catalog-run production late 1983 - current as of 1996.

Catalog-run models made from this mold:

♞ Appaloosa #9040, black blanket appaloosa, solid face, stenciled butt blanket, splashed-on black spots, 2 hind stockings with gray hooves, front hooves gray or black (1985-88). Same appaloosa pattern as #9080 except for the lack of stockings. #9040 is shown with 4 gray hooves in the 1985-87 catalogs; in the 1988 he has gray hind hooves and black front hooves, as on collector Kim Jones's 3 specimens.

♞ Appaloosa #9080, chestnut blanket appaloosa, solid face, chestnut mane and tail same color as body or darker, stenciled butt blanket, splashed-on chestnut spots, 4 stockings, gray hooves (1989-94). Same appaloosa pattern as #9040 except for the front stockings.

♞ Bay Pinto #9035, bay paint, tobiano; solid face; black mane and tail; some with solid black lower legs, some with 4 stockings; 4 gray hooves (1985-88). Same pinto pattern as #9075. In the 1985-87 catalogs #9035 has black legs; in the 1988 catalog he has 4 vague stockings and dark knees and hocks, as on my own model.

♞ "Moonglow" #1023, reddish dun, bald face, darker red dun mane and tail, 4 stockings, gray hooves (1995 - current as of 1996). Part of The Saddle Club Collection. For a full list of the horses in this group, see Saddle Club Collection. In The Saddle Club series of books by author Bonnie Bryant, "Moonglow is the wild Dun mare that Kate Devine chose to adopt and train for Western riding" (per the 1995 Breyer catalog). Strictly speaking, as a dun this model should have a dorsal stripe; since it does not, it might more properly be called a light chestnut.

♞ Paint #9075, black paint, tobiano; solid face; black mane and tail; 4 stockings; gray hooves (1989-94). Same pinto pattern as #9035.

♞ Quarter Horse Stallion #9015, bay, solid face, black points, no or various stockings, gray or black hooves (late 1983 - 1988). The bay, buckskin, and palomino regular runs all have the model number 9015. All three colors were also sold in Bitsy Breyer And Quarter Horse Western Set #1015 [late 1983 - 1987]. For discussion of release date, see the entry for #9015 palomino. The 1984 catalog shows the bay with one right hind stocking, and collectors Kim Jones and Sheryl Leisure have specimens like this (the hoof with the stocking is gray; the other hooves are black). The 1985-88 catalogs all hide the bay's hind legs, but in 1985-87 his front legs are solid and in 1988 they have vague stockings. The bay #9015 is typically a medium to light golden-brown shade, but a 4-stocking model I purchased new in packet is a very light sandy color that could just as well be called cinnamon buckskin. I am not sure whether to count him as a variation of bay #9015 or of buckskin #9015—his package says only "9015," with no color designation.

♞ Quarter Horse Stallion #9015, buckskin; solid face; black points; some with 4 stockings and gray hooves, some with 4 solid black legs and hooves (late 1983 - 1988). The bay, buckskin, and palomino regular runs all have the model number 9015. All three colors were also sold in Bitsy Breyer And Quarter Horse Western Set #1015 [late 1983 - 1987]. For discussion of release date, see the entry for #9015 palomino. Catalogs show the buckskin horse as a clear tan or yellow buckskin color, and my buckskin from set #1015 is like this. The 1984-87 catalogs show the buckskin with 4 white stockings under black joints; the 1984 also shows him with 4 black legs in the Bitsy Breyer and Quarter Horse Western Set #1015. In the 1988 catalog he again has 4 black legs. The black-legged version with a Western Bitsy Breyer was also sold through the 1983 Sears holiday catalog; see Bitsy Breyer And Quarter Horse Western Set #1015, below.

♞ Quarter Horse Stallion #9015, palomino, most with solid face, white mane and tail, various stockings, gray hooves (late 1983 - 1988). The bay, buckskin, and palomino regular run Quarter Horse Stallions all have the model number 9015. All three colors were also sold in Bitsy Breyer And Quarter Horse Western Set #1015 [late 1983 - 1987]. These horses are not in the 1983 catalog or manual, but they were evidently released late in that year, for #9015 in "assorted colors" is on the 1983 price list, and the palomino is shown in the 1983 Ward's holiday catalog in a set called New Collector Series, which also included bay Arabian Stallion #9001 and Bitsy Breyer And Thoroughbred Jockey Set #1010 with black Thoroughbred Stallion. (My description of this set is based on the Ward's photo, not their description, which is garbled and has little in common with the photo: "grey Arab, bay Morgan thoroughbred and palomino quarter horse.") The body color of palomino #9015 ranges from golden tan to vivid lemon and orange shades. The stockings can be very vague. Collector Paula DeFeyter has a palomino #9015 with a bald face.

♞ Quarter Horse Stallion #9060, blue roan, white horse with gray flecks, black points, black hooves (1989-94).

Sets:

• Bitsy Breyer And Quarter Horse Western Set #1015, horse, Bitsy rider, and tack (late 1983 - 1987). Per a 1984 ad flier from Bentley Sales Company, the horse in this set came in the same three colors as the #9015 horses made in 1983-88. This set is not in the 1983 catalog or manual, but evidently it was released late in that year, for it is on the 1983 price list, and the buckskin version of the set is also shown in the 1983 Sears holiday catalog as part of a larger set called Breyer And The Little Bits. This larger set also included bay Arabian Stallion #9001, chestnut Thoroughbred Stallion #9010, black Morgan Stallion #9005, Western Bitsy Breyer, and tack. For the doll and tack in the #1015 set see Bitsy Breyer And Quarter Horse Western Set #1015 in the Riders - Soft Or Jointed Plastic section.

♞ "Spot" And Kate, Western Set #1019, black blanket appaloosa "Spot," blaze, unstenciled blanket covering butt and half of barrel, large splashed-on black spots, 4 stockings, gray hooves, with Bitsy-mold rider and tack (1994 - current as of 1996). In the Saddle Club Series. For discussion and details on the doll and tack, see Saddle Club Series in this section and the entries for these sets under Bitsy Breyer in the Riders - Soft Or Jointed Plastic section.

Special-run models made from this mold:

♘ Quarter Horse Stallion SR, black, solid face, black mane and tail, 4 stockings, gray hooves (1989). Penney's holiday catalog. Sold in Parade Of Breeds Collector Assortment II set SR #719051. 10,000 sets made. Quantity and set number are per a Breyer company computer printout of activity 1985-92. See Parade Of Breeds Collector Assortment II for a complete list of this set.

♘ Quarter Horse Stallion SR, black leopard appaloosa, white horse with black splashed-on spots; gray muzzle; black mane, tail, knees, and hocks; 4 stockings; gray hooves (1990). Penney's holiday catalog. Sold in Parade Of Breeds Collector Assortment III set SR #711090. 8,500 sets made. Quantity and set number are per a Breyer company computer printout of activity 1985-92. See Parade Of Breeds Collector Assortment III for a complete list of this set. The spots on this model are larger than those on the SR red leopard appy.

♘ Quarter Horse Stallion SR, red leopard appaloosa, white horse with red chestnut splashed-on flecks and spots; grayish brown mane, tail, knees, and hocks; 4 stockings; gray hooves (1988). Penney's holiday catalog. Sold in Parade Of Breeds Collector Assortment I set SR #713267. The set number is per a Breyer company computer printout of activity 1985-92. See Parade Of Breeds Collector Assortment I for a complete list of this set. The spots on this model are smaller than those on the SR black leopard appy.

♘ Quarter Horse Stallion SR, smoke gray, solid upper face, light area above nose, black points, 4 stockings, gray hooves (1988). Penney's holiday catalog. Sold in Parade Of Breeds Collector Assortment I set SR #713267. The set number is per a Breyer company computer printout of activity 1985-92. See Parade Of Breeds Collector Assortment I for a complete list of this set. The stockings on the smoke gray horse can be very vague. In about 1989, collector Christi Hayes found two of these gray SRs in a toy store, packaged in the usual regular-run Little Bit packaging.

Note: The Quarter Horse Stallion mold has a "© B.M.C." engraving only.

Saddlebred — see American Saddlebred

Saddle Club Collection, Little Bits — This series, introduced in 1995, comprises four Little Bits horses, all sold separately: "Belle" (see under American Saddlebred), "Delilah" (see under Morgan Stallion), "Moonglow" (see under Quarter Horse Stallion), and "Prancer" (see under Thoroughbred Stallion). All four models represent characters in the Saddle Club series of books by author Bonnie Bryant, published by Bantam. For other Saddle Club horses by Breyer, see "Starlight" (under Jumping Horse) above in the Traditionals section, Saddle Club Series in the Little Bits section, and Saddle Club Collection below in the Stablemates section.

Saddle Club Series — This series consists of five Little Bits horse and rider sets, with riders made from the old Bitsy Breyer molds painted in mostly new colors and with tack identical to that in the old sets with Bitsy and horse. Four of the five Saddle Club sets were advertised in the 1994 catalog but were not issued until very late that year owing to production problems. The fifth set, "Cobalt" And Veronica, is not in the 1994 catalog but is listed as new in the 1995 catalog; it is also shown on the back of the boxes of the sets released in late 1994. The pieces in all five sets represent equine and human characters in the Saddle Club series of books by author Bonnie Bryant, published by Bantam. The sets are "Cobalt" And Veronica, Hunter/Jumper Set (see under Thoroughbred Stallion); "Pepper" And Lisa, Hunter/Jumper Set (see under Morgan Stallion); "Spot" And Kate, Western Set (see under Quarter Horse Stallion); "Starlight" And Carole, Cross Country Set (see under Arabian Stallion); and "Topside" And Stevie, Cross Country Set (see under Thoroughbred Stallion). For details on the dolls and tack see under Bitsy Breyer in the Riders - Soft Or Jointed Plastic section. For other Saddle Club horses by Breyer, see "Starlight" (under Jumping Horse) above in the Traditionals section, Saddle Club Collection in the Little Bits section, and Saddle Club Collection below in the Stablemates section.

Shire — see under Clydesdale

"Spot" And Kate, Western Set — see under Quarter Horse Stallion

"Starlight" And Carole, Cross Country Set — see under Arabian Stallion

Thoroughbred Stallion — ♞ Galloping on left lead. Sculpted by Chris Hess, perhaps adapted from an original Hagen-Renaker piece by Maureen Love Calvert. Mold in catalog-run production late 1983 - current as of 1996.

Catalog-run models made from this mold:

♞ "Prancer" #1022, shaded bay with light belly, star, black points, 4 stockings, pink-tan hooves (1995 - current as of 1996). Part of The Saddle Club Collection. For a full list of the horses in this group, see Saddle Club Collection. In The Saddle Club series of books by author Bonnie Bryant, "Prancer" is a former race horse being retrained by a girl named Lisa Atwood (per the 1995 Breyer catalog).

♞ Thoroughbred Stallion #9010, black; solid face; black mane and tail; most with 1 right hind stocking with gray hoof, other hooves black; some with no stockings and 4 tan/brown hooves (late 1983 - 1988). The black, chestnut, and dark/medium bay regular runs all have the model number 9010. All three colors were also sold in Bitsy Breyer And Thoroughbred Jockey Set #1010 [late 1983 - 1987]. For discussion of release date, see the entry for #9010 chestnut. The black #9010 with right hind stocking and gray hoof is shown in Breyer catalogs 1985-87 (back legs are hidden in 1988). A horse with 1 right hind stocking and tan hoof appears in the 1986 Penney's holiday catalog; collectors Paula DeFeyter and Kate Morgan wrote to me that they have such models. Paula and collectors Sheryl Leisure, Heather Hagerstrand, and Kim Jones also have horses with 4 tan hooves and no stockings; collector Heather Wells's horse from the #1010 Bitsy Breyer set has brown hooves. The tan-hoof, no stocking version appears in several pre-1985 sources: a 1983 *JAH* ad for the forthcoming regular-run Little Bit series (see *JAH* X/#1 [1983], p. 13; this issue is incorrectly printed with "1982"); the 1983 Ward's and Penney's holiday catalogs, which offered the horse in sets with Jockey Bitsy Breyer; and the 1984 Breyer catalog, although here only the front legs are visible. For the Ward's and Penney's sets see Bitsy Breyer And Thoroughbred Jockey Set #1010, below.

♞ Thoroughbred Stallion #9010, chestnut, solid face, darker chestnut mane and tail, some with solid legs and 4 brown-gray hooves, some with 1 right hind stocking with a gray hoof (late 1983 - 1988). The black, chestnut, and dark/medium bay regular-run Thoroughbred Stallions all have the model number 9010. All three colors were also sold in Bitsy Breyer And Thoroughbred Jockey Set #1010 [late 1983 - 1987]. These horses are not in the 1983 catalog or manual, but evidently they were released late in that year, for #9010 in "assorted colors" is listed on the 1983 price list, and a #9010 that is either bay or chestnut appears in the 1983 Sears holiday catalog in a set called Breyer And The Little Bits, which also included bay Arabian Stallion #9001, black Morgan Stallion #9005, and Bitsy Breyer And Quarter Horse Western Set #1015 with buckskin Quarter Horse Stallion. The chestnut #9010 varies from medium reddish-brown to light golden chestnut. The chestnuts in the 1984-87 Breyer catalogs have their back legs hidden, so it is hard to determine the dates of the no-stocking and 1-stocking versions. The version with 1 right hind stocking, which is the less common version in my experience, appears both in a 1983 *JAH* ad for the Little Bit series (see *JAH* X/#1 [1983], p. 13; the issue is incorrectly printed with "1982") and in the 1988 catalog. But evidently it was produced in some in-between years too, for collector Delana Metcalf wrote to me that she purchased her 1-stocking horse new in 1985. I have a 1-stocking horse in a Bitsy Jockey #1010 set.

♞ Thoroughbred Stallion #9010, dark/medium bay, no white markings, charcoal/black points and hooves (late 1983 - 1988). The black, chestnut, and dark/medium bay regular runs all have the model number 9010. All three colors were also sold in Bitsy Breyer And Thoroughbred Jockey Set #1010 [late 1983 - 1987]. For discussion of release date, see the entry for #9010 chestnut. The bay's body color varies from dark reddish bay to browner and sandier shades. Oddly, in the 1988 catalog the horse that is presumably "supposed" to be the bay #9010 is not a bay at all but a deep red chestnut with darker chestnut mane and tail and no black shading on the legs. Despite this photo, I would assume that normal #9010 bays were issued in this year, for all the other Little Bits in the photo are their normal colors—albeit the "normal" #9010 chestnut has an unwonted hind stocking.

♞ Thoroughbred Stallion #9055, steel gray; solid face, some with baldish lower face; black points; 2 hind stockings with gray hooves; front hooves black (1989-94).

Sets:

• Bitsy Breyer And Thoroughbred Jockey Set #1010, horse, Bitsy rider, and racing tack (late 1983 - 1987). Per a 1984 ad flier from Bentley Sales Company, the horse in this set came in the same three colors as the #9010 horses sold 1983-88. This set is not in the 1983 catalog or manual, but evidently it was released late in that year, for it is on the 1983 price list and appears in the 1983 Penney's and Ward's catalogs. The Penney's set, called Bitsy Breyer Jockey Set, included a black Thoroughbred Stallion with tan/brown hooves and no white markings, and the same doll and almost the same tack as set #1010. The Ward's set, called New Collector Series...The Little Bits, included the same tan-hoofed black Thoroughbred, doll, and tack as the Penney's set, plus palomino Quarter Horse Stallion #9015 and bay Arabian Stallion #9001. (My description of this set is based on the Ward's photo, not their description, which is garbled and has little in common with the photo: "grey Arab, bay Morgan thoroughbred and palomino quarter horse.") For details on the riders and tack in all these sets see Bitsy Breyer And Thoroughbred Jockey Set #1010 in the Riders - Soft Or Jointed Plastic section. The number 1010 had two previous assignments: originally it belonged to the Showcase Collection issue of the liver chestnut Quarter Horse Yearling (Traditional), then it went to the Dealer Starter Assortment.

♞ "Cobalt" And Veronica, Hunter/Jumper Set #1025, black "Cobalt," no white markings, black hooves, with Bitsy-mold rider and tack (1995 - current as of 1996). In the Saddle Club Series. Unlike the other 4 sets in this series, this set is not in the 1994 catalog but is listed as new in the 1995 catalog. For further discussion and details on the doll and tack, see Saddle Club Series in this section and the entries for these sets under Bitsy Breyer in the Riders - Soft Or Jointed Plastic section.

♞ "Topside" And Stevie, Cross Country Set #1017, sandy bay "Topside," no white markings, gray-shaded muzzle, black points, black hooves, with Bitsy-mold rider and tack (1994 - current as of 1996). In the Saddle Club Series. Some of these sandy bay horses have lovely body shading, while others are more flat and uniform in coloring. "Topside" is confusable with sandy specimens of #9010 dark/medium bay, but in my experience "Topside" is lighter, almost a cinnamon buckskin shade, and has soft gray shading over the whole nose and lower part of the face, whereas #9010 has little or no gray facial shading. For further discussion and details on the doll and tack, see Saddle Club Series in this section and the entries for these sets under Bitsy Breyer in the Riders - Soft Or Jointed Plastic section.

Special-run models made from this mold:

🐎 Thoroughbred Stallion SR, dappled rose gray, light grayish-tan horse with lighter dapples, solid face, darker grayish-chestnut mane and tail, gray-shaded knees and hocks, 4 stockings, gray hooves (1990). Penney's holiday catalog. Sold in Parade Of Breeds Collector Assortment III set SR #711090. 8,500 sets made. Quantity and set number are per a Breyer company computer printout of activity 1985-92. See Parade Of Breeds Collector Assortment III for a complete list of this set. The stockings on this rose gray Thoroughbred can be vague and the dappling can be very subdued. Collector Deb Moore obtained a completely undappled horse from another collector who assured her it was a 1990 SR.

🐎 Thoroughbred Stallion SR, dark bay, baldish face, black points, most with 1 right hind stocking with gray hoof, other hooves black (1988). Penney's holiday catalog. Sold in Parade Of Breeds Collector Assortment I set SR #713267. The set number is per a Breyer company computer printout of activity 1985-92. See Parade Of Breeds Collector Assortment I for a complete list of this set. My own model has a quite cleanly bald face, but collector Lani Keller's model has a nearly solid face, just a shade or two lighter than the body color. The Penney's catalog photo hides this horse's hind legs, but the models I know of typically have only a right hind stocking. Collector Kim Jones's model, however, has only a left hind stocking.

🐎 Thoroughbred Stallion SR, reddish bay, solid face, gray-shaded muzzle, black points, 2 hind stockings, 4 black hooves (1989). Penney's holiday catalog. Sold in Parade Of Breeds Collector Assortment II set SR #719051. 10,000 sets made. Quantity and set number are per a Breyer company computer printout of activity 1985-92. See Parade Of Breeds Collector Assortment II for a complete list of this set. Leftovers of this special were given to a few attendees of the "Breakfast with Peter Stone" event held at the Bon Marché store in Seattle, Washington, in 1993, because the supply of SR light bay Morgan Stallions made especially for 1993 "Breakfast" events ran short (per Peter Stone, conversation of Mar. 1995). Collector Heather Wells's Thoroughbred is from the Bon Marché event, as is collector Vicki Boehm's.

Notes:

(1) Except for its larger size, the Thoroughbred Stallion mold is nearly identical to the Stablemates "Seabiscuit," which debuted many years earlier. Breyer's Stablemate mold is a direct copy of the Hagen-Renaker company's mini "Seabiscuit" #10 by Maureen Love Calvert (see Roller, Rose, and Berkwitz 1989, p. 52), but to the best of my knowledge H-R did not issue the mold in a size larger than the mini. So evidently the adaptation of the small mold to the larger scale is a Breyer innovation.

(2) The Thoroughbred Stallion mold has a small "© B.M.C." stamp only.

"Topside" And Stevie, Cross Country Set — see under Thoroughbred Stallion

Unicorn — 🦄 Mare, standing/pacing, curly tail attached to left buttock and leg, curly mane and fetlock feathers, cloven hooves, molded-on beard and horn. Sculpted by Chris Hess. Mold in catalog-run production 1984-94.
Catalog-run models made from this mold:
🐎 Unicorn #9020, alabaster; soft gray mane, tail, beard, and hooves; gold-and-white-striped horn (1984-94). The feathers too are gray on some models but white or nearly white on others.
Special-run models made from this mold:
🐎 Unicorn SR, white; pale blue mane, tail, beard, feathers, and hooves; solid gold horn; some are carousel unicorns with a brass pole passing through the back and belly, dark pink suede saddle, white reins, and wire bit, mounted on round wooden base (1985). Carousel version (with tack, pole, and base) sold through Ward's holiday catalog, for $14.99. The carousel Unicorns were outfitted with their tack, pole, and base by Riegseckers of Indiana (see Riegseckers Models above in the Traditionals section), but I am not sure whether Breyer or Riegseckers painted the Unicorns—former Breyer executive Peter Stone could not recall who did the painting when I asked him in December 1995. Models without the tack, pole, and base were sold by Riegseckers; collector Ida Santana found a barrel full of these Unicorns and SR mauve Morgan Stallions without bases at the Riegseckers' store in the early 1990s. The Ward's catalog photo shows the Unicorn's horn as silver, but the horn is gold on my own model and the several other collectors' specimens I have seen. Also sold through this Ward's catalog, on the same page as the Unicorn, was a little merry-go-round without animals, for $24.99. It has a round wooden base, round red and white canopy with yellow trim, and wide white center pole. The carousel version of the SR Unicorn could be mounted on this merry-go-round. According to the Ward's catalog, four more animals were to be made in future years to complete the carousel (the Unicorn is the "first in annual series of five"). The accompanying photo shows the merry-go-round with the projected four models, all Little Bits molds with brass poles running through them: [a] a pink Morgan Stallion with deep pink saddle and white reins; [b] a white or pale blue Clydesdale with dark blue mane, tail, and hooves, dark blue saddle, and white or pink reins; [c] a very dark (could be black) Saddlebred with light blue (?) hooves, a saddle (color obscure), and pink reins; and [d] another model that appears to be an Arabian Stallion in a tannish color. To my knowledge these 4 horses were never produced because the Ward's catalog went out of business in 1986. The merry-go-round too was made by the Riegseckers of Indiana (the Ward's catalog says the merry-go-round is "hand-crafted in Amish country of Northern Indiana").
Note: The Unicorn mold has the "© B.M.C." stamp only.

Stablemates

GENERAL NOTE: The Stablemate scale, with adult molds averaging about 2.75 inches tall at the eartips, is the smallest of Breyer's four sizes of realistic models. There are sixteen Stablemates molds—fourteen adults and two foals—all of which were introduced in 1975. Although only seven molds are shown in the 1975 catalog and manual (two of them listed by the wrong names; see note 1 for the Morgan Stallion mold), the remaining nine are in the 1975 price list, under separate headings specifying release later in the year. All sixteen molds were sculpted by Maureen Love Calvert and had previously been produced in ceramic by the Hagen-Renaker company, where Calvert was an employee. The first Breyer catalog ever to mention the origins of these molds is the 1995, which states "A Hagen-Renaker Design" in a footnote on each page that features any Stablemates. These footnote acknowledgments reflect a refurbished licensing agreement between the two companies (per Breyer executive Peter Stone). For the most part the Breyer names for these miniature Hagen-Renaker molds are the same as the Hagen-Renaker names; the few deviations are mentioned in the notes on the particular molds below.

Also listed in the 1975 price list and a 1975 ad flier for the then-new Stablemates series are two additional Stablemates foal molds: Arabian Horse Foal and Morgan Horse Foal. These are not listed in any other Breyer publications known to me and were in fact never produced. According to the price list and ad flier, they were to be sold in sets of two foals of the same mold in different colors: #5703 Arabian Horse Foals in dapple and bay, #5704 Arabian Horse Foals in alabaster and black, #5705 Morgan Horse Foals in bay and black, and #5706 Morgan Horse Foals in chestnut and palomino. Why Breyer abandoned the plan for these foals I don't know.

Stablemates were marketed in a group as #5500 Stallion and Mare Counter Display Assortment, or Stablemates Assortment, from 1975 to 1988. (Various smaller Stablemates assortments were also offered to dealers in the early years: #5501 Stallion and Mare Assortment, #5800 Foal Assortment, and #5801 Foal Assortment.) The group number changed in 1989 to #5600, and changed again in 1995 to #5900, the latter change coinciding with a change to new colors throughout the Stablemates line. Individual model numbers are also given to Stablemates horses in all Breyer dealer catalogs and collector's manuals from 1975 through 1980. From 1981 through 1984, manuals give the numbers but catalogs omit them. Since 1985, no manual or catalog has given the individual model numbers except the 1987 catalog. Individual model numbers are, however, printed on the models' packaging.

Stablemates models, unlike other Breyers, are molded in one piece and are solid. But until 1992, Stablemates were like other Breyers in that they were made by Breyer Animal Creations in the U.S.A. of high-quality cellulose acetate plastic. Since 1992, all Stablemates except for the SR keychain Standing and Lying Foals have been manufactured in China from a lower-quality plastic to enable Breyer to reduce the price of these models. The packets in which these Stablemates are sold say "Made in China." The new material was identified as ABS plastic in a 1991 Black Horse Ranch model mail-order company newsletter that announced the upcoming change, and also in JAH 21/#4 Fall 1994 (p. 3). According to collector Elaine Lindelef, who is in real life a mechanical engineer with access to reference books on industrial materials, ABS plastic is acrylonitrile-butadiene-styrene copolymer. The 1992 holiday SR Stablemates were the first special runs to be made in China from the new plastic. Their box didn't say so, but the Sears holiday catalog calls them "imported," and they are definitely made of the new, tinny-feeling ABS plastic, which responds with a distinctive timbre when tapped with a fingernail or flittered between the fingers.

All Stablemates are matte or semigloss finish. The semigloss models can be so shiny as to appear glossy; I have seen a few models like this, but I do not believe they are genuinely glossy in the sense of having a varnish coating over the paint. However, many Stablemates—both cellulose acetate and ABS models—have been issued with factory-glossed eyes, while other have been issued with unglossed eyes. As to color design, Stablemates are even more variable than other Breyers, particularly with respect to white markings and similar details. This is understandable in view of the tiny scale of these models. On a bay leg measuring an inch in length, the achievement of a clean white stocking between a crisply blackened knee and a neat gray hoof by a mass-production painting department that turns out thousands of models per week can only be an ideal. The norm will be closer to a bay-black-gray blur. Accordingly, in the descriptions below, references to stockings, bald faces, hooves of a definite color, and so on must be taken with a grain of salt.

American Saddlebred — see Saddlebred

Appaloosa — see Appaloosa #5178 (under "Native Dancer"); also see Arabian Mare SR, semi-leopard appaloosa; "Citation" SR, brown dun blanket appaloosa; Morgan Stallion SR, black blanket appaloosa; Quarter Horse Stallion SR, red leopard appaloosa

Arabian Horse Foal — see the General Note at the start of this section

Arabian Mare — 🐎 Standing, neck arched, looking right, ears back, tail attached to left buttock and leg. Sculpted by Maureen Love Calvert. Mold in catalog-run production 1975 - current as of 1996.
Catalog-run models made from this mold:
🐎 Arabian Mare #5011, dapple gray, dappling on neck and head varies; bald, solid, or dappled face; gray mane and tail same color as body or darker; 4 or various stockings; gray hooves (1975-76). The stockings can be so oversprayed as to disappear. Often these mares are quite heavily dappled all over, but collector Sheryl Leisure found one, still in its original blister-packaging, with dapples only on the barrel and butt, and collector Kim Jones has a couple of mares with well-dappled bodies but no dappling on the neck and head. The 1975 Sears holiday catalog sold #5011 in unusual packaging: a cute little white cardboard box printed with a line drawing of the Arabian Mare mold. The printing on the box front says "Sears No. 2257 / Dapple Arabian Mare / Breyer Molding Company," with Breyer's Chicago address. The side flap says "Sears No. 2257 (Breyer No. 5011)." (Thanks to collector Sande Schneider for a photo of the box.) #5011 is similar to the dapple gray Arabian Mare in the Saddle Club Collection #5650, but there are notable differences. The dappling on the old #5011 is normally messier looking and irregular, the dapples varying greatly in shape and size and being interspersed with streaks, whereas the dapples on #5650 are more neatly rounded and uniform, giving somewhat of a polka-dot impression. Also, the older mare is made of high-quality cellulose acetate plastic, whereas #5650 is made of ABS plastic, which has a tinny feel and timbre (see the General Note at the start of the Stablemates section).
🐎 Arabian Mare #5014, bay, solid face, black mane and tail, most with black-shaded knees and hocks and 4 or various stockings, gray hooves (1975-88). The body color on this mare ranges from dark to medium bay and from browner to redder and sandier

shades. The stockings are often vague and oversprayed with gray or brown. In the 1975 catalog (group photo), this mare has black or charcoal hooves and no black on the legs, but in subsequent catalogs she does have black or at least some dark shading on the knees and hocks.

- Arabian Mare #5017 and #5130, alabaster; gray mane, tail, and hooves (as #5017 1975-87; as #5130 1989-94). This mare was discontinued for one year, 1988, then brought back with a different model number. The new number, #5130, is not given in Breyer catalogs and manuals; I have gotten it from the March 1989 Bentley Sales price list and the model's packaging. There is no difference between the #5017 and #5130 mares, except that the older models may be more yellowed with age than the newer ones. This mare was also sold through the 1989 Sears holiday catalog in Stablemate Assortment I set #495600. For a complete list of this set, see Stablemate Assortment I. Collector Kim Jones has a lovely old #5017 mare with gray lower legs as well as gray hooves, mane, and tail.
- Arabian Mare #5182, palomino, baldish face, oversprayed light palomino mane and tail, 4 stockings, gray hooves (1995 - current as of 1996). The models I have seen are a golden tan color, not yellow. The bald face may be so oversprayed as to go solid on some models; in fact the mare in the 1995 catalog looks solid-faced. My own mare's face is quite clearly bald. The model number is per the horse's packaging.

Set:

- Saddle Club Collection, Stablemates #5650, dapple gray Arabian Mare, dapples on neck and head; solid face; darker gray mane and tail; 4 stockings; gray hooves (1994-95). For a complete list of this set and a discussion of the change of models in late 1995, see Saddle Club Collection. The set is named for the Saddle Club series of books by author Bonnie Bryant, but the horses in the set do not represent particular characters in the books. The stockings on this Arabian Mare can be very vague. For differences between this mare and the old dapple gray Arabian Mare #5011, see the entry for the latter.

Special-run models made from this mold:

- Arabian Mare SR, black, solid face, black mane and tail, 2 hind stockings with gray hooves, front hooves black (1990). Sears holiday catalog. Sold in Stablemate Assortment II set SR #495601. 5,000 sets made. For a complete list of this set, see Stablemate Assortment II. Quantity and set number are per a Breyer company computer printout of activity 1985-92. Collector Heather Wells's mare has a shiny semigloss finish.
- Arabian Mare SR, chestnut, solid face, darker chestnut mane and tail, 2 hind stockings with gray hooves, front hooves brownish-gray (1991). Sears holiday catalog. Sold in Stablemate Assortment III set SR #495091. 4,400 sets made. For a complete list of this set, see Stablemate Assortment III. Quantity and set number are per a Breyer company computer printout of activity 1985-92. This mare is a fairly light reddish shade and could be called a reddish dun.
- Arabian Mare SR, semi-leopard appaloosa, white horse with chestnut spots splashed onto butt and barrel; gray-shaded head with bald face; gray-and-white striped mane and tail; gray legs; brownish-gray hooves (1995). Penney's holiday catalog. Sold in Set Of 12 Miniatures SR #710695. 10,600 sets made. The set number and quantity are per *JAH* editor Stephanie Macejko (conversations of Sept. 1995 and July 1996). For a complete list of this set, see Set Of 12 Miniatures SR. The bald face on this Arab Mare may be oversprayed with gray on some specimens. The brownish tone on my own mare's hooves is barely perceptible; I noticed it at all only because I saw that the bottoms of her hooves were solid brown.
- Arabian Mare SR, steel gray; solid face; darker gray mane, tail, knees, and hocks; 4 vague stockings; dark gray hooves (1992 and 1994). Sold through the 1992 Sears holiday catalog in Stablemate Assortment IV set #495092 and through the 1994 Penney's holiday catalog in Twelve-Piece Stablemates Set #711094. 4,500 of the Sears sets and 10,000 of the Penney's sets were made. (Quantity and set number for the Sears set are per a Breyer company computer printout of activity 1985-92; those for the Penney's set are per *JAH* editor Stephanie Macejko.) For a complete list of these sets, see Stablemate Assortment IV. The 1994 horses have glossed eyes; the 1992 horses do not. In my own sets, the 1992 mare is a medium gray, while the 1994 mare is a shade or two darker.

Notes:

(1) This mold was previously produced in ceramic by the Hagen-Renaker company as Arab Mare #46 (see Roller, Rose, and Berkwitz 1989, p. 50).

(2) The Arabian Mare mold has "Breyer Molding Co. © 1975" stamped on the belly. Some models also have a "B" stamp, on the girth beside the copyright stamp—collector Kim Jones has an unpainted Arab Mare like this.

Arabian Stallion (Morgan Stallion mold) — see under Morgan Stallion

Arabian Stallion — Standing, head up, looking left, tail attached to left buttock and leg. Sculpted by Maureen Love Calvert. Mold in catalog-run production 1975 - current as of 1996.

Catalog-run models made from this mold:

- Arabian Stallion #5010, dapple gray, dapples on neck and head; bald, solid, or dappled face; gray mane and tail same color as body or darker; 4 or various stockings; gray hooves (late 1975 - 1976). Collector Heather Wells has both bald- and solid-faced versions; collector Lori Ogozalek has a model with dappled face. The stockings can be so oversprayed as to disappear. This model's name, number, and color were incorrectly issued on the Morgan Stallion mold in the first part of 1975; see note 1 for the Morgan Stallion mold for discussion.
- Arabian Stallion #5013, bay, solid face, black-shaded points, 4 or various stockings, dark gray hooves (early 1975 as "Citation" #5020; late 1975 - 1988 as Arabian Stallion #5013). This model was first released in early 1975 but was incorrectly labeled as "Citation" #5020. In the same year, the bay Morgan Stallion mold was incorrectly issued as Arabian Stallion #5013. Late in 1975, the "Citation" name, number, and color were issued on the correct "Citation" mold, and the bay Arabian and Morgan Stallion molds were issued with their correct names and numbers, much to everyone's enduring confusion. (See note 1 for the Morgan Stallion mold for further discussion.) I count the Arab Stallion "Citation" and Arabian Stallion #5013 as the same model because the coloring is essentially the same. The body color ranges from dark to medium bay and from browner to redder and sandier shades. Collector Sheryl Leisure found a #5013 bay Arabian Stallion mounted on a little white rectangular wooden base with green felt covering the top and a red label on the front side saying "Louisville, Kentucky." A sticker on the bottom of the base says "Carey Craft Originals / Handcrafted / Versailles, Kentucky." The horse has hand-painted eyewhites in the outer corners of the eyes, which are in the style of the eyewhites on many Breyer Traditional models from the 1960s but may well have been added by Carey Craft Originals. It is highly unlikely that the eyewhites are Breyer factory original—if they were OF, they would be the only ones known to me on Stablemates. Sheryl has seen a photo of one other piece identical to hers.
- Arabian Stallion #5016, alabaster; gray mane, tail, and hooves (late 1975 - 1988). This model's name, number, and color were issued on the Morgan Stallion mold in the first part of 1975. See note 1 for the Morgan Stallion mold for discussion.
- Arabian Stallion #5120, steel gray; solid face; black or charcoal-gray mane, tail, knees, and hocks; 4 or various stockings; gray hooves (1989-94). The model number is per a March 1989 Bentley Sales price list and the model's packaging. This same horse was also sold through the 1989 Sears holiday catalog in Stablemate Assortment I set #495600. For a complete list of this set, see Stablemate Assortment I. The body color of this model ranges from a medium gray to nearly charcoal gray. In my experience the lighter horses are earlier. My own horse has 4 stockings, the left hind clearer than the others. For the #5120 in set with "Jessica" doll, see Götz "Jessica" Doll With Stablemates below in this section.
- Arabian Stallion #5181, medium chestnut, solid face, slightly darker chestnut mane and tail, 4 stockings, tan hooves (1995 - current as of 1996). The model number is per the horse's packaging.
- "Citation" #5020, bay (early 1975 as "Citation" #5020; late 1975 - 1988 as Arabian Stallion #5013). This so-called "Citation" is actually an Arabian Stallion mold that was issued under an incorrect name and number in its debut year (see note 1 for the Morgan Stallion mold for discussion). I count him as the same model as #5013 since they are essentially the same color. As shown in the 1975 Breyer catalog, this "Citation" model is a deep reddish bay with solid bay front legs and black-shaded hind legs with two little white socks. My own model, which came still sealed in his original "Citation" packet, is similarly marked, with solid bay front legs, black-shaded hocks, and 2 hind stockings, but his body is medium sandy bay, very matte. A deep red bay Arab "Citation" also appears in the 1975 Sears holiday catalog in a set with a bay Thoroughbred Mare and bay Thoroughbred Standing Foal; here the stallion's front legs are hidden, but his hind legs are visible, and only the left one has a sock. The description in the Sears catalog says "Miniature Family. Authentic reproduction of 'Citation,' the famous sire of race horses, and his family." The set came in a little white cardboard box printed with line drawings of the Arab Stallion and TB Mare and Standing Foal molds. The printing on the box front says "Sears No. 20263 / Bay Thoroughbred Mare / 'Citation' Famous Thoroughbred / Bay Thoroughbred Foal / Breyer Molding Company," with Breyer's Chicago address. The side flap says "Sears No. 20263 (Breyer No. 5670)." (Thanks to Sande Schneider for a photo of the box.) The Sears holiday catalog comes out in the fall, so these "Citations" would have been produced earlier in the year, before Breyer corrected the mold-mix-up problem.

Special-run models made from this mold:

- Arabian Stallion SR, black, solid face, black mane and tail, 2 hind stockings with gray hooves, front hooves black (1991). Sears holiday catalog. Sold in Stablemate Assortment III set SR #495091. 4,400 sets made. For a complete list of this set, see Stablemate Assortment III. Quantity and set number are per a Breyer company computer printout of activity 1985-92.
- Arabian Stallion SR, buckskin, solid face, charcoal points and hooves (1990). Sears holiday catalog. Sold in Stablemate Assortment II set SR #495601. 5,000 sets made. For a complete list of this set, see Stablemate Assortment II. Quantity and set number are per a Breyer company computer printout of activity 1985-92. This horse's body color is a medium tan buckskin. Regarding a possible earlier SR buckskin Arab Stallion, see note 3 for this mold.
- Arabian Stallion SR, dappled red chestnut, solid face, slightly darker chestnut mane and tail, 4 stockings, gray hooves (1992 and 1994). Sold through the 1992 Sears holiday catalog in Stablemate Assortment IV set #495092 and through the 1994 Penney's holiday catalog in Twelve-Piece Stablemates Set #711094. 4,500 of the Sears sets and 10,000 of the Penney's sets were made. (Quantity and set number for the Sears set are per a Breyer company computer printout of activity 1985-92; those for the Penney's set are per *JAH* editor Stephanie Macejko.) For a complete list of these sets, see Stablemate Assortment IV. The 1994 horses have glossed eyes; the 1992 horses do not. The dapples on these SR Arabian Stallions are faint since they are not white but chestnut of a slightly lighter shade than the main body color. The stockings can be vague.
- Arabian Stallion SR, light dusky chestnut, bald face, charcoal mane and tail, 4 stockings, front hooves peachy-gray, hind hooves peach (1995). Penney's holiday catalog. Sold in Set Of 12 Miniatures SR #710695. 10,600 sets made. The set number and quantity are per *JAH* editor Stephanie Macejko (conversations of Sept. 1995 and July 1996). For a complete list of this set, see Set Of 12 Miniatures SR. The bald face on this stallion may be oversprayed with chestnut on some models.
- "Emperor's Gold Bar" SR, palomino, solid face, white mane and tail with some palomino overspray, 1 left hind stocking with gray hoof, other hooves palomino-gray (sometime in the period 1975-80). Quantity unknown. The model is mounted on a transparent plastic paperweight that encases a road apple manufactured by the real horse "Emperor's Gold Bar." I first learned about this item from collector Heather Wells, who in late 1994 discovered an ad for it in the May 1980 issue of *Horse Of Course!* (p. 75). The ad explains: "Emperor's Gold Bar is the beautiful racing bred stallion who's [*sic*] advertised breeding fee soared to an incredible one-million dollars!!! Now you can own a piece of this gorgeous Palomino stallion. Genuine 'horse-hockey' from Emperor's stall artistically entombed in transparent plastic. Atop is a solid detailed statue of Emperor. . . . The conversation piece of the century, and the perfect gift. Order Now While Supply Lasts. . . . $8.50. . . The Clements Co. . . . Guntersville, AL." The black and white photo in the ad shows the "statue" to be a Stablemate Arabian Stallion; the transparent plastic paperweight is shaped like an upside-down custard cup. Subsequently I learned of a collector, Jolie Devereux, who owns one of these inviting parlor pieces. Jolie's horse and paperweight look just like those in the 1980 ad, but the collector from whom she purchased it told her it was issued circa 1975. (It could not have been issued earlier than 1975 since the mold was first issued by Breyer in that year.) Jolie's horse has the usual Breyer copyright stamp on its belly and definitely looks factory original. He was attached to the paperweight with glue on the bottoms of his hooves. He came with a little folded hang tag, the front of which says "Genuine 'Horse-Hockey' By 'Emperor's Gold Bar' A.Q.H.A. Reg. No. 786615." Inside, the tag reads: "Great grandson of world-famous 'Three Bars,' and one of the most beautiful racing bred stallions in the world. Declared undisputed world equine tetherball champion in 1971 and still holds claim to that title today. Emperor is sometimes referred to as the 'million dollar lover' since his advertised breeding fee is a whopping $1,000,000,000 [*sic*]. . . . Space-Age Products . . . Tolleson, AZ." (Thanks to Jolie for information.) When I asked Breyer executive Peter Stone about this SR in March 1995, he had no recollection of it but commented that the horse in the *Horse Of Course!* ad certainly appeared to have a Breyer factory finish.

Notes:

(1) Although this mold was first issued in 1975, it was called Arabian Stallion in catalogs only from 1976 on. See note 1 for the Morgan Stallion mold for discussion.

(2) This mold was previously produced in ceramic by the Hagen-Renaker company as Arab Stallion #47 (see Roller, Rose, and Berkwitz 1989, p. 50).

(3) Collector Karen Perkins told me about an SR buckskin Arabian Stallion made, she believed, in the 1970s. She had this model for many years and could not recall where she had gotten it, but she learned from another collector that it was originally issued in the 1970s in a set with another SR Stablemate, a black "Swaps" as she recalled. Karen's horse (now sold) is a lovely mustard yellow buckskin shade, as on the old buckskin SM Quarter Horse Mare. It also has black mane and tail, black upper legs, 4 stockings, and gray hooves. I have not heard of these horses from any other source.

(4) Nearly all models of the Arabian Stallion mold have "Breyer Molding Co. © 1975" stamped on the belly. The only specimen I know of that lacks this copyright stamp is a bay #5013 or #5020 "Citation" Arab Stallion purchased used by collector Lisa Heino, who kindly sent me photos of the horse. His belly is completely smooth, so evidently he was molded without the stamp and did not simply have it smeared in the molding process, as sometimes happens (smeared stamps can look like nothing but a few vague lumps). So I suspect that Lisa's horse is a very early #5020 (#5020 was one of the first models made from the mold), and that Breyer added the copyright stamp to the mold only after the mold debuted, as has been the case with several other Breyer molds. If this is right, Breyer must have added the stamp to the Arab Stallion just a few months after he debuted, for my own #5020 bay "Citation" Arab Stallion (purchased in packet) does have the usual copyright stamp on the belly. Lisa's horse is colored like mine, with solid bay front legs and two hind socks under black-shaded hocks. Some models of the Arabian Stallion mold might have a "B" stamp in addition to the copyright, but I am not sure.

"Citation" (Arabian Stallion mold) — see under Arabian Stallion

"Citation" — Standing, looking right, tail tip attached to right hock. Sculpted by Maureen Love Calvert. Mold in catalog-run production late 1975 - current as of 1996.

Catalog-run models made from this mold:

- "Citation" #5020, bay, solid face, black mane and tail, black or charcoal shading on the legs, 4 or various stockings, gray or black hooves (late 1975 - 1990). This model's name, number, and color were issued by mistake on the Arabian Stallion mold in the first part of 1975 (see Arabian Stallion #5013 bay), but the correct "Citation" mold was apparently released later in the same year (see note 1 for the Morgan Stallion mold). In the 1976 catalog, the first in which this mold is pictured, the model appears to have a star. This may be a test color model; to my knowledge no models with stars were produced for sale. The stockings on #5020 can be so vague as to disappear. My own specimen, an older model, has solid black hind legs and hooves and solid bay front legs with brownish gray hooves. The body color ranges from a fairly dark brown bay to orangy bay (collector Karen Perkins has a bright orange specimen) to a fairly light sandy bay.
- Standing Thoroughbred #5019, chestnut / reddish dun, solid face, dark brownish-gray mane and tail, dark gray-shaded or chestnut front legs with brownish-gray hooves, 2 hind stockings with gray hooves (pre-catalog release mid-1990, catalog run 1991-94). The model name and number are per the model's packaging. This model is not in the 1990 catalog, but he appeared in stores in mid-1990, according to Diederich 1988 (Section 3) and collector Gale Good. The horse is first shown in the 1991 catalog, which does not say he is new though he clearly is new relative to the 1990 catalog. The #5019 in the 1991-92 catalogs has dark gray-shaded front legs, but the one in the 1993-94 catalogs has chestnut front legs, the same color as the body. My older #5019 made of cellulose acetate is a reddish dun with gray-shaded front legs; my more recent #5019 (purchased new in April 1995) made of ABS plastic is a medium sandy-brown chestnut with charcoal-shaded front legs.
- Standing Thoroughbred #5175, alabaster, soft gray mane and tail, gray hooves (1995 - current as of 1996). The model name and number are per the horse's packaging. Collector Daphne Macpherson, of Cascade Models mail-order business, brought to my attention that this model comes in a pale smoke gray variation. The two specimens I purchased from her are solid soft gray, with slightly darker gray mane, tail, and hooves. My alabaster #5175 and others I have seen, as well as the horse in the 1995 catalog, have stark white bodies. The number 5175 previously belonged to the Presentation Collection edition of the Traditional-scale Indian Pony #175.

Special-run models made from this mold:

- "Citation" SR, brown dun blanket appaloosa, solid face, brown dun mane striped with dark gray, mostly white tail, unstenciled blanket covering butt and part of barrel, splashed-on black spots, 4 vague socks, pale peach hooves (1995). Penney's holiday catalog. Sold in Set Of 12 Miniatures SR #710695. 10,600 sets made. The set number and quantity are per *JAH* editor Stephanie Macejko (conversations of Sept. 1995 and July 1996). For a complete list of this set, see Set Of 12 Miniatures SR. Undoubtedly the socks on this appaloosa vary and may disappear on some models. Various hooves may be touched with dun, as are the front hooves of my own model.
- "Citation" SR, dapple gray, dapples on neck, head, and face; darker gray points and hooves (1992 and 1994). Sold through the 1992 Sears holiday catalog in Stablemate Assortment IV set #495092 and through the 1994 Penney's holiday catalog in Twelve-Piece Stablemates Set #711094. 4,500 of the Sears sets and 10,000 of the Penney's sets were made. (Quantity and set number for the Sears set are per a Breyer company computer printout of activity 1985-92; those for the Penney's set are per *JAH* editor Stephanie Macejko.) For a complete list of these sets, see Stablemate Assortment IV. The 1994 horses have glossed eyes; the 1992 horses do not. The dapples on the SR "Citation" (both years) are relatively neat and round, unlike typical Breyer dapples, which are wild and varied in shape. In my own sets, the 1992 horse has smaller dapples than the 1994 horse.
- "Citation" SR, dappled gray dun, dapples on shoulders and hindquarters only; solid face; charcoal/black points; 2 hind stockings with peach hooves; front hooves charcoal/black (1995). Penney's holiday catalog. Sold in Set Of 12 Miniatures SR #710695. 10,600 sets made. The set number and quantity are per *JAH* editor Stephanie Macejko (conversations of Sept. 1995 and July, 1996). For a complete list of this set, see Set Of 12 Miniatures SR. The dapples on this dun horse are muted, being only a shade lighter than the basic body color.
- "Citation" SR, dusty chestnut / olive dun, solid face, darker chestnut or brownish-gray mane and tail, 4 or various stockings, gray hooves (1990). Sears holiday catalog. Sold in Stablemate Assortment II set SR #495601. 5,000 sets made. For a complete list of this set, see Stablemate Assortment II. Quantity and set number are per a Breyer company computer printout of activity 1985-92. This horse has a medium chestnut color that is very un-red, described as dusty chestnut by Buchanan 1994. The specimens with grayed mane and tail might aptly be called olive dun. In the Sears catalog photo, three stockings are visible on this model, but his left hind leg is hidden. The models owned by collectors Heather Wells and Kim Jones have 4 stockings (some vague), but my own horse and collector Sheryl Leisure's have 2 hind stockings only, with the front legs the same color as the body.
- "Citation" SR, red roan; white or light tan horse with chestnut flecks; red chestnut mane and tail; gray-chestnut knees and hocks; 4 stockings; tan hooves (1989). Sears holiday catalog. Sold in Stablemate Assortment I set #495600. 4,500 sets made. For a complete list of this set, see Stablemate Assortment I. Quantity and set number are per a Breyer company computer printout of activity 1985-92. The stockings on this horse can be vague. One of my specimens of this SR has a white body with red chestnut flecks, while the other has a light tan body with browner flecks.
- "Citation" SR, steel gray, solid face, charcoal/black points and hooves (1991). Sears holiday catalog. Sold in Stablemate Assortment III set SR #495091. 4,400 sets made. For a complete list of this set, see Stablemate Assortment III. Quantity and set number are per a Breyer company computer printout of activity 1985-92. On my own horse the mane, tail, and lower legs are all the same charcoal color, but collector Heather Wells's horse has black lower legs and gray mane and tail, just a shade darker than the body.

Notes:

(1) The "Citation" mold is first pictured in the 1976 catalog and manual but evidently was released late in 1975. See note 1 for the Morgan Stallion mold for discussion.

(2) The Hagen-Renaker company mini mold of which this Stablemate is a copy was produced by H-R under the name "Citation" (with the model number 11; see Roller, Rose, and Berkwitz 1989, p. 52). Breyer introduced its copy under the same name but renamed the mold Standing Thoroughbred when the original "Citation" color was discontinued.

(3) The "Citation" mold has "Breyer Molding Co. © 1976" stamped on the belly. Some models might also have a "B" stamp, but I'm not sure.

Draft Horse — Standing. Sculpted by Maureen Love Calvert. Mold in catalog-run production late 1975 - current as of 1996.

Catalog-run models made from this mold:

- Draft Horse #5055, sorrel; bald or solid face; most with mane and tail same color as body or lighter; no or various stockings; gray hooves; matte and semigloss (late 1975 - 1988). Regarding release date, see note 1 for this mold. The color of this drafter varies from a very light tan shade with matching mane and tail to a dark sandy chestnut with lighter mane and tail. Buchanan 1995 reports a bay variation of #5055 with a black mane and tail but no black on the legs, and collector Heather Wells has a horse like this, with 4 stockings, and gray hooves. The 1976 catalog, the first catalog that pictures #5055, shows a liver chestnut horse with flaxen mane and tail, white muzzle, 4 stockings, and gray hooves. This may be a test-color piece; to my knowledge liver models were not produced for sale. The 1977-79 catalogs show #5055 with a bald face, as on my own model; catalogs 1980-88 show a horse with a solid face.
- Draft Horse #5180, dapple gray, dapples on neck and head; bald, solid, or dappled face; gray mane and tail; 4 or various stockings; gray hooves (1989-94). The model number is per the March 1989 Bentley Sales price list and the model's packaging. The body color varies from light to dark gray. The usual number of stockings is 4, but a model I bought new in 1994 has only a right hind stocking. The dappling on older models is normally messier looking and irregular, the dapples varying greatly in shape and size and being interspersed with streaks, whereas the dapples on newer models—those made in China of ABS plastic— are more neatly rounded and uniform, giving somewhat of a polka-dot impression. #5180 was also sold through the 1989 Sears holiday catalog in Stablemate Assortment I set #495600. For a complete list of this set, see Stablemate Assortment I.
- Draft Horse #5187, rose dun; bald face; charcoal mane, tail, knees, and hocks; 4 stockings; peach-tan hooves (1995 - current as of 1996). The model number is per the horse's packaging.

Set:

- Saddle Club Collection, Stablemates #5650, alabaster Draft Horse, gray mane and tail, gray hooves (1994-95). For a complete list of this set and a discussion of the change of models in late 1995, see Saddle Club Collection. The set is named for the Saddle Club series of books by author Bonnie Bryant, but the horses in the set do not represent particular characters in the books.

Special-run models made from this mold:

- Draft Horse SR, black, no white markings, black mane and tail, black hooves (1990). Sears holiday catalog. Sold in Stablemate Assortment II set SR #495601. 5,000 sets made. For a complete list of this set, see Stablemate Assortment II. Quantity and set number are per a Breyer company computer printout of activity 1985-92.
- Draft Horse SR, black, solid face, black mane and tail, 1 right hind stocking with gray hoof, other hooves black (1984). Made for the Riegseckers of Indiana. Sold in set with 6 other SR Draft Horses; see Draft Horse SR chestnut for a full list. 200 sets made (per Gutierrez 1989). Thanks to Gale Good and Sue Lehman for color details on their models.
- Draft Horse SR, buckskin, solid face, charcoal points, tan hooves (1992 and 1994). Sold through the 1992 Sears holiday catalog in Stablemate Assortment IV set #495092 and through the 1994 Penney's holiday catalog in Twelve-Piece Stablemates Set #711094. 4,500 of the Sears sets and 10,000 of the Penney's sets were made. (Quantity and set number for the Sears set are per a Breyer company computer printout of activity 1985-92; those for the Penney's set are per *JAH* editor Stephanie Macejko.) For a complete list of these sets, see Stablemate Assortment IV. The 1994 horses have glossed eyes; the 1992 horses do not.
- Draft Horse SR, chestnut ("bay"), solid or bald face, dark chestnut mane and tail, 4 stockings, gray hooves (1984). Made for the Riegseckers of Indiana. Sold in set with 6 other SR Draft Horses: black, palomino, red sorrel, smoke gray, red roan, and unpainted white. 200 sets made (per Gutierrez 1989). The published hobby sources that list this SR horse call it bay, but Heather Wells's, Gale Good's, Sue Lehman's, Sheryl Leisure's, and Sande Schneider's models have no black on them at all—their horses are a medium chestnut with dark chestnut mane and tail. Some models may have dark shading on the knees and hocks. I believe most of these models have a solid face, but Heather's horse has a bald face. My dating for this SR set is based on the Riegseckers receipt, dated December 31, 1984, that came with Heather's set.
- Draft Horse SR, medium/light bay, solid face, black points, black hooves (1991). Sears holiday catalog. Sold in Stablemate Assortment III set SR #495091. 4,400 sets made. For a complete list of this set, see Stablemate Assortment III. Quantity and set number are per a Breyer company computer printout of activity 1985-92. My own horse is a fairly light, somewhat sandy bay; but collector Heather Wells's is a medium bay.

Draft Horse SR, palomino, bald face, white mane and tail lightly oversprayed with palomino, 4 or various vague stockings, gray hooves (1984). Made for the Riegseckers of Indiana. Sold in set with 6 other SR Draft Horses; see Draft Horse SR chestnut for a full list. 200 sets made (per Gutierrez 1989). Some of the palominos may have an oversprayed or solid face, but collector Sheryl Leisure's specimen has a large bald face.

Draft Horse SR, red roan, tan horse with red chestnut dappling, roan face, dark red chestnut mane and tail, 4 vague stockings, gray hooves (1984). Made for the Riegseckers of Indiana. Sold in set with 6 other SR Draft Horses; see Draft Horse SR chestnut for a full list. 200 sets made (per Gutierrez 1989). This model may have vague stockings.

Draft Horse SR, red sorrel, solid face, flaxen/pale sorrel mane and tail, 1 right hind stocking with gray hoof, other hooves sorrel-gray, matte (1984). Made for the Riegseckers of Indiana. Sold in set with 6 other SR Draft Horses; see Draft Horse SR chestnut for a full list. 200 sets made (per Gutierrez 1989). This horse is a fairly light red-sandy color that is only somewhat redder than regular-run sorrel #5055s.

Draft Horse SR, smoke gray, bald face, darker gray mane and tail, 4 or various stockings, gray hooves (1984). Made for the Riegseckers of Indiana. Sold in set with 6 other SR Draft Horses; see Draft Horse SR chestnut for a full list. 200 sets made (per Gutierrez 1989). Collector Sande Schneider's smoke gray horse has solid front legs and 2 vague hind stockings.

Draft Horse SR, unpainted white (1984). Made for the Riegseckers of Indiana. Sold in set with 6 other SR Draft Horses; see Draft Horse SR chestnut for a full list. 200 sets made (per Gutierrez 1989). This model is just raw white plastic, with no paint detailing at all, not even on the eyes.

Draft Horse SR, yellow-olive dun; solid face; charcoal points; gray-shaded belly, chest, and dorsal stripe; yellow-tan hooves (1991). Sears holiday catalog. Sold in Stablemate Assortment III set SR #495091. 4,400 sets made. For a complete list of this set, see Stablemate Assortment III. Quantity and set number are per a Breyer company computer printout of activity 1985-92.

Notes:

(1) This mold is not in the 1975 catalog or manual, but it is on the 1975 price list, under the heading "Stablemates—September 1st releases." So apparently it was released in 1975, but later in the year than the Stablemates listed in the catalog and manual.

(2) Unlike most other Stablemates, this mold has a different name than it had when produced in ceramic by Hagen-Renaker, prior to production in plastic by Breyer. Hagen-Renaker called the mold Percheron #459 (see Roller, Rose, and Berkwitz 1989, p. 51).

(3) The Draft Horse mold has "Breyer Molding Co. © 1976" stamped on the belly. Some models might also have a "B" stamp, but I am not sure.

"Emperor's Gold Bar" SR — see under Arabian Stallion

Foals, Lying and Standing — see Thoroughbred Lying Foal; Thoroughbred Standing Foal

Götz "Jessica" doll with Stablemates — In 1995, the Götz company, a German manufacturer of collectible dolls, released a 19.5-inch equestrian doll named Jessica, whose accessories include a pair of leather saddle bags stamped with the Breyer logo, and two regular-run Breyer Stablemates: Arabian Stallion #5120 in steel gray and Thoroughbred Mare #5141 in medium chestnut. Jessica is not a Breyer product, nor is Götz affiliated with Breyer's parent company, Reeves International (per *JAH* editor Stephanie Macejko, conversation of Sept. 1995). A Jessica doll with her accessories was on display at BreyerFest 1995 at the Bentley Sales Company booth. A black and white photo of the doll appears in *JAH* 22/#4 July/Aug. 1995 (p. 3); color photos are printed in the 1995 Penney's holiday catalog (p. 487) and in the fall/winter 1995-1996 supplemental catalog of State Line Tack company in New Hampshire.

Keychain SR foals — see under Thoroughbred Lying Foal; Thoroughbred Standing Foal

Morgan Horse Foal — see the General Note at the start of this section.

Morgan Mare — Prancing, right front leg raised, head up, looking left, tail attached to left buttock and leg. Sculpted by Maureen Love Calvert. Mold in catalog-run production late 1975 - current as of 1996.

Catalog-run models made from this mold:

Morgan Mare #5038, bay, solid face, black points, 4 or various stockings, gray/charcoal hooves (late 1975 - 1988). Regarding release date, see note 1 for this mold. Some models, such as collector Kim Jones's, have black points with no stockings, but typically this mare has at least some vague stockings. Some models have no black on the legs at all, per *Quequechan Model Horse Collector*, August 1985; collector Sheryl Leisure has such a mare as well. The body color varies from dark to medium and from browner shades to sandy, reddish, and orangy bay shades. Redder specimens with stockings are indistinguishable from the 1991 SR reddish bay with stockings.

Morgan Mare #5039, black, solid face, black mane and tail, 1-4 stockings, most with 4 gray or black hooves (late 1975 - 1988). Regarding release date, see note 1 for this mold. This model is listed but not shown in the 1976 catalog. In the 1977-79 catalogs she is shown with 4 stockings and dark gray hooves, as on my own mare; in 1980-87 she has at least a right front stocking (other legs unclear) and dark gray hooves; in 1988 she has 1 clear left hind stocking with pink hoof, other legs and hooves black. This pink-hoof version was produced for sale—I own one and know of others. Collector Robin Briscoe has a mare with 1 left hind stocking and 4 black hooves; collector Kim Jones has a mare identical to Robin's except for a gray hoof on the stockinged leg.

Morgan Mare #5040, chestnut, solid face, chestnut mane and tail same color as the body or darker, 4 or various stockings, gray hooves (late 1975 - 1976). Regarding release date, see note 1 for this mold. This model is listed but not pictured in the 1976 catalog. #5040 varies from a rich medium chestnut to lighter sandy-tan chestnut and is extremely similar to the 1990 SR chestnut. Among the specimens I have seen, the regular runs tend to be a bit more matte and a bit more shaded than the SR, but such differences are not at all reliable or consistent.

Morgan Mare #5160, palomino, solid or baldish face, white mane and tail oversprayed with palomino, 4 or various stockings, gray hooves (1989-94). The model number is per the March 1989 Bentley Sales price list and the model's packaging. This horse was also sold through the 1989 Sears holiday catalog in Stablemate Assortment I set #495600; for a complete list of this set, see Stablemate Assortment I. The color varies from yellow-tan to palomino to light golden sorrel.

Morgan Mare #5185, red chestnut, solid face, mane and tail same color as body or darker, 1 left hind stocking with tan hoof, other hooves reddish-charcoal (1995 - current as of 1996). The model number is per the horse's packaging.

Special-run models made from this mold:

Morgan Mare SR, chestnut, bald face, pale chestnut/flaxen mane and tail, 4 or various stockings, gray hooves (1995). Penney's holiday catalog. Sold in Set Of 12 Miniatures SR #710695. 10,600 sets made. The set number and quantity are per *JAH* editor Stephanie Macejko (conversations of Sept. 1995 and July 1996). For a complete list of this set, see Set Of 12 Miniatures SR. This mare is a medium/light brownish chestnut shade. The bald face may be oversprayed with chestnut on some models.

Morgan Mare SR, chestnut, solid face, darker chestnut mane and tail, 4 or various stockings, gray hooves (1990). Sears holiday catalog. Sold in Stablemate Assortment II set SR #495601. 5,000 sets made. For a complete list of this set, see Stablemate Assortment II. Quantity and set number are per a Breyer company computer printout of activity 1985-92. This mare, with her medium/light sandy chestnut body color and darker mane and tail, is very similar to the old regular-run chestnut; see the entry for #5040 for discussion.

Morgan Mare SR, chocolate sorrel, solid face, flaxen mane and tail, light chestnut lower legs, charcoal hooves (1992 and 1994). Sold through the 1992 Sears holiday catalog in Stablemate Assortment IV set #495092 and through the 1994 Penney's holiday catalog in Twelve-Piece Stablemates Set #711094. 4,500 of the Sears sets and 10,000 of the Penney's sets were made. (Quantity and set number for the Sears set are per a Breyer company computer printout of activity 1985-92; those for the Penney's set are per *JAH* editor Stephanie Macejko.) For a complete list of these sets, see Stablemate Assortment IV. The 1994 horses have glossed eyes; the 1992 horses do not. In my own sets, the 1992 mare has red tones in her mane and tail, while the 1994 mare has beige tones.

Morgan Mare SR, reddish bay, solid face, black mane and tail, charcoal/black knees and hocks, 4 stockings, gray hooves (1991). Sears holiday catalog. Sold in Stablemate Assortment III set SR #495091. 4,400 sets made. For a complete list of this set, see Stablemate Assortment III. Quantity and set number are per a Breyer company computer printout of activity 1985-92. The stockings can be vague and oversprayed. This model is indistinguishable from redder, 4-stocking specimens of the regular-run #5038 bay mare.

Notes:

(1) This mold is not in the 1975 catalog or manual, but it is on the 1975 price list, under the heading "Stablemates—September 1st releases." So apparently it was released in 1975, but later in the year than the Stablemates listed in the catalog and manual.

(2) This mold was previously produced in ceramic by the Hagen-Renaker company as Morgan Mare #388 (see Roller, Rose, and Berkwitz 1989, p. 52).

(3) The Morgan Mare mold has "Breyer Molding Co. © 1976" stamped on the belly. Some models also have a "B" stamp—collector Robin Briscoe has a bay #5038 like this.

Morgan Stallion — Walking, right front leg raised, neck arched, looking right, tail tip attached to left hock. Sculpted by Maureen Love Calvert. Mold in catalog-run production 1975 - current as of 1996.

Catalog-run models made from this mold:

Arabian Stallion #5010, dapple gray, most with dapples on neck and head; bald or solid face; gray mane and tail same color as body or darker; 4 or various stockings; gray hooves (early 1975). This so-called "Arabian Stallion" is actually a Morgan Stallion mold that was issued under an incorrect name, number, and color in its debut year. Later the same year, this name, number, and color were issued on the correct Arabian Stallion mold, and the dapple Morgan Stallion was discontinued (see note 1 for this mold). This model appears to have a bald face in the group photo in the 1975 catalog, and I saw a bald-faced specimen at BreyerFest 1994. Several other specimens I know of, owned by Paula Hecker, Kristi Hale, Karen Malcor, and Sande Schneider, have solid gray faces. Kristi's model has no stockings. Normally #5010, like other Stablemates, was sold in a blister packet, but the 1975 Sears holiday catalog offered him in a cute little white cardboard box printed with a line drawing of the Morgan Stallion mold. The printing on the box front says "Sears No. 2256 / Dapple Arabian Stallion / Breyer Molding Company," with Breyer's Chicago address. The side flap says "Sears No. 2256 (Breyer No. 5010)." (Thanks to Sande Schneider for a photo of the box.) The Sears holiday catalog comes out in the fall, so these #5010s would have been produced earlier in the year, before Breyer corrected the mold-mix-up problem.

• Arabian Stallion #5013, bay, solid face, black mane and tail, 4 or various stockings, gray/charcoal hooves (early 1975 as Arabian Stallion #5013; late 1975 - 1988 as Morgan Stallion #5035). This so-called "Arabian Stallion" is actually a Morgan Stallion mold that was issued under an incorrect name and number in its debut year. For discussion see Morgan Stallion #5035 and note 1 for this mold. I count #5013 and #5035 as the same model, for they are essentially the same color. The bay "Arabian Stallion" #5013 in the group photo in the 1975 catalog has no black on the legs, nor does collector Sande Schneider's #5013, which is still in its original packaging. Collector Kim Jones's #5013, however does have black hocks. Both Sande's and Kim's horses have gray hooves, but the catalog model has charcoal/black hooves.

Arabian Stallion #5016, alabaster, gray mane and tail, gray hooves (early 1975). This so-called "Arabian Stallion" is actually a Morgan Stallion mold that was issued under an incorrect name, number, and color in its debut year. Later the same year, this name, number, and color were issued on the correct Arabian Stallion mold, and the alabaster Morgan Stallion was discontinued. See note 1 for this mold.

Morgan Stallion #5035, bay, solid face, black points, 4 or various stockings, gray/charcoal hooves (early 1975 as Arabian Stallion #5013; late 1975 - 1988 as Morgan Stallion #5035). The Morgan Stallion mold in bay was first released in 1975 but incorrectly labeled as Arabian Stallion #5013. In the same year, the true Arabian Stallion mold in bay was issued as "Citation" #5020. Apparently later in 1975, the Arabian Stallion name and number were issued on the correct Arabian Stallion mold, the correct "Citation" mold was issued in bay with its correct name and number, the bay Morgan Stallion mold got its correct name and number, and everybody lived happily ever after. The stockings on #5035 can be so vague and oversprayed as to disappear. The body color varies from dark to medium and from browner shades to sandy, reddish, and orangy bay shades.

Morgan Stallion #5036 black, solid face, black mane and tail, 1-4 stockings, most with 4 gray or black hooves (late 1975 - 1988). Regarding release date, see note 1 for this mold. The 1976 catalog shows this horse with 4 stockings and gray hooves; collector Kim Jones has a model like this. Kim also has a model with 3 vague stockings and 4 charcoal hooves. The 1977-87 catalogs show #5036 with 1 left hind stocking and 4 dark gray or black hooves, and I have seen a 1-stocking specimen with a gray hoof on the stockinged leg and black hooves on the other legs. The 1988 too shows the model with 1 left hind stocking, but that leg has a pink hoof; the other legs and hooves are black. Collectors Robin Briscoe, Gale Good, and Kim Jones all have #5036s like this 1988 model.

♠ Morgan Stallion #5037, medium/light chestnut, solid face, chestnut mane and tail same color as the body or darker, 4 or various stockings, gray hooves (late 1975 - 1976). Regarding release date, see note 1 for this mold. This model is not pictured but only listed in the 1976 catalog; my description is drawn from collectors' specimens. The color varies from a medium sandy-brown chestnut to light tan chestnut; collector Kim Jones has models of both extremes. Kim's horses and other old chestnuts I have seen are browner or tanner, less red, than typical #5150s. Typical #5150s are fairly red or salmon colored and often are light enough to count as red dun. However, some #5150s are a medium brown chestnut, virtually identical to #5037—in April 1995, at a toy store, I saw several such #5150s (one of which I purchased). But there is a difference that will help identification in some questionable cases: all #5037s are made of high-quality cellulose acetate plastic, whereas post-1991 #5150s are made of ABS plastic, with its characteristically tinny feel and timbre (see General Note at the start of the Stablemates section).

♠ Morgan Stallion #5150, medium chestnut / red dun, solid face, darker chestnut mane and tail, some with dark chestnut shading on knees and hocks, 4 or various stockings, gray hooves (1989-94). The model number is per the March 1989 Bentley Sales price list and the model's packaging. This horse was also sold through the 1989 Sears holiday catalog in Stablemate Assortment I set #495600. For a complete list of this set, see Stablemate Assortment I. I have one #5150 with darker chestnut shading on the knees and hocks and one without. See entry for #5037 for further discussion of color variations.

♠ Morgan Stallion #5184, light bay, solid face, charcoal/black points, 1 left hind stocking, 4 charcoal/black hooves (1995 - current as of 1996). The model number is per the horse's packaging.

Set:

♠ Saddle Club Collection, Stablemates #5650, medium reddish bay Morgan Stallion, solid face, black points, 1 left hind stocking with tan-pink hoof, other legs and hooves black (1994-95). For a complete list of this set and a discussion of the change of models in late 1995, see Saddle Club Collection. The set is named for the Saddle Club series of books by author Bonnie Bryant, but the horses in the set do not represent particular characters in the books.

Special-run models made from this mold:

♘ Morgan Stallion SR, black, white lower face, black-and-white striped mane and tail, 4 stockings, pale tan hooves (1995). Penney's holiday catalog. Sold in Set Of 12 Miniatures SR #710695. 10,600 sets made. The set number and quantity are per *JAH* editor Stephanie Macejko (conversations of Sept. 1995 and July 1996). For a complete list of this set, see Set Of 12 Miniatures SR. The stockings are slightly oversprayed with black on my own horse and may disappear on some models.

♘ Morgan Stallion SR, black blanket appaloosa, solid face, large white unstenciled blanket on butt and barrel, splashed-on black spots, no stockings, black hooves (1992 and 1994). Sold through the 1992 Sears holiday catalog in Stablemate Assortment IV set #495092 and through the 1994 Penney's holiday catalog in Twelve-Piece Stablemates Set #711094. 4,500 of the Sears sets and 10,000 of the Penney's sets were made. (Quantity and set number for the Sears set are per a Breyer company computer printout of activity 1985-92; those for the Penney's set are per *JAH* editor Stephanie Macejko.) For a complete list of these sets, see Stablemate Assortment IV. The 1994 horses have glossed eyes; the 1992 horses do not.

♘ Morgan Stallion SR, dark red chestnut, solid face, mane and tail same color as body or slightly darker, 4 stockings, gray hooves (1990). Sears holiday catalog. Sold in Stablemate Assortment II set SR #495601. 5,000 sets made. For a complete list of this set, see Stablemate Assortment II. Quantity and set number are per a Breyer company computer printout of activity 1985-92. The stockings can be vague.

♘ Morgan Stallion SR, palomino, solid face, white mane and tail oversprayed with palomino, vague stockings, gray hooves (1991). Sears holiday catalog. Sold in Stablemate Assortment III set SR #495091. 4,400 sets made. For a complete list of this set, see Stablemate Assortment III. (Quantity and set number are per a Breyer company computer printout of activity 1985-92.) The photo of this model in the Sears catalog shows him as yellow palomino with clean white mane and tail; my model however is a slightly darker and redder color and has color on his mane and tail. This model does not have the "Breyer Molding Co. © 1975" stamp that Morgan Stallions had as late as the first part of 1991. See note 2 for this mold.

♘ Morgan Stallion SR, seal brown, solid face, charcoal/black points and hooves, no white markings (1992 and 1994). Sold through the 1992 Sears holiday catalog in Stablemate Assortment IV set #495092 and through the 1994 Penney's holiday catalog in Twelve-Piece Stablemates Set #711094. 4,500 of the Sears sets and 10,000 of the Penney's sets were made. (Quantity and set number for the Sears set are per a Breyer company computer printout of activity 1985-92; those for the Penney's set are per *JAH* editor Stephanie Macejko.) For a complete list of these sets, see Stablemate Assortment IV. The 1994 horses have glossed eyes; the 1992 horses do not.

Notes:

(1) This mold was previously produced in ceramic by the Hagen-Renaker company as Morgan Stallion #389 (see Roller, Rose, and Berkwitz 1989, p. 52). Though Breyer's copy of the mold was first issued in 1975, it was called Morgan Stallion in catalogs only from 1976 on. In the 1975 catalog, it is labeled "Arabian Stallion" (dapple gray, bay, and alabaster), and the Arabian Stallion mold is labeled "Citation" (bay). Neither the name "Morgan Stallion" nor the proper "Citation" mold is in this catalog at all. The mislabeled models were also packaged and sold with the incorrect names, numbers, and colors. This was just a mistake on Breyer's part; in producing the Hagen-Renaker miniature horses as Stablemates, Breyer clearly meant to use H-R's names and colors, for in the 1976 Breyer catalog all three molds in question have their correct H-R names and colors. The corrections were made late in 1975, to judge from the 1975 price list and a 1975 ad flier for the new Stablemates series. Unlike the catalog and manual for 1975, the price list and ad flier include all 16 Stablemates molds, separating them into three batches: some (those in the 1975 catalog) available at the start of the year, a second batch labeled "May 1st Releases," and a final batch labeled "September 1st Releases." In this last batch are listed Morgan Stallions in bay, black, and chestnut. These would have been issued on the "Citation" mold unless the error had been corrected; but I haven't heard of "Citations" issued as Morgan Stallions, so evidently the snafu was rectified by September 1975.

(2) The front legs of the Morgan Stallion mold have become thick and crude over the years. The SR palomino (cellulose acetate) in the 1991 Sears set still has legs that are nearly as slim and elegantly contoured as older models' legs, but the two Morgan Stallions (ABS plastic) in the 1992 Sears set have noticeably thickened, coarsened front legs. A #5150 chestnut that I bought new in April 1995 has veritable sausages for front legs, particularly the right (raised) front.

(3) The Morgan Stallion's mold-mark history is bewildering, for his copyright stamp, "Breyer Molding Co. © 1975," has come and gone like the Cheshire Cat over the years. The earliest models of this mold have the stamp—collectors Sande Schneider and Kim Jones have 1975-issue bay #5013s and 1975-76 chestnut #5037s with the copyright, and I have seen it on numerous specimens of dapple gray #5010 and alabaster #5016, both issued in 1975 only. A few years later, about 1979 or 1980, the mold acquired the "B" stamp, between his front legs. Some "B" stamp models also carry the copyright—Kim has a 4-stocking black #5036 with both stamps—but some "B" models have no other stamps: I've heard of blacks like this, and Sande has a bay with only the "B." I do not know for sure which "B" models came first, but the most conservative hypothesis (the one that has the copyright stamp performing the fewest Cheshire Cat tricks) is that the models with both stamps came first, then the ones with only the "B," the copyright having been removed for the first time in the mold's life probably about 1981. Then the "B" stamp itself was removed at the end of the "B" era, about 1982 or 1983, and the mold went completely stampless, apparently for some years, for Kim's black #5036 with pink hoof, dating to 1988, and collector Heather Wells's #5150 chestnut from the 1989 Stablemate Assortment are both stampless. (Kim and I also have a stampless bays, probably #5035s, and collector Kay Schlumpf has a stampless black #5036; *ex hypothesi* these specimens were made after the "B" era, but we don't know for a fact that they were.) Then the copyright stamp reappeared—it is on my own and other collectors' 1990 SR dark red chestnuts. Then the copyright disappeared again, leaving the mold stampless once more—the several specimens of the 1991 holiday SR palomino that I know of and my cellulose acetate #5150 purchased new in March 1992 have no stamps. Then, yes, the stamp reappeared—it is back on the 1992 holiday SR black appaloosa and seal brown (both ABS plastic) and continues with the 1994 holiday SR black appy and seal brown, the 1995 SR black, and the catalog-run models that debuted 1994 and 1995. One explanation I have heard for the erratic behavior of the copyright stamp is that there are two metal injection-molds for the Morgan Stallion, one with and one without the stamp. But this is not right. The Morgan Stallion, like all other Breyer horses, has only one injection mold. For discussion, see Production Process in the Appendix near the end of this book.

"Native Dancer" — ♞ Standing, head up, looking left, tail attached to left buttock and leg. Sculpted by Maureen Love Calvert. Mold in catalog-run production mid-1975 - current as of 1996.

Catalog-run models made from this mold:

♠ Appaloosa #5178, red bay blanket appaloosa, solid face, unstenciled blanket covering butt and part of barrel, splashed-on bay spots, black points, black hooves (1995 - current as of 1996). The model name and number are per the horse's packaging. On my own specimen, the bay spots are a browner, less red shade than the basic body color.

♠ "Native Dancer" #5023, steel gray; solid face; dark gray or black mane and tail; some with black legs and hooves, some with 4 or various vague stockings and gray hooves (mid-1975 - 1994). Regarding release date, see note 1 for this mold. Body color ranges from medium gray to nearly charcoal. The models in the 1976-84 and 1988 catalogs have charcoal/black points, no white stockings. Models in 1985-87 have a couple vague stockings; those in 1989-93 have 4 fairly clear stockings. The #5023s I saw in store in December 1992 were nearly charcoal gray with some very vague stockings and mane and tail only slightly darker than the body (the packets said "Made in China"), and my own model purchased new in 1995 is also like this. The real "Native Dancer" was a famous race horse.

Special-run models made from this mold:

♘ "Native Dancer" SR, black, solid face, black mane and tail, 1 left hind stocking with charcoal hoof, other legs and hooves black (1992 and 1994). Sold through the 1992 Sears holiday catalog in Stablemate Assortment IV set #495092 and through the 1994 Penney's holiday catalog in Twelve-Piece Stablemates Set #711094. 4,500 of the Sears sets and 10,000 of the Penney's sets were made. (Quantity and set number for the Sears set are per a Breyer company computer printout of activity 1985-92; those for the Penney's set are per *JAH* editor Stephanie Macejko.) For a complete list of these sets, see Stablemate Assortment IV. The 1994 horses have glossed eyes; the 1992 horses do not.

♘ "Native Dancer" SR, palomino, solid face, white mane and tail partly oversprayed with palomino, 2 hind stockings with gray hooves, front hooves palomino-gray (1991). Sears holiday catalog. Sold in Stablemate Assortment III set SR #495091. 4,400 sets made. For a complete list of this set, see Stablemate Assortment III. Quantity and set number are per a Breyer company computer printout of activity 1985-92. The photo of this model in the Sears catalog shows him as true palomino; my model however is a slightly darker and redder color. The stockings may vary or be vague.

♘ "Native Dancer" SR, medium bay, solid face, black points, left front and left hind stockings with tan hooves, right hooves black (1995). Penney's holiday catalog. Sold in Set Of 12 Miniatures SR #710695. 10,600 sets made. The set number and quantity are per *JAH* editor Stephanie Macejko (conversations of Sept. 1995 and July 1996). For a complete list of this set, see Set Of 12 Miniatures SR.

♘ "Native Dancer" SR, red bay, solid face, black points, black hooves (1989). Sears holiday catalog. Sold in Stablemate Assortment I set #495600. 4,500 sets made. For a complete list of this set, see Stablemate Assortment I. Quantity and set number are per a Breyer company computer printout of activity 1985-92.

♘ "Native Dancer" SR, white, charcoal/black points and hooves (1990). Sears holiday catalog. Sold in Stablemate Assortment II set SR #495601. 5,000 sets made. For a complete list of this set, see Stablemate Assortment II. Quantity and set number are per a Breyer company computer printout of activity 1985-92.

Notes:

(1) The "Native Dancer" mold is not in the 1975 catalog or manual, but it is on the 1975 price list, under the heading "Stablemates—May 1st releases." So apparently it was released in 1975, but later in the year than the Stablemates that are listed in the catalog and manual.

(2) The Hagen-Renaker company mini mold of which this Stablemate is a copy was produced by H-R under the name "Native Dancer" (with the model number 12; see Roller, Rose, and Berkwitz 1989, p. 52). Breyer introduced its copy under the same name but dropped this when the original "Native Dancer" color was discontinued.

(3) The "Native Dancer" mold has "Breyer Molding Co. © 1975" stamped on the belly. Some models might also have a "B" stamp (as on Julie Hall's #5023).

Quarter Horse Mare — ♞ Prancing, right front leg up, neck arched, heavy mane and forelock swept forward, tail attached to left hock. Sculpted by Maureen Love Calvert. Mold in catalog-run production late 1975 - 1988.

Catalog-run models made from this mold:

♠ Quarter Horse Mare #5048, palomino, solid or bald face, white mane and tail oversprayed with palomino, 4 or various stockings, gray hooves (late 1975 - 1987). Regarding release date, see note 1 for this mold. The stockings can be so vague as to disappear. The palomino color of this mare varies from medium to light tan and to more orangy and yellow shades. My own #5048, a light yellowy palomino made in the mid to late 1980s, has a solid face, while collector Lori Ogozalek's mare, made in the first year of issue, has a bald face. Collector Kim Jones also has a bald-faced model. #5048 was discontinued a year before her mate, the palomino QH Stallion #5045.

Quarter Horse Mare #5049, golden chestnut, solid face, darker chestnut mane and tail, 4 or various stockings, gray hooves (late 1975 - 1976). The body color is a medium to light golden-tan chestnut. This model is pictured in the 1976 catalog, where she has 4 stockings, but on collectors' specimens the stockings can be so vague as to disappear. Regarding release date, see note 1 for this mold.

Quarter Horse Mare #5050, buckskin, solid face, black points, 4 or various stockings, gray or black hooves (late 1975 - 1988). Regarding release date, see note 1 for this mold. The stockings can be so vague as to disappear. The body color of these mares ranges from light yellowy and sandy shades to orangy buckskin to a medium brown buckskin. Some models might have a bald face. Collector Eleanor Harvey sent me photos of her brown-buckskin mare with a high semigloss finish. The number 5050 previously belonged to the Presentation Collection edition of "Adios" #50. #5050 was issued for a year longer than her mate, the buckskin QH Stallion #5047.

Set:

Stablemates Stable Set #3085, dark bay Quarter Horse Mare; solid face; black points; no or various stockings; dark gray or black hooves (1976-80). Set also includes a cardboard stable, dark bay Thoroughbred Lying and Standing Foals, and either a dark bay Quarter Horse Stallion [1976-78 only] or a dark bay "Seabiscuit" [1979-80 only]. This mare comes in mahogany, plum, and red bay shades. I have also heard of a liver chestnut variation with dark liver mane and tail. The 1976 catalog (p. 5) shows the QH Mare in this set as liver chestnut with a blaze as well as 4 stockings; to my knowledge this is a test color model that was not produced for sale. The 1977-78 catalogs show only the box, which pictures the same liver mare. (The box shown in the 1976 catalog, p. 11, must have been a rejected prototype, for the boxtop pictures a "Swaps," Arabian Mare, and two Arabian Stallions.) The 1979-80 catalogs, which show the models as well as the box, show a dark bay QH Mare with no white markings. The model number 3085 previously belonged to "Diablo" The Mustang, Golden Charm decorator (Traditional-scale Mustang mold).

Notes:

(1) This mold is not in the 1975 catalog or manual, but it is on the 1975 price list, under the heading "Stablemates—September 1st releases." So apparently it was released in 1975, but later in the year than the Stablemates that are listed in the catalog and manual. The mold has been out of circulation since 1989. When I asked *JAH* editor Stephanie Macejko about this in June 1995, she explained that the metal injection mold is damaged in such a way that the mares come out of the machine with a large plastic "growth" on their heads.

(2) This mold, unlike most other Stablemates molds, has a different name than it had when produced in ceramic by Hagen-Renaker, prior to production in plastic by Breyer. Hagen-Renaker called the mold Head Down Horse #428/61 (per Roller, Rose, and Berkwitz 1989, p. 52 and photo 124). Evidently, Hagen-Renaker did not produce a mini Quarter Horse mare, so Breyer recruited the Head Down Horse to be the partner of the Quarter Horse Stallion. Hagen-Renaker collector Sue Stewart noted that the H-R horse has male equipment, although the Breyer mold is a mare.

(3) Some models of the Quarter Horse Mare mold have no mold marks; I believe these stampless horses are the earliest models of the mold. Collectors Heather Wells, Sheryl Leisure, and others have stampless specimens of #5049 chestnut, which was made late 1975 - 1976 only. Next came models with "Breyer Molding Co. © 1976" stamped on the belly. This stamp, which has remained on the mold ever since, was apparently added late in 1976: collectors Nancy Kelly, Alison Lochwood, and Kim Lory Jones have stampless examples of dark bay #3085, whose first year of issue was 1976; but collector Jolie Devereux has a chestnut #5049 with the Breyer stamp, and collector Eleanor Harvey has a stamped buckskin #5050, which she got in the first year of issue (late 1975 - late 1976). A few years after the addition of the Breyer stamp, a "MEXICO" stamp was added to the mold, just above the Breyer stamp, sometime in the late 1970s. Many collectors own models with "MEXICO"—collector Therese Schuler, for example, has a "MEXICO" mare that she purchased around 1977-78. Nonetheless it is unlikely that any of these mares were in fact molded in Mexico, as I discuss in the Mold Stamps section in the Appendix near the end of this book. In any case it is virtually certain that the majority of "MEXICO"-stamp mares were made in the U.S., for the Breyer company's sojourn in Mexico was very brief, a matter of a few days, yet indisputable evidence indicates that the "MEXICO" stamp remained on the Quarter Horse Mare mold for several years: it was on her long enough to see the "B" stamp come and go. I have seen a palomino with "MEXICO" and "B" (in addition to the Breyer copyright stamp), and I have heard of a bay like this as well. These "B" mares would have been made sometime in the period 1979-83, the era of the "B" stamp for Breyers generally, after which time the "B" was removed from the mold. The "MEXICO" stamp evidently remained on the mold even after the removal of the "B": my palomino "MEXICO" mare with no "B" (purchased in 1995) came still sealed in her original packaging, which is an ordinary Stablemates blister-pack printed with "Reeves International, Inc." Since Reeves acquired Breyer Animal Creations late in 1984, my mare must have been packaged no earlier than 1985, which strongly suggests that she was molded no earlier than 1984 or 1985. I am not sure if the "MEXICO" stamp was removed before the QH Mare was discontinued at the end of 1988, but if it was, the last mares made, like those issued just before the "MEXICO" stamp, would have only the Breyer copyright stamp.

Quarter Horse Stallion — Pawing/walking, head up, looking right, tail flipped out behind. Sculpted by Maureen Love Calvert. Mold in catalog-run production late 1975 - 1988, 1995 - current as of 1996.

Catalog-run models made from this mold:

Quarter Horse Stallion #5045, palomino, solid or bald face, white mane and tail oversprayed with palomino, 4 or various stockings, gray hooves (late 1975 - 1988). Regarding release date, see note 1 for this mold. The stockings can be so vague as to disappear. The palomino color of this stallion varies from medium to light tan and to more orangy and yellow shades. My own old orangy-peach palomino with no mold stamp has a bald face. #5045 was issued for a year longer than his mate, the palomino QH Mare #5048.

Quarter Horse Stallion #5046, golden chestnut, solid face, darker chestnut mane and tail, 4 or various stockings, gray hooves (late 1975 - 1976). The body color is a medium to light golden-tan chestnut. This horse is shown in the 1976 catalog, which shows him with a distinct right hind stocking and vague stockings on the other legs. My own horse has no definite stockings. Regarding release date, see note 1 for this mold.

Quarter Horse Stallion #5047, buckskin, solid or bald face, black points, 4 or various stockings, gray or black hooves (late 1975 - 1987). Regarding release date, see note 1 for this mold. The stockings can be so vague as to disappear. The body color ranges from light yellowy and sandy shades to orangy buckskin to medium brown buckskin. Collector Liz Strauss has two bald-faced stallions, but solid face seems to be the norm. The number 5047 previously belonged to the Presentation Collection edition of Traditional "Man O' War" #47. #5047 was discontinued a year before his mate, the buckskin QH Mare #5050.

Quarter Horse Stallion #5186, light bay, solid face, black points, black hooves (1995 - current as of 1996). The model number is per the horse's packaging.

Set:

Stablemates Stable Set #3085, dark bay Quarter Horse Stallion, solid face, black points, no or various stockings, dark gray or black hooves (1976-78 only). The set as a whole was issued 1976-80, but in 1979-80 it had a dark bay "Seabiscuit" instead of the QH Stallion. All sets also came with a cardboard stable, dark bay Thoroughbred Lying and Standing Foals, and dark bay Quarter Horse Mare. This stallion comes in mahogany, plum, and red bay shades. The 1976 catalog (p. 5) shows the QH Stallion with blaze; this may be a test color model. His legs are not visible. The 1977-78 catalogs show only the box, which pictures the same QH Stallion with blaze. (The box shown in the 1976 catalog, p. 11, must have been a rejected prototype, for the boxtop pictures a "Swaps," Arabian Mare, and two Arabian Stallions.) The 1979-80 catalogs, which show the models themselves, show "Seabiscuit" instead of the QH Stallion. Since the QH Stallion himself is not shown in the 1977-78 catalogs, I can't say positively that "Seabiscuit" didn't replaced him before 1979, but it stands to reason that Breyer would show the new horse as soon as the switch was made. The model number 3085 previously belonged to "Diablo" The Mustang, Golden Charm decorator (Traditional scale).

Special-run models made from this mold:

Quarter Horse Stallion SR, medium chestnut, solid face, mane and tail same color as body, gray-shaded knees and hocks, 4 stockings, pale tan hooves (1995). Penney's holiday catalog. Sold in Set Of 12 Miniatures SR #710695. 10,600 sets made. The set number and quantity are per *JAH* editor Stephanie Macejko (conversations of Sept. 1995 and July 1996). For a complete list of this set, see Set Of 12 Miniatures SR. On my own Quarter Horse Stallion, the hooves are so faintly tan that they might more accurately be called white. This horse is a very un-yellow shade of chestnut, with an almost rosy cast.

Quarter Horse Stallion SR, red leopard appaloosa, white horse with red chestnut splashed-on spots, red chestnut mane and tail, gray muzzle and hooves (1992 and 1994). Sold through the 1992 Sears holiday catalog in Stablemate Assortment IV set #495092 and through the 1994 Penney's holiday catalog in Twelve-Piece Stablemates Set #711094. 4,500 of the Sears sets and 10,000 of the Penney's sets were made. (Quantity and set number for the Sears set are per a Breyer company computer printout of activity 1985-92; those for the Penney's set are per *JAH* editor Stephanie Macejko.) For a complete list of these sets, see Stablemate Assortment IV. The 1994 horses have glossed eyes; the 1992 horses do not.

Notes:

(1) This mold is not in the 1975 catalog or manual, but it is on the 1975 price list, under the heading "Stablemates—September 1st releases." So apparently it was released in 1975, but later in the year than the Stablemates that are listed in the catalog and manual.

(2) This mold was previously produced in ceramic by the Hagen-Renaker company as Quarter Horse Stallion #31 (see Roller, Rose, and Berkwitz 1989, p. 52).

(3) Some models of the Quarter Horse Stallion mold have no mold marks—collector Kim Jones has a stampless dark bay #3085, and I have stampless palimino #5045 and chestnut #5046. Since #5046 was issued only in 1975-76, my horse suggests that the stampless models were the earliest models of the mold. But the stamp must have been added to the mold just months later, for my other #5046 and one owned by collector Sheryl Leisure do have stamps. Some models have a "B" stamp in addition to the Breyer stamp.

Running Paint — see under "Seabiscuit"

Running Thoroughbred — see under "Seabiscuit"

Saddlebred — Racking, braid in mane, braided forelock. Sculpted by Maureen Love Calvert. Mold in catalog-run production 1975-90.

Catalog-run models made from this mold:

Saddlebred #5001, dapple gray, most with dapples on neck and head; bald or solid face; gray mane and tail same color as body or darker; 4 or various stockings; gray hooves (1975-76). The gray body color varies from dark to light. Some models have a lot of dark gray shading on the knees and hocks while others have virtually none. Collector Lori Ogozalek wrote to me that she has one dapple gray Saddlebred with bald face, as is shown in the 1975 catalog, and another with solid face. All four of collector Kim Jones's models, which I have seen in person, have bald or baldish faces. Collector Paula DeFeyter sent me a photo of her variant model with solid black lower legs and hooves, no stockings.

Saddlebred #5002, bay, solid face, black mane and tail, 4 or various stockings, gray hooves (1975-88). The color varies from a fairly light sandy bay to fairly dark red bay. Typically these horses have charcoal/black shading on the knees and hocks, but some models have only a whisper of grayish shading or no dark shading at all. The model in the 1975 catalog is sandy bay with dark joints and 4 vague stockings, but the model in the 1976 catalog is decidedly chestnut; see the next entry for this variation. In subsequent years the catalog models again look bay, the shade varying from lighter to darker. All catalogs seem to show at least a couple vague stockings. Collector Andrea Gurdon mentioned to me that #5002 comes in a chalky version; collector Kim Jones has one of these models, which I have seen in person. See Chalkies & Pearlies in the Appendix near the end of this book. Normally #5002, like other Stablemates, was sold in a blister packet, but the 1975 Sears holiday catalog offered him in a little white cardboard box printed with a line drawing of the Saddlebred mold. The printing on the box front says "Sears No. 2258 / Bay Saddlebred / Breyer Molding Company," with Breyer's Chicago address. The side flap says "Sears No. 2258 (Breyer No. 5002)." (Thanks to Sande Schneider for a photo of the box.)

• Saddlebred #5002, chestnut, bald face, mane and tail same chestnut as the body, 4 stockings, gray hooves (1975-76?). This model is actually a variation of #5002 bay in that it is labeled "#5002 bay" in the Breyer publications in which it appears, namely a 1975 Breyer Stablemates ad flier and the 1976 catalog and manual. But unlike typical

Breyer color variations, this one is a totally different color from what it is "supposed" to be—it has a fairly light tan chestnut body color and no black on it whatsoever. Hence I list it as a separate model. I am not sure, however, whether this chestnut horse was actually produced for sale. The only chestnut Saddlebred I know of in a collection is owned by Sandy Tomezik. Her horse, which she found at a flea market, has a solid face and is a more reddish-orange color than the tawny model shown in the Breyer catalog. So rather than a #5002 from the mid-1970s, Sandy's horse might conceivably be a relatively recent factory oddity or test—possibly a test for an SR of 1,000 chestnut Saddlebreds that was ordered by Hobby Center Toys but then canceled early in 1989 (per the Breyer company printout of activity 1985-92).

♞ Saddlebred #5110, black, no white markings, black mane and tail, gray hooves (1989-90). The model number is per the March 1989 Bentley Sales price list and the model's packaging. This horse was also sold through the 1989 Sears holiday catalog in Stablemate Assortment I set #495600. For a complete list of this set, see Stablemate Assortment I. Undoubtedly some #5110s have black or partially black hooves due to overspray.

Special-run models made from this mold:

Saddlebred SR, silver plated, no paint detailing (1975). Made for Breyer's Silver Anniversary. Probably about 1,000 models made, according to Breyer executive Peter Stone (conversation of Oct. 3, 1995). Stone also noted that these horses are made of a type of ABS plastic that can be electroplated, unlike Breyer's usual cellulose acetate. A company called B&P Electroplating plated the horses for Breyer, according to Stone (conversation of July 1995). The models were packaged in metallic-silver colored cardboard boxes containing purple-flocked molded inserts to cradle the horses. These Saddlebreds were not sold but given away as promotional items to Breyer's customers. One of these models is shown in *JAH* 17/#5 Nov./Dec. 1990 (pp. 16-17), along with a test-color Traditional "Man O' War" that was plated with sterling silver. The photo caption mentions no quantities but states: "On a number of occasions Breyer has contemplated augmenting its line with models such as this. For their Silver Anniversary, Breyer issued a limited edition #5002 Stablemates Saddlebred (see inset). The #5002s were not sold in stores, but rather were used as promotional pieces."

Notes:

(1) This mold has tiny ribbons molded into the mane, but to my knowledge they are not painted on any SR or regular-run model made from the mold. All the Saddlebreds I've seen have had ribbons the same color as the mane.

(2) This mold was previously produced in ceramic by the Hagen-Renaker company as American Saddlebred #458 (see Roller, Rose, and Berkwitz 1989, p. 51).

(3) In his presentation at the West Coast Model Horse Collector's Jamboree in August 1993, Breyer executive Peter Stone explained why this mold was discontinued. Most of the metal injection molds for the Stablemates have cavities for 2 horses (of 2 different shapes; for instance, the TB Lying and Standing Foal cavities are in the same metal injection mold, as I saw on a visit to the factory in November 1994), so that two horses can be molded at a time. The Saddlebred injection mold—the first Stablemate mold made by Breyer (per Stone, conversation of Nov. 1994)—is the only one that differs, having cavities for only one horse, so that only one can be molded at a time. This makes production of the Saddlebred more costly, since it takes as much time and energy to produce him one at a time as to produce the other horses two at a time, so the mold was taken out of production.

(4) Some models of the Saddlebred mold have no Breyer stamp or other mold mark—collector Sande Schneider has a dapple gray #5001 like this, and collector Kim Jones and I own stampless bay #5002s (Kim's is a chalky, mine is not). I believe these stampless horses are the earliest models of the mold. Later models have "Breyer Molding Co. © 1975" stamped on the belly. The stamp must have been put onto the mold within a year or so of the mold's debut, for the stamp is present on Kim's several #5001 dapple grays, and #5001 was issued only for two years, 1975-76. Some models have a "B" stamp as well as the Breyer stamp—collector Robin Briscoe has a #5002 bay with a "B."

Saddle Club Collection, Stablemates — The horses in this set as issued in 1994-95 are a dapple gray Arabian Mare; alabaster Draft Horse; medium reddish bay Morgan Stallion; red chestnut Running Thoroughbred (see under "Seabiscuit"); and black Thoroughbred Mare with no white markings. All five models were sold together in a boxed set called The Saddle Club Collection, Stablemates #5650. The name "Saddle Club" refers to the series of books by author Bonnie Bryant, published by Bantam, although these Stablemates models do not represent particular characters in the books. Near the end of 1995, all the models of the #5650 set were discontinued and replaced with new models, although the set's name and number remained the same. The new version of the set, which continues in production in 1996, is shown at the back of the 1996 Breyer catalog but does not appear at all in the 1996 collector's manual, which shows only the old version. The models in the new set (which appeared too late to be fully listed in this book) are a smoke gray Arabian Mare with charcoal/black points and various stockings (labeled simply "Arabian" on the set's packaging), sandy bay "Citation" mold (labeled "Thoroughbred"), chestnut pinto "Native Dancer" with blaze (labeled "Pinto"), dark seal brown "Silky Sullivan" with blaze (labeled "Appendix Quarter Horse"), and chestnut leopard appaloosa "Swaps" (labeled "Appaloosa"). For other Saddle Club horses by Breyer, see "Starlight" (under Jumping Horse) in the Traditionals section, and Saddle Club Collection and Saddle Club Series in the Little Bits section.

"Seabiscuit" — Galloping on left lead. Sculpted by Maureen Love Calvert. Mold in catalog-run production mid-1975 - current as of 1996.

Catalog-run models made from this mold:

♞ Running Paint #5179, chestnut pinto, overo; solid face; chestnut mane and tail same shade as body or slightly darker; 4 stockings; tan hooves (1995 - current as of 1996). The model name and number are per the horse's packaging. This horse has white pinto spots only on the barrel—one large spot on the left side and two smaller spots on the right. The basic body color is a medium/light chestnut with not much red tone.

♞ Running Thoroughbred #5025, black, no white markings, black mane and tail, gray hooves (pre-catalog release mid-1990, catalog run 1991-94). The model number is per the March 1991 Bentley Sales price list and the model's packaging. This model is not in the 1990 catalog, but it appeared in stores in mid-1990 according to Diederich 1988 (Section 3) and collector Gale Good. The horse is in the 1991 catalog, which doesn't say the model is new, though it obviously is new relative to the 1990 catalog. The hooves may be oversprayed black on some models.

♞ "Seabiscuit" #5024, dark bay, solid face, black points, no or various stockings, black or gray hooves (mid-1975 - 1990). Regarding release date, see note 2 for this mold. To my knowledge this model is the same as the "Seabiscuit" sold in the Stablemates Stable Set #3085 in 1979-80. Catalogs 1976-79 show #5024 as dark bay with no white markings, though the Stable Set horse is shown with 1 right hind stocking in 1979. In the 1980 catalog, 3-4 vague stockings appear on both #5024 and the Stable Set horse. The stockings fade in and out in the following years' catalogs, and are vaguely present in 1988-90. My own model has 4 stockings and gray hooves; collector Kim Jones has a couple of #5024s with solid black legs and hooves and a couple others with one or two vague stockings and black hooves. Kim also has a model that is not bay but liver chestnut, with dark brown mane and tail, gray-shaded knees and hocks, and 4 vague stockings. The real "Seabiscuit" was a famous race horse.

Sets:

♞ Saddle Club Collection, Stablemates #5650, red chestnut Running Thoroughbred, solid face, mane and tail same color as body or slightly darker, 4 stockings, gray hooves (1994-95). For a complete list of this set and a discussion of the change of models in late 1995, see Saddle Club Collection. The set is named for the Saddle Club series of books by author Bonnie Bryant, but the horses in the set do not represent particular characters in the books. The stockings on this red chestnut horse can be vague. The box in which the set is packaged labels this horse "Running Thoroughbred."

• Stablemates Stable Set #3085, with dark bay "Seabiscuit," solid face, black points, various stockings (1979-80 only). The set as a whole was issued 1976-80, but in 1976-78 it had a dark bay Quarter Horse Stallion instead of "Seabiscuit" (see under Quarter Horse Stallion for discussion). All sets also came with dark bay Thoroughbred Lying and Standing Foals, dark bay Quarter Horse Mare, and cardboard stable. The "Seabiscuit" in this set is essentially the same model as "Seabiscuit" #5024, to judge from catalog photos. See the entry for #5024 for discussion of stockings. The model number 3085 previously belonged to "Diablo" The Mustang, Golden Charm decorator (Traditional-scale Mustang mold).

Special-run models made from this mold:

"Seabiscuit" SR, alabaster, gray points and hooves (1992 and 1994). Sold through the 1992 Sears holiday catalog in Stablemate Assortment IV set #495092 and through the 1994 Penney's holiday catalog in Twelve-Piece Stablemates Set #711094. 4,500 of the Sears sets and 10,000 of the Penney's sets were made. (Quantity and set number for the Sears set are per a Breyer company computer printout of activity 1985-92; those for the Penney's set are per *JAH* editor Stephanie Macejko.) For a complete list of these sets, see Stablemate Assortment IV. The 1994 horses have glossed eyes; the 1992 horses do not.

"Seabiscuit" SR, dapple gray, dapples on neck and head; solid or slightly dappled face; black/charcoal points and hooves (1991). Sears holiday catalog. Sold in Stablemate Assortment III set SR #495091. 4,400 sets made. For a complete list of this set, see Stablemate Assortment III. Quantity and set number are per a Breyer company computer printout of activity 1985-92.

"Seabiscuit" SR, palomino, mane and tail oversprayed with palomino, no white markings, gray hooves (1990). Sears holiday catalog. Sold in Stablemate Assortment II set SR #495601. 5,000 sets made. For a complete list of this set, see Stablemate Assortment II. Quantity and set number are per a Breyer company computer printout of activity 1985-92. This horse is quite a bright yellow or orangy color.

"Seabiscuit" SR, red chestnut, no white markings, darker chestnut mane and tail, reddish-gray hooves (1989). Sears holiday catalog. Sold in Stablemate Assortment I set #495600. 4,500 sets made. For a complete list of this set, see Stablemate Assortment I. Quantity and set number are per a Breyer company computer printout of activity 1985-92.

Notes:

(1) The Hagen-Renaker company mini mold of which this Stablemate is a copy was produced by H-R under the name "Seabiscuit" (with the model number 10; see Roller, Rose, and Berkwitz 1989, p. 52). Breyer introduced its copy under the same name but renamed the mold Running Thoroughbred when the original "Seabiscuit" color was discontinued. Except in size, the "Seabiscuit" mold is nearly identical to the Little Bits Thoroughbred Stallion, which debuted many years later.

(2) This mold is not in the 1975 catalog or manual, but it is on the 1975 price list, under the heading "Stablemates—May 1st releases." So apparently it was released in 1975, but later in the year than the Stablemates listed in the catalog and manual.

(3) On the back cover of the 1994-95 catalogs there appears a model of the "Seabiscuit" mold that is painted differently from any regular run or SR "Seabiscuit" known to me. He is a medium reddish-sandy bay with a crisp right hind stocking and tan hoof, other legs and hooves black. Perhaps he is a test piece; whether such horses were produced for sale I don't know.

(4) The "Seabiscuit" mold has "Breyer Molding Co. © 1975" stamped on the belly. Some models might have a "B" stamp as well, but I'm not sure.

Set of 12 Miniatures SR #710695 (1995) — see Arabian Mare SR, semi-leopard appaloosa; Arabian Stallion SR, light dusky chestnut; "Citation" (Standing Thoroughbred) SR, brown dun blanket appaloosa; "Citation" SR, dappled gray dun; Morgan Mare SR, chestnut with pale mane and tail; Morgan Stallion SR, black with striped mane and tail; "Native Dancer" SR, medium bay; Quarter Horse Stallion SR, medium chestnut; "Silky Sullivan" SR, dark grulla; "Silky Sullivan" SR, pale rose gray; "Swaps" SR, grulla; Thoroughbred Mare SR, dark brown. In the sets I know of, all the horses have glossed eyes and a small gold oval "Made in China" sticker on the belly.

"Silky Sullivan" — Standing, bottom of tail swung out. Sculpted by Maureen Love Calvert. Mold in catalog-run production mid-1975 - current as of 1996.

Catalog-run models made from this mold:

♞ "Silky Sullivan" #5022, dark/medium chestnut; solid face; darker chestnut mane and tail; no or various stockings; stockinged legs have gray or black hooves, other hooves dark gray-chestnut or black (mid-1975 - 1994). Regarding release date, see note 1 for this mold. The 1976 catalog and manual switched the labels for the "Silky Sullivan" and "Swaps" models, but I don't know whether the models were packaged and sold under the wrong names too. "Silky Sullivan" is shown with no stockings in the 1976-79 catalogs. In 1980-90, various vague stockings, typically 4, appear now and again. In 1991-94, the horse is shown with 1 crisp left front stocking; I got such a model new in October 1994. The chestnut color often has a rosy or plum cast but varies to brown shades. *Quequechan Model Horse Collector* of January 1985 shows a picture of a bay variation of "Silky Sullivan," of which "about 50 were made," according to the caption (no source is cited for the quantity). Cary 1994 also reports having found "Silky Sullivans" with black mane and tail. The real "Silky Sullivan" was a famous race horse.

♞ Thoroughbred Racehorse #5177, black, no white markings, gray hooves (1995 - current as of 1996). The model name and number are per the horse's packaging. The hooves may be oversprayed with black on some models. Some models may have an inadvertent sock or two where the black of the legs has not been brought all the way down to the tops of the hooves.

Special-run models made from this mold:

- "Silky Sullivan" SR, buckskin, no white markings, black points, black hooves (1989). Sears holiday catalog. Sold in Stablemate Assortment I set #495600. 4,500 sets made. For a complete list of this set, see Stablemate Assortment I. Quantity and set number are per a Breyer company computer printout of activity 1985-92. Collector Heather Wells's horse is a quite pale peachy tone rather than the yellowish tone of a normal buckskin. The photo in the Sears catalog shows a darker buckskin horse.
- "Silky Sullivan" SR, dark grulla, dark brown head with solid face, charcoal points, 4 vague stockings, peach-tan hooves (1995). Penney's holiday catalog. Sold in Set Of 12 Miniatures SR #710695. 10,600 sets made. The set number and quantity are per *JAH* editor Stephanie Macejko (conversations of Sept. 1995 and July 1996). For a complete list of this set, see Set Of 12 Miniatures SR.
- "Silky Sullivan" SR, pale rose gray, white horse with faint tan shading; mane and tail striped light tan and pale gray; tan-gray shaded knees and hocks; tan-gray hooves (1995). Penney's holiday catalog. Sold in Set Of 12 Miniatures SR #710695. 10,600 sets made. The set number and quantity are per *JAH* editor Stephanie Macejko (conversations of Sept. 1995 and July 1996). For a complete list of this set, see Set Of 12 Miniatures SR.
- "Silky Sullivan" SR, reddish bay, solid face, charcoal/black points, 2 hind stockings with gray or black hooves, front hooves black (1991). Sears holiday catalog. Sold in Stablemate Assortment III set SR #495091. 4,400 sets made. For a complete list of this set, see Stablemate Assortment III. Quantity and set number are per a Breyer company computer printout of activity 1985-92. Collector Heather Wells's horse has brownish-charcoal mane, tail, front legs, and hocks; my own horse is a truer black in these areas.
- "Silky Sullivan" SR, reddish dun/chestnut, solid face, dark chestnut-gray mane and tail, gray-shaded knees, no dark shading on hind legs, 4 stockings, gray hooves (1990). Sears holiday catalog. Sold in Stablemate Assortment II set SR #495601. 5,000 sets made. For a complete list of this set, see Stablemate Assortment II. Quantity and set number are per a Breyer company computer printout of activity 1985-92.) My own model is quite an orangy dun, while collector Heather Wells's horse is a bit more brownish/sandy chestnut.
- "Silky Sullivan" SR, rose gray, no dapples; solid face; dark gray points; 1 vague left hind stocking with gray hoof; other hooves dark gray (1992 and 1994). Sold through the 1992 Sears holiday catalog in Stablemate Assortment IV set #495092 and through the 1994 Penney's holiday catalog in Twelve-Piece Stablemates Set #711094. 4,500 of the Sears sets and 10,000 of the Penney's sets were made. (Quantity and set number for the Sears set are per a Breyer company computer printout of activity 1985-92; those for the Penney's set are per *JAH* editor Stephanie Macejko.) For a complete list of these sets, see Stablemate Assortment IV. The 1994 horses have glossed eyes; the 1992 horses do not. In my own sets, the 1992 horse is lighter than the 1994 horse.

Notes:

(1) This mold is not in the 1975 catalog or manual, but it is on the 1975 price list, under the heading "Stablemates—May 1st releases." So apparently it was released in 1975, but later in the year than the Stablemates listed in the catalog and manual.

(2) The Hagen-Renaker company mini mold of which this Stablemate is a copy was produced by H-R under the name "Silky Sullivan" (with the model number 30; see Roller, Rose, and Berkwitz 1989, p. 52). Breyer introduced its copy under the same name but renamed the mold Thoroughbred Racehorse when the original "Silky Sullivan" color was discontinued.

(3) The "Silky Sullivan" mold has "Breyer Molding Co. © 1975" stamped on the belly. Some models have a "B" stamp as well—collector Chelle Fulk has a #5022 like this.

Stablemate Assortment I set #495600 (1989) — Only five of the horses in this set are SRs; seven are simply then-current regular runs, as is evident not only from their colors but also from a Breyer company computer printout of activity 1985-92, which lists the seven as "reg. item." See Arabian Mare #5017 and #5130, alabaster; Arabian Stallion #5120, steel gray; "Citation" (Standing Thoroughbred) SR, red roan; Draft Horse #5180, dapple gray; Morgan Mare #5160, palomino; Morgan Stallion #5150, medium chestnut / red dun; "Native Dancer" SR, red bay; Saddlebred #5110, black; "Seabiscuit" (Running Thoroughbred) SR, red chestnut; "Silky Sullivan" SR, buckskin; "Swaps" SR, blue roan; Thoroughbred Mare #5140, dark/medium bay. In the sets I've seen, the horses have glossed eyes.

Stablemate Assortment II SR #495601 (1990) — see Arabian Mare SR, black; Arabian Stallion SR, buckskin; "Citation" (Standing Thoroughbred) SR, dusty chestnut / olive dun; Draft Horse SR, black with no white markings; Morgan Mare SR, chestnut; Morgan Stallion SR, dark red chestnut; "Native Dancer" SR, white charcoal points; "Seabiscuit" (Running Thoroughbred) SR, palomino; "Silky Sullivan" SR, reddish dun/chestnut; "Swaps" SR, pale rose gray; "Swaps" SR, steel gray; Thoroughbred Mare SR, red bay. In the sets I've seen and heard reports of, the horses have unglossed eyes.

Stablemate Assortment III SR #495091 (1991) — see Arabian Mare SR, chestnut; Arabian Stallion SR, black; "Citation" (Standing Thoroughbred) SR, steel gray; Draft Horse SR, medium/light bay; Draft Horse SR, yellow-olive dun; Morgan Mare SR, reddish bay; Morgan Stallion SR, palomino; "Native Dancer" SR, palomino; "Seabiscuit" (Running Thoroughbred) SR, dapple gray; "Silky Sullivan" SR, reddish bay; "Swaps" SR, dark liver chestnut; Thoroughbred Mare SR, alabaster. In the sets I've seen, all the horses have unglossed eyes except for the black Arab Stallion, which has glossed eyes.

Stablemate Assortment IV SR #495092 (1992) and Twelve-Piece Stablemates Set SR #711094 (1994) — The 1994 set is a reissue of the 1992 set; the test-run samples created for the 1992 set were used again for the 1994 set, according to Breyer executive Peter Stone (conversation of Nov. 1994). The only systematic difference between the two sets in my experience is that the 1994 horses have glossed eyes whereas the 1992 horses do not. See Arabian Mare SR, steel gray; Arabian Stallion SR, dappled red chestnut; "Citation" (Standing Thoroughbred) SR, dapple gray; Draft Horse SR, buckskin; Morgan Mare SR, chocolate sorrel; Morgan Stallion SR, black blanket appaloosa; Morgan Stallion SR, seal brown; "Native Dancer" SR, black; Quarter Horse Stallion SR, red leopard appaloosa; "Seabiscuit" (Running Thoroughbred) SR, alabaster; "Silky Sullivan" SR, rose gray; "Swaps" SR, buckskin.

Stablemate assortment (1995) — see Set Of 12 Miniatures SR

Stablemates Stable Set — see under Quarter Horse Stallion; Quarter Horse Mare; "Seabiscuit"; Thoroughbred Lying Foal; and Thoroughbred Standing Foal

Standing and Lying Foals — see Thoroughbred Standing Foal; Thoroughbred Lying Foal

Standing Thoroughbred — see under "Citation"

"Swaps" — Standing, head up, looking right, left hind leg forward, tail attached to right buttock and leg. Sculpted by Maureen Love Calvert. Mold in catalog-run production mid-1975 - current as of 1996.

Catalog-run models made from this mold:

- "Swaps" #5021, chestnut, solid face, slightly darker chestnut mane and tail, most with 1 right hind stocking with gray hoof, other hooves dark chestnut-gray (mid-1975 - 1994). Regarding release date, see note 3 for this mold. The 1976 catalog and manual switched the labels for the "Swaps" and "Silky Sullivan" models; I don't know whether the models were actually packaged and sold under the wrong names too. The body color varies from dark to medium and from a rich brown to a pinkish or plum chestnut. The stocking can be so vague as to disappear, leaving the model with 4 solid legs. Such no-white specimens, especially if they have a plum body shade and are made of ABS plastic, may be difficult to distinguish from Thoroughbred Racehorse #5176, which has no white markings and is always made of ABS plastic (see the General Note at the start of the Stablemates section). But even a no-white "Swaps" may have at least a slight lightening on the right hind leg and should have a less red, more brown or pinky/plum body color than #5176. Some "Swaps" models have more than 1 stocking; I have an early "Swaps" with 2 stockings (right hind and left front), and a later "Swaps" (purchased new in 1989) with 4 stockings, albeit some of them vague. Collector Kim Jones has a model with 2 hind stockings.
- Thoroughbred Racehorse #5176, red chestnut, no white markings, slightly darker chestnut mane and tail, chestnut-charcoal hooves (1995 - current as of 1996). The model name and number are per the horse's packaging. This model is a dark to medium color which may be hard to distinguish from some "Swaps" models; see the entry for #5021 for discussion.

Special-run models made from this mold:

- "Swaps" SR, blue roan, white horse with gray flecks, black points, black hooves (1989). Sears holiday catalog. Sold in Stablemate Assortment I set #495600. 4,500 sets made. For a complete list of this set, see Stablemate Assortment I. Quantity and set number are per a Breyer company computer printout of activity 1985-92.
- "Swaps" SR, buckskin, solid face, gray points and hooves (1992 and 1994). Sold through the 1992 Sears holiday catalog in Stablemate Assortment IV set #495092 and through the 1994 Penney's holiday catalog in Twelve-Piece Stablemates Set #711094. 4,500 of the Sears sets and 10,000 of the Penney's sets were made. (Quantity and set number for the Sears set are per a Breyer company computer printout of activity 1985-92; those for the Penney's set are per *JAH* editor Stephanie Macejko.) For a complete list of these sets, see Stablemate Assortment IV. The 1994 horses have glossed eyes; the 1992 horses do not.
- "Swaps" SR, dark liver chestnut, solid face, liver-charcoal mane and tail, 2 front stockings with gray hooves, hind hooves liver-charcoal (1991). Sears holiday catalog. Sold in Stablemate Assortment III set SR #495091. 4,400 sets made. For a complete list of this set, see Stablemate Assortment III. Quantity and set number are per a Breyer company computer printout of activity 1985-92. This model is very dark, and the mane and tail are nearly black. Heather Wells's horse has charcoal-shaded knees and hocks and thus might be called a very dark bay. My own horse lacks this shading.
- "Swaps" SR, grulla, gray horse with dark brown head, back, chest, and belly; solid face; charcoal-brown points; light brown fetlocks, pasterns, and hooves (1995). Penney's holiday catalog. Sold in Set Of 12 Miniatures SR #710695. 10,600 sets made. The set number and quantity are per *JAH* editor Stephanie Macejko (conversations of Sept. 1995 and July 1996). For a complete list of this set, see Set Of 12 Miniatures SR. Possibly this horse was intended to have white stockings and light brown hooves, but my own specimen has light brown "stockings."
- "Swaps" SR, pale rose gray, no dapples, medium gray mane and tail, no white markings, gray hooves (1990). Sears holiday catalog. Sold in Stablemate Assortment II set SR #495601. 5,000 sets made. For a complete list of this set, see Stablemate Assortment II. Quantity and set number are per a Breyer company computer printout of activity 1985-92. This horse is very pale, a peachy-cream shade.
- "Swaps" SR, steel gray, charcoal points and hooves, no white (1990). Sears holiday catalog. Sold in Stablemate Assortment II set SR #495601. 5,000 sets made. For a complete list of this set, see Stablemate Assortment II. Quantity and set number are per a Breyer company computer printout of activity 1985-92.

Notes:

(1) This mold is nearly identical to the Classic "Swaps" mold except in size. Before being issued in plastic by Breyer, both sizes were produced in ceramic by Hagen-Renaker. H-R issued the mini size as "Swaps" #457 (see Roller, Rose, and Berkwitz 1989, p. 52 and photo 333). Breyer introduced its Stablemate copy under the same name but renamed the mold Thoroughbred Racehorse when the original "Swaps" color was discontinued.

(2) Collector Lori Ogozalek pointed out to me that a few "Swaps" models have a space between the tail and the leg above the area where the tail tip joins the leg. The models she has seen with the space have all been older ones; my own older model too has the space. On many models of this mold, the area is filled in with excess plastic.

(3) This mold is not in the 1975 catalog or manual, but it is on the 1975 price list, under the heading "Stablemates—May 1st releases." So apparently it was released in 1975, but later in the year than the Stablemates listed in the catalog and manual.

(4) Regarding a possible SR black "Swaps" from the 1970s, see note 3 for the Arabian Stallion mold.

(5) The "Swaps" mold has "Breyer Molding Co. © 1975" stamped on the belly. Some models have a "B" stamp as well.

Thoroughbred Lying Foal — Lying on belly, head raised. Sculpted by Maureen Love Calvert. Mold in catalog-run production 1975-80.

Catalog-run models made from this mold:

- Stablemates Stable Set #3085, dark bay Lying Foal, solid face, black mane and tail, no black on the legs, no or various stockings, gray or black hooves (1976-80). Set also includes a cardboard stable, dark bay TB Standing Foal, dark bay Quarter Horese Mare, and either a dark bay Quarter Horse Stallion [1976-78 only] or a dark bay "Seabiscuit" [1979-80 only]. The color of the Lying and Standing Foals varies from dark to medium mahogany, plum, and red bay shades. The 1976 catalog (p. 5) shows both foals with blaze and hind stockings. I have seen one Lying Foal like this, which also had black mane, tail, and hooves. The 1977-78 catalogs show only the box, which pictures the same foals with blazes. (The box shown in the 1976 catalog, p. 11, must have been a rejected prototype, for the boxtop pictures a "Swaps," Arabian Mare, and two Arabian Stallions.) The 1979-80 catalogs, which show the models themselves, show the foals with no white markings; my own Lying Foal is like this. The model number 3085 previously belonged to "Diablo" The Mustang, Golden Charm decorator (Traditional-scale Mustang mold).

- Thoroughbred Lying and Standing Foals set #5700, sandy bay Lying Foal; solid face; black mane and tail; no black on the legs; some with 2 hind stockings, some with no stockings; gray/charcoal hooves (1975-76). The Standing Foal in this set is also sandy bay.
- Thoroughbred Lying and Standing Foals set #5701, black Lying Foal; solid face; black mane and tail; some with 2 hind stockings, some with no stockings; black or gray hooves (1975-76). The Standing Foal in this set is also black. These foals are cast in white plastic and painted black, unlike the SR black keychain foals, which are solid black plastic. The #5701 Lying and Standing foals are shown in the 1975 catalog with bald face, but these might be test colors. In a 1975 Stablemates ad flier from Breyer, they have solid faces, as do the foals in Diederich 1988 (Section 3) and *Breyer Collector's Video*.
- Thoroughbred Lying and Standing Foals set #5702, chestnut Lying Foal; solid face; slightly darker or lighter chestnut mane and tail; some with 2 hind stockings, some with no stockings; gray hooves (1975-76). The Standing Foal in this set is also chestnut. The color varies from a medium chestnut to light reddish dun. Collector Heather Wells has a set of the dun foals in original packaging.

Special-run models made from this mold:

- Keychain Thoroughbred Lying Foal SR #411494, black, solid, no paint detailing; on gold-tone metal keychain with oblong metal tag bearing the "Breyer" cartouche logo (1994). Made for BreyerFest 1994, in Lexington, Kentucky. 250 models made. Three other SR Stablemate foals on identical keychains were also sold at BreyerFest 1994: Thoroughbred Lying and Standing Foals in transparent amber plastic and a TB Standing Foal in solid black. 250 foals of each of the 4 styles were made, for a total of 1,000 keychain foals, per Breyer executive Peter Stone in his discussion session at this BreyerFest. (The same quantity is reported in *JAH* 21/#4 Fall 1994, inside front cover. The model numbers for the foals are per *JAH* editor Stephanie Macejko, conversation of June 1995.) Stone also stated that these foals were made in the Breyer factory in Wayne, New Jersey, not in China, where most of the Stablemates models have been made since 1992 (see General Note at the start of the Stablemates section). After BreyerFest, some keychain foals were sold by model mail-order companies; Stone told me that these were leftovers from BreyerFest and that no new foals were produced after the initial 1,000 (conversation of Nov. 1994). Unlike the black regular-run foals, which are white plastic painted black, the black keychain foals are cast in black opaque plastic. The plastic of the keychain specials, both black and transparent amber, is cellulose acetate (per the *JAH* cited above), like the plastic of normal Breyers. However, whereas normal Breyers are made of opaque white cellulose acetate, the keychain foals were cast from a colorless transparent cellulose acetate to which color—amber and black—was added, according to Stephanie Macejko (conversation of March 1995). Stephanie noted that Breyer molded many experimental foals (which are now in storage) before achieving nicely colored ones, and that the black foals were made only after experiments with blue coloring failed to produce good-looking models. The hope had been to make foals of blue and yellow, matching the colors of the Breyer logo. The metal keychains are attached to the models by small metal screw eyes screwed into the foals' backs. The foals have the usual Breyer copyright stamps on the belly (see the notes for these two molds).
- Keychain Thoroughbred Lying Foal SR #411694, transparent amber, no paint detailing; on gold-tone metal keychain with oblong metal tag bearing the "Breyer" cartouche logo (1994). Made for BreyerFest 1994, in Lexington, Kentucky. 250 models made. See Keychain Thoroughbred Lying Foal SR black for discussion.

Notes:

(1) This mold, unlike most other Stablemates molds, has a different name than it had when produced in ceramic by Hagen-Renaker, prior to production in plastic by Breyer. H-R called this mold "Arab Foal lying" (with the model number 49; see to Roller, Rose, and Berkwitz 1989, p. 50). H-R did call the standing foal a Thoroughbred, however. These two foal molds are Breyer's tiniest molds.

(2) Some models of the Thoroughbred Lying Foal mold have no Breyer stamp or other mold marks (I have one like this); I believe these are the earliest ones. Others have a tiny "Breyer Molding Co. © 1975" stamp on the belly.

Thoroughbred Mare — Standing/walking, looking right, neck stretched, tail tip attached to left hock. Sculpted by Maureen Love Calvert. Mold in catalog-run production 1975 - current as of 1996.

Catalog-run models made from this mold:

- Thoroughbred Mare #5026, golden chestnut, solid face, darker chestnut mane and tail, 4 or various stockings, gray or black hooves (1975-87). #5026 is shown in a group photo in the 1975 catalog, where she has 4 clear stockings; catalogs thereafter show her with one or two clear stockings. My own mares and collector Elaine Hoffman's have gray hooves, but collector Kim Jones has one with black hooves.
- Thoroughbred Mare #5028, black, solid face, black mane and tail, 4 or various stockings, most with 4 dark gray or black hooves (1975-88). In the 1975 catalog this mare has 4 crisp stockings, but in later catalogs through 1987 the stockings are vague and various. My own mare has 4 stockings with dark gray hooves; collector Kim Jones has a mare with 2 hind stockings with black hooves and another with 1 left hind stocking with a black hoof. Kim also has a mare with 1 left hind stocking with a pink hoof (other hooves black); this version is shown only in the 1988 catalog. Buchanan 1994 reports a variation with two hind stockings with pink hooves.
- Thoroughbred Mare #5030, medium bay, solid face, charcoal/black points, 4 or various stockings, gray or black hooves (1975-88). This mare's stockings can be so vague and oversprayed as to disappear; one of my own mares has charcoal gray lower legs and hooves, no stockings at all. The color varies from a fairly dark brown bay to medium reddish and sandy bays. The darker mares are very similar to the #5140 dark/medium bay mares except for number of stockings. Also, on #5030, the hooves on dark legs are typically the same dark color as the legs, but on #5140, the hooves are typically lighter than the black legs. The 1975 Sears holiday catalog offered the #5030 mare in a "Miniature Family" set with regular-run sandy bay Thoroughbred Standing Foal (#5700) and regular-run bay Arabian Stallion (called "Citation" #5020 at that time). The set came in a cute little white cardboard box printed with line drawings of the three molds. The printing on the box front says "Sears No. 20263 / Bay Thoroughbred Mare / 'Citation' Famous Thoroughbred / Bay Thoroughbred Foal / Breyer Molding Company," with Breyer's Chicago address. The side flap says "Sears No. 20263 (Breyer No. 5670)." (Thanks to Sande Schneider for a photo of the box.)
- Thoroughbred Mare #5140, dark/medium bay, solid face, black points, 1 left hind stocking, 4 gray or tannish-gray hooves (1989-90). The model number is per a March 1989 Bentley Sales price list and the model's packaging. This horse was also sold through the 1989 Sears holiday catalog in Stablemate Assortment I set #495600. For a complete list of this set, see Stablemate Assortment I. For differences from #5030, see that entry.
- Thoroughbred Mare #5141, medium chestnut, solid face, darker chestnut mane and tail, 4 or various stockings, chestnut or tan hooves (1991-94). The model number is per the March 1991 Bentley Sales price list and the model's packaging. The 1991 catalog and manual do not say this model is new, but she clearly is—she has a different color and model number from the TB Mare in the 1990 catalog (#5140 dark/medium bay). In the 1991-92 catalogs this chestnut mare has 4 stockings and chestnut hooves that match the body color, and my own model (made of ABS plastic) is like this. But collector Robin Briscoe's 4-stocking mare has tan hooves, much lighter than the body; this version is also reported in Buchanan 1994. In the 1993-94 catalogs the mare has only 1 stocking (left hind) and 4 chestnut hooves. I also have a cellulose acetate mare with 2 hind stockings (one is vague) and 4 chestnut hooves. For the #5141 mare in set with "Jessica" doll, see Götz "Jessica" Doll With Stablemates above in this section.
- Thoroughbred Mare #5183, steel gray, solid face, darker gray mane and tail, 4 stockings, dark gray hooves (1995 - current as of 1996). The model number is per the horse's packaging.

Set:

- Saddle Club Collection, Stablemates #5650, black Thoroughbred Mare, no white markings, black mane and tail, black hooves (1994-95). For a complete list of this set and a discussion of the change of models in late 1995, see Saddle Club Collection. The set is named for the Saddle Club series of books by author Bonnie Bryant, but the horses in the set do not represent particular characters in the books. In the 1994 catalog this black mare appears to have gray hooves, but my own model and others I've seen have black hooves.

Special-run models made from this mold:

- Thoroughbred Mare SR, alabaster, gray points and hooves (1991). Sears holiday catalog. Sold in Stablemate Assortment III set SR #495091. 4,400 sets made. For a complete list of this set, see Stablemate Assortment III. Quantity and set number are per a Breyer company computer printout of activity 1985-92.
- Thoroughbred Mare SR, dark brown, solid face, brownish-charcoal points, 4 stockings, tan hooves (1995). Penney's holiday catalog. Sold in Set Of 12 Miniatures SR #710695. 10,600 sets made. The set number and quantity are per *JAH* editor Stephanie Macejko (conversations of Sept. 1995 and July 1996). For a complete list of this set, see Set Of 12 Miniatures SR.
- Thoroughbred Mare SR, red bay, no white markings, black points, black hooves (1990). Sears holiday catalog. Sold in Stablemate Assortment II set SR #495601. 5,000 sets made. For a complete list of this set, see Stablemate Assortment II. Quantity and set number are per a Breyer company computer printout of activity 1985-92. Collector Heather Wells's mare is a very red.

Notes:

(1) This mold was previously produced in ceramic by the Hagen-Renaker company as Thoroughbred Mare #24 (see Roller, Rose, and Berkwitz 1989, p. 52).

(2) Nearly all models of the Thoroughbred Mare mold have "Breyer Molding Co. © 1975" stamped on the belly. The only specimen I know of that lacks this copyright stamp is a #5030 bay purchased used by collector Lisa Heino, who kindly sent me photos of the horse. The horse's belly is completely smooth, so evidently the model was molded without the stamp and did not simply have it smeared in the molding process, as sometimes happens (smeared stamps can look like nothing but a few vague lumps). Lisa's mare could be one of the earliest models of the mold, indicating that the mold was stampless when it debuted in 1975 and had the stamp added sometime thereafter. Some models of this mold might have a "B" stamp in addition to the copyright, but I'm not sure.

Thoroughbred Racehorse — see under "Silky Sullivan" and under "Swaps"

Thoroughbred Standing Foal — Looking left. Sculpted by Maureen Love Calvert. Mold in catalog-run production 1975-80.

Catalog-run models made from this mold:

- Stablemates Stable Set #3085, dark bay Standing Foal, solid face, black mane and tail, no black on the legs, no or various stockings, gray or black hooves (1976-80). Set also includes a cardboard stable, dark bay TB Lying Foal, dark bay Quarter Horse Mare, and either dark bay Quarter Horse Stallion [1976-78 only] or dark bay "Seabiscuit" [1979-80 only]. These Standing and Lying Foals come in mahogany, plum, and red bay shades. The 1976 catalog (p. 5) shows both foals with blaze and hind stockings. I have not seen a Standing Foal with a blaze, although I have seen one Lying Foal with blaze. The 1977-78 catalogs show only the box, which pictures the same foals with blazes. (The box shown in the 1976 catalog, p. 11, must have been a rejected prototype, for the boxtop pictures a "Swaps," Arabian Mare, and two Arabian Stallions.) The 1979-80 catalogs, which show the models themselves, show them with no white markings. However, my own Standing Foal has 2 hind stockings, and collector Kim Jones has a couple of foals with 4 stockings. The model number 3085 previously belonged to "Diablo" The Mustang, Golden Charm decorator (Traditional-scale Mustang mold).
- Thoroughbred Lying and Standing Foals set #5700, sandy bay Standing Foal; solid face; black mane and tail; no black on the legs; some with 2 hind stockings, some with 4 stockings; gray/charcoal hooves (1975-76). The Lying Foal in this set is also sandy bay. The 1975 Sears holiday catalog offered this bay Standing Foal in a "Miniature Family" set with regular-run bay Thoroughbred Mare (#5030) and regular-run bay Arabian Stallion (called "Citation" #5020 at that time). The set came in a cute little white cardboard box printed with line drawings of the three molds. The printing on the box front says "Sears No. 20263 / Bay Thoroughbred Mare / 'Citation' Famous Thoroughbred / Bay Thoroughbred Foal / Breyer Molding Company," with Breyer's Chicago address. The side flap says "Sears No. 20263 (Breyer No. 5670)." (Thanks to Sande Schneider for a photo of the box.)
- Thoroughbred Lying and Standing Foals set #5701, black Standing Foal; solid face; black mane and tail; some with 4 stockings, some with no stockings; black or gray hooves (1975-76). The Lying Foal in this set is also black. For discussion see Thoroughbred Lying and Standing Foals set #5701, under Lying Foal.
- Thoroughbred Lying and Standing Foals set #5702, chestnut Standing Foal; solid face; slightly darker or lighter chestnut mane and tail; some with 2 hind stockings, some with 4 stockings; gray hooves (1975-76). The Lying Foal in this set is also chestnut. The color varies from a medium chestnut to light reddish dun. Collector Heather Wells has a set of the dun foals in original packaging.

Special-run models made from this mold:

- Keychain Thoroughbred Standing Foal SR #411394, black, solid, no paint detailing; on gold-tone metal keychain with oblong metal tag bearing the "Breyer" cartouche logo (1994). Made for BreyerFest 1994, in Lexington, Kentucky. 250 models made. See Keychain Thoroughbred Lying Foal SR black for discussion.

🔑 Keychain Thoroughbred Standing Foal SR #411594, transparent amber, no paint detailing; on gold-tone metal keychain oblong metal tag bearing the "Breyer" cartouche logo (1994). Made for BreyerFest 1994, in Lexington, Kentucky. 250 models made. See Keychain Thoroughbred Lying Foal SR black for discussion.

Notes:

(1) This mold and the TB Lying Foal are Breyer's tiniest molds. The TB Standing Foal mold was previously produced in ceramic by the Hagen-Renaker company as Thoroughbred Foal #25 (see Roller, Rose, and Berkwitz 1989, p. 52).

(2) Some models of the Thoroughbred Standing Foal mold have no Breyer stamp or other mold marks (collector Kim Jones has black #5701 and chestnut #5702 Standing Foals like this); I believe these are the earliest ones. Others have a tiny "Breyer Molding Co. © 1975" stamp on the belly.

Twelve-Piece Stablemates Set SR (1994) — see Stablemate Assortment IV SR

Dapples

GENERAL NOTE: The Dapples series, introduced in 1995, is Breyer's latest line of models and was designed specifically to appeal to young girls with a taste for fantasy-style horses. The models represent the characters in a storybook that comes in several of the Dapples sets. Although sculptor Kathleen Moody made the Dapples horses fairly realistic in overall form, they incorporate storybook-style features such as oversized eyes and synthetic hair manes and tails that flow nearly to the floor. The series includes five different horse molds (three adults and two foals), a girl doll named Darla, and a number of accessories. The entire line is manufactured for Breyer in mainland China. The horses, which are smaller than Breyer's Artist Series models but larger than Classics, are made of the same ABS plastic that has been used to make Stablemates since 1992, according to Breyer executive Peter Stone (conversation of July 1995).

The Dapples line does not appear in the regular 1995 Breyer catalog but in a separate 1995 Dapples brochure. According to the 1995 Dapples price lists that accompanied the brochure, the models are available to dealers not only singly and in sets as listed below but also in assortments #95108 and #95109.

"Amazement" — 🐎 Stallion, smiling and trotting, head high. Sculpted by Kathleen Moody. Mold in catalog-run production 1995 - current as of 1996.
   Catalog-run models made from this mold:
   ♠ "Amazement" #95102, dark chestnut pinto, tobiano; blaze with white muzzle; multi-colored eyes; long curly dark-chestnut synthetic hair mane and tail; red, blue, and gold cord fabric mane ribbons; white legs; black hooves (1995 - current as of 1996). Comes with a hot-pink plastic brush. This model represents a character called "Amazement, The Prize Winning Stallion" in the storybook that comes with sets (see below).
   Sets:
   • "Amazement's" Riding Set #95104, dark chestnut pinto stallion; Darla doll; removable soft-plastic black English bridle and saddle; red felt saddle pad; blue fabric neck ribbon; hard-plastic hot-pink bucket, yellow tackbox, gold loving-cup trophy, and hot-pink brush and comb; and Sunny's Special Wish storybook (1995 - current as of 1996). The stallion is the same as #95102. The doll and accessories in this set are identical to the doll and some of the accessories in Dapples Deluxe Rider Set #95107; see that entry for descriptions. See Darla in the Riders - Soft Or Jointed Plastic section for details on the doll.
   • Dapples Deluxe Set #95106, dark chestnut pinto stallion "Amazement"; blue fabric neck ribbon; hard-plastic hot-pink bucket, yellow tackbox, gold loving-cup trophy, hot-pink brush and comb, silver wishing-star ring, and horse-head necklace; Sunny's Special Wish storybook; and Dapples horse stickers (1995 - current as of 1996). Set also includes "Sunny" and "Sunny's" Mom foal and mare models. The stallion is the same as "Amazement" #95102. The accessories in this set are identical to some of those in Dapples Deluxe Rider Set #95107; see that entry for descriptions.
   • Dapples Deluxe Rider Set #95107, dark chestnut pinto stallion "Amazement," Darla doll, removable soft-plastic black English bridle and saddle; red felt saddle pad; blue fabric neck ribbon; hard-plastic hot-pink bucket, yellow tackbox, gold loving-cup trophy, hot-pink brush and comb, silver wishing-star ring, and horse-head necklace; Sunny's Special Wish storybook; and Dapples horse stickers (1995 - current as of 1996). Set also includes "Sunny" and "Sunny's" Mom horse models. The stallion is the same as "Amazement" #95102. The reins on the bridle are detachable. The saddle has silver-painted stirrups and a white Dapples horse-head logo on each saddle flap. The blue ribbon, which has a gold paper medallion in the center of the rosette, is designed to hang around "Amazement's" neck. The necklace, designed to hang around "Amazement's" owner's neck, consists of a Dapples horse-head pendant in white with yellow mane, on a chain of silver plastic beads. No author's name appears in the tiny paperbound Sunny's Special Wish booklet, but the cover says "The First Dapples Storybook," suggesting that more books are to follow. The stickers depict all 5 of the existing Dapples horse and foal models plus a lying foal. The colors of the hard-plastic accessories might vary; my descriptions are based on my own Dapples Deluxe Rider Set #95107 and "Dancer" And "Celestria" Set #95105. In the 1995 Dapples brochure, wishing-star ring is gold and the bucket, tackbox, and necklace pendent are all blue. But these brochure pieces are undoubtedly prototypes, for they are less elaborate in mold than the accessories in my sets. See the Riders - Soft Or Jointed Plastic section for details on the doll.
   Note: The "Amazement" mold has a stamp reading "© Reeves/Breyer Made in China" inside the hind leg. The bridle has no mold stamp, but the saddle is stamped with "© Reeves/Breyer Made in China." All the hard-plastic accessories in the sets have mold stamps as well, as follows. Bucket, loving-cup trophy, and tackbox: "© Reeves/Breyer Made in China." Brush, comb, and ring: "© Reeves China." Necklace (pendant portion): "Dapples © 1994 Reeves/Breyer China."

"Celestria" — 🐎 Filly, standing, looking slightly to one side. Sculpted by Kathleen Moody. Mold in catalog-run production 1995 - current as of 1996.
   Catalog-run models made from this mold:
   ♠ "Dancer" And "Celestria" Set #95105, pearl white filly "Celestria," turquoise-blue star, multi-colored eyes, curly blonde synthetic hair mane and tail, pink and white-with-gold fabric tail ribbons, gray-blue hooves (1995 - current as of 1996). Set also includes "Dancer" mare model, Sunny's Special Wish storybook, and accessories. For a list of accessories, see the entry for this set under "Dancer." "Celestria," unlike her dam

"Dancer," is not sold separately but only in the set. This model represents a character called "Celestria, The Star Fairy Filly" in the storybook that comes with the set.
   Note: The "Celestria" mold has a stamp reading "© Reeves/Breyer Made in China" inside the hind leg. For the mold stamps on the accessories, see the note for the "Amazement" mold.

"Dancer" — 🐎 Mare, trotting, looking slightly to one side. Sculpted by Kathleen Moody. Mold in catalog-run production 1995 - current as of 1996.
   Catalog-run models made from this mold:
   ♠ "Dancer" #95100, pearl white, turquoise-blue star, multi-colored eyes, floor-sweeping wavy blonde synthetic hair mane and tail, orange and white-with-gold fabric mane ribbons, gray-blue hooves (1995 - current as of 1996). Comes with a hot-pink plastic brush. The ribbons are braided into a lock of the mare's mane. This model represents a character called "Dancer, The Star Fairy Mare" in the storybook that comes with sets (see below).
   Set:
   • "Dancer" And "Celestria" Set #95105, pearl white mare "Dancer"; hard-plastic hot-pink bucket; yellow tack box, hot-pink brush and comb, silver wishing-star ring, and horse-head necklace; Sunny's Special Wish storybook; and Dapples horse stickers (1995 - current as of 1996). Set also includes "Celestria" filly model. The mare is the same as "Dancer" #95100. The accessories I have listed are those in my own #95105 set. The 1995 Dapples brochure shows this set with fewer accessories, some of which are differently colored, but these are undoubtedly prototypes. The accessories in this set are identical to some of those in Dapples Deluxe Rider Set #95107; see that entry under "Amazement" for discussion.
   Note: The "Dancer" mold has a stamp reading "© Reeves/Breyer Made in China" inside the hind leg. For the mold stamps on the accessories, see the note for the "Amazement" mold.

Dapples Deluxe Rider Set — see under "Amazement"

Dapples Deluxe Set — see under "Amazement"

Darla — see in the Riders - Soft Or Jointed Plastic section

Mom — see "Sunny's" Mom

"Sunny" — 🐎 Filly, standing, nose in the air. Sculpted by Kathleen Moody. Mold in catalog-run production 1995 - current as of 1996.
   Catalog-run models made from this mold:
   • Dapples Deluxe Set #95106, ocher pinto filly "Sunny," accessories, and storybook (1995 - current as of 1996). Set also includes "Amazement" stallion and "Sunny's Mom" mare models. See the entry for this set under "Amazement" for details. The foal in this set is the same as "Sunny" in set #95103.
   • Dapples Deluxe Rider Set #95107, ocher pinto filly "Sunny," Darla doll, accessories, and storybook (1995 - current as of 1996). Set also includes "Amazement" stallion and "Sunny's Mom" mare models. See the entry for this set under "Amazement" for details. The foal in this set is the same as "Sunny" in set #95103.
   ♠ "Mom" And "Sunny" Set #95103, ocher pinto filly "Sunny," star and snip, multi-colored eyes, curly strawberry blonde synthetic hair mane and tail, gold cord fabric mane ribbon, orange hooves (1995 - current as of 1996). Set also includes "Sunny's" Mom mare model and hot-pink plastic brush. This filly, unlike her dam, is not sold separately but only in sets. This model represents a character called "Sunny the Wishful Filly" in the storybook that comes with the Dapples Deluxe sets (see under "Amazement").
   Note: The "Sunny" mold has a stamp reading "© Reeves/Breyer Made in China" inside the hind leg. For the mold stamps on the accessories, see the note for the "Amazement" mold.

"Sunny's" Mom — 🐎 Mare, pawing/prancing, head tucked. Sculpted by Kathleen Moody. Mold in catalog-run production 1995 - current as of 1996.
   Catalog-run models made from this mold:
   ♠ "Sunny's" Mom #95101, light sorrel, blaze with white muzzle, multi-colored eyes, long wavy strawberry blonde synthetic hair mane and tail, teal satin mane and tail ribbons, 4 stockings, tan hooves (1995 - current as of 1996). Comes with a hot-pink plastic brush. A lock of the mare's tail comes braided. This model represents a character called "Sunny's Mom, The Beautiful Mare" in the storybook that comes with the Dapples Deluxe sets (see under "Amazement").
   Sets:
   • Dapples Deluxe Set #95106, light sorrel mare "Sunny's" Mom, accessories, and storybook (1995 - current as of 1996). Set also includes "Amazement" stallion and "Sunny" foal models. See the entry for this set under "Amazement" for details. The mare in this set is the same as "Sunny's" Mom #95101.
   • Dapples Deluxe Rider Set #95107, light sorrel mare "Sunny's" Mom, Darla doll, accessories, and storybook (1995 - current as of 1996). Set also includes "Amazement" stallion and "Sunny" foal models. See the entry for this set under "Amazement" for details. The mare in this set is the same as "Sunny's" Mom #95101.
   • "Mom" And "Sunny" Set #95103, light sorrel mare "Sunny's" Mom and hot-pink plastic brush (1995 - current as of 1996). Set also includes "Sunny" foal model. The mare is the same as "Sunny's" Mom #95101.
   Note: The "Sunny's" Mom mold has a stamp reading "© Reeves/Breyer Made in China" inside the hind leg. For the mold stamps on the accessories, see the note for the "Amazement" mold.

Hard Plastic (1950s)

General note: Breyer's old hard-plastic rider molds were issued only for a few years, from about 1954 through 1958, possibly into 1959. Several of the models made from these molds were undoubtedly inspired by popular TV programs of that era, such as *The Adventures of Robin Hood* and *The Adventures of Kit Carson*, and one model, Corky The Circus Boy, was actually licensed by a TV show. Breyer's earliest riders, the Cowboy and Indian, first appeared in the ca.1954 catalog. These two molds and all the other old rider molds are in the 1958 catalog and price list but are gone from the 1960 and later catalogs. (No catalog or price list for 1959 exists to my knowledge.) The dates given below for the specific rider sets are the best estimates I could make on the basis of the scanty documentation I have been able to find from that era.

There are six basic old rider molds, one of which—the Canadian Mountie—has two different mold versions. Three of these molds have "Howdy Doody" style faces (as collectors have designated them), with a slightly cartoonish, balloon-faced appearance: Cowboy, Indian, and one version of the Mountie. The rest have a more realistic, handsome style of face: Corky, Davy Crockett, Robin Hood, and the other Mountie mold version.

According to Breyer executive Peter Stone, all the rider, saddle, and accessory molds were sculpted by Chris Hess and produced at the old Breyer factory in Chicago. I saw the old metal injection-molds of Robin Hood and the Howdy Doody Mountie when I visited the new factory in Wayne, New Jersey, in November 1994. Although Breyer produced these models, still it is possible that Breyer adopted the basic designs for them from Hartland Plastics company, which had issued rider models since 1952 or 1953. Breyer's Canadian Mountie, for instance, is very similar in both mold and color to Hartland's Sergeant Lance O'Rourke Mountie figure, which preceded the Breyer. These early Hartland people were sculpted by Roger Williams and Alvar Backstrand. (Hartland information is per Fitch 1993, 2: 5-6, 15-16, 70, 78, 116.)

All of Breyer's old riders came in sets with mounts—in most cases with either "Fury" Prancers or Western Ponies, but in one case (Corky) with the Elephant. For details on the mounts in the rider sets, see the entries in the Traditionals and Wildlife sections. For details on the saddles in the sets with horses, see the notes for the "Fury" Prancer and Western Pony molds.

Canadian Mountie — ♞ Left hand in lap, right hand on waist; coat, pants, gloves, belt, lanyard, chest strap, and boots all molded on; handsome-face and Howdy-Doody-face mold versions. Sculpted by Chris Hess. Mold in catalog-run production 1955/57 - 1958/59

Catalog-run models made from this mold:

♞ Canadian Mountie set #P440, rider painted with dark brown or black hair, red jacket and dark blue or black pants; on dark brown or black "Fury" Prancer; with removable gray plastic Mountie hat, brown hard-plastic snap-on English saddle, and separate dark blue hard-plastic saddle blanket with yellow border (sometime in the period 1955-57). Same horses as dark brown Prancer #P40 and "Black Beauty" Prancer #P40 with blaze. For discussion of accessories and of mold and paint variations of the rider, see the notes for this mold. My dating for this set is based on the dating of the dark brown Prancer that was sold in some #P440 sets and on the fact that this set is not in the ca. 1954 catalog or the 1958 catalog or price list. The set is listed on an undated typescript sheet listing several rider sets that probably i bers. (*JAH* XIII/#2 1985, p. 13, also says the Mountie's number was #P440.) The sheet says the horse is a dark brown Prancer, and the horse in a new-in-box set found by collector Denise Deen was dark brown. But some #P440 sets did come with a black Prancer with blaze and gold bridle and breastcollar; such a set is shown in the same *JAH*. (The box for #P440 is shown in Walerius 1991, p. 14. Walerius notes that the horse pictured on the box is black, and this is true as well of the identical box in which Denise Deen's set came. But the box picture is printed in black and white, so the horse's color in the picture is irrelevant to the question of whether the ponies in these sets were black or dark brown.) Collectors Jo Kulwicki and Ida Santana both own sets with Mountie (Howdy Doody version) and black Prancer that were apparently used by Drewry's Beer company of South Bend, Indiana, as promotional items in the 1950s. These sets feature two identical tiny decals—one in each rear corner of the saddle blanket—picturing a Canadian Mountie from the hips up and black horse head. Although "Drewry's" is not printed on the decals, Jo confirmed that this is one of the beer company's logos when she sighted several other Drewry's collectible items in antique stores in southern Michigan.

• Canadian Mountie set #P445, rider on white "Fury" Prancer (1957/58 - 1958/59). Same rider and accessories as in Canadian Mountie set #P440; same horse as white Prancer #P45. This set is in the 1958 catalog and price list. Though it is conceivable that #P445 debuted earlier than 1957 and thus ran concurrently with Mountie #P440 for some time, I suspect that #P445 appeared only after #P440 was discontinued. My chief reason for thinking so is that the box in which #P440 was packaged makes no reference to any horse-color options for the Mountie. (I have thoroughly inspected the original box owned by collector Denise Deen.) Other rider models, such as Lucky Ranger, that had various horse options had these options printed on their boxes. For discussion of accessories and of mold and paint variations of the Mountie, see the notes for this mold.

Notes:

(1) Mold versions: There are two mold versions of Breyer's Mountie—the Howdy Doody version and the Handsome version. Of the models I've seen, Howdy is slightly narrower in the chest and shorter than Handsome, but otherwise the bodies are identical in molded design. (The size differences could be a result of thermoplastic shrinkage rather than of actual mold size; see Mold Variations below in the Appendix.) The real differences between them are in their faces. Howdy has a smooth, balloonish look to his facial molding (reminiscent of the Howdy Doody marionette of 1950s TV fame), a smooth forehead, and no molded-in hairline or hair texturing—he is in effect molded bald. Handsome on the other hand has a rugged, mature look to his facial molding, molded-in wrinkles on the forehead, and molded-in hairline and textured hair. The Howdy version is featured on the box lid of #P440 sets and also appears in *JAH* XIII/#2 1985 (p. 13). The Handsome version is shown in *JAH* X/#1 1982 (p. 11), and was found new in Howdy-picture box with dark brown Prancer by collector Denise Deen. The Mountie #P445 pictured in the 1958 catalog appears to be a Handsome, but I am not certain since he is turned at an angle and is grainy in my photocopy. Interestingly, the old Mountie metal injection-mold that I saw at the Breyer factory in Wayne, New Jersey, in November 1994, contained cavities for simultaneous molding of two Mountie models (unlike the Robin Hood and other old rider injection molds, which have cavities for only one model each). The two cavities appeared to be identical Howdy version Mounties—both were smooth-browed and bald. I did not see the mold for the Handsome version, but *JAH* editor Stephanie Macejko did see it on her own expedition through the mold-storage area in fall 1995. In the photo she kindly sent me, Handsome's hairline and brow furrows are clearly visible. Unlike the Howdy mold, the Handsome contains cavities for only one model.

(2) Paint variations: Many Mounties of both mold versions are cast in red plastic, but not all: collector Jo Kulwicki's Howdy Doody version is white plastic with the red coat as well as the other colors painted on. All the Howdy Mounties I know of are intricately painted, with much facial and wardrobe detailing, whereas many handsome Mounties lack almost all paint detailing. The Mountie #P445 in the 1958 catalog, which I believe is the handsome version, also seems to lack detailing. However, the handsome Mountie #P440 found new in box (with Howdy version featured on the lid) by collector Denise Deen has a fully detailed paint job, as do handsomes owned by collectors Sheryl Leisure and Sande Schneider. On the detailed models of both versions, the hair is painted dark brown or black, and the face has dark brown or black eyebrows and eyelashes, blue eyes with whites, and red mouth. The coat is red with gold buttons, lanyard, and belt buckle. The belt, chest strap, holster, and boots are black or dark brown. The pants are painted dark blue or black with yellow stripe down the legs. The painted gloves come in both gray and black. On the undetailed handsome Mounties, the face is a painted blank of Caucasian fleshtone, the coat is solid red with red buttons, straps, etc., and the pants are solid dark blue or black with no painted stripe. His gloves are painted gray.

(3) Non-Breyer Mounties: The Hartland plastics company made a Mountie rider called Sergeant Lance O'Rourke, which looks very similar to the Breyer Mountie in both mold and color. One difference between them is that the Hartland's boot tops have molded-in crinkles, while the Breyer's boot tops are smooth. Collectors Sande Schneider and Sheryl Leisure have found specimens of another Mountie model that looks much like a Breyer Mountie but was probably made by Lido, a company that made plastic horses and riders in the 1950s and 1960s (per Diederich 1988, Section 4; the Mountie in question is identified as Lido by Paula DeFeyter, per Schneider 1993). This model is made of lighter-weight plastic than Breyer's Mountie and is standing nearly upright. The Breyer by contrast (both mold versions) is in a much deeper squatting position.

(4) Saddles and blankets: The Mountie's saddle is identical to the saddle that came with Race Horse Derby Winner—a brown hard-plastic saddle with brown vinyl cinch and stirrup leathers and pale gray hard-plastic stirrups. The Mountie's hard-plastic saddle blanket, which is a separate piece (this did not come with the Race Horse), is usually dark blue with yellow border, but collector Sande Schneider found a Mountie set with a red blanket with gold border (see Schneider 1993). Possibly this red blanket was not original to Sande's set but actually came with a riderless "Fury" set with English saddle. (Regarding these riderless sets see note 6 for the "Fury" Prancer mold above in the Traditionals section.) Sande also has saddle blankets in two mold versions: the red one and a blue one have a ridge line on the underside across the withers; another blue one lacks the ridge.

(5) Other accessories: The Mountie's removable gray plastic hat came with a braided black and silver fabric hatband. The hatband is visible in the photo on the #P440 set's box and in the photo of the #P445 set in the 1958 catalog. Controversy has raged over whether the Mountie also came with a pistol. As Schneider 1993 points out, the Mountie's holster is molded closed, which suggests that he didn't have a pistol. Against this, some collectors have speculated that a pistol came hung around Mountie's neck on a string. However, there is overriding evidence against the pistol. As mentioned above, collector Denise Deen found a new-in-box #P440 set, which she kindly allowed me to inspect in person. Her set includes the usual English saddle, saddle blanket, and Mountie hat with fabric braid band, but no pistol. Furthermore, the list of components printed on the side of her set's box includes no pistol: "HAT / RIDER / HORSE & REINS / SADDLE BLANKET / SADDLE, CINCH & STIRRUPS." Finally, the 1958 Breyer catalog neither shows nor mentions a pistol in the entry for set #P445, the only Mountie model in that catalog. The entry states: "Canada's beloved crimson coated Officer on White Prancer. Removable hat, saddle and blanket. Fun for all."

(6) Breyer's Canadian Mountie may have been inspired by the popular TV program *Sergeant Preston of the Yukon*, starring Richard Simmons as Sergeant William Preston. The sergeant's horse was named "Rex." This program was syndicated in 1955. (Information per Terrace 1979, 2: 878-79.)

(7) Neither Mountie mold version has any Breyer stamp or other mold marks. The saddle, saddle blanket, and Mountie hat have no marks either.

Corky The Circus Boy — ♞ Right arm raised, left arm outstretched; smiling, handsome-style face; cap, clothing, and boots all molded on. Sculpted by Chris Hess. Mold in catalog-run production 1957/58 - 1958/59.

Catalog-run models made from this mold:

♞ Circus Boy Corky On "Bimbo" set #601, boy rider with white hair, white cap, white shirt and jodhpurs, red belt, black boots, and black string tie; riding gray Elephant (1957/58 - 1958/59). Same pachyderm as Elephant #91. For details on the Elephant see the entry for this set under Elephant below in the Wildlife section. Corky is molded in white plastic and has his Caucasian skin tones and other color details painted on. This set has no removable accessories but did come with a small hang tag suspended from the

Elephant's neck, saying "Circus Boy / starring / Corky and Bimbo." As this indicates, the set represents the characters Bimbo the elephant and his water boy Corky Wallace in the TV show *Circus Boy*. The 1958 catalog and price list—the only early Breyer publications known to me that list the set—say "Sold under license arrangements with television producers." The show ran from September 1956 through September 1958 (the latter year being reruns, per Terrace 1979, 1: 189-90; reruns continued until September 1960, per Brooks and Marsh 1992). So the set may have been released as early as 1957, though probably not earlier since Breyer would have needed time to design and produce the Corky model after the start of the show in late 1956. On the show, Corky was played by child actor Mickey Braddock, who later changed his name to Mickey Dolenz and became one of the singers in The Monkees pop band and TV show. I gleaned this information by accident one morning in October 1993, when I turned on a Cable News Network news show to pass the time while brushing my teeth. An interview segment that happened to come on featured the adult Dolenz. As the interview proceeded, up popped an old black and white photo of him as Corky, mounted on an elephant and accompanied by a chimpanzee. (The photo showed the young Dolenz in ordinary clothes, but a photo in Terrace 1979 shows him in a white circus-boy outfit like that on the Breyer model.) Though the CNN interviewer pressed for details on the "Corky" era, Dolenz inexplicably omitted to mention that he had been immortalized in plastic by the Breyer Molding Company. The model does look remarkably like Dolenz in the face. The model number 601 later belonged to regular-run Classic "Kelso."

Note: The Corky mold has no Breyer stamp or other mold marks.

Cowboy — ♞ Left hand in lap, right hand on waist; Howdy-Doody-style face; neckerchief, fringed outer shirt, fringed chaps, 2 holsters with molded-in "tooled" designs, and boots all molded on. Sculpted by Chris Hess. Mold in catalog-run production ca.1954 - 1958/59.

Catalog-run models made from this mold (also see note 1 for this mold):

♞ Cowboy & Pinto set #341, rider with dark brown hair, yellowish buckskin outer shirt and shoulder fringe, turquoise blue inner shirt, red neckerchief, dark brown chaps, silver buckle on dark brown belt with silver ammo, dark brown holsters with silver edges; on black pinto Western Pony; with removable gray cowboy hat, rifle, 2 handguns, and black old-style Western saddle (ca.1954 - pre-1958). Same horse as Western Pony #41. This set is listed only in the ca.1954 catalog, which also itemizes the accessories, all of which are plastic. The original ca. 1954 color catalog that I saw at the Breyer factory in November 1994 showed the Cowboy painted in the colors listed above, except for the inner shirt, which was an indistinguishable dark color. Models I have seen, however, have a blue inner shirt. Collector Ida Santana's Cowboy in set #342 has the usual color scheme except for his neckerchief, which is buckskin, matching the outer shirt. Hat colors may vary—the Cowboy shown in Diederich 1988, Section 1, seems to have a white hat; a Cowboy I saw at BreyerFest 1993 had a dark brown hat, as did a Cowboy #342 found by collector Sande Schneider; and a Cowboy on a white Western Pony at BreyerFest 1995 had a red-brown hat. Collector Paula DeFeyter's Cowboy in set #343 (described and shown in DeFeyter 1991b), which has a blue-gray hat, also has blue-gray firearms. I have also seen firearms in various shades of brown and red-brown, but whether these originally came with Cowboy or Lucky Ranger sets, or both, I don't know. The Cowboy in the ca. 1954 catalog has painted facial details, as do all the models I've seen: the eyebrows and eyes are brown and the mouth red. But some Cowboys might lack facial detailing, as do some Lucky Rangers. The saddle shown in the ca.1954 catalog is cinchless, and Sande Schneider has found a couple of Cowboy sets with this type of saddle, but I've heard that some models have cinch saddles. For full discussion of saddle styles see note 3 for Western Pony and note 6 for "Fury" Prancer, above in the Traditionals section. The model number 341 also belonged to the Lucky Ranger set with black pinto Western Pony, and much later was assigned to the regular-run horned Holstein Cow.

• Cowboy & Pinto set #342, rider on brown pinto Western Pony, with brown old-style Western saddle (ca.1954 - pre-1958). Same rider and accessories as in Cowboy & Pinto set #341; same horse as Western Pony #42 This set is listed only in the ca.1954 catalog. The model number 342 also belonged to the Lucky Ranger set with brown pinto Western Pony, and much later was assigned to the regular-run horned Guernsey Cow.

• Cowboy set #343, rider on palomino Western Pony, with brown old-style Western saddle (ca.1954 - pre-1958). Same rider and accessories as in Cowboy & Pinto set #341; same horse and saddle as Western Pony #43. This set is listed only in the ca.1954 catalog, where it is misleadingly placed under the heading "Cowboy & Pinto" along with #341 and #342. The model number 343 also belonged to the Lucky Ranger set with palomino Western Pony, and much later was assigned to the regular-run horned Jersey Cow.

♞ Lucky Ranger set #341, rider with dark brown hair, pale tan outer shirt with gold shoulder fringe, white inner shirt, turquoise blue neckerchief, dark brown chaps, gold buckle on dark brown belt, gold holsters; on black pinto Western Pony; with removable black or brown cowboy hat, rifle, 2 handguns, and black old-style Western saddle (1955/56 - 1957). Same horse and saddle as Western Pony #41. Lucky set #341 is not in the ca. 1954 or 1958 catalogs, but it is listed among six Lucky sets on the box in which the sets were sold. The sets consist of identical Lucky Rangers on palomino, black pinto, and brown pinto Western Ponies and "Fury" Prancers. (I have seen a photo of the box side that lists the sets; thanks to collector Gale Good for a photocopy). I date all six sets through 1957 on the basis of a 1957 Sears holiday catalog ad for a music box made from a Lucky #P343 set; #P343 is one of the sets on the Lucky box, and presumably all six were issued in the same years. The 1956 Sears holiday catalog advertises what may be the same Lucky #P343 music box, but in my Xerox of this ad it is unclear whether the rider is a Lucky or a Cowboy. (See Music Boxes below in this section for discussion.) The accessories I've listed, all of which are plastic, are per the description of Lucky set #345 in the 1958 catalog: "removable guns, sharp-shooters rifle, hat and western saddle." The same accessories appear in the picture on the Lucky box and are noted in both Sears ads. The 1957 Sears text mentions all but the hat, which is visible in the photo: "Musical Cowboy-on-Horse. Ready to draw with his 2 'six' guns and a sharpshooter rifle. Plan a real battle in strict Wild West fashion—he's all prepared for Indian fighting, etc. Trusty Palomino pony waits for is rider's commands. Form-fitting, authentic-looking Western saddle. Break-resistant plastic to withstand rough action. Imported Swiss movement plays 'Home on the Range. . . . $4.47." In my experience, most Luckies have painted facial detailing—brown eyebrows; brown or blue eyes, sometimes with eyewhites; and red mouth—and the clothing colors described above. The picture on the Lucky Ranger box (see black and white photo in Walerius 1991, p. 14) also shows Lucky's face with painted detail, his outer and inner shirts as very pale, and his chaps and hat as very dark, but oddly, it shows no paint detailing on the shoulder fringe and shows the neckerchief as very dark, apparently inconsistent with turquoise. The photo of Lucky set #345 in the 1958 catalog is also black and white, but it is clear that the rider has a dark hat and pants, very pale shirts, and medium-toned neckerchief. Collector Paula DeFeyter's Lucky in set #P343 (shown and described in DeFeyter 1991b), unlike other Luckies I've seen, has a pale gray outer shirt and black hair and eyebrows. His eyes are blue with eyewhites, and his hat and firearms are brown. Collector Jo Kulwicki has an very unusual Lucky #345: he has the normal white inner shirt, dark brown chaps, and black hat, but his outer shirt and neckerchief are white, he lacks gold detailing on shoulder fringe and holster, and his face is a blank of Caucasian fleshtone. For discussion of the saddle see note 3 for the Western Pony mold and note 6 for the "Fury" Prancer mold above in the Traditionals section. The model number 341 also belonged to the Cowboy set with black pinto Western Pony, and much later was assigned to the regular-run horned Holstein Cow.

• Lucky Ranger set #P341, rider on black pinto "Fury" Prancer, with black old-style Western saddle (1955/56 - 1957). Same rider and accessories as in Lucky Ranger set #341; same horse and saddle as "Fury" Prancer #P41. Lucky set #P341 is not in the ca. 1954 or 1958 catalogs, but it is listed on the Lucky Ranger box; see Lucky Ranger set #341 for discussion of dates. The model number P341 also belonged to the Cowboy set with black pinto Prancer.

• Lucky Ranger set #342, rider on brown pinto Western Pony, with brown old-style Western saddle (1955/56 - 1957). Same rider and accessories as in Lucky Ranger set #341; same horse and saddle as Western Pony #42. Lucky set #342 is not in the ca. 1954 or 1958 catalogs, but it is listed on the Lucky Ranger box; see Lucky Ranger set #341 for discussion of dates. The model number 342 also belonged to the Cowboy set with brown pinto Western Pony, and much later was assigned to the regular-run horned Guernsey Cow.

• Lucky Ranger set #P342, rider on brown pinto "Fury" Prancer, with brown old-style Western saddle (1955/56 - 1957). Same rider and accessories as in Lucky Ranger set #341; same horse and saddle as "Fury" Prancer #P42. Lucky set #P342 is not in the ca. 1954 or 1958 catalogs, but it is listed on the Lucky Ranger box; see Lucky Ranger set #341 for discussion of dates. The model number P342 also belonged to the Cowboy set with brown pinto Prancer.

• Lucky Ranger set #343, rider on palomino Western Pony, with brown old-style Western saddle (1955/56 - 1957). Same rider and accessories as in Lucky Ranger set #341; same horse and saddle as Western Pony #43. Lucky set #343 is not in the ca. 1954 or 1958 catalogs, but it is listed on the Lucky Ranger box; see Lucky Ranger set #341 for discussion of dates. The model number 343 also belonged to the Cowboy set with palomino Western Pony, and much later was assigned to the regular-run horned Jersey Cow.

• Lucky Ranger set #P343, rider on palomino "Fury" Prancer, with brown old-style Western saddle (1955/56 - 1957). Same rider and accessories as in Lucky Ranger set #341; same horse and saddle as Prancer #P43. Lucky set #P343 is not in the ca. 1954 or 1958 catalogs, but it is listed on the Lucky Ranger box; see Lucky Ranger set #341 for discussion of dates. For the music boxes made from this set, see Music Boxes below in this section.

• Lucky Ranger set #345, rider on white Western Pony, with black or brown old-style Western saddle (1957/58 - 1958/59). Same rider and accessories as in Lucky Ranger set #341; same horse as Western Pony #45. Since #45 came with a black saddle, one would expect Lucky set #345 to include a black saddle as well, but Jo Kulwicki's #345 set came with a brown saddle. Since she did not get her set new, however, we can't be positive her saddle is the original one. For other accessories and clothing see Lucky Ranger set #341. Lucky #345 is listed only in the 1958 Breyer catalog and price list, and he is the only Lucky there. Since he is not listed along with the other six Lucky sets on the original Lucky Ranger box (presumably he came in a different box), I believe Lucky #345 debuted after the other six sets were discontinued. The model number 345 later belonged to the regular-run horned Brown Swiss Cow.

Notes:

(1) The above listings for Cowboy and Lucky Ranger sets, as well as the listings below for the Indian mold, include only those sets for which I have found reliable evidence. It is possible, however, that Breyer issued some further sets: Indian Chief set #P240 with buckskin-pants and/or turquoise-pants rider and black Prancer; Indian sets #241 and #242 with turquoise-pants riders and pinto Western Ponies; Indian Chief sets #P241 and #P242 with buckskin-pants riders and pinto Prancers; Cowboy sets #P341, #P342, #P343, and #P345 with black pinto, brown pinto, palomino, and white Prancers; Cowboy set #345 with white Western Pony; and Lucky Ranger set #P345 with white Prancer. Most of these (all but Cowboy sets #345 and #P345) are listed by long-time collector and Breyer consultant Marney Walerius in her book (Walerius 1991, p. 31). On the same page, she states: "The Indian or Indian Chief was best known for being on Pintos. Their packaging top flap had six boxes and numbers from which you were supposed to have a color choice. . . . Same choice option was on the top of the box for the Cowboy and Lucky Ranger." I have not seen the relevant flap of the Indian box (the flap is not visible in the photo of the box on Walerius's p. 14), and I have not seen a Cowboy box at all. These boxes may well list at least some of the Indian and Cowboy sets I have omitted. The possibility that Breyer issued a Cowboy set #P343 and buckskin-pants Indian Chief sets #P241 and/or #P242 looms particularly large in view of the 1955 Sears holiday catalog, which offers one music box made from a palomino Prancer and a Cowboy-mold rider apparently painted as a Cowboy, and another music box made from a pinto Prancer and an Indian-mold rider who seems to have arm warpaint, as is standard on known buckskin-panted Indians. (See Music Boxes below in this section for discussion). I am more skeptical about the existence of Lucky Ranger set #P345. I have seen a photo of the relevant flap of the Lucky Ranger box (copy kindly sent to me by collector Gale Good), and the white Prancer is not among the six horse options listed there: palomino, black pinto, and brown pinto Prancers and Western Ponies. Nor is Lucky on white Prancer offered in any publications I know of from the 1950s, including the 1958 Breyer catalog and price list, which advertise Lucky only on a white Western Pony.

(2) The Cowboy mold has no round Breyer stamp or other mold marks. His cowboy hat and saddle have no marks either.

Davy Crockett — ♞ Hands in lap, with fingers of right hand held straight out from body; handsome-style face; powder horn, pouch, open knife-sheath, fringed jacket, straps across chest, fringed pants, and moccasins all molded on. Sculpted by Chris Hess. Mold in catalog-run production 1955 - 1958/59.

Catalog-run models made from this mold:

♞ Davy Crockett set #P540[?], rider with dark brown hair; jacket, pants, and moccasins all medium brown buckskin; dark brown straps crossing chest and back, white powderhorn; on dark brown "Fury" Prancer; with removable rubbery brown coonskin cap with white bands painted on the tail, plastic long rifle and knife, and rubbery brown cavalry-type saddle (1955 - 1956/57). Same horse as dark brown Prancer #P40. It is conceivable that some Davy sets came with #P40 black Prancers—the horse shown on the Davy set's box could be either dark brown or black. But all the reliably original collectors' sets that I know of, including the sets on MasterCrafters clocks, have dark brown Prancers (see MasterCrafters Clocks in the Appendix near the end of this book). For a description of the saddle, see note 6 for the "Fury" Prancer mold above in the Traditionals section. In my experience, Davy models have no painted facial detailing, only the Caucasian fleshtone. Typically Davy is molded in medium brown plastic, which gives his buckskin clothing its color; however, I have seen one Davy molded in white plastic, whose painted-on buckskins were more of a khaki-olive color. Evidently some Kit Carsons were issued with identical buckskin clothing; see the entry for Kit #540. Collector Lynn Hiersche owns a Davy with a blue powder horn (or "water bottle," as Lynn called it) and has seen another Davy like this. Davy Crockett is not listed in the ca. 1954 catalog or any 1950s Breyer company publications known to me, but his status as a Breyer is established by the set's box, which has the words "Breyer Molding Co. Chicago" in small print on the side. The Davy set's number is not printed on the box; my reasons for proposing the number P540 are discussed in note 2 for this mold. The Davy set is advertised for the first time to my knowledge in the 1955 Sears holiday catalog: "New! Davy Crockett astride his Horse. . . . Realistic figure of Davy complete with raccoon cap, his trusty rifle 'Old Betsy' cradled in his arms and detailed saddle on horse—all are removable. Durable plastic, authentic frontier colors. . . . $3.69." Neither the knife nor the horse's color are noted in the ad (and the photo in my bleary Xerox of the ad is no help). Nor is the knife shown or mentioned on the Davy set's box. But it only makes sense to believe he did come with a knife, since he is molded with a knife sheath open and waiting, and since many collectors have found Davy models with a knife. The long rifle, an old flintlock style, has been found with Davy sets by several collectors. The rifle and knife in a Davy set found by collector Paula DeFeyter are brown (per DeFeyter 1991c), and I have seen brown knives and rifles in person; but collector Kim Jones's Davy has a white knife, and certainly other color variations are possible, too. In all likelihood, Breyer was inspired to issue its Davy set by TV shows of the 1950s: a series of episodes about the real Davy Crockett, starring Fess Parker and produced by Walt Disney studios, first aired on *Disneyland* on December 15, 1954, and between January and December 1955; the episodes were rerun in 1956 (per Gianakos 1980, pp. 401-2). Davy's omission from the 1958 catalog and price list indicates that he was not produced after 1956/57. The real David (Davy) Crockett, 1786-1836, was a frontiersman born in Limestone, Tennessee. After serving in his state legislature, he was elected to three terms in the U.S. House of Representatives. "His dress, language, racy backwoods humor, and naive yet shrewd comments on city life and national affairs made him a popular figure in Washington," but he is most famous for fighting and dying at the Alamo during the Texas Revolution against the Mexican government, which still owned Texas at that time (*Columbia Encyclopedia*, 5th Ed.).

♠ Kit Carson set #540, rider with dark brown hair; some identical to the rider in Kit Carson set #542; others evidently have jacket, pants, and moccasins all medium brown buckskin, dark straps crossing chest and back, white powder-horn; on "Black Beauty" Western Pony with diamond star; with removable pale-colored cowboy hat, rubbery plastic neckerchief, plastic rifle and knife, and rubbery brown cavalry-type saddle (1957/58 - 1958/59). The Kits dressed in buckskin are apparently the same rider as Davy Crockett #P540[?]. Same accessories as Kit Carson #542 (see that entry). Same horse as Western Pony "Black Beauty" #40 with diamond star. The #540 set is listed only in the 1958 catalog and price list. Both of these publications call Kit's pony "Black Beauty," and the pony in the catalog photo has a star and 4 stockings. The photo, which is black and white, also shows Kit in uniformly medium-dark jacket, pants, and moccasins—the right tone to be medium brown buckskin, which is the normal color for Davy Crockett #P540[?]! This is very surprising, because the color scheme that collectors normally associate with Kit Carson is pale tan or pale gray jacket and dark chocolate brown pants, as on Kit Carson #542. I have never heard of a rider of this mold having any other color scheme besides the all-over buckskin or the pale tan or gray with dark brown, so in all probability the Kit #540 in the 1958 catalog is wearing buckskin. Assuming that Kit #540s like this were actually sold, it would be impossible to distinguish them from Davy Crocketts if they lost their distinguishing horses and accessories—Kit's neckerchief and cowboy hat (both shown as very light or white in the catalog photo) versus Davy's coonskin cap. This would help explain why Davy Crockett seems to be one of the more common 1950s rider models—some of them were sold as Kit Carsons! However, it is quite certain that at least some Kit #540s have the normal Kit #542 color scheme, for collectors Sheryl Leisure and Laura Diederich both found normal Kits on "Black Beauty" Western Ponies. Another normal Kit on a "Black Beauty" (the version with no stockings), owned by collector Paula DeFeyter, is shown in DeFeyter 1991c. Paula also notes here that her Kit's rifle and knife are brown but that some yellow knives have been found with other Kit sets; I imagine that other color variations are possible too. See the entry for Kit #542 for discussion of the normal Kit's clothing colors.

• Kit Carson set #P540, rider on dark brown or black "Fury" Prancer (1955/56 - 1956). Same rider and accessories as Kit Carson #542; same horse as dark brown Prancer #P40 or "Black Beauty" Prancer #P40. The #P540 set is not in the ca. 1954 Breyer catalog or any other Breyer company documents known to me but is in the Fall/Winter 1956 Sears catalog (for $3.69). I suspect that this set was superseded by Kit Carson set #542, which is the only Kit set listed on an old Breyer company sheet that I date to 1956/57. The #P540 set is also listed on an undated typescript sheet listing several rider sets that probably is a collector's compilation made in the 1970s or 1980s; the sheet doesn't mention the horse but gives the number as #P540, which indicates a brown or black "Fury" Prancer. The photo in the 1956 Sears catalog shows the Prancer as very dark with 4 stockings and a blaze, but since the photo is printed in sepia, I can't be sure whether the horse is dark brown or black. Nor can I be positive of Kit's clothing colors, but the photo clearly shows his hat, jacket, and powder horn as pale and his pants, moccasins, and chest straps as very dark, all consistent with the known color scheme of Kit in the #542 set. The photo also shows the neckerchief to be pale, which is consistent with one of the known colors of this accessory (see Kit Carson set #542 for discussion). A #P540 set (minus neckerchief) purchased by collector Robert Peterson from a man who worked for Breyer in the 1950s does have the usual Kit colors; as shown in the photo Robert kindly sent me, the jacket is the pale gray version. Robert's set also has a "Black Beauty" Prancer with gold bridle and breastcollar, though it is possible that some sets come with a dark brown Prancer. In any case, the Sears catalog text says: "New! Kit Carson / A famous hero of the old west rides again! Here's an authentic reproduction of Kit Carson and his horse in bright wild west colors. An ideal model for a western fan's room, fun to play with, too ... Kit comes off his horse, you can remove his gun, knife and hat, too. Finely detailed plastic. About 9 inches high. Kit's a fine room-mate for adventurous boys. They'll dream of riding on the wild open ranges. . . . $3.69." The neckerchief is plainly visible in the Sears photo, so why the text doesn't list it among Kit's removable accessories I don't know. Nor is it clear why the colors are called "bright"; at any rate I've never heard of a Kit outfitted more noisily than Kit #542 with his drab tan/gray and dark brown outfit and black or dark brown pony. Although neither the Sears ad nor the 1950s Breyer publications listing the various Kit Carson sets mention television, it is reasonable to suppose that Breyer's Kit was inspired by the popular TV program *The Adventures of Kit Carson*, starring Bill Williams. The show aired from 1951 through 1955 or 1956 (sources conflict about the ending date; see, e.g., Terrace 1979, 1: 31; Gianakos 1980, p. 86; and Brooks and Marsh 1992, p. 15). The real Christopher "Kit" Carson, 1809-68, was born in Kentucky and raised on the Missouri frontier. In his teens he ran away to Taos, New Mexico, where "he made his living as a teamster, cook, guide, and hunter for exploring parties" (*Columbia Encyclopedia*, 5th ed.). He became famous by serving as guide on John C. Frémont's exploratory expeditions into the Rocky Mountains, Oregon, Nevada, and across the Sierra Nevada into California. In 1853 Carson became U.S. Indian Agent of the federal government. During the Civil War years he helped organize and lead the New Mexican Volunteer army in battles against Apaches, Navahos, and Comanches in New Mexico and Texas.

♠ Kit Carson set #542, rider with dark brown or black hair, pale tan or pale gray jacket, dark brown pants and moccasins, dark brown straps crossing chest and back, white powder-horn; on brown pinto Western Pony; with removable gray plastic cowboy hat, rubbery plastic neckerchief, hard plastic rifle and knife, and rubbery brown cavalry-type saddle (sometime in the period 1956-57). Same horse as Western Pony #42. The #542 set is not in the ca. 1954 catalog or the 1958 catalog or price list; he is listed only on an old Breyer company sheet that probably dates to 1956/57. The list of accessories I've given is based on this old sheet, which has a full-color photo of the #542 set, and also on the 1958 Breyer catalog, which has a black and white photo of the #540 set, and the Fall/Winter 1956 Sears catalog, which has a sepia and white photo of the #P540 set. The knife is not visible in any of these photos since it would be in the sheath on the backside of the model, but it is mentioned in the Sears catalog and the 1958 Breyer catalog. The Sears catalog says, "Kit comes off his horse, you can remove his gun, knife and hat, too." The Sears photo shows the saddle and neckerchief as well as the rifle. The 1958 Breyer catalog states, "Removable hat, neckerchief, hunting knife and saddle," and the rifle is shown in the photo. The rifle is very similar to the "sharpshooter" rifle in Cowboy and Lucky Ranger sets but may differ in mold somewhat; I'm not sure.The neckerchief is made of rubbery plastic, according to collector Ida Santana, who has a Kit #542 with a pale grayish-tan neckerchief. Collector Paula DeFeyter has a Kit #540 with a rubbery red neckerchief (DeFeyter 1991c). The neckerchief in the color Breyer company sheet mentioned above is blue. The sheet shows Kit's hat as gray, but Paula's Kit came with a white hat. Ida's Kit, collector Sande Schneider's Kit, and the Kit on the Breyer sheet all have pale tan jackets with red-brown fringe. Paula's Kit, however, has a pale gray jacket, as does collector Laura Diederich's Kit #540 (shown in Diederich 1988, Section 1; Laura wrote to me about the jacket). Paula also notes in her article that her Kit's rifle and knife are brown but that some yellow knives have been found with other Kit sets. Collector Robert Peterson's #P540 Kit set has a light gray rifle, about the same color as Kit's jacket. I imagine that other color variations are possible too. Sande's Kit has no facial detailing, but Paula's and collector Sheryl Leisure's models have red mouths and black eyebrows and eyes. Ida's Kit is similar but appears to have blue eyes. For a description of the saddle, see note 6 for the "Fury" Prancer mold above in the Traditionals section.

Notes:

(1) We can be certain that no Davy Crockett or Kit Carson sets included the old-style Western saddle that came with Cowboy and Lucky Ranger sets (and with riderless Prancers and Western Ponies), for the Davy mold simply does not fit into the Western saddle. His molded-on buckskin fringe prohibits him from taking a seat. (Thanks to Heather Wells for this observation.)

(2) The model number for the Davy Crockett set with dark brown "Fury" Prancer is a mystery. Neither the number nor any mention of Davy appears in the 1950s Breyer company documents known to me, and no number is printed on the box in which the set was sold. (Thanks to collector Kim Fairbrother for color photos and a thorough description of her original Davy set box. A black and white photo of an identical box is reprinted in Walerius 1991, p. 14.) My guess as to what the number should be is #P540. This number is consistent with the known numbering system used for the other old rider sets. All these sets have numbers consisting of two smaller numbers: the model number of the horse in the set and a number designating the mold of the rider—the rider-mold numbers being 1 for Robin Hood, 2 for Indian, 3 for Cowboy, 4 for Canadian Mountie, and 6 for Corky. So, for example, the number for Robin Hood set #P145, with white "Fury" Prancer, incorporates the number P45 for the horse and the number 1 (wedged between the "P" and the "45" of the horse's number) for the rider mold. We also know that the rider-mold numbers remained the same even when different rider models were made from the same mold—for instance, the set numbers for Lucky Ranger and Cowboy sets alike incorporate the rider-mold number 3. To be consistent with all this, the number for the Davy Crockett set has to incorporate the model number of Davy's Prancer, namely, #P40 dark brown. It also has to include the number 5 for the rider mold, for this is the rider-mold number used in the documented numbers for Kit Carson sets, which were made from the Davy mold. Hence my proposed number P540 for the Davy Crockett set. Lest it be objected that #P540 already belongs to one of the Kit Carson sets, I would point out that some Cowboy and Lucky Ranger sets too have the same set numbers—so evidently this type of confusion would not have deterred Breyer with respect to the Davy and Kit sets.

(3) The only regular-run Davy Crockett set for which I have found reliable evidence is the #P540[?] set with dark brown Prancer. However, some Davys on palomino Prancers have been discovered on lamps that probably date to the 1950s. Collectors Sande Schneider and Paula DeFeyter have both found such lamps (thanks to both for sending me photos). Perhaps Breyer sold these sets to the lamp company on a special order, for I have found no evidence that Davy was issued on a palomino Prancer as a regular run. The Davy Crockett box shows a dark (black or brown) horse in the photo on the lid and makes no reference to any other horse-color options. Other rider models, such as Lucky Ranger, that had various horse options had these options printed on their boxes. For further discussion of the Davy lamps, see the Lamps & Nightlights section in the Appendix near the end of this book.

(4) The Davy Crockett mold has no round Breyer stamp or other mold marks. Nor are there any mold stamps on Davy's rubbery cavalry saddle and coonskin cap or Kit Carson's cowboy hat.

Drewry's Beer promotional Mountie set — see Canadian Mountie #P440

Indian — Left hand on hip, right hand hanging down; Howdy-Doody-style face; headband, chest strap, belt, loop for tomahawk, open knife-sheath, pants with fringe and loincloth, and moccasins all molded on; two holes molded into the Indian's back for quiver attachment; one mold version with feather hole on the side of the head, one mold version with no hole. Sculpted by Chris Hess. Mold in catalog-run production ca.1954 - 1958/59.

Catalog-run models made from this mold:

- Indian & Pinto set #241, rider with black hair, yellowy buckskin pants and leg-fringe, yellowy buckskin or red moccasins, red loincloth with self fringe, red headband with two vertical white stripes in front, black belt with light buckskin buckle, black quiver-strap across chest and back, white warpaint on face, chest, and arms; on black pinto Western Pony; with removable fuzzy cloth riding blanket; removable plastic tomahawk, quiver, knife, and 3 or 4 arrows; metal bow; and single plastic brave's feather; later sets also with paper headdress and/or plastic chief's headdress (ca.1954 - pre-1958). Same horse as Western Pony #41. This set and set #242 are listed in the ca.1954 catalog, which has a color photo of #241. These sets were heralded by an undated news release from Eastman Chemical Company, Breyer's plastic supplier, which must have been published just prior to the catalog (the news release omits mention of an accessory that the catalog lists as "newly added," as I'll discuss below). The news release does not mention any set numbers but was accompanied by a black and white photo of set #241 (photo reprinted in Walerius 1991, p. 30). The release announces: "Indians of the American West had never seen a horse until the Spanish came, but they got the idea immediately. Later, a brave's pony became as indispensable to him as his bow or his war paint. Now this famous twosome—the Indian warrior and his mount—is being reproduced in rugged Tenite acetate plastic figures which look almost real enough to circle a wagon train. Pinto pony rider, weapons and headdress feather are all molded separately to give extra play value. They fit neatly together to make a colorful statuette." *Rider*: The color photo in the ca.1954 catalog shows the Indian in light buckskin pants and red moccasins, but other buckskin-pants Indian riders that I have seen have buckskin moccasins, matching the pants. The news-release photo shows the moccasins as the same pale color as the pants, presumably buckskin. Other color details of the rider may also vary—for instance, collector Julia Harris has a buckskin-pants model with unpainted (reddish plastic) loincloth and headband. The catalog shows the rider's face painted not only with white warpaint but also with black eyes and eyebrows and red or pink lips, as appear on many collector's specimens; the news-release photo too shows this facial detailing. The catalog also shows the Indian with three white crosshatches of warpaint on his upper arm just below the shoulder; but the news-release photo shows him with a long white zigzag down the length of each arm, and the many collectors' specimens of buckskin-pants Indians that I have seen all have these zigzags. *Accessories*: The news-release and catalog photos both clearly display the accessories but differ slightly about a few of them. The catalog shows the fuzzy blanket (for discussion, see note 3 for this mold), metal bow (see note 4), and several plastic items: single white feather with dark tip (probably a red tip, as shown on the buckskin-pants Indian in *JAH* 17/#2 May/June 1990, p. 18); yellow tomahawk; red quiver; red knife; and 4 arrows, 2 red and 2 yellow. (The quiver is shaped like a small jalapeño chili with the top cut off, with molded-in "fringe" around the top rim and down one side and two molded-on plastic pegs that go into the holes on the Indian's back.) The black and white news-release photo shows the same accessories (the colors are hard to judge, of course) except that the feather is a solid color, probably red (as is collector Sande Schneider's specimen), and there are only 3 arrows, which are light colored, probably yellow. Sande has found quivers, tomahawks, and arrows in yellow and red, as well as arrows and a knife in transparent copper-colored plastic. A music-box #P241 Indian displayed at BreyerFest 1995 had not only yellow arrows and a transparent copper-colored quiver (I saw a second quiver like this at the same BreyerFest) but also a white tomahawk, which raises the possibility that other accessories came in white too. And collector Sheryl Leisure found a brown tomahawk. The mind boggles. (For the music box, see Music Boxes below in this section.) As to headdresses, apparently none were issued with the earliest sets. The Eastman news release does not show or mention a full headdress but only a "headdress feather," and collector Paula DeFeyter's #241 set, which she found in original box with the accessories still sealed, includes all the accessories listed above except for a headdress. Nor does the ca.1954 catalog show a headdress in the photo, but it does feature a large blurb saying "Newly Added: Full Indian Headdress," which implies that previous sets lacked a headdress. The catalog gives no specifics about the "Newly Added" headdress, such as whether it was paper or plastic. But presumably the paper headdress was the earlier of the two, and indeed a paper headdress came with collector Billie Parsons's #242 set, which she had on display at BreyerFest 1993 (set #242 is in the ca.1954 catalog along with set #241). Conceivably some sets came with plastic headdress instead of or along with the paper one. See note 1 for this mold for descriptions of both headdresses.
- Indian & Pinto set #242, rider on brown pinto Western Pony (ca.1954 - pre-1958). Same buckskin-pants rider and accessories as in Indian & Pinto set #241. Same horse as Western Pony #42. This set is listed in the ca.1954 catalog and probably in an old undated news release from Eastman Chemical Company. For discussion, see the entry for #241.
- Indian Chief And Pinto Pony set #P241, rider with black hair; many with turquoise pants with red, gold, and white leg-fringe; turquoise moccasins with gold detailing on top; pale tan or pinkish loincloth with red, gold, and white fringe; turquoise headband with white zigzag and red dots in front; black belt with gold buckle flanked by white designs; black quiver-strap across chest and back; white warpaint on face and chest but not arms; on black pinto "Fury" Prancer; with removable fuzzy cloth riding blanket; removable plastic tomahawk, quiver, knife, and 4 arrows; metal bow; and plastic chief's headdress; some also with single plastic brave's feather and a paper headdress (1955 - 1956/57). Same horse as Prancer #P41. The earliest #P241 sets may have buckskin-pants riders as in Indian & Pinto set #241, as I'll discuss in a moment. Neither #P241 nor #P242 is in the ca. 1954 catalog or the 1958 catalog or price list, but one or the other of these sets appears in the 1955 and 1956 Sears holiday catalogs, which advertise a pinto Prancer (color unspecified) and Indian set made into a music box (see Music Boxes below in this section for discussion). #P241 is also shown on the set's Breyer box, a photo of which is printed in Walerius 1991 (p. 14). Though the photo is black and white and the set number is not visible on the box, still it is clear that the Prancer pictured on the box is black pinto, for he is much darker than his Indian rider and much darker than a brown pinto Prancer would look in such a photo. The box calls the set Indian Chief And Pinto Pony. *Rider*: It is certain that at least some #P241 riders have turquoise pants rather than buckskin (these two versions being the only Indian models known to me) since collector Heather Wells's music-box #P241 and an identical music box on display at BreyerFest 1995 both have turquoise-pants riders. Also, a #P242 set found in original box by collector Paula DeFeyter has the turquoise-pants coloring. However, there are clues indicating that the very first #P241 and #P242 sets had buckskin-pants riders, clues that concern the paint details of the two Indian versions. Turquoise-pants Indians, like their buckskin-pants brethren in sets #241, #242, and #240, commonly have the painted facial details of black eyes and eyebrows and red or pink lips. But turquoise-pants models, with multicolor designs on their headbands, loincloths, and pants, and gold trim on their moccasins, are in general much more colorful and detailed than buckskin-pants models, which lack these pretty touches. The buckskin-pants fellows excel only in having zigzag arm warpaint; the turquoise-pants fellows are generally bare-armed. Of the many Indian models of both colors that I have seen, only one has violated these general paint schemes: a turquoise-pants Indian at BreyerFest 1995 had the paint scheme of a typical buckskin-pants model, with zigzag arm warpaint, only two vertical white lines on his turquoise headband, and no color designs on his clothing fringes. Now as to the clues concerning early #P241s and #P242s: In my Xeroxes of the Sears ads for the music box set, the Indian in the 1955 ad quite clearly has zigzag arm warpaint, consistent with buckskin pants, whereas the Indian in the 1956 ad seems to lack arm warpaint, which omission suggests he has turquoise pants. Similarly, the Indian in the black-and-white picture on #P241's box has zigzag warpaint on his arms, indicative of buckskin pants—but he also has an unusual white "necklace" of warpaint, so perhaps he was a test-color piece. *Accessories*: The 1955 Sears ad lists the Indian's accessories as arrows, tomahawk, knife, headdress, brave's feather, and "wool" riding blanket. The bow is plainly visible in the ad photo, which also shows the headdress to be the paper one; the quiver is hidden owing to the photo angle. The 1956 Sears ad includes the same accessories, except that the headdress is plastic rather than paper. The set's box pictures the rider with a bow, arrows, tomahawk, plastic headdress, and riding blanket; the knife and quiver aren't visible owing to the photo angle. Paula DeFeyter's #P242 turquoise-pants set in original box, about which she kindly wrote to me, came with the accessories still sealed in a packet and with a diagram showing where to put them on the rider. The accessories included all those listed above, including the plastic brave's feather that fits into a hole on the rider's head, and two headdresses, one paper and one plastic. In my experience, however, most turquoise-pants riders have no hole in the head, which indicates that they did not come with the brave's feather. The feather must have been discontinued at some point during the production of turquoise-pants sets and the mold altered to fill in the head hole. For discussion of tomahawk, arrows, etc., see the entry above for set #241. For the headdresses, see note 1 for this mold. For the riding blanket, see note 3. For the metal bow, see note 4.
- Indian Chief And Pinto Pony set #P242, rider on brown pinto "Fury" Prancer (1955 - 1956/57). Same turquoise-pants rider and accessories as in Indian Chief And Pinto Pony set #P241, although the earliest #P242 sets may have buckskin-pants riders as in Indian & Pinto set #241. Same horse as Prancer #P42. For discussion, see the entry for #P241.
- Indian Warrior set #240, rider on "Black Beauty" Western Pony with diamond star; with removable fuzzy cloth riding blanket and removable plastic tomahawk, quiver, knife, and arrows (1958 [maybe earlier] - 1958/59). Probably the same buckskin-pants rider as in Indian & Pinto set #241. Same horse as Western Pony "Black Beauty" #40 with diamond star. This set is in the 1958 catalog, which uses the name "Indian Warrior," and the 1959 price list, which says "Indian Chief." Both sources call the pony "Black Beauty." The photo of the set in the 1958 catalog is black and white, so I can't be certain of the color of the Warrior's pants, but presumably they are either buckskin (as on rider #241) or turquoise (as on rider #P241) since I've never heard of an Indian rider in any other colors. The photo does, however, give some strong clues that #240 is in fact a buckskin-pants model: the model in the photo has a long zigzag of white warpaint running down each arm, two vertical white stripes on his headband, no white designs on his belt, apparently no color-detailing on his loincloth and pants fringes, and a loincloth darker than the pants. All of these features are typical of buckskin-pants models and different from the features of most turquoise-pants Indians (see discussion for set #P241). This #240 set includes fewer accessories than earlier Indian sets. The 1958 catalog states: " Indian Warrior / Mounted on Black Beauty, with blanket, quiver, arrows, tomahawk and knife—all removable. Unmatched for play thrills . . . Retail $3.00." The blanket, quiver, and tomahawk are all visible in the catalog photo. The tomahawk and quiver look fairly dark and could be red (see the entry for set #241 for discussion of accessory colors; for the riding blanket, see note 3 for this mold). The photo angle is wrong to show the arrows, so I don't know how many came with this set. No bow is shown or listed for #240. How the Warrior was supposed to shoot his arrows I don't know, but it seems likely that the bow was eliminated for safety reasons (see note 4 for this mold). Nor are any head accessories for #240 listed or shown in the catalog—the photo clearly shows that this Warrior has not got even a single feather on his head. This suggests that he has no hole in his head either, since the head hole in earlier models of this mold was made to accommodate the feather (see notes 1 and 2 for this mold). Of the many buckskin-pants Indians I have seen, one, owned by collector Kim Jones, has no head hole; he could well be a #240.

Notes:

(1) Headwear: Three different removable headwear accessories came with various of the Indian sets. The earliest accessory of the three is a single plastic feather, which can be either white with a red tip or a solid color—red or yellow or possibly white or dark orange (for discussion see Indian & Pinto set #241). The other two headwear accessories are both full feather headdresses, one made of plastic, the other of heavy, coated paper. On the plastic headdress, the feathers are white with red tips and black shading at the bases, and flow back from an integral red headband. Two feathers hang down from the headband, one on either side, to frame the Indian's face. Collector Billie Parsons had a paper headdress on display at BreyerFest 1993 in a #242 buckskin-pants set, and collector Paula DeFeyter kindly sent me a photo of the paper headdress that came in her #P242 turquoise-pants set. Billie's and Paula's headdresses are identical: very colorful and elaborate, with a lower band of mustard yellow with green and black designs, a central band of orange, and a top band of mustard feathers tipped with bands of green and black. A pair of paper feathers hangs from the lower band downward on each side of the rider's face. Paula wrote to me that her headdress "had to be punched out of the paper it came on." It is fairly certain that of the two headdresses, the paper one came first: a paper headdress appears in a 1955 Sears holiday catalog ad for a music box made from an Indian and pinto Prancer set; but a plastic headdress is featured in the 1956 Sears holiday catalog ad for this music box. (See Music Boxes below in this section for discussion.) But although the paper headdress came first, it was not discontinued as soon as the plastic headdress debuted; as noted in the entries above, some Indian-mold sets came with both headdresses. Nor did Breyer discontinue the brave's feather when the first headdresses came out: some Indian-mold sets came with all three headwear accessories. So the distinction collectors sometimes draw between Indians and Chiefs—Indians supposedly being the

buckskin-pants fellows with a single feather and Chiefs being the turquoise-pants fellows with headdress—simply does not hold up. Breyer did call some buckskin-pants riders Indian, and some Indians came with only a feather, but others came with a veritable trousseau of headdresses. Likewise, Breyer did call turquoise-pants riders Chief and supplied them with a headdress or two, but Breyer also gave some of them a brave's feather, which the owner was free to put on the Chief's head in lieu of a headdress.

(2) Head holes: Some Indian models have a hole molded or punched into the right side of the head to hold the removable plastic feather; others have no hole. The models with a hole must be earlier, for it was the earlier sets that came with a feather. Later models did not come with a feather and thus must be the ones with no head hole. In my experience turquoise-pants models typically have no head hole, but specimens with the hole do exist (see the entry for #P241 above, and see Schneider 1992a). Buckskin-pants models in my experience are the reverse, the vast majority having head holes and only a few having no hole (such as the one owned by collector Kim Lory Jones). These no-hole buckskin-pants fellows may well be #240 Warriors, the last models made from this mold. At BreyerFest 1995 I saw a buckskin-pants model that was very unusual in having no hole at the side of his head but two at the back of his head, one at the level of the headband and the other just above it. Whether these holes were factory original I do not know, but the model was an older one, to judge from the fact that he had a paper headdress.

(3) The multicolored cloth riding blanket that came with all the Indian-mold sets is a small oblong of fuzzy fabric, roughly 6 inches long and 2 inches wide (the size varies a bit), with an elastic girth sewn on. The blankets vary in color—I have seen them in red and in orange with various Indian designs (the designs differ somewhat from blanket to blanket) and in a blue and green plaid; the one in the ca.1954 catalog is red and white plaid; and the one in the ca. 1958 catalog in the #240 set appears to be a solid dark color. There may be other colors and patterns as well.

(4) The bow that came in many pre-1958 Indian sets is made of metal. At BreyerFest 1994, I got to inspect one of these little accessories (a specimen now owned by collector Sande Schneider). The bow is about 3.5 inches long and quite rigid. The main shaft of the bow is round, like heavy-gauge wire, but with a flat area in the middle, where the model's owner would grip the bow as he or she drew back the string to shoot. The ends of the bow are flat and sharp-cornered, and have a notch cut out to accommodate the "string." The bow is tarnished nearly black; it could have been brass or silver colored when new. We are not sure exactly what the original bow string was like, but it can be seen to be a flat, flexible lace of some type in the photo that accompanied the ca. 1954 Eastman Chemical news release announcing the first Indian sets (photo reprinted in Walerius 1991, p. 30). A diagram of the Indian mold showing where the various accessories go, which came with collector Paula DeFeyter's Indian set in original box, does not say what the original bow string is made of but does say: "Bow string is replaceable. Knot both ends of short section of rubber band, insert in slots of bow." (Thanks to Paula for a copy of the diagram.) The ca.1954 catalog shows the metal bow very clearly in photos but does not mention it in the text describing the #241 and #242 Indian sets: "Arrows that come out of their removable quiver and shoot ... tomahawk and scalping knife that are 'usable' too—all in harmless plastic." Apparently the company thought it best to omit mention of the dangerous metal bow. What appears to be the same metal bow is also pictured on the box of the #P241 set (see photo in Walerius 1991, p. 14), but here too the text printed with the picture is telling for what it omits: "Fully equipped with all traditional regalia including harmless arrows that really shoot!" And again mention of the bow is omitted from the text of 1955 and 1956 Sears holiday catalog ads for music boxes made from Indian and Prancer sets, although the bow is plain to see in the ad photos. (See Music Boxes below in this section.) It is not impossible that the metal bow was replaced, perhaps in 1957, with a plastic bow like that issued with the Robin Hood model, but I have no solid evidence of an Indian with plastic bow. Besides, the Indian needed to have a bow with which the owner could shoot the arrows—all the advertising touts the shootability of the "harmless plastic arrows"—whereas Robin Hood's arrows, being molded into his quiver, are not shootable and thus do not require a bow tolerant of prolonged archery practice by youthful aspiring marksmen. In any case, the bow accessory was apparently discontinued altogether by 1958, for the #240 Indian Warrior in the 1958 catalog, though he does have the usual plastic arrows, has no bow at all—no bow is shown in the photo of the model, and no bow is listed in the description of his accessories ("with blanket, quiver, arrows, tomahawk and knife—all removable"). The Robin Hood model in the 1958 catalog also seems to have lost his bow.

(5) A warshield is listed among the Indian's accessories on an undated typescript sheet listing several rider sets that probably is a collector's compilation from the 1970s or 1980s. But I am highly skeptical that a warshield came in any Breyer Indian-mold sets. I have never seen such an accessory, and no 1950s Breyer publication known to me shows or mentions a warshield with any Indian-mold model. Nor is a warshield shown or listed among the accessories for the Indian and Prancer music boxes in the 1955 and 1956 Sears holiday catalogs (see Music Boxes below in this section). Nor to my knowledge is a warshield shown or mentioned on the Indian's box from the 1950s (see photo in Walerius 1991, p. 14). And no warshield is mentioned on the diagram of the Indian mold showing where the accessories go, which came with collector Paula DeFeyter's Indian set in original box. (The diagram does not mention the full headdresses or the arrows either, but then, it's pretty obvious where these would go; it is not at all obvious where a warshield would go.) As collector Sande Schneider has suggested to me, rumors of a Breyer warshield may stem from confusion about the warshield that did come with various Hartland Indian rider sets. The Hartland warshield, as shown in Fitch 1993 (1: MM), is a round white plastic item with Indian designs on the front.

(6) Breyer may have issued more Indian-mold sets than are listed above. Buckskin-pants riders may have come on black pinto and brown pinto "Fury" Prancers, and turquoise-pants riders might have been issued on black pinto and brown pinto Western Ponies. If so, these sets would have had the same numbers as the sets with these horses listed above. It is also conceivable that riders of one or both pants versions came on a black Prancer as #P240. For discussion see note 1 for the Cowboy mold.

(7) The Indian mold has no round Breyer stamp or other mold marks. None of the accessories I have seen have had any mold stamps either.

Indian Chief — see under Indian

Indian Warrior — see under Indian

Kit Carson — see under Davy Crockett

Lucky Ranger — see under Cowboy

Mountie — see Canadian Mountie

Music Boxes — These remarkable 1950s artifacts were, to my knowledge, all made from "Fury" Prancers with riders. The music-box mechanism is located inside the Prancer, with the socket for the winding key projecting through a hole in the horse's shoulder. I have seen or read reports of music boxes made from three different Prancer sets: palomino Prancer with Cowboy or Lucky Ranger (#P343), which plays "Home on the Range"; black pinto Prancer with Indian Chief (#P241), which plays a tune that nobody seems to be able to identify; and white Prancer with Robin Hood (#P145), sometimes called William Tell, which plays Rossini's "William Tell Overture."

A music box made from a palomino Prancer and Lucky Ranger #P343 set was on display at BreyerFest 1994. The pony wore a red-brown old-style Western saddle, while Lucky, with blue eyes and eyewhites, wore a black cowboy hat, carried a brown plastic rifle, and packed red-brown plastic six-shooters in his holsters. This is the only collector's specimen of the palomino music box that I know of with a rider; others have lost whatever riders they may once have had. Ads for both palomino and pinto Prancer music boxes appear in the 1955 and 1956 Sears holiday catalogs, and for the palomino Prancer music box alone in the 1957 Sears holiday catalog. All three catalogs call the palomino set "Musical Cowboy-On-Horse," but to judge from the photos in my black-and-white Xeroxes of these ads, the rider in the 1957 set and possibly in the 1956 set too is a Lucky Ranger—his outer shirt is very light and his shoulder fringe dark. The 1955 rider appears to be a Cowboy in that his shirt seems fairly dark, but it is hard to tell for sure. "'Cowboy and Indian' tunes add to the thrill of owning these hand painted authentic-looking figures," says the 1955 ad; "Western Pinto horse for Indian, Palomino for cowboy. Both figures are made of break-resistant plastic. . . . Musical Cowboy-On-Horse. Imported Swiss unit plays 'Home on the Range.' Here's a rootin' tootin' cowboy with all his Wild West gear—2 guns, a sharpshooter rifle and a form-fitting authentic Western saddle. . . . $4.98." The description is essentially the same in the 1956 ad, where the price has tumbled to $4.49, and the 1957 ad, which offers the item for the bargain price of $4.47.

A music box made from a black pinto Prancer with turquoise-pants Indian Chief #P241 is owned by collector Heather Wells. An identical piece, only minus the Chief's headdress, was on display at BreyerFest 1995. Another black pinto Prancer music box, lacking a rider, is shown in Diederich 1988, Section 1. I do not know whether music boxes were made with brown pinto Prancers, and the 1955 and 1956 Sears ads cited above do not mention the pinto pony's color. Nor do these ads shed any light on the enduring mystery of the tune. No collectors I know who have heard this music box's tune can identify it—certainly I can't—and the Sears copy-writer seems just as stumped. "Musical Indian-On-Horse. Imported Swiss music unit plays typical Indian tune," says the 1955 ad evasively. "Arrows can really shoot, tomahawk and knife are usable, too. All are made of harmless plastic. Chief headdress, brave's feather, wool blanket are removable. . . . $4.98." The photo that goes with this 1955 ad clearly shows the Chief's bow, which presumably is a far-from-harmless metal one (see note 4 for the Indian mold). The photo also shows his headdress to be the original paper one (see note 1 for the Indian mold). The 1956 ad, which offers the reduced price of $4.49, uses essentially the same descriptions but shows the Chief with a plastic headdress rather than paper. Neither ad mentions the color of the Chief's pants, but interestingly, the fellow in the 1955 ad photo appears to have arm warpaint, which is typical of Indian models with buckskin pants, whereas the fellow in the 1956 photo appears to lack arm warpaint, as is typical of the Chief models with turquoise pants.

Finally, music boxes made from white "Fury" Prancers with Robin Hood riders are mentioned by Walerius 1991 (pp. 20, 23-24, 31). The white Prancer music box is also listed by Diederich 1988, Section 1, but without reference to a rider. Neither of these sources provides a photo of this music box, and I have never seen a white Prancer music box or any 1950s documentation for them. Consequently, I have grown a bit skeptical of their existence, though of course with Breyer history one must always keep an open mind.

Until collector Andrea Gurdon unearthed the above-cited 1950s Sears ads for music boxes (see Gurdon 1996), it was purely a matter of speculation whether these artifacts are Breyer company products or not. Walerius 1991, taking the negative view, says the music boxes were made by a Breyer employee who did some of the work at home and distributed the finished pieces himself: "Once assembled and painted the employee paid Breyer for the set and in turn took it and sold it as an item or gave it as a gift to friends and family. . . . The employee released them from his home and not through Breyer's records and sales" (p. 20). Walerius cites no sources for this account, and I am skeptical of it in view of the Sears ads. It seems unlikely that a single employee working presumably in his spare time could keep Sears stocked with music boxes three years running or that the Breyer company would have allowed him to do so when it could have reaped the harvest of the sales itself. After all, the very same Sears catalogs with the music-box Prancers offer other Breyer products that Breyer itself surely sold to Sears—regular Davy Crockett and Robin Hood sets and various Western Horse and Western Pony "grooming kits," examples of which have been found in original Breyer boxes and which thus must be Breyer company products. Further, as Andrea notes (see Gurdon 1996), the music-box pages from the 1955 Sears holiday catalog particularly suggest that Sears may have instigated the music-box project—probably as a special Christmas deal—farming out musical mechanisms it had purchased elsewhere to various manufacturers of items into which the mechanisms could be stuffed. Though the 1955 Sears pages mention no manufacturers, they brim with items made into music boxes: a plastic church bank ("to save for charities, church donations"), a jewelry box, "Tuneful Tabby, the Tumbling Cat," powder boxes, dolls, an especially attractive "Davy Crockett Musical Tooth Brush Holder" (no relation to Breyer's Davy), a purse, a Santa with reindeer, a cake plate, and an "Illuminated Madonna and Rosary Box" (made by Hartland Plastics, per Gurdon 1996), to name just a few in addition to the Breyer Prancers. All these are equipped with the same type of Swiss mechanism, which is illustrated and touted at the top of the page: "These delicate musical movements were purchased from Swiss Craftsmen whose unique musical skill is handed down from generation to generation." If Sears did contract with manufacturers for these music boxes, it seems highly likely that the Breyer music-box Prancer sets are indeed "official" Breyer company products.

Robin Hood — ♞ Rides or stands, left arm extended, right arm raised reaching for molded-in arrows in quiver; handsome-style face; cap with feather, quiver with arrows, shirt, chest straps, belt, powder horn, pants, and "elf" boots all molded on. Sculpted by Chris Hess. Mold in catalog-run production 1956 - 1958/59.

Catalog-run models made from this mold:

♞ Robin Hood set #P145, rider with black or dark brown hair, <u>forest green shirt and pants</u>; some with dark green cap with red feather, dark green boots, and dark green chest straps and belt; some with red cap with green feather, red boots, and tan chest straps and belt; white powder-horn; on white "Fury" Prancer; with removable yellow or red plastic sword and bow, and rubbery brown medieval-type saddle (1956 - 1958/59). Same horse as Prancer #P45. I have heard that Robin Hood came with a hang tag, but I have not actually seen one. This set is not in the ca. 1954 catalog but is in the 1956

Sears holiday catalog, which advertised it as "Robin Hood on White Horse . . . $3.69." The Robin Hood set is also listed and pictured on an old undated Breyer sheet that I date to 1956/57 and in the 1958 catalog. For further discussion of dates, see note 2 for this mold. The version of this rider with red cap and boots is often referred to by collectors as William Tell; for discussion see note 1 for this mold. Other color details vary as well. Collectors Sande Schneider and Paula DeFeyter both have dark-green-cap Robin Hoods with silver trim on the belt buckle, black hair and eyebrows, and blue eyes with eyewhites, and I saw 2 others just like this at BreyerFest 1995. Paula has another Robin with a green cap the same shade as the shirt and pants, dark green boots, red trim on the buckle, brown hair and eyebrows, and brown eyes with no eyewhites. Sande has a red-cap Robin with brown hair and eyebrows but no other painted facial details. *Accessories*: Robin's accessories are itemized in the 1956 Sears ad: "Robin is armed with detachable sword and bow! He stands alone. Robin, saddle and reins are removable. Plastic." The 1956/57 Breyer sheet, which has color photos, does not list the accessories but does clearly show the sword and the bow, both in a dark color (red I believe), as well as the saddle and reins, which are the ordinary chain reins that came on most Prancers. As this sheet also illustrates, Robin can hold either the sword or the bow in his outstretched hand—when he holds the bow, the sword fits into a strap-loop molded onto his thigh; when he holds the sword, the bow can be slung across his chest. Both the sheet and the 1956 Sears ad show the bow with a string; what it is made of I don't know, but it would have to be removable for the bow to be slipped in and out of Robin's hand. Paula DeFeyter's Robins have red bow and sword, but I have seen a couple of Robins with yellow bows, and Walerius 1991(p. 53) mentions a yellow sword. It is possible that the bow was discontinued during the last year or two of production of Robin Hood, for the 1958 catalog's entry for this model neither shows nor mentions a bow, although it does show a sword. The Indian model in the 1958 catalog also seems to have lost his bow. Walerius 1991 (pp. 23, 31) wrongly states that Robin Hood's cap is soft rubber, which implies that it is a removable accessory. I have seen several of these models, both red-cap and green-cap versions, and the cap is part of the Robin mold, not removable, and is made of hard plastic like the rest of Robin. For a description of the saddle, see note 6 for "Fury" Prancer above in the Traditionals section. Robin Hood was a "legendary hero of 12th-century England who robbed the rich to help the poor" (*Columbia Encyclopedia*, 5th ed.).

Notes:

(1) Collectors often say there are two separate forest-green-clad models made from this mold: Robin Hood, usually identified as the version with dark green cap, boots, chest straps, and belt; and William Tell, with red cap and boots and tan chest straps and belt. However, the only model of the Robin Hood mold that is listed in early Breyer publications known to me is labeled "Robin Hood." The 1956 Sears holiday catalog, too, advertises only "Robin Hood on white horse." No model called William Tell is listed in these documents, and I know of no other solid evidence, such as an old Breyer box, identifying a model as William Tell. The only document I've seen that lists a William Tell model is an undated typescript sheet listing several rider sets that I am quite sure, for independent reasons, is not a company document but a collector's compilation from the 1970s or 1980s. In the face of this dearth of evidence for a William Tell model, collector Sande Schneider suggested to me that Breyer in fact never issued a rider under this name but only issued Robin Hood in two color variations. The designation "William Tell," according to Sande's theory, is a collector's fiction that started when the music boxes reportedly made from these horse-and-rider sets became known (see Music Boxes above in this section). These music boxes play Rossini's "William Tell Overture." Whether the riders on them have red cap and boots I'm not sure—I have never seen one of these music boxes or even a photo of one—but in any case I believe Sande is right about Breyer never issuing a William Tell but only a Robin Hood in color variations. This view is supported not only by the lack of 1950s documentation for William Tell but by color evidence from the old Breyer publications that include Robin Hood. The undated Breyer company catalog sheet that I believe dates to 1956/57, which lists and pictures Robin Hood #P145, has full-color photos. I saw the original sheet in the Reeves International archives in New Jersey in November 1994. The photo of Robin Hood, with the large caption "Robin Hood" printed beneath it, shows him with dark green boots, tan chest straps and belt, and red cap! That is, he mixes up the color details that collectors attribute to Robin and William respectively, and the mixture has more "William" details (tan straps and red cap) than Robin details (green boots). The photo of Robin Hood #P145 in the 1958 catalog, which is unfortunately printed in black and white, shows the straps as dark, which probably means they were dark green (tan straps would appear light); the cap and boots too are dark, but it's impossible to tell from the tones whether they were red or green. Whether models with the mixture of colors shown on the 1956/57 sheet were actually issued for sale I don't know, but in any event Sande's idea that Robin Hood was issued in color variations of red and green cap and boots, etc., certainly gains credibility from these Breyer publications. As to the music boxes that play "The William Tell Overture," assuming that they do exist, it is interesting to speculate that their creation was inspired by a 39-episode TV series called *The Adventures of William Tell*, starring Conrad Phillips, which was aired in syndication for only one year, 1958, but which ran for many more years on a local all-night channel in Chicago, where Breyer was located (per McNeil 1991, p. 835, and Erickson 1989, p. 19). This program was "filmed on location in Switzerland by a lot of the production people who'd worked on the CBS networker *Robin Hood* (1955-58)" (Erickson 1989, p. 19). The fact that the nationally popular, long-running TV program *The Lone Ranger* used Rossini's *William Tell Overture* as its opening theme could also have lent luster to the idea of a William Tell music box.

(2) Although the 1950s Breyer publications that list Robin Hood do not mention television, it is reasonable to suppose that this model was inspired by TV programs: *The Adventures of Robin Hood*, a series starring Richard Green, which ran from September 1955 to September 1958 (per Terrace 1979, 1: 32-33, and McFarland 1989, p. 19), and *The Story of Robin Hood*, a 1952 movie that was aired on the popular *Disneyland* TV show in November 1955 (per Gianakos 1980, p. 402). The timing of the Breyer model established by the 1956 Sears holiday catalog and the 1958 Breyer catalog and price list is too close to these program dates to be coincidental. Further, it is well known that other Breyer models of this era were based on TV programs—the "Lassie" and "Rin Tin Tin" models, for instance, were "sold under license arrangements with television producers" according to the 1958-63 catalogs and price lists. Models such as Robin Hood and Davy Crockett probably wouldn't require such licensure—providing they didn't look too much like the TV actors who played these characters—since they represent historical figures, over whom no one holds copyrights. In any case, assuming that Breyer's Robin was based on these TV shows, then the Breyer would not have been issued any earlier than 1956, since design and production time would be needed after the fall 1955 debut of the TV shows.

(3) The Robin Hood mold has no round Breyer stamp or other mold marks.

William Tell — see note 1 for the Robin Hood mold

Soft Or Jointed Plastic

GENERAL NOTE: All the dolls listed in this section are manufactured for Breyer by companies in the Orient. For details on the horses in the rider sets listed below, see the entries in the Traditionals and Little Bits sections above. For the ceramic dolls in the Miniature Collection horse-and-buggy sets, see Miniature Collection above in the Classics section.

Alec Ramsey — Traditional-scale boy doll, soft plastic with wire-core limbs, painted-on hair. Head sculpted by Chris Hess. Mold in production: pre-catalog release 1981, catalog run 1982-86.

Catalog-run models made from this mold:

Ben Breyer #550, same doll as Alec Ramsey in The Black Stallion And Alec Set #3000, but wearing blue-and-white checked long-sleeved cloth shirt, denim bluejeans, and black plastic Western boots (1983-86). Same boots as on Brenda Breyer #500. This Ben Breyer doll, with the same clothing, was sold as Paul Beebe through the fall 1993 FAO Schwarz catalog, in set #700493 with Marguerite Henry's book *Misty of Chincoteague*, "Misty" #20, and "Stormy" #19. Paul Beebe was one of the two children portrayed in the book. The model number 550 previously belonged to the Showcase Collection issue of the black pinto Western Horse.

Sets:

The Black Stallion And Alec Set #3000, Alec Ramsey doll, with painted black or dark brown hair and brown freckles, wearing black satiny jockey outfit (pre-catalog release 1981, catalog run 1982-85). Set also includes Black Stallion (same model as #401) and racing tack. The jockey outfit consists of black satiny cloth pants, black satiny long-sleeved shirt with purple and gold stripes, removable black plastic crash helmet with matching stripes, and black plastic English boots (same as Brenda Breyer's English boots). The tack includes leather racing saddle with separate purple elastic and leather surcingle, purple felt saddle blanket with white "3" in each rear corner, black plastic crop, and leather bridle with orange reins. Very similar sets were sold through the Sears, Ward's, and Penney's holiday catalogs in 1981 and 1982. All these sets included Walter Farley's book *The Black Stallion*, and the same doll, clothing, and tack as in set #3000, with a couple small differences: The 1981 Sears catalog shows the saddle blanket with the number "4" rather than "3." The 1981 Ward's catalog shows the saddle blanket with the number "3," but the surcingle is striped blue and white rather than solid purple. The Penney's 1985 holiday catalog offered a rather different set, consisting of a chestnut "Man O' War" #47 with the same doll, clothing, and tack as in set #3000.

Kelly Reno And "Little Man" Gift Set #3096, Kelly Reno is the same doll as Alec Ramsey in The Black Stallion And Alec Set #3000, but wearing solid pale gray long-sleeved cloth shirt, bluejeans, and black plastic Western boots (1984-85). Set also includes palomino Stock Horse Stallion, leather bridle, and fuzzy red bareback pad with leather surcingle. Kelly Reno is the boy actor who played the part of Alec Ramsey in the movie *The Black Stallion*.

Special-run models made from this mold:

Rearing Circus Stallion With Ringmaster set SR, same doll as Alec Ramsey in The Black Stallion And Alec Set #3000, but wearing white cloth shirt and black tie, red tailcoat, black pants, black felt top-hat, and black plastic boots (1985). Penney's holiday catalog. Set also includes SR flocked white Fighting Stallion and tack. The tack consists of a red and white leather surcingle, white leather bridle with two reins, and a removable red plume that attaches to the bridle's crownpiece by means of a small metal hook. See under Fighting Stallion above in the Traditionals section for details on the horse.

Notes:

(1) The Alec mold's head was sculpted by long-time Breyer sculptor Chris Hess, according to Breyer executive Peter Stone (conversation of Nov. 1994).

(2) The Alec mold has a stamp molded into its back that reads "Breyer Animal Creations / Made in Hong Kong."

Ben Breyer — see under Alec Ramsey

Bitsy Breyer — Little Bits-scale girl doll, jointed hard plastic body with soft plastic head, molded-on clothing (different for each of the 4 mold versions), rooted synthetic hair. Sculpted by Chris Hess. Molds in catalog-run production: Bitsy beach, late 1983 - 1985, 1994 - current as of 1996; Bitsy English, late 1983 - 1987, 1994 - current as of 1996; Bitsy jockey, late 1983 - 1987; Bitsy Western, late 1983 - 1987, 1994 - current as of 1996.

Catalog-run models made from these mold versions:

Bitsy Breyer And Arabian Stallion Beach Set #1001, Caucasian doll with long brown hair in a ponytail, molded-on red shorts and yellow T-shirt with horsehead design on chest (late 1983 - 1985). Set also includes Little Bits Arabian Stallion, brown rubber English bridle, white plastic surfboard with red center stripe, and plastic comb for Bitsy. For details on the horse and discussion of release date, see the entry for #1001 in the Little Bits section. The bridle is identical to the one in Bitsy Breyer And Morgan English Set #1005. The red stripe on the surfboard is a strip of stick-on plastic tape. A similar set was released in 1983 through the Penney's catalog; see below, Bitsy Breyer Beachcomber Set SR. The red shorts on the #1001 Bitsy are shown in the 1984-85 Breyer catalogs, but collector Sande Schneider's doll has yellow shorts with a red stripe along the bottom.

Bitsy Breyer And Morgan English Set #1005, Caucasian doll with same head as #1001, molded-on black coat, white breeches, and black boots; removable black plastic crash cap (late 1983 - 1987). Set also includes Little Bits Morgan Stallion, brown rubber English bridle and saddle, black plastic riding crop (possibly omitted from some sets), and plastic comb for Bitsy. For details on the horse and discussion of release date, see the entry for set #1005 in the Little Bits section. The crash cap is the same mold as the race cap in Bitsy Breyer And Thoroughbred Jockey Set #1010. The riding crop is not pictured or mentioned in the main listing for the #1005 set in Breyer catalogs or on the set's box, but a crop did come with collector Lynn Luther's set, and in the 1986-87 catalogs a crop is visible on the arm of the English Bitsy in the Bitsy Breyer Stable Set #9950. The English bridle is molded with two cheekpieces on each side and workable rubber "buckles" on the noseband and throatlatch. The reins are a separate piece, molded with bit "cheekpieces" at the ends, which attach to the bridle. The reins are identical to those on the Western bridle in Bitsy Breyer And Quarter Horse Western Set #1015. The English saddle has a molded-on girth, which fastens with a rubber buckle under the belly. The stirrup leathers, which are molded with decorative "tooling" and have molded-on stirrups, are separate pieces, detachable from the saddle. These stirrup pieces are identical to those on the Western saddle in set #1015 and to those on the racing saddle in Bitsy Breyer And Thoroughbred Jockey Set #1010.

♞ Bitsy Breyer And Quarter Horse Western Set #1015, Caucasian doll with same head as #1001, molded-on light blue shirt with dark blue yoke and white sleeves, tan chaps, and bluejeans; removable brown soft-plastic cowboy hat (late 1983 - 1987). Set also includes Little Bits Quarter Horse Stallion, brown rubber Western bridle, brown rubber Western saddle and breast collar, and plastic comb for Bitsy. For details on the horse and discussion of release date, see the entry for this set in the Little Bits section. The bridle is molded with a single cheekpiece on each side and workable rubber "buckles" on noseband and throatlatch. The reins are a separate piece, molded with bit "cheekpieces" at the ends, which attach to the bridle. The reins are identical to those on the English bridle in Bitsy Breyer And Morgan English Set #1005. (My description of the Western bridle is based on the #1015 set I got from collector Lani Keller, which she had purchased new in the 1980s. The bridle shown with this set in the 1984 Breyer catalog is the same as the English bridle in set #1005, though the 1985-86 catalogs do seem to show the Western bridle.) The Western saddle has a molded-on cinch and a molded-on breastcollar, which fastens at the chest. The detachable "tooled" stirrup leathers with molded-on stirrups are identical to those on the English saddle in set #1005 and on the racing saddle in set #1010.

♞ Bitsy Breyer And Thoroughbred Jockey Set #1010, Caucasian doll with same head as #1001, molded-on red and white shirt, white breeches, and black boots; removable red and white plastic race cap (late 1983 - 1987). Set also includes Little Bits Thoroughbred Stallion, brown rubber English bridle, brown rubber racing saddle, black plastic riding crop, and plastic comb for Bitsy. For details on the horse and discussion of release date, see the entry for #1010 in the Little Bits section. The race cap is the same mold as the crash cap in Bitsy Breyer And Morgan English Set #1005. The riding crop, which is also the same as in set #1005, is not pictured or listed in the main Bitsy listings of the Breyer catalogs, but it did come with the #1010 sets purchased by collectors Lynn Luther and Lani Keller. The English bridle and reins too are the same as in set #1005. The racing saddle has a molded-on brown rubber saddle blanket marked with white "3" in each rear corner, and a molded-on rubber girth that fastens under the belly. The detachable "tooled" stirrup leathers with molded-on stirrups are identical to those on the English saddle in Bitsy set #1005 and the Western saddle in Bitsy set #1015. Set #1010 is also shown in the 1983 Penney's and Ward's holiday catalogs. The Penney's set as shown in their photo includes a black Little Bits Thoroughbred Stallion with tan hooves and no white markings, same doll as #1010, comb for Bitsy, and same tack as in set #1010 except that the saddle blanket was yellow and marked with a dark "3." The Ward's set includes the same horse, doll, and tack as the Penney's set, plus some other Little Bits horses (for details, see the entry for #1010 in the Little Bits section).

♞ "Cobalt" And Veronica, Hunter/Jumper Set #1025, Veronica doll, same Caucasian doll and crash cap as in Bitsy Breyer And Morgan English Set #1005, but with molded-on red coat (1995 - current as of 1996). Set also includes black Little Bits Thoroughbred Stallion, black plastic crop, pink plastic comb for Veronica, and same brown rubber English tack as in Bitsy Breyer And Morgan English Set #1005. In the Saddle Club Series. Unlike the other 4 sets in this series, this set is not in the 1994 catalog but is listed as new in the 1995 catalog.

• "Pepper" And Lisa, Hunter/Jumper Set #1018, Lisa doll, same Caucasian doll (same mold and colors) and crash cap as in Bitsy Breyer And Morgan English set #1005 (1994 - current as of 1996). Set also includes dapple gray Little Bits Morgan Stallion, black plastic riding crop, pink plastic comb for Lisa, and same brown rubber English tack as in set #1005. In the Saddle Club Series.

♞ "Spot" And Kate, Western Set #1019, Kate doll, same Caucasian doll and brown Western hat as in Bitsy Breyer And Quarter Horse Western Set #1015, but with molded-on white shirt with russet and purple yoke, russet-red chaps, and gray jeans (1994 - current as of 1996). Set also includes black blanket appaloosa Little Bits Quarter Horse Stallion, black plastic riding crop, pink plastic comb for Kate, and same brown rubber Western tack as in set #1015. In the Saddle Club Series.

♞ "Starlight" And Carole, Cross Country Set #1016, Carole doll, African American, from the waist up is same mold as in Bitsy Breyer And Arabian Stallion Beach Set #1001 but with brown skin, long black pony tail, and molded-on green shirt; from the waist down she is same mold as in Bitsy Breyer And Thoroughbred Jockey Set #1010, but with molded-on light gray breeches and dark brown boots (1994 - current as of 1996). Set also includes dark mahogany bay Little Bits Arabian Stallion, black plastic crop, green and blue plastic race cap, white cloth competitor's vest printed with a blue "4" and the Breyer logo, pink plastic comb for Carole, and same brown rubber English tack as in Bitsy Breyer And Morgan English Set #1005. In the Saddle Club Series.

♞ "Topside" And Stevie, Cross Country Set #1017, Stevie doll, Caucasian, from the waist up is same mold as in Bitsy Breyer And Arabian Stallion Beach Set #1001, but with long blonde pony tail and molded-on red shirt; from the waist down she is same mold and colors as in Bitsy Breyer And Thoroughbred Jockey Set #1010 (1994 - current as of 1996). Set also includes sandy bay Little Bits Thoroughbred Stallion, black plastic crop, red and black plastic race cap, white cloth competitor's vest printed with a blue "8" and the Breyer logo, pink plastic comb for Stevie, and same brown rubber English tack as in Bitsy Breyer And Morgan English Set #1005. In the Saddle Club Series.

Special-run models made from this mold:

♘ Bitsy Breyer Beachcomber Set SR, same Caucasian doll as in set #1001 but with molded-on white T-shirt (1983). Penney's holiday catalog. Set also includes black Little Bits Arabian Stallion with black hooves, no white markings; rubber bridle; comb for Bitsy; and surfboard. This set is similar to the Bitsy Breyer And Arabian Stallion Beach Set #1001 issued in 1983-85, except that in the SR set the horse is apparently black and the doll has a white T-shirt rather than yellow. The bridle and surfboard are the same as in set #1001. Both the doll and horse shown in the Penney's catalog could be test colors; whether the sets actually sold were like this or were instead regular-run #1001 sets I do not know.

Notes:

(1) Chris Hess created the original sculptures for the "Bitsy Breyer" dolls, using Missy Stone, daughter of Breyer executive Peter Stone, as his real-life model (per Peter Stone, conversation of Nov. 1994; also see *JAH* 20/#3 Summer II 1993, p. 4). Now an actress, Missy appeared occasionally with her father at Breyer signing parties and has been featured in *JAH* (X/#2 1982 and XI/#4 1985) as well as on the packaging of Little Bits models and Bitsy Breyer sets.

(2) In the Bitsy Breyer sets from the 1980s, all four mold versions of Bitsy—beach, English, jockey, and Western—have two stamps molded into their backs: "Breyer Animal Creations ®" and "Molded in H.K." The box in which all four sets were packaged is printed with "Doll and accessories made in Hong Kong" and "© copyright 1983 Breyer Molding Company, Chicago, Illinois 60612." The Saddle Club set dolls from the 1990s have the same "Breyer Animal Creations ®" stamp molded into their backs, but their second back stamp says "Made in China." Through 1995 their box said "Horse and packaging made in USA / Doll & accessories made in China" and "© copyright 1994 Reeves International," but starting in 1996, when the horses, too, began to be produced overseas, the nationality statement changed to simply "Made in China." Also printed on the box is the statement "The Saddle Club is a trademark of Bonnie Bryant Hiller." None of the rubber tack in the old Bitsy Breyer sets or the new Saddle Club sets has any identifying mold stamps.

"Black Beauty" Gift Set SR — see under Brenda Breyer

Brenda Breyer — ♞ Traditional-scale girl doll, soft plastic with wire-core limbs, rooted synthetic hair. Sculpted by Eddie Mosqueda. Mold in production: pre-catalog release 1978 and 1979, catalog run 1980 - current as of 1996 (jointed limbs 1979 only; long hair 1978-87; big curly hair 1988-92; short straight hair 1993 - current as of 1996).

Catalog-run models made from this mold:

LONG STRAIGHT BROWN HAIR, BLUE EYES, MONA LISA SMILE:

♞ Brenda Breyer #500, doll with long ponytail, wearing red cloth leotard, denim bluejeans, and removable black or brown plastic Western boots (pre-catalog release 1978 and 1979, catalog run 1980-86). In the same years as the original Brenda #500 was issued, two additional outfits for her were sold separately. One was English Riding Outfit #501, with tan breeches, black hunt coat, white leotard, black plastic riding crop and English boots, black crash cap (earlier caps are black plastic; later ones are rigid felt/flock); and small white paper competitor's tag printed with "757." The other was Western Riding Outfit #502, with long-sleeved red and white checked cloth shirt, brown fake-suede chaps that zip up the back of the legs, red cloth scarf with wire scarf ring, and brown plastic cowboy hat and Western boots. Although Brenda did not appear in Breyer catalogs until 1980, she debuted two years earlier: the smooth-limbed version was advertised in the 1978 Ward's catalog, where she is sporting Western Outfit #502. The 1979 Ward's catalog offered Brenda (limb version unclear) with both Western Outfit #502 and English Outfit #501. The jointed-limbs version of Brenda #500, clad in the standard red leotard and bluejeans, was sold through the 1979 Sears and Aldens holiday catalogs and other retailers. (See note 1 for this mold for discussion of the limb versions.) Brenda #500 was reissued with big curly hair and a denim jeans jacket in 1988; see that entry below. Western Outfit #502 was reissued in 1988 as Brenda Breyer Riding Outfit #502 and in 1988-89 on Western Brenda Breyer #498. The number 501 previously belonged to the Bolo Tie (see in the Wildlife section). The number 500 previously belonged to the Showcase Collection issue of palomino Arabian Mare (Family Arabian Mare mold).

Sets:

♞ Brenda Breyer And Sulky Set #2446, doll with long ponytail, wearing satiny blue and white jockey shirt and pants, black plastic English boots and crop, and white plastic cap with blue bill (pre-catalog release 1981, catalog run 1982-87). Set also includes alabaster Pacer, brown leather bridle and harness, and plastic sulky (typically blue, but a few black) with moving black plastic tires that have transparent plastic "spoke shields," or "wheel disks," which in real harness racing keep the horse from catching a hoof in the spokes (per collector and harness racing expert Ardith Carlton). Collector Sheryl Leisure's set came with the jockey outfit in a packet and the Brenda dressed in the same outfit as Brenda #500; whether all sets were like this I don't know. Collector Sande Schneider wrote to me that the blue sulkies she has seen vary in color from turquoise to navy. The sulky in her #2446 set is black plastic (see Schneider 1992a), though Brenda's racing silks are the normal blue and white. Set #2446 debuted in the 1981 Aldens and Ward's holiday catalogs, both of which sold the doll separately from the horse and sulky. The 1981 Aldens photo shows a blue sulky of lighter design than the normal sulky; it almost looks like metal wire, as does the black sulky pictured in the 1981 Sears holiday catalog with the Brenda Breyer Harness Racing Set SR with medium bay Pacer (see below). Both of these odd sulkies could be prototypes; to my knowledge no sulkies like them were issued for sale. Ward's sold the #2446 set again in 1982, this time with the addition of a small blue cloth number-blanket with white "7" in the corner, draped over the horse's back. A different set, Sulky Kit #2400, containing only the sulky and harness, is in the 1981 Breyer catalog and on the 1981-85.

• Brenda Breyer Gift Set #3095, doll with long ponytail, same clothing as Brenda Breyer #500 (1980-85). Set also includes sorrel blanket appaloosa Performance Horse, leather bridle with snaffle rings, and fuzzy bareback pad with attached leather surcingle and metal buckle. The bareback pad is shown sometimes as dark brown and sometimes as red in the Breyer catalogs for these years. The 1980 Sears catalog, which also sold this set, shows the pad as dark blue. The model number 3095 previously belonged to the Breyer Rider Gift Set (doll with palomino "Adios").

♞ Brenda Western Gift Set #1120, doll with long ponytail, wearing Western Riding Outfit #502 (1983-85). For Outfit #502, see long-haired Brenda Breyer #500. Set also includes chestnut pinto Western Prancer with chain reins and plastic Western saddle. The tack in this set was the same as the usual tack that came with the Western Prancer without rider. The model number 1120 previously belonged to the Copenhagen decorator Running Mare.

♞ Open Top Buggy set #19841, doll with long loose hair, wearing long dress of patterned dark green fabric with white lace, white ribbon sash, white cloth headband, shoes? (1984). Set also includes buggy pulled by a flocked chestnut Proud Arabian Stallion. Brenda presumably has shoes or boots, but if so, they are hidden by the dress in the 1984 catalog photo. In 1985 this set was reissued in a whole new version, called Drive On A Sunny Day #19841, with a slightly smaller carriage, a flocked "Johar," and a ceramic doll rather than Brenda. For further details see Open Top Buggy (under Proud Arabian Stallion above in the Traditionals section); and Drive On A Sunny Day (under "Johar" above in the Classics section).

BIG CURLY BROWN HAIR AND BLUE EYES, TOOTHY SMILE 1988, MONA LISA SMILE 1989-92; SHORT STRAIGHT BROWN HAIR, BLUE EYES, MONA LISA SMILE, 1993 - CURRENT AS OF 1996 *[the heads of the following dolls vary according to the dates just given; see note 2 for this mold]*:

♞ Brenda Breyer #500, wearing red cloth leotard, blue denim jeans jacket and jeans, and removable black plastic Western boots (1988-90). This big-haired doll is a reissue of the original long-haired Brenda Breyer #500 with the addition of the jeans jacket, which the original doll did not have. An additional Western outfit for the reissued Brenda was sold separately in 1988 only: Brenda Breyer Riding Outfit #502. This outfit is identical to the Western Riding Outfit #502 that was sold as an extra for the original long-haired Brenda #500 (see the entry for her above).

♞ Dressage Brenda Breyer #510, wearing black cloth tailcoat with yellow "vest" edges, white breeches, and satiny white cap-sleeved leotard with attached cravat; and English boots, top hat, and riding crop all of black plastic (1990 - current as of 1996). The #510s that I saw in a toy store in October 1995 came in a new style of box with slots to hold two new accessories: a pink plastic brush and comb. These changes were introduced in 1995, per *JAH* editor Stephanie Macejko (conversation of Oct. 13, 1995).

- English Brenda Breyer #499, wearing same cloths and accessories as in English Riding Outfit #501 (1988-89). For Outfit #501, see long-haired Brenda Breyer #500.
- Saddle Seat Brenda Breyer #512, wearing dark blue cloth saddle suit with appliqué red rosebud on coat lapel, red vest, white shirt with blue and white striped cravat, black plastic jodhpur boots, dark blue plastic bowler, and black plastic riding crop (1993 - current as of 1996). The saddle suit consists of pants and a long tailcoat. This same Brenda (but minus the crop) was sold in Future Champion Show Set SR in 1992; see below. Sometime in 1995 or 1996, #512 is to be issued in a new style of box with slots to hold two new accessories: a plastic brush and comb (per *JAH* editor Stephanie Macejko, conversation of Oct. 13, 1995).
- Show Jumping Brenda Breyer #511, wearing red cloth hunt coat with black collar and no pockets, satiny white leotard, white cloth breeches, black plastic English boots, rigid black felt crash cap, and black plastic riding crop (1990 - current as of 1996). The hunt coat has 3 brass "buttons" and no pockets. The leotard has an attached white cravat. The #511s that I saw in a toy store in October 1995 came in a new style of box with slots to hold two new accessories: a blue plastic brush and comb. These changes were introduced in 1995, per *JAH* editor Stephanie Macejko (conversation of Oct. 13, 1995). The 1990 catalog shows what may be a test doll: her hair is much shorter and frizzier hair than the mid-length curly big hair shown in the 1991-92 catalogs. Whether Brenda simply had a bad hair day for the catalog photo or was actually produced for sale like this in 1990 I don't know. The red coat has 3 gold-colored beads for buttons but actually closes by means of Velcro strips.
- Western Brenda Breyer #498, wearing the same shirt, hat, boots, and chaps as in Brenda Breyer Riding Outfit #502 and Western Riding Outfit #502 (1988-89). For Outfit #502, see long-haired Brenda Breyer #500.
- Western Show Brenda Breyer or Western Brenda Breyer Rider #514, wearing bright pink cloth jacket with black lace lapel trim, white short-sleeved leotard with white lace trim, black satin pants, black fake-suede chaps with black fringe and attached black synthetic leather belt with silver "buckle" monogrammed "BB," black plastic Western boots, and fuzzy black cowboy hat (pre-catalog release 1994, catalog run 1995 - current as of 1996). This model was released in 1994 through State Line Tack's fall/winter supplement 1994-95 catalog, which advertised her as "Designed exclusively for State Line Tack." Despite what this ad copy might suggest, the doll sold by State Line was not a special run but an early release of the new regular-run #514 that appears in the 1995 Breyer catalog, which calls her Western Brenda Breyer Rider. (The 1996 catalog calls her simply Western Brenda.) The boxes in which the 1994 State Line dolls were packaged call her Western Show Brenda Breyer, and I have listed her by this name to avoid confusion with the earlier Western Brenda Breyer #498. The #514s that I saw in a toy store in October 1995 came in a new style of box with slots to hold two new accessories: a blue plastic brush and comb. These changes were introduced in 1995, per *JAH* editor Stephanie Macejko (conversation of Oct. 13, 1995). Brenda #514's hat is identical to Stampede Riggins's; her boots are identical to Brenda Breyer #500's.

Set:

- Princess Of Arabia set #905, wearing pale blue satin long coat hand-beaded with blue and orange beads, and "harem" pants, long-sleeved blouse, and headdress all of plain pale blue satin; Limited Edition (1995). Set also includes a light dapple gray or red roan Black Stallion (Traditional) in matching native costume consisting of bridle, body sheet, and "saddle." The doll is barefooted. Her coat is lined with silver fabric and trimmed with silver edging-ribbon. The horse's bridle is made of the same silver edging and has an attached neck-drape of beaded pale blue satin. Dark turquoise-blue tassels dangle from the neck-drape and reins. His body sheet is the same beaded pale blue satin, lined with dark turquoise blue and trimmed with silver edging-ribbon, which also forms an attached breastcollar. Dark turquoise-blue tassels adorn the breastcollar and bottom edges of the sheet. The "saddle" is a little pale blue satin brocade pillow that attaches to the sheet with Velcro. Silver edging-ribbon forms the stirrups. For details on the horse, see the two entries for #905 under Black Stallion above in the Traditionals section. On June 1, 1995, the QVC home-shopping cable TV channel offered 300 sets that were ordinary #905s with dapple gray horse but that came in boxes labeled with the special-run model number 703095 (per *JAH* editor Stephanie Macejko).

Special-run models made from this mold:

LONG STRAIGHT BROWN HAIR, BLUE EYES, MONA LISA SMILE:

- Brenda Breyer Harness Racing Set SR, same doll and outfit as in Brenda Breyer And Sulky Set #2446 (1981, 1982, 1983, 1984, and 1985). Sears holiday catalog. Set also includes medium bay Pacer and the same blue plastic sulky and leather bridle and harness as in set #2446. In 1982-85, according to the photos in the Sears catalogs, the SR set included in addition a fluffy blue shadow-guard across the Pacer's nose and a small blue cloth number-blanket with white number in the corner: "4" in 1982-84, "7" in 1985. The 1982 and 1983 photos show one further accessory: a tiny "head number"—a little round card printed with the number 4, which attaches to the bridle's crown piece and stands up between the horse's ears. The set shown in the 1981 Sears catalog has several differences from the 1982-85 sets. For one thing, the 1981 photo shows no shadow-guard, number-blanket, or head number. Also it shows Brenda in a black and white outfit (same pattern as the blue and white); whether dolls in this outfit were actually sold I don't know. Finally, the 1981 photo shows a black sulky of lighter design than the normal blue sulky—it almost looks like metal wire, though the description says "easy-to-assemble plastic racing sulky." The 1981 Aldens holiday catalog too shows a sulky that looks like metal wire in the #2446 Brenda Breyer And Sulky Set. These oddly designed sulkies are probably prototypes; but it is possible that some of the 1981 SR sets came with black plastic sulkies of normal design, for collector Sande Schneider got a black plastic sulky in her early #2446 set. However, collector Jane Chapman wrote to me that the set she got from Sears in 1981 came with a normal blue plastic sulky, as well as a Brenda in normal blue and white silks. But like the set in the 1981 Sears catalog, Jane's set lacks the shadow-guard and number blanket (she didn't mention a head number). Also the harness in her set is made of thin leather with the pieces all glued together, whereas the harness in her friend's 1982 set is made of heavier leather with stitching across the top of the girth.
- Brenda Breyer Sulky And Pacer Set SR, same doll and outfit as in Brenda Breyer And Sulky Set #2446 (1981, 1982, and 1983). Penney's holiday catalog. Set also includes light golden chestnut Pacer and the same blue plastic sulky and leather bridle and harness as in set #2446. In 1982-83, but not 1981, the set also included a small blue cloth number-blanket with a white number "2" in the corner and a fluffy blue shadow-guard across the Pacer's nose, according to the Penney's catalog photos. The 1982 photo shows, in addition, a tiny "head number"—a little round card printed with the number 2, which attaches to the bridle's crown piece and stands up between the horse's ears. My photocopy of the 1983 catalog page is blurry but does not seem to include the head number.
- "Legionario" With Brenda Breyer Rider set SR, doll in satiny short white dress with pink lace at the hem and silver rickrack at neck, waist, and cuffs; white tights; pink cloth slippers; pink ribbon around ponytail; and elastic ankle-cuff attached to metal bracket (1985). Penney's holiday catalog. Set also includes flocked and haired white "Legionario." The horse has a red and white leather surcingle, white leather bridle with two reins, and a removable red plume on top of his head, which attaches to the bridle's crownpiece. Brenda's metal foot-bracket hooks onto the horse's surcingle so that she can stand on his back like a proper circus ballerina.
- U.S. Equestrian Team Set SR, doll in red cloth hunt coat with black or blue collar and pocket rims, white turtleneck sleeveless leotard, white cloth breeches, flocked black hunt cap, black plastic English boots and crop, and small white competitor's tag printed with "757" (1980). Penney's holiday catalog. Set also includes regular-run #59 "Morganglanz," leather English saddle and bridle, and triple-bar jump. The jump, as shown in the Penney's catalog photo, consists of three separate post-and-rail fences made of wood and painted white, with bands of red on the crossbars. One fence is low, with a single crossbar; the next is medium height with two crossbars; and the last is high with three crossbars. The Penney's photo does not show Brenda's crop, crash cap, white shirt, or competitor's tag, but I believe these items did come with the set because they were included in an English riding outfit with red coat that I purchased new in cellophane pack in 1995 from a sale of old inventory. The pack has a sticker with the number 9206178, which I believe is the Penney's catalog number (I don't have the text page for this Penney's catalog). The coat has a "Made in Hong Kong" tag sewn into one seam. Such outfits were also advertised as early as January 1983 on Bentley Sales Company price lists, as "501R Red Brenda Breyer English Riding Outfit." Presumably these outfits were leftovers from the 1980 Penney's run. The crop, cap, and shirt, although not the competitor's tag, were also included with a red-coated Brenda purchased by collector Lisa Barnett from Bentley's in 1986. (Thanks to Lisa for photos of her doll.) Presumably Lisa's doll was also a leftover from the 1980 run. Lisa's red coat differs slightly from mine: hers has 2 "brass buttons" (gold-colored beads) on the front and a black collar and pocket rims, whereas mine has 3 "brass buttons" on front and a blue, almost turquoise, collar and pocket rims. (Both coats actually close by means of a snap.) A blue collar is visible in the Penney's catalog photo. The "buttons" and pocket rims are not visible in the Penney's photo because the Brenda there is slumped miserably forward over her mount's withers, head down and face hidden, as though she were about to fall off.

SHORT STRAIGHT BROWN HAIR, BLUE EYES, MONA LISA SMILE:

- "Black Beauty" Gift Set SR #700894, doll in long-sleeved red and white checked cloth shirt, denim bluejeans, and removable brown plastic Western boots (1994). Mid-year special. Set also includes glossy black Classic "Black Beauty," book, and halter and lead. Breyer promotional literature shows Brenda's hair as curly, but the dolls came with straight hair. The jeans, shirt, and boots are identical to those on Western Brenda Breyer #498. The halter is black leather with red leather brow and nose bands, and wire buckles. The lead line is black leather with a silver chain leader that circles the horse's nose. This tack, which I believe is made in China, is identical to that sold in the Future Champion Show Set SR.
- Female Rider SR #710995, doll in blue-and-white striped long-sleeved cloth shirt with embroidered yellow "B," pale yellow-tan cloth breeches with black fake-suede knee patches, black plastic English boots, fuzzy black crash cap, and black plastic riding crop (1995). Penney's holiday catalog. 6,000 dolls made. Model number and quantity are per *JAH* editor Stephanie Macejko, whose own dressage-schooling attire provided the prototype for this doll's outfit. "Female Rider" is the imaginative title given to the doll in the Penney's catalog. The shirt has a white collar and Velcro closures in the back.
- Future Champion Show Set SR #494092, same doll and clothing as Saddle Seat Brenda Breyer #512 (1992). Sears holiday catalog. Set also includes bay pinto Saddlebred Weanling and removable show halter and lead. The regular-run Saddle Seat Brenda Breyer #512 differs from the SR doll only in having a crop, which the SR lacks. The halter is black leather with red leather brow and nose bands, and wire buckles. The lead line is black leather with a silver chain leader that circles the horse's nose. This tack came sealed in a packet marked "Made in China." This tack it identical to that sold in the "Black Beauty" Gift Set SR.

Notes:

(1) Most Brenda Breyer dolls have joints only at the neck, shoulders, waist, and hips. Some early #500 Brendas, however, have additional limb joints—large, gruesome ones—at the wrists and ankles. This unusual version appears clearly in the 1979 Sears and Aldens holiday catalogs (she may be in the Penney's and Ward's catalogs for that year, too, but the photos are unclear). She was also available at toy stores; collector Sheryl Leisure got a jointed-limbs Brenda from a collector who had purchased the doll new at Toy Villa in Southern California sometime in the 1980s. At least some of these jointed-limbs dolls, like Sheryl's, came in unusual packaging, with Brenda astride a cardboard cutout of the palomino Western Prancer. (Some smooth-limbed Brendas may have come in this packaging, too.) Neither the jointed-limbs Brenda nor the unusual packaging appears in any Breyer catalogs; all catalogs that include Brenda, starting with the 1980 catalog, show the smooth-limbs version. Oddly enough, the jointed-limbs doll, though early, apparently was not the very first Brenda. The 1978 Ward's holiday catalog, the earliest Brenda venue that I know of, featured what is evidently a smooth-limbed doll—although her long sleeves cover her wrists in the Ward's photo, the text makes a point of her smooth limbs: "bendable knees and arms (without hinges and joints)." And the back cover of *JAH* Winter 1979, the first *JAH* issue for that year, shows a Brenda with no wrist joints at all, and insists, "no unsightly hinges or joints." So I believe the jointed-limbs doll was issued only in 1979, perhaps only for the holiday season. The real mystery is why she was issued at all, if the joints were thought to be so "unsightly."

(2) I am not certain whether the Brenda Breyer dolls with toothy grins shown only in the 1988 catalog were produced for sale. I don't believe I have actually seen one. But then, I don't believe I've looked real hard, either.

(3) The Brenda Breyer mold was designed by Eddie Mosqueda, of Varner Studios in Torrance, California, for Unger Toys, of Henry Unger International (per Breyer executive Peter Stone, conversation of Nov. 1994). Unger marketed the dolls, as well as Brenda's outfits #501 and #502 and Brenda Breyer Horse Stickers #510A, under license from Breyer for a few years, until Breyer took over direct control of these items. The earliest dolls, including jointed-limbs and smooth-limbs Brendas with long hair, have Unger's jack-in-the-box logo and the words "Unger Toys / Made in Hong Kong" molded into their backs. Later Brendas have only "Made in China" molded into their backs. The sulky that came in the #2446 set and SR sets has the round "Breyer Molding Co." stamp, located on the underside of the seat.

Brenda Breyer Riding Outfit #502 — see Brenda Breyer #500 (long-haired)

Brenda Breyer Sulky Kit #2400 — see Brenda Breyer And Sulky set #2446

Brenda Western Gift Set — see under Brenda Breyer

Breyer Rider — • Traditional-scale girl doll, hard plastic with jointed limbs, rooted synthetic hair. Sculptor unknown. Mold advertised in the 1976 catalog but never released (per *JAH* 15/#2 May/June 1988, p. 15).

Catalog-run models made from this mold:

- Breyer Rider #400, girl with long straight blond hair and blue eyes, wearing white cloth T-shirt with horsehead design on front and denim bluejeans (1976). Same doll and clothing as in Breyer Rider Gift Set #3095. Though advertised in the 1976 catalog, this doll was never released. The model number 400 previously belonged to the Showcase Collection issue of palomino Arabian Stallion (Family Arabian Stallion mold).

Set:

- Breyer Rider Gift Set #3095, same doll and clothing as Breyer Rider #400 (1976). Set was also to include palomino "Adios" and rubbery Western saddle and bridle. This set was never released, although it is advertised in the 1976 Breyer catalog. The tack is not shown in the catalog photo, but it does appear in *JAH* 15/#2 May/June 1988 (p. 15) and on the boxes of the few sets that were produced as samples (these boxes differ from the box shown in the catalog). For further details see Breyer Rider Gift Set under "Adios" above in the Traditionals section. The model number 3095 later belonged to the Brenda Breyer Gift Set with Brenda doll on sorrel blanket appaloosa Performance Horse.

Note: The Breyer Rider doll was to be manufactured in Hong Kong by the Mego company, to judge from the fact that the Breyer Rider in the 1976 catalog is identical to Mego dolls sold independently of Breyer. These dolls have "Mego," "Hong Kong," and the copyright date 1972 molded into the plastic on their backs. (Thanks to Sheryl Leisure for letting me examine her Mego doll.)

"Buck" And Hillary Gift Set — see under Hillary

Darla — see under Hillary

Dressage Brenda — see under Brenda Breyer

Eagle — ♞ Classic-scale girl doll, soft plastic head and wire-core limbs, rooted synthetic hair. Sculptor unknown. Mold in production 1995.

Special-run models made from this mold:

- ⊕ Eagle And "Pow Wow" set SR #705095, grinning Native American girl doll named Eagle, with painted brown eyes, white teeth, and red lips, with long black hair in two braids tied with turquoise ribbons; real feather in hair; wearing fringed orange cloth shirt with tan "burlap" collar, fringed tan "burlap" skirt with orange ribbon trim, and turquoise cloth ankle bands (1995). Mid-year special. Set also includes black pinto horse "Pow Wow" (Classic "Johar" mold), riding blanket, and tan leather halter and lead. About 4,000 sets made, per *JAH* editor stephanie Macejko (conversation of July 1996). The riding blanket is the same tan "burlap" cloth as Eagle's skirt, with a band of fringed turquoise cloth at each end. Orange diamond designs are appliquéd onto the turquoise band, and a real feather, dyed orange, is sewn onto one side of the blanket. A "Girth" of white ribbon with a Velcro closure is tacked onto the underside of the blanket. The set's name and number are per the Reeves International 1995 Mid-Year Introduction brochure and the set's box. For details on the horse, see under "Johar" in the Classics section.
- ⊕ Willow And "Shining Star" set SR #703495, Willow is same doll as Eagle in set #705095, but wears a white satin shirt with white fringe, beaded turquoise-blue "bib," beaded white satin pants with white fringe, beaded blue cloth tiara with real feather, bead-and-feather ornaments on braids, and beaded white satin slippers (1995). *Just About Horses* Retail Set for subscribers only. 5,000 sets made. Set also includes bay blanket appaloosa horse "Shining Star" (Classic Rearing Stallion mold), black leather halter with red brow and nose bands, and black leather lead with chain. To receive a set, subscribers had to submit to their Breyer retailer a coupon that came in *JAH* 22/#4 May/June 1995. The set is advertised in the Reeves International 1995 Mid-Year Introduction brochure. For details on the horse, see under Rearing Stallion in the Classics section.

Note: The Eagle doll mold has no mold stamps. She does, however, have two holes in her back, for what purpose I have no idea. The swivel joint at her waste is on an angle, so that the doll assumes different postures as you bend her right or left.

English Brenda — see under Brenda Breyer

English Riding Outfit #501 and SR — see Brenda Breyer #500 (long-haired)

Female Rider SR — see under Brenda Breyer

Future Champion Show Set SR — see under Brenda Breyer

Götz "Jessica" doll with Stablemates — see Götz "Jessica" Doll above in the Stablemates section

Hillary — ♞ Classic-scale girl doll, jointed hard plastic body with soft plastic head, molded-on English boots, rooted synthetic hair. Sculpted by William Burford. Mold in catalog-run production 1995 - current as of 1996.

Catalog-run models made from this mold:

- ♠ English Hillary Doll #515, grinning doll with painted brown eyes, white teeth, and red lips; long curly brown hair; molded-on black hunt boots; in red cloth hunt coat, silky white short-sleeved leotard and breeches; with black plastic crop, black-flocked hunt cap, and blue plastic brush and comb (1995 - current as of 1996). In the B Ranch series. Same doll and clothing as in "Buck" And Hillary Gift Set #2004 [1995 - current as of 1996]. The top portion of the doll's hair is in a pony tail secured with a red plastic band. The doll's britches end just below the knee. The hunt cap is made of a rather flimsy transparent plastic with black flocking. The red coat, which closes with Velcro, has a black collar and tiny round "brass buttons." Both the hunt coat and the leotard have a little sewn-in tag that says "Made in China." The description I've given of this doll is based on my own specimen, purchased new in August 1995 in the #2004 set. The English Hillary shown in the 1995 catalog is somewhat different—she seems to have black hair, and she has no teeth showing in her smile. Presumably this was a prototype piece not produced for sale.
- ♠ Western Hillary Doll #516, same doll as English Hillary #515, in turquoise cloth jacket, silky white short-sleeved leotard with turquoise appliqué rose, black satin pants, and black fake-suede chaps with black fringe and silver plastic-cloth "B" buckle; with black-flocked cowboy hat and pink plastic brush and comb (1995 - current as of 1996). In the B Ranch series. Except for her clothing, this doll is just the same as the English Hillary, with the same facial coloring, hair, and so on. Western Hillary's ponytail is secured with a blue plastic band rather than red. The cowboy hat is made of a rather flimsy transparent plastic with black flocking. The jacket has lacy black rickrack down the lapels. The leotard has a lace color. The jacket and the leotard each have a little sewn-in tag that says "Made in China." The description I've given of this doll is based on my own specimen, purchased new in August 1995. The Western Hillary shown in the 1995 catalog is slightly different in that she has blue eyes rather than brown, and gold rickrack on her jacket. Presumably this was a prototype piece not produced for sale.

Sets:

- "Buck" And Hillary Gift Set #2004, same doll and clothing as English Hillary #515 (1995 - current as of 1996). In the B Ranch series. Set also includes pale buckskin horse "Buck," blue leather saddle and bridle, green and white roll-top jump, and neck ribbon for "Buck." The saddle and bridle shown with this set in the 1995 catalog are brown, but those in my own set (purchased in July 1995) are blue, with a red girth and white stirrup leather on the saddle. According to *JAH* editor Stephanie Macejko, the blue tack is correct for this set; the catalog photo is wrong (conversation of Aug. 1995). The bridle's throatlatch and saddle's girth close with Velcro. The stirrups are metal wire. The seat and flaps of the saddle are stamped with "stitching" around the seat and other detailing, including a Breyer logo on each flap. The roll-top jump (as it is called in the 1995 catalog) consists of two separate parts: a roll-top part, which is a rounded length of solid wood completely covered with green felt, and a fence part, consisting of two wooden standards connected by two round wooden rails, all painted white. The roll-top part, which has a metal "Breyer" cartouche logo glued to the center, sits beneath the rails of the fence. For details on the horse and ribbon, see under "Silky Sullivan" in the Classics section.
- ♠ Darla, in "Amazement's" Riding Set #95104, same basic doll as English Hillary #515 but with painted blue eyes and hot-pink lips; long blonde hair; in hot pink cloth racing jacket with yellow appliqués, stretchy white short-sleeved leotard, stretchy white breeches, and yellow and hot-pink soft plastic racing cap (1995 - current as of 1996). Set also includes Dapples "Amazement" stallion, tack, accessories, and storybook. For a full list of tack and accessories, see the entry for this set under "Amazement" in the Dapples section.
- Darla, in Dapples Deluxe Rider Set #95107, same doll and clothing as in "Amazement's" Riding Set #95104, tack, accessories, and book (1995 - current as of 1996). Set also includes "Amazement," "Sunny," and "Sunny's" Mom horse models. For a full list of tack and accessories, see under "Amazement" in the Dapples section. Also see the Dapples section for descriptions of the horses.

Notes:

(1) This mold was designed by William Burford, of Langhorn, Pennsylvania, who used as his real-life model Mrs. Lisa Godbee, wife of the Dapples line production manager at Reeves International, according to Breyer executive Peter Stone (conversations of Nov. 1994 and July 1995). The dolls and their clothing are manufactured in China—the boxes in which they are packed say "Made in China," as do cloth tags sewn into some of their garments.

(2) The Hillary mold has two separate mold stamps, one on the back of the head that says "© Reeves China," and another on the doll's back that says "© Reeves/Breyer Made in China."

"Jessica" doll with Stablemates — see Götz "Jessica" Doll above in the Stablemates section

Kelly Reno — see under Alec Ramsey

Latigo — A Breyer rider model that didn't happen. This doll, assigned the model number 520, is listed on a Breyer company computer printout of activity 1985-92 as part of no fewer than four projects, all slated for 1991 and all designated "Proposal cancelled." He also appears on the typescript 1991 Breyer price list (issued Dec. 6, 1990), listed as "520 Latigo [price] TBA [to be announced]." I don't know whether Latigo was to be a new mold or a reissue of the Alec Ramsey doll in new guise, but according to the printout listings he was to be manufactured in the Orient. Three of the printout listings—one for Penney's, one for Sears, and one, which calls the doll Latigo Trooper, for "cust. all"—indicate that he was to be sold in a set with a black "Phar Lap" (mold #90) and a Breyer leather Western saddle (#2395). The fourth listing, which mentions no horse, calls the model "Cole 'Latigo' Cantrell doll in cowboy outfit" and specifies the outfit as a brown jacket and trousers, red hat, boots, and gun. A newsletter I received in February 1991 from the Small World toy store and mail-order company sheds a bit more light on this doll: "#520 Latigo a new male rider doll based on Stan Lynde's cartoon cowboy joins the line." The December 1991 newsletter from Horses International mail-order company provides Latigo's epitaph: "The boy doll, Latigo, has been removed from our list. Hopefully in the near future they will produce a boy doll. I know that I still get requests for Ben Breyer, so there must be a demand out there."

"Legionario" With Brenda Breyer Rider set SR — see under Brenda Breyer

Miniature Collection dolls — See Open Top Buggy (under Brenda Breyer). For the ceramic dolls in the other horse-and-buggy sets in this collection and associated SR sets, see these listings above in the Classics section: Collector's One Horse Open Sleigh SR (under "Black Beauty"); Delivery Wagon (under "Keen"); The Doctor's Buggy (under Black Stallion); Drive On A Sunny Day (under "Johar"); Family To Church On Sunday (under "Duchess" and under "Jet Run"); Joey's Pony Cart (under "Merrylegs"); Montgomery Ward Delivery Wagon SR (under "Keen"); and Pony Cart And Driver SR (under "Merrylegs"). For discussion see Miniature Collection in the Classics section.

Open Top Buggy set — see under Brenda Breyer

Paul Beebe doll — see Ben Breyer (under Alec Ramsey)

"Pepper" And Lisa, Hunter/Jumper Set — see under Bitsy Breyer

Rearing Circus Stallion With Ringmaster set SR — see under Alec Ramsey

Saddle Club Series — see the following entries under Bitsy Breyer:"Cobalt" and Veronica, Hunter/Jumper set #1025; "Pepper" And Lisa, Hunter/Jumper Set #1018; "Spot" And Kate, Western Set #1019; "Starlight" And Carole, Cross Country Set #1016; "Topside" And Stevie, Cross Country Set #1017

Saddle Seat Brenda — see under Brenda Breyer

Show Jumping Brenda — see under Brenda Breyer

"Spot" And Kate, Western Set — see under Bitsy Breyer

Stampede Riggins — 🐴 Traditional-scale man doll, soft plastic with wire-core limbs, painted-on hair. Sculpted by Barnum Models. Mold in catalog-run production 1993 - current as of 1996.
Catalog-run models made from this mold:
🐴 Stampede Riggins, Breyer Western Rider, #513, man doll with painted-on brown hair and blue eyes, wearing ankle-length off-white cloth raincoat, short-sleeved blue-and-white-striped leotard, tan pants with attached blue ribbon suspenders, red neckerchief, black plastic Western boots, and fuzzy black cowboy hat (1993 - current as of 1996). Stampede is in the 1993 catalog (hiding behind his neckerchief), which says "Available September," and indeed he was not released until late in 1993. His boots are the same as Brenda Breyer's Western boots, with an even top; they are not like the boots shown in the 1993 catalog, which must be prototypes. Stampede's hat as shown in the 1993 catalog is white, but the hat actually issued with the doll is black, as shown in subsequent catalogs. In the 1996 catalog, Stampede's full name was shortened to Western Stampede Riggins.
Special-run models made from this mold:
♻ Texas Cowboy Replica SR #711294, same doll as Stampede Riggins #513, wearing brown velour vest, long-sleeved red cloth leotard with double-breasted front with four round gold buttons down each side, light blue pants with integral black belt with gold cloth "buckle," dark plaid neckerchief, black plastic Western boots, and fuzzy black cowboy hat (1994). Penney's holiday catalog. 3,000 models made. Model number and quantity are per JAH editor Stephanie Macejko (conversation of Sept. 1995). Why Penney's deemed it necessary to specify this doll as a "Replica" I don't know. The Replica's hat and boots are identical to Stampede Riggins's.
Notes:
(1) Stampede Riggins was designed by Barnum Models, of Cincinnati, Ohio, according to Breyer executive Peter Stone (conversation of Nov. 1994). The dolls and their clothing are manufactured in China, as is indicated by the doll's mold stamp and on his packaging. (2) The Stampede Riggins mold has a mold stamp on his back that says "Breyer™ / Made in China."

"Starlight" And Carole, Cross Country Set — see under Bitsy Breyer

Sulky Kit #2400 — see Brenda Breyer And Sulky set #2446

Texas Cowboy Replica SR — see under Stampede Riggins

"Topside" And Stevie, Cross Country Set — see under Bitsy Breyer

U.S. Equestrian Team Set SR — see under Brenda Breyer

Western Brenda and Western Show Brenda — see under Brenda Breyer

Western Riding Outfit #502 — see Brenda Breyer #500 (long-haired)

Willow — see under Eagle

General note: All the cattle and hogs are Traditional scale except for two of the oldest bull molds: the polled walking Black Angus Bull and the horned walking Hereford Bull. These two are smaller than the rest, being approximately Classic scale.

Ayrshire Calf — see under Calf

Ayrshire Cow, horned — see under Cow

Ayrshire Cow SR, polled — see under Cow

"Big Red One" SR — see Red Angus Bull SR (under Black Angus Bull, polled, standing)

Black Angus Bull — Polled, standing, large bull, looking right, tail tip attached to left hock. Sculpted by Chris Hess. Mold in catalog-run production 1978 - current as of 1996.

Catalog-run models made from this mold:

- Black Angus Bull #365, black, no white markings, black hooves, matte (1978 - current as of 1996). This model replaced the old walking Black Angus #72, and is much larger than the old fellow.

Special-run models made from this mold:

- Red Angus Bull SR, nicknamed "The Big Red One," dark red chestnut; no white markings; glossy black eyes; most with dark red chestnut nose, some with pale tan-pink nose; darker chestnut hooves; matte (1983 and 1984). Made for the Iowa Red Angus Association (IRAA). 1,000 models made: 100 with tan-pink nose (called simply "pink nose" by collectors) and 900 with dark nose (same color as body or somewhat darker). The 1,000 quantity is per former IRAA secretary Ardis Heidebrink (per correspondence between Ardis Heidebrink and collectors Cheryl Mundee and Lea Dobranski; copies kindly provided to me by Cheryl). Models came with certificate of ownership issued by the IRAA. The pink-nosed bulls are a bit browner, less red, in body color than the dark-nosed bulls. Bulls of both nose colors are numbered by hand in black between the front legs. *Numbering*: The numbering was done by the IRAA, not by Breyer, according to Breyer executive Peter Stone (conversation of Mar. 1995) and Ardis Heidebrink. The numbering system, which was verified for Cheryl Mundee by Ardis Heidebrink, is complicated. The pink-nosed bulls, which were the first ones produced (1983), have an individual number written over the run-total number /100, indicating that there were 100 models made in that run. For example, collector Jo Kulwicki's pink-nosed bull is numbered 10/100, Cheryl Mundee's is 88/100, and my own is 92/100. (My bull, unlike Jo's and Cheryl's, has glossed nose and hooves; the gloss might have been added by the Angus Assn.) Of the dark-nosed bulls, 200 of them have an individual number written over a run-total number of /200 (I know of numerous specimens, among them Heather Wells's, 101/200; Cheryl Mundee's, 128/200; Jo Kulwicki's, 170/200; and Gale Good's, 182/200). 300 more dark-nosed bulls have an individual number over a run-total number of /300 (I've heard of two specimens: 249/300 and another with a number in the 200's over /300). The last 400 dark-nosed bulls have individual numbers but no run-total number (Sheryl Leisure's bull is 242; Paula DeFeyter's, 247; Deanna Schane's four specimens: 236, 237, 241, and 243). *History*: The "Big Red One" SR was originally made for the IRAA to sell at a national convention in 1983. In 1984, Ardis Heidebrink of the IRAA ran an ad in *JAH* XI/#1 1984 (p. 8) offering leftover bulls for sale for $20. The pink-nosed bulls were the first ones made: the /100 series is identified as the first by the certificates of ownership, dated 1983, that came with my and Cheryl Mundee's pink-nosed /100 series bulls: "Under Limited Edition of the first 100 Replicas of the Red Angus Bull. The first 100 will be numbered as a Collectors Item. 'The Big Red One' is authorized by the Iowa Red Angus Association." Cheryl's, Gale's, Jo's, Sheryl's, and Paula DeFeyter's dark-nosed bulls, on the other hand, came with certificates that have no date and don't mention any quantity in the printed statement: "Under limited edition / Red Angus Bull—Collectors' Series / 'The Big Red One' is authorized by / the Iowa Red Angus Association." Interestingly, the *JAH* ad, which has a black and white photo of a bull with a light nose, undoubtedly pinky-tan in real life, states: "A limited number of Red Angus bulls were made by the Breyer Molding Co. for the Iowa Red Angus Association. The National Red Angus convention in Bettendorf, Iowa was the first official offering. Each bull is authentic in appearance with a *pink nose*" (my italics). At first glance this might suggest that the pink-nosed bulls were made second, not first, for after all, they are advertised in a 1984 *JAH*. But this idea is contradicted by my 1983 certificate. And there are further clues in the ad that suggest a reading consistent with the certificate. In addition to the photo of the bull, the ad shows a copy of the 1983 certificate, identical to mine and Cheryl's. But in the photo, the small print on the certificate, which is the part I quoted above about "the first 100," is illegible, and it appears to have been made so intentionally. My theory is that the Association effaced that print because by the time they placed the ad, they had few if any of the / 100 series left and knew they would be offering the newly made, differently numbered bulls. They didn't want anybody to feel misled by the statement about "the first 100." But at the time they placed the ad, the theory continues, they did not yet have the new bulls in hand but only on order. And what the Association thought it had on order was a bunch of bulls painted just like the /100 series bulls—namely, with pink noses. This would explain why the Association put the "pink nose" description in the ad. I'd bet hard cash they were surprised when the new bulls arrived with dark noses.

Notes:

(1) To judge from my own models, the ears and scrotum on this mold are separately molded pieces. The seam around the base of the latter organ is very well effaced, but the seam joining the two halves of the organ has a side-to-side orientation, revealing that this portion can't be an integral part of the mold.

(2) The large Black Angus Bull mold has the round "Breyer Molding Co." stamp. Most and possibly all models made from this mold also have a "B" stamp. If any lack it (I've never seen one that did), they would in all likelihood be the earliest ones. This mold is one of only a few Breyer molds that still have the "B." This mold was never given the "U.S.A." stamp.

Black Angus Bull — Polled, walking, small bull, looking left, tail tip attached to right hock, molded-on halter. Probably copied from an original piece by Edward Marshall Boehm. Mold in catalog-run production 1959/60 - 1973, 1976-77 (smooth-barrel mold version 1959/60 - early to mid 1960s; semi-rough-coat mold version early to mid 1960s; full-rough-coat mold version 1967 [maybe earlier] - 1973, 1976-77).

Catalog-run models made from this mold:

Poodle-cut (smooth-barrel), semi-rough, and full-rough mold versions:

- Black Angus Bull #72, black; no white markings; black hooves; hand-painted eyewhites and/or eyepinks on early models; halter is metallic copper, brick red, or chocolate brown; early ones glossy, later ones matte (1959/60 - 1973, 1976-77). This bull is not in the 1958 catalog or price list but he is in the 1960 catalog. Most glossy #72s have a metallic copper halters, but I've heard of examples of glossies with chocolate-brown halters (see, e.g., *Quequechan Model Horse Collector*, Apr. 1985). Matte bulls have chocolate-brown or brick-red halters. All the matte-finish #72s I know of are the full-rough mold version (see note 1 for this mold) and have no eyewhites, and most have a "U.S.A." stamp, which dates them to no earlier than 1970. The one semigloss bull I have heard of, owned by collector Heather Hagerstrand, has a red halter and "U.S.A." like typical matte bulls. Collector Liz Strauss found a couple of matte bulls (one of which I now own) with no "U.S.A.," which indicates that the switch to matte finish on #72 did occur prior to 1970. The glossy models come in all three mold versions (the poodle-cut being the rarest). None of the glossies I've seen have any mold stamps, and all have eyewhites and/or eyepinks: lines of white or pale pink painted delicately along the top and bottom of the eyeballs or on the eyelid rims. Some glossies also have a white or pink mouth line, per collector Sheryl Leisure. Lemmons 1990 says the poodle-cut version is "glossy with a gold halter and eyewhites on the top eyelid and eyepinks along the bottom eyelid," while the glossy non-poodle-cut ones have gold halter and eyewhites on upper eyelids, nothing on the lower lids. But in my experience, these details vary. My own and collector Jo Kulwicki's glossy #72 poodle-cut bulls have eyewhites on upper and lower lids; no eyepinks. My glossy #72 semi-rough has whites on the uppers and pale pinks on the lowers, and my glossy full-rough has whites on uppers and lowers. Also, both of mine have copper halters, as do many others I've seen, including a pristinely mint bull with an untarnished bright copper halter, found new in box by collector Melanie Teller. I've also seen a glossy #72 with white eyebrows rather than whites in the eyes. Finally, collector Teresa Ward wrote to me that her poodle-cut bull has a gold stripe inside each ear, as well as eyewhites on the upper lids, pinks on the lowers, and a copper halter that is gold on the sections behind the ears. Since this is the only such bull we know of, we are not sure whether the gold in the ears is OF.
- Polled Hereford Bull #73, brown with white head, withers, breast, belly, and tail tip; some with dorsal stripe; pink muzzle with gray detailing; pink genitals and hooves; dark brown halter; most are glossy (1961/63 - 1965). Most #73s I've seen have a small brown patch on the upper breast, as shown on the model in the 1963 catalog (the only catalog in my possession that pictures this model); but Jo Kulwicki's #73 lacks this patch. One of my bulls has brown outlines around his inner ears, as is shown on the #73 in the 1963 catalog. All but one of the #73s known to me are glossy, have no mold stamps, and are either the full-rough or the poodle-cut mold version. The one exception, which I saw in person at BreyerFest 1996, was a semigloss #73 of the semi-rough mold version, with no mold stamps. For discussion of the evolution of the mold versions, see note 1 for this mold. The model number 73 later belonged to the Spanish Fighting Bull.

Special-run models made from this mold:

Mold version unknown:

- Black Angus Bull SR?, woodgrain (probably sometime in the period 1959/60 - 1966). This model is not listed in any Breyer catalogs or price lists in my possession, which is why I list him as an SR. He is mentioned (as "polled walking Hereford in woodgrain") on *Breyer Collector's Video*, but no specimen is shown, so I don't know what mold version he is. Evidently only a few are known to exist. My dating for this model corresponds to the introduction date of the mold and the ending date of the heyday of woodgrain models. But it is conceivable that he was made in the late 1960s or even the early 1970s.

Notes:

(1) This mold comes in three versions, all of which have to do with the bull's coat. *Smooth-barrel version*: This is often called the "poodle-cut" version. The bull's barrel, back, and croup are smooth, while the rest of the body has a rough, curly coat. This version occurs on glossy #72s and #73s and is the earliest and the rarest of the three mold versions—it is visible on the #72 in the 1960 catalog, the earliest Breyer publication in which this mold is listed. *Semi-rough-coat version*: The back and croup are smooth, but the barrel itself has a rough coat, as on the rest of the body. In my experience this version occurs on glossy #72s and semigloss #73s (I've seen only one such #73). *Full-rough-coat version*: The barrel, back, and croup all have a rough coat, as on the rest of the body. This version occurs on glossy and matte #72s and on #73s, which are, I believe, all glossy. This version is the latest and most common of the three. It is visible in the 1963 catalog on the glossy #73 and in the 1970 catalog on the matte #72 (my intervening catalogs are blurry). My guess is that the semi-rough was an intermediate version, made in 1961 and/ or 1962—years in which no catalogs were published to my knowledge. This guess fits with the evidence of earlier and later catalogs and with the evidence of finishes and mold stamps: On one hand, all semi-roughs I know of are glossy with the sole exception of a semigloss semi-rough #73, and all without exception lack the "U.S.A." stamp. Both of these characteristics indicate early models. On the other hand, some full-rough bulls are matte and have the "U.S.A." stamp, characteristics indicating late models. Oddly, the poodle-cut version appears in a 1972 Miller Stockman saddlery catalog; presumably the

photo used was old or the models being sold were old stock.

(2) Marney Walerius reports a standing version of this mold (see Walerius 1991, pp. 23, 48, 86, 90, 92), though her main listings for it, on pages 23 and 48, conflict with each other on dates (1957-58 vs. 1958-60) and on whether Polled Hereford #73 came in this version. I spoke to Marney on the phone about the alleged standing version in March 1992. She said she was sure it existed because she used to own one, a Black Angus #72, which she had gotten from another collector. Marney had given it to a boyfriend, however, and no longer had access to it, nor did she have a photo. Despite these statements, I am very skeptical of the existence of such bulls, and I think Marney must have been confused. For one thing, I have never heard of a standing version of this mold from any other source, yet if this version was made for two or three years, as Marney's book says, there should be specimens in known collections. Marney also said her model had the Breyer copyright stamp. But the walking version of this mold never had the Breyer stamp, and I don't believe that Breyer would have put this stamp on the alleged standing version only to remove it when the walking version was issued. For another thing, Marney's book does not mention that she ever owned such a bull but on the contrary registers some uncertainty about this version (and other mold versions); see particularly her "Note" regarding #72 and #73 on page 48. This "Note" raises further doubts about a standing version by stating: "There is a China Walking Hereford from England that looks very similar to Breyer's. Changes may have occurred due to copyright dispute." But if Breyer took their design from a walking china bull, modifying it to a standing position to avoid legal challenges, why would they change it back to a walking position just a couple of years later? This doesn't make sense. Breyer may indeed have taken the design for its Angus from a china bull, but I believe it was a standing china bull of American origin (see note 4 for this mold).

(3) The ears and scrotum on this bull are integral parts of the mold, judging from my own models.

(4) According to Breyer executive Peter Stone, this mold was probably adapted from a porcelain Angus Bull (5" x 8.25") by Edward M. Boehm, first released in 1950 (see Palley 1976, pp. 163-64). Stone is not completely certain of this, for although he still owns some other Boehm pieces copied by Breyer in the 1950s, he believes he does not have the Boehm Angus. But if the Breyer is based on the Boehm as Stone suspects, still it is true that of the several Breyer molds copied from Boehm originals, the Breyer Angus is least similar to its porcelain prototype, to judge from the (rather dark) photo of the porcelain in Palley 1976. The Breyer is a bit larger, has a halter (the Boehm doesn't), has its ears set at a slightly lower angle, and has its tail tip attached to the right hock (the Boehm's tail tip hangs free). Also, the Breyer has its right front leg bent in a walking position, while the Boehm's right front is straight, in a standing position. But the positions of the other three legs on the two bulls are identical.

(5) Early models of the small Black Angus Bull mold—including, to my knowledge, all smooth-barrels, all semi-roughs, and the earliest full-roughs, some of them matte—have no round Breyer stamp or other mold marks. Later models (matte full-roughs) have the "U.S.A." stamp only. This mold was never given the round "Breyer Molding Co." stamp.

Black Angus Calf SR — see under Calf

Brahma Bull — ♞ Large horns, standing, looking right, tail tip attached to right hock. Copied from an original sculpture by Edward Marshall Boehm. Mold in catalog-run production 1955/57 - current as of 1996.

Catalog-run models made from this mold:

♞ Brahma Bull #70, shaded gray, with pale gray or white barrel and darker gray hindquarters and forehand; dark gray neck; dark gray hooves; white horns with charcoal tips; glossy, matte, and semigloss (1955/57 - 1995). This model is called Brahman Bull in the first Breyer publication I know of that lists it—a single-sided Breyer catalog sheet that I date to 1956/57—but it is called Brahma Bull in the 1958 and subsequent catalogs. Collector Robert Peterson's very early bull, purchased from a man who worked for Breyer in the 1950s, came with a hang tag draped from its neck with a string, which is printed on both sides with "Breyer's Creation / Brahman Bull / Made in U.S.A." #70 was glossy from first release until well into the 1970s; even the one in the 1979 catalog looks glossy. Later models range from semigloss to matte, with recent models tending to be extremely matte and bisque-like. Typically the glossies are a shaded soft medium gray on the forehand and hindquarters, but a few are charcoal gray in these areas. The matte bulls typically have dark gray shading not only on the neck but also on the poll and forehead. Some glossies have pink on the nose, ears, eye corners, genitals, and dewlap, as shown in the 1963 catalog, but more commonly #70s, glossy and otherwise, have gray shading in these areas (thanks to Liz Strauss for pointing the pink out to me). Some bulls, glossy and matte, have charcoal dots on the dewclaws. Chalky glossy Brahmas are also known; I have seen three or four specimens in person. (See Chalkies in the Appendix near the end of this book for further discussion.)

♞ Brahma Bull #970, woodgrain, black eyes, unpainted white horns, no other color detailing, matte (1959-65). A few of these bulls have woodgrain horns, according to collector Lynn Luther (*Model Trading Post*, Sept./Oct. 1992, p. 4). Collector Sande Schneider's bull has woodgrain eyes. I date the release of #970 to 1959 because he appears with woodgrain Race Horse, Family Arabian Stallion, Proud Arabian Mare, and Clydesdale Stallion in an old Ward's catalog ad that I believe dates to that year. (For discussion of this dating, see under Woodgrains above in the Traditionals section.) The ad describes the models thus: "Simulated wood grain finish figurines. Beautifully detailed Horses and Brahma Bull. Faithfully copied from original hand-carved wood pieces. Made of Tenite Acetate high quality plastic, carefully hand finished in simulated wood grain. Buy any three figurines—get free 'Album of Horses' book [by Marguerite Henry]." The woodgrain Brahma appears again in the 1962 Ward's holiday catalog, as well as in 1960-65 Breyer catalogs and price lists. The model number 970 later belonged to the Showcase Collection issue of the Appaloosa Gelding (Quarter Horse Gelding mold).

Notes:

(1) According to Breyer executive Peter Stone, Breyer's gray Brahma #70 was copied from a porcelain Brahman Bull (12" x 10") by Edward M. Boehm, first released in 1953 (see Palley 1976, p. 164). Stone still owns the Boehm piece that was used as a model for the Breyer (conversations of May 1994 and Oct. 1995). As shown in Palley 1976, the Boehm piece is strikingly similar in both color and form to the Breyer, but there are differences. The Boehm bull has his head turned more sharply to the right and has his tail tip attached to the outside of the right hock, while the Breyer has his tail tip attached to the point of his right hock. But the two bulls are close if not identical in size and have virtually identical toplines, bottom lines, and leg positions. Palley remarks of the Boehm porcelains: "It seems that the Hereford and Brahman Bulls have been reproduced by the Japanese in plastic! And, from what we gather from the Boehm Studio, they're quite good copies. It is a compliment to any artist for someone to go to the trouble of copying his work when ready-made commercial molds of other sculptors are available. Certainly the Japanese cannot be faulted for poor taste." I suspect that what actually happened was that the Boehm Studio got hold of some early Breyer Hereford and Brahma specimens, ones without any mold stamps to identify the manufacturer, and just assumed that plastic copies must be Japanese!

(2) Collector Chris Wilder sold me a glossy #70 Brahma *steer*. His neutered condition appears to be factory original—the seams in the groin come together as though made that way, and the gloss finish over the area looks undisturbed. The scrotum on the Brahma Bull mold is a separately molded part, as indicated by its side-to-side seam, so my steer must have gotten to be a steer not by surgical removal of an integral part but by omission of a part that normally gets added on. He is fairly old, to judge from his lack of mold stamps. Whether there are other specimens like this I don't know. The horns and ears on the Brahma mold are also separately molded pieces, judging from my own specimens.

(3) The mold-stamp history of the Brahma Bull mold is eccentric. Models from the early decades have no mold marks. At some point, the round "Breyer Molding Co." stamp was added to the mold, inside the right hind leg; I am not certain when this occurred, but evidence suggests it was not until late 1983 or 1984. The round stamp was introduced into the Breyer line in general in 1960, but I have never heard of a woodgrain Brahma with this stamp, even though these bulls were made through 1965, and I don't believe I have ever come across a glossy #70 with the round stamp, even though the glossies were made well into the 1970s. In the "B" stamp era (1979-83), the Brahma mold was bedecked with four "B" stamps—one inside each hind leg and one tiny "B" on each horn, on the front near the base—but still no round stamp. Collector Sandy Carlsness wrote to me that her #70 is like this. I have seen in person a matte model with the "B" stamp inside each hind leg but no stamps on the horns (and again no round stamp), but I am quite sure that in fact the "B"s on the horns have never been removed from the metal injection mold, as I'll discuss in a moment. After the "B" stamp era, the "B"s on the Brahma's hind legs were removed and the round stamp was added—at BreyerFest 1992, I saw both a semigloss and a matte gray Brahma with no leg "B"s but with the round stamp on the leg and "B"s on both horns, and collector Chelle Fulk wrote to me that she has a Brahma with this same stamp assortment. These three bulls are among the specimens that convince me the "B"s were in fact never removed from the Brahma's horn molds—and in any case, Breyer simply would not have removed the horn "B"s only to put them back on a year or two later, when there was no longer need for them (see Mold Stamps in the Appendix near the end of this book). Another convincing specimen is a #385 Red Brahma Bull (released in 1996; not listed above) with two horn "B"s, which I saw at a tack store. So what are we to say of the bull mentioned above with "B"s on his legs but none on his horns, as well as my own #385 with a "B" on only one horn, another #385 I've seen with only the vestiges of a "B" on one horn, and my late-issue matte gray #70, purchased new in 1994, with no trace of horn "B"s? I believe the answer is that the horn "B"s often get wiped out completely or in part by the process of attaching the horns to the head after molding. A puckery or flaky "worked" area extending over the sites of the horn "B"s is visible on many models. This mold was never given the "U.S.A." stamp.

Brown Swiss Calf — see under Calf

Brown Swiss Cow, horned — see under Cow

Brown Swiss Cow SR polled — see under Cow

Calf — ♞ Standing, looking sharply left, tail tip attached to right hock. Sculpted by Chris Hess. Mold in catalog-run production 1972-95.

Catalog-run models made from this mold:

♞ Ayrshire Calf #350, dark red-brown pinto, blaze, white muzzle with gray tip, white tail tuft, white legs, gray hooves, matte (1972-73). This calf and the Guernsey and Holstein calves all have different pinto patterns.

♞ Brown Swiss Calf #351, medium coffee brown, solid face, white muzzle with gray tip, gray tail tuft, no stockings, gray hooves, matte (1972-73). The model number 351 previously belonged to the "Sugar" And "Spice" set with alabaster Running Mare and smoke Running Foal.

♞ Guernsey Calf #348, dark palomino pinto, star, white muzzle with gray tip, white tail tuft, white legs, gray hooves, matte (1972-73). This calf and the Ayrshire and Holstein calves all have different pinto patterns.

♞ Holstein Calf #347, black pinto, star, white muzzle with pink tip, white tail tuft, white legs, gray hooves, matte (1972-73). This same model was also sold in Cow Family set #3447 [1974-91] and in sets with SR polled Holstein Cow (see the entry for Holstein Cow SR, polled). This calf and the Guernsey and Ayrshire calves all have different pinto patterns. The photo of the Holstein Calf #347 in the 1972-73 catalogs and manuals—it's the same photo in both years—shows her with a slightly different pinto pattern from the Holstein Calf in Cow Family set #3447 in the 1974-91 catalogs. The #347 has a somewhat smaller star, and the black on the head goes all the way under the jowl and throatlatch, leaving the muzzle an island of white. #3447 has a larger star, and the under-jowl and throatlatch are white, joining to the white of the muzzle. I suspect that the #347 shown in the catalogs is a test-color model because I haven't heard of a collector's specimen with this pattern and because the #347 shown on the cover of the 1972 catalog has the normal pattern (i.e., the #3447 pattern). At least some #347s and #3447s have charcoal dots the dewclaws.

♞ Jersey Calf #349, dark palomino, solid face, white muzzle with gray tip, gray tail tuft, no stockings, gray hooves, matte (1972-73).

Sets:

• Cow Family set #3447, black pinto Holstein Calf, star, white muzzle with pink tip, white tail tuft, white legs, gray hooves, matte (1974-91). Set also includes horned Holstein Cow. These same models were sold separately as Holstein Calf #347 and horned Holstein Cow #341 [both 1972-73]. Set #3447 was called Cow Family Gift Set in the catalogs for 1974-75 but simply Cow Family thereafter. It is possible that at least some of the calves sold separately (#347) have a slightly different pinto pattern from calf #3447; see the entry for #347 for discussion.

♞ Jersey Cow Family set #3448, dark palomino Calf, large star, gray muzzle with pink tip, gray tail tuft, light/white underbelly and inner legs, gray hooves, matte (1992-95). Set also includes polled dark palomino Jersey Cow. At least some of these calves have charcoal dots on the dewclaws.

Special-run models made from this mold:

♘ Black Angus Calf SR #352, black, no white markings, black hooves (1977). Made for Bentley Sales Company to sell at Model Horse Congress. Probably 144 models made, per Stuart Bentley, owner of Bentley Sales. When I spoke to Mr. Bentley in December 1995, he said the quantity was probably a gross, but might possibly have been two gross (288 models). The date of this special is per a 1978 Bentley's ad flier for leftover models. The flier states: "Special Calves / Do you need a calf for stock horse events??? If so contact Mr. Bentley at once. At 1977 Congress he had a special run of Breyer calves painted Black Angus. There are about 25 left." The December 1979 *Model Horse Shower's Journal* carried the following comment by editor Linda Walter about the model number given to this SR: "According to info just in (thanks, D) the blk Angus Calf sold at MHC [Model Horse Congress] some years back was given the #352 or 353." The August 1980 *Hobby Horse*, edited by Shari Struzan, contains part of a "Complete Listing of Breyer Numbers Current and Discontinued," which gives the model number for the Black Angus Calf as #352. This number is probably correct, for the "Complete Listing" is quite accurate in general, and 352 makes sense in view of the other Calf model numbers of that era, the highest of which was #351 for the Brown Swiss Calf. The number 352 previously belonged to the "Sugar" And "Spice" set with smoke Running Mare and alabaster Running Foal.

♘ Calf SR, unpainted white (1987). Made for Model Horse Collector's Supply. These unpainted Calves, which are raw white plastic with no paint detailing at all, first appear on a MHCS price list dated July 26, 1987: "new unpainted calves." They are also listed as a 1987 issue on a Breyer company computer printout of activity 1985-92. Interestingly, the printout assigns the Calves a model number but then notes an error in that number: "7000-410347 Holstein Calf . . . Mold #347CA (scraped, buffed, unpainted). . . . Cust Model Horse Collectors Supply. Item number 7000-410347 should be 7000-420347 (42.... = scraped, buffed, unpainted)."

Note: The Calf mold has the round "Breyer Molding Co." stamp and the "U.S.A." stamp. Some models might have the "B" stamp too, but I'm not sure.

Charolais Bull — ♞ Standing, large bull, looking right, tail tip attached to right hock; one version polled, one version with small horns. Sculpted by Chris Hess. Mold in catalog-run production 1975 - current as of 1996 (horned mold version).

Catalog-run models made from this mold:

HORNED VERSION:

♞ Charolais Bull #360, white; pale tan body shading; pink inner ears, nose, and genitals; tan or brownish-gray hooves; white horns; matte (1975-95). The 1975 catalog shows a bull with fairly dark gray hooves. The unusual pattern of his heavy tan body shading suggests that he may be a test piece, but early #360s produced for sale do have dark/medium brownish-gray hooves and a lot of tan shading on the belly, legs, shoulders, chest, and dewlap (I have a bull like this and have seen several others). They also have a black dot on each dewclaw. Collector Joy Sheesley's old gray-hoofed bull, which has more brown shading than any other #360 I have seen, also has a lot of dark gray shading over the brown on his genitals and underbelly. Later bulls have some tan body shading, tan hooves, and no dewclaw dots. It's not certain when the hoof color changed—the 1976-89 catalog photos aren't clear, but the hoof color appears to vary between gray and tan. The 1990-94 catalogs all show bulls with tan hooves. Collector Paula DeFeyter has an unusual black-nosed Charolais with leather halter. He has dark gray hooves and abundant brownish shading on the belly, legs, hips, shoulders, and neck, as do the old regular-run #360s, but according to Paula he looks quite different from them. The halter is very nicely constructed of brown leather and has a leather lead with a chain that runs under the bull's chin through a ring on the halter. I asked Breyer executive Peter Stone whether this bull might have been an SR, but he had no recollection of it (conversation of Nov. 1994).

Special-run models made from this mold:

POLLED VERSION:

♘ Shorthorn Bull SR, polled dark red chestnut bull, no white markings, pink muzzle, dark red chestnut hooves, semigloss (1983 or earlier). Made for a breeders' association livestock show. Quantity unknown. My dating for this SR is based on the following report published in the February 1983 *Quequechan Model Horse Collector*: "Some of the special run cattle that Breyer has made: Using Charlais [*sic*] Bull mold with no horns[:] Simental [*sic*] Bull (Red & White) / Shorthorn Bull (dark red)." The two or three specimens of this SR that I have scrutinized have no belly numbering.

♘ Simmental Bull SR, polled dark reddish-brown pinto bull; white head; pink nose and genitals; white breast, belly, and legs; tan hooves; matte (1983 or earlier). Made for the National Simmental Association (NSA) in Montana. Approximately 144 models made. Distributor and quantity are per *JAH* 21/#3 Summer II 1994, p. 15 (*JAH* editor Stephanie Macejko told me she got the information from Breyer executive Peter Stone). *JAH* dates this SR to 1983. Although this is a possible dating, the fact that this SR was reported in *Quequechan Model Horse Collector* very early in 1983, in the February issue, suggests that the SR may have come out before 1983. *Quequechan* states: "Some of the special run cattle that Breyer has made: Using Charlais [*sic*] Bull mold with no horns[:] Simental [*sic*] Bull (Red & White) / Shorthorn Bull (dark red)." *JAH* also explains that not all the models distributed by the NSA were original factory finish. In addition to the approximately 144 factory-painted models, "a set of approx. 144 unpainted Charolais Bulls were also sold to the Simmental Association, and they painted the models themselves, in a lighter brown and white color, very similar to the Breyer original factory finish. All Simmental models were sold at various livestock shows throughout the year. It is unclear if any distinction was made between Breyer factory bulls and NSA-painted bulls when they were sold" (p. 15). Accompanying the *JAH* article are photos of a factory-finish bull (right-hand photo) and a bull painted by the NSA (left photo; the photo captions were mistakenly switched, as reported in *JAH* 21/#5 Winter 1994, p. 30). Of the factory-finish specimens I know of, all but one are like the right-hand bull in *JAH*. They have a Hereford-like pattern with a large, very dark reddish brown "blanket" on the body, the only pinto spot being a crisply outlined white patch over the withers, shaped roughly like a large, flying bird. The factory-finish bulls heads are white with brown ears. Typically they have brown patches covering the eyes, as shown in *JAH*, but the factory bull shown in Diederich 1988, Section 6, has no eye patches. The very different factory Simmental shown on *Breyer Collector's Video* has a true pinto pattern on the body, and gray hooves. He is owned by collector Karen Grimm (producer of the video), who got him from the NSA when the bulls were first issued; possibly he is a test piece that was sorted in with the production-line bulls. The non-factory, NSA-painted models I know of look much like the factory blanket-version bulls with brown covering the eyes, but there are differences. The non-factory models are a light milk chocolate color (though the one in *JAH* looks quite red), and their paint has a thick quality. Also, the white patch over their withers has a more straight-edged, less detailed outline than the patch on the factory bulls. Finally, non-factory bulls have brown paint on the area where the horns would be, whereas the factory bulls are unpainted white in that area. I got one of the non-factory bulls from another collector in mid-1990, and its paint, in addition to being thick, was sticky and came off on my fingers and on its paper wrappings, a most un-Breyer-like behavior. The collector told me she had another bull like mine with sticky paint, and collector Laura Diederich wrote to me that she once owned a non-factory bull with sticky paint. But other non-factory specimens known to me, such as collector Jo Kulwicki's, did not come sticky.

Notes:

(1) The polled version of this mold was produced in the two above-listed special runs in the 1980s but has never been produced as a regular run. To judge from my own Charolais #360s and others I've seen, the horns, as well as the ears and scrotum, are separately molded pieces affixed to the bull after molding.

(2) Chris Hess is identified as the sculptor of this mold in *JAH* 21/#3 Summer II 1994 (p. 15). According to former Breyer executive Peter Stone (conversation of Dec. 1995), Hess designed his sculpture from photos provided by Mr. Roy Birk, of the Charolais association in Houston. When the statue was nearly finished, Mr. Birk came to Hess's studio to critique the piece and worked with Hess to perfect it.

(3) The Charolais Bull mold has the round "Breyer Molding Co." stamp and the "U.S.A." stamp. Some models might also have the "B" stamp, but I'm not sure.

Cow — ♞ Standing, large udder, tail tip attached to left hock and udder; polled version and at least 4 versions of horns. Sculpted by Chris Hess. Mold in catalog-run production 1972 - current as of 1996 (Holstein-horns version 1972-91; other horn versions 1972-73; polled version 1992 - current as of 1996).

Catalog-run models made from this mold:

HORNED VERSIONS:

♞ Ayrshire Cow #344, dark red-brown pinto, blaze, white nose with gray tip, white over whole forehead and eyes, white stripe down windpipe, pink udder, white tail tuft, 4 stockings, gray hooves, white horns with gray tips, matte (1972-73). The Ayrshire's horns are the longest of the Cow horns and point almost vertically upward. This angulation and the white over her eyes make her look wild and crazy. Her pinto pattern is identical to that on the 1988 SR polled Ayrshire except that the SR has a solid face and no white stripe down the underside of the neck. Some #344s have dark red-brown inside the ears (Jo Kulwicki's is like this); others have pink inside the ears (Paula DeFeyter's is like this). At least some models have charcoal dots on the dewclaws.

♞ Brown Swiss Cow #345, medium coffee brown, solid face, white nose with gray tip, light breast, pink udder, gray or white tail tuft, 4 or various stockings, gray hooves, white horns with gray tips, matte (1972-73). The stockings can be very vague and oversprayed. At least some models have charcoal dots on the dewclaws. The Brown Swiss typically has horns quite similar to Guernsey #342's, pointing upward at about a 45° angle, though the Brown Swiss's horns are a bit larger and not quite so wide spread at the tips. One Brown Swiss I've seen, however, had horns very similar to Ayrshire #344's, long and very upward pointing, though a bit smaller than the Ayrshire's. The model number 345 previously belonged to Lucky Ranger, sold in set with white Western Pony.

♞ Guernsey Cow #342, dark palomino pinto, solid face, white nose with gray tip, white stripe down windpipe, pink udder, white tail tuft, white legs, gray hooves, white horns with gray tips, matte (1972-73). The Guernsey's horns are relatively small and slender, point upward at about a 45° angle, and have the widest-spread tips of all the Cow horns. At least some models have charcoal dots on the dewclaws. The model number 342 previously belonged to the Cowboy & Pinto set with rider and brown pinto Western Pony.

♞ Holstein Cow #341, black pinto, blaze, white nose with pink tip, white stripe down windpipe, pink udder, white tail tuft, white legs, gray hooves, white horns with black tips, matte or slightly semigloss (1972-73). This same model was also sold in Cow Family set #3447 [1974-91]. The Holstein's horns point almost horizontally forward and are a bit fatter and less wide spread at the tips than the Guernsey's and Brown Swiss's horns. At least some models have charcoal dots on the dewclaws. The model number 341 previously belonged to the Cowboy & Pinto set with rider and black pinto Western Pony.

♞ Jersey Cow #343, dark palomino, solid face, white nose with gray tip, pink and tan udder, gray tail tuft, no stockings, gray hooves, white horns with gray tips, matte (1972-73). Typically the Jersey's horns are about the same size as the Brown Swiss's but a bit plumper and slightly more upward-pointing; they are also closer together at the tips than any other Cow horns. A couple of Jerseys I've seen, however, had horns identical to Guernsey #342's; one of collector Sande Schneider's #343s is like this. At least some models have charcoal dots on the dewclaws. The model number 343 previously belonged to the Cowboy sold in set with palomino Western Pony.

Sets:

• Cow Family set #3447, horned Holstein Cow, black pinto (1974-91). Set also includes Holstein Calf. These same models were sold separately as Holstein Calf #347 and horned Holstein Cow #341 [both 1972-73].

POLLED VERSION:

♞ Jersey Cow Family set #3448, polled Jersey Cow, dark palomino, large star, white nose with pink tip, pink and tan udder, dark gray tail tuft, light/white underbelly and inner legs, gray hooves, matte (1992-95). Set also includes Jersey Calf. At least some models have charcoal dots on the dewclaws. The chief difference between this polled Cow and the SR polled Jersey Cow is that #3448 has a star while the SR has a solid face.

Special-run models made from this mold:

HORNED VERSIONS:

♘ Guernsey Cow SR, dark red-brown chestnut pinto, white spots on croup, withers, and poll; solid face with white nose; white breast, belly, and udder; white legs; tan hooves; chestnut horns; semigloss (1984). The date is per *Breyer Collector's Video*. Two specimens of this SR are known to me. One of them, which I have seen in person, is owned by collector Karen Grimm. This Cow's tail tuft is white; her white pinto spots are unstenciled and quite vague; and her horns are like the regular-run Holstein's in shape and angle. The second specimen was advertised in the March 1996 *Model Horse Trader*. In the black and white ad photo, this Cow's tail tuft looks black or very dark, and the white spots on her croup and withers look sharply outlined, as if created by tape- or wax-masking. Her horns have the forward angle of the Holstein's. Though I could be wrong, the paint job on these Guernsey Cows and on the horned Jersey Cow SR (see entry below) strikes me as a bit dubious; I am not absolutely convinced it is Breyer factory original. Conceivably these Cows were painted by cattlemen's associations, as were some of the SR Simmental Bulls issued at about the same time (see under Charolais Bull). When I asked former Breyer executive Peter Stone about the horned Guernsey and Jersey Cow SRs in March 1996, he had no recollection of them at all.

♘ Holstein Cow SR #417341, mixed horns, black pinto (1988). Sold through Small World and Black Horse Ranch. 79 models made. Model number, dealers, and quantity are per a Breyer company computer printout of activity 1985-92. These mixed-horn models are actually regular-run Holsteins, but someone at the factory goofed and put a non-

Holstein horn—a Guernsey or a Brown Swiss, I believe—on the left side. The difference between the mixed-horn and normal Holsteins is not glaring, especially since the normal Holstein horns are themselves slightly asymmetrical; but on the mixed-horn Holsteins, the left horn angles noticeably more upward than the right horn, which is virtually horizontal. Small World explained these cows in their Fall/Winter 1988 brochure: "One of the items on the special list deserves a bit more explanation ... Although not a special run we have been able to obtain a very limited number, 50, of an unusual model produced by Breyer. We think this might be classified as an extremely rare error/variation on the order of an invert in stamp collecting or a baseball card produced from a reversed negative. Because of the low numbers involved (apparently a total of 81 were produced) and the subtlety and uniqueness of the item we feel this will be a treasured addition to the serious Breyer enthusiast's collection. . . . Let us try and explain: the horned cow in the #3447 Cow Family set is a Hereford [sic; they meant Holstein] and has horns which are symmetrical. . . . The cow we are offering is confused, since she has a left horn which belongs to another breed. The left horn is slightly longer and has a more pronounced tilt." Following this item in the brochure is a hand-drawn diagram of the crooked horns from three perspectives.

⌂ Jersey Cow SR, caramel/palomino, solid face with white muzzle, black on end of nose, white or creamy breast and udder, black tail tuft, no stockings, dark gray hooves, caramel/palomino horns, semigloss (1983/84). I have seen two specimens of this SR in person: one owned by collector Karen Grimm, which is shown on Breyer Collector's Video, and another owned by collector Sande Schneider. A third one was advertised in the March 1996 Model Horse Trader. The video dates this SR to 1984. However, Sande's Cow has a "B" stamp (I don't know about Karen's), and this stamp generally dates to 1979-83 (see Mold Marks in the Appendix near the end of this book). Sande's Cow has black covering the whole tip of the nose; Karen's has a narrower, odd looking strip of black between the nostrils. This SR is lighter than the regular-run Jersey Cows. Her horns are like the regular-run Holstein's rather than the regular-run Jersey's. See the entry above for the horned Guernsey Cow SR for further discussion.

POLLED VERSION:

⌂ Ayrshire Cow SR #414341, polled, red-brown pinto, solid face, dark-shaded nose, pink udder, white tail tuft, white legs, gray hooves, matte and semigloss (1988 and 1993). Made for Bentley Sales Company in both years, but the 1988 release was sold through other companies as well. In both years, the Ayrshire was sold separately or in SR set with polled Brown Swiss, Guernsey, Holstein, and Jersey Cows (the 1993 set is called Dairy Cow Assortment SR #410693 on a Breyer company computer printout of 1993 SRs). 400 total sets made—200 in each of the two years. The polled Ayrshire's pinto pattern is identical to that on #344 horned Ayrshire except that the SR has a solid face and no white stripe running down the underside of the neck. The SR is also a bit redder than #344. The 1988 polled Ayrshire is virtually identical to the 1993. The only notable difference in my experience is that the 1988 release is matte and the 1993 is semigloss. Finish can vary from model to model however, so this is not a reliable distinction between the two runs. At least some models from both years have charcoal dots on the dewclaws. Quantity for the 1988 sets is per a Breyer company computer printout of activity 1985-92; quantity for the 1993 sets is per Bentley's ad fliers. (More of the polled Holsteins were made for other dealers, however; see Holstein Cow SR, polled.) This printout gives the model numbers for the individual SR polled Cows but no number for the set, whereas a Breyer computer printout of 1993 SRs gives the set number noted above but no individual model numbers. The 1985-92 printout names Bentley's as the customer for all 200 of the 1988 sets (except for the polled Holstein; see that entry below), but a July 1988 Bentley's price list says "We will have 100 of each model . . . and are taking orders now for future delivery." (Delivery occurred later that year; collector Heather Wells's receipt for her set from Bentley's is dated October 25, 1988.) The remaining sets were advertised by Black Horse Ranch and other dealers in early 1989.

⌂ Brown Swiss Cow SR #413341, polled, medium/light coffee brown, solid face, white nose with gray tip, white patch on the breast, pink and tan udder, gray tail tuft, 4 stockings, gray hooves, matte (1988 and 1993). For dealer, quantity, and set information see Ayrshire Cow SR #414341, polled. The 1988 release of the SR polled Brown Swiss Cow is very similar to the 1993 release. In my experience the only difference between them is taht the white breast-patch on the 1988 is larger than the patch on the 1993. The 1988's patch covers the whole breast and goes halfway up the windpipe, whereas the 1993's patch covers basically just the protruding area on the breast. At least some models from both years have some charcoal shading on the neck and charcoal dots on the dewclaws.

⌂ Guernsey Cow SR #415341, polled, dark palomino pinto, solid face, white nose with gray or pink tip, white stripe down windpipe, pink udder, white tail tuft, white legs, gray hooves, matte or slightly semigloss (1988 and 1993). For dealer, quantity, and set information see Ayrshire Cow SR #414341, polled. This SR Guernsey is same color and pattern as the regular-run #342 horned Guernsey Cow. The 1988 release of the SR polled Guernsey is extremely similar to the 1993 release. In my experience the only notable difference between them is that the 1988 has gray on her nose whereas the 1993 has pink. At least some models from both years have charcoal dots on the dewclaws.

⌂ Holstein Cow SR #411341, polled, black pinto, blaze, white nose with pink tip, white stripe down windpipe, pink udder, white tail tuft, white legs, gray hooves, slightly semigloss (1985, 1988, 1989, 1992, 1993, and 1995). Made for Nasco farm supply company of Fort Atkinson, Wisconsin, and Modesto, California; Agway; and Bentley Sales Company. Quantities for the 1985 run and for any runs that may have been produced in 1986-87 are unknown, but for the 1988-95 runs, a total of 1,560 polled Holsteins were made: 288 in 1988, 72 in 1989, 500 in 1992, 200 in 1993, and 500 in 1995. These quantities are per a Breyer company computer printout of activity 1985-92, Bentley's 1993 ad fliers, and, for the 1995 release, JAH editor Stephanie Macejko. (Stephanie found no records of further quantities produced in 1996, as of our conversation of July 2, 1996.) My earliest documentation for this SR is Nasco's winter 1985-86 Country Collection catalog, which advertises the polled Holstein Cow in a set with the regular-run Holstein Calf: "Breyer Holstein Set. Available only from Nasco. . . . $14.80." The same set also appears in Nasco catalogs for 1990-96 and probably in Nasco's 1987-89 catalogs as well, although I have not seen these. (Thanks to collector Kim Jones for copies of the 1985-86 and early 1990s Nasco catalogs.) The Breyer printout records the production of the Cows for Nasco and other companies only for 1988-92: Cow And Calf set SR #413448 for Agway in 1988 (the Cow alone is listed as #411341), Cow 'N Calf set SR #703447 with Holstein Calf for Nasco in 1989, and Cow Family set SR #702092 with Holstein Calf for Nasco in 1992. The 1993 polled Holstein was issued to Bentley's in Dairy Cow Assortment SR #410693, which was a reissue of the 1988 SR set of 5 polled Cows (see Ayrshire Cow SR #414341 for discussion). All of these SR polled Holstein Cows are identical to each other and, except for their lack of

horns, identical to the regular-run horned Holstein Cow. The Holstein Calves in the sets are not SR at all but regular run. These identities are confirmed by the photos in the Nasco catalogs I have seen, by my own and other collectors' 1988 and 1993 polled Holsteins from Bentleys, and by the Breyer computer printout, which describes the models in the 1988, 1989, and 1992 sets as follows: "item #341CO w/o horns (mold #341CO, 341HOR = use ears, no horns) / reg item 347CA." At least some models have black dots on the dewclaws.

⌂ Jersey Cow SR #416341, polled, dark palomino, solid face, white nose with gray tip, white patch on breast, pink udder, gray tail tuft, gray hooves, matte or slightly semigloss (1988 and 1993). For dealer, quantity, and set information see Ayrshire Cow SR #414341, polled. The 1988 release of the SR polled Jersey is nearly indistinguishable from the 1993 SR polled Jersey. On the specimens I know of, the only difference is that the white breast-patch on the 1988 SR is larger than the patch on the 1993. The 1988's patch covers the whole breast, in some cases going halfway up the windpipe, while the 1993's patch covers basically just the protruding area on the breast. At least some models from both years have some darker shading on the neck and charcoal dots on the dewclaws.

Notes:

(1) All the Cows are identical in mold except for the ears and horns (or lack of horns). The ear pieces on the polled Cow and the horn-plus-ear pieces on the horned Cows are separately molded pieces, which are fit into the head after molding. The polled Cow's ears are rounder and more upward-pointing than the horned Cows' ears. The horned Cow's ears are a bit flatter in shape and stick straight out, parallel to the ground, to accommodate the horns above them. There are at least 4 different styles of horns, appropriate for the different breeds (for descriptions, see the entries above for catalog-run horned Cows). The clearest difference between the styles is that they are set at different angles, ranging from the nearly horizontal angle of the Holstein's horns to the nearly vertical angle of the Ayrshire's. But the styles also differ in size and shape, albeit very subtly in some cases. Also the two horns of each style differ slightly from each other, even on Cows other than the SR mixed-horn Holstein. To make matters even more confusing, Breyer does not consistently use a single style of horns on a given breed.

(2) The existence of one specimen of a woodgrain Cow was mentioned by collector Sheryl Leisure in her presentation at the West Coast Model Horse Collector's Jamboree in August 1993. A woodgrain Cow is not listed in any Breyer publications that I know of. If there are more of them, it is possible that they were a small special run. In any case, this model, which can't have been produced before 1972 (when the Cow mold was introduced), was released late for a woodgrain. See Woodgrains above in the Traditionals section.

(3) The Cow mold has a small "CHESS .71" stamp (referring to sculptor Chris Hess and the year he created this mold) just above the round "Breyer Molding Co." stamp and the "U.S.A." stamp. Some models have the "B" stamp in addition.

Cow Family set — see under Cow, horned

Duroc Hog SR — see under "Jasper"

Guernsey Calf — see under Calf

Guernsey Cow, horned — see Guernsey Cow #342, and Guernsey Cow SR horned (both under Cow)

Guernsey Cow SR polled — see under Cow

Hampshire Hog SR — see under "Jasper"

Hereford Bull — 🐂 Horned, walking, small bull, looking left, tail tip attached to left buttock. Copied from an original sculpture by Edward Marshall Boehm. Mold in catalog-run production 1955/57 - 1981.
Catalog-run models made from this mold:

🐂 Hereford Bull #71, brown with white head, withers, breast, belly, and tail tip; pink muzzle, genitals, and hooves; pink horns with brown tips; most glossy, a few matte and semigloss (1955/57 - 1981). The color varies from dark chocolate brown, which occurs on many older models, to medium red chestnut, which is typical for later models, though I've seen this color on an old model as well. Collector Liz Strauss found a model with an unusual light coffee-with-cream color. One of my own bulls has a brown mouth line. There are two pattern versions of #71. On the rarer version, the edge of the brown low on the barrel and on the legs is unstenciled (airbrushed freehand), and the brown on the legs ends well above the hooves. In my experience these unstenciled models are typically dark brown in color and are glossy, but I have seen one in a lighter, redder color with semigloss finish (although he had no "U.S.A." stamp). Some of the glossy unstenciled models are chalky (see Chalkies & Pearlies in the Appendix near the end of this book). The unstenciled version is shown in the 1960 catalog and the 1966-69 price lists (these lists all use the same photo, which may not represent current production in all those years). On the more common version of #71, the edge of the brown on the barrel and legs is stenciled, and the brown on the legs generally goes down to the hooves. This version appears in post-1963 catalogs and in 1950s publications, including the earliest source I know of that lists #71, an old catalog sheet that I date to 1956/57. Most of the many #71s I've seen, of both patterns, have been glossy, but nonglossies do exist. I own a semigloss #71 (stenciled version), which has a "U.S.A." stamp and thus must have been made no earlier than 1970. As mentioned, I have also seen a semigloss with no "U.S.A." A couple of bulls I know of have their heads turned slightly more than normal (collector Sheryl Leisure has a #71 like this); this is the result of slight heat bloat, not a true mold variation.

🐂 Hereford Bull #971, woodgrain, black eyes, unpainted white horns, no other color detailing, matte (1959/60 - 1964). On two of these models that I've seen photos of—one in Diederich 1988 (Section 6) and one in Quequechan Model Horse Collector, April 1985—the horns are more down-turned than the horns on #71, though they are the same horn mold. (The horns on this mold are separate pieces attached after molding, so the varying horn angle doesn't indicate a different mold.)

Notes:

(1) According to Breyer executive Peter Stone, this mold is copied from the porcelain Hereford Bull (10.5" x 5.5") by Edward M. Boehm, first released in 1950 (see Palley 1976, pp. 26, 27, 163). In 1954, Helen Boehm presented one of her husband's Hereford Bulls to President and Mrs. Eisenhower at the White House. Peter Stone still owns the Boehm piece that was used as a model for the Breyer (conversations of May 1994 and Oct. 1995). Judging from the photo of the Boehm bull in Palley 1976, the Boehm and the Breyer are

nearly identical in both mold and color, the only difference being that on the Breyer the whole tail tuft is attached to the body, while on the Boehm only part of the tuft attaches to the body, with the very tip hanging free. Palley remarks of the Boehm porcelains: "It seems that the Hereford and Brahman Bulls have been reproduced by the Japanese in plastic! And, from what we gather from the Boehm Studio, they're quite good copies. It is a compliment to any artist for someone to go to the trouble of copying his work when ready-made commercial molds of other sculptors are available. Certainly the Japanese cannot be faulted for poor taste." I suspect that what actually happened was that the Boehm Studio got hold of some early Breyer Hereford and Brahma specimens, ones without any mold stamps to identify the country or manufacturer, and just assumed that plastic copies must be Japanese!

(2) Judging from my own models, the horns on this bull are separately molded pieces, though the ears and scrotum are integral parts of the mold.

(3) Early models of the Hereford Bull mold have no mold stamps. Later ones have the "U.S.A." stamp. Some "U.S.A." models might have the "B" stamp too, but I'm not sure. This mold was never given the round "Breyer Molding Co." stamp.

Hereford Bull, polled, standing — see Polled Hereford Bull

Hereford Bull, polled, walking — see under Black Angus Bull, polled, walking

Hog — see "Jasper"

Holstein Calf — see under Calf

Holstein Cow And Calf set SR — see Holstein Cow SR, polled (1988) and (1989 and 1992), under Cow

Holstein Cow, horned — see under Cow

Holstein Cow SR, mixed horns — see under Cow

Holstein Cow SR, polled — see under Cow

"Jasper" — Hog, barrow (castrated male); standing; curlicue tail; molded with ears standing straight. Sculpted by Chris Hess. Mold in catalog-run production 1974 - current as of 1996.

Catalog-run models made from this mold:

"Jasper" The Market Hog #355, white with large gray spot over rump and back, pink snout with gray nostrils, pink inner ears, pink nipples and anal area, pink hooves, matte (1974 - current as of 1996). Many models also have pink shading around the eyes. As shown in catalogs, the gray spot on "Jasper's" back varies from dark to light. The shape of the spot also varies. On the earliest pigs, the spot was evidently airbrushed free-hand, without the use of a stencil or mask, for the shape of the spot differs from pig to pig, as a comparison between my own very early "Jasper" and a couple of others found by collector Shery Leisure revealed. The spot on these earliest "Jaspers" can have an "outlined" appearance, as though the painter had first drawn the shape and then filled it in. Models with unstenciled spots are visible in the 1974-75 catalogs. Pigs with the normal, stenciled spot, with its characteristic double-lobed right side, first appear in 1976 and persist to the present. Another feature of the earliest pigs and of somewhat later, normal-spot pigs is that they sport gray outlines around their pink inner ears—the outlines are visible in the 1975 catalog (photos in other 1970s-80s catalogs are not clear). The normal-spot, ear-outline "Jaspers" can also have lavish pink shading; I call these gaudy hogs "pretty Jaspers." Sheryl's pretty pig boasts pale pink shading over his back and shoulders, abundant pink around the eyes, and brilliant coral-pink nipple rows and fundament. Collector Sande Schneider has a similarly spectacular pretty "Jasper," with pink paint daubed even on the ridges of his lower eyelids. Sheryl and Sande both got their pretties in older collections they purchased, so it is likely that these pigs date to the later 1970s. #355 is a portrait of a real pig named "Jasper," a prize-winning Hampshire - Chester White crossbred barrow (castrated male) who starred posthumously in the educational film *Profitable Pork Selection.* His coloring is called "blue-butt"—white with a patch of dark hair on the white skin of the rump. "Jasper" was bred and raised by Mr. Jack Rodibaugh, of Rensselear, Indiana. The town is located in Jasper County, whence the hog's name. Mr. Rodibaugh exhibited "Jasper" at the 1969 International Livestock Exhibition in Chicago, where the hog was named Grand Champion Barrow. "Jasper" was then sold to American Cyanamid Company, which in turn donated the pig to the Department of Animal Sciences at Purdue University "for study and carcass evaluation." The details of "Jasper's" heroic contribution to the study are recorded in the above-mentioned film, cosponsored by American Cyanamid. This company also commissioned the "Jasper" model from Breyer. The sculptor, Chris Hess, consulted with Mr. Rodibaugh as he created the original clay sculpture. (Information was generously provided to me by Jack Rodibaugh and his sister, Breyer collector Mary Margaret Fox.) On August 5, 1995, the QVC home-shopping cable TV channel offered 1,000 "Jaspers" that were ordinary regular runs but that came in boxes labeled with the special-run model number 705395 (per *JAH* editor Stephanie Macejko).

Special-run models made from this mold:

Duroc Hog SR, dark red-brown, no white markings, dark red-brown hooves, matte (1980/81). Made for sale to Midwestern state fairs and/or hog producers. Perhaps about 250 models made. Regarding quantity and origin, see note 1 for this mold. It is certain that this SR, along with the SR Hampshire and Spotted Poland China, was out by the early 1980s, for the existence of these three specials is reported in the February 1983 *Quequechan Model Horse Collector. Breyer Collector's Video* specifies the date as 1980; the October 1987 *Collector's Journal* says 1981. The SR Durocs owned by collectors Sheryl Leisure and Heather Wells are painted over regular-run "Jaspers"—the gray spot over "Jasper's" loins is faintly visible through the red-brown Duroc paint. Whether this is true of the whole Duroc run I don't know. See Hampshire Hog SR for further discussion.

Hampshire Hog SR, black with white band over shoulders and front legs, pink or gray front hooves, black hind hooves, matte (1979 and possibly 1980/81). Made for sale to Midwestern state fairs and/or hog producers. Perhaps about 250 models made. Regarding quantity and origin, see note 1 for this mold. Breyer may have produced more than one Hampshire Hog SR. The 1979 date is from the December 1979 *Model Horse Shower's Journal*, in which editor Linda Walter states: "And reported also is the 'Jasper the Market Hog' in black with white belt colors instead of the regular released version. Perhaps it was a special order?" *Breyer Collector's Video* dates the SR Hampshire to 1980, but the October 1987 *Collector's Journal,* which has a photo showing the Duroc, Hampshire, and Spotted Poland China SR hogs, says 1981. In the photo caption, editor Teena Housman states that she got the hogs "in 1981 through a friend from the Indiana State Fair. . . . I called Breyer to find out about these and they told me that they NEVER painted these models!! They said the same thing about the 2 bulls also; could they be a private person's repaints that were sold to the fair vendor?" I think whomever Teena spoke to at Breyer was confused, for according to Breyer executive Peter Stone, the SR hogs are factory original (see note 1 for this mold). Mr. Jack Rodibaugh, the Indiana hog producer who bred the real "Jasper" (see the entry for "Jasper" #355 above), also mentioned to me in a letter of January 1995 that "Breyer Molding later [that is, after releasing "Jasper" #355] made the model of Jasper a Hampshire (black with a white belt) and a Duroc (red)." The Hampshires owned by collectors Sheryl Leisure, Jo Kulwicki, and Heather Wells have pink front feet, but the Hampshire shown in Diederich 1988, Section 3, has gray front feet, as does the one owned by collector Robert Peterson, of which I've seen a photo.

Spotted Poland China Hog SR, white with black spots on face, shoulder, and rump; most with pale pink hooves; matte (1980/81). Made for sale to Midwestern state fairs and/or hog producers. Perhaps about 250 models made. Regarding quantity and origin, see note 1 for this mold. It is certain that this SR, along with the SR Duroc and Hampshire, was out by the early 1980s, for the existence of these three specials is reported in the February 1983 *Quequechan Model Horse Collector. Breyer Collector's Video* specifies the date as 1980; the October 1987 *Collector's Journal* says 1981. The large black spot over this model's loins is the same shape as the gray spot on regular-run "Jasper" and was undoubtedly made with the same paint mask. The other spots on this SR, which were airbrushed freehand, vary in quantity and position, and range from lentil-sized to half-dollar-sized. The hoof color varies as well—collector Sheryl Leisure's model has 3 pale pink hooves and 1 black hind hoof, while other models I've seen have 4 pale pink hooves. Other Spotted Poland specimens are shown in *JAH* 22/#3 May/June 1995 (p. 17) and Diederich 1988, Section 6. See Hampshire Hog SR for further discussion.

Notes:

(1) The above listings for hog special runs include only those SRs of which several specimens are known to me. In addition to these SRs, a number of oddball pigs have come to my attention, each of a different color, all apparently factory finish. A couple of them have their ears bent over in the middle. It is entirely possible that some or all of these oddballs are not just one-of-a-kinds or samples from very limited test runs but actual special runs (dating in all likelihood to the early 1980s), but all I know of is a specimen or two of each color. In November 1994 and again in October and December 1995, I asked former Breyer executive Peter Stone what he could recall about SR hogs. He emphasized that all the SR hogs had been ordered by one man, Otha Calvert, a retired engineer who had taken up chicken farming in Illinois and also owned an Iowa farm where hogs were raised. Mr. Calvert, who also tried to talk Mr. Stone into having Breyer create a chicken model, placed at least three separate orders for SR hogs, each time coming to the Breyer factory when the models were being made because he was very particular about their accuracy in representing real hog breeds. Mr. Calvert himself bent the ears on some of the models, bent ears being characteristic of certain breeds. He sold the models to breed associations, which advertised them through their various magazines. Mr. Stone could not say for certain what SRs had been made, but he thought he recalled Duroc, Hampshire, Spotted Poland China, and Chester White (solid white with some pink shading), in quantities of perhaps about 250 each. His guess as to breeds is surely right with regard to the first three. He may be right about Chester Whites too, for a white model is among the oddball hogs known to me. Further, his recollection of the bending of ears suggests that the bent-eared oddballs may be genuine SRs as well. But we may never know for sure. When I attempted to call Mr. Calvert in October 1995 to ask him about the SRs he had ordered, his wife, Marjorie, conveyed the sad news that he had passed away about a month previously. She very kindly checked his records for information on SR hogs but was unable to find anything except a 1981 Breyer dealer catalog; she feared she had already disposed of materials concerning these models. The only specific models she recalled when I spoke with her were some black and white hogs that Mr. Calvert had made into piggy banks for a local savings bank to give to 4H kids; whether the models were Hampshires or Spotted Poland Chinas she didn't say (she was not familiar with hog breeds). The oddball models known to me are as follows: [A] Bent-eared hog, black, blaze, 4 stockings, matte. Shown in Diederich 1988, Section 6; owned by collector Antina Richards. [B] Bent-eared hog, dark red-brown; solid face; lighter red-brown ear flaps, belly, and tail tip area; gray hooves; matte. Shown in Diederich 1988, Section 6; owned by collector Antina Richards. Antina had this model on display at BreyerFest 1994; she believes it is an SR made for a Midwestern hog association in 1980. [C] Straight-eared hog, dark red dun, bald face, dark gray hooves, matte. Owned by collector Jo Kulwicki. I have seen this model in person. [D] Straight-eared hog, light red dun with dark red dun dorsal band, face lighter than body but not bald, gray hooves, matte. Owned by collector Sue Lehman. Sue got it from another collector, who had owned it for many years. I have seen this model in person. [E] Straight-eared hog, light tan, bald face, tan hooves, matte. Shown in Diederich 1988, Section 6; owned by collector Antina Richards. [F] Straight-eared hog, light tan, solid face, gray hooves, matte. Owned by collector Paula DeFeyter, who sent me a photo of the model. [G] Straight-eared hog, light tan with a black rump, solid face, gray hooves. The front edge of the black area on the rump is a straight diagonal line from the top of the hind leg up to the center of the back, giving the impression that the hog sat in a tub of tar, except that his tail is partially tan. Owned by Paula DeFeyter, who sent me a photo of the model. [H] Straight-eared hog, medium red dun, white band over the shoulders, solid face, red dun hooves. Owned by collector Robert Peterson, who kindly sent me photos. Robert got the hog (and two pale gray ones; see next item) from the husband of a woman who used to work at Breyer. [I] Straight-eared hog, pale gray, darker gray nose and hooves. Two specimens, owned by Robert Peterson. [J] Straight-eared hog, white, matte; I'm not sure of the hoof color. Shown in Diederich 1988, Section 6; owned by collector Antina Richards.

(2) The "Jasper" mold has the round "Breyer Molding Co." stamp and the "U.S.A." stamp. Some models might have the "B" stamp in addition, but I have not come across a specimen like this.

Jersey Calf — see under Calf

Jersey Cow, horned — see Jersey Cow #343, and Jersey Cow SR horned (both under Cow)

Jersey Cow Family, calf and polled cow — see under Cow

Jersey Cow SR, polled — see under Cow

Longhorn — see Texas Longhorn

Pig — see "Jasper"

Polled Hereford Bull — 🐂 Standing, large bull, looking left, fluffed tail tuft hangs free. Sculpted by Chris Hess. Mold in catalog-run production 1968 - current as of 1996.
Catalog-run models made from this mold:
🐂 Polled Hereford Bull #74, brown with white head, withers, breast, belly, and tail tip; pink muzzle, genitals, and hooves; matte (1968 - current as of 1996). The body color varies from red chestnut to dark chocolate brown. At least some of the dark bulls are of recent vintage; in spring 1995 I got a dark chocolate brown specimen and saw a number of others just as dark.
Notes:
(1) Collector Antina Richards owns a Polled Hereford Bull in woodgrain with black eyes and hooves, which she had on display at BreyerFest 1994 (the bull is also shown in Diederich 1988, Section 6). He has holes drilled in the bottoms of his hooves, which suggests that he may at one time have been mounted on a base, possibly a lamp base. Antina found the bull at a flea market. Breyer catalogs list no woodgrain bull of this mold, but Antina's model does appear to be factory original. He lacks the "U.S.A." stamp, which means he was probably made prior to 1970, though of course not earlier than 1968, when the Polled Hereford Bull mold was first released. The regular-run woodgrain Fighting Stallion was still in production in the years 1968-70, although the heyday of woodgrains had passed by this time. Collector Sande Schneider wrote to me that she has heard of a second woodgrain large Polled Hereford Bull, so possibly Breyer issued a small special run of them.
(2) The ears and scrotum on this bull are integral parts of the mold, judging from my own model.
(3) Early models of the Polled Hereford Bull mold have the round "Breyer Molding Co." stamp only. Later models have the "U.S.A." stamp in addition. Since models with only the round stamp are rare in my experience, I suspect that the "U.S.A." was added to this mold in 1970, when the "U.S.A." was introduced into the Breyer line generally. Some "U.S.A." models might have the "B" stamp too, but I'm not certain.

Polled Hereford Bull, walking — see under Black Angus Bull, polled, walking

Red Angus Bull SR — see under Black Angus Bull, polled, standing

Shorthorn Bull SR — see under Charolais Bull

Simmental Bull SR — see under Charolais Bull

Spanish Fighting Bull — 🐂 Horned, standing/walking, head lowered in "charging" position. Sculpted by Chris Hess. Mold in catalog-run production 1970-85.
Catalog-run models made from this mold:
🐂 Spanish Fighting Bull #73, black, no white markings, black genitals, black or gray hooves, white horns with black tips, matte and semigloss (1970-85). In Presentation Collection mounted on American walnut wood base with brass "Fighting Bull" nameplate, 1972-73. The Presentation model is listed as #5073 Spanish Fighting Bull in the 1973 price list, but previously it apparently had the same model number as regular-run #73; see Presentation Collection above in the Traditionals section for discussion. Catalogs show that the gray-hoofed models are from the 1970s, though some models from these years may have black hooves, as do 1980s models. Some models, which are in all likelihood from the 1970s oil-crisis period, have dishwater gray or yellowish horns; Jo Kulwicki and I both have such models (mine has gray hooves; Jo's has black). For discussion of oil-crisis models, see Chalkies & Pearlies in the Appendix near the end of this book. Collector Judy Miller has a #73 with glossy finish, which she believes is factory original. The model number 73 previously belonged to the Polled Hereford Bull (polled walking Black Angus Bull mold).
Notes:
(1) The horns and ears on this bull are separately molded pieces, though the scrotum is an integral part of the body mold, to judge from my own model.
(2) Collector Sue Coffee sent me a photo of her Spanish Fighting Bull with a metallic gold-bronze finish, whose origins she knows nothing about. Except for the eyes, which are black, the whole bull is gold colored, including the horns, genitals, and hooves. It has an "antiqued" look suggesting patinated bronze, with dark shading in the crevices and muscle grooves. In addition to its round Breyer stamp, it has a "U.S.A." stamp, which dates the bull to no earlier than 1970. A couple of other Breyer animals with a similar finish have come to my attention: a bronze-colored Buffalo, which showed up at BreyerFest 1995 (I heard about it but did not see it), and a gold-colored Elephant with white tusks and "antique" dark shading on face, ears, neck, and hindquarters, owned by collector Karen Grimm, which appears in Breyer Collector's Video. None of these models are listed in any Breyer company publications known to me. But conceivably they are from a group of factory-original test models that I learned about from Breyer executive Peter Stone at BreyerFest 1995. He and Breyer sculptor Chris Hess had once obtained a quantity of

bronze paint called something like Bronze Glo (he couldn't recall the name for sure), which had to be rubbed onto the piece by hand rather than painted on. Stone recalled that he and Hess had experimented with this paint on various models—he wasn't sure which ones but thought they could have been Buffaloes and bulls and others; he believed that some Quarter Horse Yearlings were among them too. Since the Yearling mold debuted in 1970, the experiments must have been conducted in the 1970s or possibly the early 1980s. No production runs of bronze animals were made, according to Stone. He does not know what became of the test pieces.
(3) The earliest models of the Spanish Fighting Bull mold have the round "Breyer Molding Co." stamp only; I've seen a specimen or two like this. Later models have the round stamp and the "U.S.A." stamp—the "U.S.A." must have been added to the mold within a couple of years of release, for specimens without the "U.S.A." are scarce, and my old gray-hoofed, gray-horned #73 has a "U.S.A." Some "U.S.A." models may also have the "B" stamp, but I'm not sure.

Spotted Poland China Hog SR — see under "Jasper"

Texas Longhorn Bull — 🐂 Huge horns, standing, looking right, top of tail tuft attached to right hock. Sculpted by Chris Hess. Mold in catalog-run production 1961/63 - current as of 1996.
Catalog-run models made from this mold:
🐂 Texas Longhorn Bull #75, light brown, bald or partly bald face, many with pink nose and genitals, 4 stockings, gray hooves, white horns with gray rings, matte (1961/63 - 1989). In Presentation Collection mounted on American walnut wood base with brass "Texas Longhorn" nameplate, 1972-73. The Presentation model is listed as #5075 in the 1973 price list, but previously it apparently had the same model number as regular-run #75; see Presentation Collection above in the Traditionals section for discussion. Some early #75s have hand-painted eyewhites. The gray rings banding the horns vary from dark to almost nonexistent. Body color varies from coffee brown to red sorrel to palomino. Most Longhorns are matte, but there may be semiglossies too. Early Longhorns have a distinct chestnut forelock that looks stenciled, crisply contrasting with the big bald face; my Longhorn with eyewhites is like this. The stenciled forelock is clearly visible in the 1963 catalog and may have lasted all the way through the 1960s (my copies of these catalogs are blurry). A photo of a stenciled-forelock bull is printed in the May 1965 Western Horseman at the start of an article titled "An Association for Longhorns," about the formation of the Texas Longhorn Breeders Association of America. (The article makes no mention of Breyer or even of the plastic constitution of the bull, which looks very real in the photo. One wonders how many readers were fooled.) On later bulls, starting no later than the early 1970s, the forelock is not stenciled and fades out more gradually into the bald face.
🐂 Texas Longhorn Bull #370, dark red-brown pinto, blaze, large white patches over back and under belly, dark red-brown legs, charcoal-brown hooves, solid gray horns with charcoal tips, matte (1990-95). The back and belly patches are the only two pinto spots on this bull; his hindquarters and forehand (except for the blaze) are solid dark red-brown. The number 370 previously belonged to the Showcase Collection issue of gray blanket appaloosa Arabian Stallion (Family Arabian Stallion mold).
🐂 Texas Longhorn Bull #975, woodgrain; black eyes, many with hand-painted eyewhites; white (unpainted) horns with gray rings; no other color detailing; matte (1961/63 - 1965). Many #975s have hand-painted eyewhites in the outer corners of the eyes—the models of collectors Mel Price and Sande Schneider are like this, as is the #975 on the cover of the 1963 catalog.
Notes:
(1) The horns of the Longhorn are separately molded pieces, and can vary in angle depending on how they are set into the head holes. To judge from models I've seen, the horns have generally been set at a lower angle since the later 1980s. The ears and scrotum are integral parts of the body mold, to judge from my own models.
(2) The Presentation Collection Longhorns were not the only #75s to come mounted on bases. On display at BreyerFest 1995 was an old #75 mounted on a wood base with a copper-colored metal nameplate engraved with the word "Inflexible," unlike the brass Presentation nameplate, which says "Texas Longhorn." "Inflexible" also differed in having his nameplate mounted on the top of the base rather than the front, and in having beveled edges on the base rather than flat sides that angle slightly out, as on the Presentation pieces. I believe "Inflexible" pre-dates the Presentation Collection, for the bull had hand-painted eyewhites, which date him to the 1960s. Although the "Inflexible" bull was certainly a Breyer, I do not know who issued him on the base.
(3) Early models of the Texas Longhorn Bull mold have the round "Breyer Molding Co." stamp only. Later ones have the round stamp and the "U.S.A." stamp—my chalky #75 has a "U.S.A.," so it is quite certain that the mold got this stamp in the 1970s, possibly as early as 1970, when the "U.S.A." was first introduced into the Breyer line. Some "U.S.A." models might have the "B" stamp too, inside a hind leg and perhaps on the horns as well, but I am not sure.

GENERAL NOTE: The dog and cat molds are classed as Traditional scale although many of them are disproportionately large by comparison to the Traditional horses. The Kitten mold, which is life-sized, looms over many of the dog molds and is nearly as tall as the Traditional-scale Running Stallion. For discussion of the Traditional scale, see the General Note at the start of the Traditional horses section above.

Basset Hound — see "Jolly Cholly" Basset Hound (under "Jolly Cholly")

"Benji" — 🐾 Small, rough-haired mutt with longish tail, standing nearly square, head up and slightly cocked. Sculpted by Chris Hess. Mold in catalog-run production late 1977 - 1979.
Catalog-run models made from this mold:
- 🐾 "Benji" #7701, dark yellowy buckskin, ears and tail tip shaded dark brownish gray, no white markings, matte (late 1977 - 1979). This same model was also sold in "Tiffany" And "Benji" Set #3090 [late 1977]. "Benji" #7701 is not in the 1977 catalog and manual but is listed (as "new") in a Breyer company price list issued late in 1977. For discussion of the date of the #3090 set, see the entry below for "Tiffany." The real "Benji" was a TV and movie star. An article in T.V. Guide notes that he was a mixed breed, "a garden-variety mutt" (Mar. 9-15, 1991, p. 9).
Set: see under "Tiffany" below in this section.
Notes:
(1) JAH Spring 1977 specifically states that Chris Hess sculpted the "Benji" and "Tiffany" models. The article also notes that Joe Camp, president of the movie production company for which the real dogs worked, was very concerned that the models be realistic and accurate. He even worked with Hess on the nearly completed sculptures to get the final details just right.
(2) The "Benji" mold has the stamp "© MSP 1977." "MSP" stands for Mulberry Square Productions, the company that made the movie For the Love of Benji, in which the real "Benji" and "Tiffany" starred (per JAH Spring 1977). The most recent "Benji" models might also have a "B" stamp, but I'm not sure.

Bloodhound — see "Jolly Cholly" Bloodhound (under "Jolly Cholly")

Boxer — 🐾 Large, standing square, head up, cropped ears. Copied from an original sculpture by Edward Marshall Boehm. Mold in catalog-run production ca.1954 - 1973, 1995 - current as of 1996.
Catalog-run models made from this mold:
- 🐾 Boxer #66, some chestnut, some fawn; white or light chestnut chest; black muzzle or black lip band; painted-on white blaze; most with black circles around the eyes; most with eyewhites and black irises; 2 front stockings; glossy, semigloss, and matte; vinyl collar, chain collar, or no collar (ca.1954 - 1973). Regarding collars see note 1 for this mold. Many Boxers have black eartips and a dorsal stripe. Boxers tend to come in two basic versions: glossy chestnut with either a full black muzzle or a wide black lip band, and matte or semigloss fawn with a wide black lip band. But in my experience there are many variations on these two basic themes, with the body color ranging from rich medium chestnut to light fawn (tan). #66 is called "fawn" in the 1958 and 1972-73 catalogs; all other catalogs omit color description. The glossy models are the earliest—they are shown in the c. 1954, 1958, 1960, and 1963 catalogs. The text of the catalogs does not say when the glossy finish was discontinued, but the photos in the 1966 and subsequent catalogs show a dog that looks decidedly matte. The eyes of #66 also vary. Typical models have eyes painted white with a black iris, and have wide black circles around the eyes, giving the effect of a pugnacious character sporting a pair of recently inflicted shiners. A few dogs have green irises painted onto the white eyes, with a white pupil or "sparkle" painted atop the green—collectors Sheryl Leisure and Barb Ness have #66s like this, and I have seen one or two others. Collector Jo Kulwicki has two matte #66s with dark brown irises and no eyewhites; one of these dogs also has no black or dark circles around the eyes. Collectors Lisa Heino and Paula DeFeyter also have matte fawn #66s with no eyewhites or black circles. Evidently this variation was the last one made, for the 1969-73 collector's manuals show a #66 with no eyewhites and with only faint shaded circles around the eyes, although the dealer catalogs for these years show a #66 with the usual eyewhites and black circles. The model number 66 later belonged to the Traditional horse model "Stud Spider" Appaloosa.
- 🐾 Boxer #966, woodgrain; black lip band; painted-on white blaze; black around the eyes; eyes painted white with large black or green iris, sometimes topped with white dot; matte (1959/60 - 1965). The 1960 catalog, which is the only one that pictures this model, shows him without a collar and apparently with a solid woodgrain head, no facial color detailing. However, the specimens I know of do have the facial detailing listed above. Collector Sande Schneider's #966 has white eyes with black irises (no white dots); Sheryl Leisure's has white eyes with green irises (no dots); and Karen Grimm's, Paula DeFeyter's, and Paris Mangelsdorf's dogs all have white eyes with green irises topped by a white dot in the center. Whether Breyer conceived the dots as pupils or "sparkles" is a mystery.
- 🐾 "Pug" Boxer #322, brown brindle, dark brown dog with charcoal stripes; stenciled white chest and belly; charcoal lip band; charcoal face with pale pink areas beside nose; black eyes; pale pink chin; 4 stenciled stockings; no collar; matte (1995 - current as of 1996). The charcoal striping on the body varies in intensity from vivid to almost invisible. My own "Pug's" feet are painted with a pale tan that comes up a bit onto the toes; this effect is also visible on the dog in the 1995 Breyer Animals brochure.
Special-run models made from this mold:
- 🐾 Boxer SR, white, black muzzle or very wide black lip band, black around the eyes, eyes painted white with large black pupil, black eartips, gray shading on shoulders, glossy (mid to late 1950s). Of the six or seven white Boxers I have seen in person or in photos, only one has a collar, a choke-chain like that on many chestnut/fawn Boxer #66s (see note 1 for this mold). Collector Sande Schneider has seen a second white Boxer with a

choke-chain collar. The collared dog I have seen (in photos) is one of three white Boxers purchased by collector Robert Peterson in summer 1996 from a man in Chicago who had worked as a Breyer sales representative for several years during the 1950s. When I spoke to this sales rep on the phone in September 1996, he assured me that he had obtained the dogs, along with the other Breyers in his collection, during those years; hence my dating for this model. The rep also recalled that he had sold white Boxers just like any other Breyers. This suggests that the white Boxers may have been regular run, not SR as collectors have supposed. If they were regular run, their rarity today would indicate that they were issued only for a short time. (The rep thought he had been recalled selling them for as long as 3-4 years, but he was a bit confused about the white versus the chestnut/fawn dogs, so he may have been mistaken about the length of time.) However, we can't be positive that the white Boxer was regular run (the company could conceivably have sent the rep SR leftovers to dispose of), for the white Boxers are not listed in any 1950s Breyer catalogs or price lists known to me, and sadly, the rep was quite sure he had not kept any documents given to him by Breyer that might tell about this model. So I continue to list this Boxer as SR until further evidence turns up. But one thing that does seem probable is that more of these dogs must have been made than a couple of dozen, as collectors have speculated (e.g., Walerius 1991, p. 20). For although white Boxers are certainly rare today, collectors have found more of them than would likely have been found if so very few were made so long ago.
Notes:
(1) Some Boxer #66s came with a snap-on brown vinyl strap collar with metal studs, some with a choke-chain collar made of twisted-link chain like that used for the reins of Western Ponies and other Breyer horses, and some with no collar. The strap collar, which is the earlier of the two collars, is shown on the #66 Boxer in the ca.1954 catalog, the earliest Breyer publication known to me that shows the Boxer mold. #66 is shown with the choke-chain collar in an old Breyer company sheet that probably dates to 1955/57, and bare-necked in another old Breyer sheet, which is probably from the later 1950s. He is again shown with the choke-chain in the catalogs for 1958, 1960, 1963, and 1966-73, although 1973 catalog says "chain no longer available," so evidently the very last #66s were sold bare-necked. Collector Sande Schneider found an unusual collar on an old glossy #66 at a flea market in 1994. The collar is made of flexible brown vinyl like the old snap-on style collars, but is a bit wider and has a silver metal buckle rather than a snap. The buckle does not have a loose tongue like a typical belt buckle but instead an integral prong that fits through the holes punched in the vinyl strap. This collar appears to be professionally made, but it is the only one we know of, so it may not have been a Breyer issue.
(2) According to Breyer executive Peter Stone, Breyer's Boxer is a copy of an original porcelain Boxer by Edward M. Boehm. Stone still owns the Boehm piece that was used as a model for the Breyer (per conversations of May 1994 and Oct. 1995). The Boehm Boxer came in 9" x 8.5" and 5" x 4.5" versions, which were virtually identical except in size (per Palley 1976, p. 150). In size, mold, and color design, the Breyer is identical to the larger Boehm, which was first released no later than 1952, perhaps as early as 1949. To the best of my knowledge, the Boxer is Breyer's first non-horse animal mold, for he is the only such mold shown in that catalog (ca.1954), and the description of the model in that catalog calls him "new." That Breyer's Boxer #66 was released in 1954 is suggested as well by the following listing in the 1954 Playthings Directory, a toy-industry annual published by Playthings Magazine: "Breyer Molding Co., 2536 W. Lake St., Chicago 12, Ill. Plastic horses and dogs."
(3) The Boxer mold has no round Breyer stamp or other mold marks.

"Brandy" St. Bernard — see under St. Bernard

Calico Kitten — see under Kitten

"Chaser" Hound Dog — see under "Jolly Cholly"

"Cleopatra" Kitten — see under Kitten

Collie — see "Lassie"

French Poodle Sewing Kit—see note 2 for the Poodle mold

German Shepherd — see under "Rin Tin Tin"

"Grimalkin" — A Breyer mold that didn't happen. "Grimalkin" is the kitty companion to the horse "Sham" in Marguerite Henry's book King of the Wind. Breyer executive Peter Stone, at a "Breakfast with Peter Stone" event at Hi-Way Hobby House in Ramsey, New Jersey, in 1993, reported that Breyer had wanted to issue an in-scale model of "Grimalkin" to go with the Artist Series "Sham" model. A couple of sample pieces were made, but the kitty was so tiny that it proved unfeasible to mass produce. (As reported to me by collector Robin Briscoe, who attended the "Breakfast" event.) One of the prototype kitties, a gray and white tiger stripe, is shown in the 1984 Breyer catalog in a photo with the new "Sham" model.

"Honey" Collie — see under "Lassie"

"Jolly Cholly" — 🐾 Sitting basset hound, huge head, cartoonish appearance. Sculpted by Chris Hess. Mold in catalog-run production 1966-85, 1994-95.
Catalog-run models made from this mold:
- 🐾 "Chaser" Hound Dog #324, chestnut and white dog; white muzzle; eyes have black pupils, whites underneath, and red underlining; black nose, "whiskers," and lip line; chestnut tail with white tip; matte; with tartan plaid cloth cushion (1994-95). This dog is

similar to "Jolly Cholly" #326 but lacks the black "saddle" patch that is characteristic of #326. "Chaser's" chestnut color is shaded, the ears and head being somewhat darker than the body, and the belly being very pale. "Chaser's" cushion is identical to that sold with the Kitten models "Cleopatra" and "Leonardo"; the plaid colors are red, green, and dark blue, with thin lines of white and yellow. A cloth tag on the cushion identifies the materials and says "Breyer, Wayne N.J. USA / Made in China / © Reeves Internaiional, Inc." The reference to China pertains only to the cushion; the dogs themselves are made in the Breyer factory in Wayne, New Jersey.

- ♠ "Jolly Cholly" Basset Hound #326, tri-color, chestnut and white dog with black "saddle" patch; white muzzle and stripe on head; eyes with black pupils, whites underneath, and red, pink, or brown underlining; black nose and "whiskers"; black tail with white tip; matte (1968/69 - 1985). Regarding release date, see note 1 for this mold. Some models have a bit of black shading along the lips, but not a continuous black line as on "Chaser" #324. Collector Jo Kulwicki has several #326s, the color of whose eye underlining (the lower lid's rim and/or inner tissue) ranges from pink to raw-looking red to dark brown to medium brown (same color as the surrounding facial color). I have seen some models with raspberry pink dabs in the nostrils. A number of collectors have found #326's with an unusual feature: a chain entwined through 4 holes drilled into the neck, with a brown plastic card hanging from the chain. The cards have white lettering, which most commonly says "American Interinsurance Exchange." However, collector Sande Schneider found one that says "American Interstate Insurance Corporation of Wisconsin," and collector Mary Margaret Fox has one that says "American Underwriters Group." The chain is of a different type from that used for Breyer horse reins or the Boxer's collar, and evidently Breyer did not supply it or the plastic cards. Collector Thea Ryan (see Ryan 1993), who found one of the "American Interinsurance Exchange" models at a flea market, notes that the reverse side of the card is printed with the name and address of Hoosier Badge & Trophies, Inc., in Indianapolis. Thea wrote to the trophy company and received a reply in June 1992. The trophy company said they had made the cards for the insurance company at least nine years before— that would be 1983, which is consistent with the fact that these dogs have "U.S.A." stamps, dating them to no earlier than 1970. The trophy company did not have details but thought the insurance company had used the dogs as promotional items. In any case, the fact that the insurance company had the cards made indicates that Breyer had nothing to do with the creation of these insurance Chollys beyond manufacturing the basic models from which they are made. (Thanks to Thea for sending me a copy of the trophy company's letter.)
- ♠ "Jolly Cholly" Bloodhound #325, solid dark brown; eyes have black pupils, whites underneath, and red or pink underlining; black nose; matte (1966 - 1967/68). Regarding final year of production, see note 1 for this mold. Several hobby references state that this model was advertised as a "woodgrain"; but he has no woodgrain pattern, and none of the Breyer catalogs, manuals, or price lists that include this model refer to him as "woodgrain." Nor do any Breyer publications assign him a model number in the 900s, as all true woodgrain models have. Collector Jo Kulwicki's two Bloodhounds have pink underlining below the eyewhites; other models I've seen have red. I have seen some models with raspberry pink dabs in the nostrils.

Notes:

(1) The 1967 catalog and price list include Bloodhound #325. The 1968 catalog omits #325, and includes the new Basset Hound #326 instead; but the 1968 manual and price list include #325 and omit #326. The 1969 manual and price list omit #325 and include #326. In short, the 1968 records are so chaotic that it's impossible to say just when #325 was discontinued and #326 released.

(2) This big-headed, cartoonish looking fellow is the only comical Tenite mold ever produced by Breyer. He debuted with the nickname "Jolly Cholly" and kept it for some years, but the nickname was dropped from catalogs after 1970/71 and from manuals after 1975. A possible explanation for this nickname was brought to my attention by my brother, Ron Atkinson, a life-long baseball fan. It seems that there was a baseball player, one Charlie Grimm, who was nicknamed Jolly Cholly (Ron's baseball encyclopedia confirmed the spelling). He played first base for the Cubs starting in 1925, became a manager for the team in the mid-1930s, and retired from that post in 1960. The Cubs of course are and were a Chicago team. Breyer had been located in Chicago since the 1940s and was there through the 1960s and beyond. "Jolly Cholly" Bloodhound first appeared in 1966, six years after Jolly Cholly Grimm retired from the Cubs. Under the circumstances, it's hard to believe that the Breyer mold was dubbed with the same nickname as this longtime Cubs fixture by sheer coincidence. Ron's encyclopedia unfortunately does not tell how Charlie Grimm got his nickname (though obviously "Cholly" is a play on "Charlie") or relate any anecdotes that might suggest why a blimp-headed bloodhound would constitute an apt tribute to him. Ron noted, however, that Grimm "looked a little like a bloodhound." When I asked Breyer executive Peter Stone about the possible Cubs connection, he said did not know how the Breyer mold got its name. He commented that his father, who owned the Breyer company at that time with his partner Charles Schiff, was indeed a Cubs fan, but possibly the naming of the Jolly Cholly mold had to do with Charles Schiff rather than Charlie Grimm.

(3) Early models of the "Jolly Cholly" mold have the round "Breyer Molding Co." stamp only. Later ones have the round stamp and the "U.S.A." stamp. Some "U.S.A." models might have the "B" stamp too, but I have not actually heard of one like this.

Kitten — ♠ Sitting, looking up and sharply right, left paw raised. Sculpted by Chris Hess. Mold in catalog-run production 1966-73, 1994 - current as of 1996.
Catalog-run models made from this mold:

- ♠ Calico Kitten #336, orangy-tan tabby with charcoal-brown stripes, white or pale tan face, most with green eyes with black pupils, black "whiskers," pink mouth line, white or pale tan throat and front paws, matte (1966-73). Although Breyer catalogs always called this model a "Calico," it is actually a tabby. The basic body color varies from brownish tan to orange. Collector Jo Kulwicki has a #336 that is dark yellow with charcoal stripes. Some models have stripes inside the ears; others don't. A few have blue eyes, and some have iridescent green or blue eyes (per JAH 18/#3 Summer II 1991, p. 33, and 18/#4 Fall 1991, p. 33).
- ♠ "Cleopatra" Kitten #337, orange tabby with darker orange stripes, white or pale tan muzzle, green eyes with black pupils, black "whiskers," pink or orange mouth line, white throat and chest, 3 or 4 white paws, matte; with tartan plaid cloth cushion (1994-95). This kitten's cushion is identical to that sold with "Leonardo" Kitten and "Chaser" Hound Dog ("Jolly Cholly" mold); the plaid colors are red, green, and dark blue, with thin lines of white and yellow. A cloth tag on the cushion identifies the materials and says "Breyer, Wayne N.J. USA / Made in China / © Reeves International, Inc." The reference to China pertains only to the cushion; the kittens themselves are made in the Breyer factory in Wayne, New Jersey. On the "Cleopatras" I've seen, some have 4 white

paws, but others have 3, with the left front paw being orange.

- ♠ "Leonardo" Kitten #338, tawny-gray tabby with darker gray stripes, white muzzle, yellow eyes with black pupils, black "whiskers," gray or charcoal mouth line, white throat and chest, 3 or 4 white paws, matte; with tartan plaid cloth cushion (1994-95). See "Cleopatra" Kitten for discussion of the cushion. On the "Leonardos" I've seen, 4 white paws is the norm, but some models have only 3 white paws and a dark left front paw. I've also seen one or two models that were dark gray with faint charcoal gray stripes.
- ♠ Siamese Kitten #335, white with dark Siamese points (muzzle, tail, paws, and eartips); most with blue eyes with black pupils; matte (1966-70). The color of the points varies from dark gray to seal brown. A few #335s have green eyes and a few have iridescent blue or green eyes, all with black pupils (see JAH 18/#3 Summer II 1991, p. 33, and 18/#4 Fall 1991, p. 33). Collector Sheryl Leisure's and my own kittens with normal blue eyes have a pink mouth-line, while Sheryl's and collector Robin Briscoe's kittens with iridescent blue eyes have no mouth pinking.

Note: Early models of the Kitten mold have the round "Breyer Molding Co." stamp only, located on the back of the right (un-raised) front leg. Later models have the round stamp and the "U.S.A." stamp—I have seen #336 Calico Kittens with the "U.S.A.," so it is certain that this stamp was added to the mold no later than 1973.

"Lassie" — ♠ Collie, standing/prancing, panting, right front leg raised. Sculpted by Chris Hess. Mold in catalog-run production 1955/57 - 1965, 1995 - current as of 1996.
Catalog-run models made from this mold:

- ♠ "Honey" Collie #323, sandy chestnut with stenciled white neck, belly, legs, and tail; stenciled white muzzle and blaze; pale peach-pink tongue; black nose and "whiskers"; gray shading over the chestnut on ears and down sides of neck; matte (1995 - current as of 1996). This dog, unlike "Lassie" #65, has long gray-chestnut patches running down the sides of the neck from the ears.
- ♠ "Lassie" #65, red chestnut with unstenciled white neck, belly, legs, and tail tip; bald or oversprayed light chestnut face; red or dark pink tongue; black nose; most matte, some glossy (1955/57 - 1965). The "blanket" of chestnut over the dog's body varies in size, typically leaving the neck, shoulders, chest, forearms, and belly white, but sometimes covering nearly the whole body below a white neck ring (collector Paula DeFeyter kindly sent me a photo of her glossy #73 like this). Typically the tongue is red, but collector Jo Kulwicki's "Lassie," which she found in original box, has a dark pink tongue, as does my own model. My dog and others I've seen have a black outline along the lower lip. Breyer's "Lassie" represents the canine star of the TV show Lassie, and Breyer catalogs and price lists 1958-65 say "Sold under license arrangements with television producers." The show, which went through various versions, ran from September 1954 through September 1971 (per Terrace 1979, vol. 1, and Brooks and Marsh 1992), and the model's box, which features a black-and-white photo of a real collie against a blue background, says "Copr. [copyright] Robert Maxwell Associates, 1955." Thus the model could not have been introduced earlier than 1955 and might have debuted a year or two later. Collector Melanie Teller sent me a Xerox of her model's original shield-shnaped hang tag, which says: "Lassie / Wonder Dog of T.V. / Made of durable Tenite." The model number 65 later belonged to the Traditional horse model Marguerite Henry's "Justin Morgan."

Note: The "Lassie" mold has no round Breyer stamp or other mold marks.

"Leonardo" Kitten — see under Kitten

Poodle — ♠ Standing square, panting, looking left, molded-on collar. Copied from a china poodle probably manufactured by Rosenthal. Mold in catalog-run production 1955/57 - 1973.
Catalog-run models made from this mold:

- ♠ Poodle #67, black; green, blue, black, or red eyes; red or pink tongue; collar typically red, pink, or black; some with painted-on white teeth; glossy (1955/57 - 1967/68). Regarding dates and the Poodle sewing kit, see notes 2 and 3 for this mold. The green-eyed and blue-eyed Poodles have black pupils; the red-eyed ones have a dot of red in the middle of black scleras. Walerius 1991 (p. 23) says some #67s have gold collars, though I have not heard of an actual specimen like this. I've heard reliable reports of gray collars and blue collars; a gray-collar specimen reported by Schneider 1994 has no mold stamps and thus must date to the 1950s. Many collars, of whatever color, have a buckle and keeper painted on in white. Jo Kulwicki has a black Poodle with black eyes and black collar with white painted buckle. A very unusual black Poodle was offered for sale at BreyerFest 1996: he was cast in black plastic subtly marbled with small swirls of white plastic. He had a typical red collar and painted-on white teeth. His lack of mold stamps dated him to the 1950s. The model number 67 later belonged to the Traditional horse model Marguerite Henry's "San Domingo."
- ♠ Poodle #68, white; black nose and eyes; some with black eyebrows; most with either red or pink collar and tongue; glossy (1955/57 - 1967/68). Regarding dates and the Poodle sewing kit, see notes 2 and 3 for this mold. The eyebrows don't seem to follow a chronology; both older models (without mold stamps) and newer ones (with stamps) have been found with and without black eyebrows. Collector Kate Cabot sold me a glossy chalky white Poodle with eyebrows and a red collar. He is a cream color rather than stark white, and dates to the 1960s (he has the round Breyer stamp but no "U.S.A."). Some #68s have blue collars, of a turquoise or sky-blue shade. Sande Schneider's, Jo Kulwicki's, and Robin Briscoe's blue-collar models have no round Breyer stamp, which means they date to the 1950s. The eyebrows on Sande's model, oddly enough, extend out from his pupils. Walerius 1991 (p. 23) notes that some #68s have gold collars. Many collars of whatever color have a buckle and keeper painted on in white; Jo Kulwicki even has a white Poodle with unpainted (white plastic) collar with white painted buckle. Not all collars have this detail, however; Robin's and Jo's blue-collar models lack it. The model in the 1963 catalog—the only publication in my possession that shows #68 in color—has black eyebrows, a bright red tongue, and matching bright red collar with white buckle and keeper. The model number 68 later belonged to the Traditional horse model "Legionario III."
- ♠ Poodle #69, silver gray, black nose and eyes, red or deep pink collar and tongue, some with painted-on white teeth, matte (1968/69 - 1973). Regarding release date, see note 3 for this mold. "Silver gray" is the description used for this dog in Breyer catalogs; it is a realistic gray color, not metallic. I've heard that #69s have been found with green collars. Many collars, of whatever color, have a buckle and keeper painted on in white. The model number 69 later belonged to the Traditional model "Smoky" The Cow Horse.
- ♠ Poodle #967, woodgrain; black eyes, some with hand-painted eyewhites; black nose; black eyebrows; red tongue; black collar with gold buckle; matte (1961/63 - 1964). The details on this model may vary. The models owned by collectors Kate Cabot and Sande Schneider have all the details listed above.

Notes:

(1) This very early Breyer mold is a direct copy of a china poodle, according to former Breyer executive Peter Stone (conversation of March 1996). At the time of our conversation, Stone had just recently seen the china piece, which was in the possession of Mrs. Hess, widow of Chris Hess, Breyer's primary mold maker from 1950 through the mid-1980s. Stone was not sure of the manufacturer of the china poodle, but it was probably the Rosenthal company, as collector Sande Schneider recently discovered. At an antique show she visited in February 1996, Sande came upon a china poodle that was identical to the Breyer "even down to the buckle on the collar." It also appeared to be the same size as the Breyer. The china dog had no sticker or engraving on it that Sande could see, but the vendor selling the piece told her it was a Rosenthal. The Rosenthal company is particularly noted as a manufacturer of collectible plates, which it has been issuing for about 90 years, according to Breyer collector and china/ceramic aficionado Sue Stewart. Breyer evidently borrowed the colors as well as the design for the Poodle from the Rosenthal dogs, to judge from the fact that Mrs. Hess's piece is white and the dog seen by Sande gray.

(2) The earliest Breyer catalog in which the Poodle mold appears is the 1958, but it is certain that the mold was released no later than 1957 since it is advertised in the 1957 Sears holiday catalog (thanks to collector Andrea Gurdon for a Xerox). Conceivably the mold debuted as early as 1955, but probably not earlier since it is not in the ca. 1954 Breyer catalog. In the 1957 Sears catalog, the #67 black and #68 white Poodles are each offered in a "French Poodle Sewing Kit." The ad photo shows the two dogs standing side by side, with the white Poodle (and undoubtedly the black, too, but my Xerox is unclear) wearing what looks to be a short, circular cape or blanket around his neck, which reaches over his back. According to the ad text, the blanket has a pocket full of sewing items: "This adorable poodle will hold sewing needs or jewelry while it decorates your dresser or night stand. Break-resistant Tenite, looks like fine bone china. Pocket of blanket holds purse size kit with 12 assorted color cotton threads, thimble, buttons, needle, pins. . . . *State black or white*. . . . Each $2.84... 2 for $5.19." Collector Sheryl Leisure saw one of these sewing-kit Poodles at a flea market in early 1996. The dog was black, and his blanket was red felt with zigzag edges, as though it had been cut out with pinking shears. Collector Marie Ferguson found the white Poodle version in late 1996; his blanket is dark royal blue felt with slightly scalloped edges, as are visible in the Sears ad. Sadly, he had lost all of his sewing items.

(3) The 1967 catalog and price list include #67 black and #68 white only. The 1968 manual and price list likewise include #67 and #68 only. The 1968 catalog, however, omits #67 and #68, and includes the new #69 silver gray instead. The 1969 manual and price list likewise omit #67 and #68 and include #69. (There is no 1969 catalog to my knowledge.) In short, the 1968 records are chaotic, so it's impossible to be sure just when #67 and #68 were discontinued and #69 was released.

(4) The Poodle is an unusually heavy mold because of his huge hairy legs, which are solid plastic. His heftiness got him discontinued as an economy measure at the start of the oil-crisis era. Breyer's cellulose acetate plastic is not a petroleum product but did become scarce during that period. For discussion see the Breyer Company History section below in the Appendix.

(5) Collector Sande Schneider has observed that many Poodle models have an odd "seam" or "vein" running diagonally from the left flank forward and up toward the middle of the dog's back (see Schneider 1994). On some models the fault is so severe that the plastic has actually cracked, but on others it is only a faint line that does not crack the plastic. In Sande's experience and mine, this seam or crack occurs on most models that have the round "Breyer Molding Co." stamp but not on earlier models, which have no stamp. A few models with the round stamp do not have the flaw—collector Sheryl Leisure's black Poodle with stamp is an example.

(6) Sande Schneider also pointed out that the Poodle's ears are separately molded pieces that are glued to the model's head after molding. (See Schneider 1994.) The joint around the base of the ears is quite visible on some specimens. That the ears must be separate pieces is also evident from the shape of the ears, with their sharp folds and narrow passages underneath. This shape would be virtually impossible to mold if the ears were integral to the Poodle's head.

(7) In September 1996, collector Robert Peterson wrote to me about a mysterious poodle dog he had acquired only a few weeks before from a man in Chicago, who identified the dog as a Breyer that had never gone into production. The man was a retired independent sales representative who had represented Breyer for several years during the 1950s and had gotten the poodle along with a number of other Breyers during that time. As shown in the photo kindly provided by Robert, the dog is standing square like the usual Breyer Poodle but is a completely different mold, smaller, sleeker, and more finely built, with mouth shut and face, neck, paws, midriff, and tail shaft smoothly "shaved" (see the last photo in the photos for the Poodle mold). Her tail is broken but originally ended in a round tuft, according to the former sales rep. She has a molded-on collar with two small molded-on bows on the back side. The dog is molded in normal-feeling white plastic, according to Robert; and like all other Breyers from the 1950s, she has no mold stamps. As for the dog's color, her face, neck, and paws are white, and her midriff, though rubbed nearly white, bears traces of light gray paint. Her "hairy" portions—crown and ears, forehand, and hindquarters—are a medium grayish blue with a semigloss finish. The collar is pale pink with turquoisey bows. The eyes have eyewhites and black "pupils." When I spoke to the former sales rep on the phone in September 1996, he was certain that the dog was a Breyer. Although he represented other toy companies besides Breyer, Breyer was the only one that produced plastic animals. He said that he had displayed this blue poodle for Breyer at a toy show in New York City one year (toy shows, he said, were regularly held there in the New Yorker and McElfin [sp?] hotels). The rep did not know what specific decisions Breyer had made about the dog, but evidently they simply shelved it owing to lack of market interest. Nor did the rep know how many were made or whether other samples like his had been given to other sales representatives; his own piece was the only one he knew of. The dog's authenticity was confirmed by *JAH* editor Stephanie Macejko, who found the original metal injection-mold, labeled "small poodle," in storage at Breyer in January 1997. She will print photos of the mold in *JAH* May/June 1997.

(8) The earliest models of the Poodle mold have no mold stamps. Somewhat later ones have the round "Breyer Molding Co." stamp only. The latest ones—silver gray #69s made from about 1970 through 1973—have both the round stamp and the "U.S.A." stamp.

"Pug" Boxer — see under Boxer

"Rin Tin Tin" — German Shepherd, standing, panting. Sculpted by Chris Hess. Mold in production: catalog run 1955/57 - 1965, pre-catalog release 1971, catalog run 1972-73.

Catalog-run models made from this mold:

- German Shepherd #327, charcoal gray; white-and-gray shaded face, breast, and belly; many with gray stripe on head and painted-on white teeth on lower jaw; red tongue; matte (pre-catalog release 1971, catalog run 1972-73). Though this model doesn't appear in catalogs and manuals until 1972, it and #215 dapple PAM were made available to collectors in 1971, according to an old Breyer company flier of which I have a photocopy. The flier, which has photos of both models (#327 is called "Silver German Shepherd"), says: "Your Model Show Sensations for 1971 / Introductory Offer!!! - Mail Order Exclusive," pricing the mare at $3.50 and the dog at $2.50, postage paid. Most #327s have painted-on lower teeth, but a few do not—collector Jo Kulwicki has a dog like this, and I have seen one or two others. The color of #327 varies from nearly black to medium gray, with occasional dogs having a decidedly brown hue. Jo's toothless model is a dark gray-brown, as is collector Heather Wells's dog with painted-on teeth. The amount of white on #327 also varies; for instance, some dogs have no white at all on the belly. See next entry for discussion of brown dogs.
- "Rin Tin Tin" #64, brown and white dog; typically with white head, breast, belly, and legs; unpainted teeth; red or pink tongue; matte or semigloss (1955/57 - 1965). This model represents the canine star of the TV show *Adventures of Rin Tin Tin*, and Breyer catalogs and price lists 1958-65 say "Sold under license arrangements with television producers." The show ran from October 1954 through September 1964 (it was all reruns from 1959 on, per Terrace 1979, vol. 1). The model's box, which features a black-and-white photo of a real German Shepherd's head against a blue background, says "Copyright 1955 Screen Gems Inc.," so the model could not have been introduced earlier than 1955 and might have debuted a year or two later. Collector Jo Kulwicki's "Rin Tin Tin", which she found in original box, came with a hang tag suspended from his neck on a string, which says "Rin-Tin-Tin / made of durable plastic / Fighting Blue Devils." "Fighting Blue Devils" was the nickname of the cavalry company to which "Rinty" (as "Rin Tin Tin" was called for short) and his pet boy, Corporal Rusty, belonged. Some models have charcoal-gray nose, eyes, and ruff shading, contrasting with the brown body color, while others have brown nose, eyes, and shading, the same color as the body. "Rintys" comes in two extreme color patterns and all gradations in between. On one extreme is a white or pale tan dog with a medium brown to dark charcoal-brown "saddle" pattern over his back and rump and brown shading on the tail and back of the neck. This version is pictured in the 1958 catalog and in a couple of other Breyer sheets from the 1950s. On the other extreme is a dog with the medium to dark brown color over most of the body, but with the head, belly, and legs remaining basically white or pale tan. "Rin Tin Tins" of this non-saddle version, as Schneider 1992 points out, are shown in the 1960 and 1963 catalogs, and collectors have found them in "Rin Tin Tin" boxes with "Rin Tin Tin" tags around their necks. These non-saddle "Rintys" are confusable with the gray-brown version of German Shepherd #327. One distinction between them is in the teeth: all the known "Rintys" I've seen, including the non-saddle "Rinty" in the 1963 catalog, lack painted-on teeth, whereas most (though not all) #327s have some painted-on white teeth. Another difference is that even the non-saddle "Rintys" generally have more white or light areas overall; in particular the head is typically white or pale tan with only touches of brown (notably on the ears), whereas #327's head typically has a lot of dark shading, which often comes down from the top of the head and extends in a stripe between the eyes and down the nose. Collector Paula DeFeyter wrote to me that she has a saddle-pattern "Rinty" in black rather than brown; this is the only such dog I've heard of. The model number 64 later belonged to Black Foundation Stallion.

Note: The "Rin Tin Tin" mold has no mold marks.

Sewing-kit Poodles — see note 2 for the Poodle mold

Siamese Kitten — see under Kitten

St. Bernard — Standing, looking up. Sculpted by Chris Hess. Mold in catalog-run production 1972-80, 1995 - current as of 1996.

Catalog-run models made from this mold:

- "Brandy" St. Bernard #321, tawny chestnut body with white neck, belly, lower legs, and tail tip; gray dun patches covering ears and eyes; white muzzle and stripe on head; black nose; charcoal lip-lines; red tongue; black eyes with "bloodshot" pink below; matte (1995 - current as of 1996). This dog is lighter and yellower in body color than the old red-brown #328 St. Bernard. Also, on #328, the whole neck is white, but on "Brandy" the white of the neck is interrupted by long patches of tawny chestnut running down from the ear areas. A further difference is that #328 generally has charcoal toenails, but "Brandy" does not—her feet are solid white.
- St. Bernard #328, chestnut body with white neck, belly, lower legs, and tail tip; red-brown or black patches covering ears and eyes; white muzzle and stripe on head; black nose; charcoal lip-lines; red tongue; black eyes with eyewhites and "bloodshot" red below; matte (1972-80). The body color varies from dark to medium red chestnut to tawny dun and caramel shades. The 1972-75 catalogs and manuals show the patches on the head as being dark brown, contrasting with the red-brown of the body; collector Jo Kulwicki's dogs of this version have black highlights on the dark brown head patches. Subsequent manuals and catalogs show the head patches as the same color as the body. Some dogs have a dorsal stripe; others don't.

Note: The St. Bernard mold has the round "Breyer Molding Co." stamp and the "U.S.A." stamp. The last #328s made might have the "B" stamp in addition, but I'm not sure.

"Tiffany" — Small shaggy dog (Maltese or Lhasa Apso?), standing, head turned sharply to left, tail curled over back. Sculpted by Chris Hess. Mold in catalog-run production late 1977.

Catalog-run models made from this mold:

- "Tiffany" And "Benji" Set #3090, white "Tiffany," black eyes and nose, matte (late 1977). Set also includes a "Benji" dog model and a cardboard diorama of Athens, with pillars and a "stone" walkway in the foreground and a photo of the Parthenon on the Acropolis forming the background. The "Benji" in this set is the same as the "Benji" sold separately as #7701 [late 1977 - 1979]. The #3090 box calls the set "Joe Camp's Benji & Tiffany" (regarding Mr. Camp, see note 1 for this mold). This set is not in the 1977 Breyer catalog or manual but is in a Breyer company price list issued late in 1977, which says "3090 Benji/Tiffany Gift Set—DISCONTINUED." The set also appears in the 1977 Penney's holiday catalog, which lists it as "Benji and Tiffany 'On Location' Set," for $6.99. Whether the sets were distributed in 1977 to retailers other than Penney's I don't know, but *JAH* Spring 1977 states: "Benji and Tiffany set will be available in June." The release of the set was timed to coincide with the release of the second "Benji" movie, *For the Love of Benji*, which was filmed in Greece. The set was discontinued because it flopped miserably, according to former Breyer executive Peter Stone (conversation of Nov. 1994, and presentation at the Peter Stone Company's "Tribute to Christian Hess," July 27, 1996, Lexington, Ky.). Stone commented that Breyer produced some 40,000 "Benji" And "Tiffany" sets, confident that they would sell like hotcakes. But Penney's managed to sell only about 1,000 sets, sticking Breyer with vast quantities of leftovers. Consequently, #3090 sets appeared on Bentley Sales Company price lists for several years (1979-82), and "Tiffany" from the set was on Bentley's lists as late as December 1984. Many collectors who find this set keep it in its box, which revels in rococo splendor: a large, heart-shaped window in the multi-colored, flower-strewn lid showcases the models inside, which are fitted into a hot-pink background. The diorama, or "chipboard scene," as the Penney's catalog calls it, comes in disassembled sections shrink-wrapped together in the bottom of the box. Assembly is a business of folding and bending and inserting tabs A, B, C, D, E, F, etc., into slots A, B, C, D, E, F, etc.—and a frustrating business it is, according to collector Jo Kulwicki, who very kindly broke her diorama out of its plastic wrap and assembled it for my edification as I sat and watched, sipping something relaxing and offering free advice.

Notes:

(1) *JAH* Spring 1977 specifically states that Chris Hess sculpted the "Benji" and "Tiffany" models. The article also notes that Joe Camp, president of the movie production company for which the real dogs worked, was very concerned that the models be realistic and accurate. He even worked with Hess on the nearly completed sculptures to get the final details just right.

(2) The "Tiffany" mold has the stamp "© MSP 1977." "MSP" stands for Mulberry Square Productions, the company that made the movie *For the Love of Benji*, in which the real "Benji" and "Tiffany" starred (see *JAH* Spring 1977).

Donkeys & Mules

General note: All the donkey and mule models are Traditional scale. See the General Note at the start of the Traditional horses section above.

Balking Mule — ♞ Squatting on haunches, front legs braced, teeth bared, ears back, roached mane, tail tip attached to left hock, molded-on bridle with small molded-on blinkers. Sculpted by Chris Hess. Mold in catalog-run production 1968-73.

Catalog-run models made from this mold:

♞ Balking Mule #207, bay, solid face with gray-shaded white muzzle, black mane and tail tuft, brown legs (no black), gray hooves, matte or slightly semigloss (1968-73). Some have a brown bridle; others have brick red. Some have a dorsal stripe. This model is not always easy to distinguish from the seal brown #208. The bay varies from quite dark to a medium reddish color, but is always somewhat lighter and redder than seal brown #208. Either this bay Mule or the seal brown appears in the July 1973 *Western Horseman,* atop a large trophy clutched by a genial-looking man. The caption reads, "Hugh Hamilton—winner of the Hugh Pelott Memorial Award for Charm." The accompanying article tells about a guest ranch in Arizona, which held an annual Desert Caballeros trail ride in which the article's author participated. He explains: "The night before the ride was highlighted by a special trophy presentation. . . . Some years ago Hugh Hamilton changed his name from Hugh Pelott to Hugh Hamilton. Hugh and his mule, Trixie, are famous on the DC ride; so this trophy sprang into being. Part of it stemmed from the fact that I had a balky mule statue from the Breyer Molding Company that I didn't quite know what to do with. Butch Morgan, Blue Ribbon Trophies, engraved the brass plates—one stating that this was the Hugh Pelott Memorial Award ... for Charm. The other plate shows that it was won five years in a row by Hugh Hamilton, and the trophy was topped off by one of Trixie's shoes. One she had worn over miles of trails, and then Hugh carried it in his saddlebag for over a thousand miles in case Trixie threw a shoe and needed a spare. Hugh was mighty proud of his trophy."

♞ Balking Mule #208, seal brown, solid face with gray-shaded white muzzle, black mane and tail tuft, brown or black lower legs, gray or black hooves, matte or slightly semigloss (1968-70). Some #208s have a brown bridle; others have brick red. Some have a dorsal stripe. The catalogs that list this Mule call him "brown," while the manuals call him "dark brown." Collectors often refer to him as "seal brown." His color is less red than bay #207's and is darker, ranging from dark chocolate to a charcoal brown that is nearly black.

Special-run models made from this mold:

♘ Balking Mule SR, alabaster; gray mane and tail tuft; gray muzzle, knees, and hocks; gray hooves; black bridle; matte (1994). Made for Black Horse Ranch. 400 models made, per Karen Grimm of BHR and *JAH* editor Stephanie Macejko. Sold separately or in set with apricot dun, black blanket appy, black leopard appy, and chestnut Balking Mules. These 5 models plus the SR buckskin were produced by Breyer as Balking Mule Assortment SR #410894, per Stephanie Macejko. Though these SR Mules were announced in 1993 (in the October *Model Horse Trader*), they were not issued until early 1994 owing to factory delays. BHR's original announcements of the 5-Mule sets and the SR buckskin Mule gave the quantity of 300 of each color. A seventh SR Balking Mule, in steel gray, also quantity 300, was advertised by BHR in November 1993 as an exclusive to subscribers of the magazine *The Model Horse Trader*, edited by Sheryl Leisure. However, in January 1994 BHR announced that the steel gray Mule would not be produced after all, owing to a snafu at Breyer. Heather Wells explained to me that the quantity of the other 6 colors was increased to 400 each to offset the cancellation of the grays.

♘ Balking Mule SR, apricot dun, solid face, darker red dun mane and tail tuft, dun-gray muzzle and hooves, no stockings, black bridle, matte (1994). Made for Black Horse Ranch. 400 models made. Sold separately or in set with alabaster, black blanket appy, black leopard appy, and chestnut Balking Mules. These 5 plus the SR buckskin were produced by Breyer as Balking Mule Assortment SR #410894. The mane and tail tuft are very red on some of the apricot dun Mules, more brown on others. See Balking Mule SR alabaster for further discussion.

♘ Balking Mule SR, black blanket appaloosa, solid face, unstenciled blanket covering butt and half of barrel, splashed-on black spots, 4 stockings, tan hooves, brown bridle, matte (1994). Made for Black Horse Ranch. 400 models made. Sold separately or in set with alabaster, apricot dun, black leopard appy, and chestnut Balking Mules. These 5 and the SR buckskin were produced by Breyer as Balking Mule Assortment SR #410894. See Balking Mule SR alabaster for further discussion.

♘ Balking Mule SR, black leopard appaloosa, white mule with splashed-on black spots, black mane and tail tuft, gray muzzle, 4 high black "stockings," black hooves, black bridle, matte (1994). Made for Black Horse Ranch. 400 models made. Sold separately or in set with alabaster, apricot dun, black blanket appy, and chestnut Balking Mules. These 5 and the SR buckskin were produced by Breyer as Balking Mule Assortment SR #410894. The black on the leopard appy's legs comes up to the middle of the forearms and gaskins. See Balking Mule SR alabaster for further discussion.

♘ Balking Mule SR, buckskin; solid face; dun-gray mane, tail tuft, muzzle, knees, and hocks; buckskin lower legs; dun-gray hooves; black bridle; matte (1994). Made for Black Horse Ranch. 400 models made. This buckskin Mule plus the alabaster, apricot dun, black blanket appy, black leopard appy, and chestnut Mules were produced by Breyer as Balking Mule Assortment SR #410894. Unlike the other SR Mules, the buckskin was available only as an exclusive to prior customers of BHR, limit one per customer. He is a medium/pale buckskin shade but lacks the dark lower legs of true buckskin coloration. See Balking Mule SR alabaster for further discussion.

♘ Balking Mule SR, chestnut, solid face, darker gray-chestnut mane and nose, gray tail tuft, 4 cream "stockings," gray hooves, black bridle, matte (1994). Made for Black Horse Ranch. 400 models made. Sold separately or in set with alabaster, apricot dun, black blanket appy, and black leopard appy Balking Mules. These 5 and the SR buckskin were produced by Breyer as Balking Mule Assortment SR #410894. The chestnut Mule is a shaded medium brown color, not at all red. See Balking Mule SR alabaster for further discussion.

Notes:

(1) The blinkers on this mold are an integral part of the mold. The Balking Mule differs in this respect from the only other Breyer mold with blinkers, the Old Timer, whose blinkers are separately molded pieces glued onto the horse.

(2) Early models of the Balking Mule mold have the round "Breyer Molding Co." stamp only. Later ones have round stamp and the "U.S.A." stamp—I have seen seal brown #208 with the "U.S.A.," so we know this stamp was added to the mold in 1970, when the "U.S.A." was introduced into the Breyer line.

"Brighty" — ♞ Sitting burro, ears up. Sculpted by Chris Hess. Mold in catalog-run production 1974-87, 1991 - current as of 1996.

Catalog-run models made from this mold:

♞ "Brighty 1991" #376, grayish brown, solid face with white muzzle, dark primitive stripe over withers, dorsal stripe, white underside, 2 front pale tan stockings and 2 hind pale tan socks, 4 gray hooves, matte (1991 - current as of 1996). Called "Brighty 1991" in the 1991-92 catalogs, Marguerite Henry's "Brighty 1991" in 1993, "Brighty 1991" By Marguerite Henry in 1994-95, and simply "Brighty" in 1996. This donkey is essentially the same pattern as Marguerite Henry's "Brighty" #375, but in a brownish rather than gray color. On January 21 and June 1, 1995, the QVC home-shopping cable TV channel sold a total of 893 "Brighty 1991" models that were ordinary regular runs but that came in boxes labeled with the special-run model number 701395 (number is per the model's box; quantity is per *JAH* editor Stephanie Macejko). See next entry for further discussion.

♞ Marguerite Henry's "Brighty" #375, gray, solid face with white muzzle, dark primitive stripe over withers, some with dorsal stripe, white underside, 2 front stockings, 4 gray hooves, matte (1982-87). This same model was also sold in "Brighty" Gift Set #2075 [1974-81]. "Brighty" and "Brighty 1991" #376 are essentially the same pattern, but "Brighty" has a gray body color and, typically, solid hind legs, whereas "Brighty 1991" is brownish and has hind socks. However, the "Brighty" in gift set #2075 is shown with 2 hind socks in the 1974-79 catalogs. "Brighty's" gray color varies from light to fairly dark. Jo Kulwicki's #375s and others I've seen lack dorsal stripes, but Sande Schneider's two do have the dorsal stripe. All three "Brighty" issues—#2075, #375, and #376—represent the title character in Marguerite Henry's book *Brighty of the Grand Canyon*. This story is based on a real jack burro named "Brighty" (see Henry 1969, pp. 75-84). The book relates that this wild burro, whose full name was "Bright Angel," was named after Bright Angel Creek in the Grand Canyon, where he used to spend the winter, safe from the heavy snows above the canyon. He was gray with a white nose; also there was a "black stripe down Brighty's back and [a] crossbar over his shoulder" (p. 132). The Breyer mold depicts Brighty in a characteristic pose: the book says that he liked "to sit, dog fashion" (p. 9). Several of Wesley Dennis's drawings of "Brighty" in the book show him sitting down (pp. 1, 68, 112, 117) and may well have provided sculptor Chris Hess with his concept for the mold.

Set:

• "Brighty" Gift Set #2075, gray burro, earlier ones with 4 stockings, later ones with 2 front stockings only; 4 gray hooves; and book *Brighty of the Grand Canyon*, by Marguerite Henry (1974-81). This same model was also sold separately as Marguerite Henry's "Brighty" #375 [1982-87]. Catalogs 1974-79 show the gift set "Brighty" with 2 hind socks in addition to his front ones. In the 1980-81 catalogs the hind legs are solid gray, as they are on "Brighty" #375 in all the catalogs that list him.

Note: Most and perhaps all models of the "Brighty" mold have no Breyer stamp or other mold marks. Some models might have the "B" stamp only, but I haven't seen one like this.

"Brown Sunshine" Of Sawdust Valley — Walking mule mold scheduled for release in 1996. The mold will represent the title character from author Marguerite Henry's recent book *Brown Sunshine of Sawdust Valley* and is being sculpted by the book's illustrator, Bonnie Shields. For a photo of a prototype sculpture, see *JAH* 22/#4 July/Aug. 1995 (p. 5).

Donkey — ♞ Jenny (female), standing, tail tip attached to right hock. Sculpted by Chris Hess. Mold in catalog-run production 1956? - 1974, 1992.

Catalog-run models made from this mold:

♞ Donkey #81, most gray, bald or solid face, black/charcoal mane and tail tuft, some with dorsal stripe and primitive stripe over withers, 0-4 stockings, gray hooves, most matte or semigloss (1956? - 1974). This same model was also sold in Donkey With Baskets set #82 [1958 {maybe earlier} - 1958/59]; see below. The color of these jennies varies greatly, ranging from medium/light gray to gray-blue to nearly black and from grayish brown to bay. Collector Sheryl Leisure found a truly bay model, his matte reddish-brown color not at all grayed, with black mane and tail tuft (no black on the legs), gray hooves, 4 stockings, and a big bald face; he is made of a chalky-looking plastic with a slight dishwater-gray tinge. Collector Sandy Tomezik also found a true bay model, colored identically to Sheryl's (thanks to Sandy for photos), and she has seen a couple of others. Conceivably this bay version was a special run issued in the early decades of Breyer, but it could also be a version of #81. Although Breyer catalogs and manuals indicate via color photos or printed words that the Donkey was issued in gray or gray-brown in the late 1950s, early 1960s, and early 1970s, the mid to late 1960s publications leave open the possibility of a bay. Catalog photos for these years are black and white or sepia, and no catalogs, price lists, or manuals from the 1950s through 1970s state the color of the Donkey except the 1958 publications, which say "grey." My own matte gray-brown Donkey has a huge bald face, pink nose and inner ears, and glossy black mane and tail tuft. A few Donkeys are glossy all over; collector Lani Keller has one like this. Some Donkeys are molded in shiny battleship-gray plastic and are unpainted except for black mane, eyes, and tail tuft. There are also models that appear to be cast in gray plastic but are actually white plastic painted a uniform, unshaded, shiny battleship gray (Lani Keller and Sande Schneider own such models). Models of this uniform battleship-gray appearance are shown in the 1963 catalog and possibly the 1960 and earlier publications as well. I have also seen a few models of this solid, uniform coloring that had a decidedly blue hue. Regarding the release date for this model see note 1 for this mold. #81 mysteriously crops up on the 1977 price list, but this may indicate simply a sell-off of leftovers from previous years, for she is not in the catalog or manual for 1977 or in catalogs, manuals, or price lists known to me for 1975-76 or 1978 on (though I do not have a 1976 price list). This model was reissued with color variations in 1992 as #390.

♠ Donkey #390, light gray, bald face, charcoal mane, gray tail tuft, dorsal stripe and primitive stripe over withers, 4 stockings, gray hooves, matte (1992). This model is overall a lighter gray than many old #81s, and has a more defined primitive stripe than most of them. It's no coincidence that the Donkey and the Elephant were reissued in 1992 since it is an election year. The 1992 catalog pages with these models emphasize the election-year theme, and the boxes they come in have an American flag pasted onto the yellow backing behind the model. Note that the Donkey shown in the catalog appears to be the mirror image of the old Donkey mold: its tail tuft is attached to the left hock rather than the right, etc. The old and new Donkeys are in fact exactly the same mold. The catalog just shows a "flopped photo": the photo was printed from the reverse side of the negative to suit the layout design of the catalog.

Set:
• Donkey With Baskets set #82, gray Donkey with removable red plastic baskets (1958 [maybe earlier] - 1958/59). This same model was also sold separately as Donkey #81 [1956? - 1974]. Set #82 is not in the ca.1954 catalog or the 1960 or later catalogs but is in the 1958 catalog, which promotes the set thus: "with removable bright red baskets

on each side usable as planters or for holding trinkets." The two pannier baskets, which are molded together at the handles, hang on either side of the donkey and are strapped onto her by means of a removable double girth that feeds through the basket handles. The double girth, made of the same pliable red plastic as the baskets, consists of two thin girths molded together at their centers. The baskets themselves have a molded-in "woven" pattern, very similar to the red plastic howdah in the #94 Elephant With Howdah set (see below in the Wildlife section). The Donkeys in the #82 sets owned by collectors Jo Kulwicki and Paula DeFeyter are both molded in gray plastic and have painted black eyes, mane, and tail tuft. But it is entirely possible that other #82 sets came with Donkeys molded in white plastic and painted gray. The model number 82 later belonged to the regular-run dapple gray Clydesdale (Clydesdale Stallion mold).

Notes:

(1) The Donkey is not in the ca.1954 catalog but is in the 1958 catalog and price list. If, as seems likely, the Donkey was first issued along with the Elephant in an election year, then the year would have been 1956, when Dwight Eisenhower ran for his second term as president. The donkey, or jackass, as the symbol of the Democratic party originated during the presidency (1829-37) of Andrew Jackson, a man from the backwoods and a champion of ordinary people. The aristocratic Whig political faction dubbed him a jackass as a satire on his supposed country-boy ignorance. The analogy amused him, and as a result his political party adopted the jackass as its symbol. (S. E. Morison, H. S. Commager, and W. E. Leuchtenburg, Concise History of the American Republic, p. 187.) The donkey and the elephant were further popularized as political party symbols by the American caricaturist and illustrator Thomas Nast, 1840-1902 (New Columbia Encyclopedia).

(2) The Donkey mold has no mold marks. The baskets on Donkey #82 have no mold stamps either.

Mule — see Balking Mule

GENERAL NOTE: All the wildlife models are Traditional scale except for the buffalo skull on the Bolo Tie, which is Classic scale, and possibly the Elephant, which is Classic scale if it is an adult. (See the General Notes at the start of the Traditional and Classic sections above for information on these scales.)

American Bison — see American Bison #381 (under Buffalo); also see Buffalo #76 for the Presentation Collection American Bison

Antelope — see Pronghorn Antelope

Bear — 🐻 Female, walking. Sculpted by Chris Hess. Mold in catalog-run production 1967-76, 1987-88, 1992-95.
Catalog-run models made from this mold:
🐻 Bear #306, black, brown or light/white face, black nose, matte (1967-73). This model was also sold in Bear Family set #3068 [1974-76]. Some black Bears and Cubs have fairly dark reddish-brown faces, while others have light faces, varying from light tan or grayish to white. Some models of both facial versions have pink detailing on the mouth, either pink dabs or a whole pink mouth line. It is hard to say which facial version came first. The black Bear and Cub are shown in the white-faced version in all the catalogs and manuals I have that show the models in color, namely, those for 1968-75, which is nearly the full production span of these models. But the black Bear Family set's box, which is shown in catalogs and manuals for 1974-76, features a photo of models with red-brown faces. Since this set debuted in 1974, the box's picture should be of models from 1973, when Breyer would have been designing the box. This suggests that the brown-faced models were issued in these late years. But if so, why are white-faced models posed in front of the box in the 1974-75 catalogs? (Only the box, no bears, appears in the 1976 publications.) Little help is offered by the evidence of mold stamps, notably the "U.S.A." stamp, which was introduced into the Breyer line in 1970. Of the black Bears and Cubs whose stamps I know of, the light-faced ones all lack the "U.S.A.," but some of the brown-faced ones lack it too, while others have it. So at least some models of both facial versions were issued before 1970. All this rather chaotic evidence suggests that perhaps Breyer alternated the facial versions a few times over the years or even issued them simultaneously.
🐻 Bear #307, brown, lighter brown or white face, black nose, matte (1967-71). The body color ranges from dark to medium brown. The facial color varies from a brown just slightly lighter than the body to white edged with brown overspray. Some models of darker and lighter facial versions have pink detailing on the mouth, either pink dabs or a pink line.
Sets:
• Bear Family set #3068, bear and cub, both black, white face, black nose, matte (1974-76). These same models were also sold separately as Bear #306 and Bear Cub #308 [both 1967-73]. See Bear #306, black, for discussion of color variation.
🐻 Bear Family set #3071, bear and cub, both white, red-brown eyes, pink ears and nose, tan edges of feet, matte (1992-95). Catalogs don't say what type of bear this set represents. Several collectors have commented to me that these models should not be regarded as polar bears, which have a much lankier build.
🐻 Cinnamon Bear And Cub set #3069, both medium red-brown, light tan face, brown nose, matte (1987-88).
Note: Early models of the Bear mold have the round "Breyer Molding Co." stamp only. Later models have the round and "U.S.A." stamps—collector Sande Schneider has a black Bear with the "U.S.A.," so it is certain that this stamp was added to the mold no later than 1976; it may have been added as early as 1970, when the "U.S.A." was first introduced into the Breyer line.

Bear Cub — 🐻 Walking/standing with left hind foot back. Sculpted by Chris Hess. Mold in catalog-run production 1967-76, 1987-88, 1992-95.
Catalog-run models made from this mold:
🐻 Bear Cub #308, black, brown or light/white face, black nose, matte (1967-73). This model was also sold in Bear Family set #3068 [1974-76]. See Bear #306, black, for discussion of color variations.
🐻 Bear Cub #309, brown, lighter brown or white face, black nose, matte (1967-71). The body color ranges from dark to medium brown. The facial color varies from a brown just slightly lighter than the body to white edged with brown overspray. Some models of darker and lighter facial versions have pink detailing on the mouth, either pink dabs or a pink line.
Sets:
• Bear Family set #3068, bear and cub, both black (1974-76). These same models were also sold separately as Bear #306 and Bear Cub #308 [both 1967-73]. See Bear #306, black, for discussion of color variations.
🐻 Bear Family set #3071, bear and cub, both white, red-brown eyes, pink ears and nose, tan edges of feet, matte (1992-95). See Bear Family set #3071 under Bear for discussion.
🐻 Cinnamon Bear And Cub set #3069, both medium red-brown, light red-brown face, black nose, matte (1987-88).
Note: Early models of the Bear Cub mold have the round "Breyer Molding Co." stamp only. Later models have the round and "U.S.A." stamps—collector Jo Kulwicki has a #309 brown Cub with the "U.S.A.," so it is certain that this stamp was added to the mold no later than 1971; it may have been added as early as 1970, when the "U.S.A." was first introduced into the Breyer line.

Bighorn Ram — 🐏 Standing with head up; large thick horns curled under. Sculpted by Chris Hess. Mold in catalog-run production 1969-80.

Catalog-run models made from this mold:
🐏 Bighorn Ram #78, brown, white or light tan muzzle and rump, tan or gray horns, gray mouth line, gray hooves, matte (1969-80). The body color ranges from a dark coffee brown to light chestnut. The gray-horned version is shown on *Breyer Collector's Video*. The tan-horned version is shown in all catalogs that list the Bighorn, which suggests that the tan-horn version is more common. Some models have a gray stripe on the horns, running longways down the outside following the curl. One of these, with a very thin gray stripe on tan horns, is shown in *JAH* 21/#1 Spring 1994 (p. 15); another was advertised in *The Model Horse Trader*, February 1994. Regarding the release date of this model, see note 1 for the mold.
🐏 Dall Sheep #85, white; some with tan shading, tan horns, and brown mouth line; some with gray shading, gray horns, and gray mouth line; all with gray hooves; matte (1970-73). In my experience, the tan-horn version is less common. Some models, both tan-horn and gray-horn, have a dark gray stripe on the horns, running longways down the outside following the curl. #85 is not pictured in any of the catalogs or manuals that list it, so I don't know which color version came first. A gray-horned specimen is shown in *JAH* 21/#1 Spring 1994 (p. 15). The model number 85 previously belonged to "Diablo" The Mustang in albino (Mustang mold), and later belonged to the Azteca (Foundation Stallion mold).
Notes:
(1) Bighorn Ram #78 is listed as "new for 1970" in the 1970 dealer catalog, but he was actually released in 1969—he is listed in the 1969 collector's manual and pictured in an article in *Craft Model & Hobby Industry*, which states, "The 1969 additions to the fine line of Breyer Animal Creations are ready to enhance the collections of all horse and animal fanciers." Evidently when a new dealer catalog was issued in 1970 for the first time since 1968 (there is no 1969 catalog to my knowledge), Breyer decided to list the 1969 as well as the 1970 models as "new for 1970" to bring them to the attention of dealers, who would naturally suppose that any model not listed as new was something they had seen in 1968.
(2) Chris Hess is identified as the sculptor of this mold in *JAH* 21/#1 Spring 1994 (p. 15).
(3) The horns on this mold, to judge from several specimens I have examined, are integral to the mold, not separately molded as on many other Breyer ruminants.
(4) The Bighorn Ram mold has the round "Breyer Molding Co." stamp. Later models have a "B" stamp as well as the round (I saw one like this at the 1994 Jamboree in Ontario, California). I believe this mold was never given the "U.S.A." stamp; on the numerous specimens of both #78 and #85 that I've checked, none has had this stamp.

"Bimbo" — see Circus Boy Corky On "Bimbo" (under Elephant)

Bison — see Buffalo

Bolo Tie — 🐃 Buffalo skull with horns, on string tie. Sculpted by Bob Scriver. Mold in catalog-run production 1972-76.
Catalog-run models made from this mold:
🐃 Bolo Tie #501, white buffalo skull with charcoal shading, charcoal horns, matte; on black or brown braided plastic string tie with silver metal tips (1972-76). The skulls all have charcoal shading, regardless of the color of the string tie. A brass-colored metal fixture riveted to the back of the skull holds the skull onto the tie. The Bolo Tie is omitted from the 1972-73 catalogs, but the omissions were apparently oversights, for the bolo is listed in the 1972-73 manuals and price lists. Collector Jo Kulwicki's Bolo Tie came with a small gold paper label on the string tie, which says "Bob Scriver / Sculptor / Browning, Montana" on one side and "Buffalo Skull / By Bob Scriver 69' [sic] © / Breyer Molding Company• Chicago" on the other. The model number 501 later belonged to the English Riding Outfit (for Brenda Breyer #500).
Note: The Bolo Tie mold has "© B. Scriver" engraved along the right edge, below the eye socket. The letters are not too legible and look like part of the rough texturing of the skull. The 1972 manual states that the Bolo Tie was "Created by Bob Scriver, famous cowboy artist of Browning, Montana."

Buck, modernistic — see Golden Buck

Buck — 🦌 Realistic, standing/walking, looking sharply left; antlers; no male parts. Sculpted by Chris Hess. Mold in catalog-run production 1964 - current as of 1996.
Catalog-run models made from this mold:
🦌 Buck #301, tawny, solid face, black muzzle, white underside, tawny antlers about the same color as the body, black hooves, matte (1964-73). This same model was also sold in Deer Family set #304 [1964-65] and in Deer Family set #3123 [1974 - current as of 1996]. My own Buck's antler's have touches of soft gray shading.
Sets:
• Deer Family set #304, buck, doe, and fawn, all tawny (1964-65). These same models were also sold separately as Buck #301, Doe #302, and Fawn #303 [all 1964-73], and in Deer Family set #3123 [1974 - current as of 1996].
• Deer Family set #3123, buck, doe, fawn, all tawny, with cardboard carry-box (1974 - current as of 1996). These same models were also sold separately as Buck #301, Doe #302, and Fawn #303 [all 1964-73], and in Deer Family set #304 [1964-65].
Notes:
(1) The antlers on the Buck are separately molded pieces affixed to the model's head after molding.
(2) Early models of the Buck mold have the round "Breyer Molding Co." stamp only. Later ones have the round stamp and the "U.S.A." stamp. Some "U.S.A." models might have the "B" stamp too, but I'm not sure.

Buffalo — Bull with horns; standing in stretched position, looking left; tail tip attached to left hock. Sculpted by Chris Hess. Mold in catalog-run production 1965 - current as of 1996.

Catalog-run models made from this mold:

- American Bison #381, yellow dun; black head, chest, and legs; red-shading on barrel and hindquarters; black horns; black hooves; matte (1994 - current as of 1996). Models come with a small hang tag tied to the tail, telling about the American bison. The tag notes, "A large Bison Bull may stand six feet at the shoulder and weigh a ton."
- Buffalo #76, brown, solid face, black muzzle, dark brown "mane" and tail tip, dorsal stripe, white or gray-shaded horns with black tips, black hooves, matte and semigloss (1965-91). In Presentation Collection mounted on American walnut wood base with brass "American Bison" nameplate, 1972-73. The Presentation model is listed as #5076 American Bison in the 1973 price list, but previously it apparently had the same model number as regular-run #76; see Presentation Collection above in the Traditionals section for discussion. #76 is not in the 1992 catalog or manual. He is on the 1992 price list, but I believe his inclusion there was just an oversight. The color of #76 varies from deep shaded buckskin to dark brown to rich red-brown, the latter being typical of more recent models. Some #76s from the 1960s have factory-painted pink or white mouth lines and nostril lines; I have one like this (he's semigloss) and know of others. Collector Lani Keller saw a model at the 1995 BreyerFest with eyewhites and white eyebrows in addition to mouth lines. I saw a Presentation Collection Buffalo at BreyerFest 1993; he was matte and did not have the mouth or nostril detailing. Collector Tracy Phillips reports having seen a #76 with a very glossy finish (Phillips 1993).
- "Tatanka" The White Buffalo #380, white with soft gray shading on ruff, head, horns, and tail tuft; black eyes, muzzle, and horn tips; dark red handprint Indian symbol on left hip; charcoal dots on the dewclaws; gray hooves; matte (1992-93). The amount of gray shading varies; some models may have so little as to be virtually all white. The name "Tatanka," according to Breyer executive Peter Stone, means "buffalo" in some Native American languages. Regarding a possible SR "Tatanka" without hand print, see note 1 for this mold. The number 380 previously belonged to the Showcase Collection issue of gray blanket appaloosa Arabian Mare (Family Arabian Mare mold).

Special-run models made from this mold:

- Buffalo SR, light smoke gray, black nose, dorsal stripe, gray hooves, matte (mid-1970s?). Perhaps made as promotional pieces for the 1977 movie *The White Buffalo*. About 10-25 models made (per Gutierrez 1989 and collector Sheryl Leisure). These models are often reported as being alabaster (white) with gray shading. I've seen two of them, and the models are actually light smoke gray—the gray is pervasive; it's more than just shading. Also this model is often reported as having been made in the mid-1960s, around the time the mold was released. This can't be right, however, since these models have the "U.S.A." stamp, which dates them to no earlier than 1970—not to mention that the movie for which the models might have been made was released in 1977, not the 1960s. One film book describes the movie thus: "Wild Bill Hickok is haunted by the image of a buffalo that symbolized his fear of death; strange, murky film." Another film book says: "Wild Bill Hickok and Chief Crazy Horse join forces to kill a marauding white buffalo. Ridiculous symbolic Western, not helped by the very artificial looking beast of the title."
- Buffalo SR, woodgrain, black muzzle, unpainted white horns, black hooves, matte (probably sometime in the period 1965-66). This model is not listed in any Breyer catalogs or price lists in my possession, which is why I list him as an SR. I've heard of only two of these models, both mounted on lamps. One is pictured on the cover of *The Model Horse Trader*, July 1993; the model is a dark woodgrain, and the lamp is typical of the Dunning Industry lamps made in the 1960s from a variety of woodgrain and other Breyer models (see the Lamps & Nightlights section below in the Appendix). My suggested dating for the woodgrain Buffalo corresponds to the introduction date for the mold and the ending date of the heyday of woodgrain models generally. However, it is possible that he was made in the late 1960s or even the early 1970s.

Notes:

(1) A small special run of "Tatanka" models without the red handprint on the hip may have been issued early in 1995, as I learned from collector Rusty Black, who purchased one of these models in August 1995. According to Rusty, the model is identical to "Tatanka" #380 aside from the lack of the handprint symbol. Her model also has the date "95" and the number "08/65" written in green marker inside one hind leg, seemingly indicating that he is the eighth model in a run of 65. The woman who sold Rusty the buffalo had gotten two of them from a Daisy Baiman of Bozeman, Montana, who evidently had ordered the SR from Breyer. Shortly after acquiring the model, Rusty met someone else who claimed to have two of these no-handprint "Tatankas," which had been sold at an event in Montana. Both of these persons said the models had come with certificates, although the woman who sold Rusty her model did not yet have a certificate. In November 1995, the woman wrote to Rusty: "After waiting for Daisy [Baiman] to act, Breyer never did send her certificates for the White Buffaloes." In lieu of a certificate, the woman sent Rusty a copy of the letter of sale she had gotten from Daisy with the models. Dated April 1995, the letter states: "I [Daisy Baiman] do sell to . . . two of the 65 special run White Bison. These models were produced for the Buffalo Days Rodeo held on a rotating basis. The numbers sold were numbers 4 and 8 and will not be offered again." Mysteriously, when Rusty asked Breyer executive Peter Stone about this alleged SR at the West Coast Model Horse Collector's Jamboree at the end of August 1995, he said he knew nothing about it. Nor did *JAH* editor Stephanie Macejko know anything about it when I spoke to her at the same event. Whatever the story of their origin may prove to be, these models, Rusty speculates, may have been issued in celebration of the real white buffalo calf named "Miracle," born on the farm of David and Valerie Heider in Janesville, Wisconsin, in August 1994. The birth stirred much attention from Native American Indians, whose religious traditions include beliefs about the sacredness of white buffaloes. *The Journal Times* (Racine, Wisconsin), November 2, 1995, states in an article about the calf: "According to Native American legend, the birth of a female white buffalo will mark the beginning of a new spirituality throughout the world, eventually uniting the races and restoring global peace."

(2) Regarding a few test-run Buffaloes and other animals in gold-bronze finish, see note 2 for the Spanish Fighting Bull mold above in the Cattle & Hogs section.

(3) The horns on the Buffalo are separately molded pieces affixed to the model's head after molding.

(4) Early models of the Buffalo mold have the round "Breyer Molding Co." stamp only. Later ones have the round stamp and the "U.S.A." stamp. Some "U.S.A." models made prior to 1992 also have a small "B" stamp on the back side of each horn. I got a #76 brown Buffalo new in 1990, and it has a "B" on both horns, though the "B" on the right horn is blurry. "Tatanka" #380 has the "B" only on the left horn; the one on the right has disappeared. Some "U.S.A." #76 brown Buffaloes might have the "B" stamp on the leg as well as on the horns, but I'm not sure.

Cheetah — Not a Breyer product. For discussion see Wilderness Animal Series By Christian Hess, below in this section.

Cinnamon Bear — see under Bear

Cinnamon Cub — see under Bear Cub

Circus Boy Corky On "Bimbo" — see under Elephant

Cougar — Not a Breyer product. For discussion see Wilderness Animal Series By Christian Hess, below in this section.

Cub — see Bear Cub

Dall Sheep — see under Bighorn Ram

Deer Family sets — see under Buck (realistic); Doe (realistic); and Fawn

Doe, modernistic — see Golden Doe

Doe — Realistic, standing, looking sharply left, no antlers. Sculpted by Chris Hess. Mold in catalog-run production 1964 - current as of 1996.

Catalog-run models made from this mold:

- Doe #302, tawny, solid face, black muzzle, white underside, black hooves, matte (1964-73). This same model was also sold in Deer Family set #304 [1964-65] and in Deer Family set #3123 [1974 - current as of 1996].

Sets: see under Buck.

Note: Early models of the Doe mold have the round "Breyer Molding Co." stamp only. Later ones have the round stamp and the "U.S.A." stamp. Some "U.S.A." models have the "B" stamp in addition (collector Chelle Fulk has one like this).

Elephant — Small, standing, head raised, mouth open, trunk curled up over head, short tusks, tail tip attached to right hock. Sculpted by Chris Hess. Mold in catalog-run production 1956? - 1974, 1992.

Catalog-run models made from this mold:

- Elephant #91, gray, gray-shaded mouth and tip of trunk, white or gray tusks, most matte or semigloss (1956? - 1974). This same pachyderm was also sold in Elephant With Howdah set #94 [1958 {maybe earlier} - 1958/59] and Circus Boy Corky On "Bimbo" set #601 [1957/58 - 1958/59]. Many Elephants are molded in white plastic and painted gray, with the tusks left unpainted white; the body color ranges from medium gray to charcoal. A few of these Elephants are glossy; collector Lani Keller has one like this. Some Elephants are molded in a shiny bluish-gray or battleship-gray plastic and are unpainted except for black on the eyes; the tusks too are left gray. Some models that appear to be cast in gray plastic are actually white plastic painted a uniform, unshaded, shiny battleship gray, including the tusks (Lani also has one of these, and Sande Schneider used to). Models of this uniform battleship-gray are shown in the 1960 and 1963 catalogs and possibly earlier publications as well; whether they are the painted or unpainted version isn't clear. I own a #91 (with a "U.S.A." stamp, dating her to no earlier than 1970) cast in pale gray plastic and painted dark gray except for the tusks, which are unpainted. Regarding the release date of #91 see note 1 for this mold. #91 mysteriously crops up on the 1977 price list; presumably these models were leftovers from 1974, for the Elephant is not in the catalog or manual for 1977 or in catalogs, manuals, or price lists known to me for 1975-76 or 1978 on. The gray Elephant was reissued with color variations in 1992 as #391 (see below).
- Elephant #92, pink, no white markings or other detailing, semigloss (1958 [maybe earlier] - 1958/59). The only early Breyer publication I know of that lists this pink model and the blue Elephant #93 is the 1958 price list. Oddly, both models are omitted from the 1958 catalog. There must have been a small time lag between the catalog and the price list, during which time the decision was made either to add the pastel pachyderms (if the catalog came before the price list) or to discontinue them (if the catalog came after). Two pink Elephants that I know of, one of which I've seen in person, are actually made of shiny, pale-flesh-pink plastic, though at first they appear to be painted with thick shiny paint. They look like something discarded from the surgery—pale flesh-pink blobs. The eyes, tusks, and toenails are all the same pale pink as the body. Collector Ida Santana's model came in its original cardboard mailer carton with "#92 pink Elephant" stamped on the top. The model number 92 later belonged to the regular-run smoke Belgian.
- Elephant #93, blue (1958 [maybe earlier] - 1958/59). Regarding documentation, see the entry for #92 pink Elephant. I have never seen an Elephant that is certifiably a #93, but collector Lynn Hiersche's husband, Duane, found a pair of Elephants that are candidates. As Lynn told me via email in November 1996, these beasts are "a cross between a pastel baby blue and a washed out teal-blue. They are light blue with a slight teal tint to them." The color is in the plastic, not painted on, which is also the case with at least some pink #92 Elephants. And like pink #92s, Lynn's blue beasts have no paint detailing on the eyes, tusks, or other areas. Lynn's blue pachyderms lack the "U.S.A." stamp, a fact that dates them definitely to pre-1970. Unfortunately, they did not come with their original boxes, so we can't be sure that they are #93s until some solid evidence turns up. Lynn's pair are the only pale blue Elephants I have heard of, but some Elephants of a much darker and grayer shade of blue also exist. One of these is owned by collector Lillian Sutphin. He has the appearance of the battleship-gray version of #91 gray Elephant, with even, unshaded, thick-looking paint, tusks the same color as his body, and black eyes. But compared with true battleship-gray Elephants and Donkeys, he has a decidedly blue hue. Collector Laura Diederich has seen a similar model, which appeared to be molded in grayish-blue plastic. (Lillian is sure her model is painted since his white plastic shows on the bottoms of his feet.) Might these battleship-blue Elephants be #93s? Well, they could be, but there is a problem that makes me skeptical. Old Donkeys also come in a battleship-blue variation that has the appearance of the battleship-gray version of #81 gray Donkey. (I have seen one or two of these battleship-blue Donkeys in person.) Yet Breyer never issued a Donkey that it labeled as blue and sold under a different model number from gray #81. So battleship-blue Donkeys must simply be a variation of gray #81. This makes one suspect that the battleship-blue Elephants such as Lillian's are likewise simply variations of gray #91, and that true #93 blue Elephants are something different. The model number 93 later belonged to the regular-run dapple gray Belgian.
- Elephant #391, light/medium gray, pink mouth and tip of trunk, white tusks, dark gray toenails, matte (1992). This model is basically a reissue of the old gray Elephant #91,

but it has pink detailing and is lighter gray than most old #91s. It's no coincidence that the Elephant and the Donkey—symbols of the Republican and Democratic parties respectively—were reissued in 1992 since it was an election year (see note 1 for this mold). The 1992 catalog pages with these models emphasize the election-year theme, and the boxes the models came in have an American flag pasted onto the yellow backing. For the tusk mystery of #391, see note 3 for this mold. Regarding the barrel crack on many #391s, see note 4.

Sets:

- Circus Boy Corky On "Bimbo" set #601, circus boy rider on gray elephant (1957/58 - 1958/59). In about the same years this same pachyderm was sold in Elephant With Howdah set #94; in the years1956? - 1974 it was sold separately as Elephant #91. Several Corky sets I have seen, including that owned by collector Joy Sheesley, have Elephants of the solid battleship-gray version with gray tusks (see Elephant #91). But the Elephant in Jo Kulwicki's set is cast in white plastic and painted gray, with white tusks. For discussion of dates, hang card, and background, see the entry for Corky The Circus Boy in the Riders - Hard Plastic section. The model number 601 later belonged to the Classic model "Kelso," dark bay.
- Elephant With Howdah set #94, gray with detachable red plastic howdah (1958 [maybe earlier] - 1958/59). In about the same years this same Elephant was sold in Circus Boy Corky On "Bimbo" set #601; in the years 1956? - 1974 it was sold separately as Elephant #91. The howdah set is not in the ca. 1954 or 1960 or later catalogs but is in the 1958 catalog, which promotes the set thus: "comes with or without Howdah for holding jewelry and small dresser or office items." I have seen two howdah sets in person, at BreyerFest in 1994 and 1995. The Elephant in one of these sets appeared to be made of gray plastic; he was solid, unshaded battleship gray, including his tusks. The Elephant in the other set was unusual in having a shiny semigloss finish, a shaded dark brownish-gray body color, and tusks and eyes painted the same color as the body. He was made of white plastic, as a few small rubs in his paint revealed. The howdah in the #94 set is a rather tacky-looking pliable red plastic riding box molded with a "woven" pattern as though it were a basket, very similar to the baskets in the #82 Donkey with Baskets set (see above in the Donkeys & Mules section). The howdah is held onto the Elephant's back by means of a removable red plastic girth with molded-in designs, which passes through slots in the bottom edges of the howdah and then splits into two thin girth-straps going under the Elephant's belly. The model number 94 later belonged to the regular-run chestnut Belgian.

Special-run models made from this mold:

- Elephant SR, woodgrain, black eyes, unpainted white tusks, no other color detailing, matte (probably sometime in the period 1959-66). The woodgrain Elephant is not listed in any Breyer publications known to me, which is why I list it as an SR. Only a few of these models are known to exist. My suggested dating for them corresponds to the heyday of woodgrain models generally, but it is possible that they were made in the late 1960s.

Notes:

(1) The Elephant is not in the ca.1954 catalog but is in the 1958 catalog and price list. This means that if, as seems likely, the Elephant was first issued along with the Donkey in an election year, then the year would have been 1956, when Dwight Eisenhower was elected for his second term as president. The elephant was popularized as a symbol for the Republican party by the American caricaturist and illustrator Thomas Nast, 1840-1902 (*New Columbia Encyclopedia*).

(2) Hagen-Renaker expert Joan Berkwitz pointed out to me that the Breyer Elephant looks somewhat like a baby. The comparative size of the Corky rider in the Circus Boy Corky on "Bimbo" set also suggests that the elephant is young, as collector Karen Crossley wrote to me. As a baby, the Elephant mold qualifies as a Traditional piece. If indeed Breyer released this mold and the Donkey as political symbols in an election year, then perhaps the Elephant was made small in order to keep it about the same size as the Donkey. Joan Berkwitz also remarked to me that figurines of Elephants are often sculpted with the trunk raised since this is a traditional symbol of good luck in Asian cultures. Breyer too evoked this symbolism later in the 1950s: the 1958 catalog comments, "Elephant / With Trunk raised to bring you luck."

(3) The tusks on the Elephant are integral to the mold; they are not separately molded parts. Oddly, the #391 pictured in the 1992 catalog has longer, slenderer tusks than the #391s produced for sale, which have the same short stubby tusks as Elephants from earlier decades. Megan Thilman, who became editor of *JAH* in 1992, told me that the company briefly considered retooling the mold to lengthen the tusks and got as far as creating the prototype model shown in the catalog. The prototype is an ordinary Elephant with its original tusks removed and new, longer ones built up by hand from acetate beads. The retooling of the metal injection-mold proved unfeasible, however, and the idea was dropped.

(4) Many #391 Elephants have a hairline crack on their right side. When I got my #391 I noticed that it had a barely visible 3-inch-long hairline crack in the plastic, starting in the right flank and snaking up the barrel toward the ear. Pressing the plastic beside the crack caused a soft crackling noise, indicating that the defect went all the way through. When I notified my supplier of the defect, she checked several other #391s and found that they all had the crack. Several friends of mine who had gotten #391s from other dealers also discovered the crack in their models when I asked them to look carefully in strong light. The fact that this crack turns up in the same spot on so many #391s suggests that there is a defect in the metal injection-mold. Evidently the defect is something new, for the old #91s that I and others have checked do not have it.

(5) Regarding a possible test-run Elephant and other animals in gold-bronze finish, see note 2 for the Spanish Fighting Bull mold above in the Cattle & Hogs section.

(6) Early models of the Elephant mold have no mold marks. Later ones have the "U.S.A." stamp only—I have a #91 with the "U.S.A." and have seen many others like this, so we know this stamp was added to the mold no later than 1974 and possibly as early as 1970, when the "U.S.A." was first introduced into the Breyer line. This mold was never given the round Breyer stamp or the Breyer Reeves stamp. The howdah in the #94 Elephant With Howdah set has no mold stamps.

Elk — Walking, head up, mouth open; large antlers. Sculpted by Chris Hess. Mold in catalog-run production 1968 - current as of 1996.

Catalog-run models made from this mold:

- Elk #77, reddish-brown, no white markings, black-shaded nose, dark red-brown neck ruff, light tan rump, tan antlers with black tips, dark gray-brown hooves, matte (1968 - current as of 1996). Catalog photos show this model as more brown in the early years and more red in recent years. Collector Blain Kukevitch wrote to me that his old Elk with no "U.S.A." has the extra detail of black ear rims, and has a light tan lower jaw rather than the more usual black. The model was purchased new in 1970, according to the person who sold it to Blain.

Notes:

(1) The antlers on the Elk are separately molded pieces affixed to the model's head after molding.

(2) The early models of the Elk mold have the round "Breyer Molding Co." stamp only (models owned by collectors Heather Wells and Blain Kukevitch are like this). Later ones have both the round stamp and the "U.S.A." stamp. Some "U.S.A." models might have the "B" stamp as well, but I am not certain.

Fawn — Realistic, standing, looking sharply to left. Sculpted by Chris Hess. Mold in catalog-run production 1964 - current as of 1996.

Catalog-run models made from this mold:

- Fawn #303, tawny, with white spots along sides of body, solid face, black muzzle, white underside, black hooves, matte (1964-73). This same model was also sold in Deer Family set #304 [1964-65] and in Deer Family set #3123 [1974 - current as of 1996]. The Fawn's white spots are painted on over the tawny color.

Sets: see under Buck.

Note: Early models of the Fawn mold have the round "Breyer Molding Co." stamp only. Later models have the round stamp and the "U.S.A." stamp. Some "U.S.A." models might have the "B" stamp in addition, but I'm not sure.

Golden Buck — Modernistic, standing with head raised, mouth open; long knobby horns are flat on the inside; legs are also flat on the inside. Sculpted by Chris Hess or Don Manning. Mold in catalog-run production 1961/62 - 1964.

Catalog-run models made from this mold:

- Golden Buck #101, metallic gold, black eyes, semigloss (1961/62 - 1964). This Buck and the matching Golden Doe are listed in the 1963 catalog as "Golden Buck & Doe"; the 1964 price list calls them "Golden Deer—Modernistic Design." Regarding introduction date see note 1 for this mold. The model number 101 later belonged to the Quarter Horse Yearling, liver chestnut.

Notes:

(1) This mold and the Golden Doe are not in the 1960 catalog; they are in the 1963 (there apparently are no catalogs for 1961-62). It is certain, however, that these two molds were introduced no later than 1962, for the Golden Buck and Doe are advertised in the 1962 Ward's holiday catalog, in the "Furnishings" section. The item description says "Golden Buck'n Doe for shelf, table. Modern design in unbreakable plastic. . . . Pair $2.00."

(2) This mold and the matching Doe mold are highly unusual Breyers in that they are unrealistic and abstract, as is implied by the 1964 price list's designation of them as "Modernistic." Collectors in fact often refer to them as the "modernistic buck and doe."

(3) Collector Sande Schneider wrote to me with information that raises questions about the origins of the Golden Buck and Doe molds. At a flea market, Sande found a modernistic buck and doe identical in shape and size to Breyer's Golden Buck and Doe but made of colorless transparent plastic. Low inside the right hind leg of each of Sande's models is a mold stamp that reads: "Designed / Don Manning." Until we find out which came first, the Breyers or the Don Mannings, it's impossible to know who originally sculpted these molds, Don Manning or Breyer's chief sculptor, Chris Hess—and therefore who borrowed whose design. Apparently these deer designs have been used by other manufacturers as well. Collector Jo Kulwicki has two transparent bucks like Sande's except that they have no mold stamps at all. Sande has also seen a smaller-scale modernistic buck and doe in green plastic. Collector Sandy Tomezik has seen several different animals in this same modernistic style and owns a modernistic 5" antelope in transparent aqua plastic, which has no manufacturer's marks on it.

(4) The Golden Buck mold has the round "Breyer Molding Co." stamp only.

Golden Doe — Modernistic, standing, head raised but tilted down, no horns, insides of legs flat. Sculpted by Chris Hess or Don Manning. Mold in catalog-run production 1961/62 - 1964.

Catalog-run models made from this mold:

- Golden Doe #102, metallic gold, black eyes, semigloss (1961/62 - 1964). See Golden Buck #101 for discussion. The model number 102 later belonged to the Quarter Horse Yearling, palomino.

Notes:

(1) Regarding the dates, style, and sculptor of this mold, see the notes for Golden Buck.

(2) The Golden Doe mold has the round "Breyer Molding Co." stamp only.

Koala — Not a Breyer product. For discussion see Wilderness Animal Series By Christian Hess, below in this section.

Modernistic Buck — see Golden Buck

Modernistic Doe — see Golden Doe

Montana Mountain Goat — see under Rocky Mountain Goat

Moose — Walking with nose poked out; large antlers. Sculpted by Chris Hess. Mold in catalog-run production 1966 - current as of 1996.

Catalog-run models made from this mold:

- Moose #79, brown, no white markings, black-shaded nose, darker brown ruff on neck and shoulders, many with dorsal stripe from tail to nose, tan antlers with black tips, dark gray-brown or black hooves, matte or semigloss (1966 - current as of 1996). In Presentation Collection mounted on American walnut wood base with brass "Moose" nameplate, 1972-73. The Presentation model is listed as #5079 in the 1973 price list, but previously it apparently had the same number as regular-run #79; see Presentation Collection above in the Traditionals section for discussion. "Brown" is almost too general a description of the Moose to be accurate, for his color varies widely, ranging from a dark chocolate brown, as on Heather Wells's, Sande Schneider's, Blain Kukevitch's, and one of my own models, to dark grayish-tan dun, as on collector Jo Kulwicki's model, to a medium red chestnut, as on my second model. As shown in catalogs, the redder models are more recent; my red chestnut fellow, who also has charcoal dots on his dewclaws, was made in 1993 or 1994. The dark chocolate Mooses (as Sande calls them), which often have dabs of bright or pale pink in the nostrils, are older, dating to the 1960s and 1970s. (Heather's and my chocolate specimens have a "U.S.A." stamp, dating them to no earlier than 1970, and Blain's was purchased new in 1970 according to the person he bought it from.) On all colors of Moose, the antlers are typically lighter than the body, but Blain's chocolate Moose has antlers the same color as its body.

Notes:

(1) The antlers on the Moose are separately molded pieces affixed to the model's head after molding.

(2) Early models of the Moose mold have the round "Breyer Molding Co." stamp only. Later models also have the "U.S.A." stamp. Some "U.S.A." models might have the "B" stamp too, but I am not sure.

Panda — Not a Breyer product. For discussion see Wilderness Animal Series By Christian Hess, below in this section.

Panther — Not a Breyer product. For discussion see Wilderness Animal Series By Christian Hess, below in this section.

Pronghorn Antelope — ♠ Standing with head up; large, upright, two-pronged horns. Sculpted by Chris Hess. Mold in catalog-run production 1971-76.
Catalog-run models made from this mold:
♠ Pronghorn Antelope #310, brown, with white sides and belly, white on sides of face, black or gray band up the crest and down center of face, white and brown horizontal stripes on front of neck, white rump, brown tail, some with black tail tip, gray horns and hooves, matte (1971-76).
Notes:

(1) The antlers on this mold, to judge from specimens I have examined, are integral to the mold, not separately molded as on many other Breyer ruminants.

(2) The Pronghorn Antelope mold has the round "Breyer Molding Co." stamp and the "U.S.A." stamp.

Rocky Mountain Goat — ♠ Standing nearly square; sharp, upright horns. Sculpted by Marvin Morin. Mold in catalog-run production 1973-76, 1989.
Catalog-run models made from this mold:
♠ Montana Mountain Goat #312, white with reddish-brown horns; subtle light-chestnut dusting on knees, hocks, and belly; charcoal nose and beard; no painted mouth line; gray hooves; matte (1989). This model is essentially a reissue of the earlier Rocky

Mountain Goat, with the same model number but a new name. There are consistent differences, however—notably in horn color and muzzle detailing.
♠ Rocky Mountain Goat #312, white with black or dark gray horns; many with subtle light-chestnut dusting on body; white nose and beard; gray nostrils and mouth line; gray hooves; matte (1973-76). At first glance the shading on this model can look like age-related yellowing of the plastic, but on closer inspection it can be seen to be paint. These models are now old enough, however, that many of them may be somewhat yellowed as well. Collector Sande Schneider has a pure white Rocky Goat, with no chestnut shading at all. The Rocky Mountain Goat differs only in details from the later Montana Mountain Goat, and the two have the same model number.
Notes:

(1) At a signing party in 1988, Breyer executive Peter Stone told me that the Rocky Mountain Goat was sculpted for Breyer by an American Indian man from Montana. Mr. Stone repeated this statement about the Mountain Goat at BreyerFest 1990, specifying that the mold was sculpted by a Crow Indian artist named Marvin Morin (spelling per Mac Donald 1993 and JAH 21/#1 Spring 1994, p. 15). Former Breyer employee Jill Göllner also states that the sculptor of this mold was an American Indian artist (Göllner 1989-90, pp. 34-35).

(2) The horns on this goat are integral to the mold, not separately molded pieces.

(3) The Rocky Mountain Goat mold has the round "Breyer Molding Co." stamp and the "U.S.A." stamp.

"Tatanka" — see under Buffalo

Wilderness Animal Series by Christian Hess — This is a series of wild-animal models created by Breyer sculptor and mold engineer Chris Hess. These models are not Breyer products but were independently produced and marketed by Hess. The animals are a cheetah, cougar, koala, panda, panther (made from the cougar mold), and timber wolf. They were issued in the mid-1980s and may be re-released by The Peter Stone Company. For further details, see the entry on Chris Hess in the Sculptors section of the Appendix below.

Wolf — Not a Breyer product. For discussion see preceding entry, Wilderness Animal Series By Christian Hess.

Appendix

Breyer Company History

The 1940s & 1950s

Before plastic horses. The Breyer Molding Company began manufacturing plastic horse models in 1950, when the company was located in Chicago, Illinois. Breyer did not begin life as a maker of models, however, but as a manufacturer of a wide variety of plastic items, most of them components made to order for other companies and, during the Second World War, for the federal government. "During WWII, Breyer made plastic parts for airplanes and other vehicles," states an article by former *JAH* editor Steve Ryan. "After the war, Breyer made parts for TVs and radios. Breyer was also responsible for the plastic components of 'swinging clocks.' Let me explain these: an arch-shaped clock with one or two figures (male and/or female) seated on swings which moved back and forth in time with the seconds. The small light inside illuminated a forest or garden scene behind the swingers. Most of the cases were marbled plastic, that is, swirls of black and another color. There is also another clock shaped like a church with a figure pulling on the bell rope. Last of all, Breyer even made steering wheels for a truck company!"[1]

Prior to 1943, the Breyer Molding Company had been owned by the Shoecraft family.[2] In 1943 these owners sold the company to Sam J. Stone—father of Breyer executive Peter A. Stone—and a partner, Barney Smith, for $15,000. Shortly thereafter, Smith died, and Sam Stone acquired a new partner, Charles Schiff.[3] Peter Stone told me in May 1994 that his father and Smith had bought the Breyer Molding Company knowing absolutely nothing about plastics molding! They had to learn the business in a hurry. In those early days, Stone recounted, the company did not use injection molding but instead a process called compression molding, whereby a "pill" of softened plastic of a pre-measured amount was smashed into the desired shape by extremely dangerous machinery. One of Peter Stone's boyhood tasks was to bring the pills from the pill-preparation area to the compression molders. He recalled that among other items, Breyer made compression-molded checkers and poker chips, which were the company's first attempt to establish "proprietary products"—that is, products conceived and produced by the company on its own, as opposed to products commissioned by other companies. Thus the boxes containing the checkers and chips should be printed with the Breyer name and an early company logo—Stone vaguely recollected a diagonal design.[4]

MasterCrafters and the Western Horse. Breyer's first horse model, the Western Horse, made its appearance in 1950 as just one more plastic component made to order for another company: "The first horse manufactured by Breyer, the number 57 Western Horse, was originally designed as a custom molded part for a midwest clock manufacturer."[5] This manufacturer was MasterCrafters Clock Company, which needed the horses to mount on mantel clocks.[6] The horse was sculpted by Christian Hess, who would serve as Breyer's primary animal sculptor and injection-mold maker for decades to come. Hess's design for the horse was not original, however. Rather, it was adapted from the Large Western Champ, sculpted by Roger Williams of Hartland Plastics, Inc., located in Hartland, Wisconsin. Champ had likewise been Hartland's first horse mold, created in 1946 or 1947, and had likewise been used on mantel clocks by MasterCrafters Clock Company. MasterCrafters approached Breyer about supplying horses for its clocks after Hartland stopped doing so.[7]

After the Western Horses for the clocks were produced, so the story goes, MasterCrafters gave the metal mold for the horse to Breyer in lieu of payment for the creation of the mold. Breyer decided to use the molds to produce and sell the horses on its own:

> "A clock, a horse and a lot of imagination started a tradition back in 1950. MasterCrafters Clock Co. made the clock and Breyer Molding Co. designed and molded the horse. Although 2,000 of the clocks were made, it was not enough to pay for the dies; they were returned to Breyer in lieu of payment. Breyer decided to produce and market the horse as the No. 57 Western Horse. The popularity of this single item led to a line of beautifully sculpted, hand painted horses and other animals."[8]

The 1991 catalog adds a date to this turn of events: "1952: Breyer markets first model horse, the #57 Western Horse." Two aspects of these quotations are mystifying: the statement that #57 (palomino) was first and the statement that Breyer first marketed the models in 1952. These assertions fly in the face of ads placed by retail companies for free-standing Western Horses—that is, horses not on clocks—in *Western Horseman* magazine issues as early as 1950 and 1951. The earliest of these issues that I know of, the one for November 1950, has an ad not for palominos but for white horses—actually the ad says "cream" and calls the horse "Cream Puff." The ad does not mention Breyer, but the horse shown in the ad looks exactly like the horses on the earliest MasterCrafters Western Horse clocks. Further, collector Paula DeFeyter found a free-standing "Cream Puff"-style Western Horse in original box, a cardboard mailing carton printed with Breyer's name and address (no model number or name). The palomino horse was advertised for the first time to my knowledge nearly a year later, in the September 1951 *Western Horseman*, and again in the December 1951 issue. So evidently the palomino came second, and obviously both colors of models were marketed prior to 1952.[9]

In any event, the February 1952 issue of *Playthings* magazine, a toy-industry publication, discussed both the palomino and the white models in a brief article titled "Attractive Items from Breyer":

> "To satisfy the popular craze for animals the Breyer Molding Co., Chicago 12, molds an authentic Palomino, a breed of the thoroughbred class. Breyer No. 57 Palomino is executed in true-to-nature coloring and expressive detail. . . . No. 57 Palomino is a western mount with removable saddle, handsomely styled and hand decorated in gold on cow-hide brown. The head harness and loose hanging bridle gear hold special attraction for the boy or girl with Wild West aspirations. The No. 59 White Horse has the same attributes as No. 57 except that its coloring is not as detailed, therefore its price is lower."

The following issue of Playthings, March 1952, has a full-page ad by the Breyer company for palomino #57 and white #59 "Western Mounts."[10] This *Playthings* ad is a wholesale ad aimed at retailers—it offers master cartons of 6 models in self-mailer cartons (no prices mentioned)—and explicitly states "Manufactured by Breyer Molding Co." But retailers' ads for Breyer models in horse magazines throughout the 1950s and well into the 1960s were aimed at consumers and were placed not by Breyer but by saddlery shops and other businesses, which didn't bother to give the Breyer company's name. And often these advertisers invented fanciful epithets for the models. The November 1950 ad for the white/cream Western Horse, which was run again in the November 1951 *Western Horseman*, was placed by the "little joe" Wiesenfeld Co. of Baltimore, Maryland, and, as mentioned above, dubs the horse "Cream Puff." (He's $8 in the November 1950 ad but $4 in the November 1951 ad. I don't know whether "Cream Puff" flopped or the 1950 price was a typo.) The October-November 1952 *Horse Lover's Magazine* has an ad by G. J. Jedlicka Saddlery, of Santa Barbara, California, offering "Wonder Boy—A handsome Western horse over 10 inches high. . . . Your choice of Palomino with brown saddle or white with black saddle" (either for $3.95; one "wonders" indeed—what happened to the price break on the white?). The October-November 1954 *Horse Lover's Magazine* has another ad by "little joe" Wiesenfeld, this time offering "Turf Queen—the sorrel thoroughbred. Perfect in every detail—from long flowing tail and white front legs to beautiful white blazed head, pert ears, and halter . . . of strong unbreakable plastic" ($2.50). The drawing in the ad reveals the horse to be Breyer's Race Horse #36. "Little joe" strikes again in the August-September 1956 *Horse Lover's Magazine* with an ad for "Pale Face," a pony shown by the illustration to be a palomino "Fury" Prancer #P43.[11] But we are getting ahead of our story.

A much-asked question is, where did the name "Breyer" come from? As noted above, when the company was purchased by Sam Stone and his partner in 1943, it already had the name Breyer Molding Co. The origin of the name is not mentioned in early *JAH* articles on the history of the company, and apparently nobody in the company today knows for sure where it came from. But Peter Stone has a favorite speculation: the company might possibly have been named after a nineteenth-century German chemist who invented a type of cellulose plastic. Megan Thilman, former *JAH* editor, gave a few more details of this story: "[T]here was no 'Mr. Breyer' involved in the company, at any time. The best anyone alive can recall, the name honors a German chemist who developed a type of plastic called cellulosics. Way back when, cellulose plastics were used mostly to make collars for men's shirts. The cellulose (plant fiber) in the plastic makes a very resilient material. The Breyer Molding Company, where Breyer horses were first made, specialized in molding cellulosics plastics (our models are made of cellulose acetate, you know)."[12] In August 1993 I asked Peter Stone about the origins of this speculation. He said that some years previously, a British woman had contacted the company to inquire about the possibility of a connection between the company's name and her own family name, which was Breyer. Her family was German but had fled to Britain in the 1930s to escape Nazi persecution. The woman had a nineteenth-century ancestor who was a chemist, from whom she thought the company might have taken its name. No connection between the family and company names was verified, however.

Money Manager (1949-53). The white and palomino Western Horses were not Breyer's first ventures into the toy market. Advertised in the January 1951 and March 1952 issues of *Playthings* is an object called My Own Money Manager. "Money ... Money ... Money," the 1952 ad's headline announces. "Teach Children how to Manage it with this Item." The Item in question is a plastic bank in the shape of a tiny "file cabinet with four drawers in which to intelligently distribute an allowance." Measuring 4.25" x 4.25" x 4.2", the Money Manager, says the ad, comes in "Forest Green or Flag Red" with ivory-colored drawer pulls. The drawers are labeled with "Popular titles for children," namely "Charity," "Presents," "Saving," and (the only one with any child-appeal as far as I can tell) "Spending." Each Money Manager came with a booklet entitled *Grow a Self-Reliant Child*, "a money management guide for children from pre-school through high school." The 1951 ad notes that My Own Money Manager is "commended by Parent's magazine."

This educational toy had been on the market since about 1949, according to the "Attractive Items from Breyer" article in the February 1952 *Playthings*: "My Own Money Manager was designed and produced by the Breyer Molding Co. . . . On the market for 3 years its interest to parents and teaches [*sic*] continues to grow." (No mention of any interest to children.) Peter Stone, in his presentation at the August 1993 West Coast Model Horse Collector's Jamboree, said he recalled watching TV ads for the Money Manager when he was a boy. The ads featured a male character named "Two-Ton Baker," a local Chicago cabaret-style singer who sat playing a piano with one of the little file cabinets on top of it. Money Managers were sold by Walgreens Drug stores, Stone said. In a conversation in May 1994, Stone commented to me that his father and his father's business partner had in fact originally conceived of the little file cabinet not as a toy but as a cigarette case for the gracious home. The purchaser was to label the drawers with tear-out labels saying "Chesterfield," "Lucky Strike," and so on, so that guests could select their preferred brands from the drawers. The cigarette case did not sell well, however, so the item was given a fresh identity as a children's educational toy.

The Money Manager survived into 1953 but evidently was gone by 1954, to judge from *The Playthings Directory*, a toy-industry annual that listed company names, addresses, and toy products. The entries for Breyer Molding Co. in the 1951 and 1953 *Directories* list only the Money Manager as the company's toy product. Why they omit the Western Horses that had been introduced previously I don't know. But in the 1954 *Directory* the tables are turned: the Money Manager is gone and in its place are listed "plastic horses and dogs," the latter being presumably a reference to the Boxer, the sole dog in the ca.1954 Breyer catalog.

I know of no Money Managers existing in collections today. But if indeed Breyer produced these banks for something like four years, there must be specimens lurking in attics and basements somewhere in the land.

Breyer Animal Creations. Following the introduction of the #59 and #57 Western Horses in 1950-51, Breyer rapidly expanded its line of horses and other models and named the line "Breyer Animal Creations," a division of Breyer Molding Company. The second mold introduced by Breyer was the Western Pony, which appears for the first time to my knowledge in an ad in the September 1953 *Western Horseman*.[13] Four more molds were introduced the following year. The ca. 1954 catalog, the earliest Breyer catalog known to exist, contains not only the Western Horse and Western Pony but also the Cowboy and Indian riders, Race Horse, and Boxer. Each page of the catalog bears the heading "A Breyer Animal Creation" except for the Cowboy and Indian pages, which tactfully say "A Breyer Creation."

The next horse mold, the "Fury" Prancer, debuted in 1955, along with the Davy Crockett rider mold. The Davy with Prancer set appears in the 1955 Sears holiday catalog, as do the Cowboy on palomino Prancer and Indian on pinto Prancer made into music boxes, not to mention the Western Pony outfitted with a "grooming kit" for kids. Davy Crockett sets were also sold by MasterCrafters Clock Company on mantel clocks. Kit Carson on a dark Prancer turns up in the Fall/Winter 1956 Sears catalog, and Robin Hood on his white Prancer follows shortly in the 1956 Sears holiday catalog, along with more grooming kits with the Western Pony and Western Horse.[14]

Further horses and other animals debuted in the mid- to late 1950s. The 1958 catalog and price list include, in addition to all the molds already mentioned, the Proud Arabian Mare and Foal, Clydesdale Stallion, "Rin Tin Tin," "Lassie," Poodle, Brahma Bull, horned walking Hereford Bull, Donkey, Elephant, Robin Hood, Canadian Mountie, and Corky the Circus Boy molds. The Family Arabian Stallion was released perhaps late in 1958 and certainly no later than 1959; he is shown with the PAM and PAF in a Frontier Saddlery ad in the September and December 1959 issues of *Western Horseman*. One more mold, the polled walking Black Angus Bull, came out in either 1959 or 1960.

Assuming the Black Angus debuted in 1959, we have a total of 8 horse molds, 6 rider molds, and 9 other animal molds, for a grand total of 23 molds introduced in the decade of the 1950s. The number of 1950s models is of course even greater since several molds were painted in an assortment of colors. Surprisingly, not all 1950s models were painted at the Breyer factory. In its early years, Breyer Molding Company had no facilities for decorating the plastic products it molded. Consequently, until at least the mid-1950s Breyer models were painted by the company of Paul and Bill Cifioni (pronounced shiff-ON-ee) of Chicago, according to Peter Stone (conversation of July 1995).

Three interesting trends characterize this first decade of Breyer Animal Creations. One was the issuing of models based on television programs. The 1958 catalog and price list explicitly identify "Rin Tin Tin," "Lassie," black "Fury" Prancer #27, and Corky the Circus Boy as representations of TV characters. Although Breyer company publications of the time do not say so, it is likely that television programs provided the inspiration for other models as well—notably Kit Carson, Davy Crockett, Robin Hood, and the Canadian Mountie. All these models appeared about the same time as the popular TV shows that dramatized the adventures of the historical figures in question. Basing models on TV characters was a concept that Breyer would recall in future decades with models representing popular movie characters—such as "Benji" and "Tiffany," the Black Stallion and Alec, Black Beauty, Kelly Reno and "Little Man"—and of course with many models based on books by Marguerite Henry and other authors.

A second trend of the 1950s was Breyer's "borrowing" of mold designs from other manufacturers. In some instances the Breyer designs are adaptations rather than outright copies—examples of such designs are the Western Horse and Pony molds, which opened the 1950s, and the Family Arabian Stallion and Proud Arabian Mare and Foal, which closed the decade, indeed slammed it shut with a lawsuit (see the notes for the PAM mold). In other instances, the Breyers are copies with few or no modifications: Race Horse, Boxer, Poodle, Brahma Bull, and horned walking Hereford Bull.[15] In light of these numerous borrowings, the promotional blurb on the back of the 1958 Breyer catalog seems almost taunting: "Much in the manner of the fine artisans who produce similar figures in high priced china and ceramic have we captured the naturalness and lovable expression that make each animal irresistibly fascinating." Over the years since the 1950s Breyer has in turn been amply borrowed from, by Hong Kong manufacturers and others.

The third trend of Breyer's first decade has been maintained ever since—namely, the marketing of the models not simply as toys for kids but also as decorative and collectible objects for adults. This emphasis shines in the slogans on 1950s Breyer catalogs and promotional fliers: "It's a Toy, a Welcome Gift, an Art Object, because it's so real!" "A Wise Buyer Buys Breyer Animal Creations for Toys, Gifts and Art Objects." The descriptions of the individual models in these publications abound with similar comments: "A winner for wide appeal as an ornament or a plaything" (Race Horse); "Exquisitely hand decorated as is the authentic removable saddle. Smooth, lightweight, defies rough handling" (Western Horse); "Handsome desk ornament, endearing companion for any child. Collector's delight" (Boxer); "comes with or without Howdah for holding jewelry and small dresser or office items" (Elephant). The 1958 catalog stresses the models' similarity to china figurines, a feature enhanced by the high-gloss varnish put on many models of that time: "The china-like appearance of this majestic pair will surely be the pride and joy of all age groups" (Proud Arab Mare and Foal); "realistically reproduced with sparkling lustre" (Clydesdale Stallion); "simulates fine china. . . . heavy enough to use as book ends and yet light enough for any child's play" (Poodle); "having the appearance of fine china, this spectacular creation is truly a collector's item" (Brahma Bull); "its exquisite china appearance makes this magnificent animal a welcome gift for any age group" (Hereford Bull). And Breyer surely had adults rather than children in mind when, in 1959, it broke for the first time from its tradition of realistic coloration to introduced a new, unrealistic finish: woodgrain. Evidently this style enjoyed considerable popularity, for numerous woodgrain models—horses, dogs, and bulls—were issued for several more years.[16]

The 1960s

The 1960 catalog gives evidence of the first discontinuations of Breyer Animal Creations molds. All rider molds are gone from the 1960 catalog, never to reappear. The Proud Arabian Mare and Foal molds are also absent from this catalog, owing to a lawsuit by the Hagen-Renaker Company concerning copyright infringement.[17] The rest of the 1950s molds, however, continued into the 1960s and were joined by many new horse and other animal molds in that decade. Also in the 1960s a second unrealistic style of coloring made its entrée: the decorator colors.[18]

Throughout this period of expansion of its line of models, Breyer Molding Co. continued to manufacture custom-molded plastic parts for other companies, such as Zenith, Bell Electric, and International Harvester.[19] Indeed such custom molding was Breyer's main business, the models being a mere sideline, according to the biography of Peter Stone in *JAH* 20/#3 Summer II 1993 (p. 12). Stone went to work for Breyer Molding Co., his father's company, as production manager of the custom-molding operation in 1965. A year or two later, the article reports, the company considered discontinuing the entire Breyer Animal Creations line of models. This may seem surprising in view of the steady growth of the line since the early 1950s. The 1967 price list looks like a testament to the vitality of Breyer Animal Creations, including as it does 38 horse and other animal molds painted into a total of 96 different models. But despite appearances, the animal line was not very profitable and was threatened with discontinuation.[20] The day was saved by Peter Stone, who did not want to see the animals go and believed they had untapped market potential. His father transferred him to the company's Breyer Animal Creations division, and Stone thereupon began to promote the line nationwide, a campaign he pursued for over 25 years. In the mid-1970s he would become president of Breyer Animal Creations, a position he would hold until the mid-1980s, when this division of Breyer Molding Co. was sold.[21]

The end of this decade brought two interesting developments: the discontinuation of glossy finish from most of the Breyer line and the introduction of the company's first effort at display packaging, the "touchability box," a packaging option for the Family Arabians offered in 1968-70.

The 1970s

These years might be called the decade of diversity. To begin with, the original larger-scale line of models, which was first designated as the "Traditional" scale in the 1975 catalog, underwent further experimentation with packaging and with a new concept, base mounting. 1970-72 were the years of the Showcase Collection, consisting of a large number of regular-run models packaged in clear-plastic carrying cases. Another regular-run series, the Presentation Collection of Traditional-scale models mounted on wooden bases, was issued from 1971 through 1973.[22] Breyer's line of Traditional-scale cloth stable blankets, leather saddles and bridles, and other accessories also debuted in these years, with the first such items appearing in the 1971 manual.

Next, Breyer brought out two entirely new lines of horses—the Classics and the Stablemates—both of smaller scale than the original line. The Classic scale debuted in 1973 with the release of the Classic Arabian Family Gift Set #3055. The Classic group of horses increased rapidly in the following years and is still growing today, with the addition of the Messenger Series Of Kiger Mustangs. The full Stablemates line of miniature models was introduced in 1975 and 1976. Though no new Stablemates molds have been added to the line since then, most of these tiny horses are still in production today.[23]

The company also faced difficulties in the 1970s, thanks to the world-wide oil crisis, which began in 1973 and lasted for close to a decade.[24] Although the cellulose acetate plastic from which Breyers are made is not a petroleum product, it became scarce and costly during the oil-crisis era. Some U.S. plastics suppliers stopped making it, turning their efforts instead to the production of petroleum-based plastics, which became highly profitable at this time. Other suppliers, with their competitors gone, raised their prices on it. For many years Breyer had paid 40 cents per pound for top-quality cellulose acetate, but during the oil-crisis era the price more than doubled, to 96 cents per pound. In response to the squeeze, Breyer not only discontinued the weightiest molds, notably the Shire and Poodle, but also sought alternatives to its customary high-grade cellulose acetate. Lower-grade cellulose acetate—the stuff from which the so-called "chalky" and "pearly" models of the 1970s are made (see Chalkies & Pearlies below in this Appendix)—was purchased from suppliers in Belgium and Italy. Breyer also tried switching to a less expensive and lighter weight type of plastic called cellulose propionate, which was available from U.S. suppliers. But propionate caused many problems: it created fumes in the factory; it molded poorly, causing a high rate of reject models from the injection-molding equipment; and it didn't allow Breyer's tried and true paints to adhere properly, with the result that the company had to grope for new paint formulas. Consequently, Breyer's stopped using propionate after a couple of years.[25]

Another important development for hobbyists in the decade of the 1970s was the advent of the Breyer company's magazine for collectors, *Just About Horses*, first issued in late 1975. The magazine has been in publication ever since and today has several thousand subscribers.[26]

The late 1970s inaugurated the era of special runs made for the collecting hobby, an era that is still flourishing today. Although a few special runs had been made in the late 1950s, 1960s, and early 1970s, the concept of specials issued for sale to model-horse collectors was stimulated with a vengeance by the hobby's own development of live shows, which reached national proportions with the large Model Horse Congresses of the late 1970s.[27]

Last and least, in the final two years of the decade the company offered the Traditional line in display packaging once again (this time the model-icidal blister-wrap box) and loosed Brenda Breyer upon Western civilization, the founding mother of what would shortly become a new generation of rider dolls.

The 1980s

In 1981 Brenda was joined by her cousin Alec Ramsey, another Traditional-scale soft-plastic doll. Alec and his second-born identical twin Ben Breyer perished after only a few years, but Brendas continue to proliferate to the present day. The Little Bits-scale Bitsy Breyer dolls, which are jointed dolls of hard plastic, debuted in 1983 and survived for only a few years but were reincarnated in the mid-1990s as denizens of the Saddle Club Collection. Brenda, Alec, and Bitsy dolls were and are all manufactured in Asia. Along with Bitsy came the Little Bits series of horses, a fourth scale for Breyer, smaller than the Classics but larger than the Stablemates. Breyer originally manufactured the Little Bits horses in the U.S. but has had them produced in China since the end of 1995.

Also in 1983 Peter Stone began to make public appearances across the nation at promotional events called "signing parties," where he would meet with collectors and autograph their Breyers for them. These events would continue for several years to come.[28]

In 1984 Breyer inaugurated the Artist Series of models, which would showcase the work of four American equine artists: Rich Rudish, Bob Scriver, Jeanne Mellin Herrick, and Breyer's own Christian Hess. Though these molds are still in production today, they are no longer designated as "Artist Series" but have joined the Traditional herd.[29]

And also in 1984, Breyer Animal Creations was sold.

Reeves International. Until late in 1984, Breyer Animal Creations was, as noted above, a division of Breyer Molding Company, and it is identified as such on the 1984 catalog and most prior catalogs. In November 1984 this division was purchased by a company called Reeves International, Inc., of Pequannock, New Jersey,[30] and shortly thereafter Reeves commenced construction of the new factory for Breyer Animal Creations in Wayne, New Jersey, just a few miles from Pequannock. Catalogs from 1985 to the present identify Breyer as "Breyer Animal Creations, a division of Reeves International, Inc."

The president of Reeves International is Mr. Werner J. Fleischmann, who was born in Zurich, Switzerland, and emigrated to the U.S. after serving in the Swiss army during World War II. In the U.S. he became the business partner of Dr. Hazard Reeves in a company that exported precious-metal commodities to Europe and imported German goods such as Steiff toy animals. Dr. Reeves subsequently left the company, but Mr. Fleischmann remained and developed Reeves International, Inc., into an importer and distributor of fine European toys. Eventually Reeves International became a manufacturer of fine toys as well as a distributor, creating the Suzanne Gibson line of dolls.[31]

Peter Stone, who became Breyer/Reeves's director of marketing after the sale,[32] announced the acquisition of Breyer Animal Creations by Reeves in the first issue of *JAH* published in 1985 (11/#4, p. 10):

> "With the holiday season and the new year it seems an appropriate time to thank you, our Breyer customers, for your enthusiastic interest and continued support. Also it is the time to announce the advent of another sort... the acquisition of Breyer Animal Creations by Reeves International, Inc. of Pequannock, New Jersey.
>
> Reeves International is an importer and manufacturer of a variety of high quality products. As an importer and distributor of such lines as Britains Miniature Models, Gorgi [sic; should be Corgi] Die Cast Vehicles, LGB trains, Steiff Plush Animals, and Kouvalias Pre-School Wooden Toys along with the manufacture and distribution of Suzanne Gibson Dolls and now Breyer Animal Creations, Reeves will mean to you a continued source of high quality models and, in the future, more outlets offering Breyer."

In another *JAH* later that year, Mr. Stone reported: "On July 8th [1985], the first 'New Jersey' model, a No. 89 Black Beauty, was produced in our new plant in Wayne, New Jersey. By January 1, 1986, all of our products will come from this fine facility. Quality will be better than ever and, you will be pleased to know, several of our skilled craftsmen from Chicago have moved to join us" (*JAH* 12/#2 1985, p. 11). Also in 1985, a special-run horse was issued to celebrate Reeves's acquisition of Breyer: the red sorrel Little Bits American Saddlebred, which was a new mold that year and was the last Breyer mold ever to receive the old "Breyer Molding Co." round stamp. The hang-tag that came on some of these SR Saddlebreds says "1985, a special year for Breyer Animal Creations... the year the tradition of Breyer creativity and quality is joined with the strength and marketing diversity of Reeves International, Inc. Let this limited edition of Breyer's Little Bits Series remind you of a very special year and a very special company. . . . Breyer Animal Creations, now a division of Reeves International, Inc.!"

For roughly a year following the Reeves acquisition, the old Breyer Molding Company in Chicago remained in business on its own. Indeed it continued to manufacture not only custom-molded parts for such companies as Zenith and International Harvester but also Breyer models, which it sold under contract to Reeves International prior to completion of Reeves's new Breyer factory in Wayne.[33] The Breyer Molding Company finally went out of business in the latter part of 1985.[34]

The decade of the 1980s brought one more event of enormous significance for Breyer collectors, but this time deeply sad significance. Christian Hess, the company's primary sculptor and injection-mold maker since 1950, died in 1988.[35] The loss of this extraordinarily gifted man is still felt today, not only artistically but practically. For according to Peter Stone (conversation of July 1995), craftsmen capable of creating the metal injection-molds from which Breyers are made are becoming more and more scarce. Hess was a consummate craftsman and engineer as well as an artist, and Breyer depended upon his talents in all these fields for decades.

The 1990s

So far, this decade has ushered in four noteworthy developments for the model-horse hobby. The first was the establishment of BreyerFest, an annual convention organized by the company. The first Fest was held in 1990, in Lexington, Kentucky, and this has been the predominant venue ever since. These events attract hundreds of model-horse enthusiasts from across the nation.[36]

The second development was the advent of non-plastic Breyers. In the latter part of 1991, the company broke with its decades-long tradition of producing moderately priced models in cellulose acetate plastic when it issued two horses in a medium called cold-cast porcelain (which is actually plastic resin dosed with marble powder): "Spotted Bear," sold exclusively through the Sears holiday catalog, for $95, and "Galaxias," sold exclusively through the Penney's holiday catalog, for $99.99. The following year three more models were issued in this medium: "Misty," "Secretariat," and "Fashionably Late." These, however, were the last of the cold-casts, for reportedly Breyer was dissatisfied with the quality of the models, and I know that many collectors received flawed and damaged specimens. All of these models were manufactured in Asia from existing Breyer molds. Also in 1992, Breyer inaugurated a new Evolution Of The Horse series of fine-porcelain models with the introduction of the Icelandic Horse. This series continued in 1993 with the Shire Horse and in 1994 with the Spanish Barb. All three of these pieces are new molds, and like the cold-cast porcelains, they are manufactured in the Orient. In 1993 the company also issued its first ceramic piece, the Little Bits–scale Performing "Misty," created and manufactured for Breyer by the Hagen-Renaker Company, of San Dimas, California. The latest non-plastic line, the Premier Fine Porcelain Series, debuted in 1995 with the costumed Premier Arabian Mare and promises a Saddlebred in full Western parade tack in 1996.

The third notable development so far in the 1990s is Breyer's introduction of plastic models made of lower-quality plastics than its usual engineering-grade cellulose acetate. In 1992 Breyer ceased manufacturing the Stablemates models at its own U.S. factory and began to have these little horses produced in China of a material called ABS plastic. This change has allowed Breyer to reduce the price of Stablemates significantly. In 1995, Breyer introduced its Dapples line of storybook-style models, all of which are manufactured in the orient of the same ABS plastic.

Finally, in a startling turn of events for collectors, Peter Stone, who had been "Mr. Breyer" to collectors of all ages for nearly three decades, left Breyer-Reeves in the first part of October 1995. Since then he has established his own new business, The Peter Stone Company, which will produce, among other items, a line of realistic, injection-molded, cellulose acetate horse models.

Sculptors

Christian Hess

Chris Hess (1916-1988) was Breyer's primary sculptor and injection-mold maker from the time the company began to produce models, in 1950.[37] He is sorely missed by model horse collectors, for his talented hands were a source of exquisitely subtle, realistic designs. Several of his pieces remain today the most widely prized sculptures in the hobby—"Lady Phase," Hanoverian, Cantering Welsh Pony, "Legionario III," "Misty," and Shire, to name just a few favorites. His last Breyer sculpture was #435 "Secretariat," released in 1987 as part of the Artist Series of models by various American artists. This piece and others—such as "El Pastor," "Halla," and Classic Andalusian Mare—were sculpted by Hess solely from photographs of the real horses. Hess's remarkable ability to create 3-dimensional replicas of 2-dimensional images also extended to paintings and drawings. His "Sea Star" mold looks much like the foal in Wesley Dennis's painting on the cover of Marguerite Henry's *Sea Star: Orphan of Chincoteague*; Hess's "Smoky" mold very closely resembles a drawing by Will James in James's book *Smoky, the Cow Horse*; and the Foundation Stallion is based on a painting of "El Morzillo" published in a Hallmark calendar. Breyer executive Peter Stone told me that something on the order of 80 percent of Hess's molds were designed from photographs and two-dimensional artworks.[38] What makes this skill the more remarkable is that Hess was not a horseman and knew little about horse anatomy. To compensate, he referred to equine anatomical diagrams, which Stone still had in his files when I visited the Breyer factory in Wayne, New Jersey, in November 1994.

Hess made many sculptures other than Breyers. A Bentley Sales Company ad flier for some of his work states that he created, among other pieces, "many Christmas and other lawn decorations, [and] wood sculpturings for architectural moldings." The *JAH* biography of Hess notes that he was "originally a wood carver, making decorations for buildings. He then became a freelance model maker, his first being the 'Wonder Horse,' a bouncing, rideable horse." Near the end of his life he created two resin-bronze horses and a group of wildlife sculptures called the Wilderness Animal Series, all of which he sold in the years 1984-87 through Bentley's and perhaps some other retailers as well. These pieces are not Breyers; Hess produced and marketed them independently (see *JAH* 18/#1 Spring 1991, p. 13). One of the horses isdue to be re-released in 1996 by The Peter Stone Company, which may also re-issue the Wilderness animals at some point.

Hess Wilderness Animal Series. According to Bentley's ad fliers, this series comprised five molds (dimensions are given only for two): Cheetah, 3.5" tall x 8" long, yellow with black spots; Panda, 5" tall x 3.5" wide, black and white; Timber Wolf, gray with white; Cougar, yellow dun; and Koala Bear, light gray. The Koala is clinging to a thin brown tree trunk and has a light gray baby on her back. The Cheetah came in two different mold versions: one, shown on a Bentley's flier, with her spots recessed as on a golf ball, and another, smooth-bodied version with her spots filled in.[39] According to the fliers, the Wilderness sculptures are made of a material called Kraton, "an engineered thermoplastic rubber" that is "extremely break-resistant." But Kraton is actually plastic, a high-impact styrene mixed with an emulsifier, according to Peter Stone (conversation of Feb. 1996). The six animals owned by collector Joy Sheesley, which she purchased from Bentley's and which I have seen in person, are not in the least rubbery; in fact they look and feel like Breyer plastic. The 1984 Bentley's flier offers the sculptures only in painted versions, "hand-painted by the artist." The 1985 flier lists not only all the above hand-painted sculptures but also the following: the Cougar mold as a black Panther in both painted and flocked versions, and flocked versions of the dun Cougar and the Panda. Other animals were issued in flocked versions as well, although they are not listed in the Bentley's fliers. Collector Jo Kulwicki owns not only the three flocked pieces just mentioned but also a Koala, Cheetah, gray Wolf, and black Wolf, all flocked. Several of Jo's pieces came from the Riegseckers of Indiana (the company that flocked several horse special runs for Breyer in the mid-1980s), which suggests that Hess had the Riegseckers do the flocking on the Wilderness animals. Jo's flocked Panda came with a hang tag saying "The animals created in the Wilderness Animal Series (WAS), are all original reproductions by Christian Hess Inc. The original sculpturing, molds and parts are all produced at our plant in Franklin Park, Illinois. We decided on introducing the endangered species first, to draw attention to their plight." Hess's signature appears at the end of this text. The back of the hang tag is printed with "© 1982." All six of Joy's animals, which are the painted versions, have a "© 82 Hess" engraving molded into them. Regarding the quantities of these animals, old Bentley's sales record cards in my possession show that Bentley's sold the following between August 1984 and early 1987: 112 painted and 22 flocked Cougars, 78 painted and 19 flocked black Panthers, 152 painted Wolves, 112 painted Cheetahs, and 102 painted Koalas. (I have no record cards for any Pandas or for flocked Wolves, Cheetahs, or Koalas.) How many more Hess may have produced I don't know, but I would guess not more than a few hundred of each mold. All five molds may be reissued, in painted versions, by The Peter Stone Company. According to Peter Stone (conversation of April 1996), these pieces will be newly cast in Kraton; they are not remainders of 1980s production.

Hess resin-bronze horses. Less well known than the Wilderness Animal Series are two horse sculptures that Hess cast in a mixture of resin and powdered bronze and finished with a bronze patina: "Trouble" (13" tall x 9" wide), a rearing horse on a base, and "Breakaway" (9" tall x 12.5" long), a jumping horse on a base. The Bentley's photo flier I have for these pieces is not dated, but it does mention the Wilderness Animal Series, indicating that the horses were contemporary with the wildlife animals. Collector Kim Jones, who gave me a photocopy of the flier, said that the horses came out shortly after the Wilderness pieces appeared. The flier states, "These classic editions are serial numbered to ensure authenticity and are limited to just 1,000 pieces." However, I learned from Stuart Bentley that to his knowledge only two pieces of each horse figure were actually made: the two prototypes shown in the ad flyer and two more, which were the only ones that Bentley's sold. These two were purchased by long-time Breyer consultant and collector Marney Walerius. One of the molds, "Trouble," is due to be reissued without his base by The Peter Stone Company in 1996. The new issues will be injection-molded of cellulose acetate plastic and painted in a variety of colors, among them a limited-edition bronze color in commemoration of Chris Hess. The first pieces of this bronze-colored edition were presented to attendees of The Peter Stone Company's inaugural event, "A Tribute to Christian Hess," held in Lexington, Kentucky, on July 27, 1996. At the event, Mr. Stone remarked in his presentation that the bases on which the original "Trouble" pieces had been mounted each had a little molded-on rattle snake, which explains the horse's alarmed rearing stance and Hess's title for this sculpture! He also noted that Hess had created this horse on his own initiative in hopes that Breyer would want to produce it in cellulose acetate as part of its regular line. But Stone himself had turned Hess down, citing the lackluster market performance of Breyer's existing rearing mold, the Fighting Stallion. An attendee of the "Tribute" event noted afterward that the "Trouble" models given out there seem to be molded of transparent plastic—you can see through them if you hold them up to strong light.

Hess's Breyers. A few Breyer molds are identified as Hess pieces by "CHess" mold marks, and several other molds are identified as his by various *JAH* issues and Breyer catalogs. But for many molds introduced prior to the Artist Series, I have been unable to find clear statements as to the sculptor. Since it is well known that Hess was Breyer's primary sculptor from 1950 on, it is reasonable to give him the benefit of the doubt in such cases. Thus in this book I have identified Hess as the original sculptor of all molds for which I have found no information to the contrary. Among his original works I include not only those molds that appear to be based on photos of real horses but also those evidently based on paintings or drawings by other artists. I do not include molds that appear to have been copied or adapted from the original sculpture of other artists. By these criteria, Hess was, as far as I have been able to determine, the original sculptor of between 115 and 117 of Breyer's horse and other animal molds (depending on the outcome of the undecided cases; see below under Don Manning). These Hess originals include 6 Little Bits molds, 15 Classic molds, and 94-96 Traditional horse and other animal molds.

Edward Marshall Boehm

Boehm (pronounced "beem"), born in Baltimore in 1913, had become one of the most renowned creators of fine porcelain sculpture in the world prior to his death in January 1969. His studio in Trenton, New Jersey, still produces fine porcelains today. The photos and dates in *The Porcelain Art of Edward Marshall Boehm*, by Reese Palley, indicate that four Breyer molds are either direct copies or close adaptations of sculptures by Boehm. The molds are the Boxer, horned walking Hereford Bull, Brahma Bull, and polled walking Black Angus Bull. These pieces, all dating to the 1950s, are some of Breyer's oldest molds. Breyer executive Peter Stone, son of one of the founders of Breyer Animal Creations, told me that he recalls his father making occasional trips to a Chicago shop that carried Boehm porcelains and bringing back a Boehm to be rendered in plastic by the Breyer company, which was also located in Chicago at that time. Stone still has the Boehm Boxer, Hereford, and Brahma, and possibly one or two others. (Conversations of May 1994 and October 1995)

Maureen Love Calvert

Long revered by model-horse collectors, Maureen Love Calvert has sculpted equine and other animal molds for the Hagen-Renaker company since 1951. Prior to this she had attended the California School of Fine Arts in San Francisco and produced commissioned equine portraits. (Per Renaker 1977 and 1979.) Calvert has by my count contributed some 37 molds to the Breyer product line—more than any other artist except Chris Hess. All but one of these were previously produced in ceramic by the Hagen-Renaker company, which has been located in southern California since its beginnings in the mid-1940s. The first Calvert designs to appear (with modifications) in cellulose acetate were Proud Arabian Mare, Proud Arabian Foal, and Family Arabian Stallion, inducted into the Breyer line in the late 1950s. Breyer was obliged by Hagen-Renaker to cease production of the PAM and PAF molds shortly after their introduction but reintroduced them in the early 1970s under a release agreement with Hagen-Renaker.

Since the mid-1970s Breyer has leased the rights from Hagen-Renaker to produce in plastic numerous other Calvert sculptures.[40] These include the 9 molds of the Classic Arabian, Mustang, and Quarter Horse Families; 5 of the Classic Race Horses ("Kelso," "Man-O-War," "Silky Sullivan," "Swaps," and "Terrang") and all 16 of the Stablemates molds.[41] Most recently, Calvert sculpted the Little Bits-scale Performing "Misty" mold (1993), which was produced in ceramic for Breyer by Hagen-Renaker.

One further Breyer mold should perhaps be credited to Calvert: the Little Bit Thoroughbred Stallion. Except in size, this mold is nearly identical to Calvert's Stablemate "Seabiscuit."

Kitty Cantrell

Breyer's "Aristocrat" Hackney mold, introduced in 1995, is the original work of this award-winning Southern California artist. As both an artist and an environmentalist, Cantrell is widely celebrated for her sculptures of wildlife, such as eagles, wolves, and whales, according to a flyer promoting Cantrell's Ocean Realm Collection of metal sculptures set in Lucite, produced by Genesis. A further Cantrell Breyer mold is scheduled for release by Breyer in 1996—the "Henry" The Norwegian Fjord, pictured on the back cover of *JAH* 22/#3 May/June 1995.

Rowland Cheney

This painter and sculptor teaches art at the San Joaquin Delta College in Stockton, California. Cheney is also a wildlife activist who has worked to protect the wild Kiger Mustangs of Southeastern Oregon. He and Josh Warburton, the district manager of the BLM in Southeastern Oregon, co-founded Western Heritage Enterprises, an organization committed to preserving and promoting this unique strain of Mustangs. (Information is per Ryan 1992.) Cheney has sculpted six Classic-scale molds for Breyer as of 1994: "Mesteño" The Messenger (released 1992); the mare and foal molds of The Dawning Gift Set (released 1993); the rearing mold (in two versions) of The Challenger Gift Set, and the charging stallion and grazing yearling molds of The Progeny Gift Set (released 1995). These pieces constitute Breyer's "Messenger Series" of Kiger Mustangs. Cheney is scheduled to create one final piece or set for this series, to be released in 1996.

Francis Eustis

Francis Eustis, who studied at Yale University School of Fine Arts, is a widely known horse sculptor, having sold his exquisite limited-edition pieces from his studio in Ohio for many years. He exhibited his works at numerous art shows, and some of his pieces are on display at natural history museums and zoos. His brochure says that the sculptures are made of "a practically unbreakable material" (hardened latex, per Walerius 1991, p. 17). Eustis bred and raised various breeds of horses, among them Belgians and Arabians. The Breyer line includes one Eustis mold: "Roy" The Belgian Drafter, released in 1989, when Eustis was 75. (Biographical information is per *JAH* 16/#4 Sept./Oct. 1989.)

Suzann Fiedler

This artist created the "ideal American Quarter Horse" bronze sculpture for the American Quarter Horse Association to use on trophies awarded to champion Quarter Horses. Breyer used Fiedler's bronze as the inspiration for its Ideal Quarter Horse mold, introduced in 1995. (*JAH* 21/#5 Winter 1994, p. 5.) The mold bears a stamp of Fiedler's signature.

Grand Wood Carving

Grand Wood Carving, a company located in Chicago, began manufacturing wood carved statuettes in 1939, according to a Grand Wood catalog of which I have a copy. The company still exists but has not produced horses since the 1980s, according to Joan Berkwitz 1993. The heyday of Grand Wood mahogany horse figures was from the 1940s through the 1960s. These figures were carved by a machine (analogous to the machines that duplicate metal keys) and only finished by hand, according to collector Gale Good. Breyer's Race Horse, introduced ca.1954, appears to be a close adaptation of Grand Wood's "Whirlaway" model, first released in 1943. Furthermore, as Joan comments, it is possible that Breyer, which was located in Chicago from its beginnings until the mid-1980s, derived from Grand Wood the whole concept of woodgrain-look models.

Jeanne Mellin Herrick

This well-known and long-established equine painter and sculptor, who lives with her family at Saddleback Farm in New York, is also a breeder and trainer of Morgan horses and the author of several books on horses (per *JAH* XIV/#4 1987, p. 14, and 15/#2 May/June 1988, p. 13). An ad for limited-edition prints of her famous painting of the Morgan Horse pedigree appeared in the April 1966 *Western Horseman* magazine (p. 112). Herrick has sculpted six Traditional molds for Breyer, all of different breeds: "Sherman Morgan," introduced in 1987 as part of the Artist Series; "John Henry," introduced in 1988; "Roemer," introduced in 1990; "Misty's Twilight," introduced in 1991; "Pluto," introduced in 1991; and the Friesian, introduced in 1992. See Breyer dealer catalogs 1987-88 for further information on Herrick.

Don Manning

It is possible that Don Manning is the original sculptor of the Golden Buck and Doe molds, both introduced by Breyer in 1961/63. On the other hand, it's possible that they are Chris Hess originals, to which Don Manning helped himself. For further discussion see the notes for Golden Buck in the Wildlife section above.

Kathleen Moody

This Arizona artist's name was familiar to model-horse hobbyists long before it turned up in the 1992 Breyer catalog under the photo of Breyer's first fine-porcelain sculpture, the Icelandic Horse, the first piece in the Evolution Of The Horse series. This horse is Moody's first Breyer mold, but she is a longtime model-horse collector and sculptor. Among her many widely admired designs are the Peruvian Paso and "Lady Jewel" and "Jade" molds, all of which she created for Hartland Collectables prior to her work for Breyer, and a number of resin horses issued through DaBar Enterprises of Mesa, Arizona. Moody is now established as Breyer's porcelain sculptor, having designed the Shire Horse (released in 1993) and the Spanish Barb (released in 1994) in the Evolution Of The Horse Series and the 1995 Premier Arabian Mare, the first piece in the Premier Fine Porcelain Series of costumed horses. In coming years she will contribute further pieces to the latter series, such as the Saddlebred in parade tack scheduled for 1996. The Breyer line also includes several plastic molds by Moody: "Gem Twist," introduced in 1993, and the five storybook-style horse molds of Breyer's Dapples series, introduced in 1995. Her new plastic mold of the jumper "Big Ben" will debut in 1996. See *JAH* Fall 18/#4 1991 (p. 18) for further information on Moody.

MARVIN MORIN

Breyer's Rocky Mountain Goat and Saddlebred Weanling molds are the work of artist Marvin Morin.[42] The primary source if information on this sculptor is Breyer executive Peter Stone, who spoke about Morin during the auction at BreyerFest 1990, where the original wax sculpture of the Rocky Mountain Goat was sold. I was not present at the auction, but two collectors published reports on it. According to Heather Wells's report (see Wells 1990), Stone commented that the Mountain Goat was "carved by a Crow Indian named Marvin Mooran [sic] who happened to be studying art in Chicago. Pete Stone had met him and asked him to do work for Breyer. . . . Mr. Mooran also sculpted the American Saddlebred Weanling." Jill Gutierrez's report (see Gutierrez 1990), though differing about this sculptor's last name, which she gives as "Warren" (undoubtedly she just misunderstood what Stone said), concurs that at the auction Stone described him as "a Crow Indian . . . who was an artist in Chicago in the late 1960s. He was an Indian craftsman that Peter Stone knew, and he also sculpted the Saddlebred Weanling."

Rosenthal

The Rosenthal company, to the best of my knowledge, is the manufacturer of the china poodle figurine used to make the mold for Breyer's Poodle. For further discussion see the notes for the Poodle mold above in the Dogs & Cats section.

Rich Rudish

Among the accomplishments of this well-known horseman, American Horse Show Association judge, and equine artist are illustrations for the covers of several real-horse magazines and for books by Marguerite Henry, as well as work for Hallmark Cards. The bronze statues at the Kemper Arena in Kansas City are also Rudish's creations. Two of the Traditional-size molds in Breyer's Artist Series are Rudish designs, both of them representing historical horses portrayed in Mrs. Henry's beloved book *King of the Wind*: "Sham," first released in 1984, and "Lady Roxana," first released in 1986. The design for a third Breyer mold, the Foundation Stallion, might also have originated with Rudish, specifically with a painting he created for a Hallmark calendar in the 1970s (see the notes for that mold in the Traditionals section for details). Rudish died in 1989. (Biographical information is per Breyer dealer catalogs 1984-87 and *JAH* 16/#5 Nov./Dec. 1989, inside front cover.)

Bob Scriver

Bob Scriver is celebrated for his Western and rodeo sculpture. Each year a replica of one of his sculptures is awarded by the National Cowboy Hall of Fame to the Rodeo Cowboy Association's All-Around World Champion Cowboy. He is also the author of the books *No More Buffalo* and *An Honest Try* (per *JAH* X/#2 1984, p. 9). Breyer dealer catalogs 1985-87 report that Scriver was born on a Blackfoot Indian reservation in Montana. He has sculpted two molds for Breyer: the buffalo skull on the Bolo Tie, released in 1972, and the "Buckshot" mold, introduced as part of the Artist Series in 1985. Scriver also designed three belt buckles for a business venture called Stone Associates, founded by Breyer executive Peter Stone; see Belt Buckles above in the Traditionals section for discussion.

Bonnie Shields

Author Marguerite Henry introduced Breyer to artist Bonnie Shields, of Idaho, who made the illustrations for Henry's recent book *Brown Sunshine of Sawdust Valley*. Following its long tradition of rendering Henry characters in plastic, Breyer commissioned Shields to sculpt the title character of this book, a mule named "Brown Sunshine." The mold is scheduled for release in 1996. A mule aficionado for many years, Shields has made these increasingly popular hybrid beasts the subject of her sculpture, limited-edition prints, and greeting cards. (Information is per *JAH* 22/#4 July/Aug. 1995, pp. 4-5.)

Pam Talley Stoneburner

This artist contributed two Traditional molds to the Breyer line: "Rugged Lark," released in 1989, and "Khemosabi+++," released in 1990. Prior to her work for Breyer, Stoneburner worked primarily in two-dimensional media, creating commissioned equine portraits in oils and pastels as well as some limited-edition prints. Stoneburner holds a bachelor's degree (1981) in animal science from Virginia Polytechnic Institute. (Biographical information is per *Arabian Horse World*, July 1989, p. 153; the 1989 Breyer catalog.)

Martha White

This Texas artist, lawyer, and breeder of Arabian horses collected Breyers in her childhood. She studied art and equine science in college and has created several bronze sculptures. Her first and only Breyer mold so far is "Llanarth True Briton," the large Traditional-scale Welsh cob stallion, first issued in 1994. (Biographical information is per *JAH* 20/#4 Fall 1993, p. 8.)

Roger Williams

Roger Williams sculpted most of the horse molds for the original Hartland Plastics Company, including the large and small Western Champs, which were the first and second horse molds produced by Hartland. The large Champ was first issued in 1946 or 1947; the small Champ debuted later, perhaps as late as 1952. These two molds are the ones from which Chris Hess adapted the designs for Breyer's Western Horse, introduced in 1950, and Western Pony, introduced in 1953. (Hartland information is from Fitch 1993, 2: 4-6, 15-16.)

Mold Marks

Over the years, Breyer models have had various identifying marks molded into the plastic, including Breyer Molding Company and Breyer Reeves copyright marks, the "U.S.A." mark, and others. I distinguish all these marks into two types: stamps, which have raised letters and look typeset, and engravings, which have indented letters and in most cases look handwritten, as if as if they had been carved into the soft clay of the original sculpture. I use the general term "mold marks" (or simply "marks") to refer to either or both of these types. All marks ever used on Breyer molds are discussed individually below. For details on what marks a particular mold has, see the notes for the individual molds above in the main sections of this book.

Most mold marks are located inside the models' hind legs, above the hocks. But there are exceptions. For instance, the Shetland Pony and the Stablemates have their copyright marks on the belly. The Lying Down Foal wears its marks inside the forearm. And some models of the Buffalo and Brahma Bull molds sport tiny "B" stamps on their horns.

The first mold marks ever to be used on Breyers were the "CHess" engraving and the round "Breyer Molding Co." copyright stamp. Models made before the advent of these two marks, which is to say all models made in the decade of the 1950s, have no mold marks at all (although many of the 1950s injection molds from which these models were made had stamps added to them after the 1950s). But these early models are not the only ones that have no marks. In fact they are only the first of three categories of stampless models that I have discovered in my research on mold marks—which research consists mainly of peering at the undersides of as many models as I can lay my hands on without being screeched at by protective owners. The second category comprises models of a few Traditional and Classic molds that were never given any mold marks except perhaps the "B" stamp, which was taken off the molds after a brief period. (For lists of these stampless molds, see below under Classics and Traditionals.) The third category comprises the earliest models made from certain post-1960 molds that got their stamps only sometime after they'd been released. Rugged Lark is a Traditional example: he was stampless when first issued in 1989 but had acquired the "© Breyer Reeves" stamp by late 1990. A few Classic and Stablemate molds also follow this pattern.

Most mold marks are permanent—that is, once the mark is added to the metal injection-mold at the factory, it is there for good. The "U.S.A." stamp is an example. It was added to the Clydesdale Stallion and numerous other old molds in about 1970 and to many new molds introduced 1970-75. Then the stamp was discontinued, in the sense that it was not added to any more molds after 1975. But it was never removed from the molds it had been added to; hence models made from these molds today still have the stamp. (Thus in the date spans given for permanent mold marks in the listings below, the ending date is the date when the mark was last added to any Breyer mold; it does not mean that the mark disappeared altogether from the Breyer line thereafter.) This pattern of once-it's-added-it's-there-for-good is also generally true of the round "Breyer Molding Co." stamp, other Breyer copyright marks, the several non-Breyer copyright marks, and most artist's name marks. Exceptions are the copyright mark on the Stablemate Morgan Stallion, the "U.S.A." stamp on "El Pastor," the "CHess" engraving on the Shetland Pony and Family Arabian Foal, and the round stamp on the "Halla" mold, all of which were removed from the molds at some point.

Two marks were generally not permanent—the "B" stamp and the "Hecho en Mexico" stamp. Just a few years after the "B" stamp was introduced, it vanished from most of the many injection molds to which it had been added. Only a very few molds still have their "B" today. The "Hecho en Mexico" stamp too was removed from the one mold to which it had been added, "El Pastor." The "MEXICO" stamp too may have been removed from the one mold it adorned—the Stablemate Quarter Horse Mare—but I am not sure.

Stablemates

<u>"Breyer Molding Co. © 1975" stamp and "Breyer Molding Co. © 1976" stamp, both 1975 - 1976?</u> All Stablemate molds have had one or the other of these linear stamps on the belly for most or all of their lives. Despite the "© 1976" in one of these stamps, all of the Stablemates molds were introduced in 1975, though some later in the year than others. Molds introduced in early 1975 got the "Breyer Molding Co. © 1975" version of the stamp; those introduced in late 1975 got the "Breyer Molding Co. © 1976" version. The stamps vary somewhat in size, the teeniest being those on the Thoroughbred Lying and Standing Foals.

A few Stablemates molds apparently debuted in 1975 with no stamp on them but had a stamp added some months later. These were the Arabian Stallion, Saddlebred, Thoroughbred Mare, and Thoroughbred Lying and Standing Foals, all of which eventually got the "Breyer Molding Co. © 1975" version of the stamp, and the Quarter Horse Mare and Stallion, both later given the "Breyer Molding Co. © 1976" version.

I know for certain of several Stablemate molds that at one time had a "B" stamp, and it may be that most Stablemates in production during the "B" stamp period had this mark. The only molds that could not have had the "B" are the Thoroughbred Lying and Standing Foal molds, which were discontinued before the "B" stamp was introduced. See below under Traditionals for details on this stamp.

<u>"MEXICO" stamp, late 1970s - mid-1980s.</u> One Stablemate mold—the Quarter Horse Mare—had a "MEXICO" stamp in addition to her "Breyer Molding Co. © 1976" stamp for some years, starting in the late 1970s. And some of these "MEXICO" mares have a "B" stamp as well. You wouldn't think such a small belly could accommodate so many inscriptions. See below under Traditionals for discussion of the "MEXICO" and "Hecho en Mexico" stamps.

Little Bits

<u>"© B.M.C." stamp and engraving, late 1983 - 1984.</u> Six of the seven plastic Little Bits molds have a "© B.M.C." mark, which runs vertically down the inside of the gaskin. "B.M.C." stands for "Breyer Molding Company." This mark varies somewhat in size from mold to mold, and is a stamp on some molds and an engraving on others. The one LB mold that has a different stamp is the American Saddlebred (released 1985), the last of the plastic Little Bits to appear. Instead of the "© B.M.C." mark, he has the round "Breyer Molding Co." stamp, which otherwise is found only on Traditionals and Classics. Why he got the round stamp I have no idea.

The eighth mold of the Little Bits scale, the ceramic Performing "Misty," has no mold marks.

I have never heard of a Little Bits model with a "B" stamp, and it is highly unlikely that these molds ever had it. Little Bits were first released late in 1983, which was the last year for the "B" stamp. I doubt that Breyer would have added this stamp to these new molds during the year in which the company was removing the stamp from molds of other scales.

Classics

Most Classic molds introduced prior to 1990 have the round "Breyer Molding Co." stamp. But only four Classic molds have the "U.S.A." stamp as well as the round, and they are early Classics: Rearing Stallion, introduced in 1965; Arabian Family Mare and Stallion, introduced in 1973; and Quarter Horse Family Mare, introduced in 1974. I know for sure of several Classic molds that had the "B" stamp in addition to their other stamps, and it may be that most or all the Classic molds in production during the "B" stamp period had this mark. All Classic molds introduced in the 1990s so far—namely, all the molds in the Messenger Series of Kiger Mustangs—have been given the "© Breyer Reeves" stamp. Undoubtedly this stamp will be added to new Classic molds in the future as well. See below under Traditionals for details on all these marks.

Several Classic molds were originally issued without any stamps but were given the round "Breyer Molding Co." stamp a short while later. Molds that I know of are the Mustang Family Mare and Stallion, the QH Family Stallion, "Kelso," "Man-O-War," "Silky Sullivan," "Swaps," and "Terrang."

A few Classic molds were never given any stamps except perhaps, for a short time, the "B." These molds are the Arabian Family Foal, Mustang Family Foal, Quarter Horse Family Foal, and the Polo Pony.

I know of just two small stamps that occur only on a Classic mold and no molds of other scales:

<u>"L" and "R" stamps, sometime in the period mid-1983 - 1987.</u> These little stamps, which presumably are abbreviations for "Left" and "Right," occur only on the wing tabs of some Classic "Pegasus" models. I believe the mold was first issued without these stamps and then had them added sometime later, but I am not certain of this chronology.

Dapples

<u>"© Reeves/Breyer Made in China," 1995.</u> All five Dapples horse molds introduced in 1995 have this lengthy mold stamp, which runs down the inside of a hind leg. Most of the accessories that come with the Dapples sets have mold stamps as well; see the last note for the "Amazement" mold above in the Dapples section for details.

Traditionals

Traditional molds, being far more numerous and in many cases longer-lived than molds of the other scales, have the greatest variety of mold stamps. All these stamps are listed below in chronological order.

Some Traditional molds were never given any mold stamps, except perhaps, for a short time, the "B." These molds are the Proud Arabian Foal, Race Horse, Western Pony, Donkey, "Brighty," Boxer, "Lassie," "Rin Tin Tin," and of course the old hard-plastic riders (Robin Hood et al.), who were discontinued before the Breyer Molding Company began to put stamps on its models.

<u>"Breyer Molding Co." round stamp, 1960-85, 1995.</u> This round copyright stamp is the most common mark on Breyer models. It nearly always has the copyright "©" in the center, with the name "BREYER MOLDING CO." encircling it. This stamp was in all likelihood introduced in 1960 (as I'll discuss below) and added to most molds then in production. From that time through 1984, at the end of which year Breyer Animal Creations was acquired by Reeves International, the round stamp was also put on most new Traditional and Classic molds. Traditional "Sham" and Action Stock Horse Foal, the only new Traditional or Classic molds for 1984, were the last 1980s molds of either of these scales to receive the round stamp. The Little Bits American Saddlebred mold, released in 1985, was the last 1980s Breyer mold of any size to receive the round stamp and is the only mold smaller than Classic size to have it at all. Since 1986, most new molds have been issued with one form or another of the Breyer Reeves copyright mark. But in 1995, something very surprising happened: the long-discontinued round stamp appeared on the new Ideal Quarter Horse mold. He is the first new mold to be issued with this stamp since the 1985 Little Bits horse. The explanation for this anomaly is, I believe, that this "new" 1995 mold is actually a modified re-issue of a mold from the 1970s. (For discussion, see the mold notes for the Ideal Quarter Horse above in the Traditionals section.)

The round stamp has never been removed from the molds that had it, with one exception: the "Halla" mold, which lost its round stamp when it was retooled as "Bolya." "Bolya" has a Breyer Reeves stamp.

The round stamp was certainly in use in 1963, for it is plainly visible on the buckskin Quarter Horse Gelding in the 1963 catalog. It is also certain that the stamp was in use in 1962: I have seen it on glossy muscled bay Clydesdale Stallions, which dates to 1962. I have also seen the round stamp on "Fury" Prancer models that date to no later than 1960/62: Heather Wells's white Prancer, Kim Jones's brown pinto Prancer, and my own "Black Beauty" Prancer (silver-tack version). I also am sure that the round stamp was in use in 1961: I have seen the round stamp on a woodgrain no-muscle Clydesdale Stallion, a model that dates to no later than that year, and on a no-muscle dapple gray regular-run #82, which also in all probability dates to 1961.[43] My inspections of mold marks on other models from this era make me believe the round stamp was introduced in 1960. I've never seen or heard of any stampless models of the Shetland, QH Gelding, FAM, and FAF molds, all of which first appear in the 1960 catalog (for the dating of this catalog, see in the References section below); but if the stamp were introduced after 1960, there should be stampless specimens of these molds. But I don't believe that the stamp appeared any earlier than 1960, for I have seen stampless Family Arabian Stallions in woodgrain and appaloosa, which colors were introduced in 1959. If the stamp had been introduced before 1960, none of these models should lack it. Further, 1959 was in all probability the last year of production for the old-mold Proud Arabian Mare mold and the only year of production for the appaloosa and woodgrain models of that mold, yet no specimens of these models that I know of have the round stamp.

In fact I suspect that the forced discontinuation of the PAM and PAF had something to do with Breyer's decision to introduce a copyright stamp on its molds. The timing seems too close for coincidence: the company had been producing models for a whole decade with no stamps at all, and then suddenly in 1960, in the wake of the copyright suit by Hagen-Renaker over the PAM and PAF molds, Breyer models appear with the round stamp. Perhaps during that legal contretemps Breyer learned that its own interests would be easier to defend if the models wore a copyright emblem. This is only speculation on my part, however.

There are two aberrant versions of the round stamp that I know of. One is found on the belly of a few very early Family Arabian Foal models. This stamp is like the usual round stamp except that it lacks the copyright "C" inside the circle of the stamp. The second aberrant version occurs on the leg of some early Family Arabian Stallions. This stamp is a mere fragment of the round stamp, consisting of two concentric curved lines with three upside-down letters, "MOL." For further details on these stamps, see the notes for the Family Arabian Foal and Stallion molds.

"CHess" engravings and stamps, 1960-72. These marks indicate that the mold was sculpted by Christian Hess (see above in the Sculptors section of this Appendix). Only six of the many molds sculpted by Hess carry his mark. The "CHess" mark comes in both engraving and stamp versions. Most of them omit the period after the "C" and thus look like the name of a difficult board game. The stamp versions are in all capital letters, and two of them include a year date. The stamp versions are as follows: "CHESS" on the Cantering Welsh Pony (introduced 1971); "C.HESS .71" on the Shire (introduced 1972); and "CHESS .71" on the Cow (introduced 1972). On all three of these molds the stamp is located right near the round "Breyer Molding Co." stamp. The engraving versions of the "CHess" mark, composed of handwritten letters, appear on the Five-Gaiter mold (introduced 1961/63), early models of the Shetland Pony mold (introduced 1960), and early models of the Family Arabian Foal mold (introduced 1960). On the FAF, the engraving consists of mere fragments: one vertical of the "H" and an "es." The engravings were removed from the FAF and Shetland not long after they were introduced; for discussion see the notes for these molds in the Traditionals section above. All the other molds with a "CHess" mark (stamp or engraving) still carry the mark today.

"U.S.A." stamp, 1970-75. Breyer introduced the "U.S.A." to satisfy the requirements of international trade law and discontinued the stamp when the law changed, according to Breyer executive Peter Stone (conversation of Oct. 3, 1995). As he recalled, Canada in particular required imported goods to bear some mark indicating country of origin. As I will discuss in a moment, my data on individual models indicate that the "U.S.A." was added in 1970 to many molds that had been introduced prior to 1970, and that it was added subsequently to many new molds introduced in the years 1970-75. Molds that were given the "U.S.A." stamp still retain it today, with the partial exception of "El Pastor."[44] Typically this stamp sits just above or below the round "Breyer Molding Co." stamp, but there are exceptions, such as the Shetland Pony, which has the "U.S.A." inside its thigh, far from the round stamp on its belly.

All evidence I've gathered indicates that the "U.S.A." stamp was introduced in 1970. I have a #38 gray appaloosa FAM with a "U.S.A.," Sande Schneider has a #37 gray appy FAS with this stamp, and I've seen #126 charcoal Running Stallion, #34 charcoal Fighting Stallion, #121 smoke Running Mare, and #208 seal brown Balking Mule, all with the "U.S.A." stamp. Since all these models were last made in 1970, the stamp must have been introduced no later than that year. I think it was not introduced as early as 1968: I have seen matte palomino, charcoal, and appy FAMs and FASs that do not have the "U.S.A." stamp. Since matte finish was introduced on these models in 1968 (see the notes for FAM above in the Traditionals section), the stampless models must have been made no earlier than 1968. I also think the stamp was not introduced as early as 1969, for I have found "U.S.A."-less specimens of some of the models introduced in 1969 (e.g., Lying Foals, "Adios," "Jolly Cholly"), models that subsequently did get the stamp.

Although Breyer introduced the "U.S.A." in 1970, the stamp was not put on the entire Breyer line in that year. The only molds to get the stamp then were some molds that had been introduced prior to 1970, for example, the Running Stallion and others mentioned just above. Several pre-1970 molds, such as the Belgian, Pacer, and Family Arab Foal, never received the "U.S.A." At least one pre-1970 mold, the Western Prancer, apparently did not get the stamp in 1970 but did have it added within the next couple of years. Indeed, all pre-1970 molds that ever got the "U.S.A."—there are 41 such molds in all—got it, I am virtually certain, in the period 1970-75. Of the 41, I have been able to prove by reference to individual specimens that 19 got their "U.S.A." stamp in that period for sure, most of them in 1971-73, and that 4 more got their stamp no later than 1976 (particulars are mentioned in the notes for these molds above in the Traditionals section). Probative specimens for the remaining molds may well surface in the future. Meanwhile, suffice it to say that it is highly unlikely that the "U.S.A." stamp was added to any of these old molds after 1975—for after that year, the company altogether ceased putting this stamp on new molds (as I'll discuss in a moment), so it makes little sense that they would persist in adding it to old molds.

The new molds introduced in 1970—Indian Pony, Quarter Horse Yearling, Scratching Foal, and Spanish Fighting Bull—did not get the "U.S.A." immediately, but it was added to them within a year or two of their release (for specifics, see the notes for these molds in the Traditionals section). Of the molds introduced in 1971 (CWP, new-mold PAM, PAS, and Pronghorn), 1972 ("Misty," Shire, Tennessee Walker, Calf, Cow, St. Bernard, and Bolo Tie), and 1973 ("Justin Morgan," Saddlebred Weanling, Suckling Foal, TB Mare, Rocky Mountain Goat, and Classic Arabian Foal, Mare, and Stallion), all but two (Classic Arab Foal, which never had any mold marks, and Bolo Tie, copyrighted by Bob Scriver) do have the "U.S.A." and evidently were released with it—at least I've never seen any models of these molds that didn't have this stamp. The years 1974 and 1975 seem to have been phase-out years for the "U.S.A." Only four of the seven molds introduced in 1974 have this stamp, and only one mold of the several introduced in 1975 has it—the Charolais Bull. No molds introduced after 1975 have the "U.S.A." stamp.

It is important to stress again that several older molds were *never given* the "U.S.A." stamp. The molds introduced prior to 1970 that were still in production in the 1970s but never received this stamp are the Belgian, Bighorn Ram, Boxer, Brahma Bull, Bucking Bronco, Donkey, Family Arabian Foal, Pacer, Proud Arabian Foal, "Rin Tin Tin," and Western Pony. On collectors' sales lists, models are often advertised with the statement "no U.S.A," which is supposed to indicate that the model is old (pre-1970) and therefore more valuable. For many old molds this inference is true, *but not for all*. In the case of molds that were never given this stamp, the fact that a given model has no "U.S.A." of course means absolutely nothing about its age and therefore nothing about its value. A Belgian or FAF with no "U.S.A." might have been made very recently!

"© Scriver" engraving, 1972. This mark occurs only on the Bolo Tie. A very similar mark, with Scriver's name, does however occur on the "Buckshot" mold (see below).

"© MSP 1977" stamp, late 1977. This stamp occurs only on two molds, both dogs: "Benji" and "Tiffany." "MSP" stands for Mulberry Square Productions, which is the company that made the movie starring the real dogs "Benji" and "Tiffany." For discussion see the notes for these molds above in the Dogs & Cats section.

"Hecho en Mexico" ("Made in Mexico") stamp, late 1970s. The "Hecho en Mexico" stamp occurs only on "El Pastor," inside the hind leg. A similar stamp, which says only "MEXICO," occurs only on the Stablemate Quarter Horse Mare mold, on the belly. These stamps were added when production of at least one of these two molds was exported to Mexico for a very brief period in the late 1970s.

Although Stablemate QH mares with "MEXICO" are well known among collectors, I have never seen or even heard of a collector's specimen of "El Pastor" with "Hecho en Mexico" (or with "Mexico," the stamp reported by *JAH* X/#1 1982, p. 9). An explanation for this lack of specimens was provided by former Breyer executive Peter Stone, who told me about the "Hecho en Mexico" stamp (conversations of Dec. 1995 and Jan.-Mar. 1996). This stamp, according to Stone, was definitely put on about 2,000 "El Pastors" made at a molding factory in Nogales, in the state of Sonora, Mexico, sometime in the late 1970s. Stone himself orchestrated the Mexico production as part of his plan to escape Breyer's home town of Chicago and move to Arizona. But the plan fizzled almost as soon as it began. The heads of Breyer Animal Creations at that time, Sam Stone (Peter's father) and his partner Chuck Schiff, were reluctant to lose control of the manufacturing and cast a skeptical eye at Peter's youthful schemes. Confirming their worst fears, the Mexican communist labor movement called a general strike in Nogales just as Peter's project got under way. The "El Pastor" models, which were made in a period of a few days, were simply abandoned in Mexico, to the best of Stone's recollection. Stone does not believe that any Stablemate QH Mares were made in Mexico; he has no recollection at all of such production and in fact was surprised when I told him that some of these little horses have a "MEXICO" stamp. He speculated that perhaps Breyer had scheduled this mold for transfer to Mexico and added the stamp to it in preparation, but then abandoned the plan because of the "El Pastor" debacle. But evidently Breyer left the "MEXICO" stamp on the mare for some time, for specimens abound in the U.S. (see the notes for this mold above in the Stablemates section). The dearth of "El Pastors" with "Hecho en Mexico" in U.S. collections, on the other hand, indicates that this stamp was removed from the "El Pastor" metal injection-mold immediately after the Mexico adventure. Whatever the story on the QH Mares may be, all the abandoned models of either mold would have been unpainted, for the Mexico plant did only the molding, no decorating. Where the horses ended up Stone has no idea, but he did keep a painted sample "Hecho en Mexico" "El Pastor" in his personal collection for many years. Unfortunately, only a few years ago, he relinquished the model to be repainted as a test piece for Penney's or some such since there were no other "El Pastor" bodies available. The test piece might still be in the sample room at Reeves International.

To the best of Stone's recollection, the production of Breyers in Mexico occurred in the late 1970s (the 1982 *JAH* article dates the Mexico "El Pastors" to 1980)—and this dating concurs with the rest of "El Pastor's" mold stamp history (see the notes for this mold above in the Traditionals section). Although "El Pastor's" "Hecho en Mexico" stamp was removed when production returned to the U.S., evidently the Stablemate QH Mare kept her "Mexico" stamp for some time thereafter—through at least 1984 or 1985 (see the notes for this mold above in the Stablemates section).

"B" stamp, late 1979 - 1983. This mysterious stamp was used on many and perhaps all Traditional, Classic, and Stablemate molds that were in production in the period late 1979 - 1983, except for new molds introduced 1982-83. On some molds, for example "Phantom Wings," Running Stallion, Stock Horse Stallion, Western Horse, and Classic Andalusian Mare, the "B" is upside-down (or backwards, however you prefer to think of it). But on other molds the "B" is right side up.

The evidence that I have collected indicates that the "B" stamp first appeared in 1979, on at least a couple of molds. The lighter version of the 1979 SR dapple Clydesdale Mare and one version of the 1979 SR dapple gray Belgian have the "B." Not all 1979 dapple Belgians and Clyde Mares have this stamp, however, which suggests that these horses were made in successive batches (as is also indicated by the fact that both of these SRs come in more than one version) and that only the batches made later in the year got the stamp.

Of the many molds that got this stamp, most had it removed within a very few years, but not all molds had it removed at once. On some, such as the Family Arabians and Running Mare and Foal, it was gone by 1982 (the 1982 SR light chestnut FAS and SR dark chestnut FAM and FAF do not have a "B," nor do the 1982 SR Running Mare and Foal in red roan and Running Mare in palomino). Though the stamp was definitely discontinued as of 1982 in the sense that it was not put on any new molds introduced in 1982 or later, nonetheless some molds that had received the stamp hung onto it at least into 1982. For instance, the 1982 SR black Belgian with blue/white tail ribbon has the "B." Many molds that had the "B" certainly lost it by 1983—the stamp is not on the 1983 SR gray appy Stock Stallion, the 1983 SR palomino Foundation Stallion, or either version of the Penney's SR buckskin "Lady Phase" (1983 and 1984). But some molds kept their "B" into 1983. For instance, some black-point Proud Arabs have a "B" (Jo Kulwicki, Sande Schneider, and Chelle Fulk all have black-point PASs like this; Chelle also has a black-point PAF with the "B"). Since the black-points were, according to Breyer catalog photos, made 1983-84, the "B" stamp must have been used on this mold at least into 1983. But since not all black-point Proud Arabs have the "B" (Jo Kulwicki's mare, for example, does not) the stamp must have been removed from the mold no later than 1984.

A few molds that got the "B" stamp never had it removed. These molds are the Rearing Stallion (Classic scale); large Black Angus Bull; Brahma Bull, which had the "B" stamps on its legs removed but still has tiny "B"s on its horns; and Buffalo, which still has a tiny "B" stamp on its left horn (the mold used to have a "B" on the right horn too, but that eventually disappeared—"Tatanka" does not have it).

On most models with a "B" stamp, the stamp lurks on the hind leg opposite the leg with the copyright stamp. The Stablemates, however, wear their "B" stamps on their undersides. The Brahma Bull and, as just mentioned, the Buffalo have a tiny "B" on their horns. Oddly, some molds have their "B" stamp upside-down (or backwards, however you care to think of it)—the "Phantom Wings" mold, for instance, and the Western Horse, among others.

Evidently the "B" stamp was introduced when Breyer stopped using its traditional cellulose acetate plastic and began using a type of plastic called cellulose propionate. (Both types are discussed in a 1983 newsletter titled *Insights*, published by Eastman Chemical Products, which manufactured these plastics under the brand name Tenite.) This explanation of the "B" is given in a hobby publication issued in 1981 or 1982, that is, during the "B" era. The publication is a handout titled "Mold Markings and Factory Finishes in Date Order," written by collector Becky Helm as part of her Model Horse Council information service. Becky states on the handout: "'B' 1980-current / This was added to indicate the change from Acetate to Proprionate [*sic*] plastic." The technical nature of this explanation strongly suggests that it was not mere speculation but news from the factory, and the timing of the handout indicates that the news was fresh. When I asked Breyer executive Peter Stone about this account of the "B" in October 1995, he had no recollection about the "B" stamp per se, but he was certain that Breyer had indeed used propionate for virtually the whole plastic Breyer line for a couple of years during the oil-crisis era since this type of plastic cost less than acetate, which became scarce and expensive in that period (see Breyer Company History above in this Appendix). He was not sure of the precise years that Breyer used propionate, but it is well known that the oil crisis raged through 1980 and tapered off over the next two years, which timing coincides with the "B" era.[45] Furthermore, according to Stone, propionate, which is lighter weight than acetate, cannot be mixed with acetate; it has various chemical properties that make such mixing an absolute "no no." This means that in regrinding scraps of molded plastic for reuse—an economy measure that the company has always practiced—Breyer would have had to be careful not to mix propionate scraps with any acetate the company may have used in this period. Thus Stone finds it entirely plausible that the company would have added a mark to models made of propionate to distinguish them clearly from acetate products. Why they chose a "B" rather than a "P" for "propionate" isn't clear, but in any case, propionate caused Breyer many headaches and so was discontinued after roughly two years. This would certainly explain why the "B" stamp was discontinued so soon after being introduced. It is also interesting that the dates of the "B" stamp era coincide fairly neatly with the omission of all mention of plastic in the 1978-84 dealer catalogs. Most previous catalogs and all subsequent ones mention cellulose acetate.

"P^P" stamp, sometime in the period 1972-83. This mysterious stamp exists only on the saddles of later Western Prancers. It is located underneath the saddle seat. My dating for the stamp is based on two specimens. The first is Collector Sande Schneider's saddle with no stamp, which came new in a sealed Showcase Collection box; also enclosed in the box was a 1971 manual, so we know the stamp was not in use this early. The second specimen is a saddle in my possession which has a "P^P" stamp under the seat and also a "B" stamp inside one fender; the "B" tells us that the "P^P" was introduced no later than 1979-83 (see above for dating of the "B"). The stamp was never removed from the mold—collector Kay Schlumpf has a saddle with the "P^P" stamp only, which came on a chestnut pinto Western Prancer #1120, dating to 1983-85, and the "P^P" is still on the saddle of "Ranger" #889, released in 1994. Breyer executive Peter Stone does not know what this stamp means or why it was put on the saddle mold (conversation of Oct. 4, 1995).

"© B.-M." stamp, 1984. This stamp is a mere ghost that appears only on the Action Stock Horse Foal, on the hind leg opposite the round "Breyer Molding Co." stamp. It is reminiscent of the "© B.M.C." stamp on Little Bits molds. The faintness of this "© B.-M." stamp, together with the fact that this mold has the round stamp, suggests that perhaps the company first thought it would use "© B.-M." on this mold but then changed its mind and effaced it, but not thoroughly. On my models, this ghost stamp is most visible on early models but can still be discerned (in part at least) on recent models.

The years 1985 and 1986 were transitional for mold marks because of the Reeves acquisition in late 1984. Only one mold introduced in this period, the Little Bits American Saddlebred (1985), was given the round "Breyer Molding Co." stamp. All the other molds introduced in these years—"Buckshot" (1985), "Phar Lap" (1985), "Kipper" (1986), "Lady Roxana" (1986), and "Touch Of Class" (1986)—have neither the old round stamp nor the "© Breyer Reeves" stamp that has since become standard. Instead, each has a unique mark, consisting of a copyright engraving with the year and/or name of the copyright holder. The engraving on "Lady Roxana" is the only one of these five marks that even mentions Reeves. The five marks are as follows:

"© 1984 and TM 20th Century Fox" engraving, 1985. The only mold that has this mark is "Phar Lap," first released in 1985. The mark is still on the mold today. 20th Century Fox is the movie studio that released the film *Phar Lap*.

"© 1985 Bob Scriver" engraving, 1985. The only mold that has this mark is "Buckshot" (although the Bolo Tie has a very similar mark, with Scriver's name; see above). The mark was still on the "Buckshot" mold when the mold was discontinued at the end of 1995.

"©1985" engraving, 1986. The only mold that has this mark is "Touch Of Class," first released in 1986. The mark is still on the mold today.

"© 1986 Reeve Intl." engraving, 1986. The only mold that has this mark is the "Lady Roxana." The mark is still on the mold today. The omission of the letter "s" from the end of "Reeve" in this engraving is evidently a mistake, for the name of the company that owns Breyer is Reeves International.

"© 1986 •thelwell•" engraving, 1986. The only mold that has this mark is "Kipper," which was produced just briefly, in 1986.

Since 1987, several new mold marks have been introduced:

"© Breyer Reeves" stamp, 1987 - current as of 1996. This is now the company's standard stamp. The two new molds for 1987—"Sherman Morgan" and "Secretariat"—were the first molds to receive it. Most plastic molds introduced since then also have this copyright stamp (but two of these didn't get it right away; see the notes for the "Rugged Lark" and "Halla" molds in the listings above). This stamp was also added to the Western Horse mold in 1991, the last year of production for palomino #57. This ancient mold, the very first animal mold made by Breyer, never had the round "Breyer Molding Co." stamp, although it has had the "U.S.A" stamp since about 1970. The "© Breyer Reeves" stamp varies somewhat in size and comes in two basic versions. In one version, which appears for example on "Pluto," the letters are on a slightly raised, flat, oblong area, so that the stamp looks like a little plaque molded into the plastic. The other version, as on "John Henry" for example, lacks the flat plaque and is therefore less obtrusive. All molds that have gotten this stamp in either version still have it today.

"© Breyer Reeves" engraving, 1992 - current as of 1996. This engraving occurs on Breyer's fine porcelain molds: the three molds of the Evolution Of The Horse series—Icelandic Horse, released in 1992; Shire Horse, released 1993; and Spanish Barb, released 1994—and the Premier Arabian Mare, released in 1995 as the first in the Premier Fine Porcelain Series of costumed horses. Presumably it will also be on the porcelain palomino Saddlebred in Western parade tack, due out in 1996.

"92" engraving, 1992. This little engraving appears only on the fine porcelain Icelandic Horse; it is on the thigh opposite the one with the "© Breyer Reeves" engraving.

"93" engraving, 1993. This small engraving appears only on the fine porcelain Shire Horse, inside the left hind leg.

"94" engraving, 1994. This small engraving appears only on the fine porcelain Spanish Barb, inside the left hind leg.

"© Reeves Breyer" stamp, 1994. This stamp, which is a variation of the "© Breyer Reeves" stamp (plaqueless version), occurs on only one mold: "Llanarth True Briton," introduced in 1994.

"95" engraving, 1995. This small engraving appears only on the fine porcelain Premier Arabian Mare, inside the left hind leg.

"95" stamp, 1995. This stamp occurs on most specimens of the 1995 QVC special-run Western Horse and "Sham" and on some specimens of the 1996 "Tseminole Wind" SR (not listed in this book), which is also made from the "Sham" mold.

"AQHA '95" stamp, 1995. This new stamp occurs on 1995 models of the Ideal Quarter Horse mold and also, inadvertently, on the models issued in the first few months of 1996.

"Suzann Fiedler" stamp, 1995. This new stamp in script letters occurs only on the belly of the Ideal Quarter Horse mold, first released in 1995. The stamp is the signature of the sculptor of the trophy piece from which this mold was adapted.

"JEH stamp," 1995-. This tiny stamp occurs on the "Mesteño"Progeny mold (introduced 1995), two 1996 molds ("Big Ben" and "Henry" Fjord, not listed in this book), and perhaps one or two other molds. The letters in the stamp are the initials of John E. Harrold, the engineer who made the metal injection-molds for these horses.

Production Process

Sculpting

Sculptor Rowland Cheney, at the West Coast Model Horse Collector's Jamboree in August 1993, gave a very interesting presentation on the engineering challenges of sculpting a new mold for Breyer. Of first importance to a free-standing Breyer model is the consideration of balance. But an original sculpture, Cheney pointed out, is usually created from clay or similar material on an armature attached to a base; hence problems of balance simply don't arise for the original piece. Even if it were removed from the base, a solid clay sculpture would not necessarily exhibit the same properties of balance as a hollow-bodied plastic horse of the same shape. Consequently, the sculptor has to do a lot of calculating to determine whether the clay sculpture will translate into a well-balanced plastic figure, and even then he can't be sure he has succeeded until the plastic figures have been molded. Second, the sculptor has to take into account the limitations of injection molding with respect to shape. A sculpture suitable for injection molding can't have undercut angles or other contours that would cause the plastic figure to interlock with its steel mold like a hook in an eye. The molten plastic can be injected into such a mold perfectly well, but the resulting plastic figure can't be removed from the mold without being mangled. Finally, as if these engineering problems weren't enough to thwart artistic vision, Cheney learned that Breyer puts the box before the horse. Literally. Before he started work on "Mesteño," Breyer handed Cheney a box and said, "The model has to fit in here."

When the original sculpture is completed, plaster or resin castings are made from it. Plaster was used until about 1992 or 1993, when resin became the medium of choice for the castings, according to former *JAH* editor Megan Thilman Quigley (Haynet email, Feb. 26, 1996). These castings are often painted and used as photo models for the Breyer dealer catalog in the first year of release of new molds because the plastic models are not yet ready. For the same reason, as I learned from model-horse hobbyist and artist Karen Gerhardt, painted castings are also often used for display at the New York City Toy Fair, a major toy-buyers convention held in January each year. Karen was employed by Breyer in 1990 and 1991 "to paint the prototype new molds for the catalog photo shoots, and for display at the NYC Toy Fair," as she wrote to me. When she received white plaster castings of the "Pluto" and "Misty's Twilight" sculptures from Breyer in 1990, she had to "patch holes, cracks, and pits" in them before starting to paint. She created a lovely subtle dappling for "Pluto," which shows up on the plaster model on the cover of the 1991 catalog but was not adopted on the production-run plastic models. Her color design for "Misty's Twilight," however, which she developed from photos of the real horse, was followed quite closely on the production line, "even to the white/brown/black fade on the tail." Karen was told by Breyer that the plaster castings are also used to make the metal injection-molds and whatever painting masks might be needed for the planned models. Things went differently, however, with the "Bolya" mold, the prototype of which Karen painted in 1991 to be photographed for the 1992 catalog. The prototype "Bolya" was not a plaster casting but a remade "Halla" plastic model. For details see the notes for "Halla" in the Traditionals section above.

Molding

Most Breyer horses and other animals are made of high-quality cellulose acetate plastic. For many years, Breyer used a brand of cellulose acetate called Tenite, manufactured by Eastman Chemical Products, Inc., a subsidiary of Eastman Kodak Company.[46] References to Tenite cellulose acetate occur in all Breyer catalogs from ca.1954 through 1970, in the 1971 manual (there is no catalog for that year), and in catalogs 1976-77. The 1972-75 and 1978-84 catalogs omit all mention of plastic, perhaps for reasons concerning Breyer's use of lower-grade cellulose acetate and cellulose propionate during the oil-crisis era. Catalogs 1985-96 mention simply "cellulose acetate" or "durable engineering-grade plastic" or "durable, engineering-grade cellulose acetate."

The process by which the models are formed is called injection molding.[47] In this process, melted plastic is injected under high pressure into a metal mold and allowed to cool until the plastic figure solidifies. The metal molds are very costly to make, and there is only one for each Breyer horse or other figure. The metal molds for Traditionals, Classics, Little Bits, the Stablemate Saddlebred (the first Stablemate mold created), and the old Robin Hood rider have cavities for molding only one model at a time.[48] The metal molds for the other Stablemates have cavities for molding two models at a time, but the two models are different—for example, the Lying and Standing Foal cavities are side by side in a single metal mold. The only metal mold I know of that has cavities for producing two identical models at a time is the mold for the Howdy Doody version of the old Canadian Mountie rider.[49]

Prior to 1993, the metal molds were foundry-cast from Kirksite steel. The only exception was the very first horse mold, the Western Horse, which Breyer sculptor Chris Hess made from steel by carving and cutting. Since 1991 or 1992, new Breyer molds have been made from beryllium copper, a harder, more rust-resistant metal that allows a tighter seal between the parts of the mold when the plastic is injected, so that there is less "flash" (fringes of excess plastic) created by leakage of molten plastic between the metal parts. The creation of a metal mold requires great skill and craftsmanship and is extremely expensive—Breyer pays about $50,000 for a single new mold.[50]

A metal injection-mold consists of the mold base, which is a big metal case, and the mold core. For all Breyer figures except Stablemates, the core contains four metal forms that look like horse bas-reliefs or Jell-O molds: a cavity form and a core form for each of the two halves of the model. Each core-and-cavity pair of forms fits together like nested bowls. The melted plastic is injected into the narrow space between the two forms of each nested pair, so that a model comes out of the mold in hollow halves—except for Stablemates, which are molded whole and are solid. The plastic is melted at about 430 degrees F. and injected into the molds under 240 tons of pressure. The mold opens and releases the molded halves after about a minute. The warm, soft halves are put onto cooling frames that hold them in shape until they are fully cool and hard. Each different Breyer figure has to have its own cooling frames designed especially to fit it. Next, the edges of the halves are soaked briefly in acetone to re-soften them, and the halves are bonded together under pressure. Each Breyer figure also has to have its own soaking and bonding fixtures, which are made of metal. The bonded seams of the plastic model are then sanded, the surface buffed, and the model wiped carefully by hand with an acetone-moistened cloth in preparation for painting. As a quality-control measure, at least one out of every 40 models is tested and weighed to make sure it contains the proper amount of plastic.[51]

Most Breyer models have a small hole in the corner of the mouth or in one nostril. The holes are not flaws but are deliberately made—they are created in the metal injection molds.[52] The purpose of the holes is to allow hot air to escape from the hollow cavity inside the models in case the models become overheated, as they easily can if they are shipped during the summer, left in enclosed vehicles in the sun, displayed in windows facing full sunlight, and so on. Hot air trapped inside the model can ruin it by causing it to bloat into an absurd rendition of Porky Pig. It is always wise to check a model's torso, neck, and head for heat-bloat before purchasing. The effect can be subtle and is often visible only when the model is viewed from the top or the front.

Painting

The decoration of a Breyer model is a complicated process involving many steps of airbrushing and paintbrush detailing, all of which is done by hand—with the result that at least slight variations from model to model are inevitable. On many models, layers of different colors are applied to create a rich, complexly shaded color. Many models also require the use of metal stencils or "masks," as they are called, which keep the paint off of the masked area while uncovered areas are sprayed. There are two types of paint masks: small ones, called clamp masks, used for areas such as manes, tails, blazes, and molded-on halters, and larger ones, called book masks, used to make body patterns such as pinto and appaloosa.[53]

Test-color models. Experienced collectors are aware (often sorely) that when new models come out, they don't always look quite so spectacular as the specimens in Breyer catalogs. In some cases, particularly when the model is a new mold, the catalog models are painted plaster or resin castings rather than injection-molded plastic specimens. In other cases the catalog models are plastic test-color models: models on which new color and pattern ideas are tried out prior to mass-production. Such pieces appear in dealer catalogs because at the time the catalogs are prepared—months in advance of the year whose inventory they advertise—the prototype or test pieces are often the only samples of new models available to be photographed. For the same reason, test models often appear in retail catalogs that offer special runs, such as the Penney's holiday catalog.

Test-color models are carefully painted by hand with any white areas masked off with grease pencil or similar material rather than a metal mask. Thus they typically look more crisp and detailed than mass-produced models—compare the "Breezing Dixie" in the 1988 catalog with a production-line specimen, for instance. Sometimes test pieces not only look more crisp but even have a different pattern from the mass-produced models. Such discrepancies can happen when it is discovered, after the test model has been photographed, that such and such a feature of the test doesn't translate well into mass production techniques, or doesn't look right, or is too complicated, or isn't realistic, or whatever. See the entry for the chestnut pinto Running Mare above in the Traditionals section for an example of what can go awry. But the deviation of mass-produced models from test colors is sometimes a blessing. The mass-produced "Yellow Mount," for instance, to my taste anyway vastly improves upon the test color "Yellow Mount" with white spots that look like goose eggs that appears in catalogs and manuals 1970-75—an inordinate number of years for a test color to appear in catalogs under any circumstances.

Mold Variations

Variations of Shape

Numerous Breyer molds exhibit variations of shape, some trivial and some very interesting and collectible. Shape variations can be divided into three different types. What I call *true mold variations* are created by changes in the metal injection-mold. The foreleg up and foreleg down Stock Horse Mares are variations of this type. The various eye-versions of the Running Mare too are examples of this type, although some of the changes here were accidental. The second type, *separate-parts variations*, are created by the addition of separately molded parts to the model. Examples are the polled and horned versions of the Cow and the Charolais Bull, which have separately molded horn/ear parts that are glued onto the models' heads after molding. The third type, *post-molding variations*, are changes made to the individual models at the factory after molding. Examples are the whole-hoof and pared-hoof versions of the Stock Horse Stallion mold (the hoof is pared after being molded whole) and the front legs of the "Sombra" and "Mesteño" versions of the "Mesteño Challenger" mold ("Sombra's" front legs are bent further after being molded in the same position as "Mesteño's"). To my knowledge most flocked models are also examples of this type in that they have their plastic tails removed after molding to make room for their hair tails—the exception being the Saddlebred Weanling, which had her tail removed from the injection mold itself in preparation for the flocked rocking horses that were made from the mold. The following is a complete list of the mold shape-variations I know of, with the exception of most flocked models. (See Flocked Models above in the Traditionals section for a full list.) For details on the mold variations listed here, see the notes for the individual mold entries above.

Traditional horses. *Clydesdale Stallion:* muscle and no-muscle versions. *Family Arab Mare:* normal version with tail standing free and "in-between mare" version with tail attached to buttock (never released for sale). *Family Arab Stallion*: version with realistic scrotum and version with bar-like scrotum. *Family Arab Foal:* versions with rounded, in-curving eartips and with straight pointed eartips. *Fighting Stallion*: version with realistic scrotum and version with bar-like scrotum. *Five-Gaiter:* version with full tassel on the mane ribbon and version with nipped tassel; also diorchid and monorchid versions of the nipped-tassel horses. *Foundation Stallion:* full stallion version and version without sheath. *"Gem Twist"*: 39-braid version and 20-braid version. *"Halla"*: "Halla" (braided-mane) version and "Bolya" (loose-mane) version. *Hanoverian*: versions with and without brand. *Lying Down Foal*: normal foal and unicorn versions; also a foal version with no mane ridges (only one specimen known to me). *"Morganglanz"*: pared-toes and intact-toes versions; versions with brand and without brand. *Mustang:* version with pared left front hoof and version with intact hoof. *Proud Arabian Mare:* old-mold version with straight foreleg and new-mold version with foreleg splayed. *Running Foal:* versions with pared right hind hoof and with intact hoof. *Running Mare:* early normal-eye, flat-eyeball, swollen-eye, and repaired normal-eye versions. *Running Stallion:* horse version and unicorn version with horn and beard; the beards on old and new Unicorns also differ. *Saddlebred Weanling:* version with tail tip attached to butt and version with tail tip unattached. *"Sham"*: wheat-ear and no-wheat-ear versions. *Stock Horse Mare:* foreleg-raised and foreleg-down versions. *Stock Horse Stallion:* versions with pared right hind hoof and with intact right hind hoof. *Trakehner*: version with and version without brand. *Western Horse:* diamond-conchas version and normal version with rounded conchas.

Classic horses. *"Hobo" on stand:* version with and version without brand on horse and writing on stand. *Lipizzan:* regular and "Pegasus" versions. *"Mesteño" Challenger:* "Mesteño" Challenger version with right hind hoof flat on the ground, and "Sombra" version with right hind hoof cocked. *Polo Pony on stand:* old version of stand with smaller hole, etc., and new version of stand with larger hole, different woodgraining, etc.

Cattle and hogs. *Black Angus Bull (polled, walking):* poodle-cut, semi-rough-coat, and full-rough-coat versions. *Brahma Bull:* bull version and steer version (only one specimen known to me). *Charolais Bull:* polled and horned versions. *Cow:* polled and horned versions, with at least four different styles of horns. *"Jasper" the Hog:* straight-ear and bent-ear versions.

Little Bits horses. *Performing Misty:* version with stool attached to hoof and version with stool separate.

Old hard-plastic riders. *Canadian Mountie:* handsome face and Howdy Doody face versions. *Indian:* feather-hole and no-feather-hole versions.

Accessories. *Old-style saddles for the Western Horse:* numerous variations; see note 7 for Western Horse. *Old-style saddles for the Western Pony and "Fury" Prancer:* short-fender and long-fender versions. *Saddle blanket from the Canadian Mountie set and riderless "Fury" Prancers:* versions with and without ridge lines.

Variations of Size

Many collectors have been surprised to discover that different models of the same mold are different sizes. Collector Gale Good acquainted me with the size-variation phenomenon a few years ago. She had tried to put her newer Five-Gaiters on the same shelf with her older Five-Gaiters, but the newer ones wouldn't fit—their ears ran into the shelf above. Subsequently, Gale and I compared an assortment of Belgian models, only to discover that some stood more than a quarter inch taller than others at the croup, back, and ears. The taller ones were proportionally wider too; they were bigger in every direction, so none of the models appeared distorted (as they would if they were victims of heat-bloat). Various other collectors have pointed out size differences among Family Arabian Mares, Proud Arabian Stallions, Running Mares, Scratching Foals, and more. Presumably most or all Breyer molds exhibit the size-variation syndrome to some degree. Size variation is surprising because there is only one steel injection-mold per Breyer figure—thus the variations cannot be attributed to differing sizes of injection molds.

One intuitive guess about what causes size variation is that Breyer's cellulose acetate plastic might shrink with age. However, collector and mechanical engineer Elaine Lindelef thinks this is improbable. To shrink over time, models would either have to be under the right sort of physical stress, which is not likely in the typical conditions in which models are kept, or be "outgassing," that is, evaporating molecules into the air, which would create toxic gas that would poison collectors across the land. (Toxic gas is, however, a hazard for hobbyists who remake plastic models by heating.) I would add that the shrinking-with-age idea also stumbles by assuming that newer models are always bigger than older ones. This is not the case—newer models are sometimes smaller than older ones. For example, several #109 dapple Five-Gaiters (1987-88) that I know of, my own included, are smaller than older Five-Gaiters. My #109 is a good quarter of an inch shorter at the eartips than my #52 sorrel Five-Gaiter from the 1960s. So the shrinking-with-age explanation won't do. The far more likely explanation for size variation, according to Elaine, has to do with the fact that shrinkage occurs at the factory during the molding process. Molten plastic shrinks as it cools, and the rate of shrinkage varies as a result of varying humidity, temperature, and other conditions. Elaine cites the following passage on plastics from an engineering reference manual titled *Machinery's Handbook 24*: "Shrinkage in a given material can vary with thickness, direction of the flow of the plastics in the mold, and molding conditions." Thus models of the same mold may already differ in size when they emerge from the factory.

Molded-On Tack & Brands

Tack

Twelve different plastic Breyer animal molds—all of them old, first issued in the 1950s and 1960s—have tack that is part of the mold and therefore not removable. (I am not counting mane and tail ribbons or bobs as tack). "Fury" Prancer, Western Horse, and Western Pony all have molded-on bridles and breastcollars; the Western Prancer has a molded-on bridle but no breastcollar. All these horses are molded with holes through their mouths, which accommodate the addition of wire bits and chain reins to complete the bridles. All of them also come with removable plastic saddles. The Balking Mule too has a molded-on bridle, complete with small molded-on blinkers, but he has no added bit, reins, or saddle. Several molds have molded-on halters: "Man O' War" (Traditional); Pacer; Quarter Horse Gelding; Race Horse, which also came with removable plastic race saddle; and polled walking Black Angus Bull. The Poodle has a molded-on collar. The Old Timer takes the prize as the plastic Breyer with the most molded-on tack: he has a bridle, collar, and body harness all molded on. The blinkers on his bridle are separately molded parts attached after molding. He also has a removable plastic hat with two holes in it to fit over his ears.

The Balking Mule, which debuted in 1968, was the last plastic Breyer to be created with molded-on tack. One concern dissuading Breyer from creating more molds of this type may have been the labor involved in finishing such models after molding: painting the slender straps and tiny buckles and studs of molded-on tack is detail work requiring extra time and care. Breyer may also have been influenced by model-horse hobbyists' dislike of molded-on tack. Many hobbyists, particularly those interested in model-horse showing—an activity that developed to national proportions in the 1970s—craft wonderfully realistic and detailed leather tack for their models. Molded-on tack interferes with the use of leather tack and thus diminishes an original-finish model's versatility in the show ring; it is also a nuisance to sand off in the process of customizing models.

Breyer has revived its tradition of molded-on tack with the inauguration of the Premier Fine Porcelain Series of horses in costume. The first piece in this series, the Premier Arabian Mare (released in 1995), has molded-on bridle, saddle, blanket, and breastcollar, all adorned with molded-on tassels and all elaborately hand painted. Undoubtedly the costumes of the future pieces in this series will also have their outfits molded on.

Brands

Seven different Breyer molds have (or had) the interesting detail of a brand molded into the horse's thigh or shoulder: Hanoverian (whose brand, however, was removed prior to the release of the "Gifted" model), "Hobo" with removable stand (whose brand was removed prior to release of SR "Nevada Star"), "Legionario," "Morganglanz" (whose brand was removed prior to release of "Black Beauty 1991"), "Roemer," "Smoky," and Trakehner (whose brand was removed in preparation for a special run in spring 1996). "Morganglanz" and Trakehner have the same brand, but each of the other five molds has its own unique brand. When a mold has a brand, of course the brand becomes a feature of every model made from that mold. Consequently, numerous catalog-run and special-run models have molded-in brands. On some models, such as "Legionario III" #68, the brand is delicately painted in with black for emphasis, while on others, such as Trakehner #54, it is simply left the color of the horse. For descriptions of the molded-in brands, see the notes for the molds listed above.

Several Breyer models have brands that are not molded in but only painted on: SR "Mustang Lady," the SR dinner model for BreyerFest 1991, has a Bureau of Land Management freeze brand painted in white along her neck, as does regular-run #929 "Cheyenne." "Bright Zip," the SR dinner model for BreyerFest 1994, has the ranch brand of owner John Lyons painted in white on the shoulder. "Mego," the SR dinner model for BreyerFest 1995, has a diamond-D brand painted on his left thigh. Regular-run #938 "Shane" has a rocking-B brand on his left shoulder. Finally, the SR dark bay Running Mare made for State Line Tack has a white "SLT" brand painted on her left hip. See the entries for these models for further description of these brands.

Finishes

Collectors use three basic categories for the finishes on Breyer models: glossy, which is very shiny; semigloss, which is somewhat shiny; and matte, which is dull, sometimes even powdery looking.

Glossy Finish

Glossy finish properly so called consists of a coating of shiny varnish added over the paint. This finish was applied to many (but not all) early Breyers, starting with the models of the early 1950s. Gloss finish was phased out for the most part in the late 1960s. In the 1968 catalog, all colors of the Family Arabs are for the first time specified as "mat" (*sic*). A few models, notably the dapple gray Old Timer and the Brahma Bull, carried their gloss finishes into the 1970s. The company's idea in using gloss finish in the early years was to give the models the appearance of china figurines.

The glossy tradition was revived in 1988 when Breyer produced the special-run alabaster Family Arabs for Enchanted Doll House. These three models, which were advertised as commemorative reissues of the alabaster Family Arabs from the 1960s, have a glossy varnish finish. The 1990 Sears holiday catalog brought another wave of neo-glossy special runs: a set of three Traditional models—"Man O' War," "Secretariat," and "Sham"—which had their regular run colors but which were coated with a high-gloss varnish. More recent glossy revivals are the 1992 Commemorative Edition "Memphis Storm," the 1984 SR Classic "Black Beauty," and the 1994-release "CH Imperator" American Saddlebred.

Semigloss & Matte Finishes

Semigloss finish is a shiny factory finish due to shiny paint or plastic. Semigloss models can be almost as shiny as true glossies, but the shine is from the paint or the plastic itself—not from an added coat of varnish, as on a true glossy model. Semigloss finish can be silky smooth or have a textured look and feel. Matte finish is a dull, non-shiny factory finish, which can be smooth or textured, and which at its most extreme has a powdery or bisque look. But more average matte finishes can have a lot of sheen, and the line between matte and semigloss is very far from definite. In fact the term "matte" is often used loosely by collectors to mean simply "non-glossy," referring to all models, including semiglossies, that don't have a varnish coating. Whether a model emerges from the factory with a matte or a semigloss finish seems to be an entirely random matter, depending on the particular batch of paint the horse was colored with or the amount of buffing his plastic surface was given before painting, etc. Thus the first specimen of the dapple gray "Adios" special run you happen to pick up, for example, may be quite a high semigloss, but the next specimen may well be dead matte.

In my opinion, the very earliest Breyer horses—the white Western Horses with brown-shaded mane and tail, produced in 1950—are matte or semigloss, for they do not appear to have a true gloss coating. Matte and semigloss finishes were continued in the mid to late 1950s on the rider models and the Donkey, Elephant, "Rin Tin Tin," and "Lassie." Most woodgrain models, the first of which debuted in 1959, are also matte or slightly semigloss. Non-woodgrain matte and semigloss horses abounded in the early 1960s; the 1963 catalog has many of them, right along with the numerous glossies. They are such models as the smoke and alabaster Running Mare and Foal, the bay Clydesdale Stallion, and the buckskin Mustang. Since the late 1960s, matte and semigloss have had the Breyer field almost completely to themselves. Matte and semigloss finishes are far more realistic than glossy, and although it is often said that Breyer decided to phase out gloss finish as an economy measure, I can only think that the difference in realism, a quality always in demand among collectors and long touted by the company, must have contributed to that decision.

Eyes & Hooves

Eyes

The vast majority of Breyer horses have simple, monochrome black or dark gray eyes, sometimes left matte but often brought to life with a coating of glossy varnish, even on the tiny eyes of the Stablemates models. This monochrome coloring has been varied on a few models in Breyer history. Some early palomino, brown pinto, and white Western Horses, Western Ponies, and "Fury" Prancers from the 1950s have gold eyes, though these are now typically so tarnished as to look rather gray or brownish. The "albino" Five-Gaiter and Mustang of the 1960s were for a brief period given monochrome "red" eyes. The color is not the blood red of an albino laboratory rat's eyes but a dark reddish brown. Some Fighting Stallions, Five-Gaiters, and Mustangs of the 1960s have pink shading on the inside corners of the eyes.

Other forms of eye detailing have occurred more frequently. Starting in the later 1950s, many (but not all) Breyer horses and cattle were given the attractive detail of eyewhites—dabs or lines of white paint applied by hand to the outer corners of the models' black eyes. On many models, particularly earlier ones, the eyewhites are small, consisting of a couple of brushstrokes of thin white paint forming a < shape. Some later models have larger eyewhites, filling in the whole outer corner of the eye. The brush strokes used to apply these larger whites varied, to judge from my own models—a bay Running Mare and a couple of early "Man O' Wars." Early "Man O' War" #47s are particularly notable for their huge eyewhites. One of mine has his whites painted on over the black of the eyeballs, the other has the whites painted first, with the black applied over the outer edge of the white. I believe that eyewhites were probably discontinued by 1969, and almost certainly by 1970, for no eyewhites are visible on any models in Breyer collector's manuals from 1969 on. Although big whites are still visible on Pacer #46 in the 1970 dealer catalog, the photo used here is the same one used in 1967 and 1968 and thus may well not reflect 1969-70 models.

Breyer revived and improved upon the tradition of eye detailing in 1987 with the introduction of "Cips," the first Limited Edition (LE) model. This model has tri-color eyes, consisting of black pupils, brown irises outlined with black, and painted eyewhites in the outer corners. These eyes are much more detailed than the early "eyewhite" eyes. Since "Cips," several more horses have been given tri-color eyes: "Breezing Dixie" (LE 1988); "Silver" Quarter Horse SR (Commemorative Edition 1989) and most subsequent CE models; signing party SR red roan "Lady Phase" (1989); BreyerFest dinner model SR "Mego" (1995); and BreyerFest volunteer SR palomino "Lady Phase" (1995). "Domino" (CE 1993) has a tri-color eye on the left, but on the right side he introduces something new for Breyer: a "blue eye," which has a black pupil encircled by a hand-painted pale blue iris. LE models issued from 1989 on have had ordinary eyes rather than tri-color. ("Fugir Cacador," LE 1993, has tri-color eyes only in the Breyer catalog.) All the fine-porcelain pieces issued by Breyer so far—the three horses in the Evolution Of The Horse series and the Arabian Mare in the Premier Fine Porcelain Series—also have tri-color eyes, though in a somewhat different style from the eyes of the plastic models just listed. The fine porcelains' eyes are predominantly brown and black, with a "sparkle" dot of white. Finally, all five horse models in the Dapples series introduced by Breyer in 1995 also have intricately painted eyes: brown and black with white "sparkle" dot and eyewhites, augmented with black, brown, or blue eyeliner and, on some models, orange inner corners.

A simplified version of eye detailing was introduced on the Commemorative Edition for 1991, "Hyksos," which has two-color eyes. The eyeball is painted black, with a brown U-shaped iris is painted over the black, leaving a black pupil in the middle and black in the corners. There is no painted eyewhite. (It was brought to my attention by Gale Good and Heather Wells that "Hyksos's" pupils are anatomically incorrect: they are vertical rectangles, whereas real horses' pupils are horizontal rectangles. I checked many of the other models with tri-color eyes and found that they suffer the same pathology.) The Commemorative for 1994, "Gifted," also has two-color eyes, but his brown irises are O-shaped.

The 1994 BreyerFest special-run models ("Bright Zip" and "Winchester") and the 1995 BreyerFest raffle model ("Mystique") all have eyes like the oldest models with eyewhites: monochrome black with small dabbed eyewhites in the outer corners.

Hooves

Breyer has paid less attention to hooves than to eyes over the years but has not neglected them altogether. The normal Breyer hoof is airbrushed monochrome black, gray, brown, tan, or pink. Many models have a mixture of monochrome hoof colors: gray, black, or brown on the solid legs and tan or pink on the legs with stockings. A few models have hand-painted monochrome hooves, which are rather heavy and unrealistic in appearance: "Precipitado Sin Par" #116, with pink hooves; the earliest issues of "Breezing Dixie," with gray hooves; and early issue Traditional "Man O' War" #47s, also with gray hooves. The gray, black, and gold hooves of some Western Horses, Western Ponies, and "Fury" Prancers from the 1950s also have a rather heavy look and were probably hand painted.

Breaking with the monochrome norm, several models have been given hooves with vertical stripes, as are fairly common among real horses. Three of these models are from the 1970s: Appaloosa Performance Horse #99, Pony Of The Americas #155, and the SR Pony Of The Americas in black blanket appaloosa. The rest are much more recent, from the 1990s, the first among them being Family Appaloosa Mare #860 (black leopard "Lady Phase" mold), "Night Vision" SR (bay snowflake leopard SHF mold; only the front hooves are striped), "Llanarth True Briton," "Bright Zip" SR, "Martin's Dominique" #898 (only one hoof striped), the grulla Clydesdale Stallion from Circus Extravaganza set #3170, and the Fine Porcelain Spanish Barb #79194 (one hoof striped). 1995 brought a very avalanche of models with one or more striped hooves, among them some Classic-scale models.

In 1993 Breyer initiated a new style of hoof detailing, with horizontal color banding. This style is most striking on "Gem Twist" #495, which has gray bands circling the tops of his tan hooves just below the coronary bands. Wild American Horse #881 ("Phar Lap" mold in shaded brown-gray smoke) has dark brown bands around the bottom edges of his tan hooves. The hooves on "Pantomime" #884 (black blanket appy POA mold) aren't actually banded but shade from a darker tan at the bottom edges to very pale tan around the top. One model introduced in 1994 also has horizontal hoof-bands: "Promises" Rearing Stallion #890, whose hooves are like "Gem Twist's." No new-for-1995 horses sport this style of hoof detailing, however.

Further recent developments in hoof detailing appeared first on the Fine Porcelain Shire Horse #79193: she has painted-on silver shoes (a couple of them with toe clips) and molded frogs on the bottoms of the raised hooves. The Fine Porcelain Spanish Barb and Premier Arabian Mare likewise have frogs on the raised hooves, though they wear no shoes. The "Roy" and Friesian molds have molded-on shoes, but these have not been accentuated with paint so far.

Regarding the foam-rubber hoof pads used on early Fighting Stallions, see note 2 for the Fighting Stallion mold.

Chalkies & Pearlies

"Chalky" and "pearly" are collectors' terms for certain types of Breyer models that were for the most part made during the world-wide oil crisis, which began in 1973 and lasted through that decade. As mentioned above, although the cellulose acetate plastic from which Breyers are made is not a petroleum product, it became very scarce during the oil-crisis era (see Breyer Company History above in this Appendix). In response to the shortage, Breyer executive Peter Stone purchased plastics from manufacturers in Belgium and Italy, but these suppliers often had only lower-grade cellulose acetate—the stuff from which the "chalky" and "pearly" models of the 1970s are made.

Chalky & Colored-Plastic Models

When collectors speak of "chalkies," what they usually have in mind are models that have a white paint basecoat, which gives them a chalky appearance. Collectors also sometimes apply the term "chalky" to two much less common types of models, neither of which has a white paint basecoat. One of these types is made of chalky-looking white plastic; the other is made of colored plastic. For the sake of clearly distinguishing these categories of models, I prefer to use the terms "basecoat chalky," "chalky-plastic chalky," and "colored-plastic model." Most models of all three types were made during the 1970s, but several earlier examples of basecoat chalkies and chalky-plastic chalkies are known, some with glossy finish (see below).

Basecoat chalkies. Many of the lower-quality plastics used by Breyer in the oil-crisis era were colored—bright purple, green, red, gray, and so on—and others were white but adulterated with swirls or specks of color. Many models made from these plastics were first covered with a white basecoat to hide the color of the plastic, and then painted with the normal colors of the model. The white portions of these models—stockings, blazes, pinto spots, and so forth—have a chalky appearance owing to the white opaque basecoat. Unlike normal Breyers, most chalkies do not yellow; the basecoat remains bright white even today (though I do have a chalky Appaloosa Performance Horse whose white portions are a creamy color). Chalky models often have a luminous, rich appearance owing to the glimmering of the white basecoat through the surface paint. Some collectors find basecoat chalkies odd looking, but others find them beautiful and seek to add them to their collections.

Oil-crisis-era basecoat chalkies that I have seen in person or heard reliable reports of are these: red roan semi-leopard Appy Performance Horse #99, chestnut Belgian #94, glossy gray Brahma Bull #70 (I have seen several of these; some may be pre-1970, but their dating is uncertain since #70 was made glossy well into the 1970s and has an irregular mold-stamp history), "Brighty" #375, Classic Lipizzan #620, chestnut Classic QH Foal #4001, palomino Classic QH Family Stallion #3045, chestnut Clydesdale Foal #84, chestnut Clydesdale Mare #83, bay Clydesdale Stallion #80 (version D), Donkey #81, "El Pastor" #61, Elephant #91, matte palomino Family Arabian Mare #5 and Foal #6, matte charcoal Family Arabian Stallion #201, matte alabaster Fighting Stallion #30, palomino Grazing Mare #143, chestnut pinto Indian Pony #175 without warpaint, solid-faced and bald-faced versions of bay Jumping Horse #300, "Justin Morgan" #65, "Man O' War" #47, "Midnight Sun" #60, "Misty" #20, black Morgan #48, dapple PAF #213, alabaster PAF #218, mahogany PAM #216, Appaloosa Yearling #103, alabaster Rearing Stallion (Classic scale) #180, alabaster Running Mare #120, dark chestnut Saddlebred Weanling #62, bay Shetland Pony #23, Spanish Fighting Bull #73, Stablemate "Seabiscuit" #5024 and bay Stablemate Saddlebred, tan Texas Longhorn #75, chestnut Suckling Foal #3155, bay Thoroughbred Mare #3155, black pinto Western Pony #41, and "Yellow Mount" #51. I am sure that many more could be added to this list—it is entirely possible that all models in production in that era were issued in chalky at some point along the line.

Some basecoat chalkies were made earlier, in the 1950s and 1960s. To my knowledge, these models always have a glossy finish. Specimens that I have seen or gotten reliable reports of are these: glossy bay Family Arab Stallion #13 (with no Breyer stamp), glossy horned walking Hereford Bull #71 (version with unstenciled belly line; I own one of these and have seen several others), old-mold glossy bay Proud Arab Mare #14, and glossy white Poodle #68 (with Breyer stamp; I own this one). Some 1950s palomino Western Horse #71s also look chalky, but on the ones I've seen, it's hard to tell if the white is a basecoat or chalky-looking plastic.

The basecoat-chalky tradition had something of a revival in "Pluto" The Lipizzaner (introduced 1991), the Lakota Pony (1992), and perhaps one or two subsequent models. Although these models are cast in normal white cellulose acetate, they are painted white all over, with shading and markings painted on top of this basecoat.

Colored-plastic models. A few oil-crisis-era models made of bizarrely colored plastics were given no white basecoat. Understandably, most of these models are completely painted in dark colors, with no stockings or facial markings. One discovers the truth of their plastic color via chips in the paint. Elaine Lindelef has a "Midnight Sun" and a "Justin Morgan" made of gray-brown-purple plastic with no basecoat. Denise Chance reports having a "Justin Morgan" of purple plastic *sans* basecoat (Chance 1991). Several black Morgans made of red, gray, and purple plastics without basecoat are also known. Collectors Jo Kulwicki and Sally Heitkotter and I all have Spanish Fighting Bulls with unpainted dishwater-gray horns; the body of Sally's bull is made of the same gray plastic, visible through rubs in his black paint. I have a #91 Elephant (with "U.S.A." stamp) cast in pale gray plastic and painted dark gray, with the pale gray tusks left unpainted. Collectors sometimes call these colored-plastic models "chalkies," but since these pieces have no basecoat and no chalky-white appearance, it would be clearer to refer to them instead as colored-plastic models. These should not be confused, of course, with the 1950s and 1960s models cast in realistically colored plastics with no body-color painted over it except for details such as white markings: the Western Horses, Western Ponies, and "Fury" Prancers made from black or dark brown plastic and the Elephants and Donkies cast in battleship gray plastic.

Chalky-plastic chalkies. This type of chalky model, which is in my experience less common, is made from white plastic that is itself chalky and opaque in appearance. I have seen several white Western Horses from the early 1950s like this, and collector Elaine Lindelef had a "Yellow Mount" and a Classic Arabian Family Mare made of such plastic. Elaine tried to remake these models, but the plastic proved intractable.

Pearlies

Pearlies are models made of a lovely white plastic that has a translucent appearance and an iridescent sheen like a pearl's. The sheen is visible on the unpainted portions of the models, such as stockings and blazes, and occasionally glimmers through the body paint as well. The pearly models I know of are black blanket appy Lying Down Foal, chestnut Suckling Foal, bay and palomino Rearing Stallions (Classic scale), chestnut Classic Arabian Family Foal, and Classic Quarter Horse Family Foals in chestnut, palomino, and possibly bay. Examples of some of these are shown on *Breyer Collector's Video*. Pearlies, like chalkies, were produced during the oil crisis era of the 1970s.

Yellowing, Split Seams, & Mildew Dapples

Breyers are of course subject to various types of injury due to accidents and rough handling: broken parts, rubs and scratches in the paint, black marks, ink stains, heat bloating, and so forth. These types of damage can generally be avoided through careful treatment of the models. But there are three types of damage that can occur spontaneously, even to models stored out of harm's way.

Yellowing

Yellowing of the plastic is by far the most common of the spontaneous types of damage suffered by Breyers—indeed it is unusual for an older model not to have yellowed at least to some degree. The yellow color can vary in intensity from a light creamy tinge that scarcely detracts from the model's appearance to a deep yellow that ruins the model's looks. Models that share rooms with wood-burning stoves or cigarette-smoking humans can develop a deep yellow-orange hue along with an unpleasant reek. But typical cases of yellowing occur in the absence of obvious environmental pollution such as this, and seem to involve a tendency of the plastic itself to yellow with age.

Collectors have developed various methods for whitening yellowed models. Soaking the model in a bath of household bleach plus water is a widely used technique, though "recipes" vary in the proportions of bleach to water and in the length of the soak. I will not present such formulas here since I have not used them myself and have heard of cases where models' finishes have been damaged. Gold-painted areas, such as the mane and tail ribbons on Clydesdale Stallions, are said to be particularly prone to discoloration from bleach. Another de-yellowing method, safer but equally effective, is to float the yellowed model in a chlorinated swimming pool, flipping the model over every day or two so that all surfaces get equal exposure to the chlorine and the sunshine. A third technique, more appealing to collectors who may hesitate to expose the model to chlorine, is simply to give the model a sunbath: leave it in a sunny spot outside or in a window that gets long hours of bright sun, flipping the beast from time to time to assure equal exposure all around. Although this method avoids chemicals, it has a risk of its own, namely that the model may bloat from overheating. To minimize the hazard, don't sun the model on very hot days, and always make sure the model has a small hole in its nostril or in the corner of its mouth to allow hot air to escape from inside the body cavity. Floating the model in a kiddy pool of pure water while it sunbathes may also help keep it cooler and so prevent bloat. Oddly, the effectiveness of the sunbathing method varies—some models show significant whitening in two or three days, whereas others take months or may never improve. Perhaps differences in the cause of the yellowing or in the chemical composition of the plastic explain this variability.

Split Seams

In my experience, split seams are a far less common malady than yellowing and occur chiefly on very old models, from the 1950s and 1960s. Portions of the seam joining the two halves of the model have simply popped open because of a poor bond or warping of the plastic. A split can be short and narrow or long and gaping. It often occurs along the croup and top of the tail, along the crest, or on the front of the neck and breast. Closing a split seam is a risky business, liable to create more damage than it mends. The pressure or heat required to bring the warped seam-edges together can crack or otherwise deform the model and mar the paint finish. And the acetone needed to bond Breyer plastic firmly is a solvent that goes to work on paint as well as plastic.

Mildew Dapples

A plastic horse being a very different thing from a rose bush or a wedge of cheese, it may come as a surprise that Breyers can develop mildew mold. I learned of this possibility only recently. My first inkling was a couple of models—a chestnut "Morganglanz" and a chestnut Classic "Ginger"—acquired by collector Sheryl Leisure from another collector. Both models, which are supposed to be solid chestnut, were covered with lighter chestnut dapples. The dapples were so realistic they seemed to be intentionally made, leading Sheryl and me to speculate that they might be factory original. A short while later, I learned from collector Erica Leipus that she had pulled a couple of long-neglected models off her dusty shelves only to discover they were covered with "little greyish blobs of mold . . . about the same color as the dust." When she wiped the mold off the models—a Clydesdale Stallion and a Family Arab Stallion, both matte bay—she found that her horses were now covered with realistic dapples, slightly lighter than the brown body color. In the photos Erica kindly sent me, the dapples on the Clydesdale look very much like those on Sheryl's horses, though a bit smaller on average. The dapples on the FAS are very tiny, appearing in the photo more like roaning than dappling. Of course we don't know for sure that Sheryl's models were dappled by mold, but Erica's experience proves that this can happen. It is interesting to note that Erica's and Sheryl's models are all of a medium brown body color. Erica mentioned that she found a bit of mold on a black model too, but no dapples had developed. Perhaps the mold simply hadn't been there long enough—but then again, perhaps mold finds Breyer medium brown particularly tasty.

Stickers & Hang Tags

Stickers

In earlier years, some Breyer models were sold with one of two different types of Breyer Animal Creations stickers pasted onto their bodies: gold-foil stickers and blue-ribbon stickers. Although collectors today prize these stickers, young collectors back in 1960s often removed them from the models, with unfortunate results—the stickers left a residue on the model which is virtually impossible to remove completely without damaging the paint finish.

Gold foil stickers, about 1959 - mid 1960s. The earlier of the two types of sticker is gold-foil paper with black print saying "A Breyer Creation made of Tenite Acetate / U.S.A." These stickers are roughly square in shape, with scalloped edges. They were stuck to the models' shoulder, barrel, or belly, and were used chiefly on woodgrain models, though not exclusively (see Walerius 1991, p. 12, for a photo of the belly of a brown pinto Western Horse bearing a gold-foil sticker). I give 1959 as the starting date for the use of these stickers on the basis of two models that date to 1959: a woodgrain PAM with gold-foil sticker on the barrel, owned by collector Kim Jones, and a no-muscle woodgrain Clydesdale Stallion with no round Breyer stamp but with gold-foil sticker, which I saw at BreyerFest 1993. An ending date is harder to determine, but it is plausible to suppose that the discontinuation of the gold-foil sticker coincided with the end of the heyday of woodgrain models. (Plocek 1988 gives the dates of gold-foil stickers as 1963-65.)

Blue Ribbon stickers, early 1960s - early 1970s. These small paper stickers were made in several slight variations of shape and size, but all had the basic shape of a rosette ribbon with two tails, such as you might win at a horse show. All the stickers are blue with gold or yellow lettering. "Breyer Creations" is printed around the outer edge of the rosette; in the center is printed the model's number and sometimes (but not always) the model's name as well. Blue-ribbon stickers were normally glued onto the models' shoulders or hips. They were used on all sorts of models, from the Clydesdale Stallion to the Siamese Kitten. Collector Sheryl Leisure suggests that the only models that had stickers on them were those put out for display by shop owners. Customers would pick a model from the display, and the store clerk would check the number on the chosen model's sticker and go to the storeroom to fetch a box printed with that number. Sheryl remembers that this was the system in her neighborhood store during the 1960s, and the models she got in the boxes from the back room had no stickers on them. Blue-ribbon stickers were also stuck onto the clear plastic boxes of the earliest Showcase Collection models—such stickers are visible on the boxes in a Showcase Collection photo brochure dating to 1970, of which I have a Xerox (the photo is reprinted in *JAH* 18/#3 Summer II 1991, p. 30, and 18/#4 Fall 1991, p. 14). Slightly later (1971-72) photo brochures with Showcase Collection models show the boxes with a slightly different sticker: rectangular, with a the blue-ribbon logo printed on one side and the phrase "Showcase Collection by Breyer / made in USA" on the other. Collector Sande Schneider owns a Showcase Collection box with the rectangular sticker, which I have seen in person.

A clue as to the dating of blue-ribbon stickers used on the models' bodies is given by Breyer catalogs and manuals that feature a blue-ribbon logo resembling the stickers. The earliest Breyer catalog that uses this logo is the 1960: on the back cover is a drawing of a two-tailed rosette ribbon, with the word "Breyer" and a drawing of a horse approximating the Family Arabian Stallion on the rosette. One version or another of the blue-ribbon logo also appears in the 1963-70 catalogs; none appears in the 1972 or later catalogs (no 1971 catalog was published to my knowledge). The latest Breyer manual bearing a blue-ribbon logo is the 1974. Collectors' models with blue-ribbon stickers also help establish the dating. Collector Julie Harris found a Race Horse #36 with a blue-ribbon sticker saying "Breyer Creations #36," so it is certain that these stickers were in use at least as early as 1966, the last year of production for #36. It is also certain that the stickers were used on models into the early 1970s, for they have been found on the Indian Ponies and other models issued in those years. (For further details, see Gurdon 1994.)

Other stickers. Since phasing out these two types of stickers, Breyer has not to my knowledge used stickers on the models' bodies except for the tiny and easily removed "Made in Taiwan" stickers on the cold-cast resin and fine-porcelain pieces of the 1990s and "Made in China" stickers on some post-1992 Stablemates and post-1995 Little Bits. But the company has applied a considerable variety of stickers to the models' boxes. In addition to the blue-ribbon stickers on Showcase boxes mentioned above, some stickers were used on the all-cardboard picture-boxes of the 1970s and early 1980s. For example, collector Kim Lory Jones has a Western Prancer box printed with a photo of a smoke model but bearing an oval gold-foil sticker saying "Box Contains Model No. 112 Color: Palomino"; she also has a Running Mare box with a photo of a bay mare and a sticker saying "Box Contains Model No. 123 Color: Dark Dapple." In the later 1980s, the blister-packets of various regular-run Little Bits models came adorned with a red sticker advertising the "Free Bitsy Breyer Offer," and the packets of Little Bits Morgan Stallions sported a sticker of the Morgan Horse Association of America. Many different ornamental stickers have appeared on the plastic-fronted yellow boxes introduced by Reeves International in 1986, such as the "Made In U.S.A." sticker printed with an American flag. The boxes of all the Commemorative and Limited Edition horses, for instance, have come with large round stickers, typically gold foil, giving the model's name and the basic facts of the edition. Similar stickers have adorned the boxes of various regular and special runs, both Traditional and Classic. Many of the Artist Series, Classic After School Herd, and B Ranch series horses come in boxes with stickers identifying the series. A new, small gold-foil sticker saying "Retired Breyer Collectable" appeared in 1996 on the boxes of some recently discontinued models and sets. According to *JAH* editor Stephanie Macejko (conversation of July 2, 1996), these "Retired" stickers are put on the boxes not by the factory but by the retailers, who may order the stickers from Breyer if they wish. Another gold-foil sticker printed with "Discontinued / Breyer / Discontinued" turned up on the bodies of some vintage models at BreyerFest 1996; presumably these have also been recently made available to Breyer vendors to use as they wish.

Hang Tags

The little cards made of heavy paper that generally come suspended from the model's neck by a string are known as hang tags. Breyer first issued models with hang tags in the 1950s: Race Horse Derby Winner, Brahma Bull, "Lassie," "Rin Tin Tin," and Corky On "Bimbo" are the ones I know of for sure. Although the Corky set was made only for a brief period in the late 1950s, Race Horse, "Lassie," and "Rin Tin Tin" ran from the mid-1950s to mid-1960s. Whether hang tags were issued with them for the entire decade of their production I don't know. But to the best of my knowledge, after these models were discontinued, Breyer issued no more models with hang tags until 1985, following the acquisition of Breyer Animal Creations by Reeves International.

In 1985, the Little Bits SR red sorrel American Saddlebred was issued with a hang tag celebrating the Reeves acquisition. No further hang-tag models appeared in the 1980s to my knowledge, but the six Artist Series horses introduced in the mid to late 1980s came with small folded "Artist Series" brochures loose in the boxes. The 1990s are becoming the decade of the hang tag. In 1992, four models were issued with hang tags: "Bolya," Friesian, Lakota Pony, and Classic "Mesteño" The Messenger. Hang-tag models have been issued in every year since then: American Bison #381, "Aristocrat," "Gem Twist," "Ichilay," "Ponokah-Eemetah," "Llanarth," all the subsequent "Mesteño" models in the Messenger Series Of Kiger Mustangs.

Belly Numbering & Dating

Belly numbering is found on only a few special or limited runs. There are two types of belly numbering, but in both types the numbers are applied to the model's underside by hand in ink. In one type, which I refer to as "double numbering," two numbers are written: the total number of models in the run and the individual model's number in the run. For example, my 1989 Commemorative Edition "Silver" Quarter Horse SR has "0836/5000" written on his belly, supposedly indicating that he was the 836th model in a limited run of 5,000 models. (See below for a caution about the individual numbers.) In the other type of belly numbering, which I call "single numbering," only the individual model number is written, no run-total number.

The earliest belly-numbered model I know of, the Red Angus Bull SR (1983 and 1984), was numbered by the Red Angus Association, not by Breyer. Some of these bulls are double numbered between the front legs while others are single numbered. The Breyer company itself introduced belly numbering on the first *JAH* special, the chestnut Saddlebred Weanling (1984), which is double numbered. Many subsequent *JAH* specials are also numbered: dapple gray Cantering Welsh Pony (1985/86, single numbered), chestnut Trakehner (1987, single numbered), chestnut Running Stallion (1988, single numbered), and blue roan Quarter Horse Yearling (1989, double numbered). More recent *JAH* SRs have been hand-dated on the belly rather than numbered: the caramel pinto Western Horse (1990), "Pride And Vanity" (1992/93), "Steel Dust" (1993/94), "Moon Shadows" (1994), and the foals "Buster" and "Brandi" (1995) are all dated on the belly, and the black Jumping Horse (1991/92) is dated on the bottom of his jump. The horse in the 1995 *JAH* Special Retail Set, Willow And "Shining Star," is double numbered on the belly. Also double numbered are the SR cold-cast porcelain "Spotted Bear," "Galaxias," and "Misty," made for the Sears and Penney's holiday catalogs. SR "Night Deck" and "Night Vision" were both double numbered by employees of Black Horse Ranch, the company that ordered the special. The belly-numbering tradition was brought to catalog-run models via the Commemorative Editions, all of which are double numbered. Many or all of the horse-and-buggy SR sets and Miniature Collection sets from the 1980s are signed and numbered by the manufacturer, the Riegseckers of Indiana, on the undersides of the vehicles. Note that for all the numbered and dated runs just mentioned, there may be some specimens that for one reason or another are not numbered—for example, I know of chestnut Weanlings, chestnut Running Stallions, and "Gifted" CE's with blank bellies. Some of these were undoubtedly simply skipped by accident; others were overruns that Breyer did not bother to number; the "Gifteds" escaped the factory before the numbering had been done.

The point of numbering is to emphasize the scarcity of the model and thus enhance its value to collectors. While it's a nice thing to have a number on one's model indicating that the model is a limited issue, sometimes collectors get odd notions about numbering. In particular, they get excited about the fact that their models have low numbers in the run. To my mind this "the lower the number, the better" idea makes no sense. Models with lower numbers are not necessarily prettier or more carefully finished or freer of defects than those with high numbers. So what's the excitement about? Collector Jo Kulwicki suggests that the low-number fetish is a bit of Hagen-Renaker wisdom inappropriately carried over to Breyers. In the manufacture of H-Rs, the plaster molds in which the ceramic models are cast degrade quickly with use—a mold is good for only about 30 models.[54] Models produced early in the life of a particular mold are crisply defined and beautifully detailed; models made in a mold past its prime are a little vague. So it makes excellent sense in H-R collecting to prefer models made earlier in a run. But it makes no sense in Breyer collecting. For one thing, Breyer molds are made of hard metal, not plaster. Consequently, models produced today from Breyer injection molds made two or three decades ago are typically as crisp as the first models out of the mold, and certainly no mold degradation will be apparent between the first and last models of a 2,000-piece belly-numbered run made in the course of a few weeks. For another thing, the belly numbers on Breyers do not reflect the order in which the models were made—a lower number does not mean an earlier model. For example, the "Night Deck" and "Night Vision" models were numbered by the dealer as they were pulled out of their shipping boxes. (This is no secret; it was being done in a room crowded with customers at a model event in Southern California.) Obviously these numbers had nothing to do with the order in which the models were made. Breyer executive Peter Stone assured me (conversation of Nov. 1994) that the numbers put on models at the factory are likewise applied completely randomly. After all, the models in a run are not completed one at a time at the factory. Whole batches of models are put through first this phase of preparation or painting, then that phase, then another, and no attention is paid to keeping the models in a certain order as they are pulled off the racks at each new station. The concept of an "earlier model in the run" simply has no meaning in the context of such a production process.

A word of warning: I learned the hard way that belly numbers are not always indelible. One warm afternoon, I had occasion to clutch my #818 caramel pinto SB Weanling around her middle for maybe a minute. When I turned her over and pulled my thumb away to check her numbers, they were smudged.

MasterCrafters Clocks

Breyer Molding Company produced its first horse mold, the Western Horse, in 1950 as a custom order for MasterCrafters Clock Company, which used the models as ornaments on mantel clocks (for details see Breyer Company History above in this Appendix). Breyer also produced the horses' saddles and the plastic bases on which the horses and clocks were mounted, according to Breyer executive Peter Stone (conversation of Nov. 1994). These clocks with Western Horses come in two different styles, one with the horse standing over the clock (the clock is between the horse's legs, under his belly), the other with the horse standing beside the clock, to the right of it and facing it but angled slightly forward. The over-the-clock style with plastic base is earlier than the beside-the-clock style, to judge from the fact that the

Western Horses on all the over-the-clocks known to me, with only a couple of exceptions (discussed below), are the early mold version, with diamond-shaped conchas. All the beside-the-clock Western Horses known to me are of the normal, rounded-conchas mold version that is still produced today, and thus must have been made after the mold was altered. Further evidence that the over-the-clocks came first is the fact that most of these clocks so closely resemble the over-the-clock Hartland Champ MasterCrafters clocks that preceded them and from which Breyer took its design for the Western Horse.[55] Aside from the subtle mold differences between the Hartland and Breyer horses, the typical over-the-clock Western Horse clocks are virtual mirror images of the Hartland Champ clocks, being identical in color, components, and design, right down to the diamond-shaped conchas on the horses' bridles. The only striking difference is that the Hartland Champs face right while the Western Horses face left, so that everybody has his mane facing front.

A comment on the quantity of Western Horse MasterCrafters clocks is in order here. As noted above in the Breyer Company History section, statements published by Breyer about the origins of Breyer Animal Creations cite a particular quantity of horses made for MasterCrafters. A Breyer Animal Creations flier of 1976, for example, says: "In 1950, at the request of the MasterCrafters Clock Company, an acetate horse was designed to stand on the base of a clock. . . . After an initial purchase of 2,000 [horses]. . ." Similar statements specifying the same quantity appear in the 1985 and 1986 dealer catalogs and in *JAH X/#2* 1982 (p. 11), 16/#1 Feb./Mar. 1989 (p. 29), and 19/#1 Spring 1992 (p. 11). Most of these statements are accompanied by photos of the over-the-clock style clock with white diamond-conchas horse, but none of them mentions the existence of two different styles of clock, so it is not obvious from these statements what the 2,000 figure is supposed to include. However, the fact that these statements mention the quantity in the context of 1950 suggests that the quantity pertains only to the earliest style of clocks, namely the horse-over-the-clocks; for in all likelihood the beside-the-clocks were made no earlier than 1951. Furthermore, specimens of both styles of clocks, although not exactly common today, are not nearly as rare as one would expect them to be if only 2,000 total clocks of both styles had ever been made. In fact I have seen so many clocks now, of both basic styles, that I suspect the bruited 2,000 were merely the first batch of several made throughout 1950 and 1951.

In addition to the Champ clocks and the two styles of Western Horse clocks, I know of several other types of MasterCrafters horse clocks, some using Breyers and others not, all of which are described below in what I believe to be chronological order. For a Breyer clock/nightlight made by another company, see below in the section on Lamps & Nightlights.

Horse-over-the-clock Hartland Champ clock (sometime in the period 1947-49). The horse stands over the clock (with the clock between his legs), facing right so his mane shows. I know of only three Champ clocks in collections (owned by collectors Jo Kulwicki, Heather Wells, and Denise Hauck—Denise's is reported in *Hartland Market*, Apr. 1995), and all are of this style. As mentioned above, these clocks and the typical over-the-clock style Western Horse clocks are virtually identical except that the horses face opposite directions, so that the mane side always faces the front. (Western Horses have manes on the left and thus face left on their clocks.) The Champs are cast in white plastic with painted dark brown/black hooves, and at least some have "antique" brown mane and tail, as on the brown-mane-and-tail version over-the-clock Western Horses (see next entry). The removable plastic saddles on the Champs are brown with whitewashed skirts and fenders, identical to the cinchless version of the Western Horse saddles. One of the three Champ clocks I know of is missing whatever reins and bit it might have come with, but the other two have o-link chain reins attached to a cylinder-style bit with safety-pin style hooks, identical to the gear on some over-the-clock Western Horses. The Champ clock bases, clock casings and faces (except perhaps for the hands), and patent numbers engraved on the backs of the clock casings are all identical to the over-the-clock Western Horse clocks—see the next entry for details. I am not sure if the Champs are attached to their bases with screws or with plastic pegs molded to the bottoms of their hooves (Western Horse clocks use both means). The name "MasterCrafters" does not appear anywhere on these clocks. For collectors interested in Hartlands I should mention that two of the clock Champs I know of do not have holes in their backs, as some apparently later free-standing Champs do (I don't know about the third clock Champ).

The dating of the Champ clocks is not entirely clear. Fitch 1993 (2: 4) and Walerius 1991 (p. 1) agree that Hartland introduced the Champ mold around 1947. Fitch reports that Hartland created Champ for MasterCrafters, which indicates that the clocks themselves date from that time. (She also notes that Hartland and MasterCrafters had a preexisting relationship.) Walerius, however, suggests that MasterCrafters approached Hartland sometime after Hartland had issued the Champ mold on its own. In either case, to judge from the clocks I know of, the Hartland clocks are rare by comparison to either version of the Western Horse clock, and this rarity would suggest that they were produced only for a brief period.

Horse-over-the-clock Western Horse clock with plastic base (1950). The horse stands over the clock (with the clock between his legs), facing left so his mane shows. In most cases known to me (exceptions are discussed below), the horses are the earlier mold version, with diamond-shaped conchas on bridle and breastcollar, and are white or off-white with dark brown or black hooves. Typically they have "antique" brown-washed mane and tail, but some have white mane and tail—though some of the latter horses may simply have had the delicate brown antiquing worn away. The horses have old-style Western saddles[56] in brown with "antique" white-washing on skirts and fenders. Some saddles have no cinch; some have a vinyl cinch with a slip-through buckle, the cinch being attached to the saddle with high-set, nail-head style grommets. The reins are o-link chains.[57] Some have no bit (the chain simply runs through the mouth); others have cylinder-style bits; and still others have wire bits. The horse and clock stand on a plastic base shaped like a low pedestal, roughly 3 inches high at the highest point. The base is normally dark brown, but on collector Leslie Granger's clock the base is a marbled seafoam green plastic, although it is the same shape as the dark brown bases. On some over-the-clocks, the horse is attached to the base by means of plastic pegs molded onto the bottoms of the horse's hooves; on others (such as Leslie Granger's and collector Sande Schneider's), the horse is affixed by screws through the bottoms of its hooves. Sitting at the center of the base is the clock with its plain round metal casing, which is sometimes solid dark brown and sometimes mottled gray-brown. The clock face has Arabic numerals and says "Clock movement by Sessions / Made in U.S.A." at the bottom. Neither the name "MasterCrafters" nor the name "Breyer" appears anywhere on these clocks. The back of the clock casing is engraved with the following six patent numbers, stacked up as shown:

1935208	1977184
1996375	1977185
2049261	1977186

A few exceptional horse-over-the-clock clocks that have come to my attention warrant special mention. One was purchased at an antique show by collector Christina Dils, who had the clock on display at BreyerFest 1995. While completely typical in all other respects—a white diamond-conchas horse with brown-washed mane and tail, cylinder bit, o-link reins, and brown whitewashed saddle with no cinch and no grommet holes, standing on a brown base—Tina's clock came with an unusual "hang tag" suspended from the reins. The tag appears to be original to the clock, whose electrical cord was still folded and wrapped in old paper "with a few petrified spiders" when Tina got it. The tag, which is round and made of thin cardboard, has two small holes near the top, through which the rein is threaded. (The rein must have been detached from the bit to be threaded like this.) On the front side, the tag is gold-foiled with red print that says: "Authentic Western Horsemount / Removable Saddle / Unbreakable Plastic." The reverse side, which has no gold foil, states: "Clean with lukewarm water only / Polish with wax / Ceramic Clock Co. / 216 N. Clinton St. / Chicago [8? print unclear], Ill." Nary a mention of MasterCrafters! So what is the Ceramic Clock Company? An intriguing clue is provided by the label on the back of an old MasterCrafters clock featuring a little plastic girl on a swing, dating undoubtedly to the 1940s or 1950s (collector Daphne Macpherson's photos of this clock and label appear in *Hartland Market*, April 1995, p. 38). The label gives the name and address of the clock company: "MasterCrafters Clock and Radio Company / 216 N. Clinton St., Chicago 8, Ill."—the same address as for the Ceramic Clock Co. on Tina's hang tag! Absent further clues, I can only speculate that Ceramic Clock was some sort of subsidiary of MasterCrafters. In any case, to return to Tina's hang tag, the tag's reference to the horse as "Western Horsemount" is reminiscent of Breyer documents from the early 1950s, which refer to the Western Horse as "Western Mount" or "Western Mount Horse" (see note 6 for the Western Horse mold in the Traditionals section).

Also noteworthy are a handful of over-the-clock clocks with seafoam-green bases and diamond-conchas Western Horses of an extraordinary and quite hideous color, which I can only describe as bile yellow-charcoal. These clocks were first brought to my attention by collector Sande Schneider, who has seen two of them in person and kindly sent me a photo of one; she also saw a free-standing bile horse—that is, not on a clock, and with no evidence on his hooves of having ever been on a clock—at BreyerFest 1996. I managed to miss this free-standing specimen but did see a clock specimen at the same BreyerFest, and the collector who owned it said she had an identical one (though prettier, less bilious) at home. This makes a total of 4 bile-horse clocks and 1 free-standing bile horse that I've heard of. Oddly, one of the clocks Sande saw had the horse facing to the right, so that his mane was hidden from the front. But the one in the photo she sent and the one I saw in person at BreyerFest 1996 have the horse facing left, as is normal for white-horse over-the-clocks. On the bile-horse clocks, the clock face and casing are identical to those of ordinary over-the-clocks (although the hands on the one at BreyerFest were needle-shaped). The bases are seafoam-green marbled with brown, identical to the base of Leslie Granger's white-horse clock mentioned above. The horses are cast in white/creamy plastic—the one at BreyerFest felt like typical Breyer plastic to me, but the one Sande saw had an odd feel, in her opinion. Their paint color is unlike anything I've seen on a Breyer before: a sickly, bilious shade of yellow oversprayed with liberal amounts of charcoal-brown shading in the muscle grooves, flanks, and other areas of the body. The color fades out to a baldish face and 4 high white stockings. Interestingly, the mane and tail have the same "antique" brown shading as on many white clock-horses, but touched with a slight mist of the bile colors. The hooves are black; the bridle and breastcollar dark brown with gold concha-studs. The saddle is the same mold as that on normal over-the-clock horses but is white/cream plastic lightly shaded with the bile yellow-charcoal. The saddles on the bile-horse clocks had no girth or grommets, but the saddle on the free-standing horse that Sande saw had high-set nailhead-style grommets and a girth with slip-through buckle. The bile-horses' reins are typical o-links attached to a cylinder bit with "safety pin" style hooks. The bile-horse clock I saw at BreyerFest was engraved with the same six patent numbers as are listed above for the white-horse clocks, so I have no doubt these clocks are MasterCrafters. I also feel fairly sure that the horses under the paint are Breyers—at least the mold is identical to the white diamond-conchas horses. So presumably these clocks were made in 1950 (or early 1951) along with the white-horse clocks. What gives one pause is the color. Was this Breyer's doing—are these horses perhaps precursors to palomino #57? Or did the MasterCrafters company decide to add some delicious body color to white horses with "antique" brown manes and tails? Or is there some other story behind these bizarre horses?

The final two unusual over-the-clock clocks that should be mentioned here are noteworthy because their horses are normal-mold. One is a clock with a normal-mold white Western Horse with brown-shaded made and tail, black hooves, through-the-mouth o-link reins, and a high-donut-grommet snap saddle with gold touches, which I saw at BreyerFest 1996. The other is a clock with a normal-mold, normal-color palomino (not bile yellow-charcoal) with black hooves, o-link reins attached, I believe, to a wire bit, and high-donut-grommet saddle (I'm not sure of the color or girth closure), shown in the December 1994 *Western Horseman* in an article by Carol Gilbert titled "A Model Hobby" (pp. 109-112). Both clocks have the usual brown over-the-clock base and Arabic-numeral clock face, but since the horses are normal mold, I would guess these clocks were made in early 1951, just prior to the beside-the-clock MasterCrafters, many of which have white and palomino horses such as these. In any case, the normal mold version of the Western Horse had certainly replaced the old diamond-conchas version by the latter part of 1951—the normal mold version (free-standing) appears in the September 1951 *Western Horseman*.

Horse-beside-the-clock Western Horse clock (sometime in the period 1951- early 1953). The horse stands to the right of the clock and facing it (so his mane shows) but angled slightly forward. On all of these clocks that I've seen, the horses are of the normal mold version. They come in both palomino and white. The palominos in my experience typically have black hooves and solid gold bridle, although I have seen one with gold only on the bridle studs, and two others with gray hooves. The white horses on these clocks have gold only on the studs of bridle and breastcollar. Some of the white horses have white mane and tail; others have "antique" brown mane and tail. The saddle on both colors of horses is the old-style Western saddle in brown, with high-set, donut-style grommets and snap-on vinyl cinch. In my experience, the saddle on the white horses has gold-washed skirts and fenders, whereas the saddle on palominos has gold touches only on the "tooled" designs. Some of the white horses also come with a white felt saddle blanket; I've never seen a palomino beside-the-clock horse with this accessory. The reins on both colors of horses are o-link chains, which either run through the mouth *sans* bit or attach to a wire bit. The clock and horse stand on a simple rectangular base, about 1 inch high, made of mottled dark brown plastic, which I suppose was meant to look like marble. The horse is attached to the base with screws through the bottoms of his hooves. The clock casing is made of white metal and is quite ornate: a horseshoe shape, open end up, cradles the round clock, and below the horseshoe is a bas-relief of a cowhorse mounted by a cowboy, roping a steer. The clock face is identical to that on the over-the-clock style clocks, with Arabic numerals and, at the bottom, the words "Clock movement by Sessions / Made in U.S.A." The back of the clock is engraved with the same six patent numbers as on the over-the-clock style clocks. Neither the MasterCrafters nor the Breyer name appears anywhere on the clock. The beside-the-clock style of Western Horse clock is shown in Diederich 1988 (Section 1) and on *Breyer Collector's Video*.

Although these clocks were made after the horse-over-the-clock clocks, they certainly date to the early 1950s. I suggest an earliest dating of 1951 for them because my earliest definite evidence of the existence of the normal-mold version Western Horse is an ad for the palomino Western Horse (free-standing, not on clock) in the September 1951 *Western Horseman*. The o-link chain reins on beside-the-clock horses indicates that they were issued no later than early 1953, for by late 1953 Breyer had introduced the twisted-link chain reins that are still used on the Western Horse mold today.

Horse-over-the-clock Western Horse clock with metal base (sometime in the period 1953-55). I have seen only one of these unusual clocks, at BreyerFest 1994. As on the older over-the-clock MasterCrafters with plastic base, on this metal-base piece the horse stands over the clock (with the clock between his legs), facing left so his mane shows. The horse is a palomino of the normal mold version, with solid gold bridle, gold studs and upper straps on the breastcollar, and gray hooves. His old-style Western Saddle, with high-set, donut-style grommets and snap-on vinyl cinch, is a red-brown shade with abundant gold touches on the "tooled" designs. Interestingly, this horse is the first palomino clock horse I've seen with a felt saddle blanket, in red. The reins are the normal twisted-link style. The other unique feature of this clock is the base, which is dark metal, probably tarnished with age. It is rectangular, about an inch and a half high, and quite ornate, with molded-in "quilted" designs on the sides and fancy fluted "columns" molded at the corners. The plain, round clock case, made of the same dark metal, stands in the center of the base. The clock face and innards were missing from the piece at BreyerFest, but the back of the casing was engraved with the same six patent numbers as on the older over-the-clock style clocks, which is why I believe this metal-base clock is a MasterCrafters. The horse's twisted-link reins date him to no earlier than 1953, and his high-grommet snap saddle dates him to no later than 1955.

"Fury" Prancer clock with Davy Crockett rider (mid-1950s). The horse stands to the right of the clock, facing it squarely. The dark brown Prancer, Davy Crockett rider, rubbery cavalry-type saddle, and other accessories on these clocks are the same as were sold in Breyer's regular-run Davy Crockett set. The clock and horse with rider are mounted on a plain oblong wood base, varnished but not painted, about half an inch high. On the front of the base is a little metal name plate that says "Davy Crockett." The plain round clock is very similar to that on the over-the-clock Western Horse Clocks, with a plain round metal casing in gold tone. The clock face has Arabic numerals and says "Made in U.S.A." at the bottom and "MasterCrafters" below the "12." The back of the clock casing has no writing on it whatsoever. The six patent numbers found on the earlier clocks are not to be found on the Davy clocks, to judge from the specimens I know of. For a photo of the box in which Davy clocks were sold, see Walerius 1991, p.3. For my dating of these clocks, see note 3 for the "Fury" Prancer mold in the Traditionals section above.

"Fury" Prancer clock with no rider (mid-1950s). I have seen only one of these clocks, at the 1995 BreyerFest. It is very similar to the Davy Crockett clock, having the same wood base and identical round clock, complete with "MasterCrafters" printed below the "12." The chief difference, aside from the lack of a rider, is that the positions of the horse and clock are reversed: on the riderless piece, the horse stands to the left of the clock, facing it. The horse is black with painted-on blaze and stockings, black hooves, and gold bridle and breastcollar. He has the normal chain reins and wears a black Western saddle with snap cinch.

Horse-beside-the-clock "scooper-ears" pseudo-Western Horse clock (early to mid 1950s?). The horse stands to the left of the clock and facing it squarely; hence his mane does not show from the front. The plastic horse is the "scooper-eared" mold described in note 5 for Western Horse (above in the Traditionals section). On the one clock I've seen, the horse is black, with gold hooves, gold bridle and breastcollar, black plastic Western Saddle, and black plastic lace reins. Horse and clock stand on a plastic "marbled" brown base, very similar to the base of the Western Horse beside-the-clock but lighter in color, more of a rust shade. The round clock face is identical to that on the Western Horse clocks, with Arabic numerals and, at the bottom, the words "Clock movement by Sessions / Made in U.S.A." The clock is in a gold-colored casing that features a bas-relief of a cowboy on cowpony, a cowboy hat, and a gun with ammo belt. The back of the clock casing is engraved with the same patent numbers as on the over-the-clock style Western Horse clocks. The MasterCrafters name does not appear anywhere on the clock, to my knowledge. This clock is shown in Diederich 1988, Section 4.

Of course it's hard to be sure of the dating of this clock and the clock with the textured-tack horse (see below), but I place them in the early to mid 1950s on the basis of their similarities to the beside-the-clock Western Horse clocks. My guess is that after Breyer's arrangement with MasterCrafters had ended, the clock company turned to yet other plastics manufacturers to supply horse models for its clocks, the result being the clocks with scooper-eared horses and with textured-tack horses.

Horse-beside-the-clock "textured-tack" pseudo-Western Horse clock (early to mid 1950s?). The horse stands to the right of the clock and facing it squarely, so his mane shows. The plastic horse is the "textured tack" mold described in note 5 for the Western Horse mold (above in the Traditionals section). On the two clocks with this horse that I've seen in person, the horse is white, with white mane and tail, gray hooves, gold breastcollar and bridle with molded-in texture, bead-chain reins (as on some non-clock Hartland Champs), and Western saddle with textured patch. On one clock the saddle was black; on the other it was red-brown. A third clock that I've seen in a photo has a palomino horse with slightly oversprayed white mane and tail, faded gray hooves, gold breastcollar and bridle (texture not visible in the photo), bead-chain reins, and no saddle. On all three clocks, horse and clock stand on a plastic "marbled" pale orangy-tan base, similar in shape and size to the base of the Western Horse beside-the-clock but with a molded-in pattern of vertical ridges around the sides. The round clock face has Roman numerals and says "Clock Movement by Sessions * Made in U.S.A." at the bottom. The clock casing is of "marbled" pale orangy-tan plastic (a bit darker than the base), and is quite ornate, with a bas-relief at the bottom featuring two six-shooters in holsters, a pair of cowboy boots, and a saguaro cactus. The back of the clock casing is engraved with the same six patent numbers as on the Breyer Western Horse clocks, which does seem to verify this textured-tack-horse clock's authenticity as a MasterCrafters, though the name "MasterCrafters" does not appear anywhere on it. For comments on dating, see the preceding entry on the "scooper-ears" horse clock.

Clock with bas-relief resembling Breyer's Quarter Horse Yearling (early 1960s?). This clock differs radically from all the preceding. For one thing, it is designed to hang on a wall rather than to stand on a mantel. For another thing, it has no actual Breyer horse attached to it; instead, the horse (actually, just the near half of a horse), base, and clock casing are all one integral sheet of molded plastic, like a large Jell-O mold. The horse is outfitted with bead-chain reins running through a hole in her mouth. Two of these clocks that I have seen were solid metallic "antique" bronze color except for the clock face, but collector Jo Kulwicki's clock, which I've seen in person, is silver. The bas-relief of the horse bears a striking resemblance to Breyer's QH Yearling mold, although the bas-relief's neck is straight rather than turned, it has a molded-on Western saddle, and its tail attaches to the left buttock rather than the right. Evidence from Jo's clock indicates that the clock is older than the Breyer mold (which debuted in 1970) and thus could not have been copied from the Breyer. The back of Jo's clock has no patent numbers as on older MasterCrafters clocks but is engraved with "MASTERCRAFTERS CLOCK CORP. CHICAGO 12, ILL." The clue here is the "12," which is a zone number. The zone-number system was replaced by the zip-code system in the U.S. in 1963 (per *Britannica Online*). Collector Sande Schneider's bronze-colored clock, however, has a sticker on the back that does include a zip code: "MasterCrafters Clock Corp. Chicago, Ill. 60622." So evidently these clocks were made for a few years.

Lamps & Nightlights

Like MasterCrafters clocks, the lamps and at least some of the nightlights discussed below were made from Breyer models by individuals or companies other than the Breyer Molding Company. The conventional nightlights might be exceptions; it is possible that Breyer made them, but I have found no documentary evidence one way or the other on this question. Lamps sporting Breyers seem to come in innumerable varieties, certainly more than can be described here. Below are listed the best-known types of lamps along with some of the more interesting unknowns that have come to my attention.

Lamps

Dunning Industries "Ranchcraft" lamps. Table lamps with Breyer horses and other animals have been made by various companies and individuals over the years, but perhaps the best-known lamps are those with oval burlap shades and thin brass lamp poles with a torque near the top. The models on these lamps are of various molds—horses (such as Belgian, Fighting Stallion, Proud Arabian Foal, Rearing Stallion, Running Mare and Foal) and other animals (such as Texas Longhorn Bull, Bighorn Ram, Bear, and Buffalo)—and are often woodgrain but come in realistic regular-run colors as well. The model or models (some of these lamps have a mare and foal) stand in front of the brass lamp pole on a rectangular or oval wood base, which is beveled on some lamps but not all. These lamps are identified by *JAH* as "Ranchcraft" lamps, made by a company called Dunning Industries, of Greensboro, North Carolina, in the 1960s. Evidence supports the 1960s dating but also indicates that the lamps were issued into the 1970s as well. An ad for one of these lamps with a bay Fighting Stallion, priced at $24.95, appears in the September 1964 *Western Horseman* magazine (p. 12). The ad is from a store called Dutch Door, in Poughkeepsie, New York. It does not mention the Ranchcraft name or Dunning Industries, but in the photo the lamp looks like a typical Ranchcraft. The text of the ad states: "Sorrel Fighting Stallion Lamp in exciting detail. Made of durable Tenite. Each horse is screwed onto a sculptured wood base which has a walnut furniture finish. Lamp shade is 16" deep oval with natural burlap cloth covering; brown leatherette trim, top and bottom." In the photo the leatherette trim is visible around the top and bottom rims of the shade. The stallion appears to be an ordinary Breyer "bay," with black mane and tail but no black on the legs, which undoubtedly explains the ad's term "sorrel." Collector Heather Wells has a lamp with a bay Rearing Stallion; the model's lack of a "U.S.A." stamp dates him in to the 1960s. A lamp with brown Bighorn Ram found by collector Sheryl Leisure must date to no earlier than 1969, the year this model debuted. A burlap-shaded, brass-poled lamp with woodgrain Running Mare and Foal on a "hand-rubbed oak base" is offered for $37.95 in a 1972 Miller Stockman saddlery catalog, which does not mention the lamp manufacturer. Since these two woodgrain models were last produced by Breyer in 1965, I would guess that the lamps were old stock or at least made from an old stock of models. Another burlap-shaded, brass-poled lamp with "walnut base" is advertised by a New Jersey outfit called Quality Tack Service in the June 1978 *Arabian Horse World*. The lamp in the ad photo features a Proud Arabian Stallion (first issued by Breyer in 1971), but lamps with Arabian mares (presumably PAMs) were also available according to the ad text, and either mold could be ordered in "bay or grey" for $39.95. Again no manufacturer is mentioned, but the lamp in the ad looks like a typical Ranchcraft. For the *JAH* articles on Ranchcraft lamps see 17/#4 Sept./Oct. 1990 (p. 13) and 18/#2 Summer I 1991 (p. 33).

Another style of Dunning Industries lamp is the "sconce lamp," or "pin lamp," an example of which is owned by collector Sande Schneider. Designed to be mounted on a wall, this lamp has a wood back with a brass pole curving up from it. The pole pierces the belly and back of a woodgrain Running foal, and is topped by a burlap shade. The lamp has a sticker on the bottom of which is printed "Dunning Industries, Inc. / P.O. Box 9276 / Greensboro, N.C." The foal dates this lamp to the 1960s. Yet another lamp that may also be from Dunning Industries was on display at the 1994 BreyerFest. It has a smoke gray Running Foal on a pink oval base, with a thin brass pole behind the foal, and a white shade. This foal too would date its lamp to the 1960s.

"Fury" Prancer lamps. Another type of lamp features the "Fury" Prancer model with a rider, mounted on a gray plaster "desert" base that looks like a boulder or a piece of driftwood, with a tiny plaster "cactus" growing out of it. Some of these lamps have Davy Crockett and rubbery cavalry-type saddle on a dark brown or palomino Prancer and others have Lucky Ranger and plastic Western saddle on a palomino Prancer. The shades on these lamps are round or oval and come either in plain burlap or in a pale beige or dark tan heavy coated paper printed with a silhouette scene in which a coonskin-becapped frontiersman rides his Prancer through a line-drawn desert complete with cacti, cow skull, and clouds. The lamp poles look like those on the Dunning Industries Ranchcraft lamps, but the rider models and Prancers without Breyer copyright stamps would date the Prancer lamps to the mid-1950s, several years earlier than the Ranchcrafts described above.

Other 1950s and 1960s lamps. A lamp that I have not heard of elsewhere was advertised in the April 1968 *Western Horseman* (p. 165). The ad photo shows a small lamp featuring a gray blanket appaloosa Family Arabian Foal (belly-striped version); the text states that a bay foal is also available. The foal is standing on a flat oval metal base, apparently black, with a black horseshoe welded to the end behind the foal. The horseshoe stands at right angles to the base, with the ends pointing upward. The thin metal lamp pole comes up from the base beside the horseshoe. According to the ad, the lamp could be purchased with either a cylindrical burlap shade or a fluffy, lacy white shade, either one for $12.95. The advertiser is "Handcrafted Products / by War Horse Farm," in Mt. Pleasant, Texas.

A completely different lamp, of unknown origin, was found by collector Christina Dils, who had it on display at BreyerFest 1995. The lamp features a glossy white Poodle with red collar, standing on a beveled base of heavy black metal with four little brass legs. The thin, torqued brass lamp pole is topped by an oblong shade of straw thatch. The lamp has no stickers or engravings to indicate who manufactured it. The lack of mold stamps on the Poodle dates him, and thus presumably the lamp as a whole, to the late 1950s.

Glen-Tek lamps. Lamps made with Breyers in the 1970s and 1980s by a company called Glen-Tek Scientific, of Arizona, are mentioned but not described in *JAH* 18/#2 Summer I 1991 (p. 33). Collector Christina Dils kindly sent me photos of two lamps that she found, which have stickers on their bases identifying them as Glen-Tek. One lamp has a Classic "Silky Sullivan" model; the other has a Classic Lipizzan (this one was on display at BreyerFest 1995). These lamps must date to no earlier than 1975 since that is the first year of issue for both of these models. Each lamp has a rectangular wooden base with 4 short pegs or small wooden balls attached as "legs" under the corners. Each also has a slender lamp pole with a crook about half-way up; the pole comes up from the side of the base, behind the horse. The "Silky Sullivan" lamp has a small section of wood-dowel fencing mounted on the base immediately in front of the horse. The beveled edges of the base are painted milk-chocolate brown, matching the color of the lamp pole. The shade is missing. The Lipizzan lamp has a little decorative circus drum, painted red, white, blue, and yellow, mounted on the base below the horse's front hooves. The beveled edges of the base are painted white, matching the color of the lamp pole. This lamp has an ordinary pleated white shade. The stickers on the bases of Christina's lamps say "U.L. Underwriters Laboratories Inc. Portable lamp . . . / Glen-Tek Scientific Co. / P.O. Box 2701, Scottsdale, AZ 85252." The sticker on the "Silky Sullivan" lamp says "Issue no. H-8705," while the Lipizzan's sticker says "Issue no. H-8703." According to Breyer executive Peter Stone (conversation of Nov. 1994), the Glen-Tek company was co-owned by Rudy Schorsch, who later became involved in the model mail-order company Horses International.

Recent lamps. Another commercially made lamp was first brought to my attention by collector Kim David. Her lamp has an old glossy palomino Western Horse with old-style snap saddle and normal twisted-link reins. The model stands on a rectangular beveled-edge wood base in front of a brass lamp pole. The shade is remarkable. It is a square formed of four panels of rawhide or rawhide-like plastic, stitched together with lacing, as on a Western saddle. Each panel features a translucent photographic image of a Western scene: cowboys wrangling cattle in a corral, a panorama of snowy mountains, etc. The model itself appears to date to the 1950s or 1960s, but I suspect the lamp as a whole is of recent manufacture, for a lamp nearly identical to Kim's is shown in an article on contemporary Western-design furnishings printed in a 1992 newspaper magazine from Michigan sent to me by collector Jo Kulwicki. The photo caption says the lamp is from a company called Cry Baby Ranch. Collector Jennifer Pegg told me about a lamp like Kim's, but with scenes of Mount Rushmore, a river, and some wilderness on the shade. Collector Kay Schlumpf also found a lamp (minus its shade) with an old glossy palomino Western Horse standing in front of a brass pole. The base, however, is not wood but metal—a heavy rectangular sheet of black metal with the two ends curled under like the ends of a scroll. There is no sticker or engraving on the base to identify the manufacturer. Collector Sande Schneider has seen a similar scroll-based lamp with a glossy palomino Western Horse, which had a shade consisting of panels laced together.

Lamps made by collector Alison Beniush, of the model-horse mail-order business The World of Model Horse Collecting, became available in 1992. Alison's lamps feature recent Breyers mounted on bases and are topped by shades with perforated designs.

Two more lamps made with Breyers became commercially available in 1993. One, reportedly sold by Fedco for $75, is made with bay appaloosa "Stud Spiders.". This information is per the editor's notes in *The Model Horse Trader*, December 1993. The second lamp, sold through the "Expressions from Potpourri" Holiday 1993 catalog, is made with a dark red-brown pinto Texas Longhorn Bull #370 and priced at $135.

Nightlights

Conventional nightlights. A number of collectors have found nightlights apparently professionally made from original-finish Breyer models, but the Breyer company has no idea who created them.[58] Some nightlight models are mounted on oval or oblong bases made of dark-stained or blond wood, but others are free-standing (no base). The light bulb is located inside the model. A large hole is cut out of the back or belly, through which the bulb can be changed. In most cases the switch is located on the model, protruding through a small hole in the withers or shoulder.

The nightlights I have seen or heard reliable reports of are as follows: glossy gray Brahma Bull (one owned by collector Sheryl Leisure is on a redwood-stained base; another owned by collector Thea Ryan is free-standing); glossy bay Clydesdale Stallion with eyewhites on a blond base (owned by Thea Ryan); Doe and Fawn, probably together on a base (reported in DeFeyter 1991a); glossy bay FAM with eyewhites on a blond base (one was displayed at BreyerFest 1995; another appears in *JAH* 18/#2 Summer I 1991, p. 33); glossy alabaster FAM and FAF together on blond or dark base (Thea Ryan has one of each type of base; the light is in the mare); matte palomino FAM on a base, with the switch on the side of the base, not on the model; glossy palomino Fighting Stallion, free-standing (Sheryl Leisure has a photo of this); brown pinto "Fury" Prancer on a base (seen by collector Sande Schneider); walking horned Hereford Bull on a dark base (one is owned by Thea Ryan; another owned by collector Paula DeFeyter is shown in DeFeyter 1991a); glossy alabaster PAM, some on a base and others free-standing (Paula DeFeyter's free-standing one is shown in DeFeyter 1991a); glossy bay PAM and PAF together on a dark base (owned by collector Judy Miller, shown in Diederich 1988, Sec. 1); glossy bay QH Gelding with eyewhites on a dark base (one on display at BreyerFest 1995); St. Bernard (seen by Sheryl Leisure; not sure about a base); white Western Horse with snap saddle (one owned by Sande Schneider is free standing; another owned by Thea Ryan is on a dark base); black pinto Western Horse with snap saddle on a blond rectangular base (owned by Judy Miller, shown in Diederich 1988, Sec. 1); brown pinto Western Horse (not sure about saddle or base; owned by collector Andrea Gurdon); palomino Western Horse with snap saddle, on a blond base (sold to me by collector Nancy Kelly); smoke Western Prancer, free-standing (seen by collector Lani Keller); and black pinto Western Pony on base (found by collector Arlene Winter).

Most of these models were produced in the 1950s or 1960s, and presumably they were processed into nightlights in the same era. Collector Sande Schneider got her white Western Horse nightlight new at a hardware store sometime between 1959 and 1961 (see her item in the "My First Model" section of *Model Trading Post*, May/June 1992, pp. 22-23). The St. Bernard light, however, can't have been made earlier than 1972, when Breyer first issued this model.

Clock/nightlights. An unusual clock/nightlight made from an old palomino Western Horse was purchased at BreyerFest 1993 by collector Teresa Ward, who kindly sent me a photo of it. The piece is designed like a MasterCrafters clock of the horse-beside-the-clock style, with a beveled rectangular base, but the base and clock casing are made of lovely dark-blond wood, about the same color as the horse. The horse stands to the right of the clock, facing it squarely. The nightlight switch protrudes from a small hole just above the horse's withers, as is typical for ordinary Western Horse nightlights. Teresa wrote to me that this clock/nightlight was made by United Clock Corp., of Brooklyn, New York. The horse is from the later 1950s or the 1960s, to judge from his gray hooves, normal twisted-link reins, and low-grommet snap-on Western saddle. A clock/nightlight very similar in style to Teresa's was seen in person by collector Sande Schneider, who sent me a photo. This clock/nightlight features two Fighting Stallions, one matte alabaster and one glossy charcoal, facing each other and mounted on a long unbeveled oval base of blond wood. The clock face and wooden casing too are very similar to those on Teresa's clock/nightlight.

Car nightlights. And then there is the "Ministang." This bizarre item first broke upon hobby consciousness at the 1995 West Coast Model Horse Collector's Jamboree, where collector Lillian Sutphin brought for display a Ministang she had found at a Southern California flea market. It is a nightlight designed to be attached to the dashboard console of Ford Mustang cars. The Ministang, or "butt light," as Breyer executive Peter Stone dubbed it from the podium at the Jamboree, consists of the rear half of a Family Arabian Mare, into which is fitted a lightbulb and wiring. One might easily dismiss Lillian's specimen as a one-of-a-kind creation from some greaser's garage workshop—except that it came with a sales brochure, installation instructions, and a trade-marked name. "Mustanger Ministang®" lights could be ordered from the manufacturer in Zephyr Cove, Nevada—$15.95 for an alabaster (like Lillian's), $18.95 for a palomino or appaloosa. Lillian's light lacks a "U.S.A." mold stamp and has a glossy finish, both of which features date it to the 1960s. The Ministang brochure bears a copyright date of 1968, as well as several gratuitously graphic illustrations of the type of jiggling gal that the aforementioned greaser might hope to lure into his Mustang via the romantic glow of the butt light.

GENERAL NOTE: In the following list, all Breyer catalog-run and special-run models and sets made since 1950 are listed by mold name under the date when they were first released. Full production dates for each model are given in parentheses. Boldface type identifies the first model released for each mold, and thus shows when the mold itself was introduced. In these boldface entries, the mold dates given in square brackets are only for catalog-run production of the mold, not special run.

In this list, models are Traditional scale unless specified as Classic, Little Bits, Dapples or Stablemates. The listings do not include color details, mold variations, date cross-references to sets with the same model, etc. For this information see the listings above in the main sections.

1950

Western Horse #59, white (1950 - 1960/62) [mold: 1950-94, 1996-]

1951

Western Horse #57, palomino (1951-91)

1953

Western Pony mold: Western Mount Horse "Black Beauty" #44, black, gold hooves (1953 - 1955/57) [mold: 1953-76, 1995 - current as of 1996]

Ca.1954

Boxer #66, chestnut or fawn (ca.1954 - 1973) [mold: ca.1954 - 1973, 1995 - current as of 1996]
Cowboy set #343, rider on palomino Western Pony (ca.1954 - pre-1958) [rider mold: ca.1954 - 1958/59]
Cowboy & Pinto set #341, rider on black pinto Western Pony (ca.1954 - pre-1958)
Cowboy & Pinto set #342, rider on brown pinto Western Pony (ca.1954 - pre-1958)
Indian & Pinto set #241, buckskin-pants rider on black pinto Western Pony (ca.1954 - pre-1958) [rider mold: ca.1954 - 1958/59]
Indian & Pinto set #242, buckskin-pants rider on brown pinto Western Pony (ca.1954 - pre-1958)
Race Horse, Derby Winner, #36, chestnut (ca.1954 - 1966) [mold: ca.1954 - 1966]
Western Horse #55, black pinto (ca.1954 - 1973, 1975-76)
Western Horse #56, brown pinto (ca.1954 - 1966)
Western Horse mold: Western Mount Horse "Black Beauty" #58, black, gold hooves (ca.1954 - pre-1958)
Western Pony #41, black pinto (ca.1954 - 1976)
Western Pony #42, brown pinto (ca.1954 - 1966)
Western Pony #43, palomino (ca.1954 - 1973)
Western Pony #45, white (ca.1954 - 1970)

1955/57

Boxer SR, white (mid to late 1950s)
Brahma Bull #70, shaded gray (1955/57 - 1995) [mold: 1955/57 - current as of 1996]
Canadian Mountie set #P440, rider on dark brown or black "Fury" Prancer (sometime in the period 1955-57) [rider mold: 1955/57 - 1958/59]
Cowboy mold: Lucky Ranger set #341, rider on black pinto Western Pony (1955/56 - 1957)
Cowboy mold: Lucky Ranger set #P341, rider on black pinto "Fury" Prancer (1955/56 - 1957)
Cowboy mold: Lucky Ranger set #342, rider on brown pinto Western Pony (1955/56 - 1957)
Cowboy mold: Lucky Ranger set #P342, rider on brown pinto "Fury" Prancer (1955/56 - 1957)
Cowboy mold: Lucky Ranger set #343, rider on palomino Western Pony (1955/56 - 1957)
Cowboy mold: Lucky Ranger set #P343, rider on palomino "Fury" Prancer (1955/56 - 1957)
Davy Crockett set #P540[?], rider on dark brown "Fury" Prancer (1955 - 1956/57) [rider mold: 1955 - 1958/59]
Davy Crockett mold: Kit Carson set #P540, rider on dark brown or black "Fury" Prancer (1955/56 - 1956)
Davy Crockett mold: Kit Carson set #542, rider on brown pinto Western Pony (sometime in the period 1956-57)
Donkey #81, gray, standing (1956? - 1974) [mold: 1956? - 1974, 1992]
Elephant #91, gray (1956? - 1974) [mold: 1956? - 1974, 1992]
"Fury" Prancer mold: Prancer #43, palomino (1955 - 1960/62) [mold: 1955-65]
"Fury" Prancer mold: "Black Beauty" #P40, black, with blaze or bald face (1955/57 - 1960/62)

"Fury" Prancer mold: Prancer #P40, dark brown (1955 - 1956/57)
"Fury" Prancer mold: Prancer #P41, black pinto (1955 - 1960/62)
"Fury" Prancer mold: Prancer #P42, brown pinto (1955 - 1960/62)
"Fury" Prancer mold: Prancer #P45, white (1955/56 - 1960/62)
Hereford Bull #71, horned, walking; brown with white (1955/57 - 1981) [mold: 1955/57 - 1981]
Indian mold: Indian Chief And Pinto Pony set #P241, turquoise-pants rider on black pinto "Fury" Prancer (1955 - 1956/57)
Indian mold: Indian Chief And Pinto Pony set #P242, turquoise-pants rider on brown pinto "Fury" Prancer (1955 - 1956/57)
"Lassie" #65, collie dog, red chestnut and white (1955/57 - 1965) [mold: 1955/57 - 1965, 1995 - current as of 1996]
Poodle #67, black (1955/57 - 1967/68) [mold: 1955/57 - 1973]
Poodle #68, white (1955/57 - 1967/68)
"Rin Tin Tin" #64, brown and white dog (1955/57 - 1965) [mold: catalog run 1955/57 - 1965, pre-catalog release 1971, catalog run 1972-73]
Robin Hood set #P145, rider on white "Fury" Prancer (1956 - 1958/59) [rider mold: 1956 - 1958/59]
Western Pony mold: Western Pony "Black Beauty" #40, black, with bald face or diamond star (1955/58 - 1960/62)
Western Pony #40, dark brown (sometime in the period 1955-57)

1957/58

Canadian Mountie set #P445, rider on white "Fury" Prancer (1957/58 - 1958/59)
Clydesdale Stallion mold: Clydesdale #80, bay (1958 {maybe earlier} - 1989) [mold: 1958 {maybe earlier} - current as of 1996]
Corky The Circus Boy mold: Circus Boy Corky On "Bimbo" set #601, boy on Elephant (1957/58 - 1958/59) [rider mold: 1957/58 - 1958/59]
Cowboy mold: Lucky Ranger set #345, rider on white Western Pony (1957/58 - 1958/59)
Davy Crockett mold: Kit Carson set #540, rider on "Black Beauty" Western Pony (1957/58 - 1958/59)
Donkey mold: Donkey With Baskets set #82, gray, with detachable red plastic baskets (1958 {maybe earlier} - 1958/59)
Elephant #92, pink (1958 {maybe earlier} - 1958/59)
Elephant #93, blue (1958 {maybe earlier} - 1958/59)
Elephant mold: Elephant With Howdah set #94, gray, with detachable howdah (1958 {maybe earlier} - 1958/59)
"Fury" Prancer mold: "Fury" #27, black, star (1957/58 - 1965)
Indian mold: Indian Warrior set #240, buckskin-pants rider on "Black Beauty" Western Pony (1958 {maybe earlier} - 1958/59)
Proud Arabian Foal mold: Arabian Foal "Joy" #9, alabaster (1958 {possibly late 1957} - 1959) [mold: 1958 {possibly late 1957} - 1959, 1973-90]
Proud Arabian Mare mold: Arabian Mare "Pride" #8, alabaster (1958 {possibly late 1957} - 1959) [mold: catalog run 1958 {possibly late 1957} - 1959, pre-catalog release 1971, catalog run 1972-92, 1996-]
Proud Arabian Mare and Foal molds: "Pride" And "Joy" Combination #10, alabaster (1958 {possibly late 1957} - 1959)

1959

Brahma Bull #970, woodgrain (1959-65)
Clydesdale Stallion mold: Clydesdale #980, woodgrain (1959-64)
Elephant SR, woodgrain (probably sometime in the period 1959-66)
Family Arabian Stallion "Sheik" #13, bay (1959 {possibly late 1958} - 1973) [mold: 1959 {possibly late 1958} - 1990, 1993-94, 1996]
Family Arabian Stallion "Prince" #7, alabaster (1959 {possibly late 1958} - 1973)
Family Arabian Stallion #907, woodgrain (1959-66)
Family Arabian Stallion mold: Family Appaloosa Stallion "Fleck" #37, gray blanket appaloosa (1959-70)
Family Arabian Stallion and Proud Arabian Mare molds: "Prince" And "Pride" set #12, alabaster (1959)
Family Arabian Stallion and Proud Arabian Mare molds: "Sheik" And "Sheba" set #17, bay ({possibly late 1958} - 1959)
Family Arabian Stallion, Proud Arabian Mare, and Proud Arabian Foal molds: "Prince," "Pride" And "Joy" set #11, alabaster (1959)
Family Arabian Stallion, Proud Arabian Mare, and Proud Arabian Foal molds: "Sheik," "Sheba," And "Shah" set #16, bay ({possibly late 1958} - 1959)
"Fury" Prancer mold: Prancer #P945[?], woodgrain (probably 1959)
Proud Arabian Foal mold: Arabian Foal "Shah" #15, bay ({possibly late 1958} - 1959)
Proud Arabian Foal mold: Arabian Foal "Spot" #39, gray blanket appaloosa (1959)
Proud Arabian Mare mold: Arabian Mare #908, woodgrain (1959)
Proud Arabian Mare mold: Arabian Mare "Sheba" #14, bay ({possibly late 1958} - 1959)
Proud Arabian Mare mold: Arabian Mare "Speck" #38, gray blanket appaloosa (1959)
Proud Arabian Mare and Foal molds: "Sheba" And "Shah" set #18, bay ({possibly late 1958} - 1959)
Race Horse, Derby Winner, #936, woodgrain (1959-65)

1959/60

Black Angus Bull #72, polled, walking; black (1959/60 - 1973, 1976-77) [mold: 1959/60 - 1973, 1976-77]
Boxer #966, woodgrain (1959/60 - 1965)
Hereford Bull #971, horned, walking; woodgrain (1959/60 - 1964)
Western Horse #50, black, bald face (1959/60 - 1960/62)
Western Pony #945, woodgrain (1959/60 - 1964)

1960

Family Arabian Foal "Joy" #9, alabaster (1960-73) [mold: 1960-94]
Family Arabian Foal "Shah" #15, bay (1960-73)
Family Arabian Foal #909, woodgrain (1960-66)
Family Arabian Foal mold: Family Appaloosa Foal "Spot" #39, gray blanket appaloosa (1960-70)
Family Arabian Mare "Pride" #8, alabaster (1960-73) [mold: 1960-90, 1993-94]
Family Arabian Mare "Sheba" #14, bay (1960-73)
Family Arabian Mare #908, woodgrain (1960-66)
Family Arabian Mare mold: Family Appaloosa Mare "Speck" #38, gray blanket appaloosa (1960-70)
Family Arabian Mare and Foal molds: "Pride" And "Joy" set #10, alabaster (1960-64)
Family Arabian Mare and Foal molds: "Sheba" And "Shah" set #18, bay (1960-64)
Family Arabian Stallion and Mare molds: "Prince" And "Pride" set #12, alabaster (1960 - 1960/62)
Family Arabian Stallion and Mare molds: "Sheik" And "Sheba" set #17, bay (1960 - 1960/62)
Family Arabian Stallion, Mare, and Foal molds: "Prince," "Pride," And "Joy" set #11, alabaster (1960-64)
Family Arabian Stallion, Mare, and Foal molds: "Sheik," "Sheba," And "Shah" set #16, bay (1960-64)
"Fury" Prancer SR, Wedgewood Blue (sometime in the period 1960-65)
Quarter Horse Gelding mold: Quarter Horse "Two Bits" #99, bay (1960-66) [mold: 1960-80, 1995 - current as of 1996]
Quarter Horse Gelding mold: Quarter Horse "Two Bits" #999, woodgrain (1960-64)
Shetland Pony #21, black pinto (1960-73, 1976) [mold: 1960 - current as of 1996]
Shetland Pony #22, brown pinto (1960-66, 1970-73)
Shetland Pony #25, alabaster (1960-72)
Shetland Pony #925, woodgrain (1960-64)

1961

Clydesdale Stallion mold: Clydesdale #82, dapple gray (1961-66)
Fighting Stallion mold: "King" The Fighting Stallion #30, Alabaster Lipizzan (1961-85) [mold: 1961-90, 1992, 1994 - current as of 1996]
Fighting Stallion mold: "King" The Fighting Stallion #32, gray appaloosa (1961-66)
Fighting Stallion mold: "King" The Fighting Stallion #33, palomino (1961-73)
Fighting Stallion mold: "King" The Fighting Stallion #931, woodgrain (1961-73)

1961/62/63

Black Angus Bull (polled, walking) mold: Polled Hereford Bull #73, brown with white (1961/63 - 1965)
Family Arabian Foal "Charity" #6, palomino (1961/62 - 1987)
Family Arabian Foal "Doc" #203, charcoal (1961/62 - 1973)
Family Arabian Foal SR, medium chestnut, bald face (sometime in the 1960s)
Family Arabian Mare "Dickory" #202, charcoal (1961/62 - 1973)
Family Arabian Mare "Hope" #5, palomino (1961/62 - 1987)
Family Arabian Mare SR, medium chestnut, bald face (sometime in the 1960s)
Family Arabian Mare and Foal molds: "Dickory" And "Doc" set #223, charcoal (1961/62 - 1964)
Family Arabian Mare and Foal molds: "Hope" And "Charity" set #506, palomino (1961/62 - 1964)
Family Arabian Stallion "Faith" #4, palomino (1961/62 - 1987)
Family Arabian Stallion "Hickory" #201, charcoal (1961/62 - 1973)
Family Arabian Stallion SR, medium chestnut, bald face (sometime in the 1960s)
Family Arabian Stallion, Mare, and Foal molds: "Faith," "Hope," And "Charity" set #456, palomino (1961/62 - 1964)
Family Arabian Stallion, Mare, and Foal molds: "Hickory," "Dickory," And "Doc" set #213, charcoal (1961/62 - 1964)
Fighting Stallion mold: "King" The Fighting Stallion #34, charcoal (1961/63 - 1970)
Fighting Stallion mold: "King" The Fighting Stallion #35, bay (1961/63 - 1987)
Five-Gaiter mold: "Commander" The Five-Gaiter #51, albino (1961/63 - 1966) [mold: 1961/62 - 1995]
Five-Gaiter mold: "Commander" The Five-Gaiter #52, sorrel (1961/63 - 1986)
Five-Gaiter mold: "Commander" The Five-Gaiter #53, palomino (1961/62 - 1971)
Five-Gaiter mold: "Commander" The Five-Gaiter #951, woodgrain (1961/62 - 1965)
Golden Buck #101, metallic gold (1961/62 - 1964) [mold: 1961/62 - 1964]
Golden Doe #102, metallic gold (1961/62 - 1964) [mold: 1961/62 - 1964]
Mustang mold: "Diablo" The Mustang #85, albino (1961/63 - 1966) [mold: 1961/63 - 1991, 1994 - current as of 1996]
Mustang mold: "Diablo" The Mustang #86, gray appaloosa (1961/63 - 1966)
Mustang mold: "Diablo" The Mustang #87, buckskin (1961/63 - 1986)
Mustang mold: "Diablo" The Mustang #88, charcoal (1961/63 - 1970)
Mustang mold: "Diablo" The Mustang #985, woodgrain (1961/63 - 1965)
Poodle #967, woodgrain (1961/63 - 1964)
Quarter Horse Gelding mold: Quarter Horse "Two Bits" #98, buckskin (1961/63 - 1980)
Running Foal "Spice" #130, alabaster (1961/63 - 1971) [mold: 1961/63 - 1987, 1991 current as of 1996]

Running Foal "Spice" #131, smoke (solid gray) (1961/63 - 1970)
Running Foal "Spice" #133, dapple gray (1961/63 - 1973)
Running Foal "Spice" #134, bay (1961/63 - 1987)
Running Foal "Spice" #930, woodgrain (1961/63 - 1965)
Running Foal SR?, buckskin (1960s); only a couple known to exist
Running Mare "Sugar" #120, alabaster (1961/63 - 1971) [mold: 1961/63 - 1987, 1991 - current as of 1996]
Running Mare "Sugar" #121, smoke (solid gray) (1961/63 - 1970)
Running Mare "Sugar" #123, dapple gray (1961/63 - 1973)
Running Mare "Sugar" #124, bay (1961/63 - 1987)
Running Mare "Sugar" #920, woodgrain (1961/63 - 1965)
Running Mare SR?, buckskin (1960s); only a couple known to exist
Running Mare and Foal molds: "Sugar" And "Spice" #351, alabaster mare and smoke foal (1961/63 - 1964)
Running Mare and Foal molds: "Sugar" And "Spice" #352, smoke mare and alabaster foal (1961/63 - 1964)
Texas Longhorn Bull #75, light brown (1961/63 - 1989) [mold: 1961/63 - current as of 1996]
Texas Longhorn Bull #975, woodgrain (1961/63 - 1965)
Western Prancer mold: Western Prancing Horse "Cheyenne" #110, smoke (solid gray) (1961/63 - 1976) [mold: 1961/63 - 1985, 1994 - current as of 1996]
Western Prancer mold: Western Prancing Horse "Cheyenne" #111, buckskin (1961/63 - 1973)
Western Prancer mold: Western Prancing Horse "Cheyenne" #112, palomino (1961/63 - 1985)
Western Prancer mold: Western Prancing Horse "Cheyenne" #113, black pinto (1961/63 - 1966)
Western Prancer mold: Western Prancing Horse "Cheyenne" #114, bay (1961/63 - 1971)
Western Prancer mold: Western Prancing Horse "Cheyenne" #115, black leopard appaloosa (1961/63 - 1973)

1963

Fighting Stallion #1031, Copenhagen decorator, dappled blue (1963-64)
Fighting Stallion #2031, Florentine decorator, dappled metallic gold (1963-64)
Fighting Stallion #3031, Golden Charm decorator, solid metallic gold (1963-64)
Fighting Stallion #4031, Wedgewood Blue decorator, solid blue (1963-64)
Five-Gaiter mold: "Commander" The Five-Gaiter #1051, Copenhagen decorator, dappled blue (1963-64)
Five-Gaiter mold: "Commander" The Five-Gaiter #2051, Florentine decorator, dappled metallic gold (1963-64)
Five-Gaiter mold: "Commander" The Five-Gaiter #3051, Golden Charm decorator, solid metallic gold (1963-64)
Five-Gaiter mold: "Commander" The Five-Gaiter #4051, Wedgewood Blue decorator, solid blue (1963-64)
Mustang mold: "Diablo" The Mustang #1085, Copenhagen decorator, dappled blue (1963-64)
Mustang mold: "Diablo" The Mustang #2085, Florentine decorator, dappled metallic gold (1963-64)
Mustang mold: "Diablo" The Mustang #3085, Golden Charm decorator, solid metallic gold (1963-64)
Mustang mold: "Diablo" The Mustang #4085, Wedgewood Blue decorator, solid blue (1963-64)
Running Foal #1130, Copenhagen decorator, dappled blue (1963-64)
Running Foal #2130, Florentine decorator, dappled metallic gold (1963-64)
Running Foal #3130, Golden Charm decorator, solid metallic gold (1963-64)
Running Foal #4130, Wedgewood Blue decorator, solid blue (1963-64)
Running Mare #1120, Copenhagen decorator, dappled blue (1963-64)
Running Mare #2120, Florentine decorator, dappled metallic gold (1963-64)
Running Mare #3120, Golden Charm decorator, solid metallic gold (1963-64)
Running Mare #4120, Wedgewood Blue decorator, solid blue (1963-64)
Running Mare And Foal set #1351, Copenhagen decorator, dappled blue (1963-64)
Running Mare And Foal set #2351, Florentine decorator, dappled metallic gold (1963-64)
Running Mare And Foal set #3351, Golden Charm decorator, solid metallic gold (1963-64)
Running Mare And Foal set #4351, Wedgewood Blue decorator, solid blue (1963-64)

1964

Belgian #92, smoke (solid gray) (1964-71) [mold: 1964-80, 1995]
Belgian #93, dapple gray (1964-66)
Belgian #94, chestnut, lighter chestnut mane and tail (1964-80)
Belgian #992, woodgrain (1964-65)
Buck #301, tawny (1964-73) [mold: 1964 - current as of 1996]
Doe #302, tawny (1964-73) [mold: 1964 - current as of 1996]
Fawn #303, tawny with white spots (1964-73) [mold: 1964 - current as of 1996]
Fawn, Doe, and Buck molds: Deer Family set #304 (1964-65).
Morgan #48, black (1964-87) [mold: 1964-95]
Morgan #49, bay (1964-71)
Morgan #948, woodgrain (1964-65)

1965

Buffalo #76, brown (1965-91) [mold: 1965 - current as of 1996]
Buffalo SR, woodgrain (probably sometime in the period 1965-66)
Classic Rearing Stallion "Rex" #180, Alabaster Lipizzan (1965-76, 1978-85) [mold: 1965-85, 1994 - current as of 1996]
Classic Rearing Stallion "Rex" #183, palomino (1965-85)
Classic Rearing Stallion "Rex" #185, bay (1965-80)
Grazing Foal "Bows" #151, bay (1965-76, 1978-81) [mold: 1965-81, 1993-95]
Grazing Foal "Bows" #152, black (1965-70)
Grazing Foal "Bows" #153, palomino (1965-81)

Grazing Mare "Buttons" #141, bay (1965-76, 1978-80) [mold: 1965-76, 1978-80, 1993-95]
Grazing Mare "Buttons" #142, black (1965-70)
Grazing Mare "Buttons" #143, palomino (1965-76, 1978-80)
Grazing Mare and Foal molds: "Buttons" And "Bows" set #1411, both bay (1965)
Grazing Mare and Foal molds: "Buttons" And "Bows" set #1422, both black (1965)
Grazing Mare and Foal molds: "Buttons" And "Bows" set #1433, both palomino (1965)
Jumping Horse "Stonewall" #300, bay (1965-88) [mold: 1965-88, 1994]

1966

Classic Bucking Bronco #190, black (1966-73, 1975-76) [mold: 1966-73, 1975-76, 1995 - current as of 1996]
Classic Bucking Bronco #191, steel gray (1966)
"Jolly Cholly" Bloodhound #325, solid dark brown (1966 - 1967/68) [mold: 1966-85, 1994-95]
Kitten mold: Calico Kitten #336, orangy-tan tabby with charcoal-brown stripes (1966-73) [mold: 1966-73, 1994 - current as of 1996]
Kitten mold: Siamese Kitten #335, white with dark Siamese points (1966-70)
Moose #79, brown (1966 - current as of 1996) [mold: 1966 - current as of 1996]
Old Timer #200, alabaster (1966-76) [mold: 1966-93, 1995 - current as of 1996]
Old Timer #205, dapple gray (1966, 1968/70 - 1987)

1967

Bear #306, black (1967-73) [mold: 1967-76, 1987-88, 1992-95]
Bear #307, brown (1967-71)
Bear Cub #308, black (1967-73) [mold: 1967-76, 1987-88, 1992-95]
Bear Cub #309, brown (1967-71)
Classic Bucking Bronco #192, bay (1967/68 - 1970)
"Man O' War" #47, red chestnut (1967-95) [mold: 1967 - current as of 1996]
Pacer #46, liver chestnut (1967-87) [mold: 1967-87, 1990, 1996]

1968

Balking Mule #207, bay (1968-73) [mold: 1968-73]
Balking Mule #208, seal brown (1968-70)
Elk #77, reddish-brown (1968 - current as of 1996) [mold: 1968 - current as of 1996]
"Jolly Cholly" Basset Hound #326, tri-color (1968/69 - 1985)
Polled Hereford Bull #74, standing, large; brown with white (1968 - current as of 1996) [mold: 1968 - current as of 1996]
Poodle #69, silver gray (1968/69 - 1973)
Running Stallion #125, alabaster (1968-71) [mold: 1968-88, 1993 - current as of 1996]
Running Stallion #126, charcoal (1968-70)
Running Stallion #127, black blanket appaloosa (1968-81)
Running Stallion #128, red roan (1968-74)

1969

"Adios" Famous Standardbred #50, dark bay (1969-80) [mold: 1969 - current as of 1996]
Bighorn Ram #78, brown (1969-80) [mold: 1969-80]
Clydesdale Foal #84, chestnut (1969-89) [mold: 1969-91, 1994-95]
Clydesdale Mare #83, chestnut (1969-89) [mold: 1969-93]
Lying Down Foal #165, black blanket appaloosa (1969-84) [mold: 1969-88, 1996]
Lying Down Foal #166, buckskin (1969-73, 1975-76)
Lying Down Foal #167, red roan (1969-73)

1970

"Adios" mold: "Yellow Mount" Famous Paint Horse #51, chestnut paint (1970-87)
Bighorn Ram mold: Dall Sheep #85, white (1970-73)
Family Arabian Foal SR, chestnut pinto, mounted on wood base (1970/71)
Indian Pony #175, chestnut pinto (1970-76) [mold: 1970-85, 1993, 1995 - current as of 1996]
Indian Pony #176, buckskin (1970-72)
Indian Pony #177, alabaster (1970-71)
Morgan SR, bay, solid face, no white markings (early or mid 1970s)
Quarter Horse Yearling #101, liver chestnut (1970-80) [mold: 1970-88, 1995 - current as of 1996]
Quarter Horse Yearling #102, palomino (1970-80)
Scratching Foal #168, black blanket appaloosa (1970-86) [mold: 1970-86]
Scratching Foal #169, liver chestnut (1970-71)
Scratching Foal #170, red roan (1970-73)
Spanish Fighting Bull #73, black (1970-85) [mold: 1970-85]

1971

Cantering Welsh Pony #104, bay (1971-73) [mold: 1971-76, 1979-81, 1992-95]
Cantering Welsh Pony #105, chestnut (1971-76, 1979-81)
Cantering Welsh Pony #106, seal brown (1971-74)
Clydesdale Mare and Foal molds: Clydesdale Gift Set #8384, chestnut mare and foal, stable blankets (1971-90)
Presentation Collection "Adios" #50/#5050 (late 1971 - 1973)
Presentation Collection Indian Pony, alabaster (late 1971 only)
Presentation Collection "Man O' War" #47/#5047 (late 1971 - 1973)

Presentation Collection Proud Arabian Stallion "Witez II" #212/#5212 (late 1971 - 1973)
Presentation Collection Quarter Horse Yearling, palomino, #102/#5102 (late 1971 - 1973)
Presentation Collection "Yellow Mount" #51/#5051 (late 1971 - 1973)
Pronghorn Antelope #310, brown with white (1971-76) [mold: 1971-76]
Proud Arabian Mare #215, dapple gray (pre-catalog release 1971, catalog run 1972-88)
Proud Arabian Stallion #211, alabaster (1971-76, 1978-81) [mold: 1971 - current as of 1996]
Proud Arabian Stallion "Witez II" #212, mahogany bay (1971-80)
Quarter Horse Gelding mold: Appaloosa Gelding #97, sorrel blanket appaloosa (1971-80)
Quarter Horse Yearling mold: Appaloosa Yearling #103, sandy bay blanket appaloosa (1971-88)
"Rin Tin Tin" mold: German Shepherd #327, charcoal gray or gray-brown (pre-catalog release 1971, catalog run 1972-73)
Running Mare #119, red roan (1971-73)
Running Stallion #129, bay (1971-76, 1978-80)

1972

Bolo Tie #501, white buffalo skull on string tie (1972-76) [mold: 1972-76]
Calf mold: Ayrshire Calf #350, dark red-brown pinto (1972-73) [mold: 1972 95]
Calf mold: Brown Swiss Calf #351, medium coffee brown (1972-73)
Calf mold: Guernsey Calf #348, dark palomino pinto (1972-73)
Calf mold: Holstein Calf #347, black pinto (1972-73)
Calf mold: Jersey Calf #349, dark palomino (1972-73)
Cow mold: Ayrshire Cow #344, horns, dark red-brown pinto (1972-73) [mold: 1972 - current as of 1996]
Cow mold: Brown Swiss Cow #345, horns, medium coffee brown (1972-73)
Cow mold: Guernsey Cow #342, horns, dark palomino pinto (1972-73)
Cow mold: Holstein Cow #341, horns, black pinto (1972-73)
Cow mold: Jersey Cow #343, horns, dark palomino (1972-73)
"Misty" mold: "Misty" Of Chincoteague #20, chestnut pinto (1972 - current as of 1996) [mold: 1972 - current as of 1996]
"Misty" Gift Set #2055, chestnut pinto pony, book (1972-81)
Presentation Collection American Bison #76/#5076 (1972-73)
Presentation Collection Indian Pony, chestnut pinto, #175/#5175 (1972-73)
Presentation Collection Moose #79/#5079 (1972-73)
Presentation Collection Spanish Fighting Bull #73/#5073 (1972-73)
Presentation Collection Texas Longhorn #75/#5075 (1972-73)
Proud Arabian Mare #216, mahogany bay, solid face (1972-80)
Proud Arabian Mare #217, alabaster, matte (1972-76, 1978-81)
Proud Arabian Mare Gift Set #2155, dapple gray with Arab halter (1972-73)
Proud Arabian Mare Gift Set #2165, mahogany bay with Arab halter (1972-73)
Proud Arabian Mare Gift Set #2175, alabaster with Arab halter (1972-73)
Proud Arabian Stallion #213, dapple gray (1972-83)
St. Bernard #328, chestnut and white (1972-80) [mold: 1972-80, 1995 - current as of 1996]
Shire #95, dapple gray (1972-73, 1975-76) [mold: 1972-76, 1978-80]
Shire #96, honey sorrel (1972-76, 1978-80)
Tennessee Walker mold: "Midnight Sun" Famous Tennessee Walker #60, black (1972-87) [mold: 1972-89, 1992, 1995 - current as of 1996]

1973

Classic Arabian Family Foal mold: Arabian Family Gift Set #3055, chestnut foal (1973-91) [mold: 1973 - current as of 1996]
Classic Arabian Family Foal mold: Classic Arabian Foal #4000, alabaster (1973 - 1982/83)
Classic Arabian Family Foal mold: Classic Arabian Foal #4000, black (1973 - 1982/83)
Classic Arabian Family Foal mold: Classic Arabian Foal #4000, chestnut (1973 - 1982/83)
Classic Arabian Family Foal mold: Classic Arabian Foal #4000, palomino (1973 - 1982/83)
Classic Arabian Family Foal mold: Classic Arabian Foal #4000, smoke gray (1973 - 1982/83)
Classic Arabian Family Mare mold: Arabian Family Gift Set #3055, chestnut mare (1973-91) [mold: 1973 - current as of 1996]
Classic Arabian Family Stallion mold: Arabian Family Gift Set #3055, chestnut stallion (1973-91) [mold: 1973 - current as of 1996]
Indian Pony #174, bay blanket appaloosa (1973-85)
"Justin Morgan" mold: "Justin Morgan" Gift Set #2065, bay horse, book (1973-81) [mold: 1973 - current as of 1996]
Proud Arabian Foal #218, alabaster, matte (1973-76, 1978-81)
Proud Arabian Foal #219, mahogany bay, solid face (1973-80)
Proud Arabian Foal #220, dapple gray (1973-88)
Rocky Mountain Goat #312, white with charcoal or gray horns (1973-76) [mold: 1973-76, 1989]
Saddlebred Weanling #62, dark chestnut (1973-80) [mold: 1973-80, 1985-87, 1990, 1995 - current as of 1996]
Shetland Pony #23, bay (1973-88)
Suckling Foal mold: Thoroughbred Mare And Suckling Foal set #3155, chestnut foal (1973-84) [mold: 1973-84, 1994 - current as of 1996]
Thoroughbred Mare (ears back) mold: Thoroughbred Mare And Suckling Foal set #3155, bay mare (1973-84) [mold: 1973-84, 1994 - current as of 1996]

1974

Bear and Bear Cub molds: Bear Family set #3068, both black (1974-76)
"Brighty" Gift Set #2075, gray sitting burro, book (1974-81) [mold: 1974-87, 1991 - current as of 1996]
Buck, Doe, and Fawn molds: Deer Family set #3123, with carry box (1974 - current as of 1996)
Classic Quarter Horse Family Foal mold: Quarter Horse Family Gift Set #3045, bay foal (1974-93) [mold: 1974-93]
Classic Quarter Horse Family Foal mold: Quarter Horse Foal #4001, bay (1974-82)

Classic Quarter Horse Family Foal mold: Quarter Horse Foal #4001, black (1974-82)
Classic Quarter Horse Family Foal mold: Quarter Horse Foal #4001, chestnut (1974-82)
Classic Quarter Horse Family Foal mold: Quarter Horse Foal #4001, palomino (1974-82)
Classic Quarter Horse Family Mare mold: Quarter Horse Family Gift Set #3045, bay mare (1974-93) [mold: 1974-93]
Classic Quarter Horse Family Stallion mold: Quarter Horse Family Gift Set #3045, palomino stallion (1974-93) [mold: 1974-93]
Cow and Calf molds: Cow Family set #3447, polled Holstein Cow and Calf, black pinto (1974-91)
"El Pastor" Famous Paso Fino #61, bay (1974-81) [mold: 1974-81, 1987, 1992 - current as of 1996]
"Jasper" The Market Hog #355, white with large gray spot (1974 - current as of 1996) [mold: 1974 - current as of 1996]
Performance Horse mold: Appaloosa Performance Horse #99, red roan semi-leopard (1974-80) [mold: 1974-85, 1996-]

1975

Buffalo SR, light smoke gray (mid-1970s?)
Charolais Bull #360, white (1975-95) [mold: 1975 - current as of 1996]
Classic "Hobo" mold (with stand): "Hobo" Mustang Of Lazy Heart Ranch #625, buckskin (1975-80) [mold: 1975-81]
Classic "Hobo" mold (with stand): "Hobo" Of Lazy Heart Ranch Gift Set #2085, buckskin horse, book (1975-81)
Classic "Kelso" #601, dark bay (1975-90) [mold: 1975 - current as of 1996]
Classic Lipizzan Stallion #620, alabaster (1975-80) [mold: 1975-80, mid-1983 - 1987]
Classic "Man-O-War" #602, red chestnut (1975-90) [mold: 1975 - current as of 1996]
Classic "Silky Sullivan" #603, medium/dark chestnut (1975-90) [mold: 1975 - current as of 1996]
Classic "Swaps" #604, medium chestnut, star (1975-90) [mold: 1975 - current as of 1996]
Classic "Terrang" #605, dark/medium bay, no white (1975-90) [mold: 1975 - current as of 1996]
Stablemates Arabian Mare #5011, dapple gray (1975-76) [mold: 1975 - current as of 1996]
Stablemates Arabian Mare #5014, bay (1975-88)
Stablemates Arabian Mare #5017, alabaster (1975-87)
Stablemates Arabian Stallion mold: "Citation" #5020, bay (early 1975 as "Citation" #5020; late 1975 - 1988 as Arabian Stallion #5013) [mold: 1975 - current as of 1996]
Stablemates Arabian Stallion #5010, dapple gray (late 1975 - 1976)
Stablemates Arabian Stallion #5016, alabaster (late 1975 - 1988)
Stablemates Arabian Stallion mold: "Emperor's Gold Bar" SR, palomino, mounted on paperweight (sometime in the period 1975-80)
Stablemates "Citation" #5020, bay (late 1975 - 1990) [mold: late 1975 - current as of 1996]
Stablemates Draft Horse #5055, sorrel (late 1975 - 1988) [mold: late 1975 - current as of 1996]
Stablemates Morgan Mare #5038, bay (late 1975 - 1988) [mold: late 1975 - current as of 1996]
Stablemates Morgan Mare #5039, black (late 1975 - 1988)
Stablemates Morgan Mare #5040, chestnut (late 1975 - 1976)
Stablemates Morgan Stallion mold: Arabian Stallion #5010, dapple gray (early 1975) [mold: 1975 - current as of 1996]
Stablemates Morgan Stallion mold: Arabian Stallion #5013, bay (early 1975 as Arabian Stallion #5013; late 1975 - 1988 as Morgan Stallion #5035)
Stablemates Morgan Stallion mold: Arabian Stallion #5016, alabaster (early 1975)
Stablemates Morgan Stallion #5036, black (late 1975 - 1988)
Stablemates Morgan Stallion #5037, medium/light chestnut (late 1975 - 1976)
Stablemates "Native Dancer" #5023, steel gray (mid-1975 - 1994) [mold: mid-1975 - current as of 1996]
Stablemates Quarter Horse Mare #5048, palomino (late 1975 - 1987) [mold: late 1975 - 1988]
Stablemates Quarter Horse Mare #5049, golden chestnut (late 1975 - 1976)
Stablemates Quarter Horse Mare #5050, buckskin (late 1975 - 1988)
Stablemates Quarter Horse Stallion #5045, palomino (late 1975 - 1988) [mold: late 1975 - 1988, 1995 - current as of 1996]
Stablemates Quarter Horse Stallion #5046, golden chestnut (late 1975 - 1976)
Stablemates Quarter Horse Stallion #5047, buckskin (late 1975 - 1987)
Stablemates Saddlebred #5001, dapple gray (1975-76) [mold: 1975-90]
Stablemates Saddlebred #5002, bay (1975-88)
Stablemates Saddlebred SR, silver plated (1975)
Stablemates "Seabiscuit" #5024, bay (mid-1975 - 1990) [mold: mid-1975 - current as of 1996]
Stablemates "Silky Sullivan" #5022, dark/medium chestnut (mid-1975 - 1994) [mold: mid-1975 - current as of 1996]
Stablemates "Swaps" #5021, chestnut (mid-1975 - 1994) [mold: mid-1975 - current as of 1996]
Stablemates Thoroughbred Lying Foal, black, in TB Lying And Standing Foals set #5701 (1975-76) [mold: 1975-80]
Stablemates Thoroughbred Lying Foal, sandy bay, in TB Lying And Standing Foals set #5700 (1975-76)
Stablemates Thoroughbred Lying Foal, chestnut, in TB Lying And Standing Foals set #5702 (1975-76)
Stablemates Thoroughbred Mare #5026, golden chestnut (1975-87) [mold: 1975 - current as of 1996]
Stablemates Thoroughbred Mare #5028, black (1975-88)
Stablemates Thoroughbred Mare #5030, medium bay (1975-88)
Stablemates Thoroughbred Standing Foal, black, in TB Lying And Standing Foals set #5701 (1975-76) [mold: 1975-80]
Stablemates Thoroughbred Standing Foal, medium sandy bay, in TB Lying And Standing Foals set #5700 (1975-76)
Stablemates Thoroughbred Standing Foal, chestnut, in TB Lying And Standing Foals set #5702 (1975-76)

1976

"Adios" mold: Breyer Rider Gift Set #3095, palomino horse (1976); only a few horses made; no doll or tack
Breyer Rider #400, girl doll (1976) [mold: 1976]; advertised but never released
Classic Mustang Family Foal mold: Mustang Family Gift Set #3065, chestnut foal (1976-90) [mold: 1976 - current as of 1996]
Classic Mustang Family Mare mold: Mustang Family Gift Set #3065, chestnut pinto mare (1976-90) [mold: 1976-90, 1995 - current as of 1996]
Classic Mustang Family Stallion mold: Mustang Family Gift Set #3065, chestnut stallion (1976-90) [mold: 1976-91, 1995 - current as of 1996]
Classic Polo Pony #626, bay, with stand (1976-82) [mold: 1976-82]
"Lady Phase" mold: Lynn Anderson's "Lady Phase" #40, red chestnut (1976-85) [mold: 1976-85, 1988, 1992-94]
"Lady Phase" mold: Lynn Anderson's "Lady Phase" Gift Set #3075, red chestnut mare, blue ribbon, book (1976-81)
Pony Of The Americas #155, chestnut leopard appaloosa (1976-80) [mold: 1976-84, 1990-95]
Stablemates Quarter Horse Mare mold: Stablemates Stable Set #3085, dark bay mare (1976-80)
Stablemates Quarter Horse Stallion mold: Stablemates Stable Set #3085, dark bay stallion (1976-78 only)
Stablemates Thoroughbred Lying Foal mold: Stablemates Stable Set #3085, dark bay lying foal (1976-80)
Stablemates Thoroughbred Standing Foal mold: Stablemates Stable Set #3085, dark bay standing foal (1976-80)

1977

"Benji" #7701, dark yellowy buckskin dog (late 1977 - 1979) [mold: late 1977 - 1979]
Calf mold: Black Angus Calf SR #352, black (1977)
Classic "Ruffian" #606, dark brown bay (1977-90) [mold: 1977 - current as of 1996]
Family Arabian Foal SR #12, black (1977)
Family Arabian Mare SR #11, black (1977)
Family Arabian Stallion SR #10, black (1977)
Foundation Stallion mold: Black Foundation Stallion #64, black (1977-87) [mold: 1977-93, 1996-]
"Halla" Famous Jumper #63, bay (1977-85) [mold: "Halla" 1977-85, 1990-91; "Bolya" 1992-94]
"Justin Morgan" mold: Marguerite Henry's "Justin Morgan" #65, medium/dark bay (1977-89)
"Stormy" mold: Marguerite Henry's "Stormy" #19, chestnut pinto foal (1977 - current as of 1996) [mold: 1977 - current as of 1996]
"Stud Spider" Gift Set #3080, black blanket appaloosa horse, book (late 1977 - 1983) [mold: late 1977 - current as of 1996]
"Tiffany" mold: "Tiffany" And "Benji" Set #3090, white "Tiffany" dog (late 1977) [mold: late 1977]

1978

Black Angus Bull #365, polled, standing, large; black (1978 - current as of 1996) [mold: 1978 - current as of 1996]
Brenda Breyer #500, doll with long hair (pre-catalog release 1978 and 1979, catalog run 1980-86) [mold: pre-catalog release 1978 and 1979, catalog run 1980 - current as of 1996]
Classic Andalusian Family Foal mold: Andalusian Family Gift Set #3060, chestnut foal (pre-catalog release 1978, catalog run 1979-93) [mold: pre-catalog release 1978, catalog run 1979-93, 1996-]
Classic Andalusian Family Mare mold: Andalusian Family Gift Set #3060, dapple gray mare (pre-catalog release 1978, catalog run 1979-93) [mold: pre-catalog release 1978, catalog run 1979-93]
Classic Andalusian Family Stallion mold: Andalusian Family Gift Set #3060, alabaster stallion (pre-catalog release 1978, catalog run 1979-93) [mold: pre-catalog release 1978, catalog run 1979-93]
Galiceno #100, bay (1978-82) [mold: 1978-82, 1994-95]
"Legionario" mold: "Legionario III" Famous Andalusian #68, alabaster (pre-catalog release 1978, catalog run 1979-90) [mold: pre-catalog release 1978, catalog run 1979 - current as of 1996]
Mustang SR #86, black (1978)
"Phantom Wings" mold: Stock Horse Foal #18, black blanket appaloosa (1978-82) [mold: 1978-87, 1991-95]
"San Domingo" mold: Marguerite Henry's "San Domingo" #67, chestnut medicine-hat pinto (1978-87) [mold: 1978-93, 1995 - current as of 1996]
"Stud Spider" Appaloosa #66, black blanket appaloosa (1978-89)

1979

Belgian SR, black, blue/white ribbon (sometime in the period 1979-82)
Belgian SR, dapple gray, yellow/red ribbon, semigloss (1979)
"Black Beauty" #89 (stallion, cross-galloping), black (1979-88) [mold: 1979-91, 1995 - current as of 1996]
Clydesdale Mare SR, dapple gray (1979)
Clydesdale Stallion SR, dapple gray, gold bobs (1979)
Haflinger #156, chestnut (1979-84) [mold: 1979-84, 1991 - current as of 1996]
"Jasper" mold: Hampshire Hog SR, black, white band over shoulders (1979 and 1980/81)
"Lady Phase" SR, buckskin, solid face (1979)
"Legionario III" Gift Set #3070, alabaster horse, book (1979-81)
"Phantom Wings" mold: Stock Horse Foal #17, chestnut blanket appaloosa (1979-82)
Pony Of The Americas #154, bay blanket appaloosa (1979-84)

Pony Of The Americas SR, black blanket appaloosa (late 1970s or early 1980s)
Running Mare SR?, buckskin (1979); only a few pieces known
Stablemates "Seabiscuit" mold: Stablemates Stable Set #3085, dark bay "Seabiscuit" (1979-80 only)
"Stud Spider" mold: Overo Paint #88, dark chestnut paint (1979-81)
Trakehner #54, bay (1979-84) [mold: 1979-84, 1989, 1995 - current as of 1996]
Western Prancer SR, sorrel (probably sometime in the period 1979-83)

1980

"Adios" SR, unpainted white (1980)
"Black Beauty" (cross-galloping) SR, unpainted white (1980)
Brenda Breyer SR, doll in English outfit with red coat; with jumps, tack, and "Morganglanz" #59, in U.S. Equestrian Team Set (1980)
Cantering Welsh Pony SR, unpainted white (1980)
Classic "Black Beauty," black, in "Black Beauty" Family set #3040 (1980-93) [mold: 1980-93]
Classic "Duchess," bay, in "Black Beauty" Family set #3040 (1980-93) [mold: 1980-94]
Classic "Ginger," chestnut, in "Black Beauty" Family set #3040 (1980-93) [mold: 1980-93, 1996-]
Classic "Jet Run," bay, star, in U.S. Equestrian Team Gift Set #3035 (1980-93) [mold: 1980-94]
Classic "Keen," red chestnut, in U.S. Equestrian Team Gift Set #3035 (1980-93) [mold: 1980-93]
Classic "Kelso" SR?, light reddish chestnut, in U.S. Equestrian Team set (1980); probably never released
Classic "Merrylegs," dapple gray pony, in "Black Beauty" Family set #3040 (1980-93) [mold: 1980 - current as of 1996]
Classic "Might Tango," medium dapple gray, in U.S. Equestrian Team Gift Set #3035 (1980-93) [mold: 1980-93]
Classic "Ruffian" SR?, dapple gray, in U.S. Equestrian Team set (1980); probably never released
Classic "Swaps" SR?, bay, in U.S. Equestrian Team set (1980); probably never released
Clydesdale Foal SR, dapple gray, heavily dappled (1980)
Clydesdale Mare SR, unpainted white (1980)
English Riding Outfit #501, for Brenda Breyer (1980-86)
Five-Gaiter SR, unpainted white (1980)
Foundation Stallion mold: Azteca #85, dapple gray (1980-87)
Foundation Stallion SR, unpainted white (1980)
Hanoverian #58, bay (1980-84) [mold: 1980-84, 1994, 1996-]
Hanoverian SR, unpainted white (1980)
Indian Pony SR, unpainted white (1980)
"Jasper" mold: Duroc Hog SR, dark red-brown, no white (1980/81)
"Jasper" mold: Spotted Poland China Hog SR, white with black spots (1980/81)
"Lady Phase" SR, buckskin, bald face, pink or buckskin nose (1980)
"Lady Phase" SR, unpainted white (1980)
"Morganglanz" #59, chestnut (1980-87) [mold: 1980-87, 1991 - current as of 1996]
"Morganglanz" SR, unpainted white (1980)
Performance Horse mold: Brenda Breyer Gift Set #3095, sorrel blanket appaloosa, tack, doll (1980-85)
Proud Arabian Mare SR, unpainted white (1980)
Proud Arabian Stallion SR, unpainted white (1980)
Saddlebred Weanling SR, unpainted white (1980)
"Sea Star" mold: Marguerite Henry's "Sea Star" #16, red chestnut (1980-87) [mold: 1980-87, 1991-95]
"Stud Spider" SR, unpainted white (1980)
Trakehner SR, unpainted white (1980)
Western Riding Outfit #502, for Brenda Breyer (1980-86; 1988 as Brenda Breyer Riding Outfit)

1981

Alec Ramsey doll mold: The Black Stallion And Alec Set #3000, boy doll, with black horse, tack (pre-catalog release 1981, catalog run 1982-85) [doll mold: pre-catalog release 1981, catalog run 1982-86]
Black Stallion mold: Walter Farley's Black Stallion #401, black (1981-88) [mold: 1981-91, 1994-95]
Black Stallion Gift Set #2095, black horse, poster, book (1981-83)
Pacer mold: Brenda Breyer And Sulky Set #2446, with alabaster horse (pre-catalog release 1981, catalog run 1982-87)
Pacer mold: Brenda Breyer Harness Racing Set SR, with medium bay horse (1981, 1982, 1983, 1984, and 1985)
Pacer mold: Brenda Breyer Sulky And Pacer Set SR, with light golden chestnut horse (1981, 1982, and 1983)
"Smoky" The Cow Horse #69, steel gray (1981-85) [mold: 1981-85]
"Smoky" The Cow Horse Gift Set #2090, steel gray horse, book (1981-85)
Stock Horse Stallion mold: Appaloosa Stock Horse Stallion #232, bay blanket appy (1981-86) [mold: 1981-92, 1995 - current as of 1996]
Stock Horse Stallion mold: Bay Quarter Horse Stock Stallion #226, bay (1981-88)
Stock Horse Stallion mold: Tobiano Pinto Stock Horse Stallion #229, black paint (1981-88)
Western Prancer SR, brown pinto, black mane and tail (1981)

1982

Belgian mold: Percheron SR, black, yellow/red or blue/white ribbon, in SR set (1982 and 1983)
"Brighty" mold: Marguerite Henry's Brighty #375, gray sitting burro (1982-87)
Clydesdale Foal SR, true bay, in Clydesdale Family Set #8034 (1982, 1983, and 1984)
Clydesdale Mare SR, true bay, in Clydesdale Family Set #8034 (1982, 1983, and 1984)
Clydesdale Stallion SR, true bay, in Clydesdale Family Set #8034 (1982, 1983, and 1984)
Family Arabian Foal SR, dark chestnut, blaze, in Arabian Family Set With Blue Ribbon (1982)

Family Arabian Mare SR, dark chestnut, blaze, in Arabian Family Set With Blue Ribbon (1982)
Family Arabian Stallion SR, light chestnut, in Arabian Family Set With Blue Ribbon (1982)
Jumping Horse SR, seal brown (1982 and 1983)
Pacer mold: Pacing Horse, Sulky And Harness set SR, with black Pacer (1982)
Running Foal SR, dapple gray, gray mane and tail, in set (1982/83)
Running Foal SR, red roan, in set (1982)
Running Mare SR, dapple gray, dark gray mane and tail, in set (1982/83)
Running Mare SR, palomino, in set with tack (1982)
Running Mare SR, red roan, in set (1982)
Running Stallion mold variation: Unicorn #210, alabaster, gold-and-white-striped horn (1982-88)
Shire SR, dapple gray, in SR set (1982 and 1983)
Stock Horse Mare mold: Appaloosa Stock Horse Mare #233, black blanket appy (1982-88) [mold: 1982-92, 1996-]
Stock Horse Mare mold: Overo Paint Stock Horse Mare #230, bay paint (1982-88)
Stock Horse Mare mold: Sorrel Quarter Horse Stock Mare #227, deep red sorrel (1982-86)
Suckling Foal SR, bay pinto, in Pinto Mare And Suckling Foal set (1982 and 1983)
Thoroughbred Mare (ears back) SR, bay pinto, in Pinto Mare And Suckling Foal set (1982 and 1983)

1983

Alec Ramsey doll mold: Ben Breyer #550, boy doll (1983-86)
Black Angus Bull (polled, standing, large) mold: Red Angus Bull SR, dark red chestnut (1983 and 1984)
Charolais Bull mold: Shorthorn Bull SR, polled, dark red chestnut (1983 or earlier)
Charolais Bull mold: Simmental Bull SR, polled, dark reddish-brown pinto (1983 or possibly earlier)
Classic Black Stallion, black, in "The Black Stallion Returns" Set #3030 (1983-93) [mold: 1983-93]
Classic "Johar," alabaster, in "The Black Stallion Returns" Set #3030 (1983-93) [mold: 1983-93]
Classic Lipizzan mold: "Pegasus" #209, alabaster with wings (mid-1983 - 1987)
Classic "Sagr," red chestnut, in "The Black Stallion Returns" Set #3030 (1983-93) [mold: 1983-93]
Clydesdale Mare mold: Clydesdale Gelding/Stallion SR, flocked bay (1983 and 1984)
Family Arabian Foal SR, light chestnut, in Arabian Family Set With Blue Ribbon (1983)
Family Arabian Mare SR, light chestnut, in Arabian Family Set With Blue Ribbon (1983)
Family Arabian Stallion SR, dark chestnut, blaze, in Arabian Family Set With Blue Ribbon (1983)
Foundation Stallion SR, palomino, in Palomino Horse And Foal Set (1983)
"Lady Phase" SR, buckskin; bald face, solid face, or star; in Quarter Horse Mare And Foal Set (1983 and 1984)
Little Bits Arabian Stallion #9001, chestnut (late 1983 - 1988) [mold: late 1983 - current as of 1996]
Little Bits Arabian Stallion #9001, medium bay (late 1983 - 1988)
Little Bits Arabian Stallion #9001, smoke gray (late 1983 - 1988)
Little Bits Bitsy Breyer beach doll mold: Bitsy Breyer And Arabian Stallion Beach Set #1001, with accessories (late 1983 - 1985) [doll mold: late 1983 - 1985, 1994 - current as of 1996]
Little Bits Bitsy Breyer beach and Arabian Stallion molds: Bitsy Breyer Beachcomber Set SR, with black horse, accessories (1983)
Little Bits Bitsy Breyer English doll mold: Bitsy Breyer And Morgan English Set #1005, with accessories (late 1983 - 1987) [doll mold: late 1983 - 1987, 1994 - current as of 1996]
Little Bits Bitsy Breyer Jockey doll mold: Bitsy Breyer And Thoroughbred Jockey Set #1010, with accessories (late 1983 - 1987) [doll mold: late 1983 - 1987]
Little Bits Bitsy Breyer Western doll mold: Bitsy Breyer And Quarter Horse Western Set #1015, with accessories (late 1983 - 1987) [doll mold: late 1983 - 1987, 1994 - current as of 1996]
Little Bits Morgan Stallion #9005, dark/medium bay (late 1983 - 1988) [mold: late 1983 - current as of 1996]
Little Bits Morgan Stallion #9005, black (late 1983 - 1988)
Little Bits Morgan Stallion #9005, dark/medium chestnut (late 1983 - 1988)
Little Bits Quarter Horse Stallion #9015, bay (late 1983 - 1988) [mold: late 1983 - current as of 1996]
Little Bits Quarter Horse Stallion #9015, buckskin (late 1983 - 1988)
Little Bits Quarter Horse Stallion #9015, palomino (late 1983 - 1988)
Little Bits Thoroughbred Stallion #9010, black late 1983 - 1988) [mold: late 1983 - current as of 1996]
Little Bits Thoroughbred Stallion #9010, chestnut (late 1983 - 1988)
Little Bits Thoroughbred Stallion #9010, dark/medium bay (late 1983 - 1988)
"Misty," "Stormy," and "Sea Star" molds: Marguerite Henry's "Misty," "Stormy," And "Sea Star" Set #2169 (1983-85)
Old Timer SR, alabaster (1983)
"Phantom Wings," "Misty's" Foal #29, palomino pinto (1983-87)
Proud Arabian Foal SR, reddish bay, in Assorted Mare And Foals Stable Set (1983)
Proud Arabian Mare SR, reddish bay, in Assorted Mare And Foals Stable Set (1983)
Proud Arabian Stallion mold: Arabian Stallion With English Tack Set SR, reddish bay horse (1983 and 1984)
Proud Arabian Stallion SR, flocked chestnut, alone or with buggy and tack (1983)
Running Foal SR, buckskin (1983)
Stock Horse Foal (standing) mold: Appaloosa Stock Horse Foal #234, gray blanket appaloosa (1983-86) [mold: 1983-94]
Stock Horse Foal (standing) mold: Bay Quarter Horse Stock Foal #228 (1983-88)
Stock Horse Foal (standing) mold: Pinto Stock Foal #231, black paint (1983-88)
Stock Horse Foal (standing) SR, buckskin, in Quarter Horse Mare And Foal Set (1983 and 1984)
Stock Horse Foal (standing) SR, gray blanket appaloosa, in Assorted Mare And Foals Stable Set and in set with matching SHM and SHS (1983)
Stock Horse Foal (standing) SR, palomino, in Palomino Horse And Foal Set (1983)
Stock Horse Mare SR, gray blanket appaloosa, in set (1983)
Stock Horse Stallion SR, gray blanket appaloosa, in set (1983)
Western Prancer mold: Brenda Western Gift Set #1120, chestnut pinto horse, doll, tack (1983-85)

1984

Action Stock Horse Foal mold: Action American Appaloosa Stock Horse Foal #238, gray blanket appaloosa (1984-88) [mold: 1984 - current as of 1996]
Action Stock Horse Foal mold: Action American Paint Horse Foal #237, bay paint (1984-88)
Action Stock Horse Foal mold: Chestnut Stock Horse Foal #236, red sorrel (1984-86)
Action Stock Horse Foal SR, bay, in "Stallion Mare And Foal Set" (1984)
Action Stock Horse Foal SR, black paint, in Pinto Mare And Foal Set (1984 and 1985)
Action Stock Horse Foal SR, buckskin, in Collectible Stock Horse Family set (1984)
"Adios" SR, buckskin (1984)
Alec Ramsey doll mold: Kelly Reno And "Little Man" Gift Set #3096, Kelly Reno, with horse, tack (1984-85)
Belgian SR, chestnut/dark palomino, white mane and tail (1984)
Belgian SR, dapple gray, yellow/red ribbon, semigloss (1984)
Belgian SR, palomino (1984)
Belgian SR, red roan (1984)
"Black Beauty" (cross-galloping) SR, bay, in Running Horse Family set (1984)
Classic Andalusian Family Foal SR, red bay, in set (1984)
Classic Andalusian Family Mare SR, alabaster, in set (1984)
Classic Andalusian Family Stallion SR, dapple gray, in set (1984)
Classic Arabian Family Foal SR, bay, in set #21058 (1984 and 1985)
Classic Arabian Family Mare SR, rose alabaster, in set #21058 (1984 and 1985)
Classic Arabian Family Stallion SR, bay, in set #21058 (1984 and 1985)
Classic "Black Beauty" mold: Collector's One Horse Open Sleigh set SR, flocked dapple gray horse, sleigh, dolls (1984)
Classic Black Stallion mold: The Doctor's Buggy set #19842, flocked bay stallion, buggy, doctor doll (1984-87)
Classic "Duchess" and "Jet Run" molds: Family To Church On Sunday set #19843, flocked bay horses, surrey, dolls (1984-87)
Classic "Jet Run" mold: see preceding entry for #19843
Classic "Johar" mold: Drive On A Sunny Day set #19841, flocked chestnut horse, buggy, doll (1984-87)
Classic "Keen" mold: Montgomery Ward Delivery Wagon set SR, flocked chestnut horse, wagon, doll (1984)
Classic Quarter Horse Family Foal SR, black blanket appaloosa, in Appaloosa Family set (1984)
Classic Quarter Horse Family Mare SR, black blanket appaloosa, in Appaloosa Family set (1984)
Classic Quarter Horse Family Stallion SR, black blanket appaloosa, in Appaloosa Family set (1984)
Clydesdale Stallion SR, dapple gray, gold bobs (1984/85)
Cow mold: Guernsey Cow SR, horns, dark red-brown chestnut pinto (1984)
Cow mold: Jersey Cow SR, horns, caramel/palomino (1984)
"Halla," Hanoverian, Jumping Horse, "Morganglanz," and Trakehner, in U.S.E.T. Traditional Assortment #6984, for dealers; with "special packaging" (1984)
Little Bits Clydesdale #9025, bay (1984-88) [mold: 1984-95]
Little Bits Unicorn #9020, alabaster (1984-94) [mold: 1984-94]
"Misty" SR, flocked chestnut pinto, in set (1984)
Old Timer mold: McCormick Decanter With Old Timer set SR, dapple gray (1984)
Pacer SR, dapple gray (1984)
Pacer SR, dark red chestnut (1984)
Pacer SR, palomino (1984)
Performance Horse mold: Appaloosa Stallion With Western Tack Set SR, gray blanket appaloosa (1984)
Proud Arabian Stallion mold: Open Top Buggy set #19841, flocked chestnut horse, doll, buggy (1984)
Proud Arabian Stallion SR, flocked bay, with halter (1984)
Quarter Horse Gelding SR, bay, matte (1984)
Running Foal SR, bay, in Running Horse Family set (1984)
Running Foal SR, flocked palomino, in Collector's Mare And Foal Set (1984)
Running Mare SR, bay, in Running Horse Family set (1984)
Running Mare SR, flocked palomino, in Collector's Mare And Foal Set (1984)
Saddlebred Weanling SR, chestnut (1984)
"Sham" mold: Marguerite Henry's "Sham" The Godolphin Arabian #410, blood bay (1984-88) [mold: 1984-94]
"Sham" SR, golden bay (1984)
Shetland Pony mold: "Our First Pony" set SR, black pinto "Midge" pony, halter, book (1984 and 1985)
"Smoky" mold: Collector's Unicorn SR, flocked white (1984)
Stablemates Draft Horse SR, chestnut, in set (1984)
Stablemates Draft Horse SR, black, hind stocking, in set (1984)
Stablemates Draft Horse SR, palomino, in set (1984)
Stablemates Draft Horse SR, red sorrel, in set (1984)
Stablemates Draft Horse SR, smoke gray, in set (1984)
Stablemates Draft Horse SR, red roan, in set (1984)
Stablemates Draft Horse SR, unpainted white, in set (1984)
Stock Horse Mare SR, black paint, in Pinto Mare And Foal Set (1984 and 1985)
Stock Horse Mare SR, buckskin, in Collectible Stock Horse Family Set (1984)
Stock Horse Stallion SR: "Sam I Am" SR, dark bay paint (1984)
Stock Horse Stallion mold: Kelly Reno And "Little Man" Gift Set #3096, palomino horse, doll, tack (1984-85)
Stock Horse Stallion SR, bay paint (1984)
Stock Horse Stallion SR, buckskin, in Collectible Stock Horse Family set (1984)
Stock Horse Stallion SR, rose alabaster, in "Stallion Mare And Foal Set" (1984)
"Stormy" SR, flocked dark chestnut pinto, in set (1984)
Tennessee Walker SR, light/medium sorrel (1984)

1985

"Adios" SR, black (1985?); only a few made
"Buckshot" Famous Spanish Barb #415, grulla semi-leopard appaloosa (1985-88) [mold: 1985-89, 1995]
Cantering Welsh Pony SR #107, dapple gray; red mane braids (1985/86)

Classic Lipizzan mold: Sky Blue "Pegasus" SR, flocked sky blue (1985)
Classic "Merrylegs" mold: Pony Cart And Driver set SR, flocked black pinto pony, cart, doll (1985)
Classic Mustang Family Foal SR, chestnut pinto, in set #21025 (1985)
Classic Mustang Family Mare SR, bay, in set #21025 (1985)
Classic Mustang Family Stallion SR, buckskin, in set #21025 (1985)
Cow mold: Holstein Cow SR #411341, polled, black pinto; in various sets (1985, 1988, 1989, 1992, 1993, and 1995)
Fighting Stallion mold: Rearing Circus Stallion With Ringmaster Set SR, flocked white horse, Alec doll (1985)
Foundation Stallion SR, alabaster (1985)
Haflinger SR, chestnut, gray mane and tail (1985)
"Legionario" SR, chestnut (1985)
"Legionario" With Brenda Breyer Rider set SR, with flocked white horse (1985)
Little Bits American Saddlebred #9030, medium bay (1985-88) [mold: 1985 - current as of 1996]
Little Bits American Saddlebred #9030, palomino (1985-88)
Little Bits American Saddlebred #9030, red chestnut (1985-88)
Little Bits American Saddlebred SR, red sorrel, solid face (1985)
Little Bits Morgan mold: Merry-Go-Round Horse SR, mauve (1985)
Little Bits Quarter Horse Stallion mold: Appaloosa #9040, black blanket appaloosa (1985-88)
Little Bits Quarter Horse Stallion mold: Bay Pinto #9035, bay paint (1985-88)
Little Bits Unicorn SR, white; pale blue mane and tail (1985)
Lying Down Foal mold variation: Lying Down Unicorn #245, alabaster (1985-88)
"Morganglanz" SR?, dapple gray (1985); probably never released
"Phar Lap" Famous Race Horse #90, red chestnut (1985-88) [mold: 1985 - current as of 1996]
"Phar Lap" SR, dapple gray (1985)
Proud Arabian Mare SR, light reddish chestnut, solid face (1985)
Running Foal SR, flocked white, in Fanciful Mare And Pony Set (1985)
Running Mare SR, flocked white, in Fanciful Mare And Pony Set (1985)
Running Stallion mold: Sky Blue Unicorn SR, flocked sky blue (1985)
Saddlebred Weanling mold: Collector's Rocking Horse SR, flocked chestnut (1985-87)
Saddlebred Weanling mold: My Companion Rocking Horse SR, flocked white (1985)
Saddlebred Weanling mold: My Favorite Rocking Horse SR, flocked mauve (1985)
Saddlebred Weanling mold: Our Rocking Horse SR, flocked black blanket appaloosa (1985)
"San Domingo" mold: "Black Gold" SR, black, in set with book (1985)
Shetland SR?, chestnut (1985); probably never released
Shire SR, black, bald face (1985)
Shire SR, reddish bay (1985)
Shire SR, palomino, bald face (1985)
Shire SR, smoke gray (1985)

1986

Action Stock Horse Foal SR, bay peppercorn appy, in Breyer Traditional Collector's Family Set #712459 (1986)
"Adios" SR #51-1, red chestnut (1986)
Belgian SR, bay (1986/87)
Belgian SR, black, white/red ribbon (1986/87)
Belgian SR, chestnut, lighter chestnut mane and tail (1986/87)
Belgian SR, dapple gray, gold ribbon (1986)
Belgian SR, dapple gray, yellow/red ribbon (1986/87)
Belgian SR, "smoke" blue-gray semi-leopard blanket appaloosa (1986/87)
Belgian SR, unpainted white (1986)
Classic Quarter Horse Family Foal SR, chestnut blanket appaloosa, in Appaloosa Family set #21061 (1986)
Classic Quarter Horse Family Mare SR, chestnut blanket appaloosa, in Appaloosa Family set #21061 (1986)
Classic Quarter Horse Family Stallion SR, chestnut blanket appaloosa, in Appaloosa Family set #21061 (1986)
Clydesdale Mare SR, dapple gray (1986/87)
Clydesdale Stallion SR, dapple gray, red/white bobs (1986/87)
Hanoverian SR, dapple gray, white dapples splashed on gray horse (1986)
"Kipper" #9960 (regular run) and in SR set #712491, bay (1986); limited release [mold: 1986]
"Kipper" mold variation: "Midget" #9961, black pinto (1986); advertised but never released
"Kipper" mold variation: "Pumpkin" #9962, palomino (1986); advertised but never released
"Lady Roxana" mold: Marguerite Henry's "Lady Roxana" #425, alabaster (1986-88) [mold: 1986-89, 1993, 1996]
Proud Arabian Mare SR, black (1986)
Proud Arabian Mare SR, dark rose gray (1986)
Quarter Horse Gelding SR, red chestnut (1986/87)
Stock Horse Mare SR, bay peppercorn appy, in Breyer Traditional Collector's Family Set #712459 (1986)
Stock Horse Stallion SR, bay peppercorn appy, in Breyer Traditional Collector's Family Set #712459 (1986)
"Stud Spider" mold: Bay Stock Horse SR, bay (1986)
"Touch Of Class" Olympic Champion #420, medium/light bay (1986-88) [mold: 1986-94, 1996-]

1987

Action Stock Horse Foal mold: Action American Buckskin Stock Horse Foal #225 (1987-88)
"Adios" SR #410151, dapple gray (1987)
"Adios" SR #410251, palomino (1987)
"Adios" SR, red dun semi-leopard appaloosa, in Breyer Traditional Western Horse Collector Set #712848 (1987)
Bear mold: Cinnamon Bear And Cub set #3069, medium red-brown bear (1987-88)
Bear Cub mold: Cinnamon Bear And Cub set #3069, medium red-brown cub (1987-88)
Calf SR, unpainted white (1987)
Cantering Welsh Pony SR, red bay (1987)

Cantering Welsh Pony SR, red-tan dun (1987)
Cantering Welsh Pony SR #410107, dapple gray, gold braids (1987)
Classic Arabian Family Foal mold: Marguerite Henry's "Our First Pony" Gift Set #3066, bay pinto foal "Friday," possibly also a black pinto version (1987 - current as of 1996)
Classic Arabian Family Foal SR #413155, dapple gray (1987 and 1988)
Classic Arabian Family Mare SR #413255, dapple gray (1987 and 1988)
Classic Arabian Family Stallion SR #413355, dapple gray (1987 and 1988)
Classic "Jet Run" SR, medium/light chestnut, in Horse Set SR #493035 (1987)
Classic "Keen" mold: Delivery Wagon set #19846, flocked chestnut horse, wagon, doll (1987)
Classic "Keen" SR, steel gray, in Horse Set SR #493035 (1987)
Classic "Kelso" mold: "Citation" SR, medium reddish bay, in Triple Crown Winners I set #406135 (1987)
Classic "Merrylegs" mold: Joey's Pony Cart set #19845, flocked black pinto "Midge," cart, doll (1987)
Classic "Might Tango" SR, reddish bay, solid face, in Horse Set SR #493035 (1987)
Classic Mustang Family Foal mold: Marguerite Henry's "Our First Pony" Gift Set #3066, black pinto foal "Teeny" (1987 - current as of 1996)
Classic "Silky Sullivan" mold: "Whirlaway" SR, medium/light red chestnut, in Triple Crown Winners I set #406135 (1987)
Classic "Terrang" mold: "Count Fleet" SR, dark olive chestnut, in Triple Crown Winners I set #406135 (1987)
Display Unit #198700 (and #198701?), 10 Traditional horses and 2 doll riders on base (1987-88[?])
"El Pastor" mold: "Precipitado Sin Par" ("Cips") Champion Paso Fino #116, bay pinto (1987)
"El Pastor" SR #410116, bay, solid face (1987)
Five-Gaiter mold: American Saddlebred #109, dapple gray (1987-88)
Five-Gaiter mold: "Project Universe" #117, dark chestnut pinto (1987-89)
Foundation Stallion SR, liver-charcoal, in Breyer Traditional Western Horse Collector Set #712848 (1987)
Hanoverian SR #410158, black, no white (1987)
Hanoverian SR #410258, red bay (1987)
Hanoverian SR #410358, alabaster (1987)
Hanoverian SR #410458, chestnut, bright orange-red (1987)
Indian Pony SR #411175, black leopard appaloosa (1987)
Indian Pony SR #412175, dapple gray (1987)
Indian Pony SR #413175, red bay (1987)
Indian Pony SR #414175, blue roan semi-leopard appaloosa (1987)
Mustang mold: American Mustang #118, sorrel/palomino (1987-89)
Proud Arabian Stallion SR #411213, red bay, no white (1987)
Proud Arabian Stallion SR #412213, black (1987)
Proud Arabian Stallion SR #413213, light red chestnut, solid face (1987)
Running Foal SR, dapple gray, white mane and tail, in set #491212 (1987)
Running Mare SR, dapple gray, white mane and tail, in set #491212 (1987)
"San Domingo" SR, red bay, in Breyer Traditional Western Horse Collector Set #712848 (1987)
"Secretariat" Famous Race Horse #435, red chestnut (1987-95) [mold: 1987-95]
"Sherman Morgan," Son Of "Justin Morgan," #430, red chestnut (1987-90) [mold: 1987-92]
Shetland Pony mold: Marguerite Henry's "Our First Pony" Gift Set #3066, black pinto "Midge" with leather halter and two foals (1987 - current as of 1996)
Stock Horse Foal (standing) mold: American Buckskin Stock Horse Foal #224 (1987-88)
Stock Horse Mare mold: American Buckskin Stock Horse Mare #222 (1987-88)
Stock Horse Stallion mold: American Buckskin Stock Horse Stallion #221 (1987-88)
Trakehner SR, chestnut (1987)
Trakehner SR #400154, golden bay (1987)

1988

"Adios" mold: Standing Quarter Horse Stallion #705, apricot dun (1988-89)
Black Stallion SR, light coffee bay, in English Horse Collector Set #713259 (1988)
Brenda Breyer #500, doll with big curly hair (1988-90)
Brenda Breyer doll mold: English Brenda Breyer #499 (1988-89)
Brenda Breyer doll mold: Western Brenda Breyer #498 (1988-89)
"Buckshot" mold: Spanish Barb #416 , chestnut pinto (1988-89)
Cantering Welsh Pony SR #411107, fleabitten gray (1988)
Cantering Welsh Pony SR #412107, red roan (1988)
Cantering Welsh Pony SR #413107, dark chestnut (1988)
Cantering Welsh Pony SR #414107, red dun (1988)
Classic Arabian Family Foal SR, dark shaded chestnut, in set #413550 and in Foal's First Day set #403755 (1988)
Classic Bucking Bronco SR #411190, red roan (1988)
Classic Bucking Bronco SR #412190, chestnut (1988)
Classic Bucking Bronco SR #413190, black leopard appaloosa (1988)
Classic Bucking Bronco SR #414190, steel gray (1988)
Classic "Johar" SR, rose alabaster, in set #413550 and in Foal's First Day set #403755 (1988)
Classic "Man-O-War" mold: "Affirmed" SR, reddish chestnut, long star, in Triple Crown Winners II set #406254 (1988)
Classic "Swaps" mold: "Seattle Slew" SR, medium/dark chestnut, in Triple Crown Winners II set #406254 (1988)
Classic "Terrang" mold: "Secretariat" SR, red chestnut, stripe, in Triple Crown Winners II set #406254 (1988)
Clydesdale Foal SR #410184, dapple gray (1988)
Clydesdale Foal SR #410284, steel gray (1988)
Clydesdale Foal SR #410384, black (1988)
Cow mold: Ayrshire Cow SR #414341, polled, red-brown pinto; 1993 release in Dairy Cow Assortment SR #410693 (1988 and 1993)
Cow mold: Brown Swiss Cow SR #413341, polled, medium/light coffee brown; 1993 release in Dairy Cow Assortment SR #410693 (1988 and 1993)
Cow mold: Guernsey Cow SR #415341, polled, dark palomino pinto; 1993 release in Dairy Cow Assortment SR #410693 (1988 and 1993)
Cow mold: Holstein Cow SR #417341, mixed horns, black pinto (1988)
Cow mold: Jersey Cow SR #416341, polled, dark palomino; 1993 release in Dairy Cow Assortment SR #410693 (1988 and 1993)

Family Arabian Foal #708, chestnut, flaxen mane and tail (1988)
Family Arabian Foal SR, alabaster glossy, in set #400789 (1988)
Family Arabian Mare #707, chestnut, flaxen mane and tail (1988)
Family Arabian Mare SR, alabaster glossy, in set #400789 (1988)
Family Arabian Stallion #706, chestnut, flaxen mane and tail (1988)
Family Arabian Stallion SR, alabaster glossy, in set #400789 (1988)
Fighting Stallion #709, black leopard appaloosa (1988-90)
Five-Gaiter mold: "Wing Commander" #140, dark chestnut (1988-90)
Foundation Stallion mold: American Indian Pony #710, red roan (1988-91)
Indian Pony SR, red dun, in English Horse Collector Set #713259 (1988)
"John Henry" Famous Race Horse #445, dark bay (1988-90) [mold: 1988-93, 1996]
"Justin Morgan" SR, red chestnut, in English Horse Collector Set #713259 (1988)
"Lady Phase" mold: "Breezing Dixie" Famous Appaloosa Mare #711, dark bay blanket appaloosa (1988)
"Lady Roxana" mold: Prancing Arabian Mare #426, light sorrel (1988-89)
Little Bits American Saddlebred SR, dark chestnut pinto, in Parade Of Breeds Collector Assortment I #713267 (1988)
Little Bits Arabian Stallion SR, black, in Parade Of Breeds Collector Assortment I #713267 (1988)
Little Bits Morgan Stallion SR, dark shaded bay, in Parade Of Breeds Collector Assortment I #713267 (1988)
Little Bits Quarter Horse Stallion SR, red leopard appaloosa, in Parade Of Breeds Collector Assortment I #713267 (1988)
Little Bits Quarter Horse Stallion SR, smoke gray, in Parade Of Breeds Collector Assortment I #713267 (1988)
Little Bits Thoroughbred Stallion SR, dark bay, baldish face, in Parade Of Breeds Collector Assortment I #713267 (1988)
Morgan #702, light reddish bay (1988-89)
Mustang mold: "Ruby" SR #410087, dark red roan, in set (1988)
Mustang SR #410187, black leopard appaloosa (1988)
Mustang SR #410287, alabaster (1988)
Mustang SR #410387, bay blanket appaloosa (1988)
Mustang SR #410487, fleabitten gray (1988)
Mustang SR #410587, palomino (1988)
Mustang SR #410687, red dun (1988)
Old Timer #206, bay (1988-90)
"Phar Lap" SR #410190, liver chestnut, darker mane and tail (1988)
"Phar Lap" SR #410290, sorrel, flaxen mane and tail (1988)
"Phar Lap" SR #410390, dark dapple gray (1988)
"Phar Lap" SR #410490, red bay (1988)
Proud Arabian Foal SR, pink (circa 1988)
Proud Arabian Foal SR, red bay pinto, in Arabian Mare And Foal set #497679 (1988)
Proud Arabian Mare SR, red bay pinto, in Arabian Mare And Foal set #497679 (1988)
Running Stallion SR #400212, chestnut (1988)
"San Domingo" mold: Blanket Appaloosa #703, dark gray blanket appaloosa (1988-89)
"San Domingo" mold: "Wildfire" SR #410067, red chestnut pinto, in set (1988)
"Sham" mold: Prancing Arabian Stallion #411, fleabitten gray (1988-90)
Tennessee Walker mold: Tennessee Walking Horse #704, red bay (1988-89)

1989

Action Stock Horse Foal mold: Action Appaloosa Foal #810, red leopard appaloosa (1989-93)
"Black Beauty" (cross-galloping) mold: "Fade To Gray" #802 , dark dapple gray (1989-90)
Black Stallion mold: Majestic Arabian Stallion #811, leopard appaloosa (1989-90)
Classic "Black Beauty" mold: "Iltschi" SR #703440, black, in Karl May set (1989 and 1990)
Classic "Ginger" mold: "Hatatitla" SR #703240, medium bay, in Karl May set (1989 and 1990)
Classic "Jet Run" mold: "Rembrandt" SR #703235, reddish bay, in German Olympic Team set (1989 and 1990)
Classic "Keen" mold: "Ahlerich" SR #703135, reddish bay, in German Olympic Team set (1989 and 1990)
Classic "Might Tango" mold: "Orchidee" SR #703335, reddish bay, in German Olympic Team set (1989 and 1990)
Classic Quarter Horse Family Mare mold: Brown Pinto Mare SR #703245, dark chestnut paint (1989)
Classic Quarter Horse Family Stallion SR #703145, black blanket appaloosa, large blanket (1989)
Cow mold: Holstein Cow SR, polled, black pinto, in Cow 'N Calf set SR #703447 (1989) and Cow Family set SR #702092 (1992 and 1995)
Family Arabian Foal #816, bay, solid face (1989-90)
Family Arabian Mare #815, bay, solid face (1989-90)
Family Arabian Stallion #814, bay, solid face (1989-90)
Grazing Mare SR, red bay blanket appaloosa, in Mare And Foal Set #494155 (1989 and 1990)
"Halla" SR, fleabitten gray, in International Equestrian Collector Set #715963 (1989)
Hanoverian SR, dark dapple gray, in International Equestrian Collector Set #715963 (1989)
"Lady Phase" SR #410040, red roan (1989)
Little Bits American Saddlebred #9070, black pinto (1989-94)
Little Bits American Saddlebred SR, palomino pinto, in Parade Of Breeds Collector Assortment II #719051 (1989)
Little Bits Arabian Stallion #9045, alabaster (1989-94)
Little Bits Arabian Stallion SR, dapple gray, in Parade Of Breeds Collector Assortment II #719051 (1989)
Little Bits Clydesdale mold: Charger, The Great Horse, SR #419025, dapple gray (1989)
Little Bits Clydesdale mold: Shire #9065, black (1989-94)
Little Bits Clydesdale SR, golden sorrel, in Parade Of Breeds Collector Assortment II #719051 (1989)
Little Bits Morgan Stallion #9050, golden sorrel/palomino (1989-94)
Little Bits Morgan Stallion SR, rose chestnut, in Parade Of Breeds Collector Assortment II #719051 (1989)
Little Bits Quarter Horse Stallion #9060, blue roan (1989-94)
Little Bits Quarter Horse Stallion mold: Appaloosa #9080, chestnut blanket appaloosa (1989-94)

Little Bits Quarter Horse Stallion mold: Paint #9075, black paint (1989-94)
Little Bits Quarter Horse Stallion SR, black, in Parade Of Breeds Collector Assortment II #719051 (1989)
Little Bits Thoroughbred Stallion #9055, steel gray (1989-94)
Little Bits Thoroughbred Stallion SR, reddish bay, in Parade Of Breeds Collector Assortment II #719051 (1989)
"Morganglanz" SR, reddish bay with solid face, in International Equestrian Collector Set #715963 (1989)
Performance Horse SR #410099, black leopard appaloosa (1989)
Performance Horse SR #410199, alabaster (1989)
Performance Horse SR #410299, red roan (1989)
Performance Horse SR #410399, liver chestnut (1989)
"Phar Lap" mold: Galloping Thoroughbred #803, dark dappled bay (1989-90)
Proud Arabian Foal #806, dappled rose gray (1989-90)
Proud Arabian Mare #805, dappled rose gray (1989-90)
Proud Arabian Stallion #804, dappled rose gray (1989-90)
Quarter Horse Gelding mold: "Silver" Quarter Horse SR #700097, steel gray (1989)
Quarter Horse Yearling SR #400101, blue roan (1989)
Rocky Mountain Goat mold: Montana Mountain Goat #312, white with reddish brown horns (1989)
"Roy" Belgian Drafter #455, light sorrel (1989-90) [mold: 1989-93, 1996-]
"Rugged Lark" Champion American Quarter Horse Stallion #450, bay (1989-95) [mold: 1989 - current as of 1996]
Running Stallion SR #410212, bay, no black on legs (1989)
"Sham" mold: Prancing Arabian Stallion #812, dark palomino (1989-91)
Shetland Pony #801, bay pinto (1989-91)
Stablemates Arabian Mare #5130, alabaster (1989-94)
Stablemates Arabian Stallion #5120, steel gray (1989-94)
Stablemates "Citation" SR, red roan, in Stablemate Assortment I set #495600 (1989)
Stablemates Draft Horse #5180, dapple gray (1989-94)
Stablemates Morgan Mare #5160, palomino (1989-94)
Stablemates Morgan Stallion #5150, medium chestnut / red dun (1989-94)
Stablemates "Native Dancer" SR, red bay, in Stablemate Assortment I set #495600 (1989)
Stablemates Saddlebred #5110, black (1989-90)
Stablemates "Seabiscuit" SR, red chestnut, in Stablemate Assortment I set #495600 (1989)
Stablemates "Silky Sullivan" SR, buckskin, in Stablemate Assortment I set #495600 (1989)
Stablemates "Swaps" SR, blue roan, in Stablemate Assortment I set #495600 (1989)
Stablemates Thoroughbred Mare #5140, dark/medium bay (1989-90)
Stock Horse Foal (standing) mold: Paint Horse Foal #809, liver chestnut paint (1989-90)
Stock Horse Mare mold: Paint Horse Mare #808, liver chestnut paint (1989-90)
Stock Horse Stallion mold: Paint Horse Stallion #807, liver chestnut paint (1989-90)
Suckling Foal SR, red leopard appaloosa, in Mare And Foal Set #494155 (1989 and 1990)
"Touch Of Class" mold: Thoroughbred Mare #813, black (1989-90)
Trakehner mold: "Abdullah" Champion Trakehner #817, pale dapple gray (1989)

1990

"Adios" mold: Quarter Horse Stallion #830, blue roan (1990)
Brenda Breyer doll mold: Dressage Brenda Breyer #510 (1990 - current as of 1996)
Brenda Breyer doll mold: Show Jumping Brenda Breyer #511 (1990 - current as of 1996)
Cantering Welsh Pony SR, dappled rose gray, in Three Piece Horse Set #401456 (1990 and 1991)
Classic Arabian Family Foal SR, black, in Breyer Classic Collector's Arabian Family Set #713055 (1990)
Classic Arabian Family Mare SR, black, in Breyer Classic Collector's Arabian Family Set #713055 (1990)
Classic Arabian Family Stallion SR, black, in Breyer Classic Collector's Arabian Family Set #713055 (1990)
Classic "Black Beauty" mold: "King Of The Wind" Gift Set #3345, golden bay "Lath" (1990-93)
Classic Black Stallion mold: "King Of The Wind" Gift Set #3345, blood bay "Sham" (1990-93)
Classic "Duchess" mold: "King Of The Wind" Gift Set #3345, alabaster "Lady Roxana" (1990-93)
Classic "Ginger" mold: "A Pony For Keeps" Gift Set #3234, alabaster "Blue" (1990-91)
Classic "Merrylegs" mold: "A Pony For Keeps" Gift Set #3234, white "Lady Jane Grey" (1990-91)
Classic "Might Tango" mold: "A Pony For Keeps" Gift Set #3234, light dapple gray "Another" (1990-91)
Classic Mustang Family Stallion mold: "A Pony For Keeps" Gift Set #3234, chestnut "Jefferson" (1990-91)
Clydesdale Foal #826, light golden bay (1990-91)
Clydesdale Mare #825, light golden bay (1990-91)
Clydesdale Stallion #824, light golden bay (1990-91)
Five-Gaiter mold: Pinto American Saddlebred #827, black pinto (1990-91)
Haflinger SR, chestnut pinto, in Three Piece Horse Set #401456 (1990 and 1991)
"Halla" mold: Noble Jumper #820, dapple gray (1990-91)
Hanoverian mold: Vaulting Horse SR #700058 or #7000-700058, black, blaze (1990-91)
"Justin Morgan" mold: Morgan #822, dark seal brown (1990-92)
"Khemosabi+++" Champion Arabian Stallion #460, bay (1990-95) [mold: 1990-95]
"Lady Phase" SR, dapple gray, in Breyer Traditional Horse Set #717450 (1990)
Little Bits American Saddlebred SR, seal brown, in Parade Of Breeds Collector Assortment III #711090 (1990)
Little Bits Clydesdale SR, dapple gray, in Parade Of Breeds Collector Assortment III #711090 (1990)
Little Bits Morgan Stallion SR, medium bay, in Parade Of Breeds Collector Assortment III #711090 (1990)
Little Bits Quarter Horse Stallion SR, black leopard appaloosa, in Parade Of Breeds Collector Assortment III #711090 (1990)
Little Bits Thoroughbred Stallion SR, dappled rose gray, in Parade Of Breeds Collector Assortment III #711090 (1990)
"Man O' War" SR, glossy red chestnut, in Race Horse Set #497510 (1990)
"Misty" SR #410020, Florentine decorator, dappled metallic gold (1990)
Morgan mold: Show Stance Morgan #831, dark red chestnut (1990-91)

Mustang mold: Paint American Mustang #828, bay paint (1990-91)
Pacer mold: "Dan Patch" Famous Standardbred Pacer #819, red bay (1990)
Performance Horse SR, black blanket appaloosa, in Appaloosa-American Classic Set #499610 (1990)
"Phar Lap" mold: "Dr. Peaches" SR #410090, medium bay (1990)
Pony Of The Americas mold: "Rocky" Champion Connemara Stallion #821, dappled buckskin (1990-92)
Pony Of The Americas SR, black leopard appaloosa, in Three Piece Horse Set #401456 (1990 and 1991)
Quarter Horse Gelding SR, palomino, in Breyer Traditional Horse Set #717450 (1990)
"Roemer" Champion Dutch Warmblood #465, dark chestnut (1990-93) [mold: 1990-95]
"Rugged Lark" SR, red chestnut, in Breyer Traditional Horse Set #717450 (1990)
Running Stallion SR, palomino blanket appaloosa, in Appaloosa-American Classic Set #499610 (1990)
Saddlebred Weanling #818, caramel pinto (1990)
"San Domingo" mold: Comanche Pony #829, palomino (1990-92)
"Secretariat" mold: "Burmese" Her Majesty The Queen's Horse SR #700435, black (1990-91)
"Secretariat" SR #410435, Golden Charm decorator, solid metallic gold (1990)
"Secretariat" SR, glossy red chestnut, in Race Horse Set #497510 (1990)
"Sham" SR, glossy blood bay, in Race Horse Set #497510 (1990)
Stablemates Arabian Mare SR, black, in Stablemate Assortment II set #495601 (1990)
Stablemates Arabian Stallion SR, buckskin, in Stablemate Assortment II set #495601 (1990)
Stablemates "Citation" mold: Standing Thoroughbred #5019, chestnut / reddish dun (pre-catalog release mid-1990, catalog run 1991-94)
Stablemates "Citation" SR, dusty chestnut / olive dun, in Stablemate Assortment II set #495601 (1990)
Stablemates Draft Horse SR, black, no white, in Stablemate Assortment II set #495601 (1990)
Stablemates Morgan Mare SR, chestnut, in Stablemate Assortment II set #495601 (1990)
Stablemates Morgan Stallion SR, dark red chestnut, in Stablemate Assortment II set #495601 (1990)
Stablemates "Native Dancer" SR, white, charcoal points, in Stablemate Assortment II set #495601 (1990)
Stablemates "Seabiscuit" mold: Running Thoroughbred #5025, black (pre-catalog release mid-1990, catalog run 1991-94)
Stablemates "Seabiscuit" SR, palomino, in Stablemate Assortment II set #495601 (1990)
Stablemates "Silky Sullivan" SR, reddish dun/chestnut, in Stablemate Assortment II set #495601 (1990)
Stablemates "Swaps" SR, pale rose gray, in Stablemate Assortment II set #495601 (1990)
Stablemates "Swaps" SR, steel gray, in Stablemate Assortment II set #495601 (1990)
Stablemates Thoroughbred Mare SR, red bay, in Stablemate Assortment II set #495601 (1990)
"Stud Spider" mold: Blanket Appaloosa #823, red bay blanket appaloosa (1990-91)
"Stud Spider" SR, blue roan semi-leopard appaloosa, in Appaloosa-American Classic Set #499610 (1990)
Texas Longhorn Bull #370, dark red-brown pinto (1990-95)
Western Horse SR #400057, caramel pinto (1990)

1991

"Adios" mold: "Mesa" The Quarter Horse #853, dark mahogany bay (1991-92)
"Black Beauty" (cross-galloping) mold: "Dream Weaver" #833, sorrel (1991)
Black Stallion mold: "Hyksos" The Egyptian Arabian #832, ageless bronze (1991)
"Brighty 1991" #376, grayish brown sitting burro (1991 - current as of 1996)
Classic "Kelso" mold: "Norita" #251, dapple gray (1991-92)
Classic "Man-O-War" mold: "Pepe" #252 , reddish chestnut, solid face (1991-92)
Classic Quarter Horse Family Foal SR, alabaster, in Quarter Horse Family set #716091 (1991)
Classic Quarter Horse Family Mare SR, liver chestnut, in Quarter Horse Family set #716091 (1991)
Classic Quarter Horse Family Stallion SR, liver chestnut, in Quarter Horse Family set #716091 (1991)
Classic "Ruffian" mold: "Lula" #256, medium reddish bay (1991-92)
Classic "Silky Sullivan" mold: "T-Bone" #253, fleabitten gray (1991-92)
Classic "Swaps" mold: "Hawk" #254, black (1991-92)
Classic "Terrang" mold: "Gaucho" #255, red roan (1991-92)
Family Arabian Foal #841, red chestnut (1991-93)
Family Arabian Foal SR, dapple gray, in Spirit Of The Wind Set #498991 (1991)
Family Arabian Mare SR, dapple gray, in Spirit Of The Wind Set #498991 (1991)
Family Arabian Stallion SR, alabaster, black points, in Arabian Horses Of The World Set #492091 (1991 and 1992)
Grazing Foal SR, bay blanket appaloosa, in Adorable Horse Foal Set #714091 (1991)
Haflinger mold: Mountain Pony #850, light chestnut (1991-92)
Indian Pony mold: "Mustang Lady" SR #412091, shaded gray (1991)
"John Henry" mold: "Joe Patchen" #836, Sire Of "Dan Patch," black (1991-93)
Jumping Horse SR #401291, black (1991/92)
"Legionario" mold: "Spanish Pride" #851, reddish bay (1991-92)
"Legionario" SR #415091, Florentine decorator, dappled metallic gold (1991)
Lying Down Foal SR, chestnut, in Adorable Horse Foal Set #714091 (1991)
"Man O' War" SR, Golden Charm decorator (1991)
"Misty's Twilight" #470, chestnut pinto (1991-95) [mold: 1991 - current as of 1996]
"Morganglanz" mold: "Black Beauty 1991" #847, black (1991-95)
Old Timer #834, dark red roan (1991-93)
"Phantom Wings" mold: "Rough Diamond" #846, dark chestnut pinto (1991-93)
"Phar Lap" mold: "Hobo" #838, buckskin (1991-92)
"Pluto" The Lipizzaner #475, alabaster (1991-95) [mold: 1991 - current as of 1996]
Proud Arabian Mare #840, red chestnut, pale area above nose (1991-92)
Proud Arabian Mare SR, fleabitten rose gray, in Arabian Horses Of The World Set #492091 (1991 and 1992)
Proud Arabian Stallion #839, light dapple gray (1991-94)
Proud Arabian Stallion SR, red bay, blaze, in Arabian Horses Of The World Set #492091 (1991 and 1992)
"Roy" mold: Belgian Brabant #837, tan dun (1991-93)
Running Foal #849, dark chestnut pinto (1991-93)
Running Foal SR, dark rose gray, in Adorable Horse Foal Set #714091 (1991)

Running Mare #848, dark chestnut pinto (1991-93)
Saddlebred Weanling mold: "Raven" SR #701091, plum black (1991)
"San Domingo" mold: "Spotted Bear" Indian Pony SR #490465, black medicine-hat pinto, cold-cast porcelain (1991)
"San Domingo" SR #416091, Copenhagen decorator, dappled blue (1991)
Scratching Foal SR, alabaster, in Adorable Horse Foal Set #714091 (1991)
"Sea Star" mold: Chincoteague Foal #845, buckskin (1991-93)
"Sham" mold: "Galaxias" SR #710410, dapple gray, cold-cast porcelain (1991)
"Sham" SR #414091, Wedgewood Blue decorator, solid blue (1991)
"Sherman Morgan" mold: Prancing Morgan #835, black (1991-92)
Stablemates Arabian Mare SR, chestnut, in Stablemate Assortment III set #495091 (1991)
Stablemates Arabian Stallion SR, black, in Stablemate Assortment III set #495091 (1991)
Stablemates "Citation" SR, steel gray, in Stablemate Assortment III set #495091 (1991)
Stablemates Draft Horse SR, medium/light bay, in Stablemate Assortment III set #495091 (1991)
Stablemates Draft Horse SR, yellow-olive dun, in Stablemate Assortment III set #495091 (1991)
Stablemates Morgan Mare SR, reddish bay, in Stablemate Assortment III set #495091 (1991)
Stablemates Morgan Stallion SR, palomino, in Stablemate Assortment III set #495091 (1991)
Stablemates "Native Dancer" SR, palomino, in Stablemate Assortment III set #495091 (1991)
Stablemates "Seabiscuit" SR, dapple gray, in Stablemate Assortment III set #495091 (1991)
Stablemates "Silky Sullivan" SR, reddish bay, in Stablemate Assortment III set #495091 (1991)
Stablemates "Swaps" SR, dark liver chestnut, in Stablemate Assortment III set #495091 (1991)
Stablemates Thoroughbred Mare SR, alabaster, in Stablemate Assortment III set #495091 (1991)
Stablemates Thoroughbred Mare #5141, medium chestnut (1991-94)
Stock Horse Foal (standing) mold: Paint Horse Foal #844, light chestnut paint (1991-92)
Stock Horse Mare mold: Appy Mare #852, red roan leopard appaloosa (1991-92)
Stock Horse Stallion mold: "Skipster's Chief" Famous Therapeutic Riding Horse #842, sorrel (1991-92)
"Touch Of Class" mold: Selle Français #843, shaded liver chestnut (1991-92)

1992

Action Stock Horse Foal SR, pale yellow dun, in Frisky Foals set #712092 (1992)
Bear mold: Bear Family set #3071, white Bear (1992-95)
Bear Cub mold: Bear Family set #3071, white Cub (1992-95)
Belgian SR, alabaster, in Drafters Set #497092 (1992)
Buffalo mold: "Tatanka" The White Buffalo #380 (1992-93)
Calf mold: Jersey Cow Family set #3448, dark palomino calf (1992-95)
Cantering Welsh Pony mold: "Plain Pixie" #866, red roan (1992-93)
Cantering Welsh Pony SR, black, in Horses Great And Small set #496092 (1992)
Classic Andalusian Family Foal mold: Hanoverian Family set #3346, bay foal (1992-93)
Classic Arabian Family Foal mold: Desert Arabian Family set #3056, bay foal (1992-94)
Classic Arabian Family Mare mold: Desert Arabian Family set #3056, dark bay mare (1992-94)
Classic Arabian Family Stallion mold: Desert Arabian Family set #3056, bay stallion (1992-94)
Classic Bucking Bronco SR #701092, black paint (1992)
Classic "Duchess" mold: Trakehner Family set #3347, pale dapple gray mare (1992-94)
Classic "Ginger" mold: Hanoverian Family set #3346, light sandy bay mare (1992-93)
Classic "Jet Run" mold: Trakehner Family set #3347, dark chestnut stallion (1992-94)
Classic "Keen" mold: Hanoverian Family set #3346, black stallion (1992-93)
Classic "Kelso" SR, medium reddish bay, in set #493092 with book (1992)
Classic Lipizzan mold: Lipizzaner SR #620, alabaster (1992)
Classic "Merrylegs" mold: Miniature Horse SR, palomino, in Horses Great And Small set #496092 (1992)
Classic "Mesteño" Messenger mold: "Mesteño" The Messenger #480, reddish dun (1992 - current as of 1996) [mold: 1992 - current as of 1996]
Classic Mustang Family Foal mold: Trakehner Family set #3347, bay foal (1992-94)
Classic Mustang Family Foal SR, lilac grulla, in Mustang Family set #713092 (1992)
Classic Mustang Family Mare SR, dark bay, in Mustang Family set #713092 (1992)
Classic Mustang Family Stallion SR, buckskin, in Mustang Family set #713092 (1992)
Clydesdale Mare mold: Shire Mare #856, liver chestnut (1992-93)
Clydesdale Stallion mold: Highland Clydesdale #868, bay (1992-95)
Clydesdale Stallion SR, grulla, in Horses Great And Small set #496092 (1992)
Cow mold: Jersey Cow Family set #3448, dark palomino polled cow (1992-95)
Donkey #390, light gray (1992)
Elephant #391, light gray (1992)
"El Pastor" mold: "Tesoro" #867, palomino (1992-95)
Fighting Stallion mold: "Chaparral" The Fighting Stallion #855, buckskin pinto (1992)
Five-Gaiter mold: Kentucky Saddlebred #862, red chestnut (1992-93)
Foundation Stallion mold: Lakota Pony #869, white with cream shading (1992)
Friesian #485, black (1992-95) [mold: 1992 - current as of 1996]
"Halla" mold variation: "Bolya" The Freedom Horse (Akhal-Teke) #490, golden buckskin (1992-94)
Icelandic Horse mold: Fine Porcelain Icelandic Horse #79192, buckskin pinto (1992-94) [mold: 1992-94]
"John Henry" SR, liver chestnut, in Quiet Foxhunters set #491192 (1992)
"Lady Phase" mold: Family Appaloosa Mare #860, black leopard appaloosa (1992-94)
"Lady Phase" mold: "Night Deck" SR, black, in set #410392 (1992)
"Lady Phase" SR, bay paint, in Spirit Of The West set #492092 (1992)
"Misty" mold: "Misty" Of Chincoteague SR #715092, chestnut/palomino pinto cold-cast porcelain (1992)
Morgan mold: Vermont Morgan #858, chocolate sorrel (1992-93)
Mustang mold: "Turbo" The Wonder Horse SR #410592, golden palomino (1992)
Proud Arabian Foal SR, red chestnut, in Frisky Foals set #712092 (1992)
Quarter Horse Yearling SR #410492, buckskin (1992)
"Roemer" SR, seal brown, in Quiet Foxhunters set #491192 (1992)
"Roy" SR, liver chestnut, in Drafters Set #497092 (1992)
"Rugged Lark" SR, dapple gray, in Quiet Foxhunters set #491192 (1992)
Running Foal mold: Bluegrass Foal #865, blue roan (1992-94)
Running Foal SR, black blanket appaloosa, in Frisky Foals set #712092 (1992)
Saddlebred Weanling mold: Future Champion Show Set SR #494092, bay pinto, halter, and doll (1992)
"Secretariat" SR #491292, red chestnut, cold-cast porcelain (1992)
"Sham" mold: "Rana" The Arabian Stallion #863, blue chocolate (1992-93)
"Sherman Morgan" mold: "Fashionably Late" SR #498092, chocolate sorrel, cold-cast porcelain (1992)
"Sherman Morgan" mold: "Pride And Vanity" SR #400192, alabaster (1992/93)
Shetland Pony #857, dark red chestnut (1992-94)
Shire SR, palomino, in Drafters Set #497092 (1992)
Stablemates Arabian Mare SR, steel gray, in Stablemate Assortment IV set #495092 (1992) and Twelve-Piece Stablemates Set #711094 (1994)
Stablemates Arabian Stallion SR, dappled red chestnut, in Stablemate Assortment IV set #495092 (1992) and Twelve-Piece Stablemates Set #711094 (1994)
Stablemates "Citation" SR, dapple gray, in Stablemate Assortment IV set #495092 (1992) and Twelve-Piece Stablemates Set #711094 (1994)
Stablemates Draft Horse SR, buckskin, in Stablemate Assortment IV set #495092 (1992) and Twelve-Piece Stablemates Set #711094 (1994)
Stablemates Morgan Mare SR, chocolate sorrel, in Stablemate Assortment IV set #495092 (1992) and Twelve-Piece Stablemates Set #711094 (1994)
Stablemates Morgan Stallion SR, black blanket appaloosa, in Stablemate Assortment IV set #495092 (1992) and Twelve-Piece Stablemates Set #711094 (1994)
Stablemates Morgan Stallion SR, seal brown, in Stablemate Assortment IV set #495092 (1992) and Twelve-Piece Stablemates Set #711094 (1994)
Stablemates "Native Dancer" SR, black, in Stablemate Assortment IV set #495092 (1992) and Twelve-Piece Stablemates Set #711094 (1994)
Stablemates Quarter Horse Stallion SR, red leopard appaloosa, in Stablemate Assortment IV set #495092 (1992) and Twelve-Piece Stablemates Set #711094 (1994)
Stablemates "Seabiscuit" SR, alabaster, in Stablemate Assortment IV set #495092 (1992) and Twelve-Piece Stablemates Set #711094 (1994)
Stablemates "Silky Sullivan" SR, rose gray, in Stablemate Assortment IV set #495092 (1992) and Twelve-Piece Stablemates Set #711094 (1994)
Stablemates "Swaps" SR, buckskin, in Stablemate Assortment IV set #495092 (1992) and Twelve-Piece Stablemates Set #711094 (1994)
Stock Horse Foal (standing) mold: Family Appaloosa Foal #861, bay blanket appaloosa (1992-94)
Stock Horse Foal (standing) mold: "Night Vision" SR, bay snowflake leopard appaloosa, in set #410392 (1992)
Stock Horse Foal (standing) SR, bay paint, in Spirit Of The West set #492092 (1992)
"Stud Spider" mold: Family Appaloosa Stallion #859, bay blanket appaloosa (1992-94)
Suckling Foal SR, dark palomino pinto, in Frisky Foals set #712092 (1992)
Tennessee Walker mold: "Memphis Storm" Tennessee Walking Horse #854, charcoal-brown (1992)
Western Horse mold: "Tic Toc" #864, alabaster (1992-94)

1993

"Adios" mold: "Rough 'N' Ready" #885, pale yellow dun (1993-95)
"Adios" SR, bay blanket appaloosa, in Breyer Three Generations Appaloosa Set SR #710693 (1993)
Brenda Breyer doll mold: Saddle Seat Brenda Breyer #512 (1993 - current as of 1996)
Classic Andalusian Family Foal mold: Proud Mother And Newborn Foal set #3160, tan dun foal (Jan.-June 1993)
Classic Andalusian Family Foal mold: Proud Mother And Newborn Foal set #3161, dark bay foal (July-Dec. 1993)
Classic Arabian Family Foal SR, dark rose gray, in Drinkers Of The Wind set #700693 (1993)
Classic Arabian Family Stallion SR, smoke gray, in Drinkers Of The Wind set #700693 (1993)
Classic "Hobo" mold (with stand): "Nevada Star" SR #410493, smoke gray (1993)
Classic "Johar" SR, fleabitten rose gray, in Drinkers Of The Wind set #700693 (1993)
Classic "Kelso" mold: "Jeremy" #257, liver chestnut (1993-94)
Classic Lipizzan mold: Lipizzaner SR #700393, alabaster (1993 - current as of 1996)
Classic "Man-O-War" mold: "King" #258, dark mahogany brown (1993-94)
Classic "Mesteño" Dawning mold: The Dawning Gift Set, "Mesteño" And His Mother #4810, light red dun "Mesteño" foal (1993 - current as of 1996) [mold: 1993 - current as of 1996]
Classic "Mesteño's" Mother, pale buckskin mare, in The Dawning Gift Set, "Mesteño" And His Mother #4810 (1993 - current as of 1996) [mold: 1993 - current as of 1996]
Classic Rearing Stallion mold: "Little Chaparral" SR #700293, buckskin pinto (1993)
Classic Rearing Stallion SR #410593, buckskin (1993)
Classic "Ruffian" mold: "Colleen" #262, red sorrel (1993-94)
Classic "Silky Sullivan" mold: "Andrew" #259, shaded smoke gray (1993-94)
Classic "Swaps" mold: "Prince" #260, rose alabaster (1993-94)
Classic "Terrang" mold: "Ten Gallon" #261, pale tan dun (1993-94)
Clydesdale Stallion mold: "Grayingham Lucky Lad" SR #410393, black (1993)
Family Arabian Foal mold: Ara-Appaloosa Foal #874, "bay" leopard appaloosa (1993-94)
Family Arabian Mare mold: Ara-Appaloosa Mare #873, "bay" leopard appaloosa (1993-94)
Family Arabian Stallion mold: Ara-Appaloosa Stallion #872, "bay" leopard appaloosa (1993-94)
Fighting Stallion mold: Bay Fighting Stallion SR #700993 (1993)
Fighting Stallion SR, red sorrel, in Breyer Wild Horses Of America Set SR #710493 (1993)
Foundation Stallion mold: "Fugir Cacador" Lusitano Stallion #870, light buckskin (1993)
Foundation Stallion SR, bay blanket appaloosa, in Breyer Wild Horses Of America Set SR #710493 (1993)
"Gem Twist" Champion Show Jumper #495, white (1993-95) [mold: 1993 - current as of 1996]
Grazing Foal mold: "Buttons" & "Bows" set #3165, apricot dun foal "Bows" (1993-95)
Grazing Mare mold: "Buttons" & "Bows" set #3165, apricot dun mare "Buttons" (1993-95)
Haflinger mold: "Scat Cat" Children's Pony #883, bay roan leopard appaloosa (1993-94)
Hanoverian SR, dark bay with 2 stockings, in Dressage Set Of 2 Horses SR #500693 (1993)
Indian Pony mold: "Ichilay" The Crow Horse #882, grulla (1993)
"Justin Morgan" mold: "Double Take" #878, liver chestnut (1993-95)
"Lady Phase" mold: "Prairie Flower" SR #700193, red bay blanket appaloosa (1993)
"Lady Phase" SR, alabaster, in The Watchful Mare And Foal set #700593 (1993)
"Lady Roxana" mold: Proud Mother And Newborn Foal set #3160, chocolate sorrel mare (Jan.-June 1993)

"Lady Roxana" mold: Proud Mother And Newborn Foal set #3161, tan dun mare (July-Dec. 1993)

"Legionario" mold: "Medieval Knight" #880, red roan (1993-94)

Little Bits Morgan Stallion SR, light sandy bay (1993)

Little Bits Performing "Misty" #79293, ceramic, light chestnut pinto (1993) [mold: 1993]

"Misty's Twilight" SR, black, in Dressage Set Of 2 Horses SR #500693 (1993)

"Morganglanz" mold: Appaloosa Sport Horse & Canongate Saddle Set SR #700893, chestnut leopard appaloosa (1993)

Mustang SR, black, 1 stocking, in Breyer Wild Horses Of America Set SR #710493 (1993)

"Phantom Wings" mold: "Woodsprite" Pony Foal #875, reddish bay (1993-94)

"Phantom Wings" SR, bay blanket appaloosa, in Breyer Three Generations Appaloosa Set SR #710693 (1993)

"Phar Lap" mold: Wild American Horse #881, shaded brown-gray smoke (1993-94)

"Pluto" SR, pale dapple gray (1993)

Pony Of The Americas mold: "Just Justin" Quarter Pony #876, dun (1993-95)

Pony Of The Americas mold: "Pantomime" Pony Of The Americas #884, black blanket appaloosa (1993-94)

Proud Arabian Mare mold: "Steel Dust" SR #400393, pale smoke gray (1993/94)

Proud Arabian Mare SR #410293, "silver filigree" decorator, dappled metallic silver (1993)

Quarter Horse Yearling SR, bay blanket appaloosa, in Breyer Three Generations Appaloosa Set SR #710693 (1993)

Running Stallion mold: "Rumbling Thunder" #879, dark dapple gray (1993-94)

"San Domingo" mold: "Domino" The Happy Canyon Trail Horse #871, dark olive-brown paint (1993)

Shire Horse mold: Fine Porcelain Shire Horse #79193, dark dappled bay (1993-95) [mold: 1993-95]

Stampede Riggins, Breyer Western Rider #513, man doll (1993 - current as of 1996) [mold: 1993 - current as of 1996]

Stock Horse Foal (standing) SR, pale smoke gray, in The Watchful Mare And Foal set #700593 (1993)

"Touch Of Class" mold: "Guinevere" English Hack #877, red bay (1993-94)

1994

Action Stock Horse Foal mold: "Sunny" Action Foal #891, yellow dun (1994-95)

Balking Mule SR , alabaster, in Balking Mule Assortment #410894 (1994)

Balking Mule SR, apricot dun, in Balking Mule Assortment #410894 (1994)

Balking Mule SR, black blanket appaloosa, in Balking Mule Assortment #410894 (1994)

Balking Mule SR, black leopard appaloosa, in Balking Mule Assortment #410894 (1994)

Balking Mule SR, buckskin, in Balking Mule Assortment #410894 (1994)

Balking Mule SR, chestnut, in Balking Mule Assortment #410894 (1994)

Black Stallion mold: "Greystreak" Action Arabian #899, shaded smoke gray (1994-95)

Black Stallion mold: "Ofir," Sire of "Witez II," SR #700694, dark plum bay (1994)

Brenda Breyer doll mold: SR doll in Classic "Black Beauty" Gift Set #700894 (1994)

Brenda Breyer doll mold: Western Show Brenda Breyer or Western Brenda Breyer Rider #514 (pre-catalog release 1994, catalog run 1995 - current as of 1996)

"Buckshot" mold: "Winchester" SR #411194, charcoal brown (1994)

Buffalo mold: American Bison #381, yellow dun with black head (1994 - current as of 1996)

Cantering Welsh Pony mold: "Tara" Welsh Pony #892, dappled bay (1994-95)

Classic Andalusian Family Foal mold: SR steel gray foal, in Spanish-Norman Family set SR #700294 (1994)

Classic Andalusian Family Stallion mold: SR red roan stallion, in Spanish-Norman Family set SR #700294 (1994)

Classic Arabian Family Foal mold: Arabian Stallion And Frisky Foal set #3162, gray dun foal (Jan. 1 - June 30, 1994)

Classic Arabian Family Foal mold: Arabian Stallion And Frisky Foal set #3163, light sandy bay foal (July 1 - Dec. 31, 1994)

Classic "Black Beauty" SR, glossy black, in "Black Beauty" Gift Set #700894, with Brenda doll, book (1994)

Classic "Ginger" mold: SR alabaster mare with white mane and tail, in Spanish-Norman Family set #700294 (1994)

Classic "Kelso" mold: Fine Horse Family set #3348, red roan mare (1994 - current as of 1996)

Classic "Kelso" mold: "Denver" SR, dark bay, in set #410194 with foal (1994)

Classic "Merrylegs" mold: "Martin's Dominique" Champion Miniature Horse #898, black (1994-95)

Classic "Mesteño" Challenger mold: The Challenger Gift Set #4811, reddish dun "Mesteño" (1994 - current as of 1996) [mold: 1994 - current as of 1996]

Classic "Mesteño" Challenger mold variation: The Challenger Gift Set #4811, grulla "Sombra" (1994 - current as of 1996)

Classic Mustang Family Foal mold: Fine Horse Family set #3348, chestnut blanket appaloosa foal (1994 - current as of 1996)

Classic Polo Pony mold: "Silver Comet" SR #700594, dapple gray (1994)

Classic Quarter Horse Family Foal mold: "Blaze" SR, dark bay, in set #410194 with mare (1994)

Classic Rearing Stallion mold: "Promises" Rearing Stallion #890, dark chestnut pinto (1994-95)

Classic "Silky Sullivan" mold: Fine Horse Family set #3348, liver chestnut stallion (1994 - current as of 1996)

Clydesdale Foal mold: "Satin Star" Drafter Foal #894, dark chestnut (1994-95)

Clydesdale Stallion mold: Circus Extravaganza set #3170, grulla large horse (1994-95)

Fighting Stallion mold: "Ponokah-Eemetah" The Blackfeet Indian Horse #897, dark bay blanket appaloosa (1994-95)

Five-Gaiter mold: "CH Imperator" American Saddlebred #904, liver chestnut, glossy (1994-95)

Five-Gaiter mold: "Moon Shadows" SR #400294, blue roan (1994)

Friesian mold: Action Drafters Big And Small set #3175, dark dappled bay big drafter (1994-95)

Galiceño mold: "Freckle Doll" Galiceno #888, reddish bay pinto (1994-95)

Hanoverian mold: "Gifted" #887, bay with blaze (1994)

Indian Pony mold: "Chinook" SR #700194, dark dapple gray (1994)

Indian Pony SR #411294, red roan (1994)

"John Henry" mold: Dark Bay Western Horse SR #711594, dark plum bay (1994)

"Jolly Cholly" mold: "Chaser" Hound Dog #324, chestnut and white (1994-95)

Jumping Horse mold: "Starlight" #886, seal brown with large spiky star (1994)

Kitten mold: "Cleopatra" Kitten #337, orange tabby with darker orange stripes (1994-95)

Kitten mold: "Leonardo" Kitten #338, tawny-gray tabby with darker gray stripes (1994-95)

"Lady Phase" mold, chestnut leopard appaloosa, in Horse Salute Gift Set SR #711694 (1994)

Little Bits Arabian Stallion and Bitsy Breyer beach/jockey molds: "Starlight" And Carole, Cross Country Set #1016, dark mahogany bay horse, girl rider, and tack (1994 - current as of 1996)

Little Bits Clydesdale mold: Circus Extravaganza set #3170, dark dappled bay small horse (1994-95)

Little Bits Clydesdale mold: Action Drafters Big And Small set #3175, gray dun small drafter (1994-95)

Little Bits Morgan Stallion and Bitsy Breyer English molds: "Pepper" And Lisa, Hunter/Jumper Set #1018, dapple gray horse, girl rider, and tack (1994 - current as of 1996)

Little Bits Quarter Horse Stallion and Bitsy Breyer Western molds: "Spot" And Kate, Western Set #1019, black blanket appaloosa horse, girl rider, and tack (1994 - current as of 1996)

Little Bits Thoroughbred Stallion and Bitsy Breyer beach/jockey molds: "Topside" And Stevie, Cross Country Set #1017, sandy bay horse, girl rider, and tack (1994 - current as of 1996)

"Llanarth True Briton" Champion Welsh Cob #494, dark chestnut (1994 - current as of 1996) [mold: 1994 - current as of 1996]

Morgan mold: "Lippitt Pegasus" Foundation Morgan #901, blood bay (1994-95)

"Morganglanz" SR, reddish bay with blaze, in Horse Salute Gift Set SR #711694 (1994)

Mustang mold: "Rarin' To Go" #896, grulla (1994-95)

"Phantom Wings" mold: "Bright Socks" Pinto Foal #895, black pinto (1994-95)

"Phar Lap" SR, dark mahogany bay, in Horse Salute Gift Set SR #711694 (1994)

"Roemer" mold: "Domino" Gift Set #700994, black pinto horse, dressage saddle, and saddle pad (1994)

"Roemer" mold: "Vandergelder" Dutch Warmblood #900, dappled bay (1994-95)

Running Foal mold: "Little Bub," Young "Justin Morgan," #903, red bay (1994-95)

Running Foal SR, alabaster, in Spirit Of The East Gift Set SR #710294 (1994)

Running Mare mold: "Wild Diamond," "Justin Morgan's" Dam, #902, sandy bay (1994-95)

Running Mare SR, alabaster, in Spirit Of The East Gift Set SR #710294 (1994)

Running Stallion mold variation: Unicorn SR #700394, alabaster, silver-and-white-striped horn (1994)

"San Domingo" mold: "Bright Zip" SR #700794, chestnut roan blanket appaloosa (1994)

"Sea Star" mold: "Scribbles" Paint Horse Foal #893, chestnut paint (1994-95)

"Sham" mold: Arabian Stallion And Frisky Foal set #3162, dappled bay stallion (Jan. 1 - June 30, 1994)

"Sham" mold: Arabian Stallion And Frisky Foal set #3163, dappled dark yellow-gray dun stallion (July 1 - Dec. 31, 1994)

"Sham" SR #410994, liver chestnut (1994)

Spanish Barb mold: Fine Porcelain Spanish Barb #79194, pale tan dun (1994-95) [mold: 1994-95]

Stablemates Arabian Mare mold: Saddle Club Collection #5650, dapple gray (1994-95)

Stablemates Draft Horse mold: Saddle Club Collection #5650, alabaster (1994-95)

Stablemates Morgan Stallion mold: Saddle Club Collection #5650, medium reddish bay (1994-95)

Stablemates "Seabiscuit" mold: Saddle Club Collection #5650, red chestnut Running Thoroughbred (1994-95)

Stablemates Thoroughbred Lying Foal SR #411494, black, on keychain (1994)

Stablemates Thoroughbred Lying Foal SR #411694, transparent amber, on keychain (1994)

Stablemates Thoroughbred Mare mold: Saddle Club Collection #5650, black mare with no white (1994-95)

Stablemates Thoroughbred Standing Foal SR #411394, black, on keychain (1994)

Stablemates Thoroughbred Standing Foal SR #411594, transparent amber, on keychain (1994)

Stablemates molds: Twelve-Piece Stablemates Set SR #711094 (1994), reissue of Stablemate Assortment IV SR #495092 (1992) but with glossed eyes

Stampede Riggins doll mold: Texas Cowboy Replica SR #711294 (1994)

Suckling Foal mold: Medicine Hat Mare And Foal set #3180, chestnut pinto foal (1994 - current as of 1996)

Thoroughbred Mare mold: Medicine Hat Mare And Foal set #3180, chestnut pinto mare (1994 - current as of 1996)

Western Prancer mold: "Ranger" Cow Pony #889, red dun (1994-95)

1995

Action Stock Horse Foal mold: "Cricket" Quarter Horse Foal #934, chestnut (1995 - current as of 1996)

"Adios" mold: "Clayton" Quarter Horse #911, dappled palomino (1995 - current as of 1996)

"Adios" mold: "Mego" SR #707595, palomino paint (1995)

"Aristocrat" Champion Hackney #496, dark reddish bay (1995 - current as of 1996) [mold: 1995 - current as of 1996]

Belgian mold: "Goliath" The American Cream Draft Horse #906, pale palomino (1995)

"Black Beauty" (cross-galloping) mold: "Donovan" Running Appaloosa Stallion #919, gray-dun roan blanket appy (1995 - current as of 1996)

Black Stallion mold: Princess Of Arabia set #905, light dapple gray horse, doll, costume (Jan.-July 1995)

Black Stallion mold: Princess Of Arabia set #905, red roan horse, doll, costume (Aug.-Dec. 1995)

Boxer mold: "Pug" Boxer #322, brown brindle (1995 - current as of 1996)

Brenda Breyer doll mold: Female Rider SR #710995, in striped shirt and breeches (1995)

Brenda Breyer doll mold: Princess Of Arabia set #905, doll in Arabian outfit, with horse, costume (1995)

"Buckshot" mold: "Cody" #922, dark bay pinto (Jan. 1 - June 30, 1995)

"Buckshot" mold: "Hickok" SR #923, blue roan pinto (July 1 - Dec. 31, 1995)

Cantering Welsh Pony SR, bay roan, in Parade Of Horses Breeds set #705495 (1995)

Classic Arabian Family Foal mold: Bedouin Family Gift Set #3057, chestnut foal, striped mane (1995 - current as of 1996)

Classic Arabian Family Mare mold: Bedouin Family Gift Set #3057, black mare, mottled mane (1995 - current as of 1996)

Classic Arabian Family Mare mold: SR "Buckaroo," red dun, in "Buckaroo" And "Skeeter" set #700795 with medallion (1995)

Classic Arabian Family Stallion mold: Bedouin Family Gift Set #3057, dark chestnut stallion, partially striped mane (1995 - current as of 1996)

Classic Bucking Bronco mold: "Dakota" Bucking Bronco #932, dappled palomino (1995 - current as of 1996)

Classic Eagle doll mold: Eagle And "Pow Wow" set SR #705095, Native American girl, shirt and skirt, horse, tack (1995) [mold: 1995]

Classic Eagle doll mold: Willow And "Shining Star" set SR #703495, Native American girl, beaded costume, horse, tack (1995)

Classic Hillary doll mold: Darla, with racing outfit, in Dapples "Amazement's" Riding Set #95104, with horse, accessories (1995 - current as of 1996) [mold: 1995 - current as of 1996]

Classic Hillary doll mold: English Hillary Doll #515, with English outfit (1995 - current as of 1996)

Classic Hillary doll mold: Western Hillary Doll #516, with Western outfit (1995 - current as of 1996)

Classic "Hobo" mold (with stand): "Riddle" Passing Through Time, Phase One, SR #703595, bay blanket appaloosa (1995)

Classic "Hobo" mold (with stand): "Riddle" Passing Through Time, Phase Two, SR #703595, chestnut-point leopard appaloosa (1995)

Classic "Hobo" mold (with stand): "Riddle" Passing Through Time, Phase Three, SR #703595, gray-point leopard appaloosa (1995)

Classic "Johar" mold: Eagle And "Pow Wow" set SR #705095, black pinto "Pow Wow," doll, tack (1995)

Classic "Kelso" mold: "Blackjack" #263, black pinto, with ribbon (1995 - current as of 1996)

Classic "Kelso" mold: SR "Geronimo," chestnut blanket appaloosa, in "Geronimo" And "Cochise" set #700695 with medallion (1995)

Classic "Man-O-War" mold: "Apache" #264, pale grulla, with ribbon (1995 - current as of 1996)

Classic "Mesteño" Progeny mold: The Progeny Gift Set, "Mesteño" And "Rojo" #4812, reddish dun "Mesteño" stallion (1995 - current as of 1996) [mold: 1995 - current as of 1996]

Classic Mustang Family Foal mold: Appaloosa Mustang Family Gift Set #3349, chestnut blanket appy foal (1995 - current as of 1996)

Classic Mustang Family Mare mold: Appaloosa Mustang Family Gift Set #3349, black blanket appy mare (1995 - current as of 1996)

Classic Mustang Family Stallion mold: Appaloosa Mustang Family Gift Set #3349, rose dun blanket appy stallion (1995 - current as of 1996)

Classic Rearing Stallion mold: Willow And "Shining Star" set SR #703495, dark bay blanket appaloosa "Shining Star," doll, tack (1995)

Classic "Rojo," light red dun yearling, in The Progeny Gift Set, "Mesteño" And "Rojo" #4812 (1995 - current as of 1996) [mold: 1995 - current as of 1996]

Classic "Ruffian" mold: "Glory" And Plank Jump Gift Set #2003, buckskin horse, with jump, ribbon (1995 - current as of 1996)

Classic "Ruffian" mold: "Patches" #268, dark chestnut pinto, with ribbon (1995 - current as of 1996)

Classic "Silky Sullivan" mold: "Buck" And Hillary Gift Set #2004, pale buckskin horse, with doll, tack, jump, ribbon (1995 - current as of 1996)

Classic "Silky Sullivan" mold: "Spice" #265, bay blanket appaloosa, with ribbon (1995 - current as of 1996)

Classic "Swaps" mold: "Cloud" #266, dark candy-spot gray, with ribbon (1995 - current as of 1996)

Classic "Terrang" mold: "Azul" #267, blue-bay roan, with ribbon (1995-current as of 1996))

Dapples "Amazement" #95102, dark chestnut pinto stallion, with brush (1995 - current as of 1996) [mold: 1995 - current as of 1996]

Dapples "Amazement," "Sunny's Mom," "Sunny," and Hillary doll molds: Dapples Deluxe Rider Set #95107, with Darla doll, accessories, and book (1995 - current as of 1996)

Dapples "Amazement," "Sunny's Mom," and "Sunny" molds: Dapples Deluxe Set #95106, with accessories and book (1995 - current as of 1996)

Dapples "Celestria" mold: "Dancer" And "Celestria" Set #95105, pearl white filly, with mare, accessories, and book (1995 - current as of 1996) [mold: 1995 - current as of 1996]

Dapples "Dancer" #95100, pearl white mare, with brush (1995 - current as of 1996) [mold: 1995 - current as of 1996]

Dapples "Sunny" mold: Mom And "Sunny" Set #95103, ocher pinto filly, with mare and brush (1995 - current as of 1996) [mold: 1995 - current as of 1996]

Dapples "Sunny's Mom" #95101, light sorrel mare, with brush (1995 - current as of 1996) [mold: 1995 - current as of 1996]

"El Pastor" mold: "Tobe" Rocky Mountain Horse #914, dappled liver chestnut (1995 - current as of 1996)

Fighting Stallion mold: "Sierra" SR #400196, red dun (1995/96)

Grazing Mare SR, buckskin, in Serenity set #710195 (1995)

Haflinger mold: "Sargent Pepper" Appaloosa Pony #926, roaned black leopard appy (1995 - current as of 1996)

Hanoverian mold: Dressage Horse ("Art Deco") SR #710595, black pinto (1995)

Ideal Quarter Horse mold: The AQHA Ideal American Quarter Horse #497, golden-brown chestnut (1995) [mold: 1995 - current as of 1996]

Ideal Quarter Horse mold: The AQHA Ideal American Quarter Horse SR #707795, dark red chestnut (1995)

Indian Pony mold: "Cheyenne" American Mustang #929, bay roan (1995 - current as of 1996)

Jumping Horse mold: Jumping "Gem Twist" SR #702795, white (1995)

Jumping Horse mold: "Mystique" SR #707495, gray appaloosa, glossy (1995)

"Lady Phase" SR #707395, palomino (1995)

"Lassie" mold: "Honey" Collie #323, sandy chestnut and white (1995 - current as of 1996)

"Legionario" mold: "El Campeador" SR #410395, dark dapple gray (1995)

"Legionario" mold: "Promenade" Andalusian #918, liver chestnut (1995 - current as of 1996)

Little Bits American Saddlebred mold: "Belle" #1021, reddish bay (1995 - current as of 1996)

Little Bits Morgan Stallion mold: "Delilah" #1024, palomino, white mane and tail (1995 - current as of 1996)

Little Bits Quarter Horse Stallion mold: "Moonglow" #1023, reddish dun (1995 - current as of 1996)

Little Bits Thoroughbred Stallion mold: "Prancer" #1022, shaded bay, star (1995 - current as of 1996)

Little Bits Thoroughbred Stallion and Bitsy Breyer English molds: "Cobalt" And Veronica, Hunter/Jumper Set #1025, black horse with no white; girl rider and tack (1995 - current as of 1996)

Lying Down Foal mold: "Buster" SR, bay blanket appaloosa, in "Buster" And "Brandi" set #400195 (1995)

Lying Down Foal SR, buckskin, in Serenity set #710195 (1995)

"Morganglanz" mold: "Pieraz" ("Cash") SR #704695, red fleabit (1995)

Mustang mold: "Rawhide" Wild Appaloosa Mustang SR #702495, chestnut roan blanket appaloosa (1995)

Old Timer mold: "McDuff" Old Timer #935, grulla blanket appaloosa (1995 - current as of 1996)

Pacer SR, light bay, in Race Horses Of America set #710295 (1995)

"Phar Lap" mold: "Dustin" SR #700995, red dun, with medallion (1995)

"Phar Lap" mold: "Native Diver" Champion Thoroughbred #921, black (1995 - current as of 1996)

"Phar Lap" SR, medium dapple gray, in Race Horses Of America set #710295 (1995)

"Pluto" mold: "Favory" SR #702595, red fleabit (1995)

Premier Arabian Mare mold: Fine Porcelain Premier Arabian Mare #79195, alabaster, in native costume (1995) [mold: 1995]

Proud Arabian Mare SR, sandy bay, in Parade Of Horses Breeds set #705495 (1995)

Proud Arabian Stallion mold: "Sundown" Proud Arabian Stallion #933, light reddish chestnut (1995 - current as of 1996)

Quarter Horse Gelding mold: "Majesty" Quarter Horse #924, light dapple gray (1995 - current as of 1996)

Quarter Horse Yearling mold: "Calypso" Quarter Horse #937, tan dun (1995 - current as of 1996)

Quarter Horse Yearling mold: "Thunder Bay" Quarter Horse #927, dark mahogany bay (1995)

Running Mare mold: State Line Tack '95 "Special Delivery" SR #702295, dark plum bay, white "SLT" brand (1995)

Running Stallion mold: "Lone Star" #928, rose gray snowflake appaloosa (1995 - current as of 1996)

Running Stallion mold variation: Unicorn II SR #700595, black, glossy (1995)

Saddlebred Weanling mold: "Kentuckiana" Saddlebred Weanling #915, dappled liver chestnut (1995 - current as of 1996)

Saddlebred Weanling mold, alabaster, in Parade Of Horses Breeds set #705495 (1995)

St. Bernard mold: "Brandy" St. Bernard #321, tawny chestnut and white (1995 - current as of 1996)

"San Domingo" mold: "Oxidol" Rodeo Appaloosa #917, no-spot white (1995 - current as of 1996)

Scratching Foal mold: "Brandi" SR, bay blanket appaloosa, in "Buster" And "Brandi" set #400195 (1995)

"Sea Star" mold: SR "Cochise," chestnut blanket appaloosa, in "Geronimo" And "Cochise" set #700695 with medallion (1995)

"Sham" mold: "Sham" The Godolphin Arabian Horse SR #701595, blood bay, "'95" mold stamp (1995)

Stablemates Arabian Mare #5182, palomino (1995 - current as of 1996)

Stablemates Arabian Mare SR, semi-leopard appaloosa, in Set Of 12 Miniatures SR #710695 (1995)

Stablemates Arabian Stallion #5181, medium chestnut (1995 - current as of 1996)

Stablemates Arabian Stallion SR, light dusky chestnut, in Set Of 12 Miniatures SR #710695 (1995)

Stablemates "Citation" mold: Standing Thoroughbred #5175, alabaster (1995 - current as of 1996)

Stablemates "Citation" SR, brown dun blanket appaloosa, in Set Of 12 Miniatures SR #710695 (1995)

Stablemates "Citation" SR, dappled gray dun, in Set Of 12 Miniatures SR #710695 (1995)

Stablemates Draft Horse #5187, rose dun (1995 - current as of 1996)

Stablemates Morgan Mare #5185, red chestnut (1995 - current as of 1996)

Stablemates Morgan Mare SR, chestnut with pale mane and tail, in Set Of 12 Miniatures SR #710695 (1995)

Stablemates Morgan Stallion #5184, light bay (1995 - current as of 1996)

Stablemates Morgan Stallion SR, black with striped mane and tail, in Set Of 12 Miniatures SR #710695 (1995)

Stablemates "Native Dancer" mold: Appaloosa #5178, red bay blanket appy (1995 - current as of 1996)

Stablemates "Native Dancer" SR, medium bay, in Set Of 12 Miniatures SR #710695 (1995)

Stablemates Quarter Horse Stallion #5186, light bay (1995 - current as of 1996)

Stablemates Quarter Horse Stallion SR, medium chestnut, in Set Of 12 Miniatures SR #710695 (1995)

Stablemates "Seabiscuit" mold: Running Paint #5179, chestnut pinto (1995 - current as of 1996)

Stablemates "Silky Sullivan" mold: Thoroughbred Racehorse #5177, black (1995 - current as of 1996)

Stablemates "Silky Sullivan" SR, dark grulla, in Set Of 12 Miniatures SR #710695 (1995)

Stablemates "Silky Sullivan" SR, pale rose gray, in Set Of 12 Miniatures SR #710695 (1995)

Stablemates "Swaps" mold: Thoroughbred Racehorse #5176, red chestnut (1995 - current as of 1996)

Stablemates "Swaps" SR, grulla, in Set Of 12 Miniatures SR #710695 (1995)

Stablemates Thoroughbred Mare #5183, steel gray, 4 stockings (1995 - current as of 1996)

Stablemates Thoroughbred Mare SR, dark brown, in Set Of 12 Miniatures SR #710695 (1995)

Stock Horse Stallion mold: "Shane" American Ranch Horse #938, blue roan (1995 - current as of 1996)

Stock Horse Stallion SR, dappled reddish chestnut, in Race Horses Of America set #710295 (1995)

"Stormy" mold: SR "Skeeter," dark bay pinto, in "Buckaroo" And "Skeeter" set #700795 with medallion (1995)

"Stud Spider" mold: "Mister Mister" Champion Paint #916, medium chestnut paint (1995 - current as of 1996)

Tennessee Walker mold: "High Flyer" Tennessee Walker #913, chestnut pinto (1995 - current as of 1996)

Trakehner mold: "Hanover" Trakehner #912, liver chestnut (1995 - current as of 1996)

Trakehner mold: "Kaleidoscope" SR #702395, light bay pinto (1995)

Western Horse SR #701895, palomino, "'95" mold stamp (1995)

Western Pony mold: "Cisco" Western Pony With Saddle #910, buckskin (1995 - current as of 1996)

Models by Number

GENERAL NOTE: The following list includes the model numbers of all catalog-run models and sets and of some special-run models and sets. It omits not only SR model numbers that I couldn't locate but also those formed from the regular-run model number plus letters designating the SR color (e.g., #99GR for the SR gray blanket appaloosa Performance Horse). This number-plus-letters style of number for SRs was phased out in the mid-1980s and completely discontinued after 1987.

The model numbers below omit the prefixes "7000-" and "7900-," called range numbers (see JAH 19/#5 Winter 1992, p. 3), which are used on Reeves International price lists and on the bar code labels of Breyer boxes. (For example, the bar code label on the box of the Classic "Black Stallion Returns" Set #3030 says #7000-3030.) The #7000 range number was introduced by Reeves in 1985—shortly after Reeves acquired Breyer Animal Creations—to distinguish the Breyer line of plastic horses from the other lines of toys and collectibles produced or distributed by Reeves. Reeves later introduced the #7900 range number for Breyer's cold-cast porcelain (resin) and fine porcelain horses. Range numbers are always omitted from model numbers in Breyer catalogs and manuals, and almost always omitted from the name-and-number labels on the front of Breyer boxes. The only exception I know of is the SR Vaulting Horse's box, whose label has the model number 7000-700058. For consistency with all other model numbers, I omit the #7000- prefix from the Vaulting Horse's number below.

The bar code numbers consisting of the #7000- prefix plus the Breyer model number were evidently introduced in about 1988 or 1989. Previously, the bar code used the prefix #19756, followed by various numbers that are not model numbers. For instance, my "Buckshot" #415's box has a bar code with the number 19756 10056, and my "Cips" #116's bar code says 19756 10132. These numbers are not included in the list below.

In this list, models are Traditional scale unless specified as Classic, Little Bits, Dapples, or Stablemates. The listings do not include color details, mold variations, date cross-references to sets with the same model, etc. For this information see the listings above in the main sections.

#4: Family Arabian Stallion "Faith," palomino (1961/62 - 1987)
#4SP: Family Arabian Stallion "Faith," palomino, in special cardboard display carton (1968-70)
#5: Family Arabian Mare "Hope," palomino (1961/62 - 1987)
#5SP: Family Arabian Mare "Hope," palomino, in special cardboard display carton (1968-70)
#6: Family Arabian Foal "Charity," palomino (1961/62 - 1987)
#6SP: Family Arabian Foal "Charity," palomino, in special cardboard display carton (1968-70)
#7: Family Arabian Stallion "Prince," alabaster (1959 [possibly late 1958] - 1973)
#7SP: Family Arabian Stallion "Prince," alabaster, in special cardboard display carton (1968-70)
#8: Arabian Mare "Pride," alabaster (1958 [possibly late 1957] - 1959) [Proud Arabian Mare mold]
#8: Family Arabian Mare "Pride," alabaster (1960-73)
#8SP: Family Arabian Mare "Pride," alabaster, in special cardboard display carton (1968-70)
#9: Arabian Foal "Joy," alabaster (1958 [possibly late 1957] - 1959) [Proud Arabian Foal mold]
#9: Family Arabian Foal "Joy," alabaster (1960-73)
#9SP: Family Arabian Foal "Joy," alabaster, in special cardboard display carton (1968-70)
#10: "Pride" And "Joy" Combination, with Proud Arabian Mare and Foal, both alabaster (1958 [possibly late 1957] - 1959)
#10: "Pride" And "Joy" set, with Family Arabian Mare and Foal, both alabaster (1960-64)
#10: Family Arabian Stallion SR, black (1977)
#11: "Prince," "Pride," And "Joy" set, with Family Arabian Stallion, Proud Arabian Mare, and Proud Arabian Foal, all alabaster (1959)
#11: "Prince," "Pride," And "Joy" set, with Family Arabian Stallion, Mare, Foal, all alabaster (1960-64)
#11: Family Arabian Mare SR, black (1977)
#12: "Prince" And "Pride" set, with Family Arabian Stallion and Proud Arabian Mare, both alabaster (1959)
#12: "Prince" And "Pride" set, with Family Arabian Stallion and Mare, both alabaster (1960 - 1960/62)
#12: Family Arabian Foal SR, black (1977)
#13: Family Arabian Stallion "Sheik," bay (1959 [possibly late 1958] - 1973)
#13SP: Family Arabian Stallion "Sheik," bay, in special cardboard display carton (1968-70)
#14: Arabian Mare "Sheba," bay ([possibly late 1958] - 1959) [Proud Arabian Mare mold]
#14: Family Arabian Mare "Sheba," bay (1960-73)
#14: Blister-wrapped display box number for model #4 (late 1970s)
#14SP: Family Arabian Mare "Sheba," bay, in special cardboard display carton (1968-70)
#15: Arabian Foal "Shah," bay ([possibly late 1958] - 1959) [Proud Arabian Foal mold]
#15: Family Arabian Foal "Shah," bay (1960-73)
#15: Blister-wrapped display box number for model #5 (late 1970s)
#15SP: Family Arabian Foal "Shah," bay, in special cardboard display carton (1968-70)
#16: "Sheik," "Sheba," And "Shah" set, with Family Arabian Stallion, Proud Arabian Mare, and Proud Arabian Foal, all bay ([possibly late 1958] - 1959)
#16: "Sheik," "Sheba," And "Shah" set, with Family Arabian Stallion, Mare, and Foal, all bay (1960-64)
#16: Blister-wrapped display box number for model #6 (late 1970s)
#16: Marguerite Henry's "Sea Star," red chestnut (1980-87) ["Sea Star" mold]
#17: "Sheik" And "Sheba" set, with Family Arabian Stallion and Proud Arabian Mare, both bay ([possibly late 1958] - 1959)
#17: "Sheik" And "Sheba" set, with Family Arabian Stallion and Mare, both bay (1960 - 1960/62)

#17: Stock Horse Foal, chestnut blanket appaloosa (1979-82) ["Phantom Wings" mold]
#18: "Sheba" And "Shah" set, with Proud Arabian Mare and Foal, both bay ([possibly late 1958] - 1959)
#18: "Sheba" And "Shah" set, with Family Arabian Mare and Foal, both bay (1960-64)
#18: Stock Horse Foal, black blanket appaloosa (1978-82) ["Phantom Wings" mold]
#19: Marguerite Henry's "Stormy," chestnut pinto foal (1977 - current as of 1996) ["Stormy" mold]
#20: "Misty" Of Chincoteague, chestnut pinto (1972 - current as of 1996) ["Misty" mold]
#21: Shetland Pony, black pinto (1960-73, 1976)
#22: Shetland Pony, brown pinto (1960-66, 1970-73)
#23: Shetland Pony, bay (1973-88)
#25: Shetland Pony, alabaster (1960-72)
#27: "Fury," black, long vee-shaped star (1957/58 - 1965) ["Fury" Prancer mold]
#29: "Phantom Wings," "Misty's" Foal, palomino pinto (1983-87)
#30: "King" The Fighting Stallion, Alabaster Lipizzan (1961-85) [Fighting Stallion mold]
#31: No model #31 was ever issued to my knowledge, but Breyer often uses this number to designate the Fighting Stallion mold. See note 5 for the Fighting Stallion mold above in the Traditionals section.
#32: "King" The Fighting Stallion, gray appaloosa (1961-66) [Fighting Stallion mold]
#33: "King" The Fighting Stallion, palomino (1961-73) [Fighting Stallion mold]
#34: "King" The Fighting Stallion, charcoal (1961/63 - 1970) [Fighting Stallion mold]
#35: "King" The Fighting Stallion, bay (1961/63 - 1987) [Fighting Stallion mold]
#36: Race Horse, Derby Winner, chestnut (ca.1954 - 1966)
#37: Family Appaloosa Stallion "Fleck," gray blanket appaloosa (1959-70) [Family Arabian Stallion mold]
#37SP: Family Appaloosa Stallion "Fleck," gray blanket appaloosa, in special cardboard display carton (1968-70)
#38: Arabian Mare "Speck," gray blanket appaloosa (1959) [Proud Arabian Mare mold]
#38: Family Appaloosa Mare "Speck," gray blanket appaloosa (1960-70) [Family Arabian Mare mold]
#38SP: Family Appaloosa Mare "Speck," gray blanket appaloosa, in special cardboard display carton (1968-70)
#39: Arabian Foal "Spot," gray blanket appaloosa (1959) [Proud Arabian Foal mold]
#39: Family Appaloosa Foal "Spot," gray blanket appaloosa (1960-70) [Family Arabian Foal mold]
#39SP: Family Appaloosa Foal "Spot," gray blanket appaloosa, in special cardboard display carton (1968-70)
#40: Western Pony "Black Beauty," black, with bald face or diamond star (1955/58 - 1960/62)
#40: Western Pony, dark brown (sometime in the period 1955-57)
#40: Lynn Anderson's "Lady Phase," red chestnut (1976-85) ["Lady Phase" mold]
#P40: Prancer, dark brown (1955 - 1956/57) ["Fury" Prancer mold]
#P40: "Black Beauty," black, with blaze or bald face (1955/57 - 1960/62) ["Fury" Prancer mold]
#41: Western Pony, black pinto (ca.1954 - 1976)
#P41: Prancer, black pinto (1955 - 1960/62) ["Fury" Prancer mold]
#42: Western Pony, brown pinto (ca.1954 - 1966)
#P42: Prancer, brown pinto (1955 - 1960/62) ["Fury" Prancer mold]
#43: Western Pony, palomino (ca.1954 - 1973)
#P43: Prancer, palomino (1955 - 1960/62) ["Fury" Prancer mold]
#44: Western Mount Horse "Black Beauty," black, gold hooves (1953 - 1955/57) [Western Pony mold]
#45: Western Pony, white (ca.1954 - 1970)
#P45: Prancer, white (1955/56 - 1960/62) ["Fury" Prancer mold]
#46: Pacer, liver chestnut (1967-87)
#47: "Man O' War," red chestnut (1967-95)
#48: Morgan, black (1964-87)
#49: Morgan, bay (1964-71)
#50: Western Horse, black, bald face (1959/60 - 1960/62)
#50: "Adios" Famous Standardbred, dark bay (1969-80)
#51: "Commander" The Five-Gaiter, albino (1961/63 - 1966) [Five-Gaiter mold]
#51: "Yellow Mount" Famous Paint Horse, chestnut paint (1970-87) ["Adios" mold]
#51-1: "Adios" SR, red chestnut (1986)
#52: "Commander" The Five-Gaiter, sorrel (1961/63 - 1986) [Five-Gaiter mold]
#53: The Five-Gaiter, palomino (1961/62 - 1971) [Five-Gaiter mold]
#54: Trakehner, bay (1979-84)
#55: Western Horse, black pinto (ca.1954 - 1973, 1975-76)
#56: Western Horse, brown pinto (ca.1954 - 1966)
#57: Western Horse, palomino (1951-91)
#58: Western Mount Horse "Black Beauty," black, gold hooves (ca.1954 - pre-1958) [Western Horse mold]
#58: Hanoverian, bay (1980-84)
#59: Western Horse, white (1950 - 1960/62)
#59: "Morganglanz," chestnut (1980-87)
#60: "Midnight Sun" Famous Tennessee Walker, black (1972-87) [Tennessee Walker mold]
#61: "El Pastor" Famous Paso Fino, bay (1974-81)
#62: Saddlebred Weanling, dark chestnut (1973-80)
#63: "Halla" Famous Jumper, bay (1977-85)
#64: "Rin Tin Tin," brown and white dog (1955/57 - 1965)
#64: Black Foundation Stallion, black (1977-87) [Foundation Stallion mold]
#65: "Lassie," collie dog, red chestnut and white (1955/57 - 1965)
#65: Marguerite Henry's "Justin Morgan," medium/dark bay (1977-89) ["Justin Morgan" mold]
#66: Boxer, chestnut or fawn (ca.1954 - 1973)

#66: "Stud Spider" Appaloosa, black blanket appaloosa (1978-89)
#67: Poodle, black (1955/57 - 1967/68)
#67: Marguerite Henry's "San Domingo," chestnut medicine-hat pinto (1978-87) ["San Domingo" mold]
#68: Poodle, white (1955/57 - 1967/68)
#68: "Legionario III" Famous Andalusian, alabaster (pre-catalog release 1978, catalog run 1979-90)
#69: Poodle, silver gray (1968/69 - 1973)
#69: "Smoky" The Cow Horse, steel gray (1981-85)
#70: Brahma Bull, shaded gray (1955/57 - 1995)
#71: Hereford Bull, horned, walking; brown with white (1955/57 - 1981)
#72: Black Angus Bull, black (1959/60 - 1973, 1976-77) [polled, walking Black Angus Bull mold]
#73: Polled Hereford Bull, brown with white (1961/63 - 1965) [polled, walking Black Angus Bull mold]
#73: Spanish Fighting Bull, black (1970-85)
#74: Polled Hereford Bull, standing, large; brown with white (1968 - current as of 1996)
#75: Texas Longhorn Bull, light brown (1961/63 - 1989)
#76: Buffalo, brown (1965-91)
#77: Elk, reddish-brown (1968 - current as of 1996)
#78: Bighorn Ram, brown (1969-80)
#79: Moose, brown (1966 - current as of 1996)
#80: Clydesdale, bay (1958 [maybe earlier] - 1989) [Clydesdale Stallion mold]
#81: Donkey, gray, standing (1956? - 1974)
#82: Donkey With Baskets set, gray, standing, with red plastic baskets (1958 [maybe earlier] - 1958/59)
#82: Clydesdale, dapple gray (1961-66) [Clydesdale Stallion mold]
#83: Clydesdale Mare, chestnut (1969-89)
#84: Clydesdale Foal, chestnut (1969-89)
#85: "Diablo" The Mustang, albino (1961/63 - 1966) [Mustang mold]
#85: Dall Sheep, white (1970-73) [Bighorn Ram mold]
#85: Azteca, dapple gray (1980-87) [Foundation Stallion mold]
#86: "Diablo" The Mustang, gray appaloosa (1961/63 - 1966) [Mustang mold]
#86: Mustang SR, black (1978)
#87: "Diablo" The Mustang, buckskin (1961/63 - 1986) [Mustang mold]
#88: "Diablo" The Mustang, charcoal (1961/63 - 1970) [Mustang mold]
#88: Overo Paint, dark chestnut paint (1979-81) ["Stud Spider" mold]
#89: "Black Beauty" (cross-galloping), black (1979-88)
#90: "Phar Lap" Famous Race Horse, red chestnut (1985-88)
#91: Elephant, gray (1956? - 1974)
#92: Elephant, pink (1958 [maybe earlier] - 1958/59)
#92: Belgian, smoke (solid gray) (1964-71)
#93: Elephant, blue (1958 [maybe earlier] - 1958/59)
#93: Belgian, dapple gray (1964-66)
#94: Elephant With Howdah set, gray with detachable howdah (1958 [maybe earlier] - 1958/59)
#94: Belgian, chestnut, lighter chestnut mane and tail (1964-80)
#95: Shire, dapple gray (1972-73, 1975-76)
#96: Shire, honey sorrel (1972-76, 1978-80)
#97: Appaloosa Gelding, sorrel blanket appaloosa (1971-80) [Quarter Horse Gelding mold]
#98: Quarter Horse "Two Bits," buckskin (1961/63 - 1980) [Quarter Horse Gelding mold]
#99: Quarter Horse "Two Bits," bay (1960-66) [Quarter Horse Gelding mold]
#99: Appaloosa Performance Horse, red roan semi-leopard (1974-80) [Performance Horse mold]
#100: Galiceno, bay (1978-82)
#101: Golden Buck, metallic gold (1961/62 - 1964)
#101: Quarter Horse Yearling, liver chestnut (1970-80)
#102: Golden Doe, metallic gold (1961/62 - 1964)
#102: Quarter Horse Yearling, palomino (1970-80)
#103: Appaloosa Yearling, sandy bay blanket appaloosa (1971-88) [Quarter Horse Yearling mold]
#104: Cantering Welsh Pony, bay (1971-73)
#105: Cantering Welsh Pony, chestnut (1971-76, 1979-81)
#106: Cantering Welsh Pony, seal brown (1971-74)
#107: Cantering Welsh Pony SR, dapple gray with red ribbons (1985/86)
#109: American Saddlebred, dapple gray (1987-88) [Five-Gaiter mold]
#110: Western Prancing Horse "Cheyenne," smoke (solid gray) (1961/63 - 1976) [Western Prancer mold]
#111: Western Prancing Horse "Cheyenne," buckskin (1961/63 - 1973) [Western Prancer mold]
#112: Western Prancing Horse "Cheyenne," palomino (1961/63 - 1985) [Western Prancer mold]
#113: Western Prancing Horse "Cheyenne," black pinto (1961/63 - 1966) [Western Prancer mold]
#114: Western Prancing Horse "Cheyenne," bay (1961/63 - 1971) [Western Prancer mold]
#115: Western Prancing Horse "Cheyenne," black leopard appy (1961/63 - 1973) [Western Prancer mold]
#116: "Precipitado Sin Par" ("Cips") Champion Paso Fino, bay pinto (1987) ["El Pastor mold]
#117: "Project Universe" Premium Pinto American Saddlebred, dark chestnut pinto (1987-89) [Five-Gaiter mold]
#118: Blister-wrapped display box number for model #18, black blanket appy Stock Horse Foal (late 1970s) ["Phantom Wings" mold]
#118: American Mustang, sorrel/palomino (1987-89) [Mustang mold]
#119: Running Mare, red roan (1971-73)
#119: Probable blister-wrapped display box number for model #19 (late 1970s)
#120: Running Mare "Sugar," alabaster (1961/63 - 1971)
#121: Running Mare "Sugar, smoke (solid gray) (1961/63 - 1970)
#123: Running Mare "Sugar," dapple gray (1961/63 - 1973)
#123: Blister-wrapped display box number for model #23 (late 1970s)
#124: Running Mare "Sugar," bay (1961/63 - 1987)
#125: Running Stallion, alabaster (1968-71)
#126: Running Stallion, charcoal (1968-70)
#127: Running Stallion, black blanket appaloosa (1968-81)
#128: Running Stallion, red roan (1968-74)
#129: Running Stallion, bay (1971-76, 1978-80)
#0130: Showcase Collection number for model #13 (1970-72)

#130: Running Foal "Spice," alabaster (1961/63 - 1971)
#131: Running Foal "Spice," smoke (solid gray) (1961/63 - 1970)
#133: Running Foal "Spice," dapple gray (1961/63 - 1973)
#134: Running Foal "Spice," bay (1961/63 - 1987)
#140: "Wing Commander" American Saddlebred Five-Gaited World Champion 1948-1953, dark chestnut (1988-90) [Five-Gaiter mold]
#141: Grazing Mare "Buttons," bay (1965-76, 1978-80)
#142: Grazing Mare "Buttons," black (1965-70)
#143: Grazing Mare "Buttons," palomino (1965-76, 1978-80)
#P145: Robin Hood set, rider on white "Fury" Prancer (1956 - 1958/59)
#151: Grazing Foal "Bows," bay (1965-76, 1978-81)
#152: Grazing Foal "Bows," black (1965-70)
#153: Grazing Foal "Bows," palomino (1965-81)
#154: Pony Of The Americas, bay blanket appaloosa (1979-84)
#155: Pony Of The Americas, chestnut leopard appaloosa (1976-80)
#156: Haflinger, chestnut (1979-84)
#164: Blister-wrapped display box number for model #64, Black Foundation Stallion (late 1970s)
#165: Lying Down Foal, black blanket appaloosa (1969-84)
#166: Lying Down Foal, buckskin (1969-73, 1975-76)
#167: Lying Down Foal, red roan (1969-73)
#168: Scratching Foal, black blanket appaloosa (1970-86)
#168: Blister-wrapped display box number for model #68, "Legionario III" (late 1970s)
#169: Scratching Foal, liver chestnut (1970-71)
#170: Scratching Foal, red roan (1970-73)
#174: Indian Pony, bay blanket appaloosa (1973-85)
#175: Indian Pony, chestnut pinto (1970-76)
#176: Indian Pony, buckskin (1970-72)
#177: Indian Pony, alabaster (1970-71; Presentation Collection edition late 1971 only)
#180: Classic Rearing Stallion "Rex," Alabaster Lipizzan (1965-76, 1978-85)
#183: Classic Rearing Stallion "Rex," palomino (1965-85)
#185: Classic Rearing Stallion "Rex," bay (1965-80)
#188: Blister-wrapped display box number for model #88, Overo Paint (late 1970s) ["Stud Spider" mold]
#190: Classic Bucking Bronco, black (1966-73, 1975-76)
#191: Classic Bucking Bronco, steel gray (1966)
#192: Classic Bucking Bronco, bay (1967/68 - 1970)
#200: Old Timer, alabaster (1966-76)
#201: Family Arabian Stallion "Hickory," charcoal (1961/62 - 1973)
#201SP: Family Arabian Stallion "Hickory," charcoal, in special cardboard display carton (1968-70)
#202: Family Arabian Mare "Dickory," charcoal (1961/62 - 1973)
#202SP: Family Arabian Mare "Dickory," charcoal, in special cardboard display carton (1968-70)
#203: Family Arabian Foal "Doc," charcoal (1961/62 - 1973)
#203SP: Family Arabian Foal "Doc," charcoal, in special cardboard display carton (1968-70)
#205: Old Timer, dapple gray (1966, 1968/70 - 1987)
#206: Old Timer, bay (1988-90)
#207: Balking Mule, bay (1968-73)
#208: Balking Mule, seal brown (1968-70)
#209: Classic "Pegasus," alabaster with wings (mid-1983 - 1987) [Lipizzan mold]
#210: Unicorn, alabaster with gold-and-white-striped horn (1982-88) [Running Stallion mold variation]
#211: Proud Arabian Stallion, alabaster (1971-76, 1978-81)
#212: Proud Arabian Stallion "Witez II," mahogany bay (1971-80)
#213: "Hickory," "Dickory," And "Doc" set, with Family Arabian Stallion, Mare, Foal, all charcoal (1961/62 - 1964)
#213: Proud Arabian Stallion, dapple gray (1972-88)
#215: Proud Arabian Mare, dapple gray (pre-catalog release 1971, catalog run 1972-88)
#216: Proud Arabian Mare, mahogany bay, solid face (1972-80)
#217: Proud Arabian Mare, alabaster, matte (1972-76, 1978-81)
#218: Proud Arabian Foal, alabaster (1973-76, 1978-81)
#219: Proud Arabian Foal, mahogany bay, solid face (1973-80)
#220: Proud Arabian Foal, dapple gray (1973-88)
#221: American Buckskin Stock Horse Stallion (1987-88) [Stock Horse Stallion mold]
#222: American Buckskin Stock Horse Mare (1987-88) [Stock Horse Mare mold]
#223: "Dickory" And "Doc" set, with Family Arabian Mare and Foal, both charcoal (1961/62 - 1964)
#224: American Buckskin Stock Horse Foal (1987-88) [standing Stock Horse Foal mold]
#225: Action American Buckskin Stock Horse Foal (1987-88) [Action Stock Horse Foal mold]
#226: Bay Quarter Horse Stock Stallion, bay (1981-88) [Stock Horse Stallion mold]
#227: Sorrel Quarter Horse Stock Mare, deep red sorrel (1982-86) [Stock Horse Mare mold]
#228: Bay Quarter Horse Stock Foal (1983-88) [Stock Horse Foal {standing} mold]
#229: Tobiano Pinto Stock Horse Stallion, black paint (1981-88) [Stock Horse Stallion mold]
#230: Overo Paint Stock Horse Mare, bay paint (1982-88) [Stock Horse Mare mold]
#231: Pinto Stock Horse Foal, black paint (1983-88) [standing Stock Horse Foal mold]
#232: Appaloosa Stock Horse Stallion, bay blanket appaloosa (1981-86) [Stock Horse Stallion mold]
#233: Appaloosa Stock Horse Mare, black blanket appaloosa (1982-88) [Stock Horse Mare mold]
#234: Appaloosa Stock Horse Foal, gray blanket appaloosa (1983-86) [Stock Horse Foal {standing} mold]
#236: Chestnut Stock Horse Foal, red sorrel (1984-86) [Action Stock Horse Foal mold]
#237: Action American Paint Horse Foal, bay paint (1984-88) [Action Stock Horse Foal mold]
#238: Action American Appaloosa Stock Horse Foal, gray blanket appy (1984-88) [Action Stock Horse Foal mold]
#240: Indian Warrior set, rider on "Black Beauty" Western Pony (1958 [maybe earlier] - 1958/59) [Indian mold]
#241: Indian & Pinto set, rider on black pinto Western Pony (ca.1954 - pre-1958)
#P241: Indian Chief And Pinto Pony set, rider on black pinto "Fury" Prancer (1955 - 1956/57)
#242: Indian & Pinto set, rider on brown pinto Western Pony (ca.1954 - pre-1958)
#P242: Indian Chief And Pinto Pony set, rider on brown pinto "Fury" Prancer (1955 - 1956/57)
#245: Lying Down Unicorn, alabaster (1985-88) [Lying Down Foal mold variation]

#251: Classic "Norita," dapple gray (1991-92) ["Kelso" mold]
#252: Classic "Pepe," reddish chestnut, solid face (1991-92) ["Man-O-War" mold]
#253: Classic "T-Bone," fleabitten gray (1991-92) ["Silky Sullivan" mold]
#254: Classic "Hawk", black (1991-92) ["Swaps" mold]
#255: Classic "Gaucho," red roan (1991-92) ["Terrang" mold]
#256: Classic "Lula," medium reddish bay (1991-92) ["Ruffian" mold]
#257: Classic "Jeremy," liver chestnut (1993-94) ["Kelso" mold]
#258: Classic "King," dark mahogany brown (1993-94) ["Man-O-War" mold]
#259: Classic "Andrew," shaded smoke gray (1993-94) ["Silky Sullivan" mold]
#260: Classic "Prince," rose alabaster (1993-94) ["Swaps" mold]
#261: Classic "Ten Gallon," pale tan dun (1993-94) ["Terrang" mold]
#262: Classic "Colleen," red sorrel (1993-94) ["Ruffian" mold]
#263: Classic "Blackjack," black pinto, with ribbon (1995 - current as of 1996) ["Kelso" mold]
#264: Classic "Apache," pale grulla, with ribbon (1995 - current as of 1996) ["Man-O-War" mold]
#265: Classic "Spice," bay blanket appaloosa, with ribbon (1995 - current as of 1996) ["Silky Sullivan" mold]
#266: Classic "Cloud," dark candy-spot gray, with ribbon (1995 - current as of 1996) ["Swaps" mold]
#267: Classic "Azul," blue-bay roan, with ribbon (1995 - current as of 1996) ["Terrang" mold]
#268: Classic "Patches," dark chestnut pinto, with ribbon (1995 - current as of 1996) ["Ruffian" mold]
#300: Jumping Horse "Stonewall," bay (1965-88)
#301: Buck, tawny (1964-73)
#302: Doe, tawny (1964-73)
#303: Fawn, tawny with white spots (1964-73)
#304: Deer Family set, tawny Buck, Doe, and Fawn (1964-65)
#306: Bear, black (1967-73)
#307: Bear, brown (1967-71)
#308: Bear Cub, black (1967-73)
#309: Bear Cub, brown (1967-71)
#310: Pronghorn Antelope, brown with white (1971-76)
#312: Rocky Mountain Goat, white with charcoal or gray horns (1973-76)
#312: Montana Mountain Goat, white with reddish brown horns (1989) [Rocky Mountain Goat mold]
#321: "Brandy" St. Bernard, tawny chestnut and white (1995 - current as of 1996) [St. Bernard mold]
#322: "Pug" Boxer, brown brindle (1995 - current as of 1996) [Boxer mold]
#323: "Honey" Collie, sandy chestnut and white (1995 - current as of 1996) ["Lassie" mold]
#324: "Chaser" Hound Dog, chestnut and white (1994-95) ["Jolly Cholly" mold]
#325: "Jolly Cholly" Bloodhound, solid dark brown (1966 - 1967/68)
#326: "Jolly Cholly" Basset Hound, tri-color (1968/69 - 1985)
#327: German Shepherd, charcoal gray or gray-brown (pre-catalog release 1971, catalog run 1972-73) ["Rin Tin Tin" mold]
#328: St. Bernard, chestnut and white (1972-80)
#335: Siamese Kitten, white with dark Siamese points (1966-70) [Kitten mold]
#336: Calico Kitten, orangy-tan tabby with charcoal-brown stripes (1966-73) [Kitten mold]
#337: "Cleopatra" Kitten, orange tabby with darker orange stripes (1994-95) [Kitten mold]
#338: "Leonardo" Kitten, tawny-gray tabby with darker gray stripes (1994-95) [Kitten mold]
#341: Cowboy & Pinto set, rider on black pinto Western Pony (ca.1954 - pre-1958)
#341: Lucky Ranger set, rider on black pinto Western Pony (1955/56 - 1957) [Cowboy mold]
#341: Holstein Cow, horns, black pinto (1972-73) [Cow mold]
#P341: Lucky Ranger set, rider on black pinto "Fury" Prancer (1955/56 - 1957) [Cowboy mold]
#342: Cowboy & Pinto set, rider on brown pinto Western Pony (ca.1954 - pre-1958)
#342: Lucky Ranger set, rider on brown pinto Western Pony (1955/56 - 1957) [Cowboy mold]
#342: Guernsey Cow, horns, dark palomino pinto (1972-73) [Cow mold]
#P342: Lucky Ranger set, rider on brown pinto "Fury" Prancer (1955/56 - 1957) [Cowboy mold]
#343: Cowboy set, rider on palomino Western Pony (ca.1954 - pre-1958)
#343: Lucky Ranger set, rider on palomino Western Pony (1955/56 - 1957) [Cowboy mold]
#343: Jersey Cow, horns, dark palomino (1972-73) [Cow mold]
#P343: Lucky Ranger set, rider on palomino "Fury" Prancer (1955/56 - 1957) [Cowboy mold]
#344: Ayrshire Cow, horns, dark red-brown pinto (1972-73) [Cow mold]
#345: Lucky Ranger set, rider on white Western Pony (1957/58 - 1958/59) [Cowboy mold]
#345: Brown Swiss Cow, horns, medium coffee brown (1972-73) [Cow mold]
#347: Holstein Calf, black pinto (1972-73) [Calf mold]
#348: Guernsey Calf, dark palomino pinto (1972-73) [Calf mold]
#349: Jersey Calf, dark palomino (1972-73) [Calf mold]
#350: Ayrshire Calf, dark red-brown pinto (1972-73) [Calf mold]
#351: "Sugar" And "Spice" set, alabaster Running Mare and smoke Running Foal (1961/63 - 1964)
#351: Brown Swiss Calf, medium coffee brown (1972-73) [Calf mold]
#352: "Sugar" And "Spice" set, smoke Running Mare and alabaster Running Foal (1961/63 - 1964)
#352: Black Angus Calf SR [calf mold]
#355: "Jasper" The Market Hog, white with large gray spot (1974 - current as of 1996)
#360: Charolais Bull, white (1975-95)
#365: Black Angus Bull, polled, standing, large; black (1978 - current as of 1996)
#370: Showcase Collection number for model #37 (1970)
#370: Texas Longhorn Bull, dark red-brown pinto (1990-95)
#375: Marguerite Henry's "Brighty," gray sitting burro (1982-87) ["Brighty" mold]
#376: "Brighty 1991," grayish brown sitting burro (1991 - current as of 1996) ["Brighty" mold]
#380: Showcase Collection number for model #38 (1970) [Family Arabian Mare mold]
#380: "Tatanka" The White Buffalo (1992-93) [Buffalo mold]
#381: American Bison, yellow dun with black head (1994 - current as of 1996) [Buffalo mold]
#390: Donkey, light gray (1992)
#391: Elephant, light gray (1992)
#400: Showcase Collection number for model #4 (1970-72)
#400: Breyer Rider, girl doll (1976); advertised but never released

#401: Walter Farley's Black Stallion, black (1981-88) [Black Stallion mold]
#410: Showcase Collection number for model #41 (1970-72)
#410: Marguerite Henry's "Sham" The Godolphin Arabian, blood bay (1984-88) ["Sham" mold]
#411: Prancing Arabian Stallion, fleabitten gray (1988-90) ["Sham" mold]
#415: "Buckshot" Famous Spanish Barb, grulla semi-leopard appaloosa (1985-88)
#416: Spanish Barb, chestnut pinto (1988-89) ["Buckshot" mold]
#420: "Touch Of Class" Olympic Champion, medium/light bay (1986-88)
#425: Marguerite Henry's "Lady Roxana," alabaster (1986-88) ["Lady Roxana" mold]
#426: Prancing Arabian Mare, light sorrel (1988-89) ["Lady Roxana" mold]
#430: Showcase Collection number for model #43 (1970-72)
#430: "Sherman Morgan," Son Of "Justin Morgan," red chestnut (1987-90)
#435: "Secretariat" Famous Race Horse, red chestnut (1987-95)
#P440: Canadian Mountie set, rider on dark brown or black "Fury" Prancer (sometime in the period 1955-57)
#445: "John Henry" Famous Race Horse, dark bay (1988-90)
#P445: Canadian Mountie set, rider on white "Fury" Prancer (1957/58 - 1958/59)
#450: Showcase Collection number for model #45 (1970)
#450: "Rugged Lark" Champion American Quarter Horse Stallion, bay (1989-95)
#455: "Roy" Belgian Drafter, light sorrel (1989-90)
#456: "Faith," "Hope," And "Charity" set, with Family Arabian Stallion, Mare, Foal, all palomino (1961/62 - 1964)
#460: "Khemosabi+++" Champion Arabian Stallion, bay (1990-95)
#465: "Roemer" Champion Dutch Warmblood, dark chestnut (1990-93)
#470: Showcase Collection number for model #47 (1970-72)
#470: "Misty's Twilight," chestnut pinto (1991-95)
#475: "Pluto" The Lipizzaner, alabaster (1991-95)
#480: Showcase Collection number for model #48 (1970-72)
#480: Classic "Mesteño" The Messenger, reddish dun (1992 - current as of 1996)
#485: Friesian, black (1992-95)
#490: Showcase Collection number for model #49 (1970-71)
#490: "Bolya" The Freedom Horse (Akhal-Teke), golden buckskin (1992-94) ["Halla" mold variation]
#494: "Llanarth True Briton" Champion Welsh Cob, dark chestnut (1994 - current as of 1996)
#495: "Gem Twist" Champion Show Jumper, white (1993-95)
#496: "Aristocrat" Champion Hackney, dark reddish bay (1995 - current as of 1996)
#497: The AQHA Ideal American Quarter Horse, golden-brown chestnut (1995) [Ideal Quarter Horse mold]
#498: Western Brenda Breyer doll (1988-89)
#499: English Brenda Breyer doll (1988-89)
#500: Showcase Collection number for model #5 (1970-72)
#500: Brenda Breyer doll, long-haired (pre-catalog release 1978 and 1979, catalog run 1980-86)
#500: Brenda Breyer doll, big curly hair (1988-90)
#501: Bolo Tie, white buffalo skull on string tie (1972-76)
#501: English Riding Outfit, for Brenda Breyer (1979-86)
#501A: Brenda Breyer Outfit Assortment dealer package (1980 - 1984/86)
#502: Western Riding Outfit, for Brenda Breyer (1978-86)
#502: Brenda Breyer Riding Outfit, for Brenda Breyer (1988)
#506: "Hope" And "Charity" set, with Family Arabian Mare and Foal, both palomino (1961/62 - 1964)
#510: Dressage Brenda Breyer doll (1990 - current as of 1996)
#510A: Brenda Breyer Horse Stickers (1980-82)
#511: Show Jumping Brenda Breyer doll (1990 - current as of 1996)
#512: Saddle Seat Brenda Breyer doll (1993 - current as of 1996)
#513: Stampede Riggins, Breyer Western Rider doll (1993 - current as of 1996)
#514: Western Show Brenda Breyer or Western Brenda Breyer Rider (pre-catalog release 1994, catalog run 1995 - current as of 1996)
#515: Classic English Hillary Doll, with English outfit (1995 - current as of 1996) [Hillary mold]
#516: Classic Western Hillary Doll, with Western outfit (1995 - current as of 1996) [Hillary mold]
#520: Showcase Collection number for model #52 (1970-72)
#530: Showcase Collection number for model #53 (1970-71)
#540: Kit Carson set, rider on "Black Beauty" Western Pony (1957/58 - 1958/59) [Davy Crockett mold]
#P540: Kit Carson set, rider on dark brown or black "Fury" Prancer (1955/56 - 1956) [Davy Crockett mold]
#P540[?]: Davy Crockett set, rider on dark brown "Fury" Prancer (1955 - 1956/57)
#542: Kit Carson set, rider on brown pinto Western Pony (sometime in the period 1956-57) [Davy Crockett mold]
#550: Showcase Collection number for model #55 (1970-72)
#550: Ben Breyer, doll (1983-86) [Alec Ramsey mold]
#570: Showcase Collection number for model #57 (1970-72)
#601: Circus Boy Corky On "Bimbo" set, rider on gray Elephant (1957/58 - 1958/59)
#601: Classic "Kelso," dark bay (1975-90)
#602: Classic "Man-O-War," red chestnut (1975-90)
#603: Classic "Silky Sullivan," medium/dark chestnut (1975-90)
#604: Classic "Swaps," medium chestnut, star (1975-90)
#605: Classic "Terrang," dark/medium bay, no white (1975-90)
#606: Classic "Ruffian," dark brown bay (1977-90)
#620: Classic Lipizzan Stallion, alabaster (1975-80)
#620: Classic Lipizzaner SR, German export, also numbered #700192 (1992)
#625: Classic "Hobo" The Mustang Of Lazy Heart Ranch, buckskin, with brown stand (1975-80)
#626: Classic Polo Pony, bay, with stand (1976-82)
#700: Showcase Collection number for model #7 (1970-72)
#701: Collector's Rocking Horse, flocked chestnut (1985-87) [Saddlebred Weanling mold]
#702: Morgan, light reddish bay (1988-89)
#703: Blanket Appaloosa, dark gray blanket appaloosa (1988-89) ["San Domingo" mold]
#704: Tennessee Walking Horse, red bay (1988-89)
#705: Standing Quarter Horse Stallion, apricot dun (1988-89) ["Adios" mold]
#706: Family Arabian Stallion, chestnut, flaxen mane and tail (1988)
#707: Family Arabian Mare, chestnut, flaxen mane and tail (1988)
#708: Family Arabian Foal, chestnut, flaxen mane and tail (1988)

#709: Fighting Stallion, black leopard appaloosa (1988-90)

#710: American Indian Pony, red roan (1988-91) [Foundation Stallion mold]

#711: "Breezing Dixie" Famous Appaloosa Mare, dark bay blanket appy (1988) ["Lady Phase" mold]

#0800: Showcase Collection number for model #8 (1970-72) [Family Arabian Mare mold]

#800: Showcase Collection number for model #80 (1970-72)

#801: Shetland Pony, bay pinto (1989-91)

#802: "Fade To Gray," dark dapple gray (1989-90) ["Black Beauty" {cross-galloping} mold]

#803: Galloping Thoroughbred, dark dappled bay (1989-90) ["Phar Lap" mold]

#804: Proud Arabian Stallion, dappled rose gray (1989-90)

#805: Proud Arabian Mare, dappled rose gray (1989-90)

#806: Proud Arabian Foal, dappled rose gray (1989-90)

#807: Paint Horse Stallion, liver chestnut paint (1989-90) [Stock Horse Stallion mold]

#808: Paint Horse Mare, liver chestnut paint (1989-90) [Stock Horse Mare mold]

#809: Paint Horse Foal, liver chestnut paint (1989-90) [Stock Horse Foal {standing} mold]

#810: Action Appaloosa Foal, red leopard appaloosa (1989-93) [Action Stock Horse Foal mold]

#811: Majestic Arabian Stallion, leopard appaloosa (1989-90) [Black Stallion mold]

#812: Prancing Arabian Stallion, dark palomino (1989-91) ["Sham" mold]

#813: Thoroughbred Mare, black (1989-90) ["Touch Of Class" mold]:

#814: Family Arabian Stallion, bay, solid face (1989-90)

#815: Family Arabian Mare, bay, solid face (1989-90)

#816: Family Arabian Foal, bay, solid face (1989-90)

#817: "Abdullah" Champion Trakehner, pale dapple gray (1989) [Trakehner mold]

#818: Saddlebred Weanling, caramel pinto (1990)

#819: "Dan Patch" Famous Standardbred Pacer, red bay (1990) [Pacer mold]

#820: Noble Jumper, dapple gray (1990-91) ["Halla" mold]

#821: "Rocky" Champion Connemara Stallion, dappled buckskin (1990-92) [Pony Of The Americas mold]

#822: Morgan, dark seal brown (1990-92) ["Justin Morgan" mold]

#823: Blanket Appaloosa, red bay blanket appaloosa (1990-91) ["Stud Spider" mold]

#824: Clydesdale Stallion, light golden bay (1990-91)

#825: Clydesdale Mare, light golden bay (1990-91)

#826: Clydesdale Foal, light golden bay (1990-91)

#827: Pinto American Saddlebred, black pinto (1990-91) [Five-Gaiter mold]

#828: Paint American Mustang, bay paint (1990-91) [Mustang mold]

#829: Comanche Pony, palomino (1990-92) ["San Domingo" mold]

#830: Showcase Collection number for model #83 (1970-72)

#830: Quarter Horse Stallion, blue roan (1990) ["Adios" mold]

#831: Show Stance Morgan, dark red chestnut (1990-91) [Morgan mold]

#832: "Hyksos" The Egyptian Arabian, ageless bronze (1991) [Black Stallion mold]

#833: "Dream Weaver," sorrel (1991) ["Black Beauty" {cross-galloping} mold]

#834: Old Timer, dark red roan (1991-93)

#835: Prancing Morgan, black (1991-92) ["Sherman Morgan" mold]

#836: "Joe Patchen," Sire Of "Dan Patch," black (1991-93) ["John Henry" mold]

#837: Belgian Brabant, tan dun (1991-93) ["Roy" mold]

#838: "Hobo," buckskin (1991-92) ["Phar Lap" mold]

#839: Proud Arabian Stallion, light dapple gray (1991-94)

#840: Showcase Collection number for model #84 (1970-72)

#840: Proud Arabian Mare, red chestnut, pale area above nose (1991-92)

#841: Family Arabian Foal, red chestnut (1991-93)

#842: "Skipster's Chief" Famous Therapeutic Riding Horse, sorrel (1991-92) [Stock Horse Stallion mold]

#843: Selle Français, shaded liver chestnut (1991-92) ["Touch Of Class" mold]

#844: Paint Horse Foal, light chestnut paint (1991-92) [standing Stock Horse Foal mold]

#845: Chincoteague Foal, buckskin (1991-93) ["Sea Star" mold]

#846: "Rough Diamond," dark chestnut pinto (1991-93) ["Phantom Wings" mold]

#847: "Black Beauty 1991," black (1991-95) [Morganglanz mold]

#848: Running Mare, dark chestnut pinto (1991-93)

#849: Running Foal, dark chestnut pinto (1991-93)

#850: Mountain Pony, light chestnut (1991-92) [Haflinger mold]

#851: "Spanish Pride," reddish bay (1991-92) [Legionario mold]

#852: Appy Mare, red roan leopard appaloosa (1991-92) [Stock Horse Mare mold]

#853: "Mesa" The Quarter Horse, dark mahogany bay (1991-92) ["Adios" mold]

#854: "Memphis Storm" Tennessee Walking Horse, charcoal-brown glossy (1992) [Tennessee Walker mold]

#855: "Chaparral" The Fighting Stallion, buckskin pinto (1992) [Fighting Stallion mold]

#856: Shire Mare, liver chestnut (1992-93) [Clydesdale Mare mold]

#857: Shetland Pony, dark red chestnut (1992-94)

#858: Vermont Morgan, chocolate sorrel (1992-93) [Morgan mold]

#859: Family Appaloosa Stallion, bay blanket appaloosa (1992-94) ["Stud Spider" mold]

#860: Family Appaloosa Mare, black leopard appaloosa (1992-94) ["Lady Phase" mold]

#861: Family Appaloosa Foal, bay blanket appaloosa (1992-94) [standing Stock Horse Foal mold]

#862: Kentucky Saddlebred, red chestnut (1992-93) [Five-Gaiter mold]

#863: "Rana" The Arab Stallion, blue chocolate (1992-93) ["Sham" mold]

#864: "Tic Toc," alabaster (1992-94) [Western Horse mold]

#865: Bluegrass Foal, blue roan (1992-94) [Running Foal mold]

#866: "Plain Pixie," red roan (1992-93) [Cantering Welsh Pony mold]

#867: "Tesoro," palomino (1992-95) ["El Pastor" mold]

#868: Highland Clydesdale, bay (1992-95) [Clydesdale Stallion mold]

#869: Lakota Pony, white with cream shading (1992) [Foundation Stallion mold]

#870: "Fugir Cacador" Lusitano Stallion, light buckskin (1993) [Foundation Stallion mold]

#871: "Domino" The Happy Canyon Trail Horse, dark olive-brown paint (1993) ["San Domingo" mold]

#872: Ara-Appaloosa Stallion, "bay" leopard appaloosa (1993-94) [Family Arabian Stallion mold]

#873: Ara-Appaloosa Mare, "bay" leopard appaloosa (1993-94) [Family Arabian Mare mold]

#874: Ara-Appaloosa Foal, "bay" leopard appaloosa (1993-94) [Family Arabian Foal mold]

#875: "Woodsprite" Pony Foal, reddish bay (1993-94) ["Phantom Wings" mold]

#876: "Just Justin" Quarter Pony, dun (1993-95) [Pony Of The Americas mold]

#877: "Guinevere" English Hack, red bay (1993-94) ["Touch Of Class" mold]

#878: "Double Take" Morgan, liver chestnut (1993-95) ["Justin Morgan" mold]

#879: "Rumbling Thunder," dark dapple gray (1993-94) [Running Stallion mold]

#880: "Medieval Knight" Andalusian, red roan (1993-94) ["Legionario" mold]

#881: Wild American Horse, shaded brown-gray smoke (1993-94) ["Phar Lap" mold]

#882: "Ichilay" The Crow Horse, grulla (1993) [Indian Pony mold]

#883: "Scat Cat" Children's Pony, bay roan leopard appaloosa (1993-94) [Haflinger mold]

#884: "Pantomime" Pony Of The Americas, black blanket appy (1993-94) [Pony of the Americas mold]

#885: "Rough 'N' Ready" Quarter Horse, pale yellow dun (1993-95) ["Adios" mold]

#886: "Starlight," seal brown with large spiky star (1994) [Jumping Horse mold]

#887: "Gifted," bay with blaze (1994) [Hanoverian mold]

#888: "Freckle Doll" Galiceno, reddish bay pinto (1994-95) [Galiceno mold]

#889: "Ranger" Cow Pony, red dun (1994-95) [Western Prancer mold]

#890: Classic "Promises" Rearing Stallion, dark chestnut pinto (1994-95) [Rearing Stallion mold]

#891: "Sunny" Action Foal, yellow dun (1994-95) [Action Stock Horse Foal mold]

#892: "Tara" Welsh Pony, dappled bay (1994-95) [Cantering Welsh Pony mold]

#893: "Scribbles" Paint Horse Foal, chestnut paint (1994-95) ["Sea Star" mold]

#894: "Satin Star" Drafter Foal, dark chestnut (1994-95) [Clydesdale Foal mold]

#895: "Bright Socks" Pinto Foal, black pinto (1994-95) ["Phantom Wings" mold]

#896: "Rarin' To Go," grulla (1994-95) [Mustang mold]

#897: "Ponokah-Eemetah" The Blackfeet Indian Horse, dark bay blanket appaloosa (1994-95) [Fighting Stallion mold]

#898: Classic "Martin's Dominique" Champion Miniature Horse, black (1994-95) ["Merrylegs" mold]

#899: "Greystreak" Action Arabian, shaded smoke gray (1994-95) [Black Stallion mold]

#900: "Vandergelder" Dutch Warmblood, dappled bay (1994-95) ["Roemer" mold]

#901: "Lippitt Pegasus" Foundation Morgan, blood bay (1994-95) [Morgan mold]

#902: "Wild Diamond," "Justin Morgan's" Dam, sandy bay (1994-95) [Running Mare mold]

#903: "Little Bub," Young "Justin Morgan," red bay (1994-95) [Running Foal mold]

#904: "CH Imperator" American Saddlebred, liver chestnut, glossy (1994-95) [Five-Gaiter mold]

#905: Princess Of Arabia set, light dapple gray horse, doll, costume (Jan.-July 1995) [Black Stallion mold]

#905: Princess Of Arabia set, red roan horse, doll, costume (Aug.-Dec. 1995) [Black Stallion mold]

#906: "Goliath" The American Cream Draft Horse, pale palomino (1995) [Belgian mold]

#907: Family Arabian Stallion, woodgrain (1959-66)

#908: Arabian Mare, woodgrain (1959) [Proud Arabian Mare mold]

#908: Family Arabian Mare, woodgrain (1960-66)

#909: Family Arabian Foal, woodgrain (1960-66)

#910: "Cisco" Western Pony With Saddle, buckskin (1995 - current as of 1996) [Western Pony mold]

#911: "Clayton" Quarter Horse, dappled palomino (1995 - current as of 1996) ["Adios" mold]

#912: "Hanover" Trakehner, liver chestnut (1995 - current as of 1996) [Trakehner mold]

#913: "High Flyer" Tennessee Walker, chestnut pinto (1995 - current as of 1996) [Tennessee Walker mold]

#914: "Tobe" Rocky Mountain Horse, dappled liver chestnut (1995 - current as of 1996) ["El Pastor" mold]

#915: "Kentuckiana" Saddle-bred Weanling, dappled liver chestnut (1995 - current as of 1996) [Saddlebred Weanling mold]

#916: "Mister Mister" Champion Paint, medium chestnut paint (1995 - current as of 1996) ["Stud Spider" mold]

#917: "Oxidol" Rodeo Appaloosa, no-spot white (1995 - current as of 1996) ["San Domingo" mold]

#918: "Promenade" Andalusian, liver chestnut (1995 - current as of 1996) ["Legionario" mold]

#919: "Donovan" Running Appaloosa Stallion, gray-dun roan blanket appy (1995 - current as of 1996) ["Black Beauty" {cross-galloping} mold]

#920: Running Mare "Sugar," woodgrain (1961/63 - 1965)

#921: "Native Diver" Champion Thoroughbred, black (1995 - current as of 1996) ["Phar Lap" mold]

#922: "Cody," dark bay pinto (Jan. 1 - June 30, 1995) ["Buckshot" mold]

#923: "Hickok," blue roan pinto (July 1 - Dec. 31, 1995) ["Buckshot" mold]

#924: "Majesty" Quarter Horse, light dapple gray (1995 - current as of 1996) [Quarter Horse Gelding mold]

#925: Shetland Pony, woodgrain (1960-64)

#926: "Sargent Pepper" Appaloosa Pony, roaned black leopard appy (1995 - current as of 1996) [Haflinger mold]

#927: "Thunder Bay" Quarter Horse, dark mahogany bay (1995) [Quarter Horse Yearling mold]

#928: "Lone Star," rose gray snowflake appaloosa (1995 - current as of 1996) [Running Stallion mold]

#929: "Cheyenne" American Mustang, bay roan (1995 - current as of 1996) [Indian Pony mold]

#930: Running Foal "Spice," woodgrain (1961/63 - 1965)

#931: "King" The Fighting Stallion, woodgrain (1961-73) [Fighting Stallion mold]

#932: Classic "Dakota" Bucking Bronco, dappled palomino (1995 - current as of 1996) [Bucking Bronco mold]

#933: "Sundown" Proud Arabian Stallion, light reddish chestnut (1995 - current as of 1996) [Proud Arabian Stallion mold]

#934: "Cricket" Quarter Horse Foal, chestnut (1995 - current as of 1996) [Action Stock Horse Foal mold]

#935: "McDuff" Old Timer, grulla blanket appaloosa (1995 - current as of 1996) [Old Timer mold]

#936: Race Horse, Derby Winner, woodgrain (1959-65)

#937: "Calypso" Quarter Horse, tan dun (1995 - current as of 1996) [Quarter Horse Yearling mold]

#938: "Shane" American Ranch Horse, blue roan (1995 - current as of 1996) [Stock Horse Stallion mold]

#945: Western Pony, woodgrain (1959/60 - 1964)

#P945[?]: Prancer, woodgrain (probably 1959) ["Fury" Prancer mold]

#948: Morgan, woodgrain (1964-65)

#951: "Commander" The Five-Gaiter, woodgrain (1961/62 - 1965) [Five-Gaiter mold]

#966: Boxer, woodgrain (1959/60 - 1965)

#967: Poodle, woodgrain (1961/63 - 1964)

#970: Brahma Bull, woodgrain (1959-65)

#970: Showcase Collection number for model #97 (1971-72)

#971: Hereford Bull, horned, walking; woodgrain (1959/60 - 1964)
#975: Texas Longhorn Bull, woodgrain (1961/63 - 1965)
#980: Clydesdale, woodgrain (1959-64) [Clydesdale Stallion mold]
#980: Showcase Collection number for model #98 (1970-72)
#985: "Diablo" The Mustang, woodgrain (1961/63 - 1965) [Mustang mold]
#992: Belgian, woodgrain (1964-65)
#999: Quarter Horse "Two Bits," woodgrain (1960-64) [Quarter Horse Gelding mold]
#1000: Bitsy Breyer and Little Bits dealer assortment (1983 - 1984/87)
#1001: Dealer assortment of models (1974)
#1001: Little Bits Bitsy Breyer And Arabian Stallion Beach Set, horse, rider, and tack (late 1983 - 1985)
#1002: Dealer assortment of models (1974)
#1003: Dealer assortment of models (1974)
#1004: Dealer assortment of models (1975-76)
#1005: Dealer assortment of models (1975-76)
#1005: Little Bits Bitsy Breyer And Morgan English Set, horse, rider, and tack (late 1983 - 1987)
#1006: Dealer assortment of models (1975-76)
#1010: Showcase Collection number for model #101, liver chestnut Quarter Horse Yearling (1971-72)
#1010: Dealer Starter Assortment of models (1974-76)
#1010: Little Bits Bitsy Breyer And Thoroughbred Jockey Set, horse, rider, and tack (late 1983 - 1987)
#1015: Little Bits Bitsy Breyer And Quarter Horse Western Set, horse, rider, and tack (late 1983 - 1987)
#1016: Little Bits "Starlight" And Carole, Cross Country Set, dark mahogany bay Arabian Stallion, girl rider [Bitsy Breyer beach/jockey mold], and tack (1994 - current as of 1996)
#1017: Little Bits "Topside" And Stevie, Cross Country Set, sandy bay Thoroughbred Stallion, girl rider [Bitsy Breyer beach/jockey mold], and tack (1994 - current as of 1996)
#1018: Little Bits "Pepper" And Lisa, Hunter/Jumper Set, dapple gray Morgan Stallion, girl rider [Bitsy Breyer English mold], and tack (1994 - current as of 1996)
#1019: Little Bits "Spot" And Kate, Western Set, black blanket appaloosa Quarter Horse Stallion, girl rider [Bitsy Breyer Western mold], and tack (1994 - current as of 1996)
#1020: Showcase Collection number for model #102, palomino Quarter Horse Yearling (1971-72)
#1021: Little Bits "Belle," reddish bay (1995 - current as of 1996) [American Saddlebred mold]
#1022: Little Bits "Prancer," shaded bay, star (1995 - current as of 1996) [Thoroughbred Stallion mold]
#1023: Little Bits "Moonglow," reddish dun (1995 - current as of 1996) [Quarter Horse Stallion mold]
#1024: Little Bits "Delilah," palomino, white mane and tail (1995 - current as of 1996) [Morgan Stallion mold]
#1025: Little Bits "Cobalt" And Veronica, Hunter/Jumper Set, black Thoroughbred Stallion, girl rider [Bitsy Breyer English mold], and tack (1995 - current as of 1996)
#1030: Showcase Collection number for model #103 (1971-72)
#1031: Fighting Stallion, Copenhagen decorator, dappled blue (1963-64)
#1036: Set with regular-run sandy bay Appaloosa Yearling #103 and leather Western tack (1976)
#1051: "Commander" The Five-Gaiter, Copenhagen decorator, dappled blue (1963-64) [Five-Gaiter mold]
#1085: "Diablo" The Mustang, Copenhagen decorator, dappled blue (1963-64) [Mustang mold]
#1100: Showcase Collection number for model #110 (1970-72)
#1110: Showcase Collection number for model #111 (1970-72)
#1120: Running Mare, Copenhagen decorator, dappled blue (1963-64)
#1120: Showcase Collection number for model #112 (1970-72)
#1120: Brenda Western Gift Set, chestnut pinto Western Prancer and doll (1983-85)
#1124: Blister-wrapped display box number for model #124 (late 1970s)
#1130: Running Foal, Copenhagen decorator, dappled blue (1963-64)
#1134: Blister-wrapped display box number for model #134 (late 1970s)
#1140: Showcase Collection number for model #114 (1970-71)
#1150: Showcase Collection number for model #115 (1970-72)
#1174: Probable blister-wrapped display box number for model #174 (late 1970s)
#1190: Showcase Collection number for model #119 (1971-72)
#1200: Showcase Collection number for model #120 (1970-71)
#1210: Showcase Collection number for model #121 (1970)
#1216: Probable blister-wrapped display box number for model #216 (late 1970s)
#1219: Blister-wrap display box number for model #219 (late 1970s)
#1230: Showcase Collection number for model #123 (1970-72)
#1240: Showcase Collection number for model #124 (1970-72)
#1300: Showcase Collection number for model #130 (1970-71)
#1310: Showcase Collection number for model #131 (1970)
#1330: Showcase Collection number for model #133 (1970-72)
#1340: Showcase Collection number for model #134 (1970-72)
#1351: Running Mare And Foal set, both Copenhagen decorator, dappled blue (1963-64)
#1400: Showcase Collection number for model #14 (1970-72) [Family Arabian Mare mold]
#1410: Showcase Collection number for model #141 (1970-72)
#1411: "Buttons" And "Bows" set, with Grazing Mare and Foal, both bay (1965)
#1420: Showcase Collection number for model #142 (1970)
#1422: "Buttons" And "Bows" set, with Grazing Mare and Foal, both black (1965)
#1430: Showcase Collection number for model #143 (1970-72)
#1433: "Buttons" And "Bows" set, with Grazing Mare and Foal, both palomino (1965)
#1500: J.C. Penney Starter Assortment of Showcase Collection models (1971/72)
#1750: Showcase Collection number for model #175 (1970-72)
#1760: Showcase Collection number for model #176 (1970-72)
#1770: Showcase Collection number for model #177 (1970-71)
#2000: Showcase Collection number for model #200 (1970-72)
#2000: Classic After School Herd Assortment, with red roan "Gaucho" ["Terrang" mold], black "Hawk" ["Swaps" mold], medium reddish bay "Lula" ["Ruffian" mold], dapple gray "Norita" ["Kelso" mold], reddish chestnut "Pepe" ["Man-O-War" mold], and blue roan "T-Bone" ["Silky Sullivan" mold] (1991-92)
#2001: Classic After School Herd Assortment, with shaded smoke gray "Andrew" ["Silky Sullivan" mold], red sorrel "Colleen" ["Ruffian" mold], liver chestnut "Jeremy" ["Kelso" mold], dark mahogany brown "King" ["Man-O-War" mold], pale rose gray "Prince" ["Swaps" mold], and pale tan dun "Ten Gallon" ["Terrang" mold] (1993-94)

#2001-71: Dealer assortment of Traditional models (early 1970s)
#2002: B Ranch Series Assortment of horses for dealers (1995 - current as of 1996)
#2003: Classic "Glory" And Plank Jump Gift Set, buckskin horse, jump, and ribbon (1995 - current as of 1996) ["Ruffian" mold]
#2004: Classic "Buck" And Hillary Gift Set, pale buckskin horse, doll, tack, jump, and ribbon (1995 - current as of 1996) ["Silky Sullivan" mold]
#2010: Showcase Collection number for model #201 (1970-72)
#2020: Showcase Collection number for model #202 (1970-72)
#2031: Fighting Stallion, Florentine decorator, dappled metallic gold (1963-64)
#2035: Breyer necktie, red with images of "Sham" (1995 - current as of 1996)
#2036: Breyer necktie, blue with images of "Gem Twist" (1995 - current as of 1996)
#2037: Breyer necktie, green with images of Classic "Kelso" (1995 - current as of 1996)
#2050: Showcase Collection number for model #205 (1970-72)
#2051: "Commander" The Five-Gaiter, Florentine decorator, dappled metallic gold (1963-64) [Five-Gaiter mold]
#2055: "Misty" Gift Set, chestnut pinto pony and book (1972-81)
#2065: "Justin Morgan" Gift Set, bay and book (1973-81)
#2075: "Brighty" Gift Set, gray sitting burro and book (1974-81)
#2085: "Diablo" The Mustang, Florentine decorator, dappled metallic gold (1963-64) [Mustang mold]
#2085: Classic "Hobo" Of Lazy Heart Ranch Gift Set, buckskin horse, stand, and book (1975-81)
#2090: "Smoky" The Cow Horse Gift Set, horse and book (1981-85)
#2095: Black Stallion Gift Set, horse, poster, and book (1981-83)
#2110: Showcase Collection number for model #211 (1971-72)
#2120: Running Mare, Florentine decorator, dappled metallic gold (1963-64)
#2120: Showcase Collection number for model #212 (1971-72)
#2130: Running Foal, Florentine decorator, dappled metallic gold (1963-64)
#2155: Proud Arabian Mare Gift Set, dapple gray with Arabian halter (1972-73)
#2165: Proud Arabian Mare Gift Set, mahogany bay with Arabian halter (1972-73)
#2168: Set with regular-run mahogany bay Proud Arabian Mare #216 and leather English tack (1976)
#2169: Marguerite Henry's "Misty," "Stormy," And "Sea Star" Set (1983-85)
#2175: Proud Arabian Mare Gift Set, alabaster with Arabian halter (1972-73)
#2351: Running Mare And Foal set, both Florentine decorator, dappled metallic gold (1963-64)
#2400: Brenda Breyer Sulky Kit, plastic sulky and leather harness (1981 - 1984/87)
#2446: Brenda Breyer And Sulky Set, alabaster Pacer, doll, sulky, and harness (pre-catalog release 1981, catalog run 1982-87)
#3000: The Black Stallion And Alec Set, horse, doll, and tack (pre-catalog release 1981, catalog run 1982-85)
#3030: Classic "The Black Stallion Returns" Set, with black Black Stallion, alabaster "Johar," and red chestnut "Sagr" (1983-93)
#3031: Fighting Stallion, Golden Charm decorator, solid metallic gold (1963-64)
#3035: Classic U.S. Equestrian Team Gift Set, with bay "Jet Run" with star, red chestnut "Keen," and medium dapple gray "Might Tango" (1980-93)
#3040: Classic "Black Beauty" Family set, with black "Black Beauty," bay "Duchess," chestnut "Ginger," and dapple gray "Merrylegs" (1980-93)
#3045: Classic Quarter Horse Family Gift Set, bay foal, bay mare, and palomino stallion (1974-93)
#3051: "Commander" The Five-Gaiter, Golden Charm decorator, solid metallic gold (1963-64) [Five-Gaiter mold]
#3055: Classic Arabian Family Gift Set, foal, mare, and stallion, all chestnut (1973-91)
#3056: Classic Desert Arabian Family set, bay foal, dark bay mare, bay stallion (1992-94) [Arabian Family Foal, Mare, and Stallion molds]
#3057: Classic Bedouin Family Gift Set, chestnut foal with striped mane, black mare with mottled mane, and dark chestnut stallion with partially striped mane (1995 - current as of 1996) [Arabian Family Foal, Mare, and Stallion molds]
#3060: Classic Andalusian Family Gift Set, chestnut foal, dapple gray mare, alabaster stallion (pre-catalog release 1978, catalog run 1979-93)
#3065: Classic Mustang Family Gift Set, chestnut filly, chestnut pinto mare, chestnut stallion (1976-90)
#3066: Marguerite Henry's "Our First Pony" Gift Set, black pinto "Midge" [Shetland Pony mold], bay pinto "Friday" [Classic Arabian Family Foal mold], black pinto "Teeny" [Classic Mustang Family Foal mold], and halter (1987 - current as of 1996)
#3068: Bear Family set, bear and cub, both black (1974-76)
#3069: Cinnamon Bear And Cub set, both medium red-brown (1987-88)
#3070: "Legionario III" Gift Set, alabaster horse with book (1979-81)
#3071: Bear Family set, bear and cub, both white (1992-95)
#3075: Lynn Anderson's "Lady Phase" Gift Set, red chestnut "Lady Phase," blue ribbon, and book (1976-81)
#3080: "Stud Spider" Gift Set, horse and book (late 1977 - 1983)
#3085: "Diablo" The Mustang, Golden Charm decorator, solid metallic gold (1963-64) [Mustang mold]
#3085: Stablemates Stable Set, with 2 horses (horses varied), 2 foals, and stable (1976-80)
#3090: "Tiffany" And "Benji" Set, white "Tiffany" dog and dark yellowy buckskin "Benji" dog (late 1977)
#3095: Breyer Rider Gift Set, with palomino "Adios," no doll or tack (1976); only a few made
#3095: Brenda Breyer Gift Set, sorrel blanket appaloosa, tack, and rider (1980-85)
#3096: Kelly Reno And "Little Man" Gift Set, palomino Stock Horse Stallion, doll, and tack (1984-85)
#3120: Running Mare, Golden Charm decorator, solid metallic gold (1963-64)
#3123: Deer Family set, tawny Buck, Doe, and Fawn with carry-box (1974 - current as of 1996)
#3130: Running Foal, Golden Charm decorator, solid metallic gold (1963-64)
#3135: Classic "Ahlerich" SR #703135, as listed in the German edition 1989 Breyer manual
#3145: Classic Quarter Horse Family Stallion SR #703145, as listed in the German edition 1989 Breyer manual
#3155: Thoroughbred Mare And Suckling Foal set, bay mare and chestnut foal (1973-84)
#3160: Proud Mother And Newborn Foal set, with chocolate sorrel "Lady Roxana" and tan dun Classic Andalusian Family Foal (Jan. 1 - June 30, 1993)
#3161: Proud Mother And Newborn Foal set, with tan dun "Lady Roxana" and dark bay Classic Andalusian Family Foal (July 1 - Dec. 31, 1993)
#3162: Arabian Stallion And Frisky Foal set, with dappled bay "Sham" and gray dun Classic Arabian Family Foal (Jan. 1 - June 30, 1994)
#3163: Arabian Stallion And Frisky Foal set, with dappled dark yellow-gray dun stallion and

light sandy bay Classic Arabian Family Foal (July 1 - Dec. 31, 1994)

#3165: "Buttons" & "Bows" set, with Grazing Mare and Grazing Foal, both apricot dun (1993-95)

#3170: Circus Extravaganza set, with grulla large horse [Clydesdale Stallion mold] and dark dappled bay small horse [Little Bits Clydesdale mold] (1994-95)

#3175: Action Drafters Big And Small set, with dark dappled bay big drafter [Friesian mold] and gray dun small drafter [Little Bits Clydesdale mold] (1994-95)

#3180: Medicine Hat Mare And Foal set, both chestnut pinto [Thoroughbred Mare and Suckling Foal molds] (1994 - current as of 1995)

#3234: Classic "A Pony For Keeps" Gift Set, with alabaster "Blue" ["Ginger" mold], light dapple gray "Another" ["Might Tango" mold], chestnut "Jefferson" [Mustang Family Stallion mold], and white "Lady Jane Grey" ["Merrylegs" mold] (1990-91)

#3235: Classic "Rembrandt" SR #703235, as listed in the German edition 1989 Breyer manual

#3240: Classic "Hatatitla" SR #703240, as listed in the German edition 1989 Breyer manual

#3245: Classic Brown Pinto Mare SR #703245, as listed in the German edition 1989 Breyer manual

#3335: Classic "Orchidee" SR #703335, as listed in the German edition 1989 Breyer manual

#3345: Classic "King Of The Wind" Gift Set, with golden bay "Lath" ["Black Beauty" mold], blood bay "Sham" [Black Stallion mold], and alabaster "Lady Roxana" ["Duchess" mold] (1990-93)

#3346: Classic Hanoverian Family set, with bay foal [Andalusian Family Foal mold], light sandy bay mare ["Ginger" mold], and black stallion ["Keen" mold] (1992-93)

#3347: Classic Trakehner Family set, with bay foal [Mustang Family Foal mold], pale dapple gray mare ["Duchess" mold], and dark chestnut stallion ["Jet Run" mold] (1992-94)

#3348: Classic Fine Horse Family set, with chestnut blanket appaloosa foal [Mustang Family Foal mold], red roan mare ["Kelso" mold], and liver chestnut stallion ["Silky Sullivan" mold] (1994 - current as of 1996)

#3349: Classic Appaloosa Mustang Family Gift Set, with chestnut blanket appy foal, black blanket appy mare, and rose dun blanket appy stallion (1995 - current as of 1996) [Mustang Family Foal, Mare, and Stallion molds]

#3351: Running Mare And Foal set, both Golden Charm decorator, solid metallic gold (1963-64)

#3440: Classic "Iltschi" SR #703440, as listed in the German edition 1989 Breyer manual

#3447: Cow Family set, horned Holstein cow and calf, black pinto (1974-91) [Cow and Calf molds]

#3448: Jersey Cow Family set, dark palomino polled cow and calf (1992-95) [Cow and Calf molds]

#3540: Classic "Black Beauty," regular model from set #3040 sold separately to overseas companies, as listed in the German edition 1989 Breyer manual

#4000: Classic Arabian Foal, alabaster (1973 - 1982/83) [Arabian Family Foal mold]

#4000: Classic Arabian Foal, black (1973 - 1982/83) [Arabian Family Foal mold]

#4000: Classic Arabian Foal, chestnut (1973 - 1982/83) [Arabian Family Foal mold]

#4000: Classic Arabian Foal, palomino (1973 - 1982/83) [Arabian Family Foal mold]

#4000: Classic Arabian Foal, smoke gray (1973 - 1982/83) [Arabian Family Foal mold]

#4001: Classic Quarter Horse Foal, bay (1974-82) [Quarter Horse Family Foal mold]

#4001: Classic Quarter Horse Foal, black (1974-82) [Quarter Horse Family Foal mold]

#4001: Classic Quarter Horse Foal, chestnut (1974-82) [Quarter Horse Family Foal mold]

#4001: Classic Quarter Horse Foal, palomino (1974-82) [Quarter Horse Family Foal mold]

#4031: Fighting Stallion, Wedgewood Blue decorator, solid blue (1963-64)

#4051: "Commander" The Five-Gaiter, Wedgewood Blue decorator, solid blue (1963-64) [Five-Gaiter mold]

#4085: "Diablo" The Mustang, Wedgewood Blue decorator, solid blue (1963-64) [Mustang mold]

#4120: Running Mare, Wedgewood Blue decorator, solid blue (1963-64)

#4130: Running Foal, Wedgewood Blue decorator, solid blue (1963-64)

#4351: Running Mare And Foal set, both Wedgewood Blue decorator, solid blue (1963-64)

#4810: Classic The Dawning Gift Set, "Mesteño" And His Mother, with light red dun foal and pale buckskin mare (1993 - current as of 1996)

#4811: Classic The Challenger Gift Set, "Mesteño" And "Sombra," with reddish dun "Mesteño" and grulla "Sombra" (1994 - current as of 1996)

#4812: Classic The Progeny Gift Set, "Mesteño" And "Rojo," with reddish dun "Mesteño" and light red dun "Rojo" yearling (1995 - current as of 1996)

#4930: Dealer assortment (1982)

#4940: Dealer assortment (1982)

#4950: Dealer assortment (1982)

#5000: Showcase Collection number for model #50, "Adios" (1970-72)

#5001: Stablemates Saddlebred, dapple gray (1975-76)

#5002: Stablemates Saddlebred, bay (1975-88)

#5010: Stablemates Arabian Stallion, dapple gray (early 1975) [Morgan Stallion mold]

#5010: Stablemates Arabian Stallion, dapple gray (late 1975 - 1976)

#5011: Stablemates Arabian Mare, dapple gray (1975-76)

#5013: Stablemates Arabian Stallion, bay (early 1975 as "Citation" #5020; late 1975 - 1988 as Arabian Stallion #5013) [Arabian Stallion mold]

#5013: Stablemates Arabian Stallion, bay (early 1975 as Arabian Stallion #5013; late 1975 - 1988 as Morgan Stallion #5035) [Morgan Stallion mold]

#5014: Stablemates Arabian Mare, bay (1975-88)

#5016: Stablemates Arabian Stallion, alabaster (early 1975) [Morgan Stallion mold]

#5016: Stablemates Arabian Stallion, alabaster (late 1975 - 1988) [Arabian Stallion mold]

#5017: Stablemates Arabian Mare, alabaster (1975-87)

#5019: Stablemates Standing Thoroughbred, chestnut / reddish dun (pre-catalog release mid-1990, catalog run 1991-94) ["Citation" mold]

#5020: Stablemates "Citation," bay (early 1975 as "Citation," late 1975 - 1988 as Arabian Stallion #5013) [Arabian Stallion mold]

#5020: Stablemates "Citation," bay (late 1975 - 1990) ["Citation" mold]

#5021: Stablemates "Swaps," chestnut (mid-1975 - 1994)

#5022: Stablemates "Silky Sullivan," dark/medium chestnut (mid-1975 - 1994)

#5023: Stablemates "Native Dancer," steel gray (mid-1975 - 1994)

#5024: Stablemates "Seabiscuit," bay (mid-1975 - 1990)

#5025: Stablemates Running Thoroughbred, black (pre-catalog release mid-1990, catalog run 1991-94) ["Seabiscuit" mold]

#5026: Stablemates Thoroughbred Mare, golden chestnut (1975-87)

#5028: Stablemates Thoroughbred Mare, black (1975-88)

#5030: Stablemates Thoroughbred Mare, medium bay (1975-88)

#5035: Stablemates Morgan Stallion, bay (early 1975 as Arabian Stallion #5013; late 1975 - 1988 as Morgan Stallion #5035) [Morgan Stallion mold]

#5036: Stablemates Morgan Stallion black (late 1975 - 1988)

#5037: Stablemates Morgan Stallion, medium/light chestnut (late 1975 - 1976)

#5038: Stablemates Morgan Mare, bay (late 1975 - 1988)

#5039: Stablemates Morgan Mare, black (late 1975 - 1988)

#5040: Stablemates Morgan Mare, chestnut (late 1975 - 1976)

#5045: Stablemates Quarter Horse Stallion, palomino (late 1975 - 1988)

#5046: Stablemates Quarter Horse Stallion, golden chestnut (late 1975 - 1976)

#5047: Presentation Collection edition of "Man O' War" #47 (late 1971 - 1973)

#5047: Stablemates Quarter Horse Stallion, buckskin (late 1975 - 1987)

#5048: Stablemates Quarter Horse Mare, palomino (late 1975 - 1987)

#5049: Stablemates Quarter Horse Mare, golden chestnut (late 1975 - 1976)

#5050: Presentation Collection edition of "Adios" #50 (late 1971 - 1973)

#5050: Stablemates Quarter Horse Mare, buckskin (late 1975 - 1988)

#5051: Presentation Collection edition of "Yellow Mount" #51 (late 1971 - 1973) ["Adios" mold]

#5055: Stablemates Draft Horse, sorrel (late 1975 - 1988)

#5073: Presentation Collection edition of Spanish Fighting Bull #73 (1972-73)

#5075: Presentation Collection edition of Texas Longhorn #76 (1972-73)

#5076: Presentation Collection edition of Buffalo #76, called American Bison (1972-73)

#5079: Presentation Collection edition of Moose #79 (1972-73)

#5100: Showcase Collection number for model #51, "Yellow Mount" (1970-72)

#5102: Presentation Collection edition of palomino Quarter Horse Yearling #102 (late 1971 - 1973)

#5110: Stablemates Saddlebred, black (1989-90)

#5120: Stablemates Arabian Stallion, steel gray (1989-94)

#5130: Stablemates Arabian Mare, alabaster (1989-94)

#5140: Stablemates Thoroughbred Mare, dark/medium bay (1989-90)

#5141: Stablemates Thoroughbred Mare, medium chestnut (1991-94)

#5150: Stablemates Morgan Stallion, medium chestnut / red dun (1989-94)

#5160: Stablemates Morgan Mare, palomino (1989-94)

#5175: Presentation Collection edition of Indian Pony #175 (1972-73)

#5175: Stablemates Standing Thoroughbred, alabaster (1995 - current as of 1996) ["Citation" mold]

#5176: Stablemates Thoroughbred Racehorse, red chestnut (1995 - current as of 1996) ["Swaps" mold]

#5177: Stablemates Thoroughbred Racehorse, black (1995 - current as of 1996) ["Silky Sullivan" mold]

#5178: Stablemates Appaloosa, red bay blanket appy (1995 - current as of 1996) ["Native Dancer" mold]

#5179: Stablemates Running Paint, chestnut pinto (1995 - current as of 1996) ["Seabiscuit" mold]

#5180: Stablemates Draft Horse, dapple gray (1989-94)

#5181: Stablemates Arabian Stallion, medium chestnut (1995 - current as of 1996)

#5182: Stablemates Arabian Mare, palomino (1995 - current as of 1996)

#5183: Stablemates Thoroughbred Mare, steel gray, 4 stockings (1995 - current as of 1996)

#5184: Stablemates Morgan Stallion, light bay (1995 - current as of 1996)

#5185: Stablemates Morgan Mare, red chestnut (1995 - current as of 1996)

#5186: Stablemates Quarter Horse Stallion, light bay (1995 - current as of 1996)

#5187: Stablemates Draft Horse, rose dun (1995 - current as of 1996)

#5212: Presentation Collection edition of Proud Arabian Stallion "Witez II" #212 (late 1971 - 1973)

#5500: Stablemates Stallion And Mare Counter Display Assortment (1975-88)

#5501: Stablemates Stallion And Mare Assortment (1975-80)

#5600: Stablemates Counter Display Assortment (1989-94)

#5650: Stablemates Saddle Club Collection, with dapple gray Arabian Mare, alabaster Draft Horse, medium reddish bay Morgan Stallion, red chestnut Running Thoroughbred ["Seabiscuit" mold], and black Thoroughbred Mare with no white (1994-95)

#5670: Stablemates "Miniature Family" set with regular-run bay "Citation" #5020 [Arabian Stallion mold], medium bay Thoroughbred Mare #5030, and sandy bay Thoroughbred Standing Foal #5700 (1975)

#5700: Stablemates Thoroughbred Lying and Standing Foals, sandy bay (1975-76)

#5701: Stablemates Thoroughbred Lying and Standing Foals, black (1975-76)

#5702: Stablemates Thoroughbred Lying and Standing Foals, chestnut (1975-76)

#5703: Stablemates Arabian Horse Foals, dapple gray and bay (advertised 1975 but never released)

#5704: Stablemates Arabian Horse Foals, alabaster and black (advertised 1975 but never released)

#5705: Stablemates Morgan Horse Foals, bay and black (advertised 1975 but never released)

#5706: Stablemates Morgan Horse Foals, chestnut and palomino (advertised 1975 but never released)

#5800: Stablemates Foal Assortment (1975-76)

#5801: Stablemates Foal Assortment (1975-76)

#5900: Stablemates Assortment for dealers (1995 - current as of 1996)

#5930: Dealer assortment (1983)

#5940: Dealer assortment (1983)

#5950: Dealer assortment (1983)

#6071: Dealer Starter Assortment of Showcase Collection models (1971-72)

#6750: Classic Race Horse Assortment, with regular-run "Kelso," "Man-O-War," "Ruffian," "Silky Sullivan," "Swaps," and "Terrang" (1977-90)

#6930: Dealer assortment (1984)

#6940: Dealer assortment (1984)

#6950: Dealer assortment (1984)

#6984: U.S.E.T. Traditional Assortment for dealers, in "special packaging," with regular-run "Halla," Hanoverian, 2 Jumping Horses, "Morganglanz," and Trakehner (1984)

#7701: "Benji," dark yellowy buckskin dog (late 1977 - 1979)

#8034: Clydesdale Family Set SR, with Clydesdale Foal, Mare, Stallion, all true bay (1982, 1983, and 1984)

#8384: Clydesdale Gift Set, with Clydesdale Mare and Foal, both chestnut, and green blankets (1971-90)

#9000: Little Bits dealer assortment of catalog-run models (1983-88)

#9001: Little Bits Arabian Stallion, chestnut (late 1983 - 1988)

#9001: Little Bits Arabian Stallion, medium bay (late 1983 - 1988)

#9001: Little Bits Arabian Stallion, smoke (solid gray) (late 1983 - 1988)

#9005: Little Bits Morgan Stallion, dark/medium bay (late 1983 - 1988)

#9005: Little Bits Morgan Stallion, black (late 1983 - 1988)

#9005: Little Bits Morgan Stallion, dark/medium chestnut (late 1983 - 1988)
#9010: Little Bits Thoroughbred Stallion, black (late 1983 - 1988)
#9010: Little Bits Thoroughbred Stallion, chestnut (late 1983 - 1988)
#9010: Little Bits Thoroughbred Stallion, dark/medium bay (late 1983 - 1988)
#9015: Little Bits Quarter Horse Stallion, bay (late 1983 - 1988)
#9015: Little Bits Quarter Horse Stallion, buckskin (late 1983 - 1988)
#9015: Little Bits Quarter Horse Stallion, palomino (late 1983 - 1988)
#9020: Little Bits Unicorn, alabaster (1984-94)
#9025: Little Bits Clydesdale, bay (1984-88)
#9030: Little Bits American Saddlebred, medium bay (1985-88)
#9030: Little Bits American Saddlebred, palomino (1985-88)
#9030: Little Bits American Saddlebred, red chestnut, star (1985-88)
#9035: Little Bits Bay Pinto, bay paint (1985-88) [Quarter Horse Stallion mold]
#9040: Little Bits Appaloosa, black blanket appaloosa (1985-88) [Quarter Horse Stallion mold]
#9045: Little Bits Arabian Stallion, alabaster (1989-94)
#9050: Little Bits Morgan Stallion, golden sorrel/palomino (1989-94)
#9055: Little Bits Thoroughbred Stallion, steel gray (1989-94)
#9060: Little Bits Quarter Horse Stallion, blue roan (1989-94)
#9065: Little Bits Shire, black (1989-94) [Clydesdale mold]
#9070: Little Bits American Saddlebred, black pinto (1989-94)
#9075: Little Bits Paint, black paint (1989-94) [Quarter Horse Stallion mold]
#9080: Little Bits Appaloosa, chestnut blanket appaloosa (1989-94) [Quarter Horse Stallion mold]
#9100: Little Bits dealer assortment of catalog-run models (1989-94)
#9547: Grooming-kit set with glossy alabaster PAM #8, blue vinyl pack saddle, and accessories (1958)
#9548: Grooming-kit set with glossy alabaster PAF #9, blue vinyl pack saddle, and accessories (1958)
#9549: Grooming-kit set with glossy palomino Western Pony #43, large houndstooth-checked vinyl pack saddle, and accessories (1958-59)
#9593: Landrover And Horse Transporter, metal truck and horse trailer with rubber horse, all by the English company Britains Ltd.; not a Breyer product but offered through the Breyer catalogs and price lists with a Breyer model number (1986 - 1986/87)
#9900: Breyer Riding Stable, with plastic stable and several rubber horses and riders, all by the English company Britains Ltd.; not a Breyer product but offered through Breyer catalogs and price lists with a Breyer model number (1986 - 1988/89)
#9950: Little Bitsy Breyer Stable Set, vinyl-covered cardboard stable, with doll, Little Bits Morgan Stallion, and tack (1986-87)
#9960: "Kipper," bay (1986); limited release
#9961: "Midget," black pinto (1986); advertised but never released ["Kipper" mold variation]
#9962: "Pumpkin," palomino (1986); advertised but never released ["Kipper" mold variation]
#19040: "Lady Phase" SR, red roan, as listed on export price lists; same SR as #410040 (1989)
#19841: Classic Drive On A Sunny Day set, flocked chestnut "Johar," buggy, doll (1984-87)
#19841: Open Top Buggy set, flocked chestnut Proud Arabian Stallion, doll, and buggy (1984)
#19842: Classic The Doctor's Buggy set, flocked bay Black Stallion, buggy, doctor doll (1984-87)
#19843: Classic Family To Church On Sunday set, flocked bay "Duchess" and "Jet Run," surrey, dolls (1984-87)
#19845: Classic Joey's Pony Cart set, flocked black pinto "Midge," cart, doll (1987) ["Merrylegs" mold]
#19846: Classic Delivery Wagon set, flocked chestnut "Keen," wagon, doll (1987)
#21025: Classic SR set with Mustang Family: chestnut pinto Foal, bay Mare, and buckskin Stallion (1985)
#21058: Classic SR set with Arabian Family: bay Foal, rose alabaster Mare, and bay Stallion (1984 and 1985)
#21061: Classic Appaloosa Family set, all chestnut blanket appaloosa (1986) [Quarter Horse Family Foal, Mare, and Stallion molds]
#70089: Videotape, The World of Breyer Horses (1989 - current as of 1996)
#70094: Videotape, Breyer® Plant Tour with W. J. Fleischmann, President, Reeves International, Inc. (1994 - current as of 1996)
#79192: Fine Porcelain Icelandic Horse, buckskin pinto (1992-94) [Icelandic Horse mold]
#79193: Fine Porcelain Shire Horse, dark dappled bay (1993-95) [Shire Horse mold]
#79194: Fine Porcelain Spanish Barb, pale tan dun (1994-95) [Spanish Barb mold]
#79195: Fine Porcelain Premier Arabian Mare, alabaster, in native costume (1995) [Premier Arabian Mare mold]
#79293: Little Bits scale Performing "Misty," ceramic; light chestnut pinto (1993)
#95100: Dapples "Dancer," pearl white mare, with brush (1995 - current as of 1996)
#95101: Dapples "Sunny's" Mom, light sorrel mare, with brush (1995 - current as of 1996)
#95102: Dapples "Amazement," dark chestnut pinto stallion, with brush (1995 - current as of 1996)
#95103: Dapples "Mom" And "Sunny" Set, with light sorrel mare, ocher pinto filly, brush (1995 - current as of 1996)
#95104: Dapples "Amazement's" Riding Set, with stallion, Darla doll, accessories, book (1995 - current as of 1996)
#95105: Dapples "Dancer" And "Celestria" Set, with pearl white mare and filly, accessories, book (1995 - current as of 1996)
#95106: Dapples Deluxe Set, with "Amazement," "Sunny," "Sunny's Mom," accessories, book (1995 - current as of 1996)
#95107: Dapples Deluxe Rider Set, with "Amazement," "Sunny," "Sunny's Mom," Darla doll, accessories, book (1995 - current as of 1996)
#95108: Dapples dealer assortment of single horses (1995 - current as of 1996)
#95109: Dapples dealer assortment of sets (1995 - current as of 1996)
#98453: Breyer Anniversary Truck (1995)
#198500: Display Unit, base mounted with horses for dealer display (1985)
#198555: Dealer Assortment with Display Unit (1985)
#198655: Dealer Assortment with Display Unit (1986)
#198700: Display Unit, base mounted with horses for dealer display (1987)
#198701: Display Unit, base mounted with horses for dealer display (1987)
#198755: Dealer Assortment with Display Unit (1987)
#198800: Display Unit, base mounted with horses for dealer display (1988)
#198801: Display Unit, base mounted with horses for dealer display (1988)

#400057: Western Horse SR, caramel pinto (1990)
#400101: Quarter Horse Yearling SR, blue roan (1989)
#400154: Trakehner SR, golden bay (1987)
#400189: "Black Beauty" SR, bay; planned for 1989 but not issued
#400195: "Pride And Vanity" SR, alabaster (1992/93) ["Sherman Morgan" mold]
#400195: "Buster" And "Brandi" set SR, both bay blanket appaloosa (1995) [Lying Down Foal and Scratching Foal molds]
#400196: "Sierra" SR #400196, red dun (1995/96) [Fighting Stallion mold]
#400212: Running Stallion SR, chestnut (1988)
#400293: Holiday-catalog set with regular-run "Misty" #20, Stormy" #19, and book (1993)
#400294: "Moon Shadows" SR, blue roan (1994) [Five-Gaiter mold]
#400393: "Steel Dust" SR, pale smoke gray (1993) [Proud Arabian Mare mold]
#400789: Family Arabian Foal, Mare, and Stallion set SR, all alabaster glossy (1988)
#401291: Jumping Horse SR, black (1991/92)
#401456: Three Piece Horse Set SR, with dappled rose gray Cantering Welsh Pony, chestnut pinto Haflinger, and black leopard appaloosa Pony Of The Americas (1990 and 1991)
#403535: Classic German Olympic Team SR sets of "Ahlerich" #703135, "Orchidee" #703335, and "Rembrandt" #703235, made for Siwek GMBH (1989)
#403640: Classic Karl May SR sets of "Hatatitla" #703240 and "Iltschi" #703440, made for Siwek GMBH (1989)
#403755: Classic Foal's First Day set SR, with rose alabaster "Johar," dark shaded chestnut Arabian Family Foal, and Sam Savitt pail (1988)
#406135: Classic Triple Crown Winners I set SR, with medium reddish bay "Citation" ["Kelso" mold], medium/light red chestnut "Whirlaway" ["Silky Sullivan" mold], and dark olive chestnut "Count Fleet" ["Terrang" mold] (1987)
#406254: Classic Triple Crown Winners II set SR, with reddish chestnut "Affirmed" ["Man-O-War" mold], medium/dark chestnut "Seattle Slew" ["Swaps" mold], and red chestnut "Secretariat" ["Terrang" mold] (1988)
#410020: "Misty" SR, Florentine decorator, dappled metallic gold (1990)
#410040: "Lady Phase" SR, red roan (1989)
#410067: "Wildfire" SR, red chestnut pinto (1988) ["San Domingo" mold]
#410087: "Ruby" SR, dark strawberry roan (1988) [Mustang mold]
#410090: "Dr. Peaches" SR, medium bay (1990) ["Phar Lap" mold]
#410099: Performance Horse SR, black leopard appaloosa (1989)
#410107: Cantering Welsh Pony SR, dapple gray, gold mane braids (1987)
#410116: "El Pastor" SR, bay with solid face (1987)
#410151: "Adios" SR, dapple gray (1987)
#410158: Hanoverian SR, black, solid (1987)
#410184: Clydesdale Foal SR, dapple gray with little dapples (1988)
#410187: Mustang SR, black leopard appaloosa (1988)
#410190: "Phar Lap" SR, liver chestnut, darker mane and tail (1988)
#410194: Classic set with dark bay "Denver" and "Blaze" (1994) ["Kelso" and Quarter Horse Family Foal molds]
#410199: Performance Horse SR, alabaster (1989)
#410212: Running Stallion SR, bay (1989)
#410251: "Adios" SR, palomino (1987)
#410258: Hanoverian SR, red bay (1987)
#410284: Clydesdale Foal SR, steel gray (1988)
#410287: Mustang SR, alabaster (1988)
#410290: "Phar Lap" SR, sorrel, flaxen mane and tail (1988)
#410293: Proud Arabian Mare SR, "silver filigree" decorator, dappled metallic silver (1993)
#410299: Performance Horse SR, red roan (1989)
#410347: Calf SR, unpainted white (1987)
#410358: Hanoverian SR, alabaster (1987)
#410384: Clydesdale Foal SR, black (1988)
#410387: Mustang SR, bay blanket appaloosa (1988)
#410390: "Phar Lap" SR, dark dapple gray (1988)
#410392: SR set with black "Night Deck" ["Lady Phase" mold] and bay snowflake leopard appaloosa "Night Vision" [standing Stock Horse Foal mold] (1992)
#410393: "Grayingham Lucky Lad" SR, black (1993)
#410395: "El Campeador" SR, dark dapple gray (1995) ["Legionario" mold]
#410399: Performance Horse SR, liver chestnut (1989)
#410435: "Secretariat" SR, Golden Charm decorator, solid metallic gold (1990)
#410458: Hanoverian SR, chestnut, bright orange-red (1987)
#410487: Mustang SR, fleabitten gray (1988)
#410490: "Phar Lap" SR, red bay (1988)
#410492: Quarter Horse Yearling SR, buckskin (1992)
#410493: Classic "Nevada Star" SR, smoke gray (1993) ["Hobo" mold with stand]
#410587: Mustang SR, palomino (1988)
#410592: "Turbo" The Wonder Horse SR, golden palomino (1992) [Mustang mold]
#410593: Classic Rearing Stallion SR, buckskin (1993)
#410601: Classic "Citation" SR ["Kelso" mold from set #406135], as sold individually (1988)
#410605: Classic "Count Fleet" SR ["Terrang" mold from set #406135], as sold individually (1988)
#410687: Mustang SR, red dun (1988)
#410693: Dairy Cow Assortment SR, with polled Ayrshire, Brown Swiss, Guernsey, Holstein, and Jersey Cows (1993)
#410894: Balking Mule Assortment SR, with alabaster, apricot dun, black blanket appaloosa, black leopard appaloosa, buckskin, and chestnut Balking Mules (1994)
#410994: "Sham" SR, liver chestnut (1994)
#411107: Cantering Welsh Pony SR, fleabitten gray (1988)
#411175: Indian Pony SR, black leopard appaloosa (1987)
#411110: Classic Bucking Bronco SR, red roan (1988)
#411194: "Winchester" SR, charcoal brown (1994) ["Buckshot" mold]
#411213: Proud Arabian Stallion SR, red bay, solid face (1987)
#411294: Indian Pony SR, red roan (1994)
#411341: Holstein Cow SR, polled (1985, 1988, 1989, 1992, 1993, and 1995)
#411394: Stablemate Thoroughbred Standing Foal SR, black, on keychain (1994)
#411494: Stablemate Thoroughbred Lying Foal SR, black, on keychain (1994)
#411594: Stablemate Thoroughbred Standing Foal SR, transparent amber, on keychain (1994)
#411694: Stablemate Thoroughbred Lying Foal SR, transparent amber, on keychain (1994)
#412091: "Mustang Lady" SR, shaded gray (1991) [Indian Pony mold]
#412107: Cantering Welsh Pony SR, red roan (1988)
#412175: Indian Pony SR, dapple gray (1987)
#412190: Classic Bucking Bronco SR, chestnut (1988)
#412213: Proud Arabian Stallion SR, black (1987)

#413091: Man O' War SR, Golden Charm decorator, solid metallic gold (1991)
#413107: Cantering Welsh Pony SR, dark chestnut (1988)
#413155: Classic Arabian Family set SR (#413155, #413255, and #413355), all dapple gray (1987 and 1988)
#413155: Classic Arabian Foal SR, dapple gray (1987 and 1988)
#413175: Indian Pony SR, red bay (1987)
#413190: Classic Bucking Bronco SR, black leopard appaloosa (1988)
#413213: Proud Arabian Stallion SR, light red chestnut, solid face (1987)
#413255: Classic Arabian Mare SR, dapple gray (1987 and 1988)
#413341: Brown Swiss Cow SR, polled, medium/light coffee brown (1988 and 1993) [Cow mold]
#413355: Classic Arabian Stallion SR, dapple gray (1987 and 1988)
#413448: Holstein Cow And Calf set SR, black pinto polled cow and calf (1988) [Cow and Calf molds]
#413455: Classic set of SR dapple gray Classic Arabian Foal #413155, Mare #413255, and Stallion #413355 (1988)
#413550: Classic SR set with rose alabaster "Johar" and dark shaded chestnut Arabian Family Foal (1988)
#414091: "Sham" SR, Wedgewood Blue decorator, solid blue (1991)
#414107: Cantering Welsh Pony SR, red dun with metallic blue-green braids (1988)
#414175: Indian Pony SR, blue roan semi-leopard appaloosa (1987)
#414190: Classic Bucking Bronco SR, steel gray (1988)
#414341: Ayrshire Cow SR, polled, red-brown pinto (1988 and 1993) [Cow mold]
#415091: "Legionario" SR, Florentine decorator, dappled metallic gold (1991)
#415341: Guernsey Cow SR, polled, dark palomino pinto (1988 and 1993) [Cow mold]
#416091: "San Domino" SR, Copenhagen decorator, dappled blue (1991)
#416341: Jersey Cow SR, polled, dark palomino (1988 and 1993) [Cow mold]
#417341: Holstein Cow SR, mixed horns (1988) [Cow mold]
#419025: Little Bits Charger, The Great Horse, SR, dapple gray (1989) [Clydesdale mold]
#490465: "Spotted Bear" Indian Pony SR, black medicine-hat pinto, cold-cast porcelain (1991) ["San Domingo" mold]
#491192: Quiet Foxhunters set SR, with liver chestnut "John Henry," seal brown "Roemer," and dapple gray "Rugged Lark" (1992)
#491212: SR set with Running Mare and Running Foal, both dapple gray with white points (1987)
#491292: SR "Secretariat," red chestnut, cold-cast porcelain (1992)
#492091: Arabian Horses Of The World Set SR, with alabaster Family Arabian Stallion with black points, fleabitten rose gray Proud Arabian Mare, and red bay Proud Arabian Stallion with blaze (1991 and 1992)
#492092: Spirit Of The West set SR, with "Lady Phase" and standing Stock Horse Foal, both bay paint (1992)
#493035: Classic Horse Set SR, with medium/light chestnut "Jet Run," steel gray "Keen," and reddish bay "Might Tango" with solid face (1987)
#493092: Classic SR set with medium reddish bay "Kelso" and book (1992)
#493535: Classic German Olympic Team SR sets of "Ahlerich" #703135, "Orchidee" #703335, and "Rembrandt" #703235, made for Sears in the U.S. (1989)
#494092: Future Champion Show Set SR, with bay pinto Saddlebred Weanling, Brenda doll, and halter (1992)
#494155: Mare And Foal Set SR, with red bay blanket appaloosa Grazing Mare and red leopard appaloosa Suckling Foal (1989 and 1990)
#495091: Stablemate Assortment III set SR, with chestnut Arabian Mare, black Arabian Stallion, steel gray "Citation," medium/light bay Draft Horse, yellow-olive dun Draft Horse, reddish bay Morgan Mare, palomino Morgan Stallion, palomino "Native Dancer," dapple gray "Seabiscuit," reddish bay "Silky Sullivan," dark liver chestnut "Swaps," and alabaster Thoroughbred Mare (1991)
#495092: Stablemate Assortment IV set SR, with steel gray Arabian Mare, dappled red chestnut Arabian Stallion, dapple gray "Citation," buckskin Draft Horse, chocolate sorrel Morgan Mare, black blanket appaloosa Morgan Stallion, seal brown Morgan Stallion, black "Native Dancer," red leopard appaloosa Quarter Horse Stallion, alabaster "Seabiscuit," rose gray "Silky Sullivan," and buckskin "Swaps" (1992). Same set as Twelve-Piece Stablemates Set #711094 (1994).
#495600: Stablemate Assortment I set, with alabaster Arabian Mare #5017/#5130, steel gray Arabian Stallion #5120, red roan "Citation" SR, dapple gray Draft Horse #5180, palomino Morgan Mare #5160, medium chestnut / red dun Morgan Stallion #5150, red bay "Native Dancer" SR, black Saddlebred #5110, red chestnut "Seabiscuit" SR, buckskin "Silky Sullivan" SR, blue roan "Swaps" SR, and dark/medium bay Thoroughbred Mare #5140 (1989)
#495601: Stablemate Assortment II set SR, with black Arabian Mare, buckskin Arabian Stallion, dusty chestnut / olive dun "Citation," black Draft Horse with no white, chestnut Morgan Mare, dark red chestnut Morgan Stallion, white "Native Dancer" with charcoal points, palomino "Seabiscuit," reddish dun/chestnut "Silky Sullivan," pale rose gray "Swaps," steel gray "Swaps," and red bay Thoroughbred Mare (1990)
#496092: Horses Great And Small set SR, with black Cantering Welsh Pony, grulla Clydesdale Stallion, and palomino Miniature Horse [Classic "Merrylegs" mold] (1992)
#497092: Drafters Set SR, with alabaster Belgian, liver chestnut "Roy," and palomino Shire with stripe (1992)
#497510: Race Horse Set SR, with glossy red chestnut "Man O' War," glossy red chestnut "Secretariat," and glossy blood bay "Sham" (1990)
#497679: Arabian Mare And Foal set SR, with Proud Arabian Mare and Foal, both red bay pinto (1988)
#498092: SR "Fashionably Late," chocolate sorrel, cold-cast porcelain (1992) ["Sherman Morgan" mold]
#498991: Spirit Of The Wind Set SR, with Family Arabian Mare and Foal, both dapple gray (1991)
#499610: Appaloosa-American "Classic" [Traditional scale] Set SR, with black blanket appaloosa Performance Horse, palomino blanket appaloosa Running Stallion, and blue roan semi-leopard appaloosa "Stud Spider" (1990)
#500493: "Pluto" SR, pale dapple gray (1993)
#500693: Dressage Set Of 2 Horses SR #500693, with dark bay Hanoverian and black "Misty's Twilight" (1993)
#700058: or #7000-700058 Vaulting Horse SR, black, blaze (1990-91) [Hanoverian mold]
#700097: "Silver" Quarter Horse SR, steel gray (1989) [Quarter Horse Gelding mold]
#700192: Classic Lipizzaner SR, alabaster, German export, also numbered #620 (1992)
#700193: "Prairie Flower" Equitana '93 SR, red bay blanket appaloosa (1993) ["Lady Phase" mold]
#700194: "Chinook" SR, dark dapple gray (1994) [Indian Pony mold]
#700293: Classic "Little Chaparral" SR, buckskin pinto (1993) [Rearing Stallion mold]
#700294: Classic Spanish-Norman Family set SR, with steel gray foal [Andalusian Family Foal mold], red roan stallion [Andalusian Family Stallion mold], and alabaster mare with white mane and tail ["Ginger" mold] (1994)
#700393: Classic Lipizzaner SR, alabaster (1993 - current as of 1996)
#700394: Unicorn SR, alabaster with silver-and-white-striped horn (1994) [Running Stallion mold variation]
#700435: "Burmese" Her Majesty The Queen's Horse SR, black (1990-91) ["Secretariat" mold]
#700493: Holiday-catalog set with "Misty" #20, "Stormy" #19, Paul Beebe doll (Ben Breyer #550), and book (1993)
#700593: The Watchful Mare And Foal set SR, with alabaster "Lady Phase" and pale smoke gray Stock Horse Foal, standing (1993)
#700594: Classic "Silver Comet" SR, dapple gray (1994) [Polo Pony mold]
#700595: Unicorn II SR, black, glossy (1995) [Running Stallion mold variation]
#700693: Classic Drinkers Of The Wind set SR, with dark rose gray Arabian Family Foal, smoke gray Arabian Family Stallion, and fleabitten rose gray "Johar" (1993)
#700694: "Ofir," Sire of "Witez II," SR, dark plum bay (1994) [Black Stallion mold]
#700695: "Geronimo" And "Cochise" set, chestnut blanket appaloosa mare and foal, with medallion (1995) [Classic "Kelso" and Traditional "Sea Star" molds]
#700794: "Bright Zip" SR, chestnut roan blanket appaloosa (1994) ["San Domingo" mold]
#700795: "Buckaroo" And "Skeeter" set, red dun mare, dark bay pinto foal, and medallion (1995) [Classic Arabian Family Mare and Traditional "Stormy" molds]
#700893: Appaloosa Sport Horse & Canongate Saddle Set SR, chestnut leopard appaloosa (1993) ["Morganglanz" mold]
#700894: Classic "Black Beauty" Gift Set SR, glossy black horse, Brenda doll, book (1994)
#700993: Bay Fighting Stallion SR (1993) [Fighting Stallion mold]
#700994: "Domino" Gift Set SR, black pinto horse, dressage saddle, and saddle pad (1994) ["Roemer" mold]
#700995: "Dustin" SR, red dun, with medallion (1995) ["Phar Lap" mold]
#701091: "Raven" SR, plum black (1991) [Saddlebred Weanling mold]
#701092: Classic Bucking Bronco SR, black paint (1992)
#701095: Classic "Mesteño" The Messenger (same as regular-run #480), as sold on QVC (1995)
#701195: Classic The Challenger Gift Set, "Mesteño" And "Sombra" (same as regular-run #4811 set), as sold on QVC (1995)
#701295: "Misty" Of Chincoteague (same as regular-run #20), as sold on QVC (1995)
#701395: "Brighty 1991" By Marguerite Henry (same as regular-run #376), as sold on QVC (1995)
#701495: Marguerite Henry's "Stormy" (same as regular-run #19), as sold on QVC (1995)
#701595: "Sham" The Godolphin Arabian Horse SR, blood bay, most with "'95" mold stamp (1995) ["Sham" mold]
#701695: Marguerite Henry's "Our First Pony" Gift Set (same as regular-run #3066 set), as sold on QVC (1995)
#701795: "Ponokah-Eemetah" The Blackfeet Indian Horse (same as regular-run #897), as sold on QVC (1995)
#701895: Western Horse SR, palomino, most with "'95" mold stamp (1995)
#701995: "Cheyenne" American Mustang (same as regular-run #929), as sold on QVC (1995)
#702092: Cow Family SR, polled Holstein Cow and Calf (1992 and 1995) [Cow and Calf molds]
#702295: State Line Tack '95 "Special Delivery" SR, dark plum bay, white "SLT" brand (1995) [Running Mare mold]
#702395: "Kaleidoscope" SR, light bay pinto (1995) [Trakehner mold]
#702495: "Rawhide" Wild Appaloosa Mustang SR, chestnut roan blanket appaloosa (1995) [Mustang mold]
#702595: "Favory" SR, red fleabit (1995) ["Pluto" mold]
#702795: Jumping "Gem Twist" SR, white (1995) [Jumping Horse mold]
#702995: Classic The Progeny Gift Set, "Mesteño" And "Rojo" (same as regular-run #4812 set), as sold on QVC (1995)
#703095: Princess Of Arabia (same as regular-run #905 set, light dapple gray), as sold on QVC (1995)
#703135: Classic "Ahlerich" SR, reddish bay (1989 and 1990) ["Keen" mold]
#703145: Classic Quarter Horse Family Stallion SR, black blanket appaloosa, large blanket (1989)
#703195: "Cody" (same as regular-run #922), as sold on QVC (1995)
#703235: Classic "Rembrandt" SR, reddish bay (1989 and 1990) ["Jet Run" mold]
#703240: Classic "Hatatitla" SR, medium bay (1989 and 1990) ["Ginger" mold]
#703245: Classic Brown Pinto Mare SR, dark chestnut paint (1989) [Quarter Horse Family Mare mold]
#703295: "Aristocrat" (same as regular-run #496), as sold on QVC (1995)
#703335: Classic "Orchidee" SR, reddish bay, star (1989 and 1990) ["Might Tango" mold]
#703395: "Native Diver" Champion Thoroughbred (same as regular-run #921), as sold on QVC (1995)
#703440: Classic "Iltschi" SR, black (1989 and 1990) ["Black Beauty" mold]
#703447: Cow 'N Calf set SR, polled Holstein cow and calf (1989) [Cow and Calf molds]
#703495: Classic Willow And "Shining Star" set SR, dark bay blanket appaloosa horse, doll, and tack (1995) [Rearing Stallion mold]
#703540: Classic "Black Beauty," regular model from set #3040 sold separately to overseas companies (1989)
#703595: Classic Passing Through Time set SR, with bay blanket appy "Riddle" Phase One, chestnut-point leopard appy "Riddle" Phase Two, and gray-point leopard appy "Riddle" Phase Three (1995) [all Classic "Hobo" mold with stand]
#703695: Classic The Dawning Gift Set, "Mesteño" And His Mother (same as regular-run set #4810), as sold on Q2 (1995)
#703795: Classic The Challenger Gift Set, "Mesteño" And "Sombra" (same as regular-run #4811 set), as sold on Q2 (1995)
#703895: Classic "Mesteño" The Messenger (same as regular-run #480), as sold on Q2 (1995)
#703995: "Pluto" The Lipizzaner (same as regular-run #475), as sold on Q2 (1995)
#704095: "Cheyenne" American Mustang (same as regular-run #929), as sold on Q2 (1995)
#704195: "Greystreak" Action Arabian (same as regular-run #899), as sold on Q2 (1995)
#704295: "Gem Twist" Champion Show Jumper (same as regular-run #495), with saddle and bridle (1995)
#704395: "Black Beauty 1991" (same as regular-run #847), as sold on Q2 (1995)
#704495: "Ponokah-Eemetah" The Blackfeet Indian Horse" (same as regular-run #897), as

sold on Q2 (1995)

#704595: "Cody" (same as regular-run #922) , as sold on Q2 (1995)

#704695: "Pieraz" ("Cash") SR, red fleabit (1995) ["Morganglanz" mold]

#705095: Classic Eagle And "Pow Wow" set SR, black pinto horse, doll, and tack (1995) ["Johar" mold]

#705195: "Mister Mister" Champion Paint (same as regular-run #916), as sold on QVC (1995)

#705295: "Oxidol" Rodeo Appaloosa (same as regular-run #917), as sold on QVC (1995)

#705395: "Jasper" The Market Hog (same as regular-run #355), as sold on QVC (1995)

#705495: Parade Of Horses Breeds set SR, with bay roan Cantering Welsh Pony, sandy bay Proud Arabian Mare, and alabaster Saddlebred Weanling (1995)

#705595: Fine Porcelain Premier Arabian Mare (same as regular-run #79195), as sold on QVC (1995)

#705695: The AQHA Ideal American Quarter Horse (same as regular-run #497), as sold on QVC (1995)

#707395: "Lady Phase" SR, palomino (1995)

#707495: "Mystique" SR, gray appaloosa (1995) [Jumping Horse mold]

#707595: "Mego" SR, palomino paint (1995) ["Adios" mold]

#707695: "Hickok" (same as regular-run #923), as sold on Q2 (1995)

#707795: The AQHA Ideal American Quarter Horse SR, dark red chestnut (1995) [Ideal Quarter Horse mold]

#707895: "Tobe" Rocky Mountain Horse (same as regular-run #914), as sold on Q2 (1995)

#707995: "Promenade" Andalusian (same as regular-run #918), as sold on Q2 (1995)

#708095: "Lone Star" (same as regular-run #928), as sold on Q2 (1995)

#708195: "Sundown" Proud Arabian Stallion (same as regular-run #933), as sold on Q2 (1995)

#710195: Serenity set SR, with buckskin Grazing Mare and buckskin Lying Down Foal (1995)

#710294: Spirit Of The East Gift Set SR, with Running Mare and Running Foal, both alabaster (1994)

#710295: Race Horses Of America set SR, with light bay Pacer, medium dapple gray "Phar Lap," dappled reddish chestnut Stock Horse Stallion, and neck ribbon (1995)

#710410: "Galaxias" SR, dapple gray, cold-cast porcelain (1991) ["Sham" mold]

#710493: Breyer Wild Horses Of America Set SR, with red sorrel Fighting Stallion, bay blanket appy Foundation Stallion, and black Mustang with 1 stocking (1993)

#710595: Dressage Horse ("Art Deco") SR, black pinto (1995) [Hanoverian mold]

#710693: Breyer Three Generations Appaloosa Set SR, with "Adios," "Phantom Wings," and Quarter Horse Yearling, all bay blanket appy (1993)

#710694: Classic Challenger set (regular run) with watercolor print, SR for Penney's holiday catalog (1994)

#710695: Set Of 12 Miniatures SR, with Arabian Mare SR, semi-leopard appaloosa; Arabian Stallion SR, light dusky chestnut; "Citation" (Standing Thoroughbred) SR, brown dun blanket appaloosa; "Citation" SR, dappled gray dun; Morgan Mare SR, chestnut with pale mane and tail; Morgan Stallion SR, black with striped mane and tail; "Native Dancer" SR, medium bay; Quarter Horse Stallion SR, medium chestnut; "Silky Sullivan" SR, dark grulla; "Silky Sullivan" SR, pale rose gray; "Swaps" SR, grulla; Thoroughbred Mare SR, dark brown

(1995)

#710995: Female Rider SR, Brenda Breyer doll in striped shirt and breeches (1995)

#711090: Little Bits Parade Of Breeds Collector Assortment III set SR, with SR seal brown American Saddlebred, alabaster Arabian Stallion #9045, SR dapple gray Clydesdale, SR medium bay Morgan Stallion, SR black leopard appaloosa Quarter Horse Stallion, and SR dappled rose gray Thoroughbred Stallion (1990)

#711094: Twelve-Piece Stablemates Set SR (1994). Same set as Stablemate Assortment IV set SR #495092 (1992).

#711294: Texas Cowboy Replica SR #711294, man doll (1994) [Stampede Riggins mold]

#711594: Dark Bay Western Horse SR, dark plum bay (1994) ["John Henry" mold]

#711694: Horse Salute Gift Set SR, with chestnut leopard appaloosa "Lady Phase," reddish bay "Morganglanz" with blaze, and dark mahogany bay "Phar Lap" (1994)

#712092: Frisky Foals set SR, with pale yellow dun Action Stock Horse Foal, red chestnut Proud Arabian Foal, black blanket appaloosa Running Foal, and dark palomino pinto Suckling Foal (1992)

#712459: Breyer Traditional Collector's Family Set SR, with Action Stock Horse Foal, Stock Horse Mare, and Stock Horse Stallion, all bay peppercorn appaloosa (1986)

#712491: "Kipper" And Drawing Book Set SR, with bay pony, brush or comb, and book (1986)

#712848: Breyer Traditional Western Horse Collector Set SR, with red dun appaloosa "Adios," liver-charcoal Foundation Stallion, and red bay "San Domino" (1987)

#713055: Breyer Classic Collector's Arabian Family Set SR, with stallion, mare, and foal, all black (1990)

#713092: Classic Mustang Family set SR, with lilac grulla foal, dark bay mare, and buckskin stallion with primitive stripes (1992)

#713259: English Horse Collector Set SR, with light coffee bay Black Stallion, red dun Indian Pony, and red chestnut "Justin Morgan" (1988)

#713267: Little Bits Parade of Breeds Collector Assortment I set SR, with dark chestnut pinto American Saddlebred, black Arabian Stallion, dark shaded bay Morgan Stallion, red leopard appaloosa Quarter Horse Stallion, smoke gray Quarter Horse Stallion, and dark bay Thoroughbred Stallion with baldish face (1988)

#714091: Adorable Horse Foal Set SR, with bay blanket appaloosa Grazing Foal, chestnut Lying Down Foal, dark rose gray Running Foal, and alabaster Scratching Foal (1991)

#715092: "Misty" Of Chincoteague SR, chestnut/palomino pinto cold-cast porcelain (1992)

#715963: International Equestrian Collector Set SR, with fleabitten gray "Halla," dark dapple gray Hanoverian, and reddish bay "Morganglanz" with solid face (1989)

#716091: Classic Quarter Horse Family set SR, with alabaster foal, liver chestnut mare, liver chestnut stallion (1991)

#717450: Breyer Traditional Horse Set SR, with dapple gray "Lady Phase," palomino Quarter Horse Gelding, and red chestnut "Rugged Lark" (1990)

#719051: Little Bits Parade Of Breeds Collector Assortment II set SR, with palomino pinto American Saddlebred, dapple gray Arabian Stallion, golden sorrel Clydesdale, rose chestnut Morgan Stallion (some sets came with regular-run #9050 golden sorrel/palomino Morgan Stallion instead), black Quarter Horse Stallion, and reddish bay Thoroughbred Stallion (1989)

References

Breyer Company Publications

The following sections cover the four main categories of Breyer company publications: dealer catalogs, collector's manuals, annual price lists, and the magazine *Just About Horses*. Original dealer catalogs and collector's manuals for the current year, and in some cases recent past years, are available from model mail-order companies such as those listed below. When writing to them for information, enclose a business-sized self-addressed stamped envelope; when calling long distance, be sure to consider time differences.

- Bentley Sales Company, 642 Sandy Lane, Des Plaines, IL 60016; phone (708) 439-2049.
- Black Horse Ranch, 1024 Nobles Court, Minden, NV 89423; phone (909) 275-9285.
- Bravo Horse Company, 3994 Morrison Creek Rd., Gainesboro, TN 38562; phone (615) 268-2746.
- Cascade Models, 5310 136th Place SW, Edmonds, WA 98026; phone (206) 743-4650.
- Hallie Ho Farm, 1845 NW Michelbook Lane, McMinnville, OR 97128-2419; phone (503) 472-8853.
- Hi-Way Hobby House, 806 Route 17 North, Ramsey, NJ 07446; phone (201) 327-0075.
- Mission Supply House, Box 950427, Lake Mary, FL 32795; phone (407) 328-7669.
- The Model Trading Post, 314 N. Redbud Trail, Buchanan, MI 49107; phone (616) 695-6142.
- Modell-Pferde Versand, Obere Breite 8, 7895 Klettgau 1, Germany; phone (01149)-7742-4865.
- The World of Model Horse Collecting, P.O. Box 2381, Salisbury, MD 21802-2381; phone (410) 543-8972.

Copies of older dealer catalogs, collector's manuals, and price lists are available from various hobbyists, such as those listed below. When writing to them for information, enclose a business-sized self-addressed stamped envelope; when calling long distance, be sure to consider time differences.

- Laura Diederich, 3578 Berg Rd., Dodgeville, WI 53533.
- Liz Strauss, 6100 Harbord Dr., Oakland, CA 94611-3128.
- The World of Model Horse Collecting, P.O. Box 2381, Salisbury, MD 21802-2381; phone (410) 543-8972.

Dealer Catalogs

Dealer catalogs, which show the Breyer inventory for a given year, are published for distribution to wholesale purchasers, such as toy stores and mail-order companies. These catalogs contain photos of the year's models, but most of them do not give prices, which are provided instead on separate price lists (see below). Catalogs from ca. 1954 (the earliest) through 1985 are about 8.5" wide x 11" high; those from 1986 on are a bit narrower and taller, about 8.25" wide x 11.5" high. Most of them are multi-page brochures bound with staples at the center fold. Dates were not printed on or in catalogs until 1970. Fortunately, most of the undated ones can be reliably dated by reference to the pre-1970 price lists, since these have dates printed on them. My dating of undated catalogs for which there is no corresponding dated price list calls upon a variety of evidence, as discussed below.

A complete list of the catalogs known to me is given below. In this list, an asterisk (*) indicates that the date is not printed on or in the catalog but has been determined by cross-checking against Breyer price lists and/or by other evidence.

Ca.1954*: 7 pages, including back cover. No front cover, to my knowledge. The original of this catalog in the archives of Reeves International in Wayne, New Jersey, consists of four full-color 8.5" x 11" sheets, three of them printed on both sides and one on a single side. The sheets are loose and punched for a three-hole binder, but I suspect that originally they were bound together, for some of the punched holes go through printed text and were thus clearly not part of the original design. Also in the Reeves archives are four original designer's mock-up pages for the ca. 1954 catalog. These mock-ups feature color drawings in place of the photographs that would be used in the printed catalog and have blocked-in lines with bits of handwritten copy indicating where printed text would go. Two of the mock-up pages have the misspelling "Beyer Animal Creations" handwritten in the blocked-in headings. The mock-up pages have a somewhat different layout from the catalog pages but picture all the same models: Boxer with snap-on vinyl collar, various Western Horses and Ponies, the Cowboy and Indian riders on their Western Ponies, and Derby Winner (Race Horse) without saddle.

Two of the designer's mock-up pages for this catalog have the date 1954 written on them at the bottom by hand, but it is a different hand from the designer's. Whose writing it is and on what grounds they dated these pages to 1954 I don't know. Several other bits of evidence too suggest a date of 1954 for this catalog but don't actually prove it; hence my caution in dating the catalog to *circa* 1954. The catalog is surely later than 1952, for the Western Horses in it have normal reins whereas the Western Horses in Breyer's March 1952 *Playthings* magazine ad and earlier ads have the old o-link reins. Also, a write-up about Breyer in the February 1952 *Playthings* mentions only Western Horses #59 and #57 (and the Money Manager bank), but the ca. 1954 catalog includes other Western Horse models and several other molds (omitting the Money Manager). The catalog is also surely earlier than 1956, for it lacks the "Fury" Prancer mold, an ad for which appears in the August/September 1956 *Horse Lover's Magazine*. So we are left with a possible date of 1953, 1954, or 1955 for the catalog. Any of these years is consistent with the September 1953 *Western Horseman* ad for Western Pony and the October/November 1954 *Horse Lover's Magazine* ad for Race Horse, both of which models are in the catalog. It is notable that the Race Horse ad, like the catalog, shows the model without the race saddle that he would have in all later Breyer publications that list him. A 1954 dating is further suggested by listings for the Breyer Molding Co. in *The Playthings Directory*, a toy-industry annual that lists each company's major toy products. The 1954 *Directory* lists "Plastic horses and dogs" for Breyer, which is consistent with the ca. 1954 catalog's inclusion of several horses and the Boxer. (Why this *Directory* doesn't list the riders that are also in the catalog I don't know.) Yet the 1953 *Directory* lists only "Money Manger banks" for Breyer. (Inexplicably, this *Directory* omits mention of the Western Horses that were announced in the February 1952 *Playthings* magazine.)

1958*: 12 pages, including covers. Front cover: photos of horned Hereford Bull #71 and palomino Western Horse #57 placed on a large, asymmetrical shield design which is hand-drawn. This catalog has black and white photos printed on a bright yellow background (per collectors Terry and Antina Richards, who have an original). Oddly, the photo of the palomino Western Horse, which shows him with black hooves and high-grommet Western saddle, is years outdated—it is the same photo as in the earliest advertisements for #57, in the September and December 1951 *Western Horseman* and February and March 1952 *Playthings* magazines. This is the only Breyer dealer catalog known to me that contains prices for the models.

Though this old catalog has no printed date, it can be fairly reliably dated to 1958. To start with, it must be earlier than 1959 because it includes neither the FAS mold nor the bay PAM and PAF, all of which were definitely in production in 1959 and possibly in late 1958. Since the catalog does contain the alabaster PAM and PAF, which were issued at the very earliest in late 1957, the catalog can't be earlier than that date. Further, the catalog corresponds almost completely to the dated 1958 price list with respect to the models listed and the prices given for them. The only discrepancy is that the catalog omits, while the price list includes, two of Breyer's most evanescent models: the pink #92 and blue #93 Elephants. Perhaps these pastel fantasy creatures were added to the 1958 inventory only after the production of the catalog was too far along for them to be included in it; or perhaps the catalog was issued a bit later than the price list, after the decision had been made to discontinue these models.

1960*: 12 pages, including covers. Front cover: small photos of glossy Brahma and woodgrain FAS on lower right. Catalog is printed in black and sepia tones. My copy of this catalog came with the date "1961" handwritten on the cover. Although there seem to be no 1959-61 price lists to help date the catalog, still there are good reasons for believing that it was in fact published in 1960, though it might have been issued some months into the year rather than at the start. To begin with, the catalog must be later than 1959 because it does not contain the PAM and PAF molds, which were in production in 1959 (see the notes for the PAM mold above in the Traditionals section). But the catalog must also be earlier than 1961—for it does not include the Fighting Stallion mold, which was in production in 1961, as shown by a June 1961 *Western Horseman* ad for Fighting Stallions in three colors; nor does it include the no-muscle #82 dapple gray Clydesdale Stallion, which was evidently produced in 1961 (see the notes for this mold above in the Traditionals section). The catalog might not have been issued at the start of 1960, however, because it shows the FAM and FAF molds, which must have taken some months to develop following the forced discontinuation of the PAM and PAF during or just after 1959, especially since the FAM mold went through the crisis of the in-between mare mold version. In fact all three of the FAM models in this catalog have mold anomalies about them, particularly the appy (for discussion see note 1 for the FAM mold above in the Traditionals section). The earliest independent evidence of the FAM and FAF molds that I have found so far dates to mid-1961: a photo dated June 1961 that shows the very young collector Jo Kulwicki with her alabaster FAF, and a photo of the hindquarters of an appy FAM in the September 1961 *Western Horseman* (p. 83). But dated evidence from 1960 may yet surface.

1963*: 16 pages, including covers. Front cover: color photo of a bunch of Breyers, among them 2 white Fighting Stallions serving as bookends for three books. Two of the titles are legible on the books' spines: *The Hidden Heart of Baja*, by Erle Stanley Gardner (published in 1962), and *Mr. President*, by William Hillman, photos by Alfred Wagg (published in 1952; this book's subtitle, not printed on the spine, is *From the Personal Diaries, Private Letters, Papers, and Revealing Interviews of Harry S. Truman*). Catalog is full color. Dating for this catalog is established by reference to the dated 1963 price list; the models listed in the two publications coincide exactly.

1964*: 3 loose pages, inserted into the 1963 catalog. For brevity, I refer to this pages-plus-catalog combination as the 1964 catalog. I believe that in 1964 Breyer did not print a whole new catalog with the 3 new pages bound in but simply inserted the pages loose into the 1963 catalog—at least, this is suggested by the fact that the archives at Reeves International contain no 1964 catalog as such but only a 1963 catalog and the originals of these 3 pages, which are 3-hole punched. One of the pages features the Belgian, one the Morgan, and one the realistic Deer Family (Buck, Doe, and Fawn). Each page has a large color photo of the mold against a line-drawn background scene: a barn for the Belgian, a fence for the Morgan, mountains and pines for the Deer Family. Comparison of the dated 1963 price list with the dated regular 1964 price list establishes that the molds shown on these 3 pages are all new for 1964 and that the colors listed for them are the only new models for 1964. Moreover, all the models on the 3 pages plus all the models in the 1963 catalog and price list add up to precisely the models on the regular 1964 price list. (The decorator models, which are not in these loose pages or on the regular 1964 price list, do appear on the supplemental 1964 price list.)

1965*: 4 loose pages, inserted into the 1963 catalog. For brevity, I refer to this pages-plus-catalog combination as the 1965 catalog. I believe that in 1965, as in the previous year, Breyer did not print a whole new catalog with the new pages bound in but simply inserted the pages loose into the 1963 catalog. One of the pages features the Jumping Horse and the Rearing Stallion, one the Belgian and Morgan, one the realistic Deer Family (Buck, Doe, and Fawn) and Buffalo, and one the Grazing Mare and Foal. Each page features

five of the ten molds on these pages were new in 1965, and the colors listed for them are the only new models for 1965 (the remaining 5 molds were the new ones for 1964). However, all the models on the 4 pages plus all the models in the 1963 catalog and price list do not add up to precisely the models on the 1965 price list, for the price list omits a number of models—several woodgrains and the Golden Buck and Doe—all of which are in the 1963 publications. This discrepancy suggests that in 1965 Breyer may have issued a "discontinued items" list as well as the 4 loose pages with the 1964-65 models, but I have not seen such a list.

1966*: 16 pages, including covers. Front cover: full-color photo of sorrel Five-Gaiter, placed on a white background covered with black text saying "animal creations," with "Breyer" in large turquoise letters at the top. The back cover has the same black text and a large blue-ribbon logo, but the background is green. Inside, some of the pages are full color, some black and white, and some 2-toned or 3-toned. Though this catalog has no date printed in it, the original at Reeves International has several dates handwritten on the cover: "1968," which is circled and crossed out; and "1965" (also circled) with the "5" crossed out and a "6" written above it to make "1966." A 1966 dating for the catalog is established by reference to the dated 1966 price list; the models listed in the two publications coincide exactly.

1967*: 2 loose pages, inserted into the 1966 catalog. For brevity, I refer to this pages-plus-catalog combination as the 1967 catalog. Following the pattern of 1964 and 1965, Breyer evidently did not print a whole new catalog in 1967 but simply inserted these new pages loose into the 1966 catalog—at least, this is suggested by the fact that the archives at Reeves International contain no 1967 catalog as such but only a 1966 catalog and the originals of these 2 pages, which are 3-hole punched. One of the pages features the Pacer and "Man O' War" molds; the other shows the Bear and Cub and also provides a list of model numbers of items discontinued for 1967. Comparison of the dated 1966 price list with the dated 1967 price list establishes that the molds shown on the 2 pages are all new for 1967. The 1967 price list includes only one new model that the 2 pages omit, namely, the bay Bucking Bronco, which was not a new mold but only a new color. Aside from this single discrepancy, all the models and discontinuations on the 2 pages plus all the models in the 1966 catalog add up to the models on the 1967 price list.

1968*: 20 pages, including covers. Front cover: identical to the 1966 cover, except that the color of the "Breyer" heading on the 1968 catalog is, I believe, medium/dark blue. The back cover too is like the 1966 back cover except that the background of the 1968 is white. Some of the inside pages are full color, some black and white, and some 2-toned or 3-toned. Though this catalog has no date printed in it, the original at Reeves International has several dates handwritten on the cover: "1968," which is heavily crossed out; "1966" with a "7" written heavily over the final "6" to make "1967," circled and crossed out; and finally "1968" again. The confusion revealed by this cluster of pentimenti is understandable, for the catalog looks very much like its predecessors both inside and out, and worse, it has several discrepancies with the dated 1968 Breyer price list. The catalog includes 3 models that the price list omits and omits 3 models that the price list includes. Somebody at Breyer must have had a bad brain year. However, none of these discrepancies involve new molds, and molds, in my opinion, are the key to dating this catalog. The catalog and the 1968 price list agree completely on molds, among which are 4 new ones for 1968 (Balking Mule, Elk, Polled Hereford, and Running Stallion), as is established by a comparison with the dated 1967 price list, which lacks these 4 molds. The dated 1969 price list includes these molds and adds 5 new ones ("Adios," Bighorn Ram, Clydesdale Mare and Foal, and Lying Down Foal) that are not in the 1968 price list or the catalog. To my mind, these facts establish a 1968 dating for the catalog. Interestingly, this catalog is identical in content to the 20-page version of the 1970 catalog; see that listing for discussion.

1970*: 20 pages, including covers. Front cover: identical to the 1966 cover except that the background is pale blue (as is the back cover) and the "Breyer" heading dark blue. Some of the inside pages are full color, some black and white, and some 2-toned or 3-toned. This catalog identical to the 24-page 1970 catalog (see below) except that the 20-page version omits the 4 "New for 1970" pages that are included in the 24-page version. Thus the 20-page version seems to have been designed to go with the separate "New for 1970" 4-page pamphlet (see next entry), which lists the new models for both 1969 and 1970. Why the company printed two versions of the 1970 catalog, one with the "New" pages and one without, I do not know. I should also mention that the 20-page 1970 catalog, aside from the color of the cover, is identical to the 1968 catalog—the models listed are the same, the photos and page layouts are the same. So how do we know which of these catalogs dates to 1968 and which to 1970? All we have to go on is the color of the covers. I assume that the catalog with the pale blue cover dates to 1970 because this cover is completely identical to that of the 24-page 1970 catalog. It makes sense that the company would keep their catalog cover the same during a given year and vary the covers from year to year to make them distinguishable from each other.

New for 1970: Separate 4-page pamphlet, 8.5" x 11". No covers as such; the front page says "New for 1970" and shows the QH Yearling and Indian Pony. The remaining pages list not only the rest of the new models for 1970 but also the models that were new in 1969 (as a comparison of the dated 1968 and 1969 price lists shows). The latter models, however, are not identified as 1969 releases—so anyone reading the pamphlet would assume that all the models in it were new for 1970. The page with Spanish Fighting Bull has Breyer's name and address printed at the bottom. In the photos, all but one of the models are printed in sepia tones on colored backgrounds; the remaining one is black and white on a colored background.

1970: 24 pages, including covers. Front cover: photo of sorrel Five-Gaiter; identical in design to 1966 cover except that the background is pale blue and the "Breyer" heading dark blue (same cover as on the 20-page 1970 catalog). This version of the 1970 catalog is identical to the 20-page version except that it has the 4 "New for 1970" pages bound in. These "New" pages are identical to the separate "New for 1970" pamphlet except that the page with Spanish Fighting Bull lacks the Breyer name and address.

1972: 8 pages, including covers. Front cover: photo of a bunch of Breyers, books, and tack, with Proud Arabian Stallion "Witez II" on Presentation Collection base in the center. Catalog is black and white, including the covers.

1973: 8 pages, including covers. Front cover: photo of a bunch of Breyers, among them the Thoroughbred Mare and Suckling Foal. Catalog is black and white, including the covers.

1974: 12 pages, including covers (inside of back cover is blank). Front cover: photo of the Classic Arabian Family. Catalog has color covers but black and white inside pages.

1975: 12 pages, including covers. Front cover: photo of the Classic Quarter Horse Family. Catalog is full color.

1976: 12 pages, including covers. Front cover: photo montage, with shots of Lynn Anderson, Marguerite Henry, and, in the center, the Polo Pony. Catalog is full color.

1977: 8 pages, including covers. Front cover: drawing of the Polo Pony and 2 children. Catalog is full color.

1978: 8 pages, including covers. Front cover: drawing of the "San Domingo" model and a girl. Catalog is full color.

1979: 8 pages, including covers. Front cover: drawing of the clay sculpture of the Haflinger model. Catalog is full color.

1980: 16 pages, including covers. Front cover: photo of #3095 Brenda Breyer Gift Set, with sorrel appaloosa Performance Horse, doll, and tack. Catalog is full color.

1981: 16 pages, including covers. Front cover: photo of the "Smoky" model. Catalog is full color.

1982: 16 pages, including covers. Front cover: photo of #3000 The Black Stallion and Alec Set. Catalog is full color.

1983: 16 pages, including covers. Front cover: photo montage, with a shot of the "Phantom Wings" model near the center. Catalog is full color.

1984: 20 pages, including covers. Front cover: photo of a herd of Little Bits, with Western Bitsy riding heel. Catalog is full color.

1985: 20 pages, including covers. Front cover: photo of the unfinished head of the clay sculpture of the "Adios" mold. Catalog is full color.

1986: 20 pages, including covers. Front cover: blurred photo of an English rider jumping a sorrel horse. Catalog is full color.

1987: 20 pages, including covers. Front cover: slightly blurry photo (or very realistic painting?) of a herd of white horses running through shallow water. The horses look like Camargues. Catalog is full color.

1988: 20 pages, including covers. Front cover: artistic photo montage, 5 overlapping identical silhouettes of a trotting horse set against a vertical rainbow background. Catalog is full color.

1989: 20 pages, including covers. Front cover: photo of the front half of a bay horse trotting on green turf. Catalog is full color.

1990: 20 pages, including covers. Front cover: photo of a white stallion running on snow. Catalog is full color.

1990 German: 20 pages, including covers. Except for the language, this catalog is identical to the 1990 English-language version.

1991: 20 pages, including covers. Front cover: photo of the plaster casting of the "Pluto" model, painted by collector and artist Karen Gerhardt (see the entry for "Pluto" #475 above in the Traditionals section). Catalog is full color.

1991 German: 20 pages, including covers. Except for the language, this catalog is identical to the 1991 English-language version.

1992: 28 pages, including covers. Front cover: photo of the fine porcelain Içelandic Horse. Catalog is full color.

1992 German: 28 pages, including covers. Except for the language, this catalog is identical to the 1992 English-language version.

1993: 32 pages, including covers. Front cover: photo of The Dawning set. Catalog is full color.

1993 German: 32 pages, including covers. Except for the language, this catalog is identical to the 1993 English-language version.

1994: 36 pages, including covers. Front cover: photo of The Challenger set. Catalog is full color.

1994 German: 36 pages, including covers. Except for the language, this catalog is identical to the 1994 English-language version.

Mid-1994: Fold-out brochure, 8.5" x 11" folded. Front cover: bright yellow, no photos; printed with "Reeves International 1994 Mid-Year Introduction." Brochure is full color. It includes Bosun Boats and Britains models as well as Breyer items not included in the regular 1994 Breyer catalog. This was the first Mid-Year Introduction brochure, according to *JAH* editor Stephanie Macejko (conversation of Aug. 1995).

1995: 44 pages, including covers. Front cover: photo of "Aristocrat" Champion Hackney, probably the original sculpture or a resin casting. Catalog is full color. Although this is the main dealer catalog for the year, it does not include the entire regular-run line—it omits all the non-horse animals, which are covered in a separate fold-out brochure (see next entry).

1995 Animals: Fold-out brochure, 8.25" x 11.5" folded. Front cover: photo of #381 American Bison; printed with the title "Animals." Brochure is full color. This brochure includes all the regular-run non-horse animal models in production for the year.

1995 Dapples: Fold-out brochure, 8.5" x 11.5" folded. Front cover: photo of "Amazement" and two other Dapples models; printed with the title "Dapples." Brochure is full color. This brochure introduces Breyer's latest line of models, designed for young children.

Mid-1995: Fold-out brochure, 8.25" x 11" folded. Front cover: bright orange, no photos; printed with "Reeves International 1995 Mid-Year Introduction." Brochure is full color. It includes Bosun Boats and Britains and Corgi models as well as Breyer items not included in the regular 1995 Breyer catalog.

Collector's Manuals

These small annual pamphlets, which show the Breyer inventory for the given year, are published by the company for consumers and are enclosed in the box with each model. In essence they are simply miniature versions of the dealer catalogs, and like them, do not give prices. In earlier years, manuals differed somewhat from catalogs by having different covers, showing different photos of the models inside, and omitting items designed for dealers (display assortments, etc.); but in recent years, manuals have been virtually identical to dealer catalogs except in physical construction (the manuals are typically fold-out pamphlets). Collectors call them "collector's manuals" (or simply "manuals") because this is what many of the older ones call themselves: "collector's manual" is printed on the front cover of all of them from 1969 through 1980 and again in 1984. All but the earliest two manuals have a date printed on them or in them somewhere. To the best of my knowledge the manual published in 1968 was the first one ever published. Breyer has published a new manual each year since then. Manuals are always smaller than dealer catalogs, but their sizes and shapes have varied over the years, as indicated below.

In the following list, an asterisk (*) indicates that the date is not printed on or in the manual but has been determined by cross-checking against Breyer price lists and catalogs.

1968*: Fold-out, 3.75" wide x 8" high when folded. Front cover: photo of sorrel Five-Gaiter (cover design differs from that of the 1966-70 dealer catalogs). Manual is printed in sepia, black, and white. This manual coincides exactly with the dated 1968 price list.

1969*: Fold-out, 3.75" wide x 8" high when folded. Front cover: photo of red roan Running Stallion. Manual is full color. This manual has only one discrepancy from the dated 1969 price list: the manual includes, #205 dapple Old Timer, which the price list omits.

1970: Fold-out, 3.75" wide x 9.25" high when folded. Front cover: photo of chestnut Clydesdale Mare and Foal. Manual is full color.

1971: Fold-out, 6.25" wide x 8.38" high when folded. Front cover: photo of a herd of Breyers in a meadow; photo framed by black and brown borders. Manual is full color.

1972: Fold-out, 6.25" wide x 8.38" high when folded. Front cover: same cover as the 1971

manual cover, except the photo is framed by blue and yellow-green borders. Manual is full color.
1973: 8 pages, including covers; 5.38" wide x 8.5" high. Front cover: photo of sandy bay Appaloosa Yearling. Manual is full color.
1974: 8 pages, including covers; 5.38" wide x 8.38" high. Front cover: same as 1974 catalog . Manual is full color.
1975: 8 pages, including covers; 5.38" wide x 8.38" high . Front cover: same as 1975 catalog. Manual is full color.
1976: Fold-out, 5.5" wide x 4.25" high when folded. Front cover: photo montage, same central shots as on 1976 catalog. Manual is full color.
1977: Fold-out, 5.75" wide x 4" high when folded. Front cover: same drawing as on the 1977 catalog, with bottom cropped off. Manual is full color.
1978: Fold-out, 5.75" wide x 4" high when folded. Front cover: same as 1978 catalog. Manual is full color.
1979: Fold-out, 5.75" wide x 4" high when folded. Front cover: same as 1979 catalog. Manual is full color.
1980: Fold-out, 2.88" wide x 4" high when folded. Front cover: same as 1980 catalog. Manual is full color.
1981: Fold-out, 2.88" wide x 4" high when folded. Front cover: same as 1981 catalog. Manual is full color.
1982: Fold-out, 2.88" wide x 4" high when folded. Front cover: same as 1982 catalog. Manual is full color.
1983: Fold-out, 2.88" wide x 4" high when folded. Front cover: photo montage made of a portion of the photos on the 1983 catalog cover. Manual is full color.
1984: Fold-out, 5.5" wide x 5.75" high when folded. Front cover: same as the 1984 catalog. Manual is full color.
1985: Fold-out, 5.5" wide x 5.5" high when folded. Front cover: same basic design as 1985 catalog cover, but with photo of Phar Lap. Manual is full color.
1986: Fold-out, 5.5" wide x 5.5" high when folded. Front cover: same as the 1986 catalog. Manual is full color.
1987: Fold-out, 5.5" wide x 5.75" high when folded. Front cover: same as the 1987 catalog. Manual is full color.
1988: Fold-out, 3.5" wide x 5.13" high when folded. Front cover: same as the 1988 catalog. Manual is full color.
1989: Fold-out, 3.5" wide x 5.13" high when folded. Front cover: same as the 1989 catalog. Manual is full color.
1989 German: Fold-out, 3.5" wide x 5.13" high when folded. Front cover: same as the 1989 English-language manual and catalog. Unlike the English version, the German manual shows export SR Classic models: the German Olympic Team set, Karl May set, paint QH Family Mare, and large-blanket black appy QH Family Stallion. Photos and descriptions of these SR models are printed in the spots where the "Special Free Offer Coupon" and photos of the Stablemates, Little Bits, and Britains Riding Stable Set are printed in the English manual. Other than these substitutions and the difference in language, this German manual is the same as the English manual.
1990: Fold-out, 3.5" wide x 5.13" high when folded. Front cover: same as the 1990 catalog. Manual is full color.
1991: Fold-out, 3.5" wide x 5.13" high when folded. Front cover: same as the 1991 catalog. Manual is full color.
1992: Fold-out, 3.5" wide x 5.13" high when folded. Front cover: same as the 1992 catalog. Manual is full color.
1993: Fold-out, 3.5" wide x 5.13" high when folded. Front cover: same as the 1993 catalog. Manual is full color.
1994: Fold-out, 3.5" wide x 5.13" high when folded. Front cover: same as the 1994 catalog. Manual is full color.
1995: Fold-out, 3.5" wide x 5" high when folded. Front cover: same as the 1995 main catalog. Manual is full color. Like the main catalog, the manual omits the non-horse animals.
1995 Animals: Fold-out, 3.5" wide x 4.88" high when folded. Front cover: same as the 1995 Animals dealer brochure (see above in the Dealer Catalogs section). Manual is full color and has the same content as the dealer brochure. I first became aware of the "Animals" manual at BreyerFest in July 1995—it was available for free at the Breyer-Reeves company booth at the Kentucky Horse Park. These small brochures came only in the boxes of non-horse animals; the main 1995 manuals came only in the boxes of horse models.

Price Lists

Price lists are made to accompany dealer catalogs, most of which do not themselves contain prices. Typically, price lists are visually unexciting, utilitarian documents consisting of one or a few 8.5" x 11" printed pages that list the same inventory (items available) as the dealer catalog for the given year, along with the prices and payment terms. Price lists for 1966-69 have small photos of the models printed on them, but other price lists have no photos or other illustrations.

The price lists described below are the ones in my collection, which consists mainly of photocopies and is undoubtedly incomplete. In some years, Breyer evidently issued only one price list—at least that's all I have found—but in several years it issued two or more, giving different prices for different payment terms or giving updated prices that took effect later in the given year.

All pre-1985 and some post-1985 price lists have "Breyer Animal Creations" in the heading and include only Breyer items. But several post-1985 lists, as noted below, are headed "Reeves International, Inc." and cover all the lines of children's and collectible items distributed by Reeves, the company that purchased Breyer Animal Creations in late 1984.

All but two of the following price lists (the two that are actually order forms) have dates printed on them, in the heading or in the text or both. But in some cases, the printed date occurs only in a statement about the timing of orders: "Prices are effective on all orders received as of . . ." These "orders received as of" dates do not necessarily correspond to the year of the listed inventory. In these cases and in the two cases with no date (all marked by an asterisk, *, in the list below), the inventory year has been determined by cross-checking the price list against dated Breyer catalogs and manuals.

January 1, 1958: 2 main pages and at least 4 additional typescript photo pages. The two main pages are a cover page with the title "Price List / Breyer Animal Creations" and a photo of the alabaster PAM and PAF, and an inventory page headed "Price List as of January 1, 1958." The original in the archives of Reeves International in Wayne, New Jersey, is a single sheet with the cover printed on one side and the inventory page on the other. A photocopy of this price list that I got from another collector some years ago came stapled to 4 additional pages with photos of and typed information on some (but not all) of the models listed on the inventory page. These typescript pages, though not professionally produced, do seem to be authentic Breyer company documents, for the information typed on them includes quantity prices and terms of purchase. That they date to the time of the 1958 price list is confirmed by the fact that one of them lists the pink and blue Elephants, which are also listed on the 1958 inventory page but not in other Breyer publications known to me. If indeed the typescript pages were issued with the price list, then there should be more than 4 of them, because the 4 include only a fraction of the models included on the price list inventory page. Another mystery about these typescript pages is why they were produced at all, since a professionally designed and printed photo catalog was issued in 1958 (see above in the listings for dealer catalogs). Possibly the typescript pages were made a few months before the dealer catalog; or possibly they were made after the supply of dealer catalogs had run out.
January 1, 1963: 1 page, no photos.
January 1, 1964: 1 page, no photos. This is the regular price list for the year. The original is heavy off-white stock printed in black.
April 1, 1964: "Supplemental Price List," 1 page, no photos. Lists only the decorator models. There are two versions of this sheet, which list exactly the same models but give different prices. On the copy in the archives of Reeves International, the version with the lower prices has the following line typed in under the heading: "These are your ~~discount~~ prices—less 2%—10 net 30." It also has the entry for the Wedgewood Blue Mustang circled in ink with the notation "Disc" (undoubtedly for "discontinued") handwritten beside it in the margin.
January 1, 1965: 1 page, no photos.
January 1966: 4 pages, tiny photos. Original is a 2-sided 11" x 17" sheet folded in half.
January 1967: 4 pages, tiny photos. Original is a 2-sided 11" x 17" off-white sheet folded in half and printed in sepia.
January 1968: "50%" printed at top of first page. 4 pages, tiny photos. Original is a 2-sided 11" x 17" yellow sheet folded in half. This price list has higher prices than the January 1968 "50 & 10%" price list but is otherwise identical to it.
January 1968: "50 and 10%" printed at top of first page. 4 pages, tiny photos. Original is a 2-sided 11" x 17" tan sheet folded in half. This price list has lower prices than the January 1968 "50%" price list but is otherwise identical to it.
January 1969: "50%" printed at top of first page. 4 pages, tiny photos. Original is a 2-sided 11" x 17" sheet folded in half. This price list has higher prices than the January 1969 "50 & 10%" price list but is otherwise identical to it.
January 1969: "50 and 10%" printed at top of first page. 4 pages, tiny photos. Original is a 2-sided 11" x 17" sheet folded in half. This price list has lower prices than the January 1969 "50%" price list but is otherwise identical to it.
January 1970: 4 pages, no photos.
1972*: 2 pages, no photos. This might more accurately be called an order form, for it has no printed prices, although on my copy all the prices are typed in. This list has no date printed on it anywhere. The inventory on this list coincides with the dated 1972 manual, except that the list itemizes the Presentation Collection models individually while the manual only mentions them as a group.
1973*: 2 pages, no photos. This is actually an order form, for it has no printed prices. It has no date printed on it anywhere. The inventory on this list coincides with the dated 1973 manual, except that the list itemizes the Presentation Collection models individually while the manual only mentions them as a group.
1974*: 2 pages, no photos, bears a printed "orders received as of" date of January 1, 1974. This price list is incomplete: it omits the new-for-1974 models. Its listings are identical to those on the 1973 price list but with the addition of "discontinued" labels for most of the models to be discontinued for 1974 (there are some discrepancies).
1975*: 4 pages (including back "cover" with Breyer name and address only), no photos, bears a printed "orders received as of" date of January 1, 1975. The inventory on this list coincides with the dated 1975 catalog except that the list includes, while the catalog omits, two rafts of Stablemates scheduled for release later in the year: "May 1st releases" and "September 1st releases," per the price list headings.
1977*: 2 pages, no photos, bears a printed "orders received as of" date of November 1, 1976. Either "1976" is a typo for "1977" or Breyer had its new-for-1977 inventory ready amazingly early. The inventory on this list coincides with the 1977 catalog and manual except for two freakish disparities: the list includes, while the catalog and manual omit, #81 Donkey and #91 Elephant. These two models had been discontinued after 1974 according to all other contemporary Breyer documents I know of, so presumably their inclusion on this price list was an error.
Late 1977*: 2 pages, no photos, bears a printed "orders received as of" date of December 1, 1977. This list is basically the same as the earlier 1977 list (e.g., both lists flag the new-for-1977 models as "new" and include #81 and #91), but it has higher prices than the earlier list, specifies two items as "discontinued," and has listings for two new items tacked on at the very end—#3080 "Stud Spider" Gift Set and #7701 "Benji." These two models do not appear in the 1977 catalog but in the 1978.
1978*: 2 pages, no photos, bears a printed "orders received as of" date of December 1, 1977. The inventory on this list coincides with the dated 1978 catalog.
Late 1978* 2 pages, no photos, bears a printed "orders received as of" date of December 1, 1978. This list has the same inventory as the earlier 1978 price list (and the 1978 catalog) but has the items in a different order, has higher prices on many items, and omits the "new" labels from the listings for the new-for-1978 models.
1979*: 2 pages, no photos, bears a printed "orders received as of" date of December 1, 1978. The inventory on this list coincides with the dated 1979 catalog.
Late 1979*: 2 pages, no photos, bears a printed "orders received as of" date of December 1, 1979. This list is the same as the earlier 1979 list except that it has higher prices and omits the "New" labels from the new-for-1979 items.
1980*: 2 pages, no photos, bears a printed "orders received as of" date of January 1, 1980. The inventory on this list coincides with the 1980 catalog except that the list includes, while the catalog omits, item #501A English & Western Riding Outfits Assortments (for Brenda).
Late 1980*: 2 pages, no photos, bears a printed "orders received as of" date of December 1, 1980. This list has the same inventory as the earlier 1980 price list but has higher prices and omits the "New" labels from the listings for the new-for-1980 models.
1981: 2 pages, no photos. One version of this list has a band of color printed over the "1981 Price List" heading; a second version lacks the band. Otherwise they are identical. Both have a printed "orders received as of" date of December 1, 1980, as well as the heading "1981 Price List."
1982: 2 pages, no photos, bears a printed "orders received as of" date of December 1, 1981, as well as the heading "1982 Price List."
1983: First version: 2 pages, no photos. This version of the price list omits an item that the second version includes (#7500 Corral) and has lower prices for all the Bitsy Breyer sets. On the second version, these lower prices are printed but blacked out and higher prices

are printed next to them. The two price lists are otherwise identical. Both have a printed "orders received as of" date of January 1, 1983, as well as the heading "1983 Price List."

1983: Second version: 2 pages, no photos. See preceding entry for discussion.

1984: 2 pages, no photos, bears a printed "orders received as of" date of January 1, 1984, as well as the heading "1984 Price List."

1985: Reeves International price list. 1 long page, no photos. Includes dolls (Suzanne Gibson Dolls, Aithra Loetz Dolls, Heidi Ott Dolls, and others) as well as the Breyer line. This price list may well have a month printed on it as well as the year, but on my photocopy this area is cut off.

1986: Reeves International price list. Over 31 pages, including cover sheet; no photos. Lists not only Breyer but also Britains, Corgi, and other lines of toys and other children's items distributed by Reeves.

February 1986   Reeves International price list. 1 long page, no photos. Includes Corgi toy vehicles as well as the Breyer line.

1987: Reeves International price list. Over 30 pages, including cover sheet; no photos. Lists not only Breyer but also Britains, Corgi, and other lines of toys and other children's items distributed by Reeves.

1988: Export Price List. 4 pages, including cover sheet; no photos.

March 1988: Reeves International price list. 1 long page, no photos. Includes Suzanne Gibson Dolls as well as the Breyer line.

1989: Reeves International price list. Over 23 pages, including cover sheet; no photos. Lists not only Breyer but also Britains, Corgi, and other lines of toys and other children's items distributed by Reeves.

1989*: Typescript price list with Breyer items only. 3 pages. This list is dated "12/15/88" but lists the 1989 inventory.

Late 1989* Typescript price list with Breyer items only. 3 pages. This list is dated "10/23/89" and lists the 1989 inventory.

1990: Reeves International price list. Over 19 pages, including cover sheet; no photos. Lists not only Breyer but also Britains, Corgi, and other lines of toys and other children's items distributed by Reeves.

1991: Reeves International price list. Over 23 pages, including cover sheet; no photos. Lists not only Breyer but also Britains, Corgi, and other lines of toys and other children's items distributed by Reeves.

1991*: Typescript price list with Breyer items only. 4 pages. This list is dated "December 6, 1990" but lists the 1991 inventory.

1992: 1 long page, no photos.

1992: Reeves International price list. 19 pages, including cover sheet; no photos. Lists not only Breyer but also Britains, Corgi, and other lines of toys and other children's items distributed by Reeves.

January 1993: 1 long page, no photos.

March 1993: 1 long page, no photos.

January 1994: 2 pages, no photos.

March 1994: 2 pages, no photos.

July-Dec. 1994: 1 long page, no photos; titled "1994 Mid Year Catalog Price List." This list includes items that are not in the regular 1994 catalog but are in the "Reeves International 1994 Mid-Year Introduction" photo brochure (see above under Dealer Catalogs).

January 1995: 2 long pages, no photos.

February 1995: 2 long pages, no photos.

February 1995: Dapples price list. 1 page, no photos. This list and the next are identical except for pricing errors on two items: one list prices #95108 and #95109 assortments at $5.00 and $12.11 respectively; the other list corrects these prices to $60.00 and $72.66.

February 1995: Dapples price list. 1 page, no photos. See preceding entry.

Just About Horses (JAH)

This is the little magazine for collectors that was published originally by the Breyer Molding Company and then, starting with the XI/#4 1984/85 issue, by Reeves International, the New Jersey company that purchased the Breyer Animal Creations division of Breyer Molding Company in late 1984 (see in the Appendix above under Breyer Company History). The first issue of JAH appeared in late 1975, and the magazine has been published without a break ever since. The first issue and all those that followed until 1979 were two-color fold-out pamphlets. The glossy, multi-page format familiar to subscribers today began in 1979. JAH not only contains much information of interest to collectors but also has offered a special-run model exclusively to subscribers nearly every year since 1984. A subscription order form for the magazine is printed on every Breyer collector's manual. The subscription order address is Just About Horses, 14 Industrial Rd., Pequannock, NJ 07440-1991. For a full list of issues and other details, see The "Just About Horses" Index, by Nancy Young.

Over the years Just About Horses has, as mentioned, provided much information on regular-run and special-run models, though generally in a piecemeal fashion. An effort to publish a complete, alphabetical list of special runs, titled "Specialty Run Models," was initiated in 1990 by Steve Ryan, who was JAH editor at that time. Two installments made it into print, carrying the list as far as the Family Arabian molds. At his 1991 BreyerFest West presentation, Steve mentioned that his JAH list derived from a list on a computer disk he had "inherited" when he hired on with the company a few years previously. The disk, he said, was not in good shape but was salvageable. However, the project evidently was aborted after Steve's presentation, for no further installments have appeared. In fact, even the partial list provided in the original two installments is incomplete, with respect to the molds it covers. Also it contains many errors regarding quantities. Oddly, the quantity errors look systematic: in many cases the figures are precisely 100 times bigger than the quantities given in other sources. I suspect that somebody misunderstood somebody else's notation in the handing down of the disk. Nonetheless, the two published installments contain much useful information as well. See "Specialty Run Models" in the listings below.

Hobby and Other Sources

NOTE: When writing for information on the hobby publications listed below, be sure to enclose a business-sized self-addressed stamped envelope (SASE). For a partial listing of Breyer model mail-order businesses, see Breyer Company Publications above in the References section.

Algarin, Lisa. 1994. "The Lippitt Morgan." The Model Horse Gazette, May/June 1994, p. 28.

American Model Horse Collector's Digest. Now titled Equine Miniaturist; see that title below.

American Model Horse Journal. Edited and published by Sara Hauber. Publication ceased after the Winter 1991/92 issue.

Beard, Paula. 1992. Articles in Traveler's Rest Ranch Newsletter: "Halla" (July 1, 1992), "The

Morgan Horse" (July 1, 1992), and "Adios" (Sept. 1, 1992).

———. 1993. Articles in Traveler's Rest Ranch Newsletter: "Wing Commander" (Mar. 1, 1993); "Domino" (May 1, 1992); "Indian Power Symbols" (Sept. 1, 1993); and "The Kiger Mustangs" (Nov. 1, 1993).

———. 1994. "Swaps: Khaled x Iron Reward." TRR Pony Express, July/Aug. 1994, p. 25.

Berkwitz, Joan. 1993. "It Goes Against the Grain." The Glass Menagerie, June 1993.

Breyer Collector's Video. 1991. Second edition, produced by Black Horse Video. Karen Grimm, Black Horse Ranch, 1024 Nobles Court, Minden, NV 89423.

Breyer® Plant Tour with W. J. Fleischmann, President, Reeves International, Inc. 1994. Videotape. Produced by Reeves International, Inc. Listed in Breyer dealer catalogs and price lists as item #70094. Reeves International, Inc., 14 Industrial Rd., Pequannock, NJ 07440.

Brooks, Tim, and Earle Marsh. 1992. Complete Directory to Prime Time Network TV Shows: 1946-Present. 5th edition. New York: Ballantine Books.

Buchanan, Gina. 1994. "Simply Stablemates" columns in The Model Trading Post: on the "Citation" mold (Jan./Feb. 1994, p. 7), and on the Thoroughbred Mare mold (July/Aug. 1994, p. 8).

———. 1995. "Simply Stablemates" columns in The Model Trading Post: on the Draft Horse mold (Mar./Apr. 1995, p. 7) and on the Quarter Horse Mare mold (May/June 1995, p. 9).

Carlton, Ardith. 1990. Letter to the editor. The Hobby Horse News, Apr./May 1990, p. 3.

Cary, Jan. 1994. "Stablemate Trivia Quiz Answers." minis!, Feb./Mar. 1994, pp. 15-16.

Chance, Denise. 1991. "The Love of Collecting" columns in American Model Horse Journal: on chalky models (Fall 1991, p. 17), and on old-mold Proud Arabs (Spring 1991, p. 14).

The Collector's Journal Aug. 1987 - July/Aug./Sept. 1988. Titled The Model Collector's Journal after 1987. Edited and published by Teena Housman. Publication ceased after the July/Aug./Sept. 1988 issue.

Coughlin, Jamie. 1994. "More on Warmbloods" and "Warmblood Highlight: The Hanovarian [sic]." Both in Model Horse Gazette, May/June 1994, pp. 5-6 and pp. 7-8.

Cunningham, Peter. 1991. "The Genetics of Thoroughbred Horses." Scientific American, May 1991, pp. 92-98.

DeFeyter, Paula. 1991a. "Breyer Night Lights." Model Trading Post, Nov./Dec. 1991, p. 6.

———. 1991b. "The Original Finish Showcase: Breyer Riders Part I." Model Trading Post, Sept./Oct. 1991, pp. 11-13.

———. 1991c. "The Original Finish Showcase: Breyer Riders Part II." Model Trading Post, Nov./Dec. 1991, pp. 9-10.

DeFeyter, Paula, and Lynn Luther. 1991. The Model Trading Post Insurance Guide. Self-published. Lynn and Paula now issue separate insurance guides. Paula DeFeyter, 16884 James St., Holland, MI 49424. Lynn Luther, 314 N. Red Bud Trail, Buchanan, MI 49107.

Diederich, Laura. 1988. The Model Horse Book. Section 1, "Traditional Size Breyer Horses" (regular runs). Section 2, "Special Runs and Test Colors." Section 3, "Artist, Classic, Little Bits and Stablemate Series, and Flocked Christmas Specials." Section 4, "Breyer Dogs, Cats, Cattle and Wildlife." Section 6, "Breyer Dogs, Cats, Cattle and Wildlife." Self-published; no longer issued.

Edwards, Elwyn Hartley. 1994. The Encyclopedia of the Horse. First American Edition. London and New York: Dorling Kindersley.

English, Tina. 1989. "Hartland History: The Western Champ." High Stepper's Review, Sept. 1989, p. 17.

Equine Miniaturist. Formerly titled American Model Horse Collector's Digest. Edited and published by Rebecca Hileman, P.O. Box 33, Guy, AR 72061-0033.

Erickson, Hal. 1989. Syndicated Television: The First Forty Years, 1947-1987. Jefferson, N.C.: McFarland.

Fitch, Gail. 1990. Horse Colors and Gaits for Model Horse Collectors, 3rd edition, 2 vols. Self-published. Gail Fitch, 1733 N. Cambridge Ave. #109, Milwaukee, WI 53202.

———. 1993. Hartland Horses and Riders, 4th edition, 2 vols. Self-published. Gail Fitch, 1733 N. Cambridge Ave. #109, Milwaukee, WI 53202.

———. 1995a. "As Time Goes By: Hartland Clocks, Champs Impress. Hartland Market, April 1995, pp. 38-39.

———. 1995b. Hartland Horses and Riders, Nov. 1995 printing, 2 vols. Self-published. Gail Fitch, 1733 N. Cambridge Ave. #109, Milwaukee, WI 53202.

———. 1996. "Why Hasn't Someone Bought Hartland Plastics?" Collecting Figures, May 1996, pp. 17-20.

The Flying Hooves Express. Edited and published by Alison Beniush, of The World of Model Horse Collecting. The FHE ceased publication after the May 1, 1994, issue.

Geographical Collectors' Directory. Compiled by The World of Model Horse Collecting. Self-published. Alison Beniush, P.O. Box 2381, Salisbury, MD 21802-2381.

Gerhardt, Karen. 1992. "Hobby News," report on the in-between mare in the estate of Marney Walerius. The Small Horse, Nov. 1992, p. 1.

Gianakos, Larry James. 1980. Television Drama Series Programming: A Comprehensive Chronicle, 1947-1959. Metuchen, N.J.: Scarecrow Press.

The Glass Menagerie. Edited and published by Susan Candelaria, 11821 North 28th Dr., Phoenix, AZ 85029.

Göllner, Jill Ann. 1989-90. "Breyer Fact and Fantasy." The Hobby Horse News, Dec. 1989 / Jan. 1990, pp. 34-35.

Gurdon, Andrea. 1994. "Have You Got a Breyer with a Blue Ribbon Sticker?" Just About Horses, Fall 1994, p. 20.

———. 1996. "Breyer Archaeology Part One: Music Boxes." The Model Trading Post, Mar./Apr. 1996, p. 8.

[Gutierrez], Jill Rademacher. 1985. Articles in The Model Horse Gazette: "Gold Bullion—The Treasures of Special Runs," July/Aug. 1985, p. 17; and "Gold Bullion—The Treasures Move to Arabia," Nov./Dec. 1985, p. 43.

———. 1986. Articles in The Model Horse Gazette: "Test Run Breeds Native to America," Jan./Feb. 1986, pp. 32-33; and "A Horse of a Different Color," Mar./Apr. 1986, pp. 54-55.

———. 1989. List of test runs, one-of-a-kinds, special runs, and color variations. Self-published. Jill Gutierrez, 19624 Salisbury, St. Clair Shores, MI 48080.

———. 1990. BreyerFest report. Model Horse Gazette, Nov./Dec. 1990, p. 13.

Hartland Market. Edited and published by Gail Fitch. Publication ceased after the May 1996 issue.

Haynet, the model-horse mailing list on the Internet. Model-horse@qiclab.scn.rain.com. To subscribe to the list, email the message "subscribe model-horse" (without the quotation marks) to Majordomo@qiclab.scn.rain.com.

Henry, Marguerite. 1947. Misty of Chincoteague, illustrated by Wesley Dennis. First Aladdin Books edition 1991. New York: Macmillan, Aladdin Books.

———. 1948. King of the Wind, illustrated by Wesley Dennis. Chicago: Rand McNally.

———. 1949. Sea Star: Orphan of Chincoteague, illustrated by Wesley Dennis. Chicago: Rand McNally.

———. 1951. Album of Horses, illustrated by Wesley Dennis. Chicago: Rand McNally.

———. 1953. *Brighty of the Grand Canyon*, illustrated by Wesley Dennis. First Aladdin Books edition 1991. New York: Macmillan, Aladdin Books.

———. 1954. *Justin Morgan Had a Horse*, illustrated by Wesley Dennis. First Aladdin Books edition 1991. New York: Macmillan, Aladdin Books.

———. 1957. *Black Gold*, edition of 1958, illustrated by Wesley Dennis. Chicago: Rand McNally.

———. 1963. *Stormy: Misty's Foal*, illustrated by Wesley Dennis. Chicago: Rand McNally.

———. 1966. *Mustang: Wild Spirit of the West*, illustrated by Robert Lougheed. Chicago: Rand McNally.

———. 1969. *Dear Readers and Riders*. Chicago: Rand McNally.

———. 1972. *San Domingo: The Medicine Hat Stallion*, illustrated by Robert Lougheed. Chicago: Rand McNally.

———. 1976. *The Pictorial Life Story of Misty*. Chicago: Rand McNally.

———. 1984. *Our First Pony*, illustrated by Rich Rudish. Chicago: Rand McNally.

High Stepper's Review. Edited and published by Tina English. Publication ceased after the Fall 1992 issue.

Hill, Marie. 1971. *Adios: The Big Daddy of Harness Racing*. New York: Arco Publishing.

The Hobby Horse News. Edited and published by Paula Hecker, 5492 Tallapoosa Rd., Tallahassee, FL 32303.

Hollansky, Jeanette. 1990. "Breyer Current and Discontinued Models." Self-published. Jeanette no longer issues this list to my knowledge.

House, Deanna. 1995. "Adios." *TRR Pony Express*, Mar./Apr. 1995, pp. 19, 30.

James, Will. 1926. *Smoky, the Cow Horse*, illustrated by Will James. New York: Charles Scribner's Sons.

Johnson, Margie. 1990. Letter to the editor. *The Hobby Horse News*, Feb./Mar. 1990, p. 3.

Just About Horses (JAH). Edited by Stephanie Macejko. Published by Breyer, a division of Reeves International. Just About Horses, 14 Industrial Rd., Pequannock, NJ 07440-1991. For discussion see References - Breyer Publications above.

Kathman, Lesli. 1993. "Step-by-Step Repainting, Part 6: Paint/Pinto Patterns." *minis!*, July/Aug. 1993, pp. 18-24.

King, Marcia. 1990. "The Secret Life of Model Horse Collectors." *Horse Illustrated*, Dec. 1990, pp. 54-65.

Lemmons, Lyn. 1990. "VintagePoint." *Just About Horses*, Nov./Dec. 1990, p. 33.

Mac Donald, Meg. 1993. "VintagePoint" articles in *Just About Horses*: on the "Stud Spider" mold (Summer I 1993, pp. 32-33), and on the Saddlebred Weanling mold (Summer II 1993, pp. 30-33).

Maestas, Kathleen. 1987a. "Just About Breyers." *Model Horse Gazette*, Jan./Feb. 1987, pp. 22-23.

———. 1987b. "Breyer Trivia." *Model Horse Gazette*, Mar./Apr. 1987, pp. 28-29.

———. 1987c. "Just About Breyers." *Model Horse Gazette*, May/June 1987, pp. 10-11.

McNeil, Alex. 1991. *Total Television: A Comprehensive Guide to Programming from 1948 to the Present*. 3rd edition. New York: Penguin Books.

Miller, Judith L. 1993. *Know Your Breyers*. Self-published. Judith Miller, 6970 Boulder Rd., Loomis, CA 95650.

minis!. Edited and published by Lesli Kathman. Publication ceased after the Apr./May 1995 issue.

The Model Collector's Journal. See *The Collector's Journal*, above.

The Model Dispatch. Edited and published by Tierney Read. Publication ceased after the Sept./Oct. 1995 issue.

The Model Horse Gazette. Edited and published by Dawn Marie Calo. This magazine was merged into *The Hobby Horse News* (see above) in the latter part of 1996.

Model Horse News. Last edited by Jack P. Rosier. Published by Mission House model mail-order company of Floral City, FL, now called Mission Supply House, Box 950427, Lake Mary, FL 32795. The newsletter was published in the mid-1960s and ceased publication after the Nov./Dec. 1966 issue.

Model Horse Review. Edited and published by Bill and Jean Derench. Published from the mid-1970s through the early 1980s.

The Model Horse Shower's Journal. Edited and published by Linda Walter. Published from the mid to late 1960s and throughout the 1970s; publication ceased after the Jan. 1980 issue.

The Model Horse Trader. Edited and published by Sheryl Leisure, 143 Mercer Way, Upland, CA 91786. Sheryl Leisure also organizes the annual West Coast Model Horse Collector's Jamboree; for information send SASE to: Jamboree, 1034 W. "I" St. #154, Ontario CA 91762.

Model Horse World News. Edited and published by Kathleen Maestas, 508 West Maple, Farmington, NM 87401.

The Model Rag. Edited and published by Kay Fowler, Heather Wells, and Laurie Jensen. Publication ceased after the Dec. 1990 / Jan. 1991 issue.

The Model Trading Post. Edited and published by Lynn Luther, 314 N. Redbud Trail, Buchanan, MI 49107.

Motor Vehicle Manufacturers Association of the United States, Inc. 1974. *Automobiles of America: Milestones, Pioneers, Roll Call, Highlights*. 4th edition, revised. Detroit: Wayne State University Press.

Muybridge, Eadweard. 1957. *Animals in Motion*, edited by Lewis S. Brown. New York: Dover Publications.

Nack, William, with Lester Munson. 1993. "The Breaking Point," article published in an issue of *Sports Illustrated* in the latter part of 1993.

Packet of photocopied Breyer SR pages from Sears, Penney's, Ward's, and other holiday catalogs dating back to the early 1980s, and other materials. Compiled by Alison Beniush. The World of Model Horse Collecting, c/o Alison Beniush, P.O. Box 2381, Salisbury, MD 21802-2381.

Palley, Reese. 1976. *The Porcelain Art of Edward Marshall Boehm*. New York: Harry N. Abrams, Inc. A second edition of this book was published in New York in 1988 by Harrison House.

Patroonews. Edited and published by Linda Sturhann, RR 1 Box B7, Mount Upton, NY 13809.

Phillips, Tracy. 1993. Items in the "Has Anyone Noticed" column. *The Model Trading Post*, May/June 1993, pp. 15-17.

Pinkham, Lindy. 1988. "Ask Lindy." *Model Horse Gazette*, Winter 1988, pp. 21-22.

Plocek, Becky Helm. 1988. "Information Sheet." In Laura Diederich's *Model Book* (see above), Section 1, p. 3.

Quequechan Model Horse Collector. Jan. 1983 - May 1986. Edited and published by Colleen M. Brown. Publication ceased after the May 1986 issue.

Quigley, Megan Thilman. 1995. Letter to the editor. *Model Dispatch*, July/Aug. 1995, p. 5.

Renaker, Maxine. 1977. "Maureen Love Calvert: Sculptor with a Real 'Love' of Nature." *Just About Horses*, Fall 1977.

———. 1979. "The Hagen-Renaker Story." *Just About Horses*, Spring 1979, pp. 4-6.

Robinson, Joyce A. 1993. "Getting to Know 'Big Lick Tennessee Walkers.'" *Model Horse Gazette*, Nov./Dec. 1993, pp. 14-15.

Roller, Gayle; Kathleen Rose; and Joan Berkwitz. 1989. *The Hagen-Renaker Handbook*. Self-published. Kathleen Rose, 7652 Mt. Vernon Dr., Lemon Grove, CA 91945.

Rudish, Rich.. 1984. "Hello, Old Friends." *Just About Horses*, XI/#1, 1984, pp. 3-4.

———. 1985. "Thoughts on Lady Roxana." *Just About Horses*, XIII/#2, 1985 [1986], p. 20.

Ryan, Steve (former editor of JAH). 1992. "Rowland Cheney: Song of the Earth." *Equine Images*, Summer 1992, pp. 62-65.

Ryan, Thea. 1993. "Collector's Corner." *Equine Miniaturist*, Mar./Apr. 1993, p. 26.

Schlumpf, Kay. 1994. "Breyer Rearing Stallion." *TRR Pony Express*, July/Aug. 1994, p. 10.

Schneider, Sande. 1992a. Items in the "Has Anyone Noticed" column in *The Model Trading Post*: on Breyer saddles and Indian models (May/June 1992, p. 14); on FAF mold stamps, decorator/sorrel Five-Gaiter, and Breyer sulkies (July/Aug. 1992, p. 13); on dating of MasterCrafters clocks, Western Horse bridles (Sept./Oct. 1992, p. 19); on German Shepherd and "Rin Tin Tin" (Nov./Dec. 1992, p. 11).

———. 1992b. *Reference Guide to Breyer Models*. Self-published. Sande Schneider, 1927 Quincy Ave., Racine, WI 53403.

———. 1993. Items in the "Has Anyone Noticed" column in *The Model Trading Post*: on Canadian Mounties and Mountie saddle blankets (Mar./Apr. 1993, pp. 15-17); more on Canadian Mounties (May/June 1993, p. 13).

———. 1994. Items in the "Has Anyone Noticed" column in *The Model Trading Post*: on the Poodle mold (Nov./Dec. 1995, p. 15).

———. 1995. Items in the "Has Anyone Noticed" column in *The Model Trading Post*: on Jersey Cow variations (Nov./Dec. 1995, p. 8).

Self, Margaret Cabell. 1946. *The Horseman's Encyclopedia*. New and revised edition. New York: A. S. Barnes and Co.; London and Toronto: Thomas Yoseloff Ltd. Copyright 1946 and 1963.

Sewell, Anna. 1945. *Black Beauty: The Autobiography of a Horse*. Illustrated by Fritz Eichenberg. New York: Grosset & Dunlap.

Simon & Schuster's Guide to Horses & Ponies of the World. 1988. By Maurizio Bongianni; consultant editor Jane Kidd. New York: Simon & Schuster.

The Small Horse. Edited and published by Karen Gerhardt. Publication ceased after the June 1993 issue.

Snow, Melody D. 1995a. "Mego: Brains & Beauty." *Just About Horses*, 22/#3 May/June 1995, p. 7.

———. 1995b. "Mego: How He Became the 1995 BreyerFest Horse." Forthcoming in *TRR Pony Express*; advance copy provided to me by the author.

"Specialty Run Models." 1990. Two-part list of special-run models in *Just About Horses*: part one (covering Appaloosa through "Black Beauty"), 17/#4, Sept./Oct. 1990, pp. 29-20; part two (covering Cantering Welsh Pony through Family Arabian Stallion), 17/#5, Nov./Dec. 1990, pp. 29-30. For discussion of this list see the section on *JAH* above in the References section.

Sponenberg, D. Phillip, and Bonnie V. Beaver. 1983. *Horse Color*. N.p.: Breakthrough Publications.

Stoneridge, M. A. 1972. *Great Horses of Our Time*. New York: Doubleday.

Terrace, Vincent. 1979. *The Complete Encyclopedia of Television Programs, 1947-1979*. 2nd edition, revised. 2 vols. South Brunswick, N.J.: A. S. Barnes.

Traveler's Rest Ranch Newsletter. Now titled *TRR Pony Express*; see that title below.

TRR Pony Express. Formerly titled *Traveler's Rest Ranch Newsletter*. Edited and published by Paula Beard, 71 Aloha Cir., North Little Rock, AR 72120.

Walerius, Marney. 1985. "Remember When?" *Just About Horses*, VIII/#1, 1985, p. 12.

———. 1991. *Breyer Models Reference and Insurance Guide*. Self-published. Although this book bears a 1991 copyright date, it was not released until spring 1992. Marney Walerius, long-time collector and Breyer company consultant, died in April 1992, only a few weeks after releasing her book.

Waterhouse, Colleen K. 1991. *Breyer Collector's Manual*. Atkinson@cgs.edu. Colleen Waterhouse, 15917 Craddock Way, Chesterfield, MO 63005.

Wells, Heather. 1990. "People, Places & Things," report on BreyerFest 1990. *The Model Rag*, Aug./Sept. 1990, p. 30.

The World of Breyer Horses. 1989. Videotape. Produced by Reeves International, Inc. Listed in Breyer dealer catalogs and price lists as item #70089. Reeves International, Inc., 14 Industrial Rd., Pequannock, NJ 07440.

Young, Nancy Atkinson. 1990-96. *The "Just About Horses" Index*. Self-published. A detailed index for Breyer's magazine, *Just About Horses*, covering all issues from the beginning to the present. Nancy Young, 268 Ross Ct., Claremont, CA 91711-3139.

Endnotes

[1] *JAH* 19/2 Summer I 1992, p. 12. If Steve Ryan is right that Breyer manufactured plastic components for "swinging clocks," then it seems likely that the company for which these parts were made was MasterCrafters Clock Company and that Breyer took over manufacture of the parts from Hartland Plastics, Inc., after MasterCrafters stopped doing business with Hartland (as I discuss below). According to Hartland expert Gail Fitch, Hartland both designed and manufactured parts for "Girl in the Swing" clocks sold by MasterCrafters (Fitch 1995a). The clocks described by Ryan sound very much like the swing clock shown in Fitch's article.

[2] The name Shoecraft is per *JAH* 20/3 Summer II 1993, p. 12, and my August 1993 conversation with Peter Stone.

[3] "S. J. Stone and Charles Schiff, owners of Breyer Molding, came together in 1945 with the express purpose of continuing the custom molding of plastic parts for other manufacturers" (*JAH* Winter 1978). The $15,000 purchase figure and the name of Sam Stone's original partner, Barney Smith, were provided to me by Peter Stone, conversation of March 1995.

[4] In our conversation of May 1994, Peter Stone also remarked that the Breyer company in Chicago was located in an African American neighborhood. Stone's father not only employed a number of the people in the area but owned many of the houses, rather as in a traditional "company town."

[5] *JAH* Winter 1978.

[6] The MasterCrafters company was located in Chicago, Illinois, according to the address printed on the backs of some clocks. See MasterCrafters Clocks below in this Appendix. According to Breyer executive Peter Stone, Breyer manufactured not only the horses but also the saddles and the clock bases (conversation of Nov. 1994).

[7] Hartland discountinued production of Champs to devote more attention to its popular line of religious figures (per Fitch 1993, 2: 4) See note 2 for Western Horse in the Traditionals section above and MasterCrafters Clocks below in this Appendix.

[8] 1985 and 1986 Breyer catalogs, inside front cover. The statement just cited tends to suggest that MasterCrafters was having financial difficulties and thus returned the metal mold (that is, the dies) to Breyer out of necessity. When I asked Breyer executive Peter Stone about this in November 1994, he insisted that this was a misunderstanding. MasterCrafters was not floundering, and in fact Breyer continued to do business with the clock company for many years—Breyer was still manufacturing clock bases for MasterCrafters when Stone took over Breyer Animal Creations in the mid-1960s. What happened in the 1950 deal, according to Stone, was this. When Breyer manufactured the Western Horses, MasterCrafters owed Breyer for two things: the lot of 2,000 plastic horses and the metal mold that Breyer had created to produce them with. MasterCrafters paid Breyer for the 2,000 horses, but the clock company didn't want the metal mold, so simply offered to give it to Breyer instead of paying for it. This arrangement was agreeable to Breyer, since Breyer thought it could profitably produce more of the horses and market them on its own. Stone's account of the situation is supported by a Breyer Animal Creations flier of 1976, which tells the story as follows: "In 1950, at the request of the MasterCrafters Clock Company, an acetate horse was designed to stand on the base of a clock. This horse, the beginning of Breyer Animal Creations, was the #57 - Western Horse. As it happened, MasterCrafters did not pursue the horse clock and after an initial purchase of 2,000 [of the horses from Breyer], the dies were given to Breyer in lieu of payment for the tooling and Breyer was in the horse business." For discussion of the 2,000 quantity mentioned in these statements, see MasterCrafters Clocks below in this Appendix.

[9] Regarding a possible proto-#57, a Western Horse with an unpleasant bile yellow-charcoal color, see the MasterCrafters Clocks section below in this Appendix. None of the ads just cited mentions the Breyer company or Breyer model numbers, but this omission was common in ads for Breyers in later years too, as I'll discuss in a moment. Here it is also worth noting a quote from Peter Stone cited in a 1990 *Horse Illustrated* article on Breyers: "Breyer began to manufacture the horse models based on the Model #57 western horse. The first customer was F.W. Woolworth Company; they had modest success—enough that the Woolworth Company requested additional models" (King 1990, p. 55).

[10] Breyer used the name "Western Mount Horse" as late as the ca.1954 catalog, where the name refers to Western Pony models as well as to Western Horses. See note 6 for Western Horse in the Traditionals section above.

[11] The ads noted above for the palomino Western Horse in the September and December 1951 *Western Horseman* issues were placed by the Rumanco company of Denver, Colorado. These ads don't give the horse a name, instead referring to it simply as "A perfect Horse Model . . . The Popular Palomino" ($3.95). But like the other ads in horse magazines, these omit mention of Breyer. Nor do the many ads for Breyers in the mail-order catalogs of Sears and other department stores during this period mention the name Breyer.

[12] *JAH* Fall 1992, p. 4.

[13] This Western Pony ad, which offered the solid black pony with gold hooves ($2), was yet another of "little joe" Wiesenfeld's efforts. The ad does not use the designation "Western Pony" but calls the model "Black Beauty"— the nickname Breyer used for this model and the black Western Horse in the ca.1954 catalog. In view of "little joe's" penchant for devising fanciful names for the models, one wonders whether Breyer didn't simply adopt the "Black Beauty" designation from him. In any case, this ad is the earliest documentation I know of for the Western Pony and indeed for any Breyer mold other than the Western Horse.

[14] A photo of a Davy clock with its MasterCrafters box is printed in Walerius 1991, p. 3.

[15] For details on these borrowed designs, see the Sculptors section below in this Appendix and the notes for the individual molds above in the main sections of this book. Breyer executive Peter Stone has boyhood memories of a shop located not far from the Breyer company in Chicago, where his father would go to buy Boehm porcelain figurines from which to make new Breyer molds. Stone told me that he still has the Boehm pieces in his personal collection (conversation of Nov. 1994).

[16] See Woodgrains above in the Traditionals section for discussion and a list of all models with this finish.

[17] For this story see the notes for Proud Arabian Mare in the Traditionals section above.

[18] For details see Decorators (1960s) in the Traditionals section above.

[19] These customers of Breyer Molding Co. were mentioned to me by Peter Stone in various conversations of 1993-95.

[20] The Breyer Animal Creations line constituted only about an eighth of the Breyer Molding Company's business, per Peter Stone (conversation of May 1994). In this same conversation, Stone mentioned to me that his dad's partner, Charles Schiff, wanted to terminate the animal line, but Sam Stone preferred to keep it going.

[21] Although the *JAH* biography is a bit uncertain about the date of Peter Stone's move to the Breyer Animal Creations division, placing it "a year or two" after 1965, the date is given specifically as 1966 in a Breyer "Signing Party Tour" news release of 1990: "After college, in 1965, he [Stone] was appointed to the job of Production Manager in the Custom Molding division. It was not until 1966 that he was transferred to the Animal creations division to take on the job of National Sales Manager." The news release continues: "By 1975, Stone's efforts earned him the Presidency of the Animal Creations division which he held until 1985, when the company was sold to Reeves International, Inc." (A letter to collectors from Stone printed in *JAH* Winter 1977 is signed "Very truly yours, Breyer Animal Creations, Peter A. Stone, President.") Neither the news release nor the *JAH* biography mentions Stone's scholarly achievements. Prior to going to work for Breyer, Stone earned a master's degree in history from Northern Arizona University at Flagstaff, specializing in the history of the American West. While completing the program at Flagstaff he also acquired historical materials for the university library and published two articles on the Deseret period of the Mormon church. (Information per Peter Stone, conversation of May 1994.) After three decades of work for Breyer, Stone became so thoroughly identified with the company in the minds of model-horse hobbyists that one of them, Candace Liddy, who is also a renowned equine sculptor, created a statue of Stone that was issued in 1995 in resin by Stampede Resin Castings together with DaBar Enterprises, for sale to collectors. This realistic, Traditional-scale Stone, complete with cowboy hat and wire-rimmed glasses, is standing with one hand extended so that he can be conveniently used as a handler in model-horse show classes.

[22] On these two series see Presentation Collection and Showcase Collection above in the Traditionals section.

[23] For details on these two scales see the General Notes at the start of the Classic and Stablemate sections above.

[24] "In 1973, OPEC [Organization of Petroleum Exporting Countries] raised oil prices tremendously as a result of Western support for Israel during the Yom Kippur War; the price hike caused international shortages, inflation, and other problems in oil-importing nations. Increases ensued from 1975-80. However, as importing countries pursued alternate energy resources, OPEC was forced to lower prices by 1982." (*Columbia Encyclopedia*, 5th ed., s.v. "Organization of Petroleum Exporting Countries.")

[25] The information in this paragraph is from Peter Stone, conversations of Mar., Oct., and Dec. 1995 and Jan. 1996. The spelling of "propionate" is per a 1983 newsletter titled *Insights*, published by the Plastics Division of Eastman Chemical Products, Inc., Kingsport, Tennessee.

[26] For details see Just About Horses in the References section at the end of this book.

[27] For further discussion of specials see Special Runs above in the Traditionals section. For discussion of the Congresses, see Walerius 1991, p. i. The term "live show" may strike novice ears as a tad bizarre, plastic models being after all non-living, if essentially vegetable (cellulose). But the reference is to the people, not their collectibles: live shows are gatherings of hobbyists in the flesh to exhibit their models and generally disport in ways not often associated with adults. A "live show" is as opposed to a "photo show," in which participants mail photos of their models to a designated judge rather than getting together in person.

[28] For discussion, see Signing Party Special Runs above in the Traditionals section.

[29] For discussion and a list of these models see Artist Series above in the Traditionals section.

[30] The contract finalizing the sale of Breyer Animal Creations to Reeves International, which is a privately owned company, was signed on November 15, 1984, according to Peter Stone (conversation of March 1995). The 1984 date of the Reeves acquisition is also documented in several published company sources. The 1991 catalog states: "1984: Breyer becomes a division of Reeves International and moves operations to New Jersey." *JAH* 20/3 Summer II 1993, p. 13, states: "In November 1984, Breyer was sold to Reeves International. Breyer and Peter Stone would move from Chicago to New Jersey to become part of a fine quality product line." A company flier from a 1994 Reeves "dealer notebook" states: "The

company, which was acquired in 1984 by Reeves International, Inc., has built its business on one simple, unfailing principle: to produce the highest quality products possible."

[31] Suzanne Gibson dolls are no longer made, per Peter Stone, conversation of Nov. 1994.

[32] Stone is identified as Director of Marketing on various certificates of authenticity issued with SR models, such as the JAH SR caramel pinto Western Horse (1990) and JAH SR "Steel Dust" (1993/94).

[33] Information in this paragraph is per Peter Stone, conversations of August 1993, November 1994, and March 1995. Prior to completion of the Wayne factory, some of the injection molding of the models was also contracted out to other companies.

[34] The company's equipment was sold at an auction held on the premises of the Breyer Molding Co. in Chicago on January 28, 1986. Stephen L. Winternitz, Inc., Industrial Aucioneers and Appraisers, of Northbrook, Illinois, conducted the auction. A copy of the auction catalog in my possession lists 4 pages of items, ranging from hydraulic injection-molding machines to office furniture. Stuart Bentley, owner of Bentley Sales model mail-order company, told me in December 1995 that he went to the Breyer factory on the day of the equipment auction to see what memorabilia he might find. While there he spoke to Charles Schiff, one of the owners of Breyer Molding Company since the 1950s, and asked him for any Breyer Animal Creations odds and ends. Schiff gave him a number of the plaster castings that had been used to make Breyer's metal injection molds: "Misty," the Saddlebred Weanling, some bulls, and perhaps a few others.

[35] See the Sculptors section below in this Appendix.

[36] For particulars see BreyerFest SR Dinner Models above in the Traditionals section.

[37] See JAH 16/1 Feb./Mar. 1989, p. 12, for Hess's biography.

[38] JAH Spring 1977 states: "Chris [Hess] usually works from photographs. . . . As the clay model nears completion, it will sometimes need owner's approval and if necessary, Chris will travel to the owner in order to make the necessary adjustments." A Breyer Animal Creations flier that probably dates to 1976 comments, under the heading "How We Make Our Animal Creation Models": "We start from a sculptured piece that is a replica of either a drawing or a photograph. This is developed into a plaster model from which our mold is made."

[39] See JAH Summer II 1992, p. 4, for discussion of these versions.

[40] The rapprochement between the two companies was made public—albeit some years after the fact—in two JAH articles by Maxine Renaker, one of the founders of Hagen-Renaker. In the first article (Renaker 1977), Mrs. Renaker comments: "I am happy, too, to say that Maureen agrees with me that Breyer is doing a fine job of publishing her magnificent horse designs in plastic, the now material. We both feel that it is good to make copies of these beauties available to a wider public than ceramics could possibly supply." In her second article, titled "The Hagen-Renaker Story" (Renaker 1979), the author states: "Maureen Love Calvert, of whom I have written earlier for Just About Horses, must have full credit for the designs of all the fabulous horses which came out of Designers' Workshop in the 'fifties and early 'sixties and which are now enfranchised to Breyer Molding Company for publication in plastic."

[41] See Roller, Rose, and Berkwitz 1989, pp. 2ff., 72. Hagen-Renaker expert Joan Berkwitz mentioned to me that in the late 1960s or early 1970s, when Breyer approached H-R about permission to reproduce some of their sculptures, H-R supplied Breyer with a wide range of pieces cast in white bisque, with their H-R model numbers written on their sides. These pieces included all of H-R's horses and many if not all of their dogs, cats, cattle, and wildlife figures. Some of these bisques came into Marney Walerius's possession, and Joan obtained a piece or two from her.

[42] The spelling of this name is per Mac Donald 1993 and JAH 21/1 Spring 1994, p. 15.

[43] Regarding the dating of these models see the notes for Clydesdale Stallion in the Traditionals section above.

[44] For "El Pastor's" complicated mold-stamp story, see the notes for this mold in the Traditionals section above.

[45] "In 1973, OPEC raised oil prices tremendously as a result of Western support for Israel during the Yom Kippur War; the price hike caused international shortages, inflation, and other problems in oil-importing nations. Increases ensued from 1975-80. However, as importing countries pursued alternate energy resources, OPEC was forced to lower prices by 1982." (Columbia Encyclopedia, 5th ed., s.v. "Organization of Petroleum Exporting Countries.")

[46] The name "Tenite" is Eastman's registered trademark for its line of cellulosic plastics. I have copies of two old undated news releases from Eastman announcing new Breyer models. One of them must date to late 1953 or early 1954, for it announces the Indian rider with pinto Western Pony. At the bottom, the release says "Tenite is marketed by Eastman Chemical Products, Inc., Kingsport, Tenn. / Eastman Chemical Products, Inc.—Advertising Department / 260 Madison Avenue, New York 16, N.Y.—ORegon 9-1820." The second news release, which must date to late 1958 or 1959, announces "Sheik, Sheba and their foal Shah," the bay FAS, PAM, and PAF. The letterhead says "Eastman Chemical Products, Inc. / Subsidiary of Eastman Kodak Company," and gives the Madison Avenue address and phone number. At the bottom of the release is this line: "Material: Tenite acetate supplied by Eastman." It is interesting that in those early years Breyer's plastic supplier supplied at least some of Breyer's publicity, too. A 1983 ad flyer from Eastman Chemical turns the tables, using Breyer models to promote Tenite plastics. A large photo of Traditional "Man O' War" appears at the top of the flyer, followed by the headline "The legendary Man O' War / Breyer keeps the legend alive in Tenite® cellulosics." The flyer continues: "For over 30 years, Breyer Animal Creations has immortalized equine wonders like Man O' War in a remarkable, custom-tailored formulation of Tenite cellulosics from Eastman." A 1983 newsletter titled Insights, published by the Plastics Division of Eastman Chemical Products, Inc., Kingsport, Tennessee, includes an article titled "Tenite® Cellulosic Plastics," which gives a bit of history and scientific information on these materials: "The Cellulosics Department of Tennessee Eastman Company's Plastics and Polymers Division has manufactured nearly one billion pounds of cellulosic plastics in the last 10 years and every batch of that amount was prepared to meet individual customer needs. . . . Eastman developed its first cellulosic plastic, cellulose acetate, in 1932. . . . Cellulose esters are produced by the esterification of cellulose obtained from either wood pulp or cotton linters. Eastman manufactures three cellulosics—acetate, butyrate and propionate. Cellulose acetate is obtained by use of acetic acid and acetic anhydride in the esterification step. . . . To produce the plastic formulation, the cellulose ester powder is mixed with a suitable plasticizer (usually an ester of a fatty acid and an alcohol), colorants and heat stabilizers, and then melt-compounded to produce a pellet form."

[47] Most but not all of the injection molding of Breyer models has been and continues to be done at the Breyer factory—originally at the Chicago factory of Breyer Molding Company from 1950 until the mid-1980s and then at the Wayne, New Jersey, factory of Breyer/Reeves following the purchase of Breyer Animal Creations by Reeves International in the mid-1980s. However, on occasion Breyer has contracted with other injection-molding companies to do some of the molding for them. One such occasion was the period between the Reeves acquisition of Breyer and the completion of the new factory in Wayne in mid-1985, and perhaps for a few months beyond that, until the new plant was fully operational. During this period the Breyer Molding Company also continued to produce models for Reeves. (Information is per Breyer executive Peter Stone, conversations of November 1994.)

[48] Peter Stone confirmed this at the West Coast Model Horse Collector's Jamboree in August 1993.

[49] On my visit to the Breyer factory in Wayne, New Jersey, in November 1994, Peter Stone very kindly, and at risk to his back, opened up the metal injection-molds of Robin Hood and the Howdy Mountie so that I could see the actual cavities. Even these relatively small metal molds are unbelievably heavy—I tugged on them myself and could barely budge them.

[50] Information in this paragraph is per Breyer executive Peter Stone, in his presentations at the West Coast Model Horse Collector's Jamboree in August 1993 and at BreyerFest 1994, and in conversation with me in November 1994.

[51] Photos of and facts about the molding process are presented in JAH IX/#2 1982, p. 10; XIV/#3 1987, p. 18; XIV/#4 1987, p. 18; and 18/#3 Summer II 1991, pp. 15-20. The information about quality control is per Breyer executive Peter Stone, conversation of November 1994.

[52] The holes are so small that occasionally they close off before the molten plastic can harden, as Breyer executive Peter Stone explained to me on a visit to the factory in November 1994.

[53] For photos and facts see JAH XIV/#4 1987, p. 18, and 18/#3 Summer II 1991, pp. 15-20. According to former JAH editor Megan Thilman Quigley (conversation of Aug. 1995), Breyer's supplier of paint has for many years been a Chicago company named Durable Specialties, which provides custom-mixed colors of paints that are specially formulated for application to cellulose acetate plastic.

[54] Per Roller, Rose, and Berkwitz 1989, p. 4.

[55] For further discussion of this history and the mold versions see notes 2 and 3 for Western Horse above in the Traditionals section.

[56] See note 7 for Western Horse.

[57] See note 8 for Western Horse.

[58] See JAH 18/2 Summer I 1991, p. 33. As mentioned above, I think it is possible that the conventional nightlights were made by Breyer or at least commissioned by Breyer; but of course it's also conceivable that they were made by Dunning Industries (which also made the "Ranchcraft" lamps discussed above) or some other company. I simply have no evidence one way or the other at present—to my knowledge no contemporary advertisements or original nightlight packaging has been found.